RON SHANDLER'S **2014**

BASEBALL FORECASTER

AND ENCYCLOPEDIA OF FANALYTICS

TRIUMPH
BOOKS

Triumph Books and colophon are registered trademarks of Random House, Inc.

This book is available in quantity at special discounts for your group or organization. For further information, contact:

Triumph Books LLC
814 North Franklin Street
Chicago, Illinois 60610
(312) 337-0747
www.triumphbooks.com

Printed in U.S.A.
ISBN: 978-1-60078-841-3

Rotisserie League Baseball is a registered trademark of the
Rotisserie League Baseball Association, Inc.

Statistics provided by Baseball Info Solutions

Cover design by Brent Hershey
Front cover photograph by Gary A. Vasquez/USA TODAY Sports Images
Author photograph by Kevin Hurley

Ron Shandler's BASEBALL FORECASTER

Editors
Ray Murphy
Brent Hershey

Associate Editor
Brandon Kruse

· · · · · ·

Technical Wizard
Rob Rosenfeld

Design
Brent Hershey

Data and Charts
Matt Cederholm

Player Commentaries
Dave Adler
Ryan Bloomfield
Rob Carroll
Matt Cederholm
Brent Hershey
Ray Murphy
Stephen Nickrand
Kristopher Olson
Josh Paley
Brian Rudd
Jock Thompson
Rod Truesdell
Todd Zola

Research and Articles
Bob Berger
Patrick Davitt
Patrick DiCaprio
Bill Macey
David Martin
Jock Thompson
Todd Zola

Prospects
Rob Gordon
Jeremy Deloney
Tom Mulhall

Injuries
Rick Wilton

Acknowledgments

Producing the *Baseball Forecaster* has been a team effort for a number of years now; the list of credits to the left is where the heavy lifting gets done. On behalf of Ron, Brent, and Ray, our most sincere thanks to each of those key contributors.

We are just as grateful to the rest of the BaseballHQ.com staff, who do the yeoman's work in populating the website with 12 months of incredible online content: Andy Andres, Matt Beagle, Dan Becker, Alex Beckey, Brian Brickley, Ed DeCaria, Doug Dennis, Matt Dodge, Greg Fishwick, Neil FitzGerald, Colby Garrapy, Matt Gelfand, Scott Gellman, Phil Hertz, Joe Hoffer, Tom Kephart, Chris Lee, Chris Mallonee, Troy Martell, David Martin, Scott Monroe, Craig Neuman, Harold Nichols, Frank Noto, Greg Pyron, Nick Richards, Vlad Sedler, Mike Shears, Peter Sheridan, Skip Snow, Jeffrey Tomich, Michael Weddell and Joshua Weller.

Thank you to our behind-the-scenes troopers: our technical dynamic duo of Mike Krebs and Rob Rosenfeld; and to Lynda Knezovich, the patient and kind voice at the other end of your phone or email inquiries.

Thank you to all our industry colleagues, a truly impressive group. They are competitors, but they are also colleagues working to grow this industry, which is never a more evident than at our annual First Pitch Arizona gathering each November.

Thank you to Dave Morgan, Chris Pirrone, Dan Fogarty and the entire team at USA Today Sports Media Group.

Thank you for all the support from the folks at Triumph Books and Action Printing.

And of course, thank *you*, readers, for your interest in what we all have to say. Your kind words, support and (respectful) criticism move us forward on the fanalytic continium more than you know. We are grateful for your readership.

From Ray Murphy Teaming up with Ron and Brent, as well as the remarkable BHQ staff, is what keeps this job from feeling like work (well, most of the time). Back at home, my wife Jennifer has always been extremely patient with my fantasy baseball activities. I actually mentioned the topic on our first date, and somehow got a second date. Since then, she has been a true partner; always helping me find a way to take the next step on this path. Our twin girls, Grace and Bridget, missed out on a bunch of daddy/daughter time this fall, but I'll make that up to them.

From Brent Hershey When asked about my full-time job in fantasy baseball, my response is that I feel quite fortunate. Not only for writing about a game, but also working with great people. In addition to the BHQ staff, thank you, Ron, for your grace and integrity in showing a rookie the ropes. No hazing here. And Ray, thanks for your insight and collaborative spirit. Here's to many successful years ahead.

Most importantly, thanks to the three women in my midst. Though I appreciate your supportive listening to my rant about Marlon Byrd and BABIP (wife Lorie), your excitement in tagging out a runner at home plate (daughter Dillon), and your insistence that we stay for all nine innings (daughter Eden), your gifts *away* from the diamond are truly inspiring and bring me balance. Thank you.

From Ron Shandler Mega-thanks to the incredible work done by Ray and Brent. For the first time in over 20 years, I was able to carve out an afternoon to go to an Octoberfest—yay, beer!

In addition to my appreciation for all the above contributors, I always have to thank my ladies. (Take note: you can't run this organization without a household filled with women.)

Updates: Darielle graduated magna cum laude and moved back home while she looks for theater production/stage-managing work in New York. (Inquiries welcome.) Justina, now a junior, recently performed at Lincoln Center and spent the summer interning with a film scorer in L.A. And... Sue and I are building a house in Port St. Lucie! These Mets fans are coming home, sort of.

Thanks to everyone, there are more championships to be won for all of us.

TABLE OF CONTENTS

Nightmare. 1

Encyclopedia of Fanalytics 9

    Fundamentals 10

    Batters 21

    Pitchers 29

    Prospects 40

    Gaming 44

Statistical Research Abstracts 59

Gaming Research Abstracts 67

Major Leagues

    Batters 79

    Pitchers 149

    Injuries 213

Prospects

    Top Impact Prospects for 2014 229

    Top Japanese Prospects 235

    Major League Equivalents 237

Leaderboards 255

Draft Guides 267

Blatant Advertisements for Other Products 277

Nightmare

by Ron Shandler

I drive up to the Washington D.C./Baltimore area about once a month during the baseball season. It's a four-hour trip from my home in southwest Virginia but it's worth it to catch some Nats or O's action, or occasional minor league games in places like Bowie and Potomac.

The trip is cathartic for me; windows down, radio blasting. Sometimes it's classic jazz; more often it's sports talk. I do it alone; sometimes I even take in the games alone. It helps me clear my head.

For years, I've looked forward to these outings. This year was different.

This year was a nightmare.

It started back in January 2013 when I was developing the program for the First Pitch Forum spring conference series. I had decided that the theme for the event would be "Bold Statements."

After playing this game for nearly three decades, I know that fantasy leagues are often won by the team that can uncover that season's big surprise performance. Our research has shown that the most profitable players have a disproportionate impact on who is going to win your league. In 2013, more than 50% of Jose Fernandez owners finished no lower than 3rd place, and 75% finished no lower than 5th. That's huge.

The flipside works similarly. Teams that drafted first-round busts like Ryan Braun or Matt Kemp finished in the bottom third of the standings more often than not.

Identifying these players in advance—now, that's the trick. So the spring forum program was designed to go out on a limb, string together a few conditional possibilities and make some bold statements.

As author Frank Scully once said, "Why not go out on a limb? Isn't that where the fruit is?"

To be honest, this is probably the funnest part of forecasting for me. Running routine trend analyses and projecting that Paul Goldschmidt was going to improve or Fernando Rodney was going to fall off is, well, boring. Speculating that Chris Davis would have 40-HR upside and then watching him explode… that is much more fun.

So the First Pitch content developers came up with a bunch of bold statements. We suggested that you stay away from Mariners pitchers (their team ERA did spike from 3.76 in 2012 to 4.31), the saves leader on the Royals might be Luke Hochevar (right idea, wrong conclusion) and the Rockies might challenge for a wild card berth (well, they were in first place as late as May 7). There were a few others.

But the opening statement that led off the conference was the one that drew the most notice. I was the one who wrote and presented this bold statement in all seven cities:

Don't Draft Mike Trout.

Yes, it was pretty bold to defy common wisdom—and simple logic!—regarding the American League Rookie of the Year and MVP runner-up, but it was not meant to disparage the future superstar. There was no question that Trout was an exceptional player. The question was about his draftability.

After one incredible season, was it reasonable to expect him to repeat that performance? He would have to come close in order to earn back his acquisition cost. "Don't draft Mike Trout" meant that the odds were too high that you'd take a loss on your investment. That investment was very expensive—a top 3 pick in snake drafts or $40+ in auctions.

It was a cost/benefit analysis, nothing more.

I presented the case first to a tough home crowd in Los Angeles. They didn't take me seriously. I then moved on to San Francisco, Chicago and then up the East Coast. As I got deeper and deeper into the conference tour, the arguments grew stronger and stronger for me.

By the end of the tour, I had assembled a long laundry list of reasons why Mike Trout was a terrible investment for 2013. I put them together in an article for BaseballHQ.com and USAToday.com called, "12 Reasons Not to Draft Mike Trout."

The reasons touched on everything from his age to his weight. I discussed his unsustainable batting average on balls in play (BABIP) and home run to fly ball ratio. I compared his performance to others in history and charted his probable ranking in a volatile fantasy draft pool. And after I wrote about the 12 reasons, I found three more and wrote another piece.

Individually, none of the reasons was strong enough to make a case on its own. But together, they created a compelling argument for a significant fall from the upper echelons of 2013 fantasy cheat sheets.

And really, this seemed like the easiest projection I could ever make. A player whose numbers were so far off the charts had to be primed for a massive regression. So I went out on a limb with my multiple arguments, but I really thought that limb was supported by solid steel struts.

Well, the articles created a media firestorm. I was invited onto numerous radio shows to back up my contention. There was a videocast with CBS Sports. Chris Liss of Rotowire.com devoted an entire column to refute each one of my points.

Several discussion threads opened up in the BaseballHQ.com forums, one of which—"Trout's value is plummeting?"—generated more than 550 responses and more than 7,500 views. That thread exploded during the period when my laundry list was growing and Trout's projections were still being tweaked.

By mid-March, Trout had gone through eight spring training games without a home run and just one stolen base. Already there were slight murmurs about the "prophecy" coming true. I received an email from one enraged Angels fan calling me the devil. Truth.

On March 14, I had tickets to the Angels/White Sox Cactus League game at Diablo Stadium in Tempe, AZ. Tied up with some family business, I arrived late, missing the top of the first inning. When I finally made my way up the stairs and onto the concourse, the very first thing I saw was Mike Trout hitting his first home run.

I laughed. I don't believe in omens.

Trout wrapped up March with just two home runs and six stolen bases, though he did hit .350. April wasn't as kind. He opened slowly, going 2 for 11 in his first two games. After 10 games, he was batting only .227. By the end of the month, he was still batting just .261 with two home runs and four steals, a 12-HR/24-SB pace.

Some people were starting to get nervous. I have to admit, I was glued to every Angels boxscore and was getting these slight, intermittent flutters of validation.

That's when things took a nasty turn.

I decided to write a piece for USA Today, published on April 30. The headline that appeared with the online version was, "Trout's early-season struggles a matter of percentages." The headline in the print edition was a bit more pointed: "Trout's drop not shocking." I don't write the headlines.

The article itself was straightforward, looking at his current performance indicators as compared to 2012. However, the fact that I chose *that* topic at *that* time blew the first rule about small sample sizes. I was too anxious to plant the seeds of victory. Given all the attention to my earlier pieces, I was too giddy to let his April stat line pass without comment.

It defied everything I've written about exhibiting excruciating patience.

And well, you know what happened next. Trout exploded, hitting .337 over the remaining five months, with 25 HR and 29 SB. In the process, he set all sorts of offensive records, particularly for someone his age.

As Trout exploded, so did the endless online and media chatter. I became a target for derisive comments up and down the Internet. A week wouldn't go by without at least a few emails or tweets that would simply say, "Nice job projecting Trout" or "Surrender yet?"

And finally, even my monthly trips to D.C. and Baltimore became another knife in my gut.

For you see, every time I drove up Interstate 81 to northern Virginia, I had to pass a sign at exit 156 that always read:

Troutville

Now, I know that sounds silly, but consider:

- Troutville is what some fans call the left field section of Angels Stadium populated by manic Trout fans.
- The Trout Farm is the official moniker of that section. Up Route 311 from Troutville is, in fact, a trout farm.
- Troutville, VA is the only town with that name in the entire United States. Why did it have to be on my route?
- The population of Troutville is only 432 and the area is a mere 0.9 square miles, an absurdly small entity to merit its own interstate exit. Yet it was on my route.

As ridiculous as it seems, that green sign at exit 156 kept silently mocking my every trip last summer. Each time I was looking forward to putting the pedal down to John Coltrane, I had to face the reality of passing this tiny town with the evil name. *A town that has the exact same number of residents as its namesake's on base average this season.*

Karma?

Well… maybe.

My nightmare continued to grow more intense with every home run and stolen base that Trout notched in the boxscores. By mid-season, I had privately surrendered and gone into hiding to avoid all my taunters. By the end of the season, I was completely buried.

But the onslaught never let up. On October 1, I tweeted: "So much for my Tigers-Reds World Series prediction from last March. Congrats #Pirates!" The response was immediate: "About as good as your predictions on @Trouty20."

Even as late as the World Series, people were still stumbling over my March handiwork: "Wow. I just found this gem by you. Are you gonna take a year off just out of principal?? (sic) #fail."

There is an old German proverb that goes, "Lieber ein ende mit schrecken als ein schrecken ohne ende." Roughly translated, it reads, "Better to have a horrible ending than to have horrors without end."

So can I wake up now?

Awake

For me, the 2013 season was a bad dream in many respects. Two of my expert league teams finished ranked in double-digits. The other—my experts keeper league team—had been built such that 2013 was my absolute best chance for a title run. I finished third, 14.5 points out.

Mike Trout was on none of my teams. Perhaps I *was* cursed.

With the season over and with the benefit of conscious retrospect, I have to wonder where I went so far wrong.

The highest goal of forecasting is to make sure the process is sound. We can't predict the future—only general tendencies—so nailing the process is the best that we can do. Looking back at my list of 15 reasons why Trout should have fallen short of earning his draft value, was the process sound? Were the individual arguments valid? Here is how it all unraveled:

1. Trout's 2012 power had to be an outlier because he was scouted as a speed prospect. Bryce Harper was the power prospect.

Sound argument? Well, it would not be the first time that scouts were wrong, but the numbers did back it up. Trout averaged 10.5 HRs and 59 stolen bases in his previous two minor league seasons. Harper had hit 17 HRs and 26 SBs in his first pro season and was given a higher ceiling by the scouts.

However, by my establishing that comparison up front, it forced me to be on target with the projections on two players. The fact that both projections failed in opposite directions made the comparison look even worse.

And even though the process was somewhat sound, the argument was flawed. Hanley Ramirez never hit more than 8 HRs in any of his four minor league seasons yet hit 17, 29 and 33 in his first three years in the Majors. (Trout: "So there.")

Of course, we can always cherry-pick isolated examples to support or refute any argument.

2. Over the past eight years, only 3% of all 30-HR hitters had fly ball rates as low as Trout's 33%. His 27% HR/F rate in the second half was also notable (Jose Bautista's was only 22% in his 54-HR year).

Sound argument? Well, at least a sound observation. The point was that this was not a repeatable feat and thus, his home run total should fade.

But failing to repeat could mean that Trout fell short of 30 HRs or saw his fly ball rate rise. In fact, both happened. Trout's HR total did drop below 30. His fly ball rate rose from 33% to 35%. His home run to fly ball rate dropped from 22% to a more acceptable 16%.

But the net result was a loss of a just three home runs (though in 30 additional at-bats). Not exactly earth-shattering.

3. Home runs are getting scarcer each year and speed is plentiful, making the big power bats more valuable. If Trout's power was not for real, then he would have less value as a first-rounder.

Sound argument? Yes, if in fact this trend had continued. As it turned out, speed became scarcer in 2013, thereby leveling the playing field all around. We could not have known that.

But as noted, I was not trying to prove that Trout wasn't a great ballplayer; I was trying to prove that he did not merit his expected market price on Draft Day. The real question was, how much did his HR output have to drop in order for this to have any relevance? It would have to be a significant drop, and it wasn't.

So, as long as he remained a 5-category player, he was always going to end up as a first-rounder, especially if he managed to hit over .300. But that .300 average was also something I did not think he could repeat. You see…

4. Trout's .383 BABIP is typically an unsustainable level. As that regressed, so would his batting average. As his batting average regressed, so would his home run output and stolen base opportunities.

Sound argument? Yes. Solid process, bad result. This domino effect never happened because Trout managed to repeat his elevated BABIP as well as his high batting average.

Rany Jazayerli wrote: "The armies of regression from greatness and regression from luck amassed on his doorstep in the spring, and he flicked them aside as if he were Achilles."

You see, others were equally amazed.

Todd Zola wrote: "We still don't know Trout's baseline BABIP even though we now have two full seasons of data. Many will point to consecutive seasons of a BABIP north of .380 and call it Trout's established baseline. And they may be right. But the probability of sustaining a career BABIP over .380 is extremely slim."

So we're still looking for possible regression here. And that domino effect may still be around the corner.

In some ways, I see this in the same light as our analysis of Jeremy Hellickson. For two straight seasons, his ERA far exceeded his skills set. Many analysts began resigning themselves to the possibility that Hellickson had some innate quality that allowed him to consistently overachieve.

Then came 2013's disaster. The interesting takeaway from Hellickson is that, while his ERA during that three-year span was 2.95, 3.10 and 5.17, his xERA during that time was 4.58, 4.39 and 4.16. His 2013 performance was actually the best skills displayed during that period.

This is not to say that Hellickson is anywhere near the caliber of player that Trout is. It's just to note that even two seasons may not provide an accurate baseline.

By comparison, it's important to note that some of Trout's underlying skills also improved this past year. His contact rate rose from 75 to 77%. His walk rate increased from 11% to 16%. He became more patient and discriminating in the pitches he swung at. That can only lead to even better things, as incomprehensible as that sounds.

So it's also possible that—like Hellickson—Trout's skill could continue to improve even if his surface stats remain stable, or even decline.

5. Trout allegedly showed up to camp at 240 pounds. History has shown that players of that girth do not steal bases (think: Billy Butler, also 6-1, 240 lbs.).

Sound argument? I plead the Fifth.

Okay, it is true that players of those dimensions typically do not steal bases. Over the past few years, Matt Kemp and Hanley Ramirez are the only players tipping the scales at even 220 lbs who have stolen as many as 20 bases in a season. So I surmised that it would be unlikely that Trout could repeat his near-50 SB output at 240 pounds.

Of all the arguments in my articles, this was the one that drew the most ire, in good part because we could not verify Trout's actual weight. As it turned out, whether due to the weight, or batting order position, or planetary alignment, this is the projection that we beat field on.

Trout stole 33 bases. We projected he'd steal 30. All the other leading touts projected 45 and up.

In the end… Questionable process + Good result = Dumb Luck. I'll take it, though.

6. Trout's maximum-effort style of play increases the odds that a pulled hamstring or an immovable object (like an outfield wall) could send him to the disabled list.

Sound argument? More of a sound speculation. Many max-effort players face this threat and end up spending time on the DL, but of course it's not a given.

One interesting observation involves Trout's drop in defensive skill in 2013. Some surmise that he pulled back on his aggressiveness to avoid injury, thereby decreasing the number of balls he reached. However, I don't know if that's anything more than a speculation.

7. Trout had an amazing three months in 2012, but was already exhibiting signs of slowing down as the season progressed. He batted .284 in August and .257 in September.

Sound argument? Sound observation, though not terribly predictive.

Trout actually carried that lethargic performance into April this year. And then he kicked back into gear. And… he slowed down again this past September, batting just .282 that month.

But players are evaluated based on how they perform over six full months. The path they take to get to October can be pretty volatile.

I was looking for a trend in a small data sample. That trend might well have been real. But Trout's exorbitant numbers in all the other months trumped those late season "fades."

8. Opposing teams had all off-season to try to uncover a weakness they could exploit. We had yet to see how well Trout could adjust in year #2. Sophomore slumps are real.

Sound argument? Sure. Talk to Eric Hosmer, or the dozens of players who fail to adjust in season #2 and take one or more years to return to their rookie heroics. It's no guarantee to occur, but this is a game about adjustments on both sides.

It's possible that Trout's sophomore slump began in August 2012 and ended in April 2013. His explosion in May might be a testament to his ability to adjust back. Whatever the case, there have been few opposing pitchers able to neutralize him yet.

9. The 2013 projections calculated by industry touts were typically regressions off of Trout's 2012 stat line. But 2012 could not be considered a real baseline because it was just a single data point—and likely flawed—so those projections had to be flawed as well.

Sound argument? Sure, theoretically. So now we do have two data points. And they are both equally insane.

10. Trout's 2012 numbers were historic. With one more SB, he would have been only the third player in major league history to hit 30 HRs and steal 50 bases. The other two were Barry Bonds and Eric Davis, both at age 25. And neither repeated the feat.

Sound argument? Sound observation and reasonable conclusion.

And yes, Trout didn't repeat the feat. There is no question that his HR and SB totals regressed. The issue is that they didn't regress nearly as much as expected and other players didn't rise up into the first round to surpass him.

11. And Trout pulled it off at age 21. His youth could be considered either an advantage or an obstacle. He was at the green end of the growth curve, but 21-year-olds can get over-confident and not respond well to pressure.

Sound argument? Again, an observation from which I was trying to build the case. Trout ended up handling it all with aplomb. What can I say?

12. There were better picks early in the draft. There were far more players with a consistent track record of success.

Sound argument? This was really the crux of the entire argument.

In a normal season, the first round class would be composed of strong, relatively safe commodities. Truth is, many of last March's first-rounders had some warts. There were injury concerns about Kemp, Albert Pujols and Joey Votto. There were regression concerns about Andrew McCutchen and Buster Posey. Ryan Braun had the PED specter hanging over his head.

Still, I was more willing to take a chance that an established commodity like Kemp or Votto would be healthy than bet on an outlying short-termer to repeat.

And in fact, only five of the 15 projected first-rounders ended up earning their draft slot. That's a typical result. I thought Trout would have been one of the fallen 10.

In fact, given the overall weakness of the class, Trout could have regressed even more and still merited a high draft pick. You could have lopped off another $10 from his final value and he'd still finish in the top 10. He was that good.

13. Players who earn first round value in any given season have a 66% turnover each year, and players who appear on the list for the first time—as Trout did last year—are only a 14% bet to repeat.

Sound argument? Yes, though this was just more of playing the percentages. Trout ended up being one of the 14%.

It's our classic reminder that, even when you follow an overwhelming 86% percentage play, you have to be prepared to be wrong 14% of the time.

14. The arguments about Trout's historical comps were faulty. None of Mickey Mantle, Frank Robinson, Al Kaline, Jimmie Fox or Ted Williams put up the numbers Trout did in their rookie year—or ever.

Sound argument? Yes, this remains true. There are many examples of players hitting the ground running and never letting up. But nobody ever put up the *caliber* of numbers Trout had in 2012.

Some naysayers went on to compare him to more recent players who had great rookie seasons and never regressed. They wrote, "What about Albert Pujols? What about Miguel Cabrera?"

"What about Ryan Braun?"

Um, indeed.

15. And so, you can't rule out outside help.

Sound argument? Oh heck, who knows?

The PED saga took a sharp turn in 2013. For the first time, Major League Baseball suspended players without them having failed a drug test. Ryan Braun's dishonesty cast doubt on the integrity of all players throughout the sport. Despite all this, formerly suspended players were still signing lucrative new contracts, diluting the impact of the penalties, and negating the sense of magnitude and consequence that MLB has been trying to sell us for the past decade.

The reasonable conclusion is that the deterrents are insufficient and players are continuing to gain an advantage with PEDs. We don't know who they are, nor can we accurately measure the statistical gains, but that doesn't mean they don't exist. And unfortunately, human nature and logic cast our focus on the outlying performances. Barry Bonds, Roger Clemens, Alex Rodriguez, and even Braun were all outliers, and all living under the PED cloud.

So you have to at least ask the question: *How can a 22-year-old put up numbers over his first two full seasons far better than any other player in the entire history of Major League Baseball?*

Yes, maybe he is that good. Maybe we are just spectators to history. But we are living in an era when the question still needs to be asked.

This is what it looked like in the end:

Mike Trout	AB	R	HR	RBI	SB	BA	OBP	SLG	OPS
2012 actual	559	129	30	83	49	.326	.398	.564	.961
2013 Forecaster proj	597	104	25	78	41	.286	.359	.494	.853
2013 March 1 update	610	106	22	80	32	.286	.359	.471	.830
2013 Opening Day update	580	101	21	76	30	.286	.359	.471	.830
2013 actual	589	109	27	97	33	.323	.432	.557	.989

This is and will always be a game about percentage plays. You can follow the bad plays and cash in every once in awhile, but the vast majority of winners will always be the ones who follow the better percentages.

And really, the fact that Trout did defy the percentages in 2013 is not cause for celebration. You can't just revel in his greatness and proclaim, "well, of course he's that good."

What Trout has done is nothing short of incredible.

Joe Sheehan wrote: "The numbers are astounding. He led the AL in hits and walks—a combination done just four times before and just once in 50 years. No position player has ever been as good as Mike Trout has been in 2012 and 2013 and not gone on to be fully qualified for the Hall of Fame."

This was not just a great performance that someone managed to pull off twice. This was historic, and pulled off by a 22 year-old.

But can you bet on historical performances to continue, year after year?

You simply can't. That's why Miguel Cabrera did not repeat the Triple Crown. That's why Fernando Rodney fell far short of last year's ERA record. That's why Craig Kimbrel could not duplicate his 2012 record-shattering strikeout rate.

Historic performances are outliers. Roger Maris never came within 22 home runs of his record of 61. Barry Bonds never came within 24 home runs of his record of 73. Bob Gibson never came within a full run of his record 1.12 ERA. Hack Wilson never came within 32 RBIs of his record of 191. Rickey Henderson never came within 22 stolen bases of his record of 130. And Ted Williams' .406 season? It took him 13 more seasons to even come as close as .388.

You can get blindsided by an historical performance once. Betting on a repeat is just a horrible percentage play.

And so, given the chance to go back in time and redo my projection for 2013, I would do the same thing all over again. I would give the same advice all over again: don't draft Mike Trout. It was, and remains the better percentage play. The fact that it was wrong changes nothing.

There is no question that Mike Trout is a special player. He's proved that. But 2012 and 2013 are in the books. That's history. Now what?

2014

Sigh.

Does Trout's track record now make him less likely or more likely to regress? An argument can be made both ways.

Many analysts will consider him less likely to regress because he has two years of history on his side. He now wears the Badge of Honor: "Proven Player with a Track Record." That has to be the foundation of any statistically-driven forecast. It is with our projection in this book as well.

The other side of the argument is that he is still performing at a level that is unsustainable, based on history. In fact, given that he is even more of an outlier now, it's possible that the odds of a regression are greater than last year. It's the Plexiglass Principle, fighting massive resistance for two years and finally giving in, exhausted.

Either way, nobody is going to draft him outside the first round or pay less than $40 at auction anyway. He could well be the most expensive player on the board this spring.

Given our historical track record on first-rounders, we probably should not expect him to return 100% of his projected value—few first-rounders do—because that remains the better percentage play. But that will be his market price, for good or bad. Whatever happens, odds are he won't be a complete bust.

And maybe that's the way we need to approach him. We don't know whether he can continue to perform at his current level, but his age and two-year history are enough to set a pretty high floor. Odds are he won't turn into Josh Hamilton or B.J. Upton.

But a full-on three-peat? I don't know if I can go there.

No matter what anyone says, you would never bet on lightning striking the same place three times. Right?

Well…

Truth is, lightning never striking the same place is a myth anyway. The Empire State Building is struck by lightning about 100 times a year.

When you stand so tall above everything else, I suppose it makes you that much easier to find.

Welcome to the 28th Edition

If you are new to the *Baseball Forecaster*, the sheer volume of information in this book may seem daunting. We don't recommend you assessing its contents over a single commute to work, particularly if you drive. The *Forecaster* needs to be savored slowly, over time, like a fine wine. Start tonight after dinner when the kids are in bed. It's okay—Breaking Bad is already over and this week's Modern Family is a repeat. The experience is best paired with a good Merlot. Find a comfortable chair. And make sure to let your significant other know that this is where to expect to find you… for the next three months.

But where to begin?

The best place to start is with the Encyclopedia of Fanalytics, which provides the foundation concepts for everything else that appears in these pages. Take a cursory read-through, stopping at any section that looks interesting. You'll keep coming back here frequently.

Then just jump in. Close your eyes, flip to a random page, and put your finger down anywhere. Oh, look—Andrew McCutchen batted .344 in the second half and his ratio of dominating to disaster weeks was an amazing 83% to 0%—a truly superstar performance for head-to-head gamers who rely on consistency.

See, you've learned something already!

What's New in 2014?

Swinging Strikes: Pitcher boxes now contain data on Swinging Strike % (denoted as SwK in the box). Based on our research (see page 60), SwK serves as a useful validation of Dom (k/9).

Better platoon split data: Both batter and pitcher player boxes now capture platoon splits using On Base Plus Slugging (OPS) rather than Batting Average, which gives a better representation of the player's skill, rather than just reflecting what might be hit-rate noise.

Updated formulas: Our batter BPV formula now uses our Statistically Scouted Speed (Spd) metric for the speed component, rather than our old Speed Index (SX). We've also made some minor tweaks to the Mayberry Method thresholds for pitchers (to reflect the increase in strikeout rates in MLB), as well as the calculation of Health Grades for pitchers.

Answers to questions, such as: Does crossing leagues affect pitchers? How do pitch counts predict future PQS scores? Do hitters really hit HR in streaks? How do pitcher skills vary between the windup and stretch? And much more.

Updates

The Baseball Forecaster page at BaseballHQ.com is at http://www.baseballhq.com/content/ron-shandlers-baseball-forecaster-2014. This is your headquarters for all information and updates regarding this book. Here you will find links to the following:

Content Updates: In a project of this magnitude, there are occasionally items that need clarification or correction. You can find them here.

Free Projections Update: As a buyer of this book, you get one free 2014 projections update. This is a set of Excel spreadsheet files that will be posted on or about March 1, 2014. Remember to keep the book handy when you visit as the access codes are hidden within these pages.

Electronic book: The complete PDF version of the *Forecaster*—plus Excel versions of most key charts—is available free to those who bought the book directly through the BaseballHQ.com website. These files will be available in January 2014 for most of you; those who have an annual standing order will receive the files just before Thanksgiving. Contact us if you do not receive information via e-mail about accessing them. Information about the e-book version can be found at the above website.

If you purchased the book through an online vendor or bookstore, or would like these files earlier, you can purchase them from us for $9.95. Call 1-800-422-7820 for more information.

Beyond the Forecaster

The *Baseball Forecaster* is just the beginning. The following companion products and services are described in more detail in the back of the book.

BaseballHQ.com is our home website. It provides regular updates to everything in this book, including daily updated statistics and projections. A subscription to HQ gets you more than 1,000 articles over the course of a year, customized tools, access to data going back over a decade, plus much more.

First Pitch Forums are a series of conferences we run all over the country, where you can meet top industry analysts and network with fellow fantasy leaguers in your area. We'll be in cities from coast to coast in February and March. Our big annual symposium at the Arizona Fall League is the first weekend in November.

The 9th edition of the *Minor League Baseball Analyst*, by Rob Gordon and Jeremy Deloney, is the minor league companion to this book, with stat boxes for 1,000-plus prospects, and more. It is available in January.

We still have copies available of *How to Value Players for Rotisserie Baseball*, Art McGee's ground-breaking book on valuation theory. They are still on closeout at 50% off.

RotoLab is the best draft software on the market and comes pre-loaded with our projections.

Even further beyond the Forecaster

Visit us on *Facebook* at http://www.facebook.com/baseballhq. "Like" the BaseballHQ page for updates, photos from events and links to other important stuff. I do not accept requests on my personal Facebook page, but I do accept requests from those on LinkedIn.

Follow us on *Twitter*. Many BaseballHQ.com analysts are tweeting @BaseballHQ as well as in their personal accounts. You can follow me @RonShandler as long as your tweets have nothing to do with Mike Trout.

Finally, I have a new thing going on at ShandlerPark.com. Check it out.

Okay. That should have gotten you through your first glass of wine. Time to pour another; you're going to need it now.

What? You forgot the cheese? Okay, not a disaster. You can hold open your place here with the corkscrew while you hit the fridge. I'll wait.

—Ron Shandler

CONSUMER ADVISORY

AN IMPORTANT MESSAGE FOR FANTASY LEAGUERS
REGARDING PROPER USAGE OF THE *BASEBALL FORECASTER*

This document is provided in compliance with authorities to outline the prospective risks and hazards possible in the event that the Baseball Forecaster is used incorrectly. Please be aware of these potentially dangerous situations and avoid them. The publisher assumes no risk related to any financial loss or stress-induced illnesses caused by ignoring the items as described below.

1. The statistical projections in this book are intended as general guidelines, not as gospel. It is highly dangerous to use the projected statistics alone, and then live and die by them. That's like going to a ballgame, being given a choice of any seat in the park, and deliberately choosing the last row in the right field corner with an obstructed view. The projections are there, you can look at them, but there are so many better places to sit.

We have to publish those numbers, but they are stagnant, inert pieces of data. This book focuses on a live forecasting process that provides the tools so that you can understand the leading indicators and draw your own conclusions. If you at least attempt your own analyses of the data, and enhance them with the player commentaries, you can paint more robust, colorful pictures of the future.

In other words...

If you bought this book purely for the projected statistics and do not intend to spend at least some time learning about the process, then you might as well just buy an $8 magazine.

2. The player commentaries in this book are written by humans, just like you. These commentaries provide an overall evaluation of performance and likely future direction, but 60-word capsules cannot capture everything. Your greatest value will be to use these as a springboard to your own analysis of the data. Odds are, if you take the time, you'll find hidden indicators that we might have missed. Forecaster veterans say that this self-guided excursion is the best part of owning the book.

3. This book does not attempt to tackle playing time. Rather than making arbitrary decisions about how roles will shake out, the focus is on performance. The playing time projections presented here are merely to help you better evaluate each player's talent. Our online pre-season projections update provides more current AB and IP expectations based on how roles are being assigned.

4. The dollar values in this book are intended solely for player-to-player comparisons. They are not driven by a finite pool of playing time—which is required for valuation systems to work properly—so they cannot be used for bid values to be used in your own draft.

There are two reasons for this:

a. The finite pool of players that will generate the finite pool of playing time will not be determined until much closer to Opening Day. And, if we are to be brutally honest, there is really no such thing as a finite pool of players.

b. Your particular league's construction will drive the values; a $10 player in a 10-team mixed league will not be the same as a $10 player in a 12-team NL-only league.

Note that book dollar values also cannot be compared to those published at BaseballHQ.com as the online values are generated by a more finite player pool.

5. Do not pass judgment on the effectiveness of this book based on the performance of a few individual players. The test, rather, is on the collective predictive value of the book's methods. Are players with better base skills more likely to produce good results than bad ones? Years of research suggest that the answer is "yes." Does that mean that every high skilled player will do well? No. But many more of them will perform well than will the average low-skilled player. You should always side with the better percentage plays, but recognize that there are factors we cannot predict. Good decisions that beget bad outcomes do not invalidate the methods.

6. If your copy of this book is not marked up and dog-eared by Draft Day, you probably did not get as much value out of it as you might have.

7. This edition of the Forecaster is not intended to provide absorbency for spills of more than 7.5 ounces.

8. This edition is not intended to provide stabilizing weight for more than 18 sheets of 20 lb. paper in winds of more than 45 mph.

9. The pages of this book are not recommended for avian waste collection. In independent laboratory studies, 87% of migratory water fowl refused to excrete on interior pages, even when coaxed.

10. This book, when rolled into a cylindrical shape, is not intended to be used as a weapon for any purpose, including but not limited to insect extermination, canine training or to influence bidding behavior at a fantasy draft.

For new readers...

Everything begins here. The information in the following pages represents the foundation that powers everything we do.

You'll learn about the underlying concepts for our unique mode of analysis. You'll find answers to long-asked questions, interesting insights into what makes players tick, and innovative applications for all this newfound knowledge.

This Encyclopedia is organized into several logical sections:

1. Fundamentals
2. Batters
3. Pitchers
4. Prospects
5. Gaming

Enough talking. Jump in.
Remember to breathe.

For veteran readers...

As we do in each edition, this year's ever-expanding Encyclopedia includes relevant research results we've published over the past year. We've added some of the essays from the Research Abstracts and Gaming Abstracts sections in the 2013 *Forecaster* as well as some other essays from BaseballHQ.com.

And we continue to mold the content to best fit how fantasy leaguers use their information. Many readers consider this their fantasy information bible.

Okay, time to jump-start the analytical process for 2014. Remember to breathe—it's always good advice.

Abbreviations

BA	Batting average	21
BABIP	Batting average on balls-in-play (also h%, H%)	22, 30
bb%	Walk rate (hitters)	21
bb/9	Opposition walks per 9 IP (also Ctl)	29
BF/G	Batters faced per game	32
BIP	Balls-in-play	22, 30
BPI	Base performance indicator	10
BPV	Base performance value	25, 32
BPX	Base performance index	25, 33
Cmd	Command ratio (K/BB)	29
ct%	Contact rate (AB-K)/AB	21
Ctl	Control ratio (also bb/9)	29
DIS%	PQS disaster rate	36
Dom	Dominance ratio (also k/9)	29
DOM%	PQS domination rate	36
ERA	Earned run average	31
Eye	Batting eye (bb/k)	21
FB%	Fly ball percentage	21
G/L/F	Ground balls, line drives, and fly balls as a percentages of total balls in play (hits and outs)	21, 30
GB%	Ground ball percentage	21
H%	Hits allowed per balls in play (pitchers)	30
h%	Hits per balls in play (batters)	22
HCt, HctX	Hard hit ball rate x contact rate	22
HHFB%	Hard hit fly balls percentage	23
hr/9	Opposition home runs per 9 IP	31
hr/f	Home runs hit (batters), or allowed (pitchers), per fly ball	23, 31
IP/G	Innings pitched per game appearance	32
k/9	Dominance ratio (also Dom)	29
LI	Leverage index	34
LD%	Line drive percentage	21
MLE	Major league equivalency	41
OB	On base average (batters)	21
OBA	Opposition batting average (pitchers)	30
OPS	On base plus slugging average	25
PA	Plate appearances (as leading indicator)	26
PQR	Pure Quality Relief	37
PQS	Pure Quality Starts	36
Pw	Linear weighted power	23
PX	Linear weighted power index	23
QC	Quality/Consistency Score	27, 36
qERA	PQS earned run average	36
R$	Rotisserie value (also 15$, 12$, etc. for specific league sizes)	51
RAR	Runs above replacement	25, 33
RC	Runs created	26
RC/G	Runs created per game	26
REff%	Reliever efficiency percentage	36
RSpd	Roto speed	25
S%	Strand rate	31
SB%	Stolen base success rate	25
SBO	Stolen base opportunity percent	25
Slg	Slugging average	23
Spd	Statistically Scouted Speed	24
SwK	Swinging strike rate	60
Sv%	Saves conversion rate	34
WHIP	Walks plus hits divided by innings pitched	30
xBA	Expected batting average	22
xERA	Expected earned run average	31
xPX	Expected skills-based power index	23

Fundamentals

What is Fanalytics?

Fanalytics is the scientific approach to fantasy baseball analysis. A contraction of "fantasy" and "analytics," fanalytic gaming might be considered a mode of play that requires a more strategic and quantitative approach to player analysis and game decisions.

The three key elements of fanalytics are:
1. **Performance analysis**
2. **Performance forecasting**
3. **Gaming analysis**

For performance analysis, we tap into the vast knowledge of the sabermetric community. Founded by Bill James, this area of study provides objective and progressive new ways to assess skill. What we do in this book is called "component skills analysis." We break down performance into its component parts, then reverse-engineer it back into the traditional measures with which we are more familiar.

Our forecasting methodology is one part science and one part art. We start with a computer-generated baseline for each player. We then make subjective adjustments based on a variety of factors, such as discrepancies in skills indicators and historical guidelines gleaned from more than 20 years of research. We don't rely on a rigid model; our method forces us to get our hands dirty.

You might say that our brand of forecasting is more about finding logical journeys than blind destinations.

Gaming analysis is an integrated approach designed to help us win our fantasy leagues. It takes the knowledge gleaned from the first two elements and adds the strategic and tactical aspect of each specific fantasy game format.

Definitions

Base Performance Indicator (BPI): A statistical formula that measures an isolated aspect of a player's situation-independent raw skill or a gauge that helps capture the effects that random chance has on skill.

Leading Indicator: A statistical formula that can be used to project potential future performance.

Noise: Irrelevant or meaningless pieces of information that can distort the results of an analysis. In news, this is opinion or rumor that can invalidate valuable information. In forecasting, these are unimportant elements of statistical data that can artificially inflate or depress a set of numbers.

Situation Independent: Describing performance that is separate from the context of team, ballpark, or other outside variables. Strikeouts and walks, as they are unaffected by the performance of a batter's team, are often considered situation independent stats. Conversely, RBIs are situation dependent because individual performance varies greatly by the performance of other batters on the team (you can't drive in runs if there is nobody on base). Situation independent gauges are important for us to be able to isolate and judge performance on its own merits.

Soft Skills: BPIs with levels below established minimums for acceptable performance.

Surface Stats: Traditional gauges that the mainstream media uses to measure performance. Stats like batting average, wins, and ERA only touch the surface of a player's skill and often distort the truth. To uncover a player's true skill, you have to look at component skills statistics.

Component Skills Analysis

Familiar gauges like HR and ERA have long been used to measure skill. In fact, these gauges only measure the outcome of an individual event, or series of events. They represent statistical output. They are "surface stats."

Raw skill is the talent beneath the stats, the individual elements of a player's makeup. Players use these skills to create the individual events, or components, that we record using measures like HR and ERA. Our approach:

1. It's not about batting average; it's about seeing the ball and making contact. We target hitters based on elements such as their batting eye (walks to strikeouts ratio), how often they make contact and the type of contact they make. We then combine these components into an "expected batting average." By comparing each hitter's actual BA to how he should be performing, we can draw conclusions about the future.

2. It's not about home runs; it's about power. From the perspective of a round bat meeting a round ball, it may be only a fraction of an inch at the point of contact that makes the difference between a HR or a long foul ball. When a ball is hit safely, often it is only a few inches that separate a HR from a double. We tend to neglect these facts in our analyses, although the outcomes—the doubles, triples, long fly balls—may be no less a measure of that batter's raw power skill. We must incorporate all these components to paint a complete picture.

3. It's not about ERA; it's about getting the ball over the plate and keeping it in the park. Forget ERA. You want to draft pitchers who walk few batters (Control), strike out many (Dominance) and succeed at both in tandem (Command). You also want pitchers who keep the ball on the ground (because home runs are bad). All of this translates into an "expected ERA" that you can use to compare to a pitcher's actual performance.

4. It's never about wins. For pitchers, winning ballgames is less about skill than it is about offensive support. As such, projecting wins is a very high-risk exercise and valuing hurlers based on their win history is dangerous. Target skill; wins will come.

5. It's not about saves; it's about opportunity first and skills second. While the highest-skilled pitchers have the best potential to succeed as closers, they still have to be given the ball with the game on the line in the 9th inning, and that is a decision left to others. Over the past 10 years, about 40% of relievers drafted for saves failed to hold the role for the entire season. The lesson: Don't take chances on draft day. There will always be saves in the free agent pool.

Accounting for "luck"

Luck has been used as a catch-all term to describe random chance. When we use the term here, we're talking about unexplained variances that shape the statistics. While these variances may be random, they are also often measurable and projectable.

To get a better read on "luck," we use formulas that capture the external variability of the data.

Through our research and the work of others, we have learned that when raw skill is separated from statistical output, what's remaining is often unexplained variance. The aggregate totals of many of these variances, for all players, is often a constant. For instance, while a pitcher's ERA might fluctuate, the rate at which his opposition's batted balls fall for hits will tend towards 30%. Large variances can be expected to regress towards 30%.

Why is all this important? Analysts complain about the lack of predictability of many traditional statistical gauges. The reason they find it difficult is that they are trying to project performance using gauges that are loaded with external noise. Raw skills gauges are more pure and follow better defined trends during a player's career. Then, as we get a better handle on the variances—explained and unexplained—we can construct a complete picture of what a player's statistics really mean.

Baseball Forecasting

Forecasting in perspective

Forecasts. Projections. Predictions. Prognostications. The crystal ball aura of this process conceals the fact it is a process. We might define it as "the systematic process of determining likely end results." At its core, it's scientific.

However, the *outcomes* of forecasted events are what is most closely scrutinized, and are used to judge the success or failure of the forecast. That said, as long as the process is sound, the forecast has done the best job it can do. *In the end, forecasting is about analysis, not prophecy.*

Baseball performance forecasting is inherently a high-risk exercise with a very modest accuracy rate. This is because the process involves not only statistics, but also unscientific elements, from random chance to human volatility. And even from within the statistical aspect there are multiple elements that need to be evaluated, from skill to playing time to a host of external variables.

Every system is comprised of the same core elements:

- Players will tend to perform within the framework of past history and/or trends.
- Skills will develop and decline according to age.
- Statistics will be shaped by a player's health, expected role and venue.

While all systems are built from these same elements, they also are constrained by the same limitations. We are all still trying to project a bunch of human beings, each one...

- with his own individual skill set
- with his own rate of growth and decline
- with his own ability to resist and recover from injury
- limited to opportunities determined by other people
- generating a group of statistics largely affected by external noise.

Research has shown that the best accuracy rate that can be attained by any system is about 70%. In fact, a simple system that uses three-year averages adjusted for age ("Marcel") can attain

a success rate of 65%. This means all the advanced systems are fighting for occupation of the remaining 5%.

But there is a bigger question… *what exactly are we measuring?* When we search for accuracy, what does that mean? In fact, any quest for accuracy is going to run into a brick wall of paradoxes:

- If a slugging average projection is dead on, but the player hits 10 fewer HRs than expected (and likely, 20 more doubles), is that a success or a failure?
- If a projection of hits and walks allowed by a pitcher is on the mark, but the bullpen and defense implodes, and inflates his ERA by a run, is that a success or a failure?
- If the projection of a speedster's rate of stolen base success is perfect, but his team replaces the manager with one that doesn't run, and the player ends up with half as many SBs as expected, is that a success or a failure?
- If a batter is traded to a hitters' ballpark and all the touts project an increase in production, but he posts a statistical line exactly what would have been projected had he not been traded to that park, is that a success or a failure?
- If the projection for a bullpen closer's ERA, WHIP and peripheral numbers is perfect, but he saves 20 games instead of 40 because the GM decided to bring in a high-priced free agent at the trading deadline, is that a success or a failure?
- If a player is projected to hit .272 in 550 AB and only hits .249, is that a success or failure? Most will say "failure." But wait a minute! The real difference is only two hits per month. That shortfall of 23 points in batting average is because a fielder might have made a spectacular play, or a screaming liner might have been hit right at someone, or a long shot to the outfield might have been held up by the wind... once every 14 games. Does that constitute "failure"?

Even if we were to isolate a single statistic that measures "overall performance" and run our accuracy tests on it, the results will still be inconclusive.

According to OPS, these players are virtually identical:

BATTER	HR	RBI	SB	BA	OBA	SLG	OPS
Infante,O	10	51	5	.318	.347	.450	.797
Venable,W	22	53	22	.268	.310	.484	.794
Lucroy,J	18	82	9	.280	.339	.455	.794
Ibanez,R	29	65	0	.242	.306	.487	.793

If I projected Venable-caliber stats and ended up with Omar Infante's numbers, I'd hardly call that an accurate projection, especially if my fantasy team was in dire need of power and speed.

According to Roto dollars, these players are also dead-on:

BATTER	HR	RBI	Runs	SB	BA	R$
Segura,J	12	49	74	44	.294	$25
Encarnacion,E	36	104	90	7	.272	$25
Carpenter,M	11	78	126	3	.318	$25
Soriano,A	34	101	84	18	.255	$25

It's not so simple for someone to claim they have accurate projections. And so, it is best to focus on the bigger picture, especially when it comes to winning at fantasy baseball.

More on this: "The Great Myths of Projective Accuracy"

http://www.baseballhq.com/great-myths-projective-accuracy

Baseball Forecaster's forecasting process

We are all about component skills. Our approach is to assemble these evaluators in such a way that they can be used to validate our observations, analyze their relevance and project a likely future direction.

In a perfect world, if a player's raw skills improve, then so should his surface stats. If his skills decline, then his stats should follow as well. But, sometimes a player's skill indicators increase while his surface stats decline. These variances may be due to a variety of factors.

Our forecasting process is based on the expectation that events tend to move towards universal order. Surface stats will eventually approach their skill levels. Unexplained variances will regress to a mean. And from this, we can identify players whose performance may potentially change.

For most of us, this process begins with the previous year's numbers. Last season provides us with a point of reference, so it's a natural way to begin the process of looking at the future. Component skills analysis allows us to validate those numbers. A batter with few HRs but a high linear weighted power level has a good probability of improving his future HR output. A pitcher whose ERA was poor while his command ratio was solid is a good bet for ERA improvement.

Of course, these leading indicators do not always follow the rules. There are more shades of grey than blacks and whites. When indicators are in conflict—for instance, a pitcher who is displaying both a rising strikeout rate and a rising walk rate—then we have to find ways to sort out what these indicators might be saying.

It is often helpful to look at leading indicators in a hierarchy, of sorts. In fact, a hierarchy of the most important pitching base performance indicators might look like this: Command (k/bb), Dominance (k/9), Control (bb/9) and GB/FB rate. For batters, contact rate might top the list, followed by power, walk rate and speed.

Assimilating additional research

Once we've painted the statistical picture of a player's potential, we then use additional criteria and research results to help us add some color to the analysis. These other criteria include the player's health, age, changes in role, ballpark and a variety of other factors. We also use the research results described in the following pages. This research looks at things like traditional periods of peak performance and breakout profiles.

The final element of the process is assimilating the news into the forecast. This is the element that many fantasy leaguers tend to rely on most since it is the most accessible. However, it is also the element that provides the most noise. Players, management and the media have absolute control over what we are allowed to know. Factors such as hidden injuries, messy divorces and clubhouse unrest are routinely kept from us, while we are fed red herrings and media spam. *We will never know the entire truth.*

Quite often, all you are reading is just other people's opinions... a manager who believes that a player has what it takes to be a regular or a team physician whose diagnosis is that a player is healthy enough to play. These words from experts have some element of truth, but cannot be wholly relied upon to provide an accurate expectation of future events. As such, it is often helpful to develop an appropriate cynicism for what you read.

For instance, if a player is struggling for no apparent reason and there are denials about health issues, don't dismiss the possibility that an injury does exist. There are often motives for such news to be withheld from the public.

And so, as long as we do not know all the facts, we cannot dismiss the possibility that any one fact is true, no matter how often the media assures it, deplores it, or ignores it. Don't believe everything you read; use your own judgment. If your observations conflict with what is being reported, that's powerful insight that should not be ignored.

Also remember that nothing lasts forever in major league baseball. *Reality is fluid.* One decision begets a series of events that lead to other decisions. Any reported action can easily be reversed based on subsequent events. My favorite examples are announcements of a team's new bullpen closer. Those are about the shortest realities known to man.

We need the media to provide us with context for our analyses, and the real news they provide is valuable intelligence. But separating the news from the noise is difficult. In most cases, the only thing you can trust is how that player actually performs.

Embracing imprecision

Precision in baseball prognosticating is a fool's quest. There are far too many unexpected variables and noise that can render our projections useless. The truth is, the best we can ever hope for is to accurately forecast general tendencies and percentage plays.

However, even when you follow an 80% percentage play, for instance, you will still lose 20% of the time. That 20% is what skeptics use as justification to dismiss prognosticators; they conveniently ignore the more prevalent 80%. The paradox, of course, is that fantasy league titles are often won or lost by those exceptions. Still, long-term success dictates that you always chase the 80% and accept the fact that you will be wrong 20% of the time. Or, whatever that percentage play happens to be.

For fantasy purposes, playing the percentages can take on an even less precise spin. The best projections are often the ones that are just far enough away from the field of expectation to alter decision-making. In other words, it doesn't matter if I project Player X to bat .320 and he only bats .295; it matters that I project .320 and everyone else projects .280. Those who follow my less-accurate projection will go the extra dollar to acquire him in their draft.

Or, perhaps we should evaluate the projections based upon their intrinsic value. For instance, coming into 2013, would it have been more important for me to tell you that Miguel Cabrera was going to hit 40 HRs or that Chris Davis would hit 35 HRs? By season's end, the Cabrera projection would have been more accurate, but the Davis projection—even though it was off by 18 HRs—would have been far more *valuable*. The Davis projection might have persuaded you to go an extra buck on Draft Day, yielding far more profit.

And that has to be enough. Any tout who projects a player's statistics dead-on will have just been lucky with his dart throws that day.

Perpetuity

Forecasting is not an exercise that produces a single set of numbers. It is dynamic, cyclical and ongoing. Conditions are constantly changing and we must react to those changes by adjusting our expectations. A pre-season projection is just a snapshot in time. Once the first batter steps to the plate on Opening Day, that projection has become obsolete. Its value is merely to provide a starting point, a baseline for what is about to occur.

During the season, if a projection appears to have been invalidated by current performance, the process continues. It is then that we need to ask... What went wrong? What conditions have changed? In fact, has *anything* changed? We need to analyze the situation and revise our expectation, if necessary. This process must be ongoing.

When good projections go bad

We cannot predict the future; all we can do is provide a sound process for constructing a "most likely expectation for future performance." All we can control is the process.

As such, there is a limit to how much blame we can shoulder for each year's misses. If we've captured as much information as is available, used the best methodology and analyzed the results correctly, that's about the best we can do. We simply can't control outcomes.

What we *can* do is analyze all the misses to see *why* they occurred. This is always a valuable exercise each year. It puts a proper focus on the variables that were out of our control as well as providing perspective on those players that we might have done a better job with.

In general, we can organize our forecasting misses into several categories. To demonstrate, here are the players whose 2013 Rotisserie earnings varied from projections by at least $10:

The performances that exceeded expectation

Development beyond the growth trend: These are young players for whom we knew there was skill. Some of them were prized prospects in the past who have taken their time ascending the growth curve. Others were a surprise only because their performance spike arrived sooner than anyone anticipated... Domonic Brown, Andrew Cashner, Patrick Corbin, Jose Fernandez, Paul Goldschmidt, Matt Harvey, Jason Kipnis, Justin Masterson, Yasiel Puig, Hyun-Jin Ryu, Jean Segura, Julio Teheran.

Skilled players who just had big years: We knew these guys were good too; we just didn't anticipate they'd be this good... Michael Cuddyer, Chris Davis, Anibal Sanchez.

Unexpected health: We knew these players had the goods; we just didn't know whether they'd be healthy or would stay healthy all year... Jhoulys Chacin, David Ortiz.

Unexpected playing time: These players had the skills—and may have even displayed them at some time in the past—but had questionable playing time potential coming into this season. Some benefited from another player's injury, a rookie who didn't pan out or leveraged a short streak into a regular gig... Matt Carpenter, Chris Johnson, Daniel Nava.

Unexpected return to form: These players had the skills, having displayed them at some point in the past. But those skills

had been M.I.A. long enough that we began to doubt that they'd ever return; our projections model got tired of waiting. Or those previous skills displays were so inconsistent that projecting an "up year" would have been a shot in the dark; our projections model got tired of guessing. Yes, "once you display a skill, you own it" but still... Marlon Byrd, Raul Ibanez, Francisco Liriano, Nate McLouth, Ricky Nolasco, Hunter Pence, Ervin Santana, Alfonso Soriano.

Unexpected role: This category is reserved for 2013's surprise closers. There are always some every year, relievers who are on nobody's radar for saves and are suddenly thrust into the role with great success (some did not clear the $10 hurdle but all amassed at least 10 saves)... Heath Bell, Joaquin Benoit, Rex Brothers, Daniel Farquhar, Ernesto Frieri, Kevin Gregg, LaTroy Hawkins, Jim Henderson, Casey Janssen, Mark Melancon, Edward Mujica, Koji Uehara, Brad Ziegler.

The anti-regressions: After 2012, some players had regression written all over them. Sometimes it was statistical regression; sometimes a change of venue should have been foreboding. In the end, they somehow performed just like they did in 2012, or better... Bartolo Colon and Mike Trout. Two players who couldn't be more dissimilar, right?

Celebrate and claim we're geniuses: How these players put up the numbers they did is a mystery, but fantasy owners will likely chalk it up to their own superior scouting skills as they count their winnings. The truth is, who knows? However, the odds of a comparable follow-up for these players—particularly those with soft peripherals—will be small: Josh Donaldson's unexpected follow-up, Scott Feldman's sudden skills-supported uptick, Hisashi Iwakuma's excessive development at age 32, and Travis Wood's perfect trifecta of low hit rate, low hr/f rate and high strand rate.

The performances that fell short of expectation

The Biogenesis Busted: Let's start with this interesting group. There were only four players of importance who lost significant playing time to suspension. Ryan Braun was projected to earn $43 but returned only $4 this year. However, injury and underperformance were equal contributors to his disastrous season. His $39 loss was the largest of any player in 2013, but interestingly enough, he was the only one of the suspendees to cost his teams at least $10 in lost earnings.

Both Nelson Cruz and Jhonny Peralta earned about what was projected of them despite each missing 50 games. And Everth Cabrera actually earned more than projected despite missing all that time.

The DL denizens: These are players who got hurt, may not have returned fully healthy, or may have never been fully healthy (whether they'd admit it or not)... Yonder Alonso, Brett Anderson, Lance Berkman, Rafael Betancourt, Melky Cabrera, Trevor Cahill, Carl Crawford, Johnny Cueto, Curtis Granderson, Joel Hanrahan, Bryce Harper, Chase Headley, Jason Heyward, Aaron Hill, Tim Hudson, John Jaso, Derek Jeter, Josh Johnson, Matt Kemp, Jason Kubel, Ryan Ludwick, Cameron Maybin, Brandon Morrow, Michael Morse, Brett Myers, Alexi Ogando, Angel Pagan, David Price, Albert Pujols, J.J. Putz, Aramis Ramirez, Jose Reyes, Ben

Revere, Carlos Ruiz, Mark Teixeira, Jered Weaver, Rickie Weeks, Josh Willingham and Kevin Youkilis.

(Some of these players seemed to be putting up sub-par numbers before they actually hit the DL. Many were likely playing through the hurt before breaking down.)

Note that there are 39 players on this list. These were the DL denizens who lost at least $10 of value. There were dozens more that lost less, only because they started out as lesser-valued players. In all of the Top 300 coming into the season, 137 players lost time to the DL (and another 16 to demotion and suspension). The 51% attrition matched the record losses of 2009. It was not a particularly healthy year.

Accelerated skills erosion: These are players who we knew were on the downside of their careers or had soft peripherals but who we did not think would plummet so quickly. In some cases, there were injuries involved, but all in all, 2013 might be the beginning of the end for some of these guys... Michael Bourn, R.A. Dickey, Ryan Doumit, Garrett Jones, Paul Konerko, Juan Pierre, Jimmy Rollins.

Inflated expectations: Here are players who we really should not have expected much more than what they produced. Some had short or spotty track records, others had soft peripherals coming into 2013, and still others were inflated by media hype. Yes, for some of these, it was "What the heck was I thinking?" For others, we've almost come to expect players to ascend the growth curve faster these days. (You're 23 and you haven't broken out yet?? What's the problem?) The bottom line is that player performance trends simply don't progress or regress in a straight line; still, the BPI trends were intriguing enough to take a leap of faith. We were wrong... Dustin Ackley, Billy Butler, Starlin Castro, Yoenis Cespedes, Ike Davis, Andy Dirks, Alcides Escobar, Jeff Francoeur, David Freese, Aaron Hicks, Jeff Keppinger, Brett Lawrie, Kris Medlen, Will Middlebrooks, Tommy Milone, Jesus Montero, Mike Moustakas, Fernando Rodney, Josh Rutledge, Jeff Samardzija, Travis Snider, Giancarlo Stanton.

Misplaced regression: Sometimes, we're so bullish on a player that we ignore the potential for regression within the bounds of random variance. For instance, look close enough at the BPI scans of Matt Cain, Cole Hamels and Justin Verlander and you'll see that they were essentially the same pitchers this year as in 2012. There may have been a few down stretches, or some random swings of hit/strand rates, but all three arms should have little problem bouncing back in 2014. Little consolation for their 2013 owners, though.

Unexpected loss of role: This category is usually composed of closers who lost their job, sometimes through no fault of their own... John Axford, Mitchell Boggs, Jonathan Broxton, Joel Hanrahan, Brandon League, Carlos Marmol, Jason Motte, J.J. Putz, Tom Wilhelmson.

Throw our hands up and yell at the TV: These are the players for whom there is little explanation for what happened. We can speculate that they hid an injury, went off of PEDs, or just didn't have their head on right in 2013. For some, it was just the turn of an unlucky card this year: Yovani Gallardo and his possibly lingering hamstring, Jeremy Hellickson and his best skills season

of the past three, Ian Kennedy unfazed by PETCO, Miguel Montero making for a dual-Montero bust, David Murphy and his plummeting hit rate, C.C. Sabathia hitting the Girth + Workoad Wall and B.J. Upton's Dunn-esque nightmare.

About fantasy baseball touts

As a group, there is a strong tendency for all pundits to provide numbers that are publicly palatable, often at the expense of realism. That's because committing to either end of the range of expectation poses a high risk. Few touts will put their credibility on the line like that, even though we all know that those outliers are inevitable. Among our projections, you will find few .350 hitters and 70-steal speedsters. *Someone* is going to post a sub-2.50 ERA next year, but damned if any of us will commit to that. So we take an easier road. We'll hedge our numbers or split the difference between two equally possible outcomes.

In the world of prognosticating, this is called the *comfort zone.* This represents the outer tolerances for the public acceptability of a set of numbers. In most circumstances, even if the evidence is outstanding, prognosticators will not stray from within the comfort zone.

As for this book, occasionally we do commit to outlying numbers when we feel the data support it. But on the whole, most of the numbers here can be nearly as cowardly as everyone else's. We get around this by providing "color" to the projections in the capsule commentaries. That is where you will find the players whose projection has the best potential to stray beyond the limits of the comfort zone.

As analyst John Burnson once wrote: "The issue is not the success rate for one player, but the success rate for all players. No system is 100% reliable, and in trying to capture the outliers, you weaken the middle and thereby lose more predictive pull than you gain. At some level, everyone is an exception!"

Formula for consistent success

Anyone can win a league in any given season. Winning once proves very little, especially in redraft leagues. True success has to be defined as the ability to win consistently. It is a feat in itself to reach the mountaintop, but the battle isn't truly won unless you can stay atop that peak while others keep trying to knock you off.

What does it take to win that battle? We surveyed 12 of the most prolific fantasy champions in national experts league play. Here is how they rated six variables:

	Percent ranked			
	1-2	3-4	5-6	Score
Better in-draft strategy/tactics	77%	15%	7%	5.00
Better sense of player value	46%	46%	7%	4.15
Better luck	46%	23%	31%	3.85
Better grasp of contextual elements that affect players	31%	38%	31%	3.62
Better in-season roster management	31%	38%	31%	3.54
Better player projections	12%	31%	54%	2.62

Validating Performance

Performance validation criteria

The following is a set of support variables that helps determine whether a player's statistical output is an accurate reflection of his skills. From this we can validate or refute stats that vary from expectation, essentially asking, is this performance "fact or fluke?"

1. **Age:** Is the player at the stage of development when we might expect a change in performance?

2. **Health:** Is he coming off an injury, reconditioned and healthy for the first time in years, or a habitual resident of the disabled list?

3. **Minor league performance:** Has he shown the potential for greater things at some level of the minors? Or does his minor league history show a poor skill set that might indicate a lower ceiling?

4. **Historical trends:** Have his skill levels over time been on an upswing or downswing?

5. **Component skills indicators:** Looking beyond batting averages and ERAs, what do his support ratios look like?

6. **Ballpark, team, league:** Pitchers going to Texas will see their ERA spike. Pitchers going to PETCO Park will see their ERA improve.

7. **Team performance:** Has a player's performance been affected by overall team chemistry or the environment fostered by a winning or losing club?

8. **Batting stance, pitching style:** Has a change in performance been due to a mechanical adjustment?

9. **Usage pattern, lineup position, role:** Has a change in RBI opportunities been a result of moving further up or down in the batting order? Has pitching effectiveness been impacted by moving from the bullpen to the rotation?

10. **Coaching effects:** Has the coaching staff changed the way a player approaches his conditioning, or how he approaches the game itself?

11. **Off-season activity:** Has the player spent the winter frequenting workout rooms or banquet tables?

12. **Personal factors:** Has the player undergone a family crisis? Experienced spiritual rebirth? Given up red meat? Taken up testosterone?

Skills ownership

Once a player displays a skill, he owns it. That display could occur at any time—earlier in his career, back in the minors, or even in winter ball play. And while that skill may lie dormant after its initial display, the potential is always there for him to tap back into that skill at some point, barring injury or age. That dormant skill can reappear at any time given the right set of circumstances.

Caveats:

1. The initial display of skill must have occurred over an extended period of time. An isolated 1-hit shut-out in Single-A ball amidst a 5.00 ERA season is not enough. The shorter the display of skill in the past, the more likely it can be attributed to random chance. The longer the display, the more likely that any re-emergence is for real.

2. If a player has been suspected of using performance enhancing drugs at any time, all bets are off.

Corollaries:

1. Once a player displays a vulnerability or skills deficiency, he owns that as well. That vulnerability could be an old injury problem, an inability to hit breaking pitches, or just a tendency to go into prolonged slumps.

2. The probability of a player correcting a skills deficiency declines with each year that deficiency exists.

Normal Production Variance *(Patrick Davitt)*

Even if we have a perfectly accurate understanding of a player's "normal" performance level, his actual performance can and does vary widely over any particular 150-game span—including the 150-game span we call "a season." A .300 career hitter can perform in a range of .250-.350, a 40-HR hitter from 30-50, and a 3.70/1.15 pitcher from 2.60/0.95 to 6.00/1.55. And all of these results must be considered "normal."

Contract year performance *(Tom Mullooly)*

There is a contention that players step up their game when they are playing for a contract. Research looked at contract year players and their performance during that year as compared to career levels. Of the batters and pitchers studied, 53% of the batters performed as if they were on a salary drive, while only 15% of the pitchers exhibited some level of contract year behavior.

How do players fare *after* signing a large contract (minimum $4M per year)? Research from 2005-2008 revealed that only 30% of pitchers and 22% of hitters exhibited an increase of more than 15% in BPV after signing a large deal either with their new team, or re-signing with the previous team. But nearly half of the pitchers (49%) and nearly half of the hitters (47%) saw a drop in BPV of more than 15% in the year after signing.

Risk management and reliability grades

Forecasts are constructed with the best data available, but there are factors that can impact the variability. One way we manage this risk is to assign each player Reliability Grades. The more certainty we see in a data set, the higher the reliability grades assigned to that player. The following variables are evaluated:

Health: Players with a history of staying healthy and off the DL are valuable to own. Unfortunately, while the ability to stay healthy can be considered skill, it is not very projectable. We can track the number of days spent on the disabled list and draw rough conclusions. The grades in the player boxes also include an adjustment for older players, who have a higher likelihood of getting hurt. That is the only forward-looking element of the grade.

"A" level players would have accumulated fewer than 30 days on the major league DL over the past five years. "F" grades go to those who've spent more than 120 days on the DL. Recent DL stays are given a heavier weight in the calculation.

Playing Time and Experience (PT/Exp): The greater the pool of MLB history to draw from, the greater our ability to construct a viable forecast. Length of service—and consistent service—is important. So players who bounce up and down from the majors to the minors are higher risk players. And rookies are all high risk.

For batters, we simply track plate appearances. Major league PAs have greater weight than minor league PAs. "A" level players would have averaged at least 550 major league PAs per year over the past three years. "F" graded players averaged fewer than 250 major league PA per year.

For pitchers, workload can be a double-edged sword. On one hand, small IP samples are deceptive in providing a read on a pitcher's true potential. Even a consistent 65-inning reliever can be considered higher risk since it would take just one bad outing to skew an entire season's work.

On the flipside, high workload levels also need to be monitored, especially in the formative years of a pitcher's career. Exceeding those levels elevates the risk of injury, burnout, or breakdown. So, tracking workload must be done within a range of innings. The grades capture this.

Consistency: Consistent performers are easier to project and garner higher reliability grades. Players that mix mediocrity with occasional flashes of brilliance or badness generate higher risk projections. Even those who exhibit a consistent upward or downward trend cannot be considered truly consistent as we do not know whether those trends will continue. Typically, they don't.

"A" level players are those whose runs created per game level (xERA for pitchers) has fluctuated by less than half a run during each of the past three years. "F" grades go to those whose RC/G or xERA has fluctuated by two runs or more.

Remember that these grades have nothing to do with quality of performance; they strictly refer to confidence in our expectations. So a grade of AAA for Kyle Kendrick, for instance, only means that there is a high probability he will perform as poorly as we've projected.

Reliability and age

Peak batting reliability occurs at ages 29 and 30, followed by a minor decline for four years. So, to draft the most reliable batters, and maximize the odds of returning at least par value on your investments, you should target the age range of 28-34.

The most reliable age range for pitchers is 29-34. While we are forever looking for "sleepers" and hot prospects, it is very risky to draft any pitcher under 27 or over 35.

Using 3-year trends as leading indicators *(Ed DeCaria)*

It is almost irresistibly tempting to look at three numbers moving in one direction and expect that the fourth will continue that progression. However, for both hitters and pitchers riding positive trends over any consecutive three-year period, not only do most players not continue their positive trend into a fourth year, their Year 4 performance usually regresses significantly. This is true for every metric tested (whether related to playing time, batting skills, pitching skills, running skills, luck indicators, or valuation). Negative trends show similar reversals, but tend to be more "sticky," meaning that rebounds are neither as frequent nor as strong as positive trend regressions. Challenge any analysis that hints at a player's demise coming off of a negative trend or that suggests an imminent breakout following a positive trend; more often than not, such predictions do not pan out.

Health Analysis
Disabled list statistics

Year	#Players	3yr Avg	DL Days	3yr Avg
2002	337	-	23,724	-
2003	351	-	22,118	-
2004	382	357	25,423	23,755
2005	356	363	24,016	23,852
2006	347	362	22,472	23,970
2007	404	369	28,524	25,004
2008	422	391	28,187	26,394
2009	408	411	26,252	27,654
2010	393	408	22,911	25,783
2011	422	408	25,610	24,924
2012	409	408	30,408	27,038
2013	442	419	29,551	28,523

D.L. days as a leading indicator *(Bill Macey)*
Players who are injured in one year are likely to be injured in a subsequent year:

% DL batters in Year 1 who are also DL in year 2	38%
Under age 30	36%
Age 30 and older	41%
% DL batters in Year 1 and 2 who are also DL in year 3	54%
% DL pitchers in Year 1 who are also DL in year 2	43%
Under age 30	45%
Age 30 and older	41%
% DL pitchers in Yr 1 and 2 who are also DL in year 3	41%

Previously injured players also tend to spend a longer time on the DL. The average number of days on the DL was 51 days for batters and 73 days for pitchers. For the subset of these players who get hurt again the following year, the average number of days on the DL was 58 days for batters and 88 days for pitchers.

Spring training spin *(Dave Adler)*
Spring training sound bites raise expectations among fantasy leaguers, but how much of that "news" is really "noise"? Thanks to a summary listed at RotoAuthority.com, we were able to compile the stats for 2009. Verdict: Noise.

BATTERS	No.	IMPROVED	DECLINED
Weight change	30	33%	30%
Fitness program	3	0%	67%
Eye surgery	6	50%	33%
Plans more SB	6	17%	33%
PITCHERS	**No.**	**IMPROVED**	**DECLINED**
Weight change	18	44%	44%
Fitness program	4	50%	50%
Eye surgery	2	0%	50%
New pitch	5	60%	40%

In-Season Analysis
April performance as a leading indicator
We isolated all players who earned at least $10 more or $10 less than we had projected in March. Then we looked at the April stats of these players to see if we could have picked out the $10 outliers after just one month.

	Identifiable in April
Earned $10+ more than projected	
BATTERS	39%
PITCHERS	44%
Earned -$10 less than projected	
BATTERS	56%
PITCHERS	74%

Nearly three out of every four pitchers who earned at least $10 less than projected also struggled in April. For all the other surprises—batters or pitchers—April was not a strong leading indicator. Another look:

	Pct.
Batters who finished +$25	45%
Pitchers who finished +$20	44%
Batters who finished under $0	60%
Pitchers who finished under -$5	78%

April surgers are less than a 50/50 proposition to maintain that level all season. Those who finished April at the bottom of the roto rankings were more likely to continue struggling, especially pitchers. In fact, of those pitchers who finished April with a value *under -$10*, 91% finished the season in the red. Holes are tough to dig out of.

The weight of early season numbers

Early season strugglers who surge later in the year get no respect because they have to live with the weight of their early numbers all season long. Conversely, quick starters who fade late get far more accolades than they deserve.

For instance, take Ubaldo Jimenez's month-by-month ERAs. Based solely on his final 3.30 ERA, the perception is that he had a solid rebound season. Reality is different. If not for a truly horrible April, 2013 might have been considered Jimenez's career year:

Month	ERA	Cum ERA
April	7.13	7.13
May	4.23	5.57
June	3.09	4.63
July	2.83	4.17
August	3.10	3.95
Sept-Oct	1.09	3.30

Seasonal trends in hitting and pitching *(Bob Berger)*

A study of monthly trends in traditional statistical categories found:

- Batting average, HR/game and RBI/game rise from April through August, then fall in September/October.
- Stolen bases decline in July and August before rebounding in September.
- ERA tends to get worse in July/August and improve in September.
- WHIP gets worse in July/August.
- K/9 rate improves all season.

The bold statement that hitters perform better in warmer weather seems to be true broadly.

Courtship period

Any time a player is put into a new situation, he enters into what we might call a courtship period. This period might occur when a player switches leagues, or switches teams. It could be the first few games when a minor leaguer is called up. It could occur when a reliever moves into the rotation, or when a lead-off hitter is moved to another spot in the lineup. There is a team-wide courtship period when a manager is replaced. Any external situation that could affect a player's performance sets off a new decision point in evaluating that performance.

During this period, it is difficult to get a true read on how a player is going to ultimately perform. He is adjusting to the new situation. Things could be volatile during this time. For instance, a role change that doesn't work could spur other moves. A rookie hurler might buy himself a few extra starts with a solid debut, even if he has questionable skills.

It is best not to make a decision on a player who is going through a courtship period. Wait until his stats stabilize. Don't cut a struggling pitcher in his first few starts after a managerial change. Don't pick up a hitter who smacks a pair of HRs in his first game after having been traded. Unless, of course, talent and track record say otherwise.

Half-season fallacies

A popular exercise at the midpoint of each season is to analyze those players who are consistent first half to second half surgers or faders. There are several fallacies with this analytical approach.

1. Half-season consistency is rare. There are very few players who show consistent changes in performance from one half of the season to the other.

Research results from a three-year study conducted in the late-1990s: The test groups... batters with min. 300 AB full season, 150 AB first half, and pitchers with min. 100 IP full season, 50 IP first half. Of those groups (size noted):

3-year consistency in	BATTERS (98)	PITCHERS (42)
1 stat category	40%	57%
2 stat categories	18%	21%
3 stat categories	3%	5%

When the analysis was stretched to a fourth year, only 1% of all players showed consistency in even one category.

2. Analysts often use false indicators. Situational statistics provide us with tools that can be misused. Several sources offer up 3- and 5-year stats intended to paint a picture of a long-term performance. Some analysts look at a player's half-season swing over that multi-year period and conclude that he is demonstrating consistent performance.

The fallacy is that those multi-year scans may not show any consistency at all. They are not individual season performances but *aggregate* performances. A player whose 5-year batting average shows a 15-point rise in the 2nd half, for instance, may actually have experienced a BA decline in several of those years, a fact that might have been offset by a huge BA rise in one of the years.

3. It's arbitrary. The season's midpoint is an arbitrary delineator of performance swings. Some players are slow starters and might be more appropriately evaluated as pre-May 1 and post-May 1. Others bring their game up a notch with a pennant chase and might see a performance swing with August 15 as the cut-off. Each player has his own individual tendency, if, in fact, one exists at all. There's nothing magical about mid-season as the break point, and certainly not over a multi-year period.

Half-season tendencies

Despite the above, it stands to reason logically that there might be some underlying tendencies on a more global scale, first half to second half. In fact, one would think that the player population as a whole might decline in performance as the season drones on. There are many variables that might contribute to a player wearing down—workload, weather, boredom—and the longer a player is on the field, the higher the likelihood that he is going to get hurt. A recent 5-year study uncovered the following tendencies:

Batting

Overall, batting skills held up pretty well, half to half. There was a 5% erosion of playing time, likely due, in part, to September roster expansion.

Power: First half power studs (20 HRs in 1H) saw a 10% drop-off in the second half. 34% of first half 20+ HR hitters hit 15 or fewer in the second half and only 27% were able to improve on their first half output.

Speed: Second half speed waned as well. About 26% of the 20+ SB speedsters stole *at least 10 fewer bases* in the second half. Only 26% increased their second half SB output at all.

Batting average: 60% of first half .300 hitters failed to hit .300 in the second half. Only 20% showed any second half improvement at all. As for 1H strugglers, managers tended to stick with their full-timers despite poor starts. Nearly one in five of the sub-.250 1H hitters managed to hit *more than* .300 in the second half.

Pitching

Overall, there was some slight erosion in innings and ERA despite marginal improvement in some peripherals.

ERA: For those who pitched at least 100 innings in the first half, ERAs rose an average of 0.40 runs in the 2H. Of those with first half ERAs less than 4.00, only 49% were able to maintain a sub-4.00 ERA in the second half.

Wins: Pitchers who won 18 or more games in a season tended to pitch *more* innings in the 2H and had slightly better peripherals.

Saves: Of those closers who saved 20 or more games in the first half, only 39% were able to post 20 or more saves in the 2H, and 26% posted fewer than 15 saves. Aggregate ERAs of these pitchers rose from 2.45 to 3.17, half to half.

Teams

Johnson Effect *(Bryan Johnson)*: Teams whose actual won/loss record exceeds or falls short of their statistically projected record in one season will tend to revert to the level of their projection in the following season.

Law of Competitive Balance *(Bill James)*: The level at which a team (or player) will address its problems is inversely related to its current level of success. Low performers will tend to make changes to improve; high performers will not. This law explains the existence of the Plexiglass and Whirlpool Principles.

Plexiglass Principle *(Bill James)*: If a player or team improves markedly in one season, it will likely decline in the next. The opposite is true but not as often (because a poor performer gets fewer opportunities to rebound).

Whirlpool Principle *(Bill James)*: All team and player performances are forcefully drawn to the center. For teams, that center is a .500 record. For players, it represents their career average level of performance.

Other Diamonds

The Fanalytic Fundamentals

1. This is not a game of accuracy or precision. It is a game of human beings and tendencies.
2. This is not a game of projections. It is a game of market value versus real value.
3. Draft skills, not stats. Draft skills, not roles.
4. A player's ability to post acceptable stats despite lousy BPIs will eventually run out.
5. Once you display a skill, you own it.
6. Virtually every player is vulnerable to a month of aberrant performance. Or a year.
7. Exercise excruciating patience.

Aging Axioms

1. Age is the only variable for which we can project a rising trend with 100% accuracy. (Or, age never regresses.)
2. The aging process slows down for those who maintain a firm grasp on the strike zone. Plate patience and pitching command can preserve any waning skill they have left.
3. Negatives tend to snowball as you age.

Steve Avery List

Players who hang onto MLB rosters for six years searching for a skill level they only had for three.

Bylaws of Badness

1. Some players are better than an open roster spot, but not by much.
2. Some players have bad years because they are unlucky. Others have *many* bad years because they are bad... and lucky.

George Brett Path to Retirement

Get out while you're still putting up good numbers and the public perception of you is favorable. Like Mike Mussina and Billy Wagner. And Chipper Jones, Mariano Rivera and Andy Pettitte.

Steve Carlton Path to Retirement

Hang around the majors long enough for your numbers to become so wretched that people begin to forget your past successes.

Classic cases include Jose Mesa, Doc Gooden, Nomar Garciaparra and of course, Steve Carlton. Recent players who have taken this path include Ivan Rodriguez, Mike Cameron, Chone Figgins and Andruw Jones. Current players who could be on a similar course include Carlos Pena, Miguel Tejada, Travis Hafner, Jason Bay, Brian Roberts and Kevin Youkilis. Will Josh Hamilton and Albert Pujols be next?

Christie Brinkley Law of Statistical Analysis
Never get married to the model.

Employment Standards
1. If you are right-brain dominant, own a catcher's mitt and are under 40, you will always be gainfully employed.
2. Some teams believe that it is better to employ a player with any experience because it has to be better than the devil they don't know.
3. It's not so good to go *pffft* in a contract year.

Laws of Prognosticating Perspective
- *Berkeley's 17th Law:* A great many problems do not have accurate answers, but do have approximate answers, from which sensible decisions can be made.
- *Ashley-Perry Statistical Axiom #4:* A complex system that works is invariably found to have evolved from a simple system that works.
- *Baseball Variation of Harvard Law:* Under the most rigorously observed conditions of skill, age, environment, statistical rules and other variables, a ballplayer will perform as he damn well pleases.

Brad Fullmer List
Players whose leading indicators indicate upside potential, year after year, but consistently fail to reach that full potential. Players like Phil Hughes, Bud Norris, Carlos Quentin and Jeff Samardzija are on the list right now.

Ceiling
The highest professional level at which a player maintains acceptable BPIs. Also, the peak performance level that a player will likely reach, given his BPIs.

Good Luck Truism
Good luck is rare and everyone has more of it than you do. That's the law.

The Gravity Principles
1. It is easier to be crappy than it is to be good.
2. All performance starts at zero, ends at zero and can drop to zero at any time.
3. The odds of a good performer slumping are far greater than the odds of a poor performer surging.
4. Once a player is in a slump, it takes several 3-for-5 days to get out of it. Once he is on a streak, it takes a single 0-for-4 day to begin the downward spiral. *Corollary:* Once a player is in a slump, not only does it take several 3-for-5 days to get out of it, but he also has to get his name back on the lineup card.
5. Eventually all performance comes down to earth. It may take a week, or a month, or may not happen until he's 45, but eventually it's going to happen.

Health Homilies
1. Staying healthy is a skill (and "DL Days" should be a Rotisserie category).
2. A $40 player can get hurt just as easily as a $5 player but is eight times tougher to replace.
3. Chronically injured players never suddenly get healthy.

4. There are two kinds of pitchers: those that are hurt and those that are not hurt... yet.
5. Players with back problems are always worth $10 less.
6. "Opting out of surgery" usually means it's coming anyway, just later.

The Health Hush
Players get hurt and potentially have a lot to lose, so there is an incentive for them to hide injuries. HIPAA laws restrict the disclosure of health information. Team doctors and trainers have been instructed not to talk with the media. So, when it comes to information on a player's health status, we're all pretty much in the dark.

Hidden Injury Progression
1. Player's skills implode.
2. Team and player deny injury.
3. More unexplained struggles.
4. Injury revealed; surgery follows.

Law of Injury Estimation (Westheimer's Rule)
To calculate an accurate projection of the amount of time a player will be out of action due to injury, first take the published time estimate, double it and change the unit of measure to the next highest unit. Thus, a player estimated to be out two weeks will actually be out four months.

The Livan Level
The point when a player's career Runs Above Replacement level has dropped so far below zero that he has effectively cancelled out any possible remaining future value. (Similarly, the Dontrelle Demarcation.)

The Momentum Maxims
1. A player will post a pattern of positive results until the day you add him to your roster.
2. Patterns of negative results are more likely to snowball than correct.
3. When an unstoppable force meets an immovable object, the wall always wins.

Monocarp
A player whose career consists of only one productive season.

Paradoxes and Conundrums
1. Is a player's improvement in performance from one year to the next a point in a growth trend, an isolated outlier or a complete anomaly?
2. A player can play through an injury, post rotten numbers and put his job at risk... or... he can admit that he can't play through an injury, allow himself to be taken out of the lineup/rotation, and put his job at risk.
3. Did irregular playing time take its toll on the player's performance or did poor performance force a reduction in his playing time?
4. Is a player only in the game versus right-handers because he has a true skills deficiency versus left-handers? Or is his poor performance versus left-handers because he's never given a chance to face them?
5. The problem with stockpiling bench players in the hope that one pans out is that you end up evaluating

performance using data sets that are too small to be reliable.

6. There are players who could give you 20 stolen bases if they got 400 AB. But if they got 400 AB, they would likely be on a bad team that wouldn't let them steal.

Process-Outcome Matrix *(Russo and Schoemaker)*

	Good Outcome	Bad Outcome
Good Process	Deserved Success	Bad Break
Bad Process	Dumb Luck	Poetic Justice

Quack!

An exclamation in response to the educated speculation that a player has used performance enhancing drugs. While it is rare to have absolute proof, there is often enough information to suggest that, "if it looks like a duck and quacks like a duck, then odds are it's a duck."

Tenets of Optimal Timing

1. If a second half fader had put up his second half stats in the first half and his first half stats in the second half, then he probably wouldn't even have had a second half.

2. Fast starters can often buy six months of playing time out of one month of productivity.

3. Poor 2nd halves don't get recognized until it's too late.

4. "Baseball is like this. Have one good year and you can fool them for five more, because for five more years they expect you to have another good one." — Frankie Frisch

The Three True Outcomes

1. Strikeouts
2. Walks
3. Home runs

The Three True Handicaps

1. Has power but can't make contact.
2. Has speed but can't hit safely.
3. Has potential but is too old.

UGLY (Unreasonable Good Luck Year)

The driving force behind every winning team. It's what they really mean when they say "winning ugly."

Walbeckian

Possessing below replacement level stats, as in "B.J. Upton's season was downright Walbeckian." Alternate usage: "B.J. Upton's stats were so bad that I might as well have had Walbeck in there."

Wasted talent

A player with a high level skill that is negated by a deficiency in another skill. For instance, base path speed can be negated by poor on base ability. Pitchers with strong arms can be wasted because home plate is an elusive concept to them.

Zombie

A player who is indestructible, continuing to get work, year-after-year, no matter how dead his BPIs are. Like Philip Humber, Jeff Francis and Jason Marquis.

Batters

Batting Eye, Contact and Batting Average

Batting average (BA, or Avg)
This is where it starts. BA is a grand old nugget that has long outgrown its usefulness. We revere .300 hitting superstars and scoff at .250 hitters, yet the difference between the two is one hit every 20 ABs. This one hit every five games is not nearly the wide variance that exists in our perceptions of what it means to be a .300 or .250 hitter. BA is a poor evaluator of performance in that it neglects the offensive value of the base on balls and assumes that all hits are created equal.

Walk rate (bb%)
(BB / (AB + BB))
A measure of a batter's plate patience. BENCHMARKS: The best batters will have levels more than 10%. Those with poor plate patience will have levels of 5% or less.

On base average (OB)
(H + BB) / (AB + BB)
Addressing a key deficiency with BA, OB gives value to events that get batters on base, but are not hits. An OB of .350 can be read as "this batter gets on base 35% of the time." When a run is scored, there is no distinction made as to how that runner reached base. So, two-thirds of the time—about how often a batter comes to the plate with the bases empty—a walk really is as good as a hit.

The official version of this formula includes hit batsmen. We do not include it because our focus is on skills-based gauges; research has shown that HBP is not a measure of batting skill but of pitching deficiency. BENCHMARKS: We know what a .300 hitter is, but what represents "good" for OB? That comparable level would likely be .400, with .275 representing the comparable level of futility.

Ground ball, line drive, fly ball percentages (G/L/F)
The percentage of all balls in play that are hit on the ground, as line drives and in the air. For batters, increased fly ball tendency may foretell a rise in power skills; increased line drive tendency may foretell an improvement in batting average. For a pitcher, the ability to keep the ball on the ground can contribute to his statistical output exceeding his demonstrated skill level.

*BIP Type	Total%	Out%
Ground ball	45%	72%
Line drive	20%	28%
Fly ball	35%	85%
TOTAL	*100%*	*69%*

*Data only includes fieldable balls and is net of HRs.

Line drives and luck *(Patrick Davitt)*
Given that each individual batter's hit rate sets its own baseline, and that line drives (LD) are the most productive type of batted ball, a study looked at the relationship between the two. Among the findings were that hit rates on LDs are much higher than on FBs or GBs, with individual batters consistently falling into the

72-73% range. Ninety-five percent of all batters fall between the range of 60%-86%; batters outside this range regress very quickly, often within the season.

Note that batters' BAs did not always follow their LD% up or down, because some of them enjoyed higher hit rates on other batted balls, improved their contact rates, or both. Still, it's justifiable to bet that players hitting the ball with authority but getting fewer hits than they should will correct over time.

Batting eye (Eye)
(Walks / Strikeouts)
A measure of a player's strike zone judgment. BENCHMARKS: The best hitters have Eye ratios more than 1.00 (indicating more walks than strikeouts) and are the most likely to be among a league's .300 hitters. Ratios less than 0.50 represent batters who likely also have lower BAs.

Batting eye as a leading indicator
There is a strong correlation between strike zone judgment and batting average. However, research shows that this is more descriptive than predictive:

	Batting Average				
Batting Eye	2009	2010	2011	2012	2013
0.00 - 0.25	.239	.235	.232	.243	.242
0.26 - 0.50	.259	.260	.254	.255	.253
0.51 - 0.75	.272	.264	.267	.268	.265
0.76 - 1.00	.274	.272	.276	.276	.277
1.01 and over	.292	.280	.298	.292	.284

We can create percentage plays for the different levels:

For Eye	Pct who bat	
Levels of	.300+	.250-
0.00 - 0.25	7%	39%
0.26 - 0.50	14%	26%
0.51 - 0.75	18%	17%
0.76 - 1.00	32%	14%
1.01 - 1.50	51%	9%
1.51 +	59%	4%

Any batter with an eye ratio more than 1.50 has about a 4% chance of hitting less than .250 over 500 at bats.

Of all .300 hitters, those with ratios of at least 1.00 have a 65% chance of repeating as .300 hitters. Those with ratios less than 1.00 have less than a 50% chance of repeating.

Only 4% of sub-.250 hitters with ratios less than 0.50 will mature into .300 hitters the following year.

In a 1995-2000 study, only 37 batters hit .300-plus with a sub-0.50 eye ratio over at least 300 AB in a season. Of this group, 30% were able to accomplish this feat on a consistent basis. For the other 70%, this was a short-term aberration.

Contact rate (ct%)
((AB - K) / AB)
Measures a batter's ability to get wood on the ball and hit it into the field of play. BENCHMARKS: Those batters with the best contact skill will have levels of 90% or better. The hackers of society will have levels of 75% or less.

Contact rate as a leading indicator

The more often a batter makes contact with the ball, the higher the likelihood that he will hit safely.

	Batting Average				
Contact Rate	2009	2010	2011	2012	2013
0% - 60%	.189	.187	.171	.197	.203
61% - 65%	.229	.235	.199	.226	.211
66% - 70%	.241	.236	.229	.231	.232
71% - 75%	.247	.254	.243	.252	.246
76% - 80%	.263	.256	.260	.255	.261
81% - 85%	.275	.271	.268	.268	.268
86% - 90%	.281	.273	.272	.278	.272
Over 90%	.287	.270	.290	.282	.270

Contact rate and walk rate as leading indicators

A matrix of contact rates and walk rates can provide expectation benchmarks for a player's batting average:

	Walk rate (bb%)			
Contact rate (ct%)	0-5	6-10	11-15	16+
65-	.179	.195	.229	.237
66-75	.190	.248	.254	.272
76-85	.265	.267	.276	.283
86+	.269	.279	.301	.309

A contact rate of 65% or lower offers virtually no chance for a player to hit even .250, no matter how high a walk rate he has. The .300 hitters most often come from the group with a minimum 86% contact and 11% walk rate.

HCt and HctX *(Patrick Davitt)*

HCt= hard hit ball rate x contact rate
HctX= Player Hct divided by league average Hct, normalized to 100

The combination of making contact and hitting the ball hard might be the most important skills for a batter. HctX correlates very strongly with BA, and at higher BA levels often does so with high accuracy. Its success with HR was somewhat limited, probably due to GB/FB differences. **BENCHMARKS:** The average major-leaguer in a given year has a HctX of 100. Elite batters have an HctX of 135 or above; weakest batters have HctX of 55 or below.

Balls in play (BIP)

(AB – K)

The total number of batted balls that are hit fair, both hits and outs. An analysis of how these balls are hit—on the ground, in the air, hits, outs, etc.—can provide analytical insight, from player skill levels to the impact of luck on statistical output.

Batting average on balls in play *(Voros McCracken)*

(H – HR) / (AB – HR – K)

Also called hit rate (h%). The percent of balls hit into the field of play that fall for hits. **BENCHMARK:** Every hitter establishes his own individual hit rate that stabilizes over time. A batter whose seasonal hit rate varies significantly from the h% he has established over the preceding three seasons (variance of at least +/- 3%) is likely to improve or regress to his individual h% mean (with over-performer declines more likely and sharper

than under-performer recoveries). Three-year h% levels strongly predict a player's h% the following year.

P/PA as a leading indicator for BA *(Paul Petera)*

The art of working the count has long been considered one of the more crucial aspects of good hitting. It is common knowledge that the more pitches a hitter sees, the greater opportunity he has to reach base safely.

P/PA	OBA	BA
4.00+	.360	.264
3.75-3.99	.347	.271
3.50-3.74	.334	.274
Under 3.50	.321	.276

Generally speaking, the more pitches seen, the lower the BA, but the higher the OBA. But what about the outliers, those players that bucked the trend in year #1?

	YEAR TWO	
	BA Improved	BA Declined
Low P/PA and Low BA	77%	23%
High P/PA and High BA	21%	79%

In these scenarios, there was a strong tendency for performance to normalize in year #2.

Expected batting average *(John Burnson)*

$xCT\% * [xH1\% + xH2\%]$

where

$xH1\% = GB\% \times [0.0004\ PX + 0.062\ ln(SX)]$
$+ LD\% \times [0.93 - 0.086\ ln(SX)]$
$+ FB\% \times 0.12$

and

$xH2\% = FB\% \times [0.0013\ PX - 0.0002\ SX - 0.057]$
$+ GB\% \times [0.0006\ PX]$

A hitter's batting average as calculated by multiplying the percentage of balls put in play (contact rate) by the chance that a ball in play falls for a hit. The likelihood that a ball in play falls for a hit is a product of the speed of the ball and distance it is hit (PX), the speed of the batter (SX), and distribution of ground balls, fly balls, and line drives. We further split it out by non-homerun hit rate (xH1%) and homerun hit rate (xH2%). **BENCHMARKS:** In general, xBA should approximate batting average fairly closely. Those hitters who have large variances between the two gauges are candidates for further analysis. **LIMITATION:** xBA tends to understate a batter's true value if he is an extreme ground ball hitter (G/F ratio over 3.0) with a low PX. These players are not inherently weak, but choose to take safe singles rather than swing for the fences.

Expected batting average variance

xBA – BA

The variance between a batter's BA and his xBA is a measure of over- or under-achievement. A positive variance indicates the potential for a batter's BA to rise. A negative variance indicates the potential for BA to decline. **BENCHMARK:** Discount variances that are less than 20 points. Any variance more than 30 points is regarded as a strong indicator of future change.

Power

Slugging average (Slg)
(Singles + (2 x Doubles) + (3 x Triples) + (4 x HR)) / AB

A measure of the total number of bases accumulated (or the minimum number of runners' bases advanced) per at bat. It is a misnomer; it is not a true measure of a batter's slugging ability because it includes singles. Slg also assumes that each type of hit has proportionately increasing value (i.e. a double is twice as valuable as a single, etc.) which is not true. For instance, with the bases loaded, a HR always scores four runs, a triple always scores three, but a double could score two or three and a single could score one, or two, or even three. BENCHMARKS: Top batters will have levels over .500. The bottom batters will have levels less than .300.

Fly ball tendency and power *(Mat Olkin)*
There is a proven connection between a hitter's ground ball/fly ball tendencies and his power production.

1. *Extreme ground ball hitters generally do not hit for much power.* It's almost impossible for a hitter with a ground/fly ratio over 1.80 to hit enough fly balls to produce even 25 HRs in a season. However, this does not mean that a low G/F ratio necessarily guarantees power production. Some players have no problem getting the ball into the air, but lack the strength to reach the fences consistently.

2. *Most batters' ground/fly ratios stay pretty steady over time.* Most year-to-year changes are small and random, as they are in any other statistical category. A large, sudden change in G/F, on the other hand, can signal a conscious change in plate approach. And so...

3. *If a player posts high G/F ratios in his first few years, he probably isn't ever going to hit for all that much power.*

4. *When a batter's power suddenly jumps, his G/F ratio often drops at the same time.*

5. *Every so often, a hitter's ratio will drop significantly even as his power production remains level. In these rare cases, impending power development is likely, since the two factors almost always follow each other.*

Home runs to fly ball rate (hr/f)
The percent of fly balls that are hit for HRs.

hr/f rate as a leading indicator *(Joshua Randall)*
Each batter establishes an individual home run to fly ball rate that stabilizes over rolling three-year periods; those levels strongly predict the hr/f in the subsequent year. A batter who varies significantly from his hr/f is likely to regress toward his individual hr/f mean, with over-performance decline more likely and more severe than under-performance recovery.

Hard-hit flies as a sustainable skill *(Patrick Davitt)*
A study of data from 2009-2011 found that we should seek batters with a high Hard-Hit Fly Ball percentage (HHFB%). Among the findings:

- Avoiding pop-ups and hitting HHFBs are sustainable core power skills.
- Consistent HHFB% performance marks batters with power potential.

- When looking for candidates to regress, we should look at individual past levels of HR/HHFB, perhaps using a three-year rolling average.

Linear weighted power (LWPwr)
((Doubles x .8) + (Triples x .8) + (HR x 1.4)) / (At bats- K) x 100

A variation of the linear weights formula that considers only events that are measures of a batter's pure power. BENCHMARKS: Top sluggers typically top the 17 mark. Weak hitters will have a LWPwr level of less than 10.

Linear weighted power index (PX)
(Batter's LWPwr / League LWPwr) x 100

LWPwr is presented in this book in its normalized form to get a better read on a batter's accomplishment in each year. For instance, a 30-HR season today is much more of an accomplishment than 30 HRs hit in a higher offense year like 2003. BENCHMARKS: A level of 100 equals league average power skills. Any player with a value more than 100 has above average power skills, and those more than 150 are the Slugging Elite.

Expected LW power index (xPX) *(Bill Macey)*
2.6 + 269*HHLD% + 724*HHFB%

Previous research has shown that hard-hit balls are more likely to result in hits and hard-hit fly balls are more likely to end up as HRs. As such, we can use hard-hit ball data to calculate an expected skills-based power index. This metric starts with hard-hit ball data, which measures a player's fundamental skill of making solid contact, and then places it on the same scale as PX (xPX). In the above formula, HHLD% is calculated as the number of hard hit line-drives divided by the total number of balls put in play. HHFB% is similarly calculated for fly balls.

P/PA as a leading indicator for PX *(Paul Petera)*
Working the count has a positive effect on power.

P/PA	PX
4.00+	123
3.75-3.99	108
3.50-3.74	96
Under 3.50	84

As for the year #1 outliers:

	YEAR TWO	
	PX Improved	PX Declined
Low P/PA and High PX	11%	89%
High P/PA and Low PX	70%	30%

In these scenarios, there was a strong tendency for performance to normalize in year #2.

Doubles as a leading indicator for home runs *(Bill Macey)*
There is little support for the theory that hitting many doubles in year x leads to an increase in HR in year x+1. However, it was shown that batters with high doubles rates (2B/AB) also tend to hit more HR/AB than the league average; oddly, they are unable to sustain the high 2B/AB rate but do sustain their higher HR/AB rates. Batters with high 2B/AB rates and low HR/AB rates are more likely to see HR gains in the following year, but those rates will still typically trail the league average. And, batters who experience a surge in 2B/AB typically give back most of those gains in the following year without any corresponding gain in HR.

Opposite field home runs *(Ed DeCaria)*

From 2001-2008, nearly 75% of all HRs were hit to the batter's pull field, with the remaining 25% distributed roughly evenly between straight away and opposite field. Left-handers accomplished the feat slightly more often than right-handers (including switch-hitters hitting each way), and younger hitters did it significantly more often than older hitters. The trend toward pulled home runs was especially strong after age 36.

Power Quartile	AB/HR	Opp. Field	Straight Away	Pull Field
Top 25%	17.2	15.8%	16.0%	68.2%
2nd 25%	28.0	10.7%	12.2%	77.0%
3rd 25%	44.1	8.9%	10.0%	81.1%
Bot 25%	94.7	5.4%	5.9%	88.7%

Opposite field HRs serve as a strong indicator of overall home run power (AB/HR). Power hitters (smaller AB/HR rates) hit a far higher percentage of their HR to the opposite field or straight away (over 30%). Conversely, non-power hitters hit almost 90% of their home runs to their pull field.

	Performance in Y2-Y4 (% of Group)		
Y1 Trigger	<=30 AB/HR	5.5+ RC/G	$16+ R$
2+ OppHR	69%	46%	33%
<2 OppHR	29%	13%	12%

Players who hit just two or more OppHR in one season were 2-3 times as likely as those who hit zero or one OppHR to sustain strong AB/HR rates, RC/G levels, or R$ values over the following three seasons.

	Y2-Y4 Breakout Performance (% Breakout by Group, Age <=26 Only)		
	AB/HR	RC/G	R$
Y1 Trigger	>35 to <=30	<4.5 to 5.5+	<$8 to $16+
2+ OppHR	32%	21%	30%
<2 OppHR	23%	12%	10%

Roughly one of every 3-4 batters age 26 or younger experiences a *sustained three-year breakout* in AB/HR, RC/G or R$ after a season in which they hit 2+ OppHR, far better odds than the one in 8-10 batters who experience a breakout without the 2+ OppHR trigger.

Power breakout profile

It is not easy to predict which batters will experience a power spike. We can categorize power breakouts to determine the likelihood of a player taking a step up or of a surprise performer repeating his feat. Possibilities:

- Increase in playing time
- History of power skills at some time in the past
- Redistribution of already demonstrated extra base hit power
- Normal skills growth
- Situational breakouts, particularly in hitter-friendly venues
- Increased fly ball tendency
- Use of illegal performance-enhancing substances
- Miscellaneous unexplained variables

Speed

Wasted talent on the base paths

We refer to some players as having "wasted talent," a high level skill that is negated by a deficiency in another skill. Among these types are players who have blazing speed that is negated by a sub-.300 on base average.

These players can have short-term value. However, their stolen base totals are tied so tightly to their "green light" that any change in managerial strategy could completely erase that value. A higher OB mitigates that downside; the good news is that plate patience can be taught.

Players in 2013 who had at least 20 SBs with an OBP less than .300, and whose SB output could be at risk, are Emilio Bonifacio (28 SB, .291 OBP), Juan Pierre (23, .277), Elliot Johnson (22, .256), Alcides Escobar (22, .257) and Ichiro Suzuki (20, .297).

Speed score *(Bill James)*

A measure of the various elements that comprise a runner's speed skills. Although this formula (a variation of James' original version) may be used as a leading indicator for stolen base output, SB attempts are controlled by managerial strategy which makes speed score somewhat less valuable.

Speed score is calculated as the mean value of the following four elements:

1. Stolen base efficiency = $(((SB + 3)/(SB + CS + 7)) - .4) \times 20$
2. Stolen base freq. = $Square\ root\ of\ ((SB + CS)/(Singles + BB))\ /\ .07$
3. Triples rating = $(3B\ /\ (AB - HR - K))$ and the result assigned a value based on the following chart:

< 0.001	0	0.0105	6
0.001	1	0.013	7
0.0023	2	0.0158	8
0.0039	3	0.0189	9
0.0058	4	0.0223+	10
0.008	5		

4. Runs scored as a percentage of times on base = $(((R - HR)\ /\ (H + BB - HR)) - .1)\ /\ .04$

Speed score index (SX)

(Batter's speed score / League speed score) x 100

Normalized speed scores get a better read on a runner's accomplishment in context. A level of 100 equals league average speed skill. Values more than 100 indicate above average skill, more than 200 represent the Fleet of Feet Elite.

Statistically scouted speed (Spd) *(Ed DeCaria)*

$(104 + \{[(Runs–HR+10*age\_wt)/(RBI-HR+10)]/lg\_av*100\}\ /\ 5$
$+ \{[(3B+5*age\_wt)/(2B+3B+5)]/lg\_av*100\}\ /\ 5$
$+ \{[(SoftMedGBhits+25*age\_wt)/(SoftMedGB+25)]/lg\_av*100\}\ /\ 2$
$- \{[Weight\ (Lbs)/Height\ (In)^2 * 703]/lg\_av*100\}$

A skills-based gauge that measures speed without relying on stolen bases. Its components are:

- *(Runs – HR) / (RBI – HR)*: This metric aims to minimize the influence of extra base hit power and team run-scoring rates on perceived speed.

- *3B / (2B + 3B):* No one can deny that triples are a fast runner's stat; dividing them by 2B+3B instead of all balls in play dampens the power aspect of extra base hits.
- *(Soft + Medium Ground Ball Hits) / (Soft + Medium Ground Balls):* Faster runners are more likely than slower runners to beat out routine grounders. Hard hit balls are excluded from numerator and denominator.
- *Body Mass Index (BMI):* Calculated as *Weight (lbs) / Height (in)2 * 703.* All other factors considered, leaner players run faster than heavier ones.

In this book, the formula is scaled as an index with a midpoint of 100.

Stolen base opportunity percent (SBO)
(SB + CS) / (BB + Singles)

A rough approximation of how often a baserunner attempts a stolen base. Provides a comparative measure for players on a given team and, as a team measure, the propensity of a manager to give a "green light" to his runners.

Roto Speed (RSpd)
(Spd x (SBO + SB%))

An adjustment to the measure for raw speed that takes into account a runner's opportunities to steal and his success rate. This stat is intended to provide a more accurate predictive measure of stolen bases for the Mayberry Method.

Stolen base breakout profile *(Bob Berger)*
To find stolen base breakouts (first 30+ steal season in the majors), look for players that:
- are between 22-27 years old
- have 3-7 years of professional (minors and MLB) experience
- have previous steals at the MLB level
- have averaged 20+ SB in previous three seasons (majors and minors combined)
- have at least one professional season of 30+ SB

Overall Performance Analysis

On base plus slugging average (OPS)
A simple sum of the two gauges, it is considered one of the better evaluators of overall performance. OPS combines the two basic elements of offensive production—the ability to get on base (OB) and the ability to advance baserunners (Slg). **BENCHMARKS:** The game's top batters will have OPS levels more than .900. The worst batters will have levels less than .600.

Base Performance Value (BPV)
(Walk rate - 5) x 2)
+ ((Contact rate - 75) x 4)
+ ((Power Index - 80) x 0.8)
+ ((Spd - 80) x 0.3)

A single value that describes a player's overall raw skill level. This is more useful than traditional statistical gauges to track player performance trends and project future statistical output. The BPV formula combines and weights several BPIs.

This formula combines the individual raw skills of batting eye, contact rate, power and speed. **BENCHMARKS:** The best hitters will have a BPV of 50 or greater.

Base Performance Index (BPX)
BPV scaled to league average to account for year-to-year fluctuations in league-wide statistical performance. It's a snapshot of a player's overall skills compared to an average player. **BENCHMARK:** A level of 100 means a player had a league-average BPV in that given season.

Linear weights *(Pete Palmer)*
((Singles x .46) + (Doubles x .8) + (Triples x 1.02)
+ (Home runs x 1.4) + (Walks x .33) + (Stolen Bases x .3)
- (Caught Stealing x .6) - ((At bats - Hits) x Normalizing Factor)

(Also referred to as Batting Runs.) Formula whose premise is that all events in baseball are linear; that is, the output (runs) is directly proportional to the input (offensive events). Each of these events is then weighted according to its relative value in producing runs. Positive events—hits, walks, stolen bases—have positive values. Negative events—outs, caught stealing—have negative values.

The normalizing factor, representing the value of an out, is an offset to the level of offense in a given year. It changes every season, growing larger in high offense years and smaller in low offense years. The value is about .26 and varies by league.

LW is not included in the player forecast boxes, but the LW concept is used with the linear weighted power gauge.

Runs above replacement (RAR)
An estimate of the number of runs a player contributes above a "replacement level" player. "Replacement" is defined as the level of performance at which another player can easily be found at little or no cost to a team. What constitutes replacement level is a topic that is hotly debated. There are a variety of formulas and rules of thumb used to determine this level for each position (replacement level for a shortstop will be very different from replacement level for an outfielder). Our estimates appear below.

One of the major values of RAR for fantasy applications is that it can be used to assemble an integrated ranking of batters and pitchers for drafting purposes.

To calculate RAR for batters:
- Start with a batter's runs created per game (RC/G).
- Subtract his position's replacement level RC/G.
- Multiply by number of games played: (AB - H + CS) / 25.5.

Replacement levels used in this book:

POS	AL	NL
C	3.72	3.70
1B	4.61	4.59
2B	3.73	3.66
3B	3.95	4.00
SS	4.43	3.51
LF	3.98	4.06
CF	4.24	4.10
RF	4.28	4.61
DH	4.50	

RAR can also be used to calculate rough projected team won-loss records. *(Roger Miller)* Total the RAR levels for all the players on a team, divide by 10 and add to 53 wins.

Runs created *(Bill James)*

(H + BB – CS) x (Total bases + (.55 x SB)) / (AB + BB)

A formula that converts all offensive events into a total of runs scored. As calculated for individual teams, the result approximates a club's actual run total with great accuracy.

Runs created per game (RC/G)

Bill James version: *Runs Created / ((AB - H + CS) / 25.5)*

RC expressed on a per-game basis might be considered the hypothetical ERA compiled against a particular batter. Another way to look at it: A batter with a RC/G of 7.00 would be expected to score 7 runs per game if he were cloned nine times and faced an average pitcher in every at bat. Cloning batters is not a practice we recommend. BENCHMARKS: Few players surpass the level of a 10.00 RC/G, but any level more than 7.50 can still be considered very good. At the bottom are levels less than 3.00.

Plate Appearances as a leading indicator *(Patrick Davitt)*

While targeting players "age 26 with experience" as potential breakout candidates has become a commonly accepted concept, a study has found that cumulative plate appearances, especially during the first two years of a young player's career, can also have predictive value in assessing a coming spike in production. Three main conclusions:

- When projecting players, MLB experience is more important than age.
- Players who amass 800+ PAs in their first two seasons are highly likely to have double-digit value in Year 3.
- Also target young players in the season where they attain 400 PAs, as they are twice as likely as other players to grow significantly in value.

Handedness

1. While pure southpaws account for about 27% of total ABs (RHers about 55% and switch-hitters about 18%), they hit 31% of the triples and take 30% of the walks.
2. The average lefty posts a batting average about 10 points higher than the average RHer. The on base averages of pure LHers are nearly 20 points higher than RHers, but only 10 points higher than switch-hitters.
3. LHers tend to have a better batting eye ratio than RHers, but about the same as switch-hitters.
4. Pure righties and lefties have virtually identical power skills. Switch-hitters tend to have less power, on average.
5. Switch-hitters tend to have the best speed, followed by LHers, and then RHers.
6. On an overall production basis, LHers have an 8% advantage over RHers and a 14% edge over switch-hitters.

Skill-specific aging patterns for batters *(Ed DeCaria)*

Baseball forecasters obsess over "peak age" of player performance because we must understand player ascent toward and decline from that peak to predict future value. Most published aging analyses are done using composite estimates of value such as OPS or linear weights. By contrast, fantasy GMs are typically more concerned with category-specific player value (HR, SB, AVG, etc.). We can better forecast what matters most by analyzing peak age of individual baseball skills rather than overall player value.

For batters, recognized peak age for overall batting value is a player's late 20s. But individual skills do not peak uniformly at the same time:

Contact rate (ct%): Ascends modestly by about a half point of contact per year from age 22 to 26, then holds steady within a half point of peak until age 35, after which players lose a half point of contact per year.

Walk rate (bb%): Trends the opposite way with age compared to contact rate, as batters tend to peak at age 30 and largely remain there until they turn 38.

Stolen Base Opportunity (SBO): Typically, players maintain their SBO through age 27, but then reduce their attempts steadily in each remaining year of their careers.

Stolen base success rate (SB%): Aggressive runners (>14% SBO) tend to lose about 2 points per year as they age. However, less aggressive runners (<=14% SBO) actually improve their SB% by about 2 points per year until age 28, after which they reverse course and give back 1-2 pts every year as they age.

GB%/LD%/FB%: Both GB% and LD% peak at the start of a player's career and then decline as many hitters seemingly learn to elevate the ball more. But at about age 30, hitter GB% ascends toward a second late-career peak while LD% continues to plummet and FB% continues to rise through age 38.

Hit rate (h%): Declines linearly with age. This is a natural result of a loss of speed and change in batted ball trajectory.

Isolated Power (ISO): Typically peaks from age 24-26. Similarly, home runs per fly ball, opposite field HR %, and Hard Hit % all peak by age 25 and decline somewhat linearly from that point on.

Catchers and late-career performance spikes *(Ed Spaulding)*

Many catchers—particularly second line catchers—have their best seasons late in their careers. Some possible reasons why:

1. Catchers, like shortstops, often get to the big leagues for defensive reasons and not their offensive skills. These skills take longer to develop.
2. The heavy emphasis on learning the catching/ defense/ pitching side of the game detracts from their time to learn about, and practice, hitting.
3. Injuries often curtail their ability to show offensive skills, though these injuries (typically jammed fingers, bruises on the arms, rib injuries from collisions) often don't lead to time on the disabled list.
4. The time spent behind the plate has to impact the ability to recognize, and eventually hit, all kinds of pitches.

Spring training Slg as leading indicator *(John Dewan)*

A hitter's spring training Slg .200 or more above his lifetime Slg is a leading indicator for a better than normal season.

Overall batting breakout profile *(Brandon Kruse)*

We define a breakout performance as one where a player posts a Roto value of $20+ after having never posted a value of $10. These criteria are used to validate an apparent breakout in the current season but may also be used carefully to project a potential upcoming breakout:

- Age 27 or younger
- An increase in at least two of: h%, PX or Spd
- Minimum league average PX or Spd (100)
- Minimum contact rate of 75%
- Minimum xBA of .270

In-Season Analysis

Batting order facts *(Ed DeCaria)*

Eighty-eight percent of today's leadoff hitters bat leadoff again in their next game, 78% still bat leadoff 10 games later, and 68% still bat leadoff 50 games later. Despite this level of turnover after 50 games, leadoff hitters have the best chance of retaining their role over time. After leadoff, #3 and #4 hitters are the next most likely to retain their lineup slots.

On a season-to-season basis, leadoff hitters are again the most stable, with 69% of last year's primary leadoff hitters retaining the #1 slot next year.

Plate appearances decline linearly by lineup slot. Leadoff batters receive 10-12% more PAs than when batting lower in the lineup. AL #9 batters and NL #8 batters get 9-10% fewer PAs. These results mirror play-by-play data showing a 15-20 PA drop by lineup slot over a full season.

Walk rate is largely unaffected by lineup slot in the AL. Beware strong walk rates by NL #8 hitters, as much of this "skill" will disappear if ever moved from the #8 slot.

Batting order has no discernable effect on contact rate.

Hit rate slopes gently upward as hitters are slotted deeper in the lineup.

As expected, the #3-4-5 slots are ideal for non-HR RBIs, at the expense of #6 hitters. RBIs are worst for players in the #1-2 slots. Batting atop the order sharply increases the probability of scoring runs, especially in the NL.

The leadoff slot easily has the highest stolen base attempt rate. #4-5-6 hitters attempt steals more often when batting out of those slots than they do batting elsewhere. The NL #8 hitter is a SB attempt sink hole. A change in batting order from #8 to #1 in the NL could nearly double a player's SB output due to lineup slot alone.

DOMination and DISaster rates

Week-to-week consistency is measured using a batter's BPV compiled in each week. A player earns a DOMinant week if his BPV was greater or equal to 50 for that week. A player registers a DISaster if his BPV was less than 0 for that week. The percentage of Dominant weeks, DOM%, is simply calculated as the number of DOM weeks divided by the total number of weeks played.

Is week-to-week consistency a repeatable skill? *(Bill Macey)*

To test whether consistent performance is a repeatable skill for batters, we examined how closely related a player's DOM% was from year to year.

YR1 DOM%	AVG YR2 DOM%
< 35%	37%
35%–45%	40%
46%–55%	45%
56%+	56%

Quality/consistency score (QC)

$(DOM\% - (2 \times DIS\%)) \times 2$

Using the DOM/DIS percentages, this score measures both the quality of performance as well as week–to-week consistency.

Sample size reliability *(Russell Carleton)*

At what point during the season do statistics become reliable indicators of skill? Measured in plate appearances:

- 100: Contact rate
- 150: Strikeout rate, line drive rate, pitches/PA
- 200: Walk rate, ground ball rate, GB/FB
- 250: Fly ball rate
- 300: HR rate, hr/f
- 500: OBP, Slg, OPS
- 550: Isolated power

Unlisted stats did not stabilize over a full season of play.

Projecting RBIs *(Patrick Davitt)*

Evaluating players in-season for RBI potential is a function of the interplay among four factors:

- Teammates' ability to reach base ahead of him and to run the bases efficiently
- His own ability to drive them in by hitting, especially XBH
- Number of Games Played
- Place in the batting order

3-4-5 Hitters:
$(0.69 \times GP \times TOB) + (0.30 \times ITB) + (0.275 \times HR) - (.191 \times GP)$

6-7-8 Hitters:
$(0.63 \times GP \times TOB) + (0.27 \times ITB) + (0.250 \times HR) - (.191 \times GP)$

9-1-2 Hitters:
$(0.57 \times GP \times TOB) + (0.24 \times ITB) + (0.225 \times HR) - (.191 \times GP)$

...where GP = games played, TOB = team on-base pct. and ITB = individual total bases (ITB).

Apply this pRBI formula after 70 games played or so (to reduce the variation from small sample size) to find players more than 9 RBIs over or under their projected RBI. There could be a correction coming.

You should also consider other factors, like injury or trade (involving the player or a top-of-the-order speedster) or team SB philosophy and success rate.

Remember: the player himself has an impact on his TOB. When we first did this study, we excluded the player from his TOB and got better results. The formula overestimates projected RBI for players with high OBP who skew his teams' OBP but can't benefit in RBI from that effect.

Ten-Game hitting streaks as a leading indicator *(Bob Berger)*
Research of hitting streaks from 2011 and 2012 showed that a 10-game streak can reliably predict improved longer-term BA performance during the season. A player who has put together a hitting streak of at least 10 games will improve his BA for the remainder of the season about 60% of the time. This improvement can be significant, on average as much as .020 of BA.

Other Diamonds

It's a Busy World Shortcut
For marginal utility-type players, scan their PX and Spd history to see if there's anything to mine for. If you see triple digits anywhere, stop and look further. If not, move on.

Chronology of the Classic Free-Swinger with Pop
1. Gets off to a good start.
2. Thinks he's in a groove.
3. Gets lax, careless.
4. Pitchers begin to catch on.
5. Fades down the stretch.

Errant Gust of Wind
A unit of measure used to describe the difference between your home run projection and mine.

Hannahan Concession
Players with a .218 BA rarely get 500 plate appearances, but when they do, it's usually once.

Mendoza Line
Named for Mario Mendoza, it represents the benchmark for batting futility. Usually refers to a .200 batting average, but can also be used for low levels of other statistical categories. Note that Mendoza's lifetime batting average was actually a much more robust .215.

Old Player Skills
Power, low batting average, no speed and usually good plate patience. Young players, often those with a larger frame, who possess these "old player skills" tend to decline faster than normal, often in their early 30s.

Small Sample Certitude
If players' careers were judged based what they did in a single game performance, then Tuffy Rhodes and Mark Whiten would be in the Hall of Fame.

Esix Snead List
Players with excellent speed and sub-.300 on base averages who get a lot of practice running down the line to first base, and then back to the dugout. Also used as an adjective, as in "Esix-Sneadian."

Pitchers

Strikeouts and Walks

Fundamental skills

Unreliable pitching performance is a fallacy driven by the practice of attempting to project pitching stats using gauges that are poor evaluators of skill.

How can we better evaluate pitching skill? We can start with the three statistical categories that are generally unaffected by external factors. These three stats capture the outcome of an individual pitcher versus batter match-up without regard to supporting offense, defense or bullpen:

Walks Allowed, Strikeouts and Ground Balls

Even with only these stats to observe, there is a wealth of insight that these measures can provide.

Control rate (Ctl, bb/9), or opposition walks per game

BB allowed x 9 / IP

Measures how many walks a pitcher allows per game equivalent. **BENCHMARK:** The best pitchers will have bb/9 levels of 2.8 or less.

Dominance rate (Dom, k/9), or opposition strikeouts/game

Strikeouts recorded x 9 / IP

Measures how many strikeouts a pitcher allows per game equivalent. **BENCHMARK:** The best pitchers will have k/9 levels of 7.0 or higher.

Command ratio (Cmd)

(Strikeouts / Walks)

A measure of a pitcher's ability to get the ball over the plate. There is no more fundamental a skill than this, and so it is used as a leading indicator to project future rises and falls in other gauges, such as ERA. **BENCHMARKS:** Baseball's best pitchers will have ratios in excess of 3.0. Pitchers with ratios less than 1.0—indicating that they walk more batters than they strike out—have virtually no potential for long-term success. If you make no other changes in your approach to drafting pitchers, limiting your focus to only pitchers with a command ratio of 2.5 or better will substantially improve your odds of success.

Command ratio as a leading indicator

The ability to get the ball over the plate—command of the strike zone—is one of the best leading indicators for future performance. Command ratio (K/BB) can be used to project potential in ERA as well as other skills gauges.

1. Research indicates that there is a high correlation between a pitcher's Cmd ratio and his ERA.

	Earned Run Average				
Command	2009	2010	2011	2012	2013
0.0 - 1.0	6.43	5.86	5.45	6.22	5.98
1.1 - 1.5	5.10	5.14	4.84	5.03	4.91
1.6 - 2.0	4.41	4.34	4.35	4.48	4.42
2.1 - 2.5	4.19	3.95	3.89	4.09	3.96
2.6 - 3.0	3.70	3.71	3.66	3.88	3.81
3.1 - 3.5	3.40	3.36	3.58	3.67	3.46
3.6 - 4.0	3.51	3.47	3.00	3.34	3.32
4.1+	3.28	2.80	2.95	3.12	2.86

We can create percentage plays for the different levels:

For Cmd	% with ERA of	
Levels of	3.50-	4.50+
0.0 - 1.0	0%	87%
1.1 - 1.5	7%	67%
1.6 - 2.0	7%	57%
2.1 - 2.5	19%	35%
2.6 - 3.0	26%	25%
3.1 +	53%	5%

Pitchers who maintain a Cmd over 2.5 have a high probability of long-term success. For fantasy drafting purposes, it is best to avoid pitchers with sub-2.0 ratios. Avoid bullpen closers if they have a ratio less than 2.5.

2. A pitcher's Command in tandem with Dominance (strikeout rate) provides even greater predictive abilities.

	Earned Run Average	
Command	-5.6 Dom	5.6+ Dom
0.0-0.9	5.36	5.99
1.0-1.4	4.94	5.03
1.5-1.9	4.67	4.47
2.0-2.4	4.32	4.08
2.5-2.9	4.21	3.88
3.0-3.9	4.04	3.46
4.0+	4.12	2.96

This helps to highlight the limited upside potential of soft-tossers with pinpoint control. The extra dominance makes a huge difference.

3. Research also suggests that there is a strong correlation between a pitcher's command ratio and his propensity to win ballgames. Over three quarters of those with ratios over 3.0 post winning records, and the collective W/L record of those command artists is nearly .600.

The command/winning correlation holds up in both leagues, although the effect was more pronounced in the NL. Over four times more NL hurlers than AL hurlers had Cmd over 3.0, and higher ratios were required in the NL to maintain good winning percentages. A ratio between 2.0 and 2.9 was good enough for a winning record for over 70% of AL pitchers, but that level in the NL generated an above-.500 mark slightly more than half the time.

In short, in order to have at least a 70% chance of drafting a pitcher with a winning record, you must target NL pitchers with at least a 3.0 command ratio. To achieve the same odds in the AL, a 2.0 command ratio will suffice.

Power/contact rating

(BB + K) / IP

Measures the level by which a pitcher allows balls to be put into play. In general, extreme power pitchers can be successful even with poor defensive teams. Power pitchers tend to have greater longevity in the game. Contact pitchers with poor defenses behind them are high risks to have poor W-L records and ERA. **BENCHMARKS:** A level of 1.13+ describes pure throwers. A level of .93 or less describes high contact pitchers.

Balls in Play

Balls in play (BIP)
(Batters faced − (BB + HBP + SAC)) + H − K

The total number of batted balls that are hit fair, both hits and outs. An analysis of how these balls are hit—on the ground, in the air, hits, outs, etc.—can provide analytical insight, from player skill levels to the impact of luck on statistical output.

Batting average on balls in play *(Voros McCracken)*
(H − HR) / (Batters faced − (BB + HBP + SAC)) + H − K − HR

Abbreviated as BABIP; also called hit rate (H%). The percent of balls hit into the field of play that fall for hits. BENCHMARK: The league average is 30%, which is also the level that individual performances will regress to on a year to year basis. Any +/- variance of 3% or more can affect a pitcher's ERA.

BABIP as a leading indicator *(Voros McCracken)*

In 2000, Voros McCracken published a study that concluded that "there is little if any difference among major league pitchers in their ability to prevent hits on balls hit in the field of play." His assertion was that, while a Johan Santana would have a better ability to prevent a batter from getting wood on a ball, or perhaps keeping the ball in the park, once that ball was hit in the field of play, the probability of it falling for a hit was virtually no different than for any other pitcher.

Among the findings in his study were:

- There is little correlation between what a pitcher does one year in the stat and what he will do the next. This is not true with other significant stats (BB, K, HR).
- You can better predict a pitcher's hits per balls in play from the rate of the rest of the pitcher's team than from the pitcher's own rate.

This last point brings a team's defense into the picture. It begs the question, when a batter gets a hit, is it because the pitcher made a bad pitch, the batter took a good swing, or the defense was not positioned correctly?

Pitchers will often post hit rates per balls-in-play that are far off from the league average, but then revert to the mean the following year. As such, we can use that mean to project the direction of a pitcher's ERA.

Subsequent research has shown that ground ball or fly ball propensity has some impact on this rate.

Hit rate *(See Batting average on balls in play)*

Opposition batting average (OBA)
Hits allowed / (Batters faced − (BB + HBP + SAC))

The batting average achieved by opposing batters against a pitcher. BENCHMARKS: The best pitchers will have levels less than .250; the worst pitchers levels more than .300.

Opposition on base average (OOB)
(Hits allowed + BB) / ((Batters faced − (BB + HBP + SAC)) + Hits allowed + BB)

The on base average achieved by opposing batters against a pitcher. BENCHMARK: The best pitchers will have levels less than .300; the worst pitchers levels more than .375.

Walks plus hits divided by innings pitched (WHIP)

Essentially the same measure as opposition on base average, but used for Rotisserie purposes. BENCHMARKS: A WHIP of less than 1.20 is considered top level; more than 1.50 indicative of poor performance. Levels less than 1.00—allowing fewer runners than IP—represent extraordinary performance and are rarely maintained over time.

Ground ball, line drive, fly ball percentage (G/L/F)

The percentage of all balls-in-play that are hit on the ground, in the air and as line drives. For a pitcher, the ability to keep the ball on the ground can contribute to his statistical output exceeding his demonstrated skill level.

Ground ball tendency as a leading indicator *(John Burnson)*

Ground ball pitchers tend to give up fewer HRs than do fly ball pitchers. There is also evidence that GB pitchers have higher hit rates. In other words, a ground ball has a higher chance of being a hit than does a fly ball that is not out of the park.

GB pitchers have lower strikeout rates. We should be more forgiving of a low strikeout rate (under 5.5 K/9) if it belongs to an extreme ground ball pitcher.

GB pitchers have a lower ERA but a higher WHIP than do fly ball pitchers. On balance, GB pitchers come out ahead, even when considering strikeouts, because a lower ERA also leads to more wins.

Groundball and strikeout tendencies as indicators
(Mike Dranchak)

Pitchers were assembled into 9 groups based on the following profiles (minimum 23 starts in 2005):

Profile	Ground Ball Rate
Ground Ball	higher than 47%
Neutral	42% to 47%
Fly Ball	less than 42%

Profile	Strikeout Rate (k/9)
Strikeout	higher than 6.6 k/9
Average	5.4 to 6.6 k/9
Soft-Tosser	less than 5.4 k/9

Findings: Pitchers with higher strikeout rates had better ERAs and WHIPs than pitchers with lower strikeout rates, regardless of ground ball profile. However, for pitchers with similar strikeout rates, those with higher ground ball rates had better ERAs and WHIPs than those with lower ground ball rates.

Pitchers with higher strikeout rates tended to strand more baserunners than those with lower K rates. Fly ball pitchers tended to strand fewer runners than their GB or neutral counterparts within their strikeout profile.

Ground ball pitchers (especially those who lacked high-dominance) yielded more home runs per fly ball than did fly ball pitchers. However, the ERA risk was mitigated by the fact that ground ball pitchers (by definition) gave up fewer fly balls to begin with.

Extreme GB/FB pitchers *(Patrick Davitt)*

Among pitchers with normal strikeout levels, extreme GB pitchers (>3–7% of all batters faced) have ERAs about 0.4 runs lower than normal-GB% pitchers but only slight WHIP advantages. Extreme FB% pitchers (32% FB) show no ERA benefits.

Among High-K (>=24% of BF), however, extreme GBers have ERAs about 0.5 runs lower than normal-GB pitchers, and WHIPs about five points lower. Extreme FB% pitchers have ERAs about 0.2 runs lower than normal-FB pitchers, and WHIPs about 10 points lower.

Line drive percentage as a leading indicator *(Seth Samuels)*

Also beyond a pitcher's control is the percentage of balls-in-play that are line drives. Line drives do the most damage; from 1994-2003, here were the expected hit rates and number of total bases per type of BIP.

| | ┠------ Type of BIP ------┨ | | |
	GB	FB	LD
H%	26%	23%	56%
Total bases	0.29	0.57	0.80

Despite the damage done by LDs, pitchers do not have any innate skill to avoid them. There is little relationship between a pitcher's LD% one year and his rate the next year. All rates tend to regress towards a mean of 22.6%.

However, GB pitchers do have a slight ability to prevent LDs (21.7%) and extreme GB hurlers even moreso (18.5%). Extreme FB pitchers have a slight ability to prevent LDs (21.1%) as well.

Home run to fly ball rate (hr/f)

HR / FB

The percent of fly balls that are hit for home runs.

hr/f as a leading indicator *(John Burnson)*

McCracken's work focused on "balls in play," omitting home runs from the study. However, pitchers also do not have much control over the percentage of fly balls that turn into HR. Research shows that there is an underlying rate of HR as a percentage of fly balls of about 10%. A pitcher's HR/FB rate will vary each year but always tends to regress to that 10%. The element that pitchers do have control over is the number of fly balls they allow. That is the underlying skill or deficiency that controls their HR rate.

Pitchers who keep the ball out of the air more often correlate well with Roto value.

Opposition home runs per game (hr/9)

(HR Allowed x 9 / IP)

Also, expected opposition HR rate = (FB x 0.10) x 9 / IP

Measures how many HR a pitcher allows per game equivalent. Since FB tend to go yard at about a 10% rate, we can also estimate this rate off of fly balls. BENCHMARK: The best pitchers will have hr/9 levels of less than 1.0.

Runs

Expected earned run average (xERA)

Gill and Reeve version: *(.575 x H [per 9 IP]) + (.94 x HR [per 9 IP]) + (.28 x BB [per 9 IP]) – (.01 x K [per 9 IP]) – Normalizing Factor*

John Burnson version (used in this book):
(xER x 9)/IP, where xER is defined as
xER% x (FB/10) + (1-xS%) x [0.3 x (BIP – FB/10) + BB]
where xER% = 0.96 – (0.0284 x (GB/FB))
and
xS% = (64.5 + (K/9 x 1.2) – (BB/9 x (BB/9 + 1)) / 20)
+ ((0.0012 x (GB%^2)) – (0.001 x GB%) - 2.4)

xERA represents the an equivalent of what a pitcher's real ERA might be, calculated solely with skills-based measures. It is not influenced by situation-dependent factors.

Expected ERA variance

xERA – ERA

The variance between a pitcher's ERA and his xERA is a measure of over or underachievement. A positive variance indicates the potential for a pitcher's ERA to rise. A negative variance indicates the potential for ERA improvement. BENCHMARK: Discount variances that are less than 0.50. Any variance more than 1.00 (one run per game) is regarded as a indicator of future change.

Projected xERA or projected ERA?

Which should we be using to forecast a pitcher's ERA? Projected xERA is more accurate for looking ahead on a purely skills basis. Projected ERA includes *situation-dependent* events—bullpen support, park factors, etc.—which are reflected better by ERA. The optimal approach is to use both gauges as *a range of expectation* for forecasting purposes.

Strand rate (S%)

(H + BB – ER) / (H + BB – HR)

Measures the percentage of allowed runners a pitcher strands (earned runs only), which incorporates both individual pitcher skill and bullpen effectiveness. BENCHMARKS: The most adept at stranding runners will have S% levels over 75%. Those with rates over 80% will have artificially low ERAs which will be prone to relapse. Levels below 65% will inflate ERA but have a high probability of regression.

Expected strand rate *(Michael Weddell)*

*73.935 + K/9 - 0.116 * (BB/9*(BB/9+1))*
*+ (0.0047 * GB%^2 - 0.3385 * GB%)*
+ (MAX(2,MIN(4,IP/G))/2-1)
+ (0.82 if left-handed)

This formula is based on three core skills: strikeouts per nine innings, walks per nine innings, and groundballs per balls in play, with adjustments for whether the pitcher is a starter or reliever (measured by IP/G), and his handedness.

Strand rate as a leading indicator *(Ed DeCaria)*

Strand rate often regresses/rebounds toward past rates (usually 69-74%), resulting in Year 2 ERA changes:

% of Pitchers with Year 2 Regression/Rebound

Y1 S%	RP	SP	LR
<60%	100%	94%	94%
65	81%	74%	88%
70	53%	48%	65%
75	55%	85%	100%
80	80%	100%	100%
85	100%	100%	100%

Typical ERA Regression/Rebound in Year 2

Y1 S%	RP	SP	LR
<60%	-2.54	-2.03	-2.79
65	-1.00	-0.64	-0.93
70	-0.10	-0.05	-0.44
75	0.24	0.54	0.75
80	1.15	1.36	2.29
85	1.71	2.21	n/a

Starting pitchers (SP) have a narrower range of strand rate outcomes than do relievers (RP) or swingmen/long relievers (LR). **Relief pitchers** with Y1 strand rates of <=67% or >=78% are likely to experience a +/- ERA regression in Y2. **Starters and swingmen/long relievers** with Y1 strand rates of <=65% or >=75% are likely to experience a +/- ERA regression in Y2. Pitchers with strand rates that deviate more than a few points off of their individual expected strand rates are likely to experience some degree of ERA regression in Y2. Over-performing (or "lucky") pitchers are more likely than underperforming (or "unlucky") pitchers to see such a correction.

Wins

Projecting/chasing wins

There are five events that need to occur in order for a pitcher to post a single win...

1. He must pitch well, allowing few runs.
2. The offense must score enough runs.
3. The defense must successfully field all batted balls.
4. The bullpen must hold the lead.
5. The manager must leave the pitcher in for 5 innings, and not remove him if the team is still behind.

Of these five events, only one is within the control of the pitcher. As such, projecting or chasing wins based on skills alone can be an exercise in futility.

Home field advantage *(John Burnson)*

A 2006 study found that home starting pitchers get credited with a win in 38% of their outings. Visiting team starters are credited with a win in 33% of their outings.

Usage

Batters faced per game *(Craig Wright)*

$$((Batters\ faced - (BB + HBP + SAC)) + H + BB) / G$$

A measure of pitcher usage and one of the leading indicators for potential pitcher burnout.

Workload

Research suggests that there is a finite number of innings in a pitcher's arm. This number varies by pitcher, by development cycle, and by pitching style and repertoire. We can measure a pitcher's potential for future arm problems and/or reduced effectiveness (burnout):

Sharp increases in usage from one year to the next. Common wisdom has suggested that pitchers who significantly increase their workload from one year to the next are candidates for burnout symptoms. This has often been called the Verducci Effect, after writer Tom Verducci. BaseballHQ.com analyst Michael Weddell tested pitchers with sharp workload increases during the period 1988-2008 and found that no such effect exists.

Starters' overuse. Consistent "batters faced per game" (BF/G) levels of 28.0 or higher, combined with consistent seasonal IP totals of 200 or more may indicate burnout potential. Within a season, a BF/G of more than 30.0 with a projected IP total of 200 may indicate a late season fade.

Relievers' overuse. Warning flags should be up for relievers who post in excess of 100 IP in a season, while averaging fewer than 2 IP per outing.

When focusing solely on minor league pitchers, research results are striking:

Stamina: Virtually every minor league pitcher who had a BF/G of 28.5 or more in one season experienced a drop-off in BF/G the following year. Many were unable to ever duplicate that previous level of durability.

Performance: Most pitchers experienced an associated drop-off in their BPVs in the years following the 28.5 BF/G season. Some were able to salvage their effectiveness later on by moving to the bullpen.

Protecting young pitchers *(Craig Wright)*

There is a link between some degree of eventual arm trouble and a history of heavy workloads in a pitcher's formative years. Some recommendations from this research:

Teenagers (A-ball): No 200 IP seasons and no BF/G over 28.5 in any 150 IP span. No starts on three days rest.

Ages 20-22: Average no more than 105 pitches per start with a single game ceiling of 130 pitches.

Ages 23-24: Average no more than 110 pitches per start with a single game ceiling of 140 pitches.

When possible, a young starter should be introduced to the majors in long relief before he goes into the rotation.

Overall Performance Analysis

Base Performance Value (BPV)

((Dominance Rate - 5.0) x 18)
+ ((4.0 - Walk Rate) x 27))
+ (Ground ball rate as a whole number - 40%)

A single value that describes a player's overall raw skill level. This is more useful than traditional statistical gauges to track player performance trends and project future statistical output. The formula combines the individual raw skills of power, control and the ability to keep the ball down in the zone, all characteristics that are unaffected by most external factors. In tandem with a pitcher's strand rate, it provides a more complete picture of the elements that contribute to ERA, and therefore serves as an accurate tool to project likely changes in ERA. **BENCHMARKS:** A BPV of 50 is the minimum level required for long-term success. The elite of the bullpen aces will have BPVs in excess of 100 and it is rare for these stoppers to enjoy long term success with consistent levels under 75.

Base Performance Index (BPX)
BPV scaled to league average to account for year-to-year fluctuations in league-wide statistical performance. It's a snapshot of a player's overall skills compared to an average player. **BENCHMARK:** A level of 100 means a player had a league-average BPV in that given season.

Runs above replacement (RAR)
An estimate of the number of runs a player contributes above a "replacement level" player.

Batters create runs; pitchers save runs. But are batters and pitchers who have comparable RAR levels truly equal in value? Pitchers might be considered to have higher value. Saving an additional run is more important than producing an additional run. A pitcher who throws a shutout is guaranteed to win that game, whereas no matter how many runs a batter produces, his team can still lose given poor pitching support.

To calculate RAR for pitchers:

1. Start with the replacement level league ERA.
2. Subtract the pitcher's ERA. (To calculate projected RAR, use the pitcher's xERA.)
3. Multiply by number of games played, calculated as plate appearances (IP x 4.34) divided by 38.
4. Multiply the resulting RAR level by 1.08 to account for the variance between earned runs and total runs.

Handedness
1. LHers tend to peak about a year after RHers.
2. LHers post only 15% of the total saves. Typically, LHers are reserved for specialist roles so few are frontline closers.
3. RHers have slightly better command and HR rate.
4. There is no significant variance in ERA.
5. On an overall skills basis, RHers have ~6% advantage.

Skill-Specific Aging Patterns for Pitchers *(Ed DeCaria)*
Baseball forecasters obsess over "peak age" of player performance because we must understand player ascent toward and decline from that peak to predict future value. Most published aging analyses are done using composite estimates of value such as OPS or linear weights. By contrast, fantasy GMs are typically more concerned with category-specific player value (K, ERA, WHIP, etc.). We can better forecast what matters most by analyzing peak age of individual baseball skills rather than overall player value.

For pitchers, prior research has shown that pitcher value peaks somewhere in the late 20s to early 30s. But how does aging affect each demonstrable pitching skill?

Strikeout rate (k/9): Declines fairly linearly beginning at age 25.

Walk rate (bb/9): Improves until age 25 and holds somewhat steady until age 29, at which point it begins to steadily worsen. Deteriorating k/9 and bb/9 rates result in inefficiency, as it requires far more pitches to get an out. For starting pitchers, this affects the ability to pitch deep into games.

Innings Pitched per game (IP/G): Among starters, it improves slightly until age 27, then tails off considerably with age, costing pitchers nearly one full IP/G by age 33 and one more by age 39.

Hit rate (H%): Among pitchers, H% appears to increase slowly but steadily as pitchers age, to the tune of .002-.003 points per year.

Strand rate (S%): Very similar to hit rate, except strand rate decreases with age rather than increasing. GB%/LD%/FB%: Line drives increase steadily from age 24 onward, and outfield flies increase beginning at age 31. Because 70%+ of line drives fall for hits, and 10%+ of fly balls become home runs, this spells trouble for aging pitchers.

Home runs per fly ball (hr/f): As each year passes, a higher percentage of a pitcher's fly balls become home runs allowed increases with age.

Catchers' effect on pitching *(Thomas Hanrahan)*
A typical catcher handles a pitching staff better after having been with a club for a few years. Research has shown that there is an improvement in team ERA of approximately 0.37 runs from a catcher's rookie season to his prime years with a club. Expect a pitcher's ERA to be higher than expected if he is throwing to a rookie backstop.

First productive season *(Michael Weddell)*
To find those starting pitchers who are about to post their first productive season in the majors (10 wins, 150 IP, ERA of 4.00 or less), look for:

- Pitchers entering their age 23-26 seasons, especially those about to pitch their age 25 season.
- Pitchers who already have good skills, shown by an xERA in the prior year of 4.25 or less.
- Pitchers coming off of at least a partial season in the majors without a major health problem.
- To the extent that one speculates on pitchers who are one skill away, look for pitchers who only need to improve their control (bb/9).

Overall pitching breakout profile *(Brandon Kruse)*
A breakout performance is defined here as one where a player posts a Rotisserie value of $20 or higher after having never achieved $10 previously. These criteria are primarily used to validate an apparent breakout in the current season but may also be used carefully to project a potential breakout for an upcoming season.

- Age 27 or younger
- Minimum 5.6 Dom, 2.0 Cmd, 1.1 hr/9 and 50 BPV
- Maximum 30% hit rate
- Minimum 71% strand rate
- Starters should have a H% no greater than the previous year; relievers should show improved command
- Maximum xERA of 4.00

Career year drop-off *(Rick Wilton)*

Research shows that a pitcher's post-career year drop-off, on average, looks like this:

- ERA increases by 1.00
- WHIP increases by 0.14.
- Nearly 6 fewer wins

Closers

Saves

There are six events that need to occur in order for a relief pitcher to post a single save:

1. The starting pitcher and middle relievers must pitch well.
2. The offense must score enough runs.
3. It must be a reasonably close game.
4. The manager must put the pitcher in for a save opportunity.
5. The pitcher must pitch well and hold the lead.
6. The manager must let him finish the game.

Of these six events, only one is within the control of the relief pitcher. As such, projecting saves for a reliever has little to do with skill and a lot to do with opportunity. However, pitchers with excellent skills may create opportunity for themselves.

Saves conversion rate (Sv%)

Saves / Save Opportunities

The percentage of save opportunities that are successfully converted. **BENCHMARK:** We look for a minimum 80% for long-term success.

Leverage index (LI) *(Tom Tango)*

Leverage index measures the amount of swing in the possible change in win probability indexed against an average value of 1.00. Thus, relievers who come into games in various situations create a composite score and if that average score is higher than 1.00, then their manager is showing enough confidence in them to try to win games with them. If the average score is below 1.00, then the manager is using them, but not showing nearly as much confidence that they can win games.

Saves chances and wins *(Craig Neuman)*

Should the quality of a pitcher's MLB team be a consideration in drafting a closer? One school of thought says that more wins means more save opportunities. The flipside is that when poor teams win they do so by a small margin, which means more save opportunities.

A six-season correlation yielded these results for saves, save opportunities, save percentage, wins, quality starts and run differential. (Any value above .50 suggests at least a moderate correlation.)

	Sv	SvO	W	Sv%	RD	QS
SV	1					
SVO	.78	1				
W	.66	.41	1			
S%	.66	.05	.56	1		
RD	.48	.26	.92	.44	1	
QS	.41	.24	.58	.34	.60	1

Saves do correlate with wins. As for the theory that teams who play in close games would accumulate more saves, the low correlation between saves and run differential seems to dispel that a bit.

On average, teams registered one save for every two wins. However, there is a relationship between wins and the number of saves per win a team achieves:

Win Total	Saves/Win
>90	.494
80-89	.492
70-79	.505
<69	.525

Teams with fewer wins end up with more saves per win. So, when poor teams win, they are more likely to have a save chance.

Origin of closers

History has long maintained that ace closers are not easily recognizable early on in their careers, so that every season does see its share of the unexpected. Rex Brothers, Daniel Farquhar, Kevin Gregg, Jim Henderson, Mark Melancon, Edward Mjuica, Koji Uehara … who would have thought it a year ago?

Accepted facts, all of which have some element of truth:

- You cannot find major league closers from pitchers who were closers in the minors.
- Closers begin their careers as starters.
- Closers are converted set-up men.
- Closers are pitchers who were unable to develop a third effective pitch.

More simply, closers are a product of circumstance.

Are the minor leagues a place to look at all?

From 1990-2004, there were 280 twenty-save seasons in Double-A and Triple-A, accomplished by 254 pitchers.

Of those 254, only 46 ever made it to the majors at all.

Of those 46, only 13 ever saved 20 games in a season.

Of those 13, only 5 ever posted more than one 20-save season in the majors: John Wetteland, Mark Wohlers, Ricky Bottalico, Braden Looper and Francisco Cordero.

Five out of 254 pitchers, over 15 years—a rate of 2%.

One of the reasons that minor league closers rarely become major league closers is because, in general, they do not get enough innings in the minors to sufficiently develop their arms into big-league caliber.

In fact, organizations do not look at minor league closing performance seriously, assigning that role to pitchers who they do not see as legitimate prospects. The average age of minor league closers over the past decade has been 27.5.

Elements of saves success

The task of finding future closing potential comes down to looking at two elements:

Talent: The raw skills to mow down hitters for short periods of time. Optimal BPVs over 100, but not under 75.

Opportunity: The more important element, yet the one that pitchers have no control over.

There are pitchers that have Talent, but not Opportunity. These pitchers are not given a chance to close for a variety of reasons (e.g. being blocked by a solid front-liner in the pen, being left-handed, etc.), but are good to own because they will not likely hurt your pitching staff. You just can't count on them for saves, at least not in the near term.

There are pitchers that have Opportunity, but not Talent. MLB managers decide who to give the ball to in the 9th inning based on their own perceptions about what skills are required to succeed, even if those perceived "skills" don't translate into acceptable BPI levels.

Those pitchers without the BPIs may have some initial short-term success, but their long-term prognosis is poor and they are high risks to your roster. Classic examples of the short life span of these types of pitchers include Matt Karchner, Heath Slocumb, Ryan Kohlmeier, Dan Miceli, Joe Borowski and Danny Kolb. More recent examples include Brian Fuentes and Javy Guerra.

Closers' job retention *(Michael Weddell)*
Of pitchers with 20 or more saves in one year, only 67.5% of these closers earned 20 or more saves the following year. The variables that best predicted whether a closer would avoid this attrition:

- *Saves history:* Career saves was the most important factor.
- *Age:* Closers are most likely to keep their jobs at age 27. For long-time closers, their growing career saves totals more than offset the negative impact of their advanced ages. Older closers without a long history of racking up saves tend to be bad candidates for retaining their roles.
- *Performance:* Actual performance, measured by ERA+, was of only minor importance.
- *Being right-handed:* Increased the odds of retaining the closer's role by 9% over left-handers.

How well can we predict which closers will keep their jobs? Of the 10 best closers during 1989-2007, 90% saved at least 20 games during the following season. Of the 10 worst bets, only 20% saved at least 20 games the next year.

Closer volatility history

			Number of Closers		
Year	Drafted	Avg R$	Failed	%	New Sources
1999	23	$25	5	22%	7
2000	27	$25	10	37%	9
2001	25	$26	7	28%	7
2002	28	$22	8	29%	12
2003	29	$21.97	17	59%	14
2004	29	$19.78	11	38%	15
2005	28	$20.79	12	43%	15
2006	30	$17.80	10	33%	12
2007	28	$17.67	10	36%	11
2008	32	$17.78	10	31%	11
2009	28	$17.56	9	32%	13
2010	28	$16.96	7	25%	13
2011	30	$15.47	11	37%	8
2012	29	$15.28	19	66%	18
2013	29	$15.55	9	31%	13

Drafted refers to the number of saves sources purchased in both LABR and Tout Wars experts leagues each year. These only include relievers drafted for at least $10, specifically for saves speculation. *Avg R$* refers to the average purchase price of these

pitchers in the AL-only and NL-only leagues. *Failed* is the number (and percentage) of saves sources drafted that did not return at least 50% of their value that year. The failures include those that lost their value due to ineffectiveness, injury or managerial decision. *New Sources* are arms that were drafted for less than $10 (if drafted at all) but finished with at least double-digit saves.

The failed saves investments in 2013 were John Axford, Rafael Betancourt, Jonathan Broxton, Joel Hanrahan, Brandon League, Carlos Marmol, Jason Motte, J.J. Putz and Tom Wilhelmsen. The new sources in 2013 were Heath Bell, Joaquin Benoit, Rex Brothers, Daniel Farquhar, Ernesto Frieri, Kevin Gregg, LaTroy Hawkins, Jim Henderson, Casey Janssen, Mark Melancon, Edward Mujica, Koji Uehara and Brad Ziegler.

BPV as a leading indicator *(Doug Dennis)*
Research has shown that base performance value (BPV) is an excellent indicator of long-term success as a closer. Here are 20-plus saves seasons, by year:

		|----------BPV----------|	
Year	No.	100+	75+	<75
1999	26	27%	54%	46%
2000	24	25%	54%	46%
2001	25	56%	80%	20%
2002	25	60%	72%	28%
2003	25	36%	64%	36%
2004	23	61%	61%	39%
2005	25	36%	64%	36%
2006	25	52%	72%	28%
2007	23	52%	74%	26%
MEAN	*25*	*45%*	*66%*	*34%*

Though 20-saves success with a 75+ BPV is only a 66% percentage play in any given year, the below-75 group is composed of closers who are rarely able to repeat the feat in the following season:

Year	No. with BPV < 75	No. who followed up 20+ saves <75 BPV
1999	12	2
2000	11	2
2001	5	2
2002	7	3
2003	9	3
2004	9	2
2005	9	1
2006	7	3
2007	6	0

Other Relievers

Projecting holds *(Doug Dennis)*
Here are some general rules of thumb for identifying pitchers who might be in line to accumulate holds. The percentages represent the portion of 2003's top holds leaders who fell into the category noted.

1. Left-handed set-up men with excellent BPIs. (43%)
2. A "go-to" right-handed set-up man with excellent BPIs. This is the one set-up RHer that a manager turns to with a small lead in the 7th or 8th innings. These pitchers also tend to vulture wins. (43%, but 6 of the top 9)
3. Excellent BPIs, but not a firm role as the main LHed or RHed set-up man. Roles change during the season; cream rises to the top. Relievers projected to post great BPIs often overtake lesser set-up men in-season. (14%)

Reliever efficiency percent (REff%)

(Wins + Saves + Holds) / (Wins + Losses + SaveOpps + Holds)

This is a measure of how often a reliever contributes positively to the outcome of a game. A record of consistent, positive impact on game outcomes breeds managerial confidence, and that confidence could pave the way to save opportunities. For those pitchers suddenly thrust into a closer's role, this formula helps gauge their potential to succeed based on past successes in similar roles. BENCHMARK: Minimum of 80%.

Vulture

A pitcher, typically a middle reliever, who accumulates an unusually high number of wins by preying on other pitchers' misfortunes. More accurately, this is a pitcher typically brought into a game after a starting pitcher has put his team behind, and then pitches well enough and long enough to allow his offense to take the lead, thereby "vulturing" a win from the starter.

In-Season Analysis

Pure Quality Starts

We've always approached performance measures on an aggregate basis. Each individual event that our statistics chronicle gets dumped into a huge pool of data. We then use our formulas to try to sort and slice and manipulate the data into more usable information.

Pure Quality Starts (PQS) take a different approach. It says that the smallest unit of measure should not be the "event" but instead be the "game." Within that game, we can accumulate all the strikeouts, hits and walks, and evaluate that outing as a whole. After all, when a pitcher takes the mound, he is either "on" or "off" his game; he is either dominant or struggling, or somewhere in between.

In PQS, we give a starting pitcher credit for exhibiting certain skills in each of his starts. Then by tracking his "PQS Score" over time, we can follow his progress. A starter earns one point for each of the following criteria:

1. *The pitcher must go a minimum of 6 innings.* This measures stamina. If he goes less than 5 innings, he automatically gets a total PQS score of zero, no matter what other stats he produces.

2. *He must allow no more than an equal number of hits to the number of innings pitched.* This measures hit prevention.

3. *His number of strikeouts must be no fewer than two less than his innings pitched.* This measures dominance.

4. *He must strike out at least twice as many batters as he walks.* This measures command.

5. *He must allow no more than one home run.* This measures his ability to keep the ball in the park.

A perfect PQS score is 5. Any pitcher who averages 3 or more over the course of the season is probably performing admirably. The nice thing about PQS is it allows you to approach each start as more than an all-or-nothing event.

Note the absence of earned runs. No matter how many runs a pitcher allows, if he scores high on the PQS scale, he has hurled

a good game in terms of his base skills. The number of runs allowed—a function of not only the pitcher's ability but that of his bullpen and defense—will tend to even out over time.

It doesn't matter if a few extra balls got through the infield, or the pitcher was given the hook in the fourth or sixth inning, or the bullpen was able to strand their inherited baserunners. When we look at performance in the aggregate, those events do matter, and will affect a pitcher's BPIs and ERA. But with PQS, the minutia is less relevant than the overall performance.

In the end, a dominating performance is a dominating performance, whether Gerrit Cole is hurling a 3-hit shutout or giving up three runs while striking out 8 in 7 IP. And a disaster is still a disaster, whether Tyler Cloyd gets a 4th inning hook after giving up 5 runs, or "takes one for the team" and gets shelled for seven runs in one inning.

Skill versus consistency

Two pitchers have identical 4.50 ERAs and identical 3.0 PQS averages. Their PQS logs look like this:

PITCHER A:	3	3	3	3	3
PITCHER B:	5	0	5	0	5

Which pitcher would you rather have on your team? The risk-averse manager would choose Pitcher A as he represents the perfectly known commodity. Many fantasy leaguers might opt for Pitcher B because his occasional dominating starts show that there is an upside. His Achilles Heel is inconsistency—he is unable to sustain that high level. Is there any hope for Pitcher B?

- If a pitcher's inconsistency is characterized by more poor starts than good starts, his upside is limited.
- Pitchers with extreme inconsistency rarely get a full season of starts.
- However, inconsistency is neither chronic nor fatal.

The outlook for Pitcher A is actually worse. Disaster avoidance might buy these pitchers more starts, but history shows that the lack of dominating outings is more telling of future potential. In short, consistent mediocrity is bad.

PQS DOMination and DISaster rates *(Gene McCaffrey)*

DOM% is the percentage of a starting pitcher's outings that rate as a PQS-4 or PQS-5. DIS% is the percentage that rate as a PQS-0 or PQS-1.

DOM/DIS percentages open up a new perspective, providing us with two separate scales of performance. In tandem, they measure consistency.

PQS ERA (qERA)

A pitcher's DOM/DIS split can be converted back to an equivalent ERA. By creating a grid of individual DOM% and DIS% levels, we can determine the average ERA at each cross point. The result is an ERA based purely on PQS.

Quality/consistency score (QC)

(DOM% – (2 x DIS%)) x 2

Using PQS and DOM/DIS percentages, this score measures both the quality of performance as well as start-to-start consistency.

PQS correlation with Quality Starts (Paul Petera)

PQS	QS%
0	0%
1	3%
2	21%
3	51%
4	75%
5	95%

Forward-looking PQS (John Burnson)

PQS says whether a pitcher performed ably in a *past* start—it doesn't say anything about how he'll do in the *next* start. We built a version of PQS that attempts to do that. For each series of five starts for a pitcher, we looked at his average IP, K/9, HR/9, H/9, and K/BB, and then whether the pitcher won his next start. We catalogued the results by indicator and calculated the observed future winning percentage for each data point.

This research suggested that a forward-looking version of PQS should have these criteria:

- The pitcher must have lasted at least 6.2 innings.
- He must have recorded at least IP – 1 strikeouts.
- He must have allowed zero home runs.
- He must have allowed no more hits than IP+2.
- He must have had a Command (K/BB) of at least 2.5.

In-season ERA/xERA variance as a leading indicator
(Matt Cederholm)

Pitchers with large first-half ERA/xERA variances will see regression towards their xERA in the second half, if they are allowed (and are able) to finish out the season. Starters have a stronger regression tendency than relievers, which we would expect to see given the larger sample size. In addition, there is substantial attrition among all types of pitchers, but those who are "unlucky" have a much higher rate.

An important corollary: While a pitcher underperforming his xERA is very likely to rebound in the second half, such regression hinges on his ability to hold onto his job long enough to see that regression come to fruition. Healthy veteran pitchers with an established role are more likely to experience the second half boost than a rookie starter trying to make his mark.

Pure Quality Relief (Patrick Davitt)

A system for evaluating reliever outings. The scoring :

1. Two points for the first out, and one point for each subsequent out, to a maximum of four points.
2. One point for having at least one strikeout for every four full outs (one K for 1-4 outs, two Ks for 5-8 outs, etc.).
3. One point for zero baserunners, minus one point for each baserunner, though allowing the pitcher one unpenalized runner for each three full outs (one baserunner for 3-5 outs, two for 6-8 outs, three for nine outs)
4. Minus one point for each earned run, though allowing one ER for 8– or 9-out appearances.
5. An automatic PQR-0 for allowing a home run.

Avoiding relief disasters (Ed DeCaria)

Relief disasters (defined as ER>=3 and IP<=3), occur in 5%+ of all appearances. The chance of a disaster exceeds 13% in any 7-day period. To minimize the odds of a disaster, we created a model that produced the following list of factors, in order of influence:

1. Strength of opposing offense
2. Park factor of home stadium
3. BB/9 over latest 31 days (more walks is bad)
4. Pitch count over previous 7 days (more pitches is bad)
5. Latest 31 Days ERA>xERA (recent bad luck continues)

Daily league owners who can slot relievers by individual game should also pay attention to days of rest: pitching on less rest than one is accustomed to increases disaster risk.

Sample size reliability (Russell Carleton)

At what point during the season do statistics become reliable indicators of skill? Measured in batters faced:

150: K/PA, ground ball rate, line drive rate
200: Fly ball rate, GB/FB
500: K/BB
550: BB/PA

Unlisted stats did not stabilize over a full season of play. *(Note that 150 BF is roughly equivalent to six outings for a starting pitcher; 550 BF would be 22 starts, etc.)*

Pitching streaks

It is possible to find predictive value in strings of DOMinating (PQS 4/5) or DISaster (PQS 0/1) starts:

Once a pitcher enters into a DOM streak of any length, the probability is that his next start is going to be better than average. The further a player is into a DOM streak, the higher the likelihood that the subsequent performance will be high quality. In fact, once a pitcher has posted six DOM starts in a row, there is greater than a 70% probability that the streak will continue. When it does end, there is less than a 10% probability that the streak-breaker is going to be a DISaster.

Once a pitcher enters into a DIS streak of any length, the probability is that his next start is going to be below average, even if it breaks the streak. However, DIS streaks end quickly. Once a pitcher hits the skids, odds are low that he will post a good start in the short term, though the duration itself should be brief.

5-game PQS predictability (Bill Macey)

5-Game avg PQS	Avg PQS	DOM%	DIS%
Less than 1	2.1	27%	40%
Between 1 and 2	2.4	32%	32%
Between 2 and 3	2.6	36%	26%
Between 3 and 4	3.0	47%	19%
4 or greater	3.5	61%	12%

Pitchers with higher PQS scores in their previous 5 starts tended to pitch better in their next start. But the relative parity of subsequent DOM and DIS starts for all but the hottest of streaks warn us not to put too much effort into predicting any given start. That more than a quarter of pitchers who had been awful over their previous 5 starts still put up a dominating start next shows that anything can happen in a single game.

Pitch counts as a leading indicator

Workload analysis is an ongoing science. However, can we draw any conclusions from short-term trends? For this analysis, GS from 2005-2006 were isolated—looking at pitch counts and PQS scores—and compared with each pitcher's subsequent outing. We examined two-start trends, the immediate impact that the length of one performance would have on the next start.

Pitch Ct	Pct.	PQS	Next Start DOM	DIS	qERA
< 80	13%	2.5	33%	28%	4.90
80-89	14%	2.6	35%	29%	4.82
90-99	28%	2.7	37%	26%	4.82
100-109	30%	2.9	41%	23%	4.56
110-119	13%	3.1	46%	18%	4.40
120+	3%	3.0	43%	20%	4.56

There does appear to be merit to the concern over limiting hurlers to 120 pitches per start. The research shows a slight drop-off in performance in those starts following a 120+ pitch outing. However, the impact does not appear to be all that great and the fallout might just affect those pitchers who have no business going that deep into games anyway. Additional detail to this research (not displayed) showed that higher-skilled pitchers were more successful throwing over 120 pitches but less-skilled pitchers were not.

Days of rest as a leading indicator

Workload is only part of the equation. The other part is how often a pitcher is sent out to the mound. For instance, it's possible that a hurler might see no erosion in skill after a 120+ pitch outing if he had enough rest between starts:

PITCH COUNTS Three days rest	Pct.	PQS	NEXT START DOM	DIS	qERA
< 100	72%	2.8	35%	17%	4.60
100-119	28%	2.3	44%	44%	5.21
Four Days rest					
< 100	52%	2.7	36%	27%	4.82
100-119	45%	2.9	42%	22%	4.56
120+	3%	3.0	42%	20%	4.44
Five Days rest					
< 100	54%	2.7	38%	25%	4.79
100-119	43%	3.0	44%	19%	4.44
120+	3%	3.2	48%	14%	4.28
Six Days rest					
< 100	58%	2.7	39%	30%	5.00
100-119	40%	2.8	40%	26%	4.82
120+	3%	1.8	20%	60%	7.98
20+ Days rest					
< 100	85%	1.8	20%	46%	6.12
100-119	15%	2.3	33%	33%	5.08

Managers are reluctant to put a starter on the mound with any fewer than four days rest, and the results for those who pitched deeper into games shows why. Four days rest is the most common usage pattern and even appears to mitigate the drop-off at 120+ pitches.

Perhaps most surprising is that an extra day of rest improves performance across the board and squeezes even more productivity out of the 120+ pitch outings.

Performance begins to erode at six days (and continues at 7-20 days, though those are not displayed). The 20+ Days chart represents pitchers who were primarily injury rehabs and failed call-ups, and the length of the "days rest" was occasionally well over 100 days. This chart shows the result of their performance in their first start back. The good news is that the workload was limited for 85% of these returnees. The bad news is that these are not pitchers you want active. So for those who obsess over getting your DL returnees activated in time to catch every start, the better percentage play is to avoid that first outing.

Post-DL Pitching Performance *(Bill Macey)*

One question that fantasy baseball managers frequently struggle with is whether or not to start a pitcher when he first returns from the disabled list. A 2011 study compared each pitcher's PQS score in their first post-DL start against his average PQS score for that year (limited to pitchers who had at least 15 starts during the year and whose first post-DL appearance was as a starter). The findings:

- In general, exercise caution with immediate activations. Pitchers performed worse than their yearly average in the first post-DL start, with a high rate of PQS-DIS starts.

- Avoid pitchers returning from the DL due to an arm injury, as they perform significantly worse than average.

- If there are no better options available, feel comfortable activating pitchers who spent near the minimum amount of time on the DL and/or suffered a leg injury, as they typically perform at a level consistent with their yearly average.

Other Diamonds

The Pitching Postulates

1. Never sign a soft-tosser to a long-term contract.
2. Right-brain dominance has a very long shelf life.
3. A fly ball pitcher who gives up many HRs is expected. A GB pitcher who gives up many HRs is making mistakes.
4. Never draft a contact fly ball pitcher who plays in a hitter's park.
5. Only bad teams ever have a need for an inning-eater.
6. Never chase wins.

Dontrelle Willis List

Pitchers with BPIs so incredibly horrible that you have to wonder how they can possibly draw a major league paycheck year after year.

Chaconian

Having the ability to post many saves despite sub-Mendoza BPIs and an ERA in the stratosphere.

Vintage Eck Territory

A BPV greater than 200, a level achieved by Dennis Eckersley for four consecutive years.

Edwhitsonitis

A dreaded malady marked by the sudden and unexplained loss of pitching ability upon a trade to the New York Yankees.

ERA Benchmark

A half run of ERA over 200 innings comes out to just one earned run every four starts.

Gopheritis (also, Acute Gopheritis and Chronic Gopheritis)

The dreaded malady in which a pitcher is unable to keep the ball in the park. Pitchers with gopheritis have a FB rate of at least 40%. More severe cases have a FB% over 45%.

The Knuckleballers Rule: Knuckleballers don't follow no stinkin' rules.

Brad Lidge Lament

When a closer posts a 62% strand rate, he has nobody to blame but himself.

LOOGY (Lefty One Out GuY)

A left-handed reliever whose job it is to get one out in important situations.

Vin Mazzaro Vindication

Occasional nightmares (2.1 innings, 14 ER) are just a part of the game.

Meltdown

Any game in which a starting pitcher allows more runs than innings pitched.

Lance Painter Lesson

Six months of solid performance can be screwed up by one bad outing. (In 2000, Painter finished with an ERA of 4.76. However, prior to his final appearance of the year—in which he pitched 1 inning and gave up 8 earned runs—his ERA was 3.70.)

The Five Saves Certainties

1. On every team, there will be save opportunities and someone will get them. At a bare minimum, there will be at least 30 saves to go around, and not unlikely more than 45.

2. Any pitcher could end up being the chief beneficiary. Bullpen management is a fickle endeavor.

3. Relief pitchers are often the ones that require the most time at the start of the season to find a groove. The weather is cold, the schedule is sparse and their usage is erratic.

4. Despite the talk about "bullpens by committee," managers prefer a go-to guy. It makes their job easier.

5. As many as 50% of the saves in any year will come from pitchers who are unselected at the end of Draft Day.

Soft-tosser

A pitcher with a strikeout rate of 5.5 or less.

Soft-tosser land

The place where feebler arms leave their fortunes in the hands of the defense, variable hit and strand rates, and park dimensions. It's a place where many live, but few survive.

Prospects

General

Minor league prospecting in perspective

In our perpetual quest to be the genius who uncovers the next Mike Trout when he's still in high school, there is an obsessive fascination with minor league prospects. That's not to say that prospecting is not important. The issue is perspective:

1. During the 10 year period of 1996 to 2005, only 8% of players selected in the first round of the Major League Baseball First Year Player Draft went on to become stars.

2. Some prospects are going to hit the ground running (Jose Fernandez) and some are going to immediately struggle (Alex Gordon), no matter what level of hype follows them.

3. Some prospects are going to start fast (since the league is unfamiliar with them) and then fade (as the league figures them out). Others will start slow (since they are unfamiliar with the opposition) and then improve (as they adjust to the competition). So if you make your free agent and roster decisions based on small early samples sizes, you are just as likely to be an idiot as a genius.

4. How any individual player will perform relative to his talent is largely unknown because there is a psychological element that is vastly unexplored. Some make the transition to the majors seamlessly, some not, completely regardless of how talented they are.

5. Still, talent is the best predictor of future success, so major league equivalent base performance indicators still have a valuable role in the process. As do scouting reports, carefully filtered.

6. Follow the player's path to the majors. Did he have to repeat certain levels? Was he allowed to stay at a level long enough to learn how to adjust to the level of competition? A player with only two great months at Double-A is a good bet to struggle if promoted directly to the majors because he was never fully tested at Double-A, let alone Triple-A.

7. Younger players holding their own against older competition is a good thing. Older players reaching their physical peak, regardless of their current address, can be a good thing too. The R.A. Dickeys and Ryan Ludwicks can have some very profitable years.

8. Remember team context. A prospect with superior potential often will not unseat a steady but unspectacular incumbent, especially one with a large contract.

9. Don't try to anticipate how a team is going to manage their talent, both at the major and minor league level. You might think it's time to promote Byron Buxton and give him an everyday role. You are not running the Twins.

10. Those who play in shallow, one-year leagues should have little cause to be looking at the minors at all. The risk versus reward is so skewed against you, and there is so much talent available with a track record, that taking a chance on an unproven commodity makes little sense.

11. Decide where your priorities really are. If your goal is to win, prospect analysis is just a *part* of the process, not the entire process.

Factors affecting minor league stats *(Terry Linhart)*

1. Often, there is an exaggerated emphasis on short-term performance in an environment that is supposed to focus on the long-term. Two poor outings don't mean a 21-year-old pitcher is washed up.

2. Ballpark dimensions and altitude create hitters parks and pitchers parks, but a factor rarely mentioned is that many parks in the lower minors are inconsistent in their field quality. Minor league clubs have limited resources to maintain field conditions, and this can artificially depress defensive statistics while inflating stats like batting average.

3. Some players' skills are so superior to the competition at their level that you can't get a true picture of what they're going to do from their stats alone.

4. Many pitchers are told to work on secondary pitches in unorthodox situations just to gain confidence in the pitch. The result is an artificially increased number of walks.

5. The #3, #4, and #5 pitchers in the lower minors are truly longshots to make the majors. They often possess only two pitches and are unable to disguise the off-speed offerings. Hitters can see inflated statistics in these leagues.

Minor league level versus age

When evaluating minor leaguers, look at the age of the prospect in relation to the median age of the league he is in:

Low level A	Between 19-20
Upper level A	Around 20
Double-A	21
Triple-A	22

These are the ideal ages for prospects at the particular level. If a prospect is younger than most and holds his own against older and more experienced players, elevate his status. If he is older than the median, reduce his status.

Triple-A experience as a leading indicator

The probability that a minor leaguer will immediately succeed in the majors can vary depending upon the level of Triple-A experience he has amassed at the time of call-up.

	BATTERS		PITCHERS	
	< 1 Yr	Full	< 1 Yr	Full
Performed well	57%	56%	16%	56%
Performed poorly	21%	38%	77%	33%
2nd half drop-off	21%	7%	6%	10%

The odds of a batter achieving immediate MLB success was slightly more than 50-50. More than 80% of all pitchers promoted with less than a full year at Triple-A struggled in their first year in the majors. Those pitchers with a year in Triple-A succeeded at a level equal to that of batters.

Major League Equivalency (MLE) *(Bill James)*

A formula that converts a player's minor or foreign league statistics into a comparable performance in the major leagues. These are not projections, but conversions of current performance. MLEs contain adjustments for the level of play in individual leagues and teams. They work best with Triple-A stats, not quite as well with Double-A stats, and hardly at all with the lower levels. Foreign conversions are still a work in process. James' original formula only addressed batting. Our research has devised conversion formulas for pitchers, however, their best use comes when looking at BPIs, not traditional stats.

Adjusting to the competition

All players must "adjust to the competition" at every level of professional play. Players often get off to fast or slow starts. During their second tour at that level is when we get to see whether the slow starters have caught up or whether the league has figured out the fast starters. That second half "adjustment" period is a good baseline for projecting the subsequent season, in the majors or minors.

Premature major league call-ups often negate the ability for us to accurately evaluate a player due to the lack of this adjustment period. For instance, a hotshot Double-A player might open the season in Triple-A. After putting up solid numbers for a month, he gets a call to the bigs, and struggles. The fact is, we do not have enough evidence that the player has mastered the Triple-A level. We don't know whether the rest of the league would have caught up to him during his second tour of the league. But now he's labeled as an underperformer in the bigs when in fact he has never truly proven his skills at the lower levels.

Rookie playing time

Weaker-performing teams have historically (1976-2009) been far more dependent on debut rookies than stronger-performing teams. This makes sense, as non-contenders have greater incentive and flexibility to allow young players to gain experience at the MLB level. Additionally, individual player characteristics can provide clues as to which debut rookies will earn significant PA or IP:

- Rookies who can play up-the-middle (CF, 2B, SS) or on the left side (LF, 3B) are likely to see more debut playing time than those at 1B, RF, C, or DH.
- LH batters and pitchers are slightly more likely than righties to earn significant PA or IP in their debuts.
- Rookies under age 22 earn nearly twice the PAs of those aged 25-26 in their debut season. Pitchers under age 23 earn twice the innings of those aged 26-27.

Bull Durham prospects

There is some potential talent in older players—age 26, 27 or higher—who, for many reasons (untimely injury, circumstance, bad luck, etc.), don't reach the majors until they have already been downgraded from prospect to suspect. Equating potential with age is an economic reality for major league clubs, but not necessarily a skills reality.

Skills growth and decline is universal, whether it occurs at the major league level or in the minors. So a high-skills journeyman

in Triple-A is just as likely to peak at age 27 as a major leaguer of the same age. The question becomes one of opportunity—will the parent club see fit to reap the benefits of that peak performance?

Prospecting these players for your fantasy team is, admittedly, a high risk endeavor, though there are some criteria you can use. Look for a player who is/has:

- Optimally, age 27-28 for overall peak skills, age 30-31 for power skills, or age 28-31 for pitchers.
- At least two seasons of experience at Triple-A. Career Double-A players are generally not good picks.
- Solid base skills levels.
- Shallow organizational depth at their position.
- Notable winter league or spring training performance.

Players who meet these conditions are not typically draftable players, but worthwhile reserve or FAAB picks.

Batters

MLE PX as a leading indicator *(Bill Macey)*

Looking at minor league performance (as MLE) in one year and the corresponding MLB performance the subsequent year:

	Year 1 MLE	Year 2 MLB
Observations	496	496
Median PX	95	96
Percent PX > 100	43%	46%

In addition, 53% of the players had a MLB PX in year 2 that exceeded their MLE PX in year 1. A slight bias towards improved performance in year 2 is consistent with general career trajectories.

Year 1 MLE PX	Year 2 MLB PX	Pct. Incr	Pct. MLB PX > 100
<= 50	61	70.3%	5.4%
51-75	85	69.6%	29.4%
76-100	93	55.2%	39.9%
101-125	111	47.4%	62.0%
126-150	119	32.1%	66.1%
> 150	142	28.6%	76.2%

Slicing the numbers by performance level, there is a good amount of regression to the mean.

Players rarely suddenly develop power at the MLB level if they didn't previously display that skill at the minor league level. However, the relatively large gap between the median MLE PX and MLB PX for these players, 125 to 110, confirms the notion that the best players continue to improve once they reach the major leagues.

MLE contact rate as a leading indicator *(Bill Macey)*

There is a strong positive correlation (0.63) between a player's MLE ct% in Year 1 and his actual ct% at the MLB level in Year 2.

MLE ct%	Year 1 MLE ct%	Year 2 MLB ct%
< 70%	69%	68%
70% - 74%	73%	72%
75% - 79%	77%	75%
80% - 84%	82%	77%
85% - 89%	87%	82%
90% +	91%	86%
TOTAL	**84%**	**79%**

There is very little difference between the median MLE BA in Year 1 and the median MLB BA in Year 2:

MLE ct%	Year 1 MLE BA	Year 2 MLB BA
< 70%	.230	.270
70% - 74%	.257	.248
75% - 79%	.248	.255
80% - 84%	.257	.255
85% - 89%	.266	.270
90% +	.282	.273
TOTAL	.261	.262

Excluding the <70% cohort (which was a tiny sample size), there is a positive relationship between MLE ct% and MLB BA.

Pitchers

BPIs as a leading indicator for pitching success

The percentage of hurlers that were good investments in the year that they were called up varied by the level of their historical minor league BPIs prior to that year.

Pitchers who had:	Fared well	Fared poorly
Good indicators	79%	21%
Marginal or poor indicators	18%	82%

The data used here were MLE levels from the previous two years, not the season in which they were called up. The significance? Solid current performance is what merits a call-up, but this is not a good indicator of short-term MLB success, because a) the performance data set is too small, typically just a few month's worth of statistics, and b) for those putting up good numbers at a new minor league level, there has typically not been enough time for the scouting reports to make their rounds.

Minor league BPV as a leading indicator *(Al Melchior)*

There is a link between minor league skill and how a pitching prospect will fare in his first 5 starts upon call-up.

PQS Avg	MLE BPV < 50	50-99	100+
0.0-1.9	60%	28%	19%
2.0-2.9	32%	40%	29%
3.0-5.0	8%	33%	52%

Pitchers who demonstrate sub-par skills in the minors (sub-50 BPV) tend to fare poorly in their first big league starts. Three-fifths of these pitchers register a PQS average below 2.0, while only 8% average over 3.0.

Fewer than 1 out of 5 minor leaguers with a 100+ MLE BPV go on to post a sub-2.0 PQS average in their initial major league starts, but more than half average 3.0 or better.

Late season performance of rookie starting pitchers *(Ray Murphy)*

Given that a rookie's second tour of the league provides insight as to future success, do rookie pitchers typically run out of gas? We studied 2002-2005, identified 56 rookies who threw at least 75 IP and analyzed their PQS logs. The group:

All rookies	#	#GS/P	DOM%	DIS%	qERA
before 7/31	56	13.3	42%	21%	4.56
after 7/31	56	9.3	37%	29%	4.82

There is some erosion, but a 0.26 run rise in qERA is hardly cause for panic. If we re-focus our study class, the qERA variance increased to 4.44-5.08 for those who made at least 16 starts before July 31. The variance also was larger (3.97-4.56) for those who had a PQS-3 average prior to July 31. The pitchers who intersected these two sub-groups:

PQS>3+GS>15	#	#GS/P	DOM%	DIS%	qERA
before 7/31	8	19.1	51%	12%	4.23
after 7/31	8	9.6	34%	30%	5.08

While the sample size is small, the degree of flameout by these guys (0.85 runs) is more significant.

Japanese Baseball *(Tom Mulhall)*

Comparing MLB and Japanese Baseball

The Japanese major leagues are generally considered to be equivalent to very good Triple-A ball and the pitching may be even better. However, statistics are difficult to convert due to differences in the way the game is played in Japan.

1. While strong on fundamentals, Japanese baseball's guiding philosophy is risk avoidance. Mistakes are not tolerated. Runners rarely take extra bases, batters focus on making contact rather than driving the ball, and managers play for one run at a time. As a result, offenses score fewer runs per number of hits, and pitching stats tend to look better than the talent behind them.

2. Stadiums in Japan usually have shorter fences. Normally this would mean more HRs, but given #1 above, it is the American players who make up the majority of Japan's power elite. Power hitters do not make an equivalent transition to the MLB.

3. There are more artificial turf fields, which increases the number of ground ball singles. Only a few stadiums have infield grass and some still use dirt infields.

4. The quality of umpiring is questionable; there are no sanctioned umpiring schools in Japan. Fewer errors are called, reflecting the cultural philosophy of low tolerance for mistakes and the desire to avoid publicly embarrassing a player. Moreover, umpires are routinely intimidated.

5. Teams have smaller pitching staffs and use a six-man rotation. Starters usually pitch once a week, typically on the same day since Monday is an off-day for the entire league. Many starters will also occasionally pitch in relief between starts. Moreover, managers push for complete games, no matter what the score or situation. Despite superior conditioning, Japanese pitchers tend to burn out early due to overuse.

6. Japan instituted a new ball in 2011 with lower-elasticity rubber surrounding the cork, which limited offense and inflated pitching stats. A more hitter-friendly ball was used in 2013 and home runs were back up to pre-2011 levels. Continue to exercise some skepticism when analyzing pitching stats and look for possible signs of optimism in hitting stats other than the power categories.

7. Tie games are allowed. If the score remains even after 12 innings, the game goes into the books as a tie.

Japanese players as fantasy farm selections

Many fantasy leagues have large reserve or farm teams with rules allowing them to draft foreign players before they sign with a MLB team. With increased coverage by fantasy experts, the internet, and exposure from the World Baseball Classic, anyone willing to do a modicum of research can compile an adequate list of good players.

However, the key is not to identify the best Japanese players—the key is to identify impact players who have the desire and opportunity to sign with a MLB team. It is easy to overestimate the value of drafting these players. Since 1995, only about three dozen Japanese players have made a big league roster, and about half of them were middle relievers. But for owners who are allowed to carry a large reserve or farm team at reduced salaries, these players could be a real windfall, especially if your competitors do not do their homework.

A list of Japanese League players who could jump to the majors appears in the Prospects section.

Other Diamonds

Age 26 Paradox

Age 26 is when a player begins to reach his peak skill, no matter what his address is. If circumstances have him celebrating that birthday in the majors, he is a breakout candidate. If circumstances have him celebrating that birthday in the minors, he is washed up.

A-Rod 10-Step Path to Stardom

Not all well-hyped prospects hit the ground running. More often they follow an alternative path:

1. Prospect puts up phenomenal minor league numbers.
2. The media machine gets oiled up.
3. Prospect gets called up, but struggles, Year 1.
4. Prospect gets demoted.
5. Prospect tears it up in the minors, Year 2.
6. Prospect gets called up, but struggles, Year 2.
7. Prospect gets demoted.
8. The media turns their backs. Fantasy leaguers reduce their expectations.
9. Prospect tears it up in the minors, Year 3. The public shrugs its collective shoulders.
10. Prospect is promoted in Year 3 and explodes. Some lucky fantasy leaguer lands a franchise player for under $5.

Some players that are currently stuck at one of the interim steps, and may or may not ever reach Step 10, include Trevor Bauer, Mike Olt and Jesus Montero.

Developmental Dogmata

1. Defense is what gets a minor league prospect to the majors; offense is what keeps him there. *(Deric McKamey)*
2. The reason why rapidly promoted minor leaguers often fail is that they are never given the opportunity to master the skill of "adjusting to the competition."
3. Rookies who are promoted in-season often perform better than those that make the club out of spring training. Inferior March competition can inflate the latter group's perceived talent level.
4. Young players rarely lose their inherent skills. Pitchers may uncover weaknesses and the players may have difficulty adjusting. These are bumps along the growth curve, but they do not reflect a loss of skill.
5. Late bloomers have smaller windows of opportunity and much less chance for forgiveness.
6. The greatest risk in this game is to pay for performance that a player has never achieved.
7. Some outwardly talented prospects simply have a ceiling that's spelled "A-A-A."

Rule 5 Reminder

Don't ignore the Rule 5 draft lest you ignore the possibility of players like Jose Bautista, Josh Hamilton, Johan Santana, Joakim Soria, Dan Uggla, Shane Victorino and Jayson Werth. All were Rule 5 draftees.

Trout Inflation

The tendency for rookies to go for exorbitant draft prices following a year when there was a very good rookie crop.

Gaming

Standard Rules and Variations

Rotisserie Baseball was invented as an elegant confluence of baseball and economics. Whether by design or accident, the result has lasted for three decades. But what would Rotisserie and fantasy have been like if the Founding Fathers knew then what we know now about statistical analysis and game design? You can be sure things would be different.

The world has changed since the original game was introduced yet many leagues use the same rules today. New technologies have opened up opportunities to improve elements of the game that might have been limited by the capabilities of the 1980s. New analytical approaches have revealed areas where the original game falls short.

As such, there are good reasons to tinker and experiment; to find ways to enhance the experience.

Following are the basic elements of fantasy competition, those that provide opportunities for alternative rules and experimentation. This is by no means an exhaustive list, but at minimum provides some interesting food-for-thought.

Player pool

Standard: American League-only, National League-only or Mixed League. With the new MLB alignment of 15 teams per league, there has been discussion about what would constitute a new standard for the single-league fantasy player pool. The cleanest solution is to maintain the numbers of teams in AL-only leagues and to reduce the size of NL-only league by one team.

AL/NL-only typically drafts 8-12 teams (pool penetration of 49% to 74%). Mixed leagues draft 10-18 teams (31% to 55% penetration), though 15 teams (46%) is a common number.

Drafting of reserve players will increase the penetration percentages. A 12-team AL/NL-only league adding six reserves onto 23-man rosters would draft 93% of the available pool of players on all teams' 25-man rosters.

The draft penetration level determines which fantasy management skills are most important to your league. The higher the penetration, the more important it is to draft a good team. The lower the penetration, the greater the availability of free agents and the more important in-season roster management becomes.

There is no generally-accepted optimal penetration level, but we have often suggested that 75% (including reserves) provides a good balance between the skills required for both draft prep and in-season management.

Alternative pools: There is a wide variety of options here. Certain leagues draft from within a small group of major league divisions or teams. Some competitions, like home run leagues, only draft batters.

Bottom-tier pool: Drafting from the entire major league population, the only players available are those who posted a Rotisserie dollar value of $5 or less in the previous season. Intended as a test of an owner's ability to identify talent with upside. Best used as a pick-a-player contest with any number of teams participating.

Positional structure

Standard: 23 players. One at each defensive position (though three outfielders may be from any of LF, CF or RF), plus one additional catcher, one middle infielder (2B or SS), one corner infielder (1B or 3B), two additional outfielders and a utility player/designated hitter (which often can be a batter who qualifies anywhere). Nine pitchers, typically holding any starting or relief role.

Open: 25 players. One at each defensive position (plus DH), 5-man starting rotation and two relief pitchers. Nine additional players at any position, which may be a part of the active roster or constitute a reserve list.

40-man: Standard 23 plus 17 reserves. Used in many keeper and dynasty leagues.

Reapportioned: In recent years, new obstacles are being faced by 12-team AL/NL-only leagues thanks to changes in the real game. The 14/9 split between batters and pitchers no longer reflects how MLB teams structure their rosters. Of the 30 teams, each with 25-man rosters, not one contains 14 batters for any length of time. In fact, many spend a good part of the season with only 12 batters, which means teams often have more pitchers than hitters.

For fantasy purposes in AL/NL-only leagues, that leaves a disproportionate draft penetration into the batter and pitcher pools:

	BATTERS	PITCHERS
On all MLB rosters	195	180
Players drafted	168	108
Pct.	86%	60%

These drafts are depleting 26% more batters out of the pool than pitchers. Add in those leagues with reserve lists—perhaps an additional six players per team removing another 72 players—and post-draft free agent pools are very thin, especially on the batting side.

The impact is less in 15-team mixed leagues, though the FA pitching pool is still disproportionately deep.

	BATTERS	PITCHERS
On all rosters	381	369
Drafted	210	135
Pct.	55%	37%

One solution is to reapportion the number of batters and pitchers that are rostered. Adding one pitcher slot and eliminating one batter slot may be enough to provide better balance. The batting slot most often removed is the second catcher, since it is the position with the least depth.

Beginning in the 2012 season, the Tout Wars AL/NL-only experts leagues opted to eliminate one of the outfield slots and replace it with a "swingman" position. This position could be any batter or pitcher, depending upon the owner's needs at any given time. At the end of the 2012 season, 10 of 12 AL owners had batters in the swingman slot; seven of 13 NL owners had batters in that slot.

Selecting players

Standard: The three most prevalent methods for stocking fantasy rosters are:

Snake/Straight/Serpentine draft: Players are selected in order with seeds reversed in alternating rounds. This method has become the most popular due to its speed, ease of implementation and ease of automation.

In these drafts, the underlying assumption is that value can be ranked relative to a linear baseline. Pick #1 is better than pick #2, which is better than pick #3, and the difference between each pick is assumed to be somewhat equivalent. While a faulty assumption, we must believe in it to assume a level playing field.

Auction: Players are sold to the highest bidder from a fixed budget, typically $260. Auctions provide the team owner with the most control over which players will be on his team, but can take twice as long as snake drafts.

The baseline is $0 at the beginning of each player put up for bid. The final purchase price for each player is shaped by many wildly variable factors, from roster need to geographic location of the draft. A $30 player can mean different things to different drafters.

One option that can help reduce the time commitment of auctions is to force minimum bids at each hour mark. You could mandate $15 openers in hour #1; $10 openers in hour #2, etc.

Pick-a-player / Salary cap: Players are assigned fixed dollar values and owners assemble their roster within a fixed cap. This type of roster-stocking is an individual exercise which results in teams typically having some of the same players.

In these leagues, the "value" decision is taken out of the hands of the owners. Each player has a fixed value, pre-assigned based on past season performance.

Hybrid snake-auction: Each draft begins as an auction. Each team has to fill its first seven roster slots from a budget of $154. Opening bid for any player is $15. This assures that player values will be close to reality. After each team has filled seven slots, it becomes a snake draft.

If you like, you can assign fixed salaries to the snake-drafted players in such a way that rosters will still add up to about $260.

Round	Salary		Round	Salary
8	$14		16	$6
9	$13		17	$5
10	$12		18	$4
11	$11		19	$3
12	$10		20	$2
13	$9		21	$1
14	$8		22	$1
15	$7		23	$1

You can also use this chart to decide how deep you want to auction. If you want to auction the first 15 players, for instance, you'd use a budget of $238. Though not shown, if you only wanted to auction the first 5 players, your budget would be $121.

This method is intended to reduce draft time while still providing an economic component for selecting players.

Stat categories

Standard: The standard statistical categories for Rotisserie leagues are:

4x4: HR, RBI, SB, BA, W, Sv, ERA, WHIP
5x5: HR, R, RBI, SB, BA, W, Sv, K, ERA, WHIP
6x6: Categories typically added are Holds and OPS.
7x7, etc.: Any number of categories may be added.

In general, the more categories you add, the more complicated it is to isolate individual performance and manage the categorical impact on your roster. There is also the danger of redundancy; with multiple categories measuring like stats, certain skills can get over-valued. For instance, home runs are double-counted when using the categories of both HR and slugging average. (Though note that HRs are actually already triple-counted in standard 5x5—HRs, runs, and RBIs)

If the goal is to have categories that create a more encompassing picture of player performance, it is actually possible to accomplish more with less:

Modified 4x4: HR, (R+RBI-HR), SB, OBA, W+QS, (Sv+Hld), K, ERA

This provides a better balance between batting and pitching in that each has three counting categories and one ratio category. In fact, the balance is shown to be even more notable here:

	BATTING	PITCHING
Pure skill counting stat	HR	K
Ratio category	OBA	ERA
Dependent upon managerial decision	SB	(Sv+Hold)
Dependent upon team support	R+RBI-HR	W+QS

Replacing saves: The problem with the Saves statistic is that we have a scarce commodity that is centered on a small group of players, thereby creating inflated demand for those players. With the rising failure rate for closers these days, the incentive to pay full value for the commodity decreases. The higher the risk, the lower the prices.

We can increase the value of the commodity by reducing the risk. We might do this by increasing the number of players that contribute to that category, thereby spreading the risk around. One way we can accomplish this is by changing the category to Saves + Holds.

Holds are not perfect, but the typical argument about them being random and arbitrary can apply to saves these days as well. In fact, many of the pitchers who record holds are far more skilled and valuable than closers; they are often called to the mound in much higher leverage situations (a fact backed up by a scan of each pitcher's Leverage Index).

Neither stat is perfect, but together they form a reasonable proxy for overall bullpen performance.

In tandem, they effectively double the player pool of draftable relievers while also flattening the values allotted to those pitchers. The more players around which we spread the risk, the more control we have in managing our pitching staffs.

Keeping score

Standard: These are the most common scoring methods:

Rotisserie: Players are evaluated in several statistical categories. Totals of these statistics are ranked by team. The winner is the team with the highest cumulative ranking.

Points: Players receive points for events that they contribute to in each game. Points are totaled for each team and teams are then ranked.

Head-to-Head (H2H): Using Rotisserie or points scoring, teams are scheduled in daily or weekly matchups. The winner of each matchup is the team that finishes higher in more categories (Rotisserie) or scores the most points.

Hybrid H2H-Rotisserie: Rotisserie's category ranking system can be converted into a weekly won-loss record. Depending upon where your team finishes for that week's statistics determines how many games you win for that week. Each week, your team will play seven games.

*Place	Record	*Place	Record
1st	7-0	7th	3-4
2nd	6-1	8th	2-5
3rd	6-1	9th	2-5
4th	5-2	10th	1-6
5th	5-2	11th	1-6
6th	4-3	12th	0-7

* Based on overall Rotisserie category ranking for the week.

At the end of each week, all the statistics revert to zero and you start over. You never dig a hole in any category that you can't climb out of, because all categories themselves are incidental to the standings.

The regular season lasts for 23 weeks, which equals 161 games. Weeks 24, 25 and 26 are for play-offs.

Free agent acquisition

Standard: Three methods are the most common for acquiring free agent players during the season.

First to the phone: Free agents are awarded to the first owner who claims them.

Reverse order of standings: Access to the free agent pool is typically in a snake draft fashion with the last place team getting the first pick, and each successive team higher in the standings picking afterwards.

Free agent acquisition budget (FAAB): Teams are given a set budget at the beginning of the season (typically, $100 or $1000) from which they bid on free agents in a closed auction process.

Vickrey FAAB: Research has shown that more than 50% of FAAB dollars are lost via overbid on an annual basis. Given that this is a scarce commodity, one would think that a system to better manage these dollars might be desirable. The Vickrey system conducts a closed auction in the same way as standard FAAB, but the price of the winning bid is set at the amount of the second highest bid, plus $1. In some cases, gross overbids (at least $10 over) are reduced to the second highest bid plus $5.

This method was designed by William Vickrey, a Professor of Economics at Columbia University. His theory was that this process reveals the true value of the commodity. For his work,

Vickrey was awarded the Nobel Prize for Economics (and $1.2 million) in 1996.

Double-Bid FAAB: One of the inherent difficulties in the current FAAB system is that we have so many options for setting a bid amount. You can bid $47, or $51, or $23. You might agonize over whether to go $38 or $39. With a $100 budget, there are 100 decision points. And while you may come up with a rough guesstimate of the range in which your opponents might bid, the results for any individual player bidding are typically random within that range.

The first part of this process reduces the number of decision points. Owners must categorize their interest by bidding a fixed number of pre-set dollar amounts for each player. In a $100 FAAB league, for instance, those levels might be $1, $5, $10, $15, $20, $30, $40 or $50. All owners would set the general market value for free agents in these eight levels of interest. (This system sets a $50 maximum, but that is not absolutely necessary.)

The initial stage of the bidding process serves to screen out those who are not interested in a player at the appropriate market level. That leaves a high potential for tied owners, those who share the same level of interest.

The tied owners must then submit a second bid of equal or greater value than their first bid. These bids can be in $1 increments. The winning owner gets the player; if there is still a tie, then the player would go to the owner lower in the standings.

An advantage of this second bid is that it gives owners an opportunity to see who they are going up against, and adjust. If you are bidding against an owner close to you in the standings, you may need to be more aggressive in that second bid. If you see that the tied owner(s) wouldn't hurt you by acquiring that player, then maybe you resubmit the original bid and be content to potentially lose out on the player. If you're ahead in the standings, it's actually a way to potentially opt out on that player completely by resubmitting your original bid and forcing another owner to spend his FAAB.

Some leagues will balk at adding another layer to the weekly deadline process; it's a trade-off to having more control over managing your FAAB.

Fixed price free agents: In the same way as salary cap games have pre-assigned prices for players at the draft, free agents can be assigned a fixed price as well. For a player who has been in the free agent pool and available for at least two weeks, his price would be his current Rotisserie dollar value. For a player who is a recent call-up or in the pool for less than two weeks, he would be assigned a baseline (e.g. $5 in a $100 FAAB league) augmented by a pre-determined amount based on contextual factors.

For instance, claiming a current minor league call-up would cost an owner the $5 baseline, plus an additional $5 for each month the player is expected to be a full-timer, plus perhaps another $5 if he is on a .500 or better ballclub, in a favorable ballpark, etc. The final pre-set price will serve to screen out only the most interested owners. Multiple like claims would be awarded to the team lower in the standings.

The season

Standard: Leagues are played out during the course of the entire Major League Baseball season.

Split-season: Leagues are conducted from Opening Day through the All-Star break, then re-drafted to play from the All-Star break through the end of the season.

50-game split-season: Leagues are divided into three 50-game seasons with one-week break in between. The advantages:

- With dwindling attention spans over the long 162-game season, 50 games is a more accessible time frame to maintain interest. There would be fewer abandoned teams.

- There would be four shots at a title each year; the first place team from each split, plus the team with the best overall record for the entire year.

- Given that drafting is considered the most fun aspect of the game, these splits triple the opportunities to participate in some type of draft. Leagues may choose to do complete re-drafts and treat the year as three distinct mini-seasons. Or, leagues might allow teams to drop their five worst players and conduct a restocking draft at each break.

Monthly leagues: The concept of a one-month league is still something that reeks of heresy.

For three decades we've played the game six months at a time. It was a test of skill, but also a test of endurance. And from the beginning, we were always faced with the challenge of keeping non-contending owners engaged all season.

Over time, our attention spans have been growing shorter and our need for immediate gratification growing more intense. That's not necessarily a bad thing; it's just reality.

The industry responded in kind. Over the last few years, the fastest growing fantasy format has become the daily game. Set your lineup at night; claim your cash the next morning. While the element of luck plays a larger role in this game, skill can determine the better players over time. But there's no drama of following daily standings; it's a different game.

A closer look at the allure of both formats would reveal an interesting fact: We have greater accuracy projecting skill over a longer time horizon, but greater accuracy projecting playing time over a shorter horizon. Full-season leagues and one-day games feed into opposite ends of that dichotomy.

But there is a middle ground. There is a game that provides a better balance between the projectability of skill and playing time, a balance between analytical relevance and short attention spans.

One month.

Among the benefits of a monthly league over a full-season league:

- You get to have more drafts. That's the best part of playing fantasy anyway and you get to do it six times.

- If you mess up, you only have to wait a few weeks to get another shot. Had you drafted Ryan Braun, Josh Hamilton and BJ Upton last March, your season was essentially over. Muddling through six months with crappy players is the leading cause of team abandonment.

- Your opponent won't be able to ride his lucky breakout picks to a 6-month title. That guy who drafted Jean Segura and Patrick Corbin on draft day because there was nobody left? Owners shouldn't get a full-season benefit from dumb-luck picks.

- You can better plan around injuries. If you owned Matt Kemp or Johnny Cueto this season, it was frustrating waiting to see if they'd ever return to action. You shouldn't have to guess about a player's health; it's a lot easier if you can just plan around them for a month.

- Following the standings is far more fun. In full-season leagues, once categories stratify and stagnate, it can feel like you're stuck in the same spot forever. You should be able to watch your players and know that a few big games can effectively net you a handful of quick points, even in the ratio categories, every night.

- You get to have more pennant races. All that excitement you have with close races during the last week of September each year? Six times.

And there are benefits of a monthly league over a daily league:

- You can feel more long-term loyalty in ownership of your players. Part of the fun of being a fan is developing an attachment to players and following their success night after night. This can only be cultivated over time.

- It is easier to predict performance over the longer period of time. Batting champion Miguel Cabrera went hitless in more than two dozen games last season. In his 22 starts, Scott Diamond (5-10, 5.52 ERA) allowed two runs or fewer six times. Performance is highly variable on any given night.

- Daily standings provide continuity and drama. There is an excitement in following your team's rise and fall in the standings every day. It's more fun than "one and done."

- It feels more like a "season" and less like "gambling." You should be able to choose players based more on a combination of short-term variables and seasonal/career levels.

The major objection to a one month league is that it is far too short a time period to have any relevance.

Well yes, the stats may seem volatile on a player-by-player basis, but they do tend to stabilize over a roster of players, even in as little as one month's time. There will be players who have great months and players who have poor months, but in aggregate, you can still get a good sense of the overall strength of your team.

And as noted in the later essay, "What are we really chasing?," 80% of eventual 6-month winners are already sitting in a money spot after one month anyway.

Instead of dismissing the format, consider the new strategic and tactical angles that a one-month league offers:

It forces you to constantly validate each player's current performance. Faced with the surprising Aprils put up by Chris Davis and Justin Upton last year, which one would have been a better bet to sustain his numbers into May? This is vital insight for any type of game.

In-season decisions focus on optimal timing issues. Should you invest in an under-priced Troy Tulowitzki who is expected to return from the DL during the second week of the month, or draft a lesser shortstop who will play the entire month? Do you take a chance on Justin Verlander when he's coming off a month with a 6.41 ERA? Do you ride Jason Kipnis coming off a month when he batted .409?

You can draft to the schedule. Should you take a chance on a Rockies' starter in July, knowing that they are facing weak teams at home during the month? Should you overpay for Cleveland hitters in September given that they have a soft schedule against intra-division opponents?

Every month is a new game.

(Ron Shandler will be running one-month fantasy competitions during the 2014 season at ShandlerPark.com. He ran trial leagues last summer and signed up more than 750 teams. You will be able to play for real this spring, and play in April for free. Details to come.)

Single game (Quint-Inning Lite format): Played with five owners drafting from the active rosters of two major league teams in a single game. Prior to the game, 5-player rosters are snake-drafted (no positional requirements). Points are awarded based on how players perform during the game. Batters accumulate points for bases gained:

Single	+1
Double	+2
Triple	+3
HR	+4
BB	+1
HBP	+1
SB	+1

Pitchers get +1 point for each full inning completed (3 outs) and lose 1 point for each run allowed (both earned and unearned).

A deck of standard playing cards may be used as an aid for scorekeeping and to break ties.

Players may be dropped, added or traded after the first inning. However, an owner must always have 5 players by the beginning of each half inning. Any player can be cut from an owner's roster. Free agents (players not rostered by any of the owners) can be claimed by any owner, between half-innings, in reverse order of the current standings. If two owners are tied and both want to place a claim, the tie is broken by drawing high card from the scorekeeping deck. Trades can be consummated at any time, between any two or more owners.

At the beginning of the 5th inning, each owner has the option of doubling the points (positive and negative) for any one player on his roster for the remainder of the game (the "Quint"). Should that player be traded, or dropped and then re-acquired, his "Quint" status remains for the game.

Beginning in the 9th inning, all batting points are doubled.

Quint-Inning can be played as a low stakes, moderate or higher stakes competition.

- It costs ($1/$5/$55) to get in the game.
- It costs (25 cents/$1/$5) per inning to stay in the game for the first four innings.
- Beginning with the 5th inning, the stakes go up to (50 cents/$2/$10) per inning to stay in the game.
- Should the game go into extra innings, the stakes rise to ($1/$5/$25) to stay in the game until its conclusion.

Each owner has to decide whether he is still in the game at the end of each full inning. Owners can drop out at the end of any inning, thus forfeiting any monies they've already contributed to the pot. When an owner drops, his players go back into the pool and can be acquired as free agents by the other owners.

The winner is the owner who finishes with the most points.

Post-season league: Some leagues re-draft teams from among the MLB post-season contenders and play out a separate competition. It is possible, however, to make a post-season competition that is an extension of the regular season.

Start by designating a set number of regular season finishers as qualifying for the post-season. The top four teams in a league is a good number.

These four teams would designate a fixed 23-man roster for all post-season games. First, they would freeze all of their currently-owned players who are on MLB post-season teams.

In order to fill the roster holes that will likely exist, these four teams would then pick players from their league's non-playoff teams (for the sake of the post-season only). This would be in the form of a snake draft done on the day following the end of the regular season. Draft order would be regular season finish, so the play-off team with the most regular season points would get first pick. Picks would continue until all four rosters are filled with 23 men.

Regular scoring would be used for all games during October. The team with the best play-off stats at the end of the World Series is the overall champ.

Snake Drafting

Snake draft first round history

The following tables record the comparison between pre-season projected player rankings (using Average Draft Position data from Mock Draft Central) and actual end-of-season results. The 10-year success rate of identifying each season's top talent is only 36%.

2004	ADP		ACTUAL = 6
1	Alex Rodriguez	1	Ichiro Suzuki
2	Albert Pujols	2	Vlad Guerrero (5)
3	Carlos Beltran	3	Randy Johnson
4	Todd Helton	4	Albert Pujols (2)
5	Vlad Guerrero	5	Johan Santana
6	Alfonso Soriano	6	Bobby Abreu
7	N. Garciaparra	7	Adrian Beltre
8	Barry Bonds	8	Barry Bonds (8)
9	Pedro Martinez	9	Carlos Beltran (3)
10	Mark Prior	10	Ben Sheets
11	Manny Ramirez	11	Melvin Mora
12	Roy Halladay	12	Carl Crawford
13	Magglio Ordonez	13	Manny Ramirez (11)
14	Edgar Renteria	14	Miguel Tejada
15	Sammy Sosa	15	Todd Helton (4)

2005	ADP		ACTUAL = 7
1	Alex Rodriguez	1	Derrek Lee
2	Carlos Beltran	2	Alex Rodriguez (1)
3	Albert Pujols	3	Albert Pujols (3)
4	Vlad Guerrero	4	David Ortiz
5	Manny Ramirez	5	Mark Teixeira
6	Bobby Abreu	6	Carl Crawford (12)
7	Miguel Tejada	7	Chone Figgins
8	Johan Santana	8	Jason Bay
9	Todd Helton	9	Miguel Cabrera
10	Jason Schmidt	10	Manny Ramirez (5)
11	Randy Johnson	11	Michael Young
12	Carl Crawford	12	Vlad Guerrero (4)
13	Alfonso Soriano	13	Ichiro Suzuki
14	Ben Sheets	14	Bobby Abreu (6)
15	Curt Schilling	15	Johan Santana (8)

2006	ADP		ACTUAL = 4
1	Albert Pujols	1	Jose Reyes
2	Alex Rodriguez	2	Derek Jeter
3	Vlad Guerrero	3	Albert Pujols (1)
4	Mark Teixeira	4	Ryan Howard
5	Manny Ramirez	5	Johan Santana
6	Miguel Cabrera	6	Alfonso Soriano
7	Derek Lee	7	Carl Crawford (10)
8	Bobby Abreu	8	Matt Holliday
9	Miguel Tejada	9	Vlad Guerrero (3)
10	Carl Crawford	10	Miguel Cabrera (6)
11	Michael Young	11	Ichiro Suzuki
12	Carlos Beltran	12	Chase Utley
13	Jason Bay	13	Garrett Atkins
14	David Ortiz	14	Jermaine Dye
15	David Wright	15	Lance Berkman

2007	ADP		ACTUAL = 5
1	Albert Pujols	1	Alex Rodriguez (4)
2	Alfonso Soriano	2	Hanley Ramirez
3	Jose Reyes	3	Matt Holliday
4	Alex Rodriguez	4	Magglio Ordonez
5	Ryan Howard	5	David Wright (12)
6	Johan Santana	6	Jimmy Rollins
7	Carl Crawford	7	Ichiro Suzuki
8	Chase Utley	8	Jose Reyes (3)
9	Carlos Beltran	9	Jake Peavy
10	David Ortiz	10	David Ortiz (10)
11	Vlad Guerrero	11	Carl Crawford (7)
12	David Wright	12	Eric Byrnes
13	Miguel Cabrera	13	Brandon Phillips
14	Lance Berkman	14	Chipper Jones
15	Carlos Lee	15	Prince Fielder

2008	ADP		ACTUAL = 7
1	Alex Rodriguez	1	Albert Pujols (10)
2	Hanley Ramirez	2	Jose Reyes (4)
3	David Wright	3	Hanley Ramirez (2)
4	Jose Reyes	4	Manny Ramirez
5	Matt Holliday	5	Matt Holliday (5)
6	Jimmy Rollins	6	David Wright (3)
7	Miguel Cabrera	7	Lance Berkman
8	Chase Utley	8	Dustin Pedroia
9	Ryan Howard	9	Roy Halladay
10	Albert Pujols	10	Josh Hamilton
11	Prince Fielder	11	Alex Rodriguez (1)
12	Ryan Braun	12	C.C. Sabathia
13	Johan Santana	13	Carlos Beltran
14	Carl Crawford	14	Grady Sizemore
15	Alfonso Soriano	15	Chase Utley (8)

2009	ADP		ACTUAL = 5
1	Hanley Ramirez	1	Albert Pujols (2)
2	Albert Pujols	2	Hanley Ramirez (1)
3	Jose Reyes	3	Tim Lincecum
4	David Wright	4	Dan Haren
5	Grady Sizemore	5	Carl Crawford
6	Miguel Cabrera	6	Matt Kemp
7	Ryan Braun	7	Joe Mauer
8	Jimmy Rollins	8	Derek Jeter
9	Ian Kinsler	9	Zach Greinke
10	Josh Hamilton	10	Ryan Braun (7)
11	Ryan Howard	11	Jacoby Ellsbury
12	Mark Teixeira	12	Mark Reynolds
13	Alex Rodriguez	13	Prince Fielder
14	Matt Holliday	14	Chase Utley (15)
15	Chase Utley	15	Miguel Cabrera (6)

2010	ADP		ACTUAL = 5
1	Albert Pujols	1	Carlos Gonzalez
2	Hanley Ramirez	2	Albert Pujols (1)
3	Alex Rodriguez	3	Joey Votto
4	Chase Utley	4	Roy Halladay
5	Ryan Braun	5	Carl Crawford (15)
6	Mark Teixeira	6	Miguel Cabrera (9)
7	Matt Kemp	7	Josh Hamilton
8	Prince Fielder	8	Adam Wainwright
9	Miguel Cabrera	9	Felix Hernandez
10	Ryan Howard	10	Robinson Cano
11	Evan Longoria	11	Jose Bautista
12	Tom Lincecum	12	Paul Konerko
13	Joe Mauer	13	Matt Holliday
14	David Wright	14	Ryan Braun (5)
15	Carl Crawford	15	Hanley Ramirez (2)

2011	ADP		ACTUAL = 6
1	Albert Pujols	1	Matt Kemp
2	Hanley Ramirez	2	Jacoby Ellsbury
3	Miguel Cabrera	3	Ryan Braun (10)
4	Troy Tulowitzki	4	Justin Verlander
5	Evan Longoria	5	Clayton Kershaw
6	Carlos Gonzalez	6	Curtis Granderson
7	Joey Votto	7	Adrian Gonzalez (8)
8	Adrian Gonzalez	8	Miguel Cabrera (3)
9	Robinson Cano	9	Roy Halladay (15)
10	Ryan Braun	10	Cliff Lee
11	David Wright	11	Jose Bautista
12	Mark Teixeira	12	Dustin Pedroia
13	Carl Crawford	13	Jered Weaver
14	Josh Hamilton	14	Albert Pujols (1)
15	Roy Halladay	15	Robinson Cano (9)

2012	ADP		ACTUAL = 4
1	Matt Kemp	1	Mike Trout
2	Ryan Braun	2	Ryan Braun (2)
3	Albert Pujols	3	Miguel Cabrera (4)
4	Miguel Cabrera	4	Andrew McCutchen
5	Troy Tulowitzki	5	R.A. Dickey
6	Jose Bautista	6	Clayton Kershaw
7	Jacoby Ellsbury	7	Justin Verlander (8)
8	Justin Verlander	8	Josh Hamilton
9	Adrian Gonzalez	9	Fernando Rodney
10	Justin Upton	10	Adrian Beltre
11	Robinson Cano	11	Alex Rios
12	Joey Votto	12	David Price
13	Evan Longoria	13	Chase Headley
14	Carlos Gonzalez	14	Robinson Cano (11)
15	Prince Fielder	15	Edwin Encarnacion

2013	ADP		ACTUAL = 5
1	Ryan Braun	1	Miguel Cabrera (2)
2	Miguel Cabrera	2	Mike Trout (3)
3	Mike Trout	3	Clayton Kershaw (15)
4	Matt Kemp	4	Chris Davis
5	Andrew McCutchen	5	Paul Goldschmidt
6	Albert Pujols	6	Andrew McCutchen (5)
7	Robinson Cano	7	Adam Jones
8	Jose Bautista	8	Jacoby Ellsbury
9	Joey Votto	9	Max Scherzer
10	Carlos Gonzalez	10	Carlos Gomez
11	Buster Posey	11	Hunter Pence
12	Justin Upton	12	Robinson Cano (7)
13	Giancarlo Stanton	13	Alex Rios
14	Prince Fielder	14	Adrian Beltre
15	Clayton Kershaw	15	Matt Harvey

ADP attrition

Why is our success rate so low in identifying what should be the most easy-to-project players each year? We rank and draft players based on the expectation that those ranked higher will return greater value in terms of productivity and playing time, as well as being the safest investments. However, there are many variables affecting where players finish.

Earlier, it was shown that players spend an inordinate number of days on the disabled list. In fact, of the players projected to finish in the top 300 coming into each of the past four seasons, the number who lost playing time due to injuries, demotions and suspensions has been extreme:

Year	Pct. of top-ranked 300 players who lost PT
2009	51%
2010	44%
2011	49%
2012	45%
2013	51%

When you consider that about half of each season's very best players had fewer at-bats or innings pitched than we projected, it shows how tough it is to rank players each year.

The fallout? Consider: It is nearly a foregone conclusion that Chris Davis and Paul Goldschmidt— players who finished in the top 15 for the first time last year—will rank as first round picks in 2014. The above data provide a strong argument against them returning first-round value.

Yes, they are excellent players, two of the best in the game, in 2013 anyway. But the issue is not their skills profile. The issue is the profile of what makes a worthy first rounder. Note:

- Two-thirds of players finishing in the Top 15 were not in the Top 15 the previous year. There is a great deal of turnover in the first round, year-to-year.

- Of those who were first-timers, only 14% repeated in the first round the following year.

- Established superstars who finished in the Top 15 were no guarantee to repeat but occasionally reappear in a later year. These were players like David Ortiz (twice in 1st round, twice unable to repeat), Mark Teixeira (#5, 2005), Ryan Howard (#4, 2006) and Chase Utley (3 times in 1st round, only repeated once). First-time stars like Josh Hamilton (2008), Joe Mauer (2009) and Buster Posey (2012) are even less likely to repeat. Note that Carlos Gonzalez was baseball's top-ranked player in 2010. He has been drafted in the first round in each season since but has yet to return first round value again.

- From 2005 to 2007, 14 of the top 15 players were batters. In 2008, that dropped to 13. In 2009 and 2010, it dropped again to 12. In 2011 and 2012, only 10 of 15 were batters. This past season, 12 0f 15 first-rounders were batters, however, the next four players ranked outside the top 15 were all pitchers: Adam Wainwright, Jose Fernandez, Hisashi Iwakuma and Cliff Lee. As player value shifts toward pitching, more arms are appearing higher in the rankings, leaving fewer spots for the top batters.

As such, the odds are against Davis and Goldschmidt repeating in the first round, as counter-intuitive as it may seem. In past years, sudden stars like Zack Greinke, Curtis Granderson and Dustin Pedroia have failed to repeat. As talented as these players are, it's not just about skill; it's also about skill relative to the rest of a volatile player pool.

Importance of the Early Rounds *(Bill Macey)*

It's long been said that you can't win your league in the first round, but you can lose it there. An analysis of data from actual drafts reveals that this holds true—those who spend an early round pick on a player that severely under-performs expectations rarely win their league and seldom even finish in the top 3.

At the same time, drafting a player in the first round that actually returns first-round value is no guarantee of success. In fact, those that draft some of the best values still only win their league about a quarter of the time and finish in the top 3 less than half the time. Research also shows that drafting pitchers in the first round is a risky proposition. Even if the pitchers deliver first-round value, the opportunity cost of passing up on an elite batter makes you less likely to win your league.

What is the best seed to draft from?

Most drafters like mid-round so they never have to wait too long for their next player. Some like the swing pick, suggesting that getting two players at 15 and 16 is better than a 1 and a 30. Many drafters assume that the swing pick means you'd be getting something like two $30 players instead of a $40 and $20.

Equivalent auction dollar values reveal the following facts about the first two snake draft rounds:

In an AL/NL-only league, the top seed would get a $44 player (at #1) and a $24 player (at #24) for a total of $68; the 12th seed would get two $29s (at #12 and #13) for $58.

In a mixed league, the top seed would get a $47 and a $24 ($71); the 15th seed would get two $28s ($56).

Since the talent level flattens out after the 2nd round, low seeds never get a chance to catch up:

Dollar value difference between first player selected and last player selected		
Round	12-team	15-team
1	$15	$19
2	$7	$8
3	$5	$4
4	$3	$3
5	$2	$2
6	$2	$1
7-17	$1	$1
18-23	$0	$0

The total value each seed accumulates at the end of the draft is hardly equitable:

Seed	Mixed	AL/NL-only
1	$266	$273
2	$264	$269
3	$263	$261
4	$262	$262
5	$259	$260
6	$261	$260
7	$260	$260
8	$261	$260
9	$261	$258
10	$257	$260
11	$257	$257
12	$258	$257
13	$254	
14	$255	
15	$256	

Of course, the draft is just the starting point for managing your roster and player values are variable. Still, it's tough to imagine a scenario where the top seed wouldn't have an advantage over the bottom seed.

Using ADPs to determine when to select players *(Bill Macey)*

Although average draft position (ADP) data gives us a good idea of where in the draft each player is selected, it can be misleading when trying to determine how early to target a player. This chart summarizes the percentage of players drafted within 15 picks of his ADP as well as the average standard deviation by grouping of players.

ADP Rank	% within 15 picks	Standard Deviation
1-25	100%	2.5
26-50	97%	6.1
51-100	87%	9.6
100-150	72%	14.0
150-200	61%	17.4
200-250	53%	20.9

As the draft progresses, the picks for each player become more widely dispersed and less clustered around the average. Most top 100 players will go within one round of their ADP-converted round. However, as you reach the mid-to-late rounds, there is much more uncertainty as to when a player will be selected. Pitchers have slightly smaller standard deviations than do batters (i.e. they tend to be drafted in a narrower range). This suggests that drafters may be more likely to reach for a batter than for a pitcher.

Using the ADP and corresponding standard deviation, we can to estimate the likelihood that a given player will be available at a certain draft pick. We estimate the predicted standard deviation for each player as follows:

$$Stdev = -0.42 + 0.42*(ADP - Earliest\ Pick)$$

(That the figure 0.42 appears twice is pure coincidence; the numbers are not equal past two decimal points.)

If we assume that the picks are normally distributed, we can use a player's ADP and estimated standard deviation to estimate the likelihood that the player is available with a certain pick (MS Excel formula):

$$=1-normdist(x,ADP,Standard\ Deviation,True)$$

where «x» represents the pick number to be evaluated.

We can use this information to prepare for a snake draft by determining how early we may need to reach in order to roster a player. Suppose you have the 8th pick in a 15-team league draft and your target is 2009 sleeper candidate Nelson Cruz. His ADP is 128.9 and his earliest selection was with the 94th pick. This yields an estimated standard deviation of 14.2. You can then enter these values into the formula above to estimate the likelihood that he is still available at each of the following picks:

Likelihood	
Pick	Available
83	100%
98	99%
113	87%
128	53%
143	16%
158	2%

ADPs and scarcity *(Bill Macey)*

Most players are selected within a round or two of their ADP with tight clustering around the average. But every draft is unique and every pick in the draft seemingly affects the ordering of subsequent picks. In fact, deviations from "expected" sequences can sometimes start a chain reaction at that position. This is most often seen in runs at scarce positions such as the closer; once the first one goes, the next seems sure to closely follow.

Research also suggests that within each position, there is a correlation within tiers of players. The sooner players within a generally accepted tier are selected, the sooner other players within the same tier will be taken. However, once that tier is exhausted, draft order reverts to normal.

How can we use this information? If you notice a reach pick, you can expect that other drafters may follow suit. If your draft plan is to get a similar player within that tier, you'll need to adjust your picks accordingly.

Mapping ADPs to auction value *(Bill Macey)*

Reliable average auction values (AAV) are often tougher to come by than ADP data for snake drafts. However, we can estimate predicted auction prices as a function of ADP, arriving at the following equation:

$$y = -9.8ln(x) + 57.8$$

where ln(x) is the natural log function, x represents the actual ADP, and y represents the predicted AAV.

This equation does an excellent job estimating auction prices (r2=0.93), though deviations are unavoidable. The asymptotic nature of the logarithmic function, however, causes the model to predict overly high prices for the top players. So be aware of that, and adjust.

Auction Value Analysis

Auction values (R$) in perspective

R$ is the dollar value placed on a player's statistical performance in a Rotisserie league, and designed to measure the impact that player has on the standings.

There are several methods to calculate a player's value from his projected (or actual) statistics.

One method is Standings Gain Points, described in the book, *How to Value Players for Rotisserie Baseball*, by Art McGee (2nd edition available at BaseballHQ.com). SGP converts a player's statistics in each Rotisserie category into the number of points those stats will allow you to gain in the standings. These are then converted back into dollars.

Another popular method is the Percentage Valuation Method. In PVM, a least valuable, or replacement performance level is set for each category (in a given league size) and then values are calculated representing the incremental improvement from that base. A player is then awarded value in direct proportion to the level he contributes to each category.

As much as these methods serve to attach a firm number to projected performance, the winning bid for any player is still highly variable depending upon many factors:

- the salary cap limit
- the number of teams in the league
- each team's roster size
- the impact of any protected players
- each team's positional demands at the time of bidding
- the statistical category demands at the time of bidding
- external factors, e.g. media inflation or deflation of value

In other words, a $30 player is only a $30 player if someone in your draft pays $30 for him.

Roster slot valuation *(John Burnson)*

Tenets of player valuation say that the number of ballplayers with positive value—either positive projected value (before the season) or positive actual value (after the season)—must equal the total number of roster spots, and that, before the season, the value of a player must match his expected production. These propositions are wrong.

The unit of production in Rotisserie is not "the player" or "the statistic" but the player-week. If you own a player, you must own him for at least one week, and if you own him for more than one week, you must own him for multiples of one week. Moreover, you cannot break down his production—everything that a player does in a given week, you earn. (In leagues that allow daily transactions, the unit is the player-day. The point stays.)

When you draft a player, what have you bought?

"You have bought the stats generated by this player."

No. You have bought the stats generated by his slot. Initially, the drafted player fills the slot, but he need not fill the slot for the season, and he need not contribute from Day One. If you trade the player during the season, then your bid on Draft Day paid for the stats of the original player plus the stats of the new player. If the player misses time due to injury or demotion, then you bought the stats of whomever fills the weeks while the drafted player is missing. At season's end, there will be more players providing positive value than there are roster slots.

Before the season, the number of players projected for positive value has to equal the total number of roster slots—after all, we can't order owners to draft more players than can fit on their rosters. However, the projected productivity should be adjusted

by the potential to capture extra value in the slot. This is especially important for injury-rehab cases and late-season call-ups. For example, if we think that a player will miss half the season, then we would augment his projected stats with a half-year of stats from a replacement-level player at his position. Only then would we calculate prices. Essentially, we want to apportion $260 per team among the slots, not the players.

Average player value by draft round

Rd	AL/NL	Mxd
1	$34	$34
2	$26	$26
3	$23	$23
4	$20	$20
5	$18	$18
6	$17	$16
7	$16	$15
8	$15	$13
9	$13	$12
10	$12	$11
11	$11	$10
12	$10	$9
13	$9	$8
14	$8	$8
15	$7	$7
16	$6	$6
17	$5	$5
18	$4	$4
19	$3	$3
20	$2	$2
21	$1	$2
22	$1	$1
23	$1	$1

Benchmarks for auction players:

- All $30 players will go in the first round.
- All $20-plus players will go in the first four rounds.
- Double-digit value ends pretty much after Round 11.
- The $1 end game starts at about Round 21.

Dollar values by lineup position *(Michael Roy)*

How much value is derived from batting order position?

Pos	PA	R	RBI	R$
#1	747	107	72	$18.75
#2	728	102	84	$19.00
#3	715	95	100	$19.45
#4	698	93	104	$19.36
#5	682	86	94	$18.18
#6	665	85	82	$17.19
#7	645	81	80	$16.60
#8	623	78	80	$16.19
#9	600	78	73	$15.50

So, a batter moving from the bottom of the order to the clean-up spot, with no change in performance, would gain nearly $4 in value from runs and RBIs alone.

Dollar values: expected projective accuracy

There is a 65% chance that a player projected for a certain dollar value will finish the season with a final value within plus-or-minus $5 of that projection. That means, if you value a player at $25, you only have about a 2-in-3 shot of him finishing between $20 and $30.

If you want to get your odds up to 80%, the range now becomes +/- $9. You have an 80% shot that your $25 player will finish somewhere between $16 and $34.

How likely is it that a $30 player will repeat? *(Matt Cederholm)*
From 2003-2008, there were 205 players who earned $30 or more (using single-league 5x5 values). Only 70 of them (34%) earned $30 or more in the next season.

In fact, the odds of repeating a $30 season aren't good. As seen below, the best odds during that period were 42%. And as we would expect, pitchers fare far worse than hitters.

	Total>$30	# Repeat	% Repeat
Hitters	167	64	38%
Pitchers	38	6	16%
Total	205	70	34%
High-Reliability*			
Hitters	42	16	38%
Pitchers	7	0	0%
Total	49	16	33%
100+ BPV			
Hitters	60	25	42%
Pitchers	31	6	19%
Total	91	31	19%
High-Reliability and 100+ BPV*			
Hitters	12	5	42%
Pitchers	6	0	0%
Total	18	5	28%

*Reliability figures are from 2006-2008

For players with multiple seasons of $30 or more, the numbers get better. Players with consecutive $30 seasons, 2003-2008:

	Total>$30	# Repeat	% Repeat
Two Years	62	29	55%
Three+ Years	29	19	66%

Still, a player with two consecutive seasons at $30 in value is barely a 50/50 proposition. And three consecutive seasons is only a 2/3 shot. Small sample sizes aside, this does illustrate the nature of the beast. Even the most consistent, reliable players fail 1/3 of the time. Of course, this is true whether they are kept or drafted anew, so this alone shouldn't prevent you from keeping a player.

How well do elite pitchers retain their value? *(Michael Weddell)*
An elite pitcher (one who earns at least $24 in a season) on average keeps 80% of his R$ value from year 1 to year 2. This compares to the baseline case of only 52%.

Historically, 36% of elite pitchers improve, returning a greater R$ in the second year than they did the first year. That is an impressive performance considering they already were at an elite level. 17% collapse, returning less than a third of their R$ in the second year. The remaining 47% experience a middling outcome, keeping more than a third but less than all of their R$ from one year to the next.

Valuing closers
Given the high risk associated with the closer's role, it is difficult to determine a fair draft value. Typically, those who have successfully held the role for several seasons will earn the highest draft price, but valuing less stable commodities is troublesome.

A rough rule of thumb is to start by paying $10 for the role alone. Any pitcher tagged the closer on draft day should merit at least $10. Then add anywhere from $0 to $15 for support skills.

In this way, the top level talents will draw upwards of $20-$25. Those with moderate skill will draw $15-$20, and those with more questionable skill in the $10-$15 range.

Profiling the end game
What types of players are typically the most profitable in the end-game? First, our overall track record on $1 picks:

Avg Return	%Profitable	Avg Prof	Avg. Loss
$1.89	51%	$10.37	($7.17)

On aggregate, the hundreds of players drafted in the end-game earned $1.89 on our $1 investments. While they were profitable overall, only 51% of them actually turned a profit. Those that did cleared more than $10 on average. Those that didn't—the other 49%—lost about $7 apiece.

Pos	Pct.of tot	Avg Val	%Profit	Avg Prof	Avg Loss
CA	12%	($1.68)	41%	$7.11	($7.77)
CO	9%	$6.12	71%	$10.97	($3.80)
MI	9%	$3.59	53%	$10.33	($4.84)
OF	22%	$2.61	46%	$12.06	($5.90)
SP	29%	$1.96	52%	$8.19	($7.06)
RP	19%	$0.35	50%	$11.33	($10.10)

These results bear out the danger of leaving catchers to the end; only catchers returned negative value. Corner infielder returns say leaving a 1B or 3B open until late.

Age	Pct.of tot	Avg Val	%Profit	Avg Prof	Avg Loss
< 25	15%	($0.88)	33%	$8.25	($8.71)
25-29	48%	$2.59	56%	$11.10	($8.38)
30-35	28%	$2.06	44%	$10.39	($5.04)
35+	9%	$2.15	41%	$8.86	($5.67)

The practice of speculating on younger players—mostly rookies—in the end game was a washout. Part of the reason was that those that even made it to the end game were often the long-term or fringe type. Better prospects were typically drafted earlier.

	Pct.of tot	Avg Val	%Profit	Avg Prof	Avg Loss
Injury rehabs	20%	$3.63	36%	$15.07	($5.65)

One in five end-gamers were players coming back from injury. While only 36% of them were profitable, the healthy ones returned a healthy profit. The group's losses were small, likely because they weren't healthy enough to play.

Realistic expectations of $1 endgamers *(Patrick Davitt)*
Many fantasy articles insist leagues are won or lost with $1 batters, because "that's where the profits are." But are they?

A 2011 analysis showed that when considering $1 players in deep leagues, managing $1 endgamers should be more about minimizing losses than fishing for profit. In the cohort of batters projected $0 to -$5, 82% returned losses, based on a $1 bid. Two-thirds of the projected $1 cohort returned losses. In addition, when considering $1 players, speculate on speed.

Advanced Draft Strategies

Stars & Scrubs v. Spread the Risk

Stars & Scrubs (S&S): A Rotisserie auction strategy in which a roster is anchored by a core of high priced stars and the remaining positions filled with low-cost players.

Spread the Risk (STR): An auction strategy in which available dollars are spread evenly among all roster slots.

Both approaches have benefits and risks. An experiment was conducted in 2004 whereby a league was stocked with four teams assembled as S&S, four as STR and four as a control group. Rosters were then frozen for the season.

The Stars & Scrubs teams won all three ratio categories. Those deep investments ensured stability in the categories that are typically most difficult to manage. On the batting side, however, S&S teams amassed the least amount of playing time, which in turn led to bottom-rung finishes in HRs, RBIs and Runs.

One of the arguments for the S&S approach is that it is easier to replace end-game losers (which, in turn, may help resolve the playing time issues). Not only is this true, but the results of this experiment show that replacing those bottom players is critical to success.

The Spread the Risk teams stockpiled playing time, which in turn led to strong finishes in many of the counting stats, including clear victories in RBIs, wins and strikeouts. This is a key tenet in drafting philosophy; we often say that the team that compiles the most ABs will undoubtedly be among the top teams in RBI and Runs.

The danger is on the pitching side. More innings did yield more wins and Ks, but also destroyed ERA/WHIP.

So, what approach makes the most sense? **The optimal strategy might be to STR on offense and go S&S with your pitching staff.** STR buys more ABs, so you immediately position yourself well in four of the five batting categories. On pitching, it might be more advisable to roster a few core arms, though that immediately elevates your risk exposure. Admittedly, it's a balancing act, which is why we need to pay more attention to risk analysis and look closer at strategies like the RIMA Plan and Portfolio3.

The LIMA Plan

The LIMA Plan is a strategy for Rotisserie leagues (though the underlying concept can be used in other formats) that allows you to target high skills pitchers at very low cost, thereby freeing up dollars for offense. LIMA is an acronym for Low Investment Mound Aces, and also pays tribute to Jose Lima, a $1 pitcher in 1998 who exemplified the power of the strategy. In a $260 league:

1. Budget a maximum of $60 for your pitching staff.
2. Allot no more than $30 of that budget for acquiring saves. In 5x5 leagues, it is reasonable to forego saves at the draft (and acquire them during the season) and re-allocate this $30 to starters ($20) and offense ($10).
3. Ignore ERA. Draft only pitchers with:
   - Command ratio (K/BB) of 2.5 or better.
   - Strikeout rate of 7.0 or better.
   - Expected home run rate of 1.0 or less.

4. Draft as few innings as your league rules will allow. This is intended to manage risk. For some game formats, this should be a secondary consideration.
5. Maximize your batting slots. Target batters with:
   - Contact rate of at least 80%
   - Walk rate of at least 10%
   - PX or Spd level of at least 100

Spend no more than $29 for any player and try to keep the $1 picks to a minimum.

The goal is to ace the batting categories and carefully pick your pitching staff so that it will finish in the upper third in ERA, WHIP and saves (and Ks in 5x5), and an upside of perhaps 9th in wins. In a competitive league, that should be enough to win, and definitely enough to finish in the money. Worst case, you should have an excess of offense available that you can deal for pitching.

The strategy works because it better allocates resources. Fantasy leaguers who spend a lot for pitching are not only paying for expected performance, they are also paying for better defined roles—#1 and #2 rotation starters, ace closers, etc.—which are expected to translate into more IP, wins and saves. But roles are highly variable. A pitcher's role will usually come down to his skill and performance; if he doesn't perform, he'll lose the role.

The LIMA Plan says, let's invest in skill and let the roles fall where they may. In the long run, better skills should translate into more innings, wins and saves. And as it turns out, pitching skill costs less than pitching roles do.

In *snake draft leagues,* don't start drafting starting pitchers until Round 10. In *shallow mixed leagues,* the LIMA Plan may not be necessary; just focus on the BPI benchmarks. In *simulation leagues,* build your staff around BPI benchmarks.

Variations on the LIMA Plan

LIMA Extrema: Limit your total pitching budget to only $30, or less. This can be particularly effective in shallow leagues where LIMA-caliber starting pitcher free agents are plentiful during the season.

SANTANA Plan: Instead of spending $30 on saves, you spend it on a starting pitcher anchor. In 5x5 leagues where you can reasonably punt saves at the draft table, allocating those dollars to a high-end LIMA-caliber starting pitcher can work well as long as you pick the right anchor.

Total Control Drafting (TCD)

On Draft Day, we make every effort to control as many elements as possible. In reality, the players that end up on our teams are largely controlled by the other owners. Their bidding affects your ability to roster the players you want. In a snake draft, the other owners control your roster even more. We are really only able to get the players we want within the limitations set by others.

However, an optimal roster can be constructed from a fanalytic assessment of skill and risk combined with more assertive draft day demeanor.

Why this makes sense

1. Our obsession with projected player values is holding us back. If a player on your draft list is valued at $20 and you agonize when the bidding hits $23, odds are about two chances in three that he could really earn anywhere from $15 to $25. What this means is, in some cases, and within reason, you should just pay what it takes to get the players you want.

2. There is no such thing as a bargain. Most of us *don't* just pay what it takes because we are always on the lookout for players who go under value. But we really don't know which players will cost less than they will earn because prices are still driven by the draft table. The concept of "bargain" assumes that we even know what a player's true value is. Was Justin Verlander a bargain at $25 this past year?

3. "Control" is there for the taking. Most owners are so focused on their own team that they really don't pay much attention to what you're doing. There are some exceptions, and bidding wars do happen, but in general, other owners will not provide that much resistance.

How it's done

1. Create your optimal draft pool.

2. Get those players.

Start by identifying which players will be draftable based on the LIMA or Portfolio3 criteria. Then, at the draft, focus solely on your roster. When it's your bid opener, toss a player you need at about 50%-75% of your projected value. Bid aggressively and just pay what you need to pay. Of course, don't spend $40 for a player with $25 market value, but it's okay to exceed your projected value within reason.

From a tactical perspective, mix up the caliber of openers. Drop out early on some bids to prevent other owners from catching on to you.

In the end, it's okay to pay a slight premium to make sure you get the players with the highest potential to provide a good return on your investment. It's no different than the premium you might pay for a player with position flexibility or to get the last valuable shortstop. With TCD, you're just spending those extra dollars up front to ensure you are rostering your targets. In fact, TCD almost asssures that you don't leave money on the table.

The Portfolio3 Plan

The previously discussed strategies have had important roles in furthering our potential for success. The problem is that they all take a broad-stroke approach to the draft. The $35 first round player is evaluated and integrated into the plan in the same way that the end-gamer is. But each player has a different role on your team by virtue of his skill set, dollar value, position and risk profile. When it comes to a strategy for how to approach a specific player, one size does not fit all.

We need some players to return fair value more than others. A $40/first round player going belly-up is going to hurt you far more than a $1/23rd round bust. Those end-gamers are easily replaceable.

We rely on some players for profit more than others. First-rounders do not provide the most profit potential; those come from players further down the value rankings.

We can afford to weather more risk with some players than with others. Since high-priced early-rounders need to return at least fair value, we cannot afford to take on excessive risk. Our risk tolerance opens up with later-round/lower cost picks.

Players have different risk profiles based solely on what roster spot they are going to fill. Catchers are more injury prone. A closer's value is highly dependent on managerial decision. These types of players are high risk even if they have great skills. That needs to affect their draft price or draft round.

For some players, the promise of providing a scarce skill, or productivity at a scarce position, may trump risk. Not always, but sometimes. The determining factor is usually price. A $5, 20th round Michael Morse is not something you pass up, even with a Reliability Grade of DCD.

In the end, we need a way to integrate all these different types of players, roles and needs. We need to put some form to the concept of a diversified draft approach. Thus:

The Portfolio3 Plan provides a three-tiered approach to the draft. Just like most folks prefer to diversify their stock portfolio, P3 advises to diversify your roster with three different types of players. Depending upon the stage of the draft (and budget constraints in auction leagues), P3 uses a different set of rules for each tier that you'll draft from. The three tiers are:

1. Core Players
2. Mid-Game Players
3. End-Game Players

TIER 1: CORE PLAYERS

Roster			BATTERS		PITCHERS	
Slots	Budget	Rel	Ct%	PX or Spd	Rel	BPV
5-8	Max $160	BBB	80%	100 / 100	BBB	75

These are the players who will provide the foundation to your roster. These are your prime stat contributors and where you will invest the largest percentage of your budget. In snake drafts, these are the names you pick in the early rounds. There is no room for risk here. Given their price tags, there is usually little potential for profit. The majority of your core players should be batters.

The above chart shows general roster goals. In a snake draft, you need to select core-caliber players in the first 5-8 rounds. In an auction, any player purchased for $20 or more should meet the Tier 1 filters.

Since these are going to be the most important players on your roster, the above guidelines help provide a report card, of sorts, for your draft. For instance, if you leave the table with only three Tier 1 players, then you know you have likely rostered too much risk or not enough skill. If you manage to draft nine Tier 1 players, that doesn't necessarily mean you've got a better roster, just a better core. There still may be more work to do in the other tiers.

TIER 2: MID-GAME PLAYERS

Roster			BATTERS		PITCHERS	
Slots	Budget	Rel	Ct% or	PX or Spd	Rel	BPV
7-13	$50-$100	BBB	80%	100 100	BBB	50

All players must be less than $20
Batters must be projected for at least 500 AB

Tier 1 players are all about skill. Tier 2 is all about accumulating playing time, particularly on the batting side, with lesser regard to skill. This is where you can beef up on runs and RBI. If a player is getting 500 AB, he is likely going to provide positive value in those categories just from opportunity alone. And given that his team is seeing fit to give him those AB, he is probably also contributing somewhere else.

These players have value to us. And we can further filter this pool of full-timers who miss the P3 skills criteria by skimming off those with high REL grades.

TIER 3: END-GAME PLAYERS

Roster		BATTERS			PITCHERS	
Slots	Budget	Rel	Ct%	PX or Spd	Rel	BPV
5-10	Up to $50	n/a	80%	100 100	n/a	75

All players must be less than $10

Tier 3 players are your gambling chips, but every end-gamer must provide the promise of upside. For that reason, the focus must remain on skill and conditional opportunity. P3 drafters should fill the majority of their pitching slots from this group.

By definition, end-gamers are typically high risk players, but risk is something you'll want to embrace here. You probably don't want a low-risk David Dejesus-type player at the end of the draft; there is no upside or promise of profit. If a Tier 3 player does not pan out, he can be easily replaced.

As such, a Tier 3 end-gamer should possess the BPI skill levels noted above, and...

- playing time upside as a back-up to a risky front-liner
- an injury history that has depressed his value
- solid skills demonstrated at some point in the past
- minor league potential even if he has been more recently a major league bust

The Mayberry Method

The Mayberry Method—named after the fictional TV village where life was simpler—is a player evaluation method that embraces the imprecision of the forecasting process and projects performance in broad strokes rather than with precise statistics.

MM reduces every player to a 7-character code. The format of the code is 5555AAA, where the first four characters describe elements of a player's skill on a scale of 0 to 5. The three alpha characters are our reliability grades (health, experience and consistency). The skills numerics are forward-looking; the alpha characters grade reliability based on past history.

Batting

The first character in the MM code measures a batter's power skills. It is assigned using the following table:

PX	MM	Rough HR Approx
0 - 49	0	0
50 - 79	1	up to 10
80 - 99	2	up to 20
100 - 119	3	up to 30
120 - 159	4	up to 40
160+	5	up to 50+

The second character measures a batter's speed skills.

RSpd*	MM	Rough SB Approx
0-39	0	0
40-59	1	up to 10
60-79	2	up to 20
80-99	3	up to 30
100-119	4	up to 40
120+	5	up to 50+

* RSpd = Spd x (SBO + SB%).

The third character measures expected batting average.

xBA	MM
.000 - .239	0
.240 - .254	1
.255 - .269	2
.270 - .284	3
.285 - .299	4
.300+	5

The fourth character measures playing time.

Role	PA	MM
Potential full-timers	450+	5
Mid-timers	250-449	3
Fringe/bench	100-249	1
Non-factors	0-99	0

An overall MM batting score is calculated as:

MM Score = (PX score + Spd score + xBA score + PA score) x PA score

The highest score you can get is 100, so this becomes an easy scale to evaluate.

Pitching

The first character in the pitching MM code measures xERA, which captures a pitcher's overall ability and is a proxy for ERA, and even WHIP.

xERA	MM
4.81+	0
4.41 - 4.80	1
4.01 - 4.40	2
3.61 - 4.00	3
3.21 - 3.60	4
3.20-	5

The second character measures strikeout ability.

K/9	MM
0.0 - 5.3	0
5.4 - 6.3	1
6.5 - 7.3	2
7.4 - 8.3	3
8.4 - 9.3	4
9.4+	5

The third character measures saves potential.

Description	Saves est.	MM
No hope for saves; starting pitchers	0	0
Speculative closer	1-9	1
Closer in a pen with alternatives	10-24	2
Frontline closer with firm bullpen role	25+	3

The fourth character measures playing time.

Role	IP	MM
Potential #1-2 starters	180+	5
Potential #3-4 starters	130-179	3
#5 starters/swingmen	70-129	1
Relievers	0-69	0

An overall MM pitching score is calculated as:

MM Score =
((xERA score x 2) + K/9 score + Saves score + IP score) x (IP score + Saves score)

Integrating Mayberry and Portfolio3

Mayberry scores can be used as a proxy for the BPI filters in the Portfolio3 chart. Pretty much all you need to remember is the number "3."

Roster			BATTERS				PITCHERS	
Tr	Slots	Budget	Rel	PA	xBA	PX or RSpd		Rel	xERA
1	5-8	Max $160	BBB	n/a	3	3	3	BBB	3
2	7-13	$50-$100	BBB	5	3 or 3	3		BBB	2
3	5-10	Up to $50	n/a	n/a	3	3	3	n/a	3

The conversion to Mayberry is pretty straightforward. On the batting side, xBA provides a good proxy for contact rate (since ct% drives xBA), and PX and Spd stay. For pitching, xERA easily replaces BPV.

Mayberry's broad-stroke approach significantly opens up the draftable player pool, particularly for Tier 3 sleeper types. About 25% more players will be draft-worthy using these filters.

Targets

For roster budgeting purposes, here are targets for several standard leagues:

BATTING	PX	RSpd	xBA	PA	MM
12-team mixed	41	28	40	66	840
15-team mixed	41	26	39	64	790
12-team AL/NL	37	23	32	54	600
PITCHING	**ERA**	**K***	**Sv**	**IP**	**MM**
12-team mixed	23	33	7	29	460
15-team mixed	20	30	6	30	430
12-team AL/NL	17	27	5	25	320

* Make sure the majority of these points come from starting pitchers.

Mayberry reliability adjustments *(Patrick Davitt)*

Higher-reliability players met their Mayberry targets more often than their lower-reliability counterparts, and players with all "D" or "F" reliability scores underperform Mayberry projections far more often. Those results can be reflected by multiplying a player's MM Score by each of three reliability bonuses or penalties:

Grade	Bonus
A	x1.10
B	x1.05
C	x1.00
D	x0.90
F	x0.80

Note that Rel scores of "D" or "F" actually reduce MM Score.

In-Season Analyses

The efficacy of streaming *(John Burnson)*

In leagues that allow weekly or daily transactions, many owners flit from hot player to hot player. But published dollar values don't capture this traffic—they assume that players are owned from April to October. For many leagues, this may be unrealistic.

We decided to calculate these "investor returns." For each week, we identified the top players by one statistic—BA for hitters, ERA for pitchers—and took the top 100 hitters and top 50 pitchers. We then said that, at the end of the week, the #1 player was picked up (or already owned) by 100% of teams, the #2 player was picked up or owned by 99% of teams, and so on, down to the 100th player, who was on 1% of teams. (For pitchers, we stepped

by 2%.) Last, we tracked each player's performance in the next week, when ownership matters.

We ran this process anew for every week of the season, tabulating each player's "investor returns" along the way. If a player was owned by 100% of teams, then we awarded him 100% of his performance. If the player was owned by half the teams, we gave him half his performance. If he was owned by no one (that is, he was not among the top players in the prior week), his performance was ignored. A player's cumulative stats over the season was his investor return.

The results...

- 60% of pitchers had poorer investor returns, with an aggregate ERA 0.40 higher than their true ERA.
- 55% of batters had poorer investor returns, but with an aggregate batting average virtually identical to the true BA.

Sitting stars and starting scrubs *(Ed DeCaria)*

In setting your pitching rotation, conventional wisdom suggests sticking with trusted stars despite difficult matchups. But does this hold up? And can you carefully start inferior pitchers against weaker opponents? Here are the ERA's posted by varying skilled pitchers facing a range of different strength offenses:

	OPPOSING OFFENSE (RC/G)				
Pitcher (ERA)	5.25+	5.00	4.25	4.00	<4.00
3.00-	3.46	3.04	3.04	2.50	2.20
3.50	3.98	3.94	3.44	3.17	2.87
4.00	4.72	4.57	3.96	3.66	3.24
4.50	5.37	4.92	4.47	4.07	3.66
5.00+	6.02	5.41	5.15	4.94	4.42

Recommendations:

1. Never start below replacement-level pitchers.
2. Always start elite pitchers.
3. Other than that, never say never or always.

Playing matchups can pay off when the difference in opposing offense is severe.

Two-start pitcher weeks *(Ed DeCaria)*

A two-start pitcher is a prized possession. But those starts can mean two DOMinant outings, two DISasters, or anything else in between, as shown by these results:

PQS Pair	% Weeks	ERA	WHIP	Win/Wk	K/Wk
DOM-DOM	20%	2.53	1.02	1.1	12.0
DOM-AVG	28%	3.60	1.25	0.8	9.2
AVG-AVG	14%	4.44	1.45	0.7	6.8
DOM-DIS	15%	5.24	1.48	0.6	7.9
AVG-DIS	17%	6.58	1.74	0.5	5.7
DIS-DIS	6%	8.85	2.07	0.3	5.0

Weeks that include even one DISaster start produce terrible results. Unfortunately, avoiding such disasters is much easier in hindsight. But what is the actual impact of this decision on the stat categories?

ERA and WHIP: When the difference between opponents is extreme, inferior pitchers can actually be a better percentage play. This is true both for one-start pitchers and two-start pitchers, and for choosing inferior one-start pitchers over superior two-start pitchers.

Strikeouts per Week: Unlike the two rate stats, there is a massive shift in the balance of power between one-start and two-start pitchers in the strikeout category. Even stars with easy one-start matchups can only barely keep pace with two-start replacement-level arms in strikeouts per week.

Wins per week are also dominated by the two-start pitchers. Even the very worst two-start pitchers will earn a half of a win on average, which is the same rate as the very best one-start pitchers.

The bottom line: If strikeouts and wins are the strategic priority, use as many two-start weeks as the rules allow, even if it means using a replacement-level pitcher with two tough starts instead of a mid-level arm with a single easy start. But if ERA and/or WHIP management are the priority, two-start pitchers can be very powerful, as a single week might impact the standings by over 1.5 points in ERA/WHIP, positively or negatively.

Consistency *(Dylan Hedges)*
Few things are as valuable to head-to-head league success as filling your roster with players who can produce a solid baseline of stats, week in and week out. In traditional leagues, while consistency is not as important—all we care about are aggregate numbers—filling your team with consistent players can make roster management easier.

Consistent batters have good plate discipline, walk rates and on base percentages. These are foundation skills. Those who add power to the mix are obviously more valuable, however, the ability to hit home runs consistently is rare.

Consistent pitchers demonstrate similar skills in each outing; if they also produce similar results, they are even more valuable.

We can track consistency but predicting it is difficult. Many fantasy leaguers try to predict a batter's hot or cold streaks, or individual pitcher starts, but that is typically a fool's errand. The best we can do is find players who demonstrate seasonal consistency over time; in-season, we want to manage players and consistency tactically.

Consistency in points leagues *(Bill Macey)*
Previous research has demonstrated that week-to-week statistical consistency is important for Rotisserie-based head-to-head play. But one can use the same foundation in points-based games. A study showed that not only do players with better skills post more overall points in this format, but that the format caters to consistent performances on a week-to-week basis, even after accounting for differences in total points scored and playing-time.

Therefore, when drafting your batters in points-based head-to-head leagues, ct% and bb% make excellent tiebreakers if you are having trouble deciding between two players with similarly projected point totals. Likewise, when rostering pitchers, favor those who tend not to give up home runs.

Other Diamonds

Cellar value
The dollar value at which a player cannot help but earn more than he costs. Always profit here.

Crickets
The sound heard when someone's opening draft bid on a player is also the only bid.

Scott Elarton List
Players you drop out on when the bidding reaches $1.

End-game wasteland
Home for players undraftable in the deepest of leagues, who stay in the free agent pool all year. It's the place where even crickets keep quiet when a name is called at the draft.

FAAB Forewarnings
1. Spend early and often.
2. Emptying your budget for one prime league-crosser is a tactic that should be reserved for the desperate.
3. If you chase two rabbits, you will lose them both.

Fantasy Economics 101
The market value for a player is generally based on the aura of past performance, not the promise of future potential. Your greatest advantage is to leverage the variance between market value and real value.

Fantasy Economics 102
The variance between market value and real value is far more important than the absolute accuracy of any individual player projection.

Hope
A commodity that routinely goes for $5 over value at the draft table.

JA$G
Just Another Dollar Guy.

Professional Free Agent (PFA)
Player whose name will never come up on draft day but will always end up on a roster at some point during the season as an injury replacement.

RUM pick
A player who is rosterable only as a Reserve, Ultra or Minors pick.

Standings Vantage Points
First Place: It's lonely at the top, but it's comforting to look down upon everyone else.
Sixth Place: The toughest position to be in is mid-pack at dump time.
Last Place in April: The sooner you fall behind, the more time you will have to catch up.
Last Place, Yet Again: If you can't learn to do something well, learn to enjoy doing it badly.

Mike Timlin List
Players who you are unable to resist drafting even though they have burned you multiple times in the past.

Seasonal Assessment Standard
If you still have reason to be reading the boxscores during the last weekend of the season, then your year has to be considered a success.

The Three Cardinal Rules for Winners
If you cherish this hobby, you will live by them or die by them...
1. Revel in your success; fame is fleeting.
2. Exercise excruciating humility.
3. 100% of winnings must be spent on significant others.

STATISTICAL RESEARCH ABSTRACTS

Fastball Velocity and Dominance Rate

by Stephen Nickrand

It is intuitive that an increase in fastball velocity for starting pitchers leads to more strikeouts. In fact, we cite fastball velocity increases as a good thing without thinking twice. Conversely, a decline in fastball velocity is commonly used as a reason for concern.

Before accepting these conclusions as truths, let's analyze the historical link between fastball velocity and Dominance (K/9) rate. Here is a scatter plot showing the relationship between those two variables from 2009-2012 among starting pitchers (min 40 IP):

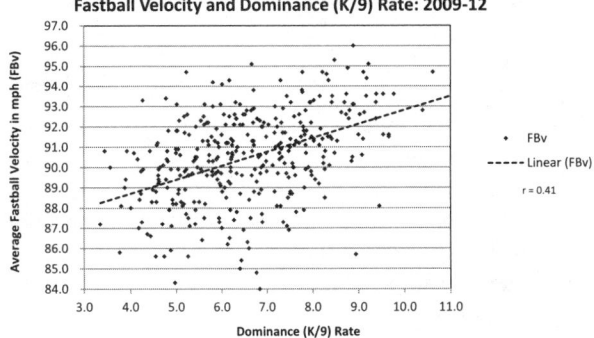

- There is a positive correlation between fastball velocity and Dom, but it's not as strong as you might think. Its correlation coefficient of r = 0.41 suggests a moderate positive correlation. It also reminds us that there are other factors at play.
- Pitch movement, pitch location, pitch mix, pitch sequencing, and deception are all additional factors that impact a SP's strikeout rate. As is the quality of a SP's other pitches.

Let's take a look at fastball velocity changes to see how they are correlated with strikeouts in more detail.

Fastball Velocity Gainers

Same Season Impact

- From 2010-12, a total of 45 starting pitchers increased their fastball velocity by at least 1.0 mph from the previous season (min 40 IP).
- Their average fastball velocity increase was +1.5 mph.
- Thirty-one (69%) also saw their Dom increase during the same season, with an average increase of 1.2 Dom.
- Fourteen (31%) saw their Dom decrease during the same season, with an average decrease of 0.6 Dom.

Next Season Impact

- A total of 28 SP increased their fastball velocity by at least 1.0 mph between 2010-2011 and 2011-2012. Eighteen threw >40 IP as a SP the following season.
- Among this group of 18 SP, 13 (72%) saw their fastball velocity decrease the following season, with an average decrease of 1.3 mph.
- Among the same group of 18 SP, only 5 (28%) saw their fastball velocity increase again the following season, with an average increase of 0.7 mph.

- Among this group of 18 SP, seven (39%) lost Dom the following season, with an average loss of 1.3 Dom.
- Among the same group of 18 SP, 11 (61%) gained Dom the following season, with an average gain of 0.5 Dom.

Fastball Velocity Losers

Same Season Impact

- From 2010-12, a total of 90 starting pitchers decreased their fastball velocity by at least 1.0 mph from the previous season (min 40 IP).
- Their average fastball velocity decrease was 1.4 mph.
- Among this group of 90 SP, 34 (38%) also saw their Dom increase during the same season, with an average increase of 0.9 Dom.
- Among the same group of 90 SP, 56 (62%) saw their Dom decrease during the same season, with an average decrease of 1.2 Dom.

Next Season Impact

- A total of 62 starting pitchers decreased their fastball velocity by at least 1.0 mph between 2010-2011 and 2011-2012. 48 pitchers threw at least 40 IP as a starter the following season. From that group:
- Twenty-four (50%) saw their fastball velocity increase the following season, with an average increase of 0.9 mph.
- Twenty-four (50%) saw their fastball velocity decrease again the following season, with an average decrease of 0.8 mph.
- Twenty-five (52%) gained Dom the following season, with an average gain of 0.9 Dom.
- Twenty-three (48%) lost Dom the following season, with an average loss of 1.0 Dom.

Conclusion

- The vast majority of SP with significant fastball velocity gains experience a significant Dom gain during the same season. A minority experience a Dom reduction. When Dom reduces, the magnitude of it usually is small.
- The vast majority of SP with significant fastball velocity gains are likely to give back those gains during the following season.
- The vast majority of SP with significant fastball velocity gains are likely to increase their Dom the following season, but the magnitude of the Dom increase usually is small. A minority experience a Dom reduction. When Dom reduces, the magnitude of it usually is significant.
- The vast majority of SP with significant fastball velocity loss are likely to experience a significant Dom decrease during the same season. A minority experience a Dom increase.
- Those SP with significant fastball velocity losses from one season to the next are just as likely to experience a fastball velocity or Dom increase as they are to experience a fastball or Dom decrease, with the amounts of the increase/decrease nearly identical.

Starting Pitchers' Swinging Strike Rates

by Stephen Nickrand

An emerging indicator for predicting starting pitching performance is swinging strike rate (SwK%), which measures the percentage of total pitches against which a batter swings and misses.

SwK% can help us validate and forecast a SP's Dominance (K/9) rate, which in turn allows us to identify surgers and faders with greater accuracy.

Let's take a multi-season look at this indicator to refine how we can apply it to starting pitchers.

First, we need to establish SwK% baselines for starting pitchers, since the rates of relievers can skew our SwK% expectations. It also seems logical that SwK% would be higher in the NL given the lack of DH, so we'll also segregate the data by league.

As such, here were the average SwK% posted by SP by league over the last 10 seasons:

SwK% baselines for SP

Year	AL	NL	MLB
2003	8.4%	9.5%	8.9%
2004	8.3%	8.8%	8.6%
2005	8.0%	8.5%	8.2%
2006	8.1%	8.1%	8.1%
2007	8.1%	8.1%	8.1%
2008	7.8%	8.4%	8.1%
2009	8.0%	8.4%	8.2%
2010	7.8%	8.3%	8.0%
2011	8.1%	8.3%	8.2%
2012	8.5%	8.8%	8.6%

Over the last five seasons, the average SwK% among SP was 8.0% in the AL and 8.4% in the NL.

Now let's examine the link between SwK% and Dom.

There were 36 SP in 2012 who increased their SwK% by at least 1.0% vs. 2011. All but three of them also increased their Dom.

Further research confirms that there is a direct link between SwK% and Dom. Among SP with at least 40 IP per year, here were the SwK% they posted by Dom level:

SwK% by Dom range

Dom Range	2008	2009	2010	2011	2012
>10.0	12.4%	11.8%	11.8%	11.3%	11.8%
9.0-9.9	10.9%	10.2%	10.9%	10.5%	10.5%
8.0-8.9	9.9%	9.5%	9.3%	9.3%	9.7%
7.0-7.9	9.2%	9.1%	8.7%	8.7%	8.8%
6.0-6.9	7.9%	8.3%	8.0%	7.8%	7.9%
5.0-5.9	7.2%	6.9%	6.7%	6.9%	7.4%
<5.0	6.1%	5.9%	5.7%	5.9%	5.8%

*min 40 IP

We can also identify a range of values for expected Dom (xDom) based on SwK% level. Using data from 2008-2012 among SP with at least 40 IP in one of those seasons, here was the Dom spread for various SwK% levels:

xDom Ranges by SwK% Level

SwK%	xDom by Percentile				
	10th	25th	50th	75th	90th
> 12.0%	8.0	8.9	9.5	10.4	11.0
11.5-11.9%	7.7	8.1	9.0	9.5	10.4
11.0-11.4%	7.4	7.8	8.6	9.4	10.0
10.5-10.9%	7.5	7.9	8.5	8.9	9.4
10.0-10.4%	7.1	7.4	8.2	9.0	9.7
9.5 - 9.9%	6.3	6.9	7.8	8.3	8.9
9.0 - 9.4%	6.5	6.9	7.5	8.0	8.7
8.5 - 8.9%	6.0	6.5	7.1	7.8	8.4
8.0 - 8.4%	5.7	6.2	6.9	7.6	8.3
7.5 - 7.9%	5.2	5.6	6.4	7.2	7.6
7.0 - 7.4%	4.7	5.2	5.9	6.5	7.1
6.5 - 6.9%	4.5	4.9	5.3	6.0	6.3
6.0 - 6.4%	4.4	4.8	5.2	5.7	6.1
5.5 - 5.9%	4.1	4.5	4.8	5.2	5.7
5.0 - 5.4%	3.5	3.8	4.3	5.2	5.8
< 5.0%	3.4	3.8	4.3	5.0	5.3

In other words, 50% of SP with a SwK% between 11.0% and 11.4% will have a Dom between 7.8 and 9.4.

One means of targeting potential Dom surgers and faders is to find SP who posted a Dom that was significantly different than what would be expected based on the above matrix.

Dom underperformers could be the result of poor or predictable pitch sequencing that limits the swings-and-misses SP induce on third strikes. Conversely, Dom that is significantly higher than xDom may suggest that a SP can get ahead of hitters without generating swings-and-misses, then may rack up whiffs when batters have two strikes on them.

It seems logical that SwK% would not regress to a league norm year-over-year. Our analysis validates this assertion. Sixty SP totaled at least 40 IP in each season from 2008 to 2012. During that period, the average SwK% variance by season for each SP was 0.98%. The SwK% of nearly all SP stayed within a range of +/- 2.0% year-over-year and did not show an obvious tendency to regress towards league norms.

Follow these rules of thumb when targeting starting pitchers based on SwK%. The few starters per year who have a 12.0% or higher SwK% are near-locks to have a 9.0 Dom or greater. Consider them elite SwK% targets. In contrast, starters with a 7.0% or lower SwK% have nearly no chance at posting even an average Dom. Finally, use an 8.5% SwK% as an acceptable threshold when searching for SP based on this metric; raise it to 9.5% to begin to find SwK% difference-makers.

Conclusion

- SwK% baselines for SP = 8.0% in AL, 8.4% in NL
- Consistent, direct correlation between SwK% and Dom
- Expected Dom (xDom) can be estimated from SwK%
- SwK% does not regress to league norms

How does Crossing Leagues Affect Pitchers?

by Bob Berger

During the off-season some pitchers move from one league to the other. Can we predict changes in an individual pitcher's statistics based on league changes? For example, every year the average ERA in the AL is higher than the average NL ERA. How does this translate to individual players? If there are consistent differences, can we quantify them? This research looks at the impact on pitcher's statistics when they change leagues. We looked at statistics of pitchers who changed leagues from 2007 through 2012.

Results 1: League Baselines

To set baselines we calculated ERA, WHIP, and K/9 averages for each league from 2007 through 2012:

League-wide averages

ERA	2007	2008	2009	2010	2011	2012	6yrAvg
AL	4.51	4.35	4.45	4.14	4.08	4.08	4.27
NL	4.43	4.29	4.19	4.02	3.81	3.95	4.12
% Diff	1.8%	1.4%	5.8%	2.9%	6.6%	3.2%	3.6%

WHIP	2007	2008	2009	2010	2011	2012	6yrAvg
AL	1.41	1.39	1.40	1.35	1.32	1.31	1.36
NL	1.40	1.39	1.38	1.35	1.31	1.31	1.36
% Diff	0.7%	0.0%	1.4%	0.0%	0.8%	0.0%	0.5%

K/9	2007	2008	2009	2010	2011	2012	6yrAvg
AL	6.64	6.64	6.86	6.83	6.94	7.41	6.89
NL	6.70	6.99	7.09	7.39	7.29	7.69	7.19
% Diff	0.9%	5.3%	3.4%	8.2%	5.0%	3.8%	4.4%

The NL had lower ERAs during all six years of the study, averaging 0.15 ERA points (3.6%) less than the AL. WHIP was remarkably consistent across the leagues during the six years and the NL K/9 rate was 0.3 K/9 (4.4%) higher than the AL rate.

Results 2: Pitchers Crossing Leagues

Do these differences translate into meaningful statistical trends for pitchers who cross leagues? We examined five data sets: pitchers who switched leagues during 2007-2008, 2008-2009, 2009-2010, 2010-2011, and 2011-2012. During each of these two-year periods, an average of about 70 pitchers switched leagues, either during the season or in the off-season. We ignored pitchers who switched leagues during the season for two reasons: First, the most actionable information is when pitchers cross leagues during the off-season, because those pitchers will often be available during drafts. Second, such pitchers often had sample sizes too small to provide meaningful data. Sample size also affected our decision to include only pitchers with at least 20 IP in each season. This resulted in an average of 26 pitchers per year who switched leagues and had at least 20 IPs in both the seasons (a total of 130 pitchers).

The first row in the following tables shows how pitchers performed during the season before they switched leagues, and the second row shows how they performed during their first season in their new league:

Season Averages for Pitchers Changing Leagues

Moving from AL to NL

Season	Wins	SV	ERA	WHIP	K/9
AL Yr1	6.8	3.5	4.28	1.37	6.8
NL Yr2	7.0	4.6	3.74	1.29	7.7
%Diff	+2.9	+31.4	-12.7	-5.9	+13.0

Moving from AL to NL

Season	Wins	SV	ERA	WHIP	K/9
NL Yr1	3.7	4.6	4.15	1.34	7.4
AL Yr2	3.1	3.7	4.43	1.39	6.6
%Diff	-16.3	-19.6	+6.7	+3.7	-10.8

The data for wins and saves were inconsistent from year to year. Saves were heavily influenced in individual years by whether a pitcher became a closer or lost his role when he switched leagues. Fantasy owners should continue to evaluate saves based on role/opportunity. But there was no such correlation for wins. The BHQ mantra of "don't chase wins" is consistent with this variability.

In contrast, the ERA, WHIP, and K/9 data are consistent for league crossers. Except in 2007-2008, pitchers moving from the NL to the AL increased their ERAs every year (averaging 6.7%), while those going from the AL to the NL decreased their ERA each year, averaging a 12.7% decrease. The effect on individual ERAs for league crossers therefore was greater than the average 3.6% difference in AL and NL league average ERAs we saw in the first table.

The league average baselines in WHIP were similar, but for individuals crossing leagues there was a 5.9% decline in WHIP when moving to the NL and a 3.7% increase when moving to the AL. In all five two-year periods, pitchers moving to the NL decreased their WHIP, and in all five periods pitchers moving to the AL increased their WHIP.

The difference in K/9 between leagues averaged 4.4%, but individual pitchers crossing leagues averaged an increase of 13% moving from the AL to the NL and a decrease of 10.8% when moving from the NL to the AL. As with WHIP, all five two-year periods showed increased K/9 rates when moving to the NL and lower K/9 rates when moving to the AL.

Conclusion

ERA and K/9 varied the most between the AL and NL. The AL has higher ERAs and lower K/9, but pitchers who cross leagues see an even greater effect on their ERA, WHIP, and K/9 during their first year in the new league than we would expect from overall league averages. Fantasy owners should consider adjusting their ERA, WHIP, and K/9 expectations for pitchers moving to the other league in this manner:

- Pitchers moving to the NL may be better than expected based on their recent career trends.
- Pitchers moving to the AL may be worse than expected based on their recent career trends.

This doesn't mean we can ignore individual pitcher skills in assessing performance potential. But we might be justified in being a little more optimistic or pessimistic, based on which way the pitcher moved.

Note: A similar study looking at hitters crossing leagues showed no significant differences in performance when hitters changed leagues.

Do Power Hitters Hit HR in Bunches?

by Patrick Davitt

Ex-ballplayers now in TV broadcast booths like to note that "big home run hitters hit 'em in bunches." If so, we could take advantage by identifying patterns that would help us stream, drop or acquire power hitters and thereby improve our counting stats.

Unfortunately, and unsurprisingly, the "homer bunch" theory is as valid as the "rising fastball" and "clutch hitter" theories—which is to say, not at all. We looked at the 23 hitter-seasons of more than 35 HR from 2010-2012, and asked how often batters had HR "bunches" or "droughts" and how often bunches followed droughts. Bunches and droughts use 10-game spans; 5+ HR and 0 HR, respectively.

A span of games excludes the first game; two straight games with a HR have a gap of 1 game, not 0. Spans, bunches and droughts excluded games the batter didn't play.

The batters averaged gaps of just over 4.0 games between HRs, in a range from 3.5 (Giancarlo Stanton, 2012 and Jose Bautista, 2010) to 5.0 (Adam Dunn, 2010 and Dan Uggla, 2011).

Both bunches and droughts were rare. There were just 22 bunches, about 0.6% of all 10-game spans, and 74 droughts, barely 2% of all 10-game spans. Only six batter-seasons had more than one bunch. And only Bautista might be characterized as prone to bunches, with five bunches over his two 35+ HR seasons.

The batters averaged about 3.2 droughts per year, ranging from five droughts for Kemp and Pujols in 2010 and Teixeira in 2011, to two droughts apiece for seven batters.

Further, we saw no evidence that once a hitter ends a drought, he begins a bunch. The average gap between the HR that ended any drought and the next HR was 3.7 games, right in line with the average gaps observed in the overall group.

Only Stanton followed a drought with a bunch, enduring a 20-game drought near the start of 2012, then hitting five HR in his next eight games.

So, notwithstanding the "expert analysis" of ex-players in broadcast booths, there is no evidence that HR hitters operate in drought-and-bunch cycles.

Simply put, HR hitters hit HRs in a random way, with game-gaps between HR that correspond roughly to their average days per HR. Assuming a 35-HR guy appears in 150 games, he will hit one HR about every four or five games, with random (and, therefore unpredictable) variation either way throughout the year.

Therefore it appears pointless to try to "time the market" by predicting the beginning or end of a drought or a bunch, or by assuming the end of one presages the beginning of the other.

Now, what's all this about rising fastballs and balls that "pick up speed" after they're hit?

April ERA as a Leading Indicator

by Stephen Nickrand

A starting pitcher's April ERA is more than just a monthly measurement. It can also act as a leading indicator for how his ERA is likely to fare during the balance of the season.

Let's look at extreme April ERA results to see what kind of in-season forecasting power they may have.

From 2010-2012, 42 SP posted an ERA in April that was at least 2.00 ER better than their career ERA:

April ERA > 2.00 ER lower than career ERA: 2010-2012*

		ERA Average		
SP Count	April	Career	May-Sep	End of Yr
42	1.77	4.50	3.95	3.59

Among SP whose April ERA was at least 2.00 ER better than their career average:

- 88% had a season-ending ERA that was lower than their career average
- Their average ERA ended up 0.91 ER lower than their career ERA
- Their May-Sept ERA was 0.55 ER lower than their career ERA

Conversely, 43 SP posted an ERA in April that was at least 2.00 ER worse than their career ERA:

April ERA > 2.00 ER higher than career ERA: 2010-2012*

		ERA Average		
SP Count	April	Career	May-Sept	End of Yr
43	7.02	3.99	4.05	4.54

*Min 20 IP in April, 40 IP total

Among SP whose April ERA was at least 2.00 ER worse than their career average:

- 67% had a season-ending ERA that was higher than their career average
- Their average ERA ended up 0.55 ER higher than their career ERA
- Their May-Sept ERA was nearly identical to their career ERA.

Conclusion

- Those who come out of the gates quickly have an excellent chance at finishing the season with an ERA much better than their career ERA.
- While April ERA gems see their in-season ERA regresses towards their career ERA, their May-Sept ERA is still significantly better than their career ERA.
- Those who stumble out of the gates have a strong chance at posting an ERA worse than their career average, but their in-season ERA improves towards their career ERA.
- April ERA disasters tend to have a May-Sept ERA that closely resembles their career ERA.

Pitch Count and PQS

by Patrick Davitt

Introduction

Many fantasy owners "stream" starting pitchers to take advantage of matchups. Owners often reflexively sit a starter coming off a high-pitch-count (PC) start, believing his next-game performance is bound to suffer from fatigue.

Similarly, owners will often start a pitcher coming off a good start to exploit his "momentum" or "confidence" or some other magical property, as we hear from broadcast booths.

We looked into these questions together and separately. Our results show that:

- We should be starting pitchers coming off high-pitch-count starts;
- We should *definitely* be starting pitchers coming off high-PQS (Pure Quality Start) outings;
- And combining PC and PQS in the first start creates a synergistic effect on the next start.

Method

We compiled PQS records from 2010-12, including only starts in which the pitcher working on three, four or five days' rest.

(PQS is "Pure Quality Start," a BaseballHQ.com metric assessing starting pitchers game-by-game. The full explanation is in the Encyclopedia, but in general, a starter earns 0-5 points per start, based on innings, hits, HRs, strikeouts and walks.)

We also eliminated starts under 50 pitches to eliminate injury-shortened starts or spot starts by relievers or call-ups.

These first-pass filters left us with 11,512 pitcher-starts, in these cohorts:

PQS			PC		
0	1605	14%	50-89	2528	22%
1	527	5%	90-99	3088	27%
2	1242	11%	100-109	3694	32%
3	2511	22%	110-119	1888	16%
4	2840	25%	120+	314	3%
5	2787	24%			

Results 1: Pitch Counts

We first got baseline PQS scores for all qualifying starts by PC cohort:

1st Game PC	50-89	90-99	100-109	110-119	120+
Next Game PQS	2.8	3.0	3.1	3.3	3.6

Overall, PQS scores rise as PC rises. This is counter-intuitive, as we might have expected the opposite: longer outings tire a pitcher, right? But the highest average score came after the longest outings, and the lowest average score comes after the shortest.

This oddity is explained in part by who threw these high-PC starts. Of 314 starts with 120+ PC, 134 were by just 13 pitchers, studs like Justin Verlander (30!), James Shields, Felix Hernandez, CC Sabathia, Cliff Lee and Max Scherzer.

But even when we removed these guys, average next-game PQS barely budged, at 3.5.

We also looked in a little more detail at the various pitch-count categories. Next-game PQS results in PC categories 90-99 and 100-109 tracked within a percentage point or two of the overall

results. For example, 24% of all next-game starts were PQS-4, and 11% were PQS-2. Those results were exactly the same in both the 90-99 and 100-109 cohorts.

This stands to reason: These cohorts figure to track an overall result of which they make almost 60%.

We did notice some large variance within the PC cohorts at the extremes, however. In the PC 50-89 category, we saw a four-point increase in next-start PQS-0 and a six-point decrease in PQS-5.

The obvious explanation is that a pitcher who threw relatively few pitches in a start was probably pulled early because he wasn't effective. This same ineffective pitcher would often follow up with another poor outing.

In the PC 110-119 and 120+ cohorts, we see the reverse. We might expect this from the results above, but isolating them makes the results pop a little more. For instance, in PC 110-119, we see a six-point gain in PQS-5 and a four-point drop in PQS-0. And in PQS 120+, we see an eight-point drop in PQS-0s, and a nine-point gain in PQS-5!

These results are nearly bar-bet material: "Does a 120-pitch outing mean the next start will be good? Or bad?"

The 120+ cohort is the smallest in the study—just 318 starts—so we'd expect and understand more variance in the outcomes. That said, it's hard to ignore these huge improvements.

PQS Scores

The second general observation was that next-game PQS rises with previous-game PQS scores. First, by aggregated outcomes:

1st Game PQS	0	1	2	3	4	5
Next Game PQS	2.7	2.8	3.0	3.0	3.1	3.3

The overall next-start PQS average in the study was 3.05, so low PQS-0 and PQS-1 starts definitely predicted follow-ups that were below average and therefore likely damaging to a fantasy team. Conversely, as the first-start PQS rose, the second followed along upwards.

The pattern also holds when we look at the percentages:

		2nd PQS					
		0	1	2	3	4	5
	0	21%	5%	13%	23%	21%	18%
	1	19%	5%	14%	23%	22%	18%
1st	2	16%	5%	11%	22%	26%	20%
PQS	3	16%	5%	11%	22%	23%	22%
	4	14%	4%	11%	21%	25%	25%
	5	13%	4%	8%	20%	25%	30%

Each intersection in the table shows the percentage of next-game PQS scores (from the top row) after a given 1st-game PQS score (from the left column).

For example, we see that 30% of all first-game PQS-5s were followed by another PQS-5, a significant gain over the overall distribution of 24%. We also see only 13% of first-game PQS-5s were followed by PQS-0, three points below the overall level.

Conversely, a pitcher who throws a PQS-0 start has a 21% likelihood of throwing a PQS-0, five points above the norm, and just an 18% chance of throwing a PQS-5, six points below.

PQS x PC

Finally, we combined first-game PC and PQS and looked at next-game results. If you guess that high-PC/high-PQS were the strongest predictors of good next-game performance (and the opposite), you're right:

1st Gm PQS		1st Game Pitch Count				
		50-89	90-99	100-109	110-119	120+
0		2.7	2.8	2.8	–	–
1		2.6	3.0	2.6	–	–
2		2.9	2.9	3.0	3.2	–
3		2.8	3.0	3.0	3.3	–
4		2.8	3.1	3.1	3.3	3.7
5		3.0	3.1	3.3	3.4	3.7

Even though a first-game PQS-5 still predicts a better second-start outcome, we see that outcome gets better as the pitch count rises. We also see you're better off starting a pitcher with a high-PC PQS-2 (3.2 average next-start PQS) than a low-PC PQS-4 (2.8) or even PQS-5 (3.0).

The explanation might be that sometimes the PQS score can be unfair. Borderline walks, checked swings not called strikes, bloop hits and wind-aided HRs can add up to low PQS scores despite decent pitching.

The mere fact that the manager left the pitcher in is a strong indicator that he was probably pitching pretty well. And there are so few high-PC/low-PQS starts (a total of just seven 120+ PC starts with PQS-0 or PQS-1) in the study that we excluded them from this table.

Analysis and Conclusion

Owners in "streaming" leagues are the obvious beneficiaries of this information. While no owner should make a decision based solely on previous-game PC/PQS data (more important to consider opponent, park, and so on), those data certainly should be considered.

And of course the biggest factor in all outcomes is the pitcher himself. Each start/next-start pair is by the same pitcher, obviously capable of throwing the same caliber of game.

Our most important finding might be that we can safely ignore the conventional wisdom that a high-PC game will make a pitcher "tired" or "worn out" and therefore less likely to be effective. The opposite is true—especially if the high-PC outing was also a strong PQS performance.

It appears these workhorse starters and their teams know what they're doing, and that they are highly likely to deliver a solid outing the next time out.

In particular, owners should be mindful of pitchers coming off low-PC/PQS-0 and high-PC/PQS-5 games.

Some caveats:

The PC categories here are arbitrary. There is no inherent advantage in a cohort of 100-109 pitches instead of, say, 96-105 or 98-107. Nor, for that matter, is there magic in 10-pitch increments.

PQS scoring itself seems to have some issues. It tends to distribute scores towards the higher end of its scale (probably because teams try not to start PQS-0 pitchers as often as PQS-5 pitchers).

Also, PQS-1s are greatly under-represented at around 4% of all outcomes. We are willing to speculate that a PQS-1 is difficult to earn because any start of less than five innings is automatically a PQS-0, and a pitcher en route to a PQS-1 is also quite likely to get pulled before reaching the five-inning minimum.

Second-half ERA Reduction Drivers

by Stephen Nickrand

It's easy to dismiss first-half-to-second-half improvement among starting pitchers as an unpredictable event. After all, the midpoint of the season is an arbitrary cutoff. Performance swings occur throughout the season.

That said, let's take a closer look at SP who experienced significant 1H-2H ERA improvement from 2010-2012 to see what indicators have proven to drive second half ERA improvement.

Twenty-two percent (79) of starting pitchers over the past three seasons had a > 1.00 ERA reduction from the first half to the second half (minimum 40 IP each half). Their average ERA improvement was 1.78 ER.

Here are the indicators that were most strongly correlated with ERA reduction for those SP.

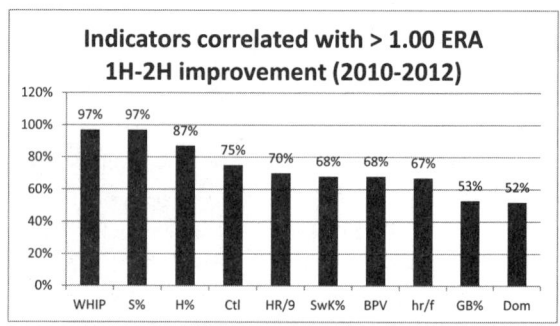

Among those 79 SP with a > 1.00 ERA 1H-2H reduction:

- 77 (97%) saw their WHIP decrease, with an average WHIP decrease of 0.26
- 77 (97%) saw their strand (S%) rate improve, with an average S% increase of 9%
- 69 (87%) saw their BABIP (H%) improve, with an average H% reduction of 5%
- 59 (75%) saw their control (bb/9) rate improve, with an average Ctl reduction of 0.8
- 55 (70%) saw their HR/9 rate improve, with an average HR/9 decrease of 0.5
- 54 (68%) saw their swinging strike (SS%) rate improve, with an average SS% increase of 1.4%
- 54 (68%) saw their BPV improve, with an average BPV increase of 37
- 53 (67%) saw their HR per fly ball rate (hr/f) improve, with an average hr/f decrease of 4%
- 42 (53%) saw their ground ball (GB%) rate improve, with an average GB% increase of 5%
- 41 (52%) saw their dominance (k/9) rate improve, with an average Dom increase of 1.3

These findings highlight the power of H% and S% regression as it relates to ERA and WHIP improvement. In fact, H% and S% are more often correlated with ERA improvement than are improved skills. They also suggest that improved control has a bigger impact on ERA reduction than does increased strikeouts.

Skills from the Wind-up vs. Skills from the Stretch

by Todd Zola

Every starting pitcher generates a body of statistics which we treat as a singular entity. But here's the problem: Each starting pitcher is actually two starting pitchers: wind-up guy and stretch guy. By lumping the numbers together, we create an inherent assumption that both skill sets are identical.

Intuitively, this seems wrong. Since every starter is two different pitchers, we must analyze each subset of data individually. Is there tangible evidence that suggests each pitcher is actually two?

The best means to confirm this dual identity is to compare the skills of starters from the wind-up versus from the stretch. Unfortunately, no one collects and archives this specific data, so some common sense is in order.

Bases-empty data will be the source of wind-up data.

Pitchers work exclusively from the stretch with runners on:

- First only
- First and second
- Second only
- First and third

These four situations will be summed together to represent stretch data. Data from 2010-12 will be used with a minimum of 90 IP per season to filter away relievers.

Results 1: Aggregate Metrics

Here's a look at various pitching metrics separated into wind-up (W) versus stretch (S):

Year	Dom W	Dom S	Ctl W	Ctl S	Cmd W	Cmd S	HR/9 W	HR/9 S	H% W	H% S
2010	7.4	6.0	2.8	2.8	2.7	2.1	1.0	0.9	.292	.302
2011	7.4	6.1	2.6	2.6	2.8	2.3	1.0	0.8	.292	.302
2012	7.9	6.1	2.5	2.7	3.1	2.3	1.1	1.0	.294	.302

Upon inspection, the hypothesis has some traction. Of note is the consistent pattern per season. Let's briefly go through each metric.

Dom—More strikeouts occur from the wind-up, though this might not be completely based on skills. With runners on base, pitchers might alter their repertoires to prevent stolen bases. They might also shun throwing put-away pitches like split-fingered fastballs, because they are more worried about passed balls.

Ctl—The fact a pitcher walks the same number of batters makes sense. If strikeouts are down from the stretch, contact is up. Batters don't extend ABs long enough to draw walks. As well, pitchers might alter their selection to help prevent walks.

Cmd—Cmd follows Dom since Ctl is the same.

HR/9—HR prevention is considered a skill and the data suggests fewer homers from the stretch.

H%—H% is markedly lower from the wind-up, which may be counter-intuitive to DIPS theory, unless there is a (likely) element of skill involved.

Results 2: Applying the Hypothesis

At the root of evaluating pitchers is contrasting surface results such as ERA to expected outcomes dictated by skills. In other words, wind-up versus stretch data can help explain the difference between ERA and xERA.

Presently, ERA is assumed to regress towards xERA. But what if a particular pitcher can maintain his wind-up Dom when working from the stretch? Or what if he has a better Ctl mark from the stretch? The result could be an ERA better than his xERA. So while some assume a correction, others are smirking sensing the delta is sustainable.

Perhaps the effect of some good luck is amplified. Consider a pitcher who is historically (assuming there is such a thing) worse from the stretch than on average. If he's enjoying some good fortune with wind-up H%, he will be forced to deliver from the stretch less often, so not only is he buoyed by a lucky H%, he isn't dragged down even more when he switches to the stretch.

Results 3: Year-to-year sustainability

If differences are random, their usefulness is going to be severely limited. They'll still be useful in explaining what has happened, which has some merit. However, the more compelling application is in explaining what will happen, so reproducibility is paramount.

In a cursory effort to shed some light on this conundrum, the 78 starting pitchers meeting the minimum 90 innings all three seasons will be investigated by comparing their skill differences between wind-up and stretch to the league average of each season respectively. The total of pitchers with better skills from the wind-up will be determined and compared to that expected randomly.

Random expectations are determined using coin-flip probability. If eight people flip a coin three times each, one (12.5 percent) should get three heads, three (37.5 percent) should get two heads, three (37.5 percent) should get one heads and one (12.5 percent) should get zero heads. Ergo, one of eight pitchers is expected to sport better or worse numbers all three years, while three of eight would be better or worse one of the three years.

Here's how the 78 qualifying pitchers fared in terms of percentage of total (years better than league average as "Yrs+"):

Yrs+	Rand	Dom	Ctl	Cmd	HR/9	H%
3	12.5%	26.9%	11.5%	16.7%	16.7%	19.2%
2	37.5%	41.0%	30.8%	42.3%	33.3%	47.4%
1	37.5%	16.7%	39.7%	28.2%	43.6%	28.2%
0	12.5%	15.4%	17.9%	12.8%	6.4%	5.1%

More pitchers exhibit the ability to sustain a better Dom, HR/9 and H% than the league average than expected via probability.

Conclusion

The hypothesis was pitching from the wind-up and from the stretch creates two different pitchers, and elements of that have been borne out in the data. Taking pitchers in aggregate, Dom, Cmd, HR/9 and H% all get worse from the stretch, though walks stay pretty stable.

As well, the same pattern of skills differences appears to be sustainable over time for individual pitchers, both in simple numbers and when compared with random probability.

With the admittance that this approach is in the embryonic stage to be refined as data collection continues to advance, chances are the chief application of this hypothesis is during the off-season, in an effort to fine-tune the upcoming season's projection, but it should have some in-season utility as well.

The Truth about Pitcher Home/Road Splits

by Stephen Nickrand

Owners use many methods to manage their pitching rosters in leagues that allow for frequent transactions. One overlooked strategy is a simple but effective one: benching pitchers when they are on the road.

Our research reveals that several pitching stats and indicators are significantly and consistently worse on the road than at home.

First, a full look at home/road stats and skills from 2010-2012:

Home Stats & Skills: 2010-2012*

Year	Lg	ERA	WHIP	Win%	Ctl	Dom	Cmd	hr/9	GB%	H%	S%	hr/f	BPV
2010	AL	3.87	1.30	.558	3.1	6.9	2.3	1.0	44%	29%	73%	9%	63
2011	AL	4.02	1.31	.534	3.0	7.0	2.3	1.0	45%	30%	72%	11%	68
2012	AL	3.90	1.27	.534	2.9	7.6	2.6	1.0	44%	30%	72%	10%	80
2010	NL	3.77	1.30	.560	3.2	7.6	2.4	0.9	45%	30%	73%	9%	74
2011	NL	3.65	1.27	.519	2.9	7.4	2.5	0.9	45%	30%	73%	9%	77
2012	NL	3.76	1.27	.532	2.9	7.8	2.7	1.0	46%	30%	73%	11%	86
2010	MLB	3.82	1.30	.559	3.1	7.3	2.3	0.9	45%	30%	73%	9%	69
2011	MLB	3.82	1.28	.526	3.0	7.2	2.4	0.9	45%	30%	73%	9%	72
2012	MLB	3.83	1.30	.533	3.1	7.3	2.3	0.9	46%	30%	73%	11%	7

*all pitchers

Road Stats & Skills: 2010-2012*

Year	Lg	ERA	WHIP	Win %	Ctl	Dom	Cmd	HR/9	GB%	H%	S%	hr/f	BPV
2010	AL	4.42	1.40	.449	3.4	6.8	2.0	1.0	44%	30%	71%	10%	51
2011	AL	4.15	1.34	.470	3.2	6.9	2.2	1.0	44%	30%	72%	10%	60
2012	AL	4.29	1.35	.481	3.2	7.3	2.3	1.2	44%	30%	71%	12%	67
2010	NL	4.30	1.40	.433	3.5	7.2	2.1	1.0	44%	31%	72%	10%	58
2011	NL	4.00	1.35	.478	3.3	7.2	2.2	1.0	45%	30%	73%	10%	62
2012	NL	4.15	1.35	.455	3.3	7.6	2.3	1.0	45%	31%	72%	11%	72
2010	MLB	4.36	1.40	.441	3.4	7.0	2.0	1.0	44%	31%	71%	10%	55
2011	MLB	4.07	1.35	.474	3.3	7.1	2.2	1.0	44%	30%	72%	10%	61
2012	MLB	4.22	1.35	.467	3.2	7.4	2.3	1.1	45%	31%	72%	12%	70

*all pitchers

In particular, the following six metrics show significant home vs. road variances:

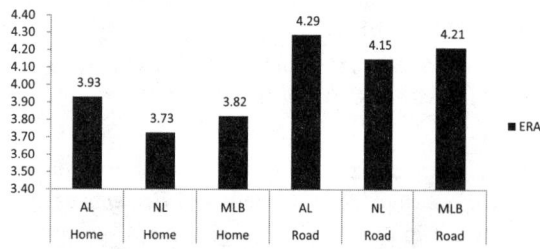

Home/Road Split 2010-12: ERA

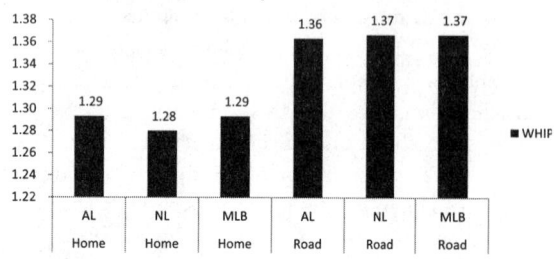

Home/Road Split 2010-12: WHIP

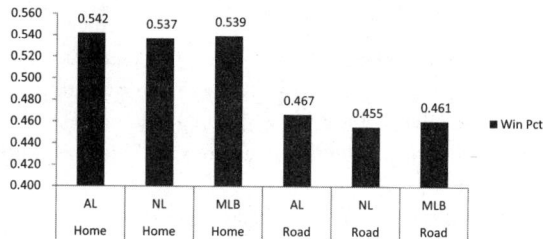

Home/Road Split 2010-12: Win Pct

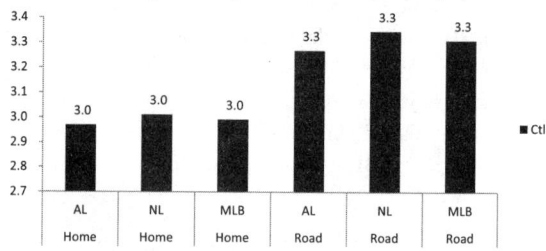

Home/Road Split 2010-12: Ctl (BB/9)

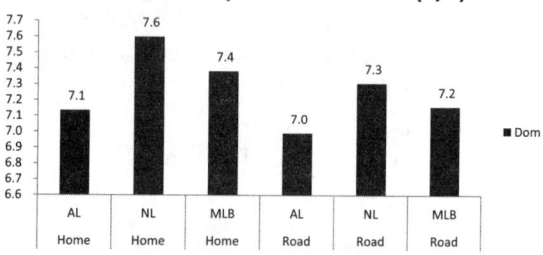

Home/Road Split 2010-12: Dom (K/9)

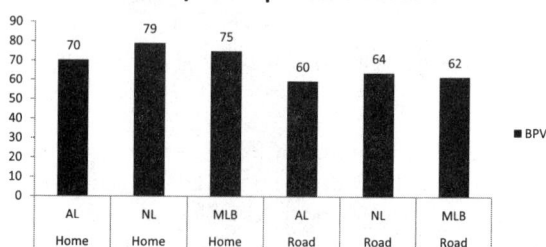

Home/Road Split 2010-12: BPV

Remember that the above are general trends and individual splits may vary. But here are some home/road rules of thumb for SP:

- If you want to gain significant ground in ERA and WHIP, keep all your average or worse SP benched on the road.
- A pitcher's win percentage drops by 15% when on the road, so don't bank on road starts as a means to catch up in wins.
- Control erodes by 10% on the road, so be especially careful with keeping wild SP in your active lineups when they are away from home.
- NL pitchers at home produce significantly more strikeouts than their AL counterparts and vs. all pitchers on the road.
- hr/9, groundball rate, hit rate, strand rate, and hr/f do not show significant home vs. road variances.

What's a player really worth?

by Ron Shandler

At the Tout Wars experts league draft in March 2013, I noticed an interesting phenomenon. The vast majority of players were purchased at very similar prices to the LABR drafts, which had been held three weeks earlier.

You might think that's an intuitively logical result given that the experts tend to have similar opinions about players. But that's not necessarily so. In the respective works of the experts, you'll read highly divergent opinions on players. Yet bidding tended to stall at near identical prices.

This was particularly notable for those players with uncertain values coming into 2013:

Player	LABR	Tout	
Berkman,Lance	13	11	Last 3 years: $8, $30, $0
Buchholz,Clay	6	8	Last 3 years: $19, $3, $1
Burnett,AJ	8	9	Last 3 years: -$5, -$5, $15
Cabrera,Melky	20	22	PED speculation
Carter,Chris	10	12	Unproven over a full season
Dickey,RA	18	20	Coming off $33 season
Gordon,Dee	9	8	Didn't even make team
Granderson,C	20	20	Injury uncertainty
Gyorko,Jed	10	12	Unproven
Hamilton,Billy	6	7	Didn't even make team
Harper,Bryce	35	33	Earned only $23 as rookie
Hart,Corey	13	15	Injury uncertainty
Johnson,Josh	13	12	Injury/new team uncertainty
Kemp,Matt	36	36	Injury uncertainty
Lawrie,Brett	25	22	Never earned more than $16
Lester,Jon	17	20	Last 3 years: $21, $14, -$3
Lincecum,Tim	16	14	Last 3 years: $17, $22, -$6
Martinez,Victor	19	20	Missed entire 2012 season
McDonald,James	4	6	Great 1st half, bad 2nd half
Medlen,Kris	19	17	Unproven over more than 138 IP
Montero,Jesus	16	18	Earned only $10 as rookie
Ryu,Hyun-Jin	5	6	Unproven yet big stats in Korea
Strasburg,Stephen	31	29	Earned only $19 in 2012
Upton,BJ	28	27	New team/league
Upton,Justin	35	35	Last 3 years: $20, $36, $25
Utley,Chase	17	19	Injury uncertainty
Votto,Joey	38	37	Injury uncertainty

How could players facing so much uncertainty get purchased at nearly identical prices? All of these players were either coming off an anomalously good or bad year, or were unproven coming into 2013. Even with the benefit of three weeks' more information, the Tout Warriors still ended up paying within +/- $3 of LABR.

Even more interesting to me was the fact that the actual bidding activity was often just a race to that perceived dollar limit. The fastest bidder to that predetermined price range won the player. As an outside observer, it seemed that purchases were just as much about bidding speed as value perception. The actual value of those players was essentially pre-set.

So... did LABR set the benchmark pricing for Tout? That would be troubling, because those drafts took place in early March, before we had the benefit of spring training games. We didn't know whether last year's hobbling players were healthy. We didn't know if "last year's bums" might seem primed for a turnaround.

We had no idea whether the rookies were even going to make their respective clubs.

Given that they were not privy to those March insights, did the LABR owners even have a real sense of player values? That seems unlikely, which makes the Tout bidding behavior even more troubling.

And now in retrospect, we can see how far off many of these values were.

So what were those players really worth?

In most March drafts, owners are working off some type of cheat sheet, populated with someone's projections. Fixed dollar values are calculated from those projections and represent a baseline for bidding behavior. Aggregate all those opinions and that is how you determine your market value.

But is that what a player is really worth?

What if we didn't have those projections? In the XFL experts keeper league, owners have to come to the table with no prep material of any kind. They draft from a list of 40-man MLB rosters. Each player's price is driven purely by demand and a very rough perception of value. In last year's draft, B.J. Upton went for $32, for one reason only: it was what the last owner to bid was willing to pay.

But is that what Upton was really worth?

Willingness to pay alone can cause some bizarre valuation behavior. That's how I once ended up with a $19 Nick Punto (many moons ago). Willingness to pay without benefit of a baseline is what causes poor money management in the standard Free Agent Acquisition Budget (FAAB) bidding process. In a blind-bidding environment, nobody knows what any player's market value is, making those bids nearly random.

In the first week of the SiriusXM/FSTA experts league, there were tons of precious FAAB dollars lost to gross overbids. Aaron Hicks was FAABed for $155 when the next highest bid was $74. Dillon Gee was FAABed for $113 when the next highest bid was $23. Jackie Bradley was FAABed for $88 when the next highest bid was $5. Chris Johnson was FAABed for $45 when the next highest bid was... well, there were no other bids.

All told in week #1, there were 32 players awarded and $1,264 spent on winning bids. All the second highest bids totaled $557.

That's a loss of $675, or an overpay rate of 53%.

In the first week alone.

That's like going to Nationals Park and willingly spending $12.75 for a beer just because you are really, really thirsty.

Consider how we place value on retail items in general. Let's say we are shopping for a camera at Best Buy. All the different models and styles are displayed across a long table in roughly price order. Prices generally run anywhere from about $150 to perhaps $500. During this shopping expedition, we examine the different features and benefits of each, and weigh that against our budget for the purchase.

If we zero in on a $250 model, we have assessed those variables and determined that particular camera meets our personal requirements for value. In our minds, we might conclude that it has comparable features to the $350 model and thus we could be getting a bargain. And so we make our purchasing decisions.

However, the manufacturers and Best Buy have set the value baseline. Without any knowledge at all, we might value a camera at $1,000, or $50, but that is not the range provided to us. Our decision-making process involves determining whether $250 is more or less what we would be willing to pay given the other options available.

That got me to thinking... perhaps figuring out what a player is worth is a task that should be left to a more objective source. Our reliance on inaccurate projections, our particular needs at a given time and personal biases are a feeble attempt to determine each player's value. And it's all a distortion; we don't know what each player's real value is. What's more, it will be different in every league.

And based on the numbers at the end of each season, we do an incredibly crappy job of it.

The fantasy game format that addresses this issue best might be the salary cap game.

The Best Buy assessment of value is how those games work. We don't have to determine what a player is really worth; we only need to determine whether we are willing to pay more or less than the price tag. That price is set by a (presumably) reputable valuation authority.

If that authority says that B.J. Upton is a $30 player, then you have to decide whether that is an appropriate price. If you think it's too high for your budget, then you can just opt for the $24 Michael Cuddyer.

Nobody is forced to overpay based on artificial demand driven by positional or categorical need. Owners do not have to adjust their values for the rest of the player pool just because one zealous owner was willing to pay $60 for Mike Trout. And bidding would not simply gravitate to a perceived pre-established end point price.

Instead, that end point is simply what the player costs. You just need to decide whether you are willing to pay it.

Of course, our attempts to determine value via auctions and snake drafts are part of the fun, even if they might be less than precise. But salary cap games level the playing field and are perhaps a better test of our ability to place a value on talent.

One thing that the Rotisserie 500 game does well is integrate the draft processes. Roto500 runs a standard snake draft, however, all players have a pre-assigned price tag. Team owners still need to fit all their rostered players under a salary cap.

It's an interesting twist that challenges us to figure out what players are really worth.

Six Tips on Category Management

by Todd Zola

TIP: Disregard whether you are near the top or the bottom of a category; focus instead on the gaps directly above and below your squad.

Sometimes we take too literally the axiom, "Trade from strength to improve weakness." The real message should be, "Trade from a category from which you can lose minimum points to improve one where you can gain maximum points."

TIP: Prorate the difference in stats between teams.

Let's say it's two-thirds of the way through and you're ninth in homers with 160 while the sixth-place team has 170. The difference is a seemingly recoverable 10 HR, so 11 HR renders four more points. Using the assumption that the present pace persists all season, that 10 HR difference is really 15, so if everything else remains the same, an additional 16 homers is necessary to vault into fifth place. Of course, roster composition is transient, so the pace is ever-changing. Even after accounting for roster changes, a prorated adjustment is necessary.

TIP: ERA tends to move towards WHIP.

On average, your team's ERA should be within three category points of its WHIP. Any bigger gap means you can anticipate your ERA moving towards your WHIP.

This regression might not occur, but it is a good idea to prepare for it when evaluating your team's position.

One exception: If your staff is dominated by either groundball or flyball pitchers. The hit rate (H%) for grounders is greater than for fly balls. As such, groundball specialists tend to sport higher WHIPs than flyball artists. However, groundball pitchers serve up fewer homers, so the ERA of a groundball pitcher with the same WHIP as a flyball pitcher should be lower.

TIP: As the season progresses, the number of at-bats and innings pitched do not preclude a gain/loss in the ratio categories.

Unlike the counting stats, you (and your opponents) can lose ground in ratios if your hitters or pitchers struggle.

From top to bottom, the ratio categories are bunched more tightly than the counting categories

Data from the Main Event leagues in the National Fantasy Baseball Championships demonstrate there are just as many points gained and lost on the last day of the season in the ratio categories as compared to the counting categories.

TIP: An opponent's point lost is a point earned.

Trades that help a team pass a close competitor in a category are just as beneficial as those that gain you a point directly.

MOST IMPORTANT TIP: Come crunch time, forget value, forget names, and forget reputation. It's all about stats and where you are situated within each category.

Each league's standings are unique with their own distribution of gaps and bunches. The key is managing your assets towards a net gain. If dealing Miguel Cabrera for Emilio Bonifacio nets more points in steals than is lost elsewhere, do the deal. It's about Bonifacio's intrinsic value to your team and not about Cabrera's ethereal value in a vacuum. Players can't breathe in a vacuum; trades shouldn't be made there.

Evaluating Reliability

by Bill Macey

Fantasy baseball owners are like investors: We're always looking for a good return. And, calculating our expected return includes assessing the risk of our draft-day investment.

Managing risk leads us to two kinds of valuation adjustments. We downgrade talented players we believe to be higher injury risks, who have a history of inconsistent performance, or whose playing time (PT) is less certain. But we upgrade players we deem more reliable with respect to health, consistency, PT, or all three.

This article analyzes what reliability is really worth—and whether the marketplace properly values that risk.

The Tools

Among the tools at BaseballHQ.com that help us quantify risk are the Reliability (Rel) grades assigned to each player. Each Rel grade has three components, assigned a letter grade A-F:
- Health (measured by days spent on the DL)
- PT/Experience (measured by MLB PT)
- Consistency (measured by runs created per game, or RC/G)

Previous research found that batters with higher reliability ratings earned more in the subsequent year, but could not find a similar effect for reliable, high-performing pitchers. This article revisits the topic of player performance compared to projected values, and measures if the market places a premium on reliability.

Result 1: Return on projected value

Over the 2011-2012 seasons, we found that the sample of batters as a whole returned a 60% return on their projected value, measured according to late March BaseballHQ.com projections (that is, a batter projected by BaseballHQ.com to earn $10 actually earned just $6 on average). Approximately 31% earned or exceeded their full projected value and 19% earned a negative value.

Pitchers were less reliable. They earned just 34% of their projected value. Fewer pitchers earned or exceeded their full projected value (28%) than those that earned a negative value (37%).

Result 2: Return by reliability ratings

We then examined the data to see if more reliable players were more likely to return their projected values, but we did not find a meaningful correlation with any of the individual reliability ratings.

This is somewhat surprising given our previous findings mentioned above—that more reliable players are also more likely to return value on a year-over-year basis. One possible explanation is that our projections are based on a player's performance over a number of years, therefore discounting the most recent year's anomalous results. Additionally, the projections also take reliability into account, particularly with respect to playing time.

Looking at the reliability ratings in concert rather than on a standalone basis, we did find that players with a B or better rating in both Health and PT/Exp (which we'll call "BB+") did return a higher percentage of their projected value.

Specifically, these BB+ batters earned a 63% return on their projected value, while their less reliable counterparts earned a 56% return. This difference is small but meaningful. It suggests that it does make sense to target more reliable batters, but the small spread cautions not to go more than the extra buck or two. To the extent that you overpay for reliability, you will very quickly erode its anticipated benefits.

This reliability threshold was more important for pitchers. BB+ pitchers earned a 50% return on their projected value, while those not meeting the criteria only earned a 14% return. While any dollar you pay greater than the expected return eats into your profits, it might still be a wiser investment than paying full projected value for a riskier pitcher who is more likely not to deliver.

Result 3: Market prices

Knowing the expected return on projected performance is only part of the equation. It's also important to consider what it will cost to acquire each player, especially if your competition also places a premium on reliability. That's why we looked at the Tout Wars mixed league auction results to see if these expert drafters were paying a premium for more reliable players.

We were not able to find any evidence suggesting that the market placed a significant price premium on more reliable players. The actual return on investment for batters generally mirrored the return on projected values, albeit slightly lower across the board: the sample of batters earned a 56% return on investment (ROI), with BB+ batters earning a 59% ROI and non-BB+ batters earning a 50% ROI.

Similarly, the ROI for pitchers was lower than the return on projected value, but still consistent: the overall sample of pitchers earned a 31% ROI, with more reliable pitchers earning a much better ROI (42%) than the less reliable sample (14% ROI).

Considering the value delivered is the same, the fact that ROI was lower than the return on projected value for all of the cohorts we analyzed implies that on average, the market price for players is higher than their projected value. However, there was no evidence to suggest that the market is paying a premium for reliability. If it had, you wouldn't expect to see similar spreads between the reliable and non-reliable cohorts.

Implications

When you head into an upcoming auction or draft, consider the following conclusions:
- Reliability grades do help identify more stable investments: players with "B" grades in both Health and PT/Experience are more likely to return a higher percentage of their projected value.
- While top-end starting pitching may be more reliable than ever, the overall pool of pitchers is fraught with uncertainty and the position represents a less reliable investment than batters.
- There does not appear to be a significant market premium for reliability, at least according to the criteria measured by BaseballHQ.com.
- There are only two types of players: risky and riskier. So while it may be worth going the extra buck for a more reliable player, be warned that even the most reliable player can falter—don't go overboard bidding up a AAA-rated player simply due to his Rel rating.

The Snake Draft PUSH List

by Ron Shandler

There is one thing missing with most published cheat sheets. While these ratings and rankings evaluate the player population, they are just an opinion about what some source believes.

What's missing is that these rankings need to be benched against the marketplace. It doesn't matter where I rank Albert Pujols. It matters where I rank Pujols in comparison to where he is likely to go in my draft. The variance in ranks—theirs to mine—is where the true draft advantage lies.

In the past, I'd incorporate these side-by-side rankings in my master draft sheet. But then I realized that it might be helpful to create a separate list with only those players who I could push up in my draft.

Thus became the PUSH List (Players Undervalued to be Selected aHead).

To create this list, we start with the average draft position (ADP) rankings from a trusted source. I typically use either Mock Draft Central (MDC) or National Fantasy Baseball Championship (NFBC), or both in tandem. The ADPs from MDC tend to be a more accurate reflection of the larger marketplace, though they break down a bit late in the draft. The ADPs from NFBC reflect a more hard-core, competitive mindset of this high-stakes league, though they tend to be more aggressive than the general marketplace.

Then with a set of projections (ours, yours, whatever source you trust), we match each player's projected round with his ADP round. We identify all those whose projection is at least two rounds earlier than their ADP. These are the players who we are projecting to be sufficiently better than the marketplace. The variance between the ADP round and projected round forms a "draft range" for each player.

Actually for us, this becomes a "target range." Drafting a player anywhere within this range is a value play. The closer a player is drafted to his ADP, the more potential profit and the less value left on the table.

The PUSH List is created by slotting players in the round just prior to their ADP. By slotting them into that round, it potentially increases the odds of drafting them, yet not too early.

For example:

CARLOS GOMEZ (in 2013 drafts)

Average Draft Position (Marketplace)	Round 17
BaseballHQ.com Projection	Round 8
Target Draft Range	Round 8-16
PUSH Round	Round 16

Chart this out for all players with at least a two-round variance.

This does not mean you absolutely have to draft these players in the PUSH Round; it just helps create a ranked list. The PUSH round is the optimal drafting spot, but anywhere in the target range—between projection and marketplace—will do.

Note that PUSH uses rounds instead of draft positions. I think using the individual player ranks is a bit too granular; there are ranges around each draft position that are essentially equivalent. By using rounds, I think it's easier to spot and process the real value differences on the fly.

Needless to say, every marketplace and every draft is different, so your PUSH list will depend upon context. But it's still instructive to look at one example, the results from Fantasy Sports Trade Association's 2013 draft. Of the PUSH players:

- 11% were drafted exactly in their ADP round.
- 62% were drafted earlier than their ADP round.
- 26% were drafted later than their ADP round.

The FSTA experts showed a strong tendency to draft players earlier than their ADPs. Should the marketplace have taken heed? Again, of the PUSH players:

- 12% were drafted exactly in their projected round.
- 17% were drafted earlier than projection.
- 70% were drafted later than projection.

This last figure offers up all sorts of opportunities to draft value. It's nice to know in retrospect; it would have been better to know in advance. Only 56% of PUSH players were drafted within the target range. This might be significant, but remember—it's data from just one league.

If the goal for a successful draft is to get as many players as possible at a potential profit over market value, the PUSH List provides an organized method for isolating those players who are your best targets.

Building a Homogeneous Head-to-Head Team

by David Martin

Introduction

Variety is the spice of life. But variety has no place in the type of players rostered on head-to-head fantasy baseball teams. Teams in head-to-head leagues need players cut from the same cloth—players that are completely homogenous.

Focusing on certain metrics helps build a homogenous team. Drafting a homogenous team inherently builds consistency into your roster. In either type of head-to-head league, week-to-week consistency is crucial.

Developing Team Homogeneity's Metric Filters

First, let's assume this team is playing in a 12-team mixed 5x5 league. Team Homogeneity will apply a LIMA-type approach where the majority of its auction dollars or high draft picks will be used on hitters. It is important to allocate these dollars/draft picks towards players that perform well in the same categories, thus providing a weekly advantage in those categories.

Second, paying attention to certain metrics can actually provide Team Homogeneity with a consistent week-to-week advantage. Bill Macey's work has established that ct%, bb% and Eye ratio are harbingers of more consistent production. Here, we use ct% and xBA in our analysis. If you play in a league that uses OPS or OBP, you should adjust your filters accordingly.

Third, because it is not possible to win every category every week, you will need to decide which categories you want to win each week. You can draft a team of speedsters that gets on base, swipes bags and scores runs. Alternatively you can go with a power-based team that has the ability to get on-base and score runs, but also hit the long ball. Below we apply the less fleet-footed Matt Holliday model. Note: this exercise can also be performed substituting Spd in place of PX.

Our filters are as follows:

- 80% and greater ct%
- .280 and greater xBA
- 120 and greater PX
- RC/G of at least 5

Based on BaseballHQ.com's 2013 projections, those filters generated a list of twenty (20) homogeneous players.

Assembling Team Homogeneity ("Team A")

Using 2013 average draft positions ("ADPs") from mockdraftcentral.com, it is possible to assemble the core of your team using players from the list of homogenous players. You can also slightly modify the PX filter to capture additional players with the requisite baseline consistency metrics.

With its first ten 2013 picks, Team A drafted eight hitters (3 OFs, C, 1B, 2B, SS, 3B) and two starting pitchers:

Player Name	ADP Round
Robinson Cano (2B, NYY)	1
Troy Tulowitzki (SS, COL)	2
Adam Jones (OF, BAL)	3
Ryan Zimmerman (3B, WAS)	4
Yoenis Cespedes (OF, OAK)	5
Zack Greinke (SP, LA)	6
Roy Halladay (SP, PHI)	7
David Ortiz (1B, BOS)	8
Jesus Montero (C, SEA)	9
Michael Cuddyer (OF, COL)	16

Note that in the process of drafting an offensive juggernaut, two starting pitchers (good ones at the time) were selected. BHQ's projected numbers for the core of Team A were as follows:

	Projected	Actual
Runs	685	557
HR	211	184
RBI	723	627
SB	53	48
AVG	.289	.293

In 2013, Team A's week-to-week DOM% consistency score (weeks where BPV > 50%) was 58%. If Team A's DOM% seems low to you, consider that in 2013, of those players that played at least one-third of the season (8 weeks worth of games), only 25% achieved a DOM% of 50% or higher for the season. For these qualifying players, the average DOM% was 36% and the median was 38%.

Assembling the Competition ("Team B")

However, these numbers are no fun in a vacuum. Instead, let's compare them to a second team—built without applying filters to create a homogeneous team, but instead using ADPs from mockdraftcentral.com. This team will even have the good fortune of drafting both Mike Trout and BHQ's 2013 projected HR leader, Giancarlo Stanton.

Importantly, Team B applies the same LIMA-type approach, loading up on offensive players early, but without regard to what categories those players might provide production in. In other words, this team is built to compete against Team A, and given its focus on hitting, will be much closer in production to Team A than the average team in the league. Here is how Team B looks:

Player Name	ADP Round
Mike Trout (OF, LAA)	1
Giancarlo Stanton (OF, MIA)	2
Hanley Ramirez (SS, LA)	3
Cole Hamels (SP, PHI)	4
Brett Lawrie (3B, TOR)	5
Jose Altuve (2B, HOU)	6
Carlos Santana (1B, CLE)	7
Miguel Montero (C, ARI)	7
Nelson Cruz (OF, TEX)	9
Matt Moore (RHP, TAM)	9

This is a very solid team. However, it was not built applying the principles of homogeneity. Here are Team B's projected core numbers:

	Projected	Actual
Runs	655	484
HR	178	141
RBI	628	484
SB	135	94
AVG	.274	.280

Comparing Teams A and B

And how do these numbers compare with those of Team A? Team A has the advantage in the following categories:

	Projected	Actual
Runs	+30	+73
HR	+33	+43
RBI	+95	+143
AVG	+.015	+.013

In 2013, Team B's DOM% consistency score was 52%. This means that Team A's 2012 DOM% consistency score is higher by 6%. Not surprisingly, Team B has the advantage in steals, but Team A could care less about winning that category. Again, it is important to remember that most teams in this league will not yield this type of hitting production.

As the draft progresses, you will need to adjust your filters. By adjusting your filters, you can effectively create tiers of target players to draft. It is recommended to keep ct%, eye ratio, and/or bb% at higher levels (the key consistency metrics), and decrease PX or Spd in later rounds. Additionally, you may wish to incorporate BHQ health grades into your decision-making process.

It should be emphasized that multiple layers of consistency have been built into this lineup as a result of the following: (1) applying metrics shown to generate consistent results; (2) allocating draft dollars/picks towards hitters, who are generally more reliable than pitchers; and (3) drafting hitters who do the same things well, which means the team is more likely to win its target categories in a given week.

Conclusion

In head-to-head fantasy baseball, the importance of drafting a homogenous team cannot be understated. The purpose here is to suggest a draft approach. Research shows that a homogeneous team is more likely to be a consistent team, which is the roster holy grail for head-to-head players.

Ratio Insulation in Head-to-Head Leagues

by David Martin

Introduction

On a week-to-week basis, inequities are inherent in the head-to-head game. Your opposition may have thirty more at-bats than your team. It may have a dozen pitchers starting versus your seven. It may have four closers in comparison to your tag team of two. One way to eliminate your competitor's advantage in the pure numbers game is through ratio insulation. By applying certain metrics, you can build a team that excels in the ratio categories (i.e. ERA, WHIP, BA, OBP, etc.). This insulates your team during those weeks when the numbers are in the competition's favor.

Target insulation categories

If you have applied the necessary metrics to build a homogenous lineup, then the hitters you drafted should provide an edge in the batting average or on-base percentage categories. In a standard 5x5 league, ERA and WHIP are the target "insulation" pitching categories. A pitcher's ERA is largely a function of his Dom and Cmd:

Resultant Earned Run Average

Cmd	-5.6 Dom	5.6+ Dom
0.0-0.9	5.36	5.99
1.0-1.4	4.94	5.03
1.5-1.9	4.67	4.47
2.0-2.4	4.32	4.08
2.5-2.9	4.21	3.88
3.0-3.9	4.04	3.46
4.0+	4.12	2.96

[From the Encyclopedia]

While a pitcher's ERA improves with increased Cmd, a concomitant increase in Dom will work to significantly lower a pitcher's ERA. WHIP is obviously a function of walks and hits, which in turn are derivatives of Cmd and Dom. As a pitcher's Cmd rises, either his walks are decreasing or his strikeouts are increasing. In either situation, WHIP is decreasing.

When to insulate during the draft

Generally speaking, you should insulate towards the end of your draft. If you have applied a LIMA approach, you will have drafted your hitters early. With your mid-round draft picks, you will have selected LIMA-quality starting pitchers, which at some point simply run out. At the time when you are faced with drafting a starting pitcher with sub-standard skills and a relief pitcher with better skills (although perhaps not a defined role), it's time to insulate by drafting the better skilled reliever.

In reviewing the last ten rounds of BaseballHQ.com's 2013 straight draft guide, there were 52 starting pitchers and 37 relief pitchers marked for those rounds. The starting pitchers selected in those rounds averaged the following statistics in 2013:

ERA	4.34
WHIP	1.33
Cmd	2.89
Dom	7.53

In comparison, the relief pitchers selected in those rounds averaged the following:

ERA	2.99
WHIP	1.12
Cmd	3.68
Dom	9.28

The relievers slotted in these later rounds have much better peripherals than the starting pitchers available. Not surprisingly, their ERA and WHIP ratios are also better. Moreover, the above numbers do not contemplate applying metric filters to determine the "best of the best" of the relievers available in those rounds.

Selecting potential insulators

To obtain a strong set of 2014 ratio insulators, apply the following filters:

Cmd > 3.0
Dom > 7.5
xERA < 3.30

Many of baseball's elite closers will make the list of potential insulators. However, the majority of these closers will not be available in the later, "insulation rounds" of the draft. (Note: It is okay to include your closers' statistics as among those insulating your team's ERA and WHIP.) Instead, focus on drafting setup men. In leagues which use holds as a category, many of these insulators are just as valuable as closers. However, even in a league where holds is not a category, these insulators should still be viewed as valuable commodities because they will lower your ERA and WHIP on a weekly basis.

Insulation at work

As mentioned, at some point during the draft, you may be faced with choosing between a starting pitcher whose peripherals are below LIMA thresholds, and a better-skilled reliever.

Based on average draft positions in the fifteen-team 2013 Straight Draft Guide, one could have netted Kenley Jansen (RHP, LA) in sixteenth round, Koji Uehara (RHP, BOS) in the twentieth round, David Robertson (RHP, NYY) in the twenty-first round, and Drew Smyly (RHP, DET) in the twenty-third round. Each of these pitchers entered 2013 as setup men.

Insulator	ERA	WHIP	Dom	Cmd	Ks
K. Jansen	2.01	.85	12.8	7.3	102
K. Uehara	1.06	.56	12.5	10.4	94
D. Robertson	2.24	1.06	10.9	4.3	73
D. Smyly	2.28	1.03	9.4	4.6	74
Average	*1.89*	*.87*	*11.4*	*6.6*	*85.8*

These insulators 2013 metrics are impressive: a 11.4 Dom and a 6.6 Cmd, as are their average ERA (1.89) and WHIP (.87). But what if you were to instead draft a starting pitcher in those same rounds; how would that affect your team's ERA and WHIP?

SP Avg.	ERA	WHIP	Dom	Cmd	Ks
SP Avg. 16	3.71	1.31	8.1	3.3	147.8
SP Avg. 20	4.93	1.39	7.6	4.0	87.6
SP Avg. 21	4.77	1.43	7.6	2.4	114.4
SP Avg. 23	3.79	1.25	7.3	2.9	116.8
SP Avg.—All	*4.30*	*1.34*	*7.6*	*3.1*	*116.7*

[note: at least four starting pitchers were averaged in a given round]

The insulators clearly have the edge in the ratio categories:

Pitcher	ERA	WHIP	Dom	Cmd	Ks
Insulators	1.89	.87	11.4	6.6	85.8
Avg. SPs	4.30	1.34	7.6	3.1	116.7

Insulator Advantage:

ERA	+ 2.41
WHIP	+ .47
Dom	+ 3.8
Cmd	+ 3.5

Opting for the insulation route will improve your team's ERA and WHIP. Now, consider the downside to drafting these insulators—the loss of strikeouts. The difference in total team strikeouts between the four insulators and the four average starting pitchers is approximately 124 strikeouts. Over the course of a twenty-six week season, this means the insulators will generate approximately 4.8 strikeouts less per week. Simply put, a properly insulated team will still be competitive in strikeouts.

Adopting this strategy may also result in the loss of wins during the course of the season. However, as is clear from the straight draft guide data above, these wins will come at a cost to your ERA and WHIP. You must ask yourself whether the cost of these wins is worth pursuing.

Conclusion

During certain weeks of the season, your head-to-head competitor will have an advantage on Day One going into your matchup. Your team should be constructed to weather this statistical storm. One strategy to minimize this advantage is to build your team's foundation around the ratio categories. ERA and WHIP should be valued like any other head-to-head statistical category. Roster space permitting, adding two to four insulators to your team will improve your team's weekly ERA and WHIP. During those weeks when your opponent has the advantage in the pure numbers game, your insulated team will be more than competitive.

A Keeper Leagues Primer

by Jock Thompson

Keeper league (KL)/dynasty formats come in all shapes and sizes, in terms of salary caps, the numbers of keepers permitted, whether there is a supplemental auction or draft, and when these drafts occur. But regardless of your particular format, there are some basic rules to live by for most KL owners as they prepare their rosters for the coming season. And whether new to dynasty play or a returning manager, serious championship seekers should review our primer.

Be realistic: Are you contending or rebuilding—and for how long? Take a backward look by reviewing your roster's reliability grades: Health, Playing Time and Consistency. Then look forward at the current season's projections. How do they stack up against other teams? How much are you relying on older players to continue at their current level, and how much are you relying on unestablished players to step up? If you don't trust your own judgment, what do the ADPs and mock drafts say about your players?

Understand and minimize your risk; identify your backup plans. Whether it's injury, age and/or inexperience, avoid excessive roster risk. Jonathan Singleton has intriguing patience-and-power upside at 1B, but his 2013 contact struggles could delay his MLB ascent. And if you're adding him to corner infield group that already includes Albert Pujols? An extreme example, but you get the picture. Likewise, Brett Anderson's skills have yet to be diminished by frequent injuries, making him a decent high-risk, high-reward play at the right price. But he's better paired with a durable Mat Latos vs. a questionable Johnny Cueto.

Ceilings vs floors: Pay attention to age. Develop replacements for your studs before they hit their mid-30s, not after they begin their descents. Take a hard look at the ceilings of your 25-year-olds; likewise, take a rational look at the floors of your 35-year-olds. Don't be afraid to sell high, but don't be afraid to rely on older players as stopgaps either, if they fit your risk profile and can be had at the right price.

Know your format; use your rules. Reserve ability and numbers, daily roster moves vs. weekly, free agent pick-up and draft days. All differ widely between leagues, all are critical as to strategy. If you're a contender, you'll need some of your reserve slots to help you win; focusing solely on the long game and prospects with an ETA past 2013 isn't going to help you.

For deep-leaguers with daily roster move capabilities, home-field advantages and platoons are your friends. Flyball pitcher Jason Vargas (sub-4 ERA in friendly home environments of Angel Stadium and Safeco Field; 5+ ERA everywhere else) illustrates the possibilities from a pitching standpoint. Almost any Colorado hitter's home/away splits deliver a similar message on offense.

Know your venues/divisions; be aware of the changes. Most fantasy owners have known for a while that the AL East isn't the place to take big risks with young pitching, but that just the opposite is true with the AL West—particularly with pitching parks in Anaheim, Oakland and Seattle that are invaded by spring marine layers. Good offensive environments and pitching venues aren't limited to the AL coasts, but you have to know your divisions and ballpark tendencies to take advantage of opportunities.

And staying abreast of changes is a must. In 2013, Safeco Field's fences were realigned, which included the elimination of the LF scoreboard that once turned HR into 2Bs for right-handed hitters. Anaheim and Oakland remain intact, but particularly with the inclusion of RHB-friendly Houston, the AL West isn't quite the pitching-friendly lock that it used to be.

Rebuilding Rule I: Know the disabled list. Competing owners are more than willing to shed their injured players, at times for pennies on the dollar, often to your league's free agent list outright. Albert Pujols, for example, should now be considered a potential buy-low target for rebuilding owners needing power in 2014.

Likewise rebuilding owners should also know the Tommy John Surgery (TJS) Stash List. The 2013 delays of Ryan Madson and Corey Luebke are making everyone reconsider the once-standard 12-month recovery window for this type of injury. But the successful rebound rates of TJS outpatients—see Jordan Zimmerman, Kris Medlen and prospect Jarrod Parker—point to one of the better fantasy pitching staff rebuild strategies.

Rebuilding Rule II: Don't be afraid to rebuild with pitching. The historical predictability of offense has always accorded second-class citizen status to pitchers, but they still count for half of the points in most formats. While other owners zig, you should zag, particularly if offense is in short supply via pre-season trade or your free agent list. At some point in-season, your well-placed pitching risks and acquisitions will make a few contenders willing to fork over 2014 offense for the pitching they hope will put them over the top.

Prospects with combined High-A and Double-A experience in 2013 are viable MLB candidates at some point this season, depending on their performance and parent club's needs. This is particularly true for organizations with Triple-A affiliates in the offense-crazed Pacific Coast League (PCL), which is no longer considered an essential development stop for pitchers. The obvious 2013 example is Jose Fernandez, who skipped both Double-A and Triple-A in his rise to stardom. Mat Latos never pitched an inning at AAA-Tucson prior to joining SD in 2009. And even after recovering from TJS, Jarrod Parker pitched only 21 innings at AAA-Sacramento before getting his 2012 MLB call.

Prospecting: Skills that succeed quickly. Selecting minor league prospects isn't easy, and is often relative to your status as a contender or rebuilder, i.e.—do you lean toward immediate results or longer-term upside? Three rules to remember: 1) A running game with plus speed can earn a profit and buy time for other skills that need seasoning (see Jonathan Villar in 2013); 2) power-plus-contact is a rare but extremely valuable thing; and 3) defense and/or versatility can mean the difference between MLB playing time and the minors.

Watch spring training games. This might be a minority view among analysts, but spring training can provide hints and even benchmarks in certain players' growth—and decide both Opening Day jobs and who gets opportunity. Julio Teheran's successful winter league campaign and terrific March suggested that he was suddenly missing more bats and walking fewer hitters—a prerequisite to harnessing his immense talent. At the same time, Domonic Brown was more than tapping into the power at which he'd hinted in years past. Particularly with respect to growth-age/ post-hype prospects, give some consideration to spring performances. But by all means, repeat the standard "spring training games don't matter" and hope that your fellow owners believe it.

Keeper Decisions

by Patrick DiCaprio

How do we make optimal keeper decisions?

For purpose of this essay, we assume a relatively common set up of keeper rules:

- You buy a player for $x at the auction.
- In his second year you can keep him at that salary.
- In the third year you either renew him at that salary for one year, at which point he goes back into the auction pool in year four. Or, you sign him to a long-term contract that increases his salary by $5 each season.

Optimal = Maximizing Dollar Profit ("DP")

You may read this and think that we mean fantasy profit. And in some sense we do. But in a more important sense, we mean actual dollars.

Let's presume you are the proud owner of a $1 Joe Keeper, who you purchased in 2012, and now you have to decide whether to renew him or sign him to a long-term contract. Many will sign him long-term. But that is the wrong decision if you want to win right now.

In a league with a $1,000 First Prize, $500 Second Prize and $100 Third Prize, you might consider the problem like this:

- Keeper is projected to average $25 production per year over the next three years.
- So, if he's simply renewed at $1, he turns a fantasy profit ("FP") of $24, but then zero over the next two years.
- A long-term deal at $16 generates a FP of $27 over three years.
- Therefore, the right decision is to sign him to long-term contract.

If you are building for the future this is likely a fair calculus. But this is only because the DP of a rebuilding team winning a cash prize in the rebuilding year is probably small. For illustrative purposes, let's say that Keeper and his $9 FP increases your chances of each cash prize by 5% for First, 10% for Second and 15% for Third. The DP of each gain is $50, $50 and $15 or $115.

If you want to win this year, you must renew Keeper at $1 and let the chips fall where they may. If a $9 FP increases DP at the rates above, then we can roughly assume a linear progression for this purpose. At a $24 FP ($25 production vs. $1 salary) Keeper will increase your chances at First by 12%, Second by 25% and Third by 40%, approximately. If you think these chances are too high, just substitute the name Mike Trout (OF, LAA) for Joe Keeper and we see that it is probably a fair assessment.

So, the actual DP gained by renewal is $120, $125 and $40, or $265 total. It is a rout.

Of course we do not expect such rigorous calculation, nor is this the full calculation; you have to consider the extra fantasy salary in year two and three from a long-term contract, compared to what you can get in the auction and the FP for each dollar spent at the auction. But this is the right way to think about the problem.

Pulling it all together

In sum, follow these rules:

- Never sign any player to a long-term deal that makes his salary more than $10 higher, unless FP will be greater than the opportunity cost.
- If you want to win this year, sign no long-term contracts unless the DP is sufficiently high.
- Never sign a pitcher whose auction price is over $10 to a long-term contract. The DP here is almost never worth it.
- When in doubt, if you are a "win-now" team make every decision in favor of minimizing opportunity cost by having more money available at the auction. The only time to deviate from this is if the player pool makes it obvious you will not have a 25-33% profit at the auction.

The Cole Hamels Revenge

by Ron Shandler

In 2013, owners of Cole Hamels suffered an unfortunate roto indignity. Despite pitching to a solid 3.60 ERA, Hamels came away with only eight wins. He earned just $9 in a season that should have generated perhaps 6-8 more wins and $8-$10 more dollars.

It's our ultimate frustration, isn't it? We watch our guys on the mound, often pitching brilliantly, but either their team's offense can't get going or the bullpen implodes.

It's a roto problem as long as the game has been in existence. I admit that I've been playing long enough to have owned Nolan Ryan during the 1987 season. That year, he led the league with a 2.76 ERA and 270 strikeouts but posted an 8-16 record, thanks to a punchless Astros offensive attack.

The problem is the Wins category. It's a team stat being applied to an individual performance. It's highly flawed for any general analysis; no less so for roto purposes. Still, it forces us to consider team context when rostering pitchers, so it does add some color to the analytical process.

But then there's the Cole Hamels problem. It's a malady that he may have contracted from his teammate Cliff Lee last year. Lee posted a 3.16 ERA in 211 innings, went winless during the first half of the season and ended up 6-9.

Over the years, there has been much written about finding a replacement for Wins. Some leagues omit it completely from their categories. Some replace it with a stat like Quality Starts. That's not a bad option. However, I find one flaw with QS; it is highly redundant with ERA. From my perspective, QS are not sufficiently different from ERA to justify its own category.

However... QS might be an interesting qualifier in tandem with Wins.

So, what would happen if we replaced Wins with Wins + Quality Starts?

For one thing, it would have raised Cole Hamels value this year. He was a top 5 pitcher in QS despite being ranked outside the top 50 in wins. Adding QS would have provided Hamels with at least a little measure of roto retribution.

Let's look at those pitchers whose roto value would have changed the most by replacing Wins with W+QS:

PITCHER	W	QS	W+Q	5x5	w/QS	+/-
			Roto value			
Hamels,Cole	8	25	33	$9	$12	+$3
Wood,Travis	9	24	33	$11	$14	+$3
Holland,Derek	10	22	32	$6	$8	+$2
Santana,Ervin	9	23	32	$11	$13	+$2
Shields,James	13	27	40	$12	$14	+$2
Strasburg,Stephen	8	18	26	$16	$18	+$2
Scherzer,Max	21	25	46	$31	$29	-$2
Miller,Shelby	15	13	28	$13	$11	-$2

The differences are not significant, but they do serve to separate the pitchers a bit.

Things start to look more different when we rank pitchers by Wins and W+QS:

	Wins		W+QS
Scherzer,Max	21	Scherzer,Max	46
Wainwright,Adam	19	Wainwright,Adam	45
Zimmermann,J	19	Kershaw,Clayton	43
Colon,Bartolo	18	Colon,Bartolo	41
Moore,Matt	17	Wilson,C.J.	41
Wilson,C.J.	17	Shields,James	40
Tillman,Chris	16	Zimmermann,J	40
Kershaw,Clayton	16	Lee,Cliff	38
Liriano,Francisco	16	Medlen,Kris	37
Lester,Jon	15	Tillman,Chris	37
Miller,Shelby	15	Corbin,Patrick	37
Greinke,Zack	15	Iwakuma,Hisashi	37
Medlen,Kris	15	Ryu/Arroyo/Minor	36

Note all the shifts in value. Matt Moore, a top 5 pitcher in wins, drops off the W+QS list (actually, to #35) thanks to only 14 quality starts. There are similar drops for Liriano, Lester, Miller and Greinke.

The biggest gainer rising into the top 12 on the W+QS list is James Shields, who had 27 quality starts despite only 13 wins. He was outside the top 25 in the Wins ranking. Even Clayton Kershaw rises five spots, appropriately.

Another benefit of W+QS is that the category provides a larger base of counting stats. Standings would potentially move more often.

Think of W+QS this way:

Your pitcher gets two points if he pitches at least 6 innings, allows 3 runs or fewer, his team scores more runs than he allows and his bullpen holds the lead.

Your pitcher gets one point if he pitches at least 5 innings, his team scores more runs than he allows—regardless of how many runs he allows—and his bullpen holds the lead.

Your pitcher gets one point if he pitches at least 6 innings and allows 3 runs or fewer, regardless of what the rest of his team does.

Cole Hamels best displays the impact this year:

- 8 wins (ranked #56)
- 25 quality starts (ranked #4)
- 33 W+QS (ranked #24).

3x3 Leagues

by Ron Shandler

When Dan Okrent and his group of French food aficionados played their first season of Rotisserie League Baseball in the early 1980s, it was a 4x4, eight-category game. It was home runs, RBIs, stolen bases, batting average, wins, saves, ERA and the ratio of hits and walks to innings pitched (which they called "Ratio").

Most of us early adopters were awed by the near-perfect elegance of these categories. It would be a full decade before anyone questioned them, or dared try to tweak them.

The 5x5 game started taking hold in the late 1990s. But why did we need to add categories anyway? The thought process was that adding categories would provide for a more robust gaming experience.

Today, 5x5 games are the standard. However, that has not kept some leagues from increasing the number of stats even more. 6x6 games have arisen, as have 7x7, 8x8 and even 12x12 games. As long as your commissioner service can support it, you can run a league with as many categories as you like.

But there are downsides to this "more is better" mentality.

The first, most obvious is the potential for redundancy. The 5x5 game, for instance, already counts home runs four times—as HRs themselves, in runs, RBI and batting average. Those leagues that add slugging average make power hitters even more dominant in the game. I also don't get leagues that use both slugging and Total Bases. Or both BA and OBP.

Similarly, leagues that include both pitcher strikeouts and K/9 make power pitchers disproportionately dominant.

But for me, the bigger downside for adding categories is that it makes managing your team more difficult. The more categories you use, the more moving parts that need to be managed. Players who contribute to multiple categories are the toughest to assess, acquire and trade.

Why would I be concerned about making things easier for fantasy managers? Because the game's uncertainty and risk have been rising over the past half-decade. Between skyrocketing DL days, MLB roster turnover and the impact of PEDs, the statistical landscape has changed and makes players much more difficult to project. This game is tough enough to play without adding more obstacles to effective roster management.

The multi-category challenges exist even in the 5x5 game. If my team needs to deal away some bags in order to beef up elsewhere, I also have to be concerned about the impact on runs. Trading for wins is nearly a fool's quest. And I don't know about you, but in all my years of playing this game, I don't think I've ever traded for a pitcher with the sole purpose of improving in WHIP alone. WHIP has always been just a tagalong category for me. Runs and RBI were mostly tagalongs as well.

A few years ago, I started toying with the possibility of getting by with less. Fewer categories would be easier to manage. The challenge would be finding categories that captured as many elements of performance as possible without sacrificing the core game.

In previous writings, I've suggested a hybrid 4x4 configuration—HR, SB, OBA, (R+RBI-HR), (W+QS), (Sv+Hld), ERA, K. But it occurred to me that this simplification may not go far enough.

Can we squeeze this down to 3x3?

It's a no-brainer on the batting side. We can pare down our regular categories to power (HR), speed (SB) and on base average (OBA). This approach would allow us to focus on individual player skills without regard to the team context of runs and RBIs.

Pitching is a little trickier. We would probably start with strikeouts and ERA. For the third category, we could do Saves plus Holds, though that would give relief pitchers a bit too much value.

Here's an interesting twist: Saves + Holds + Quality starts. We can call it "Results" (RST). Yes, it brings back team context, but it does work. While saves and holds will drive the category leaders, starters still can make some noise. In fact, bullpen arms will generate about twice as many counting stats here as starters. It's the exact opposite of strikeouts, where starters dominate the leader board by a factor of at least two. Both starters and relievers contribute to all three categories in appropriate proportions.

What type of player values does this 3x3 system generate compared to the 5x5 and 4x4 formats? Unsurprisingly similar. Here are the current top 5 batters and top 5 pitchers based on 5x5 rankings, and their accompanying 4x4 and 3x3 values.

BATTERS	5x5	4x4	3x3	HR	SB	OBA
Cabrera,M	45	49	54	44	3	.439
Trout,M	42	53	61	27	33	.429
Davis,C	39	39	40	53	4	.364
Goldschmidt,P	38	44	48	36	15	.401
McCutchen,A	34	39	44	21	27	.398
Votto,J		40	46	24	6	.436
Choo,S			41	21	20	.402
PITCHERS	**5x5**	**4x4**	**3x3**	**K**	**ERA**	**RST**
Kershaw,C	43	42	38	232	1.83	27
Scherzer,M	31	26	22	240	2.90	25
Harvey,M	26	24	22	191	2.27	20
Wainwright,A	26	25	21	219	2.94	26
Fernandez,J	26	26	23	187	2.19	20
Darvish,Y		26	23	277	2.83	21
Kimbrel,C			24	98	1.21	50
Holland,G			24	103	1.21	47

You can see the changes in the values as you compress formats, but for the most part, the best players are still the best players. The categories might still need some tweaking—particularly on the pitching side—but the names added in the 4x4 and 3x3 games still seem wholly justified.

In some ways, 3x3 is more pure, removing most of the team-dependent variables that skew individual performance metrics. But more than that, it is much easier to manage. I can more easily orchestrate a straight power-for-speed trade without worrying about the impact on runs or RBI. I can deal a starter for a reliever and have a better handle on how my team's bottom line will be affected.

I suppose you might say that it's a little cleaner.

What are we Really Chasing?

by Ron Shandler

I'm in three national experts leagues.

In one, I wallowed in the middle of the standings all season, slowly fading to an 11th place finish. There is no trading in this league, so I had to rely on the free agent pool, improving health and turnaround seasons to get me back into contention. It never happened.

In another, I finished tied for 8th place after spending nearly the entire season in 10th. It is an incredibly deep league with a barren free agent pool, so my only hope to gain ground was for my hobbling players to get healthy and the long-shot possibility of pulling off a lopsided trade. It never happened.

In my third league, I spent nearly the entire second half in 4th place, though I managed to sneak into 3rd by the final pitch. But this is a keeper league, 2013 was supposed to be my title run season and it's either first place or no place in the end. It never happened.

As always, I am in it for the long haul. I play the game for six full months; sometimes it yields results, sometimes not.

Either way, it's a lot of effort. I don't like spinning my wheels. If I am working hard at something, I need to see results. So I was wondering what the real odds were of all my effort returning its just rewards.

About 10 years ago, Scott Wilderman wrote a research article for the then *USA Today Sports Weekly Fantasy Hot Sheet* called, "Do I Still Have A Chance? Recovering from a Slow Start." The piece calculated the odds of any team finishing in the money at each of a dozen points during the season. Scott ran the TQStats commissioner service back then; he's now the proprietor of OnRoto.com.

His research showed that each league's eventual winner was in first place on May 1 only 41% of the time. However, on that date, 80% of the winners were no lower than 4th place. Consider that again: **Of the teams that eventually won their league, 80% of them were already sitting in a money spot after one month.**

As much as we dismiss the importance of April stats, that seems to be a pretty important month.

In the process of introducing my one-month league concept in 2013, I got a good amount of pushback from long-time traditional fantasy leaguers. They claim that one month is far too short a time period to have any relevance. Certainly, a full season competition is more telling of our proficiency at skills evaluation; it's also more of a testament to commitment.

But I have been parading around Scott's research as validation of the one-month concept.

Then I received the following email from one of the monthly league participants:

"I have been wondering about your 1-month statistics about winners. I wonder what it would be for two months. The reason I ask is that I also believe one month is too short. It seems that, in the leagues I was involved in this year, there was a very strong team that emerged after two months."

Intuitively, the two month time period has always made sense to me too. But as it turns out, those extra games after one month

don't have as much impact as you might think. Here are the stats for the entire season, by month:

ON DATE	% eventual winner is in top 4 spots
May 1	80%
June 1	88%
July 1	89%
Aug 1	98%
Sept 1	99.9%

The incremental improvement month-to-month after April is tiny, relatively speaking. A good portion of the season is already determined after one month.

To reinforce the dramatic implications of these results, let's flip the analysis and look at how tough it is to come back from a bad start. Here are your odds of winning your league if you are in the bottom third of the standings at the beginning of each month:

ON DATE	% chance of winning if in bottom third
May 1	9%
June 1	5%
July 1	3%
Aug 1	Less than 1%
Sept 1	Football time

According to this data, two of my three experts league teams were pretty much dead in the water from nearly the get-go.

And my contending keeper league team? When I was in 3rd place back in mid-June, I only had a 26% shot at winning. At face value, that's pretty discouraging. As strong as my team was and with more than half of the season left to play, I only had a 1-in-4 chance to win.

Does this phenomenon hold up in the major league standings? We always trumpet the need for each team to play it out for six full months. After all, where would the Dodgers be if they packed it in after their slow start this season?

As it turns out, the major league standings track fairly closely to the fantasy league research.

Let's look back at all seasons from 2002 to 2013. The teams that were in first place on May 1 each year ended up winning their division only 44% of the time. However, of the teams within three games of first place on May 1, the eventual division winner arose from that group 78% of the time.

And the flipside… if your team was more than three games out of first place on May 1, you had only a 22% chance of winning your division.

As a fan of a non-contending team, we like to cling to hope. But hope is a horrible percentage play.

Three takeaways:

1. In a six month game, winning takes substantial effort.

2. We can have a pretty good sense of who is going to win after only one month.

3. Thank goodness for the wild card.

The following section contains player boxes for every batter who had significant playing time in 2013 and/or is expected to get fantasy roster-worthy plate appearances in 2014. In most cases, high-end prospects who have yet to make their major league debuts will not appear here; you can find scouting reports for them in the Prospects section.

Snapshot Section

The top band of each player box contains the following information:

Age as of Opening Day 2014.

Bats shows which side of the plate he bats from—(L)eft, (R)ight or (B)oth.

Positions: Up to three defensive positions are listed and represent those for which he appeared a minimum of 20 games in 2013.

Ht/Wt: Each batter's height and weight.

Reliability Grades analyze each batter's forecast risk, on an A-F scale. High grades go to those who have accumulated few disabled list days (Health), have a history of substantial and regular major league playing time (PT/Exp) and have displayed consistent performance over the past three years, using RC/G (Consist).

LIMA Plan Grade evaluates how well a batter would fit into a team using the LIMA Plan draft strategy. Best grades go to batters who have excellent base skills, are expected to see regular playing time, and are in the $10-$30 Rotisserie dollar range. Lowest grades will go to poor skills, few AB and values less than $5 or more than $30.

Random Variance Score (Rand Var) measures the impact random variance had on the batter's 2013 stats and the probability that his 2014 performance will exceed or fall short of 2013. The variables tracked are those prone to regression—h%, hr/f and xBA to BA variance. Players are rated on a scale of –5 to +5 with positive scores indicating rebounds and negative scores indicating corrections. Note that this score is computer-generated and the projections will override it on occasion.

Mayberry Method (MM) acknowledges the imprecision of the forecasting process by projecting player performance in broad strokes. The four digits of MM each represent a fantasy-relevant skill—power, speed, batting average and playing time (PA)—and are all on a scale of 0 to 5.

Commentaries for each batter provide a brief analysis of BPIs and the potential impact on performance in 2014. MLB statistics are listed first for those who played only a portion of 2013 at the major league level. Note that these commentaries generally look at performance related issues only. Role and playing time expectations may impact these analyses, so you will have to adjust accordingly. Upside (UP) and downside (DN) statistical potential appears for some players; these are less grounded in hard data and more speculative of skills potential.

Player Stat Section

The past five years' statistics represent the total accumulated in the majors as well as in Triple-A, Double-A ball and various foreign leagues during each year. All non-major league stats have been converted to a major league equivalent (MLE) performance level. Minor league levels below Double-A are not included.

Nearly all baseball publications separate a player's statistical experiences in the major leagues from the minor leagues and outside leagues. While this may be appropriate for official record-keeping purposes, it is not an easy-to-analyze snapshot of a player's complete performance for a given year.

Bill James has proven that minor league statistics (converted to MLEs), at Double-A level or above, provide as accurate a record of a player's performance as major league statistics. Other researchers have also devised conversion factors for foreign leagues. Since these are adequate barometers, we include them in the pool of historical data for each year.

Team designations: An asterisk (*) appearing with a team name means that Triple-A and/or Double-A numbers are included in that year's stat line. Any stints of less than 20 AB are not included (to screen out most rehab appearances). A designation of "a/a" means the stats were accumulated at both AA and AAA levels that year. "for" represents a foreign or independent league. The designation "2TM" appears whenever a player was on more than one major league team, crossing leagues, in a season. "2AL" and "2NL" represent more than one team in the same league. Players who were cut during the season and finished 2013 as a free agent are designated as FAA (Free agent, AL) and FAN (Free agent, NL).

Stats: Descriptions of all the categories appear in the Encyclopedia.

- The leading decimal point has been suppressed on some categories to conserve space.
- Data for platoons (vL, vR), balls-in-play (G/L/F) and consistency (Wk#, DOM, DIS) are for major league performance only.
- Formulas that use BIP data, like xBA and xPX, only appear for years in which G/L/F data is available.

Batting average is presented alongside xBA. On base average and slugging average appear next, and the combined On Base Plus Slugging (OPS). OPS splits vs. left-handed and right-handed pitchers appear after the overall OPS column.

Batting eye and contact skill are measured with walk rate (bb%), contact rate (ct%) and hit rate (h%), the latter often referred to as batting average on balls-in-play (BABIP). Eye is the ratio of walks to strikeouts.

Once the ball leaves the bat, it will either be a (G)round ball, (L)ine drive or (F)ly ball. Looking at the ratio of fly balls is a good springboard to the Power gauges. Linear weighted power index (PX) measures a batter's skill at hitting extra base hits as compared to overall league levels. xPX measures power by assessing how hard the ball is being hit (rather than the outcomes of those hits). And the ratio of home runs to fly balls shows the results of those hits.

To assess speed, first look at on base average (does he get on base?), then Spd (is he fast enough to steal bases?), then SBO (how often is he attempting to steal bases?) and finally, SB% (when he attempts, what is his rate of success?).

In looking at consistency, we use weekly Base Performance Value (BPV) levels. Starting with the total number of weeks the batter accumulated stats (#Wk), the percentage of DOMinating weeks (BPV over 50) and DISaster weeks (BPV under 0) is shown. The larger the variance between DOM and DIS, the greater the consistency.

The final section includes several overall performance measures: runs created per game (RC/G). runs above replacement (RAR), Base performance value (BPV), Base performance index (BPX, which is BPV indexed to each year's league average) and the Rotisserie value (R$).

2014 Projections

Forecasts are computed from a player's trends over the past five years. Adjustments were made for leading indicators and variances between skill and statistical output. After reviewing the leading indicators, you might opt to make further adjustments.

Although each year's numbers include all playing time at the Double-A level or above, the 2014 forecast only represents potential playing time at the major league level, and again is highly preliminary.

Note that the projected Rotisserie values in this book will not necessarily align with each player's historical actuals. Since we currently have no idea who is going to close games for the Indians, or whether George Springer is going to break camp with Houston, it is impossible to create a finite pool of playing time, something which is required for valuation. So the projections are roughly based on a 12-team AL/NL league, and include an inflated number of plate appearances, league-wide. This serves to flatten the spread of values and depress individual player dollar

projections. In truth, a $25 player in this book might actually be worth $21, or $28. This level of precision is irrelevant in a process that is driven by market forces anyway. So, don't obsess over it.

Be aware of other sources that publish perfectly calibrated Rotisserie values over the winter. They are likely making arbitrary decisions as to where free agents are going to sign and who is going to land jobs in the spring. We do not make those leaps of faith here.

Bottom line… It is far too early to be making definitive projections for 2014, especially on playing time. Focus on the skill levels and trends, then consult BaseballHQ.com for playing time revisions as players change teams and roles become more defined. A free projections update will be available online in March.

Do-it-yourself analysis

Here are some data points you can look at in doing your own player analysis:

- Variance between vLH and vRH OPS
- Growth or decline in walk rate (bb%)
- Growth or decline in contact rate (ct%)
- Growth or decline in G/L/F individually, or concurrent shifts
- Variance in 2013 hit rate (h%) to 2010-2012 three-year average
- Variance between Avg and xBA each year
- Growth or decline in power index (PX) rate
- Variance between PX and xPX each year
- Variance in 2013 hr/f rate to 2010-2012 three-year average
- Growth or decline in statistically scouted speed (Spd) score
- Concurrent growth/decline of gauges like ct%, FB, PX, xPX, hr/f
- Concurrent growth/decline of gauges like OB, Spd, SBO, SB%
- Trends in DOM/DIS splits

Abreu,Jose

Age	27	Bats	R	Pos	1B	Health	A	LIMA Plan	A
Ht	6' 2"	Wt	258			PT/Exp	D	Rand Var	
						Consist	F	MM	4235

Cuban single-season HR record-holder, entering his prime years, also boasts elite plate discipline and terrific contact rate. BPIs are better than those of Cespedes and Puig when they played in Cuba. No guarantees of a smooth transition to MLB, but these skills are not to be ignored.

Yr	Tm	AB	R	HR	RBI	SB	BA	xBA	OBP	SLG	OPS	vL	vR	bb%	ct%	h%	Eye	G	L	F	PX	xPX	hr/f	Spd	SBO	SB%	#Wk	DOM	DIS	RC/G	RAR	BPV	BPX	R$
09																																		
10	for	304	81	14	72	2	331		433	570	1003			15	82	37	0.98				151			121	2%	62%				9.34	38.0	116	252	$20
11	for	252	91	18	87	2	385		484	655	1138			16	85	40	1.28				161			84	3%	62%				13.01	51.5	128	284	$27
12	for	297	72	18	91	1	339		447	582	1029			16	85	35	1.28				138			89	1%	100%				10.06	42.1	111	278	$22
13	for	285	59	10	54	2	320		406	480	886			13	84	35	0.90				103			85	8%	21%				6.76	17.0	71	178	$16
1st Half																																		
2nd Half																																		
14	Proj	406	64	19	67	2	287	279	364	504	867	867	867	11	81	31	0.65	35	22	43	139		14%	87	3%	72%				6.53	22.0	84	210	$17

Abreu,Tony

Age	29	Bats	B	Pos	2B	Health	D	LIMA Plan	D
Ht	5' 9"	Wt	200			PT/Exp	D	Rand Var	-1
						Consist	B	MM	3121

2-14-.268 in 138 AB at SF. Hit .320+ six times in Pacific Coast League despite horrifying plate discipline and marginal contact rate. In MLB those things matter. Has never shown power and doesn't run, so any value must come from batting average, which has yet to translate to MLB. Likely won't. DN: PCL All-Star.

Yr	Tm	AB	R	HR	RBI	SB	BA	xBA	OBP	SLG	OPS	vL	vR	bb%	ct%	h%	Eye	G	L	F	PX	xPX	hr/f	Spd	SBO	SB%	#Wk	DOM	DIS	RC/G	RAR	BPV	BPX	R$
09	LA *	315	36	8	41	2	279	264	306	432	738	1000	583	4	80	33	0.20	83	0	17	100	-5	0%	93	10%	33%	3	33%	67%	4.42	6.9	38	78	$7
10	ARI *	287	26	2	26	3	248	239	265	343	608	635	517	2	75	32	0.09	46	21	33	79	66	2%	84	7%	76%	22	18%	55%	3.08	-4.8	-5	-11	$2
11	aaa	483	43	5	37	6	214	229	237	302	540			3	78	26	0.14				66			103	17%	41%				2.15		5	11	$0
12	KC *	499	44	6	62	4	250	274	266	369	634	433	772	2	80	30	0.11	47	28	26	84	71	7%	86	7%	64%	9	33%	56%	3.29	-5.4	21	53	$7
13	SF *	203	27	3	20	1	261	272	284	420	705	883	650	3	74	34	0.12	46	25	28	132	61	7%	108	11%	16%	14	43%	43%	3.83	1.0	42	105	$2
1st Half		80	12	1	4	0	270	277	302	418	719	1272	581	4	72	37	0.16	48	29	23	132	50	0%	112	8%	0%	5	60%	20%	4.08	0.9	39	98	$1
2nd Half		123	15	2	15	1	255	271	273	423	696	689	675	2	75	33	0.10	45	24	31	131	65	9%	100	13%	24%	9	33%	56%	3.67	-0.1	42	105	$3
14	Proj	102	11	1	10	1	252	260	274	384	659	702	629	3	77	32	0.12	48	22	30	105	64	5%	98	11%	36%				3.37	-1.0	26	65	$2

Ackley,Dustin

Age	26	Bats	L	Pos	2B CF	Health	A	LIMA Plan	B
Ht	6' 1"	Wt	195			PT/Exp	B	Rand Var	-1
						Consist	C	MM	1415

4-31-.253 in 384 AB at SEA. Did post-hype prospect figure it out in June AAA stint? PRO: Spike in 2H LD% drove h% gains; Spd is legit; SBO should rebound; he's now "age 26 with experience." CON: 2H is an outlier compared to rest of track record. VERDICT: Treat 2013 as floor, with... UP: 10-15 HR/SB, .265 BA

Yr	Tm	AB	R	HR	RBI	SB	BA	xBA	OBP	SLG	OPS	vL	vR	bb%	ct%	h%	Eye	G	L	F	PX	xPX	hr/f	Spd	SBO	SB%	#Wk	DOM	DIS	RC/G	RAR	BPV	BPX	R$
09																																		
10	a/a	501	61	5	39	8	231	255	312	340	652			10	82	27	0.65				79			124	8%	70%				3.51		51	111	$4
11	SEA *	604	75	11	58	10	256	249	339	389	727	652	804	11	79	31	0.60	40	22	38	92	110	6%	147	8%	75%	16	50%	38%	4.51	4.8	59	131	$13
12	SEA	607	84	12	50	13	226	234	294	328	622	675	593	9	80	27	0.48	45	19	35	67	74	7%	123	10%	81%	28	29%	36%	3.22	-18.8	28	70	$8
13	SEA *	488	54	5	41	2	261	252	330	352	682	664	659	9	82	31	0.56	51	22	27	67	62	5%	110	3%	40%	24	38%	42%	3.94	-4.2	34	85	$8
1st Half		267	30	2	19	1	238	230	304	302	606	481	515	9	81	28	0.51	56	18	26	50	32	3%	101	3%	50%	11	18%	64%	3.05	-9.0	15	38	$5
2nd Half		221	24	3	22	1	290	273	362	412	774	765	775	10	82	34	0.63	48	25	28	89	83	6%	117	4%	33%	13	54%	23%	5.19	6.4	56	140	$11
14	Proj	442	53	8	38	10	253	254	325	367	692	697	690	10	81	30	0.56	47	21	32	80	74	7%	125	10%	78%				4.10	5.3	38	96	$11

Adams,Matt

Age	25	Bats	L	Pos	1B	Health	A	LIMA Plan	B
Ht	6' 3"	Wt	260			PT/Exp	C	Rand Var	-3
						Consist	C	MM	4025

Emerging slugger? Elite power numbers stand out in this otherwise-pedestrian skill set. Inepitude vL relegates him to a platoon role, so don't fall into the trap of doubling 2013 line. Still, with power getting hard to find, this is a skill set capable of yielding... UP: 450 AB, 25 HR.

Yr	Tm	AB	R	HR	RBI	SB	BA	xBA	OBP	SLG	OPS	vL	vR	bb%	ct%	h%	Eye	G	L	F	PX	xPX	hr/f	Spd	SBO	SB%	#Wk	DOM	DIS	RC/G	RAR	BPV	BPX	R$
09																																		
10																																		
11	aa	463	51	18	64	0	234	252	276	398	674			5	78	26	0.26				109			86	1%	0%				3.61		36	80	$8
12	STL *	344	38	14	50	2	267	255	300	465	765	440	739	5	74	32	0.18	44	18	39	142	126	8%	60	5%	66%	5	20%	60%	4.81	2.2	38	95	$9
13	STL	296	46	17	51	0	284	262	335	503	839	654	876	7	73	34	0.29	44	19	36	153	145	22%	70	1%	0%	26	54%	42%	5.93	11.2	52	130	$12
1st Half		98	13	6	20	0	316	280	362	571	933	1077	912	7	76	37	0.29	42	19	39	178	178	21%	69	0%	0%	13	54%	46%	7.71	8.2	81	203	$8
2nd Half		198	33	11	31	0	268	252	322	470	792	513	857	7	72	32	0.29	46	20	35	139	128	22%	78	2%	0%	13	54%	38%	5.16	3.2	38	95	$14
14	Proj	425	56	20	70	1	272	257	320	473	794	585	843	7	74	32	0.27	44	19	37	143	140	17%	66	2%	42%				5.26	8.1	37	92	$16

Almonte,Abraham

Age	25	Bats	B	Pos	CF	Health	A	LIMA Plan	C
Ht	5' 9"	Wt	205			PT/Exp	D	Rand Var	0
						Consist	B	MM	2313

2-7-.270 in 63 AB at SEA. Signed as a 16-year-old by the Yankees and overcame an alcohol problem, which is a nice feel-good story. Despite mediocre SB%, runs a lot and draws some walks. Not likely a starter, but even as a 4th OF he has the skills for... UP: double-digit HR/SB.

Yr	Tm	AB	R	HR	RBI	SB	BA	xBA	OBP	SLG	OPS	vL	vR	bb%	ct%	h%	Eye	G	L	F	PX	xPX	hr/f	Spd	SBO	SB%	#Wk	DOM	DIS	RC/G	RAR	BPV	BPX	R$
09																																		
10																																		
11																																		
12	aa	319	38	4	20	24	245	235	310	344	654			9	80	30	0.46				69			114	34%	81%				3.74		27	68	$9
13	SEA *	512	73	13	62	21	256	245	334	394	728	475	872	10	74	32	0.44	50	20	30	100	29	14%	98	20%	70%	6	50%	50%	4.44	2.4	27	68	$20
1st Half		232	36	5	31	11	249	223	328	370	698			10	71	33	0.40				93			95	23%	70%				4.06		9	23	$18
2nd Half		280	36	8	31	10	263	256	339	414	753	475	872	10	76	32	0.48	50	20	30	105	29	14%	101	18%	69%	6	50%	50%	4.76	2.6	41	103	$21
14	Proj	285	38	7	28	13	253	251	316	391	707	479	854	9	76	31	0.44	50	20	30	97	26	11%	101	22%	74%				4.29	1.0	39	96	$10

Almonte,Zoilo

Age	25	Bats	B	Pos	LF	Health	B	LIMA Plan	D
Ht	6' 0"	Wt	205			PT/Exp	D	Rand Var	0
						Consist	B	MM	1211

1-9-.236 in 106 AB at NYY. Started 7-for-12 upon callup, which earned him another 76 AB... during which he hit .211 before injuring his ankle. Old for a prospect without a history of minor-league production. His glove might earn him a bench role, but he can be safely ignored.

Yr	Tm	AB	R	HR	RBI	SB	BA	xBA	OBP	SLG	OPS	vL	vR	bb%	ct%	h%	Eye	G	L	F	PX	xPX	hr/f	Spd	SBO	SB%	#Wk	DOM	DIS	RC/G	RAR	BPV	BPX	R$
09																																		
10																																		
11	aa	175	19	3	19	3	227	228	275	338	613			6	72	30	0.24				92			93	11%	75%				3.06		5	11	$0
12	aa	419	51	19	56	12	249	253	284	438	722			5	73	30	0.18				129			83	19%	73%				4.16		31	78	$13
13	NYY *	365	34	7	40	6	260	258	318	360	678	419	638	8	80	31	0.44	53	23	24	70	99	5%	85	8%	75%	9	22%	78%	3.95	-3.0	21	53	$8
1st Half		292	28	7	36	5	273	263	338	395	733	325		9	80	32	0.49	54	21	25	85	101	14%	92	8%	83%	3	67%	33%	4.72	4.6	36	90	$11
2nd Half		73	6	0	4	1	205	228	237	219	456	455	456	4	82	25	0.23	53	23	23	13	98	0%	97	12%	50%	6	0%	100%	1.60	-6.0	-22	-55	-$7
14	Proj	165	17	2	17	3	238	241	277	314	591	406	663	6	77	30	0.26	53	23	24	59	99	6%	89	12%	69%				2.92	-5.5	-9	-21	$3

Alonso,Yonder

Age	27	Bats	L	Pos	1B	Health	B	LIMA Plan	B
Ht	6' 2"	Wt	250			PT/Exp	C	Rand Var	-2
						Consist	A	MM	2125

Should we hold out hope for this former top prospect? PRO: 2H brought elite ct% and very good Eye; just reaching prime age; 2H power loss injury-related. CON: Never much of a power hitter, PX sub-par and falling even before injury, xBA skeptical of BA. VERDICT: Wrist will get better, but PETCO remains an obstacle.

Yr	Tm	AB	R	HR	RBI	SB	BA	xBA	OBP	SLG	OPS	vL	vR	bb%	ct%	h%	Eye	G	L	F	PX	xPX	hr/f	Spd	SBO	SB%	#Wk	DOM	DIS	RC/G	RAR	BPV	BPX	R$
09	aa	105	10	2	12	1	275	286	351	431	782			10	84	31	0.74				112			88	3%	100%				5.38		76	155	$1
10	CIN *	536	55	13	56	10	253	254	310	393	703	222	600	8	79	30	0.39	47	16	37	103	139	0%	70	10%	75%	6	17%	50%	4.15	-6.8	35	76	$11
11	CIN *	446	43	15	56	4	268	268	334	435	768	651	995	9	80	31	0.48	42	22	36	113	98	21%	77	8%	44%	10	40%	50%	4.85	3.4	52	116	$12
12	SD	549	47	9	62	3	273	264	348	393	741	693	760	10	82	32	0.61	45	24	31	88	106	6%	51	2%	100%	27	44%	22%	4.83	3.7	34	85	$11
13	SD	334	34	6	45	6	281	247	341	368	710	637	736	9	86	31	0.68	46	21	33	57	84	6%	57	6%	100%	19	26%	32%	4.62	0.3	26	65	$10
1st Half		190	22	6	29	3	284	253	337	416	752	745	753	7	84	31	0.50	45	19	36	82	94	10%	64	5%	100%	9	56%	11%	5.09	2.6	38	95	$13
2nd Half		144	12	0	16	3	278	238	354	306	660	493	713	11	88	31	1.00	47	22	30	24	71	0%	63	6%	100%	10	0%	50%	3.96	-2.6	14	35	$6
14	Proj	475	45	12	61	6	275	266	343	405	747	640	784	9	84	31	0.65	45	22	32	86	92	9%	55	5%	85%				4.94	4.7	43	107	$15

JOSH PALEY

Altuve,Jose

Age	24	Bats	R	Pos	2B	Health	A	LIMA Plan	B
Ht	5' 5"	Wt	175			PT/Exp	B	Rand Var	-1
						Consist	B	MM	1425

SBs drive his value, and by that measure this was a worthy follow-up. But warning signs abound: power and speed skills dipped; RHP give him fits; value is tied to lofty AB totals. Add in a borderline SB% that could get his green light revoked, and there are plenty of reasons why his next step could be backward. DN: 20 SB.

Yr	Tm	AB	R	HR	RBI	SB	BA	xBA	OBP	SLG	OPS	vL	vR	bb%	ct%	h%	Eye	G	L	F	PX	xPX	hr/f	Spd	SBO	SB%	#Wk	DOM	DIS	RC/G	RAR	BPV	BPX	R$
09																																		
10																																		
11	HOU *	365	42	6	31	11	297	278	316	415	731	766	618	3	88	33	0.23	50	20	30	77	54	4%	118	21%	56%	11	36%	27%	4.45	7.4	56	124	$12
12	HOU	576	80	7	37	33	290	277	340	399	740	911	676	6	87	32	0.54	53	20	27	72	73	5%	137	27%	75%	27	44%	7%	4.79	17.5	62	155	$24
13	HOU	626	64	5	52	35	283	264	316	363	678	733	656	5	86	32	0.38	49	23	28	58	78	3%	97	28%	73%	27	30%	19%	4.05	5.8	33	83	$27
1st Half		312	32	3	27	18	292	268	328	375	703	772	678	5	86	33	0.38	48	25	27	60	92	4%	99	26%	78%	14	14%	29%	4.48	7.0	32	80	$28
2nd Half		314	32	2	25	17	274	259	307	350	657	702	633	5	87	31	0.38	50	20	30	56	64	2%	95	30%	68%	13	46%	8%	3.65	-0.5	33	83	$25
14	Proj	591	65	6	50	31	281	269	320	373	693	795	654	5	87	32	0.42	51	21	28	65	71	4%	111	27%	71%				4.14	7.6	46	115	$22

Alvarez,Pedro

Age	27	Bats	L	Pos	3B	Health	B	LIMA Plan	B+
Ht	6' 3"	Wt	235			PT/Exp	B	Rand Var	+1
						Consist	C	MM	5215

Adam Dunn 2.0, or something more? When you have this kind of power, any reduction in K or GB is good news; the latter drove this HR spike. That may not be the end of the growth, either: xBA says that a BA over .250 isn't out of the question. And if September's 76% contact rate sticks, then.... UP: 40 HR, .260 BA.

Yr	Tm	AB	R	HR	RBI	SB	BA	xBA	OBP	SLG	OPS	vL	vR	bb%	ct%	h%	Eye	G	L	F	PX	xPX	hr/f	Spd	SBO	SB%	#Wk	DOM	DIS	RC/G	RAR	BPV	BPX	R$
09	aa	222	35	11	34	1	306	275	384	526	909			11	72	38	0.45				158			88	1%	100%				7.44		65	133	$8
10	PIT *	589	74	25	104	3	250	246	320	450	770	644	858	9	67	33	0.32	46	15	40	156	135	18%	81	5%	40%	16	44%	38%	4.77	13.5	40	87	$16
11	PIT *	360	30	8	33	1	201	214	281	311	592	545	565	10	65	28	0.32	55	19	25	92	89	10%	75	2%	47%	16	19%	56%	2.76	-13.9	-20	-44	-$2
12	PIT	525	64	30	85	1	244	244	317	467	784	648	833	10	66	31	0.32	47	19	34	164	144	25%	73	1%	100%	27	44%	37%	5.01	15.8	37	93	$14
13	PIT	558	70	36	100	2	233	256	296	473	770	537	842	8	67	28	0.26	43	20	36	176	168	26%	77	2%	100%	27	48%	30%	4.64	10.7	48	120	$17
1st Half		257	35	20	53	1	241	255	304	510	813	551	893	8	63	29	0.24	41	21	39	204	179	31%	68	2%	100%	14	43%	29%	5.22	9.5	56	140	$19
2nd Half		301	35	16	47	1	226	256	285	442	727	525	798	8	69	27	0.27	45	20	35	155	159	22%	88	2%	100%	13	54%	31%	4.17	1.8	46	115	$15
14	Proj	554	68	31	92	2	242	250	312	462	774	606	827	9	67	30	0.30	46	19	35	165	146	24%	76	2%	81%				4.82	13.9	36	91	$17

Amarista,Alexi

Age	25	Bats	L	Pos	CF 2B	Health	A	LIMA Plan	D+
Ht	5' 8"	Wt	150			PT/Exp	D	Rand Var	+1
						Consist	A	MM	1413

Versatility in the field afforded him a long look in SD, which confirmed what we already knew: he makes contact frequently enough, but nothing good happens when bat meets ball. And based on his shaky SB success %, the red light he got this year was justified. No power, no SB skill means no path to positive value.

Yr	Tm	AB	R	HR	RBI	SB	BA	xBA	OBP	SLG	OPS	vL	vR	bb%	ct%	h%	Eye	G	L	F	PX	xPX	hr/f	Spd	SBO	SB%	#Wk	DOM	DIS	RC/G	RAR	BPV	BPX	R$
09																																		
10	a/a	256	29	1	22	6	277	250	305	333	638			4	92	30	0.49				34			129	13%	65%				3.50		43	93	$5
11	LAA *	415	35	3	39	10	227	223	258	318	576	0	491	4	83	27	0.24	43	14	43	68	53	0%	113	23%	53%	10	30%	20%	2.52	-14.7	29	64	$3
12	2 TM *	401	48	6	44	11	235	271	271	362	633	705	657	5	86	26	0.35	50	19	30	78	78	7%	140	18%	73%	22	55%	23%	3.25	-5.0	60	150	$6
13	SD	368	35	5	32	4	236	252	282	337	619	557	627	6	85	27	0.39	43	23	34	65	72	5%	125	7%	67%	27	56%	22%	3.12	-5.9	41	103	$3
1st Half		165	22	4	18	0	248	265	283	400	683	297	746	5	82	28	0.27	39	23	37	101	84	8%	117	0%	0%	14	50%	21%	3.84	0.7	54	135	$5
2nd Half		203	13	1	14	4	227	242	276	286	562	873	537	6	87	26	0.52	45	23	32	37	63	2%	132	12%	67%	13	62%	23%	2.58	-7.0	31	78	$2
14	Proj	333	33	5	31	6	244	255	282	351	633	601	638	5	85	27	0.36	46	20	34	69	71	5%	132	13%	65%				3.27	-9.0	40	100	$6

Andrus,Elvis

Age	25	Bats	R	Pos	SS	Health	A	LIMA Plan	B
Ht	6' 0"	Wt	200			PT/Exp	A	Rand Var	-1
						Consist	A	MM	1525

Just as quickly as SBO dip caused SB and R$ to plummet in 2012, everything came back in 2013. Across the board, this is a remarkably stable skill set. Strong GB tilt is a good thing for this skills profile, and 2H line shows what could happen with just a little bit more OBP... UP: 50 SB.

Yr	Tm	AB	R	HR	RBI	SB	BA	xBA	OBP	SLG	OPS	vL	vR	bb%	ct%	h%	Eye	G	L	F	PX	xPX	hr/f	Spd	SBO	SB%	#Wk	DOM	DIS	RC/G	RAR	BPV	BPX	R$
09	TEX	480	72	6	40	33	267	284	329	373	702	761	679	8	84	31	0.52	55	22	23	63	50	7%	162	28%	85%	27	48%	33%	4.37	13.3	52	106	$18
10	TEX	588	88	0	35	32	265	256	342	301	643	642	644	10	84	32	0.67	61	19	20	28	34	0%	155	23%	68%	27	22%	37%	3.49	1.1	25	54	$18
11	TEX	587	96	5	60	37	279	284	347	361	708	714	706	9	87	31	0.76	56	23	21	57	51	5%	113	26%	76%	27	48%	15%	4.41	16.6	49	109	$26
12	TEX	629	85	3	62	21	286	275	349	378	727	687	742	8	85	33	0.59	57	22	21	61	76	3%	141	16%	68%	27	48%	22%	4.59	20.8	49	123	$21
13	TEX	620	91	4	67	42	271	257	328	331	659	698	644	8	84	32	0.54	56	21	22	40	55	3%	139	26%	84%	27	30%	37%	3.99	10.1	29	73	$30
1st Half		321	42	0	28	17	243	253	300	287	586	528	608	7	83	29	0.49	60	20	20	31	46	0%	151	22%	85%	14	14%	50%	3.06	-3.9	21	53	$21
2nd Half		299	49	4	39	25	301	261	357	378	735	862	683	8	85	34	0.59	52	22	25	50	64	6%	117	29%	83%	13	46%	23%	5.16	14.2	34	85	$41
14	Proj	608	92	4	63	39	276	267	340	349	689	713	680	9	85	32	0.62	56	22	22	50	59	4%	137	26%	77%				4.22	13.3	39	98	$29

Aoki,Norichika

Age	32	Bats	L	Pos	RF	Health	A	LIMA Plan	B+
Ht	5' 9"	Wt	175			PT/Exp	A	Rand Var	0
						Consist	C	MM	1435

Nudged ct% and Eye into elite territory in 2nd MLB campaign, but got remarkably little production from those two skills. Why? Tons of GB, without the elite speed to beat throws to first. This is not the kind of skill set that will age gracefully as he moves deeper into his 30s. Don't pay for a rebound; even a repeat is questionable.

Yr	Tm	AB	R	HR	RBI	SB	BA	xBA	OBP	SLG	OPS	vL	vR	bb%	ct%	h%	Eye	G	L	F	PX	xPX	hr/f	Spd	SBO	SB%	#Wk	DOM	DIS	RC/G	RAR	BPV	BPX	R$
09	for	531	85	10	64	16	283	0	356	392	747			10	88	31	0.98				65	-5		106	16%	59%				4.75	4.7	60	122	$18
10	for	583	90	8	61	17	334	0	387	457	844			8	90	36	0.88				85	-5		100	11%	79%				6.81	36.4	77	167	$30
11	for	583	71	2	43	7	272	0	320	342	661			7	91	30	0.79				43	2		134	6%	68%				3.80	-10.7	54	120	$11
12	MIL	520	81	10	50	30	288	294	355	433	787	711	828	8	89	31	0.78	55	17	28	91	81	8%	132	27%	79%	27	63%	15%	5.35	11.0	87	218	$24
13	MIL	597	80	8	37	20	286	282	356	370	726	781	703	8	93	30	1.38	60	18	22	50	69	7%	144	16%	63%	27	56%	4%	4.43	-2.9	75	188	$22
1st Half		299	43	4	15	9	284	278	350	371	721	774	711	9	94	29	1.76	63	15	23	53	75	6%	144	17%	53%	14	64%	0%	4.33	-1.0	83	208	$20
2nd Half		298	37	4	22	11	289	284	344	369	713	793	695	8	92	30	1.09	58	21	21	47	62	7%	134	15%	73%	13	46%	8%	4.54	0.8	64	160	$24
14	Proj	547	76	8	43	19	287	283	354	387	741	745	740	8	91	30	1.02	58	18	24	62	73	6%	140	16%	69%				4.69	3.8	65	163	$22

Arcia,Oswaldo Celestino

Age	23	Bats	L	Pos	LF RF	Health	A	LIMA Plan	B
Ht	6' 0"	Wt	210			PT/Exp	F	Rand Var	-2
						Consist	D	MM	4205

14-43-.251 in 351 AB at MIN. Young and toolsy prospect had a credible big-league debut, flashing anticipated pop along with predictable strike zone issues. Those issues were exacerbated in 2H; that lack of successful adjustment casts a shadow on his short-term outlook. Still very young and worth stashing longer-term, though.

Yr	Tm	AB	R	HR	RBI	SB	BA	xBA	OBP	SLG	OPS	vL	vR	bb%	ct%	h%	Eye	G	L	F	PX	xPX	hr/f	Spd	SBO	SB%	#Wk	DOM	DIS	RC/G	RAR	BPV	BPX	R$
09																																		
10																																		
11																																		
12	aa	262	45	8	56	2	305	263	362	500	862			8	75	38	0.36				136			105	6%	53%				6.49		57	143	$12
13	MIN *	479	54	21	67	3	257	231	315	446	761	659	769	8	67	34	0.26	42	17	41	145	132	15%	99	5%	45%	19	42%	37%	4.73	6.3	32	80	$14
1st Half		250	32	10	37	2	272	233	342	458	800	708	865	10	68	36	0.34	43	16	41	144	142	13%	94	7%	33%	10	50%	40%	5.26	5.9	39	98	$17
2nd Half		229	21	11	29	1	242	228	285	432	717	621	682	6	66	32	0.18	42	19	40	145	121	17%	104	2%	100%	9	33%	33%	4.17	-1.9	23	58	$11
14	Proj	449	52	16	65	3	250	238	319	437	756	680	791	8	69	33	0.29	42	17	40	144	129	13%	112	5%	52%				4.55	7.1	32	81	$12

Arenado,Nolan

Age	23	Bats	R	Pos	3B	Health	A	LIMA Plan	A
Ht	6' 1"	Wt	205			PT/Exp	D	Rand Var	0
						Consist	B	MM	3145

10-52-.267 in 486 AB at COL. Scouting reports described him as having a mature plate approach with still-developing power. MLB debut was consistent with that take, though 2H PX dive warns at least a little caution. Needs to solve RHP next, but xBA suggests some near-term BA upside while we wait on the pop.

Yr	Tm	AB	R	HR	RBI	SB	BA	xBA	OBP	SLG	OPS	vL	vR	bb%	ct%	h%	Eye	G	L	F	PX	xPX	hr/f	Spd	SBO	SB%	#Wk	DOM	DIS	RC/G	RAR	BPV	BPX	R$
09																																		
10																																		
11																																		
12	aa	516	48	13	49	0	289	275	333	440	773			6	89	31	0.59				95			82	2%	0%				5.16		71	178	$13
13	COL *	552	58	12	65	2	274	284	307	425	732	846	652	5	85	30	0.32	43	24	34	103	103	7%	101	3%	47%	23	48%	17%	4.51	8.1	65	163	$14
1st Half		293	32	9	37	0	277	306	312	473	786	863	698	5	86	30	0.36	40	25	35	132	119	10%	92	4%	0%	10	70%	10%	5.04	8.9	88	220	$16
2nd Half		259	26	3	28	2	270	258	300	371	671	826	614	4	85	31	0.28	45	23	33	70	89	4%	114	3%	100%	13	31%	23%	3.93	-0.3	39	98	$12
14	Proj	531	53	13	57	1	279	287	316	433	749	894	693	5	87	30	0.40	43	24	33	102	101	9%	98	3%	45%				4.79	12.3	56	141	$15

RAY MURPHY

Arencibia,J.P.

Age	28	Bats	R	Pos	CA	Health	B	LIMA Plan	D+
Ht	6' 0"	Wt	200			PT/Exp	C	Rand Var	+4
						Consist	B	MM	4003

Note to self: When the hit-rate gods frown on a player with a terrible Eye, the results are disastrous (see 2H). He has the power BPI down—heavy FB tendency, consistent PX/xPX, hr/f in the teens—but plate skills do him no favors. It's not easy to smack 21 HR and end up with $1 in roto value. Draft Day tip: J.P. equals Just Power.

Yr	Tm	AB	R	HR	RBI	SB	BA	xBA	OBP	SLG	OPS	vL	vR	bb%	ct%	h%	Eye	G	L	F	PX	xPX	hr/f	Spd	SBO	SB%	#Wk	DOM	DIS	RC/G	RAR	BPV	BPX	R$
09	aaa	466	49	16	55	0	200	249	232	366	597			4	71	25	0.14				123			87	2%	0%				2.66		18	37	-$1
10	TOR *	447	48	22	54	0	225	242	265	438	703	77	772	5	74	25	0.21	29	13	58	153	161	14%	86	0%	0%	8	13%	75%	3.81	1.3	57	124	$5
11	TOR	443	47	23	78	1	219	240	282	438	720	838	682	8	70	26	0.27	35	16	50	158	153	15%	105	2%	50%	27	44%	22%	3.94	3.0	55	122	$8
12	TOR	347	45	18	56	1	233	233	275	435	710	774	688	5	69	29	0.17	37	18	45	144	128	17%	76	2%	100%	22	45%	45%	3.94	2.3	25	63	$7
13	TOR	474	45	21	55	0	194	225	227	365	592	588	594	4	69	23	0.12	37	20	44	127	133	15%	76	3%	0%	27	33%	48%	2.52	-17.9	9	23	$1
1st Half		275	31	15	36	0	215	246	239	425	665	646	678	3	68	25	0.10	37	21	42	157	129	19%	84	5%	0%	14	36%	36%	3.18	-4.5	33	83	$7
2nd Half		199	14	6	19	0	166	192	202	281	483	520	471	4	69	20	0.15	37	17	46	85	138	9%	78	0%	0%	13	31%	62%	1.74	-12.8	-20	-50	-$6
14	Proj	**421**	**43**	**19**	**56**	**0**	**205**	**228**	**246**	**388**	**633**	**667**	**621**	**5**	**69**	**25**	**0.16**	**37**	**18**	**46**	**134**	**135**	**15%**	**81**	**2%**	**36%**				**2.98**	**-9.6**	**10**	**24**	**$3**

Arias,Joaquin

Age	29	Bats	R	Pos	3B SS	Health	B	LIMA Plan	D
Ht	6' 1"	Wt	160			PT/Exp	D	Rand Var	-3
						Consist	C	MM	1511

Lasted the whole season on an MLB roster for the first time, minus time missed for an appendectomy. Two worthy pieces of his profile—very good contact and excellent Spd—are stifled by a noodle bat and utter inability to take a walk or get on base. Maybe he re-discovers some of his 2012 pop, but may not get the AB to do so.

Yr	Tm	AB	R	HR	RBI	SB	BA	xBA	OBP	SLG	OPS	vL	vR	bb%	ct%	h%	Eye	G	L	F	PX	xPX	hr/f	Spd	SBO	SB%	#Wk	DOM	DIS	RC/G	RAR	BPV	BPX	R$
09	TEX *	512	51	4	42	20	234	164	257	298	555	0	0	3	89	26	0.29	40	0	60	38	-5	0%	148	20%	85%	2	0%	50%	2.64	-13.4	39	80	$7
10	2 TM *	159	26	0	14	1	240	215	269	290	559	765	542	4	81	30	0.20	43	18	39	41	49	0%	161	3%	100%	23	13%	39%	2.65	-4.0	13	28	$0
11	aaa	241	24	2	16	5	186	249	216	276	492			4	87	21	0.28				59			121	15%	79%				1.88		39	87	-$3
12	SF *	389	39	6	45	5	275	262	302	391	693	768	625	4	85	31	0.25	47	22	32	71	84	6%	151	8%	68%	24	46%	25%	4.12	6.8	51	128	$9
13	SF	225	17	1	19	1	271	249	284	342	627	618	636	2	85	31	0.12	52	21	28	50	73	2%	139	2%	100%	24	29%	42%	3.42	-0.5	29	73	$2
1st Half		105	9	0	10	1	276	243	296	305	601	527	680	3	84	33	0.18	47	28	26	17	66	0%	150	3%	100%	14	14%	43%	3.24	-0.7	1	3	$2
2nd Half		120	8	1	9	0	267	252	273	375	648	691	591	1	87	30	0.06	56	14	30	78	79	3%	127	0%	0%	10	50%	40%	3.56	0.3	51	128	$1
14	Proj	**136**	**12**	**1**	**12**	**1**	**256**	**252**	**279**	**342**	**620**	**660**	**584**	**3**	**85**	**29**	**0.19**	**49**	**20**	**31**	**58**	**74**	**3%**	**141**	**6%**	**83%**				**3.25**	**-2.9**	**21**	**52**	**$2**

Asche,Cody

Age	24	Bats	L	Pos	3B	Health	A	LIMA Plan	B
Ht	6' 1"	Wt	180			PT/Exp	F	Rand Var	0
						Consist	B	MM	3315

5-22-.235 in 162 AB at PHI. Streaky hitter in two-month MLB debut, but impressed team with defense and overall provided more power than anticipated. Still work to do to improve contact and ABs vs. LHP, but could provide modest value with HR/SB potential for the next few seasons. Worker bee.

Yr	Tm	AB	R	HR	RBI	SB	BA	xBA	OBP	SLG	OPS	vL	vR	bb%	ct%	h%	Eye	G	L	F	PX	xPX	hr/f	Spd	SBO	SB%	#Wk	DOM	DIS	RC/G	RAR	BPV	BPX	R$
09																																		
10																																		
11																																		
12	aa	263	33	8	37	1	269	262	315	450	765			6	76	32	0.28				127			93	3%	42%				4.87		49	123	$6
13	PHI *	566	58	17	75	10	251	246	303	408	711	608	710	7	73	31	0.28	44	21	35	115	111	12%	119	10%	74%	10	40%	40%	4.19	3.2	37	93	$15
1st Half		310	30	6	37	5	248	234	296	387	682			6	71	33	0.24				110			115	11%	71%				3.84		22	55	$14
2nd Half		256	29	11	38	4	255	259	312	434	746	608	710	8	76	30	0.35	44	21	35	122	111	12%	115	8%	79%	10	40%	40%	4.64	5.0	54	135	$17
14	Proj	**489**	**56**	**14**	**68**	**5**	**259**	**252**	**311**	**416**	**727**	**642**	**748**	**7**	**75**	**32**	**0.29**	**44**	**21**	**35**	**115**	**100**	**11%**	**120**	**7%**	**71%**				**4.41**	**6.2**	**34**	**84**	**$14**

Avila,Alex

Age	27	Bats	L	Pos	CA	Health	B	LIMA Plan	D+
Ht	5' 11"	Wt	210			PT/Exp	C	Rand Var	0
						Consist	D	MM	4213

11-47-.227 in 330 AB at DET. Fact that he was banged up all season (forearm, concussion) may explain continued production drop. PRO: Patience; prominent LD swing should produce better BA; xPX hints at more power. CON: Slipping ct%; lack of FB; problems vs. LHP. Should rebound some, but don't use 2011 as the bar.

Yr	Tm	AB	R	HR	RBI	SB	BA	xBA	OBP	SLG	OPS	vL	vR	bb%	ct%	h%	Eye	G	L	F	PX	xPX	hr/f	Spd	SBO	SB%	#Wk	DOM	DIS	RC/G	RAR	BPV	BPX	R$
09	DET *	390	52	15	60	2	248	248	338	435	773	1255	910	12	74	30	0.53	43	14	43	130	193	26%	89	3%	61%	9	67%	33%	4.95	14.2	54	110	$8
10	DET	294	28	7	31	2	228	239	316	340	656	502	676	11	76	28	0.51	43	22	35	82	127	9%	61	5%	50%	27	26%	48%	3.45	-2.4	11	24	$2
11	DET	464	63	19	82	3	295	264	389	506	895	779	939	14	72	38	0.56	38	22	40	160	154	14%	91	3%	75%	27	48%	22%	7.16	44.3	71	158	$20
12	DET	367	42	9	48	2	243	245	352	384	736	539	796	14	72	35	0.59	46	24	30	106	130	11%	80	2%	100%	26	35%	38%	4.57	9.2	26	65	$5
13	DET *	374	43	12	51	0	225	238	315	369	685	455	767	12	66	31	0.39	42	28	30	116	138	17%	71	0%	0%	24	25%	42%	3.83	1.3	5	13	$4
1st Half		196	18	6	17	0	177	202	265	294	560	146	636	11	65	24	0.34	50	20	30	94	126	16%	72	0%	0%	13	23%	54%	2.42	-8.1	-21	-53	-$2
2nd Half		178	25	6	34	0	278	266	369	452	821	604	926	13	68	38	0.46	35	35	30	138	149	18%	82	0%	0%	11	27%	27%	5.90	11.0	36	90	$11
14	Proj	**390**	**47**	**13**	**57**	**1**	**249**	**250**	**345**	**416**	**760**	**581**	**817**	**13**	**70**	**32**	**0.49**	**42**	**26**	**32**	**129**	**142**	**15%**	**77**	**1%**	**79%**				**4.87**	**13.4**	**26**	**66**	**$10**

Aviles,Mike

Age	33	Bats	R	Pos	3B SS	Health	B	LIMA Plan	D+
Ht	5' 10"	Wt	205			PT/Exp	C	Rand Var	+1
						Consist	A	MM	1213

Things you can count on: Very good ct% that only yields a .250ish BA; position flexibility; 4 walks every 100 AB. Things you can't count on: Full-time AB; power and speed returning at 33; double-digit R$. Best saved for an in-season injury pickup; his years as a sneaky value play have ended.

Yr	Tm	AB	R	HR	RBI	SB	BA	xBA	OBP	SLG	OPS	vL	vR	bb%	ct%	h%	Eye	G	L	F	PX	xPX	hr/f	Spd	SBO	SB%	#Wk	DOM	DIS	RC/G	RAR	BPV	BPX	R$
09	KC	120	10	1	8	1	183	221	208	250	458	535	416	3	78	23	0.15	45	19	36	44	50	3%	107	5%	100%	7	14%	57%	1.67	-8.7	-10	-20	-$3
10	KC *	494	68	9	37	14	291	257	322	396	718	642	787	4	88	32	0.37	43	19	38	65	70	6%	150	14%	74%	24	38%	38%	4.56	8.5	58	126	$17
11	2 AL *	426	44	12	55	18	247	260	276	408	683	924	601	4	85	27	0.26	42	16	43	103	93	7%	110	33%	66%	22	55%	32%	3.61	-4.3	64	142	$12
12	BOS	512	57	13	60	14	250	254	282	381	663	753	626	4	85	27	0.30	41	19	40	84	90	7%	69	18%	70%	26	31%	19%	3.59	-5.4	38	95	$13
13	CLE	361	54	9	46	8	252	260	282	368	650	605	689	4	89	26	0.37	43	20	37	72	73	7%	60	16%	62%	27	44%	26%	3.42	-5.6	40	100	$10
1st Half		198	33	5	26	6	258	262	290	379	669	665	665	4	87	28	0.35	45	19	36	78	86	8%	63	15%	86%	14	50%	29%	3.85	-0.7	39	98	$13
2nd Half		163	21	4	20	2	245	260	272	356	628	533	718	4	91	25	0.40	41	21	38	66	58	7%	64	17%	33%	13	38%	23%	2.95	-5.1	44	110	$7
14	Proj	**336**	**42**	**8**	**40**	**8**	**248**	**255**	**279**	**369**	**648**	**651**	**645**	**4**	**87**	**27**	**0.32**	**42**	**19**	**39**	**77**	**77**	**7%**	**76**	**18%**	**62%**				**3.36**	**-6.2**	**47**	**117**	**$9**

Aybar,Erick

Age	30	Bats	B	Pos	SS	Health	B	LIMA Plan	B+
Ht	5' 10"	Wt	180			PT/Exp	A	Rand Var	+2
						Consist	A	MM	1435

With a bruised left heel, strained right hamstring, right knee soreness, and left calf cramps, there was hardly a leg ailment he did not suffer in 2013. Superb ct% and heavy GB/LD stroke remained, which bodes well for his future BA/xBA. Assuming lower-half health, his SB number should rebound.

Yr	Tm	AB	R	HR	RBI	SB	BA	xBA	OBP	SLG	OPS	vL	vR	bb%	ct%	h%	Eye	G	L	F	PX	xPX	hr/f	Spd	SBO	SB%	#Wk	DOM	DIS	RC/G	RAR	BPV	BPX	R$
09	LAA	504	70	5	58	14	312	278	353	423	776	804	762	6	89	34	0.56	46	21	33	65	62	4%	140	14%	67%	27	48%	19%	5.36	26.8	64	131	$20
10	LAA	534	69	5	29	22	253	237	306	330	636	609	646	6	85	29	0.43	49	15	36	51	54	3%	146	21%	73%	26	35%	27%	3.36	-1.1	38	83	$12
11	LAA	556	71	10	59	30	279	287	322	421	743	607	807	5	88	30	0.46	48	21	31	91	66	7%	124	27%	83%	25	64%	12%	4.81	22.1	74	164	$23
12	LAA	517	67	8	45	20	290	279	324	416	740	879	690	4	88	32	0.36	52	19	29	79	63	6%	116	19%	83%	25	52%	20%	4.84	20.5	61	153	$19
13	LAA	550	68	6	54	12	271	287	301	382	683	723	666	4	89	29	0.39	50	23	27	75	63	5%	109	15%	63%	25	52%	16%	3.90	7.5	60	150	$16
1st Half		243	25	3	31	4	284	278	304	379	683	603	714	3	91	30	0.32	52	21	27	62	78	5%	94	12%	57%	12	42%	25%	3.96	3.4	49	123	$14
2nd Half		307	43	3	23	8	261	292	297	384	682	814	628	5	88	29	0.43	48	24	28	85	52	4%	121	18%	67%	13	62%	8%	3.85	3.5	68	170	$17
14	Proj	**575**	**73**	**8**	**54**	**20**	**278**	**283**	**313**	**398**	**711**	**745**	**697**	**5**	**88**	**30**	**0.41**	**50**	**21**	**29**	**79**	**63**	**5%**	**118**	**19%**	**75%**				**4.33**	**14.3**	**65**	**163**	**$21**

Baker,Jeff

Age	33	Bats	R	Pos	1B LF	Health	C	LIMA Plan	D
Ht	6' 2"	Wt	210			PT/Exp	F	Rand Var	-4
						Consist	D	MM	3311

Ah, small sample size schizophrenia (call it SSSS). For one half, you're a 1.500-OPS platoon monster. But before you know it, nearly 40% of your swings come up empty. Without a full season of AB—Who are you, really? From here, a quickly aging cornerman who will soon be among the unemployed.

Yr	Tm	AB	R	HR	RBI	SB	BA	xBA	OBP	SLG	OPS	vL	vR	bb%	ct%	h%	Eye	G	L	F	PX	xPX	hr/f	Spd	SBO	SB%	#Wk	DOM	DIS	RC/G	RAR	BPV	BPX	R$
09	2 NL *	249	29	5	25	1	277	257	331	416	747	782	762	8	77	34	0.36	45	19	35	99	105	6%	123	2%	100%	19	42%	37%	4.88	2.1	42	86	$4
10	CHC	206	29	4	21	1	272	256	326	413	739	945	302	7	76	34	0.32	42	22	36	106	92	7%	118	2%	100%	27	41%	33%	4.72	0.6	40	87	$4
11	CHC	201	20	3	23	0	269	255	302	383	685	812	491	5	77	34	0.22	48	24	28	89	94	7%	113	0%	0%	25	48%	32%	4.05	-3.1	25	56	$2
12	3 TM	188	18	4	25	4	239	264	279	378	656	665	637	6	74	30	0.23	48	27	25	103	63	11%	94	13%	80%	27	26%	41%	3.58	-5.7	22	55	$2
13	TEX	154	21	11	21	1	279	271	360	545	905	1073	536	10	69	34	0.38	49	18	34	194	160	31%	106	2%	100%	22	50%	50%	6.89	9.9	85	213	$5
1st Half		82	13	9	16	0	317	308	378	695	1073	1491	599	9	76	32	0.40	47	15	39	240	171	38%	108	0%	0%	11	64%	36%	9.81	11.4	147	368	$9
2nd Half		72	8	2	5	1	236	219	329	375	704	769	322	12	61	36	0.36	51	22	27	129	146	18%	94	5%	100%	11	36%	64%	4.21	-0.8	2	5	$1
14	Proj	**161**	**19**	**5**	**19**	**2**	**262**	**249**	**324**	**415**	**739**	**834**	**542**	**8**	**71**	**34**	**0.31**	**48**	**22**	**30**	**119**	**118**	**14%**	**102**	**4%**	**88%**				**4.66**	**0.3**	**18**	**46**	**$5**

BRENT HERSHEY

Barmes,Clint

Barmes,Clint		Health	A	LIMA Plan	F
Age 35	Bats R Pos SS	PT/Exp	C	Rand Var	+2
Ht 6' 1"	Wt 200	Consist	B	MM	1101

His glove has helped him continue to find regular AB, but those days may be ending. Abysmal on-base skills were more tolerable when he flirted with double-digit HR. Three-year FB decline and sub-par PX have conspired to distance him from any hope of repeating 2009 glory, or even 2011, such as it was.

Yr Tm	AB	R	HR	RBI	SB	BA	xBA	OBP	SLG	OPS	vL	vR	bb%	ct%	h%	Eye	G	L	F	PX	xPX	hr/f	Spd	SBO	SB%	#Wk	DOM	DIS	RC/G	RAR	BPV	BPX	R$
09 COL	550	69	23	76	12	245	259	294	440	734	811	708	5	78	28	0.26	31	20	49	125	108	11%	104	20%	55%	26	58%	27%	4.00	8.2	56	114	$14
10 COL	387	43	8	50	3	235	243	305	351	656	748	612	8	83	27	0.53	30	21	49	82	95	5%	79	5%	60%	27	44%	44%	3.46	-0.5	40	87	$4
11 HOU	446	47	12	39	3	244	247	312	386	698	649	715	8	80	28	0.43	31	22	47	102	85	7%	81	4%	75%	23	57%	26%	3.95	5.9	45	100	$6
12 PIT	455	34	8	45	0	229	210	272	321	593	741	551	4	77	28	0.19	37	20	43	64	62	5%	97	2%	0%	27	15%	59%	2.71	-11.0	-1	-3	$1
13 PIT	304	22	5	23	0	211	228	249	309	558	529	565	4	77	26	0.20	38	22	40	77	89	5%	93	0%	0%	26	38%	46%	2.45	-9.9	8	20	-$2
1st Half	167	10	2	10	0	204	199	227	275	502	353	550	3	76	26	0.13	38	19	43	56	94	4%	95	0%	0%	14	21%	57%	2.00	-7.7	-15	-38	-$4
2nd Half	137	12	3	13	0	219	259	267	350	617	810	581	6	78	26	0.30	38	26	36	100	83	8%	92	0%	0%	12	58%	33%	3.06	-1.7	34	85	-$1
14 Proj	232	20	4	21	1	224	229	272	328	600	660	584	5	78	27	0.25	36	22	42	79	82	5%	91	2%	49%				2.84	-4.5	-1	-2	-$1

Barnes,Brandon

Barnes,Brandon		Health	A	LIMA Plan	D
Age 28	Bats R Pos CF	PT/Exp	C	Rand Var	-2
Ht 6' 2"	Wt 205	Consist	B	MM	2303

April sensation batted .226 thereafter, but managed to quadruple his previous number of lifetime MLB AB and even provided some value vs LHP. Age, Eye, poor contact skills and elevated GB% all conspire to limit his upside. Don't count on him seeing this many AB again. A 5th OF profile.

Yr Tm	AB	R	HR	RBI	SB	BA	xBA	OBP	SLG	OPS	vL	vR	bb%	ct%	h%	Eye	G	L	F	PX	xPX	hr/f	Spd	SBO	SB%	#Wk	DOM	DIS	RC/G	RAR	BPV	BPX	R$
09 aa	21	2	1	1	0	84	190	176	200	376			10	63	8	0.30				77			109	0%	0%				0.98		-32	-65	-$3
10 aaa	21	1	1	1	1	244	229	270	396	666			3	67	33	0.10				119			109	18%	100%				3.78		3	7	-$1
11 a/a	432	43	11	39	8	200	234	253	347	600			7	70	26	0.24				115			104	16%	63%				2.73		17	38	$1
12 HOU *	497	63	9	54	15	246	244	290	376	666	578	458	6	71	33	0.21	49	22	29	107	114	5%	93	22%	65%	9	22%	67%	3.56	-10.1	12	30	$11
13 HOU	408	46	8	41	11	240	217	289	346	635	791	557	5	69	33	0.17	48	20	32	86	71	9%	117	24%	50%	26	19%	58%	2.94	-16.3	-8	-20	$8
1st Half	175	20	3	17	7	263	213	310	366	676	991	515	6	70	36	0.23	48	18	35	88	73	7%	105	26%	58%	14	29%	57%	3.66	-2.7	-4	-10	$10
2nd Half	233	26	5	24	4	223	220	252	330	583	625	587	4	68	31	0.12	49	22	29	84	70	11%	125	21%	40%	12	8%	58%	2.45	-12.6	-13	-33	$7
14 Proj	265	31	4	27	7	235	226	287	344	631	743	559	5	70	32	0.19	48	21	31	92	88	8%	112	21%	56%				2.99	-9.6	-7	-17	$6

Barney,Darwin

Barney,Darwin		Health	A	LIMA Plan	C
Age 28	Bats R Pos 2B	PT/Exp	A	Rand Var	+5
Ht 5' 10"	Wt 185	Consist	B	MM	1325

2013 was second consecutive year of declining production from an already-modest source. BA and OPS lagged, and despite maintaining strong ct%, fewer LD and hard-hit balls produced career-low h%. Spd still interesting, but SBO and SB% reduce him to an offensive liability—too many AB with too few results.

Yr Tm	AB	R	HR	RBI	SB	BA	xBA	OBP	SLG	OPS	vL	vR	bb%	ct%	h%	Eye	G	L	F	PX	xPX	hr/f	Spd	SBO	SB%	#Wk	DOM	DIS	RC/G	RAR	BPV	BPX	R$
09 a/a	464	44	3	39	7	262	243	306	330	636			6	84	31	0.40				50			91	8%	76%				3.50		18	37	$6
10 CHC *	558	60	1	35	7	244	249	272	304	576	699	528	4	87	28	0.29	54	16	30	45	40	0%	114	8%	67%	9	56%	33%	2.77	-14.7	27	59	$4
11 CHC	529	66	2	43	9	276	267	313	353	666	734	650	4	87	31	0.33	49	23	28	53	36	2%	143	8%	82%	26	31%	27%	3.83	2.6	45	100	$12
12 CHC	548	73	7	44	6	254	273	299	354	653	636	659	6	89	27	0.57	48	22	30	62	58	5%	124	5%	86%	27	48%	22%	3.61	-0.7	58	145	$9
13 CHC	501	49	7	41	4	208	252	266	303	569	725	515	7	87	23	0.56	45	19	36	66	74	4%	91	6%	67%	24	38%	21%	2.53	-17.5	44	110	$0
1st Half	240	27	4	18	3	229	267	283	350	633	850	558	7	88	25	0.62	43	21	37	82	73	5%	100	8%	75%	12	50%	17%	3.28	-3.1	63	158	$4
2nd Half	261	22	3	23	1	188	233	240	261	501	594	477	6	87	21	0.51	48	17	34	51	75	4%	84	4%	50%	12	25%	25%	1.94	-14.7	27	68	-$4
14 Proj	494	54	5	43	5	246	256	295	333	628	671	614	6	88	27	0.50	48	20	32	60	61	4%	108	6%	74%				3.28	-6.1	36	90	$8

Barton,Daric

Barton,Daric		Health	A	LIMA Plan	D+
Age 28	Bats L Pos 1B	PT/Exp	D	Rand Var	0
Ht 6' 0"	Wt 205	Consist	A	MM	1201

3-16-.269 in 104 AB at OAK. Between injuries and ineptitude the previous two seasons, his time had presumably passed. But back he came, drawing his usual walks and batting over .300 in Sept. Is that enough to put him back on the fantasy radar? Only if you're happy with his 2010 line as the best-case scenario.

Yr Tm	AB	R	HR	RBI	SB	BA	xBA	OBP	SLG	OPS	vL	vR	bb%	ct%	h%	Eye	G	L	F	PX	xPX	hr/f	Spd	SBO	SB%	#Wk	DOM	DIS	RC/G	RAR	BPV	BPX	R$
09 OAK *	413	68	10	61	1	237	258	335	386	721	1083	728	13	82	27	0.83	31	20	48	101	113	5%	92	2%	28%	13	69%	23%	4.25	-4.4	65	133	$6
10 OAK	556	79	10	57	7	273	261	393	405	798	895	761	17	82	32	1.08	39	21	39	92	91	6%	119	5%	70%	27	56%	15%	5.58	15.4	71	154	$15
11 OAK *	297	33	0	24	2	199	203	311	248	558	720	533	14	78	26	0.72	38	19	43	48	103	0%	72	3%	67%	13	31%	31%	2.45	-20.1	0	0	-$3
12 OAK *	372	40	6	29	6	196	215	317	300	617	547	662	15	74	25	0.68	42	19	40	78	81	3%	91	6%	82%	11	18%	45%	3.06	-18.1	17	43	-$1
13 OAK *	495	64	7	60	1	230	239	326	323	648	653	749	12	82	27	0.78	41	22	37	68	86	9%	94	2%	20%	8	50%	25%	3.42	-17.9	36	90	$5
1st Half	232	26	4	29	1	206	212	319	317	637	0	527	14	81	24	0.88	57	7	36	84	110	20%	70	3%	33%	2	50%	50%	3.20	-10.2	43	108	$2
2nd Half	263	38	3	32	0	251	238	331	328	659	677	822	11	82	29	0.68	38	25	37	55	81	7%	111	2%	0%	6	50%	17%	3.62	-7.6	30	75	$8
14 Proj	212	26	3	27	1	230	232	333	335	668	674	666	13	79	28	0.75	38	21	40	77	91	5%	89	3%	64%				3.69	-5.8	25	63	$3

Bautista,Jose

Bautista,Jose		Health	D	LIMA Plan	B+
Age 33	Bats R Pos RF	PT/Exp	B	Rand Var	+2
Ht 6' 0"	Wt 190	Consist	D	MM	4235

PRO: Averaged 180 PX and 21% hr/f the past four years; maintained steady ct%; hit both LH and RHers.
CON: During last two years missed 117 games with wrist and hip injuries; 2011 BA an outlier; receding Eye.
VERDICT: Health permitting, bank on 30 HR—but be wary of age, injury history and h% fluctuations.

Yr Tm	AB	R	HR	RBI	SB	BA	xBA	OBP	SLG	OPS	vL	vR	bb%	ct%	h%	Eye	G	L	F	PX	xPX	hr/f	Spd	SBO	SB%	#Wk	DOM	DIS	RC/G	RAR	BPV	BPX	R$
09 TOR	336	54	13	40	4	235	244	349	408	757	919	664	14	75	28	0.66	41	17	42	110	114	12%	129	4%	100%	27	41%	41%	4.76	4.8	56	114	$5
10 TOR	569	109	54	124	9	260	322	378	617	995	843	1030	15	80	24	0.86	31	14	54	220	173	22%	106	7%	82%	27	85%	15%	7.89	59.9	158	343	$31
11 TOR	513	105	43	103	9	302	297	447	608	1056	1156	1025	20	78	31	1.19	37	16	47	191	158	23%	112	6%	64%	27	78%	7%	9.73	77.6	143	318	$35
12 TOR	332	64	27	65	5	241	280	358	527	886	718	942	15	81	22	0.94	37	14	49	165	145	20%	83	7%	71%	17	76%	12%	6.25	19.6	113	283	$14
13 TOR	452	82	28	73	7	259	281	358	498	856	910	842	13	81	26	0.82	41	16	43	150	138	18%	91	7%	78%	21	71%	5%	6.12	24.3	101	253	$20
1st Half	287	53	19	50	6	258	285	355	509	863	780	883	13	79	26	0.73	41	18	42	160	138	20%	86	7%	100%	14	79%	0%	6.34	15.8	100	250	$26
2nd Half	165	29	9	23	1	261	271	361	479	840	1129	770	14	85	26	1.04	42	13	45	133	138	14%	98	6%	33%	7	57%	14%	5.74	6.3	104	260	$11
14 Proj	487	91	31	84	5	260	276	375	506	880	916	870	15	81	26	0.94	39	15	46	152	143	17%	95	4%	67%				6.44	28.3	97	244	$22

Bay,Jason

Bay,Jason		Health	D	LIMA Plan	D
Age 35	Bats R Pos LF RF	PT/Exp	D	Rand Var	+2
Ht 6' 2"	Wt 210	Consist	D	MM	3301

Was injury free for the first time since 2009 but used sparingly in 2H before his release in August. PX and hr/f said he still had some punch, but he continued descent into "bomb or bust" territory with dwindling ct% and near microscopic h%. May hang around as a bench bat, but his days of fantasy consideration have passed.

Yr Tm	AB	R	HR	RBI	SB	BA	xBA	OBP	SLG	OPS	vL	vR	bb%	ct%	h%	Eye	G	L	F	PX	xPX	hr/f	Spd	SBO	SB%	#Wk	DOM	DIS	RC/G	RAR	BPV	BPX	R$
09 BOS	531	103	36	119	13	267	267	384	537	921	980	897	15	69	32	0.58	33	18	49	184	176	20%	101	10%	81%	27	67%	19%	7.08	47.1	88	180	$26
10 NYM	348	48	6	47	10	259	233	347	402	749	750	748	11	74	33	0.48	36	19	45	107	152	5%	156	10%	100%	17	41%	47%	4.92	9.1	52	113	$9
11 NYM	444	59	12	57	11	245	230	329	374	703	918	629	11	75	30	0.51	43	17	40	93	102	9%	107	9%	92%	24	38%	38%	4.28	3.5	33	73	$11
12 NYM	194	21	8	20	5	165	204	237	299	536	565	508	9	70	19	0.33	43	16	41	85	139	14%	86	15%	83%	18	22%	50%	2.23	-11.3	-5	-13	-$1
13 SEA	206	30	11	20	3	204	235	298	393	691	733	647	11	70	23	0.42	42	18	40	132	143	19%	90	8%	75%	17	35%	41%	3.69	-2.0	37	93	$2
1st Half	177	27	10	19	3	220	243	320	418	738	801	692	13	71	25	0.50	42	19	38	136	155	21%	92	8%	75%	14	43%	36%	4.38	1.9	46	115	$4
2nd Half	29	3	1	1	0	103	185	103	241	345	455	0	0	66	11	0.00	37	11	53	109	64	10%	84	0%	0%	3	0%	67%	0.71	-3.4	-24	-60	-$9
14 Proj	124	17	5	16	3	226	222	317	387	704	768	638	12	72	27	0.47	40	15	44	113	117	12%	93	10%	86%				4.10	0.3	29	71	$3

Beckham,Gordon

Beckham,Gordon		Health	B	LIMA Plan	B+
Age 27	Bats R Pos 2B	PT/Exp	B	Rand Var	-2
Ht 6' 0"	Wt 190	Consist	A	MM	2315

.267-5-24 in 371 AB at CHW. Around a fractured wrist, any cause for optimism? PRO: xPX shows a smidge of growth; he has a nice LD%. CON: Results have been consistently underwhelming in a large sample; no sign of him better exploiting his mildly-plus Spd. VERDICT: It doesn't quite spell bust yet, but at 27 he's at b-u-s.

Yr Tm	AB	R	HR	RBI	SB	BA	xBA	OBP	SLG	OPS	vL	vR	bb%	ct%	h%	Eye	G	L	F	PX	xPX	hr/f	Spd	SBO	SB%	#Wk	DOM	DIS	RC/G	RAR	BPV	BPX	R$
09 CHW*	553	84	18	85	9	279	282	343	469	811	890	774	9	83	31	0.57	40	17	43	127	131	10%	89	9%	69%	19	68%	16%	5.61	29.8	80	163	$19
10 CHW	444	58	9	49	4	252	249	317	378	695	667	705	8	79	30	0.40	46	17	37	91	90	7%	109	9%	40%	26	42%	31%	3.82	1.2	40	87	$8
11 CHW	499	60	10	44	5	230	230	296	337	633	541	663	7	78	28	0.32	39	20	40	79	66	6%	108	7%	63%	27	33%	26%	3.10	-9.5	22	49	$5
12 CHW	525	62	16	60	5	234	245	296	371	668	689	659	7	83	25	0.45	38	20	42	86	90	9%	92	7%	56%	27	37%	33%	3.50	-3.6	45	113	$8
13 CHW*	407	51	5	28	5	268	247	317	368	685	510	745	7	84	31	0.47	35	23	41	73	105	4%	113	6%	83%	20	40%	30%	4.09	4.3	45	113	$8
1st Half	146	17	0	11	3	301	250	331	367	699	130	875	4	83	36	0.26	35	28	37	61	117	0%	102	10%	75%	7	43%	29%	4.44	3.0	20	50	$7
2nd Half	261	34	5	17	2	249	249	310	368	678	653	690	8	85	28	0.61	35	21	43	80	100	5%	119	3%	100%	13	38%	31%	3.91	1.7	60	150	$9
14 Proj	509	63	10	46	5	255	246	312	369	681	565	716	7	83	29	0.42	37	22	41	82	97	6%	104	5%	75%				3.85	2.3	33	81	$11

ROB CARROLL

Belt,Brandon

Belt,Brandon				Health	A	LIMA Plan	A
Age	26	Bats	L	Pos 1B			
PT/Exp	C	Rand Var	-2				
Ht	6' 5"	Wt	220	Consist	B	MM	4325

You expect upside from a 26-year old, and it's here if you squint. PX and xPX hint at better power numbers, and his skills were largely better in 2H. He also hits LHP well enough to play full-time. xBA points to some BA regression, but strong LD and potential for growth ease those concerns. UP: 25+ HR.

Yr Tm	AB	R	HR	RBI	SB	BA	xBA	OBP	SLG	OPS	vL	vR	bb%	ct%	h%	Eye	G	L	F	PX	xPX	hr/f	Spd	SBO	SB%	#Wk	DOM	DIS	RC/G	RAR	BPV	BPX	R$
09																																	
10 a/a	223	30	10	40	3	288	296	367	536	904			11	76	34	0.53				165			124	7%	75%				7.03		99	215	$9
11 SF *	352	42	14	39	6	236	220	325	405	730	934	648	12	68	31	0.42	42	14	44	130	111	16%	102	12%	46%	15	47%	47%	4.16	-4.5	33	73	$7
12 SF	411	47	7	56	12	275	247	360	421	781	768	786	12	74	36	0.51	38	26	37	107	112	6%	110	11%	86%	27	41%	37%	5.42	9.7	41	103	$13
13 SF	509	76	17	67	5	289	266	360	481	841	755	867	9	75	35	0.42	34	24	41	143	130	11%	104	5%	71%	27	59%	22%	6.09	21.5	68	170	$21
1st Half	247	34	8	34	3	263	258	328	437	766	851	746	9	77	31	0.42	37	20	43	131	121	10%	87	6%	75%	14	64%	14%	4.96	2.6	58	145	$16
2nd Half	262	42	9	33	2	313	272	379	523	902	677	985	10	74	39	0.41	32	28	40	155	139	12%	120	4%	67%	13	54%	31%	7.31	19.3	78	195	$25
14 Proj	**532**	**75**	**20**	**76**	**7**	**279**	**263**	**359**	**481**	**841**	**814**	**850**	**11**	**74**	**34**	**0.45**	**36**	**24**	**41**	**147**	**122**	**12%**	**111**	**7%**	**75%**				**6.04**	**21.8**	**67**	**167**	**$20**

Beltran,Carlos

Beltran,Carlos				Health	C	LIMA Plan	B+
Age	37	Bats	B	Pos RF			
PT/Exp	A	Rand Var	-1				
Ht	6' 1"	Wt	210	Consist	B	MM	4235

Another productive season as age creeps into danger zone; how worried should we be? Seeds of doubt: four-year trend of declining OPS vs. LHP; second straight year where power fell off in 2H; 2012 SBO and hr/f are now outliers. Power and contact remain, but age, health, and declining Eye raise the risk.

Yr Tm	AB	R	HR	RBI	SB	BA	xBA	OBP	SLG	OPS	vL	vR	bb%	ct%	h%	Eye	G	L	F	PX	xPX	hr/f	Spd	SBO	SB%	#Wk	DOM	DIS	RC/G	RAR	BPV	BPX	R$
09 NYM	308	50	10	48	11	325	296	415	500	915	1013	876	13	86	35	1.09	45	20	35	109	102	11%	108	11%	92%	17	59%	6%	8.03	28.0	92	188	$16
10 NYM	220	21	7	27	3	255	271	341	427	768	1009	701	12	82	28	0.77	42	19	39	109	131	10%	101	6%	75%	12	58%	8%	5.03	2.7	73	159	$4
11 2 NL	520	78	22	84	4	300	298	385	525	910	923	903	12	83	33	0.81	40	21	39	147	147	13%	98	4%	67%	26	73%	12%	7.30	38.6	105	233	$24
12 STL	547	83	32	97	13	269	274	346	495	842	867	832	11	77	29	0.52	42	20	38	142	124	20%	74	12%	68%	27	56%	22%	5.88	20.2	68	170	$25
13 STL	554	79	24	84	2	296	282	339	491	830	729	871	6	84	32	0.42	35	24	41	122	127	13%	94	2%	67%	27	63%	11%	6.05	22.0	76	190	$25
1st Half	286	44	19	50	1	308	294	347	549	895	890	899	6	83	32	0.35	36	24	40	141	133	20%	99	3%	50%	14	64%	7%	6.93	19.4	87	218	$30
2nd Half	268	35	5	34	1	284	269	336	429	765	566	841	7	85	32	0.51	34	24	42	102	120	5%	86	1%	100%	13	62%	15%	5.15	5.3	63	158	$18
14 Proj	**519**	**74**	**21**	**81**	**7**	**288**	**277**	**347**	**480**	**827**	**775**	**846**	**8**	**82**	**32**	**0.52**	**38**	**22**	**40**	**124**	**127**	**12%**	**91**	**7%**	**68%**				**5.92**	**21.6**	**72**	**181**	**$24**

Beltre,Adrian

Beltre,Adrian				Health	B	LIMA Plan	A
Age	35	Bats	R	Pos 3B			
PT/Exp	A	Rand Var	-2				
Ht	5' 11"	Wt	220	Consist	B	MM	4145

Four years of stable production, strong DOM/DIS say "buy." But there are some minor red flags. First, his BA/xBA variance signals some BA corection. Second, expect some PT decline—at 35, a personal AB high rarely repeats. In that case, 30 HR might be tough, despite strong xPX. Bid accordingly.

Yr Tm	AB	R	HR	RBI	SB	BA	xBA	OBP	SLG	OPS	vL	vR	bb%	ct%	h%	Eye	G	L	F	PX	xPX	hr/f	Spd	SBO	SB%	#Wk	DOM	DIS	RC/G	RAR	BPV	BPX	R$
09 SEA	449	54	8	44	13	265	254	304	379	683	855	616	4	84	30	0.26	46	16	38	78	100	6%	86	15%	87%	21	38%	29%	3.95	0.1	32	65	$11
10 BOS	589	84	28	102	2	321	312	365	553	919	943	908	6	86	34	0.49	40	19	40	148	137	13%	64	2%	67%	26	73%	4%	7.54	56.5	97	211	$31
11 TEX	487	82	32	105	1	296	315	331	561	892	1075	836	5	89	28	0.47	38	18	44	156	160	16%	63	2%	50%	22	73%	5%	6.65	36.5	112	249	$27
12 TEX	604	95	36	102	1	321	299	359	561	921	737	985	6	86	33	0.44	39	21	40	136	139	17%	79	1%	100%	27	74%	7%	7.59	58.5	91	228	$33
13 TEX	631	88	30	92	1	315	287	371	509	880	948	857	7	88	32	0.64	38	22	40	115	128	14%	64	1%	100%	27	63%	7%	6.94	50.7	78	195	$32
1st Half	324	46	14	42	0	296	283	335	485	820	859	810	6	88	30	0.48	43	19	38	116	109	13%	65	0%	0%	14	71%	0%	5.89	17.1	76	190	$27
2nd Half	307	42	16	50	1	336	291	396	534	931	1029	907	9	88	34	0.82	34	24	42	115	147	14%	68	1%	100%	13	54%	15%	8.15	33.4	83	208	$38
14 Proj	**582**	**83**	**29**	**90**	**1**	**302**	**292**	**352**	**510**	**861**	**887**	**852**	**7**	**87**	**31**	**0.55**	**39**	**21**	**40**	**125**	**137**	**14%**	**69**	**1%**	**72%**				**6.47**	**39.8**	**77**	**192**	**$28**

Beltre,Engel

Beltre,Engel				Health	A	LIMA Plan	D
Age	24	Bats	L	Pos RF			
PT/Exp	B	Rand Var	-1				
Ht	6' 2"	Wt	180	Consist	B	MM	0521

0-2-1-.250 in 40 AB at TEX. These are not the skills of a good speed-only guy. With no power or patience (a 1% bb% in 2H!) and a sub-.300 OBA, he won't reach first base often. And with a 62% SB% across four seasons (MLE and MLB), that high SBO won't last in the majors. When a player aspires to be Esix Snead—pass.

Yr Tm	AB	R	HR	RBI	SB	BA	xBA	OBP	SLG	OPS	vL	vR	bb%	ct%	h%	Eye	G	L	F	PX	xPX	hr/f	Spd	SBO	SB%	#Wk	DOM	DIS	RC/G	RAR	BPV	BPX	R$
09 aa																																	
10 aa	181	12	1	12	7	246	244	280	328	608			5	86	28	0.34				46			152	20%	76%				3.12		38	83	$2
11 aa	437	49	1	21	12	211	210	248	274	522			5	76	28	0.20				48			138	20%	65%				2.15		-6	-13	$0
12 aa	564	63	12	43	28	243	240	270	385	655			3	78	29	0.16				84			159	34%	72%				3.41		35	88	$15
13 TEX *	434	50	6	27	12	258	264	291	344	636	333	580	5	78	32	0.21	48	30	21	66	23	0%	128	26%	44%	10	10%	50%	3.03	-15.9	13	33	$10
1st Half	303	35	3	16	11	271	257	314	360	674	0	800	6	79	33	0.30	56	22	22	70	41	0%	125	28%	46%	2	0%	0%	3.47	-6.5	23	58	$14
2nd Half	131	15	3	12	1	228	253	237	307	544	333	490	1	74	29	0.04	46	33	21	56	17	0%	123	18%	31%	8	13%	63%	2.13	-8.4	-16	-40	$0
14 Proj	**115**	**12**	**1**	**9**	**4**	**240**	**259**	**287**	**308**	**595**	**560**	**604**	**4**	**78**	**30**	**0.16**	**46**	**33**	**21**	**49**	**15**	**3%**	**146**	**27%**	**63%**				**2.62**	**-6.4**	**-5**	**-11**	**$2**

Berkman,Lance

Berkman,Lance				Health	F	LIMA Plan	D
Age	38	Bats	B	Pos DH			
PT/Exp	D	Rand Var	0				
Ht	6' 1"	Wt	220	Consist	D	MM	3111

Missed almost the entire 2H with hip inflammation, and still wasn't right when he returned. One can quibble over the PX/xPX variance, or point to his still-strong bb% and acceptable ct%, but the two most important numbers here are 38 (his age) and 164 (DL days, 2012-13). Take the under on 200 AB; he could even retire.

Yr Tm	AB	R	HR	RBI	SB	BA	xBA	OBP	SLG	OPS	vL	vR	bb%	ct%	h%	Eye	G	L	F	PX	xPX	hr/f	Spd	SBO	SB%	#Wk	DOM	DIS	RC/G	RAR	BPV	BPX	R$
09 HOU	460	73	25	80	7	274	290	399	509	907	710	982	17	79	30	0.99	43	18	39	150	142	17%	72	7%	64%	25	80%	4%	7.06	33.9	93	190	$18
10 2 TM	404	48	14	58	3	248	260	368	413	781	517	847	16	79	28	0.91	48	16	36	114	114	12%	77	4%	60%	23	43%	43%	5.11	7.4	64	139	$8
11 STL	488	90	31	94	2	301	295	412	547	959	804	998	16	81	32	0.99	39	22	39	153	146	20%	93	4%	25%	27	63%	22%	7.91	46.5	108	240	$27
12 STL	81	12	2	7	2	259	272	381	444	826	712	856	15	77	32	0.74	45	21	34	134	90	10%	95	8%	100%	10	60%	30%	5.81	3.1	73	183	$0
13 TEX	256	27	6	34	0	242	220	340	359	700	780	669	13	80	28	0.73	45	15	40	79	111	8%	78	0%	0%	17	29%	35%	4.11	-2.8	33	83	$2
1st Half	232	26	6	34	0	263	228	362	392	754	836	721	13	80	31	0.78	45	15	40	87	110	8%	78	0%	0%	14	36%	29%	4.91	2.8	43	108	$4
2nd Half	24	1	0	0	0	42	135	115	42	157	0	195	8	75	6	0.33	44	11	44	0	124	0%	83	0%	0%	3	0%	67%	0.13	-3.9	-58	-145	-$11
14 Proj	**178**	**24**	**5**	**28**	**1**	**267**	**250**	**381**	**416**	**797**	**710**	**823**	**15**	**80**	**31**	**0.89**	**44**	**19**	**38**	**102**	**119**	**10%**	**80**	**3%**	**51%**				**5.41**	**4.7**	**49**	**122**	**$6**

Bernadina,Roger

Bernadina,Roger				Health	B	LIMA Plan	D
Age	30	Bats	L	Pos RF LF			
PT/Exp	D	Rand Var	+5				
Ht	6' 2"	Wt	200	Consist	F	MM	2501

These BPI aren't as bad as they seem: he has below-average power, but he's not a slap hitter; speed is above average. His Achilles heel is contact, and without the plate patience to make up for it, those serviceable secondary skills are wasted. RandVar highlights rebound potential, but at age 30, will he even get that chance?

Yr Tm	AB	R	HR	RBI	SB	BA	xBA	OBP	SLG	OPS	vL	vR	bb%	ct%	h%	Eye	G	L	F	PX	xPX	hr/f	Spd	SBO	SB%	#Wk	DOM	DIS	RC/G	RAR	BPV	BPX	R$
09 WAS	4	1	0	0	1	250	345	400	500	900	1000	750	20	75	33	1.00	33	33	33	238	78	0%	110	100%	100%	1	100%	0%	8.67	0.5	165	337	-$1
10 WAS *	475	58	13	53	22	256	243	314	393	707	757	681	8	79	30	0.40	47	13	39	91	108	9%	118	21%	83%	25	40%	32%	4.32	3.1	43	93	$16
11 WAS *	473	59	11	37	27	229	249	281	351	633	461	720	7	75	28	0.29	52	20	28	89	91	11%	124	33%	75%	19	37%	37%	3.26	-12.2	24	53	$11
12 WAS	227	25	5	25	15	291	249	372	405	777	940	758	11	77	36	0.53	43	26	31	82	97	10%	104	23%	83%	27	33%	33%	5.56	9.4	27	68	$10
13 2 NL	227	26	4	11	4	181	224	250	295	545	422	565	7	71	23	0.25	51	17	32	88	81	8%	121	10%	100%	27	19%	56%	2.23	-13.6	7	18	-$3
1st Half	134	15	2	5	2	187	230	243	291	534	301	577	7	75	23	0.29	52	17	31	79	101	7%	118	8%	100%	14	21%	50%	2.28	-8.1	13	33	-$3
2nd Half	93	11	2	6	2	172	215	222	301	523	544	546	6	67	23	0.19	49	16	34	103	51	10%	113	13%	100%	13	15%	62%	2.14	-6.1	-3	-8	-$3
14 Proj	**194**	**24**	**4**	**16**	**9**	**232**	**237**	**302**	**356**	**658**	**595**	**668**	**8**	**74**	**29**	**0.33**	**48**	**19**	**33**	**91**	**84**	**9%**	**112**	**21%**	**86%**				**3.56**	**-5.2**	**23**	**57**	**$5**

Betancourt,Yuniesky

Betancourt,Yuniesky				Health	B	LIMA Plan	D+
Age	32	Bats	R	Pos 1B 3B			
PT/Exp	C	Rand Var	+2				
Ht	5' 10"	Wt	205	Consist	A	MM	2011

Consistently mediocre. The big drop in ct% could have been from swinging for the fences, but the results don't show it, and it ended up costing him BA (not that he had any extra to give up). He'll have to fight for PT, which only adds to his risk. BA may rebound some, but even so, chasing the pop here comes at a price.

Yr Tm	AB	R	HR	RBI	SB	BA	xBA	OBP	SLG	OPS	vL	vR	bb%	ct%	h%	Eye	G	L	F	PX	xPX	hr/f	Spd	SBO	SB%	#Wk	DOM	DIS	RC/G	RAR	BPV	BPX	R$
09 2 AL	470	40	6	49	3	245	255	274	351	625	772	573	4	91	26	0.48	42	17	41	61	67	3%	125	6%	50%	24	33%	0%	3.22	-19.2	59	120	$3
10 KC	556	60	16	78	2	259	268	288	405	692	778	666	4	88	27	0.36	40	18	42	90	85	8%	80	4%	40%	27	52%	19%	3.94	-10.6	60	130	$12
11 MIL	556	51	13	68	4	252	258	271	381	652	576	672	3	89	26	0.25	41	18	41	81	97	6%	88	7%	50%	27	52%	11%	3.46	-18.6	53	118	$10
12 KC *	238	22	8	40	0	238	266	266	412	678	653	658	4	88	24	0.31	38	18	44	104	91	8%	81	2%	0%	16	63%	25%	3.59	-7.1	68	170	$3
13 MIL	391	35	13	46	0	212	236	240	355	595	534	624	3	82	23	0.20	43	16	41	91	122	10%	76	0%	0%	27	37%	33%	2.76	-22.0	32	80	$2
1st Half	243	19	8	32	0	202	231	230	337	568	550	578	4	83	21	0.22	48	14	38	82	111	10%	81	0%	0%	14	29%	36%	2.48	-16.1	32	80	$2
2nd Half	148	16	5	14	0	230	245	255	385	640	507	698	3	80	26	0.17	35	19	45	107	141	9%	80	0%	0%	13	46%	31%	3.25	-6.0	37	93	$1
14 Proj	**237**	**22**	**7**	**30**	**0**	**236**	**250**	**261**	**384**	**645**	**601**	**665**	**3**	**85**	**25**	**0.23**	**40**	**17**	**43**	**95**	**109**	**8%**	**80**	**0%**					**3.35**	**-8.8**	**35**	**88**	**$4**

MATT CEDERHOLM

Betemit,Wilson

Age 32 | Bats B | Pos DH | Ht 6' 2" | Wt 220
Health F | PT/Exp D | Consist F | LIMA Plan D | Rand Var +3 | MM 4201

0-0-.000 in 10 AB at BAL. Here's hoping you didn't wait all summer long for a late-season boost. Finally returned in late August from April PCL surgery only to be released three weeks later. At 32, still young enough to resume reserve role with pop against RHP, but will need to impress during spring training.

Yr Tm	AB	R	HR	RBI	SB	BA	xBA	OBP	SLG	OPS	vL	vR	bb%	ct%	h%	Eye	G	L	F	PX	xPX	hr/f	Spd	SBO	SB%	#Wk	DOM	DIS	RC/G	RAR	BPV	BPX	R$
09 CHW *	306	31	10	42	2	201	231	255	365	619	650	561	7	66	27	0.21	47	16	38	133	50	0%	68	3%	100%	9	56%	33%	2.99	-14.4	7	14	$0
10 KC *	389	42	14	54	1	271	244	349	452	801	930	873	11	74	33	0.46	40	15	45	134	159	14%	95	2%	34%	19	53%	37%	5.47	10.8	54	117	$10
11 2 AL	323	40	8	46	4	285	238	343	452	795	607	865	9	67	40	0.30	43	19	37	139	109	10%	109	6%	80%	25	44%	36%	5.61	10.1	34	76	$10
12 BAL	341	41	12	40	0	261	244	322	422	744	405	859	8	70	34	0.30	40	25	34	121	125	14%	77	1%	0%	22	36%	36%	4.64	1.4	18	45	$7
13 BAL *	39	1	0	2	0	138	81	207	158	365	0	0	8	63	22	0.24	57	0	43	24	92	0%	83	0%	0%	3	0%	67%	0.97	-4.6	-84	-210	-$4
1st Half																																	
2nd Half	39	1	0	2	0	138	81	207	158	365	0	0	8	63	22	0.24	57	0	43	24	92	0%	83	0%	0%	3	0%	67%	0.97	-4.7	-85	-213	-$4
14 Proj	178	20	5	24	1	260	239	325	419	744	614	792	9	70	34	0.33	42	21	37	127	135	11%	90	3%	64%				4.69	1.0	20	50	$3

Bethancourt,Christian

Age 22 | Bats R | Pos CA | Ht 6' 2" | Wt 215
Health A | PT/Exp F | Consist D | LIMA Plan D+ | Rand Var 0 | MM 2211

0-0-.000 in 1 AB at ATL. A plus defender with strong arm, so he'll stick as soon as the bat plays. 2H surge in Double-A gives hope, especially ct% and PX, though bb% work in progress. Needs better SB% to assure future SBO, especially in bigs. UP: Opening day catcher with double digit HR and SB.

Yr Tm	AB	R	HR	RBI	SB	BA	xBA	OBP	SLG	OPS	vL	vR	bb%	ct%	h%	Eye	G	L	F	PX	xPX	hr/f	Spd	SBO	SB%	#Wk	DOM	DIS	RC/G	RAR	BPV	BPX	R$
09																																	
10																																	
11																																	
12 aa	268	26	2	23	7	227	211	254	270	524			3	82	27	0.19				28			103	21%	52%				2.10		-11	-28	$1
13 ATL *	359	37	10	39	10	258	260	286	401	687	0	0	4	82	29	0.22	44	20	36	98	-15	0%	80	23%	56%	1	0%	100%	3.69	0.0	40	100	$10
1st Half	183	17	3	17	6	246	232	267	354	621			3	76	31	0.12				85			86	25%	65%				3.07		4	10	$8
2nd Half	176	20	7	23	4	271	289	306	449	755	0	0	5	89	27	0.44	44	20	36	109	-15	0%	83	20%	45%	1	0%	100%	4.40	3.6	78	195	$12
14 Proj	236	24	6	24	5	248	244	277	373	650	650	650	4	83	28	0.23	41	19	40	83		8%	91	18%	57%				3.34	-2.6	28	70	$6

Bianchi,Jeff

Age 27 | Bats R | Pos 3B SS | Ht 5' 11" | Wt 180
Health B | PT/Exp D | Consist C | LIMA Plan D | Rand Var 0 | MM 1201

1-25-.236 in 235 AB in MIL. Injuries to infield starters increased at bats, but more isn't always better. Low bb% drove sub-.300 OBP; also sports an anemic PX and horrible SB%. He'll only repeat this number of AB if he's part of another health-challenged infield; these tepid skills barely warrant a bench role.

Yr Tm	AB	R	HR	RBI	SB	BA	xBA	OBP	SLG	OPS	vL	vR	bb%	ct%	h%	Eye	G	L	F	PX	xPX	hr/f	Spd	SBO	SB%	#Wk	DOM	DIS	RC/G	RAR	BPV	BPX	R$
09 aa	270	33	4	33	8	284	244	321	390	711			5	77	36	0.24				80			93	17%	63%				4.32		13	27	$8
10																																	
11 aa	444	44	1	33	14	215	220	260	276	536			6	79	27	0.28				51			98	20%	70%				2.32		-1	-2	$2
12 MIL *	395	42	7	28	11	260	234	306	363	669	358	679	6	78	32	0.31	51	18	32	71	90	17%	87	17%	60%	11	27%	36%	3.67	0.1	11	28	$8
13 MIL *	292	26	2	30	4	231	222	264	291	555	552	569	4	80	28	0.23	47	20	33	44	63	2%	114	14%	43%	22	14%	41%	2.39	-11.4	0	0	$1
1st Half	127	9	1	11	1	231	232	244	307	551	277	846	2	77	29	0.07	53	21	26	54	42	0%	135	13%	31%	10	20%	60%	2.29	-5.5	-4	-10	-$1
2nd Half	165	17	1	19	3	230	219	278	279	557	812	489	6	82	27	0.38	45	20	35	37	72	2%	90	14%	50%	12	8%	25%	2.44	-6.4	1	3	$2
14 Proj	133	13	2	12	3	241	240	280	345	624	467	695	5	79	29	0.26	49	19	32	72	72	7%	107	16%	57%				3.10	-3.5	12	30	$3

Blackmon,Charlie

Age 28 | Bats L | Pos RF CF | Ht 6' 3" | Wt 210
Health F | PT/Exp D | Consist A | LIMA Plan B | Rand Var -1 | MM 3433

6-22-.309 with 7 SB in 246 AB at COL. Bloated 2H h% (37%) in bigs fueled BA but also gave opportunity to showcase above-average PX and Spd. Low bb% limits OBP, and already 28, so growth potential is limited. Don't pay for the .309 BA, but... UP: double digit HR, SB.

Yr Tm	AB	R	HR	RBI	SB	BA	xBA	OBP	SLG	OPS	vL	vR	bb%	ct%	h%	Eye	G	L	F	PX	xPX	hr/f	Spd	SBO	SB%	#Wk	DOM	DIS	RC/G	RAR	BPV	BPX	R$
09																																	
10 aa	337	40	9	42	15	273	291	320	441	761			7	87	29	0.52				106			112	27%	65%				4.71		80	174	$13
11 COL *	341	34	7	33	11	280	256	286	380	666	905	484	4	86	28	0.27	47	16	37	79	53	3%	103	24%	61%	5	20%	20%	3.54	-5.6	48	107	$8
12 COL *	341	47	6	29	7	260	266	302	392	694	853	701	6	81	31	0.32	49	21	30	93	86	7%	111	11%	77%	8	63%	25%	4.09	0.0	46	115	$7
13 COL *	503	66	8	44	11	267	269	303	396	699	752	824	5	81	32	0.27	42	27	31	91	66	10%	133	15%	64%	16	38%	25%	4.06	-0.5	48	120	$14
1st Half	256	33	3	21	5	223	241	274	328	602	500	708	7	80	27	0.36	38	25	38	72	126	17%	134	17%	50%	3	0%	67%	2.78	-11.2	34	85	$8
2nd Half	247	33	5	23	6	312	284	333	467	800	792	835	3	81	37	0.17	42	27	31	110	61	9%	123	12%	83%	13	46%	15%	5.80	10.9	59	148	$21
14 Proj	333	42	8	31	9	272	273	316	428	744	751	742	5	82	31	0.29	44	22	34	105	82	9%	121	17%	68%				4.51	0.6	58	146	$12

Blanco,Gregor

Age 30 | Bats L | Pos CF LF | Ht 5' 11" | Wt 185
Health A | PT/Exp C | Consist B | LIMA Plan C | Rand Var -2 | MM 1503

Elevated 1H h% drove BA improvement, though regression of career-best ct% is bigger risk to 2014 BA. Drop in SB a result of a poor SB% and SBO decline. With marginal BA and no power, SB are the lynchpin of his value. Spd still rates well, but with SB% in danger zone as odometer rolls over into 30s, that's at risk too.

Yr Tm	AB	R	HR	RBI	SB	BA	xBA	OBP	SLG	OPS	vL	vR	bb%	ct%	h%	Eye	G	L	F	PX	xPX	hr/f	Spd	SBO	SB%	#Wk	DOM	DIS	RC/G	RAR	BPV	BPX	R$
09 ATL *	376	47	2	24	10	188	243	274	229	503	237	584	11	75	25	0.48	69	19	13	29	-5	0%	121	13%	73%	6	17%	67%	2.01	-24.7	-15	-31	-$2
10 2 TM *	391	50	2	22	18	262	246	340	336	676	448	813	11	78	33	0.55	54	20	26	55	66	2%	141	18%	77%	19	37%	37%	4.02	-0.3	23	50	$10
11 aaa	199	29	2	10	17	159	215	268	254	522			13	70	22	0.50				81			117	40%	87%				2.32		8	18	$0
12 SF	393	56	5	34	26	244	227	333	344	676	694	667	11	74	32	0.49	44	24	32	69	73	6%	140	26%	81%	27	19%	59%	3.99	-0.7	16	40	$12
13 SF	452	50	3	41	14	265	250	341	350	690	650	696	10	79	33	0.55	44	28	28	60	69	3%	152	16%	61%	27	19%	30%	4.01	-0.6	32	80	$12
1st Half	232	25	1	26	9	284	242	339	379	718	570	745	8	78	36	0.38	46	23	31	69	73	2%	151	20%	64%	14	21%	36%	4.42	2.7	32	80	$16
2nd Half	220	25	2	15	5	245	260	344	318	662	760	648	13	80	30	0.73	42	33	25	50	65	5%	140	12%	56%	13	15%	23%	3.58	-2.9	28	70	$8
14 Proj	397	52	4	34	17	256	234	340	343	684	645	695	11	76	33	0.54	45	24	31	64	70	4%	144	18%	72%				4.01	-1.9	17	42	$12

Blanks,Kyle

Age 27 | Bats R | Pos RF LF 1B | Ht 6' 6" | Wt 265
Health F | PT/Exp F | Consist D | LIMA Plan D | Rand Var -1 | MM 4203

8-35-.242 in 280 AB at SD. Teased us with a 5-18-.283 line in 106 June AB, then Achilles injury cost him seven weeks and never found groove upon return. Fewer flyballs cost HR, but still at age where power can re-emerge. Still chewed up LHP, but that's not enough until he stays on field awhile and resumes hitting FB.

Yr Tm	AB	R	HR	RBI	SB	BA	xBA	OBP	SLG	OPS	vL	vR	bb%	ct%	h%	Eye	G	L	F	PX	xPX	hr/f	Spd	SBO	SB%	#Wk	DOM	DIS	RC/G	RAR	BPV	BPX	R$
09 SD *	381	53	19	54	1	242	218	332	436	768	670	943	12	66	32	0.39	37	13	51	142	169	21%	75	2%	50%	11	64%	36%	4.84	8.9	25	51	$7
10 SD	102	14	3	15	1	157	202	283	324	607	865	526	13	55	25	0.33	41	14	45	165	93	12%	105	5%	100%	7	29%	57%	2.64	-4.7	11	24	-$2
11 SD *	481	65	16	65	4	231	229	288	404	692	528	789	7	69	30	0.25	40	16	45	137	115	13%	99	5%	76%	11	36%	45%	3.85	-2.9	30	67	$9
12 SD	5	0	0	0	0	200	25	333	200	533	833	0	17	60	33	0.50	33	0	67	0	-11	0%	94	0%	0%	2	0%	100%	2.13	-0.2	-96	-240	-$2
13 SD *	318	36	9	37	1	235	231	290	367	657	829	596	7	69	31	0.25	46	22	32	107	115	13%	86	3%	50%	18	22%	67%	3.51	-5.2	5	13	$4
1st Half	215	30	9	34	1	265	259	325	446	772	966	688	8	73	33	0.33	43	23	34	137	137	17%	85	4%	50%	12	33%	50%	4.97	5.9	43	108	$10
2nd Half	103	6	0	4	0	172	169	215	201	416	480	425	5	62	28	0.14	53	21	26	35	60	0%	93	0%	0%	6	0%	100%	1.33	-9.0	-82	-205	-$9
14 Proj	287	33	10	32	1	246	224	322	405	728	757	714	9	68	33	0.31	41	18	41	125	105	13%	94	3%	73%				4.29	-1.3	10	25	$6

Bloomquist,Willie

Age 36 | Bats R | Pos 2B | Ht 5' 11" | Wt 190
Health F | PT/Exp D | Consist B | LIMA Plan D+ | Rand Var -4 | MM 0321

0-14-.317 in 139 AB at ARI. Missed four months with oblique and hand injuries. In between, elite ct% and high LD buoyed BA beyond xBA. Injuries curtailed SBO though falling SB% and advancing age limit the likelihood of a SB bounceback. Only worthwhile asset is plus BA, but health grade limits the impact there.

Yr Tm	AB	R	HR	RBI	SB	BA	xBA	OBP	SLG	OPS	vL	vR	bb%	ct%	h%	Eye	G	L	F	PX	xPX	hr/f	Spd	SBO	SB%	#Wk	DOM	DIS	RC/G	RAR	BPV	BPX	R$
09 KC	434	52	4	29	25	265	250	308	355	663	666	661	6	83	31	0.37	46	21	33	51	42	3%	202	26%	81%	27	22%	41%	3.88	4.8	48	98	$13
10 2 TM	187	31	3	17	8	267	267	299	380	679	763	612	5	85	30	0.32	44	21	35	77	74	5%	106	29%	62%	27	33%	41%	3.73	1.2	45	98	$5
11 ARI	350	44	4	26	20	266	265	317	340	657	737	620	6	85	30	0.45	49	25	26	48	43	5%	127	30%	67%	24	29%	38%	3.53	0.2	32	71	$11
12 ARI	324	47	0	23	7	302	263	325	398	724	797	689	4	83	36	0.22	50	22	28	70	81	0%	154	20%	41%	20	35%	20%	4.27	7.1	44	110	$10
13 ARI *	160	19	0	19	0	317	270	354	369	723	745	719	5	91	35	0.66	49	25	26	35	63	0%	142	4%	0%	11	27%	18%	4.63	4.9	49	123	$3
1st Half	87	11	0	12	0	302	259	337	364	701	802	648	5	93	33	0.71	37	25	38	44	107	0%	115	0%	0%	5	40%	20%	4.48	2.4	53	133	$4
2nd Half	73	8	0	7	0	335	282	374	376	749	696	805	6	90	37	0.62	63	25	12	23	15	0%	143	7%	0%	6	17%	17%	4.81	2.7	35	88	$3
14 Proj	212	27	1	20	4	291	268	330	362	692	722	678	5	88	33	0.44	51	24	26	47	58	1%	148	14%	46%				3.98	1.7	31	78	$7

TODD ZOLA

Bogaerts,Xander

Bogaerts,Xander			Health	A	LIMA Plan	B+
Age 21	Bats R	Pos 3B	PT/Exp	F	Rand Var	+1
Ht 6' 3"	Wt 185		Consist	D	MM	4335

1-5-.250 in 44 AB at BOS. Precocious youngster rips thru AA-AAA during 2012-13 with .300+ BA and 20 HR in 536 AB. Age, inexperience point to initial MLB growing pains, and power is a work in progress. But patience, xBA and position say he can be profitable now. Worth more than a speculative bid, even in single-year leagues.

Yr Tm	AB	R	HR	RBI	SB	BA	xBA	OBP	SLG	OPS	vL	vR	bb%	ct%	h%	Eye	G	L	F	PX	xPX	hr/f	Spd	SBO	SB%	#Wk	DOM	DIS	RC/G	RAR	BPV	BPX	R$
09																																	
10																																	
11																																	
12 aa	92	10	4	15	1	326	300	332	581	913			1	77	39	0.04				187			80	12%	46%				7.00		84	210	$3
13 BOS *	488	64	12	58	7	278	291	351	427	778	1089	463	10	77	34	0.48	47	34	19	106	87	17%	128	7%	67%	7	43%	57%	5.26	25.4	52	130	$16
1st Half	283	39	8	36	6	277	247	354	435	790			11	75	34	0.48				108			155	8%	84%				5.49		58	145	$20
2nd Half	205	25	5	23	1	280	299	346	417	763	1089	463	9	79	34	0.47	47	34	19	103	87	17%	98	5%	32%	7	43%	57%	4.93	8.6	47	118	$11
14 Proj	423	57	19	50	5	277	274	342	480	822	899	777	10	77	32	0.48	42	22	36	137	78	16%	118	7%	61%				5.80	22.1	64	160	$14

Bogusevic,Brian

Bogusevic,Brian			Health	C	LIMA Plan	D+
Age 30	Bats L	Pos LF	PT/Exp	D	Rand Var	-3
Ht 6' 3"	Wt 220		Consist	C	MM	2411

6-16-.273 in 143 AB at CHC. Took advantage of late-season OF openings to put up nice small sample 2H vs. RHP. Flashes decent pop and running game, but too many GBs, poor contact limit his value. Upside is a deep league platoon player, but 2012 overexposure suggests caution. He's a bench player.

Yr Tm	AB	R	HR	RBI	SB	BA	xBA	OBP	SLG	OPS	vL	vR	bb%	ct%	h%	Eye	G	L	F	PX	xPX	hr/f	Spd	SBO	SB%	#Wk	DOM	DIS	RC/G	RAR	BPV	BPX	R$
09 aaa	520	59	5	46	19	244	223	304	328	632			8	73	32	0.33				65			104	16%	85%				3.47		-4	-8	$9
10 HOU *	530	70	10	43	17	224	267	291	330	621	0	584	9	73	29	0.35	69	19	13	83	73	0%	96	15%	89%	6	33%	67%	3.27	-12.8	6	13	$8
11 HOU *	382	41	6	40	18	244	255	310	378	688	421	839	9	74	32	0.36	52	21	27	104	104	12%	113	25%	76%	18	39%	44%	3.96	-1.0	31	69	$9
12 HOU	355	39	7	28	15	203	229	297	299	596	436	630	10	73	26	0.43	55	20	25	65	79	11%	103	20%	79%	27	19%	59%	2.79	-14.1	-2	-5	$3
13 CHC *	408	52	13	38	13	255	258	320	409	729	313	841	9	73	32	0.35	51	23	26	110	99	21%	110	14%	83%	11	27%	45%	4.55	5.8	33	83	$13
1st Half	281	37	7	24	12	247	261	317	381	699	0	636	9	72	32	0.36	56	25	19	102	110	0%	117	19%	82%	2	50%	50%	4.18	1.4	24	60	$16
2nd Half	127	15	6	14	1	274	277	325	471	796	333	879	7	76	32	0.32	50	23	27	128	97	24%	101	3%	100%	9	22%	44%	5.42	5.1	54	135	$6
14 Proj	224	26	6	21	7	251	249	321	383	704	375	748	9	74	32	0.36	52	21	27	95	95	13%	106	15%	80%				4.17	1.0	22	56	$7

Bonifacio,Emilio

Bonifacio,Emilio			Health	C	LIMA Plan	C
Age 29	Bats B	Pos 2B LF	PT/Exp	C	Rand Var	0
Ht 5' 11"	Wt 205		Consist	B	MM	1503

Turned year around with better 2H patience and h% gains. Plus Spd, running game and positional versatility are his strengths, which get neutralized by poor ct%, zero power, and sub-par infield defense. When he plays, he runs, so the only real variable is his role.

Yr Tm	AB	R	HR	RBI	SB	BA	xBA	OBP	SLG	OPS	vL	vR	bb%	ct%	h%	Eye	G	L	F	PX	xPX	hr/f	Spd	SBO	SB%	#Wk	DOM	DIS	RC/G	RAR	BPV	BPX	R$
09 FLA	461	72	1	27	21	252	237	303	308	611	704	571	7	79	32	0.36	53	19	28	37	23	1%	159	23%	70%	27	19%	67%	3.15	-7.9	11	22	$10
10 FLA *	344	43	0	18	18	244	239	303	310	613	827	586	8	76	32	0.35	52	22	26	51	52	0%	164	23%	79%	20	25%	55%	3.25	-4.2	10	22	$6
11 FLA	565	78	5	36	40	296	259	360	393	753	863	714	9	77	38	0.46	53	24	23	73	53	5%	146	27%	78%	27	22%	33%	5.24	24.2	32	71	$26
12 MIA	244	30	1	11	30	258	225	330	316	645	503	714	9	79	32	0.48	58	17	26	33	56	2%	175	41%	91%	12	17%	58%	4.09	2.6	14	35	$11
13 2 AL	420	54	3	31	28	243	241	295	331	625	563	651	7	75	32	0.29	53	20	27	72	44	4%	127	35%	78%	26	19%	46%	3.33	-5.0	13	33	$14
1st Half	207	25	2	13	11	203	238	233	304	537	420	584	4	75	26	0.16	52	17	31	85	55	4%	111	41%	79%	14	29%	43%	2.29	-9.3	12	30	$7
2nd Half	213	29	1	18	17	282	244	349	357	706	690	714	9	76	37	0.42	55	23	22	60	34	3%	134	31%	77%	12	8%	50%	4.51	5.1	11	28	$20
14 Proj	387	50	2	33	31	248	239	309	327	637	596	653	8	77	32	0.37	55	20	25	59	47	3%	141	35%	82%				3.60	-1.1	17	43	$16

Borbon,Julio

Borbon,Julio			Health	A	LIMA Plan	D
Age 28	Bats L	Pos CF	PT/Exp	D	Rand Var	+3
Ht 6' 0"	Wt 195		Consist	A	MM	1511

1-3-.200 with 7 SB in 105 AB at CHC. Seemed to trade contact for patience with disastrous results. And despite his running game uptick, the Spd trend doesn't look great. Without power or a plus glove, his 2010 promise is nearly gone. A SB flyer at best, he'll need another's injury and a ct% rebound to open a door to playing time.

Yr Tm	AB	R	HR	RBI	SB	BA	xBA	OBP	SLG	OPS	vL	vR	bb%	ct%	h%	Eye	G	L	F	PX	xPX	hr/f	Spd	SBO	SB%	#Wk	DOM	DIS	RC/G	RAR	BPV	BPX	R$
09 TEX *	564	90	6	50	40	297	271	347	384	731	250	848	7	87	33	0.60	54	19	27	49	54	13%	189	29%	78%	10	30%	50%	4.90	12.8	61	124	$28
10 TEX	438	60	3	42	15	276	241	309	340	649	609	660	4	87	31	0.32	56	13	31	40	32	3%	145	18%	68%	27	22%	44%	3.60	-6.2	32	70	$13
11 TEX *	224	28	0	20	17	255	274	294	352	646	733	612	5	84	30	0.36	53	23	24	63	49	0%	160	44%	72%	7	43%	43%	3.44	-4.4	49	109	$6
12 aaa	533	52	8	37	13	253	245	285	354	639			4	85	29	0.31				62			119	18%	58%				3.29		36	90	$9
13 2 TM *	178	18	1	4	11	203	231	287	271	558	594	541	10	77	26	0.51	53	19	28	54	62	5%	126	27%	83%	17	29%	41%	2.64	-8.2	13	33	$0
1st Half	65	8	1	3	4	200	208	278	262	539	579	514	10	78	24	0.50	59	11	30	41	42	8%	106	28%	80%	13	31%	38%	2.44	-3.6	0	0	$1
2nd Half	113	10	0	1	7	205	254	292	277	568	633	576	11	77	27	0.52	43	32	25	62	92	0%	128	26%	84%	4	25%	50%	2.76	-5.1	18	45	$0
14 Proj	110	12	1	6	6	231	249	295	311	606	624	599	8	81	28	0.45	52	22	27	56	58	3%	127	27%	76%				3.04	-3.8	25	62	$2

Bourjos,Peter

Bourjos,Peter			Health	F	LIMA Plan	C
Age 27	Bats R	Pos CF	PT/Exp	D	Rand Var	-2
Ht 6' 1"	Wt 185		Consist	C	MM	2503

3-12-.274 in 175 AB at LAA. Produced until 1H injuries—hamstring, thumb, wrist—and Sept. surgery torpedoed his season. Contact, bb% remain sub-par, but were in line with history prior to physical woes. Power/speed combo now MIA for two years, but still owns speed and defense. He's risky, but... UP: 10 HR, 20 SB.

Yr Tm	AB	R	HR	RBI	SB	BA	xBA	OBP	SLG	OPS	vL	vR	bb%	ct%	h%	Eye	G	L	F	PX	xPX	hr/f	Spd	SBO	SB%	#Wk	DOM	DIS	RC/G	RAR	BPV	BPX	R$
09 aa	437	65	5	46	29	269	253	335	392	726			9	82	32	0.54				72			151	32%	69%				4.42		50	102	$17
10 LAA *	595	77	15	50	29	242	237	269	382	651	480	679	4	78	29	0.17	51	10	39	86	96	12%	195	30%	77%	10	60%	20%	3.43	-14.4	50	109	$17
11 LAA	502	72	12	43	22	271	252	327	438	765	840	725	6	75	34	0.26	47	17	36	117	88	9%	191	26%	71%	26	38%	27%	4.70	6.8	66	147	$18
12 LAA *	197	30	3	21	3	223	214	285	325	610	606	607	8	74	29	0.33	52	13	35	73	64	7%	138	8%	75%	25	8%	64%	3.04	-7.1	13	33	$1
13 LAA *	223	34	4	16	6	247	222	286	355	641	608	740	5	70	33	0.18	59	14	27	77	65	9%	183	11%	100%	12	17%	50%	3.58	-4.2	10	25	$4
1st Half	143	23	4	12	4	316	239	350	439	789	676	907	5	75	40	0.21	58	15	27	78	65	12%	191	9%	100%	8	25%	25%	5.92	6.7	33	83	$9
2nd Half	80	10	1	4	2	124	190	173	205	377	250	321	6	61	19	0.15	62	10	28	74	63	0%	123	20%	100%	4	0%	100%	1.10	-8.4	-46	-115	-$6
14 Proj	391	61	6	42	15	256	224	317	369	686	699	681	7	73	34	0.28	52	15	33	82	71	7%	166	19%	78%				3.92	-2.9	17	43	$14

Bourn,Michael

Bourn,Michael			Health	B	LIMA Plan	B
Age 31	Bats L	Pos CF	PT/Exp	A	Rand Var	-1
Ht 5' 11"	Wt 180		Consist	B	MM	1515

SB% decline, rather than move to the AL, caused SBO dip. With ct% and Eye at historical lows, little reason for optimism about a BA recovery. More 50+ SB years look unlikely, but this isn't a skills free-fall just yet. With health and Spd intact, count on a mild rebound.

Yr Tm	AB	R	HR	RBI	SB	BA	xBA	OBP	SLG	OPS	vL	vR	bb%	ct%	h%	Eye	G	L	F	PX	xPX	hr/f	Spd	SBO	SB%	#Wk	DOM	DIS	RC/G	RAR	BPV	BPX	R$
09 HOU	606	97	3	35	61	285	266	354	384	738	723	742	9	77	37	0.45	58	21	21	68	49	3%	179	38%	84%	27	26%	37%	5.11	15.3	36	73	$32
10 HOU	535	84	2	38	52	265	260	341	346	686	555	723	10	80	33	0.54	59	17	23	61	54	2%	145	38%	81%	25	32%	44%	4.28	0.6	33	72	$25
11 2 NL	656	94	2	50	61	294	265	349	386	734	645	772	7	79	37	0.38	51	27	23	70	56	2%	149	38%	81%	27	33%	41%	5.01	14.5	32	71	$35
12 ATL	624	96	9	57	42	274	251	348	391	739	728	745	10	75	35	0.45	54	22	25	80	86	8%	148	28%	76%	26	38%	42%	4.80	10.3	31	78	$28
13 CLE	525	75	6	50	23	263	243	316	360	676	655	685	7	75	34	0.30	57	20	24	72	61	7%	156	24%	66%	25	28%	56%	3.79	-7.0	20	50	$19
1st Half	231	33	2	15	11	299	240	344	385	729	641	775	6	74	40	0.27	61	17	22	73	55	6%	150	23%	69%	12	25%	67%	4.70	3.5	14	35	$19
2nd Half	294	42	4	35	12	235	244	292	340	633	667	618	8	76	30	0.33	53	21	25	71	65	7%	153	25%	63%	13	31%	46%	3.17	-9.1	22	55	$19
14 Proj	546	80	6	49	34	270	250	331	372	703	676	715	8	76	35	0.37	55	21	24	74	66	6%	157	29%	74%				4.27	1.6	25	63	$24

Bradley,Jackie

Bradley,Jackie			Health	A	LIMA Plan	D+
Age 24	Bats L	Pos CF	PT/Exp	F	Rand Var	+2
Ht 5' 10"	Wt 195		Consist	B	MM	4323

3-10-.198 in 95 AB at BOS. Entered 2013 as a work-in-progress with broad skill set apart from just-average pop. 2013 line suggests he traded off contact and patience for power. Running game has yet to materialize, and the swing needs to add loft. But his handedness and athleticism suggest he could be useful now.

Yr Tm	AB	R	HR	RBI	SB	BA	xBA	OBP	SLG	OPS	vL	vR	bb%	ct%	h%	Eye	G	L	F	PX	xPX	hr/f	Spd	SBO	SB%	#Wk	DOM	DIS	RC/G	RAR	BPV	BPX	R$
09																																	
10																																	
11																																	
12 aa	229	31	5	24	7	262	255	346	414	760			11	77	32	0.56				110			97	15%	68%				4.86		52	130	$5
13 BOS *	415	62	10	37	7	240	267	308	401	710	327	722	9	73	30	0.37	63	16	22	129	79	21%	107	16%	49%	11	36%	45%	3.92	-3.9	47	118	$8
1st Half	213	30	4	20	4	252	281	322	417	739	248	679	9	76	32	0.43	60	17	23	134	71	13%	96	15%	55%	5	40%	40%	4.40	1.5	60	150	$9
2nd Half	202	32	6	17	3	226	253	294	385	678	542	759	9	70	29	0.32	66	14	21	124	89	33%	115	16%	43%	6	33%	50%	3.46	-4.5	33	83	$7
14 Proj	252	37	6	24	8	256	262	342	416	758	599	806	10	74	32	0.43	51	19	30	124	82	11%	109	17%	66%				4.58	3.0	51	127	$8

JOCK THOMPSON

Brantley,Michael

Age	27	Bats	L	Pos	LF	Health	A	LIMA Plan	A
Ht	6' 2"	Wt	200			PT/Exp	A	Rand Var	-1
						Consist	A	MM	1335

Reliability is nice, but his value depends on the color of the traffic light. Even with Spd a tick above average, he doesn't run enough for high SB totals. Turned some doubles into HRs, but xPX suggests that won't last. Strong ct% and LD% assure a nice BA, but OPS vs LHP (just two career HR) say a platoon could be in his future.

Yr	Tm	AB	R	HR	RBI	SB	BA	xBA	OBP	SLG	OPS	vL	vR	bb%	ct%	h%	Eye	G	L	F	PX	xPX	hr/f	Spd	SBO	SB%	#Wk	DOM	DIS	RC/G	RAR	BPV	BPX	R$
09	CLE *	569	76	5	41	42	254	278	323	323	646	1072	591	9	87	28	0.80	47	26	27	47	22	0%	120	30%	82%	6	0%	33%	3.74	-3.9	43	88	$19
10	CLE *	570	79	6	44	20	260	263	318	342	659	467	665	8	88	29	0.69	48	20	32	53	57	4%	114	17%	72%	17	41%	29%	3.73	-4.1	45	98	$15
11	CLE	451	63	7	46	13	266	264	318	384	702	525	782	7	83	31	0.45	49	20	31	82	82	6%	111	15%	72%	22	45%	9%	4.20	2.9	47	104	$13
12	CLE	552	63	6	60	12	288	286	348	402	750	680	785	9	90	31	0.95	49	23	29	75	76	4%	108	13%	57%	27	63%	0%	4.87	14.0	71	178	$17
13	CLE	556	66	10	73	17	284	277	332	396	728	664	757	7	88	31	0.60	47	23	30	72	76	7%	108	13%	81%	27	56%	19%	4.74	11.9	57	143	$23
1st Half		284	36	5	39	8	275	265	322	373	696	577	758	7	87	30	0.54	51	20	28	63	65	7%	104	12%	80%	14	50%	14%	4.27	2.1	45	113	$21
2nd Half		272	30	5	34	9	294	287	342	419	762	774	757	7	89	32	0.67	42	26	31	80	88	7%	112	14%	82%	13	62%	23%	5.25	9.3	69	173	$24
14	**Proj**	**550**	**67**	**8**	**63**	**16**	**281**	**276**	**335**	**390**	**725**	**665**	**751**	**8**	**88**	**31**	**0.67**	**47**	**23**	**30**	**73**	**75**	**6%**	**111**	**13%**	**76%**				**4.65**	**9.9**	**57**	**142**	**$18**

Brantly,Rob

Age	24	Bats	L	Pos	CA	Health	A	LIMA Plan	D+
Ht	6' 1"	Wt	195			PT/Exp	F	Rand Var	0
						Consist	F	MM	1013

1-18-.211 in 223 AB at MIA. Steps back in ct%, xPX, and hr/f hurt; low h% didn't help either. On the bright side, he still posted the "best" BA among five Marlins catchers. That and solid defensive skills should get him another chance, but for now, little reason to have him on your radar.

Yr	Tm	AB	R	HR	RBI	SB	BA	xBA	OBP	SLG	OPS	vL	vR	bb%	ct%	h%	Eye	G	L	F	PX	xPX	hr/f	Spd	SBO	SB%	#Wk	DOM	DIS	RC/G	RAR	BPV	BPX	R$
09																																		
10																																		
11																																		
12	MIA *	462	41	7	40	1	270	260	314	382	696	523	908	6	83	31	0.39	41	24	35	80	103	10%	90	5%	19%	8	63%	0%	4.03	4.5	38	95	$7
13	MIA *	293	18	2	20	0	199	210	245	257	502	239	583	6	79	25	0.28	49	19	32	49	57	2%	80	0%	0%	22	27%	59%	2.01	-15.5	-8	-20	-$5
1st Half		164	7	0	15	0	238	201	294	287	580	276	645	7	79	30	0.37	47	20	34	47	56	0%	81	0%	0%	14	29%	57%	2.82	-4.4	-7	-18	-$2
2nd Half		129	11	2	5	0	150	220	179	220	400	111	408	3	79	18	0.17	55	18	28	51	60	9%	100	0%	0%	8	25%	63%	1.19	-10.8	-6	-15	-$8
14	**Proj**	**365**	**28**	**7**	**26**	**0**	**230**	**242**	**272**	**337**	**609**	**332**	**666**	**5**	**80**	**27**	**0.28**	**47**	**21**	**32**	**78**	**76**	**7%**	**85**	**2%**	**20%**				**2.98**	**-8.1**	**5**	**12**	**$2**

Braun,Ryan

Age	30	Bats	R	Pos	LF	Health	A	LIMA Plan	C
Ht	6' 2"	Wt	205			PT/Exp	B	Rand Var	-2
						Consist	C	MM	4445

Suspension got all the attention, but thumb and neck injuries were already affecting his output. Rebounds in ct%, FB% and hr/f should help numbers recover, but that's a lot of "should". The $64k question: was the down year due to injury or lack of juice? UP: 2012. DN: Potentially below even the lowest market price.

Yr	Tm	AB	R	HR	RBI	SB	BA	xBA	OBP	SLG	OPS	vL	vR	bb%	ct%	h%	Eye	G	L	F	PX	xPX	hr/f	Spd	SBO	SB%	#Wk	DOM	DIS	RC/G	RAR	BPV	BPX	R$
09	MIL	635	113	32	114	20	320	303	386	551	937	1198	875	8	81	35	0.47	47	20	34	140	117	18%	128	14%	77%	27	63%	15%	7.71	62.8	93	190	$38
10	MIL	619	101	25	103	14	304	295	365	501	866	786	893	8	83	33	0.53	48	17	35	131	112	14%	105	10%	82%	27	67%	4%	6.66	44.3	87	189	$32
11	MIL	563	109	33	111	33	332	314	397	597	994	1049	979	9	83	35	0.62	42	21	37	165	154	19%	119	23%	85%	26	81%	4%	9.10	75.5	122	271	$47
12	MIL	598	108	41	112	30	319	296	391	595	987	1209	915	10	79	35	0.49	44	18	38	170	153	23%	111	21%	81%	27	74%	15%	8.57	73.3	105	263	$45
13	MIL	225	30	9	38	4	298	268	372	498	869	1053	777	11	75	36	0.48	52	16	32	142	150	16%	123	13%	44%	14	43%	14%	6.31	14.4	74	185	$10
1st Half		214	30	9	36	4	304	273	382	509	891	1069	798	11	76	37	0.52	53	16	31	143	146	18%	126	13%	44%	11	55%	9%	6.65	15.9	80	200	$11
2nd Half		11	0	0	2	0	182	168	182	273	455	667	375	0	64	29	0.00	29	14	57	108	235	0%	89	0%	0%	3	0%	33%	1.55	-0.9	-30	-75	-$11
14	**Proj**	**565**	**95**	**29**	**92**	**21**	**301**	**288**	**376**	**533**	**909**	**1029**	**867**	**10**	**78**	**34**	**0.53**	**47**	**18**	**35**	**154**	**141**	**18%**	**121**	**17%**	**73%**				**7.14**	**49.3**	**93**	**233**	**$36**

Brown,Andrew

Age	29	Bats	R	Pos	RF	Health	A	LIMA Plan	D+
Ht	6' 0"	Wt	185			PT/Exp	D	Rand Var	-1
						Consist	B	MM	4201

7-24-.227 in 150 AB at NYM. Power is his game, but 2H (PX, hr/f levels) more realistic than his first. That isn't the only red flag: he hits too many ground balls for big HR totals, and low ct% limits BA upside. At 29, he's no spring chicken; his future chances will be few.

Yr	Tm	AB	R	HR	RBI	SB	BA	xBA	OBP	SLG	OPS	vL	vR	bb%	ct%	h%	Eye	G	L	F	PX	xPX	hr/f	Spd	SBO	SB%	#Wk	DOM	DIS	RC/G	RAR	BPV	BPX	R$
09	aa	263	30	9	31	1	235	253	297	381	677			8	79	27	0.41				89			103	1%	100%				3.78		34	69	$2
10	aa	361	46	14	45	1	231	235	290	393	683			8	68	30	0.25				123			99	4%	23%				3.68		15	33	$5
11	STL *	381	45	12	51	3	213	233	286	343	629	417	400	9	64	30	0.28	50	29	21	102	91	0%	106	8%	35%	3	33%	67%	3.03	-12.3	-9	-20	$3
12	COL *	502	59	21	66	4	240	253	286	444	730	775	701	6	70	30	0.21	45	19	36	151	107	17%	107	7%	53%	10	50%	40%	4.17	1.6	46	115	$10
13	NYM *	303	38	11	47	1	233	235	293	411	704	709	666	8	70	30	0.28	46	15	39	133	124	17%	116	1%	100%	17	53%	35%	4.02	-0.3	38	95	$5
1st Half		182	27	7	27	0	233	239	291	436	728	889	333	8	69	30	0.26	50	10	40	151	172	38%	119	0%	0%	5	80%	20%	4.23	1.2	50	125	$6
2nd Half		121	11	4	20	1	231	217	295	372	667	633	695	8	71	29	0.31	45	16	38	105	113	12%	94	3%	100%	12	42%	42%	3.69	-1.2	15	38	$3
14	**Proj**	**213**	**25**	**9**	**31**	**1**	**231**	**236**	**288**	**412**	**700**	**749**	**651**	**8**	**70**	**29**	**0.27**	**46**	**16**	**38**	**135**	**125**	**16%**	**110**	**4%**	**62%**				**3.92**	**-3.4**	**25**	**62**	**$5**

Brown,Domonic

Age	26	Bats	L	Pos	LF	Health	A	LIMA Plan	A
Ht	6' 5"	Wt	205			PT/Exp	C	Rand Var	0
						Consist	C	MM	3325

Regular playing time finally allowed this post-hype prospect to live up to the hype. But don't get carried away—xPX and second half hr/f say that this power level is unlikely to hold, and that will take a bite out of his BA. While some will bet on further growth, put your money on regression.

Yr	Tm	AB	R	HR	RBI	SB	BA	xBA	OBP	SLG	OPS	vL	vR	bb%	ct%	h%	Eye	G	L	F	PX	xPX	hr/f	Spd	SBO	SB%	#Wk	DOM	DIS	RC/G	RAR	BPV	BPX	R$
09	aa	147	17	3	17	7	258	247	311	410	721			7	72	34	0.28				107			121	22%	86%				4.50		28	57	$3
10	PHI *	405	60	18	67	16	279	274	335	485	820	148	732	8	74	34	0.32	41	22	37	145	159	13%	114	24%	64%	9	33%	44%	5.47	10.2	63	137	$19
11	PHI *	322	46	7	31	13	238	242	336	362	698	705	729	13	77	29	0.66	47	18	35	90	90	9%	116	18%	70%	13	46%	31%	4.03	-5.6	44	98	$7
12	PHI *	407	48	9	49	3	243	257	303	384	687	621	746	8	80	28	0.42	46	21	33	95	90	10%	92	10%	32%	10	50%	30%	3.68	-11.4	40	100	$6
13	PHI	496	65	27	83	8	272	288	324	494	818	724	857	7	80	29	0.40	42	23	35	137	112	19%	111	9%	73%	26	54%	15%	5.58	13.9	81	203	$22
1st Half		303	43	21	57	8	274	302	321	545	866	845	873	6	79	28	0.33	42	23	35	166	121	25%	112	13%	89%	14	64%	0%	6.21	15.3	98	245	$30
2nd Half		193	22	6	26	0	269	262	332	415	746	577	830	9	82	30	0.53	43	22	35	93	100	11%	112	4%	0%	12	42%	33%	4.60	0.8	57	143	$9
14	**Proj**	**544**	**69**	**22**	**74**	**9**	**261**	**270**	**323**	**442**	**764**	**636**	**812**	**9**	**79**	**29**	**0.45**	**44**	**21**	**35**	**118**	**106**	**14%**	**109**	**9%**	**70%**				**4.90**	**14.0**	**58**	**144**	**$19**

Bruce,Jay

Age	27	Bats	L	Pos	RF	Health	A	LIMA Plan	B+
Ht	6' 3"	Wt	215			PT/Exp	A	Rand Var	0
						Consist	A	MM	5225

Consistency, thy name is Bruce. Don't confuse his rising value with rising skills; increased playing time played a part. The good news is his health and peak age, but his Eye and FB% are eroding a bit. Pay for the power, but another year like the last three is more likely than the next step up.

Yr	Tm	AB	R	HR	RBI	SB	BA	xBA	OBP	SLG	OPS	vL	vR	bb%	ct%	h%	Eye	G	L	F	PX	xPX	hr/f	Spd	SBO	SB%	#Wk	DOM	DIS	RC/G	RAR	BPV	BPX	R$
09	CIN	345	47	22	58	3	223	269	303	470	773	643	825	10	78	22	0.51	39	13	49	147	150	17%	102	8%	50%	18	61%	22%	4.50	-1.0	83	169	$7
10	CIN	509	80	25	70	5	281	261	353	493	846	899	821	10	73	34	0.43	36	20	44	145	139	15%	133	6%	56%	26	54%	35%	6.08	21.3	71	154	$20
11	CIN	585	84	32	97	8	256	251	341	474	814	804	818	11	73	30	0.45	36	17	47	151	150	16%	96	9%	53%	27	52%	26%	5.30	11.9	65	144	$22
12	CIN	560	89	34	99	9	252	270	327	514	841	754	879	10	72	29	0.40	35	20	44	178	162	19%	94	9%	75%	27	63%	26%	5.69	17.9	82	205	$22
13	CIN	626	89	30	109	7	262	264	329	478	807	734	841	9	70	33	0.34	37	24	39	165	132	17%	85	7%	70%	27	52%	30%	5.40	14.4	60	150	$25
1st Half		331	44	18	56	2	278	278	327	520	846	848	841	7	70	34	0.24	35	26	38	183	133	20%	100	5%	50%	14	50%	36%	5.88	13.5	73	183	$27
2nd Half		295	45	12	53	5	244	248	332	431	763	603	839	12	71	31	0.45	38	21	41	145	131	14%	75	8%	83%	13	54%	23%	4.86	3.7	46	115	$23
14	**Proj**	**598**	**89**	**31**	**103**	**8**	**255**	**261**	**332**	**480**	**811**	**736**	**845**	**10**	**72**	**31**	**0.40**	**37**	**21**	**43**	**163**	**143**	**17%**	**91**	**8%**	**68%**				**5.38**	**16.4**	**66**	**164**	**$24**

Buck,John

Age	33	Bats	R	Pos	CA	Health	A	LIMA Plan	D
Ht	6' 3"	Wt	230			PT/Exp	C	Rand Var	+1
						Consist	A	MM	2001

Ah, small sample sizes. Nine HR, 25 RBI with a 200 PX in April; the rest of the year, not so much. When your plate approach melds extreme hacking with only average power, you can expect to flirt with the Mendoza line repeatedly. Experienced backup catchers will always find a home, but he's invisible outside of deep leagues.

Yr	Tm	AB	R	HR	RBI	SB	BA	xBA	OBP	SLG	OPS	vL	vR	bb%	ct%	h%	Eye	G	L	F	PX	xPX	hr/f	Spd	SBO	SB%	#Wk	DOM	DIS	RC/G	RAR	BPV	BPX	R$
09	KC *	213	18	9	39	1	242	259	286	472	758	664	822	6	70	30	0.21	37	18	45	159	120	14%	101	5%	50%	22	36%	50%	4.47	4.9	52	106	$3
10	TOR	409	53	20	66	0	281	254	314	489	802	1116	718	4	73	34	0.14	39	16	45	151	138	15%	82	0%	0%	25	36%	48%	5.35	19.0	46	100	$14
11	FLA	466	41	16	57	0	227	224	316	367	683	586	716	10	75	27	0.47	41	18	41	95	133	11%	74	1%	0%	27	41%	41%	3.69	0.0	22	49	$5
12	MIA	343	29	12	41	0	192	217	297	347	644	564	680	13	70	24	0.48	43	17	40	111	123	13%	66	0%	0%	27	30%	56%	3.21	-5.2	16	40	-$1
13	2 NL	392	39	15	62	2	219	228	285	362	648	617	658	7	73	26	0.28	44	19	37	98	128	14%	76	3%	67%	27	33%	48%	3.22	-5.7	11	28	$5
1st Half		250	32	13	39	2	208	227	256	388	644	638	662	6	72	23	0.23	40	16	44	120	152	16%	83	6%	67%	14	50%	43%	3.17	-4.2	23	58	$9
2nd Half		142	7	2	23	0	239	218	303	317	620	539	652	8	76	30	0.38	50	24	26	59	87	7%	72	0%	0%	13	15%	54%	3.22	-2.1	-8	-20	$0
14	**Proj**	**224**	**19**	**7**	**32**	**0**	**222**	**224**	**299**	**358**	**657**	**603**	**675**	**9**	**73**	**27**	**0.36**	**44**	**19**	**37**	**97**	**120**	**12%**	**76**	**0%**	**0%**				**3.39**	**-2.2**	**-2**	**-5**	**$3**

DAVE ADLER

Butler,Billy

Age	28	Bats	R	Pos	DH		
Ht	6' 1"	Wt	240				
Health	A	PT/Exp	A	Consist	C		
LIMA Plan	B	Rand Var	-2	MM	3025		

A power dip was expected, but not quite to this extent. Lack of punch shows up in xBA as well, suggesting he's no longer a lock in that category. Lost 1B eligibility in many leagues (7 games there in 2013). Peak age means he'll likely rebound some, but not to 2012 levels. That may have been an early career year.

Yr	Tm	AB	R	HR	RBI	SB	BA	xBA	OBP	SLG	OPS	vL	vR	bb%	ct%	h%	Eye	G	L	F	PX	xPX	hr/f	Spd	SBO	SB%	#Wk	DOM	DIS	RC/G	RAR	BPV	BPX	R$
09	KC	608	78	21	93	1	301	291	362	492	853	966	805	9	83	33	0.56	47	18	34	126	117	12%	65	1%	100%	27	56%	19%	6.50	33.4	72	147	$21
10	KC	595	77	15	78	0	318	278	388	469	857	727	888	10	87	35	0.88	48	18	34	104	112	8%	65	0%	0%	27	70%	7%	6.81	36.8	73	159	$24
11	KC	597	74	19	95	2	291	277	361	461	822	917	790	10	84	32	0.69	46	19	36	117	131	10%	57	2%	67%	27	67%	7%	5.99	24.7	69	153	$23
12	KC	614	72	29	107	2	313	288	373	510	882	1042	827	8	82	34	0.49	47	24	29	120	118	20%	57	2%	67%	27	52%	26%	6.94	40.6	59	148	$29
13	KC	582	62	15	82	0	289	251	374	412	787	797	783	12	82	33	0.77	53	20	26	84	92	12%	48	0%	0%	27	44%	37%	5.52	16.6	37	93	$19
1st Half		269	26	6	44	0	283	244	385	409	794	828	786	14	80	33	0.85	51	20	29	93	107	10%	48	0%	0%	14	43%	36%	5.60	8.3	41	103	$15
2nd Half		313	36	9	38	0	294	257	363	415	778	773	780	10	84	33	0.69	55	21	24	76	80	14%	58	0%	0%	13	46%	38%	5.45	8.2	37	93	$22
14	**Proj**	**597**	**68**	**20**	**90**	**1**	**298**	**270**	**371**	**452**	**822**	**882**	**802**	**10**	**83**	**33**	**0.67**	**50**	**21**	**29**	**102**	**106**	**14%**	**52**	**1%**	**68%**				**6.05**	**25.5**	**44**	**111**	**$22**

Byrd,Marlon

Age	36	Bats	R	Pos	RF		
Ht	6' 0"	Wt	215				
Health	B	PT/Exp	C	Consist	F		
LIMA Plan	B	Rand Var	-5	MM	3025		

Sacrificed ct% for more power, and it worked, as he posted career high power numbers across the board. However, given his age and mediocre skills history, the swing-from-the-heels approach can't be sustainable. Let someone else pay for anything resembling a repeat, because odds are it ain't happening.

Yr	Tm	AB	R	HR	RBI	SB	BA	xBA	OBP	SLG	OPS	vL	vR	bb%	ct%	h%	Eye	G	L	F	PX	xPX	hr/f	Spd	SBO	SB%	#Wk	DOM	DIS	RC/G	RAR	BPV	BPX	R$
09	TEX	547	66	20	89	8	283	285	329	479	808	744	835	6	82	31	0.33	41	19	41	127	116	11%	83	10%	67%	26	46%	12%	5.42	12.6	68	139	$19
10	CHC	580	84	12	66	5	293	277	346	429	775	916	717	5	83	34	0.32	52	17	30	97	90	8%	97	4%	83%	27	44%	30%	5.11	8.1	51	111	$19
11	CHC	446	51	9	35	3	276	266	324	395	719	649	740	5	83	32	0.32	50	22	28	82	68	9%	105	4%	60%	22	41%	27%	4.32	-3.6	40	89	$10
12	2 TM	143	10	1	9	0	210	224	243	245	488	761	348	3	78	26	0.16	50	26	25	24	57	4%	90	9%	0%	10	0%	70%	1.66	-13.3	-31	-78	-$3
13	2 NL	532	75	24	88	2	291	272	336	511	847	959	797	6	73	36	0.22	39	24	37	159	153	16%	127	5%	33%	26	65%	19%	5.91	19.4	70	175	$24
1st Half		218	29	12	40	1	257	248	305	486	791	800	793	6	67	33	0.21	41	16	43	174	150	18%	109	7%	33%	14	50%	29%	4.91	2.9	57	143	$15
2nd Half		314	46	12	48	1	315	290	348	529	877	1157	799	5	77	38	0.22	38	28	33	150	156	15%	128	4%	33%	12	83%	8%	6.70	19.2	77	193	$30
14	**Proj**	**466**	**55**	**13**	**58**	**2**	**269**	**257**	**311**	**416**	**727**	**849**	**674**	**5**	**77**	**33**	**0.22**	**44**	**23**	**33**	**104**	**112**	**11%**	**112**	**6%**	**29%**				**4.24**	**-2.9**	**20**	**51**	**$13**

Cabrera,Asdrubal

Age	28	Bats	B	Pos	SS		
Ht	6' 0"	Wt	205				
Health	B	PT/Exp	A	Consist	B		
LIMA Plan	A	Rand Var	+1	MM	3225		

Nagging injuries were thought to be to blame for struggles late in 2012, and he tried to play through more of them in 1st half of 2013. Second-half ct%, xPX say he deserved better if not for low h%, and hint at a bounce toward prior BA and HR peaks... UP: 20 HR, .275 BA.

Yr	Tm	AB	R	HR	RBI	SB	BA	xBA	OBP	SLG	OPS	vL	vR	bb%	ct%	h%	Eye	G	L	F	PX	xPX	hr/f	Spd	SBO	SB%	#Wk	DOM	DIS	RC/G	RAR	BPV	BPX	R$
09	CLE	523	81	6	68	17	308	286	361	438	799	762	813	8	83	36	0.49	48	22	30	93	89	5%	109	14%	81%	23	57%	17%	5.89	35.3	57	116	$22
10	CLE	381	39	3	29	6	276	242	326	346	673	647	685	6	84	32	0.42	52	17	31	52	57	3%	96	9%	60%	18	33%	28%	3.82	4.3	22	48	$7
11	CLE	604	87	25	92	17	273	269	332	460	792	777	799	7	80	30	0.37	44	17	39	123	115	13%	96	15%	77%	27	56%	26%	5.20	30.7	64	142	$26
12	CLE	555	70	16	68	9	270	269	338	423	762	796	745	9	82	30	0.53	41	23	36	101	105	10%	67	9%	69%	27	48%	30%	4.88	23.3	49	123	$17
13	CLE	508	66	14	64	9	242	256	299	402	700	639	730	6	78	29	0.31	36	23	41	118	139	9%	92	11%	75%	25	32%	20%	3.92	7.5	47	118	$13
1st Half		224	35	6	26	5	268	264	311	451	762	737	793	6	74	34	0.24	36	26	39	143	106	10%	84	13%	83%	12	33%	33%	4.92	9.4	50	125	$15
2nd Half		284	31	8	38	4	222	249	275	363	638	550	684	7	80	25	0.38	37	21	42	99	161	8%	96	10%	67%	13	31%	8%	3.23	-2.0	45	113	$11
14	**Proj**	**552**	**72**	**16**	**70**	**11**	**261**	**261**	**321**	**416**	**737**	**709**	**751**	**7**	**80**	**30**	**0.38**	**40**	**22**	**38**	**110**	**120**	**9%**	**87**	**11%**	**74%**				**4.50**	**16.6**	**51**	**128**	**$18**

Cabrera,Everth

Age	27	Bats	B	Pos	SS		
Ht	5' 10"	Wt	190				
Health	B	PT/Exp	C	Consist	C		
LIMA Plan	B	Rand Var	-3	MM	1515		

Ran wild on bases again before June hamstring injury and 50-game suspension derailed his season. Improved plate approach was the key development here, as more contact yields more chances to reach base, and thus more chances to run. If he can hold those gains... UP: 60 SB.

Yr	Tm	AB	R	HR	RBI	SB	BA	xBA	OBP	SLG	OPS	vL	vR	bb%	ct%	h%	Eye	G	L	F	PX	xPX	hr/f	Spd	SBO	SB%	#Wk	DOM	DIS	RC/G	RAR	BPV	BPX	R$
09	SD *	404	63	2	31	26	256	259	334	360	693	628	733	10	76	33	0.49	63	15	23	72	57	3%	160	28%	76%	20	30%	25%	4.17	8.0	34	69	$13
10	SD *	243	27	1	24	12	207	229	278	272	550	607	545	9	71	29	0.34	54	22	23	50	70	3%	107	29%	67%	22	18%	45%	2.39	-8.6	-22	-48	$2
11	SD *	254	31	1	9	19	209	264	264	274	538	1000	143	7	78	26	0.34	100	0	0	48	2	0%	153	48%	65%	1	0%	100%	2.20	-10.7	14	31	$2
12	SD *	542	67	2	34	54	249	237	313	321	635	523	698	9	73	34	0.35	61	19	20	61	47	4%	122	37%	93%	21	10%	62%	3.88	5.9	-2	-5	$21
13	SD	381	54	4	31	37	283	273	355	381	736	934	651	10	82	34	0.59	60	21	19	65	49	7%	146	39%	76%	18	39%	33%	4.80	14.5	45	113	$23
1st Half		275	37	4	24	31	305	281	378	418	796	1060	680	10	81	37	0.62	58	24	18	74	54	11%	143	39%	82%	13	38%	31%	6.04	20.0	49	123	$32
2nd Half		106	17	0	7	6	226	248	287	283	570	527	581	8	84	27	0.53	66	12	21	42	39	0%	131	39%	55%	5	40%	40%	2.38	-3.7	26	65	-$1
14	**Proj**	**544**	**75**	**3**	**36**	**44**	**264**	**252**	**330**	**343**	**673**	**700**	**663**	**9**	**79**	**33**	**0.44**	**61**	**18**	**21**	**59**	**50**	**4%**	**141**	**37%**	**74%**				**3.89**	**6.8**	**25**	**62**	**$25**

Cabrera,Melky

Age	29	Bats	B	Pos	LF		
Ht	6' 0"	Wt	200				
Health	C	PT/Exp	B	Consist	F		
LIMA Plan	B+	Rand Var	0	MM	2335		

xPX was always skeptical of his 2011-12 power gains, though 2013 looks like an overcorrection. It may be related to leg issues that plagued him all year, and who knows what role PEDs may or may not have played. Ct% remains consistent, but with power and speed dropping, BA could be next, and that wouldn't leave much.

Yr	Tm	AB	R	HR	RBI	SB	BA	xBA	OBP	SLG	OPS	vL	vR	bb%	ct%	h%	Eye	G	L	F	PX	xPX	hr/f	Spd	SBO	SB%	#Wk	DOM	DIS	RC/G	RAR	BPV	BPX	R$
09	NYY	485	66	13	68	10	274	296	336	416	752	763	747	8	88	29	0.73	50	21	30	87	75	10%	84	9%	83%	27	63%	22%	4.93	13.1	64	131	$15
10	ATL	458	50	4	42	7	255	267	317	354	671	642	685	8	86	29	0.66	49	19	32	71	60	3%	98	6%	88%	26	42%	15%	3.91	-0.9	49	107	$7
11	KC	658	102	18	87	20	305	289	339	470	809	788	818	5	86	34	0.37	47	20	33	108	88	10%	119	18%	67%	27	63%	19%	5.70	31.5	77	171	$33
12	SF	459	84	11	60	13	346	298	390	516	906	1111	826	7	86	38	0.57	52	22	26	99	80	11%	154	12%	72%	20	65%	10%	7.84	46.1	87	218	$28
13	TOR	344	39	3	30	2	279	255	322	360	682	595	717	6	86	32	0.49	46	22	31	57	85	3%	108	4%	50%	15	27%	13%	4.07	0.9	38	95	$7
1st Half		309	34	3	29	2	278	255	324	362	687	599	716	6	86	32	0.49	46	23	32	57	86	4%	108	4%	50%	13	31%	15%	4.08	0.5	37	93	$8
2nd Half		35	5	0	1	0	286	240	324	343	667	571	729	5	89	32	0.50	55	16	29	49	74	0%	105	0%	0%	2	0%	0%	3.97	0.0	38	95	-$6
14	**Proj**	**425**	**59**	**9**	**49**	**7**	**290**	**280**	**335**	**429**	**764**	**760**	**766**	**7**	**86**	**32**	**0.51**	**51**	**20**	**30**	**89**	**79**	**9%**	**121**	**9%**	**67%**				**5.12**	**13.2**	**62**	**155**	**$17**

Cabrera,Miguel

Age	31	Bats	R	Pos	3B		
Ht	6' 4"	Wt	240				
Health	A	PT/Exp	A	Consist	C		
LIMA Plan	C	Rand Var	-3	MM	4155		

Was slowed by groin, abdominal injuries down the stretch (1 HR in Sept), so don't get too worried about the 2H skills dip. In addition to elite skills, he's remained incredibly durable, having amassed at least 148 games, 648 PA for 10 straight years. He remains the ideal low-risk player to build a team around.

Yr	Tm	AB	R	HR	RBI	SB	BA	xBA	OBP	SLG	OPS	vL	vR	bb%	ct%	h%	Eye	G	L	F	PX	xPX	hr/f	Spd	SBO	SB%	#Wk	DOM	DIS	RC/G	RAR	BPV	BPX	R$
09	DET	611	96	34	103	6	324	297	396	547	942	958	937	10	82	35	0.64	43	20	37	133	140	18%	77	4%	75%	27	63%	4%	8.06	66.9	82	167	$32
10	DET	548	111	38	126	3	328	327	420	622	1042	1000	1054	14	83	34	0.94	39	19	42	187	169	20%	66	3%	50%	26	81%	4%	9.83	85.6	130	283	$38
11	DET	572	111	30	105	2	344	317	448	586	1033	990	1047	16	84	37	1.21	44	22	34	158	140	18%	76	1%	67%	27	85%	0%	10.19	92.0	121	269	$39
12	DET	622	109	44	139	4	330	315	393	606	999	913	1027	10	84	34	0.67	42	22	36	161	161	23%	75	3%	80%	27	81%	7%	9.08	84.1	110	275	$42
13	DET	555	103	44	137	3	348	317	442	636	1078	1210	1038	14	83	36	0.96	39	24	37	170	165	25%	74	1%	100%	26	69%	19%	10.96	99.5	120	300	$46
1st Half		316	64	25	82	2	373	329	456	680	1136	1366	1079	13	82	40	0.86	39	25	36	188	164	27%	82	2%	100%	14	79%	7%	12.69	67.7	133	333	$54
2nd Half		239	39	19	55	1	314	301	416	577	994	1046	979	15	84	31	1.11	38	23	39	147	167	24%	66	1%	100%	12	58%	33%	8.97	32.1	106	265	$36
14	**Proj**	**578**	**104**	**37**	**120**	**2**	**327**	**306**	**416**	**578**	**994**	**1017**	**985**	**13**	**84**	**34**	**0.92**	**41**	**22**	**37**	**153**	**160**	**21%**	**73**	**1%**	**77%**				**9.08**	**78.1**	**98**	**246**	**$39**

Cain,Lorenzo

Age	28	Bats	R	Pos	CF RF		
Ht	6' 2"	Wt	205				
Health	D	PT/Exp	C	Consist	B		
LIMA Plan	B	Rand Var	0	MM	2515		

Missed time due to oblique, groin issues during second half, and had dismal Sept after he returned. Improvement in bb% a step in right direction, as getting on base and using his speed is clearest path to fantasy relevance. Stagnant ct%, poor Health grade are all that stands in the way of... UP: 25 SB.

Yr	Tm	AB	R	HR	RBI	SB	BA	xBA	OBP	SLG	OPS	vL	vR	bb%	ct%	h%	Eye	G	L	F	PX	xPX	hr/f	Spd	SBO	SB%	#Wk	DOM	DIS	RC/G	RAR	BPV	BPX	R$
09	aa	145	14	3	12	2	187	224	232	293	525			6	72	24	0.21				77			95	21%	42%				1.94		-8	-16	-$2
10	MIL *	478	61	3	33	27	283	233	343	379	722	668	805	8	77	36	0.40	43	21	37	70	104	2%	182	21%	86%	12	50%	25%	4.81	9.6	37	80	$18
11	KC *	509	62	10	57	11	262	260	301	393	695	167	765	5	77	32	0.24	50	22	28	95	57	0%	148	15%	61%	2	50%	50%	3.96	-4.1	39	87	$13
12	KC *	274	33	8	36	10	256	252	298	407	705	844	681	6	75	31	0.24	47	22	31	101	92	13%	119	16%	100%	12	42%	33%	4.37	1.0	31	78	$8
13	KC	399	54	4	46	14	251	247	310	348	658	617	676	8	77	31	0.37	49	22	29	76	69	4%	125	19%	70%	24	38%	42%	3.61	-7.5	25	63	$11
1st Half		253	33	3	30	9	257	266	314	375	689	577	739	8	76	33	0.34	53	24	23	95	66	7%	117	20%	69%	14	50%	36%	3.97	-1.5	32	80	$14
2nd Half		146	21	1	16	5	240	210	297	301	599	669	553	8	80	29	0.41	44	18	39	44	76	2%	135	17%	71%	10	20%	50%	3.00	-5.2	13	33	$5
14	**Proj**	**453**	**59**	**9**	**54**	**15**	**254**	**244**	**312**	**374**	**686**	**711**	**674**	**8**	**77**	**31**	**0.35**	**47**	**21**	**33**	**85**	**84**	**8%**	**132**	**17%**	**76%**				**3.97**	**-2.7**	**29**	**72**	**$15**

BRIAN RUDD

Calhoun,Kole

Age 26 Bats L Pos RF	Health A	LIMA Plan C	
Ht 5' 10" Wt 190	PT/Exp F	Rand Var 0	
	Consist D	MM 3323	

8-32-.282 in 195 AB at LAA. Opportunity's door cracked open in Aug/Sept—did he kick it down for good? Ability to hit LHP, strong arm aid playing-time prospects. 39% HH%, xPX suggest 2H hr/f not out of line. SBO, minor-league track record indicate more AB might even bring handful of SBs. Watch role. With PT... UP: 20 HR, 15 SB

Yr	Tm	AB	R	HR	RBI	SB	BA	xBA	OBP	SLG	OPS	vL	vR	bb%	ct%	h%	Eye	G	L	F	PX	xPX	hr/f	Spd	SBO	SB%	#Wk	DOM	DIS	RC/G	RAR	BPV	BPX	R$
09																																		
10																																		
11																																		
12	LAA *	433	53	8	48	9	224	253	274	354	628	0	578	6	74	29	0.26	41	29	29	95	150	0%	99	14%	71%	9	0%	33%	3.16	-14.8	15	38	$5
13	LAA *	435	59	15	62	8	272	266	333	438	771	889	782	8	81	31	0.48	41	23	36	105	131	14%	102	11%	64%	10	70%	20%	5.01	9.2	58	145	$16
1st Half		151	18	3	19	4	251	252	300	383	683			7	82	29	0.39				84			121	15%	77%				3.92		47	118	$6
2nd Half		284	40	11	43	4	283	272	350	468	818	889	782	9	81	32	0.53	41	23	36	116	131	14%	97	9%	54%	10	70%	20%	5.66	9.8	65	163	$22
14	Proj	**324**	**42**	**12**	**43**	**8**	**260**	**263**	**312**	**435**	**747**	**851**	**712**	**7**	**78**	**30**	**0.37**	**41**	**23**	**36**	**116**	**118**	**13%**	**97**	**15%**	**68%**				**4.64**	**1.8**	**55**	**138**	**$10**

Callaspo,Alberto

Age 31 Bats B Pos 3B 2B	Health A	LIMA Plan B	
Ht 5' 9" Wt 225	PT/Exp B	Rand Var +1	
	Consist B	MM 1025	

2012-2013 carbon copy seasons highlight his consistency, and with resilient bb% and ct%, xBA suggests there may still be some upside in his BA. Low PX, FB% say 10 HR is his ceiling, and ineffectiveness vs. RHP leaves his PT a bit vulnerable. But multi-position eligibility does have value. As does knowing what you are going to get.

Yr	Tm	AB	R	HR	RBI	SB	BA	xBA	OBP	SLG	OPS	vL	vR	bb%	ct%	h%	Eye	G	L	F	PX	xPX	hr/f	Spd	SBO	SB%	#Wk	DOM	DIS	RC/G	RAR	BPV	BPX	R$
09	KC	576	79	11	73	2	300	283	356	457	813	913	768	8	91	32	1.02	41	17	42	93	93	5%	90	2%	67%	27	74%	0%	5.95	35.1	85	173	$17
10	2 AL	562	61	10	56	5	265	270	302	374	675	576	701	5	93	27	0.74	45	18	38	67	64	5%	74	6%	63%	27	44%	11%	3.89	2.7	58	126	$11
11	LAA	475	54	6	46	8	288	262	366	375	740	730	745	11	90	31	1.21	41	22	37	60	64	4%	69	5%	89%	27	48%	26%	4.99	16.8	52	116	$14
12	LAA	457	55	10	53	4	252	255	331	361	692	833	634	11	87	27	0.95	44	21	36	68	77	7%	56	5%	57%	27	48%	30%	4.05	4.3	43	108	$8
13	2 AL	453	52	10	58	0	258	272	333	369	702	763	672	10	90	27	1.13	40	25	36	70	66	7%	55	1%	0%	25	68%	12%	4.18	6.0	54	135	$9
1st Half		220	28	4	30	0	268	280	340	368	708	651	723	10	92	28	1.41	44	25	32	63	45	6%	58	1%	0%	12	75%	8%	4.28	3.7	59	148	$10
2nd Half		233	24	6	28	0	249	265	332	369	701	855	621	11	87	26	0.97	36	25	39	76	86	8%	60	1%	0%	13	62%	15%	4.09	2.7	51	128	$8
14	Proj	**439**	**51**	**9**	**52**	**2**	**263**	**265**	**337**	**372**	**709**	**784**	**675**	**10**	**89**	**28**	**1.05**	**41**	**23**	**37**	**70**	**72**	**6%**	**60**	**3%**	**54%**				**4.32**	**4.4**	**49**	**122**	**$11**

Campana,Tony

Age 28 Bats L Pos CF	Health A	LIMA Plan F	
Ht 5' 8" Wt 165	PT/Exp D	Rand Var +1	
	Consist B	MM 0501	

0-0-.261-8 SB in 46 AB at ARI. Potential first-ballot Esix Snead Hall of Famer bolstered candidacy by finding even fewer AB on better team. Given ability to pile up SBs with as few as 150-175 PA, can't be ruled out as $1 end-gamer. But ct% won't allow him to be more than that.

Yr	Tm	AB	R	HR	RBI	SB	BA	xBA	OBP	SLG	OPS	vL	vR	bb%	ct%	h%	Eye	G	L	F	PX	xPX	hr/f	Spd	SBO	SB%	#Wk	DOM	DIS	RC/G	RAR	BPV	BPX	R$
09																																		
10	aa	489	55	0	28	34	274	227	318	327	645			6	81	34	0.34				43			125	40%	59%				3.30		10	22	$17
11	CHC *	263	41	1	12	29	264	248	296	321	617	490	628	4	78	34	0.20	67	16	18	46	2	6%	152	46%	90%	20	10%	60%	3.69	-3.0	5	11	$11
12	CHC *	317	43	1	8	42	247	242	291	282	573	554	620	6	73	33	0.23	69	21	9	30	-6	0%	152	61%	79%	22	14%	68%	2.95	-11.1	-22	-55	$14
13	ARI *	397	47	1	17	26	227	228	276	280	557	600	692	6	72	31	0.24	73	13	13	39	-6	0%	190	37%	69%	9	0%	67%	2.50	-19.9	-7	-18	$9
1st Half		233	23	1	13	14	218	192	258	271	529			5	71	31	0.19				43			137	34%	73%	1	0%	100%	2.29		-30	-75	$9
2nd Half		164	24	0	4	13	241	234	301	294	595	600	692	8	75	32	0.34	73	13	13	34	-6	0%	205	41%	64%	8	0%	63%	2.80	-7.1	5	13	$9
14	Proj	**99**	**13**	**0**	**4**	**9**	**245**	**237**	**293**	**295**	**588**	**507**	**608**	**6**	**75**	**33**	**0.26**	**70**	**16**	**14**	**38**		**2%**	**146**	**45%**	**74%**				**2.93**	**-3.8**	**-13**	**-33**	**$4**

Cano,Robinson

Age 31 Bats L Pos 2B	Health A	LIMA Plan C	
Ht 6' 0" Wt 210	PT/Exp A	Rand Var 0	
	Consist B	MM 4255	

In drama-filled year in the Bronx, he chugged quietly into free agency. PX slipped a bit, but xPX marks him as ridiculously consistent. Eye growth suggests he'll age gracefully. If he leaves NYY, HR total may take slight hit (though he did hit more road HR in 2013); otherwise a rock-solid performer for at least another year or two.

Yr	Tm	AB	R	HR	RBI	SB	BA	xBA	OBP	SLG	OPS	vL	vR	bb%	ct%	h%	Eye	G	L	F	PX	xPX	hr/f	Spd	SBO	SB%	#Wk	DOM	DIS	RC/G	RAR	BPV	BPX	R$
09	NYY	637	103	25	85	5	320	317	352	520	871	876	869	4	90	33	0.48	47	20	33	117	90	13%	89	8%	42%	27	67%	7%	6.58	49.2	92	188	$29
10	NYY	626	103	29	109	3	319	310	381	534	914	857	944	8	88	33	0.74	44	19	36	130	125	14%	91	3%	60%	27	70%	7%	7.47	62.7	101	220	$33
11	NYY	623	104	28	118	8	302	318	349	533	882	879	884	6	85	32	0.40	47	22	31	147	116	17%	90	7%	80%	27	67%	11%	6.65	50.1	97	216	$33
12	NYY	627	105	33	94	3	313	324	379	550	929	646	1108	9	85	33	0.64	49	26	26	145	115	24%	80	3%	60%	27	70%	7%	7.57	65.1	99	248	$32
13	NYY	605	81	27	107	7	314	312	383	516	899	788	969	10	86	33	0.76	44	26	30	128	115	17%	76	4%	88%	26	65%	19%	7.34	58.9	90	225	$34
1st Half		307	44	17	48	5	287	295	362	502	863	696	971	10	84	29	0.73	48	20	32	131	104	20%	81	5%	100%	14	64%	21%	6.60	24.9	88	220	$31
2nd Half		298	37	10	59	2	342	332	401	530	931	882	966	9	88	37	0.81	41	32	27	125	126	14%	76	3%	67%	12	67%	17%	8.19	34.7	94	235	$37
14	Proj	**620**	**92**	**28**	**107**	**6**	**315**	**318**	**379**	**530**	**909**	**783**	**985**	**9**	**86**	**33**	**0.68**	**46**	**25**	**29**	**136**	**116**	**18%**	**80**	**4%**	**75%**				**7.39**	**61.8**	**93**	**232**	**$35**

Carp,Mike

Age 28 Bats L Pos LF 1B	Health C	LIMA Plan D+	
Ht 6' 2" Wt 210	PT/Exp D	Rand Var -5	
	Consist F	MM 4121	

Resuscitated career with bearded buddies in BOS. Power has never been in dispute, but 1H hr/f couldn't last. Fewer FB in 2H also fed the HR correction. Take a picture of that .296; given ever-present ct% woes, it won't repeat. And health history suggests part-time role is best. But when he plays, always a threat to go yard.

Yr	Tm	AB	R	HR	RBI	SB	BA	xBA	OBP	SLG	OPS	vL	vR	bb%	ct%	h%	Eye	G	L	F	PX	xPX	hr/f	Spd	SBO	SB%	#Wk	DOM	DIS	RC/G	RAR	BPV	BPX	R$
09	SEA *	467	56	12	52	0	238	238	314	372	686	730	900	10	73	30	0.41	44	20	36	97	95	6%	105	1%	0%	8	63%	25%	3.87	-10.3	22	45	$4
10	SEA *	446	50	19	56	1	207	229	264	377	642	556	496	7	73	24	0.29	31	17	52	117	124	0%	93	3%	24%	4	0%	50%	3.14	-20.5	31	67	$3
11	SEA *	541	61	24	85	4	267	267	314	455	769	884	761	6	73	32	0.25	43	25	32	136	152	18%	77	6%	45%	15	47%	33%	4.83	3.5	39	87	$18
12	SEA *	303	26	6	31	2	191	220	262	292	554	722	631	9	72	24	0.34	50	21	29	75	94	14%	75	8%	31%	16	25%	38%	2.30	-22.4	-10	-25	-$2
13	BOS	216	34	9	43	1	296	273	362	523	885	745	904	9	69	39	0.33	41	24	34	181	140	17%	96	2%	100%	26	50%	35%	6.88	13.6	70	175	$9
1st Half		112	22	8	25	0	313	305	379	652	1031	690	1087	10	68	40	0.33	43	17	40	258	186	26%	107	0%	0%	13	62%	23%	9.16	13.8	131	328	$12
2nd Half		104	12	1	18	1	279	252	342	385	727	844	722	9	70	39	0.32	40	32	28	101	92	5%	85	3%	100%	13	38%	46%	4.72	0.3	7	18	$6
14	Proj	**224**	**28**	**10**	**35**	**1**	**256**	**264**	**327**	**461**	**788**	**755**	**795**	**9**	**71**	**32**	**0.33**	**43**	**23**	**34**	**154**	**121**	**18%**	**88**	**4%**	**55%**				**5.01**	**6.5**	**45**	**112**	**$7**

Carpenter,Matt

Age 28 Bats L Pos 2B 3B	Health A	LIMA Plan B+	
Ht 6' 3" Wt 215	PT/Exp B	Rand Var -4	
	Consist D	MM 3235	

Those who heeded the advice in last year's Forecaster to "take a flyer" were rewarded with strong growth year, and 2B eligibility to boot. Solid plate approach, ct%, LD% should minimize any h%, BA regression. Low FB suggests HR spike not coming. But plenty here to like and invest in.

Yr	Tm	AB	R	HR	RBI	SB	BA	xBA	OBP	SLG	OPS	vL	vR	bb%	ct%	h%	Eye	G	L	F	PX	xPX	hr/f	Spd	SBO	SB%	#Wk	DOM	DIS	RC/G	RAR	BPV	BPX	R$
09																																		
10	aa	396	55	8	39	8	259	242	338	385	723			11	74	33	0.46				97			110	9%	77%				4.50		30	65	$9
11	STL *	449	41	7	48	3	228	178	323	338	661	500	378	12	81	27	0.74	45	0	55	80	2	0%	83	6%	41%	3	33%	67%	3.49	-2.2	39	87	$2
12	STL	296	44	6	46	1	294	268	365	463	828	784	846	10	79	36	0.54	40	24	36	116	114	7%	104	2%	50%	24	58%	21%	6.07	19.9	61	153	$9
13	STL	626	126	11	78	3	318	293	392	481	873	820	897	10	84	36	0.73	39	27	34	116	103	6%	123	3%	50%	27	63%	11%	6.89	54.5	90	225	$30
1st Half		311	60	7	32	1	322	288	388	482	871	823	904	10	85	36	0.72	37	27	36	109	98	7%	139	3%	33%	14	71%	7%	6.90	26.7	90	225	$28
2nd Half		315	66	4	46	2	314	298	388	479	867	817	890	11	84	37	0.75	40	27	32	123	107	5%	105	3%	67%	13	54%	15%	6.89	27.1	89	223	$32
14	Proj	**606**	**101**	**11**	**78**	**4**	**292**	**277**	**370**	**445**	**814**	**767**	**836**	**11**	**81**	**35**	**0.65**	**39**	**26**	**35**	**110**	**108**	**6%**	**112**	**4%**	**55%**				**5.83**	**36.1**	**65**	**163**	**$23**

Carroll,Jamey

Age 40 Bats R Pos 3B	Health A	LIMA Plan D	
Ht 5' 11" Wt 175	PT/Exp C	Rand Var +5	
	Consist C	MM 0321	

As his playing days wind to a close, perhaps a Christmas "Carroll" is in order. S-i-i-lent bat... (Increasingly) ho-o-le-y bat... All is calm (5% SBO)... All hits light (sub-40 PX for third straight year)... No one quakes... at the sight (even with better h% luck). If retirement comes, may it bring you heavenly peace, Jamey.

Yr	Tm	AB	R	HR	RBI	SB	BA	xBA	OBP	SLG	OPS	vL	vR	bb%	ct%	h%	Eye	G	L	F	PX	xPX	hr/f	Spd	SBO	SB%	#Wk	DOM	DIS	RC/G	RAR	BPV	BPX	R$
09	CLE	315	53	2	26	4	276	245	355	340	695	685	698	10	80	34	0.57	46	24	30	44	54	3%	128	6%	67%	21	33%	52%	4.17	4.0	16	33	$6
10	LA	351	48	0	23	12	291	246	379	339	718	733	713	13	82	36	0.80	53	21	26	42	37	0%	136	12%	75%	27	33%	37%	4.69	9.5	29	63	$11
11	LA	452	52	0	17	10	290	260	359	347	706	751	689	9	87	33	0.81	50	24	27	39	28	0%	181	6%	100%	27	52%	22%	4.60	11.0	55	122	$10
12	MIN	470	65	1	40	9	268	265	343	317	660	839	588	10	86	31	0.80	56	24	20	37	17	1%	124	9%	64%	27	37%	19%	3.73	0.0	33	83	$10
13	2 AL	227	26	0	11	2	211	255	267	251	518	648	465	7	83	26	0.44	56	25	19	36	17	0%	102	5%	67%	25	32%	36%	2.16	-11.0	6	15	-$2
1st Half		134	15	0	6	1	216	256	276	246	522	644	492	8	84	26	0.52	63	23	14	27	16	0%	104	3%	100%	13	38%	31%	2.25	-6.0	7	18	-$2
2nd Half		93	11	0	5	1	204	252	253	258	511	652	411	6	81	25	0.33	47	27	26	50	18	0%	95	10%	50%	12	25%	42%	2.02	-4.9	5	13	-$3
14	Proj	**128**	**16**	**0**	**8**	**2**	**243**	**256**	**309**	**292**	**601**	**714**	**551**	**8**	**84**	**29**	**0.57**	**53**	**24**	**22**	**40**	**22**	**0%**	**113**	**8%**	**69%**				**3.02**	**-3.7**	**8**	**21**	**$2**

KRISTOPHER OLSON

Carter,Chris

Age 27	Bats R	Pos 1B LF DH	PT/Exp C	Rand Var -2	
Ht 6' 4"	Wt 245		Consist B	MM 5205	
			Health A	LIMA Plan C	

What's not to like about a guy approaching 30 HR in peak years? There's this little nugget: he was the only hitter in MLB to eclipse even 200 AB with a sub-60% ct%. Excellent power skills and bb% kept him in the lineup, but if these slide at all, or he runs into bad luck with h%... DN: .200 BA, and a spot on the bench.

Yr	Tm	AB	R	HR	RBI	SB	BA	xBA	OBP	SLG	OPS	vL	vR	bb%	ct%	h%	Eye	G	L	F	PX	xPX	hr/f	Spd	SBO	SB%	#Wk	DOM	DIS	RC/G	RAR	BPV	BPX	R$
09	a/a	544	87	20	87	10	278	263	355	463	817			11	73	35	0.44				133			90	11%	59%				5.63		47	96	$20
10	OAK *	535	70	22	70	2	201	213	276	377	653	520	606	9	66	26	0.30	32	14	54	139	70	11%	77	2%	59%	6	33%	67%	3.30	-20.0	18	39	$3
11	OAK *	340	39	11	48	3	204	224	269	352	621	145	448	8	64	28	0.25	17	38	46	123	33	0%	84	6%	74%	6	0%	83%	3.03	-15.6	-2	-4	$2
12	OAK *	494	70	23	75	3	225	228	316	423	739	898	837	12	65	30	0.38	34	20	46	154	126	25%	69	4%	73%	15	47%	27%	4.39	-1.5	29	73	$10
13	HOU	506	64	29	82	2	223	226	320	451	770	782	765	12	58	32	0.33	31	22	47	197	171	21%	80	2%	100%	27	44%	33%	4.72	3.4	40	100	$12
1st Half		263	38	15	40	0	228	227	321	452	774	760	780	12	58	33	0.32	34	23	44	195	159	22%	80	0%	0%	14	57%	36%	4.80	2.4	37	93	$13
2nd Half		243	26	14	42	2	218	226	314	449	763	800	748	12	58	30	0.34	28	22	50	199	183	19%	85	3%	100%	13	31%	31%	4.64	1.1	45	113	$12
14	Proj	**466**	**60**	**26**	**73**	**3**	**222**	**230**	**308**	**443**	**750**	**770**	**739**	**11**	**61**	**30**	**0.32**	**33**	**21**	**46**	**185**	**141**	**20%**	**77**	**3%**	**79%**				**4.48**	**-1.7**	**34**	**86**	**$9**

Casilla,Alexi

Age 29	Bats B	Pos 2B	PT/Exp D	Rand Var +4	
Ht 5' 9"	Wt 170		Consist B	MM 1511	
			Health B	LIMA Plan D	

We'll start with a bit of good news: excellent speed skills remained in place, so SBs could return with h% correction and a team willing to give him a shot. The rest is pretty ugly: regular ABs rarely come to slap hitters with fading ct%, and the rest of his skills are mediocre or worse. The bad far outweighs the good.

Yr	Tm	AB	R	HR	RBI	SB	BA	xBA	OBP	SLG	OPS	vL	vR	bb%	ct%	h%	Eye	G	L	F	PX	xPX	hr/f	Spd	SBO	SB%	#Wk	DOM	DIS	RC/G	RAR	BPV	BPX	R$
09	MIN *	384	42	2	31	18	240	226	296	310	606	488	559	7	84	28	0.49	52	12	36	42	38	0%	157	24%	72%	21	24%	43%	3.08	-7.5	32	65	$6
10	MIN	152	26	1	20	6	276	261	331	395	726	813	702	8	89	31	0.76	50	13	37	71	40	2%	141	16%	86%	20	40%	45%	4.76	4.5	72	157	$5
11	MIN	323	52	2	21	15	260	267	322	368	691	579	743	8	86	30	0.62	57	13	30	78	65	3%	121	22%	79%	19	53%	21%	4.11	3.6	61	136	$8
12	MIN	299	33	1	30	21	241	256	282	321	603	704	571	5	83	29	0.31	55	19	26	61	59	2%	99	32%	95%	27	30%	41%	3.32	-3.5	21	53	$8
13	BAL	112	15	1	10	9	214	247	268	295	563	555	574	7	82	25	0.45	57	17	27	55	52	4%	138	41%	82%	25	28%	40%	2.75	-3.3	31	78	$1
1st Half		81	10	1	8	5	222	255	276	321	597	539	673	7	84	25	0.46	61	13	26	64	58	6%	134	32%	83%	14	43%	29%	3.03	-1.7	43	108	$2
2nd Half		31	5	0	2	4	194	227	265	226	491	607	369	9	77	25	0.43	43	29	29	31	33	0%	122	63%	80%	11	9%	55%	2.12	-1.6	-9	-23	-$1
14	Proj	**130**	**18**	**1**	**12**	**7**	**245**	**253**	**298**	**335**	**633**	**643**	**626**	**7**	**83**	**29**	**0.43**	**53**	**19**	**29**	**64**	**50**	**2%**	**135**	**26%**	**84%**				**3.51**	**-0.7**	**41**	**101**	**$4**

Castellanos,Nick

Age 22	Bats R	Pos LF	PT/Exp D	Rand Var -1	
Ht 6' 4"	Wt 210		Consist C	MM 2213	
			Health A	LIMA Plan D+	

0-0-.278 in 18 AB at DET. His cup of coffee was decaf, but 2013 season did nothing to dim his bright future. Plate skills improved nicely at Triple-A, where he posted career highs in doubles and HR. Expect the usual bumps in the road if given a starting gig, but his bat has little left to prove in the minors.

Yr	Tm	AB	R	HR	RBI	SB	BA	xBA	OBP	SLG	OPS	vL	vR	bb%	ct%	h%	Eye	G	L	F	PX	xPX	hr/f	Spd	SBO	SB%	#Wk	DOM	DIS	RC/G	RAR	BPV	BPX	R$
09																																		
10																																		
11																																		
12	aa	322	29	6	21	4	245	225	270	345	616			3	76	30	0.15				71			98	12%	50%				3.02		0	0	$3
13	DET *	551	70	15	65	3	257	241	313	406	718	545	571	7	81	29	0.43	59	6	35	104	-15	0%	100	3%	76%	5	0%	20%	4.35	6.0	55	138	$13
1st Half		326	50	9	36	3	281	273	350	446	796			10	82	32	0.58				117			104	4%	70%				5.51		73	183	$20
2nd Half		225	21	6	29	1	224	213	256	347	603	545	571	4	81	25	0.22	59	6	35	85	-15	0%	92	2%	100%	5	0%	20%	2.94	-7.4	28	70	$4
14	Proj	**365**	**39**	**11**	**36**	**3**	**246**	**249**	**286**	**391**	**677**	**677**	**677**	**5**	**79**	**28**	**0.27**	**42**	**20**	**38**	**100**		**10%**	**99**	**7%**	**61%**				**3.73**	**-3.1**	**28**	**70**	**$8**

Castillo,Welington

Age 27	Bats R	Pos CA	PT/Exp D	Rand Var -5	
Ht 5' 10"	Wt 210		Consist B	MM 3203	
			Health C	LIMA Plan D+	

Finished strong in his first full MLB season: .311 BA, 4 HR in 45 Sept AB. Still-emerging power skills (see 2H PX) and minors history suggest double-digit HR totals are within reach as he hits peak age, but h% and xBA don't support a BA repeat. Subpar ct% caps further growth, making him a run-of-the-mill option among mid-tier CAs.

Yr	Tm	AB	R	HR	RBI	SB	BA	xBA	OBP	SLG	OPS	vL	vR	bb%	ct%	h%	Eye	G	L	F	PX	xPX	hr/f	Spd	SBO	SB%	#Wk	DOM	DIS	RC/G	RAR	BPV	BPX	R$
09	aa	319	23	10	32	1	218	247	248	361	609			4	76	26	0.17				97			82	1%	100%				2.93		16	33	$0
10	CHC *	259	27	11	46	0	224	218	264	423	687	708	1167	5	72	27	0.20	23	8	69	151	187	11%	89	5%	0%	5	60%	0%	3.51	-1.4	49	107	$3
11	CHC *	240	24	10	22	0	224	205	263	373	636	0	400	5	71	28	0.18	50	13	38	107	2	0%	83	0%	0%	3	0%	100%	3.22	-3.4	5	11	$1
12	CHC *	327	34	11	43	0	245	225	324	394	717	1199	604	10	70	32	0.39	46	20	34	111	99	12%	70	0%	0%	16	38%	38%	4.30	5.8	13	33	$5
13	CHC	380	41	8	32	2	274	240	349	397	746	707	758	8	74	35	0.35	44	22	34	99	110	8%	71	2%	100%	25	32%	40%	4.68	10.7	17	43	$8
1st Half		221	23	2	12	1	267	232	299	353	652	558	721	4	76	34	0.19	45	22	33	74	104	4%	76	2%	100%	14	21%	36%	3.69	-0.1	-3	-8	$6
2nd Half		159	18	6	20	1	283	250	377	459	836	1049	800	13	72	36	0.55	42	21	37	134	118	14%	75	2%	100%	11	45%	45%	6.20	11.1	47	118	$10
14	Proj	**384**	**40**	**10**	**42**	**1**	**255**	**234**	**329**	**390**	**719**	**905**	**664**	**9**	**72**	**33**	**0.34**	**44**	**21**	**35**	**105**	**107**	**11%**	**70**	**1%**	**88%**				**4.26**	**6.2**	**3**	**8**	**$8**

Castro,Jason

Age 27	Bats L	Pos CA	PT/Exp D	Rand Var -5	
Ht 6' 3"	Wt 215		Consist C	MM 4125	
			Health F	LIMA Plan B	

PRO: Power metrics fully backed his HR spike, which came as he maintained patient plate approach. CON: His ct% fell into the danger zone; a fortunate h% propped up his BA; and he didn't show this kind of power in the minors. VERDICT: This was a skill-supported step forward, but don't go all in on a repeat.

Yr	Tm	AB	R	HR	RBI	SB	BA	xBA	OBP	SLG	OPS	vL	vR	bb%	ct%	h%	Eye	G	L	F	PX	xPX	hr/f	Spd	SBO	SB%	#Wk	DOM	DIS	RC/G	RAR	BPV	BPX	R$
09	aa	239	31	3	24	2	268	244	325	349	674			8	84	31	0.52				55			103	4%	60%				3.91		27	55	$3
10	HOU *	406	49	5	28	1	218	236	298	296	594	223	670	10	80	26	0.58	41	22	37	56	62	4%	93	2%	40%	15	40%	27%	2.85	-10.7	17	37	-$1
11																																		
12	HOU	257	29	6	29	0	257	264	334	401	735	361	831	11	76	32	0.51	43	28	30	101	107	10%	91	0%	0%	22	55%	32%	4.63	6.8	37	93	$3
13	HOU	435	63	18	56	2	276	270	350	485	835	738	864	10	70	36	0.38	39	25	35	167	140	17%	85	3%	67%	23	61%	22%	5.96	27.8	62	155	$15
1st Half		261	33	11	27	2	268	280	330	479	809	638	843	8	74	32	0.35	39	25	36	161	134	15%	77	5%	67%	14	71%	14%	5.47	13.2	66	165	$16
2nd Half		174	30	7	29	0	287	255	380	494	874	830	898	13	64	41	0.42	41	26	34	177	149	18%	105	0%	0%	9	44%	33%	6.72	14.6	58	145	$14
14	Proj	**439**	**60**	**14**	**52**	**1**	**264**	**261**	**341**	**429**	**770**	**569**	**829**	**11**	**74**	**33**	**0.44**	**41**	**26**	**33**	**125**	**118**	**13%**	**91**	**2%**	**64%**				**5.05**	**17.0**	**36**	**90**	**$12**

Castro,Starlin

Age 24	Bats R	Pos SS	PT/Exp A	Rand Var +2	
Ht 5' 10"	Wt 190		Consist C	MM 2425	
			Health A	LIMA Plan B	

Well, this was ugly. Previously stable ct% and Spd dipped and dragged BA and SB down accordingly. xPX points to some untapped power, making a HR bump possible given his lofty AB totals. Still in growth years and has shown better skills, so a rebound is likely and a potentially significant one. UP: 15 HR, 30 SB, .300 BA.

Yr	Tm	AB	R	HR	RBI	SB	BA	xBA	OBP	SLG	OPS	vL	vR	bb%	ct%	h%	Eye	G	L	F	PX	xPX	hr/f	Spd	SBO	SB%	#Wk	DOM	DIS	RC/G	RAR	BPV	BPX	R$
09	aa	111	10	0	13	5	285	267	339	384	722			8	89	32	0.73				62			119	17%	100%				4.95		58	118	$2
10	CHC *	572	69	4	57	13	310	282	351	428	779	897	701	6	86	36	0.43	51	20	29	83	78	3%	147	16%	49%	22	36%	32%	5.17	26.6	66	143	$21
11	CHC	674	91	10	66	22	307	273	341	432	773	847	751	5	86	35	0.36	49	20	31	82	79	5%	144	17%	71%	27	63%	15%	5.34	34.1	64	142	$29
12	CHC	646	78	14	78	25	283	271	323	430	753	775	746	5	85	32	0.36	47	21	32	87	100	8%	153	23%	66%	27	63%	22%	4.72	22.6	66	165	$26
13	CHC	666	59	10	44	9	245	249	284	347	631	619	635	4	81	29	0.23	51	20	29	75	99	6%	110	10%	60%	27	33%	41%	3.18	-6.6	26	65	$9
1st Half		335	37	4	26	7	233	243	259	328	588	468	642	3	81	28	0.19	46	19	34	72	113	4%	106	13%	78%	14	36%	43%	2.84	-6.3	23	58	$10
2nd Half		331	22	6	18	2	257	251	295	366	661	803	628	5	80	31	0.27	55	20	24	78	85	9%	111	8%	33%	13	31%	38%	3.53	0.6	28	70	$8
14	Proj	**633**	**75**	**12**	**65**	**20**	**270**	**267**	**310**	**398**	**708**	**746**	**695**	**5**	**83**	**31**	**0.30**	**50**	**20**	**30**	**85**	**93**	**8%**	**132**	**19%**	**71%**				**4.18**	**13.2**	**47**	**117**	**$22**

Cedeno,Ronny

Age 31	Bats R	Pos SS	PT/Exp D	Rand Var -1	
Ht 6' 0"	Wt 195		Consist A	MM 1311	
			Health B	LIMA Plan D	

His already-shaky skill set just got shakier, as plate skills fell off the table. xBA said he was lucky to crack .240. Spd remains his biggest asset, but without playing time and ability to get on base, it's a wasted skill. Ask yourself this question: Do you really want to own a guy who was cut by the Astros?

Yr	Tm	AB	R	HR	RBI	SB	BA	xBA	OBP	SLG	OPS	vL	vR	bb%	ct%	h%	Eye	G	L	F	PX	xPX	hr/f	Spd	SBO	SB%	#Wk	DOM	DIS	RC/G	RAR	BPV	BPX	R$
09	2 TM	341	32	10	38	5	208	226	256	337	593	548	609	5	77	24	0.24	51	11	38	78	101	10%	142	10%	71%	24	29%	58%	2.70	-8.6	25	51	$1
10	PIT	468	42	8	38	12	256	251	293	382	675	767	647	5	77	32	0.22	49	16	35	96	77	7%	132	15%	80%	27	37%	33%	3.84	4.6	37	80	$9
11	PIT	413	43	2	32	2	249	241	297	339	636	577	653	7	77	32	0.32	43	23	33	75	55	2%	112	7%	29%	25	24%	40%	3.30	-2.5	19	42	$3
12	NYM *	195	19	4	23	0	239	257	302	367	670	759	718	8	78	29	0.41	52	22	26	90	94	12%	92	2%	0%	22	41%	27%	3.64	0.8	30	75	$1
13	2 TM	264	24	3	21	5	227	242	272	330	617	776	533	5	72	32	0.19	52	22	26	64	70	6%	147	14%	56%	24	25%	63%	2.99	-4.1	-2	-5	$2
1st Half		120	12	1	12	2	242	224	272	333	605	899	414	4	73	32	0.16	47	20	33	75	105	3%	116	12%	67%	14	29%	57%	3.01	-1.7	-2	-5	$2
2nd Half		144	12	2	9	3	243	230	288	326	614	629	614	6	72	33	0.22	56	24	21	55	39	10%	162	16%	50%	10	20%	70%	2.97	-2.2	-8	-20	$2
14	Proj	**197**	**19**	**3**	**18**	**3**	**242**	**240**	**293**	**350**	**643**	**723**	**596**	**6**	**75**	**31**	**0.26**	**50**	**22**	**28**	**79**	**73**	**8%**	**122**	**12%**	**60%**				**3.31**	**-0.9**	**4**	**9**	**$3**

RYAN BLOOMFIELD

Cervelli,Francisco

Age	28	Bats	R	Pos	CA	Health	F	LIMA Plan	D+
Ht	6' 1"	Wt	205			PT/Exp	F	Rand Var	+1
						Consist	F	MM	2213

Other than a broken finger, a sore elbow, and a 50-game PED suspension, it was a great season. ("Other than that, Mrs. Lincoln, how was the play?") Given the sample size and other incriminating circumstances, best to disregard this "breakout". There's some peak-age potential for improvement, but use 2010-12 as your baseline.

Yr	Tm	AB	R	HR	RBI	SB	BA	xBA	OBP	SLG	OPS	vL	vR	bb%	ct%	h%	Eye	G	L	F	PX	xPX	hr/f	Spd	SBO	SB%	#Wk	DOM	DIS	RC/G	RAR	BPV	BPX	R$
09	NYY *	221	27	4	24	0	254	249	289	353	641	724	663	5	82	29	0.28	46	20	34	65	85	4%	104	10%	0%	16	31%	44%	3.11	-4.0	23	47	$2
10	NYY	266	27	0	38	1	271	237	359	335	694	846	617	11	84	32	0.79	47	18	34	47	52	0%	130	2%	50%	26	42%	42%	4.07	2.7	37	80	$4
11	NYY	124	17	4	22	4	266	243	324	395	719	743	711	7	77	32	0.31	47	20	33	88	105	13%	94	15%	80%	19	32%	58%	4.37	2.4	21	47	$3
12	NYY *	355	34	2	30	5	205	75	268	262	531	1000	0	8	73	28	0.32	0	0	100	47	737	0%	100	5%	100%	2	50%	50%	2.32	-15.4	-21	-53	-$1
13	NYY	52	12	3	8	0	269	300	377	500	877	684	1017	13	83	28	0.89	30	28	42	145	148	17%	93	0%	0%	4	100%	0%	6.40	4.0	103	258	$0
1st Half		52	12	3	8	0	269	300	367	500	867	684	1017	13	83	28	0.89	30	28	42	145	148	17%	93	0%	0%	4	100%	0%	6.40	4.0	103	258	$0
2nd Half																																		
14	Proj	254	38	6	35	3	254	244	331	372	703	703	703	9	79	30	0.50	42	22	36	82	96	8%	93	6%	70%				4.10	2.9	26	66	$5

Cespedes,Yoenis

Age	28	Bats	R	Pos	LF DH	Health	B	LIMA Plan	A
Ht	5' 10"	Wt	210			PT/Exp	B	Rand Var	+2
						Consist	D	MM	4325

Did manage to confirm his rookie power display, but at the expense of everything else. Plate control profile is becoming disturbingly Soriano-esque (or is it "Hamiltonian" now?). But his history shows better; nagging aches likely contributed. For now, assume Eye corrects; if he can find 1H PX again, too... UP: .290, 35 HR, 20 SB

Yr	Tm	AB	R	HR	RBI	SB	BA	xBA	OBP	SLG	OPS	vL	vR	bb%	ct%	h%	Eye	G	L	F	PX	xPX	hr/f	Spd	SBO	SB%	#Wk	DOM	DIS	RC/G	RAR	BPV	BPX	R$
09	for	328	81	14	74	4	301	0	368	491	858			10	88	31	0.91				108	-5		87	8%	45%				6.32	21.1	88	180	$17
10	for	342	85	13	65	5	322	0	383	529	912			9	88	34	0.79				121	-5		132	7%	57%				7.43	31.5	106	230	$21
11	for	354	87	20	97	10	311	0	380	536	915			10	89	30	1.04				128	2		92	12%	75%				7.47	33.4	109	242	$26
12	OAK	487	70	23	82	16	292	269	356	505	861	853	864	8	79	33	0.42	40	20	40	132	114	15%	113	15%	80%	26	58%	19%	6.36	32.5	74	185	$25
13	OAK	529	74	26	80	7	240	244	294	442	737	880	672	7	74	28	0.27	38	17	46	136	127	14%	118	12%	50%	24	46%	29%	4.11	2.1	56	140	$17
1st Half		265	44	15	42	2	226	243	283	453	736	931	665	7	72	26	0.28	32	16	51	155	142	15%	109	13%	29%	12	50%	25%	3.91	-0.9	62	155	$16
2nd Half		264	30	11	38	5	254	245	296	432	728	835	680	6	76	29	0.25	43	17	40	117	112	14%	117	12%	71%	12	42%	33%	4.33	2.4	47	118	$17
14	Proj	517	85	27	92	11	272	266	333	490	823	906	785	8	78	30	0.38	39	18	43	139	120	15%	117	13%	67%				5.51	22.3	75	188	$26

Chavez,Endy

Age	36	Bats	L	Pos	RF CF	Health	B	LIMA Plan	D
Ht	5' 11"	Wt	170			PT/Exp	F	Rand Var	-3
						Consist	F	MM	0321

2-14-.267 in 266 AB at SEA. He's not running much anymore, and with that goes his only real shot at contributing anything fanalytically. It's pretty cool when they play the "Indiana Jones" theme at the ballpark when he gets a hit, though.

Yr	Tm	AB	R	HR	RBI	SB	BA	xBA	OBP	SLG	OPS	vL	vR	bb%	ct%	h%	Eye	G	L	F	PX	xPX	hr/f	Spd	SBO	SB%	#Wk	DOM	DIS	RC/G	RAR	BPV	BPX	R$
09	SEA	161	17	2	13	9	273	256	328	342	669	539	699	8	86	31	0.64	53	19	28	39	46	5%	134	19%	90%	11	36%	27%	4.22	0.0	35	71	$4
10	a/a																																	
11	TEX *	384	46	6	37	13	276	280	305	392	697	818	735	4	90	29	0.42	50	20	30	71	74	8%	139	20%	73%	21	43%	38%	4.16	-0.8	69	153	$12
12	BAL *	215	19	2	15	3	182	246	214	249	463	370	544	4	85	20	0.28	55	19	27	47	32	6%	91	13%	60%	16	13%	38%	1.62	-18.2	16	40	-$4
13	SEA *	294	27	2	15	1	272	250	298	329	626	530	646	4	88	30	0.31	53	22	25	41	74	3%	108	9%	15%	24	21%	42%	3.15	-9.3	26	65	$3
1st Half		230	22	2	12	0	278	250	299	346	645	525	672	3	87	31	0.23	51	22	28	50	89	4%	102	8%	0%	13	31%	38%	3.32	-5.7	26	65	$4
2nd Half		64	5	0	3	1	250	252	294	266	560	544	565	6	92	27	0.80	60	21	19	13	28	0%	117	11%	50%	11	9%	45%	2.55	-3.1	28	70	-$2
14	Proj	167	16	1	11	3	245	257	281	307	588	524	605	5	89	27	0.44	55	20	25	42	50	4%	115	13%	57%				2.82	-8.2	20	51	$2

Chavez,Eric

Age	36	Bats	L	Pos	3B	Health	F	LIMA Plan	D
Ht	6' 1"	Wt	215			PT/Exp	F	Rand Var	0
						Consist	C	MM	4031

This year it was a strained right oblique, a stiff right hip, and (just so his left side didn't feel neglected) a left knee strain. Still, considering we all thought he was done a few years ago, he has been very solid when on the field. But at 36 he's not going to get healthier, and you simply can't count on even 200 AB again.

Yr	Tm	AB	R	HR	RBI	SB	BA	xBA	OBP	SLG	OPS	vL	vR	bb%	ct%	h%	Eye	G	L	F	PX	xPX	hr/f	Spd	SBO	SB%	#Wk	DOM	DIS	RC/G	RAR	BPV	BPX	R$
09	OAK	30	0	0	1	0	100	137	129	133	262	222	321	3	77	13	0.14	43	13	43	31	114	0%	76	0%	0%	3	0%	67%	0.49	-3.6	-36	-73	-$3
10	OAK	111	10	1	10	0	234	227	276	333	610	322	635	7	72	32	0.26	49	19	32	92	108	4%	72	0%	0%	7	29%	29%	3.17	-2.7	0	0	-$1
11	NYY	160	16	2	26	0	263	226	320	356	676	609	687	8	79	32	0.41	46	18	36	69	78	4%	85	0%	0%	16	25%	31%	3.96	-0.1	14	31	$2
12	NYY	278	36	16	37	0	281	276	348	496	845	382	911	10	79	31	0.51	42	23	35	132	137	21%	63	0%	0%	27	52%	33%	6.17	17.0	61	153	$9
13	ARI	228	28	9	44	1	281	280	332	478	810	700	827	8	80	32	0.42	41	22	36	131	126	13%	92	2%	100%	22	50%	18%	5.72	11.1	71	178	$8
1st Half		119	18	7	25	1	319	296	362	571	934	333	998	6	83	34	0.40	44	17	40	154	141	18%	101	3%	100%	11	64%	9%	7.82	12.2	101	253	$12
2nd Half		109	10	2	19	0	239	267	308	376	684	926	626	9	77	29	0.44	39	29	32	103	109	7%	78	0%	0%	11	36%	27%	3.88	-0.3	35	88	$3
14	Proj	180	21	7	29	0	274	272	329	459	788	632	812	8	80	31	0.44	42	22	36	123	118	14%	80	0%					5.38	7.2	47	119	$6

Chisenhall,Lonnie

Age	25	Bats	L	Pos	3B	Health	B	LIMA Plan	B+
Ht	6' 2"	Wt	190			PT/Exp	D	Rand Var	0
						Consist	A	MM	4325

11-36-.225 in 289 AB at CLE. This season will be viewed as a disappointment, given he was handed the 3B job and couldn't hold it. But there are signs of hope here, PX growth foremost. While his best skills were posted in a torrid 100-AB stretch at Triple-A, they're still part of his profile. Time to buy low. UP: 20 HR, .270 BA

Yr	Tm	AB	R	HR	RBI	SB	BA	xBA	OBP	SLG	OPS	vL	vR	bb%	ct%	h%	Eye	G	L	F	PX	xPX	hr/f	Spd	SBO	SB%	#Wk	DOM	DIS	RC/G	RAR	BPV	BPX	R$
09	aa	93	12	3	12	1	170	279	225	348	573			7	81	17	0.38				109			105	7%	100%				2.44		60	122	-$2
10	aa	460	64	12	66	2	245	260	301	378	679			7	82	28	0.44				88			103	2%	100%				3.87		44	96	$9
11	CLE *	467	62	12	57	1	242	246	287	388	675	888	640	6	78	29	0.29	38	20	42	106	117	10%	107	2%	47%	14	50%	21%	3.72	-3.1	44	98	$8
12	CLE *	260	28	8	29	2	267	275	297	431	729	442	848	4	80	31	0.21	43	25	32	110	67	14%	95	5%	67%	9	44%	22%	4.43	3.6	46	115	$5
13	CLE *	394	48	16	58	3	256	263	302	446	748	408	705	6	79	29	0.31	38	20	42	130	93	11%	107	3%	100%	22	68%	23%	4.65	8.0	65	163	$11
1st Half		236	28	9	39	2	279	262	319	469	788	307	740	6	75	34	0.24	43	20	38	137	89	11%	112	3%	100%	10	60%	30%	5.33	9.1	57	143	$15
2nd Half		158	20	7	19	1	222	268	276	411	688	804	682	7	84	22	0.46	35	20	45	121	95	12%	104	3%	100%	12	75%	17%	3.76	-1.0	78	195	$5
14	Proj	428	52	17	55	3	259	266	306	441	747	555	790	6	80	29	0.31	39	21	41	123	87	12%	103	4%	84%				4.60	7.8	53	133	$13

Choice,Michael

Age	24	Bats	R	Pos	RF	Health	A	LIMA Plan	D
Ht	6' 0"	Wt	215			PT/Exp	D	Rand Var	-3
						Consist	A	MM	2201

0-0-.278 in 18 AB at OAK. MLEs don't blow you away, but despite being one of the younger players at his level, he's shown growth each year during his steady ascent through the minors. Clearly needs and will likely get more Triple-A seasoning, and there's little in his BPIs to suggest a '14 breakout. But the tools are intriguing.

Yr	Tm	AB	R	HR	RBI	SB	BA	xBA	OBP	SLG	OPS	vL	vR	bb%	ct%	h%	Eye	G	L	F	PX	xPX	hr/f	Spd	SBO	SB%	#Wk	DOM	DIS	RC/G	RAR	BPV	BPX	R$
09																																		
10																																		
11																																		
12	aa	359	45	7	43	4	241	215	292	342	634			7	72	32	0.26				73			97	5%	77%				3.36		-7	-18	$5
13	OAK *	528	65	9	62	1	245	197	311	344	655	583	700	9	73	32	0.36	58	8	33	79	131	0%	95	2%	23%	4	25%	50%	3.55	-10.7	5	13	$8
1st Half		296	42	7	37	1	233	211	306	333	639			9	72	30	0.37				75			81	4%	23%				3.29		-9	-23	$10
2nd Half		232	23	2	25	0	259	207	318	358	676	583	700	8	76	34	0.35	58	8	33	85	131	0%	98	0%	0%	4	25%	50%	3.92	-1.7	18	45	$6
14	Proj	226	27	5	26	1	245	221	303	360	663	663	663	8	73	32	0.31	40	20	40	88		7%	92	3%	65%				3.67	-5.3	0	0	$4

Choo,Shin-Soo

Age	31	Bats	L	Pos	CF	Health	B	LIMA Plan	B+
Ht	5' 11"	Wt	205			PT/Exp	A	Rand Var	-1
						Consist	C	MM	3325

This OB machine showed his injury-plagued '11 was the clear outlier. Walk rate will probably regress a bit, but nothing else in this skill set was really anything outside his norm. He's not the sexiest name on the draft board, but a look at those non-'11 R$ and RAR numbers says he's among best OF in most any format.

Yr	Tm	AB	R	HR	RBI	SB	BA	xBA	OBP	SLG	OPS	vL	vR	bb%	ct%	h%	Eye	G	L	F	PX	xPX	hr/f	Spd	SBO	SB%	#Wk	DOM	DIS	RC/G	RAR	BPV	BPX	R$
09	CLE	583	87	20	86	21	300	270	394	489	883	825	909	12	74	38	0.52	42	22	36	131	130	13%	101	12%	91%	26	58%	15%	7.00	46.7	57	116	$28
10	CLE	550	81	22	90	22	300	277	401	484	885	670	998	13	79	35	0.70	45	20	35	124	136	15%	78	15%	76%	24	63%	21%	6.89	42.9	65	141	$30
11	CLE	313	37	8	36	12	259	245	344	390	733	688	757	10	75	32	0.46	45	22	32	91	128	10%	97	18%	71%	17	35%	41%	4.44	3.2	25	56	$9
12	CLE	598	88	16	67	21	283	268	373	441	815	605	926	11	75	35	0.49	50	23	27	118	107	13%	82	15%	75%	27	48%	33%	5.64	26.4	42	105	$24
13	CIN	569	107	21	54	20	285	273	423	462	885	612	1011	16	77	34	0.84	49	21	29	126	99	16%	113	14%	65%	27	59%	15%	6.46	38.6	76	190	$29
1st Half		295	54	12	26	8	268	269	386	458	844	490	1059	16	74	33	0.74	50	20	29	138	92	19%	117	13%	57%	14	64%	14%	5.91	15.2	75	188	$25
2nd Half		274	53	9	28	12	303	276	419	467	887	750	961	17	80	35	0.98	49	22	29	113	106	14%	101	15%	71%	13	54%	15%	7.08	22.3	74	185	$33
14	Proj	573	94	19	63	21	284	268	398	450	847	650	943	14	76	34	0.68	48	22	30	119	109	14%	98	15%	70%				6.05	30.9	60	151	$28

ROD TRUESDELL

Ciriaco,Pedro

Age 28 | Bats R | Pos SS | Ht 6' 0" | Wt 180
Health A | PT/Exp D | Consist D
LIMA Plan D | Rand Var +1 | MM 1511

2-8-.224 in 125 AB at KC/SD/BOS. Turns out that 2012 glimmer of hope was nothing more than a hit rate blip. Elite Spd gives hope of 30 SB if he can get 400 AB, but that won't happen with zero pop and sub-.300 OBP. There's a reason he played for three teams in '13. At best, a MI speed end-gamer in the deepest of leagues.

Yr Tm	AB	R	HR	RBI	SB	BA	xBA	OBP	SLG	OPS	vL	vR	bb%	ct%	h%	Eye	G	L	F	PX	xPX	hr/f	Spd	SBO	SB%	#Wk	DOM	DIS	RC/G	RAR	BPV	BPX	R$
09 aa	469	45	3	44	32	272	238	292	339	631			3	84	32	0.17				44			111	36%	74%				3.43		10	20	$17
10 PIT *	482	49	4	42	14	224	269	238	321	559	0	1500	2	82	26	0.10	33	33	33	67	244	0%	156	22%	75%	4	50%	50%	2.50	-15.0	35	76	$4
11 PIT *	310	26	1	23	11	201	262	213	259	472	444	860	1	81	25	0.07	60	24	16	40	2	0%	152	38%	55%	13	23%	38%	1.58	-19.4	4	9	-$1
12 BOS *	535	65	5	35	27	278	256	294	370	664	764	678	2	80	34	0.12	50	23	27	67	39	4%	153	31%	68%	14	36%	29%	3.69	4.0	28	70	$18
13 3 TM *	285	23	3	19	12	226	239	260	312	572	574	648	4	83	26	0.27	45	20	34	58	84	6%	142	23%	84%	19	32%	37%	2.76	-5.8	31	78	$3
1st Half	103	8	2	8	6	249	238	303	375	678	535	787	7	80	30	0.38	39	23	39	78	102	7%	144	26%	86%	14	36%	43%	4.02	1.7	40	100	$5
2nd Half	182	15	1	11	6	213	249	235	276	511	778	217	3	84	25	0.19	67	13	21	47	27	0%	132	20%	83%	5	20%	20%	2.16	-7.4	23	58	$2
14 Proj	**135**	**13**	**1**	**10**	**6**	**239**	**247**	**273**	**320**	**593**	**699**	**534**	**3**	**82**	**29**	**0.19**	**53**	**19**	**28**	**57**	**51**	**3%**	**138**	**28%**	**74%**				**2.82**	**-2.7**	**17**	**42**	**$1**

Coghlan,Chris

Age 29 | Bats L | Pos LF | Ht 6' 0" | Wt 195
Health F | PT/Exp D | Consist B
LIMA Plan D | Rand Var -2 | MM 1311

Back, calf problems kept this former ROY a shell of his former self. Days of double-digit HR are long gone due to GB tilt, tiny PX. Also gone is his 2B eligibility. With no power, even good health won't make him roster-worthy. It's now safe to erase 2009 completely from your memory. Click - gone.

Yr Tm	AB	R	HR	RBI	SB	BA	xBA	OBP	SLG	OPS	vL	vR	bb%	ct%	h%	Eye	G	L	F	PX	xPX	hr/f	Spd	SBO	SB%	#Wk	DOM	DIS	RC/G	RAR	BPV	BPX	R$
09 FLA *	600	100	11	64	15	318	293	382	462	844	814	863	9	85	36	0.70	48	23	30	92	81	7%	113	11%	71%	23	52%	17%	6.53	39.7	69	141	$26
10 FLA	358	60	5	28	10	268	268	335	383	718	709	720	8	77	34	0.39	51	24	25	87	67	7%	125	13%	77%	17	35%	41%	4.42	3.3	32	70	$10
11 FLA *	341	42	6	27	9	220	269	284	345	628	307	801	8	84	25	0.54	49	20	32	92	78	7%	85	22%	55%	12	50%	25%	3.02	-11.5	51	113	$3
12 MIA *	410	40	6	32	7	209	250	287	307	594	186	451	10	83	24	0.64	63	13	23	65	28	5%	94	11%	62%	9	11%	33%	2.79	-16.8	34	85	$0
13 MIA	195	10	1	10	2	256	242	318	354	672	861	641	8	78	32	0.40	50	21	29	73	65	2%	117	4%	100%	15	33%	53%	3.90	-1.1	23	58	$0
1st Half	130	7	1	10	0	277	263	324	415	739	824	726	6	78	35	0.31	42	25	32	103	93	3%	111	0%	0%	10	50%	40%	4.74	2.1	42	105	$1
2nd Half	65	3	0	0	2	215	185	301	231	532	1000	487	11	78	27	0.57	65	12	24	15	10	0%	110	10%	100%	5	0%	80%	2.43	-3.5	-17	-43	-$3
14 Proj	**159**	**13**	**1**	**9**	**3**	**247**	**242**	**316**	**333**	**649**	**594**	**661**	**9**	**80**	**30**	**0.51**	**56**	**17**	**27**	**64**	**48**	**4%**	**108**	**9%**	**76%**				**3.58**	**-2.1**	**17**	**42**	**$2**

Colabello,Chris

Age 30 | Bats R | Pos 1B | Ht 6' 4" | Wt 220
Health A | PT/Exp D | Consist C
LIMA Plan D+ | Rand Var -1 | MM 4103

7-17-.194 in 160 AB at MIN. Independent ball vet mashed way to International League MVP at age 29. But MLB hurlers found huge holes in swing. Extreme, unrepeatable hr/f drove his MLB power, so don't read too much into those 7 HR. With chronic contact issues, chances of a storybook sequel are nil.

Yr Tm	AB	R	HR	RBI	SB	BA	xBA	OBP	SLG	OPS	vL	vR	bb%	ct%	h%	Eye	G	L	F	PX	xPX	hr/f	Spd	SBO	SB%	#Wk	DOM	DIS	RC/G	RAR	BPV	BPX	R$
09																																	
10																																	
11																																	
12 aa	496	55	12	69	0	221	240	271	359	629			6	76	27	0.29				99			76	0%	0%				3.18		21	53	$4
13 MIN *	498	53	22	68	1	243	224	311	420	731	573	655	9	65	33	0.28	64	14	23	141	71	30%	78	3%	37%	15	13%	67%	4.34	-4.0	17	43	$11
1st Half	286	31	12	44	1	264	267	318	451	769	0	364	7	67	35	0.24	78	22	0	150	13	0%	90	3%	34%	3	0%	100%	4.89	2.4	32	80	$15
2nd Half	212	22	9	24	1	215	205	303	378	681	636	685	11	63	29	0.34	62	13	25	129	77	30%	81	3%	40%	12	17%	58%	3.66	-6.1	2	5	$5
14 Proj	**321**	**35**	**12**	**43**	**1**	**231**	**229**	**298**	**396**	**694**	**679**	**700**	**8**	**69**	**30**	**0.29**	**47**	**17**	**36**	**127**	**69**	**15%**	**78**	**2%**	**50%**				**3.83**	**-7.5**	**8**	**21**	**$6**

Conger,Hank

Age 26 | Bats B | Pos CA | Ht 6' 1" | Wt 220
Health A | PT/Exp F | Consist B
LIMA Plan D+ | Rand Var -3 | MM 3013

Former top catching prospect finally got off AAA-MLB shuttle. 140+ PX in three separate months says there's a HR burst on the horizon, and he's around the age where many young backstops start to make headway at dish and increase manager's comfort with them behind it. With ct% recovery and opportunity... UP: 20 HR.

Yr Tm	AB	R	HR	RBI	SB	BA	xBA	OBP	SLG	OPS	vL	vR	bb%	ct%	h%	Eye	G	L	F	PX	xPX	hr/f	Spd	SBO	SB%	#Wk	DOM	DIS	RC/G	RAR	BPV	BPX	R$
09 aa	459	56	10	62	3	284	261	353	403	756			10	85	32	0.70				73			98	3%	56%				5.02		48	98	$12
10 LAA *	416	41	8	39	0	245	252	315	365	680	333	587	9	82	28	0.57	55	15	30	84	82	0%	85	2%	0%	5	40%	60%	3.79	0.9	42	91	$4
11 LAA *	277	23	9	36	0	221	230	285	361	646	539	644	8	79	25	0.43	39	18	44	95	92	10%	68	0%	0%	21	43%	33%	3.37	-2.9	32	71	$1
12 LAA *	282	32	6	29	1	226	189	260	336	597	0	405	4	79	27	0.22	58	0	42	77	28	0%	87	2%	100%	4	25%	0%	2.91	-6.8	15	38	$1
13 LAA	233	23	7	21	0	249	237	310	403	713	629	724	7	74	31	0.28	39	20	41	115	135	10%	84	2%	0%	27	44%	41%	4.03	2.1	28	70	$2
1st Half	102	12	4	11	0	265	240	299	431	730	277	813	5	75	32	0.19	48	16	36	119	143	15%	86	4%	0%	14	50%	36%	4.28	1.7	30	75	$3
2nd Half	131	11	3	10	0	237	234	301	382	682	937	658	8	73	30	0.34	33	22	45	112	130	7%	89	0%	0%	13	38%	46%	3.83	0.5	28	70	$1
14 Proj	**359**	**36**	**12**	**41**	**0**	**240**	**240**	**298**	**396**	**694**	**617**	**702**	**7**	**77**	**28**	**0.31**	**39**	**19**	**42**	**109**	**118**	**10%**	**75**	**2%**	**33%**				**3.83**	**1.3**	**22**	**55**	**$6**

Corporan,Carlos

Age 30 | Bats B | Pos CA | Ht 6' 2" | Wt 230
Health A | PT/Exp F | Consist B
LIMA Plan F | Rand Var -2 | MM 3001

When looking for a caddy and you're short on time, scan yearly PX and look for multiple triple digits. Nothing there? See if bb% or ct% are decent enough to mitigate likely BA damage. Still out of luck? Read player writeup for witty banter or instructive commentary such as this. If you've made it this far, why are you still reading?

Yr Tm	AB	R	HR	RBI	SB	BA	xBA	OBP	SLG	OPS	vL	vR	bb%	ct%	h%	Eye	G	L	F	PX	xPX	hr/f	Spd	SBO	SB%	#Wk	DOM	DIS	RC/G	RAR	BPV	BPX	R$
09 MIL *	180	8	1	13	0	170	88	201	233	435	0	2000	4	71	24	0.13	0	0	100	54	-5	0%	88	4%	0%	1	0%	0%	1.39	-13.5	-36	-73	-$6
10 aaa	286	23	7	30	2	229	254	265	386	651			5	74	29	0.19				116			109	9%	50%				3.29		32	70	$1
11 HOU *	234	15	2	20	0	193	201	243	278	522	673	451	6	71	26	0.23	45	17	38	74	68	0%	76	3%	0%	16	19%	69%	2.08	-12.1	-20	-44	-$4
12 HOU *	284	27	8	32	1	229	248	264	359	623	433	855	5	72	29	0.17	32	32	37	96	89	18%	64	4%	55%	9	56%	22%	3.10	-5.2	-3	-8	$2
13 HOU	191	16	7	20	0	225	210	287	361	648	660	640	5	69	29	0.17	44	20	36	99	108	15%	71	0%	0%	25	20%	64%	3.13	-3.3	-12	-30	$0
1st Half	98	12	5	11	0	276	246	317	459	776	716	918	6	64	38	0.17	46	29	25	141	104	31%	79	0%	0%	14	21%	57%	5.13	3.9	7	18	$4
2nd Half	93	4	2	9	0	172	153	206	258	464	552	446	4	73	21	0.16	42	12	46	61	112	6%	77	0%	0%	11	18%	73%	1.64	-6.3	-25	-63	-$4
14 Proj	**200**	**15**	**6**	**20**	**0**	**213**	**224**	**266**	**350**	**616**	**570**	**638**	**5**	**71**	**27**	**0.18**	**43**	**21**	**37**	**101**	**96**	**12%**	**72**	**2%**	**36%**				**2.82**	**-5.5**	**-16**	**-39**	**$1**

Cowgill,Collin

Age 28 | Bats R | Pos LF CF | Ht 5' 9" | Wt 185
Health A | PT/Exp D | Consist C
LIMA Plan D | Rand Var 0 | MM 2401

4-16-.211 in 152 AB at LAA/NYM. Four organizations before 350 AB at MLB level confirm how far this former 5th-rd pick has fallen. That decent '10 PX is clearly a blip now, and with consistent 50% GB%, any hope for power return is gone. Poor OBP, sliding ct% will keep SB upside at bay. Not worthy of a post-hype speculation.

Yr Tm	AB	R	HR	RBI	SB	BA	xBA	OBP	SLG	OPS	vL	vR	bb%	ct%	h%	Eye	G	L	F	PX	xPX	hr/f	Spd	SBO	SB%	#Wk	DOM	DIS	RC/G	RAR	BPV	BPX	R$
09																																	
10 aa	502	73	13	68	20	263	284	325	427	752			8	84	29	0.58				108			107	24%	67%				4.64		74	161	$18
11 ARI *	487	60	8	48	21	270	248	319	391	710	716	518	7	79	33	0.34	48	19	33	85	115	5%	156	20%	78%	10	20%	60%	4.39	4.6	45	100	$16
12 OAK *	364	32	3	34	8	216	241	266	290	556	844	510	6	76	28	0.28	55	23	22	57	30	6%	108	18%	57%	11	0%	64%	2.40	-17.9	-2	-5	$1
13 2 TM *	290	33	8	27	4	214	217	258	343	601	669	456	6	73	27	0.22	51	11	37	91	74	10%	123	7%	100%	21	24%	71%	2.93	-9.3	15	38	$2
1st Half	196	22	6	19	2	202	195	247	325	572	493	554	6	74	24	0.23	41	9	50	88	70	9%	105	6%	100%	8	25%	63%	2.62	-8.6	13	33	$2
2nd Half	94	11	2	8	2	241	227	283	379	662	771	372	6	70	32	0.20	59	13	29	98	77	11%	140	8%	100%	13	23%	77%	3.70	-0.9	13	33	$1
14 Proj	**131**	**15**	**2**	**13**	**3**	**235**	**234**	**284**	**351**	**634**	**753**	**496**	**6**	**75**	**30**	**0.28**	**52**	**17**	**31**	**83**	**65**	**8%**	**120**	**14%**	**75%**				**3.33**	**-2.8**	**14**	**35**	**$3**

Cozart,Zack

Age 28 | Bats R | Pos SS | Ht 6' 0" | Wt 195
Health B | PT/Exp B | Consist A
LIMA Plan B+ | Rand Var 0 | MM 2415

On surface, a solid follow-up to '12 rookie debut. But waning PX, big GB jump put double-digit HR in jeopardy. Low bb% and PX confirm that he won't be anything more than a .260 hitter. That leaves his wheels, which actually are pretty good but need green light. New manager could help. Expect more SB, fewer HR.

Yr Tm	AB	R	HR	RBI	SB	BA	xBA	OBP	SLG	OPS	vL	vR	bb%	ct%	h%	Eye	G	L	F	PX	xPX	hr/f	Spd	SBO	SB%	#Wk	DOM	DIS	RC/G	RAR	BPV	BPX	R$
09 aa	463	59	9	48	8	234	252	312	358	670			10	78	28	0.52				87			97	8%	78%				3.74		34	69	$5
10 aaa	553	68	14	50	22	216	251	257	349	606			5	77	26	0.24				93			112	25%	83%				2.98		29	63	$9
11 CIN *	360	47	8	26	6	260	248	292	389	681	667	880	4	81	30	0.24	58	10	32	92	163	20%	128	11%	73%	3	33%	33%	3.89	4.0	46	102	$7
12 CIN	561	72	15	35	4	246	254	288	399	687	699	683	5	80	28	0.27	42	20	38	102	86	9%	135	3%	100%	26	35%	19%	3.89	6.3	54	135	$8
13 CIN	567	74	12	63	0	254	255	284	381	665	686	658	4	82	29	0.25	50	18	32	88	63	8%	115	0%	0%	27	48%	19%	3.73	3.7	44	110	$11
1st Half	299	42	7	31	0	244	254	276	381	657	719	630	4	84	27	0.27	49	15	36	94	65	8%	110	0%	0%	14	50%	14%	3.55	0.7	53	133	$10
2nd Half	268	32	5	32	0	265	256	299	381	680	639	686	5	80	31	0.25	52	21	27	80	60	9%	119	0%	0%	13	46%	23%	3.95	3.7	32	80	$11
14 Proj	**565**	**72**	**9**	**52**	**4**	**251**	**254**	**288**	**366**	**655**	**659**	**653**	**5**	**81**	**30**	**0.27**	**48**	**20**	**32**	**83**	**72**	**6%**	**119**	**4%**	**83%**				**3.62**	**2.6**	**28**	**70**	**$11**

STEPHEN NICKRAND

Craig,Allen

Age	29	Bats	R	Pos	1B LF RF	Health	C	LIMA Plan	B+
						PT/Exp	C	Rand Var	-4
Ht	6' 2"	Wt	215			Consist	B	MM	3335

Slow start (no HR in April) bookended by foot injury in September kept his HR totals down. Third straight year of FB% decline also didn't help. LD% supports high BA, but h% and xBA say another .300+ BA may be a stretch. With health and skills concerns, his status as a $20 player carries a fair amount of risk.

Yr	Tm	AB	R	HR	RBI	SB	BA	xBA	OBP	SLG	OPS	vL	vR	bb%	ct%	h%	Eye	G	L	F	PX	xPX	hr/f	Spd	SBO	SB%	#Wk	DOM	DIS	RC/G	RAR	BPV	BPX	R$
09	aaa	472	61	18	65	2	272	261	314	439	753			6	77	32	0.26				108			88	2%	100%				4.85		34	69	$12
10	STL *	420	50	13	72	1	249	262	302	407	710	674	739	7	77	30	0.33	38	22	39	115	141	11%	84	2%	40%	13	38%	38%	4.15	-5.4	41	89	$9
11	STL *	241	39	12	44	5	292	291	340	508	848	1000	875	7	81	32	0.39	44	19	37	144	111	18%	97	8%	100%	17	47%	41%	6.36	11.9	85	189	$11
12	STL	469	76	22	92	2	307	293	354	522	876	1011	827	7	81	34	0.42	44	23	33	140	112	17%	80	2%	67%	22	64%	5%	6.85	28.9	77	193	$23
13	STL	508	71	13	97	2	315	277	373	457	830	779	845	7	80	37	0.40	45	27	28	99	100	11%	93	1%	100%	23	48%	17%	6.23	22.4	45	113	$25
1st Half		305	44	9	63	1	318	283	350	479	829	913	815	5	82	37	0.27	44	26	30	108	109	12%	92	1%	100%	14	50%	14%	6.29	13.8	52	130	$29
2nd Half		203	27	4	34	1	310	268	386	424	810	617	890	11	78	38	0.57	47	29	25	85	86	10%	92	1%	100%	9	44%	22%	6.08	8.2	33	83	$18
14	**Proj**	**500**	**73**	**18**	**92**	**3**	**293**	**279**	**347**	**465**	**812**	**801**	**816**	**7**	**80**	**34**	**0.40**	**44**	**24**	**32**	**118**	**106**	**14%**	**90**	**3%**	**91%**				**5.80**	**16.7**	**54**	**134**	**$21**

Crawford,Brandon

Age	27	Bats	L	Pos	SS	Health	A	LIMA Plan	C
						PT/Exp	C	Rand Var	-1
Ht	6' 2"	Wt	215			Consist	B	MM	1115

Hit five HR in April, and only four more in the remaining 407 AB. There's been no growth in xPX, so don't mistake that fluky month for the development of a power stroke. He doesn't run, and xBA doesn't project any BA upside. He's far more valuable in real life than on your fantasy squad.

Yr	Tm	AB	R	HR	RBI	SB	BA	xBA	OBP	SLG	OPS	vL	vR	bb%	ct%	h%	Eye	G	L	F	PX	xPX	hr/f	Spd	SBO	SB%	#Wk	DOM	DIS	RC/G	RAR	BPV	BPX	R$
09	aa	392	33	3	27	11	245	232	277	344	620			4	73	33	0.16				80			100	22%	58%				3.05		-2	-4	$4
10	aa	291	37	6	19	3	223	229	303	342	645			10	71	29	0.40				89			133	6%	76%				3.41		19	41	$1
11	SF *	303	30	4	27	4	197	224	266	279	545	445	608	9	82	23	0.52	51	14	35	55	79	5%	109	13%	44%	14	36%	43%	2.22	-12.5	24	53	-$2
12	SF	435	44	4	45	1	248	246	304	349	653	631	661	7	78	31	0.35	47	23	30	77	85	4%	88	5%	20%	27	26%	37%	3.44	-0.8	17	43	$4
13	SF	499	52	9	43	1	248	246	311	363	674	546	727	8	81	29	0.44	49	19	32	80	78	7%	105	2%	33%	27	41%	41%	3.72	3.1	36	90	$6
1st Half		271	34	5	28	1	269	261	324	391	715	575	802	8	81	32	0.42	55	19	25	85	65	9%	104	4%	33%	14	36%	43%	4.31	6.6	40	100	$11
2nd Half		228	18	4	15	0	224	228	286	329	615	486	654	8	81	26	0.45	42	19	40	74	94	6%	106	0%	0%	13	46%	38%	3.09	-2.6	32	80	$0
14	**Proj**	**549**	**55**	**8**	**47**	**3**	**251**	**241**	**312**	**356**	**668**	**580**	**697**	**8**	**79**	**30**	**0.41**	**48**	**19**	**33**	**76**	**83**	**6%**	**103**	**5%**	**42%**				**3.65**	**3.0**	**16**	**39**	**$9**

Crawford,Carl

Age	32	Bats	L	Pos	LF	Health	F	LIMA Plan	B
						PT/Exp	C	Rand Var	0
Ht	6' 2"	Wt	215			Consist	C	MM	3535

Even with TJS in the rear-view mirror, new injuries helped him earn that health grade. While the days of 50+ SB are gone, there are still useful skills here, especially if he can maintain the resurgent ct%. Forget Devil Ray Carl; that guy doesn't work here any more. 2013 looks like the new baseline, and it's not terrible.

Yr	Tm	AB	R	HR	RBI	SB	BA	xBA	OBP	SLG	OPS	vL	vR	bb%	ct%	h%	Eye	G	L	F	PX	xPX	hr/f	Spd	SBO	SB%	#Wk	DOM	DIS	RC/G	RAR	BPV	BPX	R$
09	TAM	606	96	15	68	60	305	286	364	452	816	704	868	8	84	35	0.52	52	19	29	88	77	10%	143	41%	79%	26	54%	27%	6.00	33.2	65	133	$40
10	TAM	600	110	19	90	47	307	284	356	495	851	696	930	7	83	35	0.44	47	16	36	116	98	11%	163	34%	82%	27	63%	15%	6.58	42.1	88	191	$42
11	BOS	506	65	11	56	18	255	261	289	405	694	566	757	4	79	30	0.22	48	18	34	104	112	8%	116	23%	75%	23	30%	26%	3.95	-1.6	46	102	$14
12	BOS *	139	26	3	20	6	285	291	310	460	771	856	750	4	82	33	0.21	54	19	27	113	95	12%	118	22%	100%	6	50%	33%	5.38	5.1	64	160	$5
13	LA	435	62	6	31	15	283	278	329	407	736	551	796	6	85	32	0.42	47	23	30	89	90	5%	124	17%	79%	23	43%	22%	4.75	8.5	62	155	$16
1st Half		183	32	5	13	9	301	293	350	470	820	891	808	7	85	33	0.52	45	24	31	110	106	10%	132	24%	75%	10	50%	10%	5.93	9.8	85	213	$19
2nd Half		252	30	1	18	6	270	266	308	361	669	298	788	5	85	32	0.36	49	22	29	73	77	2%	108	11%	86%	13	38%	31%	3.96	-0.4	41	103	$14
14	**Proj**	**498**	**77**	**11**	**50**	**21**	**282**	**283**	**323**	**438**	**761**	**667**	**798**	**5**	**83**	**32**	**0.33**	**49**	**21**	**30**	**105**	**94**	**9%**	**129**	**21%**	**83%**				**5.04**	**14.4**	**73**	**183**	**$22**

Crisp,Coco

Age	34	Bats	B	Pos	CF DH	Health	D	LIMA Plan	B+
						PT/Exp	B	Rand Var	+2
Ht	5' 10"	Wt	185			Consist	A	MM	2525

Power surge started in 2H of 2012 with 9 HR and 134 PX. Continued into 2013, with a big boost in FB% in 2H. But at no time was it supported by xPX, which casts doubt as to sustainability. Other concerns: inability to stay healthy, big drop in SBO, and flagging success vs LHP. Expect less power, maybe flat speed.

Yr	Tm	AB	R	HR	RBI	SB	BA	xBA	OBP	SLG	OPS	vL	vR	bb%	ct%	h%	Eye	G	L	F	PX	xPX	hr/f	Spd	SBO	SB%	#Wk	DOM	DIS	RC/G	RAR	BPV	BPX	R$
09	KC	180	30	3	14	13	228	281	336	378	714	678	738	14	87	25	1.26	48	18	34	83	90	6%	152	28%	87%	10	50%	30%	4.42	1.0	91	186	$4
10	OAK *	312	55	8	41	33	291	270	356	448	804	949	716	9	83	33	0.59	47	17	37	99	98	9%	136	40%	88%	14	57%	14%	6.13	16.7	72	157	$21
11	OAK	531	69	8	54	49	264	273	314	379	693	593	741	7	88	29	0.63	42	24	34	75	83	5%	108	41%	84%	26	65%	15%	4.37	2.0	60	133	$25
12	OAK	455	68	11	46	39	259	274	325	418	742	682	774	9	86	28	0.70	44	20	36	95	76	8%	125	36%	91%	26	38%	23%	5.03	10.5	77	193	$22
13	OAK	513	93	22	66	21	261	278	335	444	779	645	857	11	87	26	0.94	41	20	40	107	85	12%	108	18%	81%	25	56%	16%	5.27	15.4	90	225	$25
1st Half		237	46	9	28	13	274	292	370	456	826	753	858	13	88	28	1.29	46	19	35	111	74	12%	104	21%	81%	13	62%	8%	6.02	12.7	101	253	$26
2nd Half		276	47	13	38	8	250	266	312	435	747	549	856	8	87	25	0.68	36	20	44	103	95	13%	110	14%	80%	12	50%	25%	4.64	3.8	80	200	$24
14	**Proj**	**475**	**81**	**13**	**58**	**25**	**264**	**270**	**331**	**417**	**748**	**651**	**800**	**9**	**87**	**28**	**0.79**	**42**	**20**	**38**	**93**	**84**	**9%**	**120**	**23%**	**83%**				**4.95**	**10.8**	**85**	**212**	**$23**

Crowe,Trevor

Age	30	Bats	B	Pos	RF LF	Health	F	LIMA Plan	D
						PT/Exp	F	Rand Var	0
Ht	5' 10"	Wt	190			Consist	B	MM	1301

1-13-.218 with 6 SB in 165 AB at HOU. Had a chance at regular playing time in the anemic HOU outfield until a shoulder injury shelved him for two months. Only skill he offers is the ability to run, but that's completely undercut by terrible SB success rate. Strictly roster filler at this point, in real life and fantasy.

Yr	Tm	AB	R	HR	RBI	SB	BA	xBA	OBP	SLG	OPS	vL	vR	bb%	ct%	h%	Eye	G	L	F	PX	xPX	hr/f	Spd	SBO	SB%	#Wk	DOM	DIS	RC/G	RAR	BPV	BPX	R$
09	CLE *	368	42	2	32	17	241	251	306	330	636	683	586	9	79	30	0.45	56	16	27	64	58	3%	117	25%	67%	19	26%	42%	3.30	-7.6	22	45	$6
10	CLE *	561	62	3	45	24	238	253	282	314	596	490	679	6	83	28	0.35	53	18	29	57	70	2%	110	24%	75%	22	50%	32%	2.97	-17.1	24	52	$10
11	CLE	28	6	0	2	3	214	238	313	250	563	517	606	13	68	32	0.44	58	32	11	40	28	0%	103	33%	100%	3	0%	67%	3.13	-0.6	-38	-84	-$1
12	a/a	310	32	2	20	12	207	222	260	285	545			7	78	26	0.32				58			105	35%	51%				2.12		5	13	$1
13	HOU *	402	45	3	28	17	225	227	280	291	571	743	529	7	79	28	0.37	50	20	30	48	90	3%	112	26%	62%	12	33%	58%	2.57	-17.7	4	10	$6
1st Half		184	24	2	14	10	220	229	295	303	598	773	514	10	80	26	0.53	49	19	32	51	84	6%	132	32%	63%	7	43%	43%	2.77	-7.3	22	55	$9
2nd Half		218	21	1	14	6	229	224	267	280	547	718	541	5	78	29	0.24	51	20	29	46	94	0%	93	20%	62%	5	20%	80%	2.39	-11.0	-11	-28	$4
14	**Proj**	**130**	**14**	**1**	**9**	**5**	**225**	**230**	**280**	**291**	**571**	**616**	**557**	**7**	**79**	**28**	**0.35**	**52**	**19**	**29**	**51**	**78**	**2%**	**106**	**26%**	**60%**				**2.53**	**-7.8**	**4**	**11**	**$2**

Cruz,Nelson

Age	34	Bats	R	Pos	RF	Health	B	LIMA Plan	B
						PT/Exp	B	Rand Var	0
Ht	6' 2"	Wt	240			Consist	B	MM	4115

Boost in PX and hr/f in 1H had him on track for his first 40-HR season. It was almost as if he found some magic pill to fight off advancing age....oh, right. Prior consistency suggests he'll get back on track, but PED issue casts a shadow over everything he's done, including his aging curve.

Yr	Tm	AB	R	HR	RBI	SB	BA	xBA	OBP	SLG	OPS	vL	vR	bb%	ct%	h%	Eye	G	L	F	PX	xPX	hr/f	Spd	SBO	SB%	#Wk	DOM	DIS	RC/G	RAR	BPV	BPX	R$
09	TEX	462	75	33	76	20	260	277	332	524	856	752	898	10	74	28	0.42	38	16	46	166	154	21%	85	21%	83%	25	56%	12%	6.02	23.6	77	157	$22
10	TEX *	429	61	22	81	18	311	293	369	554	924	976	941	9	80	35	0.46	37	18	45	163	149	15%	102	19%	82%	21	57%	14%	7.60	39.0	99	215	$27
11	TEX *	497	66	31	90	9	262	278	311	512	823	1096	747	7	76	28	0.30	41	16	43	168	144	19%	71	13%	64%	24	71%	17%	5.36	15.8	76	169	$21
12	TEX	585	86	24	90	8	260	262	319	460	779	944	727	8	76	30	0.34	41	18	41	141	151	13%	80	9%	67%	27	48%	19%	4.94	11.3	58	145	$20
13	TEX	413	49	27	76	5	266	264	327	506	833	821	837	8	74	30	0.32	42	17	41	162	154	21%	58	6%	83%	20	65%	25%	5.71	17.0	59	148	$18
1st Half		295	32	20	61	5	271	268	328	525	854	808	874	8	73	31	0.32	40	16	44	175	161	21%	54	9%	83%	14	71%	21%	6.05	13.6	67	168	$24
2nd Half		118	17	7	15	0	254	250	313	458	770	854	743	8	75	28	0.33	47	18	35	131	136	23%	78	0%	0%	6	50%	33%	4.89	1.5	44	110	$3
14	**Proj**	**484**	**66**	**22**	**79**	**7**	**263**	**252**	**322**	**452**	**774**	**866**	**744**	**8**	**75**	**31**	**0.34**	**42**	**17**	**40**	**132**	**148**	**15%**	**73**	**7%**	**74%**				**5.00**	**7.7**	**45**	**114**	**$19**

Cruz,Tony

Age	27	Bats	R	Pos	CA	Health	A	LIMA Plan	D
						PT/Exp	F	Rand Var	+3
Ht	5' 11"	Wt	215			Consist	B	MM	1001

When you're a backup catcher playing behind a perennial All-Star who routinely sees 500 AB, you don't have a lot of time to make an impression. We're still waiting. No plate patience, no power, little chance at regular playing time. Unless your league awards points for warming up pitchers between innings, pass.

Yr	Tm	AB	R	HR	RBI	SB	BA	xBA	OBP	SLG	OPS	vL	vR	bb%	ct%	h%	Eye	G	L	F	PX	xPX	hr/f	Spd	SBO	SB%	#Wk	DOM	DIS	RC/G	RAR	BPV	BPX	R$
09	aa	405	34	7	37	1	187	242	236	299	535			6	77	23	0.28				80			93	1%	100%				2.22		14	29	-$5
10	a/a	163	20	5	15	0	231	251	288	367	655			7	78	27	0.37				97			100	0%	0%				3.51		37	80	$0
11	STL *	214	17	2	23	0	223	206	271	306	577	668	674	6	77	28	0.28	46	15	38	64	69	0%	101	4%	0%	15	27%	40%	2.59	-7.2	4	9	-$1
12	STL	126	11	1	11	0	254	237	267	365	632	439	724	2	85	29	0.16	46	14	40	79	92	2%	99	4%	0%	25	36%	36%	3.25	-1.6	39	98	-$1
13	STL	123	13	1	13	0	203	241	240	293	533	235	643	3	80	25	0.16	54	18	28	67	77	4%	91	0%	0%	21	29%	52%	2.14	-5.9	8	20	-$3
1st Half		33	3	0	4	0	152	200	176	212	389	0	554	3	73	21	0.11	46	17	38	63	100	0%	79	0%	0%	11	9%	64%	1.13	-2.8	-27	-68	-$4
2nd Half		90	10	1	9	0	222	257	247	322	570	333	673	3	82	26	0.19	57	19	24	69	70	6%	100	0%	0%	10	50%	40%	2.61	-3.0	23	58	-$2
14	**Proj**	**135**	**13**	**1**	**13**	**0**	**227**	**226**	**262**	**311**	**574**	**372**	**664**	**4**	**80**	**28**	**0.21**	**49**	**16**	**35**	**65**	**84**	**2%**	**94**	**2%**	**6%**				**2.59**	**-4.6**	**2**	**4**	**$1**

DAVE ADLER

Cuddyer,Michael

Age 35	Bats R	Pos RF	Health C	LIMA Plan B+	
Ht 6' 2"	Wt 220		PT/Exp B	Rand Var -5	
			Consist C	MM 4335	

The big boost in BA is enticing, but xBA shows that his skills dipped slightly; thank you, h%. While HRs have been fairly steady, xPX and GBs put that into question as well. Combine those warning signs, spotted health history and advancing age, and there's regression ahead - maybe a lot. DN: 15 HR, .270 BA.

Yr	Tm	AB	R	HR	RBI	SB	BA	xBA	OBP	SLG	OPS	vL	vR	bb%	ct%	h%	Eye	G	L	F	PX	xPX	hr/f	Spd	SBO	SB%	#Wk	DOM	DIS	RC/G	RAR	BPV	BPX	R$
09	MIN	588	93	32	94	6	276	293	342	520	862	1013	803	8	80	30	0.46	44	17	40	147	122	17%	117	5%	86%	27	67%	22%	6.19	26.4	91	186	$22
10	MIN	609	93	14	81	7	271	280	336	417	753	875	700	9	85	30	0.62	50	17	33	97	90	8%	116	6%	70%	27	63%	15%	4.85	4.2	71	154	$18
11	MIN	529	70	20	70	11	284	277	346	459	805	993	728	8	82	31	0.51	49	18	34	116	108	14%	99	8%	92%	26	54%	19%	5.71	16.3	69	153	$21
12	COL	358	53	16	58	8	260	296	317	489	806	929	760	8	78	29	0.41	49	20	31	155	125	18%	91	14%	73%	19	58%	21%	5.34	7.7	82	205	$13
13	COL	489	74	20	84	10	331	287	389	530	919	815	954	9	80	38	0.46	50	20	30	134	101	17%	117	8%	77%	26	65%	23%	7.83	41.7	80	200	$31
1st Half		244	38	14	48	6	344	303	392	590	982	1006	974	7	80	39	0.39	45	22	33	161	107	22%	115	10%	86%	13	85%	8%	9.05	29.0	99	248	$35
2nd Half		245	36	6	36	4	318	270	386	469	855	596	933	10	79	38	0.53	54	18	27	107	94	11%	114	7%	67%	13	46%	38%	6.70	14.9	59	148	$27
14	Proj	525	75	20	81	9	292	285	352	487	839	852	834	9	80	33	0.46	49	19	31	133	108	16%	108	9%	75%				6.14	24.9	73	184	$23

D Arnaud,Travis

Age 25	Bats R	Pos CA	Health F	LIMA Plan B	
Ht 6' 2"	Wt 195		PT/Exp D	Rand Var +4	
			Consist C	MM 3113	

1-5-.202 in 99 AB at NYM. Top prospect lost most of the past two years to injury—a torn PCL in 2012, broken foot in 2013. Didn't do much with his first cup of coffee in majors, but the seeds of a solid patience-and-power profile are there. Has future All-Star upside, though it may take a few years (and health) to reach it.

Yr	Tm	AB	R	HR	RBI	SB	BA	xBA	OBP	SLG	OPS	vL	vR	bb%	ct%	h%	Eye	G	L	F	PX	xPX	hr/f	Spd	SBO	SB%	#Wk	DOM	DIS	RC/G	RAR	BPV	BPX	R$
09																																		
10																																		
11	aa	424	61	19	66	3	290	275	334	504	838			6	74	35	0.25				160			83	6%	61%				5.97		63	140	$18
12	aaa	279	31	12	36	1	287	267	318	492	810			4	76	34	0.19				139			89	3%	38%				5.51		52	130	$8
13	NYM *	182	18	3	15	0	208	225	314	324	638	298	630	13	74	26	0.61	47	18	35	92	74	4%	96	0%	0%	7	43%	43%	3.27	-2.3	29	73	-$2
1st Half		36	7	1	5	0	183	254	322	337	659			17	73	23	0.75				136			104	0%	0%				3.38		68	170	-$1
2nd Half		146	10	2	10	0	212	215	308	316	624	298	630	12	75	27	0.55	47	18	35	80	74	4%	100	0%	0%	7	43%	43%	3.15	-2.5	19	48	-$2
14	Proj	407	44	10	48	2	262	248	316	412	728	329	857	8	76	32	0.34	44	20	36	112	67	9%	92	3%	57%				4.51	9.4	28	69	$10

Danks,Jordan

Age 27	Bats L	Pos CF RF	Health A	LIMA Plan D	
Ht 6' 4"	Wt 210		PT/Exp C	Rand Var 0	
			Consist D	MM 3301	

5-12-.231 with 7 SB in 160 AB at CHW. Extreme hacker is unlikely to ever hit for a decent BA, but small-sample xPX from his MLB stint hints at some latent power. 21% SBO in majors says he could be a decent SB threat, too. But age and struggles vs LHP limit future growth. Rather than budding star, think decent 4th OF.

Yr	Tm	AB	R	HR	RBI	SB	BA	xBA	OBP	SLG	OPS	vL	vR	bb%	ct%	h%	Eye	G	L	F	PX	xPX	hr/f	Spd	SBO	SB%	#Wk	DOM	DIS	RC/G	RAR	BPV	BPX	R$
09	aa	284	43	6	17	6	220	222	300	324	624			10	71	29	0.40				76			119	12%	64%				3.13		4	8	$1
10	aaa	445	47	7	32	11	209	202	263	317	580			7	60	33	0.19				105			109	19%	62%				2.60		-25	-54	$1
11	aaa	463	51	13	51	14	222	209	297	367	664			10	60	34	0.27				129			105	16%	75%				3.58		-3	-7	$8
12	CHW *	285	43	9	29	8	268	234	370	423	793	385	685	14	67	37	0.49	47	22	31	123	82	6%	104	13%	64%	17	18%	53%	5.33	9.1	26	65	$9
13	CHW *	368	41	10	33	9	232	223	306	362	667	523	707	10	65	33	0.31	39	27	33	106	137	15%	84	13%	74%	18	22%	56%	3.67	-6.3	-6	-15	$6
1st Half		163	21	5	17	3	226	217	312	353	665	250	495	11	64	32	0.35	45	25	30	97	85	17%	105	8%	69%	8	25%	63%	3.61	-2.8	-10	-25	$5
2nd Half		205	19	5	16	6	237	229	301	368	669	566	772	8	66	33	0.27	38	28	34	112	150	14%	83	17%	76%	10	20%	50%	3.71	-2.8	-2	-5	$7
14	Proj	219	26	6	20	6	229	219	308	364	672	478	732	10	65	33	0.33	44	22	34	112	107	12%	100	14%	71%				3.70	-3.1	1	3	$5

Davidson,Matthew

Age 23	Bats R	Pos 3B	Health A	LIMA Plan D	
Ht 6' 2"	Wt 225		PT/Exp D	Rand Var 0	
			Consist B	MM 4001	

3-12-.237 in 76 AB at ARI. Established a nice power profile in PCL, then hit lots of line drives in his Sept callup. But xBA points to problems - even with power and LD%, he may be hard-pressed to top a .250 BA. Just at the start of the growth curve, expect some more time on the Triple-A shuttle. Keep an eye on him, though.

Yr	Tm	AB	R	HR	RBI	SB	BA	xBA	OBP	SLG	OPS	vL	vR	bb%	ct%	h%	Eye	G	L	F	PX	xPX	hr/f	Spd	SBO	SB%	#Wk	DOM	DIS	RC/G	RAR	BPV	BPX	R$
09																																		
10																																		
11																																		
12	aa	486	65	19	62	2	244	249	320	428	747			10	72	30	0.40				130			90	5%	36%				4.47		42	105	$10
13	ARI *	519	43	14	59	1	235	240	288	392	680	641	833	7	67	33	0.22	37	27	37	134	144	16%	95	1%	39%	7	43%	43%	3.74	-3.9	17	43	$6
1st Half		299	22	7	30	1	245	223	279	387	666			5	66	35	0.14				124			88	1%	100%				3.65		0	0	$7
2nd Half		220	21	8	29	0	223	250	299	400	700	641	833	10	67	29	0.34	37	27	37	147	144	16%	94	2%	0%	7	43%	43%	3.85	-0.8	37	93	$5
14	Proj	192	20	6	23	0	237	237	311	398	709	614	759	9	69	31	0.31	40	22	39	130	130	11%	100	3%	34%				3.97	0.0	15	38	$3

Davis,Chris

Age 28	Bats L	Pos 1B	Health A	LIMA Plan B+	
Ht 6' 3"	Wt 230		PT/Exp B	Rand Var 0	
			Consist F	MM 5125	

The power was never in doubt, but THIS? Combine a big increase in fly balls with an insane hr/f, and yeah, it makes sense. He still strikes out a ton, but does it really matter? Outliers ALMOST always (Curse you, Trout!) regress, but there's room to regress and still be an elite, first-round level hitter in these power-starved times.

Yr	Tm	AB	R	HR	RBI	SB	BA	xBA	OBP	SLG	OPS	vL	vR	bb%	ct%	h%	Eye	G	L	F	PX	xPX	hr/f	Spd	SBO	SB%	#Wk	DOM	DIS	RC/G	RAR	BPV	BPX	R$
09	TEX *	556	71	26	85	0	258	237	314	456	770	546	808	8	65	35	0.23	35	21	44	147	162	20%	95	1%	0%	21	29%	43%	4.88	4.3	24	49	$13
10	TEX *	518	56	12	63	5	264	247	320	413	732	411	618	8	70	36	0.27	42	22	36	125	75	3%	74	6%	69%	11	9%	36%	4.55	-0.8	18	39	$12
11	2 AL *	398	58	26	71	2	299	278	333	559	892	906	657	5	67	39	0.16	38	25	37	202	137	10%	86	2%	100%	16	31%	56%	6.80	24.0	68	151	$20
12	BAL	515	75	33	85	2	270	252	326	501	827	792	836	7	67	34	0.22	39	23	38	162	150	25%	74	4%	40%	27	71%	30%	5.46	12.7	36	90	$20
13	BAL	584	103	53	138	4	286	297	370	634	1004	763	1142	11	66	34	0.36	32	22	46	266	199	30%	65	3%	80%	27	78%	11%	8.24	59.5	120	300	$38
1st Half		298	60	31	80	0	332	330	402	728	1131	849	1262	11	69	39	0.38	31	24	45	289	217	33%	64	0%	0%	14	86%	0%	11.19	51.4	151	378	$47
2nd Half		286	43	22	58	4	238	264	325	535	860	699	991	11	62	29	0.34	34	20	46	239	178	26%	75	8%	80%	13	69%	23%	5.82	10.5	87	218	$30
14	Proj	575	89	39	105	4	276	267	344	541	885	765	937	9	66	35	0.28	35	23	42	204	167	24%	74	4%	70%				6.43	30.1	66	166	$28

Davis,Ike

Age 27	Bats L	Pos 1B	Health D	LIMA Plan B	
Ht 6' 4"	Wt 230		PT/Exp C	Rand Var +4	
			Consist D	MM 4215	

9-33-.205 in 317 AB at NYM. The irony... Posted horrible stats by early June 2012 but then exploded. Posted nearly the same stats by June '13 and was demoted instead. The difference? His underlying skills were worse this year. 2nd half shows glimmers that there's still something here, but approach with caution.

Yr	Tm	AB	R	HR	RBI	SB	BA	xBA	OBP	SLG	OPS	vL	vR	bb%	ct%	h%	Eye	G	L	F	PX	xPX	hr/f	Spd	SBO	SB%	#Wk	DOM	DIS	RC/G	RAR	BPV	BPX	R$
09	aa	207	24	11	35	0	276	252	341	494	835			9	66	37	0.29				164			82	0%	0%				5.94		42	86	$5
10	NYM *	556	79	20	74	3	267	254	358	445	802	805	787	12	74	33	0.55	43	16	41	132	129	12%	91	3%	60%	25	60%	20%	5.49	14.5	56	122	$16
11	NYM	129	20	7	25	0	302	277	383	543	925	493	1142	12	76	35	0.55	42	17	41	165	126	17%	104	0%	0%	7	71%	29%	7.61	10.6	92	204	$5
12	NYM	519	66	32	90	0	227	262	308	462	771	560	868	11	73	25	0.43	39	21	40	157	166	21%	57	2%	0%	27	48%	30%	4.63	0.7	57	143	$12
13	NYM *	392	49	13	41	4	207	229	323	357	680	406	727	15	68	27	0.54	45	20	35	119	99	12%	75	3%	100%	20	35%	50%	3.76	-10.0	22	55	$3
1st Half		248	27	8	22	0	174	204	259	301	559	424	526	10	66	22	0.34	45	19	36	98	97	12%	80	0%	0%	12	8%	67%	2.40	-17.7	-11	-28	-$1
2nd Half		144	22	5	19	4	264	264	419	454	873	349	952	21	72	33	0.96	45	21	34	152	102	12%	82	7%	100%	8	75%	25%	6.82	9.2	79	198	$9
14	Proj	423	57	18	61	4	234	247	338	419	758	492	843	14	72	29	0.56	43	18	39	140	123	15%	75	3%	88%				4.76	2.1	45	113	$11

Davis,Khristopher

Age 26	Bats R	Pos LF	Health A	LIMA Plan C+	
Ht 5' 11"	Wt 200		PT/Exp F	Rand Var +4	
			Consist F	MM 4223	

11-27-.279 with 3 SB in 136 AB at MIL. Injuries and suspensions created an opportunity, and he took advantage. 78% ct% and 212 PX in 120 AB at MIL in 2nd half; a small sample size, but an indicator that he can hold his own in the bigs. If he gets regular playing time... UP: 25+ HR.

Yr	Tm	AB	R	HR	RBI	SB	BA	xBA	OBP	SLG	OPS	vL	vR	bb%	ct%	h%	Eye	G	L	F	PX	xPX	hr/f	Spd	SBO	SB%	#Wk	DOM	DIS	RC/G	RAR	BPV	BPX	R$
09																																		
10																																		
11	aa	124	8	2	12	0	180	233	228	281	509			6	78	22	0.29				77			94	0%	0%				2.00		17	38	-$4
12	a/a	241	36	11	37	2	305	259	387	516	903			12	70	40	0.45				160			80	6%	50%				7.13		58	145	$10
13	MIL *	379	51	21	52	7	233	266	294	456	750	1009	918	8	72	27	0.31	43	20	37	159	162	29%	90	15%	60%	16	63%	25%	4.31	3.0	60	150	$11
1st Half		218	19	7	17	4	192	249	261	331	592	673	452	9	71	24	0.33	50	25	25	105	17	0%	84	17%	55%	5	20%	40%	2.60	-10.0	13	33	$4
2nd Half		161	32	14	35	3	290	314	340	627	967	1105	951	7	73	31	0.28	42	20	38	230	175	31%	97	12%	69%	11	82%	18%	7.52	15.9	121	303	$21
14	Proj	351	47	15	49	4	253	257	335	449	784	778	786	9	72	31	0.36	42	20	38	145	158	16%	95	8%	59%				4.79	8.1	47	118	$11

DAVE ADLER

Davis,Rajai

Age	33	Bats	R	Pos	LF RF	Health	C
Ht	5' 9"	Wt	195			PT/Exp	C
						Consist	B

LIMA Plan	C+
Rand Var	-1
MM	2513

With SB outnumbering RBI, you know how he earns his paycheck. 1H BA held promise, but it was an h%-fueled mirage. Struggles against RHP already limit playing time, and as he ages, insane SBO rates may be tough to maintain. But 33 isn't ancient just yet, so give him another year of speed value.

Yr	Tm	AB	R	HR	RBI	SB	BA	xBA	OBP	SLG	OPS	vL	vR	bb%	ct%	h%	Eye	G	L	F	PX	xPX	hr/f	Spd	SBO	SB%	#Wk	DOM	DIS	RC/G	RAR	BPV	BPX	R$
09	OAK	390	65	3	48	41	305	266	360	423	784	773	789	7	82	37	0.41	46	20	34	83	72	3%	132	47%	77%	27	41%	22%	5.49	16.7	50	102	$25
10	OAK	525	66	5	52	50	284	250	320	377	697	784	666	5	85	33	0.33	48	16	37	67	58	3%	131	44%	82%	27	37%	22%	4.42	6.7	45	98	$28
11	TOR	320	44	1	29	34	238	238	273	350	623	829	551	4	80	29	0.24	44	16	40	85	50	1%	151	71%	76%	20	35%	45%	3.12	-8.5	46	102	$11
12	TOR	447	64	8	43	46	257	248	309	378	687	783	638	6	77	32	0.28	45	23	32	86	75	7%	119	54%	78%	27	26%	44%	3.95	-0.3	27	68	$22
13	TOR	331	49	6	24	45	260	241	312	375	687	857	594	6	80	31	0.31	39	23	38	81	84	6%	127	61%	88%	23	26%	30%	4.34	3.5	36	90	$23
1st Half		126	23	1	8	19	317	250	344	397	740	826	691	4	82	38	0.22	38	30	32	57	69	3%	128	55%	90%	11	9%	36%	5.75	6.0	21	53	$21
2nd Half		205	26	5	16	26	224	238	281	361	642	887	548	7	79	26	0.36	40	18	42	97	93	7%	110	67%	87%	12	42%	25%	3.63	-2.5	41	103	$24
14	Proj	**317**	**46**	**5**	**27**	**38**	**260**	**244**	**309**	**375**	**684**	**827**	**613**	**6**	**80**	**31**	**0.30**	**42**	**21**	**36**	**83**	**74**	**5%**	**129**	**59%**	**83%**				**4.12**	**0.9**	**48**	**121**	**$17**

De Aza,Alejandro

Age	30	Bats	L	Pos	CF LF	Health	A
Ht	6' 0"	Wt	190			PT/Exp	A
						Consist	B

LIMA Plan	B+
Rand Var	-1
MM	2415

Bump in FB% and hr/f led to more HRs, but xPX casts doubt on the power surge. Nice improvement vs LHP, but two-year decline in xBA suggests .280+ BA isn't coming back. He's been consistently above $20 for three seasons, but these indicators are enough to create a little uncertainty about a fourth.

Yr	Tm	AB	R	HR	RBI	SB	BA	xBA	OBP	SLG	OPS	vL	vR	bb%	ct%	h%	Eye	G	L	F	PX	xPX	hr/f	Spd	SBO	SB%	#Wk	DOM	DIS	RC/G	RAR	BPV	BPX	R$
09	FLA *	287	40	6	28	8	254	250	316	409	726	0	788	8	75	32	0.37	50	13	38	110	-5	0%	122	20%	58%	7	43%	57%	4.21	1.0	45	92	$6
10	CHW *	348	46	4	38	14	252	245	300	362	662	900	692	6	78	31	0.30	56	12	32	85	45	0%	124	22%	75%	6	17%	17%	3.70	-5.5	30	65	$9
11	CHW *	537	78	12	51	29	285	266	340	440	780	702	951	8	77	35	0.36	49	20	31	115	81	11%	142	33%	61%	10	60%	20%	4.92	10.8	59	131	$24
12	CHW	524	81	9	50	26	281	259	349	410	760	700	779	8	79	34	0.43	42	26	32	88	96	7%	126	25%	68%	24	42%	29%	4.79	8.4	43	108	$22
13	CHW	607	84	17	62	20	264	250	323	405	728	816	702	8	76	32	0.34	41	25	35	100	81	11%	118	17%	71%	27	37%	41%	4.43	3.4	36	90	$23
1st Half		303	46	10	40	10	264	245	324	419	743	852	707	8	73	33	0.33	42	22	36	114	88	13%	105	17%	71%	14	36%	36%	4.65	4.2	34	85	$25
2nd Half		304	38	7	22	10	263	254	315	391	706	782	697	7	78	32	0.35	39	27	33	86	75	9%	131	17%	71%	13	38%	46%	4.22	0.4	37	93	$20
14	Proj	**537**	**74**	**11**	**51**	**21**	**266**	**255**	**329**	**398**	**727**	**719**	**729**	**8**	**77**	**33**	**0.36**	**43**	**25**	**32**	**95**	**86**	**8%**	**126**	**21%**	**69%**				**4.36**	**3.0**	**38**	**94**	**$20**

DeJesus,David

Age	34	Bats	L	Pos	CF LF	Health	C
Ht	5' 11"	Wt	190			PT/Exp	B
						Consist	A

LIMA Plan	C
Rand Var	+1
MM	2223

His skills have been merely league-average for three years now. But low hr/f and SBO combined with decreased playing time have turned those average skills into lackluster counting stats and BA. He's been on five different teams in four seasons - he's good enough to lust for, not good enough to love.

Yr	Tm	AB	R	HR	RBI	SB	BA	xBA	OBP	SLG	OPS	vL	vR	bb%	ct%	h%	Eye	G	L	F	PX	xPX	hr/f	Spd	SBO	SB%	#Wk	DOM	DIS	RC/G	RAR	BPV	BPX	R$
09	KC	558	74	13	71	4	281	277	347	434	781	690	832	8	84	31	0.59	46	20	34	91	95	8%	116	8%	31%	25	60%	12%	4.96	11.6	64	131	$15
10	KC	352	46	5	37	3	318	282	384	443	827	725	864	9	87	36	0.72	47	21	32	86	95	5%	118	5%	50%	16	56%	19%	6.13	18.0	70	152	$13
11	OAK	442	60	10	46	4	240	252	323	376	698	459	787	9	81	28	0.52	43	20	37	91	100	8%	110	6%	57%	27	41%	33%	3.85	-5.2	49	109	$7
12	CHC	506	76	9	50	7	263	263	350	403	753	438	826	11	82	30	0.69	41	24	35	90	131	6%	121	10%	47%	27	48%	30%	4.56	4.8	62	155	$12
13	3 TM	391	52	8	38	5	251	257	327	402	729	467	772	9	80	30	0.49	42	19	39	111	110	7%	106	8%	63%	22	50%	14%	4.29	0.6	60	150	$8
1st Half		200	32	6	21	3	260	278	312	445	757	523	804	7	83	29	0.43	43	19	38	126	109	10%	114	7%	100%	11	73%	18%	4.87	4.0	81	203	$11
2nd Half		191	20	2	17	2	241	236	326	356	682	402	737	11	77	30	0.55	40	20	40	95	111	3%	93	9%	40%	11	27%	9%	3.71	-2.7	36	90	$4
14	Proj	**380**	**51**	**7**	**38**	**4**	**256**	**257**	**337**	**397**	**734**	**493**	**790**	**10**	**81**	**30**	**0.56**	**42**	**21**	**37**	**100**	**112**	**6%**	**111**	**8%**	**52%**				**4.33**	**1.8**	**53**	**132**	**$9**

Den Dekker,Matthew

Age	26	Bats	L	Pos	CF	Health	A
Ht	6' 1"	Wt	205			PT/Exp	D
						Consist	A

LIMA Plan	D
Rand Var	-1
MM	2303

1-12-.207 with 4 SB in 58 AB at NYM. Has climbed through the minors despite ct% deficiencies, though with decent speed and high SBO, he can be a contributor on the basepaths. Platoon issues may make him unlikely to stick as a full-timer (.978 OPS vs RHP in the minors, but .362 OPS vs LHP). Think 4th OFer/platoon role.

Yr	Tm	AB	R	HR	RBI	SB	BA	xBA	OBP	SLG	OPS	vL	vR	bb%	ct%	h%	Eye	G	L	F	PX	xPX	hr/f	Spd	SBO	SB%	#Wk	DOM	DIS	RC/G	RAR	BPV	BPX	R$
09																																		
10																																		
11	aa	272	35	8	23	9	179	208	232	314	546			6	62	25	0.18				113			114	30%	59%				2.12		-11	-24	$0
12	a/a	533	63	13	57	16	223	214	258	361	619			5	65	32	0.14				109			105	26%	60%				2.89		-9	-23	$9
13	NYM *	237	27	5	29	9	214	205	263	318	581	200	572	6	65	31	0.19	34	29	37	82	135	8%	106	21%	80%	6	0%	83%	2.76	-9.8	-25	-63	$3
1st Half																																		
2nd Half		237	27	5	29	9	214	205	263	318	581	200	572	6	65	31	0.19	34	29	37	82	135	8%	106	21%	80%	6	0%	83%	2.76	-10.5	-26	-65	$3
14	Proj	**330**	**40**	**7**	**34**	**9**	**212**	**200**	**269**	**331**	**599**	**302**	**622**	**6**	**64**	**31**	**0.17**	**39**	**22**	**39**	**97**	**122**	**9%**	**104**	**20%**	**67%**				**2.70**	**-15.3**	**-16**	**-40**	**$5**

Denorfia,Chris

Age	33	Bats	R	Pos	RF LF CF	Health	A
Ht	6' 0"	Wt	195			PT/Exp	C
						Consist	B

LIMA Plan	D+
Rand Var	0
MM	2433

Rising HR totals make it look like he's developing some pop, but high GB% and lack of xPX growth show that trend is being driven by more playing time. GB/Spd/ct% combo works for BA, but futility vs. RHP will continue to throttle his AB totals. And as the AB totals go, so goes his value. Best use: exploit the platoon split.

Yr	Tm	AB	R	HR	RBI	SB	BA	xBA	OBP	SLG	OPS	vL	vR	bb%	ct%	h%	Eye	G	L	F	PX	xPX	hr/f	Spd	SBO	SB%	#Wk	DOM	DIS	RC/G	RAR	BPV	BPX	R$
09	OAK *	434	44	6	35	10	202	285	240	289	529	0	0	5	85	23	0.33	100	0	0	53	-5	0%	136	21%	57%	2	0%	0%	2.10	-34.7	35	71	-$1
10	SD *	405	52	10	44	13	256	287	316	408	723	763	769	8	81	29	0.47	59	17	24	101	68	16%	132	18%	70%	21	33%	29%	4.34	-3.1	63	137	$11
11	SD	307	38	5	19	11	277	263	337	381	718	887	611	8	84	32	0.57	59	16	25	70	61	8%	132	18%	65%	23	35%	48%	4.40	-1.8	51	113	$8
12	SD	348	56	8	36	13	293	296	345	451	796	890	697	7	85	33	0.52	60	18	22	95	69	13%	146	19%	72%	27	56%	19%	5.51	8.9	76	190	$14
13	SD	473	67	10	47	11	279	271	337	395	732	834	663	8	82	32	0.50	55	21	24	79	68	11%	123	8%	100%	27	44%	19%	4.88	3.6	47	118	$17
1st Half		247	31	6	26	7	275	261	335	393	727	869	616	8	83	31	0.54	56	17	27	79	76	11%	105	10%	100%	14	50%	14%	4.81	2.5	47	118	$17
2nd Half		226	36	4	21	4	283	277	341	398	740	790	709	8	81	34	0.47	55	25	21	78	60	11%	130	6%	100%	13	38%	23%	4.96	3.2	44	110	$16
14	Proj	**258**	**37**	**6**	**24**	**7**	**278**	**278**	**333**	**407**	**740**	**836**	**670**	**8**	**83**	**32**	**0.49**	**57**	**20**	**23**	**84**	**66**	**11%**	**131**	**13%**	**78%**				**4.81**	**2.6**	**51**	**128**	**$10**

DeRosa,Mark

Age	39	Bats	R	Pos	2B 3B	Health	F
Ht	6' 1"	Wt	215			PT/Exp	F
						Consist	C

LIMA Plan	D
Rand Var	0
MM	1001

Who says that old guys can't get the job done? PX, xPX, hr/f, xBA were all reminiscent of 2009; only difference was playing time. Won't be a full-timer again, but plate patience, power, and good results vs LHP mean there might still be a platoon/bench role for him somewhere. The AARP card can wait.

Yr	Tm	AB	R	HR	RBI	SB	BA	xBA	OBP	SLG	OPS	vL	vR	bb%	ct%	h%	Eye	G	L	F	PX	xPX	hr/f	Spd	SBO	SB%	#Wk	DOM	DIS	RC/G	RAR	BPV	BPX	R$
09	2 TM	515	78	23	78	3	250	256	319	433	752	928	695	8	77	29	0.39	43	17	40	117	120	14%	79	4%	60%	26	42%	31%	4.57	9.5	42	86	$12
10	SF	93	9	1	10	0	194	228	279	258	537	840	421	9	83	22	0.56	44	19	36	46	60	4%	81	9%	0%	5	20%	60%	1.95	-5.9	12	26	-$2
11	SF *	128	12	0	14	1	259	219	303	280	583	667	639	6	78	33	0.28	58	22	20	21	38	0%	82	5%	50%	16	19%	56%	2.86	-4.2	-34	-76	$0
12	WAS	85	13	0	6	1	188	221	300	247	547	651	456	14	79	24	0.78	60	13	27	54	52	0%	88	4%	100%	15	33%	47%	2.41	-4.1	15	38	-$2
13	TOR	204	23	7	36	0	235	257	326	407	733	810	589	12	76	28	0.57	46	20	34	123	123	13%	74	0%	0%	27	48%	33%	4.44	3.0	51	128	$2
1st Half		105	14	4	21	0	210	264	303	390	693	784	511	12	75	24	0.54	48	21	31	134	106	16%	64	0%	0%	14	50%	29%	3.81	-0.5	53	133	$2
2nd Half		99	9	3	15	0	263	248	354	424	778	840	663	12	77	32	0.61	43	19	38	112	141	10%	89	0%	0%	13	46%	38%	5.19	3.5	50	125	$2
14	Proj	**190**	**20**	**3**	**27**	**0**	**244**	**232**	**318**	**347**	**665**	**757**	**561**	**10**	**77**	**30**	**0.47**	**50**	**18**	**31**	**75**	**91**	**7%**	**80**	**3%**	**31%**				**3.64**	**-0.3**	**6**	**15**	**$3**

Descalso,Daniel

Age	27	Bats	L	Pos	SS 2B 3B	Health	A
Ht	5' 10"	Wt	190			PT/Exp	C
						Consist	B

LIMA Plan	D+
Rand Var	+2
MM	2323

Surface stats have been steady and unremarkable, but his skills have been all over the map. If you could pick and choose, there are the makings of a more valuable player (2010 ct%, 2012 LD% and xPX, 2013 SBO). That's a stretch, of course, but he's too young to completely rule out skill consolidation. End-game speculation only.

Yr	Tm	AB	R	HR	RBI	SB	BA	xBA	OBP	SLG	OPS	vL	vR	bb%	ct%	h%	Eye	G	L	F	PX	xPX	hr/f	Spd	SBO	SB%	#Wk	DOM	DIS	RC/G	RAR	BPV	BPX	R$
09	a/a	438	55	7	54	2	262	268	319	388	707			8	84	30	0.54				82			103	3%	68%				4.27		52	106	$7
10	STL *	502	66	6	53	7	231	276	282	329	611	1000	559	7	88	25	0.58	61	14	25	69	30	0%	117	10%	58%	4	25%	75%	3.01	-7.6	57	124	$5
11	STL	326	35	1	28	2	264	241	334	353	687	518	724	9	80	33	0.51	47	20	33	72	61	1%	130	4%	50%	27	37%	48%	3.99	4.5	37	82	$4
12	STL	374	41	4	26	6	227	235	303	324	627	812	564	9	78	28	0.45	45	23	32	60	100	4%	144	9%	67%	27	22%	48%	3.14	-4.1	22	55	$2
13	STL	328	43	5	43	6	238	262	290	366	656	529	684	6	83	27	0.39	48	18	34	96	85	5%	89	13%	67%	27	41%	30%	3.44	-0.6	50	125	$6
1st Half		135	21	3	23	4	274	267	329	430	758	595	809	8	79	33	0.38	45	19	35	123	108	8%	94	15%	80%	14	43%	29%	4.99	5.9	58	145	$10
2nd Half		193	22	2	20	2	212	259	255	321	576	468	601	5	86	24	0.41	49	17	34	80	70	4%	89	11%	50%	13	38%	31%	2.56	-5.5	48	120	$3
14	Proj	**389**	**47**	**6**	**42**	**7**	**252**	**256**	**313**	**372**	**685**	**686**	**685**	**7**	**82**	**30**	**0.44**	**46**	**20**	**33**	**86**	**87**	**5%**	**109**	**10%**	**68%**				**3.87**	**4.7**	**41**	**103**	**$9**

DAVE ADLER

Desmond,Ian

Age 28	Bats R	Pos SS	Health	A	LIMA Plan	B+
Ht 6' 3"	Wt 210		PT/Exp	A	Rand Var	-2
			Consist	D	MM	4425

He owns the 20/20 level now, right? Probably. But PX/xPX regressed below league average in 2H. Maybe that was just due to nagging injuries (blister, back, hamstring). But xBA has rarely bought him as a .280 hitter. Should again be among NL's top SS, but minus-2 Rand Var speaks to faint whiff of uncertainty.

Yr	Tm	AB	R	HR	RBI	SB	BA	xBA	OBP	SLG	OPS	vL	vR	bb%	ct%	h%	Eye	G	L	F	PX	xPX	hr/f	Spd	SBO	SB%	#Wk	DOM	DIS	RC/G	RAR	BPV	BPX	R$
09	WAS *	430	55	10	40	19	295	266	349	453	802	633	913	8	79	36	0.39	54	12	34	108	138	17%	124	21%	77%	5	40%	20%	5.70	26.5	56	114	$17
10	WAS	525	59	10	65	17	269	257	308	392	700	799	664	5	79	32	0.26	53	16	32	88	84	8%	128	17%	77%	27	41%	37%	4.19	10.3	38	83	$16
11	WAS	584	65	8	49	25	253	239	298	358	656	642	659	6	76	32	0.25	52	18	31	79	75	6%	135	24%	71%	27	30%	52%	3.56	0.9	22	49	$15
12	WAS	513	72	25	73	21	292	279	335	511	845	902	828	6	78	33	0.27	48	18	35	142	115	18%	119	23%	78%	24	46%	33%	6.06	36.9	74	185	$27
13	WAS	600	77	20	80	21	280	265	331	453	784	766	789	7	76	34	0.30	43	22	34	126	100	13%	101	18%	78%	26	50%	31%	5.26	30.1	50	125	$28
1st Half		301	36	15	48	8	276	278	314	508	823	862	811	5	75	32	0.23	40	21	39	164	105	17%	89	16%	80%	14	64%	21%	5.62	18.6	71	178	$28
2nd Half		299	41	5	32	13	284	253	342	398	740	662	767	8	77	36	0.37	47	24	29	88	94	8%	112	19%	76%	12	33%	42%	4.86	11.9	28	70	$28
14	**Proj**	**584**	**75**	**20**	**72**	**23**	**273**	**265**	**321**	**449**	**770**	**765**	**771**	**6**	**77**	**32**	**0.29**	**46**	**20**	**34**	**124**	**100**	**13%**	**114**	**21%**	**76%**				**4.98**	**25.7**	**54**	**136**	**$24**

Dickerson,Chris

Age 32	Bats L	Pos DH	Health	B	LIMA Plan	F
Ht 6' 4"	Wt 230		PT/Exp	F	Rand Var	+1
			Consist	F	MM	2401

4-13-.238 with 5 SB in 105 AB at BAL. Another year on the fringes of an MLB roster, and for good reason: That ct% and Eye just aren't going to cut it, no matter how, um, competent his power and speed may be. LD%, FB% moved in positive direction, but at his age, the opportunities are likely to start going to younger players.

Yr	Tm	AB	R	HR	RBI	SB	BA	xBA	OBP	SLG	OPS	vL	vR	bb%	ct%	h%	Eye	G	L	F	PX	xPX	hr/f	Spd	SBO	SB%	#Wk	DOM	DIS	RC/G	RAR	BPV	BPX	R$
09	CIN	255	31	2	15	11	275	245	370	373	743	623	763	13	74	36	0.59	49	22	29	74	69	4%	137	15%	79%	21	33%	48%	4.94	7.1	25	51	$6
10	2 NL *	140	20	2	10	8	253	238	315	375	690	0	566	8	64	38	0.25	52	26	21	103	60	0%	125	25%	87%	12	8%	83%	4.22	0.7	-6	-13	$3
11	NYY *	262	34	3	19	18	207	187	276	281	557	718	637	9	64	31	0.27	45	18	36	70	55	8%	111	34%	78%	15	13%	53%	2.59	-11.5	-35	-78	$3
12	NYY *	280	45	8	23	15	249	245	338	415	753	2000	1026	12	65	36	0.39	67	11	22	137	100		115	24%	80%	6	33%	67%	4.83	7.2	30	75	$9
13	BAL *	241	34	6	19	6	211	215	268	334	601	286	693	7	67	29	0.23	36	25	39	101	105	15%	108	15%	72%	19	21%	53%	2.87	-8.3	-2	-5	$2
1st Half		106	18	4	14	4	258	231	287	429	717	286	798	4	65	36	0.12	36	27	37	138	121	18%	104	23%	80%	13	31%	54%	4.25	0.7	11	28	$8
2nd Half		135	16	2	5	2	174	174	253	258	512	0	67	10	68	24	0.34	38	13	50	73	-15	0%	103	10%	57%	6	0%	50%	1.98	-9.0	-16	-40	-$3
14	**Proj**	**95**	**14**	**1**	**7**	**4**	**222**	**222**	**294**	**334**	**627**	**421**	**656**	**9**	**66**	**32**	**0.30**	**46**	**24**	**30**	**97**	**79**	**8%**	**108**	**21%**	**78%**				**3.25**	**-3.7**	**-1**	**-3**	**$2**

Dickerson,Corey

Age 25	Bats L	Pos LF	Health	A	LIMA Plan	B
Ht 6' 1"	Wt 205		PT/Exp	F	Rand Var	0
			Consist	A	MM	4333

5-17-.263 in 194 AB at COL. Minor league standout's skills held up reasonably well in first MLB exposure, earning him PT from August on. For a player with plus power, he makes good contact. Some speed, but not likely going to be a source of big SBs. Still, with enough MLB AB and a touch more FB ... UP: 20 HR.

Yr	Tm	AB	R	HR	RBI	SB	BA	xBA	OBP	SLG	OPS	vL	vR	bb%	ct%	h%	Eye	G	L	F	PX	xPX	hr/f	Spd	SBO	SB%	#Wk	DOM	DIS	RC/G	RAR	BPV	BPX	R$
09																																		
10																																		
11																																		
12	aa	266	34	13	32	6	274	289	313	508	821			5	81	30	0.29				143			105	16%	65%				5.42		82	205	$9
13	COL *	509	68	13	47	6	297	287	338	494	832	581	819	6	81	35	0.33	40	26	34	125	107	10%	155	16%	29%	14	64%	21%	5.47	20.5	86	215	$19
1st Half		293	35	6	24	4	328	344	361	529	890	1000	795	5	81	39	0.28	44	44	11	130	152	0%	143	20%	23%	3	67%	33%	6.20	17.9	85	213	$23
2nd Half		216	33	6	23	2	257	279	307	448	755	543	821	7	81	29	0.39	40	25	35	119	104	10%	153	8%	50%	11	64%	18%	4.58	3.6	82	205	$13
14	**Proj**	**330**	**42**	**10**	**33**	**4**	**275**	**278**	**314**	**468**	**782**	**545**	**837**	**6**	**81**	**31**	**0.33**	**40**	**23**	**37**	**124**	**94**	**10%**	**142**	**12%**	**46%**				**4.96**	**9.0**	**70**	**176**	**$11**

Dietrich,Derek

Age 24	Bats L	Pos 2B	Health	A	LIMA Plan	D
Ht 6' 0"	Wt 200		PT/Exp	F	Rand Var	+2
			Consist	C	MM	4311

9-24-.214 in 215 AB at MIA. 25% h% and poor plate skills sabotaged initial opportunity after rapid rise to MLB. HR output looks intriguing at first, but 16% hr/f doesn't jibe with most scouting reports. Did end AA season with a flourish, though (.303, 6 HR in 89 AB in Aug). Needs more seasoning, but worth keeping on your radar.

Yr	Tm	AB	R	HR	RBI	SB	BA	xBA	OBP	SLG	OPS	vL	vR	bb%	ct%	h%	Eye	G	L	F	PX	xPX	hr/f	Spd	SBO	SB%	#Wk	DOM	DIS	RC/G	RAR	BPV	BPX	R$
09																																		
10																																		
11																																		
12	aa	133	18	3	14	0	233	218	263	358	622			4	69	31	0.13				95			103	4%	0%				3.01		-6	-15	$0
13	MIA *	433	61	18	54	3	227	255	288	421	708	786	644	8	70	28	0.29	40	25	35	142	114	16%	113	4%	100%	12	42%	25%	4.03	4.9	47	118	$8
1st Half		264	39	10	32	3	230	259	293	420	713	873	622	8	73	28	0.33	39	25	36	132	110	17%	122	5%	100%	9	56%	22%	4.13	3.4	53	133	$10
2nd Half		169	22	8	22	1	222	248	280	422	702	400	703	7	66	29	0.23	44	22	34	160	125	14%	99	2%	100%	3	0%	33%	3.89	1.0	38	95	$5
14	**Proj**	**197**	**27**	**7**	**23**	**1**	**230**	**245**	**299**	**407**	**706**	**672**	**715**	**6**	**69**	**30**	**0.21**	**42**	**23**	**35**	**134**	**119**	**15%**	**111**	**3%**	**83%**				**3.73**	**0.2**	**25**	**63**	**$4**

Dirks,Andy

Age 28	Bats L	Pos LF	Health	B	LIMA Plan	C+
Ht 6' 0"	Wt 195		PT/Exp	C	Rand Var	0
			Consist	D	MM	2323

Where did power go? Somehow managed to hold onto favorable side of platoon for much of season, but sub-.700 OPS vs. RHP won't cut it in that role. Low SBO in 2012 blamed on Achilles, but never came back. Last year we said It's "now-or-never time" for him. Now? "Never" looks like prohibitive favorite... DN: 200 AB, 5 HR

Yr	Tm	AB	R	HR	RBI	SB	BA	xBA	OBP	SLG	OPS	vL	vR	bb%	ct%	h%	Eye	G	L	F	PX	xPX	hr/f	Spd	SBO	SB%	#Wk	DOM	DIS	RC/G	RAR	BPV	BPX	R$
09	aa	361	37	5	36	9	229	239	286	311	597			7	82	27	0.44				54			97	16%	62%				2.86		16	33	$3
10	a/a	476	60	12	49	17	257	270	299	395	693			6	83	29	0.36				92			106	19%	79%				4.06		53	115	$14
11	DET *	376	58	13	47	15	265	249	302	423	725	871	675	5	82	29	0.30	34	19	47	105	89	8%	95	22%	77%	19	47%	37%	4.42	4.8	53	118	$14
12	DET *	351	59	9	39	3	307	268	354	470	824	751	889	7	82	35	0.42	38	24	37	101	102	8%	141	3%	71%	19	53%	21%	6.10	20.3	68	170	$14
13	DET	438	60	9	37	7	256	251	323	363	686	631	698	9	81	30	0.50	42	25	33	72	77	8%	119	6%	88%	27	48%	37%	4.05	0.9	36	90	$10
1st Half		238	29	6	21	6	248	255	304	353	656	703	649	7	81	28	0.41	44	27	30	65	83	11%	118	9%	100%	14	43%	43%	3.77	-1.7	27	68	$11
2nd Half		200	31	3	16	1	265	248	341	375	716	556	756	10	81	31	0.61	41	22	37	80	69	5%	119	3%	50%	13	54%	31%	4.38	2.1	46	115	$8
14	**Proj**	**324**	**48**	**8**	**32**	**5**	**270**	**255**	**328**	**401**	**730**	**682**	**741**	**8**	**82**	**31**	**0.44**	**40**	**23**	**37**	**88**	**86**	**8%**	**123**	**7%**	**74%**				**4.55**	**5.0**	**43**	**107**	**$10**

Dominguez,Matt

Age 24	Bats R	Pos 3B	Health	A	LIMA Plan	B+
Ht 6' 1"	Wt 215		PT/Exp	C	Rand Var	0
			Consist	B	MM	3025

Seized control of HOU 3B job with 8-HR May (25% hr/f) and never let go, not that the Astros had a lot of alternatives. PX just league average, but at his age, further growth possible. Eye, xBA histories send pretty clear message: Don't expect BA help. But if you can carry the BA, another 20 HR should be a pretty safe bet.

Yr	Tm	AB	R	HR	RBI	SB	BA	xBA	OBP	SLG	OPS	vL	vR	bb%	ct%	h%	Eye	G	L	F	PX	xPX	hr/f	Spd	SBO	SB%	#Wk	DOM	DIS	RC/G	RAR	BPV	BPX	R$
09	aa	97	9	2	8	0	178	238	277	304	582			12	73	23	0.50				102			93	0%	0%				2.62		27	55	-$3
10	aa	504	51	11	68	0	231	255	300	368	667			9	78	27	0.45				102			91	2%	0%				3.58		41	89	$4
11	FLA *	385	36	8	42	0	215	250	258	328	586	944	419	5	83	24	0.34	49	19	32	79	96	0%	74	1%	0%	4	50%	25%	2.71	-15.2	30	67	$0
12	HOU *	556	47	11	63	0	226	254	263	335	598	655	824	5	86	24	0.36	54	18	27	67	89	20%	100	1%	0%	8	38%	25%	2.88	-18.1	39	98	$3
13	HOU	543	56	21	77	0	241	253	286	403	690	627	714	5	82	26	0.31	42	19	39	104	96	12%	68	1%	0%	27	56%	30%	3.78	-2.7	45	113	$11
1st Half		278	28	11	44	0	230	255	257	399	656	676	650	3	84	24	0.23	40	18	43	107	125	11%	71	0%	0%	14	64%	29%	3.40	-4.8	53	133	$10
2nd Half		265	28	10	33	0	253	252	305	408	713	585	783	7	80	28	0.38	45	20	35	101	64	13%	74	2%	0%	13	46%	31%	4.18	1.6	40	100	$12
14	**Proj**	**563**	**54**	**25**	**70**	**0**	**238**	**266**	**283**	**421**	**704**	**612**	**736**	**5**	**83**	**25**	**0.33**	**46**	**19**	**35**	**114**	**89**	**15%**	**78**	**1%**	**0%**				**3.90**	**-1.3**	**42**	**106**	**$11**

Donaldson,Josh

Age 28	Bats R	Pos 3B	Health	A	LIMA Plan	B+
Ht 6' 0"	Wt 220		PT/Exp	B	Rand Var	-5
			Consist	F	MM	3225

Surprise season generated numbers that even zoomed past last year's upside projection (.270, 20 HR). BA gains had strong skill support, including improved bb%, ct%, but .300 not likely sustainable. xPX and low FB% cast doubt on the power spike. 2013 was likely a career year but he'll still be highly productive.

Yr	Tm	AB	R	HR	RBI	SB	BA	xBA	OBP	SLG	OPS	vL	vR	bb%	ct%	h%	Eye	G	L	F	PX	xPX	hr/f	Spd	SBO	SB%	#Wk	DOM	DIS	RC/G	RAR	BPV	BPX	R$
09	aa	455	47	6	64	5	217	245	303	325	628			11	77	27	0.54				84			82	6%	68%				3.20		24	49	$2
10	OAK *	326	35	12	48	2	180	199	252	331	583	768	0	9	67	22	0.29	50	5	45	115	70	11%	75	5%	62%	6	17%	50%	2.57	-14.4	3	7	-$1
11	aaa	444	52	10	46	8	199	228	256	317	573			7	72	25	0.27				94			84	15%	64%				2.52		5	11	$1
12	OAK *	483	59	17	62	7	247	257	291	410	701	703	680	6	79	28	0.29	40	23	38	107	107	11%	68	10%	68%	17	35%	47%	3.98	0.5	34	85	$11
13	OAK	579	89	24	93	5	301	282	384	499	883	1042	813	12	81	34	0.69	44	21	36	132	97	14%	101	4%	71%	27	48%	19%	6.92	47.4	85	213	$29
1st Half		301	44	13	53	2	316	292	387	525	912	1092	840	10	81	36	0.60	45	22	33	142	88	16%	95	4%	50%	14	50%	7%	7.43	28.2	88	220	$30
2nd Half		278	45	11	40	3	284	270	376	471	847	999	781	13	81	32	0.79	43	19	38	121	108	13%	106	3%	100%	13	46%	31%	6.39	18.9	82	205	$26
14	**Proj**	**568**	**80**	**19**	**80**	**7**	**281**	**262**	**358**	**447**	**805**	**901**	**763**	**10**	**79**	**33**	**0.52**	**42**	**21**	**37**	**115**	**103**	**12%**	**90**	**6%**	**68%**				**5.54**	**25.2**	**51**	**128**	**$23**

KRISTOPHER OLSON

Doumit,Ryan

Age	33	Bats	B	Pos	DH CA RF		
Ht	6' 1"	Wt	220				
Health	C	LIMA Plan	C	PT/Exp	C	Rand Var	+2
Consist	B	MM	3125				

BA drop attributable at least in part to dip in hit rate, but second-half PX and ct% dip (which was sandwiched around time missed with concussion) is cause for concern. Still, he caught enough to earn CA eligibility for another year. At that position, you could certainly do far worse.

Yr	Tm	AB	R	HR	RBI	SB	BA	xBA	OBP	SLG	OPS	vL	vR	bb%	ct%	h%	Eye	G	L	F	PX	xPX	hr/f	Spd	SBO	SB%	#Wk	DOM	DIS	RC/G	RAR	BPV	BPX	R$
09	PIT	280	31	10	38	4	250	268	299	414	714	686	725	7	83	27	0.41	42	18	40	104	103	11%	78	6%	100%	16	50%	25%	4.31	0.2	52	106	$5
10	PIT	406	42	13	45	1	251	246	331	406	738	532	832	9	79	29	0.47	41	16	43	108	117	9%	75	1%	100%	26	42%	31%	4.44	1.9	44	96	$7
11	PIT *	244	20	8	32	0	289	272	340	453	793	912	802	7	84	32	0.47	44	21	36	106	112	12%	86	1%	0%	19	63%	21%	5.43	5.6	62	138	$6
12	MIN	484	56	18	75	0	275	274	320	461	781	690	823	6	80	31	0.30	42	22	36	125	110	13%	66	0%	0%	27	41%	26%	5.12	11.5	52	130	$14
13	MIN	485	49	14	55	1	247	257	314	396	710	753	692	9	80	28	0.48	47	19	33	105	110	11%	85	1%	100%	27	44%	26%	4.24	-0.5	48	120	$8
1st Half		245	28	8	35	1	233	265	301	400	701	743	682	9	82	25	0.55	50	16	34	113	122	12%	82	2%	100%	14	36%	21%	4.03	-3.1	63	158	$9
2nd Half		240	21	6	20	0	263	248	330	392	721	764	702	9	77	32	0.44	44	24	32	96	95	10%	91	0%	0%	13	54%	31%	4.46	0.1	33	83	$8
14	Proj	452	46	13	56	1	267	260	325	419	744	741	746	8	80	31	0.42	44	21	35	106	108	10%	81	1%	73%				4.72	2.8	35	87	$10

Dozier,Brian

Age	27	Bats	R	Pos	2B		
Ht	5' 11"	Wt	190				
Health	A	LIMA Plan	B	PT/Exp	C	Rand Var	+1
Consist	C	MM	3315				

Plenty of reason to be skeptical of this apparent breakout... xPX doesn't believe power is for real, though 2H fly balls helped. Middling batting average shows little sign of upside. And platoon splits are huge -- he batted more than 100 points higher vs LHPs. The safe play is to drop out when the bidding hits double-digits.

Yr	Tm	AB	R	HR	RBI	SB	BA	xBA	OBP	SLG	OPS	vL	vR	bb%	ct%	h%	Eye	G	L	F	PX	xPX	hr/f	Spd	SBO	SB%	#Wk	DOM	DIS	RC/G	RAR	BPV	BPX	R$
09																																		
10																																		
11	aa	311	43	4	25	8	269	264	314	407	721			6	83	31	0.39				94			124	21%	49%				4.11		59	131	$7
12	MIN *	497	45	7	47	11	223	232	264	318	581	775	547	5	81	26	0.29	42	21	38	65	80	6%	108	15%	73%	15	20%	27%	2.74	-15.1	19	48	$4
13	MIN	558	72	18	66	14	244	256	312	414	726	978	649	8	78	28	0.43	38	21	41	118	99	10%	123	16%	67%	27	52%	33%	4.19	7.8	64	160	$16
1st Half		228	32	7	26	6	228	239	302	368	670	900	616	10	79	26	0.49	42	19	39	90	94	10%	140	20%	50%	14	36%	43%	3.40	-2.1	49	123	$10
2nd Half		330	40	11	40	8	255	268	311	445	756	1022	674	8	78	29	0.38	35	22	43	138	102	10%	113	13%	89%	13	69%	23%	4.82	10.8	75	188	$20
14	Proj	455	53	12	47	10	241	253	298	388	686	914	616	7	80	28	0.38	40	21	39	101	91	8%	125	15%	63%				3.74	0.6	46	116	$11

Drew,Stephen

Age	31	Bats	L	Pos	SS		
Ht	6' 0"	Wt	190				
Health	F	LIMA Plan	B+	PT/Exp	C	Rand Var	-1
Consist	C	MM	4315				

1H: Injuries, underachievement, prospects nipping at heels. 2H: First-rate SS production. Skills strong throughout, with PX, xPX the headliners. Hasn't run since '11 ankle injury, and three-year ct% decline has ravaged xBA. Desperately needs platoon mate wherever he lands. Buy expecting a mix of HR and DL Days.

Yr	Tm	AB	R	HR	RBI	SB	BA	xBA	OBP	SLG	OPS	vL	vR	bb%	ct%	h%	Eye	G	L	F	PX	xPX	hr/f	Spd	SBO	SB%	#Wk	DOM	DIS	RC/G	RAR	BPV	BPX	R$
09	ARI	533	71	12	65	5	261	267	320	428	748	573	810	8	84	29	0.56	39	19	42	99	106	6%	140	4%	83%	25	64%	16%	4.79	21.0	75	153	$11
10	ARI	565	83	15	61	10	278	271	352	458	810	794	817	10	81	32	0.57	40	19	41	117	108	8%	149	9%	67%	26	65%	23%	5.57	34.7	84	183	$18
11	ARI	321	44	5	45	4	252	247	317	396	713	671	728	9	77	31	0.41	39	21	40	107	109	5%	114	10%	50%	16	38%	19%	4.12	6.6	47	104	$6
12	2 TM *	328	42	8	31	1	218	237	306	346	653	563	697	11	74	27	0.49	32	28	40	89	122	8%	110	3%	33%	15	33%	40%	3.39	-1.1	25	63	$1
13	BOS	442	57	13	67	6	253	251	333	443	777	585	876	11	72	32	0.44	33	25	42	142	156	10%	115	5%	100%	23	52%	26%	5.15	22.3	60	150	$13
1st Half		232	27	5	31	2	233	242	315	409	725	593	779	11	71	31	0.42	32	25	43	131	153	7%	123	4%	100%	12	50%	42%	4.34	6.1	50	125	$8
2nd Half		210	30	8	36	4	276	264	356	481	837	579	995	11	73	34	0.46	34	25	41	153	159	13%	104	7%	100%	11	55%	9%	6.16	16.1	69	173	$17
14	Proj	438	60	12	61	5	258	249	335	426	761	612	830	11	74	32	0.46	35	24	41	122	136	9%	118	6%	74%				4.91	18.5	51	127	$13

Duda,Lucas

Age	28	Bats	L	Pos	LF 1B		
Ht	6' 4"	Wt	255				
Health	B	LIMA Plan	C	PT/Exp	C	Rand Var	0
Consist	C	MM	4005				

15-33-.223 in 318 AB at NYM. Evidence mounts that 2011's ct% was fool's gold. 1st half power impressed, but June intercostal injury derailed season and he never fully recovered. With health, power should rebound, but low BA may curtail chances.

Yr	Tm	AB	R	HR	RBI	SB	BA	xBA	OBP	SLG	OPS	vL	vR	bb%	ct%	h%	Eye	G	L	F	PX	xPX	hr/f	Spd	SBO	SB%	#Wk	DOM	DIS	RC/G	RAR	BPV	BPX	R$
09	aa	395	39	7	42	2	244	238	325	369	694			11	73	32	0.44				97			88	3%	41%				3.97		19	39	$3
10	NYM *	509	63	19	75	1	240	267	308	438	746	421	749	9	76	28	0.41	35	19	46	145	129	14%	58	1%	100%	6	50%	50%	4.54	-0.7	58	126	$9
11	NYM *	430	55	18	68	1	276	274	352	476	828	705	888	10	79	31	0.57	34	22	43	136	116	9%	89	1%	100%	20	60%	30%	5.92	16.2	76	169	$15
12	NYM *	497	52	17	63	1	233	222	313	374	687	662	745	10	71	30	0.40	35	23	42	99	134	13%	50	1%	100%	23	22%	57%	3.90	-10.2	0	0	$7
13	NYM *	380	50	15	38	1	222	221	333	388	722	610	831	14	68	29	0.52	32	20	48	129	181	14%	66	3%	16%	18	39%	33%	4.13	-5.3	25	63	$5
1st Half		226	29	11	23	0	235	239	345	438	783	602	871	14	70	29	0.56	33	18	49	154	208	14%	64	4%	0%	12	50%	25%	4.78	1.3	53	133	$7
2nd Half		154	21	4	15	1	205	197	316	316	632	630	736	14	65	29	0.47	29	24	47	91	108	14%	82	1%	100%	6	17%	50%	3.22	-6.6	-12	-30	$1
14	Proj	430	53	18	51	1	233	235	339	409	748	629	794	12	71	29	0.47	33	22	46	130	138	13%	67	2%	52%				4.41	5.1	24	61	$9

Dunn,Adam

Age	34	Bats	L	Pos	DH 1B		
Ht	6' 6"	Wt	285				
Health	A	LIMA Plan	B	PT/Exp	A	Rand Var	0
Consist	D	MM	5005				

Three sudden months of shocking competence at plate (.272, 18 HR, 51 RBI in Jun-Aug with 69%+ ct% each month) salvaged season. True colors returned in September (.159 BA, 4 HR, 51% ct%). Did at least right the ship vs. LHP in 2H. Has brushed off retirement talk, but teams may force his hand.

Yr	Tm	AB	R	HR	RBI	SB	BA	xBA	OBP	SLG	OPS	vL	vR	bb%	ct%	h%	Eye	G	L	F	PX	xPX	hr/f	Spd	SBO	SB%	#Wk	DOM	DIS	RC/G	RAR	BPV	BPX	R$
09	WAS	546	81	38	105	0	267	266	398	529	928	787	978	18	68	33	0.66	31	20	49	185	158	21%	55	1%	0%	27	59%	19%	7.25	43.2	72	147	$20
10	WAS	558	85	38	103	0	260	266	356	536	892	719	965	12	64	33	0.39	33	18	49	219	195	21%	70	1%	0%	27	59%	30%	6.41	31.0	80	174	$21
11	CHW	415	36	11	42	0	159	180	292	277	569	309	646	15	57	24	0.42	33	20	48	113	134	10%	44	1%	0%	27	15%	78%	2.39	-28.8	-33	-73	-$7
12	CHW	539	87	41	96	2	204	238	333	468	800	767	817	16	59	25	0.47	34	22	44	207	172	29%	46	2%	67%	27	59%	30%	4.99	8.2	49	123	$13
13	CHW	525	60	34	86	1	219	232	320	442	762	681	786	13	64	27	0.40	38	19	42	167	170	24%	54	1%	50%	26	35%	42%	4.56	1.0	33	83	$12
1st Half		268	36	21	52	1	198	244	302	459	761	592	819	13	65	21	0.42	36	18	46	191	201	26%	48	2%	100%	14	43%	36%	4.42	-0.6	53	133	$14
2nd Half		257	24	13	34	0	241	219	334	424	759	784	753	12	63	33	0.38	41	21	38	142	138	21%	66	1%	0%	12	25%	50%	4.69	1.5	14	35	$11
14	Proj	481	59	29	76	1	224	228	334	439	774	692	803	14	62	29	0.43	36	20	44	171	162	22%	52	1%	44%				4.77	3.9	21	54	$12

Dyson,Jarrod

Age	29	Bats	L	Pos	CF		
Ht	5' 9"	Wt	160				
Health	B	LIMA Plan	C+	PT/Exp	D	Rand Var	0
Consist	B	MM	1513				

2-17-.258 with 34 SB in 213 AB at KC. Sporadic PT, but when he's in the lineup, whoowhee, watch him fly. Splits made case for good half of platoon. If a team ever committed to using him that way, he'd be a SB title contender, but time is running out. Best to appreciate him for what he is: a reasonably-priced SB source.

Yr	Tm	AB	R	HR	RBI	SB	BA	xBA	OBP	SLG	OPS	vL	vR	bb%	ct%	h%	Eye	G	L	F	PX	xPX	hr/f	Spd	SBO	SB%	#Wk	DOM	DIS	RC/G	RAR	BPV	BPX	R$
09	aa	248	28	0	10	27	223	211	282	275	556			7	76	29	0.34				36			143	52%	80%				2.72		-6	-12	$6
10	KC *	277	38	2	22	20	219	238	273	302	575	273	783	7	80	27	0.37	67	5	28	61	116	9%	135	44%	71%	5	60%	40%	2.64	-13.9	26	57	$6
11	KC *	363	54	2	20	36	221	256	280	275	555	333	544	8	81	27	0.44	68	16	16	38	12	0%	157	41%	91%	11	9%	82%	2.89	-15.1	19	42	$10
12	KC *	355	60	0	12	34	261	250	323	332	655	510	689	8	83	32	0.52	57	19	24	44	56	0%	201	38%	85%	25	20%	40%	3.99	-2.5	44	110	$14
13	KC *	265	36	2	18	37	231	247	293	324	616	531	741	8	78	29	0.39	58	17	25	66	68	5%	152	64%	86%	21	33%	29%	3.51	-5.9	27	68	$14
1st Half		106	17	2	10	13	200	252	230	356	586	455	961	4	77	24	0.17	46	17	37	112	138	13%	131	105%	87%	10	60%	10%	2.81	-4.6	46	115	$9
2nd Half		159	19	0	8	24	252	237	331	302	633	548	663	11	78	32	0.54	63	17	20	36	42	0%	153	53%	86%	11	9%	45%	3.92	-1.2	10	25	$18
14	Proj	322	47	3	18	38	251	245	312	341	653	467	705	8	79	31	0.42	58	16	26	61	77	4%	168	49%	86%				3.95	-2.1	37	93	$17

Eaton,Adam

Age	25	Bats	L	Pos	LF CF		
Ht	5' 8"	Wt	185				
Health	D	LIMA Plan	B	PT/Exp	D	Rand Var	+4
Consist	F	MM	1425				

3-22-.252 with 5 SB in 250 AB at ARI. Elbow injury popped pre-season hype bubble. Hot August raised hopes take-off was imminent. Sept slump said "not so fast," but bad-luck h% large part of reason. Power negligible, so value hinges on getting on base and getting green light. Reversing bb% trend would help. A work in progress.

Yr	Tm	AB	R	HR	RBI	SB	BA	xBA	OBP	SLG	OPS	vL	vR	bb%	ct%	h%	Eye	G	L	F	PX	xPX	hr/f	Spd	SBO	SB%	#Wk	DOM	DIS	RC/G	RAR	BPV	BPX	R$
09																																		
10																																		
11	aa	212	22	3	20	7	268	241	333	375	709			9	82	32	0.54				68			130	22%	52%				4.00		40	89	$4
12	ARI *	613	108	7	38	32	312	274	367	440	807	890	737	8	83	37	0.51	64	12	24	90	91	13%	139	26%	67%	4	50%	25%	5.76	28.4	64	160	$31
13	ARI *	285	43	4	25	5	234	260	282	341	623	708	665	6	81	28	0.35	57	19	25	71	63	6%	130	11%	71%	13	31%	23%	3.18	-7.8	36	90	$4
1st Half		31	2	0	2	0	99	204	145	150	294			5	74	13	0.21				52			98	0%	0%				0.61		-21	-53	-$11
2nd Half		254	41	4	23	5	251	265	298	365	663	708	665	6	82	29	0.38	57	19	25	73	63	6%	135	11%	71%	13	31%	23%	3.68	-3.7	42	105	$5
14	Proj	439	62	7	37	15	274	266	346	396	742	844	702	8	82	32	0.47	57	17	25	80	74	8%	136	18%	65%				4.44	5.4	49	123	$16

KRISTOPHER OLSON

Ellis,A.J.

Age 33	Bats R	Pos CA	Health A	LIMA Plan C	
Ht 6' 3"	Wt 220		PT/Exp C	Rand Var 0	
			Consist D	MM	2005

As expected, days of .270 BA were numbered, even as ct% rose. At first blush, power took a step back, but XPX says late-career HR spike not out of question. Eschewed patience in 2H, but made contact on a good number of those extra hacks. If approach sticks, more HR could follow, though BA would hinge on whether ct% holds.

Yr Tm	AB	R	HR	RBI	SB	BA	xBA	OBP	SLG	OPS	vL	vR	bb%	ct%	h%	Eye	G	L	F	PX	xPX	hr/f	Spd	SBO	SB%	#Wk	DOM	DIS	RC/G	RAR	BPV	BPX	R$
09 LA *	293	32	0	27	1	234	199	326	274	601	0	250	12	80	29	0.68	56	11	33	33	78	0%	97	4%	34%	7	0%	43%	2.90	-7.0	1	2	-$1
10 LA *	169	12	0	20	1	240	215	323	295	617	673	688	11	80	30	0.60	52	16	32	49	59	0%	94	1%	100%	22	23%	45%	3.21	-2.4	10	22	$0
11 LA *	269	26	3	25	0	224	224	322	307	628	1069	645	13	82	26	0.82	49	16	35	60	99	8%	88	3%	0%	13	46%	31%	3.13	-4.6	31	69	-$1
12 LA	423	44	13	52	0	270	243	373	414	786	702	815	13	75	33	0.61	45	23	33	100	102	13%	102	0%	0%	27	48%	37%	5.30	19.4	38	95	$9
13 LA	390	43	10	52	0	238	238	318	364	682	671	684	10	80	27	0.58	44	19	37	86	138	9%	89	2%	0%	26	38%	27%	3.79	1.0	38	95	$5
1st Half	179	15	3	18	0	257	229	351	369	720	830	679	13	75	33	0.59	45	20	35	85	113	6%	112	0%	0%	13	31%	31%	4.44	3.8	31	78	$3
2nd Half	211	28	7	34	0	223	245	287	360	647	486	688	8	84	24	0.56	44	17	39	86	157	10%	68	4%	0%	13	46%	23%	3.25	-3.0	43	108	$7
14 Proj	403	43	11	50	0	243	239	334	374	708	738	699	11	79	28	0.62	45	19	36	90	116	10%	92	2%	9%				4.07	4.4	23	58	$5

Ellis,Mark

Age 37	Bats R	Pos 2B	Health D	LIMA Plan B	
Ht 5' 10"	Wt 190		PT/Exp B	Rand Var -2	
			Consist B	MM	1215

Hey, look: It's another Dodger named "Ellis" who has no business hitting .270. Resurgent Spd may have helped him outhit xBA, but hard to believe that will last from 37-year-old who dealt with unsurprising quad, groin injuries. The cliff looms. DN: .240 BA and regular spot on the bench

Yr Tm	AB	R	HR	RBI	SB	BA	xBA	OBP	SLG	OPS	vL	vR	bb%	ct%	h%	Eye	G	L	F	PX	xPX	hr/f	Spd	SBO	SB%	#Wk	DOM	DIS	RC/G	RAR	BPV	BPX	R$
09 OAK *	410	53	10	63	10	252	270	292	383	675	706	709	5	86	27	0.41	40	20	39	83	69	8%	79	14%	77%	19	47%	16%	3.81	1.9	47	96	$10
10 OAK	436	45	5	49	7	291	258	358	381	739	839	706	8	87	33	0.71	42	21	37	65	65	4%	88	9%	54%	24	38%	17%	4.65	12.2	46	100	$13
11 2 TM	480	55	7	41	14	248	245	288	346	634	693	614	4	84	28	0.29	46	17	37	70	66	5%	93	17%	74%	26	35%	42%	3.28	-5.4	32	71	$9
12 LA	415	62	7	31	5	258	260	333	364	697	877	612	9	83	30	0.57	39	27	34	72	80	6%	97	4%	100%	21	43%	29%	4.11	5.5	39	98	$8
13 LA	433	46	6	48	4	270	245	323	351	674	743	644	6	83	31	0.35	43	24	33	54	78	5%	116	4%	80%	24	25%	46%	3.84	2.2	23	58	$10
1st Half	185	22	4	20	3	259	239	294	346	640	737	603	5	82	30	0.27	41	24	35	55	78	7%	79	6%	100%	11	18%	36%	3.59	-0.6	8	20	$9
2nd Half	248	24	2	28	1	278	249	325	355	679	749	670	6	83	33	0.41	44	25	32	53	79	3%	132	3%	50%	13	31%	54%	4.02	2.3	31	78	$11
14 Proj	426	51	6	43	4	264	250	320	356	677	773	637	6	84	30	0.41	42	24	34	63	76	5%	102	5%	71%				3.83	1.6	22	56	$10

Ellsbury,Jacoby

Age 30	Bats L	Pos CF	Health F	LIMA Plan D+	
Ht 6' 1"	Wt 195		PT/Exp A	Rand Var -3	
			Consist F	MM	2535

The good: Spd and SB rebounded with vengeance. The bad: More nagging injuries (groin, wrist, foot). The big question: Is this a first round talent? Memories of his Troutian 2011 bias the analysis, but big SBs and 2H power surge lead to intriguing upside speculation. Just don't ignore the "Fs" to the left.

Yr Tm	AB	R	HR	RBI	SB	BA	xBA	OBP	SLG	OPS	vL	vR	bb%	ct%	h%	Eye	G	L	F	PX	xPX	hr/f	Spd	SBO	SB%	#Wk	DOM	DIS	RC/G	RAR	BPV	BPX	R$
09 BOS	624	94	8	60	70	301	275	355	415	770	785	763	7	88	33	0.66	50	18	32	66	84	5%	151	43%	85%	27	56%	15%	5.66	25.0	67	137	$41
10 BOS *	102	15	0	6	8	239	256	277	297	575	471	488	5	91	26	0.60	49	16	35	48	35	0%	103	37%	89%	6	33%	33%	3.00	-3.7	46	100	$2
11 BOS	660	119	32	105	39	321	313	376	552	928	841	965	7	85	34	0.53	43	23	34	145	115	17%	109	30%	72%	27	78%	4%	7.42	57.8	106	236	$49
12 BOS	303	43	4	26	14	271	259	313	370	682	648	701	6	86	30	0.44	47	20	33	70	91	5%	103	22%	82%	15	53%	20%	4.15	-0.7	44	110	$9
13 BOS	577	92	9	53	52	298	276	355	426	781	641	863	8	84	34	0.51	51	21	28	85	78	7%	136	33%	93%	25	56%	20%	5.90	26.6	62	155	$39
1st Half	331	51	1	29	32	296	276	356	405	761	651	826	9	86	34	0.69	52	20	27	73	67	1%	142	34%	91%	14	57%	21%	5.70	14.2	66	165	$42
2nd Half	246	41	8	24	20	301	274	344	455	799	629	917	6	81	35	0.34	49	22	30	102	95	14%	114	30%	95%	11	55%	18%	6.16	13.5	54	135	$36
14 Proj	522	83	11	52	41	283	276	335	419	753	656	805	7	85	32	0.48	48	21	31	90	88	8%	120	34%	87%				5.17	14.9	71	179	$30

Elmore,Jake

Age 27	Bats R	Pos SS	Health A	LIMA Plan D	
Ht 5' 9"	Wt 185		PT/Exp C	Rand Var +1	
			Consist C	MM	1311

2-6-.242 in 120 AB at HOU. Name sounds like a mashup of the Blues Brothers, but you were singing the blues, brother, if you rostered him. Has speed but couldn't harness it in bigs (1-for-7 SB). Plays everywhere (even caught once!), which may keep him employed. But roster only if he's the "sole man" available.

Yr Tm	AB	R	HR	RBI	SB	BA	xBA	OBP	SLG	OPS	vL	vR	bb%	ct%	h%	Eye	G	L	F	PX	xPX	hr/f	Spd	SBO	SB%	#Wk	DOM	DIS	RC/G	RAR	BPV	BPX	R$
09																																	
10 aa	388	54	2	26	21	259	242	340	327	667			11	84	30	0.78				51			122	28%	60%				3.59		39	85	$11
11 aa	381	41	2	29	10	231	227	299	298	596			9	81	28	0.50				54			95	22%	46%				2.67		14	31	$3
12 ARI *	487	58	1	51	19	264	250	330	354	684	449	515	9	85	31	0.67	56	14	31	64	48	0%	104	21%	66%	9	44%	11%	3.95	6.3	44	110	$13
13 HOU *	388	46	6	28	13	244	258	308	342	650	699	597	8	83	28	0.55	41	27	32	65	70	6%	135	24%	49%	16	44%	38%	3.21	-2.5	44	110	$8
1st Half	290	31	4	23	12	247	290	304	347	651	1100	500	8	83	29	0.47	60	27	13	67	35	0%	134	26%	59%	3	33%	67%	3.35	-1.0	41	103	$12
2nd Half	98	15	2	5	1	235	255	318	327	645	660	627	11	85	26	0.80	38	27	35	59	77	7%	112	20%	17%	13	46%	31%	2.83	-2.0	43	108	-$2
14 Proj	127	16	1	10	4	246	249	316	338	654	675	641	10	84	28	0.65	45	22	33	63	65	4%	117	22%	47%				3.29	-0.7	34	85	$3

Encarnacion,Edwin

Age 31	Bats R	Pos 1B DH	Health B	LIMA Plan C	
Ht 6' 2"	Wt 230		PT/Exp A	Rand Var +3	
			Consist A	MM	4255

Wrist surgery cut short stellar encore; expected to be OK by spring. HR total dipped slightly, but still-robust PX/xPX says "errant gusts of wind." Meanwhile, check out ct%, bb%, Eye, and xBA, particularly in 2H. Think he was seeing the ball well? SB% says he could still swipe a few. With health... UP: 45 HR, .300 BA.

Yr Tm	AB	R	HR	RBI	SB	BA	xBA	OBP	SLG	OPS	vL	vR	bb%	ct%	h%	Eye	G	L	F	PX	xPX	hr/f	Spd	SBO	SB%	#Wk	DOM	DIS	RC/G	RAR	BPV	BPX	R$
09 2 TM *	330	39	15	45	2	226	248	316	409	725	814	707	12	78	25	0.59	37	17	46	111	107	12%	83	3%	67%	18	50%	22%	4.24	-3.4	49	100	$4
10 TOR *	364	52	23	58	1	251	281	309	487	796	914	755	8	83	25	0.48	32	17	51	143	133	15%	68	1%	100%	21	57%	29%	5.14	5.6	83	180	$11
11 TOR	481	70	17	55	8	272	275	334	453	787	845	767	8	84	29	0.56	36	19	44	124	124	9%	75	8%	80%	27	63%	15%	5.29	9.4	76	169	$16
12 TOR	542	93	42	110	13	280	285	384	557	941	1086	892	13	83	27	0.89	33	18	49	157	153	19%	79	9%	81%	27	81%	7%	7.47	44.0	109	273	$31
13 TOR	530	90	36	104	7	272	311	370	534	904	859	916	13	88	25	1.32	35	22	43	150	152	18%	69	5%	88%	25	84%	8%	6.95	35.5	123	308	$28
1st Half	315	54	23	66	3	270	306	347	537	883	778	917	11	87	25	0.90	34	21	45	152	164	19%	68	4%	100%	14	79%	7%	6.56	17.7	113	283	$32
2nd Half	215	36	13	38	4	274	318	400	530	930	988	914	17	90	25	2.14	37	22	42	147	136	16%	75	7%	80%	11	91%	9%	7.48	17.7	138	345	$23
14 Proj	537	93	37	102	9	284	303	378	552	930	985	915	13	86	27	1.03	35	20	45	158	142	18%	72	7%	82%				7.42	42.7	119	298	$31

Escobar,Alcides

Age 27	Bats R	Pos SS	Health A	LIMA Plan B+	
Ht 6' 1"	Wt 195		PT/Exp A	Rand Var +2	
			Consist D	MM	1525

Negative swing of h% pendulum whacked BA, OBP, and curtailed SB chances—a shame, given SB%. Poor OBP and ineptitude vs. RHP got worse as season progressed. Would a few walks kill you, Alcides? Expect some BA recovery as h% reverts; but xBA says the recovery stops short of '12 levels.

Yr Tm	AB	R	HR	RBI	SB	BA	xBA	OBP	SLG	OPS	vL	vR	bb%	ct%	h%	Eye	G	L	F	PX	xPX	hr/f	Spd	SBO	SB%	#Wk	DOM	DIS	RC/G	RAR	BPV	BPX	R$
09 MIL *	555	80	4	38	37	270	254	308	357	664	1020	622	5	83	32	0.32	52	17	31	58	37	3%	176	35%	74%	9	22%	44%	3.79	4.6	43	88	$20
10 MIL	506	57	4	41	10	235	255	288	326	614	614	614	7	86	27	0.51	44	21	34	53	77	3%	187	11%	71%	27	41%	22%	3.10	-5.0	59	128	$5
11 KC	548	69	4	46	26	254	262	290	343	633	576	651	4	87	29	0.34	53	18	29	58	46	3%	166	27%	74%	27	41%	22%	3.34	-1.4	54	120	$14
12 KC	605	68	5	52	35	293	271	331	390	721	676	739	4	83	34	0.27	53	23	24	65	51	4%	138	25%	88%	27	33%	26%	4.73	22.1	38	95	$25
13 KC	607	57	4	52	22	234	250	259	300	559	620	532	3	86	27	0.23	46	23	31	45	60	3%	135	17%	100%	26	23%	27%	2.74	-12.5	29	73	$11
1st Half	312	32	3	25	11	253	262	281	333	614	758	559	4	88	28	0.33	47	22	31	53	62	4%	130	15%	100%	14	36%	14%	3.38	-0.8	45	113	$15
2nd Half	295	25	1	27	11	214	237	232	264	496	482	503	2	84	25	0.15	44	24	31	36	58	1%	135	19%	100%	12	8%	42%	2.14	-12.1	11	28	$7
14 Proj	606	64	4	51	27	258	257	290	337	628	640	623	4	86	30	0.28	49	22	29	53	55	3%	147	21%	88%				3.46	-0.2	35	87	$18

Escobar,Eduardo

Age 25	Bats B	Pos SS 3B	Health A	LIMA Plan D	
Ht 5' 10"	Wt 175		PT/Exp D	Rand Var -2	
			Consist C	MM	1311

3-10-.236 in 165 AB at MIN. Say something nice about him? Umm... this was a growth year? In fact, one might even consider it his career year! And at 25, there is still upside. Of course, we could say all those things about most any breathing 25-year-old. UP: $1

Yr Tm	AB	R	HR	RBI	SB	BA	xBA	OBP	SLG	OPS	vL	vR	bb%	ct%	h%	Eye	G	L	F	PX	xPX	hr/f	Spd	SBO	SB%	#Wk	DOM	DIS	RC/G	RAR	BPV	BPX	R$
09																																	
10 aa	202	19	3	19	3	241	244	270	343	613			4	81	29	0.21				68			121	6%	100%				3.18		24	52	$1
11 CHW *	496	46	4	41	11	243	296	279	321	601	667	500	5	76	31	0.21	67	33	0	62	2	0%	112	17%	56%	5	0%	40%	2.88	-8.1	0	0	$6
12 2 AL *	269	34	1	17	6	207	227	257	270	526	844	419	6	78	26	0.30	51	21	28	41	42	0%	149	11%	84%	19	26%	68%	2.28	-9.6	4	10	-$1
13 MIN *	331	39	6	30	4	250	244	301	382	683	655	619	7	77	31	0.32	42	21	37	97	94	6%	135	11%	51%	18	33%	39%	3.77	3.3	42	105	$5
1st Half	118	16	3	9	0	220	239	276	347	623	670	605	7	85	24	0.50	41	18	40	70	94	8%	165	4%	0%	14	43%	36%	3.01	-1.7	61	153	$0
2nd Half	213	23	3	21	4	267	265	315	402	717	624	657	7	73	36	0.26	43	30	27	114	94	0%	116	15%	58%	4	0%	50%	4.23	4.8	32	80	$8
14 Proj	164	19	2	14	3	237	247	285	347	632	773	577	6	78	29	0.30	46	23	31	78	73	6%	135	11%	63%				3.23	-1.2	18	45	$3

KRISTOPHER OLSON

Escobar,Yunel

Age 31 | Bats R | Pos SS | Ht 6' 2" | Wt 210
Health A | PT/Exp A | Consist C
LIMA Plan B+ | Rand Var +1 | MM 1225

Hit rate has bounced between two poles in the past five seasons, with the results showing in BA. But save for a minor 1H hr/f surge last year, all other BPIs remain steady and unspectacular. As such, expect more of the same going forward, with the only variables being playing time and that h% pendulum.

Yr	Tm	AB	R	HR	RBI	SB	BA	xBA	OBP	SLG	OPS	vL	vR	bb%	ct%	h%	Eye	G	L	F	PX	xPX	hr/f	Spd	SBO	SB%	#Wk	DOM	DIS	RC/G	RAR	BPV	BPX	R$
09	ATL	528	89	14	76	5	299	289	377	436	812	691	864	10	88	32	0.92	50	20	30	81	86	10%	92	5%	56%	27	67%	7%	5.72	33.6	67	137	$19
10	2 TM	497	60	4	35	6	256	255	337	318	655	728	634	10	89	28	0.98	54	18	28	44	64	3%	87	5%	75%	24	50%	17%	3.62	2.8	38	83	$7
11	TOR	513	77	11	48	3	290	276	369	413	782	929	740	11	86	32	0.87	57	18	25	79	79	10%	132	3%	50%	24	58%	13%	5.35	27.7	71	158	$16
12	TOR	558	58	9	51	5	253	261	300	344	644	644	643	6	87	28	0.50	56	19	25	57	69	7%	94	4%	83%	27	44%	22%	3.51	1.2	38	95	$8
13	TAM	508	61	9	56	4	256	266	332	366	698	750	674	10	86	28	0.78	53	19	27	76	98	8%	91	5%	50%	27	59%	19%	4.07	9.6	53	133	$10
1st Half		265	29	6	31	2	245	255	303	355	658	794	600	8	86	27	0.59	51	19	31	71	119	9%	87	4%	67%	14	57%	29%	3.62	1.2	44	110	$10
2nd Half		243	32	3	25	2	267	276	360	379	738	700	755	13	85	30	0.97	56	20	23	81	76	6%	95	6%	40%	13	62%	8%	4.58	7.9	61	153	$11
14	**Proj**	**519**	**65**	**9**	**53**	**4**	**264**	**267**	**336**	**370**	**706**	**736**	**694**	**10**	**86**	**29**	**0.78**	**55**	**19**	**26**	**71**	**83**	**8%**	**99**	**5%**	**56%**				**4.22**	**11.4**	**43**	**106**	**$11**

Espinosa,Danny

Age 27 | Bats B | Pos 2B | Ht 6' 0" | Wt 205
Health A | PT/Exp B | Consist C
LIMA Plan D | Rand Var +3 | MM 4303

3-12-.158 in 158 AB at WAS. History of low ct% hinted at potential downside, but this was a disaster. Trying to play through broken bone in wrist may have played role, but once it was reportedly healed, things got no better at AAA (.566 OPS). Previous power/speed combo still enticing, but probably faces uphill battle for ABs.

Yr	Tm	AB	R	HR	RBI	SB	BA	xBA	OBP	SLG	OPS	vL	vR	bb%	ct%	h%	Eye	G	L	F	PX	xPX	hr/f	Spd	SBO	SB%	#Wk	DOM	DIS	RC/G	RAR	BPV	BPX	R$
09																																		
10	WAS *	584	84	24	73	21	238	232	291	416	707	846	684	7	73	28	0.28	46	8	46	120	133	18%	116	27%	60%	6	50%	50%	3.79	2.4	40	87	$18
11	WAS	573	72	21	66	17	236	241	323	414	737	857	703	9	71	30	0.34	44	16	40	132	130	14%	115	17%	74%	27	48%	41%	4.18	9.0	44	98	$14
12	WAS	594	82	17	56	20	247	234	315	402	717	775	694	7	68	34	0.24	47	19	34	123	109	13%	106	19%	77%	27	33%	44%	4.11	8.0	19	48	$16
13	WAS *	441	33	4	27	6	169	173	199	245	444	529	448	4	63	26	0.10	51	10	39	74	95	7%	77	11%	83%	10	40%	50%	1.52	-30.8	-55	-138	-$7
1st Half		214	13	3	14	2	139	174	167	231	398	529	448	3	61	21	0.09	51	10	39	91	95	7%	70	7%	100%	10	40%	50%	1.17	-18.3	-53	-133	-$7
2nd Half																																		
14	**Proj**	**294**	**33**	**9**	**29**	**7**	**237**	**223**	**300**	**395**	**694**	**793**	**664**	**7**	**68**	**32**	**0.22**	**46**	**15**	**39**	**125**	**116**	**12%**	**99**	**16%**	**73%**				**3.75**	**0.5**	**15**	**37**	**$7**

Ethier,Andre

Age 32 | Bats L | Pos CF RF | Ht 6' 2" | Wt 205
Health A | PT/Exp A | Consist A
LIMA Plan B+ | Rand Var +1 | MM 3235

Second half power metrics and consistently high line drive rate say he's still got it. However, he's slipped a bit vs RH, and futility vs LH is fully engrained at this point. At 32, there still may be one last fling at productive numbers, but it's speculative at best.

Yr	Tm	AB	R	HR	RBI	SB	BA	xBA	OBP	SLG	OPS	vL	vR	bb%	ct%	h%	Eye	G	L	F	PX	xPX	hr/f	Spd	SBO	SB%	#Wk	DOM	DIS	RC/G	RAR	BPV	BPX	R$
09	LA	596	92	31	106	6	272	296	361	508	869	629	960	11	81	29	0.62	38	20	42	148	132	15%	92	6%	60%	27	56%	11%	6.14	35.0	92	188	$22
10	LA	517	71	23	82	2	292	286	364	493	857	625	960	10	80	33	0.58	39	22	40	135	142	14%	94	2%	67%	25	64%	16%	6.46	33.9	80	174	$21
11	LA	487	67	11	62	0	292	265	368	421	789	563	878	11	79	35	0.56	44	25	31	97	80	9%	91	1%	0%	24	46%	29%	5.52	19.2	44	98	$16
12	LA	556	79	20	89	2	284	271	351	460	812	606	945	8	78	33	0.40	43	24	33	120	106	14%	91	3%	50%	26	54%	27%	5.57	23.1	53	133	$20
13	LA	482	54	12	52	4	272	268	360	423	783	613	854	11	80	32	0.64	39	24	37	109	124	8%	104	5%	57%	25	60%	16%	5.17	14.9	64	160	$13
1st Half		266	21	5	24	1	252	248	325	372	698	584	763	10	83	29	0.64	41	20	39	84	107	6%	97	4%	33%	14	57%	14%	4.02	-1.2	50	125	$8
2nd Half		216	33	7	28	3	296	287	387	486	873	660	952	13	77	36	0.64	37	30	33	142	146	13%	109	6%	75%	11	64%	18%	6.81	15.8	82	205	$19
14	**Proj**	**457**	**60**	**14**	**58**	**3**	**278**	**274**	**360**	**445**	**805**	**605**	**895**	**11**	**79**	**33**	**0.56**	**40**	**25**	**35**	**120**	**117**	**11%**	**99**	**4%**	**59%**				**5.51**	**17.5**	**52**	**129**	**$16**

Federowicz,Tim

Age 26 | Bats R | Pos CA | Ht 5' 10" | Wt 215
Health A | PT/Exp D | Consist B
LIMA Plan D | Rand Var -5 | MM 3001

4-16-.231 in 160 AB at LA. PRO: Clubbed 8 HR in 79 early season AB at Triple-A, which hints at more power potential. CON: Troubling ct% trend and 0.12 Eye vs RH suggest he'll be a BA liability. Increased role could lead to double digit HR, but would be accompanied by a serious BA penalty.

Yr	Tm	AB	R	HR	RBI	SB	BA	xBA	OBP	SLG	OPS	vL	vR	bb%	ct%	h%	Eye	G	L	F	PX	xPX	hr/f	Spd	SBO	SB%	#Wk	DOM	DIS	RC/G	RAR	BPV	BPX	R$
09																																		
10																																		
11	LA *	435	40	9	45	1	222	213	274	332	606	400	489	7	77	27	0.30	56	11	33	84	29	0%	68	1%	100%	3	0%	67%	2.98	-9.4	9	20	$2
12	LA *	415	43	7	46	0	222	213	279	335	614	0	833	7	73	29	0.29	100	0	0	91	-11	0%	76	1%	0%	3	0%	100%	3.03	-8.5	3	8	$1
13	LA *	239	26	10	33	0	265	233	320	448	769	650	623	8	63	38	0.22	45	22	33	158	88	11%	72	0%	0%	24	33%	54%	4.98	8.8	16	40	$5
1st Half		151	18	8	27	0	267	241	327	491	818	593	558	8	64	37	0.25	51	14	35	186	83	11%	65	0%	0%	11	45%	27%	5.59	8.2	44	110	$8
2nd Half		88	8	2	6	0	261	214	309	375	684	711	669	6	60	41	0.17	39	30	31	107	92	12%	90	0%	0%	13	23%	77%	3.99	0.7	-32	-80	$0
14	**Proj**	**195**	**20**	**5**	**22**	**0**	**232**	**229**	**284**	**366**	**650**	**672**	**640**	**7**	**68**	**32**	**0.23**	**44**	**23**	**33**	**113**	**88**	**12%**	**76**	**1%**	**29%**				**3.46**	**-1.5**	**-14**	**-34**	**$3**

Fielder,Prince

Age 30 | Bats L | Pos 1B | Ht 5' 11" | Wt 275
Health A | PT/Exp A | Consist C
LIMA Plan B+ | Rand Var 0 | MM 4045

In a season full of ups and downs, the end result was much less than anticipated. He didn't crush RH as he's always done, and power levels are way off his 2007-09 peak. His durability remains impressive, and he may have another 2011 in him. But 2H PX, xPX show downside, and suggest he's a bit risky as he enters his thirties.

Yr	Tm	AB	R	HR	RBI	SB	BA	xBA	OBP	SLG	OPS	vL	vR	bb%	ct%	h%	Eye	G	L	F	PX	xPX	hr/f	Spd	SBO	SB%	#Wk	DOM	DIS	RC/G	RAR	BPV	BPX	R$
09	MIL	591	103	46	141	2	299	302	412	602	1014	943	1042	16	77	32	0.80	41	16	43	187	175	23%	43	2%	40%	27	74%	4%	8.85	69.3	102	208	$32
10	MIL	578	94	32	83	1	261	266	401	471	871	668	975	16	76	29	0.83	42	18	40	138	134	18%	28	0%	100%	27	56%	22%	6.23	27.2	58	126	$19
11	MIL	569	95	38	120	1	299	306	415	566	981	822	1046	16	81	31	1.01	43	20	37	170	145	22%	45	1%	50%	27	74%	15%	8.40	59.4	109	242	$32
12	DET	581	83	30	108	1	313	304	412	528	940	808	1017	13	86	33	1.01	41	25	33	126	128	18%	45	0%	100%	27	70%	11%	7.88	51.2	84	210	$30
13	DET	624	82	25	106	1	279	275	362	457	819	819	819	11	81	31	0.64	41	23	36	119	128	14%	36	1%	50%	27	56%	11%	5.73	19.8	55	138	$24
1st Half		307	40	13	62	0	274	269	363	469	832	1001	769	12	80	30	0.70	38	20	42	134	145	13%	33	1%	0%	14	57%	21%	5.90	11.4	64	160	$23
2nd Half		317	42	12	44	1	284	281	350	445	794	695	880	9	82	31	0.57	44	26	31	104	111	15%	46	1%	100%	13	54%	0%	5.56	8.5	47	118	$25
14	**Proj**	**583**	**84**	**29**	**105**	**1**	**291**	**287**	**386**	**497**	**882**	**799**	**929**	**12**	**82**	**31**	**0.78**	**42**	**23**	**36**	**132**	**132**	**17%**	**40**	**1%**	**62%**				**6.74**	**34.8**	**71**	**178**	**$27**

Flaherty,Ryan

Age 27 | Bats L | Pos 2B | Ht 6' 3" | Wt 210
Health A | PT/Exp D | Consist A
LIMA Plan D+ | Rand Var 0 | MM 3203

10-27-.224 in 246 AB at BAL. Saw pretty consistent AB vs RH in first half, and the results weren't pretty. Has a bit of pop in his bat, but not enough to make up for all the strikeouts, nor the dreadful BA that results. LH MIs with power get lots of chances, but not enough signs of growth here to forecast any improvement.

Yr	Tm	AB	R	HR	RBI	SB	BA	xBA	OBP	SLG	OPS	vL	vR	bb%	ct%	h%	Eye	G	L	F	PX	xPX	hr/f	Spd	SBO	SB%	#Wk	DOM	DIS	RC/G	RAR	BPV	BPX	R$
09																																		
10	aa	71	7	1	6	1	154	222	230	210	440			9	81	18	0.53				39			105	5%	100%				1.49		7	15	-$3
11	a/a	475	48	13	57	3	224	244	275	365	640			7	75	27	0.28				104			89	10%	31%				3.10		26	58	$5
12	BAL *	191	19	8	21	1	224	208	254	380	634	667	613	4	72	27	0.14	43	13	44	96	107	13%	123	3%	100%	24	25%	63%	3.20	-3.0	12	30	$1
13	BAL *	280	31	12	31	2	223	241	275	390	665	641	687	7	74	26	0.28	49	16	36	117	115	15%	90	3%	100%	24	38%	38%	3.55	-1.4	34	85	$3
1st Half		208	21	8	21	2	214	234	260	357	617	517	636	6	75	25	0.24	52	16	32	98	95	14%	87	5%	100%	13	23%	38%	3.05	-4.1	17	43	$4
2nd Half		72	10	4	10	0	250	261	316	486	803	875	811	9	74	29	0.37	42	15	43	171	164	17%	108	0%	0%	11	55%	36%	5.23	3.2	83	208	$1
14	**Proj**	**263**	**29**	**11**	**31**	**1**	**231**	**235**	**293**	**401**	**694**	**753**	**688**	**6**	**74**	**27**	**0.25**	**44**	**16**	**40**	**118**	**124**	**14%**	**109**	**3%**	**68%**				**3.69**	**0.0**	**23**	**58**	**$5**

Flores,Wilmer

Age 22 | Bats R | Pos 3B | Ht 6' 3" | Wt 190
Health A | PT/Exp F | Consist C
LIMA Plan D+ | Rand Var +1 | MM 3021

1-13-.211 in 95 AB at NYM. Injury to David Wright gave him opportunity, but after strong start, went 5 for last 45 with 17 Ks. Certainly young enough for plate patience and power to develop further, and defensive versatility could help give him another chance soon. He's a talent worth tracking, but needs more seasoning.

Yr	Tm	AB	R	HR	RBI	SB	BA	xBA	OBP	SLG	OPS	vL	vR	bb%	ct%	h%	Eye	G	L	F	PX	xPX	hr/f	Spd	SBO	SB%	#Wk	DOM	DIS	RC/G	RAR	BPV	BPX	R$
09																																		
10																																		
11																																		
12	aa	251	30	7	27	0	274	271	318	428	746			6	86	29	0.48				95			94	0%	0%				4.78		64	160	$5
13	NYM *	519	53	11	69	1	247	269	276	382	659	447	591	4	81	29	0.22	51	22	27	97	47	5%	86	4%	16%	8	50%	50%	3.47	-2.9	38	95	$9
1st Half		319	33	8	43	1	249	269	276	401	677			4	84	27	0.25				101			112	7%	16%				3.58		61	153	$11
2nd Half		200	20	3	26	0	244	244	276	353	629	447	591	4	76	31	0.18	51	22	27	90	47	5%	77	0%	0%	8	50%	50%	3.28	-2.4	9	23	$4
14	**Proj**	**233**	**25**	**6**	**28**	**0**	**258**	**270**	**291**	**402**	**693**	**542**	**770**	**5**	**82**	**29**	**0.29**	**46**	**22**	**32**	**101**	**42**	**10%**	**87**	**1%**	**25%**				**4.02**	**0.3**	**36**	**90**	**$5**

BRIAN RUDD

Florimon Jr.,Pedro

Age 27	Bats B	Pos SS		Health	A	LIMA Plan	D+
Ht 6' 2"	Wt 180			PT/Exp	C	Rand Var	-1
				Consist	B	MM	1303

Ability to record outs on defense got him a job, but between the weak OBP and times caught stealing, he also generated tons of outs on offense. Low SB% raises doubts about how much longer he'll get a green light. 2H hr/f was a positive, but xPX, Eye suggest pitchers should have no fear. There are safer options for SB.

Yr Tm	AB	R	HR	RBI	SB	BA	xBA	OBP	SLG	OPS	vL	vR	bb%	ct%	h%	Eye	G	L	F	PX	xPX	hr/f	Spd	SBO	SB%	#Wk	DOM	DIS	RC/G	RAR	BPV	BPX	R$
09 aa	22	0	0	1	0	89	120	127	89	216			4	58	15	0.10				0			106	0%	0%				0.32		-126	-257	-$3
10 aa	120	12	1	9	3	159	196	213	202	415			6	72	21	0.24				36			105	18%	73%				1.33		-37	-80	-$3
11 BAL *	462	44	7	51	12	234	310	298	347	645	1000	375	8	71	31	0.31	50	50	0	93	2	0%	109	23%	47%				3.14	-4.0	10	22	$6
12 MIN *	561	54	5	37	14	219	223	267	297	564	619	558	6	70	30	0.22	58	20	22	62	32	4%	116	19%	57%	8	13%	25%	2.48	-16.7	-19	-48	$3
13 MIN	403	44	9	44	15	221	232	281	330	611	459	661	8	71	29	0.29	47	23	30	86	80	11%	95	22%	71%	27	30%	48%	2.99	-5.4	0	0	$8
1st Half	194	19	3	24	7	232	246	297	325	622	305	713	8	76	29	0.39	47	25	28	73	74	8%	95	16%	88%	14	36%	43%	3.32	-0.8	11	28	$8
2nd Half	209	25	6	20	8	211	220	263	335	598	581	609	7	67	28	0.22	47	21	32	100	85	14%	105	29%	62%	13	23%	54%	2.69	-5.2	-5	-13	$8
14 Proj	325	35	5	33	10	228	227	284	325	608	551	632	7	71	31	0.26	50	22	28	78	61	8%	106	19%	68%				2.98	-4.9	-10	-25	$4

Flowers,Tyler

Age 28	Bats R	Pos CA		Health	A	LIMA Plan	D
Ht 6' 4"	Wt 245			PT/Exp	F	Rand Var	+2
				Consist	B	MM	4103

Continued to swing for the fences at expense of BA (and his starting job), and declining bb% says pitchers have him figured this out. xPX even raises red flags in the power department. Underwent surgery in September to repair rotator cuff, labrum, but there is no surgery that is going to fix this ct%.

Yr Tm	AB	R	HR	RBI	SB	BA	xBA	OBP	SLG	OPS	vL	vR	bb%	ct%	h%	Eye	G	L	F	PX	xPX	hr/f	Spd	SBO	SB%	#Wk	DOM	DIS	RC/G	RAR	BPV	BPX	R$
09 CHW*	369	62	15	49	3	270	243	377	469	846	775	425	15	65	38	0.49	50	13	38	160	89	0%	95	2%	100%	5	20%	80%	6.23	26.5	48	98	$11
10 CHW*	357	34	14	40	1	186	177	283	363	646	0	542	12	59	27	0.33	33	0	67	158	120	0%	100	3%	57%	5	0%	80%	3.20	-5.9	19	41	-$1
11 CHW*	332	41	19	41	2	223	210	320	432	752	431	863	13	58	32	0.34	32	16	51	179	180	13%	88	3%	61%	10	40%	50%	4.50	8.0	29	64	$6
12 CHW	136	19	7	13	2	213	225	296	412	708	905	586	8	59	30	0.21	53	18	29	165	87	30%	80	11%	67%	26	27%	62%	3.64	-0.2	10	25	$1
13 CHW	256	24	10	24	0	195	208	247	355	603	455	661	5	63	26	0.15	42	17	41	133	106	15%	72	2%	0%	22	32%	59%	2.62	-8.9	-5	-13	-$1
1st Half	197	20	8	22	0	213	222	255	386	641	473	716	5	66	28	0.17	41	17	42	138	91	15%	73	3%	0%	14	36%	50%	3.11	-3.7	11	28	$1
2nd Half	59	4	2	2	0	136	158	177	254	432	409	443	5	53	21	0.11	45	16	39	109	171	17%	89	0%	0%	8	25%	75%	1.33	-4.8	-64	-160	-$8
14 Proj	258	28	12	33	1	212	205	284	386	670	669	670	8	59	31	0.20	44	17	39	150	127	20%	70	4%	60%				3.38	-2.6	-14	-35	$4

Forsythe,Logan

Age 27	Bats R	Pos 2B		Health	D	LIMA Plan	D
Ht 6' 1"	Wt 195			PT/Exp	D	Rand Var	+2
				Consist	C	MM	2411

6-19-.214 with 6 SB in 220 AB at SD. Missed first two months due to plantar fasciitis, and much of Sept with same issue. Plus Spd, stable bb%, gains in hr/f are good signs, and after 685 MLB AB, high LD% is clearly a skill he owns. But also owns career .251 xBA, poor ct%, and can't hit RH, which limit both role and fantasy impact.

Yr Tm	AB	R	HR	RBI	SB	BA	xBA	OBP	SLG	OPS	vL	vR	bb%	ct%	h%	Eye	G	L	F	PX	xPX	hr/f	Spd	SBO	SB%	#Wk	DOM	DIS	RC/G	RAR	BPV	BPX	R$
09 aa	244	30	2	25	4	236	206	331	312	643			12	69	33	0.46				57			120	5%	100%				3.55		-13	-27	$1
10 aa	392	56	2	32	14	215	212	329	283	612			15	71	29	0.60				62			108	15%	72%				3.06		0	0	$3
11 SD *	328	36	4	32	8	226	217	297	326	623	548	577	9	70	31	0.34	43	20	37	87	98	0%	98	16%	57%	15	33%	53%	3.06	-6.0	1	2	$3
12 SD *	373	53	7	32	10	263	249	329	383	712	1010	603	9	79	32	0.46	36	29	35	77	107	7%	159	11%	83%	18	33%	28%	4.42	8.3	45	113	$9
13 SD *	245	26	7	22	6	221	253	291	360	651	651	593	9	74	27	0.39	42	28	29	93	105	13%	112	11%	86%	17	12%	35%	3.50	-1.1	25	63	$2
1st Half	99	13	4	14	2	285	274	358	486	844	693	823	10	72	36	0.40	38	33	29	141	108	19%	119	10%	67%	4	0%	25%	6.10	6.8	58	145	$7
2nd Half	146	13	3	8	4	178	239	245	274	519	627	476	8	76	21	0.37	45	26	29	63	103	9%	107	13%	100%	13	15%	38%	2.20	-7.0	5	13	$0
14 Proj	190	25	5	20	5	248	246	325	384	709	818	655	9	74	31	0.40	40	27	33	95	105	11%	116	12%	79%				4.17	2.7	25	63	$5

Fowler,Dexter

Age 28	Bats B	Pos CF		Health	B	LIMA Plan	B+
Ht 6' 4"	Wt 190			PT/Exp	B	Rand Var	0
				Consist	D	MM	4515

Hit 8 of his 12 homers in April, later missed time due to hand and knee injuries, which may explain 2H hr/f plunge. Power/speed combo shows there's potential for more, but mediocre ct% and shaky SB% are now fixtures. 20/20 still in play, though, and value is much higher in leagues that count OBP.

Yr Tm	AB	R	HR	RBI	SB	BA	xBA	OBP	SLG	OPS	vL	vR	bb%	ct%	h%	Eye	G	L	F	PX	xPX	hr/f	Spd	SBO	SB%	#Wk	DOM	DIS	RC/G	RAR	BPV	BPX	R$
09 COL	433	73	4	34	27	266	247	363	406	770	859	729	13	73	35	0.58	42	21	37	104	83	4%	165	27%	73%	26	42%	31%	5.10	12.9	54	110	$15
10 COL *	545	87	7	44	14	266	261	346	422	768	744	764	11	76	34	0.50	45	22	33	107	95	6%	171	14%	63%	24	54%	25%	4.94	13.5	63	137	$15
11 COL *	578	92	6	49	13	251	250	338	406	743	762	807	12	73	34	0.48	43	21	35	119	102	4%	161	15%	56%	22	45%	18%	4.48	6.6	60	133	$12
12 COL	454	72	13	53	12	300	249	389	474	863	857	866	13	72	39	0.53	39	27	34	115	125	12%	175	10%	71%	27	33%	33%	6.67	32.5	60	150	$20
13 COL	415	71	12	42	19	263	246	369	407	776	860	741	14	75	33	0.62	42	23	34	102	102	11%	135	20%	68%	23	48%	35%	4.99	11.0	50	125	$18
1st Half	258	49	10	26	12	291	260	380	473	853	962	818	13	75	35	0.58	41	23	36	126	117	15%	138	16%	86%	13	54%	23%	6.61	17.7	70	175	$25
2nd Half	157	22	2	16	7	217	223	335	299	634	674	619	15	74	28	0.68	44	24	32	62	79	5%	125	26%	50%	10	40%	50%	2.97	-6.2	15	38	$6
14 Proj	513	82	17	52	20	282	253	383	458	841	871	829	14	74	35	0.61	42	23	35	122	103	13%	160	17%	68%				6.06	28.0	61	152	$24

Francisco,Juan

Age 27	Bats L	Pos 1B 3B		Health	A	LIMA Plan	D+
Ht 6' 2"	Wt 240			PT/Exp	D	Rand Var	-1
				Consist	A	MM	4003

Power is legit, and small-sample 2H hints at truly elite upside. However, power spike coincided with ct% bottoming out, and lack of progress in solving LH will probably prevent him from becoming a full-timer. He's a streaky hitter with streaky skills, but overall, the year-end results are unlikely to change much.

Yr Tm	AB	R	HR	RBI	SB	BA	xBA	OBP	SLG	OPS	vL	vR	bb%	ct%	h%	Eye	G	L	F	PX	xPX	hr/f	Spd	SBO	SB%	#Wk	DOM	DIS	RC/G	RAR	BPV	BPX	R$
09 CIN *	550	73	27	87	5	284	317	314	497	811	833	1190	4	76	33	0.18	57	29	14	138	66	50%	90	6%	70%	4	50%	50%	5.51	14.3	51	104	$20
10 CIN *	363	39	16	53	1	258	269	291	477	768	444	753	4	69	33	0.15	60	11	29	168	45	10%	103	3%	44%	10	30%	60%	4.72	1.4	53	115	$9
11 CIN *	393	44	15	52	1	261	278	282	454	736	286	820	3	75	32	0.11	45	25	30	142	125	14%	79	1%	100%	8	50%	25%	4.44	-1.6	43	96	$10
12 ATL	192	17	9	32	1	234	240	278	432	710	468	768	5	64	32	0.16	43	24	33	158	114	23%	58	6%	50%	25	40%	52%	3.90	-3.9	11	28	$2
13 2 NL	348	36	18	48	0	227	216	296	422	719	425	748	8	60	32	0.23	45	18	37	160	143	23%	100	3%	0%	26	31%	54%	3.97	-6.5	18	45	$5
1st Half	173	17	9	26	0	225	219	280	410	690	314	758	7	64	29	0.21	49	17	34	134	130	24%	114	3%	0%	14	36%	50%	3.68	-4.9	14	35	$5
2nd Half	175	19	9	22	0	229	215	304	434	738	804	739	10	57	34	0.25	41	18	40	189	157	23%	91	2%	0%	12	25%	58%	4.26	-1.8	26	65	$5
14 Proj	327	34	15	47	1	239	235	292	434	726	430	769	7	64	32	0.20	46	20	35	158	125	21%	84	3%	34%				4.13	-4.6	11	27	$8

Francoeur,Jeff

Age 30	Bats R	Pos RF		Health	A	LIMA Plan	D
Ht 6' 4"	Wt 210			PT/Exp	B	Rand Var	+3
				Consist	D	MM	1301

At least he had a higher OPS than Jeff Mathis and Brendan Ryan. Plate approach has never been a strength, but ct%, Eye reached new lows. Hasn't even been serviceable vs LHP past two years. Still has a hint of Spd, but can't use it from dugout. May crack another major league roster—just don't let him find his way onto yours.

Yr Tm	AB	R	HR	RBI	SB	BA	xBA	OBP	SLG	OPS	vL	vR	bb%	ct%	h%	Eye	G	L	F	PX	xPX	hr/f	Spd	SBO	SB%	#Wk	DOM	DIS	RC/G	RAR	BPV	BPX	R$
09 2 NL	593	72	15	76	6	280	266	309	423	732	878	677	4	84	31	0.25	38	21	41	89	106	7%	115	7%	60%	26	62%	15%	4.52	-1.4	53	108	$16
10 2 TM	454	52	13	65	8	249	238	300	383	683	805	639	6	82	28	0.37	41	14	45	86	107	8%	114	10%	73%	27	41%	22%	3.83	-10.5	46	100	$10
11 KC	601	77	20	87	22	285	276	329	476	805	934	762	6	80	33	0.30	40	20	40	137	113	10%	107	23%	69%	26	62%	12%	5.36	13.0	74	164	$27
12 KC	561	58	16	49	4	235	252	287	378	665	695	652	6	79	27	0.29	45	21	34	93	106	11%	101	9%	36%	27	44%	33%	3.35	-21.5	33	83	$7
13 2 TM	245	20	3	17	3	204	219	238	298	536	539	534	4	75	26	0.15	47	17	36	71	86	5%	119	7%	100%	19	21%	58%	2.27	-17.8	2	5	-$2
1st Half	183	19	3	13	2	208	217	241	322	563	594	559	4	73	27	0.16	46	16	39	86	90	6%	131	6%	100%	13	23%	46%	2.55	-10.8	11	28	-$1
2nd Half	62	1	0	4	1	194	219	206	226	432	431	433	2	81	24	0.08	50	22	28	30	75	0%	85	9%	100%	6	17%	83%	1.53	-5.7	-23	-58	-$6
14 Proj	194	16	3	18	3	228	238	265	335	599	597	601	4	79	27	0.21	45	20	35	77	95	6%	101	11%	71%				2.85	-9.5	11	27	$2

Frandsen,Kevin

Age 32	Bats R	Pos 1B 2B		Health	A	LIMA Plan	D
Ht 6' 0"	Wt 185			PT/Exp	D	Rand Var	+2
				Consist	B	MM	1231

Saw consistent PT down the stretch for second straight year, but unlike 2012, h% did him no favors. Recent success vs LH intriguing, but it's a small 139 AB sample, and he had a .666 OPS prior to 2012. Best case looks like empty batting average in a part-time role, but BA history says we can't even count on that.

Yr Tm	AB	R	HR	RBI	SB	BA	xBA	OBP	SLG	OPS	vL	vR	bb%	ct%	h%	Eye	G	L	F	PX	xPX	hr/f	Spd	SBO	SB%	#Wk	DOM	DIS	RC/G	RAR	BPV	BPX	R$
09 SF *	477	47	8	37	2	223	252	251	315	566	421	369	4	91	23	0.39	55	14	32	53	120	0%	111	7%	28%	9	22%	0%	2.48	-22.3	47	96	-$1
10 LAA *	359	45	2	24	4	221	266	255	294	549	589	625	4	90	24	0.43	56	15	28	55	51	0%	112	8%	78%	16	56%	19%	2.47	-16.8	46	100	$0
11 a/a	288	23	4	28	7	234	244	256	320	576			3	86	26	0.20				57			98	20%	58%				2.59		25	56	$2
12 PHI *	586	52	3	39	1	271	287	295	360	655	980	762	3	90	30	0.34	54	24	22	62	48	5%	104	6%	20%	10	50%	0%	3.55	-7.6	50	125	$8
13 PHI	252	27	5	26	1	234	271	296	341	637	869	536	5	88	25	0.41	57	18	25	67	63	9%	108	2%	100%	27	37%	26%	3.08	-6.9	51	128	$1
1st Half	86	13	3	12	1	279	297	340	442	782	980	748	9	88	29	0.80	64	16	20	102	48	20%	109	4%	100%	14	50%	21%	5.40	3.5	87	218	$5
2nd Half	166	14	2	14	0	211	255	229	289	519	804	424	2	89	23	0.21	53	20	27	49	71	5%	108	0%	0%	13	23%	31%	2.14	-9.4	32	80	-$1
14 Proj	134	14	2	12	1	244	272	295	345	640	792	572	4	89	26	0.37	56	19	25	66	63	7%	105	6%	55%				3.14	-5.9	37	93	$2

BRIAN RUDD

Franklin,Nick

Age	23	Bats	B	Pos	2B	Health	A	LIMA Plan	B+
Ht	6' 1"	Wt	195			PT/Exp	D	Rand Var	+1
						Consist	B	MM	3305

12-45-.225 in 369 AB at SEA. Looked like he was on his way to AL ROY through June, then 2H ct% fell through the floor and derailed everything. xPX and FB% legitimize the HR totals, while plate patience makes for a passable OBP. Further optimism is on hold until he proves he can put the ball in play against MLB pitching.

Yr Tm	AB	R	HR	RBI	SB	BA	xBA	OBP	SLG	OPS	vL	vR	bb%	ct%	h%	Eye	G	L	F	PX	xPX	hr/f	Spd	SBO	SB%	#Wk	DOM	DIS	RC/G	RAR	BPV	BPX	R$
09																																	
10 aa																																	
11 aa	83	11	2	5	4	296	234	338	422	760			6	75	38	0.26				85			128	31%	57%				4.66		22	49	$2
12 a/a	472	53	8	45	10	239	237	300	373	673			8	74	31	0.33				98			109	13%	69%				3.71		25	63	$7
13 SEA *	511	58	15	59	11	239	238	324	383	707	599	727	11	73	30	0.47	35	24	41	109	140	11%	84	8%	92%	19	37%	37%	4.25	7.9	30	75	$12
1st Half	254	31	7	29	10	283	271	369	428	796	781	873	12	83	32	0.80	31	28	41	101	141	11%	80	13%	91%	6	83%	17%	5.80	15.1	63	158	$20
2nd Half	257	27	8	30	1	195	210	279	339	617	524	661	10	63	27	0.32	36	22	41	120	139	12%	98	2%	100%	13	15%	46%	3.01	-5.6	2	5	$4
14 Proj	537	60	16	58	11	238	237	311	394	706	645	735	10	71	30	0.37	36	24	40	118	140	10%	100	9%	82%				4.16	7.4	31	77	$10

Frazier,Todd

Age	28	Bats	R	Pos	3B	Health	A	LIMA Plan	A
Ht	6' 3"	Wt	220			PT/Exp	C	Rand Var	+3
						Consist	D	MM	4225

BA stopped him shy of a full return to '12 levels as h% fell back to earth, but positive signs remain: Stable power skills suggest 20 HR is a reasonable baseline, while steady Eye improvement and 2H ct% hint at further BA growth. At peak age with room for more, like... 25 HR, .265 BA

Yr Tm	AB	R	HR	RBI	SB	BA	xBA	OBP	SLG	OPS	vL	vR	bb%	ct%	h%	Eye	G	L	F	PX	xPX	hr/f	Spd	SBO	SB%	#Wk	DOM	DIS	RC/G	RAR	BPV	BPX	R$
09 a/a	514	57	15	64	8	268	289	323	446	768			7	83	30	0.46				118			87	14%	46%				4.74		68	139	$13
10 aaa	480	54	14	50	11	224	245	277	383	660			7	69	29	0.24				125			106	16%	70%				3.44		25	54	$7
11 CIN *	427	51	18	48	13	221	255	275	396	671	985	654	7	71	27	0.25	48	21	31	130	138	23%	93	20%	74%	12	42%	33%	3.53	-6.1	31	69	$8
12 CIN *	461	58	20	72	5	265	258	321	480	801	858	817	8	75	32	0.32	33	22	45	143	127	13%	125	7%	72%	25	60%	24%	5.32	17.6	68	170	$15
13 CIN	531	63	19	73	6	234	251	314	407	721	782	696	9	76	27	0.40	42	18	40	121	121	12%	98	9%	55%	27	41%	22%	3.95	-0.7	51	128	$12
1st Half	265	31	9	37	4	238	239	320	396	716	748	723	11	74	29	0.46	44	18	38	115	130	12%	96	8%	67%	14	36%	29%	4.20	1.8	39	98	$12
2nd Half	266	32	10	36	2	229	263	278	417	695	818	669	6	79	25	0.33	40	18	41	127	113	11%	99	10%	40%	13	46%	15%	3.68	-2.4	63	158	$11
14 Proj	537	66	21	76	7	251	258	318	441	759	837	729	8	76	29	0.34	40	20	40	133	125	13%	106	9%	63%				4.56	9.4	52	131	$17

Freeman,Freddie

Age	24	Bats	L	Pos	1B	Health	A	LIMA Plan	B+
Ht	6' 5"	Wt	225			PT/Exp	A	Rand Var	-5
						Consist	C	MM	4235

This breakout was essentially a mirror image of '12 skills, and that's a good thing. Sure, h% will fall, but not as much as you'd think given prior levels. Stable, improving plate skills and production at this age make him a keeper league gem. xPX gives room for further power growth, so if those 2H FB% gains hold... UP: 30+ HR.

Yr Tm	AB	R	HR	RBI	SB	BA	xBA	OBP	SLG	OPS	vL	vR	bb%	ct%	h%	Eye	G	L	F	PX	xPX	hr/f	Spd	SBO	SB%	#Wk	DOM	DIS	RC/G	RAR	BPV	BPX	R$
09 aa	149	14	2	23	0	238	251	291	326	617			7	86	27	0.54				60			86	0%	0%				3.17		35	71	$0
10 ATL *	485	64	16	74	5	285	272	335	457	792	1667	333	7	79	33	0.36	44	19	38	122	120	17%	97	6%	70%	5	20%	40%	5.42	11.4	59	128	$17
11 ATL	571	67	21	76	4	282	260	346	448	795	707	837	8	75	34	0.37	42	23	35	122	138	14%	79	5%	50%	27	37%	33%	5.35	12.4	41	91	$20
12 ATL	540	91	23	94	2	259	271	340	456	796	714	855	11	76	30	0.50	37	26	37	132	137	15%	88	1%	100%	27	52%	30%	5.32	11.5	60	150	$18
13 ATL	551	89	23	109	1	319	274	396	501	897	764	958	11	78	38	0.55	38	27	35	121	151	15%	95	1%	100%	25	60%	16%	7.38	41.0	61	153	$31
1st Half	264	40	9	53	0	307	276	380	470	849	793	879	11	78	36	0.54	38	29	33	112	151	13%	98	0%	0%	12	58%	17%	6.56	14.1	56	140	$25
2nd Half	287	49	14	56	1	331	273	404	530	933	740	1033	11	78	39	0.55	39	25	37	130	152	17%	96	1%	100%	13	62%	15%	8.18	27.0	67	168	$37
14 Proj	579	88	26	103	2	294	275	369	487	855	738	920	10	78	34	0.50	38	26	36	130	144	16%	90	2%	74%				6.42	29.2	55	138	$27

Freese,David

Age	31	Bats	R	Pos	3B	Health	C	LIMA Plan	C+
Ht	6' 2"	Wt	225			PT/Exp	B	Rand Var	+1
						Consist	C	MM	2025

A few benchmarks from 2012 he likely won't reach again: 1) 20 HR: heavy GB% stroke and hr/f regression make 10 HR a better bet; 2) .290+ BA: xBA continued to spiral in unison with PX and Spd; 3) 500+ AB: "C" health grade entering post-peak years. Pay for a repeat of 2013 rather than a return to his 2012 peak.

Yr Tm	AB	R	HR	RBI	SB	BA	xBA	OBP	SLG	OPS	vL	vR	bb%	ct%	h%	Eye	G	L	F	PX	xPX	hr/f	Spd	SBO	SB%	#Wk	DOM	DIS	RC/G	RAR	BPV	BPX	R$
09 STL *	247	31	8	38	1	258	228	313	422	736	387	1390	7	72	33	0.29	44	12	44	121	145	9%	80	1%	100%	4	50%	50%	4.57	4.1	25	51	$4
10 STL	240	28	4	36	1	296	248	361	404	765	873	721	8	75	38	0.36	49	22	29	83	102	8%	104	3%	50%	13	31%	54%	5.10	7.3	17	37	$7
11 STL	333	41	10	55	1	297	273	350	441	791	900	759	7	77	36	0.37	52	25	23	102	121	17%	76	1%	100%	20	30%	50%	5.54	14.1	30	67	$12
12 STL	501	70	20	79	3	293	265	372	467	839	886	824	10	76	35	0.47	52	22	26	116	119	20%	93	4%	50%	27	56%	26%	6.06	28.9	46	115	$20
13 STL	462	53	9	60	1	262	253	340	381	721	811	689	9	77	32	0.44	55	21	24	91	97	10%	74	2%	33%	25	32%	28%	4.28	3.8	24	60	$10
1st Half	220	27	5	27	1	277	257	346	400	746	739	755	9	78	34	0.47	56	21	23	87	89	13%	95	1%	100%	13	31%	31%	4.91	5.8	30	75	$11
2nd Half	242	26	4	33	0	248	247	316	364	679	885	633	9	76	31	0.42	55	21	24	94	105	9%	60	3%	0%	12	33%	25%	3.76	-1.5	19	48	$8
14 Proj	447	55	11	65	1	273	258	346	408	754	843	724	9	76	34	0.41	53	22	25	99	107	13%	78	3%	44%				4.77	10.2	19	48	$14

Freiman,Nathan

Age	27	Bats	R	Pos	1B	Health	A	LIMA Plan	D
Ht	6' 8"	Wt	250			PT/Exp	D	Rand Var	-1
						Consist	B	MM	1011

Couldn't find regular playing time; he failed to reach 40 AB in any month. The big question is: who did he bribe to win AL Rookie of the Month in May (1 HR, 3 R, 9 RBI in 37 AB)? Minimal power and no SB potential wash out respectable plate skills, and struggles vs. RHP say not to draft him... unless he pays out for that too.

Yr Tm	AB	R	HR	RBI	SB	BA	xBA	OBP	SLG	OPS	vL	vR	bb%	ct%	h%	Eye	G	L	F	PX	xPX	hr/f	Spd	SBO	SB%	#Wk	DOM	DIS	RC/G	RAR	BPV	BPX	R$
09																																	
10																																	
11																																	
12 aa	516	59	15	77	0	235	239	287	377	663			7	77	28	0.31				96			79	2%	0%				3.53		23	58	$8
13 OAK	190	10	4	24	0	274	252	327	389	716	805	406	7	84	31	0.45	38	24	39	76	92	6%	86	0%	0%	25	32%	44%	4.42	-0.9	37	93	$2
1st Half	102	7	2	17	0	275	268	327	412	739	906	284	7	83	31	0.47	29	28	43	93	84	5%	101	0%	0%	13	38%	31%	4.74	0.4	55	138	$3
2nd Half	88	3	2	7	0	273	195	319	364	683	700	620	6	84	31	0.43	48	19	33	56	102	8%	78	0%	0%	12	25%	58%	4.07	-1.3	19	48	$1
14 Proj	164	12	3	21	0	259	243	311	370	681	747	430	7	81	30	0.37	40	22	37	76	95	7%	81	1%	0%				3.88	-3.4	9	24	$3

Fuentes,Reymond

Age	23	Bats	L	Pos	CF	Health	A	LIMA Plan	D
Ht	6' 0"	Wt	160			PT/Exp	D	Rand Var	-2
						Consist	F	MM	1501

0-1-.152 in 33 AB at SD. Got a taste of MLB pitching in late September, and it didn't taste good (52% ct%). Plate approach improved nicely in the minors, though ct% still has a ways to go for a singles-hitting speedster. Lack of a plus skill beyond speed means he can safely be avoided for now, but check back in a year.

Yr Tm	AB	R	HR	RBI	SB	BA	xBA	OBP	SLG	OPS	vL	vR	bb%	ct%	h%	Eye	G	L	F	PX	xPX	hr/f	Spd	SBO	SB%	#Wk	DOM	DIS	RC/G	RAR	BPV	BPX	R$
09																																	
10																																	
11																																	
12 aa	473	42	3	27	28	189	195	255	258	514			8	68	27	0.28				58			113	35%	74%				2.10		-27	-68	$2
13 SD *	433	60	4	34	30	280	248	345	368	713	333	381	9	75	37	0.39	60	20	20	73	69	0%	130	31%	71%	6	0%	100%	4.42	4.0	16	40	$21
1st Half	235	37	4	22	20	305	238	378	427	804			10	76	39	0.48				92			135	35%	69%				5.67		40	100	$27
2nd Half	198	27	1	14	12	265	234	329	324	653	333	381	9	74	36	0.36	60	20	20	56	69	0%	122	26%	79%	6	0%	100%	3.80	-2.2	-4	-10	$13
14 Proj	127	16	0	9	8	244	209	311	301	612	693	593	9	72	34	0.35	53	17	30	54	62	0%	132	31%	74%				3.20	-3.8	-14	-35	$4

Fuld,Sam

Age	32	Bats	L	Pos	LF CF RF	Health	D	LIMA Plan	D
Ht	5' 10"	Wt	175			PT/Exp	F	Rand Var	+4
						Consist	B	MM	0521

"The Legend of Sam Fuld" is quickly becoming a distant memory as he struggles to find regular PT. Anemic PX and HctX (65; league average 100) are boat anchors on his BA. Decent bb% and elite speed skills suggest a return to 20 SB is possible, but who wants to give ABs to a Mendoza-challenged OF with no power?

Yr Tm	AB	R	HR	RBI	SB	BA	xBA	OBP	SLG	OPS	vL	vR	bb%	ct%	h%	Eye	G	L	F	PX	xPX	hr/f	Spd	SBO	SB%	#Wk	DOM	DIS	RC/G	RAR	BPV	BPX	R$
09 CHC *	425	62	3	26	19	247	295	318	348	666	900	792	10	91	27	1.13	47	25	28	60	66	4%	162	22%	72%	14	50%	21%	3.74	-4.1	80	163	$9
10 CHC *	396	45	3	19	13	200	206	278	277	555	667	374	10	87	22	0.83	43	9	48	48	114	0%	150	24%	52%	7	14%	57%	2.28	-22.8	53	115	$0
11 TAM	308	41	3	27	20	240	264	313	360	673	554	710	9	88	28	0.65	48	19	33	83	70	4%	128	35%	71%	27	37%	37%	3.71	-2.5	62	138	$8
12 TAM	98	14	0	5	7	255	268	318	327	644	623	656	8	86	30	0.57	51	26	23	43	44	0%	142	32%	78%	11	27%	36%	3.56	-1.1	37	93	$1
13 TAM	176	25	2	17	8	199	248	270	267	537	734	417	9	84	23	0.61	52	23	25	33	30	5%	167	21%	80%	27	19%	44%	2.37	-8.9	33	83	$1
1st Half	95	12	2	8	3	179	257	250	284	534	994	385	9	84	19	0.60	54	20	25	52	36	10%	145	18%	75%	14	29%	43%	2.22	-5.6	41	103	$0
2nd Half	81	13	0	9	5	222	238	292	247	539	593	475	9	84	26	0.62	49	26	25	11	22	0%	136	24%	83%	13	8%	46%	2.55	-3.7	5	13	$2
14 Proj	128	18	1	10	7	225	256	295	299	594	655	559	9	85	26	0.64	50	24	26	43	42	3%	144	27%	77%				2.94	-4.3	38	96	$3

RYAN BLOOMFIELD

Furcal,Rafael

Age	36	Bats	B	Pos	SS	Health	F
Ht	5' 8"	Wt	195			PT/Exp	D
						Consist	B
LIMA Plan	B	Rand Var	0	MM	1433		

Missed 2013 after Tommy John surgery. Took ground balls in Sept, seems to be on track for Opening Day. Prior to injury, still had great ct% and modest speed, but a year away at his age is a complication. The upside is a decent BA and a handful of steals, but that's just end-game flyer material now.

Yr	Tm	AB	R	HR	RBI	SB	BA	xBA	OBP	SLG	OPS	vL	vR	bb%	ct%	h%	Eye	G	L	F	PX	xPX	hr/f	Spd	SBO	SB%	#Wk	DOM	DIS	RC/G	RAR	BPV	BPX	R$
09	LA	613	92	9	47	12	269	274	335	375	711	815	679	9	85	30	0.69	53	19	28	66	75	6%	121	10%	67%	26	35%	27%	4.34	14.7	51	104	$14
10	LA	383	66	8	43	22	300	287	366	460	826	774	847	9	84	34	0.67	47	20	33	102	77	8%	124	22%	85%	21	52%	33%	6.30	29.7	77	167	$20
11	2 NL	333	44	8	28	9	231	276	298	348	646	634	650	8	88	24	0.72	54	18	28	75	65	10%	77	17%	64%	18	67%	22%	3.27	-2.3	54	120	$5
12	STL	477	69	5	49	12	264	261	325	346	671	737	639	8	88	29	0.77	54	19	27	51	46	4%	105	11%	75%	22	41%	27%	3.93	5.8	43	108	$12
13																																		
1st Half																																		
2nd Half																																		
14	Proj	319	49	6	31	11	271	272	336	392	727	744	721	9	86	30	0.71	51	19	29	78	65	7%	109	16%	77%				4.61	10.6	64	160	$10

Galvis,Freddy

Age	24	Bats	B	Pos	2B	Health	D
Ht	5' 10"	Wt	170			PT/Exp	C
						Consist	A
LIMA Plan	D+	Rand Var	0	MM	2313		

6-19-.234 in 205 AB at PHI. Got a bigger opportunity, with 10+ games at four different positions, but huge drop in ct% stifled him. There are hints of value here, though: xPX insists there is more life in his bat. Spd is enticing, but he has yet to use it to steal bases in the majors. With a ct% rebound... UP: 10 HR, 10 SB.

Yr	Tm	AB	R	HR	RBI	SB	BA	xBA	OBP	SLG	OPS	vL	vR	bb%	ct%	h%	Eye	G	L	F	PX	xPX	hr/f	Spd	SBO	SB%	#Wk	DOM	DIS	RC/G	RAR	BPV	BPX	R$
09	aa	61	5	1	4	0	186	229	207	230	438			3	88	20	0.23				21			108	9%	0%				1.35		8	16	-$3
10	aa	501	44	4	36	11	206	227	240	268	508			4	81	25	0.24				44			117	15%	72%				2.06		5	11	-$1
11	a/a	543	63	7	35	19	250	245	283	347	630			4	82	29	0.26				70			113	26%	57%				3.10		31	69	$11
12	PHI	190	14	3	24	0	226	265	254	363	617	735	562	4	85	25	0.24	41	21	38	95	116	5%	82	0%	0%	10	40%	30%	3.04	-3.5	49	123	-$1
13	PHI *	446	33	8	38	3	220	218	255	339	594	688	662	5	77	27	0.21	36	19	46	82	115	8%	131	5%	74%	18	39%	39%	2.83	-11.3	23	58	$1
1st Half		159	10	4	15	1	195	224	255	346	601	577	649	7	78	23	0.36	36	18	46	91	126	8%	117	3%	100%	13	46%	38%	2.82	-4.4	48	120	-$2
2nd Half		287	23	4	23	2	234	221	256	335	591	808	714	3	76	29	0.13	36	21	43	77	86	11%	117	6%	67%	5	20%	40%	2.84	-7.5	9	23	$2
14	Proj	268	22	7	24	3	235	246	269	381	649	720	614	4	80	27	0.22	38	20	42	98	108	8%	110	8%	65%				3.35	-2.8	32	80	$4

Garcia,Avisail

Age	23	Bats	R	Pos	RF CF	Health	B
Ht	6' 4"	Wt	240			PT/Exp	F
						Consist	C
LIMA Plan	B	Rand Var	-4	MM	2315		

7-31-.283 in 244 AB at DET/CHW. Has hit .289 in the majors so far, but xBA and h% cast doubt on whether it can continue. High GB% hinders his power potential. He's shown considerable Spd, but lack of plate patience and ugly SB% might limit SB opportunities. But, did YOU have it all figured out when you were 23?

Yr	Tm	AB	R	HR	RBI	SB	BA	xBA	OBP	SLG	OPS	vL	vR	bb%	ct%	h%	Eye	G	L	F	PX	xPX	hr/f	Spd	SBO	SB%	#Wk	DOM	DIS	RC/G	RAR	BPV	BPX	R$
09																																		
10																																		
11																																		
12	DET *	262	33	5	21	7	296	292	318	407	725	745	588	3	81	35	0.17	62	27	11	67	63	0%	134	20%	54%	6	0%	100%	4.36	0.6	27	68	$8
13	2 AL *	418	55	13	57	6	310	255	342	456	798	640	770	5	76	38	0.20	56	18	26	96	92	15%	140	10%	55%	17	29%	53%	5.56	14.7	35	88	$19
1st Half		131	16	3	15	0	310	237	339	431	770	490	808	4	74	40	0.17	63	14	22	86	88	14%	113	6%	0%	8	38%	63%	5.04	2.2	10	25	$5
2nd Half		287	39	10	42	6	310	261	343	468	810	818	757	5	77	38	0.21	52	20	27	100	94	15%	145	12%	67%	9	22%	44%	5.81	10.7	43	108	$26
14	Proj	504	63	12	56	9	276	253	305	403	709	599	760	4	78	33	0.19	57	18	25	83	92	13%	141	14%	52%				4.12	-4.9	19	48	$17

Garcia,Leury

Age	23	Bats	B	Pos	2B	Health	A
Ht	5' 7"	Wt	160			PT/Exp	F
						Consist	C
LIMA Plan	D	Rand Var	-1	MM	1501		

0-2-.198 with 7 SB in 101 AB at TEX/CHW. Good defender played four positions in 2013; positional flexibility is his strong suit. However, he's just a one-trick pony. While he compiled more than 150 SB in six minor league seasons, he currently lacks the plate skills to exploit his speed in the majors. Add to Esix Snead list.

Yr	Tm	AB	R	HR	RBI	SB	BA	xBA	OBP	SLG	OPS	vL	vR	bb%	ct%	h%	Eye	G	L	F	PX	xPX	hr/f	Spd	SBO	SB%	#Wk	DOM	DIS	RC/G	RAR	BPV	BPX	R$
09																																		
10																																		
11																																		
12	aa	377	45	2	24	25	280	225	312	377	690			5	78	35	0.22				60			156	33%	77%				4.19		19	48	$14
13	2 AL *	324	38	4	18	19	229	216	275	318	594	566	445	6	69	32	0.20	46	25	29	68	44	0%	160	33%	75%	17	12%	65%	2.91	-8.1	-9	-23	$7
1st Half		112	18	2	12	3	247	228	289	363	652	423	487	6	70	34	0.20	44	25	31	86	62	0%	134	17%	76%	11	18%	64%	3.56	-0.5	1	3	$4
2nd Half		212	20	2	6	16	220	211	268	295	563	800	407	6	68	32	0.21	47	25	28	59	24	0%	168	41%	75%	6	0%	67%	2.61	-7.3	-17	-43	$9
14	Proj	166	20	0	10	10	233	220	272	302	573	703	533	5	72	32	0.21	46	25	29	52	39	0%	158	32%	77%				2.80	-4.6	-9	-21	$4

Gardner,Brett

Age	30	Bats	L	Pos	CF	Health	F
Ht	5' 11"	Wt	185			PT/Exp	C
						Consist	B
LIMA Plan	B+	Rand Var	-1	MM	2515		

New plate approach (more FB and LD) led to more HR and improved BA in 1H, but xPX and xBA foresaw the 2H regression. SBO dip drove SB down; he said it was because he was not running with LH Robinson Cano up behind him for much of year. SBs should return to prior every-10-AB rate, so with health... UP: 50 SB, still.

Yr	Tm	AB	R	HR	RBI	SB	BA	xBA	OBP	SLG	OPS	vL	vR	bb%	ct%	h%	Eye	G	L	F	PX	xPX	hr/f	Spd	SBO	SB%	#Wk	DOM	DIS	RC/G	RAR	BPV	BPX	R$
09	NYY	248	48	3	23	26	270	255	345	379	724	781	708	9	84	31	0.65	49	18	33	59	43	4%	180	40%	84%	21	33%	48%	4.77	3.9	58	118	$13
10	NYY	477	97	5	47	47	277	256	383	379	762	725	776	14	79	34	0.78	53	19	28	72	34	5%	159	31%	84%	27	41%	15%	5.41	16.3	51	111	$28
11	NYY	510	87	7	36	49	259	260	345	369	713	616	738	11	82	30	0.65	52	19	28	72	48	6%	169	39%	79%	27	44%	30%	4.40	2.5	58	129	$24
12	NYY	31	7	0	3	2	323	266	417	387	804	2032	426	14	77	42	0.71	38	38	25	60	51	0%	101	31%	50%	5	20%	60%	5.24	0.9	18	45	$0
13	NYY	539	81	8	52	24	273	251	344	416	759	744	767	9	76	34	0.41	41	23	35	104	70	6%	146	22%	75%	24	42%	29%	4.89	10.1	52	130	$22
1st Half		311	45	7	31	11	286	263	345	450	795	793	798	8	77	35	0.40	41	23	35	117	70	9%	130	20%	65%	14	57%	36%	5.35	10.5	61	153	$26
2nd Half		228	36	1	21	13	254	236	325	368	694	673	726	10	75	34	0.42	42	23	35	87	70	2%	154	24%	87%	10	20%	20%	4.29	0.8	37	93	$18
14	Proj	502	85	6	45	40	267	250	350	389	739	710	751	10	79	33	0.54	47	21	32	85	56	5%	161	33%	79%				4.72	8.2	55	139	$26

Gattis,Evan

Age	27	Bats	R	Pos	LF CA	Health	A
Ht	6' 4"	Wt	230			PT/Exp	F
						Consist	B
LIMA Plan	B	Rand Var	+1	MM	4123		

21-65-.243 in 354 AB at ATL. Rags-to-riches story made great copy when he hit a bunch of moon shots in the first half, but lack of patience and hr/f regression defined his 2H. He'll keep knocking 'em out (although xPX says not as often), and xBA hints at some BA upside. With CA eligibility, even a power-only profile is plenty valuable.

Yr	Tm	AB	R	HR	RBI	SB	BA	xBA	OBP	SLG	OPS	vL	vR	bb%	ct%	h%	Eye	G	L	F	PX	xPX	hr/f	Spd	SBO	SB%	#Wk	DOM	DIS	RC/G	RAR	BPV	BPX	R$
09																																		
10																																		
11																																		
12	aa	182	19	7	29	1	221	280	283	430	714			8	81	24	0.45				130			102	6%	40%				3.90		76	190	$1
13	ATL *	375	45	22	66	0	245	264	285	483	768	808	757	5	77	26	0.24	41	14	45	163	136	17%	60	0%	0%	24	58%	21%	4.65	10.5	69	173	$11
1st Half		163	24	14	37	0	252	292	311	577	887	1079	830	8	75	25	0.34	39	14	47	219	159	24%	66	0%	0%	12	83%	8%	6.11	11.5	112	280	$14
2nd Half		212	21	8	29	0	239	243	264	412	676	596	691	3	79	27	0.16	42	15	42	121	118	11%	66	0%	0%	12	33%	33%	3.64	-0.4	40	100	$8
14	Proj	393	44	20	66	1	250	266	304	476	780	818	765	6	79	27	0.32	40	15	45	150	134	14%	80	2%	50%				4.81	9.1	67	167	$12

Gennett,Scooter

Age	24	Bats	L	Pos	2B	Health	A
Ht	5' 10"	Wt	180			PT/Exp	D
						Consist	A
LIMA Plan	D+	Rand Var	-2	MM	2313		

6-21-.324 in 213 AB at MIL. When your name is Scooter, you better have speed, and he does. But this one doesn't have a Rizutto-esque Eye, can't hit LHP, and needed a 38% hit rate in the majors to prop up his BA. 2H xPX offers a glimmer of hope, but we'll need more convincing.

Yr	Tm	AB	R	HR	RBI	SB	BA	xBA	OBP	SLG	OPS	vL	vR	bb%	ct%	h%	Eye	G	L	F	PX	xPX	hr/f	Spd	SBO	SB%	#Wk	DOM	DIS	RC/G	RAR	BPV	BPX	R$
09																																		
10																																		
11																																		
12	aa	533	54	5	36	9	267	244	299	353	652			4	85	31	0.30				61			96	11%	62%				3.59		28	70	$10
13	MIL *	534	61	9	37	9	274	240	307	380	688	329	946	5	79	33	0.23	39	24	37	72	115	10%	147	12%	58%	14	43%	29%	3.98	4.9	30	75	$14
1st Half		262	27	2	15	7	251	202	291	331	622	0	687	5	81	30	0.30	44	12	44	54	81	7%	146	17%	59%	4	25%	50%	3.15	-4.3	25	63	$9
2nd Half		272	34	7	22	3	296	253	324	428	752	376	1016	4	77	36	0.18	38	28	35	89	124	11%	134	7%	56%	10	50%	20%	4.91	9.2	31	78	$18
14	Proj	335	37	9	23	6	260	251	293	396	689	239	778	4	81	30	0.25	40	21	38	89	107	8%	129	12%	61%				3.87	1.7	35	87	$8

DAVE ADLER

Gentry,Craig

Age	30	Bats	R	Pos	CF LF	Health	B	LIMA Plan	D+
Ht	6' 2"	Wt	190			PT/Exp	F	Rand Var	-3
						Consist	C	MM	1511

Rather than follow the wild BA swings, focus on xBA, which has been steady and bad. Big 2nd half was fueled by a spike in both contact rate and hit rate, but both were just corrections from the 1st half. OBP and speed have value, even as a part-timer, but window will close quickly for a 30 year-old.

Yr	Tm	AB	R	HR	RBI	SB	BA	xBA	OBP	SLG	OPS	vL	vR	bb%	ct%	h%	Eye	G	L	F	PX	xPX	hr/f	Spd	SBO	SB%	#Wk	DOM	DIS	RC/G	RAR	BPV	BPX	R$
09	TEX *	529	79	6	41	37	255	245	306	354	660	750	277	7	85	29	0.48	33	25	42	59	57	0%	173	31%	84%	5	20%	40%	3.88	-5.6	54	110	$18
10	TEX *	292	34	3	27	9	249	183	300	323	623	348	633	7	77	31	0.32	43	9	48	48	103	0%	185	19%	60%	7	14%	57%	3.16	-9.4	18	39	$5
11	TEX *	243	38	2	19	21	232	248	281	303	585	735	648	6	80	28	0.35	50	23	27	52	62	4%	156	37%	94%	21	29%	52%	3.20	-7.6	25	56	$7
12	TEX	240	31	1	26	13	304	245	367	392	759	859	686	6	83	36	0.34	47	20	33	61	57	2%	138	28%	65%	27	30%	44%	4.67	2.9	35	88	$10
13	TEX	246	39	2	22	24	280	253	373	386	759	801	709	11	81	34	0.63	50	19	31	74	46	3%	168	34%	89%	24	42%	33%	5.30	7.4	58	145	$14
1st Half		116	16	1	9	8	216	237	300	310	610	714	501	11	76	28	0.50	59	15	26	66	58	5%	159	31%	80%	12	33%	50%	3.15	-3.7	28	70	$6
2nd Half		130	23	1	13	16	338	266	407	454	861	884	879	10	86	39	0.83	42	23	35	79	36	3%	155	35%	94%	12	50%	17%	7.95	12.9	77	193	$21
14	**Proj**	**225**	**34**	**2**	**21**	**18**	**267**	**250**	**349**	**362**	**712**	**768**	**656**	**8**	**82**	**32**	**0.50**	**48**	**20**	**31**	**67**	**52**	**3%**	**159**	**34%**	**84%**				**4.35**	**1.2**	**46**	**116**	**$9**

Getz,Chris

Age	30	Bats	L	Pos	2B	Health	D	LIMA Plan	D+
Ht	5' 11"	Wt	185			PT/Exp	D	Rand Var	+3
						Consist	B	MM	0521

1-18-.220 with 16 SB in 209 AB at KC. Part of the 2B carousel in KC. Elite ct% and high LD% give him the basis for a good BA, but utter lack of power keeps him from getting there. Runs well and frequently, but lack of OBP puts a ceiling on his SB totals. And as he enters his 30s, lack of playing time might be next.

Yr	Tm	AB	R	HR	RBI	SB	BA	xBA	OBP	SLG	OPS	vL	vR	bb%	ct%	h%	Eye	G	L	F	PX	xPX	hr/f	Spd	SBO	SB%	#Wk	DOM	DIS	RC/G	RAR	BPV	BPX	R$
09	CHW	375	49	2	31	25	261	259	324	347	670	650	675	7	86	30	0.56	47	19	33	57	46	2%	120	26%	93%	24	38%	29%	4.09	3.9	41	84	$12
10	KC	224	23	0	18	15	237	247	302	277	579	699	548	8	88	27	0.68	52	18	30	35	29	0%	108	27%	88%	23	39%	26%	2.98	-5.0	28	61	$4
11	KC	380	50	0	26	21	255	239	313	287	600	636	588	7	88	29	0.67	54	18	28	20	16	0%	150	24%	75%	26	23%	35%	3.10	-7.0	30	67	$9
12	KC *	232	26	0	22	10	263	284	304	346	650	547	714	5	91	29	0.61	43	29	28	53	50	0%	125	21%	76%	16	50%	13%	3.66	-0.4	55	138	$5
13	KC *	293	34	2	25	18	227	252	278	291	568	605	546	7	90	25	0.69	45	22	33	42	37	2%	119	30%	81%	21	38%	29%	2.77	-8.5	43	108	$7
1st Half		148	19	1	13	4	213	238	272	286	558	703	514	8	88	24	0.67	41	20	39	50	41	2%	116	14%	80%	12	50%	25%	2.57	-5.2	43	108	$3
2nd Half		145	15	1	12	14	241	282	284	295	579	399	608	6	92	26	0.71	53	25	22	35	27	0%	116	46%	81%	9	22%	33%	2.98	-3.2	42	105	$10
14	**Proj**	**216**	**25**	**0**	**18**	**13**	**245**	**262**	**295**	**304**	**599**	**559**	**612**	**7**	**90**	**27**	**0.68**	**48**	**23**	**29**	**40**	**35**	**1%**	**127**	**28%**	**81%**				**3.14**	**-3.6**	**45**	**114**	**$6**

Giavotella,Johnny

Age	26	Bats	R	Pos	2B	Health	A	LIMA Plan	D
Ht	5' 8"	Wt	180			PT/Exp	C	Rand Var	+1
						Consist	A	MM	1211

0-4-.220 in 41 AB at KC. Another rider on the Royals' 2B merry-go-round. Once-promising prospect is starting to look like an AAAA suspect. 2013 xPX is a small sample-size fluke. Spd isn't a strength, and poor SB% says he shouldn't be running anyway. Eye growth might save him, but if KC is losing interest, shouldn't you be, too?

Yr	Tm	AB	R	HR	RBI	SB	BA	xBA	OBP	SLG	OPS	vL	vR	bb%	ct%	h%	Eye	G	L	F	PX	xPX	hr/f	Spd	SBO	SB%	#Wk	DOM	DIS	RC/G	RAR	BPV	BPX	R$
09																																		
10	aa	522	68	6	48	10	284	268	340	396	736			8	86	32	0.61				78			115	12%	55%				4.62		59	128	$15
11	KC *	631	68	8	72	11	277	262	314	393	708	740	621	5	85	32	0.36	43	21	36	82	66	4%	113	12%	59%	9	33%	22%	4.23	9.1	52	116	$17
12	KC *	543	67	7	64	8	256	260	306	351	657	547	591	7	85	29	0.49	47	23	30	62	50	2%	104	6%	87%	14	14%	36%	3.73	0.0	37	93	$11
13	KC *	411	41	5	39	6	238	237	311	332	643	498	713	10	83	28	0.60	57	14	30	72	127	0%	85	10%	56%	6	50%	17%	3.37	-4.4	34	85	$5
1st Half		296	32	5	32	5	254	271	326	363	689	0	1750	10	82	30	0.59	50	25	25	81	-15	0%	88	9%	69%	1	100%	0%	4.02	2.8	39	98	$9
2nd Half		115	8	0	7	1	198	216	272	253	525	498	520	9	85	23	0.66	58	12	30	49	144	0%	89	11%	24%	5	40%	20%	2.02	-6.2	25	63	-$7
14	**Proj**	**161**	**17**	**1**	**15**	**2**	**245**	**242**	**317**	**322**	**639**	**624**	**647**	**8**	**84**	**29**	**0.55**	**49**	**18**	**33**	**60**	**89**	**2%**	**98**	**9%**	**58%**				**3.24**	**-2.2**	**24**	**61**	**$2**

Gillaspie,Conor

Age	26	Bats	L	Pos	3B	Health	A	LIMA Plan	C
Ht	6' 1"	Wt	205			PT/Exp	C	Rand Var	0
						Consist	B	MM	3025

FB% and xPX suggest that there might be a little more power in his bat, but it's still not what you want from a corner IF. Batted .159 vs LHP in 63 AB, but that might be enough to force him into a platoon. Overall, skills were marginally better in 2H than the 1H, but the ceiling is low. UP: 20 HR, .260 BA

Yr	Tm	AB	R	HR	RBI	SB	BA	xBA	OBP	SLG	OPS	vL	vR	bb%	ct%	h%	Eye	G	L	F	PX	xPX	hr/f	Spd	SBO	SB%	#Wk	DOM	DIS	RC/G	RAR	BPV	BPX	R$
09																																		
10	aa	491	49	7	58	0	268	263	312	389	701			6	85	30	0.44				78			123	4%	0%				4.06		54	117	$9
11	SF *	447	42	7	41	6	236	201	303	344	647	667	771	9	79	29	0.45	39	11	50	75	57	11%	113	14%	35%	6	33%	17%	3.20	-11.0	29	64	$4
12	SF *	433	42	8	35	0	216	284	262	315	577	0	467	6	84	24	0.40	39	33	28	62	17	0%	92	0%	0%	2	50%	50%	2.69	-17.4	29	73	$0
13	CHW	408	46	13	40	0	245	243	305	390	695	451	738	8	81	28	0.47	37	20	42	91	110	9%	117	1%	0%	27	48%	26%	4.01	0.7	49	123	$6
1st Half		203	20	5	20	0	251	234	315	374	690	333	749	9	79	30	0.44	38	21	41	84	106	7%	108	2%	0%	14	43%	29%	3.94	-0.2	34	85	$5
2nd Half		205	26	8	20	0	239	251	300	405	705	576	728	8	82	25	0.50	37	20	43	98	114	11%	123	0%	0%	13	54%	23%	4.08	0.6	63	158	$7
14	**Proj**	**420**	**45**	**17**	**40**	**1**	**239**	**257**	**295**	**411**	**706**	**479**	**746**	**8**	**82**	**26**	**0.45**	**37**	**20**	**42**	**105**	**111**	**11%**	**117**	**3%**	**27%**				**3.99**	**0.3**	**45**	**113**	**$8**

Gindl,Caleb

Age	25	Bats	L	Pos	LF	Health	A	LIMA Plan	D+
Ht	5' 7"	Wt	205			PT/Exp	B	Rand Var	0
						Consist	B	MM	4123

5-14-.242 in 132 AB at MIL. Small sample size, but surprising skills growth in majors (0.80 Eye, 140 xPX, .274 xBA) hint at possible BA and power upside. OPS vs LHP is based on only 12 AB; did better vs RHP in minors (.892 OPS). Need more data before going all in, but there's enough potential here to justify a small investment.

Yr	Tm	AB	R	HR	RBI	SB	BA	xBA	OBP	SLG	OPS	vL	vR	bb%	ct%	h%	Eye	G	L	F	PX	xPX	hr/f	Spd	SBO	SB%	#Wk	DOM	DIS	RC/G	RAR	BPV	BPX	R$
09																																		
10	aa	463	48	8	47	8	241	257	308	357	665			9	81	28	0.50				88			93	11%	59%				3.60		41	89	$6
11	aaa	472	59	11	42	4	259	240	324	387	711			9	77	32	0.41				90			110	7%	42%				4.15		32	71	$9
12	aaa	452	43	11	40	3	232	240	280	376	656			6	75	29	0.27				101			101	4%	74%				3.49		25	63	$4
13	MIL *	444	40	14	50	3	244	248	309	412	721	1083	746	9	75	30	0.37	39	21	40	120	140	12%	66	6%	45%	15	27%	40%	4.19	1.7	34	85	$7
1st Half		264	19	7	29	2	229	241	285	369	655	400	588	7	71	30	0.27	44	25	31	107	141	0%	68	7%	42%	3	0%	100%	3.38	-5.2	5	13	$6
2nd Half		180	21	7	21	1	267	277	343	474	817	1323	772	10	81	30	0.61	38	21	41	137	140	13%	80	4%	50%	12	33%	25%	5.57	8.1	80	200	$9
14	**Proj**	**286**	**29**	**11**	**29**	**2**	**254**	**258**	**320**	**441**	**761**	**741**	**763**	**9**	**77**	**30**	**0.43**	**38**	**21**	**41**	**128**	**126**	**12%**	**70**	**6%**	**54%**				**4.77**	**6.4**	**51**	**127**	**$7**

Goins,Ryan

Age	26	Bats	L	Pos	2B	Health	A	LIMA Plan	D
Ht	5' 10"	Wt	170			PT/Exp	D	Rand Var	0
						Consist	B	MM	1211

2-8-.252 in 119 AB at TOR. Making the majors is exciting, but at some point, it's time to settle down and be more patient (only two walks). Huge ct% drop is a killer for a skill set that already lacks plus power or speed. What we have here is a utility infielder ceiling.

Yr	Tm	AB	R	HR	RBI	SB	BA	xBA	OBP	SLG	OPS	vL	vR	bb%	ct%	h%	Eye	G	L	F	PX	xPX	hr/f	Spd	SBO	SB%	#Wk	DOM	DIS	RC/G	RAR	BPV	BPX	R$
09																																		
10																																		
11																																		
12	aa	546	53	6	49	12	260	247	306	362	668			6	84	30	0.41				70			96	16%	54%				3.63		35	88	$11
13	TOR *	496	43	7	43	2	229	232	264	324	588	576	628	4	75	29	0.19	56	19	25	76	53	9%	95	8%	28%	7	14%	43%	2.69	-11.1	0	0	$2
1st Half		221	21	2	23	2	246	223	291	340	632			6	74	32	0.25				81			94	14%	21%				3.00		5	13	$5
2nd Half		275	22	4	20	1	216	232	242	311	553	576	628	3	75	27	0.13	56	19	25	73	53	9%	105	1%	100%	7	14%	43%	2.46	-8.5	-2	-5	$0
14	**Proj**	**166**	**15**	**3**	**15**	**2**	**240**	**250**	**279**	**347**	**625**	**602**	**639**	**5**	**78**	**29**	**0.25**	**56**	**19**	**25**	**80**	**48**	**8%**	**106**	**12%**	**47%**				**3.09**	**-3.1**	**9**	**22**	**$2**

Goldschmidt,Paul

Age	26	Bats	R	Pos	1B	Health	A	LIMA Plan	C
Ht	6' 3"	Wt	245			PT/Exp	A	Rand Var	-2
						Consist	B	MM	5245

After his 2012 breakout, better plate patience, more power, and improvements vs RHP pushed him to the next level. Even contributes on the basepaths. Average ct% and borderline SB% are the warts here, but those are quibbles. With a bit more loft (40% FB rate, maybe?)... UP: 40-45 HR, though likely at the expense of some BA.

Yr	Tm	AB	R	HR	RBI	SB	BA	xBA	OBP	SLG	OPS	vL	vR	bb%	ct%	h%	Eye	G	L	F	PX	xPX	hr/f	Spd	SBO	SB%	#Wk	DOM	DIS	RC/G	RAR	BPV	BPX	R$
09																																		
10																																		
11	ARI *	522	87	30	92	10	260	270	354	498	852	657	855	13	70	32	0.48	42	21	37	174	155	21%	90	9%	74%	9	44%	44%	6.04	22.2	73	162	$23
12	ARI	514	82	20	82	18	286	274	359	490	850	1068	739	10	75	35	0.46	40	24	36	149	160	14%	78	15%	86%	27	56%	19%	6.41	26.5	64	160	$25
13	ARI	602	103	36	125	15	302	290	401	551	952	986	941	14	76	35	0.68	44	21	35	168	164	23%	90	11%	68%	27	67%	19%	7.94	56.1	95	238	$40
1st Half		301	53	19	67	8	306	295	387	555	942	862	969	12	77	34	0.57	44	22	33	167	168	24%	66	9%	89%	14	64%	21%	8.00	28.0	86	215	$41
2nd Half		301	50	17	58	7	299	285	414	548	962	1141	914	16	75	35	0.79	44	20	36	169	161	21%	112	12%	54%	13	69%	15%	7.88	27.9	104	260	$40
14	**Proj**	**580**	**96**	**34**	**107**	**13**	**290**	**290**	**380**	**543**	**923**	**1024**	**885**	**13**	**75**	**34**	**0.57**	**42**	**22**	**35**	**177**	**161**	**22%**	**89**	**10%**	**70%**				**7.33**	**44.7**	**94**	**235**	**$34**

DAVE ADLER

Gomes,Jonny

Age 33 · Bats R · Pos LF · Ht 6' 1" · Wt 230

Health A · PT/Exp D · Consist D · LIMA Plan D+ · Rand Var 0 · MM 4203

Hit just .168 with 2 HR in first 95 AB, but was solid the rest of the way (.281, 11 HR). Put an end to troubling ct% trend, but it came at expense of power, and he didn't hit LH as well as usual. Frankly, we prefer the old version—he's never going to hit for a high BA, so power, particularly vs LH, is his lone path to fantasy relevance.

Yr	Tm	AB	R	HR	RBI	SB	BA	xBA	OBP	SLG	OPS	vL	vR	bb%	ct%	h%	Eye	G	L	F	PX	xPX	hr/f	Spd	SBO	SB%	#Wk	DOM	DIS	RC/G	RAR	BPV	BPX	R$
09	CIN *	412	52	28	71	6	256	270	314	521	834	914	859	8	68	31	0.27	34	20	46	188	156	22%	70	9%	73%	20	70%	25%	5.55	18.1	62	127	$13
10	CIN	511	77	18	86	5	266	239	327	431	758	856	709	7	76	32	0.32	29	21	50	113	125	9%	113	6%	63%	27	44%	33%	4.70	10.7	44	96	$17
11	2 NL	311	41	14	43	7	209	219	325	389	714	863	654	13	66	27	0.46	34	18	48	138	136	14%	91	12%	70%	27	33%	44%	3.92	-0.5	31	69	$5
12	OAK	279	46	18	47	3	262	225	377	491	868	974	715	14	63	35	0.42	31	19	50	171	159	20%	99	4%	75%	28	54%	36%	6.13	17.5	47	118	$10
13	BOS	312	49	13	52	1	247	233	344	426	771	795	745	12	71	30	0.48	30	20	50	134	101	11%	72	1%	100%	27	48%	30%	4.90	8.5	41	103	$8
1st Half		147	23	5	20	0	218	217	311	374	686	730	656	12	73	26	0.51	29	16	55	117	105	8%	71	0%	0%	14	57%	29%	3.80	-1.0	35	88	$3
2nd Half		165	26	8	32	1	273	246	362	473	834	858	817	12	70	35	0.46	31	23	46	151	98	15%	75	2%	100%	13	38%	31%	6.04	9.5	48	120	$12
14	**Proj**	**307**	**47**	**14**	**51**	**3**	**258**	**229**	**357**	**447**	**804**	**875**	**738**	**12**	**68**	**33**	**0.44**	**31**	**20**	**49**	**143**	**125**	**14%**	**83**	**4%**	**76%**				**5.35**	**12.0**	**33**	**81**	**$9**

Gomes,Yan

Age 26 · Bats R · Pos CA · Ht 6' 2" · Wt 215

Health A · PT/Exp D · Consist C · LIMA Plan C+ · Rand Var -4 · MM 4423

Significant improvement in ct% and continued plus power puts him back on our radar, and helped him earn consistent AB down the stretch. xBA doesn't fully validate BA gains, will need to hold on to new ct% level to keep BA out of liability range. Still, if he can keep getting his name on the lineup card... UP: 20 HR.

Yr	Tm	AB	R	HR	RBI	SB	BA	xBA	OBP	SLG	OPS	vL	vR	bb%	ct%	h%	Eye	G	L	F	PX	xPX	hr/f	Spd	SBO	SB%	#Wk	DOM	DIS	RC/G	RAR	BPV	BPX	R$
09																																		
10																																		
11	a/a	290	24	10	36	0	206	233	252	366	618			6	68	27	0.19				130			83	0%	0%				2.96		15	33	$0
12	TOR *	403	38	13	51	3	254	237	292	427	719	701	567	5	71	33	0.19	48	15	37	133	127	16%	72	3%	100%	15	27%	47%	4.30	6.8	24	60	$8
13	CLE	293	45	11	38	2	294	261	345	481	826	934	766	6	77	35	0.27	43	18	39	131	126	12%	116	3%	100%	26	54%	38%	5.85	17.3	62	155	$11
1st Half		116	19	6	20	2	284	284	320	526	846	870	809	5	81	31	0.27	44	15	40	148	129	15%	131	8%	100%	13	62%	31%	6.10	7.8	94	235	$10
2nd Half		177	26	5	18	0	299	245	344	452	796	996	746	6	75	38	0.27	43	20	38	119	124	10%	100	0%	0%	13	46%	46%	5.66	9.5	38	95	$12
14	**Proj**	**364**	**44**	**14**	**47**	**2**	**266**	**257**	**317**	**457**	**774**	**854**	**720**	**5**	**75**	**32**	**0.23**	**45**	**17**	**38**	**138**	**126**	**14%**	**102**	**3%**	**100%**				**4.91**	**12.5**	**45**	**112**	**$12**

Gomez,Carlos

Age 28 · Bats R · Pos CF · Ht 6' 3" · Wt 215

Health B · PT/Exp C · Consist C · LIMA Plan D+ · Rand Var -4 · MM 4515

PRO: Already impressive power/speed combo got even better; made huge strides vs LH; showed in 2H that he can take a walk. CON: Second half ct%, xBA show significant BA downside, and 1H is a clear outlier against xBA history. For BA, next step more likely backward than forward. But go all-in on HRs and SBs.

Yr	Tm	AB	R	HR	RBI	SB	BA	xBA	OBP	SLG	OPS	vL	vR	bb%	ct%	h%	Eye	G	L	F	PX	xPX	hr/f	Spd	SBO	SB%	#Wk	DOM	DIS	RC/G	RAR	BPV	BPX	R$
09	MIN	315	51	3	28	14	229	241	287	337	623	608	631	7	77	29	0.31	45	19	35	74	56	4%	148	30%	67%	27	37%	37%	2.99	-10.7	27	55	$5
10	MIL *	319	43	5	25	19	246	224	292	347	639	580	694	6	74	32	0.25	48	16	36	72	48	7%	144	29%	82%	24	33%	50%	3.54	-5.2	11	24	$9
11	MIL	231	37	8	24	16	225	235	276	403	679	857	566	6	72	28	0.23	44	12	44	127	122	11%	146	40%	89%	22	45%	32%	3.79	-2.1	49	109	$7
12	MIL	415	72	19	51	37	260	250	305	463	768	778	762	5	76	30	0.20	40	17	43	128	124	14%	130	50%	86%	25	40%	32%	4.85	9.2	58	145	$24
13	MIL	536	80	24	73	40	284	263	338	506	843	993	797	6	73	35	0.25	40	21	38	153	137	16%	155	37%	85%	27	48%	30%	6.07	30.2	75	188	$36
1st Half		286	45	12	37	16	315	285	342	566	909	1042	872	4	77	38	0.18	42	20	38	165	138	15%	167	30%	84%	14	64%	14%	7.27	24.2	98	245	$38
2nd Half		250	35	12	36	24	248	238	316	436	752	902	724	9	68	31	0.32	38	22	39	137	135	18%	111	43%	86%	13	31%	46%	4.90	5.5	37	93	$35
14	**Proj**	**545**	**85**	**25**	**67**	**38**	**260**	**254**	**313**	**467**	**781**	**863**	**746**	**6**	**73**	**31**	**0.25**	**41**	**19**	**40**	**142**	**123**	**15%**	**146**	**37%**	**86%**				**5.06**	**14.3**	**71**	**179**	**$30**

Gonzalez,Adrian

Age 32 · Bats L · Pos 1B · Ht 6' 2" · Wt 225

Health A · PT/Exp A · Consist C · LIMA Plan B+ · Rand Var 0 · MM 3235

A rebound was expected after disappointing 2012 campaign—instead, we got a carbon copy. Still a good player, but a far cry from his peak. Or is he? xPX suggests that there may yet be some latent power here, so pay for another carbon copy but don't be surprised by... UP: 30 HR.

Yr	Tm	AB	R	HR	RBI	SB	BA	xBA	OBP	SLG	OPS	vL	vR	bb%	ct%	h%	Eye	G	L	F	PX	xPX	hr/f	Spd	SBO	SB%	#Wk	DOM	DIS	RC/G	RAR	BPV	BPX	R$
09	SD	552	90	40	99	1	277	305	407	551	958	770	1077	18	80	28	1.09	39	21	40	160	165	22%	67	1%	50%	27	74%	15%	7.84	51.0	107	218	$22
10	SD	591	87	31	101	0	298	286	393	511	904	937	887	14	81	33	0.82	39	21	39	138	151	16%	62	0%	0%	27	63%	15%	7.30	44.1	81	176	$26
11	BOS	630	108	27	117	1	338	296	410	548	957	787	1046	11	81	38	0.62	47	21	32	142	128	16%	79	0%	100%	27	59%	15%	8.61	65.8	85	189	$39
12	2 TM	629	75	18	108	2	299	279	344	463	806	846	783	6	83	34	0.38	40	24	36	111	134	10%	62	1%	100%	27	56%	30%	5.79	20.7	52	130	$24
13	LA	583	69	22	100	1	293	272	342	461	803	747	829	7	83	32	0.48	38	23	39	110	138	11%	71	1%	100%	27	63%	15%	5.77	19.1	59	148	$24
1st Half		284	29	10	48	0	296	277	355	465	820	741	858	8	85	32	0.59	37	23	39	112	151	10%	75	0%	0%	14	79%	7%	5.97	10.8	69	173	$21
2nd Half		299	40	12	52	1	291	267	338	458	796	753	805	7	82	32	0.39	39	22	39	108	126	13%	71	1%	100%	13	46%	23%	5.58	8.2	51	128	$27
14	**Proj**	**590**	**75**	**23**	**103**	**1**	**292**	**279**	**350**	**472**	**822**	**776**	**845**	**8**	**83**	**32**	**0.53**	**40**	**23**	**37**	**119**	**137**	**13%**	**68**	**1%**	**96%**				**6.00**	**22.9**	**57**	**143**	**$25**

Gonzalez,Carlos

Age 28 · Bats L · Pos LF · Ht 6' 1" · Wt 220

Health B · PT/Exp B · Consist B · LIMA Plan D+ · Rand Var -2 · MM 5435

Swapped contact for power, as FB%, xPX jumped significantly. It was working, with no negative impact on BA, until July finger injury ended his season early. Time out of the lineup is now the biggest risk to this five-category stud; if pattern of 500+ AB in even years holds, then... UP: 35 HR

Yr	Tm	AB	R	HR	RBI	SB	BA	xBA	OBP	SLG	OPS	vL	vR	bb%	ct%	h%	Eye	G	L	F	PX	xPX	hr/f	Spd	SBO	SB%	#Wk	DOM	DIS	RC/G	RAR	BPV	BPX	R$
09	COL *	470	82	20	69	20	290	287	349	526	875	809	896	8	78	34	0.41	38	23	39	143	113	17%	132	23%	73%	18	50%	33%	6.45	32.0	84	171	$23
10	COL	587	111	34	117	26	336	302	376	598	974	925	1003	6	77	39	0.30	43	21	37	171	140	20%	108	21%	76%	26	54%	19%	8.55	70.1	92	200	$46
11	COL	481	92	26	92	20	295	291	363	526	889	779	943	9	78	33	0.46	48	18	34	153	123	21%	100	19%	80%	24	63%	17%	6.84	37.6	85	189	$30
12	COL	518	89	22	85	20	303	285	371	510	881	742	961	10	78	35	0.49	49	22	29	134	116	19%	92	16%	80%	26	50%	23%	6.94	41.4	68	170	$30
13	COL	391	72	26	70	21	302	281	367	591	958	875	1004	9	70	37	0.35	38	22	41	206	171	24%	121	23%	88%	22	50%	45%	8.09	43.6	101	253	$30
1st Half		318	63	22	60	15	296	288	365	604	969	916	995	10	71	35	0.38	37	20	43	215	172	23%	124	20%	94%	14	71%	21%	8.23	37.2	115	288	$36
2nd Half		73	9	4	10	6	329	253	380	534	914	704	1042	8	64	47	0.23	40	30	30	160	166	29%	93	35%	75%	8	13%	88%	7.50	7.0	31	78	$3
14	**Proj**	**497**	**83**	**27**	**87**	**24**	**309**	**280**	**372**	**544**	**916**	**783**	**988**	**9**	**74**	**37**	**0.37**	**43**	**23**	**34**	**162**	**144**	**22%**	**107**	**21%**	**80%**				**7.44**	**46.9**	**83**	**207**	**$35**

Gonzalez,Marwin

Age 25 · Bats B · Pos SS · Ht 6' 1" · Wt 210

Health B · PT/Exp D · Consist A · LIMA Plan D · Rand Var +2 · MM 1221

4-14-.221 with 6 SB in 204 AB at HOU. Despite the low AB total, finished seventh in the AL in sacrifice bunts, a pretty good sign that he's not much of an offensive threat. Career home/road splits (home: 204 AB, 3 HR, .589 OPS; road: 205 AB, 3 HR, .589 OPS) show at least he's got consistency going for him.

Yr	Tm	AB	R	HR	RBI	SB	BA	xBA	OBP	SLG	OPS	vL	vR	bb%	ct%	h%	Eye	G	L	F	PX	xPX	hr/f	Spd	SBO	SB%	#Wk	DOM	DIS	RC/G	RAR	BPV	BPX	R$
09																																		
10	aa	305	18	3	31	4	220	245	251	298	549			4	86	25	0.29				51			109	14%	51%				2.34		26	57	$0
11	a/a	413	37	3	27	5	246	255	286	335	621			5	87	28	0.43				67			95	9%	59%				3.18		43	96	$3
12	HOU *	244	22	3	19	3	241	262	286	342	628	296	713	6	85	28	0.41	54	20	27	74	67	4%	81	11%	50%	20	35%	30%	3.17	-1.9	36	90	$1
13	HOU *	376	34	5	25	9	221	241	251	308	559	575	570	4	83	26	0.24	54	15	30	63	84	8%	95	16%	74%	20	25%	35%	2.53	-10.3	21	53	$2
1st Half		196	23	4	16	6	230	234	252	327	579	681	575	3	82	26	0.16	57	12	31	66	92	9%	100	19%	74%	13	31%	38%	2.71	-4.5	18	45	$6
2nd Half		180	12	1	10	3	212	273	251	287	538	381	522	5	84	25	0.33	42	31	27	59	43	0%	85	12%	74%	7	14%	29%	2.33	-6.4	21	53	-$2
14	**Proj**	**133**	**11**	**2**	**10**	**2**	**236**	**262**	**272**	**330**	**602**	**404**	**678**	**5**	**84**	**27**	**0.32**	**50**	**22**	**28**	**68**	**65**	**5%**	**94**	**12%**	**65%**				**2.95**	**-2.1**	**24**	**59**	**$2**

Gordon,Alex

Age 30 · Bats L · Pos LF · Ht 6' 1" · Wt 220

Health A · PT/Exp A · Consist B · LIMA Plan B+ · Rand Var 0 · MM 4325

Did George Brett "fix" him too? 2H FB% spike resulted in bunch of HR. BA took an accompanying nosedive, as lost LDs triggered a long-overdue h% correction; xBA never saw a .300 hitter here. Capable of going back to hitting LDs and approaching .300, or sticking with FBs and chasing 30 HR... but not both.

Yr	Tm	AB	R	HR	RBI	SB	BA	xBA	OBP	SLG	OPS	vL	vR	bb%	ct%	h%	Eye	G	L	F	PX	xPX	hr/f	Spd	SBO	SB%	#Wk	DOM	DIS	RC/G	RAR	BPV	BPX	R$
09	KC *	261	44	9	38	5	254	238	342	410	752	635	731	12	75	31	0.53	44	14	42	106	133	12%	99	6%	100%	13	38%	46%	4.91	7.1	39	80	$6
10	KC *	502	76	17	51	6	239	250	332	405	736	704	660	12	71	30	0.48	38	23	39	125	134	11%	82	9%	45%	15	40%	33%	4.31	5.0	36	78	$10
11	KC	611	101	23	87	17	303	276	376	502	879	829	901	10	77	36	0.48	40	22	38	144	117	13%	85	14%	68%	26	65%	27%	6.69	46.1	71	158	$32
12	KC	642	93	14	72	10	294	272	368	455	822	668	908	10	78	36	0.52	42	25	33	116	103	8%	85	8%	67%	27	56%	15%	5.95	35.4	54	135	$24
13	KC	633	90	20	81	11	265	247	327	422	749	877	683	8	78	31	0.37	40	20	39	104	125	10%	121	8%	79%	26	42%	38%	4.71	13.5	48	120	$22
1st Half		312	43	7	42	4	285	251	344	410	754	993	654	8	78	35	0.41	45	23	32	88	98	9%	104	5%	80%	14	36%	43%	5.06	9.1	32	80	$22
2nd Half		321	47	13	39	7	246	243	299	433	732	788	715	7	78	28	0.33	36	17	46	120	151	11%	132	12%	78%	12	50%	33%	4.37	3.4	62	155	$23
14	**Proj**	**618**	**92**	**21**	**77**	**12**	**281**	**259**	**350**	**455**	**805**	**814**	**801**	**9**	**77**	**33**	**0.43**	**40**	**21**	**38**	**121**	**122**	**11%**	**104**	**9%**	**72%**				**5.54**	**26.8**	**58**	**144**	**$26**

BRIAN RUDD

Gordon,Dee

Age	26	Bats	L	Pos	SS	Health	C	LIMA Plan	D
Ht	5' 11"	Wt	160			PT/Exp	D	Rand Var	-1
						Consist	B	MM	0501

1-6-.234 with 10 SB in 94 AB at LA. Tantalizing speed still stuck in neutral due to inabiliy to hit enough to stay in MLB. Value of taking BBs seems to be slowly sinking in (.385 OBP in minors), giving hope. But ct% suggests he may continue to be a BA drag. Dabbled with 2B, which may help clear path to job. With PT... UP: 40 SB, still.

Yr	Tm	AB	R	HR	RBI	SB	BA	xBA	OBP	SLG	OPS	vL	vR	bb%	ct%	h%	Eye	G	L	F	PX	xPX	hr/f	Spd	SBO	SB%	#Wk	DOM	DIS	RC/G	RAR	BPV	BPX	R$
09																																		
10	aa	555	65	1	29	40	236	226	274	291	565			5	82	29	0.28				38			147	45%	64%				2.47		13	28	$14
11	LA *	512	64	0	25	42	277	266	301	329	630	595	727	3	85	32	0.23	56	23	21	38	14	0%	166	39%	78%	11	55%	18%	3.56	0.8	30	67	$20
12	LA *	333	40	1	18	33	226	246	272	276	548	415	632	6	80	28	0.32	59	21	21	36	20	2%	146	53%	75%	18	17%	56%	2.51	-10.4	8	20	$9
13	LA *	468	53	1	28	43	234	224	301	294	595	577	623	9	77	30	0.42	49	21	30	45	33	5%	168	44%	74%	12	33%	33%	2.98	-7.6	16	40	$17
1st Half		273	32	1	18	22	213	234	282	287	569	481	546	9	76	27	0.41	43	28	30	55	35	8%	152	43%	73%	5	40%	40%	2.64	-7.3	15	38	$17
2nd Half		195	21	0	10	21	264	202	327	304	631	750	791	9	79	33	0.44	61	9	30	32	29	0%	164	45%	75%	7	29%	29%	3.52	0.3	9	23	$18
14	**Proj**	**193**	**22**	**1**	**11**	**18**	**242**	**237**	**306**	**303**	**609**	**507**	**649**	**8**	**80**	**30**	**0.43**	**56**	**19**	**25**	**43**	**25**	**2%**	**152**	**44%**	**74%**				**3.12**	**-2.1**	**14**	**34**	**$5**

Gose,Anthony

Age	23	Bats	L	Pos	CF	Health	A	LIMA Plan	D
Ht	6' 1"	Wt	195			PT/Exp	B	Rand Var	0
						Consist	B	MM	2501

2-12-.259 with 4 SB in 147 AB in TOR. Not a lot of growth to be found from this unpolished speed source, and in some metrics that matter most for a would-be base thief (OBP, bb%, Eye), a step backward. Did post a 75% ct% at TOR, albeit with a 3% bb%. At only 23, there's still time, but for now, skills say SB will come with penalty.

Yr	Tm	AB	R	HR	RBI	SB	BA	xBA	OBP	SLG	OPS	vL	vR	bb%	ct%	h%	Eye	G	L	F	PX	xPX	hr/f	Spd	SBO	SB%	#Wk	DOM	DIS	RC/G	RAR	BPV	BPX	R$
09																																		
10																																		
11	aa	509	74	15	50	59	239	225	309	389	698			9	67	33	0.31				115			129	57%	79%				4.09		20	44	$25
12	TOR *	586	85	5	41	39	243	241	302	349	651	710	601	8	71	33	0.29	60	19	21	79	51	5%	164	36%	70%	11	18%	73%	3.46	-14.0	14	35	$18
13	TOR *	540	65	5	33	21	228	227	274	333	607	425	788	6	69	33	0.20	52	22	26	82	100	7%	173	32%	55%	11	45%	45%	2.74	-25.4	5	13	$9
1st Half		258	39	2	12	8	209	193	281	286	567	917	630	9	65	31	0.29	47	18	35	72	88	0%	153	24%	51%	3	33%	33%	2.39	-14.8	-15	-38	$6
2nd Half		282	26	3	21	13	246	245	267	375	643	212	804	3	71	34	0.10	53	23	24	90	102	10%	173	41%	58%	8	50%	50%	3.04	-9.8	17	43	$13
14	**Proj**	**163**	**21**	**2**	**12**	**10**	**236**	**238**	**291**	**351**	**643**	**396**	**706**	**7**	**69**	**33**	**0.24**	**56**	**21**	**23**	**88**	**82**	**8%**	**154**	**39%**	**66%**				**3.20**	**-5.0**	**9**	**24**	**$5**

Grandal,Yasmani

Age	25	Bats	B	Pos	CA	Health	D	LIMA Plan	D
Ht	6' 2"	Wt	215			PT/Exp	F	Rand Var	+5
						Consist	D	MM	3011

.216-1-9 in 88 AB at SD. Lost season began with 50-game PED suspension; ended with early July ACL reconstruction. In short window, it was much like '12: league-average power held back by GB%. Initial timetable extended rehab into 2014 season, but now hopes to be ready by spring. Still in growth mode.

Yr	Tm	AB	R	HR	RBI	SB	BA	xBA	OBP	SLG	OPS	vL	vR	bb%	ct%	h%	Eye	G	L	F	PX	xPX	hr/f	Spd	SBO	SB%	#Wk	DOM	DIS	RC/G	RAR	BPV	BPX	R$
09																																		
10																																		
11	a/a	168	16	3	20	0	267	242	319	409	728			7	72	35	0.28				124			81	3%	0%				4.41		29	64	$2
12	SD *	386	55	12	60	0	281	248	374	432	806	971	821	13	79	33	0.69	53	17	30	102	87	17%	105	0%	0%	15	53%	33%	5.73	22.1	55	138	$12
13	SD *	124	15	1	10	0	223	256	328	331	659	752	635	13	77	28	0.69	48	24	28	95	112	5%	90	0%	0%	6	50%	0%	3.56	-0.4	42	105	-$2
1st Half		113	15	1	10	0	236	263	343	345	688	754	719	14	79	29	0.77	47	25	28	94	110	6%	94	0%	0%	6	50%	0%	3.95	0.8	48	120	-$1
2nd Half		11	0	0	0	0	91	152	167	182	348	733	0	8	64	14	0.25	57	14	29	108	128		97	0%	0%				0.85	-1.1	-11	-28	-$6
14	**Proj**	**199**	**24**	**4**	**23**	**0**	**251**	**253**	**335**	**381**	**716**	**742**	**697**	**11**	**76**	**31**	**0.52**	**49**	**22**	**29**	**106**	**101**	**8%**	**93**	**1%**	**0%**				**4.27**	**3.3**	**22**	**55**	**$4**

Granderson,Curtis

Age	33	Bats	L	Pos	CF	Health	F	LIMA Plan	B+
Ht	6' 1"	Wt	195			PT/Exp	B	Rand Var	0
						Consist	C	MM	4515

7-15-.229 with 8 SB in 214 AB at NYY. Two HBP (broken forearm, fractured pinkie) derailed season. Showed resurgent speed when on the field, but at age 33, odds of a return to 20+ SB are remote. Sub-70 ct% promises further BA damage, and recent PX/xPX suggests 40 HR isn't coming back, no matter where he's plying his trade.

Yr	Tm	AB	R	HR	RBI	SB	BA	xBA	OBP	SLG	OPS	vL	vR	bb%	ct%	h%	Eye	G	L	F	PX	xPX	hr/f	Spd	SBO	SB%	#Wk	DOM	DIS	RC/G	RAR	BPV	BPX	R$
09	DET	631	91	30	71	20	249	254	327	453	780	484	897	10	78	28	0.51	29	21	49	122	133	13%	121	15%	77%	27	67%	22%	5.01	14.4	67	137	$19
10	NYY	466	76	24	67	12	247	258	324	468	792	647	866	10	75	28	0.46	33	20	47	142	150	14%	122	12%	86%	24	54%	21%	5.19	13.1	73	159	$16
11	NYY	583	136	41	119	25	262	272	364	552	916	944	902	13	71	30	0.50	34	18	48	198	161	21%	125	22%	71%	27	67%	11%	6.64	41.4	107	238	$36
12	NYY	596	102	43	106	10	232	251	319	492	811	762	839	11	67	27	0.38	33	23	44	175	132	24%	101	9%	77%	27	52%	19%	5.17	16.8	64	160	$22
13	NYY *	240	33	8	17	8	238	231	322	412	734	792	695	11	69	31	0.40	34	23	44	134	135	11%	146	16%	80%	12	42%	33%	4.48	1.7	50	125	$5
1st Half		48	7	2	3	1	281	236	320	418	739	700	696	5	77	33	0.25	59	14	27	87	110	17%	110	7%	100%	2	50%	50%	4.88	1.0	23	58	-$1
2nd Half		192	27	6	14	7	227	228	323	411	733	795	694	12	67	31	0.42	29	24	47	148	139	11%	144	18%	78%	10	40%	30%	4.40	1.3	54	135	$7
14	**Proj**	**471**	**77**	**25**	**58**	**14**	**249**	**247**	**332**	**471**	**803**	**805**	**801**	**10**	**71**	**30**	**0.39**	**34**	**21**	**44**	**154**	**135**	**17%**	**135**	**15%**	**80%**				**5.24**	**15.0**	**68**	**169**	**$19**

Green,Grant

Age	26	Bats	R	Pos	2B	Health	A	LIMA Plan	D+
Ht	6' 3"	Wt	180			PT/Exp	B	Rand Var	-2
						Consist	A	MM	2203

1-17-.250 in 140 AB at OAK/LAA. Slashed .326/.380/.493 on two AAA teams; results not as exciting in majors. Spd suggests he could steal a few, but low success rate has dried up his opportunities. Could not sustain '12 ct% and doesn't walk much, creating BA downside. At 26, time running out to stake claim to full-time work.

Yr	Tm	AB	R	HR	RBI	SB	BA	xBA	OBP	SLG	OPS	vL	vR	bb%	ct%	h%	Eye	G	L	F	PX	xPX	hr/f	Spd	SBO	SB%	#Wk	DOM	DIS	RC/G	RAR	BPV	BPX	R$
09																																		
10																																		
11	aa	530	53	6	43	4	235	218	273	322	596			5	73	31	0.20				75			88	11%	31%				2.73		-7	-16	$4
12	aaa	524	50	9	52	9	235	245	268	348	616			4	83	27	0.26				71			102	18%	45%				2.88		30	75	$6
13	2 AL *	542	57	7	49	2	243	226	280	344	624	334	804	5	74	32	0.19	43	21	36	82	102	3%	134	4%	49%	11	18%	45%	3.20	-8.5	13	33	$6
1st Half		330	37	6	30	2	239	234	273	355	628			4	76	30	0.19				87			120	5%	66%				3.23		20	50	$8
2nd Half		212	21	1	19	0	249	209	291	328	619	334	804	6	70	35	0.20	43	21	36	73	102	3%	133	2%	0%	11	18%	45%	3.15	-3.4	-8	-20	$2
14	**Proj**	**333**	**33**	**5**	**31**	**3**	**246**	**235**	**284**	**354**	**638**	**304**	**811**	**5**	**77**	**31**	**0.22**	**43**	**21**	**36**	**81**	**92**	**6%**	**140**	**9%**	**41%**				**3.25**	**-4.5**	**5**	**13**	**$5**

Gregorius,Didi

Age	24	Bats	L	Pos	SS	Health	A	LIMA Plan	C
Ht	6' 1"	Wt	185			PT/Exp	D	Rand Var	-1
						Consist	B	MM	1113

7-28-.252 in 357 AB at ARI. A hot start (4-12-.319 in 119 AB through May 31) made ARI look smart for acquiring him; by season's end, grip on SS job was in jeopardy. Not a base stealer despite good Spd. Not particularly powerful, struggles vs. LHP. Still time to develop, but unless/until that happens, PT on shaky ground.

Yr	Tm	AB	R	HR	RBI	SB	BA	xBA	OBP	SLG	OPS	vL	vR	bb%	ct%	h%	Eye	G	L	F	PX	xPX	hr/f	Spd	SBO	SB%	#Wk	DOM	DIS	RC/G	RAR	BPV	BPX	R$
09																																		
10																																		
11	aa	148	12	2	11	2	230	234	261	322	583			4	81	27	0.22				61			119	13%	48%				2.64		18	40	-$1
12	CIN *	521	60	7	47	3	247	256	293	357	650	1000	556	6	82	29	0.36	67	13	20	67	-11	0%	164	7%	28%	4	0%	50%	3.37	-2.0	45	113	$6
13	ARI *	388	51	8	29	1	258	245	324	384	708	512	789	9	83	29	0.58	37	21	42	83	87	6%	143	2%	24%	23	52%	26%	4.20	7.8	61	153	$6
1st Half		237	34	5	18	1	291	252	339	430	769	503	885	7	84	33	0.46	33	22	45	91	84	5%	150	2%	39%	11	55%	18%	5.17	11.3	71	178	$11
2nd Half		151	17	3	11	0	205	233	302	311	614	524	662	12	81	24	0.72	43	20	38	70	92	7%	126	2%	0%	12	50%	33%	2.94	-2.5	43	108	-$1
14	**Proj**	**400**	**46**	**8**	**32**	**2**	**248**	**241**	**316**	**371**	**687**	**518**	**760**	**8**	**82**	**29**	**0.47**	**39**	**21**	**41**	**79**	**89**	**6%**	**146**	**5%**	**35%**				**3.74**	**3.2**	**32**	**80**	**$7**

Grossman,Robert

Age	24	Bats	B	Pos	LF CF	Health	A	LIMA Plan	D
Ht	6' 0"	Wt	205			PT/Exp	D	Rand Var	-2
						Consist	A	MM	2303

4-21-.268 with 6 SB in 257 AB at HOU. In subpar SB%, another example of "speed is wasted on the young." Second MLB tour went far better than first (4-18-.321 in 136 AB after July 26 callup), but low ct%, 42% h% say, "Don't get too excited." If others want to bid based on 2H "breakout," say, "Be my guest." Likely a year away.

Yr	Tm	AB	R	HR	RBI	SB	BA	xBA	OBP	SLG	OPS	vL	vR	bb%	ct%	h%	Eye	G	L	F	PX	xPX	hr/f	Spd	SBO	SB%	#Wk	DOM	DIS	RC/G	RAR	BPV	BPX	R$
09																																		
10																																		
11																																		
12	aa	485	60	8	35	10	228	222	311	346	657			11	71	31	0.42				89			115	17%	44%				3.29		14	35	$5
13	HOU *	510	61	6	36	17	254	224	332	339	671	785	669	11	71	35	0.40	47	23	30	73	90	7%	113	21%	52%	12	25%	58%	3.56	-6.5	0	0	$13
1st Half		282	29	0	11	9	195	186	300	236	537	742	497	13	67	29	0.45	50	19	31	44	92	0%	111	21%	53%	6	0%	67%	2.13	-17.5	-37	-93	$3
2nd Half		228	31	6	25	8	328	266	375	467	842	809	820	7	77	41	0.32	45	26	28	104	89	13%	112	21%	51%	6	50%	50%	6.03	12.7	39	98	$24
14	**Proj**	**252**	**31**	**4**	**19**	**7**	**255**	**237**	**333**	**369**	**702**	**766**	**676**	**10**	**72**	**34**	**0.40**	**47**	**23**	**29**	**90**	**90**	**8%**	**120**	**20%**	**49%**				**3.83**	**-1.4**	**9**	**22**	**$7**

KRISTOPHER OLSON

Gutierrez,Franklin

Age	31	Bats	R	Pos	RF	Health	F	LIMA Plan	D
Ht	6' 2"	Wt	195			PT/Exp	F	Rand Var	0
						Consist	C	MM	3303

10-24-.248 in 145 AB at SEA. Poor health continues to wreak havoc. This time it was his hamstring, but Health grade shows these issues are chronic. Power gains the last two years are nice, but not at the expense of free-falling ct% and bb%. Extreme BA risk, OPS history vs. RHP, and lack of durability deter a return to 2009-10 peak.

Yr	Tm	AB	R	HR	RBI	SB	BA	xBA	OBP	SLG	OPS	vL	vR	bb%	ct%	h%	Eye	G	L	F	PX	xPX	hr/f	Spd	SBO	SB%	#Wk	DOM	DIS	RC/G	RAR	BPV	BPX	R$
09	SEA	565	85	18	70	16	283	255	339	425	764	963	681	8	78	33	0.38	45	19	36	91	114	11%	113	13%	76%	27	41%	30%	5.09	13.7	37	76	$21
10	SEA	568	61	12	64	25	245	228	303	363	666	704	653	8	76	30	0.36	42	16	42	86	108	7%	124	19%	89%	27	41%	30%	3.90	-5.6	28	61	$15
11	SEA *	362	30	1	22	13	220	220	260	273	533	561	529	5	82	27	0.30	48	17	36	44	76	1%	115	18%	87%	17	18%	53%	2.42	-20.2	10	22	$1
12	SEA *	212	25	5	22	3	236	250	284	382	666	1160	397	6	77	28	0.29	43	21	36	104	125	9%	102	12%	57%	9	44%	33%	3.52	-4.6	36	90	$2
13	SEA *	339	34	12	39	5	190	206	223	347	569	664	846	4	63	26	0.11	44	13	43	135	122	23%	98	18%	60%	11	45%	27%	2.35	-20.5	0	0	$1
1st Half		155	18	7	21	2	203	219	237	385	622	905	857	4	66	26	0.13	47	9	44	146	118	25%	99	15%	63%	6	50%	17%	2.85	-6.5	23	58	$3
2nd Half		184	16	5	18	3	180	196	211	314	525	516	837	4	60	26	0.10	42	16	42	126	126	21%	96	21%	58%	5	40%	40%	1.97	-13.2	-19	-48	-$1
14	Proj	266	28	8	27	5	224	225	265	369	634	719	587	5	71	29	0.18	44	16	40	114	115	11%	102	15%	70%				3.15	-10.6	10	24	$2

Guzman,Jesus

Age	30	Bats	R	Pos	1B LF	Health	A	LIMA Plan	D+
Ht	6' 1"	Wt	200			PT/Exp	D	Rand Var	+1
						Consist	A	MM	3213

Another step back in what used to be a promising skill set. His ct% continued its descent for the third straight year, taking BA down to a career low. Failed to reach 300 AB again, due to struggles vs. RHP. PX/xPX offers up HR potential, and he's owned better skills, so there's still potential for some end-game profit. Barely.

Yr	Tm	AB	R	HR	RBI	SB	BA	xBA	OBP	SLG	OPS	vL	vR	bb%	ct%	h%	Eye	G	L	F	PX	xPX	hr/f	Spd	SBO	SB%	#Wk	DOM	DIS	RC/G	RAR	BPV	BPX	R$
09	SF *	472	51	10	49	0	266	288	302	396	698	462	571	5	79	32	0.25	76	18	6	85	10	0%	123	2%	0%	7	0%	43%	4.06	0.1	34	69	$7
10	aaa	445	45	12	49	4	260	262	300	397	697			5	82	29	0.32				93			93	9%	46%				3.95		42	91	$9
11	SD *	491	55	9	76	11	270	264	328	411	739	892	820	8	79	32	0.42	42	22	36	108	97	7%	97	15%	61%	16	75%	0%	4.56	7.1	51	113	$15
12	SD	287	32	9	48	3	247	246	319	418	737	942	580	9	75	30	0.41	42	18	40	120	102	10%	95	8%	50%	27	48%	41%	4.35	2.5	46	115	$6
13	SD	288	33	9	35	3	226	244	297	378	675	691	661	9	73	28	0.34	42	22	36	118	120	12%	82	5%	100%	27	37%	52%	3.70	-3.1	28	70	$3
1st Half		133	16	3	13	1	218	231	273	338	611	645	588	7	75	27	0.30	44	19	37	92	138	8%	98	3%	100%	14	36%	43%	3.05	-4.0	20	50	$1
2nd Half		155	17	6	22	2	232	254	308	413	721	748	703	10	70	29	0.37	40	24	36	142	104	15%	73	5%	100%	13	38%	62%	4.30	1.3	39	98	$5
14	Proj	256	29	8	35	3	242	250	308	402	710	789	648	8	75	29	0.37	42	21	38	119	109	11%	90	7%	68%				4.09	-3.9	35	87	$6

Gyorko,Jedd

Age	25	Bats	R	Pos	2B	Health	B	LIMA Plan	B+
Ht	5' 10"	Wt	210			PT/Exp	C	Rand Var	+1
						Consist	B	MM	4125

Successful MLB debut in which he flashed big-time power (15 HR in Aug-Sept) with full support from PX and hr/f. Plate skills should prevent you from going all-in though, especially given that ugly 2H Eye. Pay for a repeat of 20+ HR in the short-term, though BA is likely to hold back value for now. Long-term? A fine MI building block.

Yr	Tm	AB	R	HR	RBI	SB	BA	xBA	OBP	SLG	OPS	vL	vR	bb%	ct%	h%	Eye	G	L	F	PX	xPX	hr/f	Spd	SBO	SB%	#Wk	DOM	DIS	RC/G	RAR	BPV	BPX	R$
09																																		
10																																		
11	aa	236	30	5	29	1	231	222	291	330	622			8	74	29	0.33				77			86	1%	100%				3.21		3	7	$1
12	a/a	499	58	19	72	4	249	247	302	409	712			7	77	29	0.33				106			75	7%	43%				4.07		30	75	$12
13	SD	486	62	23	63	1	249	261	301	444	745	829	715	6	75	29	0.27	38	23	40	138	140	16%	85	2%	50%	24	54%	29%	4.45	11.3	49	123	$13
1st Half		232	36	8	25	1	284	275	341	461	802	899	761	8	77	34	0.37	37	27	36	131	132	13%	100	2%	100%	11	64%	18%	5.64	12.6	59	148	$15
2nd Half		254	26	15	38	0	217	246	255	429	684	744	676	5	73	24	0.19	38	18	44	144	147	19%	73	2%	0%	13	46%	38%	3.49	-1.6	40	100	$11
14	Proj	509	62	25	69	2	251	258	306	446	753	832	724	7	75	29	0.29	38	22	41	134	141	16%	81	4%	48%				4.51	12.3	36	89	$15

Hafner,Travis

Age	37	Bats	L	Pos	DH	Health	D	LIMA Plan	D
Ht	6' 3"	Wt	240			PT/Exp	D	Rand Var	+4
						Consist	C	MM	3201

Hot start in April (.318 BA, 6 HR in 66 AB) quickly went south as poor health reared its ugly head again (shoulder, foot). Moderate power remained, but ct% drop was the red flag that highlights further downside. Age, health, and inability to hit lefties all say his window for any remaining fantasy value is closing fast.

Yr	Tm	AB	R	HR	RBI	SB	BA	xBA	OBP	SLG	OPS	vL	vR	bb%	ct%	h%	Eye	G	L	F	PX	xPX	hr/f	Spd	SBO	SB%	#Wk	DOM	DIS	RC/G	RAR	BPV	BPX	R$
09	CLE *	377	50	17	55	0	271	278	352	462	814	696	866	11	81	29	0.67	39	21	40	120	121	15%	76	0%	0%	22	64%	23%	5.69	12.8	68	139	$9
10	CLE	396	46	13	50	2	278	264	374	449	824	706	863	11	76	34	0.54	43	19	38	129	106	11%	67	3%	67%	25	48%	32%	5.70	13.5	53	115	$11
11	CLE	325	41	13	57	0	280	253	361	449	811	638	886	10	76	33	0.46	43	21	36	119	121	14%	58	0%	0%	22	50%	36%	5.60	10.1	39	87	$11
12	CLE	219	23	12	34	0	228	254	346	438	784	748	798	13	79	24	0.68	43	17	39	122	123	17%	79	0%	0%	17	65%	29%	4.73	1.5	63	158	$3
13	NYY	262	31	12	37	2	202	226	301	378	679	664	682	11	70	24	0.41	37	19	44	124	117	15%	80	3%	100%	18	39%	50%	3.53	-7.8	26	65	$2
1st Half		202	27	12	35	2	223	237	314	436	750	721	764	12	70	25	0.45	34	19	47	143	134	18%	89	4%	100%	14	50%	36%	4.55	0.3	48	120	$6
2nd Half		60	4	0	2	0	133	182	200	183	383	508	390	8	68	20	0.26	49	17	34	55	59	0%	69	0%	0%	4	0%	100%	1.08	-7.0	-45	-113	-$11
14	Proj	156	16	5	19	0	211	229	313	356	669	643	678	11	73	25	0.45	43	18	39	104	105	11%	71	1%	95%				3.40	-5.3	14	35	$2

Hairston,Jerry

Age	38	Bats	R	Pos	3B LF	Health	D	LIMA Plan	D
Ht	5' 10"	Wt	195			PT/Exp	D	Rand Var	+3
						Consist	C	MM	1111

Sure, you could point to his strong contact rate and unlucky h% and maybe say a BA rebound is in the cards. But when you don't hit the ball with any authority, don't have the wheels anymore to steal bags, don't have the ability to stay healthy... well, you get the picture.

Yr	Tm	AB	R	HR	RBI	SB	BA	xBA	OBP	SLG	OPS	vL	vR	bb%	ct%	h%	Eye	G	L	F	PX	xPX	hr/f	Spd	SBO	SB%	#Wk	DOM	DIS	RC/G	RAR	BPV	BPX	R$
09	2 TM	383	62	10	39	7	251	272	315	394	710	741	694	8	86	27	0.59	34	23	43	90	74	7%	95	12%	64%	27	44%	33%	4.05	0.6	61	124	$8
10	SD	430	53	10	50	9	244	241	299	353	652	678	642	7	87	26	0.57	40	16	44	65	71	6%	106	14%	60%	22	50%	23%	3.41	-7.6	49	107	$8
11	2 NL	337	43	5	31	3	270	256	344	383	727	706	735	9	86	30	0.72	39	20	41	80	62	4%	88	5%	60%	25	40%	24%	4.43	4.2	56	124	$7
12	LA	238	19	4	26	1	273	269	342	387	729	800	683	9	89	29	0.85	36	25	39	72	82	5%	83	4%	33%	18	50%	17%	4.44	3.0	57	143	$3
13	LA	204	17	2	22	0	211	218	265	275	539	445	597	6	89	23	0.64	43	16	41	44	57	3%	84	0%	0%	24	38%	38%	2.32	-10.5	32	80	-$2
1st Half		102	7	1	11	0	265	232	312	333	645	571	704	6	92	28	0.88	40	19	41	46	51	3%	77	0%	0%	12	42%	17%	3.61	-1.1	43	108	$0
2nd Half		102	10	1	11	0	157	205	211	216	427	264	511	6	86	17	0.50	46	13	40	41	64	3%	94	0%	0%	12	33%	58%	1.38	-8.8	21	53	-$5
14	Proj	130	13	2	14	1	234	240	294	323	617	580	637	7	88	25	0.66	40	19	40	60	66	4%	87	3%	51%				3.07	-3.6	30	76	$1

Hairston,Scott

Age	34	Bats	R	Pos	RF	Health	B	LIMA Plan	D
Ht	6' 0"	Wt	205			PT/Exp	F	Rand Var	+5
						Consist	C	MM	4201

Excellent power remains his biggest asset, though xPX throws some cold water on even that. Rest of skill profile is truly bleak: rare sub-20% h% didn't help, but don't expect a full BA rebound given ct% erosion and poor bb%. Inability to hit righties continues to cap AB total, relegating him to late-round flyer status.

Yr	Tm	AB	R	HR	RBI	SB	BA	xBA	OBP	SLG	OPS	vL	vR	bb%	ct%	h%	Eye	G	L	F	PX	xPX	hr/f	Spd	SBO	SB%	#Wk	DOM	DIS	RC/G	RAR	BPV	BPX	R$
09	2 TM	430	50	17	64	11	265	256	307	456	763	920	694	5	81	29	0.30	34	15	51	121	101	10%	98	15%	79%	23	70%	17%	4.83	9.6	62	127	$13
10	SD	295	34	10	36	6	210	218	295	346	640	655	633	10	77	24	0.45	34	15	51	92	81	9%	94	10%	86%	25	36%	32%	3.24	-7.4	29	63	$3
11	NYM	132	20	7	24	1	235	251	303	470	773	702	886	8	74	26	0.32	32	13	55	165	131	13%	102	8%	50%	22	50%	41%	4.48	1.7	77	171	$2
12	NYM	377	52	20	57	8	263	273	299	504	803	867	739	5	78	29	0.23	33	21	46	155	117	15%	90	14%	80%	27	56%	19%	5.19	12.4	74	185	$14
13	2 NL	157	18	10	26	2	191	228	237	414	651	743	276	5	72	19	0.20	26	14	59	150	100	14%	76	8%	100%	27	41%	41%	3.12	-4.6	44	110	$1
1st Half		94	11	6	16	2	160	224	218	372	590	645	417	7	74	14	0.29	30	12	58	135	66	14%	78	14%	100%	14	50%	36%	2.54	-4.6	45	113	$1
2nd Half		63	7	4	10	0	238	240	262	476	738	886	0	3	68	28	0.10	20	18	61	175	156	15%	81	0%	0%	13	31%	46%	4.17	0.3	45	113	$0
14	Proj	192	24	9	31	2	228	239	272	428	700	763	579	5	74	26	0.22	31	18	51	139	118	13%	88	9%	81%				3.82	-3.7	44	109	$5

Hamilton,Billy

Age	23	Bats	B	Pos	CF	Health	A	LIMA Plan	D+
Ht	6' 0"	Wt	160			PT/Exp	F	Rand Var	+3
						Consist	C	MM	1503

0-1-.368 with 13 SB in 19 AB with CIN. We all know he can fly. Focus instead on the huge bb% drop and subpar ct% in Triple-A, which calls into question his ability to stick in the majors at all. However, even with part-time ABs and pinch-running role, his wheels have the potential for... UP: 60 SB. With full playing time? Sky's the limit.

Yr	Tm	AB	R	HR	RBI	SB	BA	xBA	OBP	SLG	OPS	vL	vR	bb%	ct%	h%	Eye	G	L	F	PX	xPX	hr/f	Spd	SBO	SB%	#Wk	DOM	DIS	RC/G	RAR	BPV	BPX	R$
09																																		
10																																		
11																																		
12	aa	175	29	1	13	45	271	207	383	360	744			15	73	37	0.67				56			157	89%	73%				4.66		17	43	$16
13	CIN *	523	72	6	36	76	238	277	284	318	603	0	950	6	77	30	0.29	50	36	14	59	-15	0%	163	72%	81%	5	20%	40%	3.23	-14.1	20	50	$34
1st Half		312	42	5	24	41	225	221	273	314	587			6	77	28	0.29				63			141	69%	81%				2.98		14	35	$36
2nd Half		211	30	1	12	35	257	277	300	326	626	0	950	6	78	32	0.28	50	36	14	53	-15	0%	164	76%	82%	5	20%	40%	3.63	-3.5	19	48	$31
14	Proj	265	40	1	18	49	246	225	303	318	621	621	621	8	76	32	0.34	48	22	30	52		2%	168	85%	78%				3.38	-6.6	18	45	$20

RYAN BLOOMFIELD

Hamilton,Josh

Age 33	Bats L	Pos RF DH	Health A	LIMA Plan B+	
Ht 6' 4"	Wt 225		PT/Exp A	Rand Var +3	
			Consist C	MM 4325	

Last year's "DN: .270 BA, 20 HR" commentary didn't go far enough. His ct% remained dismal and xBA dipped even further, but the story here was the hr/f drop in his new park. Power skills are still above average, and 2H rebound showed he can be a productive hitter, so expect a mild rebound.

Yr	Tm	AB	R	HR	RBI	SB	BA	xBA	OBP	SLG	OPS	vL	vR	bb%	ct%	h%	Eye	G	L	F	PX	xPX	hr/f	Spd	SBO	SB%	#Wk	DOM	DIS	RC/G	RAR	BPV	BPX	R$
09	TEX *	368	46	10	55	9	259	250	310	412	723	898	664	7	76	32	0.31	36	22	42	105	115	9%	94	14%	76%	18	39%	33%	4.39	4.5	32	65	$9
10	TEX	518	95	32	100	8	359	326	411	633	1044	789	1163	8	82	39	0.45	42	22	36	176	135	21%	101	6%	89%	24	79%	0%	10.35	83.1	115	250	$39
11	TEX	487	80	25	94	8	298	297	346	536	882	825	904	7	81	33	0.42	41	21	38	154	126	16%	104	7%	89%	22	73%	9%	6.86	38.8	95	211	$26
12	TEX	562	103	43	128	7	285	282	354	577	930	853	965	10	71	33	0.37	38	21	41	196	166	26%	84	8%	64%	27	63%	30%	7.15	50.5	88	220	$33
13	LAA	576	73	21	79	4	250	251	307	432	739	596	802	8	73	31	0.30	39	22	39	133	128	13%	112	3%	100%	27	52%	30%	4.55	9.6	47	118	$15
1st Half		296	43	10	29	2	223	246	279	392	671	352	801	7	73	27	0.28	41	21	38	125	107	12%	110	3%	100%	14	57%	29%	3.62	-3.6	40	100	$10
2nd Half		280	30	11	50	2	279	257	336	475	811	813	803	8	73	35	0.31	36	24	40	142	150	13%	114	3%	100%	13	46%	31%	5.68	13.2	56	140	$21
14	**Proj**	**547**	**80**	**24**	**96**	**6**	**269**	**262**	**327**	**472**	**799**	**714**	**838**	**8**	**74**	**32**	**0.34**	**39**	**22**	**39**	**144**	**139**	**15%**	**104**	**6%**	**81%**				**5.42**	**15.2**	**59**	**148**	**$20**

Hanigan,Ryan

Age 33	Bats R	Pos CA	Health C	LIMA Plan D	
Ht 6' 0"	Wt 210		PT/Exp D	Rand Var +5	
			Consist C	MM 0013	

Multiple DL stints (wrist, ankle) cut into playing time, but he was the same hitter he's always been. The BA plunge was a result of a h% swoon, though last three years of xBA say he hasn't been a .270 hitter for a while anyway. With no power or speed, even tremendous plate discipline can't save him.

Yr	Tm	AB	R	HR	RBI	SB	BA	xBA	OBP	SLG	OPS	vL	vR	bb%	ct%	h%	Eye	G	L	F	PX	xPX	hr/f	Spd	SBO	SB%	#Wk	DOM	DIS	RC/G	RAR	BPV	BPX	R$
09	CIN	251	22	3	11	0	263	264	361	331	692	745	677	13	88	29	1.19	48	24	27	40	62	5%	96	0%	0%	26	46%	27%	4.09	2.8	39	80	$1
10	CIN *	249	29	5	41	0	278	271	369	392	761	993	771	13	88	30	1.24	48	21	31	75	79	9%	82	0%	0%	21	62%	14%	5.11	9.9	65	141	$6
11	CIN	266	27	6	31	0	267	249	356	357	714	871	685	12	88	29	1.09	48	22	30	54	69	9%	77	0%	0%	25	32%	40%	4.37	5.2	44	98	$4
12	CIN	317	25	2	24	0	274	241	365	338	703	840	661	12	88	31	1.19	53	21	26	45	48	3%	76	0%	0%	27	44%	22%	4.30	5.5	39	98	$3
13	CIN	222	17	2	21	0	198	243	306	261	567	608	555	12	88	22	1.07	49	22	29	44	55	4%	74	2%	0%	22	32%	36%	2.37	-9.2	34	85	-$4
1st Half		131	11	2	13	0	183	238	262	260	522	572	515	10	89	19	0.93	48	19	33	49	69	5%	78	3%	0%	12	42%	33%	2.05	-7.0	38	95	-$3
2nd Half		91	6	0	8	0	220	253	330	264	594	668	603	14	87	25	1.25	51	26	23	38	34	0%	76	0%	0%	10	20%	40%	2.85	-2.4	31	78	-$4
14	**Proj**	**246**	**20**	**2**	**23**	**0**	**259**	**246**	**360**	**323**	**683**	**772**	**658**	**12**	**88**	**29**	**1.15**	**50**	**22**	**28**	**46**	**53**	**4%**	**74**	**0%**	**0%**				**3.86**	**1.1**	**19**	**49**	**$3**

Hannahan,Jack

Age 34	Bats L	Pos 3B	Health A	LIMA Plan D	
Ht 6' 2"	Wt 210		PT/Exp D	Rand Var 0	
			Consist B	MM 1001	

Years of terrible skills finally caught up and cost him playing time. There are two reasons why he won't get it back: PX in continual decline coupled with heavy GB% profile; poor ct% essentially locks in a low BA. Age says he's on the downside, at least he doesn't have far to fall. (You can't fall off the floor.)

Yr	Tm	AB	R	HR	RBI	SB	BA	xBA	OBP	SLG	OPS	vL	vR	bb%	ct%	h%	Eye	G	L	F	PX	xPX	hr/f	Spd	SBO	SB%	#Wk	DOM	DIS	RC/G	RAR	BPV	BPX	R$
09	2 AL *	348	32	5	26	1	202	216	274	314	589	535	666	9	70	27	0.33	40	18	42	90	96	5%	101	4%	31%	24	38%	54%	2.69	-14.3	2	4	-$4
10	aaa	334	33	6	31	2	190	221	268	296	564			10	70	25	0.35				87			94	3%	100%				2.53		-1	-2	-$3
11	CLE	320	38	8	40	2	250	241	331	388	719	811	673	11	75	31	0.48	52	16	32	101	85	10%	97	3%	67%	26	38%	42%	4.33	3.1	33	73	$5
12	CLE	287	23	4	29	0	244	232	312	341	654	481	712	9	78	30	0.43	40	23	38	74	99	5%	68	3%	0%	25	32%	44%	3.45	-4.6	11	28	$1
13	CIN	139	12	1	14	0	216	209	317	288	605	606	605	12	73	29	0.50	53	19	28	58	81	3%	101	0%	0%	26	38%	50%	2.90	-4.6	-6	-15	-$2
1st Half		80	5	0	7	0	188	210	253	250	503	800	480	8	74	25	0.33	57	17	27	51	77	0%	107	0%	0%	14	50%	43%	1.98	-5.1	-14	-35	-$3
2nd Half		59	7	1	7	0	254	208	380	339	719	333	767	17	71	34	0.71	48	21	31	67	86	8%	88	0%	0%	12	25%	58%	4.41	0.7	1	3	-$1
14	**Proj**	**124**	**12**	**2**	**13**	**0**	**232**	**219**	**326**	**324**	**650**	**584**	**665**	**11**	**74**	**30**	**0.49**	**47**	**20**	**33**	**73**	**88**	**6%**	**89**	**1%**	**36%**				**3.41**	**-2.1**	**-8**	**-21**	**$1**

Hardy,J.J.

Age 31	Bats R	Pos SS	Health B	LIMA Plan A	
Ht 6' 1"	Wt 190		PT/Exp A	Rand Var 0	
			Consist C	MM 3225	

Good things happen when you put the ball in play over 520 times. Unfortunately, declining xPX and increasing GB% say HR total has nowhere to go but down. Stable skill set gives a nice floor, though his value is heavily tied to ABs. Tread carefully as he enters his post-peak years.

Yr	Tm	AB	R	HR	RBI	SB	BA	xBA	OBP	SLG	OPS	vL	vR	bb%	ct%	h%	Eye	G	L	F	PX	xPX	hr/f	Spd	SBO	SB%	#Wk	DOM	DIS	RC/G	RAR	BPV	BPX	R$
09	MIL *	485	58	14	56	0	225	232	292	356	648	539	689	9	80	25	0.47	46	14	40	81	124	8%	118	1%	0%	25	44%	32%	3.39	-1.7	40	82	$3
10	MIN	340	44	6	38	1	268	264	320	394	714	614	759	8	84	30	0.52	49	17	34	85	89	6%	127	2%	50%	23	61%	30%	4.40	9.5	60	130	$7
11	BAL	527	76	30	80	0	269	274	310	491	801	794	803	6	83	28	0.34	40	16	43	139	130	16%	83	0%	0%	23	74%	4%	5.32	28.5	80	178	$19
12	BAL	663	85	22	68	0	238	249	282	389	671	767	639	5	84	25	0.36	43	17	40	91	109	10%	104	0%	0%	27	56%	19%	3.64	4.2	53	133	$10
13	BAL	601	66	25	76	2	263	267	306	433	738	783	720	6	88	26	0.52	45	17	38	101	99	12%	96	2%	67%	27	63%	19%	4.58	20.0	75	188	$17
1st Half		316	32	15	46	1	266	279	305	456	761	768	756	5	87	26	0.45	44	19	37	113	109	14%	84	3%	50%	14	64%	14%	4.78	12.0	78	195	$19
2nd Half		285	34	10	30	1	260	253	308	407	715	795	673	7	88	26	0.61	47	14	39	88	87	10%	112	1%	100%	13	62%	23%	4.34	7.2	73	183	$15
14	**Proj**	**592**	**72**	**23**	**71**	**1**	**256**	**260**	**301**	**421**	**722**	**763**	**706**	**6**	**86**	**27**	**0.45**	**44**	**16**	**39**	**101**	**105**	**12%**	**101**	**1%**	**67%**				**4.33**	**14.9**	**51**	**128**	**$16**

Harper,Bryce

Age 21	Bats L	Pos LF	Health B	LIMA Plan A	
Ht 6' 2"	Wt 230		PT/Exp C	Rand Var 0	
			Consist C	MM 4335	

Knee injury in June, hip problem in Sept suppressed overall numbers, but this was another solid step forward. Plate skills are developing nicely, with power that's inching toward elite levels long before his physical peak. Needs to stay healthy, but with a few more fly balls... UP: 35 HR, .300 BA.

Yr	Tm	AB	R	HR	RBI	SB	BA	xBA	OBP	SLG	OPS	vL	vR	bb%	ct%	h%	Eye	G	L	F	PX	xPX	hr/f	Spd	SBO	SB%	#Wk	DOM	DIS	RC/G	RAR	BPV	BPX	R$
09																																		
10																																		
11	aa	129	12	3	10	6	245	251	311	372	684			9	80	29	0.48				91			101	24%	75%				3.91		42	93	$1
12	WAS *	607	105	23	61	19	265	272	334	459	793	715	869	9	78	31	0.47	45	23	33	122	107	16%	134	16%	73%	24	54%	8%	5.27	21.4	70	175	$23
13	WAS	424	71	20	58	11	274	281	368	486	854	648	947	13	78	31	0.65	47	20	33	142	118	18%	89	12%	73%	22	64%	27%	6.18	26.0	79	198	$20
1st Half		150	29	12	23	2	287	311	389	587	975	617	1128	14	80	29	0.83	51	15	34	182	138	29%	99	8%	50%	10	70%	20%	7.86	16.4	126	315	$15
2nd Half		274	42	8	35	9	266	265	352	431	782	662	847	12	77	32	0.56	44	23	33	119	106	11%	86	13%	82%	12	58%	33%	5.33	10.4	53	133	$22
14	**Proj**	**579**	**92**	**27**	**90**	**16**	**272**	**282**	**355**	**486**	**840**	**670**	**921**	**11**	**78**	**31**	**0.57**	**46**	**21**	**33**	**140**	**114**	**18%**	**101**	**13%**	**71%**				**5.92**	**31.9**	**83**	**207**	**$28**

Harrison,Josh

Age 26	Bats R	Pos RF	Health A	LIMA Plan D+	
Ht 5' 8"	Wt 195		PT/Exp D	Rand Var 0	
			Consist B	MM 2431	

3-14-.250 in 88 AB at PIT. Excellent ct% remained stable yet again; growing xPX hints at some untapped power here. However, poor plate patience makes for a tougher transition to MLB pitching, and '12 Spd is looking like an outlier. Seeds of upside are there, but only as a late-round flyer.

Yr	Tm	AB	R	HR	RBI	SB	BA	xBA	OBP	SLG	OPS	vL	vR	bb%	ct%	h%	Eye	G	L	F	PX	xPX	hr/f	Spd	SBO	SB%	#Wk	DOM	DIS	RC/G	RAR	BPV	BPX	R$
09																																		
10	aa	520	59	3	59	15	268	265	302	352	654			5	89	29	0.46				61			100	18%	66%				3.61		48	104	$13
11	PIT *	421	48	5	34	14	269	257	293	381	674	593	685	3	87	30	0.26	45	17	38	78	88	2%	115	22%	67%	16	31%	38%	3.78	-2.6	54	120	$11
12	PIT	249	34	3	16	7	233	241	279	345	624	580	647	4	85	26	0.27	37	22	41	66	111	3%	156	20%	70%	27	33%	41%	2.96	-7.8	50	125	$2
13	PIT *	356	48	6	40	16	262	277	295	416	711	981	466	4	85	30	0.30	47	19	35	105	122	12%	101	34%	66%	18	33%	28%	4.03	0.3	64	160	$13
1st Half		263	36	3	26	14	260	245	299	401	700	500	311	5	83	30	0.33	9	36	55	105	76	0%	107	39%	67%	5	20%	20%	3.91	-0.5	60	150	$16
2nd Half		93	12	3	14	2	270	299	283	458	742	1034	502	2	90	27	0.19	53	16	31	106	130	15%	110	18%	63%	13	38%	31%	4.37	1.1	84	210	$3
14	**Proj**	**203**	**26**	**4**	**21**	**6**	**258**	**273**	**297**	**411**	**707**	**804**	**648**	**4**	**87**	**28**	**0.28**	**46**	**18**	**36**	**96**	**108**	**7%**	**119**	**24%**	**67%**				**3.87**	**-3.5**	**73**	**181**	**$7**

Hart,Corey

Age 32	Bats R	Pos 1B	Health F	LIMA Plan B+	
Ht 6' 6"	Wt 235		PT/Exp C	Rand Var 0	
			Consist A	MM 4225	

Surgeries on both his right (January) and left (June) knees shelved him all year. The pre-injury power was consistent and elite, so 20+ HR should return depending on AB total. But his ct% dip in '12 raised some warning flags, and health certainly raises more, so don't just assume a full return to 2010-12 levels.

Yr	Tm	AB	R	HR	RBI	SB	BA	xBA	OBP	SLG	OPS	vL	vR	bb%	ct%	h%	Eye	G	L	F	PX	xPX	hr/f	Spd	SBO	SB%	#Wk	DOM	DIS	RC/G	RAR	BPV	BPX	R$
09	MIL	419	64	12	48	11	260	252	335	418	753	690	773	9	78	31	0.47	41	17	42	105	118	9%	129	15%	65%	21	48%	24%	4.62	0.3	55	112	$11
10	MIL	558	91	31	102	7	283	279	340	525	865	973	827	7	75	33	0.32	38	18	44	166	160	17%	116	10%	54%	27	74%	22%	6.09	23.9	84	183	$26
11	MIL	492	80	26	63	7	285	283	356	510	866	1057	814	9	77	32	0.45	45	21	35	150	156	20%	121	10%	54%	23	83%	13%	6.18	22.4	84	187	$22
12	MIL	562	91	30	83	5	270	267	334	507	841	893	825	7	73	32	0.29	40	19	41	161	162	18%	105	4%	100%	27	59%	26%	5.79	19.3	69	173	$22
13																																		
1st Half																																		
2nd Half																																		
14	**Proj**	**450**	**73**	**21**	**73**	**2**	**272**	**263**	**337**	**487**	**824**	**903**	**799**	**8**	**75**	**32**	**0.34**	**40**	**19**	**41**	**151**	**154**	**16%**	**108**	**4%**	**56%**				**5.58**	**12.7**	**63**	**156**	**$18**

RYAN BLOOMFIELD

Headley,Chase

Age	30	Bats	B	Pos	3B
Ht	6' 2"	Wt	220		
Health	B	PT/Exp	A	Consist	D
LIMA Plan	B+	Rand Var	+1	MM	4225

Knee bothered him intermittently all year, requiring post-season surgery. Also had fractured thumb in March, calf injury in June, and sore back in August, which conspired to cripple his season. That might seem to merit a mulligan, but now he has an injury history. 2012 a huge outlier in this box. Don't pay for more than 20 HR.

Yr	Tm	AB	R	HR	RBI	SB	BA	xBA	OBP	SLG	OPS	vL	vR	bb%	ct%	h%	Eye	G	L	F	PX	xPX	hr/f	Spd	SBO	SB%	#Wk	DOM	DIS	RC/G	RAR	BPV	BPX	R$
09	SD	543	62	12	64	10	262	240	342	392	734	671	765	10	76	33	0.47	45	17	38	94	111	8%	89	8%	83%	27	37%	33%	4.62	9.7	27	55	$12
10	SD	610	77	11	58	17	264	240	327	375	702	589	753	8	77	33	0.40	46	18	36	82	85	6%	106	13%	77%	27	33%	30%	4.26	4.7	25	54	$16
11	SD	381	43	4	44	13	289	249	374	399	773	891	729	12	76	37	0.57	46	22	32	95	101	4%	78	12%	87%	21	43%	19%	5.49	16.0	29	64	$13
12	SD	604	95	31	115	17	286	268	376	498	875	801	906	12	74	34	0.55	48	19	32	141	134	21%	84	12%	74%	27	56%	37%	6.64	45.2	61	153	$32
13	SD	520	59	13	50	8	250	253	347	400	747	764	740	11	73	32	0.47	46	23	31	119	107	11%	85	8%	67%	25	48%	28%	4.52	8.0	36	90	$11
1st Half		258	28	6	25	5	221	238	304	345	649	659	667	11	74	28	0.46	47	21	32	93	98	10%	73	9%	83%	12	33%	33%	3.49	-3.9	14	35	$8
2nd Half		262	31	7	25	3	279	266	366	454	820	923	799	12	72	36	0.49	46	24	31	145	116	12%	100	8%	50%	13	62%	23%	5.70	13.0	59	148	$15
14	**Proj**	**557**	**70**	**18**	**69**	**10**	**265**	**259**	**357**	**432**	**788**	**792**	**787**	**12**	**74**	**33**	**0.50**	**47**	**21**	**32**	**126**	**113**	**13%**	**85**	**9%**	**69%**				**5.22**	**20.1**	**45**	**112**	**$17**

Hechavarria,Adeiny

Age	25	Bats	R	Pos	SS
Ht	6' 0"	Wt	185		
Health	A	PT/Exp	B	Consist	C
LIMA Plan	D+	Rand Var	+2	MM	1315

Good slap-hitting, contact/speed profile didn't translate to hits (.227 on grounders, .167 bunting). The rest of his BPI are dismal; so his job depends on defense, which is occasionally flashy, but with subpar range. If he were Ozzie Smith with that BPV, it might be a different story. DN: Back to the minors.

Yr	Tm	AB	R	HR	RBI	SB	BA	xBA	OBP	SLG	OPS	vL	vR	bb%	ct%	h%	Eye	G	L	F	PX	xPX	hr/f	Spd	SBO	SB%	#Wk	DOM	DIS	RC/G	RAR	BPV	BPX	R$
09																																		
10	aa	253	28	2	26	5	239	238	266	314	580			4	82	28	0.21				54			105	14%	58%				2.71		12	26	$2
11	a/a	572	53	6	41	14	229	239	259	327	586			4	81	27	0.21				70			117	26%	46%				2.51		23	51	$5
12	TOR *	569	64	6	58	5	264	236	300	360	660	590	677	5	77	33	0.23	48	21	31	68	98	7%	128	5%	71%	10	30%	50%	3.72	3.5	14	35	$11
13	MIA	543	30	3	42	11	227	240	267	298	565	589	555	5	82	27	0.31	52	20	28	46	55	2%	160	16%	52%	26	31%	50%	2.49	-17.1	27	68	$3
1st Half		236	17	2	20	3	203	245	248	288	536	536	533	6	84	23	0.38	55	18	27	47	51	4%	176	16%	38%	13	31%	46%	2.10	-10.4	41	103	-$1
2nd Half		307	13	1	22	8	244	236	282	306	588	631	572	5	81	30	0.27	49	22	28	45	59	1%	135	17%	62%	13	31%	54%	2.82	-6.0	11	28	$5
14	**Proj**	**466**	**37**	**5**	**40**	**8**	**238**	**243**	**276**	**326**	**603**	**598**	**604**	**5**	**81**	**29**	**0.26**	**50**	**21**	**29**	**60**	**73**	**4%**	**141**	**15%**	**54%**				**2.87**	**-8.4**	**10**	**25**	**$6**

Heisey,Chris

Age	29	Bats	R	Pos	LF
Ht	6' 1"	Wt	210		
Health	C	PT/Exp	D	Consist	B
LIMA Plan	D+	Rand Var	+2	MM	3413

1H wrecked by hamstring injury on April 27, but not a full-time player prior to that anyway. OPS against lefties and new ct% are stable and assure a bad-side platoon job. Terrible plate discipline and mounting struggles vR assure nothing more than that. Gone are the years hoping for 450 AB.

Yr	Tm	AB	R	HR	RBI	SB	BA	xBA	OBP	SLG	OPS	vL	vR	bb%	ct%	h%	Eye	G	L	F	PX	xPX	hr/f	Spd	SBO	SB%	#Wk	DOM	DIS	RC/G	RAR	BPV	BPX	R$
09	a/a	516	73	20	62	17	278	288	329	465	794			7	83	30	0.44				116			98	16%	83%				5.46		68	139	$19
10	CIN *	280	37	11	30	2	239	234	292	410	702	546	925	7	70	30	0.25	35	19	45	127	135	13%	113	7%	55%	23	39%	43%	3.93	-1.0	31	67	$4
11	CIN	279	44	18	50	6	254	249	309	487	797	553	865	6	72	29	0.24	32	19	49	157	129	19%	116	11%	86%	24	54%	33%	5.08	8.3	63	140	$11
12	CIN	347	44	7	31	6	265	234	315	401	715	827	680	5	77	33	0.22	37	22	41	90	71	7%	144	11%	67%	27	44%	41%	4.12	0.6	34	85	$8
13	CIN	224	29	9	23	3	237	245	279	415	694	810	622	4	77	27	0.18	40	16	44	121	109	12%	102	7%	100%	19	42%	47%	3.76	-1.9	46	115	$4
1st Half		83	7	2	6	2	181	228	218	313	532	725	375	5	75	22	0.19	45	15	40	103	81	8%	77	17%	100%	6	50%	50%	2.22	-4.8	15	38	-$2
2nd Half		141	22	7	17	1	270	254	295	475	770	869	748	3	79	30	0.17	37	16	46	131	124	14%	118	3%	100%	13	38%	46%	4.93	3.7	64	160	$7
14	**Proj**	**267**	**35**	**10**	**30**	**4**	**247**	**243**	**296**	**423**	**718**	**749**	**703**	**5**	**76**	**29**	**0.21**	**38**	**18**	**44**	**119**	**104**	**11%**	**114**	**10%**	**83%**				**4.08**	**0.5**	**42**	**105**	**$8**

Helton,Todd

Age	40	Bats	L	Pos	1B
Ht	6' 2"	Wt	220		
Health	D	PT/Exp	C	Consist	B
LIMA Plan	F	Rand Var	+1	MM	0000

From 1998 to 2004, he was a monster, especially in 2000 and 2001: 91 HR, 293 RBI, and 270 runs over two years, 400+ total bases in each year. Others to have 400+ TB in consecutive years: Chuck Klein, Jimmy Foxx, Lou Gehrig. That's it. And his best feature might be a career .418 OBP. Heck of a career, Todd.

Yr	Tm	AB	R	HR	RBI	SB	BA	xBA	OBP	SLG	OPS	vL	vR	bb%	ct%	h%	Eye	G	L	F	PX	xPX	hr/f	Spd	SBO	SB%	#Wk	DOM	DIS	RC/G	RAR	BPV	BPX	R$
09	COL	544	79	15	86	0	325	299	416	489	904	741	986	14	87	36	1.22	40	25	36	102	97	9%	90	0%	0%	26	77%	15%	7.72	45.1	85	173	$22
10	COL	398	48	8	37	0	256	237	362	367	728	714	735	14	77	31	0.74	34	23	43	81	119	6%	85	0%	0%	23	30%	39%	4.57	-0.1	31	67	$5
11	COL	421	59	14	69	0	302	288	385	466	850	794	879	12	83	34	0.83	35	27	38	112	128	10%	70	1%	0%	25	56%	12%	6.53	22.4	70	156	$17
12	COL	240	31	7	37	1	238	277	343	400	743	590	826	14	82	26	0.89	41	25	34	108	126	10%	68	3%	50%	18	56%	33%	4.56	-0.1	63	158	$3
13	COL	397	41	15	61	0	249	265	314	423	738	749	735	9	78	28	0.46	34	25	41	120	135	12%	67	0%	0%	25	44%	28%	4.57	-0.1	49	123	$8
1st Half		170	14	6	27	0	241	240	306	382	689	631	691	9	82	26	0.53	34	20	45	89	115	9%	55	0%	0%	12	50%	33%	3.94	-3.3	36	90	$5
2nd Half		227	27	9	34	0	256	279	327	454	780	799	772	10	75	30	0.42	33	29	38	145	152	14%	81	0%	0%	13	38%	23%	5.08	3.2	61	153	$11
14	Proj																																	

Hernandez,Cesar

Age	24	Bats	B	Pos	CF
Ht	5' 10"	Wt	175		
Health	A	PT/Exp	D	Consist	A
LIMA Plan	D	Rand Var	-2	MM	1411

0-10-.289 in 121 AB at PHI. He's fast. However, xBA warns against BA repeat; shaky plate discipline, unrepeatable h%, and SB% suggest he could use more seasoning in the minors. Can play 2B and OF, so utility role might be his path to a big-league career. More likely is a volume discount on Triple-A shuttle tickets.

Yr	Tm	AB	R	HR	RBI	SB	BA	xBA	OBP	SLG	OPS	vL	vR	bb%	ct%	h%	Eye	G	L	F	PX	xPX	hr/f	Spd	SBO	SB%	#Wk	DOM	DIS	RC/G	RAR	BPV	BPX	R$
09																																		
10																																		
11																																		
12	a/a	532	53	2	48	18	264	244	299	361	660			5	84	31	0.30				65			117	27%	53%				3.41		34	85	$12
13	PHI *	522	64	2	38	25	276	243	329	341	670	581	722	7	77	36	0.35	52	25	23	48	48	0%	158	23%	68%	7	14%	57%	3.86	-3.6	11	28	$19
1st Half		288	29	2	19	19	260	246	318	337	655	571	524	8	78	33	0.39	57	22	22	51	61	0%	155	30%	73%	2	50%	50%	3.69	-4.1	17	43	$20
2nd Half		234	35	0	20	7	298	238	347	350	696	583	788	7	76	39	0.31	51	26	23	46	43	0%	139	16%	57%	5	0%	60%	4.19	0.2	-2	-5	$17
14	**Proj**	**131**	**15**	**0**	**11**	**5**	**276**	**252**	**326**	**342**	**667**	**612**	**693**	**6**	**80**	**35**	**0.33**	**53**	**24**	**23**	**50**	**50**	**0%**	**138**	**23%**	**61%**				**3.68**	**-1.9**	**9**	**23**	**$4**

Herrera,Jonathan

Age	29	Bats	B	Pos	SS 2B
Ht	5' 9"	Wt	180		
Health	B	PT/Exp	F	Consist	B
LIMA Plan	D	Rand Var	-4	MM	1311

Excellent contact rate, but zero punch. Stopped hitting grounders, which did nothing except neutralize his speed. Not an effective base stealer, so his value is solely tied to average. 2H BA looks pretty, but xBA, Rand Var and BPV all say it won't repeat. Classic backup infielder. Avoid.

Yr	Tm	AB	R	HR	RBI	SB	BA	xBA	OBP	SLG	OPS	vL	vR	bb%	ct%	h%	Eye	G	L	F	PX	xPX	hr/f	Spd	SBO	SB%	#Wk	DOM	DIS	RC/G	RAR	BPV	BPX	R$
09	aaa	381	41	1	22	11	225	236	284	283	567			8	85	26	0.57				35			137	16%	64%				2.59		28	57	$1
10	COL *	444	52	2	31	4	245	233	308	298	606	722	680	8	85	29	0.59	50	18	32	36	26	2%	129	7%	40%	17	29%	35%	2.98	-9.0	24	52	$3
11	COL	281	28	3	14	4	242	246	313	299	612	615	610	9	86	27	0.70	49	23	28	35	48	5%	121	9%	50%	23	22%	39%	3.02	-5.4	27	60	$1
12	COL *	254	31	4	13	4	248	260	293	340	633	638	677	6	84	28	0.40	52	22	26	59	39	6%	113	8%	80%	23	30%	30%	3.40	-1.9	32	80	$2
13	COL	195	16	1	16	3	292	255	336	364	701	564	747	7	88	33	0.58	39	26	35	47	51	2%	117	8%	60%	26	46%	35%	4.37	3.9	39	98	$3
1st Half		100	9	0	7	1	270	252	318	340	658	345	747	7	89	30	0.64	33	29	38	42	46	0%	117	7%	50%	14	43%	29%	3.67	-0.1	40	100	$2
2nd Half		95	7	1	9	2	316	253	363	389	752	739	746	7	86	36	0.54	46	23	31	53	56	4%	107	9%	67%	12	50%	42%	5.20	3.9	35	88	$5
14	**Proj**	**195**	**19**	**2**	**13**	**3**	**271**	**253**	**322**	**346**	**668**	**623**	**684**	**7**	**86**	**31**	**0.55**	**46**	**23**	**31**	**50**	**46**	**4%**	**116**	**9%**	**63%**				**3.84**	**2.1**	**23**	**57**	**$4**

Herrmann,Chris

Age	26	Bats	L	Pos	CA RF
Ht	6' 0"	Wt	200		
Health	A	PT/Exp	C	Consist	A
LIMA Plan	F	Rand Var	+1	MM	2100

4-18-.204 in 187 AB at MIN. Mom said to say something nice or say nothing at all, so let's note his league average speed and generic walk rate. 2H PX was OK. xBA says BA is kinda sorta underrated. BPV projects to be above zero. Let's quit while we're ahead.

Yr	Tm	AB	R	HR	RBI	SB	BA	xBA	OBP	SLG	OPS	vL	vR	bb%	ct%	h%	Eye	G	L	F	PX	xPX	hr/f	Spd	SBO	SB%	#Wk	DOM	DIS	RC/G	RAR	BPV	BPX	R$
09																																		
10																																		
11	aa	337	38	4	33	6	216	227	310	312	622			12	77	27	0.60				68			116	10%	65%				3.12		24	53	$1
12	MIN *	508	70	7	48	2	229	245	293	317	610	0	237	8	79	28	0.43	69	15	15	63	46	0%	89	2%	57%				3.05	-10.2	12	30	$4
13	MIN *	404	38	5	34	2	193	202	258	280	537	545	624	8	70	26	0.29	43	19	38	69	156	10%	103	6%	39%	14	29%	43%	2.21	-19.4	-14	-35	-$3
1st Half		214	20	1	16	2	208	224	258	273	530	0	1303	6	76	27	0.28	25	33	42	51	339	20%	109	7%	64%	3	67%	0%	2.25	-9.8	-8	-20	-$2
2nd Half		190	18	4	18	0	175	194	258	288	545	545	546	10	64	25	0.30	45	18	38	94	134	8%	99	5%	0%	11	18%	55%	2.17	-9.6	-18	-45	-$5
14	**Proj**	**64**	**7**	**1**	**6**	**0**	**207**	**219**	**278**	**319**	**597**	**615**	**591**	**9**	**74**	**26**	**0.37**	**45**	**18**	**38**	**83**	**121**	**7%**	**106**	**5%**	**49%**				**2.80**	**-1.8**	**3**	**6**	**$0**

JOSH PALEY

Heyward,Jason

Age 24 | Bats L | Pos RF CF | Ht 6' 5" | Wt 240

Health C | PT/Exp B | Consist C | LIMA Plan B+ | Rand Var +3 | MM 4335

1H appendectomy, 2H hamstring and jaw injuries all suppressed AB, and probably SBs in particular. Breakout coming? PRO: concurrent 2H ct% growth and PX recovery; GBs slowly converting to LDs. CON: xPX doesn't buy into 2H PX surge; still too few balls in air. VERDICT: He's still just 24, with lots to like here.... UP: 30 HR, 20 SB.

Yr Tm	AB	R	HR	RBI	SB	BA	xBA	OBP	SLG	OPS	vL	vR	bb%	ct%	h%	Eye	G	L	F	PX	xPX	hr/f	Spd	SBO	SB%	#Wk	DOM	DIS	RC/G	RAR	BPV	BPX	R$
09 a/a	173	32	6	29	5	338	312	433	560	993			14	87	36	1.27				127			120	10%	84%				9.42		116	237	$9
10 ATL	520	83	18	72	11	277	278	393	456	849	755	895	15	75	34	0.71	55	18	27	126	100	17%	115	9%	65%	25	60%	28%	6.08	22.0	69	150	$20
11 ATL	396	50	14	42	9	227	251	319	389	708	577	754	11	77	26	0.55	54	13	33	112	106	14%	93	10%	82%	24	42%	21%	4.09	-6.2	48	107	$7
12 ATL	587	93	27	82	21	269	261	335	479	814	635	934	9	74	32	0.38	44	19	37	138	133	17%	112	19%	72%	27	59%	19%	5.51	15.3	60	150	$26
13 ATL	382	67	14	38	2	254	272	349	427	776	801	766	11	81	28	0.66	44	21	35	116	95	13%	104	6%	33%	20	65%	20%	4.75	1.6	72	180	$10
1st Half	212	29	6	17	1	231	258	312	373	685	573	759	11	79	27	0.57	40	23	36	101	109	10%	88	7%	25%	11	64%	27%	3.66	-5.1	47	118	$6
2nd Half	170	38	8	21	1	282	293	368	494	862	1142	773	12	83	30	0.79	48	19	33	134	79	17%	117	4%	50%	9	67%	11%	6.36	9.2	100	250	$14
14 Proj	528	88	21	78	13	263	273	352	453	805	764	824	11	79	30	0.60	47	19	34	127	105	15%	103	12%	72%				5.37	14.2	74	184	$20

Hicks,Aaron

Age 24 | Bats B | Pos CF | Ht 6' 2" | Wt 190

Health A | PT/Exp D | Consist D | LIMA Plan D+ | Rand Var +2 | MM 3501

8-27-.192 in 281 AB at MIN. Every promotion since 2010 has resulted in initial struggles, with bb% and ct% issues ruining everything else. Rushed to majors from AA, he needs more seasoning. Spd and PX hint at a nice power/speed blend... in 2015. Nice stash candidate in keeper leagues.

Yr Tm	AB	R	HR	RBI	SB	BA	xBA	OBP	SLG	OPS	vL	vR	bb%	ct%	h%	Eye	G	L	F	PX	xPX	hr/f	Spd	SBO	SB%	#Wk	DOM	DIS	RC/G	RAR	BPV	BPX	R$
09																																	
10																																	
11																																	
12 aa	472	80	10	49	26	258	232	347	401	748			12	73	33	0.51				96			141	26%	68%				4.63		37	93	$18
13 MIN *	353	42	8	31	10	192	218	258	328	586	713	566	8	70	25	0.29	45	17	38	102	104	11%	146	18%	76%	16	44%	44%	2.68	-17.5	22	55	$2
1st Half	211	25	6	20	4	177	210	247	314	561	898	488	8	71	22	0.32	44	13	43	97	122	11%	139	14%	67%	12	42%	42%	2.37	-12.4	24	60	$1
2nd Half	142	17	2	10	6	215	235	276	348	624	311	728	8	67	31	0.26	48	25	28	109	67	12%	141	22%	85%	4	50%	50%	3.21	-4.2	15	38	$3
14 Proj	221	31	5	20	9	224	232	304	375	679	583	704	10	71	29	0.36	45	19	36	111	89	9%	151	23%	73%				3.65	-3.6	35	88	$6

Hill,Aaron

Age 32 | Bats R | Pos 2B | Ht 5' 11" | Wt 205

Health D | PT/Exp B | Consist F | LIMA Plan A | Rand Var -3 | MM 3235

11-41-.290 in 327 AB at ARI. His litany of 2013 injuries read like instructions in the old "Operation" game: quad, hand, hamstring, groin. Despite that, good contact still sets a nice skills base and xPX remains strong. Double-digit SB unlikely to return, but a 2B with power and BA is plenty valuable.

Yr Tm	AB	R	HR	RBI	SB	BA	xBA	OBP	SLG	OPS	vL	vR	bb%	ct%	h%	Eye	G	L	F	PX	xPX	hr/f	Spd	SBO	SB%	#Wk	DOM	DIS	RC/G	RAR	BPV	BPX	R$
09 TOR	682	103	36	108	6	286	294	330	499	829	897	806	6	86	29	0.43	39	20	41	122	120	15%	87	5%	75%	27	63%	11%	5.81	41.2	80	163	$27
10 TOR	528	70	26	68	2	205	245	271	394	665	451	729	7	84	20	0.48	35	11	54	115	132	11%	79	4%	50%	25	60%	4%	3.26	-6.4	68	148	$5
11 2 TM	520	61	8	61	21	246	250	299	356	655	678	648	6	86	27	0.49	37	21	42	75	85	4%	95	22%	75%	25	44%	24%	3.53	-1.9	48	107	$13
12 ARI	609	93	26	85	14	302	286	360	522	882	839	901	8	86	32	0.60	34	21	45	132	145	11%	113	12%	74%	27	63%	7%	6.75	52.1	101	253	$30
13 ARI *	351	49	11	44	1	290	275	345	455	800	911	789	8	85	31	0.57	39	22	40	108	120	10%	93	5%	20%	18	67%	22%	5.39	17.2	72	180	$12
1st Half	80	13	3	11	0	283	302	352	485	837	641	1005	10	89	29	0.95	45	20	35	124	88	17%	88	5%	0%	5	80%	0%	5.77	4.8	102	255	$1
2nd Half	271	36	8	33	1	292	268	342	446	789	965	744	7	84	32	0.49	37	22	41	103	127	9%	94	5%	25%	13	62%	31%	5.28	12.1	63	158	$15
14 Proj	517	74	20	68	7	284	281	345	475	820	798	827	8	86	30	0.59	38	21	41	120	117	11%	99	8%	62%				5.62	28.2	83	208	$22

Hoes,LJ

Age 24 | Bats R | Pos RF | Ht 6' 0" | Wt 190

Health A | PT/Exp C | Consist B | LIMA Plan C+ | Rand Var 0 | MM 1313

1-10-.282 in 170 AB at BAL and HOU. Key piece in Bud Norris trade owns decent plate discpline and contact skills. Strong OBP suggests could fit near the top of a lineup. Spd says he has the wheels to rack up SB to provide significant fanalytic value. A nice fourth OF, maybe more.... UP: 20 SB.

Yr Tm	AB	R	HR	RBI	SB	BA	xBA	OBP	SLG	OPS	vL	vR	bb%	ct%	h%	Eye	G	L	F	PX	xPX	hr/f	Spd	SBO	SB%	#Wk	DOM	DIS	RC/G	RAR	BPV	BPX	R$
09																																	
10 aa																																	
11 aa	344	41	6	48	14	292	247	361	394	754			10	83	34	0.64				72			87	19%	65%				4.96		37	82	$14
12 BAL *	514	67	5	45	17	267	275	338	357	695	0	0	10	84	31	0.68	100	0	0	59	-11	0%	128	19%	57%	1	0%	0%	3.98	-4.6	44	110	$14
13 2 AL *	535	74	4	42	13	278	268	350	365	714	669	710	10	82	33	0.61	62	20	18	67	35	4%	113	12%	59%	9	56%	44%	4.37	1.4	37	93	$16
1st Half	286	39	3	28	5	276	245	353	370	723			11	83	33	0.69				73			102	11%	47%				4.37		43	108	$17
2nd Half	249	35	1	14	8	280	263	346	358	704	669	710	9	81	34	0.53	62	20	18	61	35	4%	131	14%	71%	9	56%	44%	4.37	-0.6	33	83	$16
14 Proj	316	42	3	28	10	276	251	349	366	715	715	714	10	83	33	0.63	54	18	28	66	32	4%	117	16%	61%				4.33	-1.1	35	87	$11

Holliday,Matt

Age 34 | Bats R | Pos LF | Ht 6' 4" | Wt 250

Health B | PT/Exp A | Consist A | LIMA Plan A | Rand Var 0 | MM 4245

Excellent and broad-based year-to-year skills. He was even consistent week-to-week (0% DIS). Mashed everyone in 2H, with Eye spike and ct% paving the way. 2H H% won't sustain, but these plate skills support BA. Age becoming a concern, but this skill set doesn't show any sign of fading... yet.

Yr Tm	AB	R	HR	RBI	SB	BA	xBA	OBP	SLG	OPS	vL	vR	bb%	ct%	h%	Eye	G	L	F	PX	xPX	hr/f	Spd	SBO	SB%	#Wk	DOM	DIS	RC/G	RAR	BPV	BPX	R$
09 2 TM	581	94	24	109	14	313	286	394	515	909	807	944	11	83	35	0.71	44	17	39	125	120	13%	96	11%	67%	27	52%	15%	7.29	51.4	83	169	$30
10 STL	596	95	28	103	9	312	298	390	532	922	982	900	10	84	33	0.74	42	17	41	142	133	14%	77	8%	64%	27	74%	4%	7.44	55.0	97	211	$32
11 STL	446	83	22	75	2	296	298	388	525	912	883	918	12	79	33	0.65	46	21	34	160	128	18%	73	2%	67%	25	64%	12%	7.18	38.6	92	204	$22
12 STL	599	95	27	102	4	295	270	379	497	877	1021	827	11	78	34	0.57	46	19	35	132	145	16%	90	4%	50%	27	52%	22%	6.61	42.6	69	173	$27
13 STL	520	103	22	94	6	300	288	389	490	879	799	903	12	83	33	0.80	46	21	34	123	126	15%	80	4%	86%	25	68%	0%	6.86	40.1	82	205	$29
1st Half	288	59	11	41	2	267	267	345	431	775	615	826	11	83	29	0.71	50	17	33	101	131	14%	90	3%	67%	14	64%	0%	5.14	9.3	64	160	$24
2nd Half	232	44	11	53	4	341	312	427	565	992	1003	1001	13	84	37	0.92	41	26	34	149	120	17%	76	5%	100%	11	73%	0%	9.48	32.8	105	263	$35
14 Proj	525	95	23	96	6	299	288	389	505	893	899	891	12	81	33	0.72	45	21	35	136	130	16%	81	5%	74%				6.99	43.2	84	209	$29

Hosmer,Eric

Age 24 | Bats L | Pos 1B | Ht 6' 4" | Wt 220

Health A | PT/Exp A | Consist F | LIMA Plan B+ | Rand Var -3 | MM 3335

Monthly BA log: Apr: .250; May: .269; Jun: .303; Jul: .324; Aug: .323; Sep: .324. George Brett was hired as hitting coach on May 30 and left on July 25. Coincidence? 2H xBA unpersuaded, but xPX gains and GB reduction are excellent signs, and at 24 there's more room for growth, so... UP: 25 HR, 15 SB, .300 BA.

Yr Tm	AB	R	HR	RBI	SB	BA	xBA	OBP	SLG	OPS	vL	vR	bb%	ct%	h%	Eye	G	L	F	PX	xPX	hr/f	Spd	SBO	SB%	#Wk	DOM	DIS	RC/G	RAR	BPV	BPX	R$
09																																	
10 aa	195	30	9	27	2	282	314	321	514	835			5	85	29	0.40				142			117	8%	68%				5.79		103	224	$7
11 KC *	621	82	21	89	13	309	279	359	471	830	585	886	7	84	34	0.49	50	19	32	104	106	13%	90	10%	73%	22	59%	23%	6.18	26.8	63	140	$30
12 KC	535	65	14	60	16	232	262	304	359	663	591	700	9	82	26	0.59	54	18	28	80	95	11%	88	12%	94%	26	54%	27%	3.76	-13.6	40	100	$11
13 KC	623	86	17	79	11	302	287	353	448	801	797	803	8	84	34	0.51	53	22	25	96	105	13%	103	8%	73%	26	50%	8%	5.77	20.0	61	153	$28
1st Half	289	39	7	33	7	277	289	330	412	742	802	719	7	84	31	0.51	57	22	21	87	89	13%	112	13%	70%	14	36%	14%	4.74	1.1	58	145	$22
2nd Half	334	47	10	46	4	323	285	376	479	855	795	891	8	84	36	0.51	49	23	28	104	119	13%	97	5%	80%	12	67%	0%	6.80	19.5	64	160	$34
14 Proj	600	81	18	77	11	285	283	340	440	780	718	811	8	84	32	0.52	52	21	27	100	103	13%	100	8%	78%				5.36	12.8	61	152	$25

Howard,Ryan

Age 34 | Bats L | Pos 1B | Ht 6' 4" | Wt 240

Health F | PT/Exp C | Consist C | LIMA Plan B | Rand Var -1 | MM 5115

July meniscus tear ended season, but striking out 1/3 of the time and ineptitude vs. LHs were already problems. All of that says his days as everyday player would be over, were it not for that contract. Bill James noted that the decline of someone with "old player skills" (power, no speed) can be swift, harsh and come early. Indeed.

Yr Tm	AB	R	HR	RBI	SB	BA	xBA	OBP	SLG	OPS	vL	vR	bb%	ct%	h%	Eye	G	L	F	PX	xPX	hr/f	Spd	SBO	SB%	#Wk	DOM	DIS	RC/G	RAR	BPV	BPX	R$
09 PHI	616	105	45	141	8	279	291	360	571	931	653	1088	11	70	33	0.40	36	23	41	199	202	25%	76	6%	89%	26	69%	0%	7.27	46.8	85	173	$30
10 PHI	550	87	31	108	1	276	273	353	505	859	826	876	10	71	33	0.38	40	23	37	157	153	21%	105	1%	50%	26	46%	31%	6.14	24.2	64	139	$23
11 PHI	557	81	33	116	1	253	264	346	488	835	634	921	12	69	31	0.44	40	21	39	175	175	22%	53	1%	100%	27	48%	41%	5.71	18.3	58	129	$21
12 PHI	260	28	14	56	0	219	237	295	423	718	604	784	9	62	29	0.25	43	26	31	159	143	27%	54	0%	0%	13	38%	54%	3.98	-4.8	11	28	$4
13 PHI	286	34	11	43	0	266	251	319	465	784	539	878	7	67	36	0.24	39	24	38	163	160	15%	86	0%	0%	14	36%	43%	5.17	4.8	40	100	$7
1st Half	273	31	10	41	0	264	248	319	462	780	509	881	7	66	36	0.24	38	23	39	165	163	14%	82	0%	0%	14	36%	43%	5.09	3.9	39	98	$8
2nd Half	13	3	1	2	0	308	325	357	538	896	1000	819	7	77	33	0.33	50	40	10	132	110		94	0%	0%				7.08	0.9	58	145	-$7
14 Proj	412	55	19	79	1	256	251	328	462	791	616	873	9	67	33	0.32	40	23	37	160	164	19%	71	1%	82%				5.15	6.7	35	88	$14

JOSH PALEY

Hundley,Nick

Age	30	Bats	R	Pos	CA	Health	D	LIMA Plan	D+
Ht	6' 1"	Wt	195			PT/Exp	D	Rand Var	0
						Consist	F	MM	3103

Avoiding injuries led to more AB. Mix in PX to get double-digit HR. Eye and ct% still need work, but 2H showed good progress in those areas. Unfortunately, those are still poor, he's still a health risk, BA will always be subpar, and PETCO suppresses his plus power. A 2013 repeat is entirely possible, but don't pay for more.

Yr	Tm	AB	R	HR	RBI	SB	BA	xBA	OBP	SLG	OPS	vL	vR	bb%	ct%	h%	Eye	G	L	F	PX	xPX	hr/f	Spd	SBO	SB%	#Wk	DOM	DIS	RC/G	RAR	BPV	BPX	R$
09	SD	256	23	8	30	5	238	236	313	406	719	587	768	10	70	31	0.37	31	22	47	123	127	9%	110	9%	83%	20	40%	40%	4.30	4.6	34	69	$3
10	SD	273	33	8	43	0	249	259	308	418	726	830	692	8	76	30	0.38	41	19	40	124	116	10%	109	8%	0%	26	38%	31%	4.09	3.2	54	117	$4
11	SD *	315	36	10	32	1	272	249	329	449	779	768	839	8	71	35	0.30	41	21	38	132	107	12%	147	2%	50%	19	47%	32%	5.14	13.0	53	118	$7
12	SD *	246	16	3	26	0	153	193	209	235	444	306	568	7	72	20	0.26	39	18	43	59	100	5%	106	10%	0%	14	14%	79%	1.34	-19.6	-15	-38	-$7
13	SD	373	35	13	44	1	233	240	290	389	679	553	721	7	74	28	0.27	43	20	37	115	99	13%	92	1%	100%	27	37%	48%	3.68	-0.2	29	73	$5
1st Half		176	18	5	18	0	239	236	268	392	660	438	766	4	70	31	0.13	40	21	40	126	98	10%	97	0%	0%	14	29%	50%	3.52	-1.0	22	55	$3
2nd Half		197	17	8	26	1	228	242	296	386	682	696	685	9	77	26	0.41	45	19	36	105	99	15%	91	2%	100%	13	46%	46%	3.81	0.6	37	93	$6
14	Proj	**325**	**29**	**10**	**37**	**1**	**242**	**232**	**301**	**388**	**689**	**542**	**747**	**7**	**73**	**30**	**0.29**	**41**	**20**	**39**	**107**	**103**	**10%**	**108**	**4%**	**34%**				**3.79**	**0.8**	**9**	**23**	**$3**

Hunter,Torii

Age	38	Bats	R	Pos	RF	Health	A	LIMA Plan	B
Ht	6' 2"	Wt	225			PT/Exp	A	Rand Var	-2
						Consist	B	MM	3225

Does lineup protection matter? In this case, perhaps. Spent 2012 2H between Trout/Pujols, and bb% plummeted as he got pitches to hit (w/crazy 43% h%). Found himself in front of Cabrera/Fielder in 2013, and hacktastic plate approach brought more big results. Age-related risk balances against that contextual value.

Yr	Tm	AB	R	HR	RBI	SB	BA	xBA	OBP	SLG	OPS	vL	vR	bb%	ct%	h%	Eye	G	L	F	PX	xPX	hr/f	Spd	SBO	SB%	#Wk	DOM	DIS	RC/G	RAR	BPV	BPX	R$
09	LAA	451	74	22	90	18	299	284	366	508	873	978	837	9	80	34	0.51	47	16	36	130	134	17%	85	17%	82%	22	55%	27%	6.80	31.7	69	141	$25
10	LAA	573	76	23	90	9	281	283	354	464	819	775	838	10	82	31	0.58	48	18	34	123	102	15%	77	13%	43%	27	52%	15%	5.40	18.6	69	150	$22
11	LAA	580	80	23	82	5	262	264	336	429	765	886	715	10	78	30	0.50	46	21	33	111	136	15%	90	7%	42%	27	41%	19%	4.76	8.2	51	113	$18
12	LAA	534	81	16	92	9	313	257	365	451	817	868	798	7	75	39	0.29	52	23	25	96	88	16%	83	6%	90%	25	36%	52%	6.08	26.0	17	43	$26
13	DET	606	90	17	84	3	304	276	334	465	800	829	788	4	81	35	0.23	49	20	31	110	99	11%	106	3%	60%	26	50%	23%	5.61	22.2	56	140	$26
1st Half		300	44	4	31	1	297	266	332	410	742	720	758	5	83	35	0.31	53	19	27	85	81	6%	97	3%	50%	14	43%	21%	4.89	3.7	41	103	$19
2nd Half		306	46	13	53	2	310	283	332	520	852	895	823	3	80	35	0.16	46	20	34	135	118	15%	112	4%	67%	12	58%	25%	6.34	15.7	69	173	$33
14	Proj	**560**	**83**	**16**	**82**	**4**	**281**	**264**	**327**	**430**	**758**	**803**	**739**	**6**	**79**	**33**	**0.30**	**49**	**21**	**30**	**103**	**106**	**12%**	**98**	**4%**	**67%**				**4.92**	**7.4**	**39**	**96**	**$21**

Iannetta,Chris

Age	31	Bats	R	Pos	CA	Health	C	LIMA Plan	D
Ht	6' 0"	Wt	230			PT/Exp	D	Rand Var	0
						Consist	B	MM	3003

If he could stay healthy, he'd be a beautiful Moneyball hitter with .350 OBP and some pop. Contact has been trending south for years, taking BPV with it. Those persistent dings, problems with RHPs, and poor defense (81% SB against) restrict him to part-time work. Expect more of the same.

Yr	Tm	AB	R	HR	RBI	SB	BA	xBA	OBP	SLG	OPS	vL	vR	bb%	ct%	h%	Eye	G	L	F	PX	xPX	hr/f	Spd	SBO	SB%	#Wk	DOM	DIS	RC/G	RAR	BPV	BPX	R$
09	COL	289	41	16	52	0	228	256	344	460	804	986	734	13	74	25	0.57	32	16	52	150	152	14%	88	1%	0%	24	54%	29%	4.93	10.6	70	143	$5
10	COL *	251	30	12	39	1	217	251	314	418	732	737	683	12	76	24	0.60	41	13	45	134	126	14%	75	2%	100%	22	45%	36%	4.30	4.6	61	133	$3
11	COL	345	51	14	55	6	238	245	370	414	785	990	718	17	74	28	0.79	35	20	44	126	104	12%	73	8%	67%	27	48%	30%	5.04	13.7	55	122	$9
12	LAA *	243	29	9	27	1	235	228	321	385	706	636	756	11	71	29	0.44	44	20	36	100	115	16%	85	6%	25%	16	31%	44%	3.94	1.6	16	40	$3
13	LAA	325	40	11	39	0	225	218	358	372	731	835	663	17	69	29	0.68	37	19	43	115	126	11%	70	1%	0%	27	41%	56%	4.34	6.2	26	65	$3
1st Half		182	25	6	26	0	214	226	367	357	724	880	640	19	69	28	0.79	38	22	40	111	127	12%	73	0%	0%	14	50%	43%	4.26	3.1	29	73	$4
2nd Half		143	15	5	13	0	238	208	347	392	739	792	700	14	69	31	0.55	36	15	48	120	124	10%	71	2%	0%	13	31%	69%	4.43	3.1	25	63	$2
14	Proj	**257**	**32**	**8**	**32**	**1**	**231**	**221**	**346**	**375**	**721**	**789**	**687**	**15**	**71**	**29**	**0.59**	**38**	**19**	**43**	**108**	**121**	**11%**	**74**	**3%**	**37%**				**4.18**	**3.6**	**15**	**37**	**$5**

Ibanez,Raul

Age	42	Bats	L	Pos	LF DH	Health	A	LIMA Plan	D+
Ht	6' 2"	Wt	225			PT/Exp	B	Rand Var	0
						Consist	A	MM	4223

This is so hard to explain that it's like the Underpants Gnomes' business plan on South Park. Phase 1: 41-year-old in decline. Phase 2: ??? Phase 3: Profit! But what was the ???. Whatever fueled his success—stockpiling underpants, use of dark magic, or Fountain of Youth, do not expect anything resembling a repeat.

Yr	Tm	AB	R	HR	RBI	SB	BA	xBA	OBP	SLG	OPS	vL	vR	bb%	ct%	h%	Eye	G	L	F	PX	xPX	hr/f	Spd	SBO	SB%	#Wk	DOM	DIS	RC/G	RAR	BPV	BPX	R$
09	PHI	500	93	34	93	4	272	297	347	552	899	998	859	10	76	29	0.47	43	15	42	177	179	21%	87	3%	100%	25	60%	16%	6.73	39.3	95	194	$21
10	PHI	561	75	16	83	4	275	273	349	444	793	728	822	11	81	32	0.63	45	18	37	116	121	9%	91	4%	57%	27	63%	26%	5.44	23.5	67	146	$17
11	PHI	535	65	20	84	2	245	270	289	419	707	585	747	6	80	27	0.31	46	19	35	119	117	13%	64	2%	100%	27	48%	33%	4.10	1.9	49	109	$12
12	NYY	384	50	19	62	3	240	278	308	453	761	492	812	8	83	24	0.52	41	19	39	126	112	15%	79	3%	100%	27	63%	15%	4.65	7.7	73	183	$9
13	SEA	454	54	29	65	0	242	265	306	487	793	802	790	8	72	27	0.33	36	21	43	168	144	21%	67	0%	0%	27	44%	33%	5.02	14.0	61	153	$13
1st Half		228	30	19	45	0	246	285	292	544	836	851	831	6	74	25	0.25	35	21	44	189	142	25%	81	0%	0%	14	50%	14%	5.37	9.1	86	215	$17
2nd Half		226	24	10	20	0	239	246	320	429	749	756	746	11	69	30	0.39	36	22	41	147	146	15%	66	0%	0%	13	38%	54%	4.60	3.9	39	98	$8
14	Proj	**329**	**41**	**15**	**48**	**1**	**245**	**260**	**306**	**443**	**749**	**702**	**764**	**8**	**76**	**28**	**0.36**	**40**	**20**	**40**	**135**	**133**	**15%**	**73**	**2%**	**92%**				**4.57**	**5.4**	**49**	**122**	**$9**

Iglesias,Jose

Age	24	Bats	R	Pos	SS 3B	Health	A	LIMA Plan	B
Ht	5' 11"	Wt	185			PT/Exp	D	Rand Var	-2
						Consist	B	MM	0405

3-29-.303 in 350 AB at BOS/DET. Elite defensive prospect surprised by hitting .403 through first 135 AB; fueled by ct%, Spd, GB%, and an unsustainable h%. Poor bb% and Eye, lack of pop, and natural regression brought reality in 2H. Great bunter (11-for-18) and young enough to improve at plate, but xBA caps 2014 upside.

Yr	Tm	AB	R	HR	RBI	SB	BA	xBA	OBP	SLG	OPS	vL	vR	bb%	ct%	h%	Eye	G	L	F	PX	xPX	hr/f	Spd	SBO	SB%	#Wk	DOM	DIS	RC/G	RAR	BPV	BPX	R$
09																																		
10	aa	221	22	0	10	4	267	226	287	335	622			3	77	35	0.12				58			126	11%	64%				3.28		0	0	$2
11	BOS *	363	33	1	27	10	228	285	264	262	526	2000	400	5	83	27	0.28	75	25	0	28	2	0%	92	16%	71%	4	0%	50%	2.29	-12.7	-7	-16	$2
12	BOS *	421	44	2	22	11	235	233	281	279	560	536	284	6	85	27	0.42	59	16	25	32	23	8%	110	13%	78%	7	0%	43%	2.65	-9.8	11	28	$3
13	2 AL *	469	52	6	41	9	272	250	304	357	662	769	716	4	83	32	0.28	56	18	26	59	37	4%	134	11%	63%	22	23%	32%	3.72	4.0	31	78	$12
1st Half		251	36	4	21	6	301	273	343	408	751	1055	948	6	85	34	0.42	55	21	25	71	47	4%	170	14%	58%	9	44%	0%	4.90	10.1	62	155	$18
2nd Half		218	16	2	20	3	239	223	259	298	557	600	570	3	81	29	0.14	58	16	26	45	30	5%	94	8%	75%	13	8%	54%	2.59	-5.7	-6	-15	$5
14	Proj	**571**	**57**	**4**	**42**	**10**	**252**	**238**	**305**	**315**	**621**	**677**	**586**	**4**	**82**	**30**	**0.24**	**57**	**17**	**25**	**47**	**31**	**4%**	**123**	**10%**	**71%**				**3.02**	**-7.5**	**2**	**6**	**$10**

Infante,Omar

Age	32	Bats	R	Pos	2B	Health	C	LIMA Plan	A
Ht	5' 11"	Wt	195			PT/Exp	A	Rand Var	-4
						Consist	B	MM	1435

Superior contact props up BA and sets a nice value floor. But Rand Var screams regression, while xBA, 2H Eye, and injury problems suggest the beginning of the gentle fade that comes with age. Don't pay for a rebound to 2012. Don't pay for a repeat of last year's BA either.

Yr	Tm	AB	R	HR	RBI	SB	BA	xBA	OBP	SLG	OPS	vL	vR	bb%	ct%	h%	Eye	G	L	F	PX	xPX	hr/f	Spd	SBO	SB%	#Wk	DOM	DIS	RC/G	RAR	BPV	BPX	R$
09	ATL	203	24	2	27	2	305	259	361	389	750	730	759	9	86	35	0.68	32	27	41	55	77	3%	114	3%	100%	16	44%	31%	5.29	8.6	42	86	$5
10	ATL	471	65	8	47	7	321	255	359	416	775	665	827	6	87	36	0.47	47	19	34	59	65	6%	148	8%	54%	27	41%	26%	5.44	21.9	53	115	$20
11	FLA	579	55	7	49	4	276	263	315	382	696	729	685	6	88	30	0.51	42	22	36	66	64	4%	145	4%	67%	26	50%	12%	4.23	8.3	63	140	$12
12	2 TM	554	69	12	53	17	274	267	300	419	719	872	656	4	88	29	0.32	41	20	39	86	97	6%	129	16%	85%	27	52%	22%	4.49	12.1	70	175	$18
13	DET	453	54	10	51	5	318	278	345	450	795	831	778	4	90	34	0.45	38	24	38	82	76	6%	119	6%	71%	22	59%	9%	5.81	25.3	73	183	$19
1st Half		281	35	5	24	4	299	272	334	423	758	815	729	5	90	32	0.52	38	23	38	80	83	5%	116	8%	67%	14	64%	7%	5.09	10.9	70	175	$19
2nd Half		172	19	5	27	1	349	286	367	494	861	852	866	3	91	36	0.33	38	24	37	85	65	9%	114	2%	100%	8	50%	13%	7.15	15.2	75	188	$19
14	Proj	**502**	**58**	**10**	**56**	**6**	**290**	**270**	**319**	**419**	**738**	**788**	**716**	**4**	**89**	**31**	**0.41**	**40**	**23**	**38**	**80**	**77**	**6%**	**127**	**6%**	**76%**				**4.82**	**15.8**	**58**	**144**	**$18**

Izturis,Cesar

Age	34	Bats	B	Pos	SS 2B	Health	D	LIMA Plan	D
Ht	5' 9"	Wt	180			PT/Exp	F	Rand Var	+5
						Consist	C	MM	1221

Slightly above average defense must justify his roster spot, because his hitting never has. Beautiful ct% and xBA say BA was unlucky, but uninspiring across-the-board skills position him below replacement value offensively. Three years of negative fanalytic earnings will indeed repeat. UP: $0.

Yr	Tm	AB	R	HR	RBI	SB	BA	xBA	OBP	SLG	OPS	vL	vR	bb%	ct%	h%	Eye	G	L	F	PX	xPX	hr/f	Spd	SBO	SB%	#Wk	DOM	DIS	RC/G	RAR	BPV	BPX	R$
09	BAL	387	34	2	30	12	256	269	294	328	622	705	580	4	90	28	0.47	49	20	30	44	23	2%	120	16%	75%	22	50%	18%	3.26	-2.8	43	88	$6
10	BAL	473	42	1	28	11	230	235	277	268	545	504	561	5	89	26	0.47	46	19	35	28	26	1%	100	13%	69%	27	26%	26%	2.38	-16.2	20	43	$2
11	BAL *	55	6	0	3	0	196	200	244	211	454	667	360	6	71	28	0.21	50	25	25	16	48	0%	94	9%	0%	8	0%	88%	1.44	-3.6	-62	-138	-$3
12	2 NL	166	13	2	11	1	241	286	254	343	598	392	682	2	92	25	0.23	55	21	24	59	28	6%	108	6%	50%	17	29%	18%	2.87	-3.1	54	135	-$1
13	CIN	129	6	0	11	0	209	250	259	271	530	621	497	7	90	23	0.69	52	22	27	52	35	0%	72	0%	0%	27	37%	30%	2.28	-4.8	38	95	-$4
1st Half		75	3	0	3	0	187	237	256	227	483	745	383	9	91	21	1.00	51	22	26	33	41	0%	76	0%	0%	14	43%	29%	1.82	-3.9	31	78	-$4
2nd Half		54	3	0	8	0	241	268	268	333	601	429	652	4	89	27	0.33	52	21	27	79	27	0%	84	0%	0%	13	31%	31%	3.00	-0.8	53	133	-$2
14	Proj	**100**	**7**	**0**	**9**	**1**	**230**	**266**	**266**	**306**	**572**	**530**	**588**	**5**	**90**	**25**	**0.50**	**51**	**21**	**28**	**55**	**30**	**2%**	**88**	**6%**	**66%**				**2.67**	**-2.4**	**33**	**81**	**$0**

JOSH PALEY

Izturis,Maicer

Age	33	Bats	B	Pos	2B 3B SS		
Ht	5' 8"	Wt	170				
Health	C	PT/Exp	C	Consist	B		
LIMA Plan	D+	Rand Var	+3	MM	0223		

Elite ct% and solid Eye, but unlucky h% and no pop killed his BA. As such, he rarely had the opportunity to run, and when he did, he was a special kind of awful. His only SB came in his last game of the season (8/20), after 5 failed attempts. The coup de grace: He sprained his ankle in that game and missed the rest of the season.

Yr	Tm	AB	R	HR	RBI	SB	BA	xBA	OBP	SLG	OPS	vL	vR	bb%	ct%	h%	Eye	G	L	F	PX	xPX	hr/f	Spd	SBO	SB%	#Wk	DOM	DIS	RC/G	RAR	BPV	BPX	R$
09	LAA	387	74	8	65	13	300	278	359	434	794	975	766	8	89	32	0.85	43	19	38	81	77	6%	114	15%	72%	26	58%	19%	5.60	20.2	75	153	$18
10	LAA	212	27	3	27	7	250	261	321	363	684	697	680	9	87	27	0.78	42	18	40	78	86	4%	105	18%	70%	15	60%	20%	3.88	0.9	63	137	$4
11	LAA	449	51	5	38	9	276	267	334	388	722	780	687	7	86	31	0.51	39	23	38	87	71	3%	84	13%	60%	27	41%	33%	4.32	7.6	52	116	$11
12	LAA	289	35	2	20	17	256	252	320	315	634	503	682	8	87	29	0.66	47	23	30	42	39	3%	98	22%	89%	26	23%	35%	3.64	-0.6	28	70	$7
13	TOR	365	33	5	32	1	236	261	288	310	597	606	594	7	90	25	0.71	52	22	26	48	45	6%	88	6%	17%	21	38%	10%	2.81	-10.2	39	98	$2
1st Half		231	23	5	18	0	229	279	267	338	605	635	584	5	89	24	0.48	53	23	24	69	34	10%	88	4%	0%	14	50%	0%	2.86	-5.9	50	125	$2
2nd Half		134	10	0	14	1	246	233	322	261	583	499	602	10	90	27	1.15	50	22	28	12	65	0%	99	9%	25%	7	14%	29%	2.63	-4.3	23	58	$0
14	Proj	322	34	3	30	7	262	257	323	333	656	635	663	8	88	29	0.73	48	22	30	50	55	4%	93	10%	66%				3.64	-0.5	30	74	$6

Jackson,Austin

Age	27	Bats	R	Pos	CF		
Ht	6' 1"	Wt	185				
Health	B	PT/Exp	A	Consist	D		
LIMA Plan	B	Rand Var	0	MM	3515		

Posted personal best plate discipline in 1H, then personal best PX in 2H. If only he could do both at same time. This is not out of the question—he's the perfect age for a breakout. Hamstring injury in June may have suppressed 2H SB, which should rebound. All of the needed elements are in place for... UP: 20 HR, 20 SB.

Yr	Tm	AB	R	HR	RBI	SB	BA	xBA	OBP	SLG	OPS	vL	vR	bb%	ct%	h%	Eye	G	L	F	PX	xPX	hr/f	Spd	SBO	SB%	#Wk	DOM	DIS	RC/G	RAR	BPV	BPX	R$
09	aaa	504	64	4	62	23	283	225	336	375	711			7	74	38	0.30				67			120	18%	84%				4.61		1	2	$18
10	DET	618	103	4	41	27	293	249	345	400	745	600	798	7	72	40	0.28	48	24	27	86	94	3%	204	18%	82%	27	33%	41%	5.03	13.8	36	78	$25
11	DET	591	90	10	45	22	249	218	317	374	690	732	672	9	69	34	0.31	47	17	36	94	96	7%	204	17%	81%	27	26%	52%	4.05	-3.2	33	73	$15
12	DET	543	103	16	66	12	300	260	377	479	856	856	856	11	75	37	0.50	42	24	34	118	117	11%	179	12%	57%	25	48%	20%	6.33	31.9	73	183	$25
13	DET	552	99	12	49	8	272	263	337	417	754	681	784	9	77	34	0.40	42	28	31	103	101	9%	157	8%	67%	22	45%	18%	4.83	9.3	55	138	$18
1st Half		207	47	4	18	6	290	263	372	401	773	752	780	12	80	35	0.64	45	23	32	78	89	9%	144	10%	86%	10	50%	10%	5.46	7.5	49	123	$18
2nd Half		345	52	8	31	2	261	264	311	426	737	649	787	7	75	33	0.29	40	28	32	120	108	10%	150	6%	40%	12	42%	25%	4.43	2.6	56	140	$18
14	Proj	584	103	15	56	16	286	253	354	442	796	753	813	9	75	36	0.41	41	25	34	110	103	10%	174	12%	73%				5.52	22.3	49	123	$25

Jaso,John

Age	30	Bats	L	Pos	CA		
Ht	6' 2"	Wt	205				
Health	D	PT/Exp	D	Consist	F		
LIMA Plan	C	Rand Var	-3	MM	2223		

Catchers have perilous jobs, and the concussion he experienced on July 24 knocked him out for the season. In real baseball terms, he is a useful offensive player because of his monster OBP and success vs. RHP. Fanalytically, if he's healthy, he is useful as a do-no-harm 2nd C. Check on health in spring before investing.

Yr	Tm	AB	R	HR	RBI	SB	BA	xBA	OBP	SLG	OPS	vL	vR	bb%	ct%	h%	Eye	G	L	F	PX	xPX	hr/f	Spd	SBO	SB%	#Wk	DOM	DIS	RC/G	RAR	BPV	BPX	R$
09	aaa	331	34	4	24	1	225	239	302	307	609			10	82	26	0.63				53			109	1%	100%				3.07		27	55	-$1
10	TAM	339	57	5	44	4	263	266	372	378	750	610	772	15	88	28	1.51	46	17	37	75	81	5%	109	3%	100%	25	68%	8%	4.94	11.9	78	170	$8
11	TAM	246	26	5	27	1	224	256	298	354	651	574	662	9	85	24	0.69	43	18	39	90	89	6%	79	5%	33%	27	50%	23%	3.33	-2.9	58	129	$0
12	SEA	294	41	10	50	5	276	294	394	456	850	393	927	16	83	30	1.10	46	25	28	115	86	14%	92	5%	100%	26	73%	15%	6.41	22.5	84	210	$10
13	OAK	207	31	3	21	2	271	247	387	372	759	442	802	16	78	33	0.84	40	25	35	80	58	5%	93	4%	67%	17	35%	35%	4.97	7.5	38	95	$4
1st Half		174	24	2	19	0	276	246	373	368	741	432	789	13	79	34	0.73	40	26	34	74	64	4%	94	0%	0%	14	36%	36%	4.83	5.5	31	78	$5
2nd Half		33	7	1	2	2	242	256	432	394	826	500	864	25	76	29	1.38	40	24	36	113	25	11%	99	19%	67%	3	33%	33%	5.66	2.0	75	188	-$1
14	Proj	336	44	9	41	2	268	267	362	410	773	477	816	13	82	30	0.81	43	23	34	98	63	9%	90	3%	76%				5.15	14.0	52	131	$10

Jay,Jon

Age	29	Bats	L	Pos	CF		
Ht	5' 11"	Wt	195				
Health	B	PT/Exp	B	Consist	A		
LIMA Plan	B	Rand Var	-3	MM	1335		

Plate discipline a mixed bag, both walking and striking out more. The combination of marginal power, league average Spd, and inability to hit lefties (2H vL notwithstanding) say he's on the cusp of being a fourth outfielder or the good side of a platoon. DN: 350 AB and single-digit HR, SB.

Yr	Tm	AB	R	HR	RBI	SB	BA	xBA	OBP	SLG	OPS	vL	vR	bb%	ct%	h%	Eye	G	L	F	PX	xPX	hr/f	Spd	SBO	SB%	#Wk	DOM	DIS	RC/G	RAR	BPV	BPX	R$
09	aaa	505	57	7	43	16	243	253	281	331	612			5	86	27	0.37				56			101	21%	64%				3.02		30	61	$8
10	STL *	452	68	7	49	11	284	275	337	407	743	741	791	7	83	33	0.47	49	19	32	91	76	5%	112	12%	73%	21	33%	29%	4.85	9.6	56	122	$15
11	STL	455	56	10	37	6	297	278	344	424	768	727	779	6	82	34	0.35	54	23	23	88	69	11%	105	10%	46%	27	48%	30%	4.94	10.8	44	98	$15
12	STL	443	70	4	40	19	305	278	373	400	773	697	804	7	84	36	0.48	59	22	19	64	53	6%	126	19%	73%	23	39%	22%	5.15	13.0	41	103	$19
13	STL	548	75	7	67	10	276	270	351	370	721	620	749	9	81	33	0.50	50	27	23	70	58	7%	96	9%	67%	27	37%	30%	4.36	4.2	29	73	$18
1st Half		275	41	4	33	2	244	255	311	331	642	478	702	9	81	29	0.53	50	23	26	61	67	7%	97	4%	67%	14	36%	29%	3.46	-5.8	24	60	$12
2nd Half		273	34	3	34	8	308	285	366	410	776	768	796	8	81	37	0.48	50	30	19	79	48	7%	98	14%	67%	13	38%	31%	5.42	9.4	35	88	$24
14	Proj	453	63	6	48	12	281	273	348	385	734	664	755	7	82	33	0.46	52	24	24	75	59	7%	107	13%	67%				4.51	4.4	36	90	$17

Jennings,Desmond

Age	27	Bats	R	Pos	CF		
Ht	6' 2"	Wt	200				
Health	B	PT/Exp	B	Consist	A		
LIMA Plan	B+	Rand Var	0	MM	3515		

Tantalizing power/speed combination once conjured hopes of a young Carl Crawford. While he won't steal 50 bases, he is developing a more balanced skills set with a lot to like. 2H broken finger, hamstring injuries held him back in 2013. Marry 1H power to 2H speed, and you get... UP: 2011 season, with .265 BA

Yr	Tm	AB	R	HR	RBI	SB	BA	xBA	OBP	SLG	OPS	vL	vR	bb%	ct%	h%	Eye	G	L	F	PX	xPX	hr/f	Spd	SBO	SB%	#Wk	DOM	DIS	RC/G	RAR	BPV	BPX	R$
09	a/a	497	81	9	54	46	291	278	365	443	808			10	85	33	0.78				92			131	34%	86%				6.09		76	155	$29
10	TAM *	420	68	2	30	30	236	229	300	335	636	879	350	8	80	29	0.47	47	12	41	72	142	0%	165	35%	82%	6	33%	50%	3.51	-9.3	48	104	$12
11	TAM *	585	96	19	55	33	242	248	318	404	722	791	811	10	74	30	0.43	47	18	35	113	100	16%	158	26%	82%	11	64%	18%	4.42	3.2	56	124	$21
12	TAM	505	85	13	47	31	246	236	314	388	702	735	691	8	76	30	0.38	42	20	38	92	99	9%	163	25%	94%	24	54%	33%	4.32	1.3	46	115	$19
13	TAM	527	82	14	54	20	252	258	334	414	748	857	697	11	78	30	0.56	47	17	36	113	110	10%	134	19%	71%	25	72%	20%	4.65	6.4	67	168	$19
1st Half		302	48	9	29	9	252	260	313	430	744	983	644	8	77	30	0.40	46	17	38	125	119	10%	138	21%	60%	14	79%	21%	4.37	1.8	70	175	$20
2nd Half		225	34	5	25	11	253	253	359	391	750	711	769	14	79	30	0.79	49	18	34	96	98	9%	121	17%	85%	11	64%	18%	4.95	5.2	60	150	$18
14	Proj	534	85	15	53	28	251	253	332	410	742	785	723	10	78	30	0.52	45	18	36	108	103	10%	147	23%	83%				4.68	8.0	65	161	$22

Jeter,Derek

Age	40	Bats	R	Pos	SS		
Ht	6' 3"	Wt	195				
Health	F	PT/Exp	B	Consist	F		
LIMA Plan	B	Rand Var	+5	MM	1335		

Not everyone gets to go out gracefully and gloriously like Mariano Rivera and Andy Pettitte. Injuries headline his portfolio and at his age, they may already be career-ending. If healthy, this projection is a fair bet, but there is a significant chance that The Captain will set sail. DN: retirement.

Yr	Tm	AB	R	HR	RBI	SB	BA	xBA	OBP	SLG	OPS	vL	vR	bb%	ct%	h%	Eye	G	L	F	PX	xPX	hr/f	Spd	SBO	SB%	#Wk	DOM	DIS	RC/G	RAR	BPV	BPX	R$
09	NYY	634	107	18	66	30	334	295	406	465	871	1010	817	10	86	37	0.80	57	20	23	78	86	15%	112	15%	86%	27	52%	19%	7.35	65.7	62	127	$37
10	NYY	663	111	10	67	18	270	282	340	370	710	874	632	9	84	31	0.59	65	16	18	68	57	10%	127	12%	78%	27	44%	22%	4.34	17.4	48	104	$21
11	NYY	546	84	6	61	16	297	279	355	388	743	946	666	8	85	34	0.57	62	19	19	63	63	7%	138	13%	73%	25	36%	20%	4.93	22.9	50	111	$22
12	NYY	683	99	15	58	9	316	290	362	429	791	941	723	6	87	35	0.50	62	22	16	71	44	16%	108	6%	69%	27	30%	15%	5.69	41.8	51	128	$28
13	NYY	63	8	1	7	0	190	255	288	254	542	940	348	11	84	21	0.80	70	20	9	39	27	20%	99	0%	0%	4	25%	50%	2.25	-2.3	22	55	-$3
1st Half																																		
2nd Half		63	8	1	7	0	190	255	282	254	536	940	348	11	84	21	0.80	70	20	9	39	27	20%	99	0%	0%	4	25%	50%	2.25	-2.4	22	55	-$3
14	Proj	415	61	9	43	5	273	277	342	377	719	975	606	9	85	30	0.65	63	20	18	67	50	14%	114	5%	77%				4.48	12.0	37	92	$13

Jimenez,Luis

Age	26	Bats	R	Pos	3B		
Ht	6' 1"	Wt	205				
Health	A	PT/Exp	C	Consist	B		
LIMA Plan	D	Rand Var	0	MM	1201		

0-5-.260 in 104 AB at LAA. At 26, he's not young for a prospect, and really, his anemic Eye, bb%, PX, say he's not a legitimate prospect anyway. Classic case study of a player whose skills erode at each promotion - the Peter Principle! He's an example of the lack of organizational depth that ruined LAA in 2013.

Yr	Tm	AB	R	HR	RBI	SB	BA	xBA	OBP	SLG	OPS	vL	vR	bb%	ct%	h%	Eye	G	L	F	PX	xPX	hr/f	Spd	SBO	SB%	#Wk	DOM	DIS	RC/G	RAR	BPV	BPX	R$
09																																		
10																																		
11	aa	490	52	15	79	13	256	279	288	420	708			4	84	28	0.28				114			76	20%	65%				4.02		59	131	$15
12	aaa	485	52	10	57	11	242	255	260	367	627			2	83	28	0.14				86			82	22%	58%				3.04		30	75	$9
13	LAA *	301	32	2	31	7	229	220	251	300	551	577	620	3	80	28	0.15	47	17	36	55	34	0%	104	20%	55%	8	25%	38%	2.35	-14.8	3	8	$3
1st Half		197	20	2	15	5	226	204	254	291	545	222	648	4	77	29	0.16	47	16	38	50	24	0%	120	19%	59%	6	17%	50%	2.33	-10.1	-6	-15	$4
2nd Half		104	12	1	16	2	234	248	247	317	564	1136	561	2	86	27	0.12	47	19	34	63	48	0%	84	21%	45%	2	50%	0%	2.40	-5.1	23	58	$1
14	Proj	170	18	1	22	4	238	237	283	322	605	745	548	3	83	28	0.17	47	17	36	66	38	2%	93	20%	58%				2.67	-6.8	20	51	$3

JOSH PALEY

Johnson,Chris

Age 29	Bats R	Pos 3B		Health	A	LIMA Plan	B+
				PT/Exp	B	Rand Var	-5
Ht 6' 3"	Wt 220			Consist	C	MM	3225

Nobody could have looked at the 2009-12 h% column and guessed that "40" would be the next number in the series. The rest of his skills remained about the same, with xBA on different planet from BA. To borrow from the late Al Davis, "The regression must go down and go down hard." Nobody maintains a 40% hit rate.

Yr Tm	AB	R	HR	RBI	SB	BA	xBA	OBP	SLG	OPS	vL	vR	bb%	ct%	h%	Eye	G	L	F	PX	xPX	hr/f	Spd	SBO	SB%	#Wk	DOM	DIS	RC/G	RAR	BPV	BPX	R$
09 HOU *	406	42	12	37	2	245	242	279	397	676	125	267	4	73	31	0.17	81	0	19	103	-5	0%	119	3%	60%	4	0%	75%	3.71	-3.4	19	39	$4
10 HOU *	490	59	17	76	3	297	274	326	474	800	735	848	4	76	36	0.18	41	24	35	127	117	13%	90	3%	100%	18	44%	50%	5.65	22.2	42	91	$19
11 HOU *	459	45	10	53	3	246	248	282	382	664	635	681	5	72	32	0.18	46	23	31	108	110	8%	97	6%	46%	23	26%	48%	3.55	-6.0	16	36	$7
12 2 NL	488	48	15	76	5	281	254	326	451	777	672	819	6	73	36	0.23	39	26	35	120	112	12%	108	5%	83%	27	33%	44%	5.19	16.5	34	85	$16
13 ATL	514	54	12	68	0	321	268	358	457	816	939	772	5	77	40	0.25	46	27	28	104	101	11%	71	0%	0%	26	42%	38%	6.13	29.2	27	68	$21
1st Half	217	23	5	23	0	323	261	369	465	835	992	769	7	76	41	0.31	45	25	30	113	116	10%	80	0%	0%	14	50%	36%	6.47	14.4	34	85	$15
2nd Half	297	31	7	45	0	320	275	348	451	800	888	774	4	78	39	0.20	46	29	26	98	91	12%	70	0%	0%	12	33%	42%	5.89	15.2	24	60	$25
14 Proj	**504**	**52**	**14**	**68**	**2**	**285**	**264**	**325**	**437**	**762**	**807**	**745**	**5**	**75**	**36**	**0.22**	**44**	**26**	**31**	**114**	**107**	**12%**	**88**	**2%**	**72%**				**5.01**	**14.7**	**23**	**57**	**$15**

Johnson,Elliot

Age 30	Bats B	Pos 2B		Health	A	LIMA Plan	D
				PT/Exp	D	Rand Var	+2
Ht 6' 1"	Wt 190			Consist	C	MM	1501

KC let him go after hitting .179 in 79 games. ATL picked him up and threw gasoline on the flames by deciding that he was better than Dan Uggla down the stretch and into the playoffs. Defense will keep him in the majors, Spd will get him a handful of SB, and the rest of his skills will keep him from being a starter. Pass.

Yr Tm	AB	R	HR	RBI	SB	BA	xBA	OBP	SLG	OPS	vL	vR	bb%	ct%	h%	Eye	G	L	F	PX	xPX	hr/f	Spd	SBO	SB%	#Wk	DOM	DIS	RC/G	RAR	BPV	BPX	R$
09 aaa	233	25	9	29	6	226	242	269	380	649			6	72	28	0.21				102			99	16%	71%				3.32		12	24	$3
10 aaa	427	53	8	42	22	263	237	308	384	692			6	74	34	0.25				90			121	27%	76%				4.07		17	37	$14
11 TAM	160	20	4	17	6	194	216	257	338	595	647	543	8	67	26	0.26	48	13	39	114	116	10%	127	41%	46%	25	20%	60%	2.35	-6.9	15	33	$0
12 TAM	297	32	6	33	18	242	226	304	350	654	586	688	7	72	32	0.29	47	22	31	76	81	10%	129	31%	75%	26	19%	54%	3.53	-1.1	3	8	$8
13 2 TM	254	27	2	19	22	209	212	255	283	538	579	526	6	74	28	0.24	46	20	34	54	65	3%	159	42%	92%	27	19%	63%	2.62	-8.2	0	0	$6
1st Half	128	17	2	9	11	219	200	248	297	545	556	541	4	71	29	0.14	47	18	35	54	71	6%	148	39%	100%	14	21%	64%	2.79	-3.6	-19	-48	$8
2nd Half	126	10	0	10	11	198	225	263	270	533	612	512	8	76	26	0.37	46	22	32	55	60	0%	146	45%	85%	13	15%	62%	2.46	-5.0	11	28	$4
14 Proj	**163**	**18**	**2**	**15**	**11**	**217**	**220**	**272**	**317**	**589**	**603**	**584**	**7**	**72**	**29**	**0.27**	**47**	**20**	**33**	**74**	**78**	**6%**	**140**	**37%**	**79%**				**2.88**	**-4.2**	**5**	**13**	**$4**

Johnson,Kelly

Age 32	Bats L	Pos LF 2B		Health	A	LIMA Plan	D+
				PT/Exp	B	Rand Var	0
Ht 6' 1"	Wt 200			Consist	A	MM	3303

1st half power exciting, but mediocre contact rate brought OBP to its knees and will limit BA. Traded LD% for FB% to generate power; age means no more double-digit SB. Has some limited utility as a part-timer with pop, at least when injuries or a random hot streak give him temporary bursts of regular playing time.

Yr Tm	AB	R	HR	RBI	SB	BA	xBA	OBP	SLG	OPS	vL	vR	bb%	ct%	h%	Eye	G	L	F	PX	xPX	hr/f	Spd	SBO	SB%	#Wk	DOM	DIS	RC/G	RAR	BPV	BPX	R$
09 ATL *	355	54	10	41	8	229	266	298	402	700	968	595	9	82	25	0.55	39	18	43	108	102	8%	103	12%	80%	25	52%	36%	3.98	-0.7	65	133	$5
10 ARI	585	93	26	71	13	284	277	370	496	865	953	825	12	75	34	0.53	41	21	38	149	139	16%	115	11%	65%	26	69%	15%	6.38	40.0	78	170	$25
11 2 TM	545	75	21	58	16	222	245	304	413	717	626	750	10	70	28	0.37	39	20	40	141	156	14%	114	17%	73%	27	48%	41%	4.01	0.5	49	109	$12
12 TOR	507	61	16	55	14	225	226	313	365	678	607	705	11	69	30	0.39	45	21	34	102	113	14%	93	12%	88%	27	37%	48%	3.80	-2.6	8	20	$9
13 TAM	366	41	16	52	7	235	227	305	410	715	686	723	9	73	28	0.35	39	15	46	119	116	13%	107	12%	64%	26	50%	35%	4.03	0.6	38	95	$9
1st Half	226	28	11	39	6	235	230	308	429	737	694	758	10	72	28	0.38	36	16	48	131	137	14%	112	16%	67%	14	64%	36%	4.30	1.9	48	120	$14
2nd Half	140	13	5	13	1	236	214	291	379	670	667	672	7	74	28	0.31	44	14	43	100	82	11%	96	6%	50%	12	33%	33%	3.60	-1.8	23	58	$2
14 Proj	**317**	**38**	**12**	**37**	**7**	**233**	**232**	**307**	**398**	**705**	**684**	**713**	**9**	**72**	**28**	**0.37**	**41**	**18**	**41**	**117**	**116**	**13%**	**104**	**12%**	**72%**				**4.00**	**-0.2**	**31**	**77**	**$8**

Johnson,Reed

Age 37	Bats R	Pos RF		Health	C	LIMA Plan	D
				PT/Exp	F	Rand Var	0
Ht 5' 10"	Wt 180			Consist	C	MM	2211

Lackluster results are some combination of poor Eye, inability to hit line drives, and no longer crushing lefties. It's the last one that used to give him platoon value. Milked his skills for all they were worth (which is a goodly sum of cash), but he's nearing the end of the line if he hasn't already crossed it.

Yr Tm	AB	R	HR	RBI	SB	BA	xBA	OBP	SLG	OPS	vL	vR	bb%	ct%	h%	Eye	G	L	F	PX	xPX	hr/f	Spd	SBO	SB%	#Wk	DOM	DIS	RC/G	RAR	BPV	BPX	R$
09 CHC	165	23	4	22	2	255	280	330	412	742	903	628	7	84	28	0.48	50	17	33	98	91	9%	118	8%	67%	18	44%	28%	4.31	-1.4	65	133	$2
10 LA	202	24	2	15	2	262	234	291	366	657	790	520	2	75	34	0.10	43	19	37	82	75	4%	154	9%	50%	24	33%	54%	3.43	-6.9	20	43	$2
11 CHC	246	33	5	28	2	309	263	348	467	816	797	829	2	74	40	0.08	43	21	35	132	89	8%	114	6%	67%	25	40%	44%	5.52	6.1	43	96	$8
12 2 NL	269	30	3	20	2	290	263	337	398	735	798	654	5	77	37	0.21	57	24	19	77	58	8%	132	6%	50%	27	48%	37%	4.51	-0.7	22	55	$5
13 ATL	123	13	1	11	0	244	223	311	341	653	673	637	5	74	32	0.19	56	15	29	81	70	4%	124	0%	0%	20	15%	50%	3.21	-5.0	9	23	-$1
1st Half	74	6	1	8	0	257	218	286	378	664	712	704	4	73	34	0.15	57	13	30	108	103	6%	90	0%	0%	13	15%	46%	3.71	-1.6	15	38	$0
2nd Half	49	7	0	3	0	224	213	269	286	555	594	555	6	76	30	0.25	56	17	28	41	20	0%	152	0%	0%	7	14%	57%	2.53	-2.9	-6	-15	-$3
14 Proj	**100**	**12**	**1**	**9**	**0**	**263**	**241**	**319**	**371**	**690**	**736**	**651**	**5**	**76**	**34**	**0.20**	**53**	**19**	**28**	**83**	**63**	**5%**	**128**	**3%**	**56%**				**3.78**	**-2.0**	**6**	**16**	**$2**

Jones,Adam

Age 28	Bats R	Pos CF		Health	A	LIMA Plan	D+
				PT/Exp	A	Rand Var	0
Ht 6' 3"	Wt 225			Consist	A	MM	4345

Followed 2012 breakout with more of the same. Skills were stable across the board, although he didn't hit lefties as hard. There are negatives (bb%, OBP, weak defender), but this sort of production should continue throughout his prime. About as reliable an investment as you can make on a 5-category cash cow.

Yr Tm	AB	R	HR	RBI	SB	BA	xBA	OBP	SLG	OPS	vL	vR	bb%	ct%	h%	Eye	G	L	F	PX	xPX	hr/f	Spd	SBO	SB%	#Wk	DOM	DIS	RC/G	RAR	BPV	BPX	R$
09 BAL	473	83	19	70	10	277	287	335	457	792	665	864	7	80	31	0.39	55	17	28	110	104	18%	113	11%	71%	22	41%	32%	5.23	13.4	59	120	$18
10 BAL	581	76	19	69	7	284	260	325	442	767	666	804	4	80	33	0.19	46	17	37	103	99	11%	134	10%	50%	27	41%	30%	4.71	7.8	50	109	$20
11 BAL	567	68	25	83	12	280	273	319	466	785	665	829	5	80	31	0.26	49	18	33	120	106	17%	103	12%	75%	27	52%	22%	5.17	15.0	59	131	$23
12 BAL	648	103	32	82	16	287	290	334	505	839	800	852	5	81	31	0.27	46	21	33	136	108	19%	109	16%	70%	27	59%	19%	5.70	26.9	76	190	$30
13 BAL	653	100	33	108	14	285	284	318	493	811	732	846	4	79	32	0.18	48	20	32	137	127	20%	95	12%	82%	26	62%	19%	5.49	23.0	64	160	$34
1st Half	346	56	15	57	9	292	286	308	486	793	775	809	2	81	32	0.12	49	19	32	130	129	17%	92	14%	90%	14	64%	21%	5.47	12.5	62	155	$36
2nd Half	307	44	18	51	5	277	282	315	502	816	700	895	5	77	31	0.24	47	20	32	145	123	23%	100	10%	71%	12	58%	17%	5.51	11.7	67	168	$32
14 Proj	**636**	**94**	**34**	**105**	**13**	**283**	**286**	**323**	**502**	**825**	**732**	**863**	**4**	**79**	**31**	**0.23**	**47**	**20**	**33**	**141**	**116**	**20%**	**100**	**13%**	**74%**				**5.57**	**25.2**	**71**	**177**	**$32**

Jones,Garrett

Age 33	Bats L	Pos 1B RF		Health	A	LIMA Plan	C
				PT/Exp	B	Rand Var	+3
Ht 6' 4"	Wt 230			Consist	D	MM	4223

Has made a career out of killing righties, but didn't do that in 2013. xBA says his BA should rebound, but the real story here is noticeable drop in FB%. He needs those to support his power (note xPX collapse). Along with mediocre plate discipline and age, loss of FBs will mean loss of ABs... DN: 250 AB, 10 HR.

Yr Tm	AB	R	HR	RBI	SB	BA	xBA	OBP	SLG	OPS	vL	vR	bb%	ct%	h%	Eye	G	L	F	PX	xPX	hr/f	Spd	SBO	SB%	#Wk	DOM	DIS	RC/G	RAR	BPV	BPX	R$
09 PIT *	591	78	30	81	21	273	277	333	488	821	698	1046	8	78	31	0.40	40	18	41	139	146	21%	88	19%	75%	15	67%	13%	5.63	17.6	67	137	$24
10 PIT	592	64	21	86	7	247	261	306	414	720	621	775	8	79	28	0.43	44	17	39	115	116	11%	77	7%	70%	27	52%	22%	4.29	-5.5	51	111	$13
11 PIT	423	51	16	58	6	243	258	321	433	753	460	808	10	75	29	0.46	36	20	45	141	140	11%	69	9%	67%	27	56%	26%	4.62	0.1	58	129	$10
12 PIT	475	68	27	86	2	274	277	317	516	832	532	888	6	78	30	0.32	40	18	42	152	155	17%	94	2%	100%	27	70%	19%	5.84	16.6	78	195	$19
13 PIT	403	41	15	51	2	233	266	289	419	708	317	730	7	75	28	0.31	40	24	36	135	96	14%	73	2%	100%	27	48%	30%	4.04	-6.8	46	115	$6
1st Half	234	24	7	32	1	256	263	304	419	723	192	761	6	73	33	0.25	38	28	35	130	97	12%	66	2%	100%	14	43%	29%	4.39	-0.4	29	73	$9
2nd Half	169	17	8	19	1	201	275	266	420	686	619	687	8	78	21	0.41	44	19	38	143	94	16%	91	3%	100%	13	54%	31%	3.60	-4.5	73	183	$2
14 Proj	**356**	**41**	**16**	**50**	**3**	**243**	**269**	**299**	**449**	**747**	**520**	**778**	**8**	**77**	**27**	**0.35**	**40**	**20**	**39**	**143**	**120**	**15%**	**82**	**5%**	**81%**				**4.54**	**-0.6**	**60**	**149**	**$10**

Joyce,Matt

Age 29	Bats L	Pos LF RF DH		Health	B	LIMA Plan	B
				PT/Exp	B	Rand Var	+3
Ht 6' 2"	Wt 205			Consist	B	MM	4213

Calling card has been feasting on RHP, but disturbing 3-year vR plummet bottomed out with 2H power outage. He justifiably lost his full-time gig, but still has broad, above-average skill set and at prime age. May need to get off to a good start to regain PT, but there's bounceback potential here... UP: 20 HR, .260 BA.

Yr Tm	AB	R	HR	RBI	SB	BA	xBA	OBP	SLG	OPS	vL	vR	bb%	ct%	h%	Eye	G	L	F	PX	xPX	hr/f	Spd	SBO	SB%	#Wk	DOM	DIS	RC/G	RAR	BPV	BPX	R$
09 TAM *	449	63	16	61	13	232	237	320	415	735	750	773	11	73	28	0.47	38	12	50	132	197	23%	97	16%	68%	3	67%	33%	4.34	4.9	51	104	$10
10 TAM *	308	43	12	49	3	240	259	358	448	806	263	910	16	74	29	0.70	33	18	49	151	179	13%	94	9%	33%	16	69%	19%	5.08	10.3	77	167	$7
11 TAM	462	69	19	75	13	277	269	347	478	825	657	866	10	77	32	0.46	36	21	42	144	128	12%	90	11%	93%	27	59%	22%	5.98	26.3	72	160	$20
12 TAM	399	55	17	59	4	241	244	341	429	769	631	810	12	74	28	0.54	38	19	43	124	117	13%	97	6%	57%	24	50%	29%	4.71	8.7	52	130	$9
13 TAM	413	61	18	47	7	235	259	328	419	747	499	783	13	79	26	0.68	37	20	43	124	91	13%	80	9%	70%	27	44%	41%	4.58	7.5	66	165	$11
1st Half	243	43	14	31	6	243	274	324	469	793	605	825	11	80	25	0.59	39	18	43	146	110	17%	81	11%	86%	14	50%	29%	5.17	8.4	84	210	$17
2nd Half	170	18	4	16	1	224	242	340	347	687	268	727	15	78	27	0.79	33	24	43	91	63	7%	89	5%	33%	13	38%	54%	3.74	-1.5	42	105	$1
14 Proj	**367**	**51**	**15**	**48**	**6**	**249**	**253**	**344**	**429**	**773**	**544**	**815**	**13**	**77**	**29**	**0.62**	**36**	**21**	**44**	**125**	**107**	**12%**	**89**	**8%**	**65%**				**4.94**	**10.1**	**57**	**141**	**$11**

JOSH PALEY

Kawasaki,Munenori

Age	33	Bats	L	Pos	SS		
Ht	5' 10"	Wt	165				
Health	A	LIMA Plan	D	PT/Exp	D	Rand Var	+3
Consist	D	MM	0511				

1-24-.220 with 7 SB in 240 AB at TOR. Reyes injury created a 1H opportunity, and xBA says it didn't go as badly as surface stats would indicate. Clearly he can run, and there's enough bb%/ct% skill here to support decent SB totals. It just didn't happen for him in 153 1st half ABs, and at his age that window may not open again.

Yr	Tm	AB	R	HR	RBI	SB	BA	xBA	OBP	SLG	OPS	vL	vR	bb%	ct%	h%	Eye	G	L	F	PX	xPX	hr/f	Spd	SBO	SB%	#Wk	DOM	DIS	RC/G	RAR	BPV	BPX	R$
09	for	540	71	2	33	40	242	0	291	349	640			7	84	28	0.44				66	-5		150	46%	68%				3.24	-3.8	50	102	$15
10	for	602	72	2	52	27	294	0	333	376	709			5	86	34	0.43				56	-5		127	22%	69%				4.41	16.2	42	91	$23
11	for	603	69	1	36	28	249	0	283	319	603			5	87	29	0.36				45	2		147	26%	72%				3.04	-7.8	39	87	$12
12	SEA	104	13	0	7	2	192	224	257	202	459	255	503	7	83	23	0.44	61	19	20	8	30	0%	108	15%	50%	25	16%	52%	1.52	-6.3	-13	-33	-$2
13	TOR *	300	33	1	26	9	222	251	316	285	602	438	681	12	81	27	0.73	58	22	20	39	29	3%	165	10%	90%	22	32%	32%	3.09	-3.0	32	80	$2
1st Half		162	22	1	18	8	236	272	339	328	667	416	725	14	83	28	0.94	67	17	16	54	31	5%	160	16%	89%	13	38%	31%	3.91	2.2	54	135	$8
2nd Half		138	11	0	8	1	206	230	289	235	524	471	602	10	79	26	0.54	41	30	29	21	27	0%	140	3%	100%	9	22%	33%	2.23	-5.3	-4	-10	-$4
14	Proj	**223**	**25**	**1**	**16**	**7**	**220**	**248**	**296**	**271**	**567**	**382**	**609**	**9**	**83**	**26**	**0.56**	**55**	**23**	**22**	**33**	**29**	**1%**	**149**	**15%**	**72%**				**2.58**	**-6.2**	**11**	**28**	**$0**

Kelly,Don

Age	34	Bats	L	Pos	LF CF 3B		
Ht	6' 4"	Wt	190				
Health	A	LIMA Plan	D	PT/Exp	F	Rand Var	+1
Consist	C	MM	1401				

PRO: ct%, FB%, and PX all recovered from 2012 losses; held on to bb% gains; Spd holding up well given his age. CON: h% didn't rebound, likely due to anemic LD%; PX remains substandard; Spd doesn't translate into SBs. That leaves him with a best-case offering of some empty OBP. Pass.

Yr	Tm	AB	R	HR	RBI	SB	BA	xBA	OBP	SLG	OPS	vL	vR	bb%	ct%	h%	Eye	G	L	F	PX	xPX	hr/f	Spd	SBO	SB%	#Wk	DOM	DIS	RC/G	RAR	BPV	BPX	R$
09	DET *	428	52	5	34	22	269	270	327	377	704	375	694	8	83	31	0.51	46	24	30	68	49	0%	131	22%	81%	11	27%	45%	4.39	5.2	44	90	$13
10	DET	238	30	9	27	3	244	233	272	374	646	487	663	3	82	26	0.19	32	19	49	76	91	9%	109	6%	100%	27	30%	44%	3.45	-3.7	31	67	$4
11	DET	257	35	7	28	2	245	248	291	381	672	381	698	5	88	26	0.44	29	23	48	79	72	7%	137	5%	67%	27	48%	22%	3.63	-2.5	67	149	$4
12	DET *	186	20	2	15	5	184	193	270	241	511	298	551	11	77	23	0.52	40	18	42	38	44	3%	123	12%	79%	24	21%	50%	2.08	-11.3	0	0	-$2
13	DET	216	33	6	23	2	222	230	309	343	652	574	674	11	87	23	0.96	39	15	46	70	44	7%	130	3%	100%	27	44%	26%	3.52	-2.9	67	168	$2
1st Half		100	16	3	12	2	220	236	316	360	676	733	666	12	86	23	1.00	37	16	47	81	57	7%	127	7%	100%	14	50%	21%	3.83	-0.6	73	183	$3
2nd Half		116	17	3	11	0	224	221	302	328	630	464	681	10	88	23	0.93	40	14	45	61	33	6%	121	0%	0%	13	38%	31%	3.26	-2.7	59	148	$1
14	Proj	**190**	**26**	**4**	**19**	**3**	**219**	**223**	**295**	**320**	**614**	**493**	**638**	**9**	**84**	**24**	**0.66**	**38**	**18**	**45**	**62**	**50**	**5%**	**129**	**7%**	**86%**				**3.10**	**-5.4**	**34**	**86**	**$3**

Kemp,Matt

Age	29	Bats	R	Pos	CF		
Ht	6' 4"	Wt	215				
Health	F	LIMA Plan	D+	PT/Exp	B	Rand Var	-1
Consist	F	MM	5335				

Off-season shoulder surgery led to slow start, then hamstring/shoulder/ankle injuries forced three separate DL stints plus an early shutdown. Best skill sign here is that xPX held up despite shoulder issues. Leg problems seem chronic; days of 30+ SB likely over. BA/power combo still provide a nice skill foundation, though.

Yr	Tm	AB	R	HR	RBI	SB	BA	xBA	OBP	SLG	OPS	vL	vR	bb%	ct%	h%	Eye	G	L	F	PX	xPX	hr/f	Spd	SBO	SB%	#Wk	DOM	DIS	RC/G	RAR	BPV	BPX	R$
09	LA	606	97	26	101	34	297	268	352	490	842	1045	782	8	77	35	0.37	40	21	38	119	124	14%	148	24%	81%	27	48%	11%	6.31	37.7	66	135	$35
10	LA	602	82	28	89	19	249	257	310	450	760	809	743	8	72	30	0.31	41	20	39	139	146	16%	126	24%	56%	27	56%	26%	4.41	5.7	54	117	$21
11	LA	602	115	39	126	40	324	284	399	586	986	1142	940	11	74	39	0.47	36	23	41	181	164	21%	127	26%	78%	27	74%	19%	8.73	75.9	101	224	$51
12	LA	403	74	23	69	9	303	277	367	538	906	1105	818	9	74	36	0.39	43	22	35	155	158	22%	103	11%	69%	21	48%	19%	7.08	33.3	73	183	$23
13	LA	263	35	6	33	9	270	237	328	395	723	853	671	8	71	36	0.29	40	25	35	103	142	9%	78	13%	100%	14	29%	50%	4.72	4.7	8	20	$9
1st Half		209	27	2	19	9	254	213	307	335	642	711	612	7	68	36	0.24	41	25	34	76	124	4%	84	16%	100%	11	18%	64%	3.76	-2.5	-24	-60	$10
2nd Half		54	8	4	14	0	333	332	400	630	1030	2042	853	10	81	35	0.60	36	27	36	189	201	25%	81	0%	0%	3	67%	0%	9.63	7.7	124	310	$4
14	Proj	**477**	**82**	**28**	**94**	**14**	**296**	**282**	**361**	**536**	**897**	**1165**	**810**	**9**	**74**	**35**	**0.39**	**39**	**24**	**36**	**166**	**163**	**21%**	**91**	**13%**	**80%**				**6.99**	**37.5**	**80**	**201**	**$30**

Kendrick,Howie

Age	30	Bats	R	Pos	2B		
Ht	5' 10"	Wt	205				
Health	B	LIMA Plan	B	PT/Exp	A	Rand Var	-1
Consist	B	MM	2335				

1H looked like the beginnings of a career year, before being scuttled by a cold July and an August knee injury. He breathed life into a stale skill set by turning GBs into LDs, results validated by xBA. SBO should bounce back with healthy legs, but low FB% dampens any optimism about HR total, despite erratic hr/f. UP: .300 BA, finally.

Yr	Tm	AB	R	HR	RBI	SB	BA	xBA	OBP	SLG	OPS	vL	vR	bb%	ct%	h%	Eye	G	L	F	PX	xPX	hr/f	Spd	SBO	SB%	#Wk	DOM	DIS	RC/G	RAR	BPV	BPX	R$
09	LAA *	452	69	11	69	14	290	284	327	439	767	831	745	5	81	34	0.29	54	19	27	97	86	12%	109	18%	68%	25	52%	16%	5.04	16.8	47	96	$18
10	LAA	616	67	10	75	14	279	285	313	407	721	673	741	4	85	32	0.30	53	19	28	90	93	7%	96	12%	78%	27	41%	19%	4.48	13.2	51	111	$19
11	LAA	537	86	18	63	14	285	284	338	464	802	840	782	6	78	34	0.28	52	22	27	123	127	17%	117	15%	70%	26	46%	27%	5.30	24.0	58	129	$23
12	LAA	550	57	8	67	14	287	265	325	400	725	797	694	5	79	35	0.25	59	21	21	81	87	9%	99	14%	70%	27	37%	37%	4.56	13.0	23	58	$18
13	LAA	478	55	13	54	6	297	289	335	439	775	862	745	5	81	34	0.26	51	27	21	93	88	16%	112	7%	67%	23	48%	26%	5.19	19.4	45	113	$18
1st Half		312	36	9	38	6	317	297	356	471	828	952	796	6	82	37	0.33	51	29	20	97	99	18%	122	9%	75%	14	57%	7%	6.25	21.5	55	138	$25
2nd Half		166	19	4	16	0	259	267	276	380	656	718	640	2	81	30	0.13	52	24	24	84	69	13%	85	3%	0%	9	33%	56%	3.51	-0.9	22	55	$5
14	Proj	**566**	**68**	**14**	**65**	**13**	**289**	**278**	**330**	**426**	**756**	**818**	**730**	**5**	**80**	**34**	**0.26**	**54**	**23**	**23**	**94**	**90**	**13%**	**104**	**12%**	**72%**				**4.92**	**19.4**	**38**	**96**	**$23**

Keppinger,Jeff

Age	34	Bats	R	Pos	2B 3B 1B		
Ht	6' 0"	Wt	185				
Health	C	LIMA Plan	D	PT/Exp	C	Rand Var	+2
Consist	F	MM	1031				

When your raison d'etre is to hit southpaws, and you suddenly forget how to do that, you have a serious problem. It was only 113 AB, so there might have been some sample-size flukiness contributing to the downturn. But this is why farmers diversify their crops, so they aren't left with nothing in the bad years.

Yr	Tm	AB	R	HR	RBI	SB	BA	xBA	OBP	SLG	OPS	vL	vR	bb%	ct%	h%	Eye	G	L	F	PX	xPX	hr/f	Spd	SBO	SB%	#Wk	DOM	DIS	RC/G	RAR	BPV	BPX	R$
09	HOU	305	35	7	29	0	256	282	320	387	707	802	660	8	89	27	0.82	53	18	29	74	75	9%	119	2%	0%	26	54%	23%	4.08	1.1	70	143	$3
10	HOU	514	62	6	59	4	288	292	351	393	744	810	719	9	93	30	1.42	51	20	30	72	79	4%	92	3%	80%	26	69%	4%	4.97	14.7	77	167	$14
11	2 NL *	423	43	7	37	0	273	287	297	370	667	776	645	3	94	28	0.55	47	24	29	62	61	6%	75	1%	0%	19	63%	5%	3.81	-1.6	57	127	$8
12	TAM *	406	49	9	41	1	319	283	361	429	790	923	755	6	92	33	0.80	49	23	27	63	57	9%	103	1%	100%	23	65%	13%	5.82	20.3	63	158	$14
13	CHW	423	38	4	40	0	253	259	283	317	600	586	605	5	90	27	0.49	45	24	31	41	45	3%	105	1%	0%	26	46%	31%	3.07	-10.9	37	93	$4
1st Half		242	17	2	23	0	248	250	275	298	572	567	571	4	90	27	0.39	44	25	32	29	44	3%	132	2%	0%	14	36%	36%	2.72	-9.0	34	85	$3
2nd Half		181	21	2	17	0	260	271	302	343	645	601	657	6	90	28	0.61	46	24	30	58	46	4%	80	0%	0%	12	58%	25%	3.56	-2.2	44	110	$4
14	Proj	**198**	**21**	**3**	**19**	**0**	**275**	**273**	**314**	**365**	**680**	**729**	**661**	**5**	**91**	**29**	**0.66**	**47**	**23**	**29**	**57**	**54**	**6%**	**97**	**1%**	**38%**				**4.03**	**1.9**	**35**	**88**	**$5**

Kinsler,Ian

Age	32	Bats	R	Pos	2B		
Ht	6' 0"	Wt	200				
Health	C	LIMA Plan	A	PT/Exp	A	Rand Var	0
Consist	B	MM	2335				

Turned some 2012 FBs into 2013 LDs, yielding more BA at the expense of HR. As R$ indicates, such adjustments don't materially affect value. But what will is erosion of SBs: Spd's ongoing decline has fallen to an average level, with SB% dipping into red-light territory. Days as a 5-category contributor may be at an end.

Yr	Tm	AB	R	HR	RBI	SB	BA	xBA	OBP	SLG	OPS	vL	vR	bb%	ct%	h%	Eye	G	L	F	PX	xPX	hr/f	Spd	SBO	SB%	#Wk	DOM	DIS	RC/G	RAR	BPV	BPX	R$
09	TEX	566	101	31	86	31	253	276	327	488	814	1011	738	9	86	24	0.77	30	16	54	132	133	12%	113	27%	86%	26	77%	4%	5.50	29.8	106	216	$26
10	TEX	391	73	9	45	15	286	257	382	412	794	957	743	13	85	32	0.98	40	18	42	83	90	7%	111	14%	75%	20	60%	20%	5.54	20.2	68	148	$17
11	TEX	620	121	32	77	30	255	286	355	477	832	880	816	13	89	24	1.25	35	18	47	130	125	12%	109	19%	88%	27	85%	0%	5.86	38.9	118	262	$30
12	TEX	655	105	19	72	21	256	268	326	423	749	988	671	8	86	27	0.67	38	20	42	103	88	8%	107	19%	70%	27	52%	15%	4.54	15.8	78	195	$22
13	TEX	545	85	13	72	15	277	275	344	413	757	814	733	9	89	29	0.86	37	24	39	87	109	7%	101	17%	58%	24	75%	8%	4.71	15.5	76	190	$23
1st Half		219	32	7	29	4	283	277	343	434	777	681	832	8	90	29	0.95	39	21	41	92	100	9%	81	11%	57%	11	82%	9%	5.12	8.9	78	195	$16
2nd Half		326	53	6	43	11	273	272	336	399	735	909	668	9	88	29	0.82	36	26	39	82	115	5%	114	20%	58%	13	69%	8%	4.44	7.2	73	183	$27
14	Proj	**571**	**95**	**17**	**72**	**19**	**268**	**272**	**342**	**426**	**768**	**877**	**728**	**9**	**88**	**28**	**0.86**	**37**	**21**	**42**	**99**	**106**	**8%**	**104**	**18%**	**68%**				**4.89**	**20.0**	**86**	**214**	**$24**

Kipnis,Jason

Age	27	Bats	L	Pos	2B		
Ht	5' 11"	Wt	190				
Health	A	LIMA Plan	B+	PT/Exp	A	Rand Var	-2
Consist	B	MM	4435				

PRO: Couldn't sustain 1H power surge, but xPX validates the full-season power output; lots of LDs drove BA gains; strong SB% despite average Spd. CON: xBA skeptical of BA gains due to ct% regression; 2nd consecutive 2H collapse. VERDICT: Threat of BA regression casts doubt on a repeat; he's likely to be overvalued.

Yr	Tm	AB	R	HR	RBI	SB	BA	xBA	OBP	SLG	OPS	vL	vR	bb%	ct%	h%	Eye	G	L	F	PX	xPX	hr/f	Spd	SBO	SB%	#Wk	DOM	DIS	RC/G	RAR	BPV	BPX	R$
09																																		
10	aa	315	49	7	33	5	270	261	323	417	741			7	78	33	0.36				104			121	8%	83%				4.75		48	104	$8
11	CLE *	479	74	16	61	14	248	262	312	424	736	744	878	8	76	30	0.38	45	21	34	121	126	21%	108	13%	93%	8	50%	38%	4.61	12.4	51	113	$15
12	CLE	591	86	14	76	31	257	259	335	379	714	581	787	10	82	29	0.61	47	23	30	76	91	10%	106	21%	82%	27	48%	26%	4.44	12.4	41	103	$23
13	CLE	564	86	17	84	30	284	264	366	452	818	850	801	12	75	35	0.53	43	25	32	125	128	12%	99	21%	81%	27	48%	44%	6.03	37.0	54	135	$32
1st Half		274	44	12	51	19	299	285	387	533	919	951	898	12	74	37	0.55	41	24	35	171	141	17%	92	29%	79%	14	50%	43%	7.51	29.4	88	220	$40
2nd Half		290	42	5	33	11	269	246	352	376	728	748	712	11	75	34	0.51	45	25	29	82	116	8%	106	14%	85%	13	46%	46%	4.74	8.7	23	58	$25
14	Proj	**565**	**85**	**20**	**75**	**25**	**269**	**270**	**344**	**444**	**789**	**735**	**816**	**10**	**77**	**32**	**0.49**	**45**	**24**	**32**	**120**	**114**	**15%**	**107**	**19%**	**83%**				**5.42**	**28.3**	**65**	**161**	**$27**

RAY MURPHY

Konerko,Paul

Age 38 | Bats R | Pos 1B DH | Ht 6' 2" | Wt 220
Health B | PT/Exp A | Consist D
LIMA Plan D+ | Rand Var +4 | MM 2023

A year ago in this space, we noted his 2H 2012 power outage and wondered if it signaled the beginning of his decline. He answered that in the affirmative, and with authority. xBA, xPX, and h% all say skills weren't quite as bad as results, but RHPs ate him up. Now entering the "hanging on as a platoon guy" phase of his career.

Yr	Tm	AB	R	HR	RBI	SB	BA	xBA	OBP	SLG	OPS	vL	vR	bb%	ct%	h%	Eye	G	L	F	PX	xPX	hr/f	Spd	SBO	SB%	#Wk	DOM	DIS	RC/G	RAR	BPV	BPX	R$
09	CHW	546	75	28	88	1	277	281	353	489	842	1006	779	10	84	29	0.65	36	19	46	125	140	13%	65	1%	100%	26	62%	15%	5.98	21.2	75	153	$17
10	CHW	548	89	39	111	0	312	301	393	584	977	1102	941	12	80	33	0.65	35	20	45	170	164	20%	78	1%	0%	27	59%	7%	8.43	56.6	104	226	$31
11	CHW	543	69	31	105	1	300	289	388	517	906	847	924	12	84	31	0.87	37	22	41	133	136	16%	52	1%	50%	27	56%	19%	7.26	39.7	83	184	$27
12	CHW	533	66	26	75	0	298	274	371	486	857	846	861	10	84	31	0.67	41	22	37	108	96	16%	74	0%	0%	27	63%	15%	6.45	26.9	67	168	$21
13	CHW	467	41	12	54	0	244	252	313	355	669	923	600	9	84	27	0.61	36	24	39	71	94	8%	70	0%	0%	25	48%	32%	3.72	-12.2	34	85	$6
1st Half		249	25	7	30	0	253	263	314	373	687	902	630	8	83	28	0.52	31	28	41	77	100	8%	68	0%	0%	14	50%	36%	4.00	-4.4	33	83	$8
2nd Half		218	16	5	24	0	234	236	307	335	642	952	566	10	85	25	0.72	42	21	37	64	86	7%	78	0%	0%	11	45%	27%	3.42	-7.7	37	93	$3
14	**Proj**	**347**	**34**	**11**	**45**	**0**	**258**	**257**	**335**	**395**	**730**	**856**	**693**	**10**	**84**	**28**	**0.69**	**38**	**23**	**39**	**86**	**105**	**10%**	**70**	**0%**	**0%**				**4.50**	**-1.0**	**33**	**82**	**$6**

Kottaras,George

Age 31 | Bats L | Pos CA | Ht 6' 0" | Wt 200
Health A | PT/Exp F | Consist A
LIMA Plan D | Rand Var +2 | MM 4201

Talk about your three true outcomes: 56% of his PA ended in BB, K, or HR. And his BA/OBP combo might have set a record for "lowest BA that still results in a better-than-average OBP." Oh, and more walks (24) than hits (18). All of this makes for a fun "pick him up if he's starting today" option in daily transaction leagues.

Yr	Tm	AB	R	HR	RBI	SB	BA	xBA	OBP	SLG	OPS	vL	vR	bb%	ct%	h%	Eye	G	L	F	PX	xPX	hr/f	Spd	SBO	SB%	#Wk	DOM	DIS	RC/G	RAR	BPV	BPX	R$
09	BOS *	117	16	1	10	0	247	257	339	395	734	394	769	12	73	33	0.52	30	23	48	134	129	3%	86	0%	0%	22	36%	50%	4.53	2.8	52	106	-$1
10	MIL	212	24	9	26	2	203	258	305	396	701	726	691	13	79	21	0.75	43	12	45	129	120	12%	90	4%	100%	27	56%	26%	3.98	1.7	76	165	$1
11	MIL *	213	27	8	30	0	257	253	322	439	760	513	837	9	70	33	0.32	51	19	30	140	126	19%	90	4%	0%	20	45%	50%	4.63	5.8	38	84	$4
12	2 TM	171	20	9	31	0	211	246	351	415	766	736	770	18	72	24	0.77	45	19	36	134	120	20%	78	0%	0%	27	37%	37%	4.71	5.2	56	140	$1
13	KC	100	13	5	12	1	180	216	349	370	719	614	735	19	58	25	0.57	42	21	37	166	117	24%	81	3%	100%	22	32%	45%	3.96	0.8	30	75	-$2
1st Half		49	6	2	9	1	143	196	288	327	615	536	627	17	51	22	0.42	40	16	44	196	135	18%	76	8%	100%	12	42%	33%	2.90	-1.3	20	50	-$2
2nd Half		51	7	3	3	0	216	237	385	412	796	643	836	22	65	27	0.78	44	25	31	143	102	30%	103	0%	0%	10	20%	60%	5.15	2.3	49	123	-$2
14	**Proj**	**145**	**18**	**7**	**19**	**1**	**221**	**237**	**359**	**418**	**776**	**657**	**799**	**17**	**66**	**28**	**0.60**	**44**	**20**	**36**	**152**	**119**	**20%**	**82**	**2%**	**76%**				**4.84**	**5.0**	**34**	**85**	**$3**

Kozma,Pete

Age 26 | Bats R | Pos SS | Ht 6' 0" | Wt 190
Health A | PT/Exp C | Consist B
LIMA Plan D | Rand Var 0 | MM 1201

Good place for the "scan the box for above-average skills" test: ct% has scraped 80% just once. Neither PX nor xPX has ever sniffed 100. Spd has been there a few times, but SBO and SB% history pretty much rule out any speed-related value. Oh, and BA/OBP tell us he can't find 1st base anyway. Scan complete; move along.

Yr	Tm	AB	R	HR	RBI	SB	BA	xBA	OBP	SLG	OPS	vL	vR	bb%	ct%	h%	Eye	G	L	F	PX	xPX	hr/f	Spd	SBO	SB%	#Wk	DOM	DIS	RC/G	RAR	BPV	BPX	R$
09	aa	407	41	4	29	3	191	224	252	266	518			7	77	24	0.35				52			112	6%	59%				2.09		1	2	-$5
10	aa	503	53	9	55	10	208	239	272	317	589			8	76	26	0.36				82			97	11%	82%				2.82		17	37	$3
11	STL *	415	36	2	34	1	175	204	231	231	462	583	556	7	75	23	0.29	54	15	31	48	2	0%	97	4%	39%	5	20%	60%	1.61	-25.5	-17	-38	-$8
12	STL *	520	55	9	60	7	211	266	263	320	583	1011	933	7	80	25	0.36	42	31	27	69	66	13%	131	10%	61%	6	50%	17%	2.67	-13.6	31	78	$3
13	STL	410	44	1	35	3	217	221	275	273	548	536	554	8	78	28	0.37	41	23	36	51	35	1%	93	4%	75%	27	22%	41%	2.47	-13.0	-2	-5	$0
1st Half		262	27	1	27	1	244	224	293	309	602	641	583	6	79	30	0.33	40	22	38	57	39	1%	99	3%	50%	14	29%	36%	3.02	-3.5	8	20	$3
2nd Half		148	17	0	8	2	169	217	250	209	459	407	492	10	75	23	0.43	45	24	31	41	27	0%	93	6%	100%	13	15%	46%	1.66	-8.7	-18	-45	-$7
14	**Proj**	**226**	**24**	**3**	**20**	**2**	**207**	**237**	**265**	**298**	**563**	**500**	**589**	**8**	**77**	**25**	**0.37**	**42**	**24**	**33**	**68**	**46**	**6%**	**104**	**6%**	**70%**				**2.56**	**-6.4**	**3**	**7**	**$1**

Kratz,Erik

Age 34 | Bats R | Pos CA | Ht 6' 4" | Wt 255
Health B | PT/Exp F | Consist B
LIMA Plan D+ | Rand Var +1 | MM 4003

Did a credible job filling in for Ruiz absences (suspension and injury) in 1H, then hit the DL himself with a knee injury and never got untracked upon return. Power is his one plus skill, and it's enough to keep him employed and fanalytically-relevant, at least as an injury fill-in when he earns stretches of regular playing time.

Yr	Tm	AB	R	HR	RBI	SB	BA	xBA	OBP	SLG	OPS	vL	vR	bb%	ct%	h%	Eye	G	L	F	PX	xPX	hr/f	Spd	SBO	SB%	#Wk	DOM	DIS	RC/G	RAR	BPV	BPX	R$
09	aaa	319	33	8	32	5	216	253	267	366	633			6	73	27	0.25				117			83	9%	100%				3.26		24	49	$1
10	PIT *	264	22	6	28	1	194	211	258	327	585	286	284	8	71	25	0.30	28	16	56	109	65	0%	71	6%	20%	3	0%	67%	2.55	-9.6	12	26	-$2
11	PHI *	364	40	11	38	1	226	307	280	362	642	0	2500	7	74	28	0.29	0	60	40	100	102	0%	67	2%	100%	1	100%	0%	3.36	-3.6	13	29	$3
12	PHI *	265	27	15	48	0	231	264	281	467	748	877	780	7	77	24	0.31	42	17	41	154	134	20%	48	0%	0%	16	44%	38%	4.35	5.2	63	158	$5
13	PHI	197	21	9	26	0	213	229	280	386	666	406	729	8	77	23	0.40	44	14	42	113	125	14%	61	0%	0%	21	38%	57%	3.49	-1.2	36	90	$1
1st Half		140	18	8	22	0	229	246	289	436	725	587	752	8	79	24	0.40	46	13	41	130	141	17%	56	0%	0%	10	50%	50%	4.17	1.9	53	133	$3
2nd Half		57	3	1	4	0	175	186	254	263	517	158	661	10	74	22	0.40	40	17	43	67	81	6%	79	0%	0%	11	27%	64%	2.07	-3.0	-7	-18	-$6
14	**Proj**	**258**	**25**	**12**	**35**	**0**	**222**	**237**	**286**	**404**	**690**	**559**	**736**	**8**	**76**	**25**	**0.35**	**42**	**16**	**42**	**126**	**117**	**14%**	**64**	**0%**	**0%**				**3.75**	**0.3**	**27**	**66**	**$4**

Krauss,Marc

Age 26 | Bats L | Pos LF | Ht 6' 2" | Wt 235
Health A | PT/Exp C | Consist A
LIMA Plan D | Rand Var +2 | MM 4111

4-13-.209 in 134 AB at HOU. There are hints of a workable patience-and-power skill set in this older prospect, but warts are there too: Not enough contact, no particular Spd or defensive value. His September in HOU was a bit better (.765 OPS), which might be enough to afford him another look. Don't expect much, though.

Yr	Tm	AB	R	HR	RBI	SB	BA	xBA	OBP	SLG	OPS	vL	vR	bb%	ct%	h%	Eye	G	L	F	PX	xPX	hr/f	Spd	SBO	SB%	#Wk	DOM	DIS	RC/G	RAR	BPV	BPX	R$
09																																		
10																																		
11	aa	433	48	11	45	1	210	233	281	366	647			9	68	28	0.31				123			111	5%	29%				3.22		24	53	$1
12	a/a	432	61	14	54	5	217	233	312	382	694			12	67	29	0.42				129			89	10%	48%				3.74		26	65	$6
13	HOU *	387	38	11	41	4	222	250	310	377	686	333	669	11	72	28	0.45	42	24	33	119	119	13%	73	8%	54%	14	29%	43%	3.74	-2.8	29	73	$4
1st Half		224	27	7	25	1	220	269	317	380	696	0	300	12	74	27	0.54	25	38	38	118	141	0%	88	8%	29%	3	0%	67%	3.71	-2.1	43	108	$5
2nd Half		163	11	5	16	3	226	238	300	373	673	357	701	10	69	30	0.34	44	23	33	121	116	15%	66	7%	100%	11	36%	36%	3.78	-1.2	14	35	$3
14	**Proj**	**187**	**21**	**6**	**21**	**2**	**220**	**243**	**308**	**377**	**685**	**383**	**721**	**11**	**69**	**29**	**0.40**	**44**	**23**	**33**	**126**	**104**	**13%**	**78**	**8%**	**53%**				**3.67**	**-2.0**	**20**	**51**	**$3**

Kubel,Jason

Age 32 | Bats L | Pos LF | Ht 6' 0" | Wt 220
Health B | PT/Exp C | Consist D
LIMA Plan D+ | Rand Var 0 | MM 4003

Spent a chunk of April on DL for a quad problem, then never got going. Injury doesn't seem to be an excuse for the sudden power outage that caused him to lose his job in ARI. 2H contact dip looks like he was pressing; xPX says the power is still there. Excellent rebound candidate, if he can find a job... UP: 20 HR.

Yr	Tm	AB	R	HR	RBI	SB	BA	xBA	OBP	SLG	OPS	vL	vR	bb%	ct%	h%	Eye	G	L	F	PX	xPX	hr/f	Spd	SBO	SB%	#Wk	DOM	DIS	RC/G	RAR	BPV	BPX	R$
09	MIN	514	73	28	103	1	300	292	369	539	907	643	1016	10	79	33	0.53	39	20	42	151	139	16%	61	1%	50%	27	70%	22%	7.19	38.1	78	159	$22
10	MIN	518	68	21	92	0	249	256	323	427	750	655	792	10	78	28	0.48	38	19	43	117	128	12%	68	1%	0%	27	44%	22%	4.63	2.0	46	100	$13
11	MIN	366	37	12	58	1	273	250	332	434	766	731	783	8	77	33	0.37	35	21	43	117	144	10%	59	2%	50%	19	42%	37%	5.02	5.4	35	78	$10
12	ARI	506	75	30	90	1	253	265	327	506	833	736	888	10	70	30	0.38	33	23	44	176	179	19%	73	2%	50%	27	52%	26%	5.64	17.0	65	163	$17
13	2 TM	259	21	5	32	0	216	203	293	317	610	414	642	10	64	31	0.32	33	27	41	85	149	7%	70	1%	0%	22	27%	50%	2.99	-12.0	-30	-75	-$1
1st Half		162	17	4	25	0	259	230	330	383	712	392	767	9	69	35	0.34	27	32	41	94	147	9%	77	2%	0%	12	25%	42%	4.23	-1.3	-4	-10	$4
2nd Half		97	4	1	7	0	144	138	239	206	445	452	441	11	57	24	0.29	43	16	41	65	155	4%	70	0%	0%	10	30%	60%	1.47	-9.9	-76	-190	-$8
14	**Proj**	**398**	**39**	**16**	**56**	**0**	**239**	**230**	**313**	**410**	**723**	**673**	**739**	**10**	**68**	**31**	**0.34**	**36**	**22**	**42**	**132**	**156**	**14%**	**66**	**1%**	**0%**				**4.26**	**2.8**	**9**	**21**	**$8**

Lagares,Juan

Age 25 | Bats R | Pos CF | Ht 6' 1" | Wt 175
Health A | PT/Exp C | Consist C
LIMA Plan D+ | Rand Var 0 | MM 1403

4-34-.242 with 6 SB in 392 AB at NYM. An unremarkable skill set overall, but he started getting more mileage out of it in 2H: more walks, better contact, more GBs to use his speed, even started running a bit. If you double the 2H line, add a little patience and growth, you could have a decent little player. A lot of IFs, still .. UP: 20 SB.

Yr	Tm	AB	R	HR	RBI	SB	BA	xBA	OBP	SLG	OPS	vL	vR	bb%	ct%	h%	Eye	G	L	F	PX	xPX	hr/f	Spd	SBO	SB%	#Wk	DOM	DIS	RC/G	RAR	BPV	BPX	R$
09																																		
10																																		
11	aa	162	16	2	17	8	302	243	318	410	728			2	80	37	0.11				79			108	25%	77%				4.75		21	47	$5
12	aa	499	55	3	38	17	240	226	282	323	605			6	78	30	0.27				62			107	24%	60%				2.90		8	20	$8
13	NYM *	470	43	6	40	7	247	228	281	360	641	657	620	5	76	31	0.20	49	16	36	84	81	4%	153	13%	52%	24	25%	42%	3.27	-11.6	28	70	$7
1st Half		195	18	3	13	1	241	228	261	360	621	613	528	3	75	31	0.11	36	23	41	90	110	3%	129	16%	21%	11	18%	36%	2.82	-8.1	17	43	$2
2nd Half		275	25	3	27	6	251	230	295	360	655	696	643	6	77	32	0.27	54	13	33	80	70	4%	160	12%	75%	13	31%	46%	3.61	-4.6	32	80	$10
14	**Proj**	**414**	**41**	**4**	**35**	**11**	**253**	**230**	**290**	**356**	**646**	**670**	**631**	**5**	**77**	**32**	**0.22**	**48**	**17**	**35**	**77**	**86**	**4%**	**148**	**19%**	**61%**				**3.37**	**-10.0**	**15**	**38**	**$9**

RAY MURPHY

Laird,Gerald

Age	34	Bats	R	Pos	CA	Health	B	LIMA Plan	D
Ht	6' 1"	Wt	225			PT/Exp	F	Rand Var	-5
						Consist	B	MM	1111

His thoroughly unremarkable 2013 line earns a RandVar score that basically screams "there's no way he can do THIS again." When "THIS" is 1-13-.281 in 121 AB, that's just insulting. But the real slap in the face is that sterling '1111' MM score, which is a kind of binary shorthand for "does everything equally poorly."

Yr	Tm	AB	R	HR	RBI	SB	BA	xBA	OBP	SLG	OPS	vL	vR	bb%	ct%	h%	Eye	G	L	F	PX	xPX	hr/f	Spd	SBO	SB%	#Wk	DOM	DIS	RC/G	RAR	BPV	BPX	R$
09	DET	413	49	4	33	5	225	229	306	320	626	730	591	9	84	26	0.59	41	14	44	66	67	3%	95	5%	100%	27	41%	33%	3.15	-6.8	35	71	$1
10	DET	270	22	5	25	3	207	218	263	304	567	501	611	6	79	25	0.32	43	15	42	70	106	6%	73	7%	75%	25	24%	48%	2.51	-9.9	8	17	-$1
11	STL	95	11	1	12	1	232	229	302	358	660	902	610	9	80	28	0.47	38	14	49	98	76	3%	88	9%	50%	20	45%	40%	3.43	-0.7	44	98	-$1
12	DET	174	24	2	11	0	282	256	337	374	710	622	828	7	88	31	0.67	40	23	37	59	80	4%	98	0%	0%	25	44%	40%	4.44	3.6	45	113	$2
13	ATL	121	12	1	13	1	281	247	367	372	739	667	781	10	81	34	0.61	46	22	32	75	50	3%	82	5%	50%	25	44%	44%	4.60	3.1	31	78	$1
1st Half		60	5	1	8	1	283	271	348	400	748	561	901	9	85	32	0.67	51	22	27	85	64	7%	73	6%	100%	14	43%	36%	5.07	2.3	50	125	$2
2nd Half		61	7	0	5	0	279	222	362	344	707	781	673	12	77	36	0.57	41	22	37	64	34	0%	92	5%	0%	11	45%	55%	4.14	0.8	12	30	$0
14	Proj	**190**	**22**	**2**	**18**	**1**	**257**	**242**	**333**	**353**	**686**	**655**	**705**	**9**	**82**	**30**	**0.58**	**43**	**20**	**37**	**74**	**63**	**3%**	**89**	**4%**	**48%**				**3.87**	**0.9**	**27**	**66**	**$1**

Lake,Junior

Age	24	Bats	R	Pos	LF CF	Health	A	LIMA Plan	D+
Ht	6' 3"	Wt	215			PT/Exp	D	Rand Var	-3
						Consist	B	MM	3513

6-16-.284 in 236 AB at CHC. Classic profile of a raw, toolsy prospect. PRO: Power and speed skills both into the triple-digits and still emerging. CON: No concept of what's a ball, what's a strike, and which he should swing at. Elevated h% and xBA both point to some BA regression. Worth stashing longer-term—or, check back in a year.

Yr	Tm	AB	R	HR	RBI	SB	BA	xBA	OBP	SLG	OPS	vL	vR	bb%	ct%	h%	Eye	G	L	F	PX	xPX	hr/f	Spd	SBO	SB%	#Wk	DOM	DIS	RC/G	RAR	BPV	BPX	R$
09																																		
10																																		
11	aa	242	31	5	13	14	220	223	250	326	576			4	73	28	0.15				79			123	34%	87%				2.80		2	4	$3
12	aa	405	46	8	41	17	253	231	303	385	688			7	71	34	0.25				102			96	31%	57%				3.65		12	30	$11
13	CHC *	392	49	9	30	15	274	257	311	416	727	956	692	5	73	35	0.20	42	28	30	112	79	13%	135	26%	61%	12	42%	42%	4.27	2.0	35	88	$14
1st Half		100	14	2	10	6	281	239	314	391	705			5	77	35	0.21				88			95	38%	65%				4.07		19	48	$6
2nd Half		292	35	8	20	9	272	257	310	424	735	956	692	5	72	36	0.20	42	28	30	120	79	13%	141	22%	58%	12	42%	42%	4.35	1.5	38	95	$17
14	Proj	**298**	**37**	**8**	**25**	**10**	**258**	**249**	**309**	**410**	**718**	**911**	**651**	**5**	**73**	**33**	**0.21**	**45**	**22**	**33**	**116**	**71**	**11%**	**138**	**23%**	**66%**				**4.05**	**0.3**	**29**	**73**	**$10**

Lambo,Andrew

Age	25	Bats	L	Pos	RF	Health	A	LIMA Plan	D+
Ht	6' 3"	Wt	210			PT/Exp	D	Rand Var	0
						Consist	B	MM	4101

1-2-.233 in 30 AB at PIT. Power surge breathed life into fading prospect status. Contact issues remain a significant concern, but now that issue is at least countered by legitimate HR potential. Need to see a repeat before we can fully buy in, but he's worked his way back onto our radar as a possible impact bat.

Yr	Tm	AB	R	HR	RBI	SB	BA	xBA	OBP	SLG	OPS	vL	vR	bb%	ct%	h%	Eye	G	L	F	PX	xPX	hr/f	Spd	SBO	SB%	#Wk	DOM	DIS	RC/G	RAR	BPV	BPX	R$
09	aa	492	61	9	53	3	234	260	281	368	649			6	78	28	0.30				99			89	7%	52%				3.37		34	69	$4
10	aa	272	31	5	29	1	246	228	296	350	646			7	74	32	0.27				78			110	3%	43%				3.46		6	13	$3
11	a/a	437	42	8	46	4	206	233	262	320	581			7	74	26	0.29				92			80	8%	54%				2.63		11	24	$0
12	aa	92	11	3	13	0	216	240	300	358	657			11	78	25	0.53				87			103	5%	0%				3.31		35	88	-$1
13	PIT *	474	55	23	78	5	234	247	286	443	730	2000	661	7	68	30	0.23	47	16	37	157	130	14%	106	8%	71%	8	38%	50%	4.20	-5.8	45	113	$13
1st Half		290	35	14	51	5	248	258	303	462	765			7	71	30	0.27				152			109	10%	82%				4.76		54	135	$18
2nd Half		184	21	8	26	0	213	232	261	414	674	2000	661	6	63	29	0.17	47	16	37	165	130	14%	101	3%	0%	8	38%	50%	3.40	-6.0	30	75	$4
14	Proj	**227**	**26**	**8**	**32**	**1**	**222**	**235**	**281**	**386**	**667**	**2114**	**619**	**8**	**72**	**28**	**0.29**	**47**	**16**	**37**	**121**	**117**	**13%**	**110**	**6%**	**45%**				**3.48**	**-6.7**	**21**	**53**	**$4**

LaRoche,Adam

Age	34	Bats	L	Pos	1B	Health	C	LIMA Plan	B+
Ht	6' 2"	Wt	200			PT/Exp	B	Rand Var	0
						Consist	F	MM	4215

It was erosion, not collapse, that turned 2012's career year into 2013's disappointment: ct%, FB%, hr/f, and h% all gave back a few ticks, yielding a big decline in end results. The lesson: Regression is a powerful force. His true skill level lies somewhere between 2012 and 2013, so set your expectations there.

Yr	Tm	AB	R	HR	RBI	SB	BA	xBA	OBP	SLG	OPS	vL	vR	bb%	ct%	h%	Eye	G	L	F	PX	xPX	hr/f	Spd	SBO	SB%	#Wk	DOM	DIS	RC/G	RAR	BPV	BPX	R$
09	3 TM	555	78	25	83	2	277	271	355	488	843	706	902	11	74	33	0.49	35	22	43	145	157	14%	82	3%	50%	27	56%	30%	6.10	23.8	62	127	$17
10	ARI	560	75	25	100	0	261	253	320	468	788	758	802	8	69	33	0.28	38	18	44	160	172	15%	81	1%	0%	26	50%	38%	5.11	8.5	47	102	$17
11	WAS	151	15	3	15	1	172	211	288	258	546	395	603	14	75	21	0.68	43	19	38	62	119	7%	77	2%	100%	8	13%	38%	2.34	-10.9	5	11	-$3
12	WAS	571	76	33	100	1	271	274	343	510	853	825	864	11	76	31	0.49	34	22	44	157	164	17%	76	1%	50%	27	63%	15%	6.18	25.9	75	188	$22
13	WAS	511	70	20	62	4	237	241	332	403	735	566	791	12	74	28	0.55	37	22	42	113	134	13%	100	3%	80%	26	50%	31%	4.47	-1.7	45	113	$11
1st Half		265	37	12	36	2	257	247	343	445	789	650	836	12	72	31	0.47	37	23	40	131	154	16%	103	3%	100%	14	50%	29%	5.29	5.4	48	120	$15
2nd Half		246	33	8	26	2	215	234	318	358	676	463	745	13	77	25	0.66	36	20	43	95	114	10%	96	4%	67%	12	50%	33%	3.68	-7.0	42	105	$7
14	Proj	**524**	**68**	**23**	**81**	**3**	**252**	**249**	**341**	**433**	**774**	**652**	**819**	**12**	**75**	**30**	**0.55**	**37**	**21**	**42**	**125**	**140**	**14%**	**82**	**3%**	**74%**				**5.04**	**6.9**	**44**	**109**	**$16**

Lavarnway,Ryan

Age	26	Bats	R	Pos	CA	Health	A	LIMA Plan	D
Ht	6' 4"	Wt	240			PT/Exp	D	Rand Var	+2
						Consist	B	MM	2001

1-14-.299 in 77 AB at BOS. There was real promise in the 2011 minor-league power surge, but that HR swing has disappeared as quickly as it arrived. Or has it? xPX trend provides an interesting counterpoint to this empty skill set. It's like that one lone clue in a mystery novel that ultimately reveals the killer. Tuck it away.

Yr	Tm	AB	R	HR	RBI	SB	BA	xBA	OBP	SLG	OPS	vL	vR	bb%	ct%	h%	Eye	G	L	F	PX	xPX	hr/f	Spd	SBO	SB%	#Wk	DOM	DIS	RC/G	RAR	BPV	BPX	R$
09																																		
10	aa	158	18	6	28	0	253	245	333	417	750			11	71	32	0.41				128			89	0%	0%				4.74		36	78	$3
11	BOS *	474	62	25	79	1	254	237	321	467	788	980	553	9	73	30	0.36	31	14	55	153	113	13%	86	2%	40%	6	33%	67%	5.09	19.0	59	131	$15
12	BOS *	472	53	8	47	1	233	212	297	349	645	506	437	8	77	29	0.39	43	13	44	89	120	4%	61	1%	100%	10	20%	60%	3.44	-3.8	14	35	$4
13	BOS *	257	25	3	31	0	240	249	295	337	632	724	778	7	82	28	0.43	43	23	34	75	153	5%	78	0%	0%	14	36%	36%	3.34	-2.8	28	70	$1
1st Half		157	18	2	19	0	230	311	307	343	651	808	708	10	83	26	0.67	38	38	25	88	157	0%	85	0%	0%	5	60%	40%	3.49	-1.0	51	128	$2
2nd Half		100	7	1	12	0	256	207	274	326	601	667	788	2	80	31	0.12	44	18	38	54	152	6%	79	0%	0%	9	22%	33%	3.07	-1.9	-6	-15	$0
14	Proj	**195**	**22**	**5**	**26**	**0**	**246**	**232**	**304**	**381**	**685**	**627**	**711**	**7**	**78**	**29**	**0.34**	**42**	**17**	**41**	**99**	**139**	**8%**	**72**	**0%**					**3.85**	**0.8**	**17**	**42**	**$4**

Lawrie,Brett

Age	24	Bats	R	Pos	3B	Health	D	LIMA Plan	A
Ht	6' 0"	Wt	225			PT/Exp	C	Rand Var	+2
						Consist	C	MM	3425

11-46-.254 with 9 SB in 401 AB at TOR. In between two DL stints (oblique, ankle), all of the problems that plagued him in 2012 carried over: Acceptable ct% is undermined by a heavy GB tilt and only average power and speed. That initial hot streak upon 2011 callup is becoming less and less relevant. Time to lower expectations.

Yr	Tm	AB	R	HR	RBI	SB	BA	xBA	OBP	SLG	OPS	vL	vR	bb%	ct%	h%	Eye	G	L	F	PX	xPX	hr/f	Spd	SBO	SB%	#Wk	DOM	DIS	RC/G	RAR	BPV	BPX	R$
09	aa	52	5	0	0	0	254	183	254	286	540			0	71	36	0.00				16			138	17%	0%				1.99		-60	-122	-$2
10	aa	554	73	7	51	24	263	255	312	407	719			7	76	33	0.30				103			140	29%	64%				4.16		45	98	$17
11	TOR *	442	67	21	64	15	297	282	345	546	891	786	1022	7	79	33	0.35	38	17	45	162	147	17%	129	18%	82%	8	63%	38%	6.86	35.8	101	224	$23
12	TOR	494	73	11	48	13	273	265	324	405	729	813	697	6	83	31	0.38	50	20	30	85	78	9%	106	16%	62%	23	43%	35%	4.37	6.0	45	113	$16
13	TOR *	422	45	12	48	10	252	254	308	393	701	613	742	7	82	28	0.43	49	17	34	91	89	10%	112	14%	66%	20	60%	25%	4.04	1.1	49	123	$11
1st Half		139	11	5	14	2	209	235	257	374	631	641	641	6	74	24	0.25	49	14	37	108	129	13%	135	11%	67%	7	57%	43%	3.05	-4.0	37	93	-$1
2nd Half		283	34	7	34	8	274	264	332	403	734	591	793	8	85	30	0.59	48	19	33	84	71	8%	96	15%	66%	13	62%	15%	4.59	5.0	55	138	$17
14	Proj	**502**	**63**	**15**	**56**	**14**	**262**	**262**	**321**	**422**	**743**	**708**	**755**	**7**	**81**	**30**	**0.38**	**48**	**18**	**34**	**105**	**96**	**11%**	**122**	**16%**	**67%**				**4.46**	**7.2**	**56**	**139**	**$17**

LeMahieu,DJ

Age	25	Bats	R	Pos	2B	Health	A	LIMA Plan	B
Ht	6' 4"	Wt	205			PT/Exp	C	Rand Var	-1
						Consist	A	MM	1535

2-28-.280 with18 SB in 404 AB at COL. Nice job of maximizing the value of his one skill: Makes a lot of contact without hitting many fly balls, which allows him to exploit his speed. He finally got the green light on the bases, and made most of that too. Not much room for growth, but he should be able to repeat this a few more times.

Yr	Tm	AB	R	HR	RBI	SB	BA	xBA	OBP	SLG	OPS	vL	vR	bb%	ct%	h%	Eye	G	L	F	PX	xPX	hr/f	Spd	SBO	SB%	#Wk	DOM	DIS	RC/G	RAR	BPV	BPX	R$
09																																		
10																																		
11	CHC *	474	40	4	38	6	266	260	294	341	635	667	465	4	86	30	0.27	65	17	19	54	38	0%	117	13%	40%	9	11%	56%	3.24	-5.8	30	67	$7
12	COL *	484	46	3	41	9	281	261	318	370	689	681	764	5	85	33	0.37	56	19	25	61	72	4%	145	14%	50%	17	41%	35%	3.96	4.2	44	110	$11
13	COL *	547	59	3	41	23	286	286	317	375	692	652	682	4	84	34	0.28	55	27	18	64	64	3%	141	22%	71%	20	30%	30%	4.17	8.0	39	98	$20
1st Half		277	31	2	22	16	294	295	331	398	730	746	704	5	84	35	0.35	56	28	17	73	59	6%	156	25%	82%	8	38%	25%	4.87	9.2	53	133	$24
2nd Half		270	28	1	19	7	278	279	301	352	653	596	672	3	84	33	0.21	54	27	19	56	66	2%	119	19%	54%	12	25%	33%	3.51	-1.5	25	63	$15
14	Proj	**442**	**44**	**3**	**35**	**20**	**280**	**271**	**310**	**370**	**680**	**668**	**686**	**4**	**85**	**33**	**0.29**	**55**	**22**	**23**	**64**	**63**	**3%**	**139**	**25%**	**72%**				**4.01**	**4.0**	**35**	**87**	**$16**

RAY MURPHY

Lind,Adam

Age	30	Bats	L	Pos 1B DH	Health	B	LIMA Plan B
Ht	6' 2"	Wt	220		PT/Exp	B	Rand Var -3
					Consist	C	MM 4225

Improving patience, Eye are fueling BA trend. But that 1H h% was huge and suggests at least a mild pullback. Apart from 2012 back woes, power metrics are gyrating within a productive range, making 20 HR a good bet. LHP issues are cutting those AB (96), but he remains a productive 1B option. A H2Her who won't hurt you.

Yr	Tm	AB	R	HR	RBI	SB	BA	xBA	OBP	SLG	OPS	vL	vR	bb%	ct%	h%	Eye	G	L	F	PX	xPX	hr/f	Spd	SBO	SB%	#Wk	DOM	DIS	RC/G	RAR	BPV	BPX	R$
09	TOR	587	93	35	114	1	305	311	370	562	932	780	992	9	81	33	0.53	43	20	37	161	141	20%	63	1%	50%	26	73%	12%	7.54	48.8	93	190	$27
10	TOR	569	57	23	72	0	237	258	287	425	712	341	829	6	75	28	0.26	41	19	40	133	135	13%	69	0%	0%	27	44%	26%	4.05	-7.5	40	87	$8
11	TOR	499	56	26	87	1	251	263	295	439	734	639	771	6	79	27	0.30	40	22	38	119	135	17%	66	2%	50%	24	50%	38%	4.39	-1.6	43	96	$14
12	TOR *	457	45	17	65	1	274	250	332	445	778	553	795	8	78	32	0.40	48	17	35	110	101	12%	89	1%	100%	18	56%	17%	5.21	9.2	45	113	$12
13	TOR	465	67	23	67	1	288	279	357	497	854	573	924	10	78	33	0.50	46	21	33	140	141	19%	81	1%	100%	27	52%	19%	6.40	24.6	69	173	$19
1st Half		223	34	11	33	1	327	288	393	547	940	864	950	10	79	38	0.51	44	22	34	147	157	18%	91	1%	100%	14	64%	21%	8.18	21.7	82	205	$23
2nd Half		242	33	12	34	0	252	267	327	450	778	335	900	10	77	28	0.48	48	20	32	134	125	20%	74	0%	0%	13	38%	15%	5.02	3.7	59	148	$16
14	Proj	479	60	22	72	1	274	267	336	467	803	567	876	9	78	31	0.43	45	20	35	129	128	17%	78	1%	83%				5.53	12.7	47	118	$15

Lobaton,Jose

Age	29	Bats	B	Pos CA	Health	C	LIMA Plan D+
Ht	6' 0"	Wt	210		PT/Exp	F	Rand Var -1
					Consist	C	MM 2003

Health woes (knee, shoulder) may have factored into poor 2011-12. But really, the minor league track record (.250 BA) speaks volumes, as does the fact that the only time he's batted higher than .225 was 139 AB in the 1st half. He might have good skill waiting on pitches, but we don't need to wait around for him.

Yr	Tm	AB	R	HR	RBI	SB	BA	xBA	OBP	SLG	OPS	vL	vR	bb%	ct%	h%	Eye	G	L	F	PX	xPX	hr/f	Spd	SBO	SB%	#Wk	DOM	DIS	RC/G	RAR	BPV	BPX	R$
09	SD *	234	23	5	16	0	213	215	277	324	601	0	353	8	71	28	0.31	50	17	33	85	-5	0%	101	0%	0%	2	0%	100%	2.91	-5.8	1	2	-$2
10	a/a	265	22	5	27	1	214	221	279	309	588			8	74	27	0.35				72			91	1%	100%				2.81		0	0	-$1
11	TAM *	218	20	6	23	0	216	237	314	344	658	390	349	12	68	29	0.44	46	27	27	102	21	0%	72	0%	0%	7	14%	57%	3.52	-1.3	1	2	-$1
12	TAM *	195	17	2	21	0	201	200	295	291	586	751	584	12	71	27	0.47	48	16	36	78	100	5%	69	2%	0%	21	29%	52%	2.68	-6.3	-5	-13	-$3
13	TAM	277	38	7	32	0	249	256	320	394	714	653	745	10	77	30	0.46	44	23	32	104	82	10%	101	1%	0%	27	52%	22%	4.25	4.3	41	103	$4
1st Half		139	20	4	18	0	273	253	331	417	748	733	753	8	79	32	0.41	41	22	38	103	100	10%	92	0%	0%	14	50%	21%	4.85	4.5	44	110	$6
2nd Half		138	18	3	14	0	225	259	314	370	684	579	738	12	74	28	0.50	48	25	26	105	61	11%	106	3%	0%	13	54%	23%	3.71	0.0	37	93	$2
14	Proj	312	35	6	34	0	232	234	316	352	668	671	667	11	73	30	0.45	45	22	33	93	86	8%	89	1%	5%				3.64	-0.7	6	15	$4

Lombardozzi,Steve

Age	25	Bats	B	Pos 2B LF	Health	A	LIMA Plan D
Ht	6' 0"	Wt	200		PT/Exp	C	Rand Var 0
					Consist	A	MM 1321

PRO: Excellent ct%, still young. CON: Everything else. Poor patience, zero power, declining Spd and a poor running game. 2H produced a small-sample glimmer, but he offers empty BA at best. Even his new positional versatility won't help much.

Yr	Tm	AB	R	HR	RBI	SB	BA	xBA	OBP	SLG	OPS	vL	vR	bb%	ct%	h%	Eye	G	L	F	PX	xPX	hr/f	Spd	SBO	SB%	#Wk	DOM	DIS	RC/G	RAR	BPV	BPX	R$
09																																		
10	aa	105	17	4	10	3	276	294	341	477	818			9	85	29	0.65				118			131	20%	62%				5.47		93	202	$3
11	WAS *	587	73	7	43	24	273	244	310	371	681	0	459	5	85	31	0.35	44	19	37	64	29	0%	125	22%	73%	4	25%	50%	3.99	5.7	41	91	$18
12	WAS	384	40	3	27	5	273	252	317	354	671	532	715	5	88	30	0.41	47	20	33	52	46	3%	118	8%	63%	27	26%	26%	3.77	1.2	41	103	$7
13	WAS	290	25	2	22	4	259	258	278	338	616	659	601	3	88	29	0.24	50	20	31	57	45	3%	101	11%	57%	27	41%	30%	3.15	-4.3	36	90	$3
1st Half		175	15	0	14	2	234	250	251	297	549	556	539	2	87	27	0.18	52	19	29	49	41	0%	112	14%	40%	14	43%	29%	2.32	-7.4	29	73	$2
2nd Half		115	10	2	8	2	296	269	319	400	719	897	682	3	90	32	0.33	46	21	32	70	51	6%	90	7%	100%	13	38%	31%	4.73	3.3	50	125	$5
14	Proj	168	17	2	13	3	272	258	307	361	668	649	673	4	88	30	0.35	48	20	32	60	47	3%	113	12%	67%				3.77	0.3	34	86	$4

Loney,James

Age	30	Bats	L	Pos 1B	Health	A	LIMA Plan B
Ht	6' 3"	Wt	220		PT/Exp	B	Rand Var -2
					Consist	F	MM 1135

Suddenly productive again, just in time to save everyday role. A close look reveals no skill changes—apart from some serious LD%-and-h% inflation, and some brief 1H success vs. LHP. Regression is a lock; see 2010-2011 for benchmarks. And be mindful that the AB of a power-challenged 30-year-old 1Bman are always at risk.

Yr	Tm	AB	R	HR	RBI	SB	BA	xBA	OBP	SLG	OPS	vL	vR	bb%	ct%	h%	Eye	G	L	F	PX	xPX	hr/f	Spd	SBO	SB%	#Wk	DOM	DIS	RC/G	RAR	BPV	BPX	R$
09	LA	576	73	13	90	7	281	276	357	399	756	779	750	11	88	30	1.03	43	22	35	70	65	7%	81	5%	70%	27	59%	15%	5.07	7.5	57	116	$17
10	LA	588	67	10	88	10	267	284	329	395	723	575	785	8	84	30	0.55	43	25	32	92	79	6%	77	10%	67%	27	56%	7%	4.43	-3.0	50	109	$16
11	LA	531	56	12	65	4	288	272	339	416	755	561	816	7	87	31	0.63	41	22	37	85	79	7%	87	3%	100%	27	48%	15%	5.12	7.6	60	133	$16
12	2 TM	434	37	6	41	0	249	266	293	336	630	508	662	6	88	27	0.55	46	25	29	58	65	5%	62	3%	0%	27	33%	26%	3.26	-17.3	32	80	$4
13	TAM	549	54	13	75	3	299	297	348	430	778	729	797	7	86	33	0.57	42	30	28	89	77	10%	66	2%	75%	27	48%	22%	5.48	13.2	52	130	$20
1st Half		278	35	9	40	3	313	306	368	475	842	957	799	8	87	34	0.65	42	29	29	106	82	13%	77	5%	75%	14	71%	14%	6.47	14.1	73	183	$25
2nd Half		271	19	4	35	0	284	289	333	384	717	529	795	7	85	32	0.50	42	31	27	72	71	6%	62	0%	0%	13	23%	31%	4.56	-0.3	33	83	$15
14	Proj	454	43	9	57	2	281	279	331	396	727	629	761	7	87	31	0.59	44	26	30	78	73	8%	68	3%	60%				4.64	0.6	37	92	$13

Longoria,Evan

Age	28	Bats	R	Pos 3B	Health	D	LIMA Plan B+
Ht	6' 2"	Wt	210		PT/Exp	B	Rand Var -1
					Consist	A	MM 4125

Contact trend doesn't bode well for BA improvement, but that's our only quibble. Power is his game, and all of his power and FB metrics climbed to elite levels in 2013. Perfect health fueled his season, and the record shows that this is really his only risk. If your roster construction can handle that exposure, he's still a top 3B pick.

Yr	Tm	AB	R	HR	RBI	SB	BA	xBA	OBP	SLG	OPS	vL	vR	bb%	ct%	h%	Eye	G	L	F	PX	xPX	hr/f	Spd	SBO	SB%	#Wk	DOM	DIS	RC/G	RAR	BPV	BPX	R$
09	TAM	584	100	33	113	9	281	289	364	526	889	909	881	11	76	32	0.51	39	19	42	164	148	18%	80	6%	100%	27	67%	19%	6.81	47.2	83	169	$26
10	TAM	574	96	22	104	15	294	283	372	507	879	956	845	11	78	34	0.58	37	20	43	150	142	11%	123	12%	75%	25	76%	4%	6.80	45.8	95	207	$29
11	TAM	483	78	31	99	3	244	286	355	495	850	943	819	14	81	24	0.86	37	18	45	158	137	18%	85	4%	60%	23	70%	17%	5.82	26.9	105	233	$18
12	TAM *	303	39	17	57	2	276	264	357	491	848	1064	842	11	76	31	0.53	38	22	40	137	147	20%	83	6%	40%	14	57%	21%	5.99	17.7	64	160	$11
13	TAM	614	91	32	88	1	269	264	343	498	842	950	799	10	74	32	0.43	37	19	45	164	173	16%	83	1%	100%	27	63%	33%	5.98	35.8	73	183	$23
1st Half		302	52	17	47	0	298	275	371	550	921	1062	861	10	75	35	0.47	34	18	48	175	189	15%	90	0%	0%	14	64%	36%	7.41	28.5	92	230	$28
2nd Half		312	39	15	41	1	240	253	317	449	766	845	737	10	72	29	0.40	40	19	41	152	156	16%	80	1%	100%	13	62%	31%	4.79	7.6	55	138	$18
14	Proj	592	86	32	99	2	266	269	349	495	844	951	805	11	76	30	0.51	38	19	43	157	156	17%	83	2%	68%				5.96	34.0	70	174	$24

Lough,David

Age	28	Bats	L	Pos RF	Health	A	LIMA Plan D+
Ht	5' 11"	Wt	180		PT/Exp	C	Rand Var -4
					Consist	C	MM 1411

5-33-.286 in 315 AB at KC. Inflated h% and AB translated into profit. He has impressive Spd, but doesn't look close to translating it into more than a handful of SBs. Without power or patience, he still profiles as a 4th OF. No longer a youngster, and barring improvement in something other than ct%, 2013 was his peak.

Yr	Tm	AB	R	HR	RBI	SB	BA	xBA	OBP	SLG	OPS	vL	vR	bb%	ct%	h%	Eye	G	L	F	PX	xPX	hr/f	Spd	SBO	SB%	#Wk	DOM	DIS	RC/G	RAR	BPV	BPX	R$
09	aa	236	32	6	24	10	297	281	324	445	770			4	87	32	0.30				89			108	25%	69%				5.07		59	120	$9
10	aaa	460	48	7	43	10	245	254	290	367	657			6	83	28	0.37				72			155	14%	64%				3.51		50	109	$7
11	aaa	456	60	6	45	10	269	268	307	398	705			5	88	30	0.45				79			132	17%	51%				4.00		67	149	$12
12	KC *	550	55	6	48	18	224	229	252	327	579	452	614	4	85	25	0.24	40	18	42	60	49	0%	142	21%	79%	6	17%	0%	2.73	-26.1	38	95	$6
13	KC *	469	57	7	46	9	285	257	311	406	718	745	718	4	84	33	0.24	42	23	35	79	46	5%	136	14%	52%	21	38%	24%	4.28	0.0	48	120	$15
1st Half		275	36	4	27	5	297	266	324	427	751	665	824	4	85	34	0.27	51	18	31	84	44	6%	149	17%	40%	8	38%	13%	4.57	1.0	61	153	$19
2nd Half		194	21	3	19	4	268	247	294	376	670	765	638	3	82	31	0.20	36	26	38	72	47	5%	114	11%	80%	13	38%	31%	3.87	-3.2	29	73	$10
14	Proj	236	27	3	22	6	264	245	297	370	666	665	667	4	84	30	0.26	41	21	38	68	47	3%	134	16%	65%				3.64	-5.6	39	97	$6

Lowrie,Jed

Age	30	Bats	B	Pos SS 2B	Health	F	LIMA Plan B+
Ht	6' 0"	Wt	190		PT/Exp	B	Rand Var -2
					Consist	B	MM 4225

FB% decline clipped power more than new home venue. But aggressiveness, ct%-and-LD upticks and inflated h% fueled BA spike. When combined with health, his AB and value soared. A good bet to be productive again, albeit with more power and less BA. But be mindful that one healthy year doesn't remove the risk.

Yr	Tm	AB	R	HR	RBI	SB	BA	xBA	OBP	SLG	OPS	vL	vR	bb%	ct%	h%	Eye	G	L	F	PX	xPX	hr/f	Spd	SBO	SB%	#Wk	DOM	DIS	RC/G	RAR	BPV	BPX	R$
09	BOS *	141	14	4	20	0	171	191	260	311	571	687	391	11	76	19	0.50	24	10	66	95	155	6%	87	0%	0%	10	40%	50%	2.49	-4.2	29	59	-$3
10	BOS	171	31	9	24	1	287	292	381	526	907	1025	823	13	85	29	1.00	29	16	54	153	166	11%	88	4%	50%	12	67%	8%	6.99	17.2	118	257	$6
11	BOS	309	40	6	36	1	252	226	303	382	685	876	582	7	81	30	0.38	33	18	49	87	120	5%	125	3%	50%	20	35%	40%	3.92	4.5	45	100	$5
12	HOU	340	43	16	42	2	244	253	331	438	769	623	819	11	81	26	0.66	29	19	51	121	162	11%	93	2%	100%	18	50%	17%	4.90	14.8	73	183	$7
13	OAK	603	80	15	75	1	290	272	344	446	791	772	800	8	85	32	0.55	33	23	43	108	99	7%	93	1%	100%	26	69%	8%	5.53	35.3	71	178	$21
1st Half		298	37	5	34	1	309	280	380	433	812	727	858	10	86	35	0.81	35	27	38	91	86	5%	83	1%	100%	14	50%	14%	6.09	21.2	64	160	$20
2nd Half		305	43	10	41	0	272	268	308	459	767	813	740	5	84	30	0.33	32	20	49	125	112	8%	105	0%	0%	12	92%	0%	4.96	13.0	79	198	$21
14	Proj	448	59	18	56	1	265	265	327	455	783	795	777	9	83	29	0.54	32	20	48	125	125	10%	98	1%	79%				5.18	22.1	67	168	$14

JOCK THOMPSON

Lucas,Edward

Age 32	Bats R	Pos 3B 1B 2B	Health A	LIMA Plan D
Ht 6' 3"	Wt 210		PT/Exp C	Rand Var -3
			Consist C	MM 1103

4-28-.256 in 351 AB at MIA. Career minor-leaguer got opportunity created by injuries to rebuilding team. Versatility and h% earned him AB, and fueled small profit as a lefty-killer. Minor league numbers—.278/.350/.399 in 3300 AB—aren't awful. But combination of sub-par ct%, bb%, PX and running game doesn't get our hopes up.

Yr	Tm	AB	R	HR	RBI	SB	BA	xBA	OBP	SLG	OPS	vL	vR	bb%	ct%	h%	Eye	G	L	F	PX	xPX	hr/f	Spd	SBO	SB%	#Wk	DOM	DIS	RC/G	RAR	BPV	BPX	R$
09	a/a	363	46	7	44	13	241	243	318	360	678			10	75	30	0.46				87			95	17%	79%				3.90		21	43	$7
10	aaa	352	35	8	34	5	243	244	310	362	672			9	77	30	0.42				87			96	6%	79%				3.80		26	57	$4
11	a/a	421	39	7	38	3	180	196	234	266	500			7	65	26	0.20				76			86	3%	100%				1.96		-36	-80	-$5
12	aaa	412	35	6	30	3	180	209	210	263	473			4	73	23	0.14				61			90	12%	35%				1.61		-21	-53	-$5
13	MIA *	532	62	8	38	2	250	240	297	341	638	883	544	6	76	32	0.28	47	25	29	71	40	5%	99	3%	52%	19	16%	47%	3.40	-9.3	4	10	$7
1st Half		268	33	5	16	1	258	228	306	352	658	863	676	6	75	33	0.28	39	24	37	74	31	4%	104	4%	53%	6	17%	33%	3.65	-2.5	6	15	$8
2nd Half		264	29	3	22	1	242	245	288	330	618	886	498	6	77	31	0.27	49	25	26	68	43	6%	98	3%	50%	13	15%	54%	3.16	-6.4	4	10	$6
14	Proj	395	41	5	31	3	228	222	277	309	586	791	500	6	74	30	0.24	47	22	31	66	38	5%	95	5%	56%				2.75	-14.8	-20	-49	$1

Lucroy,Jonathan

Age 28	Bats R	Pos CA	Health B	LIMA Plan B+
Ht 6' 0"	Wt 195		PT/Exp B	Rand Var 0
			Consist F	MM 3335

Expected h% regression brought BA back to earth, but Eye, bb% continued march forward. Picked his spots to run in the 2H and killed it. Held ct% and LD/FB swing, and two consecutive seasons of 130+ xPX suggests power breakout looming. Already one of the better bets at his position, with health... UP: .300 BA, 25 HR.

Yr	Tm	AB	R	HR	RBI	SB	BA	xBA	OBP	SLG	OPS	vL	vR	bb%	ct%	h%	Eye	G	L	F	PX	xPX	hr/f	Spd	SBO	SB%	#Wk	DOM	DIS	RC/G	RAR	BPV	BPX	R$
09	aa	419	50	8	54	1	236	264	341	367	707			14	82	27	0.86				92			91	2%	42%				4.14		57	116	$3
10	MIL *	399	36	6	38	4	256	237	298	336	634	735	589	6	84	29	0.36	44	19	38	56	79	5%	89	6%	67%	20	30%	30%	3.41	-3.3	20	43	$5
11	MIL	430	45	12	59	2	265	248	313	391	703	869	662	6	77	32	0.29	42	24	34	87	83	11%	92	3%	67%	25	36%	40%	4.21	6.3	20	44	$10
12	MIL	316	46	12	58	4	320	284	368	513	881	1169	782	7	86	34	0.50	41	21	37	112	130	12%	123	6%	80%	20	60%	15%	7.00	27.9	86	215	$16
13	MIL	521	59	18	82	9	280	281	340	455	795	859	775	8	87	29	0.67	39	23	38	104	135	10%	109	7%	90%	27	48%	7%	5.53	26.9	81	203	$21
1st Half		239	21	8	42	2	268	271	311	435	746	749	750	6	86	28	0.45	40	22	39	95	135	10%	128	5%	67%	14	36%	7%	4.68	6.7	73	183	$15
2nd Half		282	38	10	40	7	291	290	361	472	833	1065	790	10	87	31	0.86	39	24	38	112	134	11%	97	8%	100%	13	62%	8%	6.30	20.3	89	223	$26
14	Proj	517	62	19	80	7	285	276	342	461	803	961	755	8	85	31	0.55	40	22	38	108	120	11%	110	6%	85%				5.63	27.9	71	178	$22

Ludwick,Ryan

Age 35	Bats R	Pos LF	Health F	LIMA Plan C+
Ht 6' 2"	Wt 215		PT/Exp C	Rand Var +3
			Consist F	MM 3013

2-12-.240 in 129 AB at CIN. Opening Day shoulder injury shelved him until Aug, and predictably, his power was out for the year. Stable baseline skills, xPX suggest that the HR may rebound with health. But the volatile bottom lines and age warn to not bet the house on it. Inconsistency is a threat to his playing time.

Yr	Tm	AB	R	HR	RBI	SB	BA	xBA	OBP	SLG	OPS	vL	vR	bb%	ct%	h%	Eye	G	L	F	PX	xPX	hr/f	Spd	SBO	SB%	#Wk	DOM	DIS	RC/G	RAR	BPV	BPX	R$
09	STL	486	63	22	97	4	265	251	329	447	775	742	787	8	78	30	0.39	33	19	48	112	126	12%	86	5%	67%	26	35%	38%	4.96	12.7	46	94	$15
10	2 NL	490	63	17	69	0	251	255	325	418	743	609	800	9	75	30	0.40	32	23	45	120	126	10%	115	3%	0%	24	42%	42%	4.37	4.6	52	113	$10
11	2 NL	490	56	13	75	1	237	222	310	363	674	763	644	9	75	29	0.41	34	19	47	95	124	7%	72	2%	50%	26	27%	35%	3.73	-4.8	17	38	$8
12	CIN	422	53	26	80	0	275	288	346	531	877	937	853	9	77	30	0.43	33	24	43	166	127	18%	68	1%	0%	27	59%	26%	6.30	26.9	81	203	$16
13	CIN *	167	8	3	15	0	209	219	254	295	549	783	577	6	76	26	0.25	36	24	41	64	62	5%	70	0%	0%	9	11%	44%	2.41	-8.4	-10	-25	-$3
1st Half		0	0	0	0	0	0	0	1000	0	1000			100	0	0	0.00				0	-15	0%	87	0%	0%	1	0%	100%	0.00	0.0	-172	-430	-$3
2nd Half		167	8	3	15	0	209	219	245	295	540	783	564	5	76	26	0.20	36	24	41	64	62	5%	70	0%	0%	8	13%	38%	2.33	-8.7	-14	-35	-$3
14	Proj	387	41	14	61	1	252	243	313	410	723	787	701	8	76	30	0.35	34	22	44	111	107	11%	74	2%	34%				4.29	3.1	20	51	$10

Machado,Manny

Age 21	Bats R	Pos 3B	Health A	LIMA Plan B
Ht 6' 2"	Wt 180		PT/Exp C	Rand Var 0
			Consist A	MM 3325

Precocious youngster's season started fast and went downhill, culminating in knee surgery that casts a shadow on April readiness. Skill set is a work-in-progress; he's living on raw athleticism (but you need two good knees for that). H% reversal killed 2H; but sub-par bb%, PX volatility, raw running game say a breakout isn't imminent.

Yr	Tm	AB	R	HR	RBI	SB	BA	xBA	OBP	SLG	OPS	vL	vR	bb%	ct%	h%	Eye	G	L	F	PX	xPX	hr/f	Spd	SBO	SB%	#Wk	DOM	DIS	RC/G	RAR	BPV	BPX	R$
09																																		
10																																		
11																																		
12	BAL *	593	73	17	74	13	254	251	310	417	727	801	716	8	81	29	0.44	46	14	40	103	100	12%	133	12%	75%	9	44%	44%	4.40	8.0	64	160	$16
13	BAL	667	88	14	71	6	283	277	314	432	746	762	738	4	83	32	0.26	47	21	32	107	73	8%	121	9%	46%	26	62%	12%	4.64	13.2	65	163	$22
1st Half		358	53	6	42	6	321	301	349	489	837	739	877	4	84	37	0.25	47	24	29	127	72	7%	115	12%	60%	14	79%	0%	6.22	21.7	80	200	$31
2nd Half		309	35	8	29	0	239	244	272	366	638	781	555	4	83	27	0.26	47	17	36	83	75	9%	129	5%	0%	12	42%	25%	3.19	-7.4	46	115	$11
14	Proj	435	52	12	46	4	258	265	290	418	708	751	690	4	82	29	0.25	47	17	36	110	84	9%	128	7%	56%				4.09	1.5	50	124	$11

Maldonado,Martin

Age 27	Bats R	Pos CA	Health A	LIMA Plan D
Ht 6' 0"	Wt 235		PT/Exp D	Rand Var +5
			Consist B	MM 2001

A year ago, BPI were pessimistic despite a small-sample HR burst upon arrival in MIL. Apart from hr/f and some bad luck, little changed in 2013 as his offense fell apart. His h% will rebound, and he's not this awful. But BA/xBA and mediocre power history says he's a poor fantasy bet, even for the catching-starved.

Yr	Tm	AB	R	HR	RBI	SB	BA	xBA	OBP	SLG	OPS	vL	vR	bb%	ct%	h%	Eye	G	L	F	PX	xPX	hr/f	Spd	SBO	SB%	#Wk	DOM	DIS	RC/G	RAR	BPV	BPX	R$
09	aaa																																	
10	a/a	277	21	7	28	1	214	225	261	337	598			6	70	28	0.22				97			88	7%	18%				2.69		0	0	-$1
11	MIL *	343	33	8	42	1	236	225	288	353	641	0	0	7	73	30	0.27	44	20	36	91	2	0%	63	3%	55%	3	0%	100%	3.36	-3.4	-2	-4	$3
12	MIL *	354	30	11	40	1	233	230	281	370	651	612	766	6	72	29	0.24	43	23	34	97	78	14%	68	5%	23%	19	37%	53%	3.32	-4.0	0	0	$3
13	MIL	183	13	4	22	0	169	195	236	284	520	446	543	7	71	21	0.25	42	14	44	87	101	7%	80	0%	0%	26	27%	65%	1.96	-10.3	-6	-15	-$4
1st Half		116	8	3	14	0	190	213	236	328	563	324	682	6	71	24	0.21	42	16	42	103	106	9%	88	0%	0%	14	29%	57%	2.43	-4.7	5	13	-$3
2nd Half		67	5	1	8	0	134	160	205	209	414	817	339	8	72	17	0.32	43	9	48	59	93	5%	72	0%	0%	12	25%	75%	1.26	-5.6	-26	-65	-$6
14	Proj	163	13	5	19	0	217	209	277	342	620	604	624	7	71	28	0.26	43	16	41	94	90	9%	72	2%	29%				2.98	-3.7	-13	-33	$1

Marisnick,Jake

Age 23	Bats R	Pos CF	Health A	LIMA Plan D+
Ht 6' 3"	Wt 225		PT/Exp F	Rand Var 0
			Consist C	MM 3411

1-5-.183 in 109 AB at MIA. Toolsy prospect was overmatched in 2H callup after leap-frogging Triple-A; Double-A power from 1H didn't translate. Once-outstanding running game (career 84/20 SB/CS) regressed all year; he'll need it to compensate for sub-par bb% and ct%. Has an MLB future, but needs more minor league time now.

Yr	Tm	AB	R	HR	RBI	SB	BA	xBA	OBP	SLG	OPS	vL	vR	bb%	ct%	h%	Eye	G	L	F	PX	xPX	hr/f	Spd	SBO	SB%	#Wk	DOM	DIS	RC/G	RAR	BPV	BPX	R$
09																																		
10																																		
11																																		
12	aa	223	21	2	12	12	221	232	251	319	569			4	79	27	0.19				69			118	37%	73%				2.58		14	35	$2
13	MIA *	374	43	11	45	12	246	243	288	392	680	431	498	6	72	32	0.21	42	25	33	105	55	4%	116	23%	62%	9	22%	67%	3.63	-4.7	19	48	$11
1st Half		201	27	7	32	9	257	243	296	436	733			5	71	33	0.19				128			120	32%	61%				4.13		33	83	$16
2nd Half		173	16	4	13	4	234	231	278	340	618	431	498	6	73	30	0.23	42	25	33	78	55	4%	109	15%	65%	9	22%	67%	3.08	-5.0	0	0	$4
14	Proj	233	24	7	20	8	238	245	278	387	666	581	701	5	74	30	0.20	42	23	35	106	50	11%	118	24%	65%				3.42	-5.3	25	62	$6

Markakis,Nick

Age 30	Bats L	Pos RF	Health B	LIMA Plan B+
Ht 6' 1"	Wt 190		PT/Exp A	Rand Var 0
			Consist D	MM 1135

Here are his year-by-year Rotisserie values since his 2007 breakout: $31, $27, $22, $21, $21, $15, $15 and that last value was purely playing-time driven. I'd call that a trend. You can scan his various indicators and try to pick things apart, but you'd be hard-pressed to find a reason to bet on much improvement.

Yr	Tm	AB	R	HR	RBI	SB	BA	xBA	OBP	SLG	OPS	vL	vR	bb%	ct%	h%	Eye	G	L	F	PX	xPX	hr/f	Spd	SBO	SB%	#Wk	DOM	DIS	RC/G	RAR	BPV	BPX	R$
09	BAL	642	94	18	101	6	293	272	347	453	801	682	882	8	85	32	0.57	43	17	41	103	118	8%	112	4%	75%	27	67%	4%	5.71	25.5	73	149	$22
10	BAL	629	79	12	60	7	297	274	370	436	805	906	762	10	85	33	0.78	46	18	36	97	82	6%	129	5%	78%	27	67%	7%	5.86	27.6	80	174	$21
11	BAL	641	72	15	73	12	284	275	351	406	756	628	809	9	88	30	0.83	43	23	34	78	96	8%	92	8%	80%	27	59%	15%	5.04	13.9	63	140	$21
12	BAL	420	59	13	54	1	298	303	363	471	834	877	816	9	88	31	0.82	42	27	31	105	111	11%	103	2%	50%	18	78%	6%	6.15	21.7	87	218	$15
13	BAL	634	89	10	59	1	271	259	329	356	685	651	704	8	88	30	0.72	47	23	31	56	71	6%	100	2%	33%	27	48%	19%	4.07	-3.8	45	113	$15
1st Half		333	49	8	42	0	282	283	332	405	738	592	803	7	89	30	0.71	48	23	29	78	79	9%	91	2%	0%	14	64%	14%	4.67	2.1	64	160	$20
2nd Half		301	40	2	17	1	259	232	326	302	629	701	579	9	86	29	0.73	45	22	33	30	63	2%	117	1%	100%	13	31%	23%	3.42	-9.0	25	63	$10
14	Proj	608	82	12	63	1	277	270	340	391	732	712	742	9	88	30	0.76	44	23	32	74	87	7%	105	2%	43%				4.65	3.5	44	110	$17

JOCK THOMPSON

Marte,Starling

Age 25	Bats R	Pos LF	Health B	LIMA Plan B+
Ht 6' 2"	Wt 185		PT/Exp B	Rand Var -2
			Consist B	MM 4525

Outstanding first full season for lefty-killer. Could have been even better had hand injury not shelved him for a month late in 2H. Tremendous physical tools transcended deep flaws in plate approach. Ceiling is a tough call, but legs, improving running game provide nice value floor. With better pitch selection, the sky is his limit.

Yr	Tm	AB	R	HR	RBI	SB	BA	xBA	OBP	SLG	OPS	vL	vR	bb%	ct%	h%	Eye	G	L	F	PX	xPX	hr/f	Spd	SBO	SB%	#Wk	DOM	DIS	RC/G	RAR	BPV	BPX	R$
09																																		
10																																		
11	aa	536	74	9	40	19	297	260	319	436	755			3	80	36	0.16				100			118	26%	59%				4.71		45	100	$21
12	PIT *	555	71	14	68	29	255	262	294	430	723	1042	627	5	73	32	0.21	57	18	25	112	83	18%	187	40%	61%	9	33%	44%	3.94	-1.9	52	130	$20
13	PIT	510	83	12	35	41	280	259	343	441	784	1053	724	5	73	36	0.18	51	22	28	116	98	12%	195	47%	73%	24	29%	33%	4.73	10.0	55	138	$30
1st Half		313	52	8	26	22	288	269	316	466	782	1111	744	4	76	36	0.17	52	19	29	121	94	12%	199	42%	73%	14	29%	29%	5.09	9.7	69	173	$35
2nd Half		197	31	4	9	19	269	245	311	401	712	961	692	6	69	37	0.19	49	26	25	106	106	13%	157	53%	73%	10	30%	40%	4.19	1.0	19	48	$23
14	**Proj**	**586**	**87**	**16**	**49**	**39**	**272**	**260**	**329**	**445**	**774**	**1046**	**698**	**5**	**73**	**35**	**0.19**	**50**	**20**	**30**	**121**	**94**	**13%**	**184**	**43%**	**69%**				**4.53**	**8.9**	**52**	**129**	**$27**

Martin,Leonys

Age 26	Bats L	Pos CF RF	Health A	LIMA Plan B+
Ht 6' 2"	Wt 190		PT/Exp D	Rand Var -2
			Consist D	MM 2525

Running game surprised and drove value in first complete MLB season. Power was a disappointment, though xPX says not totally unexpected. Ct% and PX history say gains are possible, but work vs. LHPs and 2H fade are worrisome. Speculate that the pitch selection improves; at 26, he should have figured it out by now.

Yr	Tm	AB	R	HR	RBI	SB	BA	xBA	OBP	SLG	OPS	vL	vR	bb%	ct%	h%	Eye	G	L	F	PX	xPX	hr/f	Spd	SBO	SB%	#Wk	DOM	DIS	RC/G	RAR	BPV	BPX	R$
09																																		
10																																		
11	TEX *	295	38	3	29	13	262	314	306	364	669	0	875	6	88	29	0.52	57	29	14	68	37	0%	122	33%	54%	4	25%	25%	3.45	-7.0	57	127	$8
12	TEX *	277	40	10	35	10	291	294	341	496	837	500	624	7	80	34	0.37	47	24	29	135	55	0%	102	30%	49%	12	42%	42%	5.39	9.3	74	185	$12
13	TEX	457	66	8	49	36	260	255	313	385	698	573	749	6	77	32	0.27	51	21	28	88	62	8%	140	40%	80%	27	30%	26%	4.09	-1.9	35	88	$23
1st Half		188	32	5	15	16	293	275	338	452	790	494	870	6	79	35	0.33	52	22	25	101	66	14%	168	35%	89%	14	43%	14%	5.82	8.7	61	153	$23
2nd Half		269	34	3	34	20	238	240	278	338	616	603	644	5	76	30	0.23	50	20	30	78	58	5%	116	45%	74%	13	15%	38%	3.11	-8.8	15	38	$23
14	**Proj**	**526**	**75**	**10**	**59**	**31**	**264**	**268**	**317**	**404**	**721**	**595**	**773**	**6**	**79**	**32**	**0.31**	**51**	**21**	**28**	**98**	**61**	**9%**	**131**	**36%**	**68%**				**4.10**	**-1.2**	**53**	**134**	**$23**

Martin,Russell

Age 31	Bats R	Pos CA	Health B	LIMA Plan C
Ht 5' 10"	Wt 205		PT/Exp B	Rand Var 0
			Consist A	MM 3115

Even with slow leak in ct%, consistent history indicates there's not much guesswork here. He still offers decent power, good patience, and a handful of SB while dragging your BA down. That scares off some owners, but there is profit potential at a scarce position if you can snag him cheaply enough.

Yr	Tm	AB	R	HR	RBI	SB	BA	xBA	OBP	SLG	OPS	vL	vR	bb%	ct%	h%	Eye	G	L	F	PX	xPX	hr/f	Spd	SBO	SB%	#Wk	DOM	DIS	RC/G	RAR	BPV	BPX	R$
09	LA	505	63	7	53	11	250	254	352	329	680	756	660	12	84	28	0.86	49	21	31	53	81	5%	91	10%	65%	26	31%	19%	3.75	0.8	33	67	$8
10	LA	331	45	5	26	6	248	253	347	332	679	682	678	13	82	29	0.79	51	21	28	61	69	6%	84	7%	75%	18	39%	33%	3.89	1.8	28	61	$5
11	NYY	417	57	18	65	8	237	268	324	408	732	684	750	11	81	25	0.62	47	19	33	110	110	16%	67	9%	80%	27	41%	19%	4.37	8.5	54	120	$11
12	NYY	422	50	21	53	6	211	264	311	403	713	880	643	11	77	22	0.56	48	19	33	121	107	20%	57	7%	86%	27	52%	22%	3.93	3.0	48	120	$6
13	PIT	438	51	15	55	9	226	244	327	377	703	610	729	12	75	27	0.54	51	17	33	108	104	14%	69	12%	64%	26	38%	35%	3.86	2.2	34	85	$9
1st Half		226	29	8	30	5	248	275	328	416	744	820	742	11	81	27	0.64	54	17	29	115	116	15%	75	11%	71%	14	57%	21%	4.59	6.0	64	160	$13
2nd Half		212	22	7	25	4	203	210	305	335	639	422	715	13	69	26	0.47	46	16	37	99	89	13%	69	12%	57%	12	17%	50%	3.17	-3.6	3	8	$5
14	**Proj**	**420**	**50**	**16**	**53**	**8**	**224**	**249**	**324**	**379**	**703**	**695**	**706**	**12**	**77**	**26**	**0.57**	**49**	**18**	**33**	**107**	**101**	**15%**	**65**	**10%**	**69%**				**3.89**	**2.3**	**36**	**91**	**$9**

Martinez,J.D.

Age 26	Bats R	Pos LF RF	Health C	LIMA Plan D
Ht 6' 3"	Wt 220		PT/Exp C	Rand Var 0
			Consist C	MM 2103

Lost power reappeared in 1H, but both bb% and ct% collapsed in the process. Health (knee, wrist) finally aborted his season in late July. First-half PX/xPX metrics look interesting, but he's never shown enough primary plate skills to take consistent advantage of it. Age remains a plus, but he's running out of chances.

Yr	Tm	AB	R	HR	RBI	SB	BA	xBA	OBP	SLG	OPS	vL	vR	bb%	ct%	h%	Eye	G	L	F	PX	xPX	hr/f	Spd	SBO	SB%	#Wk	DOM	DIS	RC/G	RAR	BPV	BPX	R$
09																																		
10	aa	189	21	3	22	2	281	230	327	379	706			6	75	36	0.28				75			106	7%	45%				4.24		7	15	$4
11	HOU *	525	66	16	88	1	283	277	339	444	783	1119	620	8	78	33	0.39	37	28	36	117	124	10%	78	1%	42%	10	50%	30%	5.31	19.7	48	107	$18
12	HOU *	485	38	11	58	0	230	224	292	349	641	690	683	8	76	28	0.37	52	17	32	81	79	12%	96	3%	0%	22	36%	32%	3.28	-10.2	16	40	$3
13	HOU	296	24	7	36	2	250	236	272	378	650	621	664	3	72	32	0.12	44	22	34	103	109	9%	84	3%	100%	18	33%	61%	3.57	-3.5	5	13	$4
1st Half		214	21	7	30	2	248	241	278	402	680	710	663	4	72	31	0.15	45	20	35	119	122	13%	85	5%	100%	12	42%	50%	3.84	-1.2	19	48	$7
2nd Half		82	3	0	6	0	256	225	265	317	582	487	667	1	73	35	0.05	42	27	32	63	73	0%	90	0%	0%	6	17%	83%	2.88	-2.7	-26	-65	-$4
14	**Proj**	**266**	**21**	**5**	**31**	**1**	**243**	**238**	**280**	**361**	**641**	**637**	**643**	**5**	**75**	**31**	**0.20**	**45**	**22**	**33**	**92**	**93**	**8%**	**89**	**3%**	**53%**				**3.38**	**-5.1**	**-4**	**-9**	**$4**

Martinez,Victor

Age 35	Bats B	Pos DH	Health F	LIMA Plan B+
Ht 6' 2"	Wt 210		PT/Exp C	Rand Var -1
			Consist C	MM 2035

Back from torn ACL and lost 2012, it was like he'd never left. Started slowly due to to unfortunate h%, roared back and then some in 2H when his luck turned. Even with age and inactivity, the basic hitting skills haven't changed. xPX even suggests the HR may return. Catcher eligibility likely gone for good, but... UP: 20 HR

Yr	Tm	AB	R	HR	RBI	SB	BA	xBA	OBP	SLG	OPS	vL	vR	bb%	ct%	h%	Eye	G	L	F	PX	xPX	hr/f	Spd	SBO	SB%	#Wk	DOM	DIS	RC/G	RAR	BPV	BPX	R$
09	2 AL	588	88	23	108	1	303	294	381	480	861	847	866	11	87	32	1.01	43	21	35	103	108	13%	78	1%	100%	27	70%	4%	6.71	35.5	80	163	$23
10	BOS	493	64	20	79	1	302	291	351	493	844	1173	694	8	89	31	0.77	41	17	42	116	112	11%	86	1%	100%	23	70%	9%	6.40	25.7	94	204	$20
11	DET	540	76	12	103	1	330	298	380	470	850	823	861	8	91	35	0.90	43	24	33	95	94	7%	73	1%	100%	26	58%	8%	6.85	33.4	78	173	$27
12																																		
13	DET	605	68	14	83	0	301	275	355	430	785	735	813	8	90	32	0.87	42	22	35	84	126	7%	76	1%	0%	26	62%	8%	5.54	17.3	67	168	$22
1st Half		297	29	6	40	0	232	240	296	337	633	531	670	8	88	25	0.75	44	18	38	68	132	6%	67	1%	0%	14	43%	14%	3.27	-11.1	45	113	$9
2nd Half		308	39	8	43	0	367	309	418	519	937	881	980	8	92	38	1.04	40	27	33	99	120	9%	89	1%	0%	12	83%	0%	8.64	31.8	90	225	$34
14	**Proj**	**610**	**78**	**16**	**97**	**1**	**315**	**284**	**368**	**461**	**830**	**839**	**825**	**8**	**90**	**33**	**0.88**	**42**	**22**	**36**	**95**	**114**	**8%**	**76**	**1%**	**36%**				**6.33**	**30.1**	**62**	**156**	**$28**

Mastroianni,Darin

Age 28	Bats R	Pos LF	Health F	LIMA Plan D
Ht 5' 11"	Wt 190		PT/Exp F	Rand Var 0
			Consist D	MM 1501

0-5-.185 with 2 SB in 65 AB at MIN. Lost out to Aaron Hicks experiment in March, then shelved by ankle injury in mid-April. Post-surgery rehab was interrupted by hyper-extended knee, showed little in Sept return. His legs are his game, but now these are questionable. A return to health offers an outside chance of a small profit.

Yr	Tm	AB	R	HR	RBI	SB	BA	xBA	OBP	SLG	OPS	vL	vR	bb%	ct%	h%	Eye	G	L	F	PX	xPX	hr/f	Spd	SBO	SB%	#Wk	DOM	DIS	RC/G	RAR	BPV	BPX	R$
09	aa	247	36	1	23	35	251	228	347	320	667			13	79	32	0.69				50			118	52%	80%				4.08		17	35	$13
10	aa	525	72	3	33	33	248	229	320	328	648			10	78	31	0.48				59			139	29%	74%				3.58		21	46	$15
11	TOR *	490	60	2	24	22	214	88	274	298	571	0	0	8	80	26	0.42	0	0	100	61	2	0%	158	30%	65%	1	0%	100%	2.55	-22.2	35	78	$4
12	MIN *	276	34	3	25	32	246	232	308	325	634	710	653	8	73	33	0.33	46	29	25	52	59	10%	172	46%	85%	21	33%	57%	3.72	-2.1	4	10	$12
13	MIN *	115	11	0	8	5	186	172	250	210	460	500	415	8	68	27	0.27	40	21	40	27	84	0%	101	20%	83%	8	13%	88%	1.75	-8.2	-56	-140	-$2
1st Half		9	1	0	0	1	222	266	300	222	522	0	583	10	89	25	1.00	63	25	13	0	79	0%	112	67%	50%	3	33%	67%	1.63	-0.8	11	28	-$2
2nd Half		106	10	0	8	4	183	159	246	209	455	524	377	8	67	27	0.25	34	20	46	30	85	0%	94	15%	100%	5	0%	100%	1.75	-7.7	-64	-160	-$2
14	**Proj**	**224**	**27**	**3**	**16**	**15**	**237**	**214**	**308**	**323**	**631**	**708**	**583**	**9**	**74**	**31**	**0.37**	**40**	**22**	**38**	**64**	**75**	**4%**	**140**	**28%**	**84%**				**3.44**	**-3.9**	**7**	**17**	**$7**

Mathis,Jeff

Age 31	Bats R	Pos CA	Health C	LIMA Plan D
Ht 6' 0"	Wt 205		PT/Exp F	Rand Var +1
			Consist C	MM 2101

Forecaster veterans should turn the page. For newcomers who find themselves needing a #2 catcher in-season, you may run across this name in a hot stretch; like his .290 BA (62 AB) in June, followed by two HR to begin July. Lightning-in-a-bottle opportunity? Don't even think about it. Just scan the BA/xBA and R$ history.

Yr	Tm	AB	R	HR	RBI	SB	BA	xBA	OBP	SLG	OPS	vL	vR	bb%	ct%	h%	Eye	G	L	F	PX	xPX	hr/f	Spd	SBO	SB%	#Wk	DOM	DIS	RC/G	RAR	BPV	BPX	R$
09	LAA	237	26	5	28	2	211	196	288	308	596	625	582	8	69	28	0.30	37	17	46	73	77	7%	100	8%	40%	27	22%	63%	2.65	-7.7	-15	-31	-$1
10	LAA *	238	23	4	21	3	193	184	221	280	500	580	467	3	70	26	0.12	39	13	48	66	72	4%	126	7%	100%	19	11%	68%	2.00	-12.7	-19	-41	-$2
11	LAA	247	18	3	22	1	174	196	225	259	484	469	494	6	70	24	0.20	39	18	43	76	81	4%	81	7%	33%	27	26%	59%	1.71	-16.0	-22	-49	-$5
12	TOR	211	25	8	27	1	218	229	249	393	642	660	635	4	68	28	0.13	36	20	44	136	118	13%	79	3%	100%	26	38%	46%	3.23	-3.0	14	35	$1
13	MIA	232	14	5	29	0	181	199	251	284	535	698	464	8	67	25	0.28	43	20	37	81	87	9%	98	0%	0%	20	25%	60%	2.21	-11.0	-17	-43	-$4
1st Half		62	4	2	11	0	129	239	182	306	488	521	478	6	74	14	0.25	45	15	40	123	113	11%	99	0%	0%	8	50%	50%	1.63	-4.4	39	98	-$4
2nd Half		170	10	3	18	0	200	183	273	276	549	809	460	9	65	29	0.28	42	22	36	63	76	8%	90	0%	0%	12	8%	67%	2.40	-7.0	-44	-110	-$4
14	**Proj**	**210**	**17**	**5**	**26**	**1**	**206**	**209**	**258**	**330**	**588**	**657**	**554**	**6**	**69**	**27**	**0.22**	**40**	**19**	**41**	**99**	**95**	**9%**	**90**	**2%**	**61%**				**2.70**	**-6.6**	**-18**	**-44**	**$1**

JOCK THOMPSON

Mauer,Joe

Age 31	Bats L	Pos CA DH	Health D	LIMA Plan B+	
Ht 6' 5"	Wt 230		PT/Exp B	Rand Var -5	
			Consist C	MM 3045	

A case study in the roto-importance of context. 2012/2013 skills were nearly identical, but loss of 100 AB, drops in Runs and RBI took a bite out of his dollar value. Soaring LD% and h% held firm all year until concussion ended season in mid-August. Durability remains a value-capper, which continues to elevate risk.

Yr	Tm	AB	R	HR	RBI	SB	BA	xBA	OBP	SLG	OPS	vL	vR	bb%	ct%	h%	Eye	G	L	F	PX	xPX	hr/f	Spd	SBO	SB%	#Wk	DOM	DIS	RC/G	RAR	BPV	BPX	R$
09	MIN	523	94	28	96	4	365	325	444	587	1031	910	1103	13	88	38	1.21	48	23	30	124	118	20%	83	2%	80%	24	75%	8%	10.51	88.7	103	210	$35
10	MIN	510	88	9	75	1	327	310	402	469	871	711	978	11	90	35	1.23	47	24	29	98	126	7%	88	3%	20%	27	67%	4%	6.98	44.4	88	191	$23
11	MIN	296	38	3	30	0	287	270	360	368	729	562	829	10	87	32	0.84	55	23	22	60	75	5%	93	0%	0%	17	47%	18%	4.70	8.1	46	102	$6
12	MIN	545	81	10	85	8	319	286	416	446	861	754	918	14	84	37	1.02	53	25	22	83	113	10%	95	5%	67%	27	67%	7%	6.89	46.6	61	153	$25
13	MIN	445	62	11	47	0	324	288	404	476	880	882	879	12	80	39	0.69	47	28	25	115	113	12%	91	1%	0%	21	57%	24%	7.22	41.4	65	163	$18
1st Half		300	49	8	26	0	320	288	404	480	884	947	863	12	79	39	0.66	46	28	26	121	124	13%	100	0%	0%	14	57%	29%	7.26	28.4	68	170	$22
2nd Half		145	13	3	21	0	331	287	409	469	878	783	917	12	83	38	0.76	49	27	24	102	92	10%	84	2%	0%	7	57%	14%	7.12	13.1	63	158	$11
14	Proj	491	66	13	65	1	315	290	398	464	863	770	908	12	84	36	0.88	50	25	25	103	104	12%	88	2%	32%				6.81	41.1	57	141	$19

Maxwell,Justin

Age 30	Bats R	Pos RF CF	Health D	LIMA Plan D+	
Ht 6' 5"	Wt 220		PT/Exp D	Rand Var +1	
			Consist B	MM 4503	

7-25-.252 with 6 SB in 234 AB at KC and HOU. April broken hand shelved him 8 weeks, then ended 1H on DL with a concussion. His 2012 power returned in 2H vs. RHP, but falling FB% curbed HR output. Running game still has upside, despite SBO trend. But consistently awful ct% casts a giant shadow over that power/speed combo.

Yr	Tm	AB	R	HR	RBI	SB	BA	xBA	OBP	SLG	OPS	vL	vR	bb%	ct%	h%	Eye	G	L	F	PX	xPX	hr/f	Spd	SBO	SB%	#Wk	DOM	DIS	RC/G	RAR	BPV	BPX	R$
09	WAS *	473	67	14	42	34	214	201	295	351	646	615	897	10	61	32	0.29	48	14	38	106	120	19%	172	36%	76%	10	30%	60%	3.39	-18.2	1	2	$12
10	WAS *	334	42	8	28	17	209	195	315	338	653	729	407	13	61	32	0.39	35	16	49	125	110	10%	107	29%	65%	18	28%	44%	3.31	-13.8	3	7	$5
11	aaa	177	28	14	27	8	222	240	302	507	810			10	51	33	0.24				268			95	28%	78%				4.98		71	158	$6
12	HOU	315	46	18	53	9	229	239	304	460	764	892	697	9	64	30	0.28	44	16	39	171	134	23%	128	19%	69%	25	56%	40%	4.46	1.8	51	128	$10
13	2 AL *	283	39	8	28	7	224	235	289	383	672	710	797	8	66	31	0.27	48	20	32	131	77	14%	142	14%	77%	19	47%	37%	3.64	-5.5	30	75	$4
1st Half		137	17	2	9	3	195	217	255	305	559	863	601	7	70	27	0.27	47	19	34	86	32	4%	149	13%	73%	6	33%	50%	2.45	-8.7	10	25	$0
2nd Half		146	22	6	19	4	252	249	320	457	777	644	986	9	62	36	0.27	49	21	30	178	113	23%	119	15%	80%	13	54%	31%	5.00	2.4	48	120	$8
14	Proj	254	37	10	32	8	227	226	303	410	713	706	717	9	62	32	0.27	45	18	37	152	102	17%	132	19%	75%				4.00	-3.5	28	71	$8

Mayberry,John

Age 30	Bats R	Pos RF CF	Health A	LIMA Plan D+	
Ht 6' 6"	Wt 225		PT/Exp C	Rand Var +5	
			Consist B	MM 4213	

Began the year as the weak part of a platoon, but an uptick vs. RHP earned more consideration. Then he couldn't sustain 1H gains, as depressed h% turned 2H into a nightmare. xPX is skeptical of his power, and in this case, bb% / ct% consistency isn't a good thing. A part-timer unless something changes—which is unlikely.

Yr	Tm	AB	R	HR	RBI	SB	BA	xBA	OBP	SLG	OPS	vL	vR	bb%	ct%	h%	Eye	G	L	F	PX	xPX	hr/f	Spd	SBO	SB%	#Wk	DOM	DIS	RC/G	RAR	BPV	BPX	R$
09	PHI *	373	43	15	42	5	219	224	275	402	676	831	527	7	64	30	0.21	35	18	47	143	164	25%	115	10%	67%	12	33%	50%	3.56	-5.7	21	43	$4
10	PHI *	507	63	14	57	16	226	194	270	353	623	1500	952	6	73	28	0.23	50	0	50	94	182	50%	116	19%	78%	5	40%	60%	3.16	-13.9	16	35	$9
11	PHI *	380	49	18	60	9	256	273	310	466	775	953	785	7	78	28	0.36	42	18	40	144	109	17%	82	15%	76%	23	52%	22%	4.91	9.6	68	151	$13
12	PHI	441	53	14	46	1	245	248	301	395	695	811	626	7	75	30	0.31	52	20	28	106	74	15%	92	1%	100%	27	33%	48%	4.00	-0.7	28	70	$7
13	PHI	353	47	11	39	5	227	253	286	391	677	756	646	7	75	27	0.30	43	20	37	124	81	11%	113	11%	63%	27	44%	33%	3.56	-5.3	47	118	$6
1st Half		180	28	6	21	5	256	268	313	439	752	792	733	8	76	31	0.34	43	22	35	136	97	13%	115	20%	63%	14	57%	29%	4.53	2.7	63	158	$11
2nd Half		173	19	5	18	0	197	233	249	341	590	719	555	6	73	24	0.26	43	19	39	111	64	10%	104	0%	0%	13	31%	38%	2.69	-7.2	29	73	$0
14	Proj	326	41	11	38	4	232	255	290	401	691	795	632	7	74	28	0.29	44	20	35	125	90	13%	102	8%	69%				3.76	-6.8	36	90	$7

Maybin,Cameron

Age 27	Bats R	Pos CF	Health F	LIMA Plan B	
Ht 6' 3"	Wt 205		PT/Exp C	Rand Var +5	
			Consist C	MM 2515	

1-5-.157 in 51 AB with SD. Injury-riddled season (wrist, knee) finally ended by Sept wrist surgery. He should enter March healthy, but remains a question mark. BPIs looked stagnant even pre-injury. GB% caps any power potential. Running game, defense, and age keep him relevant. Buy the SBs and hope his legs fuel a BA spike.

Yr	Tm	AB	R	HR	RBI	SB	BA	xBA	OBP	SLG	OPS	vL	vR	bb%	ct%	h%	Eye	G	L	F	PX	xPX	hr/f	Spd	SBO	SB%	#Wk	DOM	DIS	RC/G	RAR	BPV	BPX	R$
09	FLA *	474	65	6	44	7	275	259	342	412	754	646	767	9	75	35	0.41	55	17	28	97	80	12%	152	9%	59%	12	50%	42%	4.84	10.1	44	90	$10
10	FLA *	421	62	11	45	13	252	230	308	379	687	584	697	8	71	33	0.28	53	14	33	90	100	13%	170	14%	80%	16	31%	56%	4.02	-0.9	25	54	$11
11	SD	516	82	9	40	40	264	251	323	393	716	751	703	8	76	33	0.35	55	16	29	93	93	8%	175	35%	83%	25	44%	36%	4.54	6.7	48	107	$22
12	SD	507	67	8	45	26	243	242	306	349	656	630	666	8	78	30	0.40	55	16	28	71	88	7%	139	25%	79%	27	37%	33%	3.62	-7.2	30	75	$14
13	SD *	97	11	3	8	5	176	249	257	298	555	435	481	10	79	19	0.52	55	19	26	75	45	9%	101	30%	68%	5	20%	60%	2.31	-5.7	28	70	-$1
1st Half		82	11	3	8	5	191	254	268	315	584	435	481	10	80	21	0.52	55	19	26	77	45	9%	101	35%	68%	5	20%	60%	2.58	-4.3	32	80	-$1
2nd Half																																		
14	Proj	416	59	8	38	22	257	243	328	374	701	672	713	9	77	32	0.40	55	17	28	81	77	9%	144	25%	77%				4.16	-0.1	29	73	$16

McCann,Brian

Age 30	Bats L	Pos CA	Health B	LIMA Plan B+	
Ht 6' 3"	Wt 230		PT/Exp B	Rand Var +1	
			Consist C	MM 3025	

A solid recovery from torn labrum. LD% and xBA say it could have been even better with a little h% luck. But his power rebounded fully, and his plate skills look identical to the pre-injury version. Concerns over slippage vs. LHP somewhat abated by that 2H. Healthy again, he's still a Top 10 contributor at catcher.

Yr	Tm	AB	R	HR	RBI	SB	BA	xBA	OBP	SLG	OPS	vL	vR	bb%	ct%	h%	Eye	G	L	F	PX	xPX	hr/f	Spd	SBO	SB%	#Wk	DOM	DIS	RC/G	RAR	BPV	BPX	R$
09	ATL	488	63	21	94	4	281	291	349	486	834	634	932	9	83	30	0.59	38	21	41	128	137	13%	61	4%	80%	26	65%	12%	5.97	31.3	73	149	$17
10	ATL	479	63	21	77	5	269	268	375	453	828	783	845	13	80	30	0.76	37	20	43	122	144	13%	69	4%	71%	27	59%	26%	5.79	28.8	65	141	$16
11	ATL	466	51	24	71	3	270	252	351	466	817	794	826	11	81	29	0.64	38	16	47	123	162	14%	65	4%	60%	25	56%	28%	5.64	26.0	65	144	$16
12	ATL	439	44	20	67	3	230	252	300	399	698	673	711	9	83	24	0.58	40	19	41	98	131	13%	57	3%	100%	27	48%	37%	4.00	4.0	47	118	$8
13	ATL	356	43	20	57	0	256	273	336	461	796	616	869	10	81	26	0.59	35	22	42	125	150	16%	70	1%	0%	21	67%	29%	5.13	15.0	69	173	$11
1st Half		136	14	9	24	0	250	289	346	478	824	445	979	13	82	25	0.80	35	25	40	134	168	20%	63	2%	0%	9	78%	22%	5.47	7.1	80	200	$7
2nd Half		220	29	11	33	0	259	263	318	450	768	719	799	8	81	27	0.46	36	21	44	119	139	14%	86	0%	0%	12	58%	33%	4.92	7.8	64	160	$13
14	Proj	453	52	23	72	2	253	264	332	447	779	666	830	10	82	26	0.61	37	20	43	119	146	15%	64	2%	60%				4.99	17.0	53	134	$15

McCutchen,Andrew

Age 27	Bats R	Pos CF	Health A	LIMA Plan C	
Ht 5' 10"	Wt 185		PT/Exp A	Rand Var -3	
			Consist D	MM 4545	

Contact, line drive spikes helped hold most of 2012 gains. Aggressive approach produced slow start, but career-best plate skills in 2nd half fueled terrific finish (huge 46% h% in August helped). But he remains at a prime age, with many paths to value... UP: 30 HR/30 SB.

Yr	Tm	AB	R	HR	RBI	SB	BA	xBA	OBP	SLG	OPS	vL	vR	bb%	ct%	h%	Eye	G	L	F	PX	xPX	hr/f	Spd	SBO	SB%	#Wk	DOM	DIS	RC/G	RAR	BPV	BPX	R$
09	PIT *	634	108	15	71	30	283	273	352	457	810	921	811	10	83	32	0.62	42	19	39	104	114	9%	184	21%	81%	19	68%	11%	5.79	30.6	91	186	$27
10	PIT	570	94	16	56	33	286	279	365	449	814	903	784	11	84	32	0.79	43	19	38	106	115	9%	154	24%	77%	27	67%	22%	5.84	28.5	92	200	$28
11	PIT	572	87	23	89	23	259	266	364	456	820	945	779	13	78	30	0.71	38	20	42	135	142	12%	115	19%	70%	27	63%	15%	5.52	24.2	83	184	$24
12	PIT	593	107	31	96	20	327	281	400	553	953	1144	900	11	78	38	0.53	44	22	34	140	147	19%	142	16%	63%	27	56%	19%	7.99	62.8	89	223	$40
13	PIT	583	97	21	84	27	317	288	404	508	911	1130	864	12	83	36	0.77	41	24	35	125	123	12%	131	19%	73%	26	69%	12%	7.44	53.4	96	240	$40
1st Half		301	50	9	42	16	292	288	353	462	814	984	787	9	84	33	0.57	40	25	35	119	110	10%	97	24%	80%	14	57%	21%	5.91	14.8	78	195	$36
2nd Half		282	47	12	42	11	344	289	443	557	1000	1275	945	15	82	39	0.96	41	24	34	131	137	15%	165	15%	65%	12	83%	0%	9.25	38.0	113	283	$43
14	Proj	585	100	26	89	24	306	285	393	516	909	1088	863	12	81	34	0.71	41	23	36	136	133	15%	140	17%	71%				7.23	50.0	93	234	$37

McLouth,Nate

Age 32	Bats L	Pos LF	Health C	LIMA Plan B+	
Ht 5' 11"	Wt 180		PT/Exp C	Rand Var -1	
			Consist A	MM 2415	

Terrific 1H was sparked by outlier ct% and SBO, favorable h% and unsustainable success vs. LHP. 2H crash-and-burn was much more in line with recent history, although 2H xBA and xPX say it wasn't as bad as it looked. If you level out the half-over-half occillation, you're left with line drives, aggressive SBO, and average power.

Yr	Tm	AB	R	HR	RBI	SB	BA	xBA	OBP	SLG	OPS	vL	vR	bb%	ct%	h%	Eye	G	L	F	PX	xPX	hr/f	Spd	SBO	SB%	#Wk	DOM	DIS	RC/G	RAR	BPV	BPX	R$
09	2 NL	507	86	20	70	19	256	262	352	436	788	688	833	12	80	28	0.69	40	17	43	112	100	11%	94	17%	76%	25	64%	8%	5.15	17.5	65	133	$18
10	ATL *	370	43	10	37	12	187	226	277	309	586	378	685	11	77	21	0.55	40	16	44	83	120	8%	96	15%	86%	18	33%	44%	2.77	-15.2	29	63	$1
11	ATL	267	35	4	16	4	228	237	344	333	677	531	743	14	81	27	0.85	47	17	36	74	82	5%	118	7%	67%	15	47%	20%	3.70	-2.2	47	104	$1
12	2 TM *	446	61	15	45	16	225	250	291	380	671	581	731	9	79	25	0.45	43	20	37	97	116	9%	102	16%	94%	18	33%	33%	3.78	-2.6	44	110	$10
13	BAL	531	76	12	36	30	258	269	329	399	729	640	753	9	84	29	0.62	39	25	37	95	96	7%	122	26%	81%	27	59%	15%	4.55	9.0	68	170	$21
1st Half		273	49	6	15	24	282	280	355	410	766	864	750	10	87	31	0.86	44	25	32	84	65	8%	126	33%	86%	14	64%	7%	5.46	11.3	75	188	$32
2nd Half		258	27	6	21	6	233	259	293	388	680	494	757	8	81	27	0.44	33	25	42	107	132	7%	113	16%	67%	13	54%	23%	3.70	-2.5	60	150	$11
14	Proj	442	60	11	36	19	239	253	318	375	693	569	734	10	81	27	0.58	40	22	38	92	105	8%	113	20%	83%				4.03	0.1	57	143	$13

JOCK THOMPSON

Mercer,Jordy

Age 27	Bats R	Pos SS 2B	Health A	LIMA Plan D+
Ht 6' 3"	Wt 210		PT/Exp C	Rand Var -3
			Consist C	MM 2123

8-27-.285 in 333 AB at PIT. He earned lion's share of SS job with consistent offensive production. His patience is nothing special but he brings just enough contact and pop to be productive. xBA points out some BA risk, but LD swing and xPX say he can keep this up. 2014 opportunity will hinge mostly on his sometimes-shaky defense.

Yr	Tm	AB	R	HR	RBI	SB	BA	xBA	OBP	SLG	OPS	vL	vR	bb%	ct%	h%	Eye	G	L	F	PX	xPX	hr/f	Spd	SBO	SB%	#Wk	DOM	DIS	RC/G	RAR	BPV	BPX	R$
09																																		
10	aa	485	53	2	51	5	246	250	282	323	605			5	85	29	0.32				61			97	6%	83%				3.11		28	61	$5
11	a/a	491	60	14	52	7	214	263	254	355	609			5	83	23	0.31				96			91	15%	49%				2.78		47	104	$5
12	PIT *	271	29	4	27	2	236	249	287	356	643	367	690	7	76	30	0.30	47	22	31	91	86	7%	90	15%	26%	17	24%	53%	3.07	-3.6	20	50	$2
13	PIT *	429	41	9	41	5	282	269	330	419	749	1152	654	7	81	33	0.37	47	23	30	98	117	10%	111	7%	62%	23	52%	26%	4.84	16.2	51	128	$12
1st Half		230	22	5	25	5	279	261	330	412	742	1328	625	7	80	33	0.38	50	20	30	95	126	13%	117	12%	70%	10	50%	30%	4.76	8.5	46	115	$14
2nd Half		199	19	4	16	0	286	277	330	427	757	1046	673	6	82	33	0.37	44	25	31	101	112	8%	104	2%	0%	13	54%	23%	4.93	8.2	56	140	$9
14	**Proj**	**394**	**42**	**8**	**39**	**4**	**265**	**268**	**316**	**403**	**719**	**912**	**669**	**6**	**81**	**31**	**0.33**	**47**	**23**	**30**	**99**	**105**	**9%**	**104**	**9%**	**44%**				**4.16**	**8.0**	**36**	**90**	**$8**

Mesoraco,Devin

Age 26	Bats R	Pos CA	Health A	LIMA Plan C
Ht 6' 1"	Wt 230		PT/Exp D	Rand Var 0
			Consist B	MM 2015

Bottom-line improvement was due primarily to h% rebound; BPIs say real gains are more elusive. 2H aggressiveness was accompanied by increased ct% and GBs, which added nothing to his xBA or power. He still has age, health, and power history on his side. But his struggles vs. RHP are starting to look chronic.

Yr	Tm	AB	R	HR	RBI	SB	BA	xBA	OBP	SLG	OPS	vL	vR	bb%	ct%	h%	Eye	G	L	F	PX	xPX	hr/f	Spd	SBO	SB%	#Wk	DOM	DIS	RC/G	RAR	BPV	BPX	R$
09																																		
10	a/a	239	37	14	35	1	255	293	310	501	811			7	76	28	0.34				161			115	4%	42%				5.23		85	185	$7
11	CIN *	486	50	15	60	1	244	245	304	409	713	625	579	8	78	28	0.40	40	15	45	121	83	11%	77	2%	40%	5	60%	20%	4.16	6.7	51	113	$8
12	CIN	165	17	5	14	1	212	238	288	352	640	803	590	9	80	24	0.52	45	17	38	92	80	10%	69	5%	50%	22	45%	32%	3.19	-2.5	35	88	-$1
13	CIN	323	31	9	42	0	238	246	287	362	649	874	576	7	81	27	0.39	45	21	34	83	78	10%	56	3%	0%	27	41%	37%	3.43	-2.5	24	60	$4
1st Half		147	15	4	19	0	231	248	311	361	672	814	595	10	79	27	0.55	42	23	35	91	92	10%	59	3%	0%	14	43%	36%	3.61	-0.4	29	73	$2
2nd Half		176	16	5	23	0	244	245	273	364	637	963	562	4	83	27	0.23	48	20	33	76	67	10%	67	3%	0%	13	38%	38%	3.26	-2.4	22	55	$4
14	**Proj**	**419**	**44**	**13**	**50**	**1**	**242**	**248**	**300**	**383**	**683**	**895**	**622**	**8**	**81**	**27**	**0.44**	**44**	**20**	**37**	**95**	**79**	**10%**	**62**	**3%**	**30%**				**3.80**	**1.2**	**27**	**67**	**$8**

Middlebrooks,Will

Age 25	Bats R	Pos 3B	Health C	LIMA Plan B
Ht 6' 3"	Wt 220		PT/Exp C	Rand Var +4
			Consist F	MM 4225

17-49-.227 in 348 AB at BOS. Sub-par bb% and ct% look chronic, but depressed h% also contributed to 1H struggles and demotion. 2H return to BOS brought better results, as 32% h% and 7% bb% fueled .803 OPS. PX and xBA history say he has enough to overcome deficient plate skills. Use 2H as your baseline.

Yr	Tm	AB	R	HR	RBI	SB	BA	xBA	OBP	SLG	OPS	vL	vR	bb%	ct%	h%	Eye	G	L	F	PX	xPX	hr/f	Spd	SBO	SB%	#Wk	DOM	DIS	RC/G	RAR	BPV	BPX	R$
09																																		
10																																		
11	a/a	427	45	15	68	7	258	248	288	425	713			4	71	33	0.15				131			78	9%	86%				4.24		23	51	$12
12	BOS *	360	49	22	76	6	293	276	328	530	857	906	798	5	75	34	0.21	44	22	35	152	119	21%	78	10%	75%	15	40%	33%	6.22	22.8	57	143	$18
13	BOS *	527	60	24	75	4	229	246	273	410	683	782	656	6	73	27	0.23	41	20	39	127	127	17%	70	5%	79%	19	42%	37%	3.70	-3.9	29	73	$11
1st Half		244	24	12	34	0	202	248	244	401	645	675	591	5	73	23	0.20	40	19	41	144	127	15%	69	3%	0%	10	50%	30%	3.06	-7.0	39	98	$5
2nd Half		283	35	12	41	4	252	246	298	417	715	926	747	6	74	30	0.25	42	22	36	113	129	21%	81	6%	100%	9	33%	44%	4.31	2.8	24	60	$17
14	**Proj**	**478**	**57**	**25**	**81**	**6**	**256**	**262**	**297**	**465**	**762**	**850**	**719**	**5**	**74**	**30**	**0.21**	**42**	**21**	**37**	**144**	**125**	**20%**	**75**	**7%**	**80%**				**4.69**	**10.0**	**42**	**106**	**$18**

Miller,Bradley

Age 24	Bats L	Pos SS	Health A	LIMA Plan B+
Ht 6' 2"	Wt 185		PT/Exp F	Rand Var 0
			Consist B	MM 2415

8-36-.265 with 5 SB in 306 AB at SEA. Brought career .334/.409/.516 line to his MLB debut and held his own in SEA lead-off spot. Should reach double-digit HR and SB, and Spd points to more upside if green-lighted. Growing pains are possible, but live bat with history of patience and 80+% ct% suggest he'll contribute from the get-go.

Yr	Tm	AB	R	HR	RBI	SB	BA	xBA	OBP	SLG	OPS	vL	vR	bb%	ct%	h%	Eye	G	L	F	PX	xPX	hr/f	Spd	SBO	SB%	#Wk	DOM	DIS	RC/G	RAR	BPV	BPX	R$
09																																		
10																																		
11																																		
12	aa	147	19	3	11	4	284	242	371	411	782			12	79	34	0.67				82			115	9%	76%				5.45		43	108	$3
13	SEA *	563	82	17	77	10	268	263	330	422	752	674	767	8	80	31	0.47	46	22	32	96	79	10%	146	11%	56%	15	53%	13%	4.69	20.7	61	153	$21
1st Half		268	42	9	42	7	268	305	342	423	765	500	673	10	77	32	0.49	50	38	13	105	17	0%	115	14%	59%	2	50%	50%	4.86	11.0	49	123	$22
2nd Half		295	40	8	35	3	268	266	319	420	739	674	772	7	83	30	0.45	46	21	33	89	81	10%	167	8%	50%	13	54%	8%	4.52	9.1	71	178	$19
14	**Proj**	**518**	**72**	**12**	**57**	**12**	**275**	**253**	**346**	**406**	**753**	**682**	**788**	**10**	**80**	**32**	**0.55**	**46**	**21**	**33**	**85**	**73**	**9%**	**142**	**11%**	**68%**				**4.89**	**21.2**	**43**	**106**	**$19**

Molina,Jose

Age 39	Bats R	Pos CA	Health A	LIMA Plan D
Ht 6' 2"	Wt 250		PT/Exp D	Rand Var +1
			Consist C	MM 1101

A career of offensive mediocrity, now past the window for the mid-30s catcher HR spike. It's all rising GB%, declining power and already-glacial speed, and stagnant BPIs. A h%-fueled BA like 2011 or HR spike like 2012 are long-shots, as is another 250+ AB season. Glove may extend career into his 40s, but safe for us to ignore.

Yr	Tm	AB	R	HR	RBI	SB	BA	xBA	OBP	SLG	OPS	vL	vR	bb%	ct%	h%	Eye	G	L	F	PX	xPX	hr/f	Spd	SBO	SB%	#Wk	DOM	DIS	RC/G	RAR	BPV	BPX	R$
09	NYY	138	15	1	11	0	217	206	292	268	560	539	569	9	80	27	0.50	39	19	42	37	69	2%	79	0%	0%	19	32%	63%	2.53	-4.9	-7	-14	-$2
10	TOR	167	13	6	12	1	246	249	304	377	681	464	763	5	78	28	0.25	43	22	35	83	123	13%	71	3%	100%	26	31%	50%	3.65	-0.2	14	30	$1
11	TOR	171	19	3	15	2	281	249	342	415	757	754	759	8	74	36	0.34	43	22	35	109	90	7%	79	6%	67%	26	35%	46%	4.94	5.9	26	58	$3
12	TAM	251	27	8	32	3	223	239	286	355	640	469	680	7	76	26	0.33	52	18	29	87	83	14%	52	7%	75%	27	26%	59%	3.26	-3.4	6	15	$2
13	TAM	283	26	2	18	2	233	231	290	304	594	628	577	7	78	29	0.35	55	20	26	60	51	4%	58	4%	67%	27	19%	56%	2.91	-6.9	-6	-15	$0
1st Half		139	16	1	8	2	259	228	309	324	632	703	609	7	79	32	0.34	54	18	28	53	73	3%	63	5%	100%	14	29%	57%	3.52	-0.8	-7	-18	$3
2nd Half		144	10	1	10	0	208	231	269	285	554	569	542	8	76	27	0.35	55	21	24	67	29	4%	58	3%	0%	13	8%	54%	2.39	-6.0	-6	-15	-$3
14	**Proj**	**194**	**19**	**3**	**16**	**2**	**235**	**232**	**297**	**325**	**621**	**603**	**629**	**8**	**77**	**29**	**0.35**	**53**	**19**	**28**	**70**	**67**	**6%**	**62**	**5%**	**67%**				**3.16**	**-3.2**	**-4**	**-10**	**$2**

Molina,Yadier

Age 31	Bats R	Pos CA	Health A	LIMA Plan B
Ht 5' 11"	Wt 220		PT/Exp B	Rand Var -2
			Consist B	MM 3145

2012's hr/f and SBO evaporated, but 1st half h% propped him up until regression and a knee injury pulled his 2nd half numbers down to earth. Terrific ct% and healthy LD% are core skills at this point. He can keep doing this, but injury risk is now slightly elevated.

Yr	Tm	AB	R	HR	RBI	SB	BA	xBA	OBP	SLG	OPS	vL	vR	bb%	ct%	h%	Eye	G	L	F	PX	xPX	hr/f	Spd	SBO	SB%	#Wk	DOM	DIS	RC/G	RAR	BPV	BPX	R$
09	STL	481	45	6	54	9	293	278	366	383	749	717	759	9	92	31	1.28	51	19	30	56	70	5%	70	7%	75%	27	52%	15%	4.97	17.1	54	110	$13
10	STL	465	34	6	62	8	262	269	329	342	671	570	714	8	89	28	0.82	51	21	28	54	85	5%	63	9%	67%	25	40%	16%	3.79	1.2	37	80	$9
11	STL	475	55	14	65	4	305	291	349	465	814	842	806	6	91	31	0.75	45	20	35	101	101	9%	66	7%	44%	27	67%	7%	5.79	27.4	79	176	$19
12	STL	505	65	22	76	12	315	300	373	501	874	1021	833	8	89	32	0.82	40	25	35	107	112	14%	71	10%	80%	27	74%	0%	6.93	44.2	82	205	$26
13	STL	505	68	12	80	3	319	301	359	477	836	883	823	6	89	34	0.55	42	24	34	109	111	8%	67	4%	60%	26	65%	23%	6.32	35.5	77	193	$24
1st Half		290	35	6	44	3	345	299	385	497	882	859	890	6	90	37	0.63	40	24	35	106	125	6%	78	6%	60%	14	71%	7%	7.32	27.2	81	203	$28
2nd Half		215	33	6	36	0	284	304	319	451	770	917	733	5	88	30	0.44	45	24	31	113	91	10%	57	0%	0%	12	58%	42%	5.12	8.5	73	183	$18
14	**Proj**	**471**	**60**	**14**	**71**	**5**	**302**	**296**	**350**	**460**	**811**	**877**	**792**	**7**	**89**	**32**	**0.67**	**43**	**23**	**34**	**103**	**103**	**10%**	**64**	**6%**	**68%**				**5.81**	**27.3**	**72**	**181**	**$21**

Montero,Jesus

Age 24	Bats R	Pos CA	Health A	LIMA Plan D+
Ht 6' 3"	Wt 230		PT/Exp C	Rand Var +4
			Consist C	MM 3023

3-9-.208 in 101 AB at SEA. Disaster, in four parts: Poor start, demotion, DL stint (torn meniscus), capped in Aug by 50-game PED suspension. Still young and owns that power history (we think), but must regain higher ct% level and keep hiking the FB%. He's a buying opp for risk tolerant owners, esp. while he retains C eligibility.

Yr	Tm	AB	R	HR	RBI	SB	BA	xBA	OBP	SLG	OPS	vL	vR	bb%	ct%	h%	Eye	G	L	F	PX	xPX	hr/f	Spd	SBO	SB%	#Wk	DOM	DIS	RC/G	RAR	BPV	BPX	R$
09	aa	167	19	10	33	0	318	302	373	557	930			8	87	32	0.68				134			82	0%	0%				7.76		98	200	$7
10	aaa	453	58	21	66	0	275	291	336	495	831			8	79	31	0.43				149			96	0%	0%				5.85		82	178	$14
11	NYY *	481	55	22	70	0	281	273	336	469	804	1181	877	8	75	33	0.33	39	27	34	130	155	27%	84	0%	0%	5	60%	40%	5.58	14.7	46	102	$16
12	SEA	515	46	15	62	0	260	253	298	386	685	830	609	5	81	30	0.29	43	25	33	80	92	11%	70	2%	0%	28	36%	36%	3.92	-8.6	21	53	$10
13	SEA *	174	14	4	15	0	203	216	261	324	584	531	615	7	71	26	0.27	42	20	38	87	87	10%	119	3%	0%	8	25%	50%	2.63	-10.2	6	15	-$3
1st Half		129	9	3	10	0	206	223	260	326	586	531	615	7	75	25	0.29	42	20	38	79	87	10%	119	4%	0%	8	25%	50%	2.62	-7.6	15	38	-$3
2nd Half																																		
14	**Proj**	**325**	**32**	**13**	**41**	**0**	**258**	**259**	**314**	**431**	**745**	**880**	**672**	**7**	**78**	**30**	**0.35**	**40**	**23**	**37**	**113**	**115**	**14%**	**93**	**1%**	**0%**				**4.54**	**7.9**	**30**	**75**	**$8**

JOCK THOMPSON

Montero,Miguel

Age	30	Bats	L	Pos	CA	Health	B
Ht	5' 11"	Wt	210			PT/Exp	B
						Consist	C
LIMA Plan	C+	Rand Var	+1	MM	3005		

He was reversing a horrific start when July back strain resulted in a month-long DL stint. Poor Sept (.208 BA) capped disappointing season. Bb% trend and 2H hr/f offer power hope, just needs expected FB% rebound. But the stagnant ct% and periodic futility vs. LHP say BA may not fully recover. Lower your previous expectations.

Yr	Tm	AB	R	HR	RBI	SB	BA	xBA	OBP	SLG	OPS	vL	vR	bb%	ct%	h%	Eye	G	L	F	PX	xPX	hr/f	Spd	SBO	SB%	#Wk	DOM	DIS	RC/G	RAR	BPV	BPX	R$
09	ARI	425	61	16	59	1	294	281	355	478	832	844	830	8	82	33	0.49	44	20	36	119	126	13%	81	3%	33%	27	63%	19%	5.98	27.0	65	133	$14
10	ARI	297	36	9	43	0	266	257	332	438	770	661	811	9	76	32	0.41	38	19	43	126	134	9%	84	1%	0%	18	39%	39%	4.97	10.9	50	109	$7
11	ARI	493	65	18	86	1	282	281	351	469	820	534	904	9	80	32	0.48	42	22	36	131	136	13%	60	2%	50%	27	59%	19%	5.70	27.8	64	142	$18
12	ARI	486	65	15	88	0	286	239	391	438	829	767	859	13	73	36	0.56	43	21	36	108	121	12%	98	0%	0%	27	41%	41%	5.94	30.4	37	93	$17
13	ARI	413	44	11	42	0	230	224	318	344	662	492	719	11	73	29	0.46	47	21	31	83	107	11%	66	0%	0%	23	22%	48%	3.58	-1.4	4	10	$3
1st Half		261	26	5	27	0	226	223	311	322	632	604	642	11	75	28	0.49	47	21	31	72	111	8%	63	0%	0%	14	21%	43%	3.29	-3.3	1	3	$4
2nd Half		152	18	6	15	0	237	226	322	382	703	253	842	11	70	30	0.42	47	21	31	102	99	18%	83	0%	0%	9	22%	56%	4.10	1.8	12	30	$3
14	Proj	468	57	14	64	0	269	240	355	408	763	581	827	11	74	33	0.48	45	21	34	102	116	12%	77	0%	37%				4.95	16.6	14	34	$11

Moore,Tyler

Age	27	Bats	R	Pos	LF	Health	A
Ht	6' 2"	Wt	220			PT/Exp	D
						Consist	D
LIMA Plan	D+	Rand Var	-1	MM	4311		

4-21-.222 in 167 AB at WAS. Couldn't repeat power or bb% uptick from promising 2012. AAA line—.318 BA, 10 HR, 23/39 BB/K in 173 AB—didn't carry over to WAS (8/58 BB/K). Only an inflated 2H h% kept his BA within reason. Contact is a huge obstacle, but those power metrics still give him an outside shot at an MLB career.

Yr	Tm	AB	R	HR	RBI	SB	BA	xBA	OBP	SLG	OPS	vL	vR	bb%	ct%	h%	Eye	G	L	F	PX	xPX	hr/f	Spd	SBO	SB%	#Wk	DOM	DIS	RC/G	RAR	BPV	BPX	R$
09																																		
10																																		
11	aa	519	56	25	72	2	237	265	269	453	722			4	71	29	0.15				162			88	2%	100%				4.09		49	109	$11
12	WAS *	257	31	17	49	4	264	273	323	523	846	780	929	8	71	31	0.30	40	22	38	178	148	24%	81	6%	100%	22	45%	41%	5.94	13.9	68	170	$10
13	WAS *	340	34	11	54	1	242	230	291	406	697	508	687	6	70	32	0.23	40	18	42	131	117	9%	92	1%	100%	21	19%	62%	3.99	-0.6	26	65	$6
1st Half		147	13	4	20	0	153	185	203	288	491	419	560	6	63	21	0.17	43	12	45	118	131	10%	84	0%	0%	12	17%	50%	1.76	-11.0	-16	-40	-$4
2nd Half		193	22	7	34	1	311	272	358	497	856	655	882	7	75	39	0.29	36	27	38	139	96	6%	99	1%	100%	9	22%	78%	6.63	13.6	57	143	$14
14	Proj	228	25	9	38	2	251	247	306	437	743	672	816	7	70	32	0.25	39	21	40	142	126	14%	92	3%	100%				4.54	3.5	29	73	$7

Morales,Kendrys

Age	31	Bats	B	Pos	DH 1B	Health	F
Ht	6' 1"	Wt	225			PT/Exp	C
						Consist	A
LIMA Plan	B	Rand Var	0	MM	4035		

PX dip is slightly disconcerting, but 2H hr/f rebounded nicely and xPX looks positive. Contact and bb% upticks are setting a nice floor. Solid effort vs. LHP in career-high 209 AB adds to good news. Finally ready for a return to 2009 pre-injury form? With just a bit more of an FB uptick... UP: One final shot at 2009.

Yr	Tm	AB	R	HR	RBI	SB	BA	xBA	OBP	SLG	OPS	vL	vR	bb%	ct%	h%	Eye	G	L	F	PX	xPX	hr/f	Spd	SBO	SB%	#Wk	DOM	DIS	RC/G	RAR	BPV	BPX	R$
09	LAA	566	86	34	108	3	306	300	355	569	924	801	962	8	79	33	0.39	42	17	41	166	159	18%	82	7%	30%	27	70%	15%	7.15	41.5	92	188	$27
10	LAA	193	29	11	39	0	290	289	346	487	833	548	1002	6	84	30	0.39	48	21	31	113	110	22%	66	2%	0%	8	88%	0%	5.68	6.4	60	130	$8
11																																		
12	LAA	484	61	22	73	0	273	267	320	467	787	761	791	6	76	32	0.27	51	20	28	129	109	21%	67	1%	0%	27	48%	37%	5.14	8.8	41	103	$15
13	SEA	602	64	23	80	0	277	260	336	449	785	794	780	8	81	31	0.43	49	19	33	115	134	14%	70	0%	0%	27	56%	30%	5.25	12.8	54	135	$19
1st Half		300	31	9	42	0	277	253	326	433	759	873	711	7	80	32	0.37	49	18	33	112	136	11%	71	0%	0%	14	57%	21%	4.98	4.1	48	120	$17
2nd Half		302	33	14	38	0	278	266	337	464	801	715	848	8	82	30	0.49	48	20	32	118	132	18%	74	0%	0%	13	54%	38%	5.53	8.8	62	155	$21
14	Proj	567	70	26	87	0	281	271	336	473	808	734	839	7	80	31	0.38	48	19	32	125	126	18%	67	1%	17%				5.49	15.8	46	114	$22

Moreland,Mitch

Age	28	Bats	L	Pos	1B	Health	B
Ht	6' 2"	Wt	240			PT/Exp	B
						Consist	B
LIMA Plan	B	Rand Var	+3	MM	4025		

Power is progressing nicely, supported by hr/f, xPX. But declining ct% is chipping away at BA metrics. Ugly h% following June DL return torpedoed potential career year. Age, skill set offer value, but in-season volatility has limited his AB. If someone just plugs him into lineup and leaves him there... UP: 25-30 HR, .260 BA.

Yr	Tm	AB	R	HR	RBI	SB	BA	xBA	OBP	SLG	OPS	vL	vR	bb%	ct%	h%	Eye	G	L	F	PX	xPX	hr/f	Spd	SBO	SB%	#Wk	DOM	DIS	RC/G	RAR	BPV	BPX	R$
09	aa	301	40	7	46	1	291	273	331	436	767			6	84	33	0.38				90			105	2%	41%				5.12		54	110	$8
10	TEX *	498	57	18	72	4	249	273	329	425	754	604	869	11	78	28	0.55	40	23	38	121	152	21%	61	5%	67%	11	45%	27%	4.72	1.7	52	113	$11
11	TEX	464	60	16	51	2	259	250	320	414	733	577	783	8	80	29	0.42	42	18	40	104	105	11%	77	3%	50%	27	48%	30%	4.44	-2.2	44	98	$11
12	TEX	327	41	15	50	1	275	262	321	468	789	737	798	7	78	31	0.32	42	20	38	125	128	15%	72	3%	50%	22	45%	27%	5.26	6.1	50	125	$10
13	TEX	462	60	23	60	0	232	255	299	437	736	701	752	9	75	26	0.38	43	17	39	143	136	17%	66	0%	0%	26	50%	31%	4.35	-3.5	53	133	$9
1st Half		231	28	12	32	0	268	276	321	506	828	775	860	7	76	31	0.32	43	17	40	168	137	17%	85	0%	0%	13	46%	23%	5.67	7.1	79	198	$13
2nd Half		231	32	11	28	0	195	233	279	368	647	595	661	10	74	21	0.44	44	17	39	116	135	16%	52	0%	0%	13	54%	38%	3.25	-9.8	26	65	$5
14	Proj	419	54	20	56	1	249	260	309	445	754	676	778	8	77	28	0.38	42	19	39	132	131	16%	68	2%	53%				4.66	0.7	46	115	$12

Morneau,Justin

Age	33	Bats	L	Pos	1B	Health	D
Ht	6' 4"	Wt	220			PT/Exp	B
						Consist	C
LIMA Plan	B+	Rand Var	+1	MM	3325		

Power surge in Aug (9 HR, 181 PX) vanished in Sept (zero HR, 45 PX); xPX was skeptical all season. 1H/2H BA volatility due to extreme h% swings. Still productive, but his pre-concussion power-and-patience game looks long gone. Venue change may help this FA, but vL futility suggests fewer AB. 2012-13 is the new benchmark.

Yr	Tm	AB	R	HR	RBI	SB	BA	xBA	OBP	SLG	OPS	vL	vR	bb%	ct%	h%	Eye	G	L	F	PX	xPX	hr/f	Spd	SBO	SB%	#Wk	DOM	DIS	RC/G	RAR	BPV	BPX	R$
09	MIN	508	85	30	100	0	274	289	363	516	878	836	906	12	83	28	0.84	41	16	43	143	141	16%	75	0%	0%	23	83%	13%	6.59	28.9	96	196	$19
10	MIN	296	53	18	56	0	345	312	437	618	1055	966	1113	14	79	39	0.81	33	22	45	185	187	17%	100	0%	0%	14	93%	7%	10.57	45.5	125	272	$19
11	MIN *	294	25	5	36	0	233	238	281	345	626	401	728	6	84	26	0.42	35	18	46	84	97	4%	70	0%	0%	15	40%	33%	3.23	-12.0	39	87	$1
12	MIN	505	63	19	77	1	267	263	333	440	773	569	902	9	80	30	0.48	41	22	37	110	115	13%	84	1%	100%	26	42%	23%	5.09	7.3	52	130	$14
13	2 TM	572	62	17	77	0	259	258	323	411	734	525	819	8	81	29	0.45	41	21	38	107	94	10%	85	0%	0%	26	54%	15%	4.50	-1.4	52	130	$13
1st Half		282	34	4	48	0	291	259	340	411	751	649	796	7	82	34	0.41	40	23	37	95	96	5%	95	0%	0%	14	50%	7%	5.03	3.4	48	120	$17
2nd Half		290	28	13	29	0	228	255	298	410	708	398	840	9	80	24	0.49	42	19	39	120	91	14%	78	0%	0%	12	58%	25%	4.03	-5.0	58	145	$10
14	Proj	512	59	19	72	0	261	264	328	435	763	563	862	9	81	29	0.49	40	21	40	118	106	12%	81	0%	100%				4.87	4.0	47	116	$14

Morrison,Logan

Age	26	Bats	L	Pos	1B	Health	F
Ht	6' 3"	Wt	245			PT/Exp	D
						Consist	B
LIMA Plan	B+	Rand Var	+2	MM	3225		

6-36-.242 in 293 AB at MIA. Returned from off-season surgery in June. PRO: No in-season setbacks; prior plate skills intact; .261/.354/.423 vs. RHP. CON: Few signs of 2011 power; .183 BA, zero HR vs. LHP (71 AB). After two knee operations, he'll enjoy his first healthy winter since 2010. If he can stay whole... UP: .270 BA, 20 HR.

Yr	Tm	AB	R	HR	RBI	SB	BA	xBA	OBP	SLG	OPS	vL	vR	bb%	ct%	h%	Eye	G	L	F	PX	xPX	hr/f	Spd	SBO	SB%	#Wk	DOM	DIS	RC/G	RAR	BPV	BPX	R$
09	aa	278	42	7	42	8	260	271	389	411	800			17	81	30	1.11				100			99	12%	65%				5.42		71	145	$7
10	FLA *	482	69	6	51	1	273	277	375	425	800	926	797	14	81	33	0.84	48	20	32	108	100	3%	109	3%	18%	11	45%	27%	5.47	12.2	72	157	$10
11	FLA *	486	56	24	75	2	241	281	318	457	776	723	827	10	79	26	0.53	47	18	35	143	129	18%	78	3%	67%	24	71%	13%	4.88	4.1	75	167	$12
12	MIA	296	30	11	36	1	230	252	308	399	707	659	723	9	80	25	0.53	41	18	41	107	117	11%	63	1%	100%	17	47%	29%	4.01	-5.0	47	118	$3
13	MIA *	326	36	8	41	0	233	255	316	367	683	491	778	11	81	27	0.65	48	20	32	86	97	8%	102	0%	0%	17	41%	41%	3.86	-7.1	48	120	$3
1st Half		83	13	3	10	0	253	295	301	428	729	388	1105	6	84	27	0.44	48	26	26	101	128	9%	131	0%	0%	4	75%	0%	4.40	-0.5	72	180	$1
2nd Half		243	23	5	31	0	226	242	321	346	667	518	718	12	80	26	0.71	48	19	33	80	90	8%	85	0%	0%	13	31%	54%	3.66	-6.9	37	93	$4
14	Proj	496	58	16	64	1	251	267	332	418	750	601	804	10	81	28	0.60	46	20	34	108	111	12%	94	2%	69%				4.66	0.8	54	136	$12

Morse,Michael

Age	32	Bats	R	Pos	RF	Health	D
Ht	6' 5"	Wt	245			PT/Exp	C
						Consist	D
LIMA Plan	C+	Rand Var	+5	MM	4013		

13-27-.215 in 312 AB with SEA and BAL. Torrid April (8 HR, 167 PX) was soon forgotten. Injuries (finger, oblique, wrist) wrecked his season and drove ct%, h% to new lows. PX/xPX remained attractive, but hardly vintage; FB rebound was immaterial. Health is THE #1 issue here; October wrist surgery keeps the red flag up.

Yr	Tm	AB	R	HR	RBI	SB	BA	xBA	OBP	SLG	OPS	vL	vR	bb%	ct%	h%	Eye	G	L	F	PX	xPX	hr/f	Spd	SBO	SB%	#Wk	DOM	DIS	RC/G	RAR	BPV	BPX	R$
09	WAS *	477	50	15	77	2	267	255	310	425	735	583	827	6	78	32	0.28	61	11	28	104	127	30%	95	2%	56%	8	50%	38%	4.56	-0.6	36	73	$11
10	WAS *	317	45	17	47	0	276	269	335	495	829	999	806	6	76	32	0.36	46	16	38	144	141	19%	118	1%	0%	22	50%	41%	5.75	10.3	71	154	$10
11	WAS	522	73	31	95	2	303	287	360	550	910	892	915	6	76	35	0.29	44	20	37	173	154	21%	62	4%	40%	27	59%	22%	6.85	37.0	75	167	$27
12	WAS	406	53	18	62	0	291	263	321	470	791	755	804	4	76	34	0.16	55	20	25	116	111	23%	88	1%	0%	19	37%	26%	5.31	11.7	33	83	$15
13	2 AL *	336	36	14	28	0	212	233	261	374	635	667	642	6	72	25	0.23	45	19	36	117	115	16%	72	0%	0%	21	33%	57%	3.16	-11.5	16	40	$1
1st Half		207	24	11	23	0	251	247	305	454	759	958	671	7	72	29	0.28	44	19	37	142	119	20%	76	0%	0%	12	50%	50%	4.72	1.6	43	108	$7
2nd Half		129	12	3	5	0	149	213	188	245	434	276	562	5	70	19	0.16	45	21	33	76	105	8%	74	0%	0%	9	11%	67%	1.39	-13.2	-24	-60	-$8
14	Proj	377	44	16	43	0	261	253	307	438	745	649	795	6	75	31	0.23	48	19	32	124	120	18%	74	1%	31%				4.53	0.9	22	54	$11

JOCK THOMPSON

Moss,Brandon

Age	30	Bats	L	Pos 1B RF	Health	A	LIMA Plan	B+
Ht	6' 0"	Wt	210		PT/Exp	C	Rand Var	-2
					Consist	C	MM	5125

Continued to pound righties, nearly doubling his career HR output. Even in the context of severe RH/LH splits, years with regular PT have produced consistent BA/xBA and h%. In past two seasons, elite FB% and PX has emerged at the expense of contact, a positive trade-off that supports a repeat in 2014.

Yr	Tm	AB	R	HR	RBI	SB	BA	xBA	OBP	SLG	OPS	vL	vR	bb%	ct%	h%	Eye	G	L	F	PX	xPX	hr/f	Spd	SBO	SB%	#Wk	DOM	DIS	RC/G	RAR	BPV	BPX	R$
09	PIT	385	47	7	41	1	236	251	304	364	668	646	672	8	78	29	0.40	44	20	36	86	88	6%	90	6%	17%	27	41%	33%	3.43	-13.7	27	55	$2
10	PIT *	526	53	15	69	8	208	245	250	347	598	0	392	5	73	26	0.21	55	15	30	106	145	0%	89	18%	49%	5	20%	80%	2.64	-32.5	16	35	$4
11	PHI *	442	49	17	60	3	219	196	293	399	693	0	0	9	64	30	0.29	50	0	50	154	2	0%	72	10%	29%	2	0%	50%	3.58	-13.8	21	47	$6
12	OAK *	461	68	29	73	4	254	259	314	505	819	770	1006	8	69	30	0.28	33	21	46	178	176	26%	72	4%	78%	18	61%	28%	5.42	10.9	59	148	$16
13	OAK	446	73	30	87	4	256	255	337	522	859	649	904	10	69	30	0.36	30	18	52	193	174	19%	92	6%	67%	27	70%	19%	5.86	16.4	78	195	$20
1st Half		241	37	14	41	1	232	234	312	465	777	627	824	10	66	29	0.34	31	21	49	169	155	18%	111	2%	100%	14	57%	21%	4.84	1.8	53	133	$15
2nd Half		205	36	16	46	3	283	282	352	590	943	684	993	10	72	32	0.39	30	15	55	219	193	20%	79	10%	60%	13	85%	15%	7.21	15.3	109	273	$25
14	Proj	**433**	**67**	**28**	**78**	**4**	**250**	**261**	**324**	**507**	**831**	**664**	**868**	**9**	**69**	**30**	**0.32**	**33**	**19**	**48**	**189**	**164**	**19%**	**79**	**7%**	**56%**				**5.37**	**9.9**	**71**	**178**	**$15**

Moustakas,Mike

Age	25	Bats	L	Pos 3B	Health	A	LIMA Plan	B+
Ht	6' 0"	Wt	210		PT/Exp	B	Rand Var	+1
					Consist	A	MM	3015

Suffered three sub-.200 months during seemingly lost season, but the furrows aren't irreversible. bb% and ct% didn't regress, and 2H featured flashes of 2012 power while h% normalized. Building on 2H gains vs. LHP is essential to avoid ceding more PT to right-handers. Now would be a good time to start showing his upside.

Yr	Tm	AB	R	HR	RBI	SB	BA	xBA	OBP	SLG	OPS	vL	vR	bb%	ct%	h%	Eye	G	L	F	PX	xPX	hr/f	Spd	SBO	SB%	#Wk	DOM	DIS	RC/G	RAR	BPV	BPX	R$
09																																		
10	a/a	484	72	25	95	2	286	316	322	520	842			5	85	29	0.36				149			83	3%	58%				5.94		97	211	$21
11	KC *	561	54	11	62	3	256	249	301	380	681	494	741	6	82	29	0.36	38	20	41	88	83	4%	83	3%	71%	17	35%	24%	3.92	-0.4	39	87	$10
12	KC	563	69	20	73	5	242	236	296	412	708	704	710	6	78	28	0.31	34	16	50	115	109	9%	74	6%	71%	27	48%	33%	4.01	1.0	41	103	$12
13	KC	472	42	12	42	2	233	241	287	364	651	546	682	6	82	26	0.39	37	19	45	91	86	7%	66	6%	33%	26	46%	23%	3.30	-9.2	37	93	$4
1st Half		237	19	5	15	1	215	227	265	325	590	461	636	6	85	23	0.46	39	16	45	74	81	5%	80	8%	25%	14	36%	29%	2.65	-9.8	39	98	$1
2nd Half		235	23	7	27	1	251	254	299	404	703	633	728	6	80	29	0.33	34	22	44	110	91	8%	64	4%	50%	12	58%	17%	4.06	0.6	40	100	$8
14	Proj	**513**	**59**	**18**	**64**	**3**	**246**	**251**	**295**	**415**	**710**	**630**	**738**	**6**	**81**	**27**	**0.34**	**36**	**18**	**47**	**114**	**94**	**9%**	**69**	**5%**	**52%**				**4.02**	**0.7**	**46**	**116**	**$12**

Murphy,Daniel

Age	29	Bats	L	Pos 2B	Health	C	LIMA Plan	B+
Ht	6' 2"	Wt	205		PT/Exp	A	Rand Var	-2
					Consist	A	MM	2335

Skilled batsman added more punch and speed to repertoire. Increase in FB% helped power (as hr/f remained stable). When on basepaths he combined superb SB% with more running opps. Had third most AB in MLB, so you have to temper excitement over the big counting stats. Still, a solid MI profile.

Yr	Tm	AB	R	HR	RBI	SB	BA	xBA	OBP	SLG	OPS	vL	vR	bb%	ct%	h%	Eye	G	L	F	PX	xPX	hr/f	Spd	SBO	SB%	#Wk	DOM	DIS	RC/G	RAR	BPV	BPX	R$
09	NYM	508	60	12	63	4	266	280	313	427	741	682	754	7	86	29	0.55	40	19	41	103	96	7%	89	5%	67%	27	59%	19%	4.67	14.8	71	145	$10
10	aaa	34	3	1	6	1	238	294	254	370	624			2	93	24	0.30				87			99	13%	100%				3.24		77	167	-$1
11	NYM	391	49	6	49	5	320	289	362	448	809	755	825	6	89	35	0.57	47	22	31	88	95	6%	97	9%	50%	20	45%	10%	5.80	22.8	70	156	$16
12	NYM	571	62	6	65	10	291	285	332	403	735	680	761	6	86	33	0.44	51	24	25	79	55	5%	92	8%	83%	27	48%	30%	4.86	19.2	47	118	$17
13	NYM	658	92	13	78	23	286	266	319	415	733	616	790	5	86	32	0.34	42	21	36	87	100	6%	107	16%	88%	27	52%	19%	4.84	21.9	55	138	$30
1st Half		314	45	5	32	9	277	268	312	401	713	531	818	5	86	31	0.36	44	21	35	86	112	5%	112	16%	75%	14	50%	21%	4.40	6.3	57	143	$23
2nd Half		344	47	8	46	14	294	263	325	427	752	709	767	4	85	33	0.32	41	21	38	87	89	7%	102	16%	100%	13	54%	15%	5.28	15.0	53	133	$35
14	Proj	**597**	**76**	**11**	**72**	**17**	**291**	**272**	**327**	**421**	**748**	**662**	**784**	**5**	**86**	**32**	**0.40**	**43**	**22**	**35**	**89**	**87**	**6%**	**100**	**14%**	**81%**				**4.99**	**21.7**	**61**	**152**	**$25**

Murphy,David

Age	32	Bats	L	Pos LF	Health	A	LIMA Plan	B+
Ht	6' 4"	Wt	210		PT/Exp	B	Rand Var	+5
					Consist	F	MM	3235

He'll never be a star, but we thought he'd hold more of his 2012 gains. What happened? The hit rate took ill, which also seemed to infect SB and SB%. xBA tells the real story. Stable yet unexceptional skill set was largely immune; Eye, G/L/F, PX all within career norms. Given his age and solid ct%, bet on a partial rebound.

Yr	Tm	AB	R	HR	RBI	SB	BA	xBA	OBP	SLG	OPS	vL	vR	bb%	ct%	h%	Eye	G	L	F	PX	xPX	hr/f	Spd	SBO	SB%	#Wk	DOM	DIS	RC/G	RAR	BPV	BPX	R$
09	TEX	432	61	17	57	9	269	255	338	447	785	627	833	10	75	32	0.46	38	19	43	120	97	12%	102	11%	69%	27	48%	37%	5.28	16.3	51	104	$13
10	TEX	419	54	12	65	14	291	277	358	449	806	696	847	10	83	33	0.63	44	19	36	106	95	9%	103	13%	88%	26	73%	23%	5.94	22.9	69	150	$18
11	TEX	404	46	11	46	11	275	264	328	401	729	507	809	8	85	30	0.54	54	17	29	78	82	11%	117	15%	65%	27	52%	37%	4.53	6.4	54	120	$13
12	TEX	457	65	15	61	10	304	279	380	479	859	845	862	11	84	34	0.73	43	21	35	110	109	11%	106	10%	67%	27	59%	15%	6.52	32.2	78	195	$20
13	TEX	436	51	13	45	1	220	271	282	374	656	562	685	8	86	23	0.63	43	19	38	100	98	9%	88	5%	20%	26	62%	23%	3.31	-9.0	70	175	$4
1st Half		270	27	8	27	1	219	271	275	370	645	570	679	7	87	22	0.60	41	21	39	96	81	9%	86	9%	20%	14	71%	21%	3.11	-7.6	67	168	$4
2nd Half		166	24	5	18	0	223	267	291	380	671	532	694	9	86	23	0.67	47	17	36	105	128	10%	94	0%	0%	12	50%	25%	3.63	-2.0	74	185	$2
14	Proj	**440**	**57**	**14**	**52**	**6**	**274**	**270**	**339**	**433**	**772**	**651**	**804**	**9**	**85**	**30**	**0.64**	**44**	**19**	**37**	**104**	**104**	**10%**	**100**	**8%**	**60%**				**5.05**	**13.1**	**63**	**158**	**$15**

Murphy,Donnie

Age	31	Bats	R	Pos 3B	Health	D	LIMA Plan	D
Ht	5' 10"	Wt	190		PT/Exp	F	Rand Var	-1
					Consist	D	MM	4201

11-23-.255 in 149 AB at CHC. Achieved highs in AB as well as most counting categories. MLEs never showed extraordinary pop; approaching 24% hr/f again is a pipe dream. Ct% and Eye continue to be anemic and overall hitting skills lag, so those HR will come at a stiff cost. Let him bask in 2013 while you look elsewhere.

Yr	Tm	AB	R	HR	RBI	SB	BA	xBA	OBP	SLG	OPS	vL	vR	bb%	ct%	h%	Eye	G	L	F	PX	xPX	hr/f	Spd	SBO	SB%	#Wk	DOM	DIS	RC/G	RAR	BPV	BPX	R$
09	aaa																																	
10	FLA *	250	30	11	40	0	234	281	273	439	711	1571	844	5	71	29	0.18	32	32	36	154	214	33%	107	0%	0%	9	67%	33%	3.98	0.0	51	111	$4
11	FLA *	115	12	2	10	0	160	209	200	276	476	627	535	5	77	19	0.23	39	13	49	84	109	6%	101	0%	0%	9	22%	33%	1.68	-8.7	19	42	-$4
12	MIA *	222	27	12	29	2	223	243	286	448	733	430	816	8	67	28	0.26	40	18	41	162	104	9%	105	6%	63%	17	24%	53%	4.15	1.0	47	118	$3
13	CHC *	451	44	19	50	5	219	228	262	400	663	950	818	6	68	28	0.18	35	19	45	140	157	24%	83	11%	58%	9	44%	22%	3.34	-9.1	21	53	$6
1st Half		201	13	5	20	3	200	218	254	325	579			7	69	26	0.23				97			92	18%	46%				2.45		-4	-10	$0
2nd Half		250	31	14	30	2	234	246	270	460	730	950	818	5	67	29	0.15	35	19	45	175	157	24%	84	5%	100%	9	44%	22%	4.17	1.5	43	108	$11
14	Proj	**197**	**21**	**7**	**23**	**2**	**224**	**228**	**291**	**396**	**687**	**647**	**704**	**6**	**69**	**29**	**0.21**	**39**	**17**	**44**	**131**	**125**	**12%**	**94**	**6%**	**60%**				**3.49**	**-2.9**	**19**	**47**	**$3**

Myers,Wil

Age	23	Bats	R	Pos RF	Health	A	LIMA Plan	B
Ht	6' 3"	Wt	205		PT/Exp	B	Rand Var	-3
					Consist	C	MM	4325

13-53-.293 in 335 AB at TAM. Impact was immediate after June callup as he hit for average and thunder vs both LHP and RHP. Eye, ct% and bb% improved during 2H, leaving few warts remaining; maybe elevated GB will stifle power. A rising star, but resist the urge to bid irrationally for 2014. (That's standard advice with young players.)

Yr	Tm	AB	R	HR	RBI	SB	BA	xBA	OBP	SLG	OPS	vL	vR	bb%	ct%	h%	Eye	G	L	F	PX	xPX	hr/f	Spd	SBO	SB%	#Wk	DOM	DIS	RC/G	RAR	BPV	BPX	R$
09																																		
10																																		
11	aa	354	37	5	37	7	225	233	301	334	636			10	74	29	0.43				90			89	10%	76%				3.33		18	40	$3
12	a/a	522	75	26	83	5	278	257	337	497	833			8	71	34	0.31				147			106	6%	58%				5.81		52	130	$21
13	TAM *	587	86	24	100	11	274	254	338	460	798	821	834	9	71	35	0.33	46	20	34	142	120	15%	94	9%	78%	16	50%	25%	5.46	19.8	44	110	$26
1st Half		306	42	14	56	6	257	246	313	445	757	867	762	7	69	33	0.26	43	23	35	137	98	21%	112	10%	73%	3	0%	33%	4.74	2.6	36	90	$25
2nd Half		281	44	10	44	5	292	263	364	477	841	811	848	10	73	37	0.42	47	20	34	146	125	14%	87	7%	83%	13	62%	23%	6.29	14.5	56	140	$27
14	Proj	**588**	**83**	**25**	**91**	**9**	**270**	**259**	**333**	**464**	**797**	**825**	**784**	**9**	**72**	**34**	**0.34**	**45**	**21**	**34**	**143**	**114**	**17%**	**105**	**8%**	**75%**				**5.40**	**16.1**	**49**	**122**	**$24**

Napoli,Mike

Age	32	Bats	R	Pos 1B	Health	B	LIMA Plan	B+
Ht	6' 0"	Wt	220		PT/Exp	B	Rand Var	-2
					Consist	F	MM	5115

Despite yearly fluctuations in BA/xBA and h%, he's been a solid run producer against lefties and righties with near equal aplomb. Dip in value due to loss of C eligibility is counterbalanced by jump in PT. Ct% may be deteriorating past the point that bb% can mitigate the damage. But take the power to the bank.

Yr	Tm	AB	R	HR	RBI	SB	BA	xBA	OBP	SLG	OPS	vL	vR	bb%	ct%	h%	Eye	G	L	F	PX	xPX	hr/f	Spd	SBO	SB%	#Wk	DOM	DIS	RC/G	RAR	BPV	BPX	R$
09	LAA	382	60	20	56	3	272	265	350	492	842	1023	782	9	73	32	0.39	38	19	43	149	138	17%	102	6%	50%	27	48%	33%	5.75	12.6	63	129	$12
10	LAA	453	60	26	68	4	238	264	316	468	784	966	700	8	70	28	0.31	38	20	42	168	148	19%	58	6%	67%	26	54%	31%	4.71	1.3	50	109	$12
11	TEX	369	72	30	75	4	320	312	414	631	1046	1049	1044	14	77	35	0.68	39	20	41	207	187	25%	74	5%	67%	24	67%	17%	9.66	50.1	125	278	$26
12	TEX	352	53	24	56	1	227	239	343	469	812	706	861	14	64	28	0.45	40	19	41	169	157	26%	102	1%	100%	23	43%	48%	5.17	6.0	53	133	$9
13	BOS	498	79	23	92	1	259	251	360	482	842	899	816	13	62	37	0.39	37	24	39	195	156	19%	72	1%	50%	27	56%	41%	5.84	17.8	55	138	$18
1st Half		283	38	9	54	1	261	242	337	438	775	710	811	10	64	38	0.31	36	28	36	158	143	14%	68	3%	50%	14	43%	50%	5.04	3.6	23	58	$18
2nd Half		215	41	14	38	0	256	264	375	540	915	1110	822	16	61	35	0.49	38	19	43	245	174	25%	80	0%	0%	13	69%	31%	6.93	14.6	98	245	$18
14	Proj	**456**	**75**	**27**	**80**	**2**	**262**	**254**	**365**	**505**	**870**	**910**	**852**	**13**	**64**	**35**	**0.43**	**38**	**21**	**41**	**195**	**162**	**22%**	**79**	**2%**	**65%**				**6.23**	**21.6**	**62**	**154**	**$19**

ROB CARROLL

Nava,Daniel

Age 31	Bats B	Pos RF LF	Health	B	LIMA Plan	D+
Ht 5' 11"	Wt 200		PT/Exp	C	Rand Var	-5
			Consist	C	MM	3123

Surprise name among BA/OBP leaders as ct% and xPX continued upward trends, with high h% and LD% providing the fuel. Track record and age don't support a repeat, and vL/vR splits likely to stand in the way of full-time work. Even if 2013 is his peak, he's a nice complementary piece.

Yr	Tm	AB	R	HR	RBI	SB	BA	xBA	OBP	SLG	OPS	vL	vR	bb%	ct%	h%	Eye	G	L	F	PX	xPX	hr/f	Spd	SBO	SB%	#Wk	DOM	DIS	RC/G	RAR	BPV	BPX	R$
09	aa	118	19	3	18	0	328	302	422	505	927			14	89	35	1.42				112			98	0%	0%				8.08		103	210	$
10	BOS *	445	53	8	62	4	245	226	307	374	681	637	727	8	73	32	0.33	39	16	45	106	102	2%	85	7%	54%	16	25%	56%	3.80	-2.3	20	43	$
11	aaa	441	52	7	36	7	226	238	307	339	646			10	76	28	0.49				89			95	9%	67%				3.41		27	60	$
12	BOS *	366	53	9	46	4	248	258	337	400	736	613	797	12	78	30	0.60	38	23	38	111	104	8%	74	5%	75%	17	47%	35%	4.57	6.3	47	118	$
13	BOS	458	77	12	66	0	303	263	385	445	831	647	894	10	80	36	0.55	34	26	40	103	131	8%	96	1%	0%	26	42%	19%	5.99	25.2	52	130	$1
1st Half		263	45	10	49	0	285	260	369	441	810	648	880	12	78	33	0.61	32	27	41	104	132	11%	80	2%	0%	14	43%	14%	5.64	12.1	46	115	$2
2nd Half		195	32	2	17	0	328	268	379	451	830	646	913	8	82	39	0.44	38	25	38	102	130	3%	117	0%	0%	12	42%	25%	6.49	12.7	60	150	$1
14	Proj	364	55	8	44	2	269	257	363	412	775	627	826	10	79	32	0.56	37	23	40	107	117	7%	94	3%	59%				4.92	5.0	42	105	$

Navarro,Dioner

Age 30	Bats B	Pos CA	Health	A	LIMA Plan	D+
Ht 5' 9"	Wt 205		PT/Exp	F	Rand Var	-5
			Consist	D	MM	2221

OK, who saw this coming? Who even knew he was still in the majors? A 1.123 OPS vs lefties? (Asking more questions defers having to come up with the answers.) Lifetime .251 hitter got more knocks than usual, nearly 20% of FB cleared the fence. Can he do it again? Will he do it again? No, and heck no.

Yr	Tm	AB	R	HR	RBI	SB	BA	xBA	OBP	SLG	OPS	vL	vR	bb%	ct%	h%	Eye	G	L	F	PX	xPX	hr/f	Spd	SBO	SB%	#Wk	DOM	DIS	RC/G	RAR	BPV	BPX	R$
09	TAM	376	38	8	32	5	218	248	261	322	583	740	490	5	86	23	0.35	37	20	43	64	57	6%	66	9%	71%	26	31%	23%	2.65	-12.1	28	57	$
10	TAM *	265	25	2	23	2	213	223	291	287	579	518	535	10	81	26	0.58	47	16	37	58	44	3%	70	5%	69%	18	39%	33%	2.71	-8.0	13	28	-$
11	LA	176	13	5	17	0	193	221	276	324	600	616	597	10	80	21	0.57	43	14	43	85	94	8%	80	0%	0%	18	44%	39%	2.82	-4.8	35	78	-$
12	CIN *	276	23	6	35	0	262	280	307	380	687	750	754	6	85	29	0.42	34	31	34	74	96	10%	58	0%	0%	9	22%	33%	4.03	2.7	29	73	$
13	CHC	240	31	13	34	0	300	289	365	492	856	1123	764	9	85	31	0.64	41	25	34	110	91	19%	73	1%	0%	26	54%	31%	6.36	17.7	69	173	$
1st Half		96	13	8	18	0	260	292	336	521	857	1568	647	10	83	24	0.69	43	21	36	141	126	28%	75	4%	0%	14	43%	36%	5.79	5.9	91	228	$
2nd Half		144	18	5	16	0	326	289	378	472	850	881	847	8	86	35	0.60	40	28	32	90	69	13%	82	0%	0%	12	67%	25%	6.76	11.6	59	148	$1
14	Proj	225	24	8	28	0	266	266	327	408	735	868	688	8	84	29	0.56	40	24	36	87	89	11%	72	0%	100%				4.62	5.9	33	82	$

Nelson,Chris

Age 28	Bats R	Pos 3B	Health	C	LIMA Plan	D
Ht 5' 11"	Wt 205		PT/Exp	D	Rand Var	0
			Consist	F	MM	2311

3-20-.221 in 145 AB at COL, NYY, and LAA. Failed to impress any of three employers in another season of disappointment. Poor ct%, lots of GB, and painfully weak Eye conspired to keep him off the bases, and history provides few bright spots from which to build. At 28 with a BPV of 1, further opps will be increasingly scarce.

Yr	Tm	AB	R	HR	RBI	SB	BA	xBA	OBP	SLG	OPS	vL	vR	bb%	ct%	h%	Eye	G	L	F	PX	xPX	hr/f	Spd	SBO	SB%	#Wk	DOM	DIS	RC/G	RAR	BPV	BPX	R$
09	aa	107	17	3	13	4	260	271	320	437	757			8	80	30	0.42				106			124	23%	64%				4.61		58	118	$
10	COL *	344	43	8	33	5	259	267	296	383	679	889	485	5	82	30	0.29	52	19	29	81	42	0%	108	11%	60%	8	0%	38%	3.80	-1.9	36	78	$
11	COL *	469	46	10	48	4	249	264	273	386	658	655	667	3	81	29	0.17	47	21	32	95	101	9%	108	10%	49%	13	54%	31%	3.44	-7.7	39	87	$
12	COL *	396	52	9	58	3	293	266	340	441	781	787	819	7	75	37	0.29	50	25	25	106	105	14%	115	4%	54%	24	33%	29%	5.32	14.6	36	90	$1
13	3 TM *	345	31	6	38	4	229	227	266	340	606	662	579	5	72	30	0.18	50	20	30	81	99	7%	124	7%	81%	15	13%	67%	3.01	-9.7	1	3	$
1st Half		169	13	1	12	3	221	233	246	297	543	677	541	3	71	30	0.11	58	23	19	60	61	0%	120	8%	100%	10	0%	70%	2.46	-7.8	-23	-58	$
2nd Half		176	18	5	26	2	237	219	286	382	668	641	616	6	73	30	0.25	41	16	43	100	143	10%	118	6%	61%	5	40%	60%	3.60	-2.0	21	53	$
14	Proj	166	18	3	20	2	252	246	292	381	673	697	664	5	75	32	0.22	49	21	30	93	107	9%	117	8%	68%				3.74	-1.1	14	36	$

Nieuwenhuis,Kirk

Age 26	Bats L	Pos CF	Health	A	LIMA Plan	D
Ht 6' 3"	Wt 215		PT/Exp	D	Rand Var	+5
			Consist	B	MM	3201

3-14-.189 in 95 AB at NYM. Lousy follow-up to so-so rookie year earned him a demotion by mid-season. Two-year MLB line vs LHP: .159/.266/.203; big problem is that .717 level vs. RHP isn't exactly gripping either. Eye and ct% uniformly weak. Triple-digit PX and Spd are enough to keep a candle lit, but it's a flickering one.

Yr	Tm	AB	R	HR	RBI	SB	BA	xBA	OBP	SLG	OPS	vL	vR	bb%	ct%	h%	Eye	G	L	F	PX	xPX	hr/f	Spd	SBO	SB%	#Wk	DOM	DIS	RC/G	RAR	BPV	BPX	R$
09	aa	32	7	1	2	1	371	267	428	592	1021			9	67	54	0.30				170			123	18%	42%				9.25		61	124	$
10	a/a	514	65	12	55	9	228	248	271	379	650			6	71	30	0.20				124			102	18%	54%				3.23		25	54	$
11	aaa	188	26	5	11	4	236	231	324	396	721			12	64	34	0.36				143			114	13%	63%				4.20		30	67	$
12	NYM	282	40	7	28	4	252	222	315	376	691	515	740	8	65	36	0.26	51	22	27	99	90	14%	98	11%	50%	17	18%	71%	3.85	-2.0	-11	-28	$
13	NYM *	377	45	12	36	6	182	215	252	319	571	111	661	9	65	24	0.27	46	19	35	109	100	14%	107	10%	69%	11	36%	64%	2.49	-19.6	0	0	$
1st Half		192	24	7	16	3	156	213	229	291	520	0	457	9	65	19	0.27	53	17	30	100	85	11%	103	11%	69%	8	38%	63%	2.00	-13.9	-10	-25	-$
2nd Half		185	21	4	19	3	209	217	275	349	624	167	860	8	66	29	0.27	39	21	39	117	114	15%	112	10%	69%	3	33%	67%	3.07	-6.4	9	23	$
14	Proj	128	16	4	12	2	247	226	310	390	700	378	752	9	66	35	0.27	48	21	32	118	97	14%	102	10%	64%				4.03	-0.5	1	3	$

Nieves,Wil

Age 36	Bats R	Pos CA	Health	B	LIMA Plan	D
Ht 5' 11"	Wt 190		PT/Exp	F	Rand Var	-5
			Consist	D	MM	1111

This is the year that many of those grounders found holes. Check out the string of xBA and GB%; 2013 could have just as easily been a rerun of 2009. Actually, MLB BA has hovered around .300 for the past few years, and his ct% has been pretty steady. Status as a "2nd C that won't hurt you" hinges on the vagaries of h%.

Yr	Tm	AB	R	HR	RBI	SB	BA	xBA	OBP	SLG	OPS	vL	vR	bb%	ct%	h%	Eye	G	L	F	PX	xPX	hr/f	Spd	SBO	SB%	#Wk	DOM	DIS	RC/G	RAR	BPV	BPX	R$
09	WAS	224	20	1	26	1	259	233	313	299	612	483	643	7	80	32	0.38	62	19	19	31	59	3%	83	1%	100%	25	20%	60%	3.23	-3.0	-14	-29	$
10	WAS	158	10	3	16	0	203	229	244	310	554	621	537	5	82	23	0.28	54	15	31	77	75	8%	77	0%	0%	26	38%	42%	2.39	-6.4	23	50	-$
11	MIL *	209	10	1	9	1	162	210	201	206	407	343	382	5	80	19	0.25	71	13	16	34	8	0%	80	2%	100%	12	17%	67%	1.27	-16.6	-14	-31	-$
12	2 NL *	194	15	4	17	1	260	256	287	353	640	939	667	4	79	31	0.17	66	24	10	62	41	29%	92	6%	19%	15	33%	47%	3.31	-2.1	1	3	$
13	ARI	195	16	1	22	0	297	233	320	369	690	720	670	4	84	35	0.25	61	17	21	59	40	3%	91	0%	0%	27	26%	41%	4.36	3.5	19	48	$
1st Half		55	9	0	10	0	382	269	424	436	860	845	864	7	85	45	0.50	58	25	17	48	22	0%	102	0%	0%	14	36%	36%	7.63	5.2	27	68	$
2nd Half		140	7	1	12	0	264	207	285	343	628	613	628	3	83	31	0.17	63	14	23	63	47	4%	84	0%	0%	13	15%	46%	3.38	-1.3	15	38	$
14	Proj	134	11	2	14	0	268	244	298	349	646	721	606	4	82	32	0.26	63	19	18	60	37	9%	90	2%	46%				3.62	-0.4	-5	-13	$

Nix,Jayson

Age 31	Bats R	Pos SS 3B	Health	D	LIMA Plan	D
Ht 5' 11"	Wt 195		PT/Exp	F	Rand Var	-3
			Consist	B	MM	2301

Talk about a bizarre year. LD% was double that of 2012 while PX dropped by half, producing career-low XBH. But SB and SB% were career highs. Low BA, lousy ct% and poor Eye were familiar pitfalls, before 2H was ended by hamstring and wrist injuries. This was his clearest MLB opportunity since 2010; may not get another like this.

Yr	Tm	AB	R	HR	RBI	SB	BA	xBA	OBP	SLG	OPS	vL	vR	bb%	ct%	h%	Eye	G	L	F	PX	xPX	hr/f	Spd	SBO	SB%	#Wk	DOM	DIS	RC/G	RAR	BPV	BPX	R$
09	CHW *	285	40	12	39	11	236	236	315	403	718	822	621	10	78	26	0.52	39	13	48	106	118	13%	97	17%	84%	23	43%	35%	4.33	7.8	47	96	$
10	2 AL	331	32	14	34	1	224	231	281	396	676	681	674	6	74	26	0.23	36	15	49	122	104	12%	99	5%	33%	26	38%	42%	3.39	-0.3	35	76	$
11	TOR *	299	31	9	32	6	181	196	231	328	559	998	464	6	69	23	0.21	36	9	55	114	115	8%	100	13%	85%	11	27%	64%	2.39	-10.0	11	24	-$
12	NYY *	207	28	4	21	6	234	216	289	369	658	726	645	7	69	32	0.25	46	12	42	117	107	8%	81	20%	67%	22	41%	55%	3.47	0.2	10	25	$
13	NYY	267	32	3	24	13	236	209	308	311	619	687	579	8	70	33	0.30	39	26	35	62	87	4%	111	19%	93%	18	11%	61%	3.31	-0.8	-17	-43	$
1st Half		232	23	2	20	11	237	203	300	302	602	665	572	8	70	33	0.30	40	25	36	53	83	3%	111	17%	100%	14	7%	57%	3.29	-1.2	-25	-63	$
2nd Half		35	9	1	4	2	229	241	289	371	661	765	614	8	69	30	0.27	33	33	33	118	110	13%	101	38%	67%	4	25%	75%	3.38	-0.1	17	43	-$
14	Proj	195	22	4	20	6	220	218	293	340	633	722	570	7	71	29	0.27	39	21	41	95	105	8%	98	15%	85%				3.14	-2.0	5	12	$

Norris,Derek

Age 25	Bats R	Pos CA	Health	A	LIMA Plan	D+
Ht 6' 0"	Wt 210		PT/Exp	D	Rand Var	-2
			Consist	C	MM	4313

Wouldn't it be great to live in a world of second halves and LHP? The reality has been a modicum of success against southpaws, some sock, and a nice bb%. Other truths have been impotence against RHP and a shaky ct%. Still young enough to emerge from platoon role, but he'll have to give someone a reason first.

Yr	Tm	AB	R	HR	RBI	SB	BA	xBA	OBP	SLG	OPS	vL	vR	bb%	ct%	h%	Eye	G	L	F	PX	xPX	hr/f	Spd	SBO	SB%	#Wk	DOM	DIS	RC/G	RAR	BPV	BPX	R$
09																																		
10																																		
11	aa	334	62	17	38	11	190	240	314	392	706			15	63	24	0.49				164			104	17%	71%				3.85		48	107	$
12	OAK *	427	47	13	61	9	212	235	274	359	633	618	630	8	74	26	0.32	40	22	39	102	93	13%	101	12%	80%	16	31%	63%	3.20	-6.8	24	60	$
13	OAK	264	41	9	30	5	246	241	345	409	754	990	445	12	73	30	0.52	36	21	43	124	95	11%	85	6%	100%	26	46%	38%	4.81	8.5	44	110	$
1st Half		169	23	3	15	3	195	216	299	308	607	769	456	13	72	25	0.53	35	20	45	94	91	5%	79	7%	100%	14	43%	36%	3.01	-3.7	16	40	$
2nd Half		95	18	6	15	2	337	283	411	589	1001	1273	415	11	75	40	0.50	37	23	41	175	101	21%	100	6%	100%	12	50%	42%	9.50	14.3	93	233	$1
14	Proj	249	38	10	33	5	243	242	331	417	749	944	528	11	72	30	0.44	37	21	42	130	95	13%	97	8%	84%				4.62	6.8	42	106	$

ROB CARROLL

Nunez,Eduardo

Age 27	Bats R	Pos SS	Health C	LIMA Plan C+	
Ht 6' 0"	Wt 185		PT/Exp D	Rand Var -1	
			Consist C	MM 1513	

Misfired in April before missing May/June with a strained ribcage. Better contact and h% upon 2H return got him on base at a decent rate, but SBO held down SB total and thus his value. Not necessarily a skill set that merits a full time job, but if an extended opportunity should arise... UP: 30 SB.

Yr	Tm	AB	R	HR	RBI	SB	BA	xBA	OBP	SLG	OPS	vL	vR	bb%	ct%	h%	Eye	G	L	F	PX	xPX	hr/f	Spd	SBO	SB%	#Wk	DOM	DIS	RC/G	RAR	BPV	BPX	R$
09	aa	497	68	10	54	19	310	266	340	420	760			4	86	34	0.33				70			95	18%	71%				5.18		41	84	$22
10	NYY *	514	59	5	50	25	265	247	307	348	655	692	662	6	87	30	0.46	65	6	29	57	52	7%	130	22%	82%	7	29%	0%	3.80	5.5	45	98	$16
11	NYY	309	38	5	30	22	265	274	313	385	698	742	673	7	88	29	0.59	45	21	34	80	70	5%	121	35%	79%	26	54%	8%	4.25	7.5	68	151	$11
12	NYY *	252	28	3	23	23	229	216	262	299	562	860	539	4	83	27	0.26	44	16	39	46	90	3%	131	50%	81%	12	33%	50%	2.72	-5.4	17	43	$7
13	NYY	304	38	3	28	10	260	250	307	372	679	652	693	6	83	30	0.39	41	21	38	78	81	3%	143	17%	77%	20	45%	35%	3.93	4.4	52	130	$7
1st Half		80	9	0	4	2	200	219	273	275	548	342	687	9	80	25	0.50	39	20	41	59	88	0%	124	16%	67%	7	14%	43%	2.37	-2.8	25	63	-$5
2nd Half		224	29	3	24	8	281	261	318	406	724	772	694	5	84	32	0.34	42	22	36	85	79	4%	144	18%	80%	13	62%	31%	4.62	7.3	61	153	$12
14	Proj	**395**	**47**	**5**	**36**	**20**	**250**	**241**	**296**	**350**	**646**	**678**	**624**	**6**	**84**	**29**	**0.39**	**44**	**18**	**38**	**69**	**80**	**4%**	**135**	**27%**	**78%**				**3.55**	**1.0**	**44**	**109**	**$11**

Olt,Mike

Age 25	Bats R	Pos 3B	Health A	LIMA Plan D	
Ht 6' 2"	Wt 210		PT/Exp F	Rand Var +2	
			Consist F	MM 4203	

Was a TEX untouchable after 28-82-.288 Double-A season in 2012. Then he crashed his own Pacific Coast League party with .197 BA/.368 Slg and 70% ct% (62% vs RHP), and woke up in Chicago. Spring eye problems may have contributed. He still owns those 2012 skills, but may need some time to re-establish them.

Yr	Tm	AB	R	HR	RBI	SB	BA	xBA	OBP	SLG	OPS	vL	vR	bb%	ct%	h%	Eye	G	L	F	PX	xPX	hr/f	Spd	SBO	SB%	#Wk	DOM	DIS	RC/G	RAR	BPV	BPX	R$
09																																		
10																																		
11																																		
12	TEX *	387	52	25	69	4	254	255	342	492	834	387	473	12	68	31	0.42	45	18	36	166	125	0%	108	5%	80%	8	13%	75%	5.76	20.0	64	160	$14
13	a/a	373	36	11	31	0	167	199	251	305	556			10	59	25	0.27				127			93	0%	0%				2.35		-12	-30	-$5
1st Half		186	21	7	18	0	179	203	260	340	601			10	56	27	0.25				157			88	0%	0%				2.75		-2	-5	-$5
2nd Half																																		
14	Proj	**281**	**34**	**9**	**36**	**2**	**236**	**213**	**318**	**382**	**700**	**700**	**700**	**11**	**63**	**34**	**0.33**	**42**	**20**	**38**	**126**		**13%**	**87**	**3%**	**88%**				**4.08**	**0.9**	**-7**	**-17**	**$6**

Ortiz,David

Age 38	Bats L	Pos DH	Health D	LIMA Plan B+	
Ht 6' 4"	Wt 250		PT/Exp B	Rand Var 0	
			Consist C	MM 5155	

Take a tour of his numbers these past three years while "living on borrowed time:" mirror-image BA/xBA, hefty OBP/Slg/OPS, steady Eye and ct%. PX and hr/f confirm that he's still mashing. Added career high SB this year just for fun. Age and health grade remind us this could go south at anytime, but the skills remain vintage.

Yr	Tm	AB	R	HR	RBI	SB	BA	xBA	OBP	SLG	OPS	vL	vR	bb%	ct%	h%	Eye	G	L	F	PX	xPX	hr/f	Spd	SBO	SB%	#Wk	DOM	DIS	RC/G	RAR	BPV	BPX	R$
09	BOS	541	77	28	99	0	238	262	332	462	794	716	828	12	75	27	0.55	32	17	50	149	153	13%	59	1%	0%	27	63%	26%	5.03	8.6	64	131	$12
10	BOS	518	86	32	102	0	270	279	370	529	899	599	1059	14	72	32	0.57	38	17	45	188	168	19%	62	1%	0%	27	70%	19%	6.79	34.0	86	187	$21
11	BOS	525	84	29	96	1	309	311	398	554	953	989	934	13	84	32	0.94	41	21	37	158	167	17%	63	1%	50%	27	63%	15%	8.10	51.3	110	244	$28
12	BOS	324	65	23	60	0	318	318	415	611	1026	985	1050	15	84	32	1.10	37	21	42	175	150	20%	60	1%	0%	17	82%	6%	9.46	43.1	127	318	$19
13	BOS	518	84	30	103	4	309	308	395	564	959	733	1092	13	83	33	0.86	39	23	39	162	173	18%	68	2%	100%	25	64%	12%	8.33	53.7	110	275	$31
1st Half		240	40	16	57	2	317	316	406	604	1010	769	1154	13	84	32	0.95	42	18	40	175	194	20%	72	3%	100%	12	75%	0%	9.22	30.3	126	315	$31
2nd Half		278	44	14	46	2	302	305	390	529	919	700	1040	13	82	33	0.80	35	27	38	151	154	16%	69	2%	100%	13	54%	23%	7.59	23.5	97	243	$31
14	Proj	**485**	**83**	**29**	**87**	**1**	**301**	**307**	**393**	**559**	**952**	**817**	**1029**	**13**	**82**	**32**	**0.88**	**38**	**22**	**40**	**166**	**164**	**18%**	**65**	**1%**	**60%**				**8.03**	**47.0**	**106**	**264**	**$27**

Overbay,Lyle

Age 37	Bats L	Pos 1B	Health A	LIMA Plan D+	
Ht 6' 2"	Wt 235		PT/Exp D	Rand Var +1	
			Consist B	MM 3213	

AB total underscores the year-long infirmary that was the 2013 NYY clubhouse. Dialed up some power in 1H, but 2H collapse casts doubt on return to even average levels. Career-worst Eye and bb% also suggest his former (and modest at that) skill set has atrophied. You can't spell Overbay without the O-V-E-R.

Yr	Tm	AB	R	HR	RBI	SB	BA	xBA	OBP	SLG	OPS	vL	vR	bb%	ct%	h%	Eye	G	L	F	PX	xPX	hr/f	Spd	SBO	SB%	#Wk	DOM	DIS	RC/G	RAR	BPV	BPX	R$
09	TOR	423	57	16	64	0	265	280	372	466	838	534	905	15	78	31	0.78	42	20	37	139	123	13%	55	0%	0%	27	56%	22%	6.05	17.5	70	143	$10
10	TOR	534	75	20	67	1	243	264	329	433	762	700	781	11	75	29	0.51	45	16	39	138	129	13%	70	1%	100%	27	44%	26%	4.79	2.9	58	126	$10
11	2 NL	394	43	9	47	2	234	243	310	360	670	651	677	10	78	28	0.48	46	19	35	94	120	8%	69	3%	67%	26	35%	38%	3.67	-11.0	28	62	$4
12	2 NL *	138	14	2	12	0	250	266	332	383	716	552	751	11	70	35	0.40	43	33	24	119	157	10%	64	0%	0%	20	35%	55%	4.34	-0.9	17	43	$0
13	NYY	445	43	14	59	2	240	251	295	393	688	516	746	7	75	29	0.32	44	22	35	112	119	12%	72	2%	100%	27	33%	48%	3.95	-8.7	28	70	$8
1st Half		242	24	9	34	0	240	268	281	434	715	536	786	5	77	28	0.25	44	20	37	141	145	13%	79	0%	0%	14	43%	36%	4.09	-3.7	57	143	$8
2nd Half		203	19	5	25	2	241	229	316	345	660	483	703	10	73	31	0.40	44	25	32	75	88	10%	65	3%	100%	13	23%	62%	3.72	-5.3	-7	-18	$6
14	Proj	**317**	**33**	**8**	**38**	**1**	**244**	**251**	**314**	**385**	**699**	**552**	**739**	**9**	**74**	**31**	**0.40**	**44**	**24**	**32**	**109**	**125**	**11%**	**66**	**2%**	**91%**				**4.12**	**-4.5**	**17**	**42**	**$6**

Owings,Christopher

Age 22	Bats R	Pos SS	Health A	LIMA Plan D	
Ht 5' 10"	Wt 180		PT/Exp D	Rand Var -1	
			Consist C	MM 2411	

0-5-.291 in 55 AB at ARI. Was both ROY and MVP of Pacific Coast League with .330/.359/.482 line. Wasn't overmatched during Sept callup, although decent pop and good speed are undermined by lousy bb% and weak Eye. Needs more seasoning before he can replicate this 2013 full-season line in the majors.

Yr	Tm	AB	R	HR	RBI	SB	BA	xBA	OBP	SLG	OPS	vL	vR	bb%	ct%	h%	Eye	G	L	F	PX	xPX	hr/f	Spd	SBO	SB%	#Wk	DOM	DIS	RC/G	RAR	BPV	BPX	R$
09																																		
10																																		
11																																		
12	aa	297	28	5	23	3	246	222	267	350	617			3	75	31	0.12				70			116	10%	50%				3.04		0	0	$2
13	ARI *	601	72	8	57	15	281	261	304	397	701	250	932	3	80	34	0.16	47	24	29	83	63	0%	126	16%	65%	4	50%	25%	4.16	11.3	31	78	$20
1st Half		363	44	5	36	8	303	236	316	409	725			2	78	38	0.09				81			115	17%	49%				4.39		16	40	$26
2nd Half		238	28	3	21	7	250	273	288	378	666	250	932	5	83	29	0.31	47	24	29	86	63	0%	138	14%	100%	4	50%	25%	3.86	2.7	53	133	$12
14	Proj	**135**	**15**	**3**	**12**	**3**	**261**	**252**	**286**	**394**	**679**	**373**	**802**	**3**	**78**	**31**	**0.16**	**44**	**22**	**34**	**91**	**57**	**8%**	**126**	**14%**	**68%**				**3.81**	**1.4**	**26**	**65**	**$4**

Ozuna,Marcell

Age 23	Bats R	Pos RF CF	Health C	LIMA Plan D+	
Ht 6' 1"	Wt 220		PT/Exp F	Rand Var 0	
			Consist F	MM 2511	

3-32-.265 in 275 AB at MIA. Jumped from Double-A and rode freakishly high h% and LD% through mid-June, making 2H tumble look worse than it was. Bb%, ct%, and Eye were actually peaking when thumb injury ended season in late July. He displayed a broad skill base in this debut, but plan on another uneven year or two.

Yr	Tm	AB	R	HR	RBI	SB	BA	xBA	OBP	SLG	OPS	vL	vR	bb%	ct%	h%	Eye	G	L	F	PX	xPX	hr/f	Spd	SBO	SB%	#Wk	DOM	DIS	RC/G	RAR	BPV	BPX	R$
09																																		
10																																		
11																																		
12																																		
13	MIA *	317	36	7	45	6	270	267	305	431	735	838	647	5	79	32	0.23	46	21	33	112	89	4%	120	10%	85%	13	31%	38%	4.63	0.2	52	130	$9
1st Half		249	30	6	39	5	300	278	332	476	807	955	696	5	78	36	0.21	44	23	33	129	94	4%	103	10%	83%	10	40%	40%	5.78	9.1	57	143	$14
2nd Half		68	6	1	6	1	162	224	208	265	473	368	511	6	81	19	0.31	53	15	33	51	72	6%	170	8%	100%	3	0%	33%	1.73	-6.1	29	73	-$8
14	Proj	**231**	**25**	**6**	**29**	**4**	**243**	**255**	**293**	**402**	**695**	**737**	**684**	**6**	**80**	**28**	**0.29**	**46**	**19**	**35**	**97**	**81**	**10%**	**160**	**8%**	**91%**				**3.93**	**-3.5**	**45**	**112**	**$6**

Pacheco,Jordan

Age 28	Bats R	Pos 1B	Health A	LIMA Plan D	
Ht 6' 1"	Wt 200		PT/Exp D	Rand Var +5	
			Consist F	MM 1331	

1-22-.239 in 247 AB at COL. xBA, ct%, LD% say he was the same batsman he was the year before; hit rates are fickle beasts. Power drop and high GB% slashed productivity and reduced PT. With this high-contact, low-impact profile, 2013 is probably a truer measure than 2012.

Yr	Tm	AB	R	HR	RBI	SB	BA	xBA	OBP	SLG	OPS	vL	vR	bb%	ct%	h%	Eye	G	L	F	PX	xPX	hr/f	Spd	SBO	SB%	#Wk	DOM	DIS	RC/G	RAR	BPV	BPX	R$
09																																		
10	aa	78	8	1	15	1	303	271	341	397	738			5	92	32	0.71				65			93	8%	41%				4.72		60	130	$2
11	COL *	447	33	4	39	1	225	277	255	297	552	946	572	4	86	25	0.28	53	27	20	51	49	13%	96	4%	29%	4	50%	25%	2.43	-21.4	23	51	$0
12	COL *	542	57	7	60	8	316	283	344	432	776	822	739	4	88	35	0.36	42	26	31	78	83	4%	95	6%	79%	23	43%	13%	5.55	22.7	52	130	$20
13	COL *	301	27	2	25	2	241	276	275	325	600	556	614	5	86	27	0.35	49	25	26	66	64	2%	89	3%	100%	24	33%	46%	3.03	-8.6	35	88	$1
1st Half		162	18	1	17	0	259	270	286	340	625	607	659	4	85	30	0.24	52	25	23	65	68	3%	81	0%	0%	14	36%	50%	3.34	-3.0	24	60	$3
2nd Half		139	9	1	8	2	219	275	263	308	571	435	542	6	88	24	0.51	42	26	32	67	57	0%	105	6%	100%	10	30%	40%	2.70	-5.4	51	128	-$2
14	Proj	**167**	**15**	**2**	**15**	**2**	**273**	**277**	**311**	**373**	**684**	**692**	**680**	**5**	**87**	**31**	**0.38**	**46**	**25**	**29**	**72**	**67**	**4%**	**98**	**5%**	**83%**				**4.03**	**-2.7**	**36**	**89**	**$4**

ROB CARROLL

Pagan,Angel

Age 32 | Bats B | Pos CF | Ht 6' 2" | Wt 200

Health F | PT/Exp B | Consist B | LIMA Plan A | Rand Var 0 | MM 2535

Strained a hamstring completing inside-the-park HR in late May; didn't play again until late Aug. SBO understandably impacted upon return, but plate skills were stable on both sides of DL stint. Those skills set a nice OBP floor and ensure continued SB opps, opening the door to... UP: full 2012 repeat.

Yr	Tm	AB	R	HR	RBI	SB	BA	xBA	OBP	SLG	OPS	vL	vR	bb%	ct%	h%	Eye	G	L	F	PX	xPX	hr/f	Spd	SBO	SB%	#Wk	DOM	DIS	RC/G	RAR	BPV	BPX	R$
09	NYM	343	54	6	32	14	306	283	350	487	837	807	848	7	84	35	0.45	41	21	38	108	101	6%	150	23%	67%	18	61%	11%	6.08	19.0	82	167	$14
10	NYM	579	80	11	69	37	290	251	340	425	765	692	788	7	83	33	0.45	36	20	44	89	99	5%	139	28%	80%	27	44%	33%	5.27	19.3	62	135	$29
11	NYM	478	68	7	56	32	262	256	322	372	694	672	702	8	87	29	0.71	35	24	41	74	93	4%	114	29%	82%	22	55%	9%	4.30	2.8	61	136	$19
12	SF	605	95	8	56	29	288	270	338	440	778	736	799	7	84	33	0.49	42	23	35	95	96	4%	151	22%	81%	27	59%	15%	5.40	22.4	74	185	$26
13	SF	280	44	5	30	9	282	277	334	414	749	807	725	8	87	31	0.64	43	23	34	86	77	6%	132	17%	69%	14	79%	0%	4.87	6.2	74	185	$10
1st Half		187	30	3	24	6	262	264	317	374	691	596	722	7	87	29	0.60	42	23	36	76	60	5%	115	20%	60%	8	75%	0%	3.91	-1.5	59	148	$12
2nd Half		93	14	2	6	3	323	302	376	495	871	1143	730	8	88	35	0.73	45	24	30	106	110	8%	142	11%	100%	6	83%	0%	7.26	7.6	98	245	$7
14	Proj	505	77	7	49	22	284	272	337	421	758	814	733	8	86	32	0.59	42	23	35	89	93	5%	147	20%	80%				5.12	13.6	77	193	$20

Paredes,Jimmy

Age 25 | Bats B | Pos RF | Ht 6' 3" | Wt 200

Health A | PT/Exp C | Consist A | LIMA Plan D | Rand Var +2 | MM 1401

1-10-.192 with 4 SB in 125 AB at HOU. AAAA player? MLEs and 2011 debut both showed some promise, but combined 2012-13 MLB line is .191/.237/.243 in 199 AB with 6/5 SB/CS. Add to that a lifetime 69% ct% and 0.19 Eye. Sure, he's young, but to borrow a phrase, there's really no there there. Next.

Yr	Tm	AB	R	HR	RBI	SB	BA	xBA	OBP	SLG	OPS	vL	vR	bb%	ct%	h%	Eye	G	L	F	PX	xPX	hr/f	Spd	SBO	SB%	#Wk	DOM	DIS	RC/G	RAR	BPV	BPX	R$
09																																		
10																																		
11	HOU *	553	67	10	49	27	250	253	276	371	647	500	773	4	74	32	0.14	54	21	25	92	96	7%	131	38%	60%	9	22%	56%	3.19	-18.4	19	42	$16
12	HOU *	581	70	9	43	27	252	224	278	361	639	220	546	4	75	32	0.15	47	16	36	77	98	0%	131	31%	68%	6	0%	83%	3.29	-17.2	12	30	$16
13	HOU *	452	45	7	37	16	228	250	271	343	614	282	565	6	72	30	0.22	60	19	20	90	73	6%	115	29%	56%	13	0%	69%	2.84	-20.3	9	23	$8
1st Half		241	25	6	26	8	252	259	304	408	712	279	610	7	72	33	0.26	57	19	24	123	101	8%	100	29%	50%	8	0%	50%	3.81	-4.7	30	75	$13
2nd Half		211	20	2	12	8	200	245	233	271	504	286	464	4	73	26	0.16	66	21	14	53	20	0%	140	29%	65%	5	0%	100%	1.93	-17.1	-11	-28	$2
14	Proj	100	11	0	8	4	236	230	266	313	579	331	670	4	74	31	0.17	56	19	25	63	75	3%	122	30%	63%				2.67	-5.5	-8	-20	$2

Parmelee,Chris

Age 26 | Bats L | Pos RF 1B | Ht 6' 1" | Wt 220

Health A | PT/Exp C | Consist F | LIMA Plan D+ | Rand Var +2 | MM 3103

8-24-.228 in 294 AB at MIN. Didn't carry over last year's power outburst at either AAA or MLB level, making 2012 PX look like an outlier. He's apt to take a walk, but that isn't enough; needs to be accompanied by either that 2010-11 ct% or 2012 PX to hold our attention. Age says it's put-up-or-shut-up time.

Yr	Tm	AB	R	HR	RBI	SB	BA	xBA	OBP	SLG	OPS	vL	vR	bb%	ct%	h%	Eye	G	L	F	PX	xPX	hr/f	Spd	SBO	SB%	#Wk	DOM	DIS	RC/G	RAR	BPV	BPX	R$
09																																		
10	aa	411	39	4	34	2	246	249	304	340	644			8	82	29	0.47				72			102	4%	51%				3.44		34	74	$3
11	MIN *	606	64	12	75	0	259	239	328	386	714	935	1069	9	81	30	0.53	38	19	43	90	132	15%	102	1%	0%	4	75%	0%	4.32	-5.0	45	100	$11
12	MIN *	420	56	18	61	1	268	250	355	473	828	681	667	12	74	32	0.51	38	18	44	141	106	8%	79	2%	43%	20	30%	55%	5.81	14.5	57	143	$13
13	MIN *	467	38	10	40	2	215	230	290	334	623	526	696	10	75	27	0.42	39	21	40	91	99	9%	77	2%	63%	19	32%	63%	3.13	-21.3	16	40	$0
1st Half		202	17	7	17	1	228	236	307	376	683	512	727	10	75	27	0.45	38	21	41	106	125	11%	65	4%	50%	14	43%	50%	3.76	-5.2	26	65	$3
2nd Half		265	21	3	23	1	205	230	276	302	578	554	627	9	75	26	0.39	43	22	35	80	37	5%	103	1%	100%	5	0%	100%	2.69	-15.8	14	35	-$2
14	Proj	316	31	8	33	1	244	240	324	388	711	664	726	10	76	30	0.46	39	20	41	105	93	9%	85	2%	58%				4.14	-2.9	26	65	$5

Parra,Gerardo

Age 27 | Bats L | Pos RF CF | Ht 5' 11" | Wt 200

Health A | PT/Exp B | Consist B | LIMA Plan B | Rand Var +2 | MM 2333

Used a monster AB total to inch his way over double-digit HR/SB thresholds; without that PT, his numbers look pedestrian. Solid ct% and steady BA/xBA are his calling cards, but dead-average power and speed, plus poor SB% and ineptitude vs. LHP all cap any further value gains. This is very likely as good as he gets.

Yr	Tm	AB	R	HR	RBI	SB	BA	xBA	OBP	SLG	OPS	vL	vR	bb%	ct%	h%	Eye	G	L	F	PX	xPX	hr/f	Spd	SBO	SB%	#Wk	DOM	DIS	RC/G	RAR	BPV	BPX	R$
09	ARI *	563	79	8	70	11	301	264	351	417	768	470	801	7	82	36	0.43	53	18	29	72	97	5%	123	13%	49%	22	36%	36%	5.05	15.7	38	78	$19
10	ARI *	400	36	4	35	3	270	263	311	384	695	701	674	6	80	33	0.30	51	20	29	83	92	4%	108	4%	72%	26	38%	42%	4.16	1.2	31	67	$6
11	ARI	445	55	8	46	15	292	272	357	427	784	790	782	9	82	34	0.52	50	22	28	88	84	8%	132	12%	94%	27	44%	26%	5.64	19.6	56	124	$17
12	ARI	385	58	7	36	15	273	267	335	392	727	631	754	8	80	33	0.43	53	22	24	83	101	9%	103	22%	63%	27	30%	33%	4.34	3.1	35	88	$13
13	ARI	601	79	10	48	10	268	283	323	403	726	501	820	7	83	31	0.48	55	20	25	97	97	8%	100	13%	50%	27	56%	19%	4.30	4.2	58	145	$16
1st Half		322	47	7	26	6	301	288	361	453	814	694	865	9	82	35	0.52	55	21	24	109	107	11%	103	16%	40%	14	57%	14%	5.45	13.2	65	163	$23
2nd Half		279	32	3	22	4	229	276	276	344	620	263	768	6	85	26	0.43	55	19	26	84	86	5%	96	9%	80%	13	54%	23%	3.16	-7.3	50	125	$8
14	Proj	408	54	7	36	10	270	275	327	397	724	541	786	8	82	31	0.46	54	21	26	90	95	8%	107	14%	63%				4.39	-0.7	50	125	$13

Pastornicky,Tyler

Age 24 | Bats R | Pos 2B | Ht 5' 11" | Wt 190

Health B | PT/Exp D | Consist B | LIMA Plan D | Rand Var 0 | MM 1411

0-0-.300 in 30 AB at ATL. Missed a possible PT opportunity in Aug when knee injury ended season. Speed is most advanced skill, but to date it hasn't helped produce a high h% nor SB total. Makes decent contact, but there's really not much happening when bat meets ball.

Yr	Tm	AB	R	HR	RBI	SB	BA	xBA	OBP	SLG	OPS	vL	vR	bb%	ct%	h%	Eye	G	L	F	PX	xPX	hr/f	Spd	SBO	SB%	#Wk	DOM	DIS	RC/G	RAR	BPV	BPX	R$
09																																		
10	aa	134	18	2	12	9	231	244	301	326	627			9	82	27	0.55				62			129	31%	81%				3.38		36	78	$3
11	a/a	459	52	6	36	22	281	248	319	362	681			5	89	31	0.51				50			120	26%	64%				3.91		44	98	$16
12	ATL *	322	32	3	28	4	239	270	280	335	615	536	651	5	83	28	0.33	64	18	17	71	36	8%	105	11%	56%	22	32%	45%	3.06	-4.3	31	78	$2
13	ATL *	318	38	3	21	7	259	282	307	337	644	1100	577	6	81	31	0.37	60	28	12	57	85	0%	121	11%	76%	8	13%	50%	3.58	0.6	21	53	$6
1st Half		248	28	3	19	5	270	279	301	367	668	667	583	4	81	32	0.24	58	25	17	70	152	0%	112	13%	71%	5	20%	40%	3.83	2.6	25	63	$8
2nd Half		70	9	0	2	2	220	265	326	233	559	2000	571	14	81	27	0.81	62	31	8	12	24	0%	120	6%	100%	3	0%	67%	2.61	-1.8	-3	-8	-$4
14	Proj	161	19	3	11	5	256	254	318	359	677	612	709	8	82	29	0.50	50	20	30	68	32	7%	122	14%	76%				3.90	1.0	30	75	$4

Paul,Xavier

Age 29 | Bats L | Pos LF | Ht 5' 9" | Wt 205

Health A | PT/Exp D | Consist C | LIMA Plan D | Rand Var 0 | MM 3211

Part-timer appears to be transitioning from a running game to power game, such as they are. Speed drop resulted in career-low SBO and swipes (zero), while rising PX, hr/f wrought career-high XBH by plenty. Profile remodel make sense as Basque meaning for Xavier is "new house." It's not a buyer's market, though.

Yr	Tm	AB	R	HR	RBI	SB	BA	xBA	OBP	SLG	OPS	vL	vR	bb%	ct%	h%	Eye	G	L	F	PX	xPX	hr/f	Spd	SBO	SB%	#Wk	DOM	DIS	RC/G	RAR	BPV	BPX	R$
09	LA *	130	12	2	13	6	265	200	312	410	722	400	1030	6	76	33	0.29	40	0	60	106	70	17%	96	30%	63%	3	33%	33%	4.19	0.5	34	69	$2
10	LA *	349	43	7	33	7	238	262	275	371	646	590	591	5	78	29	0.24	41	23	36	100	62	0%	101	17%	60%	12	42%	58%	3.30	-8.0	36	78	$5
11	2 NL	243	30	2	20	16	255	224	292	346	638	175	697	5	74	34	0.21	46	22	32	61	85	4%	148	35%	73%	26	19%	62%	3.41	-4.7	3	7	$6
12	CIN *	324	32	10	42	10	282	261	330	440	770	250	867	7	77	34	0.31	46	22	31	109	82	10%	84	19%	65%	12	50%	33%	4.98	8.6	35	88	$11
13	CIN	209	24	7	32	0	244	256	339	402	741	396	775	11	75	30	0.51	49	22	28	117	107	16%	66	2%	0%	27	41%	48%	4.40	2.1	37	93	$3
1st Half		150	19	5	25	0	253	264	337	413	751	393	792	11	75	31	0.51	49	24	27	118	131	16%	63	2%	0%	14	50%	36%	4.64	2.7	39	98	$5
2nd Half		59	5	2	7	0	220	228	313	373	686	400	733	12	73	27	0.50	51	19	30	114	43	15%	87	0%	0%	13	31%	62%	3.82	-0.4	35	88	-$3
14	Proj	160	17	4	20	3	250	250	323	388	711	366	743	9	75	31	0.39	48	21	31	102	79	11%	90	12%	64%				4.09	0.3	24	60	$4

Pearce,Steve

Age 31 | Bats R | Pos DH | Ht 5' 11" | Wt 210

Health F | PT/Exp F | Consist C | LIMA Plan D | Rand Var -2 | MM 2201

Missing 61 games (wrist tendinitis) likely cost him most extensive action with one team since 2009. Power and hr/f continue to inch upward, as does ct%, while batting eye reversed slide. The reality, however, is that he's defined by his limitations and has turned the corner on 30. Not the best place to be if you're a big leaguer.

Yr	Tm	AB	R	HR	RBI	SB	BA	xBA	OBP	SLG	OPS	vL	vR	bb%	ct%	h%	Eye	G	L	F	PX	xPX	hr/f	Spd	SBO	SB%	#Wk	DOM	DIS	RC/G	RAR	BPV	BPX	R$
09	PIT *	438	48	14	58	3	229	258	303	397	700	867	562	10	78	26	0.49	38	19	43	114	136	8%	66	11%	29%	15	53%	33%	3.71	-4.7	46	94	$4
10	PIT *	158	22	2	16	5	264	266	360	418	777	964	583	13	76	34	0.63	44	20	36	121	85	0%	115	16%	67%	4	25%	50%	5.11	4.9	64	139	$3
11	PIT *	124	12	3	14	0	203	197	246	304	550	589	437	5	75	25	0.22	43	15	43	73	98	3%	77	0%	0%	14	21%	64%	2.39	-6.4	-7	-16	-$2
12	3 TM *	351	42	13	47	3	247	240	325	420	745	760	657	10	77	29	0.49	38	17	45	117	128	7%	78	7%	49%	15	40%	40%	4.51	5.5	46	115	$7
13	BAL	119	14	4	13	1	261	243	362	420	782	802	749	11	79	30	0.60	39	17	44	112	129	10%	79	3%	100%	19	47%	37%	5.03	3.6	54	135	$1
1st Half		81	9	3	9	1	235	221	295	383	678	723	649	8	75	28	0.35	36	16	48	102	133	10%	76	5%	100%	11	45%	36%	3.83	-0.5	23	58	$1
2nd Half		38	5	1	4	0	316	286	435	500	935	932	1012	17	87	34	1.60	45	18	36	131	122	8%	88	0%	0%	8	50%	38%	8.10	4.2	115	288	$0
14	Proj	128	14	3	15	1	241	226	321	371	692	738	633	9	76	30	0.39	40	17	42	96	124	8%	86	6%	67%				3.79	-2.7	18	46	$3

ROB CARROLL

Pedroia,Dustin

Age 30	Bats R	Pos 2B	Health	B	LIMA Plan	A
Ht 5' 8"	Wt 165		PT/Exp	A	Rand Var	-1
			Consist	B	MM	2445

Led the AL in PA while playing through a torn ligament in his left thumb. That last tidbit tells us not to get too worked up over the dip in FB%, PX, and hr/f. Hasn't had a sub-30% h% since his rookie year and lifetime 1.04 Eye is bona fide rarity. Maybe 20 HR is out of reach, but he should again be one of the first 2B off the board.

Yr	Tm	AB	R	HR	RBI	SB	BA	xBA	OBP	SLG	OPS	vL	vR	bb%	ct%	h%	Eye	G	L	F	PX	xPX	hr/f	Spd	SBO	SB%	#Wk	DOM	DIS	RC/G	RAR	BPV	BPX	R$
09	BOS	626	115	15	72	20	296	295	371	447	819	765	839	11	93	30	1.64	39	20	41	93	92	6%	117	14%	71%	27	85%	0%	5.93	38.7	104	212	$26
10	BOS	302	53	12	41	9	288	310	367	493	860	700	910	11	87	30	0.97	39	22	39	131	97	11%	104	11%	90%	13	69%	15%	6.59	24.3	110	239	$14
11	BOS	635	102	21	91	26	307	288	387	474	861	1010	800	12	87	33	1.01	48	19	33	106	115	11%	122	15%	76%	27	70%	15%	6.80	53.9	94	209	$36
12	BOS	563	81	15	65	20	290	288	347	449	797	848	775	8	89	30	0.80	46	20	35	98	108	9%	108	17%	77%	26	65%	12%	5.56	29.2	86	215	$24
13	BOS	641	91	9	84	17	301	284	372	415	787	937	722	10	88	33	0.97	50	22	28	80	83	6%	123	10%	77%	26	65%	19%	5.67	34.4	77	193	$29
1st Half		323	53	5	47	11	322	282	403	443	846	968	795	12	86	36	1.00	50	22	28	86	90	6%	130	11%	85%	14	64%	29%	6.84	27.3	79	198	$35
2nd Half		318	38	4	37	6	280	285	340	387	727	908	640	8	90	30	0.94	51	21	28	74	76	5%	113	10%	67%	12	67%	8%	4.60	8.2	73	183	$23
14	**Proj**	**614**	**90**	**16**	**78**	**17**	**296**	**292**	**364**	**450**	**813**	**916**	**770**	**10**	**89**	**31**	**0.94**	**48**	**21**	**32**	**99**	**95**	**9%**	**117**	**11%**	**78%**				**5.94**	**38.4**	**84**	**211**	**$27**

Pena,Brayan

Age 32	Bats B	Pos CA	Health	A	LIMA Plan	D+
Ht 5' 9"	Wt 230		PT/Exp	F	Rand Var	-5
			Consist	C	MM	1021

Flirtation with .300 BA was bound to happen sometime due to consistent, contact-based skill set with solid LD%. But vanishing bb%/Eye and the absence of punch and wheels make regression a given. Still, with second catchers, it's all about damage control. His impact may again not be as catastrophic as most. Ah, faint praise.

Yr	Tm	AB	R	HR	RBI	SB	BA	xBA	OBP	SLG	OPS	vL	vR	bb%	ct%	h%	Eye	G	L	F	PX	xPX	hr/f	Spd	SBO	SB%	#Wk	DOM	DIS	RC/G	RAR	BPV	BPX	R$
09	KC *	253	26	9	32	2	269	310	311	442	753	668	817	6	89	27	0.54	51	22	28	101	61	15%	52	5%	57%	22	55%	14%	4.73	7.4	65	133	$5
10	KC	158	11	1	19	2	253	233	306	335	642	509	701	7	83	30	0.44	45	16	39	67	93	2%	55	5%	100%	24	25%	54%	3.58	-0.6	18	39	$1
11	KC	222	17	3	24	0	248	262	288	338	625	600	636	5	89	27	0.50	44	23	33	62	60	5%	43	0%	0%	25	44%	36%	3.28	-2.8	31	69	$1
12	KC	212	16	2	25	0	236	271	262	321	583	645	554	4	89	26	0.38	48	25	27	56	92	4%	50	2%	0%	27	33%	44%	2.79	-5.8	25	63	$0
13	DET	229	19	4	22	0	297	257	315	397	713	608	801	3	89	32	0.23	52	20	28	67	38	7%	60	3%	0%	25	40%	32%	4.36	4.1	33	83	$4
1st Half		122	11	2	14	0	295	244	317	385	703	500	896	3	89	32	0.29	56	17	28	59	34	7%	63	3%	0%	13	46%	31%	4.26	1.9	28	70	$5
2nd Half		107	8	2	8	0	299	276	312	411	723	745	703	2	89	32	0.17	48	23	29	75	42	7%	64	4%	0%	12	33%	33%	4.47	2.3	40	100	$4
14	**Proj**	**202**	**16**	**3**	**21**	**0**	**271**	**266**	**296**	**370**	**667**	**632**	**688**	**4**	**88**	**29**	**0.33**	**49**	**22**	**29**	**67**	**59**	**6%**	**54**	**3%**	**15%**				**3.76**	**0.3**	**26**	**65**	**$4**

Pena,Carlos

Age 36	Bats L	Pos 1B DH	Health	B	LIMA Plan	D
Ht 6' 2"	Wt 225		PT/Exp	B	Rand Var	+1
			Consist	C	MM	4001

A tanking FB% and soaring GB% would be fine for Rajai Davis, but for someone whose power is his only asset, they presage the end days. Even ct% and LD% uptick couldn't stall the decline. Waning PX, advancing age, impotence vs LHP... Well, we're piling it on. Even a mild rebound can't dress this one up.

Yr	Tm	AB	R	HR	RBI	SB	BA	xBA	OBP	SLG	OPS	vL	vR	bb%	ct%	h%	Eye	G	L	F	PX	xPX	hr/f	Spd	SBO	SB%	#Wk	DOM	DIS	RC/G	RAR	BPV	BPX	R$
09	TAM	471	91	39	100	3	227	270	356	537	893	814	936	16	65	25	0.53	29	17	54	221	202	24%	67	5%	50%	23	70%	22%	6.06	22.4	92	188	$15
10	TAM	484	64	28	84	5	196	242	325	407	732	675	759	15	67	22	0.55	45	14	41	155	149	21%	58	4%	83%	25	56%	24%	4.14	-5.4	43	93	$7
11	CHC	493	72	28	80	2	225	248	357	462	819	594	892	17	67	27	0.63	37	15	47	181	201	18%	67	3%	50%	27	56%	33%	5.38	13.2	70	156	$12
12	TAM	497	72	19	61	2	197	207	330	354	684	636	705	15	63	27	0.48	37	20	43	120	128	14%	94	3%	40%	27	37%	56%	3.50	-15.6	9	23	$3
13	2 AL	280	38	8	25	1	207	231	321	346	668	836	629	13	67	28	0.47	50	22	28	112	116	15%	87	5%	25%	18	28%	50%	3.35	-10.0	13	33	$0
1st Half		249	37	8	25	1	221	244	324	378	702	867	671	13	69	29	0.49	49	22	29	123	115	17%	87	6%	25%	14	36%	36%	3.84	-5.1	29	73	$2
2nd Half		31	1	0	0	0	97	109	222	97	319	0	339	14	52	19	0.33	56	19	25	0	126	0%	85	0%	0%	4	0%	100%	0.61	-4.3	-138	-345	-$11
14	**Proj**	**179**	**27**	**6**	**25**	**1**	**214**	**228**	**338**	**376**	**713**	**736**	**707**	**15**	**67**	**28**	**0.53**	**45**	**19**	**36**	**128**	**141**	**15%**	**80**	**4%**	**43%**				**3.97**	**-3.5**	**21**	**53**	**$3**

Pena,Ramiro

Age 28	Bats B	Pos 3B	Health	F	LIMA Plan	D
Ht 5' 11"	Wt 185		PT/Exp	F	Rand Var	-3
			Consist	D	MM	1211

If you owned him through May (.320/.381/.480), don't pretend you knew something we didn't. That eye-popping jump in PX was just one of those happy accidents. In all probability, season-ending shoulder injury in June staved off the inevitable crash. What you can fess up to is knowing that lightning won't strike here twice.

Yr	Tm	AB	R	HR	RBI	SB	BA	xBA	OBP	SLG	OPS	vL	vR	bb%	ct%	h%	Eye	G	L	F	PX	xPX	hr/f	Spd	SBO	SB%	#Wk	DOM	DIS	RC/G	RAR	BPV	BPX	R$
09	NYY *	271	33	3	18	9	242	246	299	334	633	274	817	8	81	29	0.43	37	24	39	65	63	3%	122	15%	80%	21	19%	43%	3.41	-0.7	30	61	$3
10	NYY	154	18	0	18	7	227	198	258	247	504	343	545	4	82	28	0.22	41	19	40	12	30	0%	134	21%	88%	27	0%	67%	2.22	-6.0	-10	-22	$1
11	NYY *	256	27	5	20	2	215	218	266	313	579	205	403	7	79	25	0.34	55	10	34	70	79	10%	100	8%	50%	8	25%	50%	2.63	-6.9	18	40	-$1
12	NYY *	364	30	2	22	1	212	227	263	266	529	0	667	7	76	28	0.29	50	25	25	41	-11	0%	107	5%	17%	1	0%	0%	2.17	-15.2	-16	-40	-$3
13	ATL	97	14	3	12	0	278	284	330	443	773	328	869	8	81	32	0.44	48	25	27	107	96	14%	107	8%	0%	12	50%	33%	4.79	3.6	61	153	$1
1st Half		97	14	3	12	0	278	284	333	443	777	328	869	8	81	32	0.44	48	25	27	107	96	14%	107	8%	0%	12	50%	33%	4.79	3.7	61	153	$1
2nd Half																																		
14	**Proj**	**105**	**12**	**2**	**10**	**1**	**238**	**240**	**288**	**340**	**628**	**293**	**711**	**7**	**80**	**28**	**0.35**	**42**	**23**	**35**	**70**	**66**	**6%**	**110**	**10%**	**51%**				**3.17**	**-2.5**	**16**	**40**	**$2**

Pence,Hunter

Age 31	Bats R	Pos RF	Health	A	LIMA Plan	B+
Ht 6' 4"	Wt 220		PT/Exp	A	Rand Var	0
			Consist	D	MM	4435

Impressive for age 30 season, playing 162 games and setting career highs in both HR and SB. Surges in FB%, SB% nourished those marks while other BPIs were upper norms across the board. PX and xBA stability are his core skills; bank on those. As for SB? SBO says it's in his hands, but that's the place to bet on regression.

Yr	Tm	AB	R	HR	RBI	SB	BA	xBA	OBP	SLG	OPS	vL	vR	bb%	ct%	h%	Eye	G	L	F	PX	xPX	hr/f	Spd	SBO	SB%	#Wk	DOM	DIS	RC/G	RAR	BPV	BPX	R$
09	HOU	585	76	25	72	14	282	280	346	472	818	895	798	9	81	31	0.53	53	15	33	112	100	16%	134	15%	56%	27	63%	11%	5.53	15.6	75	153	$21
10	HOU	614	93	25	91	18	282	284	325	461	786	820	776	6	83	31	0.39	53	15	32	112	96	15%	123	17%	67%	27	52%	19%	5.19	10.3	72	157	$27
11	2 NL	606	84	22	97	8	314	282	370	502	871	990	836	8	80	37	0.45	51	18	31	129	115	15%	130	6%	80%	27	63%	11%	6.93	38.1	79	176	$31
12	2 NL	617	87	24	104	5	253	254	319	425	743	731	748	8	76	29	0.39	51	17	32	110	96	16%	117	4%	71%	27	44%	37%	4.55	-1.0	48	120	$18
13	SF	629	91	27	99	22	283	280	339	483	822	976	769	8	82	31	0.45	47	17	36	128	112	15%	118	15%	88%	27	52%	11%	5.92	23.3	82	205	$34
1st Half		320	47	13	42	13	284	292	332	488	820	1028	748	7	83	31	0.41	48	18	33	134	117	15%	106	17%	100%	14	50%	7%	6.04	14.3	84	210	$33
2nd Half		309	44	14	57	9	282	267	343	479	822	926	791	9	81	31	0.49	46	16	38	122	108	15%	130	14%	75%	13	54%	15%	5.80	11.9	79	198	$35
14	**Proj**	**610**	**87**	**25**	**98**	**12**	**280**	**272**	**340**	**469**	**809**	**899**	**779**	**8**	**80**	**31**	**0.45**	**49**	**17**	**34**	**123**	**107**	**15%**	**122**	**9%**	**83%**				**5.66**	**21.0**	**68**	**170**	**$28**

Pennington,Cliff

Age 30	Bats B	Pos SS 2B	Health	A	LIMA Plan	D
Ht 5' 10"	Wt 195		PT/Exp	C	Rand Var	0
			Consist	B	MM	1301

Modest expectations had been based on his wheels, but seasons of low xBA and PX caused him to stall. Now those limitations have reduced him to a part-timer, throwing his SBO into full-throttle reverse. Those 29 swipes in 2009 look like a misprint now, and a return to the teens seems a stretch. No bags, no value.

Yr	Tm	AB	R	HR	RBI	SB	BA	xBA	OBP	SLG	OPS	vL	vR	bb%	ct%	h%	Eye	G	L	F	PX	xPX	hr/f	Spd	SBO	SB%	#Wk	DOM	DIS	RC/G	RAR	BPV	BPX	R$
09	OAK *	568	63	6	51	27	239	241	304	340	644	532	841	9	81	29	0.49	42	18	39	70	67	6%	109	25%	74%	11	45%	36%	3.46	-0.8	32	65	$11
10	OAK	508	64	6	46	29	250	242	319	368	687	655	697	9	81	30	0.52	36	21	43	81	70	3%	119	25%	85%	27	48%	41%	4.13	9.4	45	98	$15
11	OAK	515	57	8	58	14	264	243	319	369	687	670	695	8	80	32	0.40	36	25	40	78	76	5%	85	16%	61%	26	38%	42%	3.94	6.6	24	53	$14
12	OAK	418	50	6	28	15	215	233	278	311	589	420	646	8	78	26	0.39	41	23	37	67	63	5%	104	21%	71%	26	27%	54%	2.77	-9.6	16	40	$4
13	ARI	269	25	1	18	2	242	229	310	309	618	637	608	9	80	30	0.48	42	22	36	55	68	1%	97	3%	100%	25	40%	48%	3.24	-2.0	12	30	$0
1st Half		172	18	1	14	2	227	224	300	291	591	501	643	9	78	28	0.49	41	23	36	54	79	2%	77	4%	100%	14	29%	64%	2.94	-2.8	1	3	$1
2nd Half		97	7	0	4	0	268	235	324	340	664	924	549	8	82	33	0.47	43	22	35	57	49	0%	122	0%	0%	11	55%	27%	3.84	1.0	29	73	-$1
14	**Proj**	**161**	**16**	**1**	**11**	**4**	**244**	**235**	**307**	**330**	**637**	**646**	**633**	**8**	**80**	**30**	**0.45**	**40**	**22**	**37**	**65**	**65**	**3%**	**104**	**13%**	**78%**				**3.43**	**-0.2**	**17**	**44**	**$3**

Peralta,Jhonny

Age 32	Bats R	Pos SS	Health	A	LIMA Plan	B+
Ht 6' 2"	Wt 215		PT/Exp	B	Rand Var	-5
			Consist	F	MM	3015

It's doubtful that 2013 will bring anything to mind but his 50-game Biogenesis-related suspension. The specter of PEDs aside, he rode career-best LD% and highest PX in five years to first .300 season. While BA and G/L/F fluctuations tweak an otherwise steady profile, the veracity behind recent exploits comes into question.

Yr	Tm	AB	R	HR	RBI	SB	BA	xBA	OBP	SLG	OPS	vL	vR	bb%	ct%	h%	Eye	G	L	F	PX	xPX	hr/f	Spd	SBO	SB%	#Wk	DOM	DIS	RC/G	RAR	BPV	BPX	R$
09	CLE	582	57	11	83	0	254	245	316	375	690	661	701	8	77	31	0.38	50	19	31	88	78	8%	80	1%	0%	27	30%	52%	3.97	9.2	21	43	$8
10	2 AL	551	60	15	81	1	249	260	311	392	703	771	677	9	81	28	0.51	34	22	43	98	99	8%	96	1%	100%	26	42%	15%	4.20	12.4	52	113	$10
11	DET	525	68	21	86	0	299	262	345	478	824	765	848	7	82	33	0.42	36	20	44	114	116	11%	95	1%	0%	27	48%	30%	5.97	36.9	63	140	$22
12	DET	531	58	13	63	1	239	257	305	384	689	692	688	8	80	28	0.47	41	20	37	98	124	8%	82	2%	33%	27	56%	33%	3.85	6.8	43	108	$7
13	DET	409	50	11	55	3	303	263	358	457	815	964	750	8	76	38	0.36	39	25	36	119	136	10%	76	5%	50%	21	57%	24%	5.87	27.5	40	100	$16
1st Half		283	35	7	36	2	314	266	374	463	837	1012	773	9	76	39	0.40	40	27	34	117	114	10%	79	5%	50%	14	50%	29%	6.32	21.9	41	103	$20
2nd Half		126	15	4	19	1	278	257	321	444	765	887	685	6	76	34	0.27	38	22	41	126	186	10%	78	7%	50%	7	71%	14%	4.91	5.2	43	108	$7
14	**Proj**	**530**	**62**	**14**	**70**	**2**	**259**	**255**	**315**	**405**	**720**	**784**	**691**	**8**	**78**	**31**	**0.38**	**39**	**22**	**38**	**107**	**136**	**8%**	**80**	**4%**	**44%**				**4.32**	**13.2**	**32**	**80**	**$14**

ROB CARROLL

Perez,Salvador

Age	24	Bats	R	Pos	CA	Health	C	LIMA Plan	B
Ht	6' 3"	Wt	245			PT/Exp	C	Rand Var	-1
						Consist	B	MM	2035

PRO: Strong ct%, LD%; consistency; still at a pre-peak age; 2H skills set reached multiple career-high levels.
CON: Below-average power and low FB% will limit HR for now; lacks patience; large LH/RH split.
VERDICT: Target! A near-.300 BA with pop from a CA is valuable, and there's still some upside in these skills.

Yr	Tm	AB	R	HR	RBI	SB	BA	xBA	OBP	SLG	OPS	vL	vR	bb%	ct%	h%	Eye	G	L	F	PX	xPX	hr/f	Spd	SBO	SB%	#Wk	DOM	DIS	RC/G	RAR	BPV	BPX	R$
09																																		
10																																		
11	KC *	482	50	10	61	0	280	296	307	401	708	1285	711	4	88	30	0.33	42	29	29	79	86	8%	93	1%	0%	8	50%	38%	4.31	8.1	53	118	$12
12	KC *	339	46	11	44	0	301	291	327	450	778	1021	711	4	90	31	0.41	44	24	32	87	116	13%	77	0%	0%	16	69%	25%	5.37	15.4	64	160	$12
13	KC	496	48	13	79	0	292	272	323	433	757	867	714	4	87	31	0.33	47	21	33	88	96	9%	80	0%	0%	25	52%	28%	5.02	17.8	54	135	$17
1st Half		246	23	4	31	0	301	271	320	419	739	682	766	3	87	33	0.21	45	23	32	78	92	6%	88	0%	0%	13	54%	38%	4.89	8.0	43	108	$14
2nd Half		250	25	9	48	0	284	272	322	448	770	1043	663	5	88	29	0.47	48	18	34	99	100	12%	75	0%	0%	12	50%	17%	5.14	10.0	66	165	$19
14	**Proj**	**491**	**55**	**15**	**72**	**0**	**299**	**285**	**327**	**446**	**774**	**976**	**699**	**4**	**89**	**31**	**0.37**	**45**	**23**	**32**	**91**	**102**	**10%**	**78**	**0%**	**0%**				**5.30**	**21.4**	**49**	**123**	**$17**

Phegley,Joshua

Age	26	Bats	R	Pos	CA	Health	A	LIMA Plan	D+
Ht	5' 10"	Wt	220			PT/Exp	C	Rand Var	+2
						Consist	B	MM	2213

4-22-.206 in 204 AB at CHW. His 1st half HR breakout at Triple-A was the first real power he's shown, but none of that followed him to the majors (63 PX). Was overmatched vs. RHP, and marginal contact and poor plate discipline will keep BA down regardless. Not worth a flyer until he can show he owns that 1st half pop.

Yr	Tm	AB	R	HR	RBI	SB	BA	xBA	OBP	SLG	OPS	vL	vR	bb%	ct%	h%	Eye	G	L	F	PX	xPX	hr/f	Spd	SBO	SB%	#Wk	DOM	DIS	RC/G	RAR	BPV	BPX	R$
09																																		
10	aa	72	6	2	11	0	267	217	285	399	684			2	66	38	0.07				113			96	0%	0%				3.96		-10	-22	$0
11	a/a	443	43	9	46	1	217	243	263	332	595			6	80	25	0.31				84			89	3%	27%				2.78		26	58	$1
12	aaa	394	35	6	41	3	245	243	280	347	627			5	83	28	0.28				71			82	3%	100%				3.32		23	58	$4
13	CHW *	435	44	18	54	3	245	259	274	421	695	668	479	4	80	27	0.21	39	19	41	117	72	6%	70	5%	71%	14	21%	57%	3.88	2.1	45	113	$9
1st Half		221	29	13	30	1	279	301	316	529	845			5	81	30	0.28				164			74	4%	40%	1	0%	100%	5.80		88	220	$16
2nd Half		214	15	5	24	2	209	224	230	310	540	668	479	3	80	24	0.13	39	19	41	69	72	6%	68	5%	100%	13	23%	54%	2.33	-9.1	2	5	$3
14	**Proj**	**368**	**34**	**9**	**42**	**2**	**248**	**241**	**279**	**376**	**655**	**841**	**601**	**4**	**81**	**28**	**0.24**	**39**	**19**	**41**	**89**	**65**	**7%**	**73**	**4%**	**81%**				**3.59**	**-1.3**	**23**	**58**	**$7**

Phillips,Brandon

Age	33	Bats	R	Pos	2B	Health	A	LIMA Plan	B+
Ht	6' 0"	Wt	200			PT/Exp	A	Rand Var	0
						Consist	B	MM	2225

Apparently, he's the guy to go to if you want exactly 18 HR. Hitting cleanup boosted RBI, but cut into SBO. Spd held up, so SB could return if he reverts to former role. 2H hr/f dip is a minor concern, but xPX stayed steady and other skills remained intact. Plus, we all know how many bombs he'll hit anyway.

Yr	Tm	AB	R	HR	RBI	SB	BA	xBA	OBP	SLG	OPS	vL	vR	bb%	ct%	h%	Eye	G	L	F	PX	xPX	hr/f	Spd	SBO	SB%	#Wk	DOM	DIS	RC/G	RAR	BPV	BPX	R$
09	CIN	584	78	20	98	25	276	291	329	447	776	883	740	7	87	29	0.59	50	17	33	98	103	12%	109	23%	74%	27	67%	11%	5.06	23.7	76	155	$25
10	CIN	626	100	18	59	16	275	283	332	430	762	810	741	7	87	29	0.55	51	15	33	96	97	10%	127	17%	57%	27	59%	11%	4.66	18.3	77	167	$22
11	CIN	610	94	18	82	14	300	282	353	457	810	851	798	7	86	33	0.52	45	20	35	104	112	10%	94	14%	61%	27	67%	11%	5.59	33.0	71	158	$28
12	CIN	580	86	18	77	15	281	277	321	429	750	741	754	5	86	30	0.35	47	21	32	90	79	11%	92	12%	88%	27	52%	19%	4.87	19.8	56	140	$23
13	CIN	606	80	18	103	5	261	258	310	396	706	746	689	6	84	29	0.40	46	19	34	85	92	10%	93	5%	63%	26	58%	23%	4.13	8.3	45	113	$19
1st Half		299	41	11	61	1	268	260	316	421	737	865	687	7	83	29	0.42	47	18	35	98	89	13%	82	4%	33%	14	64%	21%	4.52	7.1	51	128	$21
2nd Half		307	39	7	42	4	254	254	295	371	667	620	690	6	84	28	0.38	46	20	34	74	95	8%	104	7%	80%	12	50%	25%	3.77	0.6	41	103	$18
14	**Proj**	**598**	**84**	**18**	**89**	**10**	**273**	**268**	**322**	**415**	**736**	**757**	**728**	**6**	**85**	**30**	**0.43**	**47**	**19**	**34**	**90**	**93**	**10%**	**95**	**9%**	**70%**				**4.56**	**14.8**	**54**	**136**	**$23**

Pierre,Juan

Age	36	Bats	L	Pos	LF	Health	A	LIMA Plan	D
Ht	5' 11"	Wt	180			PT/Exp	A	Rand Var	+4
						Consist	D	MM	0531

Speed is still there, but elite contact is no longer enough to make up for poor plate patience and lack of power. Can't hit lefties and can barely hit righties. Obviously, he can generate steals if he gets the playing time, but 2013 looks like his absolute upside. And downside? Japan or retirement.

Yr	Tm	AB	R	HR	RBI	SB	BA	xBA	OBP	SLG	OPS	vL	vR	bb%	ct%	h%	Eye	G	L	F	PX	xPX	hr/f	Spd	SBO	SB%	#Wk	DOM	DIS	RC/G	RAR	BPV	BPX	R$
09	LA	380	57	0	31	30	308	302	365	392	757	814	736	7	93	33	1.00	51	24	24	49	45	0%	155	35%	71%	27	52%	19%	4.98	9.9	73	149	$19
10	CHW	651	96	1	47	68	275	277	341	316	657	700	642	6	93	30	0.96	59	19	23	28	21	1%	135	43%	79%	27	33%	0%	3.75	-5.9	49	107	$34
11	CHW	639	80	2	50	27	279	270	329	327	657	766	621	6	94	30	1.05	53	21	26	31	34	1%	131	22%	61%	27	44%	19%	3.57	-9.0	53	118	$20
12	PHI	394	59	1	25	37	307	291	351	371	721	418	778	6	93	33	0.85	56	24	20	35	23	1%	168	35%	84%	27	37%	19%	4.98	10.1	64	160	$22
13	MIA	308	36	1	8	23	247	278	284	305	589	426	632	4	91	27	0.48	51	25	25	40	5	2%	138	39%	79%	27	37%	26%	2.95	-10.2	48	120	$9
1st Half		248	31	1	8	18	242	278	280	298	578	428	635	5	91	26	0.57	53	24	22	36	5	2%	143	38%	75%	14	43%	36%	2.83	-9.0	47	118	$12
2nd Half		60	5	0	0	5	267	281	267	333	600	400	618	0	93	29	0.00	40	27	33	54	4	0%	93	42%	100%	13	31%	15%	3.52	-0.9	46	115	-$2
14	**Proj**	**100**	**12**	**0**	**4**	**8**	**266**	**277**	**308**	**328**	**636**	**536**	**657**	**5**	**92**	**29**	**0.63**	**51**	**23**	**26**	**42**	**16**	**1%**	**119**	**35%**	**83%**				**3.62**	**-1.2**	**52**	**129**	**$4**

Pierzynski,A.J.

Age	37	Bats	L	Pos	CA	Health	B	LIMA Plan	B
Ht	6' 3"	Wt	235			PT/Exp	B	Rand Var	0
						Consist	C	MM	2035

For second straight season, ramped up power at the expense of contact rate; the difference in results was hr/f. Age and the inability to wait for ball four are risks, but BA has remained amazingly steady. If he stays healthy, expect another year at this level.

Yr	Tm	AB	R	HR	RBI	SB	BA	xBA	OBP	SLG	OPS	vL	vR	bb%	ct%	h%	Eye	G	L	F	PX	xPX	hr/f	Spd	SBO	SB%	#Wk	DOM	DIS	RC/G	RAR	BPV	BPX	R$
09	CHW	504	57	13	49	1	300	277	331	425	755	680	781	5	90	31	0.46	47	20	33	72	81	9%	78	1%	50%	26	50%	23%	5.09	19.1	51	104	$14
10	CHW	474	43	9	56	3	270	268	300	388	688	642	702	3	92	28	0.38	49	16	36	77	80	6%	58	7%	43%	27	56%	15%	3.84	1.7	54	117	$10
11	CHW	464	38	8	48	0	287	285	323	405	728	808	711	5	93	30	0.70	51	21	29	78	72	6%	64	0%	0%	25	52%	8%	4.64	11.9	65	144	$10
12	CHW	479	68	27	77	0	278	289	326	501	827	673	874	6	84	28	0.36	42	22	36	125	104	19%	86	0%	0%	27	56%	11%	5.62	25.7	74	185	$18
13	TEX	503	48	17	70	1	272	273	297	425	722	718	724	2	85	29	0.14	42	22	35	97	101	11%	62	2%	50%	26	50%	27%	4.26	7.8	42	105	$14
1st Half		217	25	7	26	0	286	280	311	442	754	690	800	4	85	31	0.25	43	24	34	99	95	11%	86	2%	0%	13	46%	31%	4.81	6.7	55	138	$12
2nd Half		286	23	10	44	1	262	266	270	413	682	741	668	1	85	28	0.07	42	22	36	95	106	11%	47	2%	100%	13	54%	23%	3.87	1.3	33	83	$16
14	**Proj**	**473**	**50**	**15**	**65**	**1**	**277**	**275**	**310**	**428**	**738**	**708**	**750**	**4**	**86**	**29**	**0.27**	**44**	**22**	**34**	**94**	**96**	**11%**	**69**	**1%**	**50%**				**4.55**	**11.3**	**44**	**111**	**$15**

Pill,Brett

Age	29	Bats	R	Pos	1B	Health	A	LIMA Plan	D
Ht	6' 4"	Wt	225			PT/Exp	D	Rand Var	0
						Consist	B	MM	3121

3-13-.224 in 85 AB at SF. PRO: Makes hard contact (124 HctX); crushes PCL pitching. CON: Terrible plate patience; heavy GB%. Bottom line, he's not even quite a Quad-A guy, as minor league equivalents fail to excite. At least he still has his health. If that's a scoring category, buy.

Yr	Tm	AB	R	HR	RBI	SB	BA	xBA	OBP	SLG	OPS	vL	vR	bb%	ct%	h%	Eye	G	L	F	PX	xPX	hr/f	Spd	SBO	SB%	#Wk	DOM	DIS	RC/G	RAR	BPV	BPX	R$
09	aa	527	59	15	90	5	266	280	305	419	724			5	85	29	0.37				98			80	7%	59%				4.36		54	110	$13
10	aaa	520	43	11	57	5	220	263	250	336	585			4	85	24	0.26				79			84	7%	66%				2.71		39	85	$3
11	SF *	586	56	16	73	4	237	289	258	383	641	740	1057	3	87	25	0.22	42	26	33	93	118	14%	86	12%	30%	4	50%	0%	3.09	-26.8	55	122	$9
12	SF *	351	32	10	39	1	208	226	238	342	581	588	691	4	81	23	0.21	48	12	41	87	73	11%	86	2%	100%	15	33%	33%	2.64	-21.2	31	78	$0
13	SF *	361	41	12	61	1	242	256	271	407	678	567	808	4	80	27	0.20	51	14	35	111	119	13%	86	1%	100%	14	43%	50%	3.72	-9.2	46	115	$7
1st Half		230	26	7	41	1	234	272	262	401	663	533	464	4	81	26	0.21	52	17	30	117	148	14%	75	2%	100%	5	40%	40%	3.51	-7.5	49	123	$9
2nd Half		131	15	5	20	0	258	237	286	417	703	576	1069	4	80	29	0.20	50	13	37	100	105	12%	104	0%	0%	9	44%	56%	4.10	-1.9	39	98	$5
14	**Proj**	**135**	**14**	**5**	**19**	**0**	**244**	**259**	**279**	**415**	**693**	**623**	**829**	**4**	**82**	**26**	**0.22**	**48**	**15**	**36**	**110**	**104**	**13%**	**95**	**3%**	**56%**				**3.79**	**-3.3**	**43**	**107**	**$3**

Pinto,Josmil

Age	25	Bats	R	Pos	CA	Health	A	LIMA Plan	D+
Ht	5' 11"	Wt	210			PT/Exp	F	Rand Var	-1
						Consist	A	MM	3021

4-12-.342 in 76 AB at MIN. SMALL SAMPLE ALERT. He does make hard contact (124 HctX), but there's no way he can sustain that 22% hr/f. Plate patience is there (ct% and bb% are acceptable), but defense is an issue, which will limit PT. UP: A serviceable backup, in both fantasy and "real" life.

Yr	Tm	AB	R	HR	RBI	SB	BA	xBA	OBP	SLG	OPS	vL	vR	bb%	ct%	h%	Eye	G	L	F	PX	xPX	hr/f	Spd	SBO	SB%	#Wk	DOM	DIS	RC/G	RAR	BPV	BPX	R$
09																																		
10																																		
11																																		
12	aa	47	6	1	7	0	267	274	315	478	793			7	77	32	0.30				143			105	0%	0%				5.24		67	168	-$1
13	MIN *	532	59	14	68	0	276	261	345	422	767	745	1026	10	78	33	0.49	43	24	33	107	143	22%	69	1%	0%	4	75%	25%	5.04	20.0	40	100	$14
1st Half		284	38	8	41	0	271	245	355	414	769			11	76	33	0.55				105			85	3%	0%				4.98		40	100	$16
2nd Half		248	20	7	27	0	280	267	334	432	765	745	1026	7	80	33	0.40	43	24	33	110	143	22%	65	0%	0%	4	75%	25%	5.10	9.8	45	113	$13
14	**Proj**	**211**	**22**	**6**	**26**	**0**	**268**	**258**	**338**	**416**	**754**	**632**	**789**	**9**	**79**	**32**	**0.44**	**44**	**22**	**34**	**108**	**129**	**10%**	**72**	**1%**	**0%**				**4.75**	**6.3**	**28**	**71**	**$5**

MATT CEDERHOLM

Plouffe,Trevor

Age 28	Bats R	Pos 3B	Health B	LIMA Plan C+	
Ht 6' 2"	Wt 205		PT/Exp B	Rand Var -1	
			Consist A	MM 3115	

Spent three weeks on DL with a concussion and sore calf. PRO: Power drop-off not as bad as it seems—he traded FB for LD, and xPX held steady. CON: Below-grade ct%; OPS vs. RHP could limit PT. He can return to the 20-HR level if PT holds steady, and there's still some room for growth. But don't pay for more than 2013.

Yr	Tm	AB	R	HR	RBI	SB	BA	xBA	OBP	SLG	OPS	vL	vR	bb%	ct%	h%	Eye	G	L	F	PX	xPX	hr/f	Spd	SBO	SB%	#Wk	DOM	DIS	RC/G	RAR	BPV	BPX	R$
09	aaa	430	44	8	50	3	233	259	279	359	638			6	82	27	0.36				80			108	10%	27%				3.12		40	82	$3
10	MIN *	443	46	11	42	4	201	230	237	339	576	400	468	4	75	24	0.19	50	11	39	100	173	18%	108	13%	39%	11	18%	55%	2.43	-21.4	22	48	$0
11	MIN *	478	72	18	56	5	248	256	307	433	741	782	665	8	76	29	0.35	43	17	40	132	128	10%	123	9%	56%	17	53%	24%	4.41	6.6	63	140	$12
12	MIN	422	56	24	55	1	235	262	301	455	756	911	691	8	78	25	0.40	38	18	44	136	114	17%	92	4%	25%	24	58%	33%	4.36	5.3	67	168	$9
13	MIN	477	44	14	52	2	254	249	309	392	701	826	663	7	77	30	0.30	39	25	37	98	113	10%	104	3%	67%	25	44%	32%	4.05	1.4	31	78	$9
1st Half		187	23	7	30	1	273	280	327	455	781	1021	734	7	81	31	0.42	35	27	38	121	122	12%	102	2%	100%	12	67%	8%	5.24	6.8	67	168	$12
2nd Half		290	21	7	22	1	241	227	288	352	640	722	613	6	74	30	0.25	41	23	36	82	106	9%	103	3%	50%	13	23%	54%	3.37	-5.2	6	15	$7
14	Proj	508	57	19	59	3	248	253	306	417	722	856	675	7	77	29	0.32	39	21	40	115	115	12%	105	5%	48%				4.17	2.9	33	83	$10

Polanco,Placido

Age 38	Bats R	Pos 3B	Health D	LIMA Plan D+	
Ht 5' 10"	Wt 190		PT/Exp C	Rand Var +1	
			Consist A	MM 0321	

Some quick fanalytic math:
"A" consistency + 90% ct% + 48% GB% + 32 PX = Hitting a whole slew of ground outs, over and over and over.
Empty BA is all you get, and not much of it. DN: More math... HR + SB = 0

Yr	Tm	AB	R	HR	RBI	SB	BA	xBA	OBP	SLG	OPS	vL	vR	bb%	ct%	h%	Eye	G	L	F	PX	xPX	hr/f	Spd	SBO	SB%	#Wk	DOM	DIS	RC/G	RAR	BPV	BPX	R$
09	DET	618	82	10	72	7	285	279	331	396	727	738	723	6	93	30	0.78	43	20	37	66	50	5%	111	5%	78%	27	59%	11%	4.59	10.3	69	141	$16
10	PHI	554	76	6	52	5	298	272	339	386	726	668	749	5	92	32	0.68	45	20	35	59	39	3%	112	3%	100%	25	44%	12%	4.78	11.8	60	130	$17
11	PHI	469	46	5	50	3	277	265	335	339	674	828	622	8	91	30	0.95	42	26	32	41	44	4%	78	2%	100%	23	30%	26%	4.07	0.9	37	82	$10
12	PHI	303	28	2	19	0	257	262	302	327	629	611	638	6	92	28	0.72	56	21	24	48	22	3%	87	0%	0%	20	45%	10%	3.36	-5.6	45	113	$1
13	MIA	377	33	1	23	2	260	265	315	302	617	731	563	6	92	28	0.74	48	25	27	32	33	1%	85	2%	100%	25	24%	28%	3.18	-8.8	32	80	$3
1st Half		239	24	1	12	1	238	258	286	285	571	756	508	6	92	26	0.80	48	23	29	34	26	2%	85	2%	100%	14	21%	21%	2.75	-8.7	34	85	$2
2nd Half		138	9	0	11	1	297	276	331	333	664	693	665	5	92	32	0.64	49	28	23	30	43	0%	90	2%	100%	11	27%	36%	4.05	0.3	31	78	$4
14	Proj	231	21	1	18	1	272	267	322	327	649	701	626	6	92	29	0.75	49	24	27	40	35	2%	87	2%	97%				3.63	-2.2	25	62	$4

Pollock IV,A.J.

Age 26	Bats R	Pos CF	Health A	LIMA Plan B	
Ht 6' 1"	Wt 195		PT/Exp B	Rand Var 0	
			Consist C	MM 2523	

There's some hidden upside in what seems like a pedestrian full-season debut. Most skills jumped in 2H, and a low hr/f hurt his PX (xPX was fine). Doesn't hit enough FB to be a real power source, but his legs have value and if SB success continues, should lead to higher SBO. UP: 15 HR, 25 SB.

Yr	Tm	AB	R	HR	RBI	SB	BA	xBA	OBP	SLG	OPS	vL	vR	bb%	ct%	h%	Eye	G	L	F	PX	xPX	hr/f	Spd	SBO	SB%	#Wk	DOM	DIS	RC/G	RAR	BPV	BPX	R$
09																																		
10																																		
11	aa	550	72	6	51	25	266	257	304	382	686			5	82	31	0.31				87			104	26%	76%				4.02		42	93	$17
12	ARI *	509	47	4	39	14	250	253	289	334	623	808	535	5	86	29	0.37	50	20	30	57	110	10%	100	20%	54%	10	40%	20%	3.07	-15.7	30	75	$8
13	ARI	443	64	8	38	12	269	262	322	409	730	811	678	7	81	31	0.40	48	18	34	98	112	7%	143	14%	80%	27	48%	22%	4.58	6.1	63	158	$14
1st Half		239	33	6	24	6	259	272	292	418	710	840	620	4	80	30	0.23	49	18	33	120	107	10%	98	17%	75%	14	57%	21%	4.18	0.1	56	140	$15
2nd Half		204	31	2	14	6	279	248	350	397	747	773	740	10	83	33	0.65	46	19	35	73	118	3%	191	11%	86%	13	38%	23%	5.01	4.9	71	178	$13
14	Proj	391	49	9	32	12	263	270	312	409	721	805	641	7	83	30	0.44	48	19	33	96	112	8%	139	17%	73%				4.39	2.5	61	153	$12

Posey,Buster

Age 27	Bats R	Pos CA 1B	Health C	LIMA Plan B+	
Ht 6' 1"	Wt 220		PT/Exp B	Rand Var 0	
			Consist F	MM 3135	

A worthy follow-up to 2012 until 2H power outage. A 7% drop in 2H FB% and poor hr/f didn't help, nor did nagging injuries. Contact rate bump held all season, and xPX improved overall, so there's legitmate hope for a rebound. But the Consistency grade reminds us of the perils of catching. Don't get caught in a bidding war.

Yr	Tm	AB	R	HR	RBI	SB	BA	xBA	OBP	SLG	OPS	vL	vR	bb%	ct%	h%	Eye	G	L	F	PX	xPX	hr/f	Spd	SBO	SB%	#Wk	DOM	DIS	RC/G	RAR	BPV	BPX	R$
09	SF *	148	16	3	16	0	264	236	319	395	714	0	333	8	80	31	0.41	62	8	31	85	53	0%	109	3%	0%	4	0%	50%	4.22	2.3	39	80	$1
10	SF *	578	81	22	90	1	305	291	360	493	853	955	832	8	85	33	0.57	49	18	33	119	121	15%	95	2%	19%	20	70%	20%	6.38	42.6	80	174	$24
11	SF	162	17	4	21	3	284	243	368	389	756	681	786	10	81	33	0.60	53	18	29	69	84	10%	84	5%	100%	9	44%	33%	5.05	6.2	28	62	$4
12	SF	530	78	24	103	1	336	301	408	549	957	1262	822	12	82	38	0.72	47	25	29	137	104	19%	81	1%	50%	27	70%	15%	8.65	68.5	87	218	$30
13	SF	520	61	15	72	2	294	279	371	450	821	891	792	10	87	32	0.86	47	20	33	103	116	10%	79	2%	67%	27	56%	7%	5.95	32.5	75	188	$19
1st Half		276	34	12	48	1	322	305	393	543	936	1127	864	10	87	34	0.91	45	19	36	141	142	13%	79	1%	100%	14	71%	0%	8.07	31.9	109	273	$26
2nd Half		244	27	3	24	1	262	252	338	344	682	633	710	10	86	30	0.80	50	21	29	59	86	5%	83	3%	50%	13	38%	15%	3.99	2.0	37	93	$11
14	Proj	509	63	17	74	3	304	280	378	467	845	946	804	10	84	33	0.71	48	21	31	107	105	13%	81	2%	70%				6.39	37.4	59	148	$22

Prado,Martin

Age 30	Bats R	Pos 3B 2B LF	Health A	LIMA Plan B+	
Ht 6' 1"	Wt 190		PT/Exp A	Rand Var +1	
			Consist D	MM 2245	

Consistent producer, apart from his 2012 SB and 2011 BA. Skills in 2H were a step up, especially Eye and PX. If they carry over into 2014, he could top his previous highs. Strong DOM/DIS and position flexibility make him a great H2H and sim league pick. UP: Return to 2010 levels.

Yr	Tm	AB	R	HR	RBI	SB	BA	xBA	OBP	SLG	OPS	vL	vR	bb%	ct%	h%	Eye	G	L	F	PX	xPX	hr/f	Spd	SBO	SB%	#Wk	DOM	DIS	RC/G	RAR	BPV	BPX	R$
09	ATL	450	64	11	49	1	307	289	358	464	822	923	774	7	87	33	0.61	44	20	37	105	108	8%	97	3%	25%	27	56%	15%	5.97	24.3	78	159	$14
10	ATL	599	100	15	66	5	307	295	350	459	809	747	834	6	86	34	0.47	48	21	31	102	91	9%	125	5%	63%	24	58%	21%	5.86	30.5	76	165	$24
11	ATL *	577	69	13	59	4	255	259	299	374	673	673	692	6	90	27	0.62	51	15	35	75	71	8%	120	8%	33%	23	52%	4%	3.63	-6.2	69	153	$11
12	ATL	617	81	10	70	17	301	291	359	438	796	864	760	9	89	33	0.84	48	23	29	86	76	6%	125	11%	81%	27	63%	7%	5.82	31.1	81	203	$25
13	ARI	609	70	14	82	3	282	290	333	417	750	852	716	7	91	29	0.89	48	22	30	85	89	8%	90	5%	38%	27	67%	4%	4.81	14.1	77	193	$19
1st Half		305	32	6	26	1	246	271	297	348	644	693	622	7	90	26	0.69	49	22	29	65	85	8%	85	6%	20%	14	64%	0%	3.30	-6.2	51	128	$10
2nd Half		304	38	8	56	2	319	309	371	487	858	1072	801	8	93	32	1.19	47	21	32	104	92	9%	97	3%	67%	13	69%	8%	6.72	22.4	102	255	$29
14	Proj	583	73	13	74	6	289	288	341	427	768	844	739	8	90	30	0.82	48	21	31	88	84	8%	106	7%	58%				5.15	19.3	71	177	$21

Presley,Alex

Age 28	Bats L	Pos CF	Health A	LIMA Plan C+	
Ht 5' 10"	Wt 190		PT/Exp C	Rand Var 0	
			Consist B	MM 2433	

3-15-.276 with 1 SB in 185 AB at PIT and MIN. That Spd is very tempting, but with just-average ct%, middling bb% and sub-standard power, he does little to get on base. And once he does reach, he's thrown out too much to sustain that SBO. Temper expectations—even if he's playing every day.

Yr	Tm	AB	R	HR	RBI	SB	BA	xBA	OBP	SLG	OPS	vL	vR	bb%	ct%	h%	Eye	G	L	F	PX	xPX	hr/f	Spd	SBO	SB%	#Wk	DOM	DIS	RC/G	RAR	BPV	BPX	R$
09																																		
10	PIT *	541	67	9	64	11	272	261	312	401	712	1500	511	5	83	31	0.34	64	7	29	83	13	0%	130	16%	51%	4	25%	75%	4.12	0.4	51	111	$15
11	PIT *	557	70	10	50	25	285	275	325	419	744	599	893	6	82	33	0.33	50	23	27	89	89	8%	135	26%	67%	10	70%	20%	4.66	8.9	52	116	$22
12	PIT *	499	65	13	42	14	242	270	293	397	690	690	682	7	80	28	0.35	60	17	23	91	85	16%	143	20%	61%	22	45%	45%	3.74	-5.4	49	123	$11
13	2 TM *	527	58	6	34	13	251	256	300	346	646	634	705	7	80	30	0.35	52	23	25	65	45	9%	141	18%	54%	14	21%	64%	3.32	-12.3	29	73	$10
1st Half		237	32	5	13	8	234	251	290	342	631	429	824	7	76	29	0.34	75	11	14	76	66	50%	116	21%	63%	6	33%	67%	3.17	-7.3	18	45	$10
2nd Half		290	26	1	22	5	265	260	308	350	657	666	666	6	83	32	0.36	46	26	27	56	40	3%	146	16%	44%	8	13%	63%	3.46	-6.2	34	85	$10
14	Proj	374	44	8	30	9	257	270	306	388	694	611	719	6	81	30	0.35	57	20	23	84	68	11%	138	18%	57%				3.84	-3.7	40	100	$10

Profar,Jurickson

Age 21	Bats B	Pos 2B	Health A	LIMA Plan B	
Ht 6' 0"	Wt 165		PT/Exp D	Rand Var 0	
			Consist D	MM 2325	

6-26-.234 with 2 SB in 286 AB at TEX. Yes, not every rookie is Mike Trout but 2013 should have been better. This is what happens when you're shuttled between 5 different positions, going from 20 AB one week to 5 AB another. Structure and consistency build better foundations. But this is still a future star -- invest.

Yr	Tm	AB	R	HR	RBI	SB	BA	xBA	OBP	SLG	OPS	vL	vR	bb%	ct%	h%	Eye	G	L	F	PX	xPX	hr/f	Spd	SBO	SB%	#Wk	DOM	DIS	RC/G	RAR	BPV	BPX	R$
09																																		
10																																		
11																																		
12	TEX *	497	66	14	55	14	276	255	349	447	796	0	846	10	83	31	0.67	54	8	38	105	123	20%	128	12%	77%	4	25%	75%	5.50	29.5	78	195	$17
13	TEX *	430	51	10	41	7	245	247	313	361	674	541	696	9	80	29	0.49	41	23	35	80	88	8%	114	10%	57%	19	26%	26%	3.71	3.7	37	93	$8
1st Half		249	31	7	24	5	262	250	328	399	727	624	731	9	81	30	0.52	37	23	40	90	110	9%	126	11%	61%	7	29%	29%	4.41	6.9	53	133	$13
2nd Half		181	20	3	17	2	221	237	291	309	601	501	674	9	78	27	0.45	44	24	32	66	75	7%	104	8%	50%	12	25%	25%	2.87	-3.4	16	40	$2
14	Proj	444	55	11	45	10	253	258	333	388	721	615	774	9	81	29	0.55	41	23	35	91	89	9%	119	12%	69%				4.23	7.1	46	114	$12

MATT CEDERHOLM

Puig,Yasiel

Puig,Yasiel				Health	A	LIMA Plan	B+
Age 23	Bats R	Pos RF		PT/Exp	F	Rand Var	-2
Ht 6' 3"	Wt 245			Consist	F	MM	4335

19-42-.319 with 11 SB in 382 AB at LA. What a first month! But lots of holes: 1H PX inflated by absurd hr/f; ct% and SBO fell in 2H but high GB% remained. DOM/DIS highlights the inconsistency. Still, has tools galore and some idea of what he's doing. A 30/30 year with .300 BA is possible—eventually. Exercise caution for now.

Yr	Tm	AB	R	HR	RBI	SB	BA	xBA	OBP	SLG	OPS	vL	vR	bb%	ct%	h%	Eye	G	L	F	PX	xPX	hr/f	Spd	SBO	SB%	#Wk	DOM	DIS	RC/G	RAR	BPV	BPX	R$
09																																		
10																																		
11																																		
12																																		
13	LA *	529	89	26	74	22	309	284	368	533	901	1001	897	9	76	37	0.38	50	19	31	154	106	22%	124	24%	62%	18	56%	28%	6.83	32.9	82	205	$35
1st Half		248	42	14	48	15	345	314	388	604	992	1339	1110	7	79	39	0.33	53	21	27	168	117	33%	137	31%	70%	5	80%	20%	8.69	28.1	106	265	$43
2nd Half		281	47	12	26	7	278	261	351	470	821	860	827	10	73	34	0.42	49	19	32	140	102	18%	114	17%	50%	13	46%	31%	5.43	8.1	59	148	$28
14	Proj	**543**	**88**	**24**	**76**	**17**	**287**	**274**	**363**	**493**	**856**	**940**	**824**	**9**	**75**	**34**	**0.39**	**49**	**19**	**32**	**145**	**108**	**18%**	**120**	**19%**	**61%**				**5.86**	**22.1**	**67**	**168**	**$26**

Pujols,Albert

Pujols,Albert				Health	C	LIMA Plan	A
Age 34	Bats R	Pos DH 1B		PT/Exp	A	Rand Var	+3
Ht 6' 3"	Wt 230			Consist	C	MM	4135

Missed 2+ months with plantar fasciitis, which affected him all year. Plate skills held steady from 2012, and strong xPX makes PX drop less of a concern. Still has contact and power skills needed to hit 30 HR, but his base stealing days are all but over. Expected to be ready to start the season, but he is now—officially—an injury risk.

Yr	Tm	AB	R	HR	RBI	SB	BA	xBA	OBP	SLG	OPS	vL	vR	bb%	ct%	h%	Eye	G	L	F	PX	xPX	hr/f	Spd	SBO	SB%	#Wk	DOM	DIS	RC/G	RAR	BPV	BPX	R$
09	STL	568	124	47	135	16	327	343	443	658	1101	1161	1080	17	89	30	1.80	39	16	46	182	155	20%	81	10%	80%	27	89%	7%	11.00	96.7	160	327	$43
10	STL	587	115	42	118	14	312	323	414	596	1011	1076	983	15	87	30	1.36	38	17	44	167	146	18%	71	9%	78%	27	85%	4%	9.14	72.4	135	293	$40
11	STL	579	105	37	99	9	299	311	366	541	906	946	897	10	90	28	1.05	45	17	38	137	140	18%	82	6%	90%	26	85%	4%	7.25	42.2	115	256	$33
12	LAA	607	85	30	105	8	285	303	343	516	859	926	836	8	87	29	0.68	41	19	40	140	126	14%	61	6%	89%	27	78%	11%	6.32	29.2	98	245	$27
13	LAA	391	49	17	64	1	258	270	330	437	767	690	790	9	86	26	0.73	38	20	42	109	135	12%	69	2%	50%	17	59%	12%	4.88	3.1	72	180	$11
1st Half		317	41	13	49	0	249	272	322	429	751	667	780	10	86	25	0.77	36	20	44	113	133	11%	70	1%	0%	14	57%	14%	4.63	0.3	77	193	$13
2nd Half		74	8	4	15	1	297	264	350	473	823	833	828	8	85	31	0.55	46	19	35	96	144	18%	77	4%	100%	3	67%	0%	6.10	3.1	57	143	$3
14	Proj	**539**	**76**	**27**	**98**	**2**	**287**	**283**	**357**	**490**	**847**	**865**	**842**	**9**	**87**	**29**	**0.79**	**42**	**19**	**39**	**121**	**137**	**15%**	**68**	**2%**	**60%**				**6.18**	**25.3**	**77**	**192**	**$25**

Punto,Nick

Punto,Nick				Health	D	LIMA Plan	D
Age 36	Bats B	Pos SS 3B 2B		PT/Exp	F	Rand Var	-1
Ht 5' 9"	Wt 195			Consist	B	MM	1211

Defensively, he was the #9 third baseman in the NL last year. How does that help your fantasy team? It doesn't (well, perhaps in sim leagues). Reasonable plate skills, but lacking in power, speed, consistency, age, power, playing time, base running and power. Unless you think his 2013 HR "breakout" is real...

Yr	Tm	AB	R	HR	RBI	SB	BA	xBA	OBP	SLG	OPS	vL	vR	bb%	ct%	h%	Eye	G	L	F	PX	xPX	hr/f	Spd	SBO	SB%	#Wk	DOM	DIS	RC/G	RAR	BPV	BPX	R$
09	MIN	359	56	1	38	16	228	234	337	284	621	642	613	15	81	28	0.87	48	19	33	44	31	1%	90	15%	84%	26	31%	35%	3.36	-1.5	15	31	$6
10	MIN	252	24	1	20	6	238	225	313	302	615	608	618	10	80	29	0.56	52	15	33	51	20	2%	89	11%	75%	21	19%	52%	3.20	-2.2	10	22	$2
11	STL *	172	24	1	21	2	260	294	364	375	738	798	814	14	85	30	1.07	46	31	23	75	41	4%	114	4%	61%	14	64%	36%	4.65	5.8	63	140	$2
12	2 TM	160	20	1	10	6	219	222	321	281	602	720	580	14	74	29	0.60	46	24	30	54	78	3%	88	12%	100%	27	22%	56%	3.20	-1.4	-5	-13	$0
13	LA	294	34	2	21	3	255	247	328	327	655	723	622	10	77	32	0.49	40	30	30	61	75	3%	69	7%	50%	26	27%	50%	3.60	0.8	1	3	$3
1st Half		180	21	1	12	3	261	254	332	322	654	770	597	10	79	33	0.50	43	31	26	52	49	3%	68	7%	75%	14	21%	57%	3.71	1.3	-1	-3	$5
2nd Half		114	13	1	9	0	246	239	328	333	661	650	663	11	75	32	0.48	35	29	37	78	116	3%	79	6%	0%	12	33%	42%	3.44	-0.1	8	20	$0
14	Proj	**216**	**26**	**1**	**17**	**4**	**243**	**243**	**331**	**322**	**653**	**700**	**635**	**12**	**77**	**31**	**0.60**	**42**	**27**	**31**	**65**	**73**	**3%**	**88**	**8%**	**69%**				**3.62**	**1.0**	**10**	**26**	**$4**

Quentin,Carlos

Quentin,Carlos				Health	F	LIMA Plan	B+
Age 31	Bats R	Pos LF		PT/Exp	C	Rand Var	-1
Ht 6' 2"	Wt 240			Consist	A	MM	4033

August knee injury mercifully ended season in which he also missed time due to a wrist, shoulder, suspension, and the birth of his son. When he played, skills were intact, featuring near-elite power and nice LD trend. Time to employ the J.D. Drew Plan: Pay for 275 AB and tactically plan out your 12 weeks of replacements.

Yr	Tm	AB	R	HR	RBI	SB	BA	xBA	OBP	SLG	OPS	vL	vR	bb%	ct%	h%	Eye	G	L	F	PX	xPX	hr/f	Spd	SBO	SB%	#Wk	DOM	DIS	RC/G	RAR	BPV	BPX	R$
09	CHW *	388	55	22	63	3	245	277	308	457	765	716	802	8	86	23	0.65	37	16	47	118	143	15%	56	3%	100%	20	50%	15%	4.79	8.4	74	151	$10
10	CHW	453	73	26	87	2	243	277	342	479	821	764	838	10	82	24	0.60	37	14	49	147	125	14%	83	4%	50%	26	73%	0%	5.06	13.6	91	198	$14
11	CHW	421	53	24	77	1	254	273	340	499	838	943	804	7	80	27	0.40	32	14	54	165	143	13%	71	2%	50%	22	64%	23%	5.24	14.6	91	202	$14
12	SD	284	44	16	46	0	261	290	374	504	877	1018	820	11	86	26	0.88	35	18	47	146	165	14%	51	1%	0%	19	74%	16%	5.89	15.1	99	248	$9
13	SD	276	42	13	44	0	275	276	363	493	855	863	852	10	80	30	0.56	36	20	45	149	143	13%	70	0%	0%	17	65%	12%	6.04	15.6	83	208	$9
1st Half		185	29	9	25	0	270	267	354	481	835	716	909	11	79	30	0.63	34	19	47	142	145	13%	77	0%	0%	13	69%	15%	5.95	10.2	80	200	$11
2nd Half		91	13	4	19	0	286	295	337	516	853	1240	742	7	81	31	0.41	39	20	41	163	139	13%	64	0%	0%	4	50%	0%	6.21	5.6	91	228	$6
14	Proj	**331**	**49**	**17**	**58**	**0**	**267**	**284**	**354**	**497**	**851**	**970**	**809**	**9**	**82**	**28**	**0.56**	**35**	**19**	**46**	**152**	**147**	**13%**	**61**	**1%**	**40%**				**5.76**	**16.5**	**81**	**203**	**$13**

Quintanilla,Omar

Quintanilla,Omar				Health	A	LIMA Plan	D
Age 32	Bats L	Pos SS		PT/Exp	D	Rand Var	0
Ht 5' 9"	Wt 185			Consist	A	MM	1201

2-21-.222 in 315 AB at NYM. Lack of power and marginal plate skills keep him off the bases, preventing him from using his good speed. That would hurt most players' value, but he runs so poorly, it doesn't have much of an effect. However, he IS worth 70+ points on a triple-word score.

Yr	Tm	AB	R	HR	RBI	SB	BA	xBA	OBP	SLG	OPS	vL	vR	bb%	ct%	h%	Eye	G	L	F	PX	xPX	hr/f	Spd	SBO	SB%	#Wk	DOM	DIS	RC/G	RAR	BPV	BPX	R$
09	COL	58	7	0	2	0	172	153	273	207	480	298	528	12	53	32	0.30	39	23	39	46	59	0%	102	0%	0%	24	13%	79%	1.74	-3.5	-92	-188	-$3
10	aaa	119	8	1	8	1	187	219	225	259	484			5	75	24	0.19				60			104	9%	30%				1.74		-10	-22	-$3
11	TEX *	230	29	3	16	2	205	222	248	309	558	0	364	5	78	25	0.26	58	8	33	69	126	0%	132	6%	57%	6	17%	67%	2.43	-8.8	20	44	-$2
12	2 TM *	325	37	8	34	1	225	241	281	356	638	589	705	7	76	27	0.32	56	17	27	91	88	12%	90	8%	12%	18	22%	50%	3.08	-5.7	20	50	$2
13	NYM *	441	42	3	31	3	223	225	301	292	593	500	617	10	76	29	0.47	54	20	27	52	33	3%	112	3%	65%	18	17%	61%	2.88	-10.5	2	5	$0
1st Half		227	25	3	19	1	231	213	291	333	624	523	704	8	76	29	0.35	51	12	37	76	43	7%	106	3%	29%	6	33%	33%	3.14	-3.8	13	33	$2
2nd Half		214	17	0	12	2	215	225	311	248	559	484	582	12	77	28	0.60	55	23	22	28	27	0%	109	3%	100%	12	8%	75%	2.56	-7.5	-12	-30	-$3
14	Proj	**225**	**22**	**3**	**17**	**1**	**216**	**229**	**282**	**303**	**586**	**487**	**619**	**8**	**76**	**27**	**0.38**	**52**	**19**	**29**	**65**	**56**	**5%**	**109**	**5%**	**51%**				**2.72**	**-5.2**	**-3**	**-6**	**$1**

Quintero,Humberto

Quintero,Humberto				Health	B	LIMA Plan	D
Age 34	Bats R	Pos CA		PT/Exp	F	Rand Var	0
Ht 5' 9"	Wt 215			Consist	B	MM	2001

4-13-.237 in 131 AB at PHI and SEA. Power is trending up, but age, plate skills, and FB% make that almost irrelevant. He's a double-edged sword: if he plays enough for power production to matter, he kills your BA. Lucky for you, that's not likely to happen.

Yr	Tm	AB	R	HR	RBI	SB	BA	xBA	OBP	SLG	OPS	vL	vR	bb%	ct%	h%	Eye	G	L	F	PX	xPX	hr/f	Spd	SBO	SB%	#Wk	DOM	DIS	RC/G	RAR	BPV	BPX	R$
09	HOU	157	11	4	14	0	236	226	286	376	662	840	614	4	74	29	0.17	57	10	32	99	88	11%	73	0%	0%	25	32%	40%	3.36	-1.6	7	14	-$1
10	HOU	265	13	4	20	0	234	212	262	317	579	375	665	3	78	29	0.14	47	19	34	62	50	6%	61	0%	0%	27	22%	70%	2.71	-8.0	-12	-26	-$1
11	HOU	262	22	2	25	1	240	231	258	317	575	650	555	2	80	29	0.11	52	18	30	60	78	3%	67	2%	100%	22	18%	55%	2.76	-7.4	-5	-11	$0
12	KC *	248	14	2	30	0	214	221	233	309	542	473	637	2	76	27	0.10	47	18	35	82	95	3%	51	3%	0%	12	33%	25%	2.28	-10.8	-7	-18	-$2
13	2 TM *	155	13	5	16	0	234	246	275	376	651	794	570	5	76	27	0.24	48	23	29	97	105	14%	53	0%	0%	20	25%	60%	3.45	-1.1	12	30	$0
1st Half		80	7	2	8	0	217	225	260	354	614	1514	467	6	74	26	0.23	52	17	31	101	110	8%	51	0%	0%	11	18%	55%	3.00	-1.7	7	18	-$1
2nd Half		75	6	3	8	0	253	266	291	400	691	676	702	5	79	29	0.25	45	28	28	93	102	19%	68	0%	0%	9	33%	67%	3.98	0.6	22	55	$0
14	Proj	**168**	**12**	**4**	**18**	**0**	**231**	**236**	**267**	**346**	**613**	**676**	**588**	**4**	**77**	**28**	**0.18**	**49**	**20**	**31**	**85**	**95**	**9%**	**57**	**1%**	**36%**				**3.00**	**-3.6**	**-6**	**-15**	**$2**

Raburn,Ryan

Raburn,Ryan				Health	B	LIMA Plan	C
Age 33	Bats R	Pos RF		PT/Exp	D	Rand Var	-2
Ht 6' 0"	Wt 185			Consist	F	MM	4113

That hr/f outlier—xPX shows power in line with trend—inflated his results. But he's always had punch. Does bb% jump signal some maturation? Candidate for a late-career surge—if he can crack the lineup. Aside from marginal defense, it's tough to see why he didn't play more often.

Yr	Tm	AB	R	HR	RBI	SB	BA	xBA	OBP	SLG	OPS	vL	vR	bb%	ct%	h%	Eye	G	L	F	PX	xPX	hr/f	Spd	SBO	SB%	#Wk	DOM	DIS	RC/G	RAR	BPV	BPX	R$
09	DET *	308	53	20	52	7	279	269	346	531	877	976	793	9	75	31	0.42	38	15	48	155	143	17%	125	14%	56%	25	52%	32%	6.21	17.2	84	171	$13
10	DET *	398	58	15	63	3	285	265	333	478	811	929	753	7	76	34	0.30	39	18	44	142	128	12%	113	6%	45%	27	48%	33%	5.52	14.0	66	143	$14
11	DET	387	53	14	49	1	256	238	297	432	729	807	681	5	71	33	0.18	35	21	45	135	142	11%	124	2%	50%	27	48%	37%	4.31	0.4	40	89	$9
12	DET *	265	20	4	20	2	176	201	224	277	500	477	482	6	73	23	0.23	43	14	43	82	138	2%	87	6%	63%	19	26%	47%	1.90	-20.4	-1	-3	-$5
13	CLE	243	40	16	55	0	272	282	357	543	901	1020	806	11	72	31	0.43	45	18	38	197	145	24%	70	0%	0%	26	62%	27%	6.64	16.4	92	230	$10
1st Half		141	22	9	26	0	262	268	342	525	867	905	859	11	70	31	0.40	45	16	39	198	176	24%	78	0%	0%	14	57%	21%	6.20	7.2	83	208	$10
2nd Half		102	18	7	29	0	284	301	360	569	928	1168	727	11	76	31	0.50	44	19	37	196	105	24%	73	0%	0%	12	67%	33%	7.29	8.1	108	270	$11
14	Proj	**295**	**41**	**13**	**52**	**1**	**259**	**254**	**328**	**459**	**787**	**891**	**706**	**9**	**73**	**31**	**0.35**	**42**	**17**	**41**	**149**	**136**	**15%**	**82**	**3%**	**60%**				**5.05**	**5.2**	**46**	**115**	**$10**

MATT CEDERHOLM

Ramirez,Alexei

Age 32	Bats R	Pos SS	Health A	LIMA Plan B+
Ht 6' 2"	Wt 180		PT/Exp A	Rand Var 0
			Consist B	MM 1435

A walk's as good as a hit? Career best ct% says phooey. BA benefitted, and remains an asset, but now big SB numbers have ushered in his second act. Always had plus Spd, but improved SB% turned the light green. If 2H PX uptick portends return to double-digit HR, there's another path to value. Invest with confidence.

Yr Tm	AB	R	HR	RBI	SB	BA	xBA	OBP	SLG	OPS	vL	vR	bb%	ct%	h%	Eye	G	L	F	PX	xPX	hr/f	Spd	SBO	SB%	#Wk	DOM	DIS	RC/G	RAR	BPV	BPX	R$
09 CHW	542	71	15	68	14	277	251	333	389	723	960	649	8	88	29	0.74	46	16	38	62	71	8%	117	11%	74%	27	48%	26%	4.61	18.4	54	110	$17
10 CHW	585	83	18	70	13	282	281	313	431	744	725	751	4	86	30	0.33	48	19	33	93	82	11%	128	15%	62%	27	63%	11%	4.64	20.3	68	148	$22
11 CHW	614	81	15	70	7	269	266	328	399	727	715	731	8	86	29	0.61	45	19	35	85	77	8%	115	7%	58%	27	56%	11%	4.43	17.9	65	144	$17
12 CHW	593	59	9	73	20	265	254	287	364	651	724	631	3	87	29	0.21	46	20	34	61	69	5%	129	20%	74%	27	37%	33%	3.56	2.3	43	108	$17
13 CHW	637	68	6	48	30	284	278	313	380	693	701	691	4	89	31	0.38	49	22	29	68	51	4%	121	24%	77%	27	52%	15%	4.23	14.7	58	145	$25
1st Half	314	32	1	17	18	280	256	305	344	649	691	643	3	86	32	0.25	49	22	29	52	45	1%	123	27%	82%	14	43%	21%	3.82	3.2	31	78	$24
2nd Half	323	36	5	31	12	288	299	320	415	734	709	740	4	93	30	0.63	49	22	29	83	56	6%	116	22%	71%	13	62%	8%	4.65	10.9	82	205	$27
14 Proj	**630**	**81**	**10**	**63**	**25**	**277**	**270**	**309**	**384**	**693**	**722**	**685**	**4**	**88**	**30**	**0.38**	**47**	**21**	**32**	**71**	**62**	**5%**	**124**	**22%**	**74%**				**4.13**	**12.1**	**55**	**137**	**$22**

Ramirez,Aramis

Age 36	Bats R	Pos 3B	Health C	LIMA Plan B+
Ht 6' 1"	Wt 205		PT/Exp B	Rand Var -2
			Consist B	MM 4135

After two healthy seasons, injury bug (knee) returned and cost him two months. When healthy, production as good as ever; he improved bb%, but downward trending FB% a concern. 2H ct% and still excellent xPX say age has not dimmed skills. "C" Health grade could present buying opportunity, but have a contingency plan.

Yr Tm	AB	R	HR	RBI	SB	BA	xBA	OBP	SLG	OPS	vL	vR	bb%	ct%	h%	Eye	G	L	F	PX	xPX	hr/f	Spd	SBO	SB%	#Wk	DOM	DIS	RC/G	RAR	BPV	BPX	R$
09 CHC	306	46	15	65	2	317	285	389	516	905	1083	878	8	86	33	0.65	35	21	44	112	105	13%	94	3%	67%	18	56%	17%	7.17	26.1	80	163	$15
10 CHC	465	61	25	83	0	241	255	294	452	745	816	722	7	81	25	0.38	27	16	57	132	147	12%	73	0%	0%	26	54%	27%	4.44	6.1	66	143	$11
11 CHC	565	80	26	93	1	306	297	361	510	871	824	884	7	88	31	0.62	34	23	43	125	129	12%	96	1%	50%	27	74%	11%	6.62	40.4	96	213	$27
12 MIL	570	92	27	105	9	300	299	360	540	901	1049	853	7	86	31	0.54	39	19	42	148	164	13%	93	8%	82%	27	74%	7%	6.90	45.7	105	263	$29
13 MIL	304	43	12	49	0	283	265	370	461	831	887	811	11	82	31	0.65	41	19	39	118	144	12%	78	1%	0%	19	53%	16%	5.80	15.5	69	173	$10
1st Half	165	20	5	24	0	273	242	344	424	769	689	816	10	79	32	0.51	44	17	39	109	157	10%	81	2%	0%	11	36%	9%	5.00	4.9	48	120	$9
2nd Half	139	23	7	25	0	295	291	376	504	879	1346	807	11	86	30	0.90	38	22	40	128	130	15%	79	0%	0%	8	75%	25%	6.84	11.0	93	233	$12
14 Proj	**510**	**76**	**20**	**88**	**2**	**292**	**278**	**366**	**480**	**846**	**946**	**816**	**9**	**84**	**31**	**0.62**	**39**	**20**	**41**	**122**	**143**	**12%**	**85**	**2%**	**64%**				**6.11**	**30.4**	**73**	**182**	**$23**

Ramirez,Hanley

Age 30	Bats R	Pos SS	Health D	LIMA Plan B+
Ht 6' 2"	Wt 225		PT/Exp B	Rand Var -5
			Consist F	MM 4345

Lost a half season with hamstring, back and shoulder woes. In betwen, enjoyed BA renaissance. He'll be hard-pressed to repeat, as gravity will affect hr/f, and age and injuries likely continue to ding SB. Will probably still command top dollar - even 1st round consideration - but shaky reliability makes him a high-risk investment.

Yr Tm	AB	R	HR	RBI	SB	BA	xBA	OBP	SLG	OPS	vL	vR	bb%	ct%	h%	Eye	G	L	F	PX	xPX	hr/f	Spd	SBO	SB%	#Wk	DOM	DIS	RC/G	RAR	BPV	BPX	R$
09 FLA	576	101	24	106	27	342	287	410	543	954	793	1014	10	82	38	0.60	39	20	42	128	105	12%	113	18%	77%	26	65%	19%	8.48	75.4	87	178	$40
10 FLA	543	92	21	76	32	300	285	378	475	853	838	858	11	83	33	0.69	51	16	33	112	108	14%	120	24%	76%	26	54%	35%	6.44	44.8	80	174	$33
11 FLA	338	55	10	45	20	243	255	333	379	712	994	633	12	80	27	0.67	51	16	33	94	96	11%	84	30%	67%	18	33%	22%	4.05	5.6	47	104	$12
12 2 NL	604	79	24	92	21	257	262	322	437	759	794	745	8	78	29	0.41	47	18	34	115	115	15%	95	18%	75%	27	52%	33%	4.73	21.8	51	128	$23
13 LA	304	62	20	57	10	345	326	402	638	1040	1142	1001	8	83	37	0.52	41	22	37	186	164	21%	100	14%	83%	18	67%	22%	9.94	50.7	129	323	$25
1st Half	75	15	6	18	4	387	363	432	707	1139	1028	1182	7	87	39	0.60	44	29	27	191	137	33%	87	17%	100%	6	67%	17%	13.22	17.6	142	355	$10
2nd Half	229	47	14	39	6	332	313	388	616	1004	1187	948	8	82	36	0.50	39	20	41	184	174	18%	102	13%	75%	12	67%	25%	9.02	33.8	123	308	$30
14 Proj	**495**	**87**	**22**	**86**	**14**	**297**	**291**	**358**	**508**	**866**	**932**	**842**	**8**	**82**	**33**	**0.49**	**45**	**20**	**35**	**138**	**133**	**16%**	**96**	**14%**	**80%**				**6.56**	**42.6**	**90**	**224**	**$29**

Ramirez,Wilkin

Age 28	Bats R	Pos CF	Health D	LIMA Plan D
Ht 6' 2"	Wt 230		PT/Exp D	Rand Var 0
			Consist A	MM 2301

0-6-.272 in 81 AB at MIN. Made club with strong camp, but lost four months with concussion, fractured tibia. Just 28 but skills in decline: bb% and ct% both horrid, xBA history a downer, and plummeting FB% is sapping PX. Once had SB potential, but no longer. Value limited to Ramirez-only leagues; even there an end-gamer.

Yr Tm	AB	R	HR	RBI	SB	BA	xBA	OBP	SLG	OPS	vL	vR	bb%	ct%	h%	Eye	G	L	F	PX	xPX	hr/f	Spd	SBO	SB%	#Wk	DOM	DIS	RC/G	RAR	BPV	BPX	R$
09 DET *	445	65	16	47	29	240	219	296	415	711	1253	1000	7	64	34	0.22	33	22	44	128	106	25%	152	39%	72%	7	43%	43%	3.99	-3.3	22	45	$16
10 a/a	448	50	17	54	11	198	211	252	370	623			7	56	30	0.17				149			127	24%	54%				2.77		-1	-2	$4
11 ATL *	314	36	8	30	15	224	230	265	366	631	641	625	5	69	30	0.18	53	13	33	112	85	0%	121	39%	62%	8	25%	50%	2.95	-11.3	16	36	$6
12 a/a	419	39	13	46	7	239	229	266	393	659			4	69	31	0.12				110			97	19%	45%				3.23		4	10	$7
13 MIN *	110	7	0	6	1	235	242	264	315	579	810	592	4	72	32	0.14	53	25	22	74	83	0%	100	3%	100%	11	27%	55%	2.81	-4.6	-10	-25	-$2
1st Half	45	3	0	5	0	244	226	261	311	572	414	658	2	69	35	0.07	59	25	16	73	48	0%	81	0%	0%	8	25%	63%	2.74	-1.9	-35	-88	-$2
2nd Half	65	4	0	1	1	229	241	267	318	584	1158	488	5	75	31	0.21	44	26	30	74	124	0%	112	5%	100%	3	33%	33%	2.85	-2.6	5	13	-$3
14 Proj	**166**	**16**	**2**	**13**	**5**	**227**	**219**	**271**	**338**	**610**	**785**	**497**	**5**	**69**	**32**	**0.18**	**46**	**21**	**34**	**91**	**94**	**6%**	**114**	**22%**	**65%**				**2.88**	**-6.6**	**-5**	**-12**	**$3**

Ramos,Wilson

Age 26	Bats R	Pos CA	Health F	LIMA Plan B
Ht 6' 0"	Wt 220		PT/Exp D	Rand Var 0
			Consist A	MM 3025

Another injury (hamstring) wiped out 2 months; still has not played a full MLB season. What we know: Provides solid ct% at prime position but can be allergic to walks. What we don't know: If he'll learn to hit more FB, which would turn PX and elite hr/f into HRs. Bankable BA makes taking chance on power and health more palatable.

Yr Tm	AB	R	HR	RBI	SB	BA	xBA	OBP	SLG	OPS	vL	vR	bb%	ct%	h%	Eye	G	L	F	PX	xPX	hr/f	Spd	SBO	SB%	#Wk	DOM	DIS	RC/G	RAR	BPV	BPX	R$
09 aa	205	28	3	26	0	294	277	312	419	731			2	88	32	0.21				85			88	0%	0%				4.73		52	106	$4
10 2 TM *	436	38	8	37	1	241	226	265	349	614	1375	544	3	82	28	0.18	43	13	43	77	118	3%	85	3%	28%	8	38%	50%	3.04	-8.6	24	52	$3
11 WAS	389	48	15	52	0	267	257	334	445	779	789	776	9	80	30	0.50	50	15	36	120	119	13%	79	2%	0%	27	52%	22%	5.04	15.1	61	136	$10
12 WAS	83	11	3	10	0	265	224	354	398	752	762	748	13	77	31	0.63	66	14	20	82	96	23%	74	0%	0%	6	50%	33%	4.94	3.0	24	60	$0
13 WAS	287	29	16	59	0	272	279	307	470	777	700	803	5	85	27	0.36	57	20	24	114	108	28%	67	1%	0%	18	61%	17%	4.99	10.7	65	163	$10
1st Half	48	4	2	6	0	250	262	308	438	745	593	802	8	83	26	0.50	68	10	23	123	85	22%	77	9%	0%	6	67%	33%	4.17	0.7	72	180	-$6
2nd Half	239	25	14	53	0	276	282	308	477	785	724	803	4	86	27	0.32	55	21	24	112	113	29%	72	0%	0%	12	58%	8%	5.18	9.9	65	163	$13
14 Proj	**462**	**49**	**20**	**69**	**0**	**265**	**267**	**307**	**449**	**756**	**761**	**755**	**6**	**84**	**28**	**0.37**	**58**	**15**	**26**	**115**	**105**	**20%**	**64**	**3%**	**5%**				**4.66**	**12.8**	**47**	**118**	**$15**

Rasmus,Colby

Age 27	Bats L	Pos CF	Health B	LIMA Plan A
Ht 6' 2"	Wt 190		PT/Exp B	Rand Var -5
			Consist C	MM 4215

Lost 5 weeks with oblique, eye injuries. His 2013 h%, hr/f and poor ct% were eerily close to 2010 levels. But as years in between demonstrate, those lofty levels are tenuous. Despite power potential, risk abounds since SB value is gone and BA contribution is unreliable. He could earn $20. He could earn $10.

Yr Tm	AB	R	HR	RBI	SB	BA	xBA	OBP	SLG	OPS	vL	vR	bb%	ct%	h%	Eye	G	L	F	PX	xPX	hr/f	Spd	SBO	SB%	#Wk	DOM	DIS	RC/G	RAR	BPV	BPX	R$
09 STL	474	72	16	52	3	251	250	307	407	714	474	783	7	80	28	0.38	35	20	46	98	114	9%	109	3%	75%	27	48%	30%	4.21	-0.3	47	96	$9
10 STL	464	85	23	66	12	276	251	361	498	859	810	875	12	68	36	0.43	32	19	49	170	130	15%	124	15%	60%	27	56%	33%	6.12	25.3	72	157	$21
11 2 TM	471	75	14	53	5	225	233	298	391	688	670	695	10	75	27	0.43	36	16	48	117	139	8%	124	6%	71%	25	44%	40%	3.84	-5.7	54	120	$7
12 TOR	565	75	23	75	4	223	237	289	400	689	554	740	8	74	26	0.32	38	20	42	115	123	13%	114	6%	57%	27	37%	33%	3.66	-10.0	38	95	$10
13 TOR	417	57	22	66	0	276	253	338	501	840	712	893	8	68	36	0.27	33	22	45	175	148	17%	103	1%	0%	22	64%	27%	5.85	19.1	60	150	$16
1st Half	264	33	14	38	0	242	231	310	455	765	614	837	9	64	32	0.27	31	21	48	167	157	17%	118	2%	0%	14	64%	21%	4.67	3.9	45	113	$15
2nd Half	153	24	8	28	0	333	289	378	582	960	903	986	7	74	41	0.28	36	23	41	187	136	17%	88	0%	0%	8	63%	38%	8.41	17.0	87	218	$17
14 Proj	**508**	**74**	**23**	**74**	**3**	**256**	**253**	**321**	**464**	**785**	**686**	**823**	**8**	**72**	**31**	**0.32**	**35**	**21**	**44**	**151**	**136**	**14%**	**106**	**4%**	**57%**				**5.01**	**12.4**	**51**	**128**	**$17**

Recker,Anthony

Age 30	Bats R	Pos CA	Health A	LIMA Plan D
Ht 6' 2"	Wt 240		PT/Exp F	Rand Var -1
			Consist B	MM 4001

Once an intriguing prospect with strong patience (career .360 OBP, 11 bb% in AAA). Now, he's a reserve who played his first full MLB season (all 135 AB of it) at age 29. Consistently subterranean ct% makes even .220 a reach. Lone asset might be PX, but it's not worth sticking around to see whether 2013's hr/f is for real.

Yr Tm	AB	R	HR	RBI	SB	BA	xBA	OBP	SLG	OPS	vL	vR	bb%	ct%	h%	Eye	G	L	F	PX	xPX	hr/f	Spd	SBO	SB%	#Wk	DOM	DIS	RC/G	RAR	BPV	BPX	R$
09 a/a	329	29	10	38	1	210	214	267	346	613			7	63	30	0.21				106			96	2%	100%				3.00		-16	-33	-$1
10 a/a	288	30	7	30	1	213	228	263	346	608			6	68	29	0.21				109			100	3%	35%				2.89		3	7	$0
11 OAK *	362	41	9	30	4	209	208	287	341	629	730	450	10	69	28	0.35	50	10	40	109	76	0%	84	12%	41%	4	25%	75%	2.98	-8.2	10	22	$1
12 2 TM *	271	25	8	26	2	189	187	262	307	569	417	550	9	64	26	0.27	38	18	44	94	99	7%	65	5%	61%	11	27%	45%	2.50	-10.3	-30	-75	-$2
13 NYM	135	17	6	19	0	215	226	280	400	680	783	623	9	64	29	0.27	38	20	42	153	124	16%	69	3%	0%	24	46%	46%	3.57	-0.5	18	45	$0
1st Half	51	4	2	8	0	157	226	232	333	565	637	481	9	57	22	0.23	23	30	47	169	135	14%	60	0%	0%	12	50%	33%	2.34	-2.3	1	3	-$3
2nd Half	84	13	4	11	0	250	232	315	440	756	951	681	9	68	32	0.30	45	16	40	146	119	17%	83	5%	0%	12	42%	58%	4.49	1.9	33	83	$2
14 Proj	**159**	**18**	**6**	**19**	**1**	**212**	**217**	**279**	**369**	**647**	**727**	**602**	**9**	**65**	**29**	**0.28**	**36**	**21**	**42**	**129**	**125**	**13%**	**70**	**5%**	**35%**				**3.28**	**-2.1**	**-5**	**-14**	**$2**

TODD ZOLA

Reddick,Josh

Age 27	Bats L	Pos RF	Health B	LIMA Plan B+
Ht 6' 2"	Wt 180		PT/Exp B	Rand Var +1
			Consist A	MM 4415

Lost about seven weeks as early April wrist injury sapped his power. 2H PX bounceback tempered as 5 HR came in consecutive games in early August. Relies more on lots of FB to drive HR, hr/f is quite middling. With low BA and limited SB, 2014 value depends on whether offseason surgery contributes to hr/f (read: HR) rebound.

Yr Tm	AB	R	HR	RBI	SB	BA	xBA	OBP	SLG	OPS	vL	vR	bb%	ct%	h%	Eye	G	L	F	PX	xPX	hr/f	Spd	SBO	SB%	#Wk	DOM	DIS	RC/G	RAR	BPV	BPX	R$
09 BOS *	386	49	13	36	5	234	243	296	422	719	733	530	8	76	28	0.37	31	17	52	126	161	9%	134	13%	42%	9	22%	33%	3.93	-4.0	62	127	$4
10 BOS *	513	53	15	57	4	241	259	271	408	680	1000	488	4	82	27	0.23	45	13	43	113	69	5%	107	13%	36%	9	44%	56%	3.50	-12.1	60	130	$8
11 BOS *	445	71	18	57	4	249	268	319	449	767	766	787	9	79	28	0.49	31	23	46	135	121	7%	121	7%	58%	16	56%	25%	4.77	6.5	81	180	$12
12 OAK	611	85	32	85	11	242	249	305	463	768	751	778	8	75	27	0.36	29	21	50	141	131	14%	126	9%	92%	28	64%	21%	4.82	9.8	70	175	$19
13 OAK	385	54	12	56	9	226	240	307	379	686	667	695	11	78	26	0.53	36	20	44	106	110	9%	113	11%	82%	24	58%	25%	3.90	-4.4	53	133	$9
1st Half	189	21	3	25	6	217	245	299	328	627	606	634	10	80	26	0.59	38	24	39	81	101	5%	103	12%	100%	12	58%	17%	3.36	-6.3	40	100	$6
2nd Half	196	33	9	31	3	235	238	318	429	747	709	761	11	75	27	0.49	33	17	50	132	119	12%	126	10%	60%	12	58%	33%	4.44	0.0	67	168	$12
14 Proj	**410**	**59**	**18**	**57**	**7**	**240**	**251**	**314**	**435**	**749**	**755**	**746**	**10**	**77**	**27**	**0.48**	**33**	**20**	**47**	**131**	**118**	**12%**	**122**	**10%**	**75%**				**4.58**	**1.6**	**64**	**161**	**$11**

Reimold,Nolan

Age 30	Bats R	Pos DH	Health F	LIMA Plan D+
Ht 6' 4"	Wt 205		PT/Exp F	Rand Var +3
			Consist F	MM 3313

5-12-.195 in 128 AB at BAL. Second straight season ended with neck woes; opted for surgery to fuse vertebrae. Rare FFF reliability means he has much to prove as he re-embarks on once-promising career at age 30. When healthy, sub-par ct% and suspect LD% torpedoed BA, so power is the primary path to recoup value.

Yr Tm	AB	R	HR	RBI	SB	BA	xBA	OBP	SLG	OPS	vL	vR	bb%	ct%	h%	Eye	G	L	F	PX	xPX	hr/f	Spd	SBO	SB%	#Wk	DOM	DIS	RC/G	RAR	BPV	BPX	R$
09 BAL *	467	67	23	68	13	297	279	379	515	894	815	841	12	78	34	0.59	48	14	37	139	98	14%	119	11%	80%	19	63%	16%	7.10	40.6	82	167	$21
10 BAL *	453	47	11	41	7	206	218	285	312	598	735	519	10	78	24	0.51	49	12	39	72	65	8%	89	8%	73%	11	36%	45%	2.87	-15.7	20	43	$1
11 BAL *	406	51	18	61	8	228	238	298	410	708	680	830	9	73	27	0.37	45	14	41	124	107	15%	134	12%	72%	20	50%	25%	4.01	0.4	52	116	$9
12 BAL	67	10	5	10	1	313	333	333	627	960	1076	922	3	79	33	0.14	43	26	30	201	92	31%	104	8%	100%	5	60%	20%	7.86	7.0	116	290	$2
13 BAL *	174	19	6	15	0	183	194	238	305	543	595	579	7	67	24	0.22	48	13	38	88	140	15%	125	3%	0%	8	25%	50%	2.20	-9.9	-8	-20	-$3
1st Half	147	16	5	12	0	176	192	241	293	534	689	533	8	68	22	0.27	47	14	40	81	126	14%	122	3%	0%	7	29%	43%	2.11	-9.1	-7	-18	-$2
2nd Half	27	3	1	3	0	222	196	222	370	593	412	900	0	59	33	0.00	56	13	31	130	204	20%	115	0%	0%	1	0%	100%	2.70	-1.1	-22	-55	-$3
14 Proj	**254**	**29**	**12**	**27**	**2**	**235**	**245**	**308**	**415**	**723**	**625**	**788**	**9**	**74**	**27**	**0.41**	**49**	**16**	**35**	**119**	**134**	**18%**	**138**	**6%**	**61%**				**4.20**	**-2.4**	**33**	**83**	**$6**

Rendon,Anthony

Age 24	Bats R	Pos 2B	Health A	LIMA Plan B
Ht 6' 0"	Wt 195		PT/Exp F	Rand Var 0
			Consist F	MM 3225

7-35-.265 in 351 AB at WAS. A 3B by trade, called up in early June to play 2B and held his own with the bat. Minor league 23% walk rate and .531 Slg point to discipline and power upside. He has the tools to be a plus-BA-with-pop guy at maturity. History of shoulder/ankle problems, if he can stay healthy... UP: 20 HR, .290 BA.

Yr Tm	AB	R	HR	RBI	SB	BA	xBA	OBP	SLG	OPS	vL	vR	bb%	ct%	h%	Eye	G	L	F	PX	xPX	hr/f	Spd	SBO	SB%	#Wk	DOM	DIS	RC/G	RAR	BPV	BPX	R$
09																																	
10																																	
11																																	
12 aa	68	11	2	2	0	148	250	242	320	562			11	76	15	0.51				111			124	0%	0%				2.31		52	130	-$3
13 WAS *	478	55	12	54	2	267	272	342	422	765	830	682	10	79	32	0.55	41	26	34	113	115	7%	113	2%	64%	20	45%	20%	5.02	18.7	64	160	$12
1st Half	243	29	6	27	2	291	294	375	465	840	759	803	12	78	35	0.62	35	33	32	132	129	3%	103	2%	100%	7	43%	14%	6.33	17.8	76	190	$15
2nd Half	235	26	6	27	0	243	254	307	379	686	861	620	9	80	28	0.47	43	22	35	94	108	9%	118	2%	0%	13	46%	23%	3.85	1.1	50	125	$8
14 Proj	**497**	**57**	**12**	**61**	**2**	**270**	**262**	**348**	**420**	**768**	**876**	**724**	**10**	**79**	**32**	**0.55**	**42**	**22**	**36**	**108**	**116**	**9%**	**110**	**2%**	**56%**				**5.03**	**19.0**	**42**	**106**	**$14**

Revere,Ben

Age 26	Bats L	Pos CF	Health C	LIMA Plan B
Ht 5' 9"	Wt 170		PT/Exp C	Rand Var -3
			Consist A	MM 0535

Broken foot just before ASB cost the rest of the season; should be full speed in the spring. League change had no impact, maintained his SBO pace and should be sustainable if healthy. Elite Spd, ct% and a heavy GB/LD approach yields plus BA and many SB. This is wise, as power is microscopic. Just hit, run, steal. UP: 50 SB.

Yr Tm	AB	R	HR	RBI	SB	BA	xBA	OBP	SLG	OPS	vL	vR	bb%	ct%	h%	Eye	G	L	F	PX	xPX	hr/f	Spd	SBO	SB%	#Wk	DOM	DIS	RC/G	RAR	BPV	BPX	R$
09																																	
10 MIN *	389	35	1	20	28	267	262	316	314	631	368	450	7	88	30	0.58	68	14	18	31	40	0%	143	37%	65%	5	20%	80%	3.27	-9.7	33	72	$12
11 MIN *	582	68	1	37	40	267	291	304	311	615	609	624	5	91	29	0.58	69	20	12	27	18	0%	153	31%	78%	22	36%	18%	3.38	-12.2	43	96	$20
12 MIN *	605	78	0	37	45	294	278	330	337	667	676	675	5	90	33	0.53	67	19	15	26	23	0%	158	30%	80%	24	29%	21%	4.15	0.9	40	100	$27
13 PHI	315	37	0	17	22	305	277	338	352	691	858	641	5	89	34	0.44	59	23	17	32	31	0%	152	30%	73%	15	27%	33%	4.34	2.2	37	93	$15
1st Half	266	32	0	11	20	289	269	330	331	661	842	616	6	88	33	0.48	62	21	17	29	33	0%	151	32%	74%	14	21%	36%	3.93	-1.9	32	80	$18
2nd Half	49	5	0	6	2	388	315	388	469	857	900	828	0	94	41	0.00	48	33	20	49	23	0%	134	19%	67%	1	100%	0%	7.28	3.8	57	143	$0
14 Proj	**529**	**61**	**0**	**29**	**38**	**289**	**279**	**330**	**331**	**660**	**702**	**640**	**6**	**89**	**32**	**0.55**	**60**	**24**	**16**	**28**	**24**	**0%**	**161**	**30%**	**75%**				**3.93**	**-3.6**	**30**	**75**	**$24**

Reyes,Jose

Age 31	Bats B	Pos SS	Health F	LIMA Plan C
Ht 6' 1"	Wt 195		PT/Exp A	Rand Var -2
			Consist C	MM 2545

Lost 10 weeks due to an ankle sprain that curtailed SBO and SB%. Reasonable to wonder if, at 31, he gets it all back. However, hr/f increased, perhaps in part from friendlier hitting venue and team approach, but needs to show it is sustainable. Solid ct% still renders plus BA with goodly runs, HR and SB. If (capital I) healthy.

Yr Tm	AB	R	HR	RBI	SB	BA	xBA	OBP	SLG	OPS	vL	vR	bb%	ct%	h%	Eye	G	L	F	PX	xPX	hr/f	Spd	SBO	SB%	#Wk	DOM	DIS	RC/G	RAR	BPV	BPX	R$
09 NYM	147	18	2	15	11	279	259	355	395	750	1086	662	11	87	31	0.95	41	19	40	70	76	4%	150	27%	85%	7	71%	14%	5.22	7.6	73	149	$5
10 NYM	563	83	11	54	30	282	274	321	428	749	744	750	5	89	30	0.49	43	18	40	88	67	6%	138	29%	75%	25	52%	12%	4.81	22.3	79	172	$24
11 NYM	537	101	7	44	39	337	290	384	493	877	842	888	7	92	36	1.05	42	21	37	91	88	4%	182	27%	85%	23	74%	4%	7.53	58.3	114	253	$36
12 MIA	642	86	11	57	40	287	291	347	433	780	753	792	9	91	30	1.13	46	22	32	84	83	6%	130	27%	78%	27	78%	4%	5.46	37.3	91	228	$29
13 TOR	382	58	10	37	15	296	275	353	427	780	705	804	8	88	32	0.72	46	21	33	84	82	9%	101	18%	71%	17	59%	24%	5.38	21.1	67	168	$18
1st Half	58	9	2	8	5	328	313	400	466	866	1171	752	11	88	35	1.00	49	31	20	81	49	20%	89	23%	100%	4	50%	25%	7.78	6.6	67	168	$1
2nd Half	324	49	8	29	10	290	269	345	420	764	616	813	8	88	31	0.68	45	19	36	85	87	8%	107	17%	63%	13	62%	23%	5.01	14.3	68	170	$21
14 Proj	**524**	**79**	**13**	**52**	**31**	**303**	**290**	**362**	**453**	**814**	**838**	**806**	**9**	**89**	**32**	**0.90**	**45**	**23**	**32**	**90**	**77**	**9%**	**129**	**23%**	**82%**				**6.12**	**38.8**	**89**	**222**	**$31**

Reynolds,Mark

Age 30	Bats R	Pos 1B 3B	Health A	LIMA Plan D+
Ht 6' 2"	Wt 220		PT/Exp B	Rand Var 0
			Consist B	MM 4103

Second half power outage temporarily cost MLB job as downward trending hr/f made it tougher to compensate for terrible ct%. HR, RBI and R are still fantasy viable even with low BA. But a continuation of the plummeting PX puts his job security in peril. Consider yourself warned.

Yr Tm	AB	R	HR	RBI	SB	BA	xBA	OBP	SLG	OPS	vL	vR	bb%	ct%	h%	Eye	G	L	F	PX	xPX	hr/f	Spd	SBO	SB%	#Wk	DOM	DIS	RC/G	RAR	BPV	BPX	R$
09 ARI	578	98	44	102	24	260	257	349	543	892	894	889	12	61	34	0.34	35	17	47	217	169	26%	98	22%	73%	27	63%	15%	6.34	40.9	74	151	$29
10 ARI	499	79	32	85	7	198	218	320	433	753	913	694	14	58	26	0.39	32	13	55	196	149	20%	91	8%	64%	26	46%	38%	4.24	4.7	46	100	$10
11 BAL	534	84	37	86	6	221	248	323	483	806	781	814	12	63	27	0.38	39	13	48	209	171	23%	73	8%	60%	27	56%	15%	4.92	16.0	69	153	$16
12 BAL	457	65	23	69	1	221	236	335	429	763	722	778	14	65	28	0.46	37	20	42	161	138	18%	71	3%	25%	25	32%	44%	4.50	7.8	41	103	$8
13 2 AL	445	55	21	67	3	220	217	306	393	699	725	684	10	65	29	0.33	39	18	42	132	125	17%	77	4%	75%	27	44%	48%	3.86	-1.1	13	33	$9
1st Half	275	38	15	46	3	233	222	319	422	741	816	706	11	65	30	0.36	40	19	42	140	118	20%	88	4%	100%	14	50%	43%	4.54	4.7	23	58	$14
2nd Half	170	17	6	21	0	200	206	269	347	616	605	643	9	66	26	0.28	39	17	44	118	135	13%	67	3%	0%	13	38%	54%	2.89	-5.8	-3	-8	-$1
14 Proj	**341**	**45**	**17**	**51**	**2**	**218**	**226**	**314**	**416**	**731**	**718**	**737**	**11**	**65**	**28**	**0.37**	**38**	**18**	**44**	**156**	**140**	**18%**	**74**	**5%**	**56%**				**4.12**	**-5.1**	**22**	**56**	**$8**

Rios,Alex

Age 33	Bats R	Pos RF	Health A	LIMA Plan B+
Ht 6' 5"	Wt 210		PT/Exp A	Rand Var -1
			Consist F	MM 3535

Someone missed the every other year memo. Career high SB from concurrent spike in SBO and SB%. Increased Spd at 33 an exception, not the rule, so a giveback is likely. "F" Consistency emanates from oscillating h% and hr/f (ct%, bb% quite stable). Reputation will scare some off—but he HAS produced back-to-back $30 seasons.

Yr Tm	AB	R	HR	RBI	SB	BA	xBA	OBP	SLG	OPS	vL	vR	bb%	ct%	h%	Eye	G	L	F	PX	xPX	hr/f	Spd	SBO	SB%	#Wk	DOM	DIS	RC/G	RAR	BPV	BPX	R$
09 2 AL	582	63	17	71	24	247	256	296	395	691	723	679	6	82	28	0.35	43	16	41	94	103	9%	100	22%	83%	27	48%	30%	3.98	-5.1	46	94	$16
10 CHW	567	89	21	88	34	284	277	334	457	791	717	814	6	84	31	0.41	45	17	38	109	107	12%	120	33%	71%	26	58%	19%	5.16	14.4	72	157	$31
11 CHW	537	64	13	44	11	227	255	265	348	613	704	578	5	87	24	0.40	42	18	39	76	76	7%	108	15%	65%	27	48%	26%	2.96	-21.6	54	120	$7
12 CHW	605	93	25	91	23	304	288	334	516	850	857	848	4	85	33	0.28	40	22	38	125	111	13%	127	21%	79%	27	59%	19%	6.27	33.3	87	218	$34
13 2 AL	616	83	18	81	42	278	269	324	432	756	889	714	6	82	31	0.38	44	21	35	102	83	10%	117	31%	86%	27	52%	26%	5.09	14.3	61	153	$36
1st Half	302	42	11	36	14	268	271	326	444	770	842	754	8	82	30	0.47	43	20	38	117	90	12%	99	25%	74%	14	50%	36%	4.97	4.6	68	170	$29
2nd Half	314	41	7	45	28	287	267	319	420	740	919	670	5	83	33	0.28	45	23	32	87	76	8%	132	38%	93%	13	54%	15%	5.21	6.7	53	133	$43
14 Proj	**582**	**80**	**18**	**76**	**28**	**281**	**271**	**322**	**443**	**765**	**846**	**737**	**5**	**84**	**31**	**0.36**	**43**	**21**	**37**	**103**	**90**	**10%**	**120**	**25%**	**79%**				**5.05**	**10.1**	**69**	**172**	**$29**

TODD ZOLA

Rizzo,Anthony

Age	24	Bats	L	Pos	1B	Health	A	LIMA Plan	B+
Ht	6' 3"	Wt	240			PT/Exp	B	Rand Var	+4
						Consist	F	MM	4125

Be ready: Narrative-seekers will point to his .218/.315/.382 slash after signing a 7-yr, $41M contract in mid-May and scream causation. But the coin didn't affect his BPI: more patience, better FB% with solid power peripherals, nearly identical BPV. Hit rate, xBA, RandVar and age all point to a rebound. Profit city.

Yr	Tm	AB	R	HR	RBI	SB	BA	xBA	OBP	SLG	OPS	vL	vR	bb%	ct%	h%	Eye	G	L	F	PX	xPX	hr/f	Spd	SBO	SB%	#Wk	DOM	DIS	RC/G	RAR	BPV	BPX	R$
09																																		
10	aa	414	49	14	60	5	242	270	299	422	722			8	75	29	0.32				138			86	7%	83%				4.27		51	111	$8
11	SD *	484	49	16	72	6	222	228	294	396	690	618	495	9	68	29	0.32	43	13	44	146	126	3%	59	14%	44%	11	27%	73%	3.61	-14.7	26	58	$7
12	CHC *	594	80	32	94	4	290	291	340	510	849	599	892	7	79	32	0.37	45	24	30	136	119	18%	82	6%	51%	15	60%	20%	6.09	25.0	67	168	$26
13	CHC	606	71	23	80	6	233	269	323	419	742	625	796	11	79	26	0.60	43	20	38	130	124	13%	67	7%	55%	27	63%	7%	4.34	-4.5	65	163	$13
1st Half		301	41	12	48	5	252	287	328	465	793	796	806	10	80	28	0.57	42	21	37	147	121	13%	62	11%	63%	14	71%	7%	5.10	4.5	79	198	$20
2nd Half		305	30	11	32	1	213	246	308	374	682	406	788	12	78	24	0.63	43	18	38	112	126	12%	77	4%	33%	13	54%	8%	3.65	-9.0	51	128	$7
14	Proj	600	76	24	90	5	274	267	351	461	812	665	872	10	78	32	0.48	44	20	36	131	123	14%	73	6%	52%				5.46	14.9	53	134	$20

Roberts,Brian

Age	36	Bats	B	Pos	2B	Health	F	LIMA Plan	D+
Ht	5' 9"	Wt	175			PT/Exp	F	Rand Var	0
						Consist	D	MM	2213

Heard this before? A torn knee tendon wiped out almost his entire 1H after just 12 Apr AB. Plate skills really haven't changed, and he showed adequate power upon his return. But his wheels are shot, and he is now a 36-year-old who has averaged 190 AB the past four seasons. Risky end-gamer.

Yr	Tm	AB	R	HR	RBI	SB	BA	xBA	OBP	SLG	OPS	vL	vR	bb%	ct%	h%	Eye	G	L	F	PX	xPX	hr/f	Spd	SBO	SB%	#Wk	DOM	DIS	RC/G	RAR	BPV	BPX	R$
09	BAL	632	110	16	79	30	283	279	356	451	807	781	820	10	82	32	0.66	36	22	42	117	106	7%	100	21%	81%	27	67%	19%	5.82	37.8	76	155	$28
10	BAL	230	28	4	15	12	278	248	354	391	745	801	726	10	83	32	0.65	34	22	45	83	112	5%	102	19%	86%	12	50%	25%	5.04	8.6	50	109	$8
11	BAL	163	18	3	19	6	221	240	273	331	604	583	613	7	87	24	0.57	29	23	49	71	121	4%	98	19%	86%	8	50%	13%	3.07	-3.2	50	111	$1
12	BAL *	103	6	1	8	1	186	202	254	248	502	607	370	8	80	23	0.45	45	16	39	48	25	0%	84	8%	50%	4	0%	100%	1.92	-5.9	2	5	-$3
13	BAL	265	33	8	39	3	249	262	312	392	704	768	665	9	83	27	0.59	36	24	39	92	119	9%	89	6%	75%	15	53%	27%	4.21	3.8	54	135	$6
1st Half		14	1	0	2	1	429	342	429	500	929	583	1000	0	93	46	0.00	36	43	21	58	57	0%	92	20%	100%	2	50%	50%	10.31	2.1	48	120	-$5
2nd Half		251	32	8	37	2	239	258	310	386	697	775	642	9	83	26	0.60	36	23	41	94	123	9%	89	5%	67%	13	54%	23%	4.00	2.3	54	135	$6
14	Proj	288	33	7	32	4	234	245	297	358	655	736	620	9	83	26	0.56	36	21	43	84	100	6%	90	6%	77%				3.58	-1.0	40	100	$5

Roberts,Ryan

Age	33	Bats	R	Pos	2B	Health	A	LIMA Plan	D
Ht	5' 11"	Wt	185			PT/Exp	C	Rand Var	-1
						Consist	C	MM	2201

5-17-.247 in 162 AB at TAM. Sure looks like the 2010-13 bell curve is now complete. Back to terrible contact, a LD deficiency, and more CS than SB. Sure, there's a little bit of punch, but when you're handed three Tampa-to-Durham round trip tickets in a six-week span, an Aug DFA is not a surprise. Might not get another chance.

Yr	Tm	AB	R	HR	RBI	SB	BA	xBA	OBP	SLG	OPS	vL	vR	bb%	ct%	h%	Eye	G	L	F	PX	xPX	hr/f	Spd	SBO	SB%	#Wk	DOM	DIS	RC/G	RAR	BPV	BPX	R$
09	ARI *	347	47	8	31	11	274	249	355	407	761	953	678	11	82	32	0.70	38	19	43	85	118	6%	119	13%	79%	24	29%	33%	5.11	14.5	56	114	$10
10	ARI *	413	42	8	39	9	192	205	252	315	567	420	849	7	73	24	0.30	39	10	51	96	142	8%	90	21%	53%	11	36%	45%	2.36	-17.3	14	30	-$1
11	ARI	482	86	19	65	18	249	266	341	427	768	881	724	12	80	28	0.67	35	24	41	119	119	12%	100	19%	67%	27	63%	11%	4.79	15.5	70	156	$18
12	2 TM	439	51	12	52	10	235	229	296	360	656	648	663	8	79	27	0.43	38	19	43	83	122	8%	81	14%	63%	27	37%	30%	3.49	-3.2	26	65	$8
13	TAM *	286	23	6	26	2	208	199	273	301	574	845	494	8	73	27	0.33	43	16	40	71	116	10%	91	8%	39%	17	24%	65%	2.54	-10.6	-6	-15	-$1
1st Half		156	13	3	16	0	231	202	289	326	615	891	421	8	78	28	0.38	43	15	43	68	119	7%	93	5%	0%	13	31%	54%	2.95	-3.6	13	33	$0
2nd Half		130	10	3	10	2	180	210	254	272	525	726	917	9	66	25	0.29	48	24	29	76	104	33%	89	11%	62%	4	0%	100%	2.11	-6.7	-28	-70	-$3
14	Proj	159	17	4	16	2	218	227	290	340	629	656	606	9	75	27	0.40	41	20	39	88	116	9%	92	7%	66%				3.19	-2.5	8	19	$2

Robinson,Derrick

Age	26	Bats	B	Pos	LF	Health	A	LIMA Plan	D
Ht	5' 11"	Wt	190			PT/Exp	C	Rand Var	-3
						Consist	A	MM	0501

0-8-.255 with 4 SB in 192 AB at CIN. MLEs say the legs are worth watching—so we do. But along the way, we run into poor ct%, a string of sub-.300 OBPs, and the fact that he gets thrown out stealing at a frightening clip. Which sort of undermines the whole point. Quad-A filler for now.

Yr	Tm	AB	R	HR	RBI	SB	BA	xBA	OBP	SLG	OPS	vL	vR	bb%	ct%	h%	Eye	G	L	F	PX	xPX	hr/f	Spd	SBO	SB%	#Wk	DOM	DIS	RC/G	RAR	BPV	BPX	R$
09																																		
10	aa	511	54	1	35	37	253	242	297	333	631			6	82	31	0.35				59			132	43%	66%				3.18		29	63	$15
11	aa	419	40	1	18	40	213	195	269	238	507			7	77	27	0.34				19			129	50%	70%				2.07		-20	-44	$8
12	aaa	422	50	1	19	16	219	204	276	263	540			7	77	28	0.35				33			128	23%	60%				2.27		-8	-20	$3
13	CIN *	251	25	0	10	6	239	222	296	300	596	742	575	8	73	33	0.30	47	25	28	51	25	0%	163	17%	56%	25	28%	48%	2.85	-9.2	-1	-3	$1
1st Half		109	9	0	5	2	266	246	344	330	675	775	562	11	74	36	0.46	51	29	20	56	10	0%	134	14%	40%	14	29%	64%	3.64	-1.2	6	15	$1
2nd Half		142	16	0	5	4	218	197	256	277	534	636	585	5	72	30	0.18	41	21	38	48	43	0%	164	20%	69%	11	27%	27%	2.29	-7.7	-13	-33	$0
14	Proj	130	14	0	6	6	230	218	288	280	568	658	516	7	76	30	0.32	45	24	31	40	30	0%	150	26%	62%				2.55	-6.0	-15	-37	$2

Robinson,Shane

Age	29	Bats	R	Pos	RF CF LF	Health	A	LIMA Plan	D
Ht	5' 9"	Wt	165			PT/Exp	F	Rand Var	0
						Consist	A	MM	1511

Finally stuck around all year as a reserve, and provided a bit of big-league value, including an elite Eye and some speed. But there was only one month with more than 25 AB, calling his patience and OBP gains into question. And at 29 without guaranteed PT, he's just another 4th-5th-6th-8th OFer.

Yr	Tm	AB	R	HR	RBI	SB	BA	xBA	OBP	SLG	OPS	vL	vR	bb%	ct%	h%	Eye	G	L	F	PX	xPX	hr/f	Spd	SBO	SB%	#Wk	DOM	DIS	RC/G	RAR	BPV	BPX	R$
09	STL *	370	37	3	32	13	203	288	246	286	533	286	596	5	87	23	0.43	67	17	17	54	26	0%	114	23%	79%	3	0%	33%	2.30	-21.0	37	76	$0
10	aaa	86	6	1	9	2	216	243	257	305	562			5	82	25	0.30				65			97	31%	35%				2.13		21	46	-$1
11	STL *	205	27	4	19	6	237	262	292	347	639	200	0	7	89	25	0.69	80	0	20	67	2	0%	124	16%	69%	5	20%	40%	3.34	-4.6	62	138	$3
12	STL *	236	30	3	18	4	246	227	304	342	645	694	633	8	79	30	0.38	57	12	31	68	45	7%	144	7%	100%	25	44%	32%	3.62	-3.3	29	73	$2
13	STL	144	22	2	16	5	250	257	345	319	664	598	746	14	88	27	1.35	45	25	30	39	73	5%	136	11%	83%	25	44%	40%	3.96	-0.5	54	135	$2
1st Half		60	12	2	8	3	217	225	356	333	689	595	805	18	82	23	1.18	44	15	40	69	101	10%	104	13%	100%	14	43%	57%	4.18	0.0	51	128	$3
2nd Half		84	10	0	8	2	274	284	351	310	661	602	711	11	93	29	1.67	46	32	23	19	55	0%	142	10%	67%	11	45%	18%	3.79	-0.9	52	130	$2
14	Proj	157	22	2	15	5	243	249	317	326	643	608	683	10	86	27	0.82	50	20	31	52	63	5%	136	12%	82%				3.62	-3.9	37	93	$4

Rodriguez,Alex

Age	38	Bats	R	Pos	3B	Health	F	LIMA Plan	C+
Ht	6' 3"	Wt	225			PT/Exp	C	Rand Var	+1
						Consist	A	MM	4213

7-19-.244 with 4 SB in 156 AB at NYY. Well, where to start? His risk stretches far beyond his off-the-field drama: He's 38, and becoming injured almost as frequently as he's swinging through pitches. Power was notable after hip surgery, but without a ct% reversal, he's reduced to a low-BA slugger. If he puts on the uniform.

Yr	Tm	AB	R	HR	RBI	SB	BA	xBA	OBP	SLG	OPS	vL	vR	bb%	ct%	h%	Eye	G	L	F	PX	xPX	hr/f	Spd	SBO	SB%	#Wk	DOM	DIS	RC/G	RAR	BPV	BPX	R$
09	NYY	444	78	30	100	14	286	290	402	532	933	939	931	15	78	31	0.82	42	20	38	145	138	23%	78	10%	88%	23	61%	22%	7.62	45.9	85	173	$25
10	NYY	522	74	30	125	4	270	287	341	506	847	755	883	10	81	28	0.60	46	14	40	148	139	17%	81	5%	57%	25	68%	16%	5.99	30.8	90	196	$23
11	NYY	373	67	16	62	4	276	261	362	461	823	750	848	11	79	31	0.59	49	14	37	127	116	15%	84	4%	80%	21	57%	33%	5.82	19.8	65	144	$15
12	NYY	463	74	18	57	13	272	250	353	430	783	924	717	10	75	33	0.44	45	22	32	103	118	16%	97	10%	93%	22	45%	32%	5.33	18.2	33	83	$18
13	NYY *	177	24	9	24	4	243	247	342	443	784	585	856	13	71	29	0.51	40	20	40	142	166	16%	79	11%	67%	8	50%	50%	5.01	5.7	49	123	$4
1st Half																																		
2nd Half		177	24	9	24	4	243	247	342	443	784	585	856	13	71	29	0.51	40	20	40	142	166	16%	79	11%	67%	8	50%	50%	5.01	5.5	49	123	$4
14	Proj	346	54	15	57	6	248	249	331	425	755	696	779	10	75	29	0.45	44	18	38	123	137	15%	81	8%	74%				4.66	7.1	43	107	$12

Rodriguez,Sean

Age	29	Bats	R	Pos	LF 1B	Health	A	LIMA Plan	D
Ht	6' 0"	Wt	200			PT/Exp	D	Rand Var	-3
						Consist	B	MM	3201

Once a promising super-utility type, now a platoon cornerman with anti-cornerman power. AB vs. RHP following same yearly trend as AB (just 40 in 2013); xBA and declining Spd seal the deal. We're smart enough to ignore that 2009 line by now. But I made you look, didn't I? And now you can't forget it. (Maybe you shouldn't?)

Yr	Tm	AB	R	HR	RBI	SB	BA	xBA	OBP	SLG	OPS	vL	vR	bb%	ct%	h%	Eye	G	L	F	PX	xPX	hr/f	Spd	SBO	SB%	#Wk	DOM	DIS	RC/G	RAR	BPV	BPX	R$
09	LAA *	410	77	26	86	8	257	261	336	518	854	630	786	11	64	33	0.33	63	0	37	186	74	29%	152	9%	77%	6	33%	33%	5.96	16.3	75	153	$17
10	TAM	343	53	9	40	13	251	239	308	397	705	817	642	6	72	32	0.22	42	19	39	112	120	10%	108	21%	81%	27	37%	48%	4.01	-6.0	22	48	$10
11	TAM	373	45	8	36	11	223	235	323	357	679	864	567	9	77	27	0.44	41	17	41	98	91	7%	115	20%	61%	27	52%	26%	3.31	-15.0	40	89	$5
12	TAM	301	36	6	32	5	213	220	281	326	607	655	575	8	75	26	0.36	47	15	38	82	76	7%	104	7%	100%	25	20%	48%	3.01	-14.8	15	38	$1
13	TAM	195	21	5	23	1	246	227	320	385	704	745	545	8	70	33	0.29	36	23	41	110	81	9%	90	8%	25%	27	33%	44%	3.76	-4.9	12	30	$2
1st Half		86	10	2	11	1	233	222	283	372	655	744	473	7	72	30	0.25	30	24	46	103	53	7%	108	11%	50%	14	36%	43%	3.37	-3.2	18	45	$1
2nd Half		109	11	3	12	0	257	227	325	394	719	746	618	9	68	35	0.31	41	23	36	115	105	11%	80	7%	0%	13	31%	46%	4.07	-1.7	8	20	$2
14	Proj	205	24	5	24	3	235	226	312	369	681	753	581	8	72	30	0.32	41	20	40	103	87	8%	97	10%	55%				3.57	-2.8	12	29	$4

BRENT HERSHEY

Rollins,Jimmy

Age	35	Bats	B	Pos	SS	Health	B	LIMA Plan	A
Ht	5' 8"	Wt	180			PT/Exp	A	Rand Var	0
						Consist	A	MM	2325

Two years ago, the concern was his health; since then he's put together consecutive 600-AB seasons. But with slowly declining power and speed, it becomes more difficult to gloss over that .250 BA anchor. A low hr/f points to a mild HR rebound, but his 20/20 past might be history. A couple more years at this level.

Yr	Tm	AB	R	HR	RBI	SB	BA	xBA	OBP	SLG	OPS	vL	vR	bb%	ct%	h%	Eye	G	L	F	PX	xPX	hr/f	Spd	SBO	SB%	#Wk	DOM	DIS	RC/G	RAR	BPV	BPX	R$
09	PHI	672	100	21	77	31	250	290	296	423	719	692	728	6	90	25	0.63	40	19	41	101	95	8%	100	27%	79%	26	69%	8%	4.27	15.3	84	171	$22
10	PHI	350	48	8	41	17	243	276	320	374	694	773	657	10	91	25	1.25	46	17	37	78	82	7%	98	18%	94%	17	71%	6%	4.28	8.0	78	170	$10
11	PHI	567	87	16	63	30	268	263	338	399	736	609	779	9	90	28	0.98	39	20	41	78	94	8%	101	22%	79%	26	62%	12%	4.72	20.2	72	160	$24
12	PHI	632	102	23	68	30	250	266	316	427	743	612	804	9	85	26	0.65	39	19	42	106	95	10%	98	22%	86%	27	67%	15%	4.73	22.8	73	183	$24
13	PHI	600	65	6	39	22	252	251	318	348	667	648	674	9	85	29	0.63	38	24	39	72	60	3%	94	17%	79%	27	44%	19%	3.84	5.8	44	110	$15
1st Half		312	31	4	28	8	263	247	327	362	690	680	692	9	85	30	0.64	40	21	39	71	68	4%	93	14%	62%	14	43%	14%	3.99	4.8	44	110	$16
2nd Half		288	34	2	11	14	240	254	309	333	642	616	653	9	84	28	0.63	36	26	38	73	52	2%	97	20%	93%	13	46%	23%	3.68	1.8	44	110	$14
14	Proj	542	72	11	46	23	252	258	318	377	696	637	719	9	86	28	0.69	39	22	40	84	76	6%	97	19%	82%				4.19	11.6	66	164	$15

Romine,Austin

Age	25	Bats	R	Pos	CA	Health	F	LIMA Plan	F
Ht	6' 0"	Wt	215			PT/Exp	F	Rand Var	-2
						Consist	A	MM	1101

1-10-.207 in 135 AB at NYY. Missed most of 2012 with back injury, then used sparingly in 2013 until September concussion ended his season. Has not shown the same contact ability in NY (73% career) that he had in the minors. Still young, but the trend says backup CA—and now health is a significant hurdle.

Yr	Tm	AB	R	HR	RBI	SB	BA	xBA	OBP	SLG	OPS	vL	vR	bb%	ct%	h%	Eye	G	L	F	PX	xPX	hr/f	Spd	SBO	SB%	#Wk	DOM	DIS	RC/G	RAR	BPV	BPX	R$
09																																		
10	aa	455	50	9	56	2	243	249	291	366	657			6	78	29	0.30				93			87	2%	100%				3.61		26	57	$6
11	NYY *	370	38	6	40	2	248	254	301	326	628	250	375	7	80	30	0.38	43	29	29	55	73	0%	72	4%	43%	3	0%	67%	3.27	-4.8	2	4	$4
12	aaa	61	5	3	7	0	189	242	265	350	615			9	82	19	0.57				93			91	0%	0%				2.92		50	125	-$2
13	NYY *	177	19	2	13	1	229	233	275	312	587	576	540	6	71	31	0.22	55	23	22	74	61	5%	76	2%	100%	19	26%	47%	2.87	-4.5	-17	-43	-$1
1st Half		104	10	1	5	1	206	215	231	263	494	412	330	3	71	28	0.11	56	22	22	48	13	0%	82	5%	100%	10	10%	50%	1.99	-5.6	-47	-118	-$2
2nd Half		73	9	1	8	0	260	254	333	384	717	681	728	10	73	35	0.40	54	24	22	110	101	8%	81	0%	0%	9	44%	44%	4.41	1.5	25	63	$0
14	Proj	163	18	1	16	1	242	240	297	318	615	629	608	7	75	31	0.31	54	23	22	65	66	5%	75	2%	70%				3.16	-2.7	-16	-40	$2

Rosales,Adam

Age	31	Bats	R	Pos	SS	Health	C	LIMA Plan	F
Ht	6' 1"	Wt	195			PT/Exp	F	Rand Var	+5
						Consist	B	MM	2101

5-12-.190 in 147 AB at OAK/TEX/OAK/TEX. Kids, check out the latest carnival game: "Waiver Chicken"! Take a inconsequential MIF with sloppy contact, minimal power, and declining speed. How long can YOU roster him before DFA? Two days? Three days? CRAZY!! Only takes two to play, and even contenders can do it!!

Yr	Tm	AB	R	HR	RBI	SB	BA	xBA	OBP	SLG	OPS	vL	vR	bb%	ct%	h%	Eye	G	L	F	PX	xPX	hr/f	Spd	SBO	SB%	#Wk	DOM	DIS	RC/G	RAR	BPV	BPX	R$
09	CIN *	339	44	8	35	4	242	251	315	383	698	693	598	10	81	28	0.56	45	16	40	90	85	5%	133	7%	68%	22	27%	45%	4.03	5.3	58	118	$4
10	OAK	255	31	7	31	2	271	252	321	400	721	794	681	7	75	34	0.29	38	28	34	88	68	11%	139	6%	50%	19	37%	37%	4.39	7.1	26	57	$6
11	OAK *	208	19	4	22	1	166	191	213	244	457	486	184	6	74	21	0.23	46	14	40	54	91	10%	104	5%	33%	12	17%	50%	1.55	-12.8	-16	-36	-$4
12	OAK *	374	41	7	38	3	207	236	262	317	579	558	757	7	74	26	0.28	34	28	38	85	91	7%	95	7%	49%	16	38%	50%	2.62	-9.5	7	18	$0
13	2 AL *	185	17	5	16	1	182	218	231	297	528	721	401	6	77	21	0.28	48	15	37	81	87	12%	83	6%	32%	21	33%	33%	2.08	-8.0	11	28	-$3
1st Half		137	12	4	8	1	185	227	242	309	551	756	395	7	77	21	0.33	46	17	37	86	93	12%	88	2%	100%	11	45%	36%	2.36	-4.8	20	50	-$3
2nd Half		48	6	1	8	0	172	191	199	264	462	545	444	3	75	21	0.14	55	5	40	66	60	13%	92	18%	0%	10	20%	30%	1.35	-3.4	-10	-25	-$4
14	Proj	99	11	3	11	1	209	227	262	329	591	661	516	6	75	25	0.24	42	20	38	84	88	10%	95	7%	35%				2.59	-2.7	0	0	$1

Rosario,Wilin

Age	25	Bats	R	Pos	CA	Health	A	LIMA Plan	B
Ht	5' 11"	Wt	220			PT/Exp	C	Rand Var	-3
						Consist	C	MM	4125

Not often that you see a .292 BA alongside a 0.14 Eye, but here it is. Of course, h% played a part, so xBA is a better BA reference going forward. The power, though, is real, which makes him a rare .270, 20-HR CA. And with sustained gains vRHP and a few more walks (like in 1H)... UP: 30 HR.

Yr	Tm	AB	R	HR	RBI	SB	BA	xBA	OBP	SLG	OPS	vL	vR	bb%	ct%	h%	Eye	G	L	F	PX	xPX	hr/f	Spd	SBO	SB%	#Wk	DOM	DIS	RC/G	RAR	BPV	BPX	R$
09																																		
10	aa	270	34	17	42	1	275	297	316	520	837			6	79	29	0.29				155			98	1%	100%				5.81		83	180	$9
11	COL *	459	43	20	42	1	225	251	250	406	656	1089	546	3	75	26	0.14	40	20	40	121	137	21%	104	4%	24%	4	50%	25%	3.27	-6.0	38	84	$5
12	COL	396	67	28	71	4	270	278	312	530	843	1140	726	6	75	29	0.25	46	17	37	165	142	25%	76	11%	44%	27	67%	15%	5.55	21.4	69	173	$18
13	COL	449	63	21	79	4	292	266	315	486	801	901	760	3	76	34	0.14	41	23	36	133	122	17%	82	5%	80%	25	44%	28%	5.50	22.5	42	105	$21
1st Half		251	33	13	41	3	275	268	308	486	794	808	791	5	77	31	0.21	37	22	41	140	138	16%	86	7%	75%	14	50%	21%	5.24	11.0	56	140	$21
2nd Half		198	30	8	38	1	313	264	323	485	808	1011	718	1	74	39	0.06	46	24	30	123	102	18%	79	2%	100%	11	36%	36%	5.85	11.4	24	60	$21
14	Proj	471	66	24	80	3	273	267	300	479	779	995	693	4	76	32	0.16	43	21	36	139	128	19%	84	6%	61%				5.00	17.4	44	109	$20

Ross,Cody

Age	33	Bats	R	Pos	LF RF	Health	D	LIMA Plan	B+
Ht	5' 10"	Wt	195			PT/Exp	C	Rand Var	0
						Consist	B	MM	4125

Complained of vision problems in mid-June; 1H bb%/ct% looks fine although his power tanked. Was heating up in 2H, but ugly hip injury and subsequent surgery ended season in early Aug. Still exhibits value as a lefty-killer, and his improved plate approach could extend his career. But check injury status in the spring.

Yr	Tm	AB	R	HR	RBI	SB	BA	xBA	OBP	SLG	OPS	vL	vR	bb%	ct%	h%	Eye	G	L	F	PX	xPX	hr/f	Spd	SBO	SB%	#Wk	DOM	DIS	RC/G	RAR	BPV	BPX	R$
09	FLA	559	73	24	90	5	270	266	321	469	790	959	736	6	78	31	0.28	33	19	48	131	128	11%	81	6%	71%	25	56%	24%	5.08	7.6	55	112	$17
10	2 NL	525	71	14	65	9	269	261	322	413	735	883	687	7	77	33	0.31	46	21	34	103	94	10%	105	8%	82%	27	33%	37%	4.59	-0.2	37	80	$15
11	SF	405	54	14	52	5	240	241	325	405	730	698	740	11	76	28	0.51	34	18	48	122	120	9%	81	7%	71%	22	41%	41%	4.35	-3.1	51	113	$8
12	BOS	476	70	22	81	2	267	262	326	481	807	1010	729	8	73	32	0.33	36	22	42	153	118	15%	80	4%	40%	23	57%	30%	5.34	10.1	56	140	$16
13	ARI	317	33	8	38	3	278	264	331	413	745	1012	603	7	84	31	0.50	43	21	35	90	103	8%	73	6%	60%	19	37%	26%	4.75	1.3	48	120	$8
1st Half		211	19	3	20	0	256	252	314	351	665	994	495	8	83	30	0.50	45	23	32	66	83	5%	81	3%	0%	13	31%	31%	3.63	-5.1	26	65	$6
2nd Half		106	14	5	18	3	321	291	363	538	901	1044	824	6	87	33	0.50	40	17	42	137	143	13%	72	11%	100%	6	50%	17%	7.54	8.7	93	233	$12
14	Proj	420	54	15	61	5	277	264	334	454	788	971	708	8	80	31	0.42	39	20	41	122	118	11%	75	7%	73%				5.30	15.4	56	141	$16

Ross,David

Age	37	Bats	R	Pos	CA	Health	D	LIMA Plan	D
Ht	6' 2"	Wt	230			PT/Exp	F	Rand Var	0
						Consist	B	MM	4101

Had all four HR by May 2, then 10 days later a concussion effectively took him out of commission until late August. Metrics have always supported his power, but he's had two seasons of 200+ AB in his 12-year career. With ct% and xBA in the danger zone, that trend is unlikely to change.

Yr	Tm	AB	R	HR	RBI	SB	BA	xBA	OBP	SLG	OPS	vL	vR	bb%	ct%	h%	Eye	G	L	F	PX	xPX	hr/f	Spd	SBO	SB%	#Wk	DOM	DIS	RC/G	RAR	BPV	BPX	R$
09	ATL	128	18	7	20	0	273	267	380	508	888	648	997	14	70	34	0.54	30	22	49	171	106	16%	75	0%	0%	22	59%	36%	6.70	10.9	68	139	$3
10	ATL	121	15	2	28	0	289	281	392	479	871	886	834	14	77	36	0.71	38	21	41	150	125	5%	88	3%	0%	26	35%	46%	6.51	9.5	84	183	$3
11	ATL	152	14	6	23	0	263	236	333	428	761	613	833	10	66	36	0.31	28	26	45	132	154	14%	70	2%	0%	24	38%	50%	4.80	4.8	13	29	$2
12	ATL	176	18	9	23	1	256	233	321	449	770	712	818	9	66	34	0.30	34	23	43	142	152	18%	68	2%	100%	25	44%	48%	5.03	6.7	18	45	$3
13	BOS	102	11	4	10	1	216	199	298	382	681	804	544	10	59	32	0.26	39	15	46	151	121	15%	57	4%	100%	16	50%	50%	3.68	0.0	-4	-10	-$1
1st Half		65	8	4	6	1	185	205	274	400	674	728	603	11	57	24	0.29	30	16	54	183	147	20%	68	7%	100%	10	50%	50%	3.50	-0.4	19	48	$0
2nd Half		37	3	0	4	0	270	179	325	351	676	974	461	8	62	43	0.21	55	14	32	98	76	0%	64	0%	0%	6	50%	50%	3.99	0.3	-37	-93	-$2
14	Proj	187	21	7	27	1	243	223	331	414	745	801	699	11	65	33	0.36	38	19	42	140	125	14%	62	3%	67%				4.54	4.6	13	32	$5

Ruf,Darin

Age	27	Bats	R	Pos	1B RF LF	Health	A	LIMA Plan	C+
Ht	6' 3"	Wt	220			PT/Exp	D	Rand Var	-1
						Consist	F	MM	5113

14-30-.247 in 251 AB at PHI. Dropped the ball in March, but got called up in July and filled in with better-than expected results. The holes in the swing, and the shots when he connects, are mammoth. He'll take a walk and punish LHP, but lack of defensive mobility, age, and all those Ks make it tough to secure a full-time job.

Yr	Tm	AB	R	HR	RBI	SB	BA	xBA	OBP	SLG	OPS	vL	vR	bb%	ct%	h%	Eye	G	L	F	PX	xPX	hr/f	Spd	SBO	SB%	#Wk	DOM	DIS	RC/G	RAR	BPV	BPX	R$
09																																		
10																																		
11																																		
12	PHI *	522	72	32	86	1	267	265	331	514	844	1326	845	9	74	30	0.37	39	17	43	163	260	30%	80	1%	100%	4	50%	0%	5.93	20.1	70	175	$19
13	PHI *	556	67	19	63	1	228	214	302	384	685	656	863	10	64	32	0.30	41	19	41	133	155	21%	91	2%	23%	13	38%	38%	3.76	-14.0	12	30	$8
1st Half		285	31	5	31	1	216	206	278	328	606			8	64	32	0.24				106			81	5%	23%	1	0%	100%	2.86		-17	-43	$4
2nd Half		271	37	14	32	0	240	229	326	442	768	656	863	11	64	32	0.35	41	19	41	161	155	21%	96	0%	0%	12	42%	33%	4.84	1.9	39	98	$13
14	Proj	381	50	20	51	1	244	247	328	460	788	635	846	9	68	30	0.32	41	19	41	164	140	19%	97	1%	48%				4.86	2.9	38	94	$11

BRENT HERSHEY

Ruggiano,Justin

Age 32	Bats R	Pos CF LF	Health A	LIMA Plan D+	
Ht 6' 1"	Wt 210		PT/Exp D	Rand Var +4	
			Consist F	MM 4213	

Hit rate overcorrected, but he never made enough contact to expect .250 BA, let alone 2012's .290. Tasty power-speed combo produces value when given playing time. This is a 4th OF profile, but as 2012 shows, even they can get a good number of AB some years. If that happens again in 2013... UP: full repeat.

Yr Tm	AB	R	HR	RBI	SB	BA	xBA	OBP	SLG	OPS	vL	vR	bb%	ct%	h%	Eye	G	L	F	PX	xPX	hr/f	Spd	SBO	SB%	#Wk	DOM	DIS	RC/G	RAR	BPV	BPX	R$
09 aaa	471	56	11	57	18	208	212	270	334	603			8	62	31	0.22				108			88	22%	79%				2.93		-20	-41	$6
10 aaa	457	55	10	50	17	223	216	271	343	614			6	64	32	0.18				108			90	25%	69%				2.98		-16	-35	$8
11 TAM *	273	31	9	37	9	238	233	285	392	677	576	748	6	70	31	0.22	53	13	35	119	108	14%	96	22%	73%	15	27%	53%	3.69	-3.3	20	44	$6
12 MIA *	405	51	16	54	17	291	261	355	499	853	1129	806	9	71	37	0.34	41	21	38	157	165	17%	102	27%	59%	17	59%	24%	5.90	21.1	61	153	$19
13 MIA	424	49	18	50	15	222	241	298	396	694	833	631	9	73	26	0.36	45	17	39	123	147	15%	84	23%	65%	27	41%	44%	3.63	-6.1	36	90	$11
1st Half	227	29	11	28	8	233	248	290	423	713	723	720	7	73	27	0.29	47	17	36	129	151	19%	97	22%	73%	14	50%	29%	4.01	-1.1	40	100	$14
2nd Half	197	20	7	22	7	208	233	291	365	656	975	534	10	74	25	0.44	43	16	41	116	144	12%	74	26%	58%	13	31%	62%	3.22	-6.0	32	80	$7
14 Proj	**353**	**41**	**14**	**44**	**11**	**239**	**243**	**305**	**416**	**722**	**853**	**656**	**8**	**71**	**30**	**0.31**	**44**	**17**	**38**	**133**	**147**	**14%**	**89**	**21%**	**63%**				**4.05**	**-1.3**	**36**	**91**	**$9**

Ruiz,Carlos

Age 35	Bats R	Pos CA	Health C	LIMA Plan C	
Ht 5' 10"	Wt 205		PT/Exp C	Rand Var +1	
			Consist F	MM 2233	

Profile of an aging player: 2012 plantar fasciitis followed by off-season amphetmaine suspension followed by 2013 hamstring. Elite contact rate remains intact, but bb% has crashed and burned while 2012 power spike was huge outlier. Age/health combo says that this is a risky investment.

Yr Tm	AB	R	HR	RBI	SB	BA	xBA	OBP	SLG	OPS	vL	vR	bb%	ct%	h%	Eye	G	L	F	PX	xPX	hr/f	Spd	SBO	SB%	#Wk	DOM	DIS	RC/G	RAR	BPV	BPX	R$
09 PHI	322	32	9	43	3	255	290	355	425	780	894	741	13	88	27	1.21	42	19	39	108	96	8%	72	5%	60%	24	67%	8%	5.03	12.6	87	178	$5
10 PHI	371	43	8	53	0	302	279	400	447	847	940	808	13	85	34	1.02	45	20	35	102	87	7%	84	1%	0%	25	64%	24%	6.34	27.0	77	167	$12
11 PHI	410	49	6	40	1	283	258	371	383	754	716	766	10	88	31	1.00	42	21	37	70	95	4%	72	1%	100%	26	65%	23%	4.89	13.8	54	120	$9
12 PHI	372	56	16	68	4	325	313	394	540	935	906	946	7	87	34	0.58	43	24	33	135	131	15%	59	4%	100%	22	82%	14%	7.72	39.6	88	220	$20
13 PHI	310	30	5	37	1	268	254	320	368	688	836	636	5	87	29	0.46	47	20	34	69	78	5%	77	1%	100%	19	32%	37%	3.96	2.3	41	103	$5
1st Half	88	7	0	4	1	261	221	309	295	604	804	527	6	82	32	0.38	51	20	28	31	56	0%	100	4%	100%	7	14%	43%	3.21	-1.3	-3	-8	-$2
2nd Half	222	23	5	33	0	270	264	308	396	704	850	676	5	90	28	0.52	45	19	36	82	87	7%	68	0%	0%	12	42%	33%	4.26	3.5	57	143	$8
14 Proj	**324**	**37**	**8**	**41**	**2**	**276**	**273**	**343**	**412**	**755**	**832**	**726**	**7**	**87**	**30**	**0.60**	**45**	**21**	**34**	**91**	**93**	**8%**	**73**	**2%**	**93%**				**4.80**	**10.0**	**51**	**128**	**$10**

Rutledge,Josh

Age 25	Bats R	Pos 2B	Health A	LIMA Plan B	
Ht 6' 1"	Wt 190		PT/Exp D	Rand Var 0	
			Consist C	MM 3533	

7-19-.235, 12 SB in 285 AB at COL. What could possibly go wrong? Lovely 2012 power/speed combo combined with Coors spawned hopes of a 20/20 upside. Poor glove, no plate discipline, and .298 OBP on May 20 put an end to that, at least temporarily. Still young, has shown skills, so... UP: 15/15, or 20/20 for the brave bidder.

Yr Tm	AB	R	HR	RBI	SB	BA	xBA	OBP	SLG	OPS	vL	vR	bb%	ct%	h%	Eye	G	L	F	PX	xPX	hr/f	Spd	SBO	SB%	#Wk	DOM	DIS	RC/G	RAR	BPV	BPX	R$
09																																	
10																																	
11																																	
12 COL *	633	86	21	67	19	291	290	313	492	805	798	766	3	81	33	0.17	49	20	31	131	113	12%	132	18%	82%	13	54%	23%	5.56	33.7	75	188	$27
13 COL *	428	59	10	33	13	261	252	308	387	695	533	684	6	80	31	0.34	49	18	32	87	90	10%	130	14%	84%	19	32%	53%	4.19	6.6	44	110	$13
1st Half	272	41	7	21	7	240	247	296	365	660	501	679	7	81	27	0.42	52	15	33	85	90	11%	115	10%	100%	12	42%	50%	3.75	0.4	43	108	$14
2nd Half	156	19	2	12	6	299	263	331	426	756	605	698	4	79	37	0.22	40	28	32	92	89	5%	137	20%	72%	7	14%	57%	5.03	5.8	41	103	$12
14 Proj	**333**	**45**	**10**	**29**	**11**	**272**	**275**	**313**	**438**	**752**	**703**	**776**	**5**	**80**	**32**	**0.26**	**47**	**22**	**32**	**114**	**99**	**11%**	**137**	**17%**	**82%**				**4.78**	**10.4**	**60**	**149**	**$13**

Ryan,Brendan

Age 32	Bats R	Pos SS	Health A	LIMA Plan D+	
Ht 6' 2"	Wt 195		PT/Exp C	Rand Var +1	
			Consist B	MM 1303	

My editor would like me to tell you about his poor plate discipline, lack of power, modest speed, mediocre SB%, etc. I vote for a limerick: There once was a shortstop named Ryan, Who once left Chris Carpenter cryin': "Get out of my sight! For more'n a fortnight!" And Seattle-bound he was a-flyin'.

Yr Tm	AB	R	HR	RBI	SB	BA	xBA	OBP	SLG	OPS	vL	vR	bb%	ct%	h%	Eye	G	L	F	PX	xPX	hr/f	Spd	SBO	SB%	#Wk	DOM	DIS	RC/G	RAR	BPV	BPX	R$
09 STL	390	55	3	37	14	292	273	340	400	740	664	780	6	86	34	0.43	51	19	30	67	45	3%	159	19%	67%	25	48%	36%	4.67	13.7	57	116	$13
10 STL	439	50	2	36	11	223	247	279	294	573	568	575	7	86	25	0.55	47	18	35	51	43	2%	134	14%	73%	27	37%	30%	2.69	-10.0	42	91	$3
11 SEA	436	51	3	39	13	248	232	313	326	639	708	616	7	80	30	0.39	45	20	35	59	60	2%	133	14%	81%	23	35%	48%	3.40	-0.3	24	53	$8
12 SEA	407	42	3	31	11	194	215	277	278	555	637	503	10	76	25	0.45	41	20	39	64	60	2%	123	16%	69%	28	32%	50%	2.39	-13.5	13	33	-$1
13 2 AL	319	30	4	22	4	197	211	255	273	528	495	544	7	77	24	0.32	39	20	41	58	64	4%	93	9%	67%	26	27%	42%	2.17	-12.7	-1	-3	-$2
1st Half	216	17	2	15	4	199	209	254	259	514	529	510	7	76	25	0.31	39	22	39	48	58	3%	90	12%	67%	14	21%	57%	2.08	-9.5	-13	-33	-$1
2nd Half	103	13	2	7	0	194	215	245	301	546	439	625	6	79	23	0.32	41	15	44	79	76	6%	102	0%	0%	12	33%	25%	2.34	-3.7	23	58	-$4
14 Proj	**389**	**43**	**4**	**29**	**7**	**210**	**220**	**274**	**294**	**568**	**557**	**574**	**7**	**78**	**26**	**0.37**	**42**	**19**	**39**	**64**	**63**	**4%**	**115**	**11%**	**71%**				**2.54**	**-11.3**	**9**	**24**	**$2**

Saltalamacchia,Jarrod

Age 29	Bats B	Pos CA	Health A	LIMA Plan B	
Ht 6' 4"	Wt 235		PT/Exp C	Rand Var -5	
			Consist B	MM 5215	

Catchers sometimes learn hitting later in their careers. Lofty h% means BA won't repeat, but 2H plate discipline could represent real growth. Still whiffs a lot, but with his immense power, reducing K from 1/3 to 1/4 of AB can make all the difference. 2012 hr/f won't repeat, so if 2013 2H is new level, UP: 20 HR, .260 BA.

Yr Tm	AB	R	HR	RBI	SB	BA	xBA	OBP	SLG	OPS	vL	vR	bb%	ct%	h%	Eye	G	L	F	PX	xPX	hr/f	Spd	SBO	SB%	#Wk	DOM	DIS	RC/G	RAR	BPV	BPX	R$
09 TEX	283	34	9	34	0	233	222	290	371	661	657	663	7	66	32	0.23	36	23	41	107	99	12%	98	3%	0%	20	15%	45%	3.45	-2.2	-5	-10	$2
10 2 AL *	298	34	9	32	1	217	216	285	381	666	654	573	9	72	27	0.35	42	5	53	127	8	0%	94	1%	100%	6	67%	33%	3.55	-1.5	39	85	$1
11 BOS	358	52	16	56	1	235	245	288	450	737	635	786	6	67	30	0.20	32	21	47	172	145	14%	85	2%	100%	27	44%	33%	4.25	5.7	45	100	$8
12 BOS	405	55	25	59	0	222	242	288	454	742	494	779	9	66	27	0.27	31	23	47	168	160	20%	79	1%	0%	27	48%	33%	4.26	6.7	40	100	$8
13 BOS	425	68	14	65	4	273	260	338	466	804	628	873	9	67	38	0.31	33	29	39	170	154	13%	68	5%	80%	27	52%	26%	5.56	22.4	46	115	$15
1st Half	225	32	8	31	0	262	245	328	453	781	589	841	9	61	40	0.25	29	31	40	182	179	15%	66	2%	0%	14	50%	36%	5.04	8.7	29	73	$13
2nd Half	200	36	6	34	4	285	280	353	480	833	659	914	10	75	36	0.41	36	27	37	159	132	11%	76	8%	100%	13	54%	15%	6.18	13.9	69	173	$19
14 Proj	**415**	**62**	**17**	**62**	**3**	**251**	**252**	**316**	**453**	**769**	**623**	**820**	**9**	**68**	**33**	**0.30**	**33**	**25**	**42**	**165**	**147**	**14%**	**76**	**4%**	**78%**				**4.88**	**14.3**	**44**	**110**	**$13**

Sanchez,Gaby

Age 30	Bats R	Pos 1B	Health A	LIMA Plan D	
Ht 6' 1"	Wt 230		PT/Exp C	Rand Var 0	
			Consist D	MM 2111	

His problem is simple: he can't hit righties. He stomps on lefties, but hard to milk fanalytic value out of 150 AB/year. Improved plate discipline implies continued excellence against southpaws, so he'll own wrong side of platoon. Not a signal to buy, but if management completely avoids playing him against righties, UP: .290 BA.

Yr Tm	AB	R	HR	RBI	SB	BA	xBA	OBP	SLG	OPS	vL	vR	bb%	ct%	h%	Eye	G	L	F	PX	xPX	hr/f	Spd	SBO	SB%	#Wk	DOM	DIS	RC/G	RAR	BPV	BPX	R$
09 FLA *	339	42	13	44	4	238	252	306	385	691	1167	694	9	83	25	0.57	44	17	39	84	134	29%	68	4%	100%	8	38%	25%	4.00	-5.9	38	78	$5
10 FLA	572	72	19	85	5	273	265	341	448	788	925	742	9	82	30	0.56	37	17	46	117	144	9%	96	3%	100%	27	59%	15%	5.37	12.7	72	157	$18
11 FLA	572	72	19	78	3	266	261	352	427	779	901	742	11	83	29	0.76	36	20	45	109	103	9%	59	2%	75%	27	52%	19%	5.18	9.8	62	138	$16
12 2 NL *	415	44	10	42	2	222	228	292	348	640	729	566	9	79	26	0.47	41	17	42	88	111	7%	74	5%	48%	21	43%	29%	3.27	-16.7	28	70	$2
13 PIT	264	29	7	36	1	254	260	361	402	762	987	619	14	81	29	0.86	36	23	41	107	125	8%	74	1%	100%	27	52%	33%	4.97	2.9	61	153	$4
1st Half	160	19	7	24	1	238	261	348	431	779	1054	647	14	79	26	0.79	34	20	46	133	136	12%	69	2%	100%	14	57%	43%	5.05	2.2	73	183	$6
2nd Half	104	10	0	12	0	279	260	380	356	736	920	561	14	84	33	1.00	40	26	34	69	109	0%	83	0%	0%	13	46%	23%	4.78	0.5	45	113	$1
14 Proj	**154**	**17**	**3**	**19**	**1**	**252**	**247**	**343**	**378**	**721**	**890**	**627**	**12**	**81**	**29**	**0.72**	**38**	**21**	**41**	**92**	**118**	**6%**	**76**	**2%**	**67%**				**4.39**	**-1.0**	**35**	**88**	**$3**

Sanchez,Hector

Age 24	Bats B	Pos CA	Health A	LIMA Plan D	
Ht 6' 0"	Wt 235		PT/Exp F	Rand Var +1	
			Consist C	MM 1011	

3-19-.248 in 129 AB at SF. Bum shoulder caused him trouble all year, restricting his already-limited playing time. Hitting lefties is his plus asset, so he can give a starter some days off. Nondescript, across-the-board skills, resulting in negative BPV, means he won't be a regular. Okay to fold when bidding hits $1.

Yr Tm	AB	R	HR	RBI	SB	BA	xBA	OBP	SLG	OPS	vL	vR	bb%	ct%	h%	Eye	G	L	F	PX	xPX	hr/f	Spd	SBO	SB%	#Wk	DOM	DIS	RC/G	RAR	BPV	BPX	R$
09																																	
10																																	
11 SF *	184	10	1	18	0	221	197	266	283	550	348	809	6	83	26	0.37	52	12	36	53	161	0%	58	3%	0%	7	29%	43%	2.40	-7.3	6	13	-$2
12 SF	218	22	3	34	0	280	237	295	390	685	727	661	2	76	36	0.10	44	22	34	88	101	5%	62	0%	0%	25	36%	48%	4.09	2.4	0	0	$4
13 SF *	214	15	5	26	0	235	246	285	335	620	860	552	7	78	28	0.32	43	27	31	70	74	10%	66	0%	0%	19	11%	47%	3.18	-3.2	4	10	$0
1st Half	87	5	1	7	0	241	207	295	299	594	250	575	7	75	32	0.31	44	22	33	50	4	0%	85	0%	0%	9	0%	44%	2.96	-1.9	-19	-48	-$1
2nd Half	127	9	4	19	0	231	268	279	360	639	1004	539	6	80	26	0.34	42	28	30	83	100	14%	65	0%	0%	10	20%	50%	3.33	-1.5	22	55	$1
14 Proj	**167**	**13**	**3**	**22**	**0**	**248**	**242**	**291**	**349**	**640**	**747**	**589**	**5**	**78**	**30**	**0.23**	**43**	**24**	**32**	**76**	**76**	**7%**	**67**	**0%**	**0%**				**3.35**	**-1.7**	**-9**	**-22**	**$3**

JOSH PALEY

Sanchez,Jorge Tony

Age 26 Bats R Pos CA | Ht 5' 11" Wt 225
Health A | PT/Exp C | Consist B
LIMA Plan D+ | Rand Var 0 | MM 4121

2-5-.233 in 60 AB at PIT. Hit .288 with 10 HR in AAA, where he posted .857 OPS vL. Lacks an overwhelming minor league resumé and poor plate discipline means a crippled batting average. The power is real and could hit double-digit HR, but inability to hit righties limits him to backup role. Typical BA-wrecking second catcher.

Yr Tm	AB	R	HR	RBI	SB	BA	xBA	OBP	SLG	OPS	vL	vR	bb%	ct%	h%	Eye	G	L	F	PX	xPX	hr/f	Spd	SBO	SB%	#Wk	DOM	DIS	RC/G	RAR	BPV	BPX	R$
09																																	
10																																	
11 aa	402	37	4	35	4	213	220	279	277	555			8	80	26	0.46				47			92	9%	42%				2.39		5	11	-$1
12 a/a	347	35	6	35	1	220	238	287	345	632			9	76	28	0.38				97			84	3%	42%				3.20		24	60	$0
13 PIT *	337	37	9	37	0	237	253	286	398	685	765	655	7	75	29	0.28	45	19	36	130	139	12%	75	0%	0%	10	40%	30%	3.81	1.1	42	105	$3
1st Half	198	23	6	27	0	254	253	306	448	754	2000	429	7	74	31	0.29	43	14	43	158	199	0%	60	0%	0%	1	100%	0%	4.68	5.6	58	145	$7
2nd Half	139	15	3	10	0	213	237	260	331	591	688	694	6	76	26	0.27	45	20	35	93	129	14%	89	0%	0%	9	33%	33%	2.79	-3.9	21	53	-$1
14 Proj	227	24	8	22	1	228	259	303	401	704	687	703	7	76	27	0.34	45	20	35	127	116	13%	89	3%	44%				3.74	0.2	35	87	$1

Sandoval,Pablo

Age 27 Bats B Pos 3B | Ht 5' 11" Wt 240
Health C | PT/Exp B | Consist C
LIMA Plan A | Rand Var 0 | MM 3035

With 43 of 49 HR in past three years against RHP, he's looking more like a platoon player. Has played through a number of dings (ankle/elbow/foot/heel/back), and weight remains a concern. His brother the chef (no, really) helped him shed over 20 lb. in season. Driver of 2H recovery? If so, he's at right age for... UP: 2011 redux

Yr Tm	AB	R	HR	RBI	SB	BA	xBA	OBP	SLG	OPS	vL	vR	bb%	ct%	h%	Eye	G	L	F	PX	xPX	hr/f	Spd	SBO	SB%	#Wk	DOM	DIS	RC/G	RAR	BPV	BPX	R$
09 SF	572	79	25	90	5	330	310	387	556	943	1028	914	8	85	35	0.63	45	19	36	136	115	14%	85	6%	50%	27	74%	19%	7.97	60.4	95	194	$28
10 SF	563	61	13	63	3	268	267	323	409	732	589	779	8	86	29	0.58	44	17	38	93	106	7%	65	3%	60%	27	56%	22%	4.58	9.5	54	117	$12
11 SF	426	55	23	70	2	315	301	357	552	909	723	961	7	85	33	0.51	42	19	39	145	125	16%	73	5%	33%	21	67%	19%	7.19	37.1	95	211	$22
12 SF	396	59	12	63	1	283	274	342	447	789	745	809	9	85	31	0.64	43	20	37	103	117	10%	66	2%	50%	21	48%	24%	5.45	16.3	62	155	$13
13 SF	525	52	14	79	0	278	262	341	417	758	686	786	8	85	31	0.59	41	21	37	90	92	8%	56	0%	0%	25	44%	20%	4.97	14.4	47	118	$15
1st Half	248	26	8	37	0	274	253	313	399	712	751	699	5	86	29	0.41	43	21	35	74	90	10%	56	0%	0%	12	25%	33%	4.39	2.9	34	85	$14
2nd Half	277	26	6	42	0	282	268	358	433	791	628	862	11	84	32	0.73	40	21	39	106	93	7%	59	0%	0%	13	62%	8%	5.51	12.0	61	153	$16
14 Proj	543	64	17	83	1	285	273	347	449	797	713	829	9	85	31	0.63	42	20	38	106	105	10%	64	2%	43%				5.52	23.7	60	149	$20

Santana,Carlos

Age 28 Bats B Pos CA DH 1B | Ht 5' 11" Wt 210
Health A | PT/Exp A | Consist B
LIMA Plan A | Rand Var 0 | MM 4125

OBP machine has stable, terrific control of strike zone. Other BPIs are a mixed bag. Declining FB% trend reflected in xPX suggests that 2011 HR may have been outlier. xBA shows potential he had as a prospect and 2H shift from GB to LD is progress. Treat the projection as baseline; if he rediscovers FB%... UP: .280, 25 HR.

Yr Tm	AB	R	HR	RBI	SB	BA	xBA	OBP	SLG	OPS	vL	vR	bb%	ct%	h%	Eye	G	L	F	PX	xPX	hr/f	Spd	SBO	SB%	#Wk	DOM	DIS	RC/G	RAR	BPV	BPX	R$
09 aa	429	82	19	87	2	265	284	384	472	856			16	78	30	0.88				135			90	3%	45%				6.20		81	165	$14
10 CLE *	346	52	15	60	7	263	280	389	469	858	582	1002	17	79	30	0.96	35	21	44	144	147	11%	66	6%	100%	9	67%	22%	6.48	27.5	85	185	$12
11 CLE	552	84	27	79	5	239	268	351	457	808	964	732	15	76	27	0.73	45	15	40	153	137	16%	66	5%	63%	27	67%	15%	5.35	27.0	78	173	$15
12 CLE	507	72	18	76	3	252	256	365	420	785	808	772	15	80	28	0.90	43	19	38	108	104	12%	83	5%	38%	26	50%	27%	5.10	20.8	64	160	$13
13 CLE	541	75	20	74	3	268	277	377	455	832	864	815	15	80	30	0.85	42	22	36	131	100	13%	71	2%	75%	27	67%	4%	5.95	34.7	76	190	$18
1st Half	264	37	10	34	1	269	272	377	458	836	812	849	15	79	31	0.82	46	19	35	136	94	14%	71	2%	50%	14	79%	7%	5.98	17.3	77	193	$16
2nd Half	277	38	10	40	2	267	280	373	451	825	917	783	15	81	30	0.87	39	24	37	127	105	12%	78	2%	100%	13	54%	0%	5.92	17.6	78	195	$19
14 Proj	534	77	20	78	4	265	270	376	451	828	852	815	15	79	30	0.86	42	20	38	129	112	13%	74	3%	62%				5.86	33.3	69	172	$19

Santiago,Ramon

Age 34 Bats B Pos 2B 3B 3B | Ht 5' 11" Wt 175
Health A | PT/Exp F | Consist C
LIMA Plan D | Rand Var +3 | MM 1111

When a player has a 29% LD% and hits .151 as he did in 1H, that is really unlucky. Trouble is, even if he got lucky (pardon the expression), it still wouldn't get him to second base (pardon that, too). Good contact rate, decent Eye, defensive flexibility and average speed cannot mask hideous, gorgon-esque everything else.

Yr Tm	AB	R	HR	RBI	SB	BA	xBA	OBP	SLG	OPS	vL	vR	bb%	ct%	h%	Eye	G	L	F	PX	xPX	hr/f	Spd	SBO	SB%	#Wk	DOM	DIS	RC/G	RAR	BPV	BPX	R$
09 DET	262	29	7	35	1	267	235	318	385	704	622	716	6	78	32	0.30	46	18	36	71	98	10%	122	4%	33%	27	30%	48%	4.07	4.8	21	43	$4
10 DET	320	38	3	22	2	263	241	337	325	662	763	635	9	83	31	0.54	49	21	30	43	30	4%	129	4%	50%	26	27%	42%	3.60	1.6	22	48	$4
11 DET	258	29	5	30	0	260	262	311	384	695	832	662	6	85	29	0.45	43	21	35	79	55	7%	115	0%	0%	26	31%	35%	4.04	4.5	53	118	$3
12 DET	228	19	2	17	1	206	224	283	272	555	482	580	8	83	24	0.51	52	17	31	44	53	4%	107	2%	100%	24	25%	50%	2.38	-7.3	17	43	-$3
13 DET	205	27	1	14	0	224	254	298	288	586	591	584	9	84	26	0.66	49	24	27	47	23	2%	110	2%	0%	24	29%	33%	2.75	-4.2	29	73	-$1
1st Half	53	3	0	2	0	151	261	224	245	469	580	426	9	81	19	0.50	40	29	31	70	51	0%	104	0%	0%	11	45%	36%	1.65	-3.2	31	78	-$7
2nd Half	152	24	1	12	0	250	249	321	303	624	596	636	10	86	29	0.73	52	23	25	39	14	3%	103	2%	0%	13	15%	31%	3.22	-1.1	25	63	$0
14 Proj	224	24	2	17	0	222	246	294	301	595	602	593	8	83	26	0.56	48	22	30	55	42	4%	113	2%	37%				2.82	-6.0	16	40	$1

Satin,Josh

Age 29 Bats R Pos 1B | Ht 6' 2" Wt 200
Health A | PT/Exp C | Consist B
LIMA Plan D | Rand Var -2 | MM 2001

3-17-.279 and .376 OBP in 190 AB at NYM. Organizational soldier got his chance and played quite well when opportunity arose. Career minor league .436 OBP confirms he's got some utility, but regulars at 1B need to produce more pop, average, or both to be of value fanalytically. Pass.

Yr Tm	AB	R	HR	RBI	SB	BA	xBA	OBP	SLG	OPS	vL	vR	bb%	ct%	h%	Eye	G	L	F	PX	xPX	hr/f	Spd	SBO	SB%	#Wk	DOM	DIS	RC/G	RAR	BPV	BPX	R$
09																																	
10 aa	286	32	4	26	1	238	229	298	355	653			8	69	33	0.28				103			100	1%	100%				3.56		7	15	$1
11 NYM *	508	58	9	56	2	235	229	304	353	657	700	369	9	68	33	0.31	50	21	29	106	2	0%	95	6%	30%	4	0%	100%	3.45	-17.6	4	9	$5
12 NYM *	442	50	10	42	2	217	208	301	329	630	0	0	11	68	30	0.37	44	20	36	88	-11	0%	95	6%	29%	1	0%	100%	3.09	-20.5	-6	-15	$2
13 NYM *	410	49	8	35	1	241	219	329	360	689	880	706	12	71	32	0.46	47	18	36	100	107	6%	107	4%	21%	17	41%	47%	3.85	-9.0	22	55	$4
1st Half	252	32	5	22	0	229	223	315	344	659	1079	885	11	73	30	0.46	44	20	36	92	45	0%	102	4%	0%	4	75%	25%	3.43	-9.0	19	48	$5
2nd Half	158	17	3	13	1	259	220	350	386	736	819	678	12	69	36	0.45	47	17	35	112	122	8%	103	4%	50%	13	31%	54%	4.58	-0.1	23	58	$4
14 Proj	188	21	4	17	1	232	216	312	348	660	727	601	11	69	32	0.39	46	18	36	100	91	8%	106	5%	32%				3.51	-6.2	-7	-17	$2

Saunders,Michael

Age 27 Bats L Pos CF RF LF | Ht 6' 4" Wt 225
Health A | PT/Exp C | Consist C
LIMA Plan B | Rand Var 0 | MM 4315

Missed a month with a shoulder injury. He strikes out too much to hit for average, but 2H PX, ct% combination is sufficient for plenty of HR without an accompanying BA drag. He draws some walks, steals some bags, and is at an age where breakouts frequently occur. His home park does him no favors, but... UP: 25 HR, 20 SB, .260 BA.

Yr Tm	AB	R	HR	RBI	SB	BA	xBA	OBP	SLG	OPS	vL	vR	bb%	ct%	h%	Eye	G	L	F	PX	xPX	hr/f	Spd	SBO	SB%	#Wk	DOM	DIS	RC/G	RAR	BPV	BPX	R$
09 SEA *	370	56	9	28	8	249	229	297	386	683	436	615	6	74	31	0.26	48	13	39	90	52	0%	137	14%	66%	12	8%	58%	3.80	-5.2	22	45	$6
10 SEA *	369	33	10	37	9	201	208	284	325	609	601	686	10	72	25	0.41	36	16	48	89	81	11%	96	13%	75%	22	45%	36%	2.96	-15.4	10	22	$1
11 SEA *	397	47	6	31	12	187	167	266	273	540	330	474	10	63	28	0.29	36	15	50	76	78	4%	104	18%	68%	14	7%	79%	2.27	-25.8	-33	-73	-$1
12 SEA	507	71	19	57	21	247	259	306	432	738	774	718	8	74	30	0.33	45	20	35	130	136	15%	104	22%	84%	28	39%	32%	4.54	4.0	49	123	$17
13 SEA	406	59	12	46	13	236	241	323	397	720	654	751	12	71	30	0.46	41	22	37	123	129	11%	106	16%	72%	25	48%	44%	4.29	0.1	39	98	$11
1st Half	194	26	4	15	10	211	209	301	320	621	602	623	11	69	28	0.42	40	21	39	84	116	8%	117	22%	83%	12	42%	50%	3.25	-7.3	4	10	$9
2nd Half	212	33	8	31	3	259	271	349	467	816	713	857	12	73	32	0.50	41	23	36	157	141	15%	96	10%	50%	13	54%	38%	5.39	5.9	71	178	$14
14 Proj	428	59	15	50	13	246	241	321	420	740	685	768	10	71	31	0.38	41	20	39	130	118	13%	105	16%	72%				4.52	4.5	41	103	$14

Schafer,Jordan

Age 27 Bats L Pos CF RF | Ht 6' 1" Wt 190
Health C | PT/Exp D | Consist A
LIMA Plan D | Rand Var -1 | MM 1501

3-21-.247 with 22 SB in 231 AB at ATL. Newton's Third Law of Physics applied: 1H/2H hit rates demonstrate equal and opposite reaction. Averages 1 SB per 12 AB, but epic horror vL limits him to a platoon, not that he pounds RHP either. He is bench speed incarnate.

Yr Tm	AB	R	HR	RBI	SB	BA	xBA	OBP	SLG	OPS	vL	vR	bb%	ct%	h%	Eye	G	L	F	PX	xPX	hr/f	Spd	SBO	SB%	#Wk	DOM	DIS	RC/G	RAR	BPV	BPX	R$
09 ATL *	202	23	4	10	4	203	193	302	296	599	619	592	12	63	30	0.39	44	18	39	80	77	5%	113	11%	68%	9	22%	78%	2.86	-7.8	-21	-43	-$1
10 a/a	252	18	1	10	8	166	200	220	209	429			6	73	22	0.26				37			114	35%	44%				1.20		-28	-61	-$5
11 2 NL *	486	65	3	31	29	240	237	298	308	606	568	645	8	78	30	0.37	44	26	30	53	84	3%	125	28%	77%	16	13%	44%	3.14	-14.1	7	16	$11
12 HOU	313	40	4	23	27	211	196	297	294	591	356	636	10	66	31	0.34	44	21	35	66	76	6%	127	42%	75%	23	9%	65%	2.84	-12.6	-21	-53	$7
13 ATL *	263	32	3	22	22	223	220	302	317	618	285	735	10	70	31	0.38	48	21	30	73	77	7%	144	39%	79%	21	19%	67%	3.25	-6.9	5	13	$8
1st Half	123	22	3	14	9	309	235	397	463	861	301	941	13	72	41	0.51	42	20	38	114	87	10%	159	27%	75%	14	29%	50%	6.75	8.9	53	133	$15
2nd Half	140	10	0	8	13	147	213	213	187	400	267	495	8	69	21	0.27	56	23	21	36	65	0%	113	58%	81%	7	0%	100%	1.34	-13.6	-42	-105	$3
14 Proj	190	22	2	14	15	214	214	292	295	587	402	626	10	70	30	0.36	47	22	31	65	76	4%	130	39%	77%				2.87	-7.8	-5	-13	$5

JOSH PALEY

Schafer,Logan

Age 27	Bats L	Pos LF CF	Health A	LIMA Plan D
Ht 6' 1"	Wt 180		PT/Exp D	Rand Var +3
			Consist A	MM 1411

In his first full season, took a step back at an age when he should be stepping up. Yes, hit rate was a little lower than his norm, but xBA paints the true picture, and it's consistent and not all that pretty. Without any other outstanding offensive skill, he's a fourth OF and defensive replacement waiting to happen.

Yr	Tm	AB	R	HR	RBI	SB	BA	xBA	OBP	SLG	OPS	vL	vR	bb%	ct%	h%	Eye	G	L	F	PX	xPX	hr/f	Spd	SBO	SB%	#Wk	DOM	DIS	RC/G	RAR	BPV	BPX	R$
09	aa	23	3	0	0	1	192	229	296	259	555			13	85	23	0.97				28			133	11%	100%				2.60		30	61	-$2
10																																		
11	MIL *	362	46	4	30	11	262	269	311	369	679	0	833	7	85	30	0.48	0	50	50	73	2	0%	129	21%	53%	4	0%	75%	3.68	-4.1	53	118	$8
12	MIL *	487	58	10	36	12	240	248	276	379	655	250	933	5	81	28	0.26	29	29	43	85	143	0%	151	21%	57%	5	40%	20%	3.32	-10.9	50	125	$8
13	MIL	298	29	4	33	7	211	246	279	322	601	497	625	8	80	25	0.42	46	20	34	79	82	5%	107	12%	88%	27	33%	37%	2.91	-10.6	32	80	$2
1st Half		135	10	0	11	1	207	234	241	281	523	358	568	4	78	27	0.20	49	21	31	65	67	0%	112	4%	100%	14	29%	36%	2.22	-7.6	7	18	-$3
2nd Half		163	19	4	22	6	215	255	297	356	653	567	677	10	82	24	0.63	45	20	36	91	95	9%	106	17%	86%	13	38%	38%	3.53	-2.5	54	135	$5
14	Proj	197	22	3	19	5	229	251	285	347	632	536	654	6	81	27	0.37	46	20	34	80	84	5%	118	17%	68%				3.15	-5.3	39	98	$1

Schierholtz,Nate

Age 30	Bats L	Pos RF	Health B	LIMA Plan B+
Ht 6' 2"	Wt 215		PT/Exp C	Rand Var +2
			Consist A	MM 3225

Tempting to say power explosion was just getting out of SF, but career SLG splits—.408 at AT&T, .433 elsewhere—aren't huge, and both numbers pale to this year's. No, look closely at xPX: it says that he's done this before, and also implies that he'll give a chunk of it back. Let someone else bid on a power repeat.

Yr	Tm	AB	R	HR	RBI	SB	BA	xBA	OBP	SLG	OPS	vL	vR	bb%	ct%	h%	Eye	G	L	F	PX	xPX	hr/f	Spd	SBO	SB%	#Wk	DOM	DIS	RC/G	RAR	BPV	BPX	R$
09	SF	285	33	5	29	3	267	264	302	400	702	1026	626	5	80	32	0.28	45	21	35	94	101	6%	104	6%	75%	25	36%	32%	4.25	-2.9	38	78	$4
10	SF	227	34	3	17	4	242	260	311	366	676	671	678	8	83	28	0.53	44	18	37	85	85	4%	124	16%	44%	27	30%	33%	3.48	-7.8	56	122	$2
11	SF	335	42	9	41	7	278	269	326	430	756	562	801	6	82	32	0.34	40	22	38	107	114	9%	80	13%	64%	22	50%	23%	4.74	1.2	51	113	$10
12	2 NL	241	20	6	21	3	257	253	321	407	728	444	826	9	81	30	0.50	46	20	34	87	67	9%	121	8%	60%	26	31%	42%	4.41	-1.3	49	123	$3
13	CHC	462	56	21	68	6	251	282	301	470	770	553	799	6	80	27	0.31	40	20	40	147	115	14%	84	10%	67%	27	56%	15%	4.66	0.6	75	188	$14
1st Half		224	33	11	34	5	286	314	333	536	869	514	913	7	84	30	0.44	43	21	36	161	110	16%	101	15%	71%	14	64%	0%	6.28	11.6	110	275	$20
2nd Half		238	23	10	34	1	218	251	259	408	667	582	687	5	76	25	0.22	36	19	44	132	121	13%	70	5%	50%	13	46%	31%	3.39	-7.7	41	103	$9
14	Proj	457	51	15	56	5	261	266	313	439	752	560	793	7	80	30	0.36	41	20	38	119	101	11%	95	7%	65%				4.63	2.5	57	141	$13

Schumaker,Skip

Age 34	Bats L	Pos 2B LF CF	Health C	LIMA Plan D+
Ht 5' 10"	Wt 195		PT/Exp D	Rand Var 0
			Consist A	MM 1133

"Baseball is like this: Have one good year and you can fool them for five more, because for five more years, they expect you to have another good one." - Frankie Frisch
His five years are now up.

Yr	Tm	AB	R	HR	RBI	SB	BA	xBA	OBP	SLG	OPS	vL	vR	bb%	ct%	h%	Eye	G	L	F	PX	xPX	hr/f	Spd	SBO	SB%	#Wk	DOM	DIS	RC/G	RAR	BPV	BPX	R$
09	STL	532	85	4	35	2	303	294	364	393	757	518	812	9	87	34	0.75	61	22	17	65	40	5%	111	2%	50%	27	41%	15%	5.19	22.4	53	108	$13
10	STL	476	66	5	42	5	265	279	328	338	667	541	691	8	87	30	0.67	59	22	20	51	58	6%	92	6%	63%	27	48%	22%	3.78	1.7	33	72	$9
11	STL	367	34	2	38	0	283	257	333	351	685	714	682	7	86	32	0.54	52	23	25	54	51	2%	69	2%	0%	22	36%	41%	4.06	4.2	25	56	$6
12	STL *	293	40	1	28	2	271	262	338	361	700	496	741	9	82	33	0.55	54	23	23	64	52	2%	115	3%	62%	23	43%	43%	4.25	5.0	32	80	$5
13	LA	319	31	2	30	2	263	271	332	332	665	632	671	8	83	31	0.52	54	27	18	56	45	4%	78	4%	50%	27	33%	41%	3.65	0.0	19	48	$4
1st Half		174	16	0	15	2	241	256	313	282	594	546	606	9	84	29	0.64	58	24	18	36	37	0%	80	6%	67%	14	29%	36%	2.95	-3.9	9	23	$3
2nd Half		145	15	2	15	0	290	289	335	393	729	700	757	6	82	34	0.38	50	31	19	79	55	9%	82	2%	0%	13	38%	46%	4.60	3.7	31	78	$6
14	Proj	303	34	2	29	1	273	271	335	354	689	605	705	8	83	32	0.51	54	25	21	62	49	4%	90	3%	47%				4.04	3.0	18	45	$7

Scott,Luke

Age 36	Bats L	Pos DH	Health F	LIMA Plan D+
Ht 6' 0"	Wt 220		PT/Exp D	Rand Var 0
			Consist A	MM 4113

Remarkable consistency, from his skills on the field to the time spent off it with injuries. At 36, he's not going to raise that Health grade. But if your league's rosters are deep enough to stash him when necessary, he'll smack those 9-12 HR and draw his walks. In short: worth owning, at the right price.

Yr	Tm	AB	R	HR	RBI	SB	BA	xBA	OBP	SLG	OPS	vL	vR	bb%	ct%	h%	Eye	G	L	F	PX	xPX	hr/f	Spd	SBO	SB%	#Wk	DOM	DIS	RC/G	RAR	BPV	BPX	R$
09	BAL	449	61	25	77	0	258	272	340	488	828	837	823	11	77	28	0.53	40	17	43	147	138	17%	66	0%	0%	26	46%	27%	5.69	15.5	69	141	$12
10	BAL	447	70	27	72	2	284	295	368	535	902	787	935	12	78	31	0.60	40	19	41	166	147	19%	67	2%	100%	25	68%	12%	7.03	31.8	91	198	$19
11	BAL	209	24	9	22	1	220	244	301	402	703	781	686	10	74	25	0.44	43	16	41	131	134	14%	56	4%	50%	16	44%	38%	3.89	-3.8	41	91	$1
12	TAM	314	35	14	55	5	229	261	285	439	724	475	820	6	75	26	0.26	42	17	40	147	132	15%	46	9%	100%	21	52%	33%	4.12	-3.5	44	110	$7
13	TAM	253	27	9	40	1	241	245	326	415	741	745	740	11	75	29	0.48	38	19	42	122	130	11%	76	3%	50%	20	45%	40%	4.44	-0.4	44	110	$4
1st Half		153	18	5	28	0	242	237	322	405	727	684	747	11	76	29	0.49	35	19	46	115	154	9%	84	0%	0%	10	50%	20%	4.38	-0.5	44	110	$5
2nd Half		100	9	4	12	1	240	258	321	430	751	827	728	11	74	29	0.46	44	21	36	133	91	15%	71	8%	50%	10	40%	60%	4.51	0.0	47	118	$2
14	Proj	284	31	11	42	2	238	252	317	424	741	699	757	10	75	28	0.43	41	18	40	132	125	13%	62	5%	68%				4.40	-0.9	46	115	$7

Scutaro,Marco

Age 38	Bats R	Pos 2B	Health B	LIMA Plan A
Ht 5' 10"	Wt 185		PT/Exp B	Rand Var -2
			Consist A	MM 1325

Back hurt all year, then developed a malady called "mallet finger" in his pinkie (which certainly sounds painful). So it's a testament to his plate skills that he managed even this. With health, modest power should rebound, and with it a return to '11-'12 production. One small caution flag on that health thing: he is 38 now.

Yr	Tm	AB	R	HR	RBI	SB	BA	xBA	OBP	SLG	OPS	vL	vR	bb%	ct%	h%	Eye	G	L	F	PX	xPX	hr/f	Spd	SBO	SB%	#Wk	DOM	DIS	RC/G	RAR	BPV	BPX	R$
09	TOR	574	100	12	60	14	282	262	379	409	789	809	782	14	87	31	1.20	37	19	44	82	92	6%	106	9%	74%	25	64%	4%	5.52	30.4	74	151	$19
10	BOS	632	92	11	56	5	275	258	333	388	721	743	711	8	89	30	0.75	41	17	42	77	69	5%	106	5%	56%	26	46%	8%	4.45	14.3	66	143	$16
11	BOS	395	59	7	54	4	299	279	358	423	781	775	784	9	91	32	1.06	46	19	35	83	74	6%	99	5%	67%	23	65%	4%	5.50	20.1	79	176	$14
12	2 NL	620	87	7	74	9	306	281	348	405	753	718	768	6	92	32	0.82	41	26	33	61	93	4%	122	7%	69%	27	59%	7%	5.15	25.4	68	170	$23
13	SF	488	57	2	31	2	297	269	357	369	726	758	713	8	93	32	1.32	49	21	30	49	41	1%	129	1%	100%	25	60%	12%	4.80	15.3	69	173	$12
1st Half		276	35	2	18	0	319	281	371	417	788	813	779	8	93	34	1.15	48	22	30	66	55	3%	128	0%	0%	14	64%	7%	5.79	15.4	79	198	$15
2nd Half		212	22	0	13	2	269	251	338	307	644	680	631	9	93	29	1.57	50	20	30	27	23	0%	120	3%	100%	11	55%	18%	3.67	-0.2	52	130	$7
14	Proj	527	68	4	48	5	294	269	351	378	730	738	726	8	92	31	1.12	46	22	33	57	60	3%	119	4%	75%				4.81	16.3	55	138	$17

Seager,Kyle

Age 26	Bats L	Pos 3B	Health A	LIMA Plan A
Ht 6' 0"	Wt 215		PT/Exp A	Rand Var 0
			Consist A	MM 3225

Solid follow-up, with bb% spike an encouraging addition. So-so BA skills limit his overall upside, but he's on the right side of the growth curve, so a high floor comes with that package, too. Power is where a profit could show: FB growth worth watching, and there's more power potential as he continues to mature... UP: 25-30 HR.

Yr	Tm	AB	R	HR	RBI	SB	BA	xBA	OBP	SLG	OPS	vL	vR	bb%	ct%	h%	Eye	G	L	F	PX	xPX	hr/f	Spd	SBO	SB%	#Wk	DOM	DIS	RC/G	RAR	BPV	BPX	R$
09																																		
10																																		
11	SEA *	554	62	8	51	11	264	261	313	383	697	570	719	7	82	31	0.40	30	28	42	91	118	5%	85	14%	57%	12	33%	58%	4.01	1.0	43	96	$12
12	SEA	594	62	20	86	13	259	259	316	423	738	658	783	7	81	29	0.42	36	22	42	106	115	10%	72	13%	72%	28	46%	18%	4.51	9.7	49	123	$18
13	SEA	615	79	22	69	9	260	252	338	426	764	690	808	10	80	29	0.56	34	21	45	111	106	10%	81	7%	75%	27	56%	22%	4.90	17.0	56	140	$19
1st Half		317	39	11	36	3	268	272	328	448	775	630	863	8	80	30	0.45	36	23	41	125	93	11%	66	8%	50%	14	64%	14%	4.97	9.2	60	150	$19
2nd Half		298	40	11	33	6	252	229	340	403	743	751	749	12	80	28	0.67	33	18	50	96	120	9%	103	6%	100%	13	46%	31%	4.80	7.2	53	133	$20
14	Proj	607	72	24	73	10	259	262	328	438	766	703	800	9	81	29	0.50	34	22	44	118	113	11%	80	9%	71%				4.85	15.5	60	149	$20

Segura,Jean

Age 24	Bats R	Pos SS	Health A	LIMA Plan B
Ht 5' 10"	Wt 165		PT/Exp C	Rand Var -1
			Consist B	MM 1525

OPS by month: 979/904/718/671/584/552. PX by month: 109/109/78/54/47/46. Did he wear down? Or was Apr/May simply an aberration? Nothing in history suggests he owns those 1H power skills. Needed huge 2H SBO or SB would've dipped. Likely overvalued—and risky business. DN: .250/.300/.350, 25 SB

Yr	Tm	AB	R	HR	RBI	SB	BA	xBA	OBP	SLG	OPS	vL	vR	bb%	ct%	h%	Eye	G	L	F	PX	xPX	hr/f	Spd	SBO	SB%	#Wk	DOM	DIS	RC/G	RAR	BPV	BPX	R$
09	aaa																																	
10																																		
11																																		
12	2 TM *	555	66	7	50	38	274	263	318	365	683	290	756	6	84	32	0.39	66	15	19	54	57	0%	176	33%	71%	10	30%	40%	3.98	7.7	44	110	$23
13	MIL	588	74	12	49	44	294	282	329	423	752	865	716	4	86	33	0.30	59	18	23	76	69	10%	195	37%	77%	26	46%	23%	4.91	23.5	72	180	$35
1st Half		321	46	11	32	24	327	305	353	508	861	975	819	4	87	35	0.31	57	20	23	98	85	18%	227	30%	89%	14	57%	0%	7.06	30.9	104	260	$45
2nd Half		267	28	1	17	20	255	251	287	322	609	597	616	4	84	30	0.29	60	15	24	49	49	2%	135	45%	67%	12	33%	50%	2.97	-4.1	27	68	$23
14	Proj	593	71	5	49	35	264	263	302	348	650	553	679	5	85	30	0.33	60	18	23	54	61	4%	181	31%	72%				3.54	1.4	37	92	$22

ROD TRUESDELL

Shoppach,Kelly

Age	34	Bats	R	Pos	CA		
Ht	6' 0"	Wt	220				
Health	B	PT/Exp	F	Consist	D		
LIMA Plan	F	Rand Var	0	MM	4301		

3-9-.193 in 109 AB at SEA/CLE. As a player who's made his living hitting lefties, OPS trend vL the last five years looks ominous. Of course, being released by three teams in one season can't be a good sign, either. xPX shows the raw power is still there, but he simply doesn't make enough contact. Probably has one more shot.

Yr	Tm	AB	R	HR	RBI	SB	BA	xBA	OBP	SLG	OPS	vL	vR	bb%	ct%	h%	Eye	G	L	F	PX	xPX	hr/f	Spd	SBO	SB%	#Wk	DOM	DIS	RC/G	RAR	BPV	BPX	R$
09	CLE	271	33	12	40	0	214	236	335	399	734	1045	652	11	64	29	0.34	41	22	37	145	123	18%	73	0%	0%	26	42%	42%	3.87	1.3	17	35	$1
10	TAM	158	17	5	17	0	196	180	308	342	650	823	432	11	55	32	0.28	44	11	44	145	173	13%	89	0%	0%	20	20%	55%	3.11	-3.0	-12	-26	-$1
11	TAM	221	23	11	22	0	176	185	268	339	607	788	431	8	64	21	0.24	37	12	51	119	153	15%	95	0%	0%	26	31%	54%	2.54	-8.3	0	0	-$2
12	2 TM	219	23	8	27	1	233	217	309	425	733	717	751	7	59	35	0.18	35	21	44	167	142	14%	111	2%	100%	27	33%	44%	4.05	2.2	20	50	$2
13	2 AL *	170	13	3	12	0	183	162	254	282	536	639	623	9	59	29	0.24	34	14	52	98	130	9%	68	0%	0%	12	33%	58%	2.24	-8.0	-43	-108	-$4
1st Half		107	11	3	9	0	196	187	277	346	623	639	638	10	58	31	0.27	33	14	52	149	132	9%	71	0%	0%	11	36%	55%	3.04	-2.3	-6	-15	-$2
2nd Half		63	2	0	3	0	160	93	214	172	387	0	0	6	62	26	0.18	100	0	0	16	-15	0%	74	0%	0%	1	0%	100%	1.12	-5.4	-103	-258	-$7
14	Proj	**142**	**12**	**5**	**13**	**0**	**206**	**191**	**291**	**357**	**648**	**746**	**578**	**8**	**61**	**30**	**0.21**	**37**	**15**	**48**	**130**	**145**	**12%**	**86**	**1%**	**100%**				**3.08**	**-2.8**	**-25**	**-63**	**-$2**

Shuck,J.B.

Age	27	Bats	L	Pos	LF		
Ht	5' 11"	Wt	195				
Health	A	PT/Exp	C	Consist	C		
LIMA Plan	D+	Rand Var	-4	MM	0323		

Clearly, we all saw him getting 400 AB and nearly hitting .300 this time last year, right? Slaps it on the ground enough to use his speed, and can spray some line drives, but xBA shows there was some luck involved. Fine ct% puts a floor on BA, but low PX, Rand Var both suggest this is its ceiling as well—and BA is all he brings.

Yr	Tm	AB	R	HR	RBI	SB	BA	xBA	OBP	SLG	OPS	vL	vR	bb%	ct%	h%	Eye	G	L	F	PX	xPX	hr/f	Spd	SBO	SB%	#Wk	DOM	DIS	RC/G	RAR	BPV	BPX	R$
09																																		
10	a/a	528	55	2	29	13	263	231	327	313	639			9	85	31	0.62				35			131	16%	49%				3.31		26	57	$9
11	HOU *	435	55	0	26	17	260	264	341	317	658	909	646	11	90	29	1.28	47	25	29	35	60	0%	153	20%	58%	9	44%	22%	3.54	-5.7	59	131	$9
12	aaa	315	33	0	22	8	238	238	297	280	577			8	92	26	1.08				28			111	19%	46%				2.54		42	105	$2
13	LAA	437	60	2	39	8	293	264	331	366	697	745	682	6	88	33	0.50	55	20	25	52	44	2%	125	9%	67%	27	48%	22%	4.36	4.6	43	108	$14
1st Half		163	21	0	19	2	288	274	341	362	703	828	657	7	91	32	0.93	57	19	25	56	39	0%	108	10%	40%	14	64%	14%	4.17	0.7	60	150	$7
2nd Half		274	39	2	20	6	296	258	330	369	698	679	696	5	85	34	0.35	53	21	26	50	47	3%	137	9%	86%	13	31%	31%	4.47	3.5	34	85	$18
14	Proj	**298**	**37**	**2**	**23**	**7**	**271**	**267**	**323**	**347**	**670**	**756**	**649**	**7**	**89**	**30**	**0.72**	**51**	**22**	**27**	**49**	**50**	**3%**	**130**	**15%**	**55%**				**3.76**	**-2.3**	**40**	**101**	**$8**

Sierra,Moises

Age	25	Bats	R	Pos	RF		
Ht	6' 0"	Wt	230				
Health	A	PT/Exp	C	Consist	A		
LIMA Plan	D	Rand Var	-1	MM	3201		

1-13-.290 in 107 AB at TOR. Has some interesting tools, but not enough to offset horrific Eye and its affect on his overall production. With his thick, muscular body, he seems the type who may gain some power (and lose speed) as he matures. But for now, he's just another free-swinger who can be safely ignored.

Yr	Tm	AB	R	HR	RBI	SB	BA	xBA	OBP	SLG	OPS	vL	vR	bb%	ct%	h%	Eye	G	L	F	PX	xPX	hr/f	Spd	SBO	SB%	#Wk	DOM	DIS	RC/G	RAR	BPV	BPX	R$
09	aa	34	1	1	6	0	342	218	361	461	822			3	73	44	0.11				80			96	10%	0%				5.64		-5	-10	$0
10																																		
11	aa	495	67	16	55	13	252	251	297	396	693			6	79	29	0.30				95			105	24%	46%				3.60		37	82	$14
12	TOR *	524	56	18	57	6	236	229	282	377	659	815	545	6	73	29	0.23	53	17	30	96	134	19%	58	10%	45%	10	40%	50%	3.39	-14.1	0	0	$9
13	TOR *	486	54	10	52	10	242	238	280	385	665	786	845	5	69	33	0.17	48	20	32	117	80	4%	117	15%	69%	7	29%	57%	3.56	-10.4	17	43	$10
1st Half		280	32	5	23	5	231	223	254	359	613			3	69	32	0.10				103			115	15%	70%				2.98		0	0	$9
2nd Half		206	22	5	29	5	256	248	313	420	733	786	845	8	69	35	0.27	48	20	32	135	80	4%	102	15%	68%	7	29%	57%	4.42	-0.2	33	83	$11
14	Proj	**197**	**22**	**5**	**22**	**4**	**244**	**239**	**292**	**383**	**675**	**739**	**641**	**6**	**72**	**32**	**0.23**	**50**	**19**	**31**	**105**	**102**	**11%**	**100**	**14%**	**58%**				**3.61**	**-5.0**	**14**	**35**	**$5**

Simmons,Andrelton

Age	24	Bats	R	Pos	SS		
Ht	6' 2"	Wt	170				
Health	B	PT/Exp	D	Consist	B		
LIMA Plan	A	Rand Var	+2	MM	2535		

PRO: Real 2H growth, muscling up with improving Eye, an excellent combo to support higher BA. Great speed.
CON: Poor basestealer red-lighted too much to use that speed. 2H out of previous character; can he repeat?
This projection shows the likely regression scenario, but what if the growth is sustainable? UP: .300/20/20

Yr	Tm	AB	R	HR	RBI	SB	BA	xBA	OBP	SLG	OPS	vL	vR	bb%	ct%	h%	Eye	G	L	F	PX	xPX	hr/f	Spd	SBO	SB%	#Wk	DOM	DIS	RC/G	RAR	BPV	BPX	R$
09																																		
10																																		
11																																		
12	ATL *	340	41	5	37	9	278	271	335	396	731	796	726	8	87	31	0.66	56	17	27	72	45	8%	139	12%	81%	11	45%	18%	4.74	11.9	65	163	$10
13	ATL	606	76	17	59	6	248	272	296	396	692	692	691	6	91	25	0.73	42	18	39	86	89	8%	150	8%	55%	27	59%	7%	3.85	6.2	92	230	$13
1st Half		317	41	6	23	5	240	246	278	331	610	583	619	5	90	25	0.53	46	17	37	57	65	6%	121	12%	56%	14	50%	14%	2.99	-4.6	54	135	$11
2nd Half		289	35	11	36	1	256	298	311	467	778	851	764	7	92	25	1.00	38	20	42	117	116	10%	161	3%	50%	13	69%	0%	4.92	12.3	127	318	$15
14	Proj	**600**	**74**	**15**	**63**	**9**	**261**	**276**	**312**	**406**	**718**	**751**	**706**	**7**	**90**	**27**	**0.70**	**47**	**18**	**35**	**86**	**75**	**8%**	**153**	**9%**	**70%**				**4.33**	**15.2**	**74**	**185**	**$17**

Singleton,Jonathan

Age	22	Bats	L	Pos	1B		
Ht	6' 2"	Wt	235				
Health	A	PT/Exp	D	Consist	D		
LIMA Plan	D	Rand Var	0	MM	3203		

Power prospect missed 50 games due to marijuana suspension, and never got untracked. HOU promoted him to their 40-man anyway, and he may be just a hot Triple-A start away from a 1B platoon. Contact rate is a huge red flag, though, and almost certainly means an initial struggle at least. Speculate for '15, not '14.

Yr	Tm	AB	R	HR	RBI	SB	BA	xBA	OBP	SLG	OPS	vL	vR	bb%	ct%	h%	Eye	G	L	F	PX	xPX	hr/f	Spd	SBO	SB%	#Wk	DOM	DIS	RC/G	RAR	BPV	BPX	R$
09																																		
10																																		
11																																		
12	aa	461	72	17	61	5	252	236	350	428	777			13	68	34	0.47				131			100	5%	71%				5.08		35	88	$12
13	a/a	283	28	6	31	1	200	194	308	322	630			13	58	32	0.37				117			92	1%	100%				3.17		-15	-38	-$1
1st Half		96	7	2	9	0	213	182	325	353	678			14	51	39	0.34				148			96	0%	0%				3.72		-18	-45	-$1
2nd Half																																		
14	Proj	**292**	**31**	**5**	**32**	**1**	**232**	**196**	**332**	**359**	**691**	**691**	**691**	**13**	**60**	**37**	**0.37**	**42**	**19**	**39**	**119**		**8%**	**96**	**2%**	**71%**				**3.96**	**-5.6**	**-16**	**-41**	**$4**

Sizemore,Scott

Age	29	Bats	R	Pos	2B		
Ht	6' 0"	Wt	185				
Health	F	PT/Exp	F	Consist	F		
LIMA Plan	D	Rand Var	+5	MM	4311		

Tore his ACL in 2012, then tore the "new" ACL in the same knee last April. So he's now missed essentially two entire seasons. If he'd been really superb before, maybe we'd speculate on third time being a charm. But other than just-okay pop and a few walks, he offers little even if he's healthy. There's no reason to take the risk.

Yr	Tm	AB	R	HR	RBI	SB	BA	xBA	OBP	SLG	OPS	vL	vR	bb%	ct%	h%	Eye	G	L	F	PX	xPX	hr/f	Spd	SBO	SB%	#Wk	DOM	DIS	RC/G	RAR	BPV	BPX	R$
09	a/a	520	73	15	55	17	277	276	343	446	789			9	80	32	0.50				112			108	15%	79%				5.43		62	127	$18
10	DET *	442	57	10	42	2	244	237	304	376	680	671	610	8	71	32	0.30	38	22	40	107	87	7%	102	4%	40%	12	33%	50%	3.79	0.8	19	41	$6
11	2 AL *	474	69	13	68	8	254	239	350	405	754	828	700	13	70	34	0.49	44	20	36	122	119	12%	111	9%	60%	21	43%	38%	4.74	14.2	39	87	$13
12																																		
13	OAK	6	0	0	0	0	167	236	167	333	500	600	0	0	67	25	0.00	75	25	0	189	48	0%	101	0%	0%	2	50%	0%	1.70	-0.3	50	125	-$3
1st Half		6	0	0	0	0	167	236	167	333	500	600	0	0	67	25	0.00	75	25	0	189	48	0%	101	0%	0%	2	50%	0%	1.70	-0.4	50	125	-$3
2nd Half																																		
14	Proj	**189**	**26**	**5**	**22**	**4**	**261**	**249**	**337**	**421**	**758**	**825**	**724**	**10**	**74**	**33**	**0.44**	**41**	**21**	**38**	**121**	**106**	**10%**	**113**	**10%**	**70%**				**4.84**	**6.3**	**43**	**109**	**$6**

Smith,Seth

Age	31	Bats	L	Pos	DH LF		
Ht	6' 3"	Wt	210				
Health	A	PT/Exp	B	Consist	B		
LIMA Plan	D+	Rand Var	-1	MM	3113		

Lot's of uh-oh's: production vs RHP, his raison d'etre in baseball, slid for a second straight year, and that ct% dip didn't rebound after all. Add to that the growing GB%, dwindling PX, now sub-average wheels, and lack of a true defensive position, and it all implies that the PT will continue to erode. DN: <200 AB, looking for work.

Yr	Tm	AB	R	HR	RBI	SB	BA	xBA	OBP	SLG	OPS	vL	vR	bb%	ct%	h%	Eye	G	L	F	PX	xPX	hr/f	Spd	SBO	SB%	#Wk	DOM	DIS	RC/G	RAR	BPV	BPX	R$
09	COL	335	61	15	55	4	293	282	378	510	889	868	893	12	80	33	0.69	39	19	42	134	112	13%	118	5%	80%	27	67%	26%	6.97	23.0	89	182	$13
10	COL	358	55	17	52	2	246	275	314	469	783	393	848	9	81	26	0.52	36	16	48	139	132	12%	111	4%	67%	27	63%	30%	4.94	4.7	89	193	$9
11	COL	476	67	15	59	10	284	276	347	483	830	576	891	9	80	33	0.49	38	22	40	133	127	10%	123	10%	83%	27	67%	19%	6.00	20.2	85	189	$18
12	OAK	383	55	14	52	2	240	258	333	420	754	521	805	12	74	29	0.51	41	23	36	126	130	14%	84	4%	50%	26	58%	35%	4.56	0.7	49	123	$8
13	OAK	368	49	8	40	0	253	243	329	391	721	621	748	10	74	32	0.41	45	20	35	113	102	8%	87	0%	0%	27	37%	41%	4.33	-1.7	35	88	$6
1st Half		248	34	6	32	0	278	253	347	427	774	708	805	9	74	35	0.41	44	22	34	121	99	10%	86	0%	0%	14	36%	43%	5.24	5.2	40	100	$11
2nd Half		120	15	2	8	0	200	221	278	317	595	205	652	10	75	25	0.43	49	14	37	96	107	6%	94	0%	0%	13	38%	38%	2.81	-6.4	26	65	-$4
14	Proj	**315**	**44**	**9**	**36**	**1**	**245**	**253**	**325**	**406**	**731**	**536**	**774**	**10**	**76**	**30**	**0.47**	**43**	**20**	**37**	**119**	**116**	**10%**	**97**	**2%**	**49%**				**4.38**	**-1.2**	**41**	**103**	**$7**

ROD TRUESDELL

Smoak,Justin

Age 27	Bats B	Pos 1B	Health	B	LIMA Plan	B+
Ht 6' 4"	Wt 220		PT/Exp	C	Rand Var	0
			Consist	B	MM	4205

20-50-.238 in 454 AB at SEA. PRO: xPX shows he's ready to take a step up as a power source; solid walk rate. CON: Sub-par contact rate is not unusual for a power bat, but caps his BA upside. It is possible that he'll never quite be the hitter SEA expected. Still, with blossoming power, 30-35 HR is a legitimate upside.

Yr	Tm	AB	R	HR	RBI	SB	BA	xBA	OBP	SLG	OPS	vL	vR	bb%	ct%	h%	Eye	G	L	F	PX	xPX	hr/f	Spd	SBO	SB%	#Wk	DOM	DIS	RC/G	RAR	BPV	BPX	R$
09	a/a	380	45	9	43	0	259	239	362	380	742			14	77	32	0.69				85			87	0%	0%				4.73		31	63	$5
10	2 AL *	531	64	19	70	1	222	251	318	376	694	651	691	12	74	26	0.54	38	23	39	112	140	13%	61	1%	100%	19	47%	42%	3.93	-10.9	30	65	$6
11	SEA	427	38	15	55	0	234	222	323	396	719	720	719	11	75	28	0.52	44	14	43	119	129	11%	75	0%	0%	25	48%	32%	4.24	-4.7	44	98	$5
12	SEA *	549	56	19	54	2	213	224	291	352	643	703	627	10	76	25	0.46	40	18	42	90	116	12%	76	1%	100%	26	38%	50%	3.33	-21.6	21	53	$3
13	SEA *	475	54	20	51	0	235	234	326	405	731	548	839	12	74	28	0.51	35	20	46	120	152	13%	85	0%	0%	25	44%	36%	4.40	-2.9	42	105	$8
1st Half		209	21	6	14	0	238	220	333	364	698	391	857	13	73	30	0.54	40	20	40	93	149	11%	92	0%	0%	12	33%	33%	4.07	-3.3	23	58	$3
2nd Half		266	33	14	37	0	233	245	320	436	756	636	823	11	74	26	0.49	31	19	49	140	154	14%	88	0%	0%	13	54%	38%	4.64	0.3	58	145	$12
14	**Proj**	**527**	**62**	**24**	**69**	**1**	**240**	**239**	**327**	**417**	**745**	**653**	**789**	**11**	**75**	**28**	**0.51**	**37**	**19**	**45**	**122**	**138**	**13%**	**77**	**0%**	**100%**				**4.58**	**-0.4**	**30**	**74**	**$10**

Snider,Travis

Age 26	Bats L	Pos RF	Health	C	LIMA Plan	D
Ht 6' 0"	Wt 235		PT/Exp	D	Rand Var	0
			Consist	D	MM	3101

5-25-.215 in 261 AB at PIT. Five years ago, he was free and 21 and looked like a star in the making. Slowly, pitchers realized they didn't have to throw him anything good to get him out. Now he seemingly can't loft the ball enough to cash in on his one bankable skill, the once-stellar power. And the star flickers ever fainter.

Yr	Tm	AB	R	HR	RBI	SB	BA	xBA	OBP	SLG	OPS	vL	vR	bb%	ct%	h%	Eye	G	L	F	PX	xPX	hr/f	Spd	SBO	SB%	#Wk	DOM	DIS	RC/G	RAR	BPV	BPX	R$
09	TOR *	416	58	20	60	3	266	251	345	482	827	608	775	11	68	34	0.38	44	15	41	159	125	14%	79	6%	37%	15	47%	40%	5.58	11.8	47	96	$11
10	TOR *	379	47	18	45	8	256	279	298	463	760	702	783	6	73	31	0.22	41	24	35	152	129	18%	78	16%	67%	16	38%	19%	4.61	0.0	49	107	$11
11	TOR *	435	52	6	56	16	247	239	290	367	658	300	708	6	75	32	0.24	47	17	37	102	97	6%	72	22%	80%	10	30%	50%	3.65	-12.4	17	38	$11
12	2 TM *	373	56	13	55	3	268	259	337	437	774	1110	595	10	74	33	0.41	56	19	26	119	74	13%	79	8%	42%	12	25%	58%	4.93	3.5	36	90	$11
13	PIT *	299	32	5	29	3	224	216	290	331	621	291	644	8	72	30	0.33	52	15	33	83	78	8%	82	9%	40%	22	32%	59%	3.01	-14.7	-1	-3	$1
1st Half		210	25	3	22	2	229	230	302	343	645	317	679	9	72	30	0.37	52	17	30	91	81	7%	89	9%	40%	14	29%	57%	3.26	-7.7	8	20	$3
2nd Half		89	7	2	7	1	214	163	261	303	564	0	502	6	72	27	0.23	49	6	46	64	64	13%	72	9%	40%	8	38%	63%	2.44	-5.6	-25	-63	-$3
14	**Proj**	**162**	**19**	**5**	**18**	**2**	**240**	**228**	**298**	**380**	**678**	**692**	**676**	**8**	**73**	**30**	**0.30**	**50**	**14**	**35**	**105**	**81**	**11%**	**75**	**11%**	**54%**				**3.68**	**-3.8**	**14**	**34**	**$4**

Sogard,Eric

Age 28	Bats L	Pos 2B	Health	B	LIMA Plan	D+
Ht 5' 10"	Wt 190		PT/Exp	D	Rand Var	-1
			Consist	A	MM	1313

A slugging 1B in a middle infielder's body—if only he had the muscles to launch some of those FB and LD into the bleachers! Alas, in this reality he simply flies out a lot. So he's a sketchy bet to hit even this well again, as xBA, Rand Var imply. On the other hand, you can take those whopping 9 SB to the bank. Hold me back.

Yr	Tm	AB	R	HR	RBI	SB	BA	xBA	OBP	SLG	OPS	vL	vR	bb%	ct%	h%	Eye	G	L	F	PX	xPX	hr/f	Spd	SBO	SB%	#Wk	DOM	DIS	RC/G	RAR	BPV	BPX	R$
09	aa	458	63	4	41	8	243	255	314	324	638			9	87	27	0.82				53			109	11%	54%				3.31		45	92	$5
10	OAK *	521	55	3	44	9	243	362	312	320	632	2000	533	9	84	28	0.64	50	50	0	55	78	0%	123	14%	45%	3	33%	33%	3.15	-9.1	39	85	$6
11	OAK *	385	44	5	29	9	229	230	287	318	605	154	652	8	86	26	0.58	37	19	44	60	71	8%	100	13%	71%	12	42%	42%	3.01	-8.4	39	87	$3
12	OAK *	259	28	5	22	9	223	256	282	327	609	450	487	8	85	24	0.56	39	26	35	60	61	7%	103	20%	72%	14	29%	36%	3.01	-5.7	38	95	$3
13	OAK	368	45	2	35	10	266	256	322	364	686	640	695	7	86	30	0.53	35	25	40	73	44	2%	104	16%	67%	27	56%	19%	3.93	2.2	50	125	$9
1st Half		181	25	0	9	7	265	249	332	337	669	564	705	9	86	31	0.69	41	23	36	58	55	0%	123	20%	64%	14	50%	21%	3.76	0.3	46	115	$9
2nd Half		187	20	2	26	3	267	262	301	390	691	720	684	5	87	30	0.36	30	26	44	86	34	3%	87	10%	75%	13	62%	15%	4.08	2.1	53	133	$9
14	**Proj**	**357**	**41**	**4**	**33**	**9**	**248**	**253**	**305**	**349**	**654**	**561**	**673**	**7**	**86**	**28**	**0.55**	**36**	**25**	**39**	**69**	**53**	**4%**	**100**	**16%**	**66%**				**3.51**	**-2.0**	**46**	**116**	**$8**

Solano,Donovan

Age 26	Bats R	Pos 2B	Health	B	LIMA Plan	D+
Ht 5' 9"	Wt 195		PT/Exp	D	Rand Var	-1
			Consist	B	MM	1323

3-34-.249 in 361 AB at MIA. Forecaster Fun Time—review this skill set, and make your own projection! Finished already?... Well done! You keenly noted the nonexistent power, middling speed, and poor batting Eye, and peg a sub-replacement performance to come. Yet seemingly his current team has missed ALL this. Trust yourself.

Yr	Tm	AB	R	HR	RBI	SB	BA	xBA	OBP	SLG	OPS	vL	vR	bb%	ct%	h%	Eye	G	L	F	PX	xPX	hr/f	Spd	SBO	SB%	#Wk	DOM	DIS	RC/G	RAR	BPV	BPX	R$
09	a/a	415	39	1	24	3	223	224	267	262	529			6	83	27	0.35				30			104	3%	100%				2.33		0	0	-$2
10	aaa	330	29	3	19	1	210	242	228	268	496			2	88	23	0.20				39			109	4%	55%				1.95		23	50	-$3
11	a/a	330	18	2	22	1	209	241	244	296	539			4	82	25	0.26				72			83	2%	100%				2.34		22	49	-$4
12	MIA *	426	39	2	38	10	270	248	317	342	659	683	736	6	79	34	0.32	45	28	27	53	72	3%	124	8%	100%	20	20%	45%	3.93	3.3	8	20	$8
13	MIA *	427	39	5	41	3	261	253	304	338	642	544	652	6	83	30	0.37	50	23	27	54	52	4%	96	3%	75%	18	22%	44%	3.54	-1.3	19	48	$6
1st Half		174	14	3	12	1	295	267	339	375	713	625	669	6	83	34	0.39	52	27	21	51	38	5%	112	2%	100%	6	33%	33%	4.63	4.5	22	55	$7
2nd Half		253	25	2	29	2	237	247	280	312	592	507	644	6	83	28	0.36	49	22	30	55	58	3%	86	5%	67%	12	17%	50%	2.91	-6.0	17	43	$6
14	**Proj**	**330**	**28**	**3**	**28**	**3**	**250**	**257**	**299**	**327**	**626**	**582**	**646**	**6**	**82**	**30**	**0.34**	**48**	**26**	**26**	**56**	**59**	**4%**	**105**	**5%**	**89%**				**3.29**	**-3.9**	**9**	**24**	**$5**

Solano,Jhonatan

Age 28	Bats R	Pos CA	Health	C	LIMA Plan	F
Ht 5' 9"	Wt 205		PT/Exp	F	Rand Var	+5
			Consist	B	MM	1101

0-2-.146 in 48 AB at WAS. If only he had the wheels to turn all those groundballs into infield hits! Alas, he has precious little speed. Hmm, nor any power. Wow, and no clue of the strike zone, either. If he was in Shakespeare's Richard III, he'd say: "My kingdom for a .230 batting average."

Yr	Tm	AB	R	HR	RBI	SB	BA	xBA	OBP	SLG	OPS	vL	vR	bb%	ct%	h%	Eye	G	L	F	PX	xPX	hr/f	Spd	SBO	SB%	#Wk	DOM	DIS	RC/G	RAR	BPV	BPX	R$
09	a/a	276	20	2	24	2	203	246	229	277	506			3	84	24	0.21				56			85	6%	60%				2.01		16	33	-$3
10	aa	317	23	5	34	1	220	257	259	308	568			5	90	23	0.52				58			86	3%	42%				2.58		43	93	$0
11	aaa	255	20	4	25	1	229	241	268	320	588			5	84	26	0.33				66			81	3%	39%				2.79		24	53	$0
12	WAS *	128	15	3	13	1	221	236	245	328	572	1389	758	3	80	26	0.16	60	13	27	73	122	25%	83	4%	100%	8	50%	25%	2.66	-4.0	10	25	-$1
13	WAS *	188	8	0	9	0	162	223	184	208	392	400	343	3	85	19	0.19	61	15	24	38	16	0%	84	4%	0%	14	21%	21%	1.12	-15.9	5	13	-$7
1st Half		84	3	0	2	0	145	201	177	187	364	500	377	4	77	19	0.17	67	13	20	41	19	0%	79	8%	0%	9	33%	22%	0.91	-8.0	-25	-63	-$8
2nd Half		104	5	0	7	0	175	235	190	225	415	0	250	2	92	19	0.23	45	18	36	36	8	0%	93	0%	0%	5	0%	20%	1.32	-8.0	31	78	-$7
14	**Proj**	**135**	**9**	**1**	**10**	**0**	**220**	**237**	**246**	**289**	**535**	**620**	**466**	**3**	**84**	**25**	**0.22**	**67**	**13**	**20**	**51**	**17**	**4%**	**82**	**3%**	**48%**				**2.30**	**-5.9**	**1**	**3**	**$0**

Soriano,Alfonso

Age 38	Bats R	Pos LF	Health	A	LIMA Plan	B+
Ht 6' 1"	Wt 195		PT/Exp	A	Rand Var	0
			Consist	B	MM	4225

Remarkably led all of MLB in post-All Star HR, RBI. Is the Fountain of Youth hidden in Monument Park? xPX says he really just rebounded to usual power levels. So 30 HR, yes, but not 40+. Hard to see a SBO repeat, so SB will regress. Otherwise, as young a 38 as you'll find. "Psst... hey, Derek. It's behind the Babe Ruth plaque."

Yr	Tm	AB	R	HR	RBI	SB	BA	xBA	OBP	SLG	OPS	vL	vR	bb%	ct%	h%	Eye	G	L	F	PX	xPX	hr/f	Spd	SBO	SB%	#Wk	DOM	DIS	RC/G	RAR	BPV	BPX	R$
09	CHC	477	64	20	55	9	241	247	303	423	726	569	767	8	75	28	0.34	33	19	48	121	108	11%	96	10%	82%	22	45%	27%	4.29	4.4	44	90	$10
10	CHC	496	67	24	79	5	258	269	322	496	818	944	764	8	75	30	0.37	29	16	54	171	159	12%	104	6%	83%	27	67%	11%	5.47	21.5	87	189	$16
11	CHC	475	50	26	88	2	244	263	289	469	759	812	741	5	76	27	0.24	29	20	51	154	148	14%	74	3%	67%	26	50%	27%	4.49	7.2	63	140	$13
12	CHC	561	68	32	108	6	262	262	322	499	821	831	818	7	73	31	0.29	36	20	44	161	153	18%	85	6%	75%	27	52%	30%	5.43	23.6	62	155	$21
13	2 TM	581	84	34	101	18	255	267	302	489	791	904	735	6	73	29	0.23	38	20	42	164	127	19%	79	23%	67%	26	50%	35%	4.81	14.4	61	153	$28
1st Half		292	34	9	35	8	257	255	279	428	707	864	638	3	76	31	0.13	38	21	41	129	109	10%	86	21%	73%	14	50%	43%	4.04	0.1	40	100	$19
2nd Half		289	50	25	66	10	253	279	316	550	867	945	831	9	71	27	0.32	38	19	43	202	148	28%	75	25%	63%	12	50%	25%	5.62	13.9	86	215	$37
14	**Proj**	**555**	**75**	**27**	**91**	**8**	**258**	**258**	**312**	**467**	**779**	**848**	**750**	**7**	**73**	**30**	**0.27**	**38**	**20**	**42**	**148**	**140**	**16%**	**83**	**11%**	**61%**				**4.81**	**13.0**	**51**	**127**	**$22**

Soto,Geovany

Age 31	Bats R	Pos CA	Health	C	LIMA Plan	D
Ht 6' 1"	Wt 235		PT/Exp	D	Rand Var	-3
			Consist	D	MM	4011

Star of a new reality show: "Baseball's Most Extreme Skills." No hitter with as many AB posted a higher xPX, yet only three had a lower ct%. Extreme! So what does it all mean? The number to note is the less-than-extreme AB: he's a part-timer now. Bid with that in mind, and that prodigious power can provide value as a second CA.

Yr	Tm	AB	R	HR	RBI	SB	BA	xBA	OBP	SLG	OPS	vL	vR	bb%	ct%	h%	Eye	G	L	F	PX	xPX	hr/f	Spd	SBO	SB%	#Wk	DOM	DIS	RC/G	RAR	BPV	BPX	R$
09	CHC	331	27	11	47	1	218	250	321	381	702	767	682	13	77	25	0.65	41	18	41	110	147	10%	57	1%	100%	24	42%	38%	3.99	2.7	40	82	$1
10	CHC	322	47	17	53	0	280	281	393	497	890	1072	796	16	74	33	0.75	36	24	40	153	179	18%	70	1%	0%	22	59%	27%	6.89	28.9	75	163	$11
11	CHC	421	46	17	54	0	228	241	310	411	721	971	643	10	71	28	0.36	41	19	40	143	125	14%	64	0%	0%	25	36%	36%	4.11	4.9	37	82	$6
12	2 TM	324	45	11	39	1	198	237	270	343	613	677	589	8	77	22	0.39	40	21	40	94	139	11%	79	1%	100%	23	30%	26%	2.91	-8.2	24	60	$1
13	TEX	163	20	9	22	1	245	240	328	466	794	656	874	11	63	33	0.33	32	22	46	181	201	19%	78	7%	33%	25	32%	52%	4.95	6.0	45	113	$3
1st Half		83	11	3	6	0	181	192	277	325	602	225	802	12	61	25	0.34	33	18	49	122	171	12%	80	5%	0%	13	31%	62%	2.65	-2.9	-7	-18	-$1
2nd Half		80	9	6	16	1	313	287	382	613	995	1060	953	10	65	41	0.32	31	27	42	239	230	27%	80	9%	50%	12	33%	42%	8.37	10.2	98	245	$7
14	**Proj**	**188**	**23**	**9**	**26**	**1**	**238**	**248**	**320**	**443**	**763**	**779**	**755**	**10**	**69**	**29**	**0.38**	**36**	**22**	**42**	**155**	**173**	**17%**	**74**	**4%**	**43%**				**4.62**	**5.1**	**35**	**88**	**$5**

ROD TRUESDELL

Span,Denard

Age	30	Bats	L	Pos	CF	Health	C	LIMA Plan	A
Ht	6' 0"	Wt	210			PT/Exp	B	Rand Var	0
						Consist	B	MM	1535

Much made of a "return to '09 swing" during spring; this is why you ignore pre-season noise. Essentially the same guy as every other year—Spd spike was driven by anomolous 11 triples. The only real skills change is a continued bb% decline; this should regress, but any further drop would harm SB. So monitor bb% closely.

Yr	Tm	AB	R	HR	RBI	SB	BA	xBA	OBP	SLG	OPS	vL	vR	bb%	ct%	h%	Eye	G	L	F	PX	xPX	hr/f	Spd	SBO	SB%	#Wk	DOM	DIS	RC/G	RAR	BPV	BPX	R$
09	MIN	578	97	8	68	23	311	266	392	415	807	877	774	11	85	36	0.79	53	19	28	58	39	6%	159	15%	70%	26	46%	23%	5.85	28.0	56	114	$27
10	MIN	629	85	3	58	26	264	271	331	348	679	696	670	9	88	30	0.81	54	18	28	53	48	2%	131	16%	87%	27	59%	11%	4.10	0.1	54	117	$18
11	MIN *	322	40	2	17	8	253	267	311	339	650	657	698	8	87	29	0.64	53	21	26	55	55	3%	130	10%	89%	15	33%	20%	3.70	-3.7	48	107	$4
12	MIN	516	71	4	41	17	283	290	342	395	738	739	737	8	88	32	0.76	54	21	24	78	48	4%	110	16%	74%	26	58%	19%	4.81	10.4	66	165	$16
13	WAS	610	75	4	47	20	279	285	327	380	707	539	765	6	87	31	0.55	54	23	23	65	41	3%	152	15%	77%	26	46%	12%	4.39	5.1	62	155	$20
1st Half		305	33	0	20	8	262	277	312	361	673	388	783	7	86	31	0.50	54	22	23	66	36	0%	151	14%	73%	14	36%	14%	3.87	-2.7	56	140	$14
2nd Half		305	42	4	27	12	295	291	338	400	738	711	749	6	89	32	0.61	54	24	22	64	46	7%	139	17%	80%	12	58%	8%	4.95	6.7	64	160	$27
14	Proj	583	76	3	45	21	282	280	336	378	714	655	737	7	88	32	0.64	54	22	24	64	46	3%	137	16%	77%				4.52	5.8	58	145	$19

Springer,George

Age	24	Bats	R	Pos	CF	Health	A	LIMA Plan	C
Ht	6' 3"	Wt	200			PT/Exp	F	Rand Var	-1
						Consist	F	MM	4303

Terrific power/speed prospect, with outstanding athleticism—and that one huge bugaboo, contact rate. HOU did well letting him develop in the minors all year, and bb% is encouraging, showing at least a clue of the strike zone. Exciting 30/30 potential, but for a while, it'll come at the expense of a low BA and lots of Ks.

Yr	Tm	AB	R	HR	RBI	SB	BA	xBA	OBP	SLG	OPS	vL	vR	bb%	ct%	h%	Eye	G	L	F	PX	xPX	hr/f	Spd	SBO	SB%	#Wk	DOM	DIS	RC/G	RAR	BPV	BPX	R$
09																																		
10																																		
11																																		
12	aa	73	6	2	4	3	186	187	233	284	518			6	61	28	0.16				86			97	37%	57%				1.89		-45	-113	-$2
13	a/a	492	81	29	82	34	261	247	346	499	845			12	61	36	0.34				194			100	32%	79%				5.96		56	140	$32
1st Half		292	46	16	43	19	256	240	335	480	816			11	59	38	0.29				202			92	34%	73%				5.39		48	120	$32
2nd Half																																		
14	Proj	315	45	9	42	13	241	207	316	382	698	698	698	10	63	35	0.30	37	19	44	128		10%	92	24%	66%				3.93	-2.3	3	7	$11

Stanton,Giancarlo

Age	24	Bats	R	Pos	RF	Health	C	LIMA Plan	A
Ht	6' 6"	Wt	240			PT/Exp	B	Rand Var	+1
						Consist	D	MM	5225

Awful April, then missed May with hammy. After that, the power mostly returned, but saw very few strikes to hit in that MIA lineup. Barring a change of address, that's likely an issue again. But make no mistake: this is still a slugger of the highest, most-frightening caliber. Grab him now while his stock is (somewhat) down. UP: 50 HR.

Yr	Tm	AB	R	HR	RBI	SB	BA	xBA	OBP	SLG	OPS	vL	vR	bb%	ct%	h%	Eye	G	L	F	PX	xPX	hr/f	Spd	SBO	SB%	#Wk	DOM	DIS	RC/G	RAR	BPV	BPX	R$
09	aa	299	45	14	48	1	222	244	292	428	720			9	63	30	0.27				157			100	3%	47%				4.05		29	59	$4
10	FLA *	551	80	39	103	6	269	280	355	551	906	644	889	12	67	33	0.40	43	16	41	214	138	23%	111	5%	75%	18	39%	44%	6.79	34.7	96	209	$24
11	FLA	516	79	34	87	5	262	276	356	537	893	1042	849	12	68	32	0.42	45	16	38	205	172	25%	109	7%	50%	27	63%	19%	6.31	25.7	94	209	$21
12	MIA	449	75	37	86	6	290	288	361	608	969	1024	950	9	68	35	0.32	36	22	42	226	163	29%	84	7%	75%	23	65%	17%	7.72	39.1	99	248	$25
13	MIA	425	62	24	62	1	249	253	365	480	845	1006	789	15	67	31	0.53	43	18	38	180	139	22%	83	1%	100%	22	45%	27%	5.90	16.1	69	173	$13
1st Half		146	17	8	22	1	260	251	333	479	813	846	813	10	72	31	0.39	49	14	37	158	133	21%	69	3%	100%	9	44%	33%	5.55	4.7	57	143	$7
2nd Half		279	45	16	40	0	244	252	374	480	854	1079	776	17	65	32	0.59	40	20	39	193	143	23%	99	0%	0%	13	46%	23%	6.05	13.3	79	198	$16
14	Proj	553	84	37	90	4	261	270	357	528	885	981	853	12	67	32	0.43	42	19	39	202	150	25%	89	4%	70%				6.39	31.2	77	192	$24

Stewart,Chris

Age	32	Bats	R	Pos	CA	Health	A	LIMA Plan	D
Ht	6' 5"	Wt	210			PT/Exp	F	Rand Var	0
						Consist	B	MM	1303

Again stumbled into a chunk of playing time as the CA ahead of him fell injured. That he didn't suffer a similar fate is the best thing we can say about this season. He'll surely never see 300 PA again, and it's just as well. To paraphrase Uecker, the more playing time he gets, the sooner GMs will realize he's not worth rostering.

Yr	Tm	AB	R	HR	RBI	SB	BA	xBA	OBP	SLG	OPS	vL	vR	bb%	ct%	h%	Eye	G	L	F	PX	xPX	hr/f	Spd	SBO	SB%	#Wk	DOM	DIS	RC/G	RAR	BPV	BPX	R$
09	aaa	232	28	1	15	1	238	234	305	289	594			9	85	28	0.65				38			97	3%	42%				2.91		20	41	-$1
10	SD *	266	21	4	26	1	180	240	242	275	516	0	0	7	81	21	0.43	44	20	36	65	-5	0%	120	1%	100%	2	0%	100%	2.08	-13.8	29	63	-$4
11	SF *	257	25	3	16	2	185	215	250	266	515	801	511	8	85	21	0.57	35	16	49	59	64	5%	102	5%	57%	19	47%	16%	2.05	-13.5	35	78	-$4
12	NYY	141	15	1	13	2	241	224	292	319	611	579	633	7	85	28	0.48	34	19	47	59	43	2%	97	6%	100%	26	27%	46%	3.20	-2.1	32	80	$0
13	NYY	294	28	4	25	4	211	214	293	272	566	503	591	9	83	24	0.61	42	19	40	40	62	4%	90	5%	100%	26	27%	35%	2.57	-10.4	13	33	$0
1st Half		139	16	3	11	3	259	217	322	338	660	557	704	9	82	30	0.52	42	19	39	48	56	7%	109	7%	100%	14	21%	36%	3.88	0.7	18	45	$5
2nd Half		155	12	1	14	1	168	209	250	213	463	455	488	10	85	19	0.71	41	19	40	33	67	2%	80	3%	100%	12	33%	33%	1.66	-10.4	10	25	-$5
14	Proj	256	25	3	21	3	215	217	288	287	575	567	579	8	84	25	0.58	38	19	44	51	56	3%	91	5%	93%				2.67	-8.2	13	33	$1

Stubbs,Drew

Age	29	Bats	R	Pos	RF CF	Health	A	LIMA Plan	C+
Ht	6' 4"	Wt	205			PT/Exp	A	Rand Var	0
						Consist	B	MM	3505

His one useful skill - speed - declined for the third straight year. More troubling, he continues to wail away like the power hitter he clearly isn't. Still young enough that Spd should rebound—that is, if he doesn't lose even more playing time. With his frustrating lack of any skills improvement, that's a big if.

Yr	Tm	AB	R	HR	RBI	SB	BA	xBA	OBP	SLG	OPS	vL	vR	bb%	ct%	h%	Eye	G	L	F	PX	xPX	hr/f	Spd	SBO	SB%	#Wk	DOM	DIS	RC/G	RAR	BPV	BPX	R$
09	CIN *	591	73	11	49	47	244	227	311	354	665	833	740	9	71	33	0.33	42	21	37	83	139	17%	149	38%	78%	8	38%	25%	3.79	-14.7	15	31	$21
10	CIN	514	91	22	77	30	255	237	329	444	773	789	765	10	67	34	0.33	44	16	40	138	139	16%	176	26%	83%	27	56%	30%	5.07	12.1	54	117	$24
11	CIN	604	92	15	44	40	243	216	321	364	686	896	636	9	66	34	0.31	47	20	33	98	115	11%	168	29%	80%	27	33%	56%	3.96	-5.7	14	31	$21
12	CIN	493	75	14	40	30	213	206	277	333	610	788	541	8	66	29	0.25	51	15	34	87	85	13%	146	31%	81%	25	24%	60%	3.05	-19.0	-3	-8	$12
13	CLE	430	59	10	45	17	233	222	305	360	665	718	637	9	67	32	0.31	47	20	34	106	88	10%	123	17%	89%	27	33%	52%	3.78	-6.4	11	28	$12
1st Half		257	32	6	30	8	241	217	296	381	677	783	617	7	67	34	0.24	43	18	39	116	97	9%	129	13%	100%	14	43%	36%	3.96	-3.7	16	40	$13
2nd Half		173	27	4	15	9	220	227	315	329	644	619	662	12	68	30	0.43	52	22	26	90	74	13%	106	22%	82%	13	23%	69%	3.51	-5.0	1	3	$9
14	Proj	413	61	11	38	20	229	221	303	359	662	743	629	9	67	31	0.31	48	19	33	103	94	12%	133	22%	85%				3.69	-9.5	10	24	$13

Suzuki,Ichiro

Age	40	Bats	L	Pos	RF	Health	A	LIMA Plan	B
Ht	5' 11"	Wt	170			PT/Exp	A	Rand Var	+1
						Consist	B	MM	1533

Can still flash the wheels most younger men would envy. Of course, he's always been a physical freak. But the inevitable signs of age are there, as an across-the-board 2H skills drop shows—including that vaunted Spd. R$ fell below $20 for the first time. If the skills continue to erode... DN: retirement before season's end.

Yr	Tm	AB	R	HR	RBI	SB	BA	xBA	OBP	SLG	OPS	vL	vR	bb%	ct%	h%	Eye	G	L	F	PX	xPX	hr/f	Spd	SBO	SB%	#Wk	DOM	DIS	RC/G	RAR	BPV	BPX	R$
09	SEA	639	88	11	46	26	352	288	386	465	851	829	863	5	89	38	0.45	56	18	26	68	48	7%	164	17%	74%	26	46%	15%	6.94	44.1	71	145	$35
10	SEA	680	74	6	43	42	315	271	359	394	754	684	789	6	87	35	0.52	57	17	25	55	44	4%	141	23%	82%	27	44%	19%	5.39	20.7	50	109	$34
11	SEA	677	80	5	47	40	272	275	310	335	645	648	644	5	90	30	0.57	60	19	21	42	29	4%	132	24%	85%	27	37%	11%	3.83	-8.7	45	100	$23
12	2 AL	629	77	9	55	29	283	292	307	390	696	649	724	3	90	30	0.36	51	25	24	63	40	7%	133	23%	81%	28	64%	14%	4.31	0.5	60	150	$24
13	NYY	520	57	7	35	20	262	264	297	342	639	753	590	5	88	29	0.41	52	21	27	50	33	6%	140	18%	83%	26	38%	27%	3.59	-10.3	45	113	$15
1st Half		267	27	5	18	12	270	264	309	367	676	819	603	5	89	29	0.50	50	20	29	56	37	7%	144	21%	80%	14	57%	21%	4.01	-3.4	56	140	$18
2nd Half		253	30	2	17	8	253	262	284	316	600	667	577	4	87	28	0.33	54	22	24	43	29	4%	125	14%	89%	12	17%	33%	3.18	-9.5	30	75	$12
14	Proj	401	47	5	29	17	267	273	300	351	651	684	635	4	89	29	0.41	54	21	25	53	35	5%	137	19%	82%				3.74	-8.3	43	107	$13

Suzuki,Kurt

Age	30	Bats	R	Pos	CA	Health	A	LIMA Plan	D+
Ht	5' 11"	Wt	205			PT/Exp	C	Rand Var	+2
						Consist	B	MM	1213

A full skills rebound, but tough luck kept the stats from showing it. Granted, it's a rebound from poor to merely adequate, and playing time is again a question mark. A sterling reputation with pitchers, though, could net him another starting gig. So role is key, but with enough at-bats, xBA & xPX point to a reasonable UP: .260, 15 HR.

Yr	Tm	AB	R	HR	RBI	SB	BA	xBA	OBP	SLG	OPS	vL	vR	bb%	ct%	h%	Eye	G	L	F	PX	xPX	hr/f	Spd	SBO	SB%	#Wk	DOM	DIS	RC/G	RAR	BPV	BPX	R$
09	OAK	570	74	15	88	8	274	290	313	421	734	727	737	5	90	28	0.47	44	19	36	90	99	8%	80	8%	80%	27	67%	11%	4.56	13.7	66	135	$16
10	OAK	495	55	13	71	3	242	259	303	366	669	575	701	6	90	25	0.67	42	17	41	72	87	7%	86	4%	60%	24	50%	17%	3.53	-2.7	58	126	$8
11	OAK	460	54	14	44	2	237	262	301	385	686	617	713	8	86	25	0.59	36	20	44	97	80	8%	78	4%	50%	27	63%	11%	3.75	0.4	63	140	$6
12	2 TM	408	36	6	43	2	235	223	276	328	605	628	598	5	82	27	0.27	41	17	42	66	102	4%	80	2%	100%	28	21%	46%	2.99	-8.8	17	43	$3
13	2 TM	285	25	5	32	2	232	255	290	337	627	653	619	7	88	25	0.63	37	23	40	69	100	5%	89	3%	100%	26	38%	31%	3.24	-4.0	49	123	$2
1st Half		199	16	3	19	2	226	248	287	332	619	595	624	8	87	25	0.65	37	21	42	71	90	4%	97	4%	100%	14	50%	36%	3.19	-3.1	51	128	$2
2nd Half		86	9	2	13	0	244	271	286	349	635	762	609	5	90	25	0.56	38	26	36	64	123	7%	75	0%	0%	12	25%	25%	3.36	-0.9	45	113	$0
14	Proj	362	36	8	43	2	247	252	298	358	656	679	649	6	87	27	0.48	39	21	40	73	102	6%	78	2%	83%				3.55	-1.7	34	85	$7

ROD TRUESDELL

Sweeney,Ryan

Age 29 Bats L Pos CF	Health F	LIMA Plan D+	
Ht 6' 4" Wt 225	PT/Exp F	Rand Var +1	
	Consist B	MM 2223	

6-19-.266 in 192 AB at CHC. Fractured rib cost him two months. You get the feeling he would've regressed enough anyway for this season to end up like most. True, 8 1H HR would exceed his highest season total, but xPX says it wasn't fully supported. Watch FB% to see if he has another power spike in him. But bet against.

Yr	Tm	AB	R	HR	RBI	SB	BA	xBA	OBP	SLG	OPS	vL	vR	bb%	ct%	h%	Eye	G	L	F	PX	xPX	hr/f	Spd	SBO	SB%	#Wk	DOM	DIS	RC/G	RAR	BPV	BPX	R$
09	OAK	484	68	6	53	6	293	284	348	407	755	719	766	8	86	33	0.60	45	24	31	76	84	5%	100	8%	55%	25	40%	20%	4.97	11.9	53	108	$14
10	OAK	303	41	1	36	1	294	274	342	383	725	623	754	7	86	34	0.59	52	20	28	68	36	1%	102	2%	50%	15	47%	13%	4.73	5.4	48	104	$7
11	OAK	264	34	1	25	1	265	241	346	341	687	404	743	11	82	32	0.69	48	21	31	55	65	1%	122	2%	50%	25	32%	32%	4.07	-0.2	32	71	$3
12	BOS	204	22	0	16	0	260	264	303	373	675	332	713	6	79	33	0.28	47	24	29	94	60	0%	88	0%	0%	15	67%	33%	3.86	-1.3	30	75	$1
13	CHC *	275	27	10	30	2	267	283	323	456	779	824	755	8	82	29	0.46	48	21	31	120	90	12%	116	3%	100%	13	69%	15%	5.16	8.4	75	188	$6
1st Half		195	21	8	26	2	284	290	331	505	836	930	842	7	81	32	0.36	41	24	35	141	98	12%	122	4%	100%	8	75%	0%	6.01	10.1	87	218	$10
2nd Half		80	6	2	4	0	225	234	303	338	641	567	651	10	85	24	0.75	57	17	26	72	79	11%	96	0%	0%	5	60%	40%	3.37	-2.0	49	123	-$3
14	Proj	**244**	**25**	**3**	**21**	**1**	**266**	**261**	**325**	**380**	**706**	**645**	**719**	**8**	**82**	**31**	**0.50**	**49**	**21**	**30**	**83**	**74**	**5%**	**102**	**2%**	**73%**				**4.31**	**1.0**	**32**	**81**	**$3**

Swisher,Nick

Age 33 Bats B Pos 1B RF	Health A	LIMA Plan A	
Ht 6' 0" Wt 200	PT/Exp A	Rand Var +2	
	Consist B	MM 4125	

Stunning drop in production vs RHP likely due to left shoulder bothering him most of the year. He's generally been healthy, and skills are otherwise solid. Thus, a return to form is probable; if so, a BA and PX regression will again make him a near-$20, high-RAR hitter. Undervalued on draft day (in non-Forecaster leagues).

Yr	Tm	AB	R	HR	RBI	SB	BA	xBA	OBP	SLG	OPS	vL	vR	bb%	ct%	h%	Eye	G	L	F	PX	xPX	hr/f	Spd	SBO	SB%	#Wk	DOM	DIS	RC/G	RAR	BPV	BPX	R$
09	NYY	498	84	29	82	0	249	276	371	498	869	868	868	16	75	28	0.77	38	16	46	167	146	17%	76	0%	0%	27	63%	15%	6.28	24.5	90	184	$13
10	NYY	566	91	29	89	1	288	272	359	511	870	848	879	9	75	30	0.42	36	20	45	153	163	15%	89	2%	33%	27	63%	11%	6.40	28.4	72	157	$23
11	NYY	526	81	23	85	2	260	264	374	449	822	957	763	15	76	30	0.76	39	22	39	133	133	14%	72	2%	50%	27	63%	26%	5.73	17.1	65	144	$17
12	NYY	537	75	24	93	2	272	261	364	473	837	769	873	13	74	33	0.55	39	22	39	142	127	15%	80	3%	40%	27	48%	30%	5.92	20.2	60	150	$19
13	CLE	549	74	22	63	1	246	255	341	423	763	918	680	12	75	29	0.56	38	23	39	124	138	14%	79	1%	100%	26	54%	23%	4.85	3.9	49	123	$13
1st Half		251	38	8	29	0	235	258	336	398	734	797	704	13	75	28	0.60	37	25	37	120	136	11%	80	0%	0%	13	62%	23%	4.46	-1.1	48	120	$9
2nd Half		298	36	14	34	1	255	252	341	443	784	1033	661	12	75	30	0.52	39	21	40	127	140	16%	82	1%	100%	13	46%	23%	5.20	5.2	51	128	$16
14	Proj	**530**	**75**	**24**	**80**	**1**	**263**	**262**	**360**	**461**	**821**	**891**	**785**	**13**	**75**	**31**	**0.59**	**38**	**22**	**40**	**140**	**136**	**16%**	**76**	**2%**	**55%**				**5.69**	**16.7**	**52**	**131**	**$18**

Tabata,Jose

Age 25 Bats R Pos RF LF	Health C	LIMA Plan D+	
Ht 5' 11" Wt 210	PT/Exp D	Rand Var 0	
	Consist C	MM 1433	

6-33-3-.282 in 308 AB at PIT. Yes, a power uptick, but he still hit 3 of 5 balls on the ground, so there's no HR breakout coming. And 4 SB with that Spd? PIT shut him down after 2012's 46% SB%. Still, any value here will have to come from his legs. Earning his Mgr's faith again would help; he still has the tools for... UP: 25 SB.

Yr	Tm	AB	R	HR	RBI	SB	BA	xBA	OBP	SLG	OPS	vL	vR	bb%	ct%	h%	Eye	G	L	F	PX	xPX	hr/f	Spd	SBO	SB%	#Wk	DOM	DIS	RC/G	RAR	BPV	BPX	R$
09	a/a	362	44	4	30	9	273	267	319	373	692			6	88	30	0.56				67			102	19%	52%				3.91		50	102	$8
10	PIT *	629	94	6	50	38	290	277	338	389	727	682	767	7	85	33	0.49	59	16	25	69	82	5%	145	28%	74%	18	50%	28%	4.69	11.3	55	120	$28
11	PIT *	367	58	4	23	16	269	270	347	371	718	819	679	11	82	32	0.67	61	17	22	79	89	7%	110	22%	63%	18	44%	33%	4.32	2.9	48	107	$11
12	PIT *	491	60	3	28	12	250	268	303	339	641	706	650	7	84	29	0.47	62	18	20	65	52	6%	107	21%	46%	21	29%	29%	3.18	-13.1	35	88	$7
13	PIT *	336	36	6	33	4	271	283	322	408	730	742	778	7	84	31	0.48	59	18	23	89	78	10%	136	5%	79%	22	50%	14%	4.61	5.3	65	163	$7
1st Half		104	10	2	6	2	244	254	305	358	663	500	863	8	80	29	0.45	56	18	26	85	72	12%	95	7%	100%	9	67%	22%	3.78	-0.7	36	90	$0
2nd Half		232	26	4	27	2	284	293	330	430	760	908	753	6	86	32	0.50	60	19	22	91	79	10%	147	5%	67%	13	38%	8%	5.02	6.6	77	193	$11
14	Proj	**324**	**39**	**4**	**25**	**10**	**265**	**275**	**328**	**379**	**706**	**682**	**714**	**7**	**84**	**30**	**0.49**	**60**	**18**	**22**	**80**	**73**	**7%**	**120**	**17%**	**67%**				**4.11**	**-3.3**	**48**	**120**	**$9**

Taveras,Oscar

Age 22 Bats L Pos RF	Health A	LIMA Plan C+	
Ht 6' 2" Wt 180	PT/Exp F	Rand Var 0	
	Consist D	MM 3333	

A May high-ankle injury essentially wrecked this season, which was supposed to be his last development step. So it seems likely he'll return to Triple-A to work on last remaining issues (see bb%). He's still considered a star in the making, and those '12 MLEs (posted at age 20) hint at what he could become. UP: 2012, but in MLB.

Yr	Tm	AB	R	HR	RBI	SB	BA	xBA	OBP	SLG	OPS	vL	vR	bb%	ct%	h%	Eye	G	L	F	PX	xPX	hr/f	Spd	SBO	SB%	#Wk	DOM	DIS	RC/G	RAR	BPV	BPX	R$
09																																		
10																																		
11																																		
12	aa	477	67	17	76	8	290	296	338	492	830			7	87	30	0.58				120			96	8%	88%				6.02		90	225	$20
13	aaa	173	20	4	25	4	271	266	301	398	699			4	86	30	0.30				88			83	13%	78%				4.20		50	125	$4
1st Half		173	20	4	25	4	271	266	301	398	699			4	86	30	0.30				88			99	13%	78%				4.20		55	138	$4
2nd Half																																		
14	Proj	**266**	**33**	**9**	**40**	**5**	**275**	**280**	**312**	**446**	**758**	**758**	**758**	**5**	**87**	**29**	**0.40**	**46**	**17**	**37**	**110**		**10%**	**105**	**11%**	**83%**				**4.93**	**3.6**	**74**	**185**	**$11**

Teixeira,Mark

Age 34 Bats B Pos 1B	Health F	LIMA Plan B+	
Ht 6' 3" Wt 215	PT/Exp C	Rand Var +5	
	Consist C	MM 4135	

Torn right wrist tendon sheath delayed, then ended season before it began. He's expected to be ready for spring training, but this is just the latest in a series of health issues (calf, left wrist, knee, vocal cords!) to cut both PT and production. Chronically-injured players never suddenly become healthy.

Yr	Tm	AB	R	HR	RBI	SB	BA	xBA	OBP	SLG	OPS	vL	vR	bb%	ct%	h%	Eye	G	L	F	PX	xPX	hr/f	Spd	SBO	SB%	#Wk	DOM	DIS	RC/G	RAR	BPV	BPX	R$
09	NYY	609	103	39	122	2	292	308	383	565	948	911	963	12	81	30	0.71	36	20	44	165	156	18%	80	1%	100%	27	70%	7%	7.66	51.6	107	218	$28
10	NYY	601	113	33	108	0	256	281	365	481	846	940	804	13	80	27	0.76	36	19	45	147	147	15%	73	1%	0%	27	78%	19%	5.83	21.4	87	189	$21
11	NYY	589	90	39	111	4	248	281	341	494	835	967	773	11	81	24	0.69	35	18	47	151	133	17%	69	3%	80%	27	63%	19%	5.60	17.2	92	204	$23
12	NYY	451	66	24	84	2	251	281	332	475	807	865	770	11	82	26	0.65	41	19	39	137	120	16%	69	3%	67%	24	67%	21%	5.32	9.4	80	200	$14
13	NYY	53	5	3	12	0	151	239	270	340	609	935	432	13	64	16	0.42	29	29	43	139	128	20%	73	0%	0%	3	33%	67%	2.68	-3.3	18	45	-$2
1st Half		53	5	3	12	0	151	239	262	340	602	935	432	13	64	16	0.42	29	29	43	139	128	20%	73	0%	0%	3	33%	67%	2.68	-3.4	18	45	-$2
2nd Half																																		
14	Proj	**431**	**61**	**25**	**86**	**1**	**255**	**271**	**351**	**479**	**830**	**957**	**766**	**12**	**80**	**27**	**0.68**	**35**	**20**	**45**	**141**	**133**	**17%**	**59**	**1%**	**72%**				**5.66**	**13.4**	**71**	**177**	**$17**

Tejada,Ruben

Age 24 Bats R Pos SS	Health C	LIMA Plan D+	
Ht 5' 11" Wt 185	PT/Exp C	Rand Var +5	
	Consist C	MM 1213	

0-10-.202 in 208 AB at NYM. So the good news: Rand Var shows he's almost a lock to improve his numbers in '14. The bad news, of course, is that it would be almost impossible to do worse. With no power, a continued poor Eye, and merely average speed, there's little upside in this skill set -- and we've all seen the downside.

Yr	Tm	AB	R	HR	RBI	SB	BA	xBA	OBP	SLG	OPS	vL	vR	bb%	ct%	h%	Eye	G	L	F	PX	xPX	hr/f	Spd	SBO	SB%	#Wk	DOM	DIS	RC/G	RAR	BPV	BPX	R$
09	aa	488	49	4	38	16	265	254	307	348	655			6	86	30	0.45				55			105	15%	83%				3.78		35	71	$10
10	NYM *	434	47	2	27	3	228	239	283	290	572	729	541	7	82	27	0.42	41	23	36	52	71	2%	93	7%	34%	19	42%	47%	2.59	-12.2	14	30	$0
11	NYM *	535	52	2	53	8	252	255	316	316	632	704	692	9	85	29	0.61	45	26	30	47	39	0%	115	7%	72%	18	39%	44%	3.41	-1.5	30	67	$7
12	NYM	464	53	1	25	4	289	264	333	351	685	760	647	5	84	34	0.37	40	30	30	51	55	1%	118	6%	50%	21	33%	33%	4.03	6.8	26	65	$9
13	NYM *	448	44	1	25	3	210	239	250	270	520	719	432	5	86	24	0.39	47	19	34	49	62	0%	101	5%	54%	11	45%	18%	2.15	-18.9	27	68	-$3
1st Half		191	20	0	11	2	224	242	277	281	559	742	427	7	88	25	0.61	46	19	35	49	62	0%	102	7%	67%	9	33%	22%	2.55	-5.3	37	93	-$1
2nd Half		257	24	1	14	1	202	243	231	265	496	0	463	4	85	23	0.25	50	20	30	49	60	0%	95	4%	34%	2	100%	0%	1.92	-12.5	18	45	-$4
14	Proj	**395**	**41**	**1**	**25**	**4**	**240**	**250**	**294**	**305**	**599**	**685**	**565**	**6**	**85**	**28**	**0.43**	**46**	**23**	**31**	**51**	**54**	**1%**	**110**	**6%**	**61%**				**2.89**	**-6.8**	**17**	**42**	**$4**

Thole,Josh

Age 27 Bats L Pos CA	Health A	LIMA Plan D	
Ht 6' 0" Wt 215	PT/Exp D	Rand Var +1	
	Consist B	MM 1001	

1-8-.175 in 120 AB at TOR. A lefty-hitting catcher can be quite valuable. Of course, there's a large-but-subtle difference between that and a lefty-SWINGING catcher—precious little actual hitting has occurred the past two years. Previously solid contact used to set a BA floor, but ct% trend is ominous for job security.

Yr	Tm	AB	R	HR	RBI	SB	BA	xBA	OBP	SLG	OPS	vL	vR	bb%	ct%	h%	Eye	G	L	F	PX	xPX	hr/f	Spd	SBO	SB%	#Wk	DOM	DIS	RC/G	RAR	BPV	BPX	R$
09	NYM *	437	40	1	46	7	291	323	347	373	720	600	783	8	90	32	0.82	46	34	20	58	85	0%	84	9%	62%	6	50%	17%	4.58	10.8	48	98	$10
10	NYM *	367	32	4	29	1	251	273	325	359	685	343	783	10	85	28	0.74	44	23	33	78	73	5%	108	1%	100%	16	38%	13%	4.00	3.2	58	126	$2
11	NYM	340	22	3	40	0	268	257	345	344	690	525	709	10	86	30	0.81	49	25	26	58	55	4%	51	2%	0%	27	48%	41%	3.99	2.7	28	62	$4
12	NYM	321	24	1	21	0	234	228	294	290	584	562	591	8	84	27	0.54	58	19	24	45	58	2%	80	0%	0%	25	24%	32%	2.83	-8.5	15	38	-$1
13	TOR *	269	24	6	31	0	227	229	285	340	626	477	502	8	79	26	0.40	44	19	37	72	73	3%	84	2%	0%	17	18%	59%	3.14	-4.6	18	45	$1
1st Half		171	13	5	24	0	246	186	295	378	673	0	282	7	79	28	0.34	41	6	53	82	161	0%	85	3%	0%	5	0%	60%	3.65	-0.3	24	60	$3
2nd Half		98	11	1	7	0	194	231	269	276	544	523	558	9	80	23	0.50	44	22	34	56	54	4%	96	0%	0%	12	25%	58%	2.34	-4.2	12	30	-$4
14	Proj	**115**	**10**	**1**	**11**	**0**	**233**	**236**	**301**	**307**	**607**	**498**	**630**	**8**	**83**	**27**	**0.53**	**48**	**20**	**31**	**54**	**61**	**3%**	**85**	**1%**	**26%**				**3.01**	**-2.4**	**7**	**17**	**$1**

ROD TRUESDELL

Torrealba,Yorvit

Age	35	Bats	R	Pos	CA	Health	A	LIMA Plan	F
Ht	5' 11"	Wt	200			PT/Exp	D	Rand Var	+1
						Consist	B	MM	1001

7 unis in 12 MLB seasons—does that make him wanted or unwanted? Looks like the latter now. He used to get work because of his throwing, but recent sub-20% CS numbers eliminate that value. Steep and steady erosion in power and production makes him a BA liability with no HR upside. Still the best Yorvit in the game, though.

Yr	Tm	AB	R	HR	RBI	SB	BA	xBA	OBP	SLG	OPS	vL	vR	bb%	ct%	h%	Eye	G	L	F	PX	xPX	hr/f	Spd	SBO	SB%	#Wk	DOM	DIS	RC/G	RAR	BPV	BPX	R$
09	COL	213	27	2	31	1	291	259	351	380	732	610	778	9	80	36	0.50	50	23	28	65	92	4%	109	3%	50%	22	32%	36%	4.79	6.5	26	53	$4
10	SD	325	31	7	37	7	271	258	343	378	721	698	729	9	79	32	0.49	55	20	25	77	75	11%	80	12%	58%	27	30%	33%	4.33	6.0	24	52	$8
11	TEX	396	40	7	37	0	273	281	306	399	705	612	744	5	84	31	0.31	48	25	27	92	81	8%	82	2%	0%	27	48%	30%	4.21	5.8	44	98	$7
12	3 TM	194	19	4	14	1	227	231	293	330	623	567	661	8	79	27	0.43	51	18	31	70	67	8%	83	4%	50%	23	35%	39%	3.10	-3.5	17	43	-$1
13	COL	179	10	0	16	0	240	228	295	285	580	687	547	7	87	28	0.54	49	21	30	39	47	0%	74	0%	0%	25	28%	52%	2.79	-4.8	15	38	-$2
1st Half		93	7	0	9	0	290	251	365	344	709	973	630	11	87	33	0.92	50	24	26	47	57	0%	90	0%	0%	14	29%	57%	4.52	2.1	36	90	$1
2nd Half		86	3	0	7	0	186	202	205	221	425	316	456	2	86	22	0.17	49	18	34	31	36	0%	63	0%	0%	11	27%	45%	1.42	-6.3	-5	-13	-$5
14	Proj	**131**	**10**	**1**	**12**	**0**	**240**	**240**	**291**	**317**	**608**	**598**	**612**	**6**	**84**	**28**	**0.42**	**50**	**20**	**30**	**58**	**59**	**4%**	**78**	**2%**	**46%**				**3.04**	**-2.6**	**5**	**12**	**-$1**

Torres,Andres

Age	36	Bats	B	Pos	LF CF	Health	D	LIMA Plan	D
Ht	5' 10"	Wt	195			PT/Exp	C	Rand Var	-1
						Consist	A	MM	1401

One of the biggest blips of the last five seasons has to be his '10 breakout. It can safely be forgotten. Knee, calf, Achilles injuries in '13 didn't help, but as he enters late 30s, they'll become even more commonplace. With three straight years below replacement level, even spot duty won't hide his faults. Look for a 5th OF elsewhere.

Yr	Tm	AB	R	HR	RBI	SB	BA	xBA	OBP	SLG	OPS	vL	vR	bb%	ct%	h%	Eye	G	L	F	PX	xPX	hr/f	Spd	SBO	SB%	#Wk	DOM	DIS	RC/G	RAR	BPV	BPX	R$
09	SF *	195	34	7	24	7	261	228	319	486	805	1116	667	8	65	37	0.24	34	16	49	152	165	13%	154	17%	87%	20	35%	45%	5.43	7.8	46	94	$6
10	SF	507	84	16	63	26	268	280	343	479	823	659	881	10	75	33	0.44	39	22	39	157	117	11%	105	26%	79%	26	50%	15%	5.70	24.4	78	170	$22
11	SF *	403	56	6	25	20	217	216	296	336	632	550	657	10	72	29	0.40	40	16	44	100	83	4%	111	26%	77%	21	43%	48%	3.27	-9.8	24	53	$6
12	NYM	374	47	3	35	13	230	247	327	337	664	763	600	12	76	30	0.58	48	25	28	74	65	4%	129	16%	72%	24	33%	38%	3.62	-5.0	28	70	$5
13	SF	272	33	2	21	4	250	228	302	342	644	718	564	7	78	32	0.36	42	19	38	77	70	2%	104	10%	57%	21	38%	43%	3.47	-4.7	20	50	$3
1st Half		190	23	2	18	3	268	236	319	379	698	811	587	7	76	35	0.30	40	21	39	97	71	4%	88	10%	60%	14	43%	50%	4.11	0.5	23	58	$6
2nd Half		82	10	0	3	1	207	207	278	256	534	555	491	9	82	25	0.53	46	16	37	34	67	0%	129	9%	50%	7	29%	29%	2.22	-4.7	12	30	-$4
14	Proj	**190**	**25**	**2**	**14**	**5**	**232**	**229**	**306**	**335**	**641**	**686**	**607**	**10**	**76**	**29**	**0.45**	**44**	**20**	**37**	**78**	**77**	**3%**	**122**	**15%**	**69%**				**3.37**	**-3.7**	**25**	**62**	**$3**

Tracy,Chad

Age	34	Bats	L	Pos	3B	Health	C	LIMA Plan	D
Ht	6' 1"	Wt	205			PT/Exp	F	Rand Var	+3
						Consist	F	MM	2001

So much for that small-sample LH-mashing production in '12. The '13 version couldn't stay healthy, and when he did, pop was well below average. Correction of tiny h% will likely send BA north, but xBA history confirms he'll be a liability regardless. Might stick on a bench, but no longer a guy who gets interesting with more PT.

Yr	Tm	AB	R	HR	RBI	SB	BA	xBA	OBP	SLG	OPS	vL	vR	bb%	ct%	h%	Eye	G	L	F	PX	xPX	hr/f	Spd	SBO	SB%	#Wk	DOM	DIS	RC/G	RAR	BPV	BPX	R$
09	ARI *	292	31	8	41	1	235	249	302	377	679	514	736	9	84	26	0.58	35	18	48	90	95	8%	86	3%	44%	23	61%	30%	3.74	-2.2	52	106	$2
10	2 NL *	305	37	11	42	0	272	265	312	434	747	533	631	6	82	30	0.32	39	19	42	110	72	2%	76	2%	0%	18	28%	50%	4.66	5.8	52	113	$8
11																																		
12	WAS	93	7	3	14	0	269	245	343	441	784	1000	760	10	84	29	0.67	35	16	48	114	172	8%	72	0%	0%	18	50%	28%	5.22	3.3	70	175	$0
13	WAS	129	6	4	11	0	202	206	243	326	568	778	553	5	81	22	0.28	31	15	54	80	72	7%	68	8%	0%	26	35%	42%	2.33	-6.8	19	48	-$3
1st Half		75	4	3	5	0	133	177	177	253	431	667	411	5	75	13	0.21	23	14	63	71	66	9%	80	18%	0%	14	79%	50%	1.10	-7.6	-8	-20	-$4
2nd Half		54	2	1	6	0	296	226	333	426	759	1000	745	5	89	32	0.50	40	17	44	90	79	5%	77	0%	0%	12	42%	33%	5.14	1.7	63	158	-$1
14	Proj	**98**	**7**	**2**	**12**	**0**	**247**	**231**	**299**	**379**	**678**	**798**	**667**	**7**	**83**	**28**	**0.42**	**35**	**17**	**49**	**90**	**100**	**6%**	**72**	**3%**	**5%**				**3.71**	**-0.8**	**26**	**65**	**$2**

Trout,Mike

Age	22	Bats	R	Pos	CF LF	Health	A	LIMA Plan	C
Ht	6' 2"	Wt	230			PT/Exp	B	Rand Var	-3
						Consist	D	MM	4535

Time to address lightning striking twice: Bb% and ct% crept up, which increased both BA floor and theoretical SB ceiling. In practice, future SB totals will be tied to both SBO and lineup spot. 30 HR could be in play again if 2H FB spike sticks. We'll concede that he's really good, but regression remains the world's most powerful force.

Yr	Tm	AB	R	HR	RBI	SB	BA	xBA	OBP	SLG	OPS	vL	vR	bb%	ct%	h%	Eye	G	L	F	PX	xPX	hr/f	Spd	SBO	SB%	#Wk	DOM	DIS	RC/G	RAR	BPV	BPX	R$
09																																		
10																																		
11	LAA *	476	93	15	50	33	282	253	349	460	808	773	605	9	77	34	0.44	39	21	40	119	105	14%	159	32%	76%	11	55%	36%	5.63	19.3	70	156	$26
12	LAA *	636	144	31	92	53	328	276	398	555	953	862	999	10	75	40	0.47	44	23	33	144	113	22%	153	28%	90%	24	63%	13%	8.75	76.7	85	213	$54
13	LAA	589	109	27	97	33	323	287	432	557	988	954	1000	16	77	38	0.81	41	23	36	159	133	16%	153	18%	83%	27	74%	11%	9.11	77.6	114	285	$47
1st Half		330	57	13	52	20	315	301	392	545	938	974	925	11	81	36	0.66	46	22	32	152	130	15%	149	23%	87%	14	79%	7%	8.18	36.0	113	283	$48
2nd Half		259	52	14	45	13	332	269	471	571	1042	918	1092	21	72	42	0.94	35	25	40	167	136	18%	142	14%	76%	13	69%	15%	10.25	42.2	109	273	$45
14	Proj	**575**	**110**	**25**	**91**	**35**	**302**	**274**	**400**	**520**	**921**	**861**	**944**	**14**	**76**	**36**	**0.64**	**41**	**23**	**36**	**147**	**122**	**16%**	**153**	**21%**	**84%**				**7.70**	**56.5**	**96**	**240**	**$41**

Trumbo,Mark

Age	28	Bats	R	Pos	1B	Health	A	LIMA Plan	B+
Ht	6' 4"	Wt	235			PT/Exp	A	Rand Var	+1
						Consist	B	MM	4115

Career high marks in HR, RBI will keep him among upper echelon at 1B, but now's not the time to jump in. Already spotty contact tanked in 2H, putting even a .240 BA at risk. All of his power came against lefties; Slg was 200 points lower vs. righties, so he's far from a 30 HR lock. Bid, but heed DN: .220 BA, 25 HR.

Yr	Tm	AB	R	HR	RBI	SB	BA	xBA	OBP	SLG	OPS	vL	vR	bb%	ct%	h%	Eye	G	L	F	PX	xPX	hr/f	Spd	SBO	SB%	#Wk	DOM	DIS	RC/G	RAR	BPV	BPX	R$
09	aa	533	48	13	78	5	272	266	314	419	733			6	80	32	0.30				100			86	7%	62%				4.55		39	80	$12
10	LAA *	547	71	24	84	2	237	275	287	421	709	167	200	7	72	29	0.25	43	29	29	130	31	0%	100	6%	30%	5	0%	100%	3.91	-9.7	36	78	$11
11	LAA	539	65	29	87	9	254	276	291	477	768	748	778	4	78	28	0.21	46	16	38	150	135	18%	78	13%	69%	27	56%	15%	4.61	1.7	65	144	$19
12	LAA	544	66	32	95	4	268	248	317	491	808	808	808	6	72	32	0.24	45	16	39	144	132	21%	92	7%	44%	27	52%	37%	5.20	11.0	45	113	$21
13	LAA	620	85	34	100	5	234	256	294	453	747	923	685	8	70	28	0.29	46	17	37	158	132	21%	82	5%	71%	27	52%	26%	4.43	-1.1	50	125	$19
1st Half		319	48	18	51	2	251	263	323	470	793	832	778	10	73	29	0.40	49	17	34	154	117	23%	75	5%	50%	14	50%	29%	5.07	5.4	59	148	$22
2nd Half		301	37	16	49	3	216	246	265	435	700	1012	581	6	67	26	0.20	42	18	40	163	150	19%	93	6%	100%	13	54%	23%	3.80	-6.5	42	105	$16
14	Proj	**582**	**74**	**29**	**95**	**5**	**246**	**252**	**297**	**448**	**745**	**834**	**710**	**7**	**72**	**29**	**0.25**	**46**	**17**	**38**	**143**	**135**	**18%**	**86**	**7%**	**63%**				**4.42**	**-3.1**	**41**	**103**	**$19**

Tuiasosopo,Matt

Age	28	Bats	R	Pos	LF	Health	A	LIMA Plan	F
Ht	6' 2"	Wt	225			PT/Exp	C	Rand Var	-5
						Consist	C	MM	3101

Mashed in small 1H sample, then became big liability down stretch. Truth is in the middle. Massive holes in swing, inflated h% make even .240-ish BA fool's gold. Sexy power minimized by huge GB tilt, so more AB won't yield linear HR gains. An end-gamer in the deepest of leagues, mainly those with vowels as a scoring category.

Yr	Tm	AB	R	HR	RBI	SB	BA	xBA	OBP	SLG	OPS	vL	vR	bb%	ct%	h%	Eye	G	L	F	PX	xPX	hr/f	Spd	SBO	SB%	#Wk	DOM	DIS	RC/G	RAR	BPV	BPX	R$
09	SEA *	248	34	9	28	2	219	193	302	381	683	800	200	11	58	34	0.28	50	6	44	144	120	13%	78	5%	66%	3	67%	33%	3.73	-1.8	-4	-8	$1
10	SEA *	270	31	7	26	1	190	212	278	309	587	487	571	11	66	26	0.36	44	19	37	96	107	14%	101	6%	39%	20	15%	65%	2.63	-11.6	-3	-7	-$2
11	aaa	439	43	8	45	6	164	194	242	264	506			9	62	24	0.28				87			104	10%	73%				1.95		-28	-62	-$5
12	aaa	418	34	9	41	2	191	189	256	281	537			8	66	27	0.25				70			80	7%	31%				2.17		-39	-98	-$3
13	DET	164	26	7	30	0	244	232	351	415	765	706	892	13	65	33	0.44	58	19	23	136	116	28%	97	0%	0%	24	33%	50%	4.81	4.0	27	68	$3
1st Half		71	12	3	17	0	338	304	453	563	1017	977	1104	17	73	43	0.79	42	31	27	178	158	21%	87	0%	0%	12	58%	25%	9.84	10.7	98	245	$6
2nd Half		93	14	4	13	0	172	181	252	301	554	521	633	10	59	24	0.26	73	7	20	96	76	36%	114	0%	0%	12	8%	75%	2.34	-5.1	-31	-78	$0
14	Proj	**187**	**24**	**5**	**26**	**1**	**223**	**208**	**314**	**346**	**660**	**633**	**694**	**11**	**64**	**32**	**0.34**	**53**	**18**	**29**	**101**	**109**	**16%**	**98**	**3%**	**47%**				**3.45**	**-3.3**	**-24**	**-59**	**$3**

Tulowitzki,Troy

Age	29	Bats	R	Pos	SS	Health	F	LIMA Plan	B+
Ht	6' 3"	Wt	215			PT/Exp	C	Rand Var	-3
						Consist	D	MM	4145

When healthy, a top SS option due to steady, elite power and solid Eye. Continued fading green light means days of double-digit SB are likely over, but you don't draft him for wheels anyway. Two quibbles: .850 OPS on road reflects dependence on thin air, and has yet to post consecutive 500-AB seasons. Okay, BIG quibbles.

Yr	Tm	AB	R	HR	RBI	SB	BA	xBA	OBP	SLG	OPS	vL	vR	bb%	ct%	h%	Eye	G	L	F	PX	xPX	hr/f	Spd	SBO	SB%	#Wk	DOM	DIS	RC/G	RAR	BPV	BPX	R$
09	COL	543	101	32	92	20	297	293	377	552	930	901	941	12	79	32	0.65	42	18	40	149	134	18%	149	18%	65%	26	62%	23%	7.31	58.5	107	218	$30
10	COL	470	89	27	95	11	315	309	381	568	949	990	930	9	83	33	0.62	45	15	40	158	142	17%	114	10%	85%	21	76%	0%	8.05	57.7	115	250	$30
11	COL	537	81	30	105	9	302	307	372	544	916	1049	864	10	85	31	0.75	42	20	39	150	126	17%	90	8%	75%	26	81%	19%	7.33	56.6	110	244	$30
12	COL *	208	35	10	31	2	286	288	348	501	849	671	918	9	88	29	0.76	46	17	37	118	98	13%	124	7%	50%	9	67%	0%	6.05	15.0	101	253	$8
13	COL	446	72	25	82	1	312	288	391	540	931	906	938	11	81	34	0.67	42	21	38	148	147	18%	84	1%	100%	24	75%	17%	7.82	51.9	92	230	$25
1st Half		222	41	16	51	0	347	316	408	635	1043	970	1082	9	84	36	0.64	41	20	39	178	176	22%	86	0%	0%	11	91%	0%	10.12	37.8	124	310	$31
2nd Half		224	31	9	31	1	277	259	372	446	819	803	816	13	78	32	0.69	42	21	36	115	117	14%	86	1%	100%	13	62%	31%	5.89	15.4	59	148	$19
14	Proj	**470**	**76**	**26**	**81**	**2**	**305**	**292**	**378**	**532**	**911**	**874**	**924**	**10**	**84**	**32**	**0.71**	**43**	**19**	**38**	**141**	**128**	**17%**	**101**	**3%**	**53%**				**7.27**	**49.1**	**88**	**219**	**$26**

STEPHEN NICKRAND

Turner,Justin

Age 29	Bats R	Pos 3B	Health B	LIMA Plan D	
Ht 6' 0"	Wt 210		PT/Exp D	Rand Var -3	
			Consist A	MM 2121	

This once was a place you'd look to fill out your middle-infield in deep leagues with a bat that wouldn't harm. Now as a 3B with minimal power, mediocre speed, and eroding plate control, damage avoidance is his only value now. Don't fall in love with BA trend; it's a h% product, not a reflection of skill.

Yr	Tm	AB	R	HR	RBI	SB	BA	xBA	OBP	SLG	OPS	vL	vR	bb%	ct%	h%	Eye	G	L	F	PX	xPX	hr/f	Spd	SBO	SB%	#Wk	DOM	DIS	RC/G	RAR	BPV	BPX	R$
09	BAL *	405	48	2	40	8	266	327	321	342	663	929	214	7	89	29	0.74	67	27	7	56	28	0%	87	11%	63%	5	40%	40%	3.74	1.0	45	92	$7
10	2 TM *	413	49	8	30	5	243	269	286	366	652	143	273	6	84	27	0.38	57	14	29	86	84	0%	91	9%	57%	4	50%	50%	3.45	-2.5	46	100	$5
11	NYM *	475	53	4	52	7	257	276	315	355	671	629	715	8	86	29	0.61	49	23	28	75	60	4%	87	7%	78%	24	46%	33%	3.86	2.8	48	107	$8
12	NYM	171	20	2	19	1	269	283	319	392	711	650	768	5	86	30	0.38	47	24	29	86	68	5%	93	5%	50%	25	40%	20%	4.10	2.2	52	130	$2
13	NYM	200	12	2	16	0	280	257	319	385	704	668	735	5	83	33	0.32	46	22	32	80	132	4%	92	2%	0%	22	45%	32%	4.24	3.3	36	90	$1
1st Half		94	3	0	6	0	266	212	310	330	640	642	630	6	85	31	0.43	51	20	30	57	121	0%	87	0%	0%	12	42%	33%	3.55	-0.4	26	65	-$1
2nd Half		106	9	2	10	0	292	269	324	434	758	700	804	5	81	35	0.25	42	24	34	101	142	7%	93	4%	0%	10	50%	30%	4.87	3.5	44	110	$3
14	Proj	**165**	**15**	**2**	**15**	**1**	**272**	**269**	**322**	**382**	**705**	**655**	**743**	**6**	**84**	**31**	**0.39**	**46**	**23**	**30**	**82**	**100**	**4%**	**91**	**5%**	**47%**				**4.13**	**0.8**	**33**	**82**	**$1**

Uggla,Dan

Age 34	Bats R	Pos 2B	Health A	LIMA Plan D+	
Ht 5' 11"	Wt 205		PT/Exp A	Rand Var +4	
			Consist B	MM 4205	

One of the things we don't talk about in these days of rising pitcher dominance is the inverse effect this has on certain batters. Players who have holes in their skills set -- especially free-swingers -- are most vulnerable to being cut down by the rising tide of strikeout hurlers. For Uggla, this news is not good. DN: 350 AB, 15 HR.

Yr	Tm	AB	R	HR	RBI	SB	BA	xBA	OBP	SLG	OPS	vL	vR	bb%	ct%	h%	Eye	G	L	F	PX	xPX	hr/f	Spd	SBO	SB%	#Wk	DOM	DIS	RC/G	RAR	BPV	BPX	R$
09	FLA	564	84	31	90	2	243	255	354	459	813	752	832	14	73	28	0.61	37	17	46	142	135	16%	85	2%	67%	27	48%	26%	5.39	29.0	63	129	$13
10	FLA	589	100	33	105	4	287	269	369	508	877	983	845	12	75	33	0.52	40	18	43	152	146	17%	90	3%	80%	27	59%	19%	6.73	50.7	73	159	$27
11	ATL	600	88	36	82	1	233	252	311	453	764	648	808	9	74	25	0.40	41	15	43	147	127	19%	100	3%	25%	27	63%	26%	4.51	15.5	64	142	$16
12	ATL	523	86	19	78	4	220	222	348	384	732	776	710	15	68	29	0.56	34	20	46	127	119	11%	80	4%	57%	27	44%	37%	4.21	8.9	30	75	$10
13	ATL	448	60	22	55	2	179	201	309	362	671	599	692	15	62	23	0.45	40	13	47	140	138	17%	119	2%	100%	26	31%	54%	3.38	-3.9	26	65	$2
1st Half		254	41	14	32	0	205	210	327	413	740	790	729	15	60	28	0.45	37	17	46	161	163	20%	147	0%	0%	14	36%	43%	4.33	5.0	45	113	$7
2nd Half		194	19	8	23	2	144	184	262	294	556	359	643	14	64	17	0.45	43	9	48	115	107	13%	67	4%	100%	12	25%	67%	2.34	-8.8	-1	-3	-$4
14	Proj	**393**	**55**	**18**	**53**	**2**	**213**	**215**	**331**	**390**	**721**	**669**	**739**	**14**	**65**	**28**	**0.46**	**39**	**16**	**45**	**135**	**128**	**15%**	**91**	**3%**	**71%**				**4.06**	**4.4**	**19**	**47**	**$7**

Upton,B.J.

Age 29	Bats R	Pos CF	Health B	LIMA Plan B+	
Ht 6' 3"	Wt 185		PT/Exp A	Rand Var +2	
			Consist C	MM 3405	

A matter of adjusting to a new league? More likely, nagging groin injury likely zapped power and speed. Steadiness of those skills in prior three seasons provides rationale for a sizable bounceback. BA recovery to .240 norm a solid bet with likely h% correction, ct% recovery. Mine here for profit... UP: 20 HR, 30 SB.

Yr	Tm	AB	R	HR	RBI	SB	BA	xBA	OBP	SLG	OPS	vL	vR	bb%	ct%	h%	Eye	G	L	F	PX	xPX	hr/f	Spd	SBO	SB%	#Wk	DOM	DIS	RC/G	RAR	BPV	BPX	R$
09	TAM	560	79	11	55	42	241	233	313	373	686	572	734	9	73	31	0.38	44	15	40	99	113	7%	144	39%	75%	26	35%	46%	3.89	-3.5	34	69	$20
10	TAM	536	89	18	62	42	237	247	322	424	745	919	664	11	69	31	0.41	40	17	44	149	119	11%	135	38%	82%	27	44%	22%	4.68	9.5	62	135	$23
11	TAM	560	82	23	81	36	243	244	331	429	759	746	763	11	71	30	0.44	41	18	41	136	134	14%	133	31%	75%	27	52%	26%	4.70	10.2	58	129	$24
12	TAM	573	79	28	78	31	246	246	298	454	752	792	737	7	71	30	0.27	40	19	41	145	105	17%	126	29%	84%	25	48%	28%	4.70	10.3	52	130	$24
13	ATL	391	30	9	26	12	184	190	268	289	557	449	598	10	61	27	0.29	45	19	36	93	112	10%	97	18%	71%	25	12%	72%	2.40	-21.5	-28	-70	$0
1st Half		243	19	8	19	7	177	205	275	317	592	493	634	12	64	24	0.38	46	16	38	117	117	13%	99	19%	64%	14	21%	57%	2.64	-12.3	4	10	$1
2nd Half		148	11	1	7	5	196	169	252	243	495	370	539	7	57	33	0.17	43	24	33	51	104	4%	101	17%	83%	11	0%	91%	2.02	-10.1	-83	-208	-$3
14	Proj	**507**	**71**	**18**	**64**	**27**	**236**	**229**	**307**	**394**	**701**	**650**	**720**	**9**	**69**	**31**	**0.33**	**43**	**19**	**38**	**120**	**113**	**14%**	**114**	**26%**	**78%**				**4.06**	**-1.7**	**26**	**66**	**$20**

Upton,Justin

Age 26	Bats R	Pos LF RF	Health A	LIMA Plan A	
Ht 6' 2"	Wt 205		PT/Exp A	Rand Var 0	
			Consist B	MM 4325	

Looked like an elite bat in April (1.134 OPS, 297 PX) and Aug (1.010 OPS, 219 PX), but couldn't manage an OPS above .760 or PX above 109 in any other month. 2011-12 shows he can make decent contact. With 2nd half consistency, skills say there is an age 26 breakout in there... UP: 40 HR

Yr	Tm	AB	R	HR	RBI	SB	BA	xBA	OBP	SLG	OPS	vL	vR	bb%	ct%	h%	Eye	G	L	F	PX	xPX	hr/f	Spd	SBO	SB%	#Wk	DOM	DIS	RC/G	RAR	BPV	BPX	R$
09	ARI	526	84	26	86	20	300	282	366	532	899	1208	805	9	74	36	0.40	45	19	36	152	122	19%	141	17%	80%	25	60%	20%	7.12	44.8	81	165	$28
10	ARI	495	73	17	69	18	273	243	356	442	799	768	808	11	69	36	0.42	41	19	39	131	134	12%	125	17%	69%	25	44%	36%	5.42	19.6	44	96	$20
11	ARI	592	105	31	88	21	289	280	369	529	898	929	889	9	79	32	0.47	37	18	45	160	142	15%	124	19%	70%	27	81%	15%	6.53	41.7	100	222	$33
12	ARI	554	107	17	67	18	280	250	355	430	785	830	766	10	78	33	0.52	44	21	36	96	107	11%	126	15%	69%	27	48%	22%	5.29	19.6	50	125	$24
13	ATL	558	94	27	70	8	263	254	354	464	818	994	762	12	71	32	0.47	41	22	38	145	110	18%	108	5%	89%	27	56%	33%	5.69	26.4	59	148	$22
1st Half		282	50	15	37	6	245	241	353	447	799	1002	734	14	68	30	0.53	44	17	38	146	115	20%	117	8%	86%	14	50%	36%	5.39	11.5	56	140	$22
2nd Half		276	44	12	33	2	283	268	349	482	831	984	789	9	74	34	0.39	37	25	37	144	105	16%	100	3%	100%	13	62%	31%	6.02	15.6	61	153	$22
14	Proj	**564**	**98**	**29**	**88**	**16**	**276**	**270**	**356**	**496**	**852**	**969**	**812**	**10**	**75**	**32**	**0.47**	**41**	**21**	**38**	**150**	**115**	**18%**	**112**	**14%**	**75%**				**6.09**	**33.7**	**76**	**191**	**$29**

Uribe,Juan

Age 35	Bats R	Pos 3B	Health C	LIMA Plan D+	
Ht 6' 0"	Wt 235		PT/Exp D	Rand Var -5	
			Consist D	MM 3213	

A resurgence at age 34 after two years of futility? Not so fast. Hit rate gods deserve full credit for highest BA since '09. Power rebound is more sustainable given good PX. That pop is enough to make him rosterable, but the lack of a second rosterable skill relegates him to the ranks of the end-gamers and injury replacements.

Yr	Tm	AB	R	HR	RBI	SB	BA	xBA	OBP	SLG	OPS	vL	vR	bb%	ct%	h%	Eye	G	L	F	PX	xPX	hr/f	Spd	SBO	SB%	#Wk	DOM	DIS	RC/G	RAR	BPV	BPX	R$
09	SF	398	50	16	55	3	289	282	329	495	824	760	843	6	79	33	0.30	39	21	40	131	117	13%	101	4%	75%	27	52%	30%	5.86	20.7	67	137	$13
10	SF	521	64	24	85	1	248	264	310	440	749	682	766	8	82	26	0.49	40	15	44	119	115	12%	77	2%	33%	27	59%	26%	4.51	8.0	66	143	$13
11	LA	270	21	4	28	2	204	216	264	293	557	485	582	6	78	25	0.28	42	17	41	69	76	5%	46	4%	100%	15	13%	47%	2.38	-13.5	-5	-11	-$2
12	LA	162	15	2	17	0	191	218	258	284	542	385	640	7	77	24	0.35	48	17	35	72	81	5%	53	3%	0%	20	15%	45%	2.18	-9.3	0	0	-$3
13	LA	388	47	12	50	5	278	259	331	438	769	781	765	7	79	33	0.37	43	20	37	111	118	11%	96	5%	100%	27	37%	41%	5.19	13.1	50	125	$13
1st Half		151	20	3	16	1	265	236	351	384	735	645	761	12	78	32	0.61	46	18	36	91	132	7%	79	2%	100%	14	43%	36%	4.72	3.2	34	85	$5
2nd Half		237	27	9	34	4	287	270	316	473	788	880	766	4	80	33	0.21	41	22	38	123	110	13%	102	7%	100%	13	31%	46%	5.44	9.7	58	145	$18
14	Proj	**325**	**35**	**10**	**39**	**3**	**244**	**251**	**301**	**397**	**698**	**619**	**729**	**7**	**79**	**28**	**0.35**	**44**	**19**	**38**	**106**	**103**	**10%**	**74**	**4%**	**81%**				**3.99**	**0.2**	**36**	**89**	**$7**

Urrutia,Henry

Age 27	Bats L	Pos DH	Health A	LIMA Plan D	
Ht 6' 5"	Wt 200		PT/Exp F	Rand Var +1	
			Consist F	MM 1421	

0-2-.276 in 58 AB at BAL. Former Cuban star showed good plate control, extra-base power at Double-A prior to his recall. xBA says BA is his best skill at the moment. HR ceiling limited by lack of loft in swing; 2H Spd was silenced by red light on bases. For now, buy for BA/SB and look elsewhere for pop.

Yr	Tm	AB	R	HR	RBI	SB	BA	xBA	OBP	SLG	OPS	vL	vR	bb%	ct%	h%	Eye	G	L	F	PX	xPX	hr/f	Spd	SBO	SB%	#Wk	DOM	DIS	RC/G	RAR	BPV	BPX	R$
09																																		
10																																		
11																																		
12																																		
13	BAL *	372	41	7	39	1	291	305	334	408	742	286	627	6	81	34	0.34	55	34	11	82	39	0%	127	2%	38%	7	0%	57%	4.85	9.0	41	103	$10
1st Half		214	27	6	28	1	301	255	359	450	810			8	78	36	0.42				111			96	3%	38%				5.80		50	125	$14
2nd Half		158	15	2	11	0	277	297	297	351	648	286	627	3	84	32	0.18	55	34	11	45	39	0%	158	0%	0%	7	0%	57%	3.68	-1.5	27	68	$5
14	Proj	**200**	**21**	**3**	**19**	**3**	**287**	**266**	**322**	**388**	**710**	**805**	**698**	**5**	**82**	**34**	**0.29**	**52**	**24**	**24**	**68**	**35**	**8%**	**140**	**9%**	**71%**				**4.44**	**-0.4**	**20**	**49**	**$7**

Utley,Chase

Age 35	Bats L	Pos 2B	Health F	LIMA Plan A	
Ht 6' 1"	Wt 200		PT/Exp C	Rand Var -2	
			Consist A	MM 3425	

Nice bounce back from '11-'12 knee woes, even tapped into some long-dormant elite power in 1H. With 400 AB average last four years, days of 10+ SB or 20+ HR are probably gone. There's enough left here for him to remain a top 2B choice, just not a cornerstone. In short, heed health grade before betting on a repeat.

Yr	Tm	AB	R	HR	RBI	SB	BA	xBA	OBP	SLG	OPS	vL	vR	bb%	ct%	h%	Eye	G	L	F	PX	xPX	hr/f	Spd	SBO	SB%	#Wk	DOM	DIS	RC/G	RAR	BPV	BPX	R$
09	PHI	571	112	31	93	23	282	273	397	508	905	962	877	13	81	30	0.80	34	18	48	134	152	14%	118	12%	100%	26	65%	12%	7.11	55.5	94	192	$30
10	PHI	425	75	16	65	13	275	279	387	445	832	1003	752	13	85	29	1.00	41	20	39	104	127	11%	105	11%	87%	21	48%	5%	5.89	27.1	83	180	$18
11	PHI	398	54	11	44	14	259	258	344	425	769	607	829	9	88	27	0.83	41	13	46	100	132	7%	121	13%	100%	19	58%	5%	4.96	15.1	89	198	$12
12	PHI	301	48	11	45	11	256	278	365	429	793	679	869	13	86	27	1.00	42	21	36	102	110	12%	91	13%	92%	15	60%	13%	5.29	14.4	79	198	$11
13	PHI	476	73	18	69	8	284	269	348	475	823	754	855	9	83	31	0.57	38	20	43	119	126	11%	115	8%	73%	24	67%	21%	5.80	28.9	82	205	$21
1st Half		201	33	11	30	6	284	278	345	517	863	816	886	9	84	29	0.58	35	18	46	140	159	14%	99	15%	75%	11	82%	9%	6.30	14.9	95	238	$21
2nd Half		275	40	7	39	2	284	263	346	444	789	714	832	9	83	32	0.57	40	20	40	103	102	8%	121	4%	67%	13	54%	31%	5.43	13.4	71	178	$21
14	Proj	**421**	**65**	**15**	**60**	**8**	**272**	**269**	**358**	**454**	**811**	**735**	**850**	**10**	**85**	**29**	**0.75**	**40**	**19**	**41**	**112**	**124**	**10%**	**111**	**8%**	**82%**				**5.56**	**22.5**	**84**	**211**	**$17**

STEPHEN NICKRAND

Valbuena,Luis

Age 28	Bats L	Pos 3B	Health A	LIMA Plan C	
Ht 5' 10"	Wt 170		PT/Exp C	Rand Var +3	
			Consist A	MM 3015	

Low BA, repeated MLB failures will keep many away, but surging plate control, h% correction are recipes for turning historically poor BA into an acceptable one. Continued small-but-steady growth in power skills also points to a HR spike, especially if xPX or new flyball trend holds. UP: .270 BA, 20 HR

Yr	Tm	AB	R	HR	RBI	SB	BA	xBA	OBP	SLG	OPS	vL	vR	bb%	ct%	h%	Eye	G	L	F	PX	xPX	hr/f	Spd	SBO	SB%	#Wk	DOM	DIS	RC/G	RAR	BPV	BPX	R$
09	CLE *	446	64	12	41	4	255	269	315	420	735	661	720	8	78	30	0.40	41	22	37	111	92	10%	124	10%	40%	23	57%	30%	4.30	4.1	56	114	$8
10	CLE *	371	39	6	39	2	209	234	290	312	602	855	467	10	77	26	0.49	47	18	35	79	67	3%	81	5%	55%	23	30%	61%	2.89	-12.8	17	37	$0
11	CLE *	463	51	13	56	5	244	205	296	368	664	750	412	7	73	31	0.28	42	12	45	93	100	7%	107	8%	60%	9	22%	56%	3.61	-5.2	15	33	$8
12	CHC *	476	52	9	49	1	228	242	309	361	670	624	657	10	75	28	0.47	43	21	35	102	82	5%	89	3%	17%	17	41%	24%	3.59	-5.8	33	83	$3
13	CHC	331	34	12	37	1	218	239	331	378	708	647	715	14	81	23	0.84	40	16	45	104	131	10%	95	5%	20%	22	64%	27%	3.84	-1.6	65	163	$2
1st Half		204	22	6	23	1	235	240	339	387	726	596	743	14	81	26	0.82	36	17	47	103	142	8%	99	5%	33%	14	64%	21%	4.24	1.7	65	163	$5
2nd Half		127	12	6	14	0	189	228	304	362	666	718	668	14	81	19	0.88	46	13	41	106	115	14%	96	6%	0%	8	63%	38%	3.25	-3.0	68	170	-$1
14	Proj	**421**	**48**	**14**	**50**	**1**	**245**	**240**	**335**	**401**	**736**	**761**	**732**	**12**	**79**	**28**	**0.61**	**41**	**17**	**42**	**107**	**103**	**10%**	**90**	**4%**	**12%**				**4.32**	**4.4**	**35**	**87**	**$7**

Valencia,Danny

Age 29	Bats R	Pos DH	Health A	LIMA Plan D	
Ht 6' 2"	Wt 220		PT/Exp C	Rand Var 0	
			Consist D	MM 3021	

8-23-.304 in 161 AB at BAL. Power burst captures attention, but thank Camden Yards (.676 Slg) and first-time surge against LHP (.639 Slg) for that. Power collapsed on road and vs. RHP, making '13 PX more of an outlier than an upside to chase. 3B/DH types who can only be used at home against lefties don't get PT spikes.

Yr	Tm	AB	R	HR	RBI	SB	BA	xBA	OBP	SLG	OPS	vL	vR	bb%	ct%	h%	Eye	G	L	F	PX	xPX	hr/f	Spd	SBO	SB%	#Wk	DOM	DIS	RC/G	RAR	BPV	BPX	R$
09	a/a	487	65	11	58	0	247	272	292	399	691			6	82	28	0.35				102			99	4%	0%				3.78		52	106	$6
10	MIN *	484	46	7	57	3	285	253	327	397	723	967	713	6	82	33	0.36	43	19	38	84	89	7%	81	3%	100%	19	63%	26%	4.67	2.3	35	76	$12
11	MIN	564	63	15	72	2	246	252	294	383	677	822	626	7	82	28	0.39	46	18	36	93	85	9%	92	6%	25%	27	41%	26%	3.68	-13.8	45	100	$10
12	2 AL *	471	39	9	55	1	210	228	237	326	563	592	448	3	79	25	0.16	43	18	39	82	114	6%	77	8%	11%	13	23%	62%	2.34	-31.9	12	30	$0
13	BAL *	423	48	19	59	1	258	278	292	471	763	1031	672	5	78	29	0.22	38	22	40	148	142	15%	92	5%	18%	17	47%	35%	4.57	0.8	69	173	$11
1st Half		218	29	13	33	0	245	283	280	494	774	870	754	5	75	27	0.19	32	23	45	177	167	20%	76	3%	0%	7	43%	57%	4.56	0.4	77	193	$12
2nd Half		205	19	6	26	1	272	272	304	448	752	1127	630	5	81	31	0.25	41	21	38	121	129	13%	104	7%	24%	10	50%	20%	4.56	0.3	63	158	$11
14	Proj	**166**	**17**	**5**	**21**	**0**	**247**	**261**	**281**	**417**	**698**	**857**	**562**	**5**	**80**	**28**	**0.25**	**41**	**20**	**39**	**118**	**122**	**10%**	**91**	**6%**	**24%**				**3.85**	**-3.3**	**42**	**104**	**$4**

Van Slyke,Scott

Age 27	Bats R	Pos LF	Health A	LIMA Plan D+	
Ht 6' 5"	Wt 250		PT/Exp C	Rand Var -4	
			Consist D	MM 4111	

7-19-.240 in 129 AB at LA. AAA masher finally got extended MLB look. PROs: Crazy 1H PX and FB rate with LA showcase power potential, 2H bb% spike. CONs: Holes in swing make him a BA drag, power merely average in 2H. With opportunity, consistency, a tantalizing end-game power speculation... UP: 20+ HR

Yr	Tm	AB	R	HR	RBI	SB	BA	xBA	OBP	SLG	OPS	vL	vR	bb%	ct%	h%	Eye	G	L	F	PX	xPX	hr/f	Spd	SBO	SB%	#Wk	DOM	DIS	RC/G	RAR	BPV	BPX	R$
09	aaa																																	
10	a/a	255	21	3	22	3	188	232	222	270	491			4	79	22	0.21				58			110	11%	52%				1.82		8	17	-$3
11	aa	457	57	14	65	4	281	265	345	464	809			9	74	35	0.37				144			85	9%	41%				5.45		55	122	$15
12	LA *	412	45	13	47	4	234	249	285	396	681	538	483	7	77	27	0.31	44	18	38	115	85	13%	70	9%	51%	7	29%	14%	3.65	-5.0	36	90	$6
13	LA *	333	49	15	50	6	257	233	358	460	818	764	850	14	66	35	0.46	36	17	47	166	147	16%	80	10%	64%	18	44%	44%	5.55	14.7	48	120	$11
1st Half		200	32	12	33	2	270	251	350	531	881	1005	775	11	65	36	0.35	29	16	55	212	206	21%	66	6%	61%	8	63%	25%	6.40	13.7	74	185	$15
2nd Half		133	17	3	18	4	236	207	370	354	724	509	941	18	66	33	0.63	44	19	37	98	78	6%	99	13%	65%	10	30%	60%	4.32	1.2	10	25	$5
14	Proj	**218**	**27**	**10**	**29**	**3**	**248**	**249**	**331**	**446**	**777**	**730**	**823**	**11**	**72**	**30**	**0.44**	**40**	**18**	**42**	**147**	**113**	**15%**	**79**	**10%**	**60%**				**4.89**	**5.7**	**47**	**118**	**$7**

Venable,Will

Age 31	Bats L	Pos RF CF	Health A	LIMA Plan B+	
Ht 6' 2"	Wt 210		PT/Exp C	Rand Var 0	
			Consist B	MM 3525	

3 reasons to bet against a strong follow-up to this 20/20 breakout: 1) HR spike driven by unsustainable hr/f, still no loft in swing; 2) xPX in line with previous power skills, making high PX an anomaly; 3) Inflated 2H h% was primary reason for late BA, OBP, SB jumps. So bank on 20 SB, but 10 HR is more likely than another 20.

Yr	Tm	AB	R	HR	RBI	SB	BA	xBA	OBP	SLG	OPS	vL	vR	bb%	ct%	h%	Eye	G	L	F	PX	xPX	hr/f	Spd	SBO	SB%	#Wk	DOM	DIS	RC/G	RAR	BPV	BPX	R$
09	SD *	493	63	20	61	7	233	240	291	415	706	534	836	8	70	29	0.27	44	16	40	126	119	15%	109	7%	87%	18	39%	39%	4.05	-8.2	30	61	$8
10	SD	392	60	13	51	29	245	218	324	408	732	523	764	10	67	33	0.35	39	17	44	116	109	11%	160	33%	81%	25	40%	48%	4.54	-0.7	33	72	$17
11	SD *	428	56	10	50	28	237	241	293	385	678	436	742	7	74	30	0.31	43	21	36	101	100	9%	144	30%	90%	26	35%	35%	3.99	-7.9	38	84	$14
12	SD	417	62	9	45	24	264	270	335	429	765	684	780	9	77	32	0.44	48	22	29	111	97	10%	128	28%	80%	27	52%	26%	4.96	4.3	57	143	$16
13	SD	481	64	22	53	22	268	277	312	484	796	833	786	6	75	31	0.25	47	21	32	142	107	20%	131	26%	79%	27	52%	30%	5.20	8.3	68	170	$23
1st Half		217	28	10	29	9	221	260	262	424	686	618	704	5	75	25	0.22	48	17	34	127	124	19%	126	30%	75%	14	36%	36%	3.58	-5.9	52	130	$15
2nd Half		264	36	12	24	13	307	291	349	534	883	955	860	6	76	37	0.27	46	25	29	155	93	21%	132	24%	81%	13	69%	23%	6.87	17.6	81	203	$30
14	Proj	**501**	**69**	**14**	**56**	**24**	**262**	**256**	**317**	**426**	**744**	**708**	**752**	**7**	**75**	**32**	**0.30**	**46**	**21**	**33**	**114**	**103**	**11%**	**136**	**24%**	**83%**				**4.69**	**3.6**	**54**	**134**	**$21**

Viciedo,Dayan

Age 25	Bats R	Pos LF	Health A	LIMA Plan B+	
Ht 5' 11"	Wt 230		PT/Exp B	Rand Var -1	
			Consist A	MM 3125	

Nice raw power ceiling remains dormant due to poor pitch recognition, continued groundball tilt, early '13 oblique issue. xPX growth underscores HR upside, as does growing OPS vs. RHers. Power dip vs. LHP stands out as an anomaly. Still just 25; with a little more consistency, there's a power breakout lurking... UP: 30 HR.

Yr	Tm	AB	R	HR	RBI	SB	BA	xBA	OBP	SLG	OPS	vL	vR	bb%	ct%	h%	Eye	G	L	F	PX	xPX	hr/f	Spd	SBO	SB%	#Wk	DOM	DIS	RC/G	RAR	BPV	BPX	R$
09	aa	504	65	12	70	5	267	248	297	377	675			4	81	31	0.22				70			85	5%	68%				3.88		16	33	$12
10	CHW *	447	50	23	50	2	264	265	282	467	749	960	729	2	75	30	0.10	42	19	39	138	124	16%	77	3%	62%	13	38%	46%	4.53	7.1	40	87	$12
11	CHW *	554	61	20	72	3	271	251	332	433	765	1020	469	8	79	31	0.43	58	13	29	112	62	4%	68	2%	71%	5	20%	80%	5.02	16.4	45	100	$16
12	CHW	505	64	25	78	0	255	261	300	444	744	1033	650	5	76	29	0.23	47	22	31	118	97	20%	69	2%	0%	27	48%	41%	4.39	6.1	33	83	$14
13	CHW	441	43	14	56	0	265	253	304	426	731	709	738	5	78	31	0.24	47	19	34	111	102	12%	92	0%	0%	25	44%	40%	4.49	6.4	40	100	$10
1st Half		207	19	5	23	0	237	248	272	377	649	786	601	5	78	28	0.22	43	21	35	97	110	9%	95	0%	0%	12	42%	42%	3.42	-3.7	28	70	$4
2nd Half		234	24	9	33	0	291	254	331	470	801	637	856	6	78	34	0.27	51	16	33	123	95	15%	88	0%	0%	13	46%	38%	5.59	10.2	49	123	$15
14	Proj	**515**	**56**	**21**	**70**	**1**	**258**	**258**	**304**	**436**	**740**	**877**	**688**	**6**	**78**	**29**	**0.27**	**48**	**18**	**34**	**120**	**96**	**16%**	**81**	**1%**	**49%**				**4.47**	**6.8**	**33**	**83**	**$14**

Victorino,Shane

Age 33	Bats B	Pos RF	Health B	LIMA Plan B+	
Ht 5' 9"	Wt 190		PT/Exp A	Rand Var -3	
			Consist C	MM 2535	

It's easy to see the 15 HR, 20 SB, near-.300 BA and view him as a $25 lock, but that BA won't repeat with dwindling plate control. Waning Spd, age make 20 SB his new baseline. xPX casts pessimistic shadow on 2H power surge. Still a premium multi-category producer, but ground your expectations at .280, 10 HR, 20 SB.

Yr	Tm	AB	R	HR	RBI	SB	BA	xBA	OBP	SLG	OPS	vL	vR	bb%	ct%	h%	Eye	G	L	F	PX	xPX	hr/f	Spd	SBO	SB%	#Wk	DOM	DIS	RC/G	RAR	BPV	BPX	R$
09	PHI	620	102	10	62	25	292	296	358	445	803	844	787	9	89	32	0.85	45	22	33	90	59	5%	136	18%	76%	27	70%	11%	5.66	24.3	87	178	$25
10	PHI	587	84	18	69	34	259	281	327	429	756	921	692	8	87	27	0.67	45	17	38	100	86	9%	125	26%	85%	26	62%	15%	4.87	10.2	82	178	$24
11	PHI	519	95	17	61	19	279	286	355	491	847	1032	789	10	88	29	0.87	42	16	42	121	91	9%	147	16%	86%	25	72%	12%	6.16	27.8	114	253	$23
12	2 NL	595	72	11	55	39	255	260	321	383	704	906	627	8	87	28	0.66	46	18	36	78	72	6%	126	28%	87%	27	48%	30%	4.35	1.2	65	163	$22
13	BOS	477	82	15	61	21	294	276	351	451	801	861	769	5	84	32	0.33	43	22	35	102	70	11%	104	20%	88%	25	40%	24%	5.48	16.0	62	155	$27
1st Half		206	32	3	21	9	291	265	336	393	730	658	771	6	87	32	0.52	46	22	32	68	57	5%	114	18%	82%	13	38%	31%	4.85	2.3	51	128	$18
2nd Half		271	50	12	40	12	295	284	323	494	817	994	768	4	82	32	0.23	40	23	37	129	80	15%	92	21%	92%	12	42%	17%	5.96	11.4	70	175	$33
14	Proj	**490**	**78**	**12**	**57**	**20**	**280**	**270**	**343**	**431**	**774**	**885**	**724**	**7**	**86**	**31**	**0.50**	**44**	**20**	**36**	**95**	**74**	**8%**	**124**	**18%**	**84%**				**5.11**	**9.3**	**77**	**191**	**$23**

Villar,Jonathan

Age 23	Bats B	Pos SS	Health A	LIMA Plan C+	
Ht 6' 1"	Wt 195		PT/Exp C	Rand Var -2	
			Consist A	MM 1505	

1-8-.243-18 in 210 AB at HOU. Speedster put slick wheels to use quickly. Solid walk rate should foster continued OBP growth, which will keep those swipes coming. Pop he showed in high minors isn't surfacing with that sky-high GB rate, and low BA floor will remain due to poor contact. So for now, a SB-only play... UP: 50 SB.

Yr	Tm	AB	R	HR	RBI	SB	BA	xBA	OBP	SLG	OPS	vL	vR	bb%	ct%	h%	Eye	G	L	F	PX	xPX	hr/f	Spd	SBO	SB%	#Wk	DOM	DIS	RC/G	RAR	BPV	BPX	R$
09																																		
10																																		
11	aa	324	40	8	20	11	210	220	261	341	602			7	67	29	0.21				108			114	26%	63%				2.74		2	4	$2
12	aa	326	41	9	38	30	230	209	289	339	628			8	70	30	0.28				73			108	45%	77%				3.30		-11	-28	$13
13	HOU *	549	63	7	40	42	246	249	308	360	668	673	627	8	68	35	0.28	66	20	14	91	54	6%	145	40%	73%	11	18%	64%	3.70	4.5	7	18	$22
1st Half		312	31	6	30	21	249	223	291	388	678			6	69	34	0.19				104			140	40%	73%				3.73		14	35	$25
2nd Half		237	31	1	10	21	242	234	330	324	653	673	627	12	67	36	0.39	66	20	14	73	54	6%	144	39%	73%	11	18%	64%	3.60	1.0	-6	-15	$18
14	Proj	**480**	**58**	**4**	**39**	**37**	**238**	**221**	**303**	**318**	**621**	**675**	**601**	**8**	**68**	**34**	**0.29**	**59**	**19**	**22**	**66**	**49**	**5%**	**137**	**38%**	**74%**				**3.23**	**-3.5**	**-11**	**-28**	**$17**

STEPHEN NICKRAND

Vogt,Stephen

Age	29	Bats	L	Pos	CA	Health	A	LIMA Plan	D+
Ht	6' 0"	Wt	215			PT/Exp	C	Rand Var	0
						Consist	C	MM	2013

4-16-.252 in 135 AB at OAK. 3 reasons why he'll be a solid second catcher on draft day: 1) Sept power, flyball explosion w/OAK shows some power upside; 2) Good plate control in high minors; 3) Caught stealing rate 5% higher than league average, so he's not a liability behind the dish. On right side of platoon too. UP: 15 HR.

Yr	Tm	AB	R	HR	RBI	SB	BA	xBA	OBP	SLG	OPS	vL	vR	bb%	ct%	h%	Eye	G	L	F	PX	xPX	hr/f	Spd	SBO	SB%	#Wk	DOM	DIS	RC/G	RAR	BPV	BPX	R$
09																																		
10																																		
11	a/a	510	48	12	75	3	236	258	270	381	651			4	80	27	0.24				99			96	5%	54%				3.38		40	89	$7
12	TAM *	374	35	6	31	1	197	168	261	300	561	0	80	8	79	23	0.40	26	9	65	68	54	0%	90	1%	100%	9	11%	33%	2.50	-14.3	14	35	-$3
13	OAK *	431	53	11	53	0	241	247	296	383	679	667	698	7	80	28	0.39	30	24	46	97	109	8%	101	2%	0%	13	38%	46%	3.72	0.0	44	110	$6
1st Half		244	26	6	29	0	232	211	285	374	660	0	621	7	82	26	0.41	38	8	54	95	120	14%	97	0%	0%	2	50%	50%	3.55	-1.2	48	120	$6
2nd Half		187	27	5	23	0	252	245	309	395	704	750	706	8	77	30	0.36	29	27	45	100	108	7%	100	5%	0%	11	36%	45%	3.95	1.3	36	90	$7
14	**Proj**	**260**	**29**	**7**	**29**	**0**	**227**	**243**	**281**	**368**	**649**	**695**	**641**	**7**	**79**	**26**	**0.37**	**30**	**25**	**46**	**95**	**97**	**7%**	**104**	**2%**	**32%**				**3.38**	**-2.6**	**28**	**71**	**$1**

Votto,Joey

Age	30	Bats	L	Pos	1B	Health	B	LIMA Plan	A
Ht	6' 2"	Wt	220			PT/Exp	A	Rand Var	-1
						Consist	F	MM	4145

Owners will keep chasing 2010, but it's not likely coming back. HR limited by sharply dropping flyball rate, and he's never even reached 30 in any other season. Batting average seems like a .300 lock...until you look at that xBA. Elite and steady, but very little profit potential once the bidding hits $25. DN: Second half x 2

Yr	Tm	AB	R	HR	RBI	SB	BA	xBA	OBP	SLG	OPS	vL	vR	bb%	ct%	h%	Eye	G	L	F	PX	xPX	hr/f	Spd	SBO	SB%	#Wk	DOM	DIS	RC/G	RAR	BPV	BPX	R$
09	CIN	469	82	25	84	4	322	299	414	567	981	931	1002	13	77	37	0.66	39	22	39	163	153	17%	77	3%	80%	24	67%	17%	8.75	52.0	91	186	$24
10	CIN	547	106	37	113	16	324	313	424	600	1024	863	1115	14	77	36	0.73	45	20	35	183	150	25%	89	11%	76%	27	81%	4%	9.44	71.3	112	243	$40
11	CIN	599	101	29	103	8	309	299	416	531	947	987	930	16	78	35	0.85	39	28	33	152	145	18%	81	6%	57%	27	70%	15%	7.98	55.8	93	207	$33
12	CIN	374	59	14	56	5	337	311	474	567	1041	887	1109	20	77	41	1.11	38	30	32	171	161	15%	74	5%	63%	21	76%	10%	10.12	54.4	110	275	$20
13	CIN	581	101	24	73	6	305	279	435	491	926	824	977	19	76	37	0.98	44	27	29	128	128	18%	107	4%	67%	27	67%	0%	7.80	51.2	79	198	$29
1st Half		307	56	14	38	3	326	285	436	518	954	890	991	16	78	38	0.87	45	27	28	128	120	21%	99	4%	60%	14	57%	0%	8.44	31.5	77	193	$33
2nd Half		274	45	10	35	3	281	272	436	460	895	752	962	21	75	34	1.09	42	28	30	127	136	16%	113	3%	75%	13	77%	0%	7.11	19.5	80	200	$25
14	**Proj**	**544**	**92**	**25**	**90**	**6**	**303**	**293**	**431**	**522**	**953**	**851**	**1001**	**18**	**77**	**36**	**0.96**	**40**	**27**	**32**	**155**	**142**	**18%**	**87**	**4%**	**62%**				**8.13**	**52.9**	**88**	**221**	**$29**

Walker,Neil

Age	28	Bats	B	Pos	2B	Health	B	LIMA Plan	A
Ht	6' 3"	Wt	210			PT/Exp	B	Rand Var	+3
						Consist	A	MM	3125

16-53-.251 in 478 AB at PIT. On surface, a big fade. Reason to worry? Nope. Dip in BA was fully the result of h% swoon. Blame dearth of SB on red light; speed skills are good enough for his usual 5-10 bags. Only bugaboo is steadily declining OPS vs. LHers, but 2H suggests it's not reason for alarm yet. There's a sneaky 20 HR here.

Yr	Tm	AB	R	HR	RBI	SB	BA	xBA	OBP	SLG	OPS	vL	vR	bb%	ct%	h%	Eye	G	L	F	PX	xPX	hr/f	Spd	SBO	SB%	#Wk	DOM	DIS	RC/G	RAR	BPV	BPX	R$
09	PIT *	392	36	11	56	5	230	249	275	396	671	286	544	6	81	26	0.32	32	16	52	113	125	0%	104	10%	69%	6	17%	67%	3.58	-0.9	58	118	$4
10	PIT *	594	75	16	85	9	288	275	341	460	801	809	813	7	80	34	0.40	36	22	41	122	125	9%	109	9%	69%	20	65%	15%	5.56	31.8	68	148	$22
11	PIT	596	76	12	83	9	273	262	334	408	742	672	767	8	81	32	0.48	44	21	35	96	120	7%	96	9%	60%	27	44%	30%	4.68	17.5	49	109	$18
12	PIT	472	62	14	69	7	280	259	342	426	768	602	824	9	78	33	0.45	42	24	34	101	115	11%	86	9%	58%	25	44%	28%	5.08	19.2	39	98	$16
13	PIT *	499	62	16	54	1	252	268	322	415	738	518	805	9	82	28	0.59	39	23	39	106	115	11%	101	2%	33%	22	50%	27%	4.50	12.4	65	163	$10
1st Half		244	27	6	26	1	250	256	331	389	720	401	825	11	79	29	0.59	37	26	38	95	97	9%	103	4%	33%	12	42%	42%	4.26	4.1	48	120	$8
2nd Half		255	35	10	28	0	253	279	313	441	754	685	785	8	85	26	0.59	40	21	39	116	130	12%	100	0%	0%	10	60%	10%	4.72	7.6	81	203	$13
14	**Proj**	**549**	**69**	**19**	**69**	**4**	**271**	**270**	**342**	**441**	**783**	**628**	**824**	**9**	**81**	**30**	**0.51**	**39**	**23**	**38**	**114**	**118**	**11%**	**96**	**5%**	**56%**				**5.08**	**21.9**	**56**	**140**	**$18**

Wallace,Brett

Age	27	Bats	L	Pos	1B	Health	A	LIMA Plan	D+
Ht	6' 2"	Wt	235			PT/Exp	C	Rand Var	-3
						Consist	B	MM	4103

13-36-.221 in 262 AB at HOU. Former first rounder flashed top-tier power for first time. But PX growth not supported by xPX, and he wouldn't be able to sustain it anyway with his new extreme hacker approach. Inflated hr/f casts further doubt on likelihood of a sustained power burst. Bid, but only in your end game.

Yr	Tm	AB	R	HR	RBI	SB	BA	xBA	OBP	SLG	OPS	vL	vR	bb%	ct%	h%	Eye	G	L	F	PX	xPX	hr/f	Spd	SBO	SB%	#Wk	DOM	DIS	RC/G	RAR	BPV	BPX	R$
09	a/a	532	57	14	47	1	246	237	293	368	661			6	76	30	0.28				84			90	2%	25%				3.58		11	22	$5
10	HOU *	529	52	13	49	1	228	218	262	356	618	576	623	4	71	30	0.16	39	17	44	98	122	5%	96	2%	33%	11	18%	64%	3.05	-24.9	3	7	$3
11	HOU *	440	49	6	47	2	269	238	340	378	718	549	735	10	72	36	0.38	52	21	27	98	92	8%	71	2%	64%	23	35%	52%	4.48	-1.6	8	18	$8
12	HOU *	539	59	20	61	0	243	232	290	399	688	711	757	6	66	33	0.20	38	27	35	118	138	16%	71	1%	0%	12	33%	33%	3.85	-12.1	-4	-10	$9
13	HOU *	495	61	21	62	2	241	230	292	433	725	450	787	7	61	35	0.18	41	22	37	165	118	22%	80	3%	63%	17	47%	41%	4.22	-5.6	17	43	$11
1st Half		277	30	9	31	1	239	218	289	403	692	143	488	7	61	36	0.18	59	14	27	142	99	17%	88	1%	100%	4	50%	50%	3.91	-5.7	-3	-8	$9
2nd Half		218	31	12	31	1	243	249	295	472	767	549	838	7	62	33	0.20	38	24	39	194	121	23%	73	5%	50%	13	46%	38%	4.62	0.2	42	105	$13
14	**Proj**	**358**	**42**	**13**	**42**	**1**	**245**	**232**	**311**	**410**	**721**	**533**	**775**	**7**	**65**	**34**	**0.22**	**44**	**21**	**34**	**137**	**117**	**16%**	**76**	**2%**	**55%**				**4.11**	**-5.2**	**3**	**7**	**$8**

Weeks,Jemile

Age	27	Bats	B	Pos	2B	Health	A	LIMA Plan	D+
Ht	5' 9"	Wt	160			PT/Exp	C	Rand Var	+3
						Consist	C	MM	1501

0-0-.111 in 9 AB at OAK. '12 struggles sent him to Triple-A for nearly entire season. Mediocre .745 OPS in PCL says he's still not ready, but those wheels sure are shiny. Two years of good bb%, nice contact history give him the right approach. With opportunity, a post-hype one-trick-pony to target in your end game. UP: 40 SB.

Yr	Tm	AB	R	HR	RBI	SB	BA	xBA	OBP	SLG	OPS	vL	vR	bb%	ct%	h%	Eye	G	L	F	PX	xPX	hr/f	Spd	SBO	SB%	#Wk	DOM	DIS	RC/G	RAR	BPV	BPX	R$
09	aa	105	7	1	9	3	197	243	250	277	527			7	83	22	0.42				54			93	13%	100%				2.32		20	41	-$2
10	aa	273	34	2	26	9	232	258	289	341	630			7	85	27	0.52				70			138	23%	56%				3.07		53	115	$3
11	OAK *	590	71	4	51	29	290	253	337	400	736	704	788	7	83	34	0.41	40	23	37	76	66	2%	155	27%	65%	17	59%	18%	4.60	14.9	54	120	$23
12	OAK *	489	57	2	27	17	225	242	302	307	610	669	578	10	84	27	0.68	49	19	32	52	49	2%	157	16%	77%	26	38%	23%	3.10	-9.3	46	115	$5
13	OAK *	529	67	2	27	11	210	237	284	278	561	0	250	9	76	27	0.44	50	25	25	48	-15	0%	179	10%	82%	5	0%	60%	2.59	-18.6	19	48	$1
1st Half		299	38	1	15	7	206	219	287	277	565			10	79	26	0.55				47			177	10%	86%				2.64		31	78	$3
2nd Half		230	28	1	12	4	214	226	278	278	557	0	250	8	73	29	0.33	50	25	25	51	-15	0%	153	9%	77%	5	0%	60%	2.54	-8.3	-5	-13	$0
14	**Proj**	**205**	**24**	**1**	**13**	**12**	**227**	**228**	**298**	**303**	**601**	**610**	**596**	**9**	**79**	**28**	**0.46**	**46**	**21**	**34**	**54**	**56**	**2%**	**153**	**26%**	**86%**				**3.10**	**-3.8**	**23**	**57**	**$5**

Weeks,Rickie

Age	31	Bats	R	Pos	2B	Health	D	LIMA Plan	C
Ht	5' 10"	Wt	215			PT/Exp	B	Rand Var	+4
						Consist	A	MM	4315

Three years of 20+ HR made us forget how fragile his skill set is. Bad hammy mercifully cut short horrific 2nd half. Hope for return to 20 HR, 10 SB norm is dashed by pessimistic xPX, below average Spd. Even when healthy, OPS has nosedived four straight seasons. May need a change of scenery. Don't chase former upside.

Yr	Tm	AB	R	HR	RBI	SB	BA	xBA	OBP	SLG	OPS	vL	vR	bb%	ct%	h%	Eye	G	L	F	PX	xPX	hr/f	Spd	SBO	SB%	#Wk	DOM	DIS	RC/G	RAR	BPV	BPX	R$
09	MIL	147	28	9	24	2	272	267	340	517	857	783	874	8	73	31	0.31	38	19	44	151	138	19%	158	11%	50%	7	43%	14%	5.67	8.6	79	161	$5
10	MIL	651	112	29	83	11	269	259	366	464	830	1025	769	10	72	33	0.41	49	15	36	140	115	17%	117	8%	73%	27	48%	26%	5.56	35.8	57	124	$24
11	MIL	453	77	20	49	9	269	270	350	468	818	832	814	10	76	31	0.47	48	17	35	138	109	16%	105	9%	82%	22	64%	32%	5.61	25.5	69	153	$17
12	MIL	588	85	21	63	16	230	236	328	400	728	740	723	11	71	29	0.44	45	17	38	120	114	13%	116	12%	84%	27	41%	33%	4.24	10.4	40	100	$14
13	MIL	350	40	10	24	7	209	237	306	357	663	705	644	10	70	27	0.38	49	18	33	119	99	13%	95	12%	70%	19	42%	47%	3.31	-3.7	26	65	$2
1st Half		237	32	8	19	4	228	241	312	384	696	777	666	11	69	29	0.40	46	22	32	120	107	15%	103	10%	67%	14	43%	50%	3.91	1.6	27	68	$6
2nd Half		113	8	2	5	3	168	226	242	301	543	408	609	9	72	22	0.34	56	10	35	116	81	7%	76	21%	75%	5	40%	40%	2.24	-5.4	22	55	-$6
14	**Proj**	**409**	**56**	**13**	**36**	**9**	**233**	**240**	**327**	**392**	**719**	**722**	**718**	**10**	**72**	**29**	**0.40**	**47**	**17**	**36**	**122**	**103**	**12%**	**103**	**12%**	**76%**				**4.05**	**4.4**	**37**	**93**	**$9**

Wells,Vernon

Age	35	Bats	R	Pos	LF RF DH	Health	C	LIMA Plan	D+
Ht	6' 1"	Wt	230			PT/Exp	C	Rand Var	0
						Consist	A	MM	2213

.914 OPS in April gave some hope of return to 2010. In the end, 40 PX or lower in three of six months netted him third straight year of sub-replacement value. Sub-.600 OPS vs. RH in two of last three seasons will close door on 400 AB, while his overall skills slide slams it shut on him having any double-digit value again.

Yr	Tm	AB	R	HR	RBI	SB	BA	xBA	OBP	SLG	OPS	vL	vR	bb%	ct%	h%	Eye	G	L	F	PX	xPX	hr/f	Spd	SBO	SB%	#Wk	DOM	DIS	RC/G	RAR	BPV	BPX	R$
09	TOR	630	84	15	66	17	260	260	311	400	711	602	748	7	86	28	0.56	43	15	42	87	90	6%	98	13%	81%	27	48%	15%	4.35	6.8	61	124	$16
10	TOR	590	79	31	88	6	273	307	331	515	847	643	895	8	86	27	0.60	42	16	42	150	126	15%	82	8%	60%	26	77%	4%	5.85	31.8	105	228	$22
11	LAA	505	60	25	66	9	218	250	248	412	660	851	569	4	83	22	0.23	40	12	48	114	107	12%	112	15%	69%	24	58%	25%	3.27	-11.1	66	147	$10
12	LAA *	269	37	12	31	5	229	253	272	399	671	671	686	6	84	23	0.37	42	16	42	99	110	13%	73	10%	83%	19	53%	37%	3.61	-2.9	50	125	$5
13	NYY	424	45	11	50	7	233	237	282	349	631	697	580	7	83	26	0.41	42	18	40	76	104	8%	76	10%	70%	27	33%	37%	3.28	-9.0	30	75	$7
1st Half		269	29	10	31	4	223	237	264	364	628	733	561	5	83	24	0.32	42	16	42	87	124	11%	80	12%	57%	14	43%	43%	3.06	-8.0	36	90	$9
2nd Half		155	16	1	19	3	252	237	318	323	640	652	620	9	83	30	0.58	40	22	37	57	71	2%	72	7%	100%	13	23%	31%	3.61	-1.9	20	50	$4
14	**Proj**	**295**	**35**	**9**	**36**	**5**	**237**	**245**	**285**	**373**	**658**	**690**	**638**	**6**	**84**	**26**	**0.42**	**41**	**17**	**42**	**87**	**100**	**9%**	**79**	**10%**	**78%**				**3.58**	**-3.9**	**42**	**104**	**$7**

STEPHEN NICKRAND

Werth,Jayson

Age	35	Bats	R	Pos	RF	Health	D	LIMA Plan	B+
Ht	6' 5"	Wt	225			PT/Exp	B	Rand Var	-5
						Consist	D	MM	4325

Another year removed from wrist woes and boom, 2010 revisited. Elite pop comes with full support and tons of line drives, so put 20 HR in stone. Speed and average are his risks, since regression of that 2H h% will send BA south, and waning Spd, age put double-digit SB in jeopardy. Buy the .280-20-80; any SB are now gravy.

Yr Tm	AB	R	HR	RBI	SB	BA	xBA	OBP	SLG	OPS	vL	vR	bb%	ct%	h%	Eye	G	L	F	PX	xPX	hr/f	Spd	SBO	SB%	#Wk	DOM	DIS	RC/G	RAR	BPV	BPX	R$
09 PHI	571	98	36	99	20	268	267	373	506	879	1080	806	14	73	31	0.58	36	20	44	155	143	19%	96	13%	87%	27	48%	26%	6.62	33.1	73	149	$27
10 PHI	554	106	27	85	13	296	278	388	532	921	881	937	13	73	36	0.56	37	18	45	176	163	14%	116	9%	81%	27	67%	22%	7.49	44.4	97	211	$29
11 WAS	561	69	20	58	19	232	233	330	389	718	675	730	12	71	29	0.46	43	17	40	118	132	12%	95	14%	86%	27	44%	33%	4.25	-6.0	34	76	$13
12 WAS *	321	45	5	34	8	292	249	381	428	809	1037	755	13	80	35	0.73	42	19	39	96	88	5%	125	9%	80%	16	69%	13%	5.93	11.8	63	158	$11
13 WAS	462	84	25	82	10	318	281	398	532	931	1092	884	11	78	36	0.59	36	26	38	142	142	18%	83	7%	91%	22	64%	14%	8.01	42.1	76	190	$31
1st Half	184	30	8	21	2	272	247	330	440	770	781	771	8	73	33	0.32	45	21	34	118	136	17%	89	4%	100%	10	30%	30%	5.16	3.7	30	75	$11
2nd Half	278	54	17	61	8	349	303	438	594	1031	1313	954	14	82	38	0.86	31	29	40	155	146	18%	85	8%	89%	12	92%	0%	10.32	41.9	105	263	$43
14 Proj	524	85	23	81	8	282	268	371	479	850	987	807	12	77	33	0.60	39	22	39	135	128	15%	98	6%	80%				6.28	27.1	69	171	$22

Wieters,Matt

Age	28	Bats	B	Pos	CA	Health	A	LIMA Plan	A
Ht	6' 5"	Wt	240			PT/Exp	A	Rand Var	+3
						Consist	A	MM	4225

Another 20 HR lock. This one's second half xPX suggests he hasn't reached his power ceiling yet. Mystery is why he keeps switch-hitting with continued power zap as a LHer. xBA history profiles him as a .260-.270 hitter, so don't be swayed by low h%-induced '13 mark. Seems like we've been waiting forever for... UP: 30 HR, .275 BA.

Yr Tm	AB	R	HR	RBI	SB	BA	xBA	OBP	SLG	OPS	vL	vR	bb%	ct%	h%	Eye	G	L	F	PX	xPX	hr/f	Spd	SBO	SB%	#Wk	DOM	DIS	RC/G	RAR	BPV	BPX	R$
09 BAL *	495	57	14	70	0	289	241	348	431	780	671	804	8	76	35	0.39	42	19	40	95	101	8%	87	0%	0%	20	30%	45%	5.39	23.0	26	53	$13
10 BAL	446	37	11	55	0	249	231	319	377	695	564	741	10	79	29	0.50	46	15	38	90	108	8%	76	1%	0%	25	48%	36%	4.06	4.5	32	70	$6
11 BAL	500	72	22	68	1	262	273	328	450	778	1124	665	9	83	28	0.57	43	18	39	122	130	14%	72	1%	100%	27	48%	19%	5.09	19.8	72	160	$15
12 BAL	526	67	23	83	3	249	265	329	435	764	908	715	10	79	28	0.54	44	20	35	119	113	16%	64	2%	100%	27	59%	26%	4.85	17.6	52	130	$14
13 BAL	523	59	22	79	2	235	256	287	417	704	872	628	8	80	25	0.41	39	18	44	122	124	12%	68	2%	100%	26	62%	27%	4.10	5.9	56	140	$11
1st Half	271	29	10	39	1	232	260	295	406	701	743	677	8	81	25	0.47	41	18	41	118	105	11%	72	2%	100%	14	64%	21%	4.00	2.3	59	148	$10
2nd Half	252	30	12	40	1	238	249	292	429	720	988	571	7	79	26	0.36	36	17	47	125	145	12%	71	2%	100%	12	58%	33%	4.20	3.7	53	133	$13
14 Proj	513	65	25	87	2	258	265	318	456	775	956	700	8	80	28	0.46	41	18	41	130	123	15%	67	2%	97%				5.05	20.0	57	142	$18

Willingham,Josh

Age	35	Bats	R	Pos	LF DH	Health	C	LIMA Plan	B
Ht	6' 2"	Wt	230			PT/Exp	B	Rand Var	+2
						Consist	D	MM	4105

Blame nagging knee woes for collapse. Power skills remain consistently strong, so 25-30 HR are still in play over a full season. Problem is, at age 35 and with chronic knee concerns, you can't use 500 AB as your baseline anymore. That means it's time to lower his counting stats proportionately. If bidding hits $15, stay silent.

Yr Tm	AB	R	HR	RBI	SB	BA	xBA	OBP	SLG	OPS	vL	vR	bb%	ct%	h%	Eye	G	L	F	PX	xPX	hr/f	Spd	SBO	SB%	#Wk	DOM	DIS	RC/G	RAR	BPV	BPX	R$
09 WAS	427	70	24	61	4	260	285	367	496	863	1049	819	13	76	29	0.59	36	22	42	157	148	17%	85	6%	57%	27	52%	30%	5.93	24.4	81	165	$13
10 WAS	370	54	16	56	8	268	256	389	459	848	909	828	15	77	31	0.79	31	20	49	129	149	11%	92	6%	100%	20	55%	20%	6.23	24.0	72	157	$13
11 OAK	488	69	29	98	4	246	251	332	477	810	783	823	10	69	29	0.37	35	17	48	173	161	17%	72	4%	80%	25	56%	32%	5.23	18.1	60	133	$17
12 MIN	519	85	35	110	3	260	272	366	524	890	920	877	13	73	29	0.54	38	19	43	176	136	21%	72	3%	60%	26	65%	19%	6.35	35.9	81	203	$22
13 MIN	389	42	14	48	1	208	217	342	368	709	696	714	15	67	27	0.52	37	18	45	129	134	12%	76	1%	100%	22	41%	45%	3.84	-1.6	25	63	$2
1st Half	246	32	10	37	1	224	220	330	398	728	757	753	14	69	28	0.51	37	15	48	136	134	12%	75	1%	100%	14	43%	43%	4.34	2.4	36	90	$7
2nd Half	143	10	4	11	0	182	213	312	315	626	604	643	16	64	25	0.53	35	24	41	115	136	11%	79	0%	0%	8	38%	50%	3.06	-4.4	7	18	-$6
14 Proj	435	54	20	66	2	241	238	358	438	795	803	792	14	69	30	0.52	36	19	45	149	141	15%	75	2%	76%				5.08	13.8	39	97	$12

Wong,Kolten

Age	23	Bats	L	Pos	2B	Health	A	LIMA Plan	D+
Ht	5' 9"	Wt	185			PT/Exp	D	Rand Var	+2
						Consist	B	MM	1523

0-0-.153 BA in 59 AB at STL. One extra-base hit over parts of two months with STL proves he was overmatched. As a slap hitter, his value to you will be SB anyway. Strong contact rate gives him solid foundation for that. Near 1,000 AB in high minors bodes well for him being able to adjust to MLB pitching. Assuming so... UP: 30 SB

Yr Tm	AB	R	HR	RBI	SB	BA	xBA	OBP	SLG	OPS	vL	vR	bb%	ct%	h%	Eye	G	L	F	PX	xPX	hr/f	Spd	SBO	SB%	#Wk	DOM	DIS	RC/G	RAR	BPV	BPX	R$
09																																	
10																																	
11																																	
12 aa	523	62	7	40	16	251	242	298	344	642			6	85	29	0.43				59			113	21%	57%				3.29		34	85	$11
13 STL *	471	58	7	35	18	248	272	300	358	658	0	410	7	83	28	0.44	61	17	22	72	18	0%	137	16%	94%	8	0%	75%	3.82	2.2	47	118	$12
1st Half	285	35	4	19	8	273	254	318	389	707			6	84	31	0.42				77			133	13%	88%				4.44		53	133	$15
2nd Half	186	23	4	15	10	209	261	273	311	583	0	410	8	82	24	0.47	61	17	22	65	18	0%	126	22%	100%	8	0%	75%	2.99	-4.1	34	85	$8
14 Proj	294	36	3	22	13	252	258	303	338	641	207	697	7	83	29	0.44	54	20	26	58	16	5%	128	20%	82%				3.59	-0.9	32	80	$9

Wright,David

Age	31	Bats	R	Pos	3B	Health	D	LIMA Plan	C
Ht	6' 0"	Wt	210			PT/Exp	B	Rand Var	-2
						Consist	C	MM	4335

Hamstring cost him nearly two months, but a look at his best-in-years skills shows what might've been. Surging contact has raised his BA floor, so even with regression, he'll continue to help you there. Wheels remain in tip-top shape even with leg issues, so double-digit SB remain secure. As close to a $25-$30 lock as they come.

Yr Tm	AB	R	HR	RBI	SB	BA	xBA	OBP	SLG	OPS	vL	vR	bb%	ct%	h%	Eye	G	L	F	PX	xPX	hr/f	Spd	SBO	SB%	#Wk	DOM	DIS	RC/G	RAR	BPV	BPX	R$
09 NYM	535	88	10	72	27	307	258	390	447	837	1142	754	12	74	40	0.53	38	26	36	108	113	7%	110	19%	75%	25	44%	36%	6.41	35.8	41	84	$27
10 NYM	587	87	29	103	19	283	267	354	503	856	1066	798	11	73	35	0.43	38	19	43	158	147	16%	89	18%	63%	27	59%	30%	6.16	36.5	66	143	$29
11 NYM	389	60	14	61	13	254	252	345	427	771	806	761	12	75	31	0.54	42	18	40	126	142	12%	76	13%	87%	19	53%	21%	5.11	12.7	49	109	$14
12 NYM	581	91	21	93	15	306	278	391	492	883	917	867	12	81	35	0.72	42	22	35	123	134	13%	90	13%	60%	27	59%	19%	6.83	45.9	75	188	$30
13 NYM	430	63	18	58	17	307	280	390	514	904	1072	836	11	82	34	0.70	38	23	39	130	141	13%	142	14%	85%	21	67%	5%	7.40	40.2	98	245	$26
1st Half	289	42	12	41	14	304	280	383	522	906	1012	866	11	79	35	0.62	36	25	39	142	141	13%	139	16%	93%	14	64%	7%	7.62	28.9	97	243	$32
2nd Half	141	21	6	17	3	312	277	390	496	886	1242	782	11	87	33	0.95	41	20	39	108	142	13%	124	10%	60%	7	71%	0%	6.96	11.6	94	235	$13
14 Proj	545	83	24	90	17	299	279	381	505	886	1045	829	11	81	33	0.67	40	21	38	134	139	14%	110	14%	73%				6.89	44.4	85	212	$31

Yelich,Christian S.

Age	22	Bats	L	Pos	LF	Health	A	LIMA Plan	C+
Ht	6' 4"	Wt	195			PT/Exp	F	Rand Var	0
						Consist	F	MM	3523

4-16-.288 with 10 SB in 240 AB at MIA. Top OF prospect flashed 110+ Spd in each of three months with MIA, putting good walk rate to use. That's a good thing, because power will remain in mothballs with extreme groundball tilt. Nice BA w/MIA was hit rate-fueled; he's not a .280 hitter yet. Everything but SB is a year away.

Yr Tm	AB	R	HR	RBI	SB	BA	xBA	OBP	SLG	OPS	vL	vR	bb%	ct%	h%	Eye	G	L	F	PX	xPX	hr/f	Spd	SBO	SB%	#Wk	DOM	DIS	RC/G	RAR	BPV	BPX	R$
09																																	
10																																	
11																																	
12																																	
13 MIA *	433	62	10	41	14	275	273	357	427	784	476	941	11	71	37	0.44	63	23	14	117	83	17%	149	15%	73%	10	30%	20%	5.32	15.8	46	115	$16
1st Half	164	21	5	24	3	244	256	320	464	784			10	67	33	0.34				172			143	15%	61%				4.86		71	178	$7
2nd Half	269	41	5	17	11	295	262	379	404	783	476	941	12	73	39	0.51	63	23	14	86	83	17%	140	15%	77%	10	30%	20%	5.58	11.8	30	75	$22
14 Proj	373	53	7	36	12	255	256	340	395	735	446	909	11	71	34	0.43	56	22	22	109	75	12%	149	15%	73%				4.56	6.0	34	84	$12

Youkilis,Kevin

Age	35	Bats	R	Pos	3B	Health	F	LIMA Plan	D+
Ht	6' 1"	Wt	220			PT/Exp	C	Rand Var	+1
						Consist	C	MM	3213

Herniated disk led to back surgery, which wiped out most of season. Some will still bid hoping for 2009, but it's not coming back. Eroding power, marginal loft in swing make 20 HR a reach even without a bum back. xBA trend gives no hope for any meaningful BA rebound. His $20 days are long gone, his $10 days might well be too.

Yr Tm	AB	R	HR	RBI	SB	BA	xBA	OBP	SLG	OPS	vL	vR	bb%	ct%	h%	Eye	G	L	F	PX	xPX	hr/f	Spd	SBO	SB%	#Wk	DOM	DIS	RC/G	RAR	BPV	BPX	R$
09 BOS	491	99	27	94	7	305	282	413	548	961	953	964	14	75	36	0.62	35	21	44	164	161	16%	86	6%	78%	26	65%	23%	8.04	55.0	84	171	$26
10 BOS	362	77	19	62	4	307	297	411	564	975	1311	863	14	81	33	0.87	37	16	47	164	166	14%	127	4%	80%	18	78%	6%	8.35	43.4	125	272	$20
11 BOS	431	68	17	80	3	258	275	373	459	833	987	764	14	77	30	0.68	42	20	38	146	136	13%	88	2%	100%	24	63%	25%	5.71	22.0	80	178	$14
12 2AL	438	72	19	60	0	235	247	336	409	745	878	693	10	75	27	0.47	43	21	36	110	119	16%	93	0%	0%	24	38%	29%	4.29	4.5	40	100	$9
13 NYY	105	12	2	8	0	219	223	305	343	648	314	816	7	70	29	0.26	39	20	41	107	141	7%	63	0%	0%	7	43%	57%	3.07	-2.7	3	8	-$2
1st Half	105	12	2	8	0	219	223	274	343	617	314	816	7	70	29	0.26	39	20	41	107	141	7%	63	0%	0%	7	43%	57%	3.07	-2.9	3	8	-$2
2nd Half																																	
14 Proj	293	46	8	41	1	243	245	347	399	746	731	751	11	75	30	0.50	40	20	40	117	141	9%	81	2%	85%				4.41	3.8	41	103	$7

STEPHEN NICKRAND

Young Jr.,Eric

Age 29 | Bats B | Pos LF RF | Ht 5' 10" | Wt 180
Health C | PT/Exp C | Consist F
LIMA Plan B | Rand Var +2 | MM 1515

Ran wild in the second half after finally getting extended full-time look, with consistently elite speed and a great SB success rate. As a slap hitter with okay plate control, he will live or die wherever his OBP takes him. The big question: Would .310 be enough to hold down a job? UP: 60 SB. If he goes back to part-time... DN: 20 SB.

Yr Tm	AB	R	HR	RBI	SB	BA	xBA	OBP	SLG	OPS	vL	vR	bb%	ct%	h%	Eye	G	L	F	PX	xPX	hr/f	Spd	SBO	SB%	#Wk	DOM	DIS	RC/G	RAR	BPV	BPX	R$
09 COL *	529	86	6	30	42	257	277	311	361	672	783	495	7	82	31	0.42	59	20	22	64	68	11%	176	44%	68%	7	43%	57%	3.65	-6.6	47	96	$20
10 COL *	308	41	1	14	24	230	223	293	279	572	552	623	8	78	29	0.40	54	17	29	39	55	0%	148	34%	80%	11	27%	45%	2.85	-11.4	4	9	$7
11 COL *	421	64	1	24	35	264	262	335	355	691	618	653	10	81	32	0.56	58	19	23	64	69	0%	158	32%	87%	17	24%	29%	4.43	4.6	44	98	$16
12 COL	174	36	4	15	14	316	257	377	448	825	974	770	7	82	37	0.42	49	19	32	81	73	9%	147	29%	88%	20	25%	55%	6.37	11.0	54	135	$10
13 2 NL	539	70	2	32	46	249	260	310	336	645	642	647	8	81	30	0.46	54	21	25	64	66	2%	148	40%	81%	27	37%	37%	3.65	-6.5	39	98	$23
1st Half	212	27	1	13	9	259	265	305	363	669	792	583	6	81	32	0.35	55	20	25	78	103	2%	137	25%	69%	14	57%	36%	3.73	-1.8	42	105	$10
2nd Half	327	43	1	19	37	242	256	309	318	627	493	679	9	82	29	0.53	54	21	24	56	41	2%	147	48%	84%	13	15%	38%	3.60	-4.2	35	88	$31
14 Proj	516	80	3	33	40	267	255	330	357	687	716	674	8	81	32	0.46	54	20	26	64	68	3%	158	33%	81%				4.19	2.6	42	106	$21

Young,Chris

Age 30 | Bats R | Pos CF RF LF | Ht 6' 2" | Wt 190
Health A | PT/Exp B | Consist B
LIMA Plan B | Rand Var +4 | MM 4413

Transformation from undervalued 20/20 bat to one of game's biggest enigmas is complete. PROs: Power, speed skills intact; plenty of walks; h% has to regress at some point. CONs: Can't blame latest collapse on injuries; toolsy hackers overmatched by RHers aren't going to get steady AB. Bid $10 and cross fingers and toes.

Yr Tm	AB	R	HR	RBI	SB	BA	xBA	OBP	SLG	OPS	vL	vR	bb%	ct%	h%	Eye	G	L	F	PX	xPX	hr/f	Spd	SBO	SB%	#Wk	DOM	DIS	RC/G	RAR	BPV	BPX	R$
09 ARI *	487	65	17	48	12	223	229	314	414	728	920	639	12	70	28	0.44	26	18	56	141	141	9%	125	16%	66%	26	42%	31%	4.17	1.1	54	110	$7
10 ARI	584	94	27	91	28	257	250	341	452	793	826	781	11	75	30	0.51	34	17	50	137	135	12%	98	21%	80%	26	69%	8%	5.33	18.8	64	139	$26
11 ARI	567	89	20	71	22	236	247	331	420	751	939	694	12	75	28	0.58	32	20	49	135	137	10%	125	20%	71%	27	63%	22%	4.57	5.8	74	164	$18
12 ARI	325	36	14	41	8	231	259	311	434	745	810	707	10	76	26	0.46	31	22	47	143	136	12%	79	15%	73%	24	46%	38%	4.38	1.4	63	158	$7
13 OAK	335	46	12	40	10	200	231	280	379	659	712	614	10	72	24	0.39	29	22	50	131	120	10%	119	19%	77%	26	50%	31%	3.36	-9.2	51	128	$5
1st Half	184	25	7	27	6	190	239	270	370	639	521	708	10	74	22	0.42	31	21	48	129	108	11%	99	19%	86%	13	62%	23%	3.21	-5.7	50	125	$7
2nd Half	151	21	5	13	4	212	222	287	391	678	866	452	10	70	27	0.36	26	22	52	133	135	9%	140	18%	67%	13	38%	38%	3.55	-2.9	50	125	$3
14 Proj	345	46	13	41	10	233	240	316	421	737	829	678	10	73	28	0.44	29	21	50	138	130	10%	112	17%	73%				4.36	2.0	58	145	$10

Young,Delmon

Age 28 | Bats R | Pos RF DH | Ht 6' 3" | Wt 240
Health B | PT/Exp C | Consist A
LIMA Plan D+ | Rand Var -1 | MM 2013

11-38-.260 in 334 AB at TAM/PHI. Drafted 1st overall 10 years ago and still on right side of 30, so some will keep speculating. While sexy 1H xPX conjures 2010, steadily declining ct% will keep him from sustaining power spikes anyway. Best shot is as full-time DH, but teams aren't that dumb. Heed BPV trend; gamble elsewhere.

Yr Tm	AB	R	HR	RBI	SB	BA	xBA	OBP	SLG	OPS	vL	vR	bb%	ct%	h%	Eye	G	L	F	PX	xPX	hr/f	Spd	SBO	SB%	#Wk	DOM	DIS	RC/G	RAR	BPV	BPX	R$
09 MIN	395	50	12	60	2	284	246	308	425	733	833	685	3	77	34	0.13	50	16	34	92	94	11%	103	7%	29%	25	36%	44%	4.38	4.5	19	39	$11
10 MIN	570	77	21	112	5	298	291	333	493	826	927	781	5	86	32	0.35	45	15	40	129	119	11%	68	7%	56%	27	70%	7%	5.81	29.0	78	170	$25
11 2 AL *	504	58	13	68	1	267	251	300	397	696	759	670	5	82	30	0.26	47	18	35	88	88	9%	86	1%	100%	23	35%	30%	4.14	2.4	35	78	$12
12 DET	574	54	18	74	0	267	255	296	411	707	833	649	3	80	30	0.18	43	22	35	93	107	11%	62	2%	0%	27	33%	33%	4.10	1.9	24	60	$13
13 2 TM *	381	34	12	41	0	253	239	291	389	680	684	724	5	76	31	0.23	42	22	36	97	142	12%	75	0%	0%	20	50%	35%	3.87	-1.2	16	40	$6
1st Half	181	16	7	26	0	254	235	296	418	715	743	743	6	75	30	0.24	42	18	40	117	177	14%	72	0%	0%	10	50%	40%	4.23	1.1	29	73	$7
2nd Half	200	18	5	15	0	252	244	287	362	649	639	705	5	77	31	0.21	43	26	32	80	109	10%	85	0%	0%	10	50%	30%	3.54	-2.8	7	18	$5
14 Proj	334	33	10	40	0	261	248	299	400	699	738	683	5	79	31	0.22	44	21	35	96	119	11%	75	1%	35%				4.05	-3.9	12	31	$8

Young,Michael

Age 37 | Bats R | Pos 3B 1B | Ht 6' 1" | Wt 200
Health A | PT/Exp A | Consist D
LIMA Plan C+ | Rand Var 0 | MM 1333

If he were 10 years younger, that Spd bump would convince some skipper to give him the green light. Alas, as a contact hitter in his late 30s with no loft in swing, his value lies entirely in versatility and leadership. Massive AB totals have long been a big part of his value proposition; even that firewall has now been breached.

Yr Tm	AB	R	HR	RBI	SB	BA	xBA	OBP	SLG	OPS	vL	vR	bb%	ct%	h%	Eye	G	L	F	PX	xPX	hr/f	Spd	SBO	SB%	#Wk	DOM	DIS	RC/G	RAR	BPV	BPX	R$
09 TEX	541	76	22	68	8	322	302	374	518	892	855	906	8	83	35	0.52	45	22	33	121	140	15%	104	7%	73%	24	54%	21%	7.27	47.4	79	161	$25
10 TEX	656	99	21	91	4	284	276	330	444	774	871	739	7	82	32	0.43	47	18	34	105	104	11%	97	3%	67%	27	56%	22%	5.25	23.1	59	128	$23
11 TEX	631	88	11	106	6	338	301	380	474	854	902	838	7	88	37	0.60	47	26	27	91	112	7%	116	4%	75%	27	67%	4%	6.98	49.2	74	164	$33
12 TEX	611	79	8	67	2	277	277	312	370	682	794	643	5	89	30	0.47	53	23	24	59	68	6%	111	2%	50%	27	37%	22%	4.05	0.9	47	118	$14
13 2 NL	519	52	8	46	1	279	275	335	395	730	730	729	8	84	32	0.52	53	23	24	78	82	8%	127	1%	100%	27	44%	22%	4.69	10.1	54	135	$11
1st Half	286	33	5	21	1	287	277	344	409	753	801	737	8	84	33	0.56	56	21	23	81	89	9%	134	1%	100%	14	36%	14%	5.06	8.7	60	150	$13
2nd Half	233	19	3	25	0	270	272	323	378	700	654	719	7	84	31	0.47	51	25	24	74	74	6%	112	0%	0%	13	54%	31%	4.26	1.9	44	110	$9
14 Proj	392	45	6	44	2	276	279	324	393	716	745	706	7	86	31	0.50	51	23	25	78	86	8%	116	2%	70%				4.48	5.7	41	103	$11

Zimmerman,Ryan

Age 29 | Bats R | Pos 3B | Ht 6' 3" | Wt 230
Health C | PT/Exp A | Consist A
LIMA Plan B+ | Rand Var 0 | MM 4335

As steady a $25 lock at 3B as they come. Hope for more is dashed by low loft in swing, as last time he hit 30 HR was also last time he hit more FB than GB—five years ago. His steady .280-ish BA is now at risk due to Eye slide, but xBA says his BA floor still has sturdy footing, so no reason to panic. There's value in consistently good.

Yr Tm	AB	R	HR	RBI	SB	BA	xBA	OBP	SLG	OPS	vL	vR	bb%	ct%	h%	Eye	G	L	F	PX	xPX	hr/f	Spd	SBO	SB%	#Wk	DOM	DIS	RC/G	RAR	BPV	BPX	R$
09 WAS	610	110	33	106	2	292	289	364	525	888	825	906	11	80	32	0.61	40	19	42	142	131	16%	104	1%	100%	27	63%	7%	6.95	49.9	90	184	$26
10 WAS	525	85	25	85	4	307	280	388	510	899	957	879	12	81	34	0.70	41	18	41	133	139	14%	86	3%	80%	25	52%	20%	7.28	46.9	83	180	$26
11 WAS	395	52	12	49	3	289	261	355	443	798	919	773	9	82	33	0.56	50	16	34	104	114	11%	108	3%	75%	18	56%	17%	5.64	18.2	63	140	$13
12 WAS	578	93	25	95	5	282	274	346	478	824	861	810	9	80	32	0.49	48	18	33	126	144	16%	87	4%	71%	25	64%	16%	5.85	30.3	66	165	$24
13 WAS	568	84	26	79	6	275	267	344	465	809	850	794	10	77	32	0.45	45	21	34	127	144	18%	100	4%	100%	25	48%	24%	5.69	27.3	59	148	$23
1st Half	246	34	9	41	3	272	268	354	467	821	925	786	11	74	33	0.49	45	21	34	143	137	14%	92	4%	100%	13	54%	23%	5.88	13.4	64	160	$18
2nd Half	322	50	17	38	3	276	266	336	463	799	787	801	8	78	31	0.41	44	22	33	116	149	20%	100	3%	100%	12	42%	25%	5.54	14.3	54	135	$27
14 Proj	571	86	25	83	5	281	270	348	469	818	859	803	9	79	32	0.48	46	20	34	125	139	16%	96	4%	87%				5.83	29.9	60	149	$24

Zobrist,Ben

Age 33 | Bats B | Pos 2B RF SS | Ht 6' 3" | Wt 210
Health A | PT/Exp A | Consist B
LIMA Plan B+ | Rand Var -1 | MM 3335

Hard to find a more consistent $20 producer at MI than this one, but he's on shaky ground now. HR dip shouldn't come as a surprise given fast decline in power skills. We can't assume green light will return in mid-30s, so double-digit SB in jeopardy too. Can still fill you up, just now with fewer calories.

Yr Tm	AB	R	HR	RBI	SB	BA	xBA	OBP	SLG	OPS	vL	vR	bb%	ct%	h%	Eye	G	L	F	PX	xPX	hr/f	Spd	SBO	SB%	#Wk	DOM	DIS	RC/G	RAR	BPV	BPX	R$
09 TAM	501	91	27	91	17	297	295	405	543	948	1035	905	15	79	33	0.88	42	20	39	148	132	18%	126	13%	74%	27	63%	15%	7.92	58.8	106	216	$27
10 TAM	541	77	10	75	24	238	246	346	353	699	695	700	15	80	28	0.86	44	18	38	82	93	6%	100	15%	89%	27	44%	26%	4.32	9.6	48	104	$15
11 TAM	588	99	20	91	19	269	284	353	469	822	907	783	12	78	31	0.60	45	20	35	144	120	12%	96	15%	76%	27	67%	19%	5.77	34.9	82	182	$25
12 TAM	560	88	20	74	14	270	285	377	471	848	879	835	15	82	30	0.94	43	22	35	128	114	13%	109	13%	61%	27	67%	19%	6.03	37.7	93	233	$21
13 TAM	612	77	12	71	11	275	260	354	402	756	643	812	11	85	31	0.79	43	20	37	87	98	6%	104	7%	79%	27	63%	15%	4.98	21.9	64	160	$20
1st Half	300	44	5	43	5	273	252	357	393	750	592	827	12	84	31	0.80	43	19	38	86	103	5%	99	6%	83%	14	57%	14%	4.98	11.0	58	145	$20
2nd Half	312	33	7	28	6	276	266	345	410	755	685	795	10	87	30	0.79	42	21	37	87	93	7%	108	9%	75%	13	69%	15%	4.98	11.5	69	173	$20
14 Proj	565	80	15	72	10	272	274	363	434	796	764	811	12	83	31	0.82	43	21	36	109	106	9%	107	8%	70%				5.46	28.7	72	181	$20

Zunino,Mike

Age 23 | Bats R | Pos CA | Ht 6' 2" | Wt 220
Health B | PT/Exp F | Consist F
LIMA Plan D+ | Rand Var +1 | MM 2403

5-14-.214 in 173 AB at SEA. Top backstop prospect dazzled in spring and early minors before hitting wall in PCL and MLB. As a young CA with already-plus defense and leadership qualities, his bat won't be blocked by normal catching growing pains, but poor ct% proves it's not ready yet. Leave him for 2015 in non-keeper leagues.

Yr Tm	AB	R	HR	RBI	SB	BA	xBA	OBP	SLG	OPS	vL	vR	bb%	ct%	h%	Eye	G	L	F	PX	xPX	hr/f	Spd	SBO	SB%	#Wk	DOM	DIS	RC/G	RAR	BPV	BPX	R$
09																																	
10																																	
11																																	
12 aa	51	6	2	7	0	303	283	363	520	884			9	84	32	0.60				134			89	0%	0%				6.92		90	225	$0
13 SEA *	376	49	12	44	1	199	216	255	347	603	650	609	7	67	26	0.23	43	19	39	115	108	10%	98	1%	100%	12	33%	67%	2.83	-10.4	4	10	$1
1st Half	229	27	8	33	0	202	218	242	375	617	548	625	5	65	27	0.15	36	18	45	140	114	7%	83	0%	0%	4	25%	75%	2.90	-5.8	10	25	$3
2nd Half	147	22	4	12	1	195	206	275	305	580	688	603	10	69	25	0.35	45	19	36	79	106	12%	120	3%	100%	8	38%	63%	2.69	-4.7	-4	-10	-$1
14 Proj	386	53	10	41	2	225	206	294	350	644	662	637	8	67	31	0.27	42	18	40	96	109	10%	112	2%	100%				3.32	-4.6	-11	-27	$6

STEPHEN NICKRAND

The following section contains player boxes for every pitcher who had significant playing time in 2013 and/or is expected to get fantasy roster-worthy innings in 2014. In most cases, high-end prospects who have yet to make their major league debuts will not appear here; you can find scouting reports for them in the Prospects section.

Snapshot Section

The top band of each player box contains the following information:

Age as of Opening Day 2014.

Throws right (R) or left (L).

Role: Starters (SP) are those projected to face 20+ batters per game; the rest are relievers (RP).

Ht/Wt: Each batter's height and weight.

Type evaluates the extent to which a pitcher allows the ball to be put into play and his ground ball or fly ball tendency. CON (contact) represents pitchers who allow the ball to be put into play a great deal. PWR (power) represents those with high strikeout and/or walk totals who keep the ball out of play. GB are those who have a ground ball rate more than 50%; xGB are those who have a GB rate more than 55%. FB are those who have a fly ball rate more than 40%; xFB are those who have a FB rate more than 45%.

Reliability Grades analyze each pitcher's forecast risk, on an A-F scale. High grades go to those who have accumulated few disabled list days (Health), have a history of substantial and regular major league playing time (PT/Exp) and have displayed consistent performance over the past three years, using xERA (Consist).

LIMA Plan Grade evaluates how well that pitcher would be a good fit for a team using the LIMA Plan draft strategy. Best grades go to pitchers who have excellent base skills and had a 2013 dollar value less than $20. Lowest grades will go to poor skills and values more than $20.

Random Variance Score (Rand Var) measures the impact random variance had on the pitcher's 2013 stats and the probability that his 2014 performance will exceed or fall short of 2013. The variables tracked are those prone to regression—H%, S%, hr/f and xERA to ERA variance. Players are rated on a scale of –5 to +5 with positive scores indicating rebounds and negative scores indicating corrections. Note that this score is computer-generated and the projections will override it on occasion.

Mayberry Method (MM) acknowledges the imprecision of the forecasting process by projecting player performance in broad strokes. The four digits of MM each represent a fantasy-relevant skill—ERA, strikeout rate, saves potential and playing time (IP)—and are all on a scale of 0 to 5.

Commentaries for each pitcher provide a brief analysis of BPIs and the potential impact on performance in 2014. MLB statistics are listed first for those who played only a portion of 2013 at the major league level. Note that these commentaries generally look at performance related issues only. Role and playing time expectations may impact these analyses, so you will have to adjust accordingly. Upside (UP) and downside (DN) statistical potential appears for some players; these are less grounded in hard data and more speculative of skills potential.

Player Stat Section

The past five years' statistics represent the total accumulated in the majors as well as in Triple-A, Double-A ball and various foreign leagues during each year. All non-major league stats have been converted to a major league equivalent (MLE) performance level. Minor league levels below Double-A are not included.

Nearly all baseball publications separate a player's statistical experiences in the major leagues from the minor leagues and outside leagues. While this may be appropriate for official record-keeping purposes, it is not an easy-to-analyze snapshot of a player's complete performance for a given year.

Bill James has proven that minor league statistics (converted to MLEs), at Double-A level or above, provide as accurate a record of a player's performance as Major league statistics. Other researchers have also devised conversion factors for foreign leagues. Since these are adequate barometers, we include them in the pool of historical data for each year.

Team designations: An asterisk (*) appearing with a team name means that Triple-A and/or Double-A numbers are included in that year's stat line. Any stints of less than 10 IP are not included (to screen out most rehab appearances). A designation of "a/a" means the stats were accumulated at both AA and AAA levels that year. "for" represents a foreign or independent league. The designation "2TM" appears whenever a player was on more than one major league team, crossing leagues, in a season. "2AL" and "2NL" represent more than one team in the same league. Players who were cut during the season and finished 2013 as a free agent are designated as FAA (Free agent, AL) and FAN (Free agent, NL).

Stats: Descriptions of all the categories appear in the Encyclopedia.

- The leading decimal point has been suppressed on some categories to conserve space.
- Data for platoons (vL, vR), balls-in-play (G/L/F) and consistency (Wk#, DOM, DIS) are for major league performance only.
- Formulas that use BIP data, like xERA and BPV, are used for years in which G/L/F data is available. Where feasible, older versions of these formulas are used otherwise.

Earned run average is presented alongside skills-based xERA. WHIP appears next, followed by opponents' overall OPS (oOPS). OPS splits vs. left-handed and right-handed batters appear to the right of oOPS. Batters faced per game (BF/G) provide a quick view of a pitcher's role—starters will generally have levels over 20.

Basic pitching skills are measured with Control, or walk rate (Ctl), Dominance, or strikeout rate (Dom), and Command, or strikeout-to-walk rate (Cmd). Swinging strikeout rate (SwK) is also presented with these basic skills. Our research shows that SwK serves as a useful tool for validating Dom.

Once the ball leaves the bat, it will either be a (G)round ball, (L)ine drive or (F)ly ball.

Random variance indicators include hit rate (H%)—often referred to as batting average on balls-in-play (BABIP)—which tends to regress to 30%. Normal strand rates (S%) fall within the tolerances of 65% to 80%. The ratio of home runs to fly balls (hr/f) is another sanity check; levels far from 10% are prone to regression.

In looking at consistency for starting pitchers, we track games started (GS), average pitch counts (APC) for all outings (for starters and relievers), the percentage of DOMinating starts (PQS 4 or 5) and DISaster starts (PQS 0 or 1). The larger the variance between DOM and DIS, the greater the consistency.

For relievers, we look at their saves success rate (Sv%) and Leverage Index (LI). A Doug Dennis study showed little correlation between saves success and future opportunity. However, you can increase your odds by prospecting for pitchers who have *both* a high saves percentage (80% or better) *and* high skills. Relievers with LI levels over 1.0 are being used more often by managers to win ballgames.

The final section includes several overall performance measures: runs above replacement (RAR), Base performance value (BPV), Base performance index (BPX, which is BPV indexed to each year's league average) and the Rotisserie value (R$).

2014 Projections

Forecasts are computed from a player's trends over the past five years. Adjustments were made for leading indicators and variances between skill and statistical output. After reviewing the leading indicators, you might opt to make further adjustments.

Although each year's numbers include all playing time at the Double-A level or above, the 2014 forecast only represents potential playing time at the major league level, and again is highly preliminary.

Note that the projected Rotisserie values in this book will not necessarily align with each player's historical actuals. Since we currently have no idea who is going to close games for the Indians, or whether Yordano Ventura is going to break camp with Kansas City, it is impossible to create a finite pool of playing time, something which is required for valuation. So the projections are roughly based on a 12-team AL/NL league, and include an inflated number of innings, league-wide. This serves to flatten the spread of values and depress individual player dollar projections. In truth, a $25 player in this book might actually be worth $21, or $28. This level of precision is irrelevant in a process that is driven by market forces anyway. So, don't obsess over it.

Be aware of other sources that publish perfectly calibrated Rotisserie values over the winter. They are likely making arbitrary decisions as to where free agents are going to sign and who is going to land jobs in the spring. We do not make those leaps of faith here.

Bottom line… It is far too early to be making definitive projections for 2014, especially on playing time. Focus on the skill levels and trends, then consult BaseballHQ.com for playing time revisions as players change teams and roles become more defined. A free projections update will be available online in March.

Do-it-yourself analysis

Here are some data points you can look at in doing your own player analysis:

- Variance between vLH and vRH opposition OPS
- Variance in 2013 hr/f rate from 10%
- Variance in 2013 hit rate (H%) from 30%
- Variance in 2013 strand rate (S%) to tolerances (65% - 80%)
- Variance between ERA and xERA each year
- Growth or decline in Base Performance Value (BPV)
- Spikes in innings pitched
- Trends in average pitch counts (APC)
- Trends in DOM/DIS splits
- Trends in saves success rate (Sv%)
- Variance between Dom changes and corresponding SwK levels

Aardsma,David

Age: 32 Th: R Role RP | Health F | LIMA Plan D+
Ht: 6' 3" Wt: 205 Type Pwr xFB | PT/Exp F | Rand Var -2
Consist C | MM 1300

2-2, 4.31 ERA in 40 IP at NYM. Even when he was closing, he didn't really have a closer's skill set—too many walks and fly balls. Now, after missing 2011/12 with injuries, he's back with lower Dom and struggles vs RH. Ugly 2H line (which was all time spent in majors) suggests that he's unlikely to return to relevance.

Yr	Tm	W	L	Sv	IP	K	ERA	xERA	WHIP	oOPS	vL	vR	BF/G	Ctl	Dom	Cmd	SwK	G	L	F	H%	S%	hr/f	GS	APC	DOM%	DIS%	Sv%	LI	RAR	BPV	BPX	R$
09	SEA	3	6	38	71	80	2.52	4.07	1.16	555	557	551	4.1	4.3	10.1	2.4	12%	25	21	54	27%	80%	4%	0	17			90	1.35	15.8	69	129	$23
10	SEA	0	6	31	50	49	3.44	3.89	1.17	631	688	568	3.8	4.5	8.9	2.0	10%	36	19	45	24%	74%	9%	0	16			86	1.46	3.9	52	83	$13
11																																	
12	NYY	0	0	0	1	1	9.00	5.54	2.00	1400	0	5000	5.0	9.0	9.0	1.0	17%	67	0	33	0%	0%	100%	0	24			0	0.01	-0.6	-36	-47	-$5
13	NYM *	3	2	3	62	53	3.48	4.41	1.43	800	627	897	4.3	4.9	7.8	1.6	12%	33	26	41	27%	82%	15%	0	17			60	0.83	2.9	45	58	$0
1st Half		1	0	3	32	26	1.93	2.83	1.16	494	429	536	4.5	4.3	7.4	1.7	15%	38	27	35	22%	91%	11%	0	14			100	0.50	7.6	65	84	$5
2nd Half		2	2	0	30	27	5.16	5.09	1.72	888	688	997	4.2	5.5	8.2	1.5	11%	31	26	43	32%	76%	15%	0	18			0	0.93	-4.7	9	12	-$7
14	**Proj**	**2**	**4**	**0**	**51**	**44**	**4.41**	**4.50**	**1.47**	**765**	**688**	**828**	**4.1**	**4.7**	**7.8**	**1.7**	**11%**	**30**	**22**	**48**	**29%**	**73%**	**9%**	**0**						**-3.4**	**22**	**28**	**-$3**

Affeldt,Jeremy

Age: 35 Th: L Role RP | Health F | LIMA Plan C
Ht: 6' 4" Wt: 225 Type Pwr xGB | PT/Exp D | Rand Var -2
Consist B | MM 4300

When healthy, he's death to left-handed hitters, but oblique strain and recurring groin injury eroded his Dom and tanked his Cmd last year. So we'll give him a mulligan. But that doesn't change the fact that he's missed time in four straight seasons, nor does it reverse the aging process. DN: Another 2013.

Yr	Tm	W	L	Sv	IP	K	ERA	xERA	WHIP	oOPS	vL	vR	BF/G	Ctl	Dom	Cmd	SwK	G	L	F	H%	S%	hr/f	GS	APC	DOM%	DIS%	Sv%	LI	RAR	BPV	BPX	R$
09	SF	2	2	0	62	55	1.73	3.20	1.17	581	683	501	3.4	4.5	7.9	1.8	10%	65	17	18	24%	87%	10%	0	13			0	1.44	19.9	65	122	$6
10	SF	4	3	4	50	44	4.14	3.87	1.60	795	815	784	4.3	4.3	7.9	1.8	8%	56	19	26	35%	75%	11%	0	15			57	1.17	-0.4	60	97	$0
11	SF	3	2	3	62	54	2.63	3.18	1.15	625	406	764	3.9	3.5	7.9	2.3	10%	62	16	22	26%	80%	14%	0	15			50	1.18	10.0	87	131	$5
12	SF	1	2	3	63	57	2.70	3.31	1.26	640	621	656	4.0	3.3	8.1	2.5	8%	60	20	20	32%	77%	3%	0	15			75	1.22	10.3	96	125	$3
13	SF	1	5	0	34	21	3.74	4.22	1.31	642	524	743	3.7	4.5	5.6	1.2	8%	55	25	20	25%	71%	10%	0	13			0	1.35	0.5	11	15	-$3
1st Half		1	4	0	27	17	3.29	3.90	1.28	660	511	783	3.8	4.0	5.6	1.4	8%	60	23	17	26%	76%	14%	0	13			0	1.40	1.9	32	41	-$2
2nd Half		0	1	0	6	4	5.68	5.68	1.42	546	580	496	3.5	7.1	5.7	0.8	7%	29	35	35	22%	56%	0%	0	15			0	1.16	-1.4	-82	-106	-$6
14	**Proj**	**2**	**4**	**0**	**51**	**43**	**3.51**	**3.29**	**1.28**	**662**	**569**	**729**	**3.7**	**3.8**	**7.6**	**2.0**	**9%**	**60**	**19**	**20**	**29%**	**73%**	**11%**	**0**						**2.2**	**72**	**94**	**$0**

Albers,Andrew

Age: 28 Th: L Role SP | Health A | LIMA Plan C
Ht: 6' 1" Wt: 195 Type Con FB | PT/Exp D | Rand Var -1
Consist C | MM 2001

2-5, 4.05 ERA in 60 IP at MIN. Averaged only 86 mph on his fastball, and it shows in anemic SwK and 3.8 Dom in majors. Needed pinpoint 1.1 Ctl in MIN just to get to 4.51 xERA. 17 shutout IP in first two starts, 5.69 ERA after that. If those aren't enough red flags, big IP increase creates burnout risk. You've been warned.

Yr	Tm	W	L	Sv	IP	K	ERA	xERA	WHIP	oOPS	vL	vR	BF/G	Ctl	Dom	Cmd	SwK	G	L	F	H%	S%	hr/f	GS	APC	DOM%	DIS%	Sv%	LI	RAR	BPV	BPX	R$
09																																	
10																																	
11	aa	4	1	0	43	27	3.25	3.61	1.33				13.8	1.5	5.6	3.8					35%	73%								3.7	109	164	$0
12	aa	4	3	0	98	56	4.81	5.43	1.53				22.5	1.2	5.1	4.2					37%	69%								-9.6	88	115	-$9
13	MIN *	13	10	0	192	112	3.69	4.43	1.35	698	689	702	25.0	2.0	5.3	2.7	7%	44	20	37	31%	75%	8%	10	92	30%	40%			4.1	57	74	$5
1st Half		7	3	0	92	60	3.87	5.27	1.52				24.9	2.6	5.9	2.3					34%	78%	0%	0						0.0	44	57	$0
2nd Half		6	7	0	100	52	3.53	3.65	1.19	698	689	702	25.1	1.4	4.7	3.3	7%	44	20	37	29%	73%	8%	10	92	30%	40%			4.1	74	96	$9
14	**Proj**	**5**	**7**	**0**	**114**	**63**	**4.42**	**4.18**	**1.36**	**720**	**697**	**729**	**21.4**	**1.9**	**5.0**	**2.6**	**7%**	**44**	**20**	**37**	**31%**	**71%**	**10%**	**22**						**-7.8**	**60**	**78**	**-$2**

Albers,Matt

Age: 31 Th: R Role RP | Health B | LIMA Plan B
Ht: 6' 1" Wt: 225 Type xGB | PT/Exp C | Rand Var -2
Consist A | MM 3100

Several years of scattershot results and skills, but xERA is remarkably consistent. Plunging Dom is a concern, though emergence of sinker and resulting GB profile mitigate that somewhat. 2nd half Ctl, Dom bear watching: further tinkering, hidden injury, or random variance? Ah, life in middle relief.

Yr	Tm	W	L	Sv	IP	K	ERA	xERA	WHIP	oOPS	vL	vR	BF/G	Ctl	Dom	Cmd	SwK	G	L	F	H%	S%	hr/f	GS	APC	DOM%	DIS%	Sv%	LI	RAR	BPV	BPX	R$
09	BAL	3	6	0	67	49	5.51	4.81	1.73	797	929	694	5.5	4.8	6.6	1.4	8%	48	20	31	35%	66%	4%	0	21			0	1.01	-9.8	14	26	-$7
10	BAL	5	3	0	76	49	4.52	4.27	1.48	726	819	662	5.3	4.0	5.8	1.4	8%	56	15	29	30%	70%	9%	0	21			0	0.82	-4.1	30	48	-$2
11	BOS	4	4	0	65	68	4.73	3.74	1.44	735	834	667	5.2	4.3	9.5	2.2	7%	46	18	35	32%	69%	11%	0	21			0	0.83	-6.3	78	117	-$3
12	2 TM	3	1	0	60	44	2.39	3.72	1.13	642	702	600	3.8	3.3	6.6	2.0	9%	55	19	26	23%	88%	20%	0	14			0	1.02	12.1	63	82	$4
13	CLE	3	1	0	63	35	3.14	3.77	1.27	621	683	573	4.7	3.3	5.0	1.5	8%	64	19	17	28%	74%	6%	0	17			0	0.71	5.6	43	56	$0
1st Half		2	0	0	28	21	2.22	3.63	1.34	619	822	476	4.9	4.4	6.7	1.5	9%	67	19	14	28%	84%	8%	0	19			0	0.75	5.7	45	58	$2
2nd Half		1	1	0	35	14	3.89	3.86	1.21	622	574	662	4.5	2.3	3.6	1.6	7%	61	19	19	28%	66%	5%	0	15			0	0.68	-0.1	42	54	-$1
14	**Proj**	**3**	**2**	**0**	**65**	**44**	**3.42**	**3.67**	**1.29**	**658**	**724**	**610**	**4.5**	**3.5**	**6.1**	**1.7**	**8%**	**58**	**19**	**23**	**28%**	**75%**	**11%**	**0**						**3.6**	**51**	**66**	**$1**

Alburquerque,Al

Age: 28 Th: R Role RP | Health F | LIMA Plan C
Ht: 6' 0" Wt: 195 Type Pwr | PT/Exp D | Rand Var +4
Consist A | MM 5500

The real Nook Laloosh? Brings serious heat, but isn't always sure where the ball is going. Big SwK supports elite Dom, but the problem is the pitches they DON'T swing at. H% and S%-based ERA regression came as expected, but high LD%, hr/f and FB% made it worse than necessary. Hit the bull, Al.

Yr	Tm	W	L	Sv	IP	K	ERA	xERA	WHIP	oOPS	vL	vR	BF/G	Ctl	Dom	Cmd	SwK	G	L	F	H%	S%	hr/f	GS	APC	DOM%	DIS%	Sv%	LI	RAR	BPV	BPX	R$
09	aa	1	3	0	26	25	5.02	3.92	1.57				5.0	4.6	8.4	1.8					36%	65%								-2.3	89	167	-$4
10	aa	2	4	3	34	25	6.69	4.90	1.72				6.2	5.2	6.5	1.3					35%	58%								-11.1	52	84	-$5
11	DET	6	1	0	43	67	1.87	2.59	1.15	438	468	412	4.4	6.0	13.9	2.3	16%	57	14	30	28%	82%	0%	0	19			0	1.08	11.1	123	185	$6
12	DET	0	0	0	13	18	0.68	2.75	1.05	420	345	484	6.6	5.4	12.2	2.3	18%	63	11	26	23%	93%	0%	0	29			0	1.55	5.5	114	149	-$1
13	DET	4	3	0	49	70	4.59	3.53	1.49	674	662	683	4.2	6.2	12.9	2.1	16%	40	25	34	33%	71%	13%	0	17			0	0.98	-4.4	81	105	-$3
1st Half		0	1	0	19	32	2.37	3.72	1.68	610	592	623	4.5	8.5	15.2	1.8	15%	33	36	31	39%	84%	0%	0	19			0	1.05	3.5	54	70	-$3
2nd Half		4	2	0	30	38	6.00	3.45	1.37	713	712	713	3.9	4.8	11.4	2.4	17%	44	20	36	30%	58%	19%	0	15			0	0.95	-7.9	98	126	-$3
14	**Proj**	**6**	**3**	**0**	**58**	**79**	**3.48**	**3.17**	**1.34**	**588**	**593**	**583**	**4.2**	**5.7**	**12.3**	**2.1**	**16%**	**43**	**21**	**35**	**31%**	**74%**	**7%**	**0**						**2.7**	**88**	**115**	**$3**

Allen,Cody

Age: 25 Th: R Role RP | Health A | LIMA Plan B+
Ht: 6' 1" Wt: 210 Type Pwr xFB | PT/Exp D | Rand Var -3
Consist A | MM 4520

Dom growth was outstanding, even if xERA says that the ERA improvement that came with it was a bit of a stretch. BPV has reached elite levels and now denote closer-worthiness, but high LD% and FB% will have to be tamed before he can find sustained success in that role. Still... UP: 35 Saves.

Yr	Tm	W	L	Sv	IP	K	ERA	xERA	WHIP	oOPS	vL	vR	BF/G	Ctl	Dom	Cmd	SwK	G	L	F	H%	S%	hr/f	GS	APC	DOM%	DIS%	Sv%	LI	RAR	BPV	BPX	R$
09																																	
10																																	
11																																	
12	CLE *	3	3	3	68	65	3.05	3.18	1.19	710	776	654	4.9	3.2	8.5	2.7	10%	39	24	37	28%	78%	6%	0	20			50	0.44	8.2	91	119	$5
13	CLE	6	1	2	70	88	2.43	3.48	1.25	679	691	669	3.9	3.3	11.3	3.4	12%	30	25	45	33%	85%	9%	0	16			50	1.11	12.4	121	158	$7
1st Half		2	0	1	33	40	2.16	3.32	1.08	623	633	612	4.3	3.0	10.8	3.6	12%	37	19	44	29%	85%	8%	0	17			50	0.70	7.0	129	167	$7
2nd Half		4	1	1	37	48	2.68	3.61	1.41	729	739	719	3.6	3.6	11.7	3.2	12%	24	29	46	37%	85%	9%	0	15			50	1.40	5.4	114	147	$6
14	**Proj**	**4**	**2**	**23**	**58**	**66**	**3.15**	**3.36**	**1.24**	**667**	**676**	**658**	**4.1**	**3.3**	**10.2**	**3.1**	**12%**	**29**	**25**	**45**	**32%**	**78%**	**8%**	**0**						**5.1**	**102**	**133**	**$12**

Alvarez,Henderson

Age: 24 Th: R Role SP | Health F | LIMA Plan B+
Ht: 6' 0" Wt: 210 Type Con GB | PT/Exp B | Rand Var -2
Consist B | MM 3003

Shoulder injury kept him shelved until July. No-hitter was fun, but don't confuse it with skil—it was more about luck, as was the ridiculously low hr/f that resulted in only two HR on the year. Can't seem to turn 93 mph fastball into strikeouts, and without more Dom (or luck), don't expect another mid-3s ERA.

Yr	Tm	W	L	Sv	IP	K	ERA	xERA	WHIP	oOPS	vL	vR	BF/G	Ctl	Dom	Cmd	SwK	G	L	F	H%	S%	hr/f	GS	APC	DOM%	DIS%	Sv%	LI	RAR	BPV	BPX	R$
09																																	
10																																	
11	TOR *	9	7	0	152	99	3.51	3.84	1.20	717	698	738	24.4	1.5	5.9	4.0	7%	53	20	26	30%	74%	15%	10	98	50%	0%			8.1	91	137	$9
12	TOR	9	14	0	187	79	4.85	4.53	1.44	812	885	725	26.0	2.6	3.8	1.5	5%	57	19	24	29%	70%	18%	31	92	32%	19%			-19.3	33	43	-$9
13	MIA	5	6	0	103	57	3.59	3.79	1.14	636	753	524	24.6	2.4	5.0	2.1	7%	53	22	25	27%	66%	3%	17	85	35%	18%			3.4	57	74	$4
1st Half																																	
2nd Half		5	6	0	103	57	3.59	3.79	1.14	636	753	524	24.6	2.4	5.0	2.1	7%	53	22	25	27%	66%	3%	17	85	35%	18%			3.4	57	74	$4
14	**Proj**	**7**	**11**	**0**	**179**	**98**	**4.02**	**3.76**	**1.27**	**721**	**775**	**660**	**24.7**	**2.4**	**4.9**	**2.1**	**7%**	**54**	**20**	**25**	**29%**	**70%**	**11%**	**30**						**-3.5**	**57**	**74**	**$4**

DAVE ADLER

Alvarez,Jose

Alvarez,Jose		Health	A	LIMA Plan	D+
Age: 25	Th: L Role SP	PT/Exp	D	Rand Var	+1
Ht: 5' 11"	Wt: 180 Type	Consist	B	MM	2100

1-5, 5.82 ERA in 39 IP at DET. Spent the season on the AAA shuttle. Minor league success (2.80 ERA) was new, given poor 2011/12 MLEs. It also didn't translate to the majors. SwK and 7.2 Dom with DET shows that there are skills, but issued too many free passes (3.7 Ctl). Still needs work, so shuttle rides will continue.

Yr Tm	W	L	Sv	IP	K	ERA	xERA	WHIP	oOPS	vL	vR	BF/G	Ctl	Dom	Cmd	SwK	G	L	F	H%	S%	hr/f	GS	APC	DOM%	DIS%	Sv%	LI	RAR	BPV	BPX	R$
09																																
10																																
11 aa	2	6	0	66	39	5.57	5.68	1.62				24.3	2.9	5.3	1.8					35%	67%								-13.2	31	46	-$8
12 aa	6	9	0	136	63	5.15	4.43	1.40				23.0	1.9	4.2	2.2					32%	62%								-19.1	51	66	-$8
13 DET *	9	11	1	167	122	4.11	4.29	1.32	866	851	872	19.8	2.2	6.5	2.9	11%	40	23	37	31%	72%	16%	6	50	17%	50%	100	1.22	-5.1	69	90	$2
1st Half	6	5	0	98	79	3.61	3.76	1.18	784	863	757	24.4	1.9	7.3	3.9	9%	45	20	35	30%	74%	22%	3	96	33%	33%			3.1	96	125	$9
2nd Half	3	6	1	70	42	4.82	5.03	1.50	925	846	968	15.8	2.7	5.5	2.0	12%	37	25	38	33%	69%	12%	3	37	0%	67%	100	1.34	-8.2	41	53	-$8
14 Proj	**2**	**4**	**0**	**62**	**41**	**4.51**	**4.11**	**1.37**	**778**	**742**	**795**	**20.3**	**2.7**	**5.9**	**2.2**	**11%**	**40**	**23**	**37**	**31%**	**68%**	**8%**	**13**						**-4.9**	**52**	**67**	**-$3**

Anderson,Brett

Anderson,Brett		Health	F	LIMA Plan	C
Age: 26	Th: L Role SP	PT/Exp	D	Rand Var	+5
Ht: 6' 4"	Wt: 235 Type Pwr xGB	Consist	A	MM	4201

Stat to know: He has spent the equivalent of two years on the disabled list since 2011. xERA shows that the skills are intact; hr/f and H% conspired against him in 2013. He remains an xGBer with fine Ctl. BPV says "buy," but how much do you want to spend on a guy made of glass?

Yr Tm	W	L	Sv	IP	K	ERA	xERA	WHIP	oOPS	vL	vR	BF/G	Ctl	Dom	Cmd	SwK	G	L	F	H%	S%	hr/f	GS	APC	DOM%	DIS%	Sv%	LI	RAR	BPV	BPX	R$
09 OAK	11	11	0	175	150	4.06	3.61	1.28	710	788	682	24.5	2.3	7.7	3.3	8%	51	15	34	32%	71%	11%	30	94	50%	20%			5.8	105	197	$11
10 OAK	7	6	0	112	75	2.80	3.55	1.19	655	685	646	24.7	1.8	6.0	3.4	7%	55	17	28	30%	77%	6%	19	95	58%	11%			17.7	94	151	$9
11 OAK	3	6	0	83	61	4.00	3.50	1.33	721	761	700	27.4	2.7	6.6	2.4	7%	57	18	25	31%	72%	13%	13	104	54%	31%			-0.6	81	121	-$1
12 OAK *	5	3	0	58	40	3.28	3.47	1.20	565	515	581	21.3	1.8	6.2	3.4	9%	60	24	17	30%	74%	6%	6	88	83%	17%			5.3	91	118	$2
13 OAK	1	4	3	45	46	6.04	3.36	1.61	794	853	774	12.5	4.2	9.3	2.2	9%	63	16	21	37%	63%	18%	5	48	40%	60%	100	0.78	-12.0	94	122	-$7
1st Half	1	4	0	29	29	6.21	3.64	1.62	781	827	766	22.0	4.7	9.0	1.9	8%	63	13	24	35%	61%	14%	5	85	40%	60%	0	0.99	-8.4	78	100	-$8
2nd Half	0	0	3	16	17	5.74	2.87	1.60	819	898	790	6.8	3.4	9.8	2.8	11%	62	22	16	38%	65%	29%	0	26			100	0.66	-3.6	123	159	-$5
14 Proj	**5**	**5**	**0**	**95**	**75**	**3.58**	**3.40**	**1.34**	**679**	**708**	**668**	**21.0**	**3.2**	**7.1**	**2.2**	**9%**	**58**	**19**	**22**	**31%**	**74%**	**10%**	**30**						**3.3**	**77**	**100**	**$2**

Archer,Chris

Archer,Chris		Health	A	LIMA Plan	C+
Age: 25	Th: R Role SP	PT/Exp	D	Rand Var	0
Ht: 6' 3"	Wt: 200 Type Pwr	Consist	C	MM	4303

9-7, 3.22 ERA in 129 IP at TAM. Another thoroughbred from the Tampa pitching stable. Showed his youth when he struggled with Ctl in 1H, but got it together after the break. H% says 2H ERA isn't going to repeat, but Cmd improvement gets your attention. With GB% bent and dominance vs RHB, this is one to invest in.

Yr Tm	W	L	Sv	IP	K	ERA	xERA	WHIP	oOPS	vL	vR	BF/G	Ctl	Dom	Cmd	SwK	G	L	F	H%	S%	hr/f	GS	APC	DOM%	DIS%	Sv%	LI	RAR	BPV	BPX	R$
09																																
10 aa	8	2	0	70	57	2.02	2.69	1.29				22.1	4.8	7.4	1.5					27%	85%								17.7	81	130	$7
11 a/a	9	7	0	147	112	4.36	4.74	1.63				24.3	4.9	6.9	1.4					33%	73%								-7.7	51	76	-$6
12 TAM *	8	12	0	157	154	4.19	3.21	1.32	624	915	435	21.0	4.2	8.8	2.1	10%	44	18	38	30%	68%	11%	4	82	75%	0%	0	0.99	-3.3	90	118	$3
13 TAM *	14	10	0	179	144	3.61	3.76	1.26	660	801	455	22.1	3.1	7.3	2.4	9%	47	19	34	29%	75%	12%	23	91	43%	35%			5.7	67	87	$10
1st Half	7	6	0	81	68	4.53	5.02	1.58	763	809	655	22.2	4.6	7.6	1.7	8%	49	23	28	33%	74%	15%	6	96	17%	50%			-6.6	47	60	-$3
2nd Half	7	4	0	98	76	2.85	3.49	1.00	624	796	406	22.7	1.8	7.0	3.8	10%	46	18	36	25%	77%	11%	17	90	53%	29%			12.3	100	129	$20
14 Proj	**13**	**9**	**0**	**174**	**146**	**3.67**	**3.57**	**1.26**	**681**	**794**	**499**	**21.8**	**3.2**	**7.6**	**2.3**	**9%**	**47**	**20**	**33**	**29%**	**73%**	**9%**	**33**						**4.2**	**75**	**97**	**$11**

Arrieta,Jake

Arrieta,Jake		Health	C	LIMA Plan	D+
Age: 28	Th: R Role SP	PT/Exp	C	Rand Var	+1
Ht: 6' 4"	Wt: 225 Type Pwr	Consist	A	MM	2203

5-4, 4.58 ERA in 75 IP at BAL and CHC. Been waiting four years for the breakout—did the league swap make it happen? Better GB% and Dom in the 2H, but he's still issuing too many walks, and DOM/DIS shows he's still not a dominant starter. At this point, he's at risk of becoming long relief fodder or an AAAA player.

Yr Tm	W	L	Sv	IP	K	ERA	xERA	WHIP	oOPS	vL	vR	BF/G	Ctl	Dom	Cmd	SwK	G	L	F	H%	S%	hr/f	GS	APC	DOM%	DIS%	Sv%	LI	RAR	BPV	BPX	R$
09 a/a	11	11	0	151	120	5.02	5.48	1.60				23.8	3.6	7.2	2.0					35%	71%								-13.0	45	85	-$3
10 BAL *	12	8	0	173	104	3.67	3.87	1.41	767	898	594	24.5	4.3	5.4	1.3	6%	42	19	39	28%	75%	7%	18	95	17%	33%			8.8	44	71	$5
11 BAL	10	8	0	119	93	5.05	4.45	1.46	791	856	715	23.8	4.4	7.0	1.6	8%	46	16	39	28%	70%	15%	22	95	32%	23%			-16.3	30	45	-$4
12 BAL *	8	13	0	171	151	6.13	4.74	1.47	763	846	664	21.5	3.6	8.0	2.2	8%	44	24	32	33%	58%	15%	18	82	44%	50%	0	0.79	-44.6	62	81	-$15
13 2 TM *	12	9	0	155	120	4.98	4.36	1.48	718	664	775	22.1	4.3	7.0	1.6	7%	40	25	34	30%	67%	12%	14	90	14%	21%			-21.3	51	67	-$6
1st Half	6	5	0	73	53	6.12	4.76	1.56	857	698	1047	22.7	4.0	6.5	1.6	7%	33	33	33	33%	60%	9%	5	89	0%	40%			-20.2	47	61	-$12
2nd Half	6	4	0	82	68	3.97	4.01	1.40	648	641	654	21.7	4.6	7.4	1.6	7%	44	22	35	28%	75%	14%	9	91	22%	11%			-1.1	55	71	-$1
14 Proj	**7**	**9**	**0**	**145**	**114**	**4.81**	**4.27**	**1.46**	**764**	**779**	**748**	**22.2**	**4.3**	**7.1**	**1.6**	**7%**	**42**	**21**	**37**	**30%**	**68%**	**10%**	**28**						**-16.9**	**30**	**39**	**-$4**

Arroyo,Bronson

Arroyo,Bronson		Health	A	LIMA Plan	C+
Age: 37	Th: R Role SP	PT/Exp	A	Rand Var	+1
Ht: 6' 4"	Wt: 195 Type Con	Consist	A	MM	3105

Despite advanced age, he remains affective. CON: Doesn't throw very hard (87 mph); doesn't go deep into games; low SwK confirms poor Dom. PRO: Low Ctl; mastery of RH hitters; solid DOM/DIS. Don't get carried away; xERA says to expect an ERA closer to 4.00. Fade coming, but likely has another year at this level.

Yr Tm	W	L	Sv	IP	K	ERA	xERA	WHIP	oOPS	vL	vR	BF/G	Ctl	Dom	Cmd	SwK	G	L	F	H%	S%	hr/f	GS	APC	DOM%	DIS%	Sv%	LI	RAR	BPV	BPX	R$
09 CIN	15	13	0	220	127	3.84	4.42	1.27	737	790	687	28.0	2.7	5.2	2.0	7%	45	19	37	27%	75%	12%	33	103	45%	18%			13.1	45	84	$15
10 CIN	17	10	0	216	121	3.88	4.31	1.15	679	786	576	26.7	2.5	5.0	2.1	7%	43	16	40	25%	71%	11%	33	99	52%	21%			5.3	45	73	$15
11 CIN	9	12	0	199	108	5.07	4.57	1.37	855	976	745	26.7	2.0	4.9	2.4	6%	39	19	43	29%	71%	16%	32	97	38%	22%			-27.6	50	75	-$6
12 CIN	12	10	0	202	129	3.74	4.19	1.21	721	794	642	26.1	1.6	5.7	3.7	7%	41	21	37	29%	73%	11%	32	92	50%	9%			6.8	80	105	$11
13 CIN	14	12	0	202	124	3.79	3.92	1.15	735	856	607	25.7	1.5	5.5	3.6	6%	44	20	35	27%	74%	14%	32	90	56%	19%			2.0	81	105	$12
1st Half	6	6	0	105	57	3.61	4.27	1.21	736	829	634	27.2	1.7	4.9	2.9	6%	42	21	37	28%	75%	10%	16	91	50%	13%			3.3	62	80	$10
2nd Half	8	6	0	97	67	3.98	3.56	1.09	735	886	579	24.3	1.3	6.2	4.8	7%	47	20	34	26%	72%	19%	16	89	63%	25%			-1.3	101	131	$13
14 Proj	**13**	**11**	**0**	**203**	**125**	**4.00**	**3.78**	**1.20**	**748**	**855**	**638**	**25.3**	**1.7**	**5.5**	**3.3**	**7%**	**43**	**20**	**37**	**28%**	**73%**	**14%**	**32**						**-3.3**	**75**	**97**	**$11**

Aumont,Phillippe

Aumont,Phillippe		Health	A	LIMA Plan	D
Age: 25	Th: R Role RP	PT/Exp	D	Rand Var	-1
Ht: 6' 7"	Wt: 260 Type Pwr xGB	Consist	B	MM	2400

1-3, 4.19 ERA in 19 IP at PHI. It's fair to call him a post-hype prospect as long as we point out the hype dates back to 2007. With high Dom, he would be interesting if he could just figure out the Ctl thing, but it just keeps getting worse. Still surprisingly young—which is good because he's far away from being a contributor.

Yr Tm	W	L	Sv	IP	K	ERA	xERA	WHIP	oOPS	vL	vR	BF/G	Ctl	Dom	Cmd	SwK	G	L	F	H%	S%	hr/f	GS	APC	DOM%	DIS%	Sv%	LI	RAR	BPV	BPX	R$
09 aa	1	4	4	18	22	6.09	6.09	1.96				5.6	5.7	11.4	2.0					45%	67%								-3.9	86	160	-$4
10 aa	1	6	0	50	33	7.93	5.77	1.89				21.3	6.4	5.9	0.9					34%	56%								-23.6	30	48	-$12
11 a/a	2	5	7	54	68	3.10	3.34	1.37				5.2	4.1	11.4	2.8					36%	77%								5.6	122	184	$4
12 PHI *	3	2	17	59	64	4.97	3.97	1.60	544	578	527	4.4	6.8	9.8	1.4	14%	74	3	23	31%	68%	0%	0	14			81	1.10	-7.0	82	106	$1
13 PHI *	1	5	2	55	54	4.50	4.82	1.97	818	1048	679	4.9	8.4	8.9	1.1	10%	49	29	22	36%	75%	0%	0	17			67	0.72	-4.3	77	100	-$9
1st Half	1	3	2	28	29	4.96	5.16	2.08	716	913	585	4.5	9.1	9.4	1.0	10%	58	23	19	37%	73%	0%	0	17			100	0.74	-3.7	78	101	-$8
2nd Half	0	2	0	27	25	4.03	4.49	1.86	1448	2333	1150	5.3	7.6	8.3	1.1	9%	9	55	36	35%	76%	0%	0	14			0	0.60	-0.6	75	97	-$9
14 Proj	**1**	**3**	**0**	**44**	**44**	**4.67**	**4.14**	**1.58**	**590**	**743**	**488**	**5.0**	**6.6**	**9.1**	**1.4**	**10%**	**51**	**23**	**26**	**31%**	**68%**	**4%**	**0**						**-4.3**	**15**	**19**	**-$5**

Avilan,Luis

Avilan,Luis		Health	A	LIMA Plan	B
Age: 24	Th: L Role RP	PT/Exp	A	Rand Var	-5
Ht: 6' 2"	Wt: 195 Type GB	Consist	B	MM	3100

Extreme GBer posted an ERA that might make you think of a bigger role—but hold that thought. Perfect storm of S%, H%, and hr/f, more than raw skill, was the reason. xERA points to a solid but unspectacular reliever, and there's likely to be very little fanalytic profit come draft day. OK, time to release that thought.

Yr Tm	W	L	Sv	IP	K	ERA	xERA	WHIP	oOPS	vL	vR	BF/G	Ctl	Dom	Cmd	SwK	G	L	F	H%	S%	hr/f	GS	APC	DOM%	DIS%	Sv%	LI	RAR	BPV	BPX	R$
09																																
10																																
11 aa	4	8	1	105	68	4.82	4.62	1.46				12.5	2.9	5.9	2.0					33%	67%								-11.4	51	77	-$5
12 ATL *	4	6	1	97	81	3.31	3.60	1.31	547	528	559	8.6	3.9	7.5	1.9	11%	47	20	33	28%	77%	3%	0	18			100	0.91	8.5	68	89	$3
13 ATL	5	0	0	65	38	1.52	3.68	0.95	478	383	557	3.4	3.0	5.3	1.7	9%	58	19	24	21%	84%	2%	0	13			0	1.07	18.8	48	63	$9
1st Half	2	0	0	34	18	1.60	3.94	0.89	412	332	484	3.3	3.5	4.8	1.4	8%	53	19	28	18%	80%	0%	0	13			0	1.00	9.4	24	31	$9
2nd Half	3	0	0	31	20	1.44	3.41	1.02	543	438	621	3.6	2.6	5.7	2.2	10%	62	18	20	24%	87%	5%	0	13			0	1.14	9.4	74	95	$9
14 Proj	**4**	**2**	**0**	**64**	**44**	**3.63**	**3.74**	**1.31**	**690**	**600**	**757**	**5.2**	**3.3**	**6.2**	**1.9**	**10%**	**54**	**19**	**27**	**29%**	**72%**	**7%**	**0**						**1.9**	**55**	**71**	**$0**

DAVE ADLER

Axelrod,Dylan

Age: 28	Th: R	Role RP	Health A	LIMA Plan D+
Ht: 6' 0"	Wt: 185	Type	PT/Exp C	Rand Var +3
			Consist B	MM 1101

Few strikeouts means more balls in play; that's when bad things can happen... as in 2nd-half bad. His H% and hr/f blew up, sending ERA through the roof. xERA and BPV show that the foundation is weak anyway. At this age, we should have seen some growth by now, and it's just not happening.

Yr	Tm	W	L	Sv	IP	K	ERA	xERA	WHIP	oOPS	vL	vR	BF/G	Ctl	Dom	Cmd	SwK	G	L	F	H%	S%	hr/f	GS	APC	DOM%	DIS%	Sv%	LI	RAR	BPV	BPX	R$
09																																	
10																																	
11	CHW *	10	3	0	169	128	3.54	3.58	1.35	699	682	725	23.5	2.7	6.8	2.5	10%	41	22	37	33%	72%	5%	3	79	67%	33%	0	0.62	8.3	86	129	$6
12	CHW *	9	7	0	148	114	4.82	5.29	1.55	807	861	760	21.5	3.8	6.9	1.8	11%	45	19	36	32%	72%	13%	7	68	14%	43%	0	0.73	-14.6	39	51	-$8
13	CHW	4	11	0	128	73	5.68	5.05	1.66	890	876	913	19.5	3.0	5.1	1.7	8%	40	21	39	34%	70%	13%	20	76	25%	40%	0	0.84	-28.7	29	37	-$17
1st Half		3	4	0	91	51	4.57	4.81	1.44	807	795	831	24.6	3.0	5.1	1.7	8%	41	19	40	30%	73%	12%	16	97	31%	25%			-7.8	30	39	-$12
2nd Half		1	7	0	38	22	8.36	5.60	2.18	1060	1080	1036	13.8	3.1	5.3	1.7	8%	38	26	36	42%	64%	16%	4	52	0%	100%	0	0.92	-20.9	27	35	-$29
14	**Proj**	**3**	**6**	**0**	**73**	**47**	**4.77**	**4.45**	**1.56**	**811**	**827**	**792**	**17.9**	**3.3**	**5.8**	**1.8**	**9%**	**42**	**21**	**37**	**32%**	**74%**	**13%**	**14**						**-8.1**	**36**	**47**	**-$6**

Axford,John

Age: 31	Th: R	Role RP	Health A	LIMA Plan C+
Ht: 6' 5"	Wt: 220	Type Pwr	PT/Exp B	Rand Var +3
			Consist A	MM 4510

April implosion cost him the closer's job, which given his 2012 struggles, wasn't too surprising. While Dom fell, it was matched by better Ctl; his troubles were mostly H% and hr/f-driven. Future saves? While others see 2010-2012 and say, "sure," you look at the Ctl track record and say, "it wouldn't last."

Yr	Tm	W	L	Sv	IP	K	ERA	xERA	WHIP	oOPS	vL	vR	BF/G	Ctl	Dom	Cmd	SwK	G	L	F	H%	S%	hr/f	GS	APC	DOM%	DIS%	Sv%	LI	RAR	BPV	BPX	R$
09	MIL *	5	0	2	48	47	4.22	3.72	1.48	538	192	885	6.3	5.6	8.8	1.6	9%	33	22	44	30%	72%	0%	0	20			67	0.19	0.6	75	141	$1
10	MIL	8	2	24	58	76	2.48	2.86	1.19	588	692	483	4.8	4.2	11.8	2.8	12%	48	19	33	32%	78%	2%	0	20			89	1.37	11.4	125	203	$17
11	MIL	2	2	46	74	86	1.95	3.00	1.14	557	481	621	4.1	3.1	10.5	3.4	10%	50	15	35	31%	85%	6%	0	17			96	1.15	18.1	135	202	$26
12	MIL	5	8	35	69	93	4.67	3.43	1.44	717	671	767	4.1	5.1	12.1	2.4	11%	46	24	30	33%	71%	19%	0	19			80	1.22	-5.6	105	136	$12
13	2 NL	7	7	0	65	65	4.02	3.74	1.52	796	838	761	3.9	3.6	9.0	2.5	10%	45	24	31	35%	79%	17%	0	16			0	1.11	-1.2	88	114	-$2
1st Half		3	3	0	34	37	3.93	3.76	1.43	778	917	664	3.9	3.4	9.7	2.8	11%	40	21	40	33%	79%	16%	0	15			0	1.04	-0.3	100	130	-$1
2nd Half		4	4	0	31	28	4.11	3.72	1.63	815	753	866	3.8	3.8	8.2	2.2	10%	51	28	21	36%	78%	20%	0	16			0	1.19	-0.9	74	96	-$3
14	**Proj**	**6**	**6**	**2**	**61**	**68**	**3.82**	**3.21**	**1.34**	**670**	**666**	**672**	**3.9**	**4.0**	**10.0**	**2.5**	**11%**	**47**	**23**	**30**	**32%**	**74%**	**13%**	**0**						**0.4**	**97**	**125**	**$2**

Badenhop,Burke

Age: 31	Th: R	Role RP	Health A	LIMA Plan B+
Ht: 6' 5"	Wt: 220	Type Con GB	PT/Exp C	Rand Var 0
			Consist A	MM 4100

2013 was a virtual carbon copy of 2012—a good thing. Kept his Ctl gains, and maintained a GB profile. But the fact that he does great against RH hitters while getting cuffed around by lefties means that he's becoming less useful. There's no sign of an expanded role on the horizon.

Yr	Tm	W	L	Sv	IP	K	ERA	xERA	WHIP	oOPS	vL	vR	BF/G	Ctl	Dom	Cmd	SwK	G	L	F	H%	S%	hr/f	GS	APC	DOM%	DIS%	Sv%	LI	RAR	BPV	BPX	R$
09	FLA	7	4	0	72	57	3.75	3.66	1.32	679	718	640	8.7	3.0	7.1	2.4	7%	54	20	26	31%	72%	9%	2	34	50%	50%	0	1.06	5.1	79	148	$3
10	FLA *	2	6	1	84	54	3.87	3.57	1.31	681	700	667	5.3	3.1	5.9	1.9	7%	57	14	29	30%	70%	8%	0	20			33	0.88	2.2	63	101	$1
11	FLA	2	3	1	64	51	4.10	3.48	1.40	689	706	677	5.5	3.4	7.2	2.1	7%	58	21	21	33%	68%	2%	0	20			100	1.03	-1.2	74	112	-$2
12	TAM	3	2	0	62	42	3.03	3.73	1.20	687	844	610	4.0	1.7	6.1	3.5	4%	53	23	25	30%	78%	12%	0	14			0	0.78	7.6	93	122	$2
13	MIL	2	3	1	62	42	3.47	3.56	1.19	694	918	574	4.0	1.7	6.1	3.5	6%	51	22	27	30%	74%	12%	0	15			25	1.01	3.1	91	119	$0
1st Half		1	3	1	37	27	3.38	3.23	1.02	623	750	547	3.7	2.2	6.5	3.0	7%	54	23	23	24%	71%	17%	0	14			50	1.15	2.3	91	118	$3
2nd Half		1	0	0	25	15	3.60	4.03	1.44	786	1173	606	4.5	1.1	5.4	5.0	5%	47	21	32	36%	76%	7%	0	16			0	0.79	0.8	93	121	-$3
14	**Proj**	**2**	**2**	**0**	**58**	**40**	**3.51**	**3.46**	**1.28**	**708**	**882**	**612**	**4.3**	**2.0**	**6.2**	**3.1**	**6%**	**53**	**21**	**26**	**31%**	**74%**	**9%**	**0**						**2.6**	**87**	**113**	**$0**

Bailey,Andrew

Age: 30	Th: R	Role RP	Health F	LIMA Plan B+
Ht: 6' 3"	Wt: 240	Type Pwr xFB	PT/Exp D	Rand Var +1
			Consist D	MM 3510

In 2012, it was a thumb injury; in 2013, he lost most of 2H to shoulder surgery. Dom rose in limited action, but still hasn't recovered his pre-thumb Ctl. With high FB%, he always walked a fine line, anyway. Rehab could cost him the first part of 2014, so odds of closing - anywhere - may have to wait, perhaps until 2015.

Yr	Tm	W	L	Sv	IP	K	ERA	xERA	WHIP	oOPS	vL	vR	BF/G	Ctl	Dom	Cmd	SwK	G	L	F	H%	S%	hr/f	GS	APC	DOM%	DIS%	Sv%	LI	RAR	BPV	BPX	R$
09	OAK	6	3	26	83	91	1.84	3.20	0.88	479	470	487	4.8	2.6	9.8	3.8	14%	42	13	45	23%	82%	6%	0	19			87	1.05	25.6	127	238	$27
10	OAK	1	3	25	49	42	1.47	3.58	0.96	544	569	523	4.0	2.4	7.7	3.2	11%	39	16	45	24%	89%	5%	0	16			89	1.44	15.8	91	148	$16
11	OAK	0	4	24	42	41	3.24	3.61	1.10	631	709	529	4.0	2.6	8.9	3.4	10%	37	17	46	29%	72%	6%	0	17			92	1.27	3.6	104	157	$10
12	BOS	1	1	6	15	14	7.04	5.33	1.89	862	1084	636	3.9	4.7	8.2	1.8	7%	33	23	44	39%	63%	9%	0	16			67	1.20	-5.7	32	42	-$5
13	BOS	3	1	8	29	39	3.77	3.32	1.22	761	661	872	3.9	3.8	12.2	3.3	12%	22	24	54	28%	82%	21%	0	16			62	1.21	0.3	119	155	$2
1st Half		3	1	8	23	32	4.63	3.72	1.37	844	715	990	3.8	4.2	12.3	2.9	12%	15	26	59	29%	80%	22%	0	16			62	1.14	-2.2	100	130	$4
2nd Half		0	0	0	5	7	0.00	1.47	0.56	302	347	250	4.3	1.7	11.8	7.0	14%	67	11	22	20%	100%	0%	0	16			0	1.66	2.5	212	274	-$4
14	**Proj**	**2**	**2**	**5**	**29**	**31**	**3.76**	**3.76**	**1.34**	**735**	**724**	**747**	**4.2**	**3.9**	**9.6**	**2.4**	**11%**	**32**	**19**	**49**	**31%**	**77%**	**10%**	**0**						**0.4**	**77**	**100**	**$0**

Bailey,Homer

Age: 28	Th: R	Role SP	Health B	LIMA Plan C+
Ht: 6' 4"	Wt: 230	Type	PT/Exp A	Rand Var 0
			Consist B	MM 4305

Came alive with improved Cmd in 2H 2012; held it in 2013. Gained a couple mph on his fastball; SwK continues to creep up. Best of all, with two uninterrupted seasons, he's beginning to shake the "injury-prone" label. DOM/DIS indicates that he's a blossoming ace, and BPV trend confirms it. Invest.

Yr	Tm	W	L	Sv	IP	K	ERA	xERA	WHIP	oOPS	vL	vR	BF/G	Ctl	Dom	Cmd	SwK	G	L	F	H%	S%	hr/f	GS	APC	DOM%	DIS%	Sv%	LI	RAR	BPV	BPX	R$
09	CIN *	16	10	0	203	157	4.09	4.82	1.48	740	776	704	25.7	3.6	7.0	1.9	8%	43	21	37	32%	76%	9%	20	101	30%	20%			5.8	48	90	$8
10	CIN *	6	3	0	128	113	4.22	3.89	1.34	744	677	781	23.2	3.2	7.9	2.5	9%	42	21	37	32%	69%	9%	19	102	58%	21%			-2.2	80	129	$3
11	CIN *	11	8	0	162	124	4.26	4.38	1.32	728	777	687	24.0	2.2	6.9	3.2	10%	39	22	38	32%	71%	12%	22	96	45%	18%			-6.3	76	114	$3
12	CIN	13	10	0	208	168	3.68	3.92	1.24	718	682	747	26.5	2.3	7.3	3.2	10%	45	20	35	30%	75%	12%	33	101	52%	24%			8.6	93	121	$12
13	CIN	11	12	0	209	199	3.49	3.29	1.12	660	746	575	26.5	2.3	8.6	3.7	11%	46	19	34	29%	72%	10%	32	103	66%	9%			9.7	115	150	$16
1st Half		4	6	0	102	102	3.88	3.05	1.15	655	784	509	26.0	2.2	9.0	4.1	11%	49	22	29	31%	66%	9%	16	100	69%	13%			-0.2	129	167	$12
2nd Half		7	6	0	107	97	3.11	3.52	1.10	665	704	632	27.1	2.4	8.2	3.3	11%	43	17	40	27%	77%	11%	16	106	63%	6%			9.9	102	133	$20
14	**Proj**	**15**	**8**	**0**	**203**	**177**	**3.24**	**3.33**	**1.17**	**681**	**717**	**650**	**25.1**	**2.3**	**7.8**	**3.5**	**10%**	**44**	**20**	**36**	**29%**	**76%**	**11%**	**32**						**15.6**	**102**	**133**	**$20**

Baker,Scott

Age: 32	Th: R	Role SP	Health F	LIMA Plan C
Ht: 6' 4"	Wt: 215	Type xFB	PT/Exp D	Rand Var -5
			Consist C	MM 3201

Perennial elbow issues shelved him back in summer 2011; he finally returned to start a few games down the stretch. When healthy, can be counted on for fine Cmd and lots of fly balls. xERA history says an ERA around 4.00 is about right. If you feel like gambling, he makes an intriguing stash, but beware the extreme risk.

Yr	Tm	W	L	Sv	IP	K	ERA	xERA	WHIP	oOPS	vL	vR	BF/G	Ctl	Dom	Cmd	SwK	G	L	F	H%	S%	hr/f	GS	APC	DOM%	DIS%	Sv%	LI	RAR	BPV	BPX	R$
09	MIN	15	9	0	200	162	4.37	4.16	1.19	709	607	805	25.1	2.2	7.3	3.4	10%	33	19	47	29%	67%	10%	33	99	58%	15%			-1.1	84	157	$15
10	MIN	12	9	0	170	148	4.49	3.93	1.34	793	830	756	25.0	2.3	7.8	3.4	10%	36	21	43	33%	70%	10%	29	92	48%	28%			-8.7	93	151	$4
11	MIN	8	6	0	135	123	3.14	3.63	1.17	687	743	595	23.8	2.1	8.2	3.8	11%	34	21	45	30%	78%	9%	21	93	48%	10%	0	0.72	13.3	102	154	$11
12																																	
13	CHC	0	0	0	15	6	3.60	5.05	0.87	636	723	581	19.0	2.4	3.6	1.5	9%	28	13	59	14%	70%	11%	3	67	33%	33%			0.5	6	8	-$3
1st Half																																	
2nd Half		0	0	0	15	6	3.60	5.05	0.87	636	723	581	19.0	2.4	3.6	1.5	9%	28	13	59	14%	70%	11%	3	67	33%	33%			0.5	6	8	-$3
14	**Proj**	**5**	**3**	**0**	**98**	**76**	**3.93**	**3.82**	**1.14**	**715**	**750**	**682**	**22.2**	**2.3**	**7.0**	**3.1**	**10%**	**33**	**18**	**49**	**27%**	**71%**	**11%**	**17**						**-0.8**	**76**	**98**	**$4**

Balfour,Grant

Age: 36	Th: R	Role RP	Health B	LIMA Plan C
Ht: 6' 2"	Wt: 200	Type Pwr FB	PT/Exp B	Rand Var -3
			Consist A	MM 4530

While Ctl has been rising, big jump in Dom and plummeting FB% have led to his success. xERA and H% say the ERA should be higher, but the skills remains strong. LI argues that managers have long liked using him in high-leverage situations; no reason to think that won't continue, wherever he ends up.

Yr	Tm	W	L	Sv	IP	K	ERA	xERA	WHIP	oOPS	vL	vR	BF/G	Ctl	Dom	Cmd	SwK	G	L	F	H%	S%	hr/f	GS	APC	DOM%	DIS%	Sv%	LI	RAR	BPV	BPX	R$
09	TAM	5	4	4	67	69	4.81	4.15	1.37	681	701	667	4.0	4.4	9.2	2.1	9%	36	21	43	30%	65%	8%	0	17			44	1.26	-4.1	61	114	$2
10	TAM	2	1	0	55	56	2.28	3.67	1.08	619	771	496	3.9	2.8	9.1	3.3	10%	31	20	50	29%	81%	4%	0	17			0	1.25	12.3	98	159	$5
11	OAK	5	2	2	62	59	2.47	3.53	1.03	605	579	630	3.9	2.9	8.6	3.0	7%	38	17	45	24%	84%	11%	0	16			29	1.18	11.3	92	138	$8
12	OAK	3	2	24	75	72	2.53	3.70	0.92	495	476	516	3.9	3.4	8.7	2.6	10%	36	24	41	21%	74%	5%	0	17			92	1.33	13.7	79	103	$19
13	OAK	1	3	38	63	72	2.59	3.54	1.20	610	548	682	4.0	3.9	10.3	2.7	11%	38	23	39	28%	84%	11%	0	18			93	1.23	9.9	97	127	$18
1st Half		0	1	19	32	33	1.97	3.67	1.09	601	597	605	3.9	3.4	9.3	2.8	11%	34	24	42	25%	90%	11%	0	17			100	1.23	7.5	88	114	$20
2nd Half		1	2	19	31	39	3.23	3.38	1.30	619	505	771	4.1	4.4	11.4	2.6	11%	42	22	36	32%	78%	11%	0	19			86	1.23	2.4	107	139	$16
14	**Proj**	**2**	**3**	**35**	**65**	**70**	**2.72**	**3.29**	**1.12**	**587**	**546**	**632**	**3.8**	**3.6**	**9.7**	**2.7**	**10%**	**37**	**22**	**41**	**26%**	**80%**	**9%**	**0**						**9.2**	**91**	**118**	**$19**

DAVE ADLER

Bass,Anthony

Age:	26	Th:	R	Role	RP	Health	D	LIMA Plan	D+
Ht:	6' 2"	Wt:	195	Type		PT/Exp	C	Rand Var	+1
						Consist	C	MM	2100

0-0, 5.36 ERA in 42 IP at SD. H% argues that his struggles were due to bad luck, but LD% says he really was hit hard. Lower Dom means more balls in play, adding to his woes. Had a stint as a starter in 2012, but didn't excel in that role, either. What you're left with is a fungible long reliever, but not much else.

Yr	Tm	W	L	Sv	IP	K	ERA	xERA	WHIP	oOPS	vL	vR	BF/G	Ctl	Dom	Cmd	SwK	G	L	F	H%	S%	hr/f	GS	APC	DOM%	DIS%	Sv%	LI	RAR	BPV	BPX	R$
09																																	
10																																	
11	SD *	9	4	0	123	81	2.55	3.04	1.20	655	646	660	12.1	2.9	5.9	2.0	9%	46	23	31	27%	80%	6%	3	27	0%	0%	0	0.67	21.1	69	104	$11
12	SD	2	8	1	97	80	4.73	4.09	1.32	719	749	690	17.1	3.6	7.4	2.1	10%	48	20	32	29%	65%	11%	15	64	47%	27%	100	1.13	-8.6	62	81	-$3
13	SD *	4	6	0	121	81	5.19	5.77	1.65	829	881	785	13.9	2.7	6.0	2.2	12%	45	27	28	37%	69%	10%	0	30			0	0.38	-19.9	45	58	-$14
1st Half		1	1	0	54	40	5.79	5.63	1.71	755	782	731	10.2	3.1	6.6	2.1	12%	47	25	28	38%	65%	7%	0	29			0	0.41	-12.8	56	73	-$16
2nd Half		3	5	0	67	41	4.71	5.89	1.60	1068	1188	962	19.9	2.3	5.5	2.3	11%	39	33	27	35%	74%	22%	0	33			0	0.26	-7.0	36	47	-$12
14	Proj	1	2	0	29	20	4.61	4.14	1.46	812	828	798	14.7	3.0	6.2	2.0	11%	43	23	34	32%	70%	9%	4						-2.7	50	65	-$4

Bastardo,Antonio

Age:	28	Th:	L	Role	RP	Health	A	LIMA Plan	A
Ht:	5' 11"	Wt:	200	Type	Pwr xFB	PT/Exp	D	Rand Var	-5
						Consist	A	MM	4510

Great growth year before being fingered by Biogenesis, right? Not so fast—still walked too many, high FB% didn't kill him due to S% and hr/f, and velocity remained down from its 2010 high. On the bright side, Dom will probably rebound. Expect regression, and the PED issue justs adds uncertainty.

Yr	Tm	W	L	Sv	IP	K	ERA	xERA	WHIP	oOPS	vL	vR	BF/G	Ctl	Dom	Cmd	SwK	G	L	F	H%	S%	hr/f	GS	APC	DOM%	DIS%	Sv%	LI	RAR	BPV	BPX	R$
09	PHI *	5	5	3	73	63	3.70	3.27	1.17	833	846	827	15.3	2.4	7.8	3.3	9%	23	25	52	29%	70%	10%	5	74	40%	40%	100	0.70	5.5	98	183	$6
10	PHI *	3	1	3	36	48	3.59	3.31	1.37	669	660	678	3.4	3.9	11.9	3.1	13%	32	15	53	38%	72%	4%	0	14			75	0.60	2.2	134	217	$2
11	PHI	6	1	8	58	70	2.64	3.49	0.93	524	558	506	3.5	4.0	10.9	2.7	16%	25	16	59	19%	77%	8%	0	15			80	1.47	9.3	90	135	$11
12	PHI	2	5	1	52	81	4.33	3.27	1.27	662	569	732	3.4	4.5	14.0	3.1	14%	28	22	50	33%	69%	13%	0	15			20	1.37	-2.0	137	178	$0
13	PHI	3	2	2	43	47	2.32	4.00	1.27	637	598	662	3.7	4.4	9.9	2.2	14%	31	18	50	30%	83%	4%	0	15			40	1.04	8.1	68	88	$2
1st Half		2	2	1	28	27	2.93	4.56	1.48	751	793	722	3.6	4.6	8.8	1.9	13%	32	18	50	33%	82%	5%	0	14			25	1.09	3.2	45	58	$1
2nd Half		1	0	1	15	20	1.20	3.05	0.87	395	186	535	4.0	4.2	12.0	2.9	16%	31	17	52	21%	85%	0%	0	16			100	0.93	4.9	112	145	$4
14	Proj	4	3	5	58	74	3.56	3.34	1.23	662	580	717	3.7	4.2	11.5	2.7	15%	29	19	52	30%	74%	9%	0						2.2	100	130	$5

Bauer,Trevor

Age:	23	Th:	R	Role	SP	Health	A	LIMA Plan	D
Ht:	6' 1"	Wt:	190	Type	Pwr xFB	PT/Exp	D	Rand Var	0
						Consist	F	MM	1301

1-2, 5.29 ERA in 17 IP at CLE. 2011 bonus baby has gotten a few chances to strut his stuff in the majors, but lack of Ctl keeps sending him back down. Dom drop is a concern, but with age on his side, he'll likely figure it out sooner or later. High ceiling, but you'll have to continue to be patient.

Yr	Tm	W	L	Sv	IP	K	ERA	xERA	WHIP	oOPS	vL	vR	BF/G	Ctl	Dom	Cmd	SwK	G	L	F	H%	S%	hr/f	GS	APC	DOM%	DIS%	Sv%	LI	RAR	BPV	BPX	R$
09																																	
10																																	
11	aa	1	1	0	17	23	8.11	5.80	1.70				18.9	3.9	12.4	3.2					44%	51%								-8.6	101	152	-$6
12	ARI *	13	4	0	147	154	2.91	3.41	1.32	795	851	729	23.4	4.1	9.4	2.3	7%	45	25	30	31%	80%	15%	4	81	25%	75%			20.0	93	121	$13
13	CLE *	7	9	0	138	103	5.09	5.50	1.73	840	908	778	24.2	5.7	6.7	1.2	7%	35	20	45	32%	73%	13%	4	88	25%	25%			-20.9	29	37	-$14
1st Half		4	4	0	82	69	5.09	5.20	1.63	840	908	778	22.9	5.6	7.6	1.4	7%	35	20	45	30%	72%	13%		88	25%	25%			-12.4	35	45	-$13
2nd Half		3	5	0	56	34	5.09	5.95	1.88				26.3	5.8	5.5	0.9					34%	74%	0%							-8.5	21	27	-$17
14	Proj	6	5	0	87	73	4.44	4.77	1.59	738	749	728	24.3	5.1	7.6	1.5	7%	35	20	45	32%	74%	7%	16						-6.2	12	16	-$4

Beachy,Brandon

Age:	27	Th:	R	Role	SP	Health	F	LIMA Plan	B
Ht:	6' 3"	Wt:	215	Type	Pwr FB	PT/Exp	C	Rand Var	+1
						Consist	B	MM	3303

2-1, 4.50 ERA in 30 IP at ATL. Return from June 2012 TJS looked good, but he missed September after elbow discomfort. In between, his last four starts were PQS-DOM, but SwK and Dom said he wasn't all the way back. Cleanup surgery should have him ready for spring training, but the health risk makes him a dicey option.

Yr	Tm	W	L	Sv	IP	K	ERA	xERA	WHIP	oOPS	vL	vR	BF/G	Ctl	Dom	Cmd	SwK	G	L	F	H%	S%	hr/f	GS	APC	DOM%	DIS%	Sv%	LI	RAR	BPV	BPX	R$
09																																	
10	ATL *	5	3	2	134	140	2.19	2.94	1.19	677	654	704	14.2	2.4	9.4	3.9	10%	36	29	36	33%	82%	0%	3	93	33%	33%			31.3	133	216	$15
11	ATL	7	3	0	142	169	3.68	3.29	1.21	679	707	660	23.6	2.9	10.7	3.7	13%	34	21	45	32%	73%	10%	25	97	60%	12%			4.5	126	190	$9
12	ATL	5	5	0	81	68	2.00	3.96	0.96	507	446	553	24.5	3.2	7.6	2.3	8%	41	18	41	21%	83%	7%	13	102	69%	8%			20.1	68	89	$12
13	ATL *	4	5	0	65	47	4.49	4.45	1.37	705	736	680	20.9	3.5	6.5	1.9	9%	42	17	42	28%	71%	14%	5	90	80%	20%			-5.0	41	54	-$3
1st Half		1	1	0	17	15	5.68	7.07	1.84				19.8	6.5	8.1	1.2					30%	77%	0%	0						-3.8	-3	-4	-$8
2nd Half		3	4	0	48	32	4.07	3.53	1.20	705	736	680	21.4	2.4	6.0	2.5	9%	42	17	42	28%	68%	14%	5	90	80%	20%			-1.2	65	84	-$1
14	Proj	9	7	0	131	114	3.88	3.88	1.30	722	730	715	20.8	3.5	7.8	2.2	10%	38	19	43	29%	74%	11%	26						-0.3	63	82	$6

Beckett,Josh

Age:	34	Th:	R	Role	SP	Health	F	LIMA Plan	C
Ht:	6' 5"	Wt:	225	Type	Pwr	PT/Exp	B	Rand Var	+5
						Consist	A	MM	3301

Another season with injury woes; this time, it was thorarcic surgery that shelved him for most of the year. When he pitched, results were hurt by hr/f and H%. SwK boost helped Dom get back into its normal range. Should be ready for spring training, but health grade should make you think twice before taking the risk.

Yr	Tm	W	L	Sv	IP	K	ERA	xERA	WHIP	oOPS	vL	vR	BF/G	Ctl	Dom	Cmd	SwK	G	L	F	H%	S%	hr/f	GS	APC	DOM%	DIS%	Sv%	LI	RAR	BPV	BPX	R$
09	BOS	17	6	0	212	199	3.86	3.39	1.19	691	696	683	27.6	2.3	8.4	3.6	9%	47	21	32	30%	71%	13%	32	105	78%	6%			12.2	114	213	$21
10	BOS	6	6	0	128	116	5.78	3.94	1.54	848	940	726	27.5	3.2	8.2	2.6	9%	46	19	35	35%	65%	14%	21	103	43%	19%			-26.8	86	138	-$7
11	BOS	13	7	0	193	175	2.89	3.46	1.03	608	562	671	25.6	2.4	8.2	3.4	11%	40	18	42	25%	77%	10%	30	100	70%	7%			25.0	99	149	$24
12	2 TM	7	14	0	170	132	4.65	4.25	1.33	741	801	672	26.1	2.7	7.0	2.5	9%	43	21	37	31%	67%	11%	28	94	50%	18%			-13.3	72	94	-$2
13	LA	0	5	0	43	41	5.19	4.04	1.50	844	896	790	24.4	3.1	8.5	2.7	12%	39	24	37	34%	70%	16%	8	92	38%	38%			-7.1	86	112	-$7
1st Half		0	5	0	43	41	5.19	4.04	1.50	845	896	790	24.4	3.1	8.5	2.7	12%	39	24	37	34%	70%	16%	8	92	38%	38%			-7.1	86	112	-$7
2nd Half																																	
14	Proj	7	6	0	116	102	4.31	3.73	1.35	752	780	717	25.0	3.0	7.9	2.6	10%	40	22	38	31%	72%	12%	19						-6.3	78	102	$1

Bedard,Erik

Age:	35	Th:	L	Role	SP	Health	F	LIMA Plan	D+
Ht:	6' 1"	Wt:	200	Type	Pwr FB	PT/Exp	B	Rand Var	0
						Consist	A	MM	2401

With his health history, three straight years of 120+ IP is a minor miracle. While he maintains an ability to strike batters out, Ctl, OBA, and FB% are all heading into dangerous territory. The end is near, making the 2008 deal that sent him to SEA for Adam Jones, Chris Tillman, et al look like a slam dunk for the Orioles.

Yr	Tm	W	L	Sv	IP	K	ERA	xERA	WHIP	oOPS	vL	vR	BF/G	Ctl	Dom	Cmd	SwK	G	L	F	H%	S%	hr/f	GS	APC	DOM%	DIS%	Sv%	LI	RAR	BPV	BPX	R$
09	SEA	5	3	0	83	90	2.82	3.59	1.19	627	648	618	23.2	3.7	9.8	2.6	9%	42	17	40	28%	80%	9%	15	97	40%	27%			15.4	96	180	$8
10																																	
11	2 AL	5	9	0	129	125	3.62	3.65	1.28	681	671	685	22.5	3.3	8.7	2.6	8%	42	20	38	30%	75%	10%	24	93	54%	25%			5.2	86	130	$5
12	PIT	7	14	0	126	118	5.01	4.19	1.47	758	628	786	23.2	4.0	8.5	2.1	8%	43	23	33	33%	67%	11%	24	89	38%	33%			-15.5	65	85	-$6
13	HOU	4	12	1	151	138	4.59	4.52	1.48	773	832	755	20.7	4.5	8.2	1.8	9%	36	18	46	31%	71%	9%	26	84	35%	38%	33	0.81	-13.5	41	54	-$7
1st Half		3	3	1	75	66	4.44	4.51	1.44	805	795	807	20.5	4.0	7.9	2.0	8%	34	20	46	30%	74%	12%	14	82	29%	43%	100	0.77	-5.3	48	62	-$3
2nd Half		1	9	0	76	72	4.74	4.52	1.53	741	853	694	20.9	5.0	8.5	1.7	9%	39	16	45	32%	69%	6%	12	85	42%	33%	0	0.85	-8.2	36	47	-$10
14	Proj	4	9	0	102	95	4.48	4.01	1.45	741	750	739	21.4	4.3	8.4	1.9	9%	40	19	41	31%	71%	9%	20						-7.6	53	69	-$2

Belisario,Ronald

Age:	31	Th:	R	Role	RP	Health	A	LIMA Plan	C
Ht:	6' 3"	Wt:	240	Type	Pwr xGB	PT/Exp	D	Rand Var	0
						Consist	B	MM	4200

Brings the heat and keeps the ball on the ground, two things you want from your set-up man. High oOPS and ERA in first half was due to freakish H%. That over-corrected in the 2nd half, but drop in Dom decreases his margin for error. Risky Ctl makes 1st half a barely sustainable skill set; 2nd half not so much.

Yr	Tm	W	L	Sv	IP	K	ERA	xERA	WHIP	oOPS	vL	vR	BF/G	Ctl	Dom	Cmd	SwK	G	L	F	H%	S%	hr/f	GS	APC	DOM%	DIS%	Sv%	LI	RAR	BPV	BPX	R$
09	LA	4	3	0	71	64	2.04	3.51	1.15	580	720	486	4.3	3.7	8.2	2.2	10%	56	16	28	26%	84%	8%	0	16			0	1.03	19.9	81	152	$8
10	LA	3	1	2	55	38	5.04	3.55	1.28	702	793	649	3.9	3.1	6.2	2.0	9%	61	17	22	28%	62%	16%	0	15			50	1.08	-6.6	67	108	-$1
11																																	
12	LA	8	1	1	71	69	2.54	2.91	1.07	558	725	440	4.2	3.7	8.7	2.4	11%	64	21	15	25%	77%	11%	0	16			20	1.12	13.0	100	131	$9
13	LA	5	7	1	68	49	3.97	3.74	1.47	725	811	684	3.9	3.7	6.5	1.8	10%	61	21	18	33%	72%	8%	0	14			20	1.45	-0.9	56	73	-$2
1st Half		3	5	1	35	31	4.33	3.70	1.70	830	847	820	4.1	3.6	7.9	2.2	11%	60	20	21	39%	75%	13%	0	15			20	1.30	-2.0	84	108	-$4
2nd Half		2	2	0	33	18	3.58	3.77	1.22	594	762	522	3.6	3.9	5.0	1.3	8%	63	22	14	26%	68%	0%	0	13			0	1.61	1.1	26	34	-$1
14	Proj	5	4	0	65	51	3.53	3.32	1.28	653	769	588	3.9	3.6	7.0	1.9	10%	62	20	18	29%	72%	9%	0						2.7	68	88	$2

DAVE ADLER

Belisle,Matt

Age: 34	Th: R	Role RP	Health	A	LIMA Plan	C+
Ht: 6' 4"	Wt: 225	Type	PT/Exp	C	Rand Var	+2
			Consist	A	MM	5311

Dip in S%, bump in hr/f fueled higher ERA, but BPV says he's been the same pitcher since 2011. Closer-worthy, but at his age, may be typecast as setup man. 2H skill surge restores confidence in his reliability, though LD% a bit concerning. Buy to help keep your ERA in check, and if saves come, so much the better.

Yr	Tm	W	L	Sv	IP	K	ERA	xERA	WHIP	oOPS	vL	vR	BF/G	Ctl	Dom	Cmd	SwK	G	L	F	H%	S%	hr/f	GS	APC	DOM%	DIS%	Sv%	LI	RAR	BPV	BPX	R$
09	COL *	4	2	9	89	55	4.45	4.82	1.44	780	721	831	6.7	2.1	5.5	2.6	8%	40	21	40	34%	70%	15%	0	22			100	0.56	-1.4	57	107	$2
10	COL	7	5	1	92	91	2.93	2.93	1.09	646	620	659	4.8	1.6	8.9	5.7	10%	46	20	33	31%	75%	9%	0	19			50	1.03	13.0	142	230	$10
11	COL	10	4	0	72	58	3.25	3.27	1.26	721	656	760	4.1	1.8	7.3	4.1	9%	53	19	28	33%	76%	8%	0	16			0	1.20	6.1	114	172	$5
12	COL	3	8	3	80	69	3.71	3.56	1.36	722	789	672	4.4	2.0	7.8	3.8	9%	51	24	26	35%	73%	8%	0	16			30	1.42	3.0	114	149	$0
13	COL	5	7	0	73	62	4.32	3.27	1.25	707	750	679	4.2	1.8	7.6	4.1	11%	49	26	25	33%	66%	11%	0	16			0	1.16	-4.0	115	149	-$1
1st Half		4	5	0	41	29	4.79	3.58	1.19	670	828	551	4.3	2.4	6.3	2.6	10%	54	18	28	29%	59%	9%	0	16			0	1.23	-4.7	81	104	$0
2nd Half		1	2	0	32	33	3.69	2.89	1.33	752	640	817	4.0	1.1	9.4	8.3	12%	42	37	21	38%	74%	15%	0	15			0	1.08	0.7	158	205	-$2
14	Proj	**5**	**6**	**3**	**73**	**61**	**3.60**	**3.17**	**1.24**	**683**	**693**	**677**	**4.1**	**2.0**	**7.6**	**3.7**	**10%**	**48**	**26**	**26**	**32%**	**72%**	**10%**	**0**						**2.4**	**108**	**140**	**$3**

Bell,Heath

Age: 36	Th: R	Role RP	Health	A	LIMA Plan	A
Ht: 6' 3"	Wt: 250	Type Pwr	PT/Exp	B	Rand Var	+5
			Consist	B	MM	5410

Skills returned, even if full-time closer gig did not. Results obscured by hr/f spike, and high H% looks like part of his package. But many positives here, led by near double-digit Dom and career-best Ctl, possibly due to mechanical flaw fixed in June. With opps, no reason saves couldn't return. A buck or two could pay off big.

Yr	Tm	W	L	Sv	IP	K	ERA	xERA	WHIP	oOPS	vL	vR	BF/G	Ctl	Dom	Cmd	SwK	G	L	F	H%	S%	hr/f	GS	APC	DOM%	DIS%	Sv%	LI	RAR	BPV	BPX	R$
09	SD	6	4	42	70	79	2.71	3.05	1.12	568	730	372	4.1	3.1	10.2	3.3	10%	48	18	35	30%	76%	5%	0	18			88	1.40	13.8	126	236	$26
10	SD	6	1	47	70	86	1.93	3.07	1.20	585	554	612	4.3	3.6	11.1	3.1	11%	44	18	38	33%	83%	2%	0	18			94	1.42	18.6	124	200	$28
11	SD	3	4	43	63	51	2.44	3.74	1.15	588	726	451	4.0	3.0	7.3	2.4	9%	43	21	35	27%	81%	6%	0	17			90	1.45	11.6	71	107	$22
12	MIA	4	5	19	64	59	5.09	4.15	1.55	780	678	861	3.9	4.1	8.3	2.0	8%	47	23	30	35%	67%	9%	0	16			70	1.09	-8.4	64	84	$1
13	ARI	5	2	15	66	72	4.11	3.30	1.37	802	732	849	4.2	2.2	9.9	4.5	10%	43	23	34	35%	77%	18%	0	16			68	1.17	-2.0	139	182	$5
1st Half		2	1	14	31	34	4.70	3.61	1.57	906	907	905	4.2	2.9	10.0	3.4	9%	41	25	34	37%	78%	23%	0	17			82	1.09	-3.1	120	155	$8
2nd Half		3	1	1	35	38	3.60	3.04	1.20	707	531	804	4.1	1.5	9.8	6.3	11%	45	22	34	34%	76%	15%	0	16			20	1.23	1.1	157	203	$3
14	Proj	**4**	**3**	**10**	**58**	**59**	**3.58**	**3.17**	**1.25**	**688**	**649**	**717**	**3.8**	**2.9**	**9.2**	**3.2**	**9%**	**44**	**22**	**33**	**31%**	**75%**	**13%**	**0**						**2.1**	**110**	**143**	**$6**

Benoit,Joaquin

Age: 36	Th: R	Role RP	Health	A	LIMA Plan	C+
Ht: 6' 3"	Wt: 220	Type Pwr FB	PT/Exp	C	Rand Var	-5
			Consist	A	MM	4530

On whole, rose to the challenge, in part by cutting down on FB. Some cracks (rising Ctl, falling Dom) appeared in 2H, but only blown saves came on Sept. 23, 28, with David Ortiz ALCS grand slam the exclamation point. If he can wash out that bad taste and arm is sound, skills say he can do the job.

Yr	Tm	W	L	Sv	IP	K	ERA	xERA	WHIP	oOPS	vL	vR	BF/G	Ctl	Dom	Cmd	SwK	G	L	F	H%	S%	hr/f	GS	APC	DOM%	DIS%	Sv%	LI	RAR	BPV	BPX	R$
09																																	
10	TAM	1	2	1	60	75	1.34	2.54	0.68	454	491	419	3.4	1.6	11.2	6.8	15%	39	12	49	20%	91%	9%	0	15			25	1.11	20.4	174	282	$12
11	DET	4	3	2	61	63	2.95	3.26	1.05	581	639	517	3.7	2.5	9.3	3.7	14%	39	18	43	28%	75%	7%	0	15			29	1.26	7.5	117	175	$6
12	DET	5	3	2	71	84	3.68	3.36	1.14	720	721	720	3.9	2.8	10.6	3.8	18%	36	20	44	28%	78%	18%	0	17			33	1.05	3.0	130	170	$5
13	DET	4	1	24	67	73	2.01	3.17	1.03	575	524	645	4.0	3.0	9.8	3.3	15%	42	20	38	27%	84%	8%	0	16			92	1.19	15.3	117	152	$17
1st Half		2	0	5	33	41	1.89	2.86	1.05	586	560	628	4.1	2.7	11.1	4.1	15%	39	24	37	30%	85%	7%	0	18			100	1.08	8.1	144	186	$12
2nd Half		2	1	19	34	32	2.14	3.49	1.01	564	484	661	3.9	3.2	8.6	2.7	15%	45	15	39	23%	84%	9%	0	15			90	1.30	7.2	91	117	$22
14	Proj	**4**	**2**	**31**	**65**	**69**	**2.93**	**3.24**	**1.15**	**650**	**634**	**670**	**3.9**	**3.2**	**9.5**	**3.0**	**15%**	**40**	**18**	**41**	**28%**	**79%**	**10%**	**0**						**7.5**	**105**	**136**	**$17**

Bettis,Chad

Age: 25	Th: R	Role RP	Health	F	LIMA Plan	D+
Ht: 6' 1"	Wt: 200	Type	PT/Exp	F	Rand Var	+1
			Consist	F	MM	2201

1-3, 5.64 ERA in 45 IP at COL. Made debut after missing all of '12 (shoulder), but welcome was a bit rude. Posted 68/13 K/BB in 63 IP at AA, but had HR issues that followed him to COL. Team believes in his future, moved him to bullpen late to limit IP, leading to brief Dom spike (5.5 as SP, 9.0 as RP). Keep an eye on him.

Yr	Tm	W	L	Sv	IP	K	ERA	xERA	WHIP	oOPS	vL	vR	BF/G	Ctl	Dom	Cmd	SwK	G	L	F	H%	S%	hr/f	GS	APC	DOM%	DIS%	Sv%	LI	RAR	BPV	BPX	R$
09																																	
10																																	
11																																	
12																																	
13	COL *	4	7	0	108	83	5.57	5.92	1.55	859	812	906	16.8	2.9	6.9	2.4	8%	47	21	32	34%	69%	12%	8	49	0%	50%	0	0.91	-22.6	35	45	-$12
1st Half		2	2	0	36	29	5.94	6.27	1.55				22.5	1.4	7.2	5.2					38%	65%	0%	0						-9.2	92	120	-$9
2nd Half		2	5	0	72	54	5.38	5.74	1.55	859	812	906	14.9	3.6	6.8	1.9	8%	47	21	32	31%	70%	12%	8	49	0%	50%	0	0.91	-13.4	24	31	-$13
14	Proj	**3**	**5**	**0**	**73**	**52**	**4.65**	**4.17**	**1.48**	**727**	**686**	**770**	**10.4**	**3.3**	**6.5**	**2.0**	**8%**	**45**	**21**	**34**	**32%**	**71%**	**10%**	**2**						**-7.0**	**51**	**66**	**-$4**

Billingsley,Chad

Age: 29	Th: R	Role SP	Health	F	LIMA Plan	C
Ht: 6' 1"	Wt: 240	Type Pwr	PT/Exp	B	Rand Var	-4
			Consist	B	MM	3301

Entered last spring training with "no concerns" about elbow that had bothered him late in '12. Oops. Groin, thumb injuries delayed start of '13, then lasted only two starts before TJS. Started throwing in Sept, so spring return possible. Has shown skills to succeed, but health questions mean you should probably only take a flyer.

Yr	Tm	W	L	Sv	IP	K	ERA	xERA	WHIP	oOPS	vL	vR	BF/G	Ctl	Dom	Cmd	SwK	G	L	F	H%	S%	hr/f	GS	APC	DOM%	DIS%	Sv%	LI	RAR	BPV	BPX	R$
09	LA	12	11	0	196	179	4.03	3.91	1.32	703	712	693	24.9	3.9	8.2	2.1	11%	45	18	36	29%	71%	9%	32	98	63%	9%	0	0.77	7.0	64	120	$12
10	LA	12	11	0	192	171	3.57	3.62	1.28	668	703	629	26.4	3.2	8.0	2.5	9%	50	18	32	31%	71%	4%	31	101	48%	10%			12.1	85	138	$12
11	LA	11	11	0	188	152	4.21	4.18	1.45	729	797	670	25.9	4.0	7.3	1.8	8%	45	21	34	32%	71%	7%	32	101	41%	19%			-6.3	45	68	$0
12	LA	10	9	0	150	128	3.55	3.88	1.29	725	744	703	25.4	2.7	7.7	2.8	9%	45	21	33	32%	74%	7%	25	95	72%	16%			8.6	88	115	$8
13	LA	1	0	0	12	6	3.00	4.68	1.42	766	828	684	24.5	3.8	4.5	1.2	8%	42	25	33	28%	81%	8%	2	91	0%	0%			1.3	0	0	-$3
1st Half		1	0	0	12	6	3.00	4.68	1.42	767	828	684	24.5	3.8	4.5	1.2	8%	42	25	33	28%	81%	8%	2	91	0%	0%			1.3	-1	-1	-$3
2nd Half																																	
14	Proj	**4**	**4**	**0**	**70**	**61**	**3.76**	**3.62**	**1.32**	**703**	**735**	**669**	**25.0**	**3.3**	**7.8**	**2.3**	**9%**	**47**	**20**	**33**	**31%**	**72%**	**7%**	**12**						**0.9**	**75**	**98**	**$1**

Black,Victor

Age: 26	Th: R	Role RP	Health	A	LIMA Plan	B
Ht: 6' 4"	Wt: 215	Type Pwr xFB	PT/Exp	F	Rand Var	0
			Consist	A	MM	3510

3-0, 3.71 ERA with 1 SV in 17 IP at PIT/NYM. Minor-league closer slowly but surely reining in walks. MLB sample is small, but if high FB% is legit, that could hold him back a bit. Still, September pretty promising (2.8 Ctl, 8.3 Dom, 3.0 Cmd in 13 IP). Deserves a spot on any closers-in-waiting list.

Yr	Tm	W	L	Sv	IP	K	ERA	xERA	WHIP	oOPS	vL	vR	BF/G	Ctl	Dom	Cmd	SwK	G	L	F	H%	S%	hr/f	GS	APC	DOM%	DIS%	Sv%	LI	RAR	BPV	BPX	R$
09																																	
10																																	
11																																	
12	aa	2	3	13	60	67	2.00	2.63	1.25				4.8	4.3	10.0	2.4					30%	84%								14.9	113	147	$10
13	2 NL *	8	3	18	64	64	3.17	2.60	1.20	687	609	741	4.6	3.8	9.0	2.4	10%	30	23	47	29%	73%	4%	0	16			75	1.04	5.5	103	135	$12
1st Half		0	2	12	27	28	2.77	2.01	1.09				4.8	3.6	9.3	2.6					27%	74%	0%	0						3.7	116	150	$12
2nd Half		8	1	6	37	36	3.47	3.03	1.28	687	609	741	4.4	3.9	8.8	2.3	10%	30	23	47	30%	73%	4%	0	16			55	1.04	1.8	95	123	$12
14	Proj	**6**	**3**	**8**	**65**	**68**	**3.34**	**3.75**	**1.23**	**542**	**484**	**582**	**4.7**	**4.0**	**9.4**	**2.4**	**10%**	**30**	**23**	**47**	**30%**	**72%**	**3%**	**0**						**4.2**	**71**	**92**	**$7**

Blackley,Travis

Age: 31	Th: L	Role RP	Health	B	LIMA Plan	D+
Ht: 6' 3"	Wt: 205	Type Pwr	PT/Exp	D	Rand Var	+3
			Consist	C	MM	2200

Journeyman pitcher comes complete with soundtrack: Move from OAK to HOU to TEX suggests he was not greeted with "Open Arms." "Don't Stop Believin'?" At 31, with marginal skills, hardly. And after another year of gopheritis (12 HR in 50.1 IP) and subpar Ctl, it's plenty time to go our "Separate Ways."

Yr	Tm	W	L	Sv	IP	K	ERA	xERA	WHIP	oOPS	vL	vR	BF/G	Ctl	Dom	Cmd	SwK	G	L	F	H%	S%	hr/f	GS	APC	DOM%	DIS%	Sv%	LI	RAR	BPV	BPX	R$
09	aaa	4	7	3	111	76	5.59	6.24	1.76				13.4	3.2	6.2	1.9					38%	69%								-17.4	37	70	-$9
10	aaa	2	1	0	42	30	3.71	4.91	1.70				10.0	6.2	6.4	1.0					31%	80%								1.9	39	63	-$3
11																																	
12	2 TM *	9	4	1	131	85	3.44	3.02	1.13	694	630	719	16.2	2.4	5.8	2.4	10%	48	18	35	26%	71%	9%	15	59	47%	33%	100	0.65	9.3	72	94	$10
13	2 AL	2	2	0	50	40	4.83	4.17	1.35	804	723	858	4.6	3.9	7.2	1.8	11%	44	21	35	25%	73%	24%	3	18	33%	67%	0	1.12	-6.0	45	58	-$4
1st Half		0	0	0	26	23	5.54	4.38	1.50	868	617	1100	3.8	5.2	8.0	1.5	11%	45	18	37	25%	72%	27%	0	15			0	0.98	-5.4	26	34	-$7
2nd Half		2	2	0	24	17	4.07	3.94	1.19	736	897	662	6.1	2.6	6.3	2.4	12%	42	23	34	25%	75%	20%	3	24	33%	67%	0	1.38	-0.6	64	83	-$2
14	Proj	**3**	**2**	**0**	**51**	**37**	**4.29**	**4.17**	**1.45**	**799**	**761**	**818**	**7.2**	**3.7**	**6.5**	**1.8**	**11%**	**45**	**20**	**35**	**30%**	**74%**	**13%**	**0**						**-2.7**	**42**	**54**	**-$3**

KRISTOPHER OLSON

Blanton,Joe

Age: 33	Th: R	Role RP	Health F	LIMA Plan C	
Ht: 6' 3"	Wt: 220	Type	PT/Exp B	Rand Var +5	
			Consist A	MM 3203	

Feel daring? Try telling anyone who's owned him, "You know, his skills say his results should be better"... then duck. For him, good Cmd just means he's in high demand at Home Run Derby. H%, S%, hr/f tell much of the story. Owed $7.5 million, so he'll likely be serving meatballs somewhere. Make sure it's not on your roster.

Yr Tm	W	L	Sv	IP	K	ERA	xERA	WHIP	oOPS	vL	vR	BF/G	Ctl	Dom	Cmd	SwK	G	L	F	H%	S%	hr/f	GS	APC	DOM%	DIS%	Sv%	LI	RAR	BPV	BPX	R$
09 PHI	12	8	0	195	163	4.05	4.06	1.32	759	721	792	27.0	2.7	7.5	2.8	8%	41	20	39	30%	74%	13%	31	105	55%	16%			6.4	81	151	$11
10 PHI	9	6	0	176	134	4.82	4.08	1.42	796	774	815	26.4	2.2	6.9	3.1	10%	42	19	39	33%	70%	12%	28	95	50%	14%	0	0.74	-16.0	84	136	-$1
11 PHI	1	2	0	41	35	5.01	3.36	1.48	839	791	873	16.4	2.0	7.6	3.9	10%	55	17	28	37%	68%	14%	8	53	25%	50%	0	0.66	-5.4	117	176	-$4
12 2 NL	10	13	0	191	166	4.71	3.61	1.26	759	799	718	26.0	1.6	7.8	4.9	10%	45	23	32	32%	67%	15%	30	94	63%	10%	0	0.83	-16.4	121	157	$2
13 LAA	2	14	0	133	108	6.04	4.14	1.61	904	844	976	21.8	2.3	7.3	3.2	10%	44	22	33	36%	68%	19%	20	79	30%	35%	0	0.69	-35.5	92	119	-$18
1st Half	2	10	0	98	81	5.07	3.85	1.47	848	821	879	27.3	1.7	7.5	4.5	11%	45	22	34	36%	70%	15%	16	98	38%	25%			-14.5	112	146	-$15
2nd Half	0	4	0	35	27	8.74	4.99	2.00	1051	896	1263	14.5	4.1	6.9	1.7	9%	43	25	32	37%	62%	29%	4	54	0%	75%	0	0.55	-21.1	35	45	-$27
14 Proj	**4**	**10**	**0**	**131**	**107**	**4.77**	**3.71**	**1.44**	**791**	**752**	**832**	**18.3**	**2.5**	**7.4**	**2.9**	**10%**	**43**	**22**	**34**	**33%**	**71%**	**15%**	**25**						**-14.5**	**87**	**113**	**-$4**

Blevins,Jerry

Age: 30	Th: L	Role RP	Health A	LIMA Plan B+	
Ht: 6' 6"	Wt: 175	Type Pwr xFB	PT/Exp D	Rand Var -3	
			Consist A	MM 3300	

Strand rate regression was only reason for uptick in ERA as xERA shows the skills were mostly flat. Improved Ctl a good sign, though he couldn't sustain it all season. Rising FB% trend is potentially concerning, though mitigated by his home park so far. Lots of little small-sample-size volatility.

Yr Tm	W	L	Sv	IP	K	ERA	xERA	WHIP	oOPS	vL	vR	BF/G	Ctl	Dom	Cmd	SwK	G	L	F	H%	S%	hr/f	GS	APC	DOM%	DIS%	Sv%	LI	RAR	BPV	BPX	R$
09 OAK *	5	3	2	86	71	4.58	4.33	1.40	651	719	617	5.6	2.6	7.5	2.9	9%	32	17	52	34%	68%	6%	0	19			33	0.36	-2.8	82	153	$1
10 OAK	2	1	1	49	46	3.70	4.10	1.48	758	598	892	3.5	3.3	8.5	2.6	10%	38	23	39	34%	80%	12%	0	13			50	1.19	2.3	79	128	-$1
11 OAK *	2	0	0	58	53	4.13	3.50	1.28	688	759	636	4.5	3.3	8.2	2.5	9%	38	18	44	30%	69%	6%	0	17			0	0.62	-1.3	86	129	-$1
12 OAK	5	1	1	65	54	2.48	4.10	1.07	637	575	693	4.1	3.4	7.4	2.2	11%	38	18	44	23%	83%	9%	0	16			100	0.92	12.4	57	74	$7
13 OAK	5	0	0	60	52	3.15	4.00	1.07	651	741	581	3.7	2.6	7.8	3.1	10%	31	19	50	25%	75%	8%	0	15			0	0.97	5.3	81	105	$4
1st Half	5	0	0	35	28	3.12	4.00	1.07	675	781	597	3.9	2.1	7.3	3.5	10%	34	17	48	26%	76%	8%	0	15			0	1.12	3.2	87	113	$6
2nd Half	0	0	0	25	24	3.20	4.01	1.07	618	689	554	3.4	3.2	8.5	2.7	10%	27	21	52	24%	75%	9%	0	14			0	0.78	2.1	72	93	$0
14 Proj	**4**	**1**	**0**	**65**	**57**	**3.52**	**3.79**	**1.21**	**698**	**690**	**705**	**3.8**	**3.0**	**7.9**	**2.6**	**10%**	**34**	**19**	**47**	**28%**	**74%**	**8%**	**0**						**2.8**	**73**	**94**	**$2**

Boggs,Mitchell

Age: 30	Th: R	Role RP	Health A	LIMA Plan D+	
Ht: 6' 4"	Wt: 235	Type GB	PT/Exp D	Rand Var +5	
			Consist F	MM 2100	

0-3, 8.10 ERA with 2 Sv in 23 IP at STL/COL. So much for three years of ascendant BPV. Easy to forget he began year as a closer, given how it crumbled. Change of scenery helped little, as Ctl, Dom remained AWOL. Robust GB% is last vestige of former self. Still owns skills, but feel free to wait to see if he can find them.

Yr Tm	W	L	Sv	IP	K	ERA	xERA	WHIP	oOPS	vL	vR	BF/G	Ctl	Dom	Cmd	SwK	G	L	F	H%	S%	hr/f	GS	APC	DOM%	DIS%	Sv%	LI	RAR	BPV	BPX	R$
09 STL *	8	7	0	134	92	5.14	5.92	1.81	856	1096	667	20.7	4.4	6.2	1.4	10%	53	18	29	37%	72%	6%	9	64	11%	33%	0	0.77	-13.6	36	67	-$10
10 STL	2	3	0	67	52	3.61	3.84	1.29	696	763	664	4.7	3.6	7.0	1.9	10%	53	16	31	29%	73%	8%	0	18			0	0.72	3.9	59	95	$1
11 STL	2	3	4	61	48	3.56	3.70	1.37	711	715	710	5.1	3.1	7.1	2.3	9%	51	21	28	32%	75%	8%	0	19			50	0.62	2.9	73	110	$1
12 STL	4	1	0	73	58	2.21	3.53	1.05	572	661	510	3.8	2.6	7.1	2.8	9%	53	19	28	26%	82%	9%	0	14			0	1.21	16.3	90	117	$8
13 2 NL *	1	9	3	69	33	8.37	8.65	2.30	970	794	1115	5.8	5.8	4.3	0.7	8%	54	22	24	39%	64%	26%	0	17			33	0.63	-38.5	-21	-28	-$25
1st Half	0	5	2	34	19	8.55	7.38	2.22	1007	863	1151	5.2	6.7	5.1	0.8	9%	50	27	23	38%	60%	25%	0	17			33	0.81	-19.8	9	12	-$25
2nd Half	1	4	1	35	13	7.63	9.52	2.29	891	580	1060	6.4	4.8	3.4	0.7	6%	63	11	26	38%	70%	29%	0	16			33	0.27	-16.2	-49	-63	-$26
14 Proj	**1**	**3**	**0**	**44**	**27**	**4.53**	**4.31**	**1.55**	**842**	**953**	**775**	**5.0**	**3.7**	**5.5**	**1.5**	**9%**	**52**	**18**	**29**	**32%**	**73%**	**12%**	**0**						**-3.6**	**29**	**38**	**-$5**

Brach,Brad

Age: 28	Th: R	Role RP	Health A	LIMA Plan C	
Ht: 6' 6"	Wt: 215	Type Pwr	PT/Exp D	Rand Var -4	
			Consist C	MM 3400	

1-0, 3.19 ERA in 31 IP at SD. Another year of strained relations with the strike zone (19 BB in 31 IP), leading to some serious San-Diego-to-Tucson frequent flier miles (I dunno; maybe he drove). Where did 2011's top-notch command go? RHB teed off on him, too. Needs to reconcile with home plate soon; time is running short.

Yr Tm	W	L	Sv	IP	K	ERA	xERA	WHIP	oOPS	vL	vR	BF/G	Ctl	Dom	Cmd	SwK	G	L	F	H%	S%	hr/f	GS	APC	DOM%	DIS%	Sv%	LI	RAR	BPV	BPX	R$
09																																
10																																
11 SD *	3	7	34	79	91	2.78	2.59	1.11	747	833	709	4.1	2.1	10.4	5.0	13%	26	53	21	34%	75%	0%	0	17			92	1.06	11.3	165	248	$20
12 SD	2	4	0	67	75	3.78	3.98	1.25	674	718	646	4.2	4.5	10.1	2.3	11%	35	20	45	26%	76%	15%	0	17			0	1.17	1.9	75	98	$1
13 SD *	5	3	3	75	67	2.92	4.64	1.52	819	647	972	5.0	3.9	8.0	2.0	9%	38	23	39	34%	84%	9%	0	19			100	0.62	8.8	65	84	$1
1st Half	3	1	0	38	36	3.95	5.17	1.58	864	766	928	4.9	3.7	8.5	2.3	9%	41	23	36	36%	78%	10%	0	18			0	0.68	-0.4	64	83	-$2
2nd Half	2	2	3	37	31	1.87	4.09	1.46	746	503	1045	5.0	4.0	7.4	1.8	10%	32	24	44	32%	90%	7%	0	21			100	0.52	9.2	66	85	$4
14 Proj	**2**	**3**	**0**	**46**	**47**	**3.70**	**3.73**	**1.38**	**684**	**656**	**701**	**4.5**	**4.1**	**9.1**	**2.2**	**10%**	**39**	**22**	**39**	**31%**	**76%**	**10%**	**0**						**0.9**	**70**	**91**	**-$1**

Breslow,Craig

Age: 33	Th: L	Role RP	Health C	LIMA Plan B	
Ht: 6' 1"	Wt: 190	Type	PT/Exp C	Rand Var -5	
			Consist B	MM 3200	

Worked himself into key setup role in storybook season, but soft skills foretold postseason struggles. Dom took a serious dive, but fortunate strand rate helped pick him up. Hit rate low, too, but not out of line with his past history. May continue to outpitch xERA, but you assume the risk if you want to chase that.

Yr Tm	W	L	Sv	IP	K	ERA	xERA	WHIP	oOPS	vL	vR	BF/G	Ctl	Dom	Cmd	SwK	G	L	F	H%	S%	hr/f	GS	APC	DOM%	DIS%	Sv%	LI	RAR	BPV	BPX	R$
09 2 AL	8	7	0	70	55	3.36	4.38	1.11	613	632	597	3.6	3.7	7.1	1.9	10%	32	20	48	22%	74%	9%	0	14			0	1.07	8.3	37	69	$7
10 OAK	4	4	5	75	71	3.01	4.13	1.10	620	586	637	4.1	3.5	8.6	2.4	11%	30	15	56	24%	78%	8%	0	16			71	1.03	9.8	68	109	$8
11 OAK	0	2	0	59	44	3.79	4.44	1.52	773	866	714	3.9	3.2	6.7	2.1	10%	38	20	41	35%	76%	5%	0	15			0	0.78	1.1	50	75	-$4
12 2 TM	3	0	0	63	61	2.70	3.66	1.17	645	597	683	4.1	3.1	8.7	2.8	12%	45	19	36	29%	80%	8%	0	17			0	0.83	10.3	95	123	$4
13 BOS	5	2	0	60	33	1.81	4.17	1.12	635	704	581	3.9	2.7	5.0	1.8	9%	45	21	34	25%	86%	5%	0	14			0	1.14	15.1	39	51	$5
1st Half	2	1	0	25	14	2.84	4.15	1.18	670	687	659	4.0	2.5	5.0	2.0	7%	51	15	34	28%	76%	4%	0	15			0	0.92	3.2	52	67	$2
2nd Half	3	1	0	34	19	1.05	4.18	1.08	608	714	510	3.8	2.9	5.0	1.7	10%	40	26	35	24%	94%	6%	0	14			0	1.30	11.9	29	38	$8
14 Proj	**4**	**2**	**0**	**58**	**42**	**3.38**	**3.91**	**1.24**	**684**	**721**	**656**	**3.9**	**3.0**	**6.4**	**2.2**	**10%**	**42**	**20**	**37**	**29%**	**74%**	**6%**	**0**						**3.5**	**56**	**72**	**$1**

Britton,Zach

Age: 26	Th: L	Role SP	Health D	LIMA Plan D	
Ht: 6' 3"	Wt: 195	Type xGB	PT/Exp D	Rand Var +2	
			Consist B	MM 1000	

2-3, 4.95 ERA in 40 IP at BAL. Dom, Cmd went backwards, leading to year on fringe of rotation. Even in minors, skills, stats showed little promise. Again induced GB at high rate, but that's about it for positives. Equally ineffective vs. LHB, RHB, so LOOGY duty not likely in his future. Rotation spot may not be, either.

Yr Tm	W	L	Sv	IP	K	ERA	xERA	WHIP	oOPS	vL	vR	BF/G	Ctl	Dom	Cmd	SwK	G	L	F	H%	S%	hr/f	GS	APC	DOM%	DIS%	Sv%	LI	RAR	BPV	BPX	R$
09																																
10 a/a	10	7	0	153	103	3.28	3.91	1.37				23.8	2.9	6.0	2.1					32%	77%								15.1	65	105	$7
11 BAL *	11	14	0	171	112	4.70	4.44	1.45	735	698	748	22.8	3.4	5.9	1.7	7%	53	19	28	31%	68%	9%	28	90	36%	21%			-16.0	46	70	-$3
12 PIT *	10	5	0	124	92	5.34	4.77	1.53	756	714	778	23.4	4.2	6.7	1.6	10%	61	16	23	32%	66%	14%	11	89	45%	45%	0	0.73	-20.2	45	59	-$9
13 BAL *	8	8	0	143	77	5.52	5.93	1.82	837	849	832	24.6	4.3	4.8	1.1	7%	58	20	22	36%	69%	13%	7	83	14%	43%	0	0.75	-29.2	23	30	-$20
1st Half	5	4	0	82	44	4.43	5.57	1.76	823	942	769	25.2	4.0	4.8	1.2	5%	52	21	27	36%	74%	9%	4	92	0%	25%			-5.8	29	38	-$15
2nd Half	3	4	0	61	33	6.98	6.41	1.89	856	725	910	24.0	4.7	4.9	1.1	8%	66	18	16	36%	62%	20%	3	74	33%	67%	0	0.74	-23.4	14	18	-$27
14 Proj	**4**	**4**	**0**	**64**	**36**	**4.77**	**4.46**	**1.60**	**761**	**728**	**776**	**23.5**	**4.5**	**5.2**	**1.1**	**8%**	**57**	**18**	**25**	**31%**	**71%**	**11%**	**12**						**-7.1**	**7**	**9**	**-$5**

Brothers,Rex

Age: 26	Th: L	Role RP	Health A	LIMA Plan C+	
Ht: 6' 0"	Wt: 210	Type Pwr	PT/Exp C	Rand Var -5	
			Consist A	MM 5530	

Much-anticipated closer audition came and he responded, converting 19 of 21 opps. No looking back now, right? Well, maybe. Big SwK is a start, but still walking too many batters, and struggles vs. RHB resurfaced in 2H. First-half S% couldn't last, either. Has enough skill to hold the job, but until Ctl improves, a cut below elite.

Yr Tm	W	L	Sv	IP	K	ERA	xERA	WHIP	oOPS	vL	vR	BF/G	Ctl	Dom	Cmd	SwK	G	L	F	H%	S%	hr/f	GS	APC	DOM%	DIS%	Sv%	LI	RAR	BPV	BPX	R$
09																																
10 aa	2	1	4	23	21	5.15	3.96	1.53				4.2	7.2	8.4	1.2					25%	68%								-3.0	57	92	-$1
11 COL *	4	4	1	69	94	2.74	3.69	1.38	644	594	673	4.0	4.3	12.3	2.9	12%	46	16	37	36%	83%	12%	0	15			20	1.01	10.2	118	177	$4
12 COL	8	2	0	68	83	3.86	3.55	1.48	732	587	832	3.9	4.9	11.0	2.2	15%	47	23	30	35%	75%	10%	0	15			0	1.09	1.3	91	118	$0
13 COL	2	1	19	67	76	1.74	3.49	1.29	618	463	686	3.9	4.8	10.2	2.1	13%	49	19	33	29%	90%	9%	0	16			90	1.20	17.7	80	104	$12
1st Half	2	0	4	34	37	0.52	3.40	1.17	542	458	579	3.7	4.5	9.7	2.2	13%	48	18	34	27%	97%	4%	0	15			80	1.16	14.2	80	103	$12
2nd Half	0	1	15	33	39	3.00	3.57	1.42	692	468	787	4.1	5.2	10.6	2.1	13%	50	19	31	31%	84%	15%	0	16			94	1.24	3.5	80	103	$12
14 Proj	**4**	**2**	**36**	**68**	**81**	**3.30**	**3.17**	**1.30**	**631**	**504**	**699**	**3.8**	**4.8**	**10.8**	**2.3**	**14%**	**48**	**20**	**32**	**30%**	**76%**	**11%**	**0**						**4.7**	**91**	**118**	**$17**

KRISTOPHER OLSON

Broxton,Jonathan

Age: 30 Th: R Role RP	Health F	LIMA Plan C	
Ht: 6' 4" Wt: 310 Type Pwr	PT/Exp C	Rand Var 0	
	Consist C	MM 3300	

Once-dominant closer lost much of another season to elbow/forearm woes. Even if six-month recovery from late-August surgery stays on track, he's now four years removed from last double-digit Dom. GB tilt reversed course, too. Thus, save chances unlikely to return. But first let's see him get through a season healthy.

Yr Tm	W	L	Sv	IP	K	ERA	xERA	WHIP	oOPS	vL	vR	BF/G	Ctl	Dom	Cmd	SwK	G	L	F	H%	S%	hr/f	GS	APC	DOM%	DIS%	Sv%	LI	RAR	BPV	BPX	R$
09 LA	7	2	36	76	114	2.61	2.17	0.96	479	414	541	4.1	3.4	13.5	3.9	15%	56	16	28	29%	74%	9%	0	17			86	1.32	16.1	184	345	$28
10 LA	5	6	22	62	73	4.04	3.32	1.48	718	626	794	4.2	4.0	10.5	2.6	12%	47	21	32	37%	73%	8%	0	17			76	1.31	0.3	106	171	$9
11 LA	1	2	7	13	10	5.68	5.21	1.89	840	670	951	4.4	6.4	7.1	1.1	9%	42	33	26	34%	73%	18%	0	18			88	1.04	-2.7	-25	-37	-$2
12 2 TM	4	5	27	58	45	2.48	3.55	1.26	676	628	715	4.0	2.6	7.0	2.6	9%	54	22	24	31%	80%	5%	0	16			82	1.33	11.0	86	113	$14
13 CIN	2	2	0	31	25	4.11	4.09	1.27	712	779	656	3.9	3.5	7.3	2.1	13%	46	16	37	27%	71%	12%	0	15			0	1.24	-0.9	61	79	-$3
1st Half	2	2	0	27	20	4.33	4.34	1.30	701	716	690	4.1	3.7	6.7	1.8	12%	47	16	37	27%	69%	10%	0	15			0	1.26	-1.6	46	60	-$2
2nd Half	0	0	0	4	5	2.45	2.51	1.09	795	1262	393	3.0	2.5	12.3	5.0	15%	38	25	38	27%	100%	33%	0	13			0	1.17	0.6	170	220	-$4
14 Proj	**3**	**3**	**0**	**44**	**36**	**3.81**	**3.72**	**1.30**	**671**	**621**	**712**	**4.0**	**3.6**	**7.5**	**2.1**	**12%**	**47**	**20**	**33**	**30%**	**71%**	**7%**	**0**						**0.3**	**63**	**81**	**-$1**

Buchholz,Clay

Age: 29 Th: R Role SP	Health F	LIMA Plan C	
Ht: 6' 3" Wt: 190 Type	PT/Exp B	Rand Var -5	
	Consist B	MM 3203	

Stellar 1H not entirely supported—high S%, low H%, hr/f helped—but Dom spike, career-best skills were also part of the package. Then old bugaboo—injuries—reared its ugly head. "Minor" neck strain led to bursitis and a three-month absence. Should be at peak, but tough to have faith that his health will cooperate.

Yr Tm	W	L	Sv	IP	K	ERA	xERA	WHIP	oOPS	vL	vR	BF/G	Ctl	Dom	Cmd	SwK	G	L	F	H%	S%	hr/f	GS	APC	DOM%	DIS%	Sv%	LI	RAR	BPV	BPX	R$
09 BOS *	14	6	0	191	138	4.06	4.11	1.34	729	763	697	24.1	3.4	6.5	1.9	10%	54	18	29	29%	73%	16%	16	95	38%	25%			6.2	51	95	$11
10 BOS	17	7	0	174	120	2.33	3.93	1.20	615	651	571	25.4	3.5	6.2	1.8	10%	51	18	32	26%	82%	6%	28	100	43%	21%			37.4	47	76	$21
11 BOS	6	3	0	83	60	3.48	4.16	1.29	706	706	706	25.2	3.4	6.5	1.9	9%	51	11	39	28%	77%	10%	14	97	43%	21%			4.7	55	83	$3
12 BOS	11	8	0	189	129	4.56	4.27	1.33	757	761	751	27.7	3.0	6.1	2.0	9%	48	20	33	29%	69%	13%	29	100	52%	21%			-12.8	54	71	$0
13 BOS	12	1	0	108	96	1.74	3.31	1.02	546	536	560	26.0	3.0	8.0	2.7	10%	48	21	32	25%	84%	5%	16	102	69%	0%			28.3	89	116	$18
1st Half	9	0	0	84	81	1.71	3.15	1.02	535	535	535	27.1	3.1	8.6	2.8	10%	49	21	30	26%	83%	3%	12	104	83%	0%			22.4	99	128	$23
2nd Half	3	1	0	24	15	1.88	3.87	1.04	587	536	657	22.8	2.6	5.6	2.1	9%	44	19	37	23%	87%	8%	4	96	25%	0%			5.9	52	68	$1
14 Proj	**14**	**8**	**0**	**174**	**127**	**3.40**	**3.74**	**1.23**	**677**	**663**	**694**	**25.5**	**3.0**	**6.6**	**2.2**	**9%**	**48**	**18**	**34**	**28%**	**75%**	**9%**	**28**						**9.9**	**62**	**81**	**$13**

Buehrle,Mark

Age: 35 Th: L Role SP	Health A	LIMA Plan B+	
Ht: 6' 2" Wt: 245 Type Con	PT/Exp A	Rand Var 0	
	Consist A	MM 3105	

Tempted to write, "See last year's book." But then, that's what we wrote last year... and in '12... and in '11. Only 12 wins? Major deviation! Dom has seen a bit of late-career renaissance. Nothing crazy, mind you; wouldn't be Buehrle-like. We'll go out on a limb and say, "More of the same in '14."

Yr Tm	W	L	Sv	IP	K	ERA	xERA	WHIP	oOPS	vL	vR	BF/G	Ctl	Dom	Cmd	SwK	G	L	F	H%	S%	hr/f	GS	APC	DOM%	DIS%	Sv%	LI	RAR	BPV	BPX	R$
09 CHW	13	10	0	213	105	3.84	4.34	1.25	756	839	725	26.5	1.9	4.4	2.3	7%	45	19	36	28%	73%	11%	33	97	33%	18%			12.7	51	96	$13
10 CHW	13	13	0	210	99	4.28	4.59	1.40	751	749	751	27.2	2.1	4.2	2.0	6%	46	16	38	32%	70%	6%	33	100	33%	15%			-5.2	44	71	$2
11 CHW	13	9	0	205	109	3.59	4.22	1.30	728	683	746	27.7	2.0	4.8	2.4	7%	45	20	35	30%	75%	9%	31	101	45%	10%			8.8	56	84	$8
12 MIA	13	13	0	202	125	3.74	4.19	1.17	710	645	731	26.7	1.8	5.6	3.1	8%	41	22	36	28%	73%	11%	31	99	55%	13%			7.0	71	93	$13
13 TOR	12	10	0	204	139	4.15	4.11	1.35	754	724	764	26.5	2.3	6.1	2.7	10%	45	21	34	31%	72%	11%	33	100	45%	18%			-7.2	73	95	$2
1st Half	4	5	0	103	68	4.81	4.37	1.40	770	714	790	26.6	2.6	5.9	2.3	7%	44	21	35	31%	68%	11%	17	101	41%	24%			-11.9	58	75	-$5
2nd Half	8	5	0	101	71	3.49	3.85	1.29	738	737	738	26.5	1.9	6.3	3.4	7%	47	20	33	32%	76%	10%	16	99	50%	13%			4.7	89	115	$8
14 Proj	**12**	**10**	**0**	**189**	**118**	**3.89**	**3.87**	**1.29**	**738**	**708**	**748**	**26.1**	**2.0**	**5.6**	**2.8**	**7%**	**44**	**21**	**35**	**30%**	**73%**	**10%**	**30**						**-0.5**	**69**	**90**	**$7**

Bumgarner,Madison

Age: 24 Th: L Role SP	Health A	LIMA Plan C	
Ht: 6' 5" Wt: 235 Type Pwr	PT/Exp A	Rand Var -2	
	Consist A	MM 5305	

Ho, hum. Just another 200-IP, triple-digit-BPV year. Dom continues to improve, though perhaps at the expense of a bit of Ctl. Exciting DOM/DIS trend shouts consistency. There is only one data point that raises any warning flag - the number of innings he's thrown by age 24. Just be aware when you go the extra buck..

Yr Tm	W	L	Sv	IP	K	ERA	xERA	WHIP	oOPS	vL	vR	BF/G	Ctl	Dom	Cmd	SwK	G	L	F	H%	S%	hr/f	GS	APC	DOM%	DIS%	Sv%	LI	RAR	BPV	BPX	R$
09 SF *	9	1	0	117	70	2.38	2.91	1.13	739	160	1037	19.2	2.5	5.4	2.2	9%	58	15	27	26%	82%	29%	1	39	0%	0%	0	0.38	28.0	67	125	$15
10 SF *	14	7	0	194	137	3.12	4.12	1.33	732	678	751	25.1	2.1	6.4	3.0	8%	45	17	38	32%	79%	8%	18	96	50%	22%			23.0	78	126	$13
11 SF	13	13	0	205	191	3.21	3.25	1.21	670	602	685	25.6	2.0	8.4	4.2	10%	46	21	33	33%	74%	6%	33	97	70%	15%			18.5	121	181	$17
12 SF	16	11	0	208	191	3.37	3.44	1.11	670	581	694	26.5	2.1	8.3	3.9	10%	48	19	33	29%	74%	12%	32	102	66%	13%			16.6	117	153	$23
13 SF	13	9	0	201	199	2.77	3.25	1.03	577	487	602	25.9	2.8	8.9	3.2	11%	47	18	35	26%	76%	8%	31	103	81%	6%			27.2	110	144	$26
1st Half	8	5	0	111	107	3.08	3.35	1.00	581	618	568	26.0	2.7	8.7	3.2	11%	44	19	37	25%	73%	10%	17	104	88%	6%			10.7	106	137	$28
2nd Half	5	4	0	90	92	2.39	3.12	1.07	573	303	641	25.8	2.9	9.2	3.2	12%	51	16	33	28%	78%	5%	14	102	71%	7%			16.4	116	150	$23
14 Proj	**17**	**10**	**0**	**218**	**203**	**2.93**	**3.12**	**1.11**	**625**	**522**	**653**	**24.8**	**2.5**	**8.4**	**3.4**	**11%**	**47**	**18**	**34**	**29%**	**76%**	**8%**	**34**						**25.0**	**110**	**143**	**$27**

Burnett,A.J.

Age: 37 Th: R Role SP	Health B	LIMA Plan B	
Ht: 6' 4" Wt: 230 Type Pwr GB	PT/Exp A	Rand Var 0	
	Consist A	MM 5405	

The further Yankee Stadium is in his rear view mirror, the stronger his skills become. Ability to maintain extreme GB% encouraging, as are career-best Dom, SwK. At 37, you'd expect some skills erosion but there is little sign of that here. At this writing, some "retirement" murmurs, but if not, a worthwhile investment.

Yr Tm	W	L	Sv	IP	K	ERA	xERA	WHIP	oOPS	vL	vR	BF/G	Ctl	Dom	Cmd	SwK	G	L	F	H%	S%	hr/f	GS	APC	DOM%	DIS%	Sv%	LI	RAR	BPV	BPX	R$
09 NYY	13	9	0	207	195	4.04	4.14	1.40	729	654	816	27.2	4.2	8.5	2.0	8%	43	18	39	30%	74%	11%	33	105	58%	12%			7.1	60	112	$11
10 NYY	10	15	0	187	145	5.26	4.30	1.51	824	820	827	25.1	3.8	7.0	1.9	8%	45	18	37	32%	67%	12%	33	94	45%	33%			-27.1	47	77	-$6
11 NYY	11	11	0	190	173	5.15	3.84	1.43	802	777	831	25.4	3.9	8.2	2.1	10%	49	18	32	30%	68%	17%	32	98	47%	16%	0	0.76	-28.4	68	103	-$5
12 PIT	16	10	0	202	180	3.51	3.38	1.24	668	695	641	27.5	2.8	8.0	2.9	10%	57	19	24	30%	74%	13%	31	98	55%	6%			12.5	105	137	$16
13 PIT	10	11	0	191	209	3.30	2.92	1.21	639	735	547	26.7	3.2	9.8	3.1	11%	57	19	24	32%	73%	9%	30	101	70%	10%			13.4	127	166	$14
1st Half	4	6	0	89	99	3.12	2.96	1.13	619	753	500	26.1	3.5	10.0	2.8	11%	55	18	27	27%	75%	14%	14	103	79%	7%			8.2	117	152	$16
2nd Half	6	5	0	102	110	3.45	2.89	1.29	655	720	588	27.2	2.8	9.7	3.4	12%	58	20	22	35%	72%	5%	16	99	63%	13%			5.2	135	174	$12
14 Proj	**11**	**10**	**0**	**189**	**185**	**3.63**	**3.11**	**1.28**	**686**	**731**	**641**	**25.7**	**3.2**	**8.8**	**2.7**	**10%**	**54**	**19**	**27**	**31%**	**73%**	**12%**	**30**						**5.4**	**104**	**135**	**$12**

Burton,Jared

Age: 33 Th: R Role RP	Health D	LIMA Plan C	
Ht: 6' 5" Wt: 225 Type Pwr	PT/Exp D	Rand Var 0	
	Consist C	MM 4310	

Groin injury may have contributed to May-June swoon. Once healthy, was able to right the ship, skills-wise at least. Low S% hurt results, causing some lower-leverage usage, but mastery of RHB returned. Since 2H looks a lot like 2012, with health, should be able to restore status as top setup man with outside shot at saves.

Yr Tm	W	L	Sv	IP	K	ERA	xERA	WHIP	oOPS	vL	vR	BF/G	Ctl	Dom	Cmd	SwK	G	L	F	H%	S%	hr/f	GS	APC	DOM%	DIS%	Sv%	LI	RAR	BPV	BPX	R$
09 CIN	1	0	0	59	45	4.40	4.60	1.42	759	636	850	5.0	3.5	6.8	2.0	11%	43	15	42	31%	70%	6%	0	20			0	0.76	-0.6	50	93	-$2
10 CIN *	3	2	4	41	27	3.19	4.09	1.35	0	0	0	4.7	4.0	5.8	1.4	14%	44	11	44	26%	82%	0%	0	11			67	0.47	4.5	37	60	$2
11 CIN	0	0	0	5	3	3.86	5.96	1.93	988	1625	670	3.8	5.8	5.8	1.0	9%	38	19	44	33%	88%	14%	0	16			0	0.46	0.0	-36	-54	-$4
12 PIT	3	2	5	62	55	2.18	3.40	0.92	549	748	421	3.8	2.3	8.0	3.4	14%	49	17	35	23%	81%	9%	0	15			56	1.13	14.1	108	141	$10
13 MIN	2	9	2	66	61	3.82	3.80	1.26	688	713	665	4.0	3.0	8.3	2.8	13%	41	20	39	31%	71%	8%	0	15			29	1.14	0.4	88	114	$0
1st Half	1	5	2	35	33	3.57	4.18	1.42	729	648	797	4.4	4.1	8.4	2.1	13%	43	18	38	32%	77%	8%	0	16			33	1.32	1.3	63	81	$0
2nd Half	1	4	0	31	28	4.11	3.38	1.08	638	786	485	3.5	1.8	8.2	4.7	14%	39	21	39	29%	63%	9%	0	14			0	0.96	-0.9	118	152	$0
14 Proj	**3**	**5**	**3**	**65**	**56**	**3.42**	**3.52**	**1.18**	**664**	**740**	**602**	**3.9**	**2.9**	**7.7**	**2.7**	**13%**	**44**	**18**	**38**	**28%**	**74%**	**9%**	**0**						**3.6**	**83**	**108**	**$3**

Cahill,Trevor

Age: 26 Th: R Role SP	Health D	LIMA Plan B	
Ht: 6' 4" Wt: 220 Type Pwr xGB	PT/Exp A	Rand Var 0	
	Consist A	MM 3205	

8-10, 3.99 ERA in 147 IP at ARI. Took step back in '13 that even mid-season DL respite (bruised hip) couldn't fix. ERA improvement in 2H solely due to better S%. Ability to induce GB lessens risk, but stable Dom is not a good thing when there are league-wide gains, so these skills are getting relatively less interesting.

Yr Tm	W	L	Sv	IP	K	ERA	xERA	WHIP	oOPS	vL	vR	BF/G	Ctl	Dom	Cmd	SwK	G	L	F	H%	S%	hr/f	GS	APC	DOM%	DIS%	Sv%	LI	RAR	BPV	BPX	R$
09 OAK	10	13	0	179	90	4.63	4.89	1.44	810	920	689	24.2	3.6	4.5	1.3	7%	48	18	34	28%	72%	13%	32	94	22%	34%			-6.9	10	18	$1
10 OAK	18	8	0	197	118	2.97	3.76	1.11	619	630	605	26.1	2.9	5.4	1.9	6%	56	15	29	24%	77%	11%	30	101	47%	10%			26.8	53	86	$22
11 OAK	12	14	0	208	147	4.16	3.88	1.43	738	754	720	26.5	3.6	6.4	1.8	8%	56	19	25	31%	72%	12%	34	100	47%	26%			-5.6	53	79	$1
12 ARI	13	12	0	200	156	3.78	3.60	1.29	706	696	718	26.2	3.3	7.0	2.1	10%	61	16	23	29%	72%	12%	32	99	59%	19%			5.8	75	98	$9
13 ARI *	8	12	0	163	113	4.18	4.16	1.43	745	769	719	23.9	4.0	6.2	1.5	8%	56	20	24	29%	72%	12%	25	91	28%	16%	0	0.85	-6.4	47	61	-$3
1st Half	3	10	0	97	69	4.66	3.88	1.41	765	772	757	24.8	3.6	6.4	1.8	8%	58	19	23	30%	68%	15%	17	91	35%	24%			-9.4	53	69	-$5
2nd Half	5	2	0	67	44	3.50	4.07	1.46	707	764	657	23.8	4.6	5.9	1.3	8%	53	21	26	28%	78%	8%	8	92	13%	0%	0	0.99	3.0	43	56	$0
14 Proj	**11**	**11**	**0**	**189**	**134**	**3.93**	**3.80**	**1.38**	**735**	**759**	**709**	**24.7**	**3.8**	**6.4**	**1.7**	**8%**	**56**	**19**	**25**	**29%**	**73%**	**12%**	**32**						**-1.6**	**47**	**62**	**$5**

KRISTOPHER OLSON

Cain,Matt

Age: 29	Th: R	Role: SP	Health: B	LIMA Plan: B
Ht: 6' 3"	Wt: 230	Type: FB	PT/Exp: A	Rand Var: 0
			Consist: A	MM: 4305

xERA never bought into sub-3.00 ERAs. Still, 1H crash, fueled by low S%, was a bit harsh. Just as he was getting on 2H roll (five straight PQS-5s), hit DL for first time in 261 starts. Stay was short and good results resumed, though Sept skills not quite as strong. Poised for rebound, which could come at a discount.

Yr	Tm	W	L	Sv	IP	K	ERA	xERA	WHIP	oOPS	vL	vR	BF/G	Ctl	Dom	Cmd	SwK	G	L	F	H%	S%	hr/f	GS	APC	DOM%	DIS%	Sv%	LI	RAR	BPV	BPX	R$
09	SF	14	8	0	218	171	2.89	4.11	1.18	670	649	693	26.8	3.0	7.1	2.3	9%	39	19	42	27%	80%	8%	33	102	61%	9%			38.3	63	117	$26
10	SF	13	11	0	223	177	3.14	3.95	1.08	646	663	629	27.2	2.5	7.1	2.9	9%	36	17	47	26%	75%	7%	33	106	67%	6%			25.8	76	123	$23
11	SF	12	11	0	222	179	2.88	3.71	1.08	597	523	674	27.5	2.6	7.3	2.8	10%	42	19	39	27%	73%	4%	33	106	73%	3%			29.0	82	123	$24
12	SF	16	5	0	219	193	2.79	3.71	1.04	635	711	563	27.4	2.1	7.9	3.8	10%	37	21	42	27%	77%	8%	32	105	63%	0%			33.1	101	132	$32
13	SF	8	10	0	184	158	4.00	3.87	1.16	678	644	704	25.3	2.7	7.7	2.9	9%	38	22	40	27%	69%	11%	30	97	53%	13%			-3.1	82	107	$8
1st Half		5	4	0	109	101	4.29	3.62	1.07	663	610	709	26.1	2.5	8.3	3.4	10%	38	21	41	26%	64%	13%	17	102	53%	6%			-5.8	99	128	$11
2nd Half		3	6	0	75	57	3.58	4.23	1.27	698	696	699	24.4	3.0	6.8	2.3	9%	38	24	39	29%	74%	8%	13	92	54%	23%			2.6	58	75	$4
14	**Proj**	**11**	**10**	**0**	**202**	**168**	**3.28**	**3.58**	**1.15**	**664**	**658**	**670**	**25.3**	**2.6**	**7.5**	**2.9**	**9%**	**38**	**21**	**40**	**28%**	**75%**	**8%**	**32**						**14.7**	**82**	**106**	**$18**

Capps,Carter

Age: 23	Th: R	Role: RP	Health: A	LIMA Plan: C+
Ht: 6' 5"	Wt: 220	Type: Pwr	PT/Exp: D	Rand Var: +5
			Consist: C	MM: 4510

A funny thing happened on his way to closer role: LHB feasted; balls started flying out of park (9 HR in first 35 IP), bumping him to AAA and back of pecking order. HR abated after month-long exile thanks to sharp GB% rise, but then Ctl became issue. At 23, plenty of time to round into form, but may not arrive this year, either.

Yr	Tm	W	L	Sv	IP	K	ERA	xERA	WHIP	oOPS	vL	vR	BF/G	Ctl	Dom	Cmd	SwK	G	L	F	H%	S%	hr/f	GS	APC	DOM%	DIS%	Sv%	LI	RAR	BPV	BPX	R$
09																																	
10																																	
11																																	
12	SEA *	2	3	19	76	96	2.13	2.58	1.17	667	798	552	5.3	2.6	11.3	4.3	12%	41	28	32	35%	81%	0%	0	26			90	0.50	17.7	160	209	$15
13	SEA	3	3	0	59	66	5.49	3.79	1.63	878	1029	776	5.1	3.5	10.1	2.9	13%	40	24	36	38%	71%	19%	0	20			0	1.05	-11.8	104	136	-$8
1st Half		2	2	0	32	40	5.97	3.64	1.58	930	1170	796	4.7	2.6	11.4	4.4	14%	29	23	48	39%	71%	20%	0	19			0	1.16	-8.2	143	185	-$7
2nd Half		1	1	0	27	26	4.94	3.98	1.68	814	893	748	5.6	4.6	8.6	1.9	12%	52	25	24	36%	72%	15%	0	21			0	0.90	-3.6	59	77	-$8
14	**Proj**	**3**	**3**	**3**	**65**	**72**	**3.93**	**3.30**	**1.31**	**669**	**771**	**595**	**5.0**	**3.7**	**10.0**	**2.7**	**13%**	**41**	**24**	**35**	**31%**	**73%**	**13%**	**0**						**-0.5**	**98**	**127**	**$1**

Capuano,Chris

Age: 35	Th: L	Role: RP	Health: D	LIMA Plan: C
Ht: 6' 3"	Wt: 215	Type:	PT/Exp: A	Rand Var: +2
			Consist: A	MM: 4201

Thrice, LA tried to demote him to bullpen, only to reinstate as SP out of necessity. Roller-coaster year also included June DL stint (calf), Sept groin strain. When he pitched, skills were there, especially in 2H, when Cmd leapt. Relief work (4 IP, 0 ER, 7 K), health woes, increasing struggles vs. RHB suggest pen may be good fit.

Yr	Tm	W	L	Sv	IP	K	ERA	xERA	WHIP	oOPS	vL	vR	BF/G	Ctl	Dom	Cmd	SwK	G	L	F	H%	S%	hr/f	GS	APC	DOM%	DIS%	Sv%	LI	RAR	BPV	BPX	R$
09																																	
10	MIL *	5	5	0	91	66	3.48	3.92	1.29	755	685	780	13.3	2.5	6.5	2.6	9%	43	17	40	30%	76%	11%	9	44	44%	33%	0	0.65	6.7	70	112	$4
11	NYM	11	12	0	186	168	4.55	3.78	1.35	781	653	818	24.3	2.6	8.1	3.2	11%	43	17	40	32%	70%	12%	31	90	45%	6%	0	0.82	-13.9	98	147	$1
12	LA	12	12	0	198	162	3.72	4.00	1.22	715	602	745	24.8	2.5	7.4	3.0	12%	40	21	39	29%	74%	11%	33	90	55%	18%			7.2	84	110	$12
13	LA	4	7	0	106	81	4.26	3.91	1.41	781	566	858	19.0	2.0	6.9	3.4	10%	46	20	33	34%	72%	10%	20	71	40%	50%	0	0.80	-5.1	93	121	-$4
1st Half		2	5	0	48	37	4.72	4.08	1.43	774	500	893	19.0	2.6	7.0	2.6	9%	46	20	34	33%	70%	13%	9	70	44%	56%	0	0.89	-5.0	78	102	-$5
2nd Half		2	2	0	58	44	3.88	3.77	1.40	787	637	832	19.1	1.6	6.8	4.4	11%	47	21	33	36%	73%	6%	11	71	36%	45%	0	0.72	-0.1	106	137	-$3
14	**Proj**	**5**	**7**	**0**	**106**	**84**	**3.90**	**3.60**	**1.28**	**732**	**577**	**782**	**19.3**	**2.2**	**7.2**	**3.2**	**11%**	**44**	**20**	**36**	**31%**	**73%**	**10%**	**21**						**-0.4**	**90**	**117**	**$2**

Carpenter,David

Age: 28	Th: R	Role: RP	Health: A	LIMA Plan: A
Ht: 6' 2"	Wt: 215	Type: Pwr	PT/Exp: D	Rand Var: -3
			Consist: F	MM: 4400

4-1, 1.78 ERA in 66 IP at ATL. Destined to be trivia answer: What player accompanied manager John Farrell to BOS? Relief work in ATL after waiver claim was anything but trivial. Trendy pre-'12 saves sleeper finally woke up, adding Ctl to K ability. Needs to repeat 2H, but there's a chance he's a late bloomer. Don't ignore.

Yr	Tm	W	L	Sv	IP	K	ERA	xERA	WHIP	oOPS	vL	vR	BF/G	Ctl	Dom	Cmd	SwK	G	L	F	H%	S%	hr/f	GS	APC	DOM%	DIS%	Sv%	LI	RAR	BPV	BPX	R$
09																																	
10																																	
11	HOU *	1	4	15	61	60	2.55	4.40	1.39	809	697	889	3.8	3.3	8.9	2.7	11%	38	24	38	33%	87%	11%	0	14			83	0.95	10.4	78	118	$7
12	2 TM *	1	3	4	59	50	6.01	5.96	1.70	953	1123	842	4.7	3.5	7.7	2.2	13%	42	23	35	38%	65%	13%	0	19			67	0.77	-14.4	51	67	-$10
13	ATL *	5	3	0	81	83	2.32	2.78	1.12	558	643	506	5.2	2.7	9.2	3.4	13%	38	23	39	29%	83%	8%	0	19			0	0.97	15.4	115	150	$8
1st Half		2	2	0	35	27	3.06	3.96	1.46	598	700	516	7.1	4.2	6.8	1.6	11%	39	20	41	31%	80%	5%	0	23			0	0.22	3.5	61	80	$0
2nd Half		3	1	0	46	56	1.76	2.57	0.87	540	608	502	4.2	1.6	11.0	7.0	14%	38	24	38	28%	86%	10%	0	17			0	1.25	11.9	171	221	$14
14	**Proj**	**2**	**3**	**0**	**58**	**58**	**3.46**	**3.37**	**1.25**	**665**	**779**	**592**	**4.6**	**3.0**	**9.0**	**3.0**	**13%**	**40**	**23**	**38**	**31%**	**75%**	**9%**	**0**						**2.9**	**98**	**128**	**$1**

Carrasco,Carlos

Age: 27	Th: R	Role: RP	Health: F	LIMA Plan: C
Ht: 6' 3"	Wt: 210	Type:	PT/Exp: D	Rand Var: +2
			Consist: B	MM: 3210

1-4, 6.75 ERA in 47 IP at CLE. Rocky return from '11 TJS, as 6 of 7 starts were PQS-DIS, though minor-league numbers solid. But for some wildness, was far better in bullpen (11/5 K/BB, 2 ER in 13.2 IP). Velocity back and then some, so late innings not out of realm, especially given GB%. Role aside, too talented to give up on yet.

Yr	Tm	W	L	Sv	IP	K	ERA	xERA	WHIP	oOPS	vL	vR	BF/G	Ctl	Dom	Cmd	SwK	G	L	F	H%	S%	hr/f	GS	APC	DOM%	DIS%	Sv%	LI	RAR	BPV	BPX	R$
09	CLE *	11	14	0	179	141	5.79	4.97	1.46	1125	1038	1208	24.8	2.8	7.1	2.5	7%	48	27	25	34%	61%	27%	5	80	0%	80%			-32.5	58	109	-$4
10	CLE *	12	8	0	195	151	3.87	4.04	1.31	816	581	1042	25.2	2.7	6.9	2.6	10%	57	14	29	31%	73%	16%	7	97	57%	0%			5.0	70	114	$9
11	CLE	8	9	0	125	85	4.62	4.08	1.36	754	888	600	25.5	2.9	6.1	2.1	9%	49	17	34	30%	68%	11%	21	94	52%	24%			-10.4	59	89	-$1
12																																	
13	CLE *	4	5	1	118	93	5.18	4.79	1.50	864	980	745	16.5	3.1	7.1	2.3	9%	50	22	28	34%	66%	9%	7	52	14%	86%	100	0.59	-19.2	62	81	-$9
1st Half		2	3	1	73	53	5.61	5.00	1.56	876	995	730	21.3	3.3	6.5	2.0	7%	50	23	27	34%	64%	8%	5	91	20%	80%			-15.7	51	67	-$12
2nd Half		2	2	0	45	40	4.49	4.47	1.42	847	955	761	12.0	2.7	8.0	3.0	13%	51	20	29	35%	70%	10%	2	33	0%	100%	0	0.48	-3.5	83	107	-$5
14	**Proj**	**3**	**3**	**1**	**60**	**46**	**4.21**	**3.78**	**1.39**	**741**	**809**	**671**	**18.2**	**3.1**	**7.0**	**2.2**	**10%**	**49**	**19**	**32**	**31%**	**72%**	**10%**	**11**						**-2.5**	**67**	**88**	**-$2**

Cashner,Andrew

Age: 27	Th: R	Role: RP	Health: F	LIMA Plan: C+
Ht: 6' 6"	Wt: 220	Type: Pwr GB	PT/Exp: C	Rand Var: -1
			Consist: A	MM: 4305

xERA suggests ERA was over his head, but plenty to be excited about, beginning with health (though SD wisely didn't push their luck). In 2H, added more swinging strikes and Ks, better work vs. LHB. Injuries will always be issue, but with return of Dom, bigger breakout could come... UP: 15 W, sub-3.00 ERA, 200 K

Yr	Tm	W	L	Sv	IP	K	ERA	xERA	WHIP	oOPS	vL	vR	BF/G	Ctl	Dom	Cmd	SwK	G	L	F	H%	S%	hr/f	GS	APC	DOM%	DIS%	Sv%	LI	RAR	BPV	BPX	R$
09	aa	3	4	0	58	35	4.55	3.28	1.43				20.7	4.5	5.4	1.2					30%	65%								-1.6	62	117	-$2
10	CHC *	8	7	0	111	98	3.54	3.48	1.29	795	904	726	7.2	3.6	8.0	2.2	11%	48	19	33	29%	74%	16%	0	18			0	0.90	7.4	79	127	$6
11	CHC	0	0	0	11	8	1.69	3.29	0.66	351	167	440	5.6	3.4	6.8	2.0	11%	59	7	33	8%	83%	11%	1	21	0%	0%	0	0.56	3.0	67	101	-$1
12	SD *	5	5	0	70	77	3.58	3.15	1.22	688	525	815	7.2	3.1	9.9	3.2	13%	53	23	24	32%	72%	17%	5	24	40%	60%	0	1.25	3.7	116	151	$3
13	SD	10	9	0	175	128	3.09	3.56	1.13	639	703	578	22.8	2.4	6.6	2.7	9%	53	19	29	28%	74%	8%	26	87	65%	12%	0	0.73	16.8	84	110	$14
1st Half		5	3	0	92	62	3.31	3.72	1.17	674	754	593	20.8	2.2	6.0	2.7	8%	53	16	31	28%	74%	9%	13	78	69%	15%	0	0.68	6.3	79	102	$13
2nd Half		5	6	0	83	66	2.83	3.39	1.09	600	642	562	25.6	2.6	7.2	2.8	10%	52	22	26	27%	74%	7%	13	99	62%	8%			10.6	89	115	$16
14	**Proj**	**14**	**11**	**0**	**195**	**164**	**3.40**	**3.24**	**1.18**	**631**	**618**	**642**	**12.0**	**2.8**	**7.6**	**2.7**	**11%**	**52**	**21**	**27**	**29%**	**72%**	**8%**	**13**						**11.2**	**92**	**119**	**$17**

Casilla,Santiago

Age: 33	Th: R	Role: RP	Health: F	LIMA Plan: B
Ht: 6' 0"	Wt: 210	Type: Pwr GB	PT/Exp: C	Rand Var: -5
			Consist: A	MM: 3210

Surgery to remove cyst on knee cost him eight weeks, but chronic health woes not sole reason save opps didn't return. Couldn't hold Ctl gains, and Dom fell off after injury. Gets by on ability to induce GB and strand runners, which works fine in setup role. But if others want to go extra buck chasing saves potential, let them.

Yr	Tm	W	L	Sv	IP	K	ERA	xERA	WHIP	oOPS	vL	vR	BF/G	Ctl	Dom	Cmd	SwK	G	L	F	H%	S%	hr/f	GS	APC	DOM%	DIS%	Sv%	LI	RAR	BPV	BPX	R$
09	OAK	1	2	0	48	35	5.96	4.91	1.78	866	970	769	5.1	4.7	6.5	1.4	10%	50	20	30	35%	68%	12%	0	19			0	0.80	-9.8	20	37	-$8
10	SF	7	2	2	55	56	1.95	3.28	1.19	600	678	564	4.3	4.2	9.1	2.2	11%	51	21	29	28%	84%	5%	0	17			67	1.22	14.5	79	127	$7
11	SF	2	2	6	52	45	1.74	3.60	1.12	534	632	481	4.3	4.4	7.8	1.8	12%	52	20	29	24%	84%	3%	0	17			86	0.95	14.0	54	80	$7
12	SF	7	6	25	63	55	2.84	3.78	1.22	656	727	608	3.7	3.1	7.8	2.5	10%	55	15	30	28%	83%	14%	0	14			81	1.37	9.2	89	116	$15
13	SF	7	2	2	50	38	2.16	4.03	1.28	627	652	611	3.6	4.5	6.8	1.5	10%	54	17	29	26%	84%	5%	0	14			67	1.66	10.5	34	44	$4
1st Half		3	2	1	19	16	1.89	4.13	1.21	578	655	511	3.6	6.2	7.6	1.2	10%	53	14	33	19%	86%	7%	0	15			100	2.12	4.6	2	2	$4
2nd Half		4	0	1	31	22	2.32	3.98	1.32	653	648	656	3.7	3.5	6.4	1.8	9%	54	19	27	30%	83%	4%	0	14			50	1.39	5.9	53	68	$5
14	**Proj**	**5**	**4**	**3**	**52**	**42**	**3.31**	**3.75**	**1.34**	**673**	**737**	**632**	**3.8**	**4.2**	**7.3**	**1.8**	**10%**	**53**	**17**	**29**	**29%**	**76%**	**7%**	**0**						**3.6**	**51**	**67**	**$2**

KRISTOPHER OLSON

Cecil,Brett

Age: 27 Th: L Role RP | Ht: 6' 1" Wt: 215 Type Pwr
Health A | PT/Exp C | Consist B
LIMA Plan B+ | Rand Var 0 | MM 4510

Transition to bullpen was a success, as he significantly increased velocity and GB%, and LH couldn't touch him. Season ended early due to elbow soreness, but outside of short stretch in July (7.8 Ctl), he was lights out. As long as he remains in relief role, looks like an attractive, albeit somewhat risky, LIMA target.

Yr Tm	W	L	Sv	IP	K	ERA	xERA	WHIP	oOPS	vL	vR	BF/G	Ctl	Dom	Cmd	SwK	G	L	F	H%	S%	hr/f	GS	APC	DOM%	DIS%	Sv%	LI	RAR	BPV	BPX	R$
09 TOR *	8	9	0	142	98	5.54	5.58	1.61	894	881	899	23.4	3.5	6.2	1.7	8%	43	20	38	34%	67%	15%	17	89	35%	41%	0	0.71	-21.4	32	61	-$8
10 TOR	15	7	0	173	117	4.22	4.21	1.33	733	597	773	25.9	2.8	6.1	2.2	9%	44	18	38	30%	70%	9%	28	97	50%	18%			-3.0	56	90	$6
11 TOR *	12	13	0	202	139	4.80	4.94	1.37	779	522	876	26.5	2.8	6.2	2.2	9%	38	18	43	29%	70%	13%	20	96	50%	10%			-21.5	36	54	-$2
12 TOR *	6	8	0	144	104	4.50	4.78	1.46	855	603	934	17.1	2.8	6.5	2.4	10%	37	22	41	33%	71%	14%	9	49	44%	22%	0	0.72	-8.5	58	76	-$5
13 TOR	5	1	1	61	70	2.82	2.96	1.10	594	458	736	4.2	3.4	10.4	3.0	12%	51	20	29	28%	76%	9%	0	15			33	0.89	7.8	124	161	$5
1st Half	3	0	0	41	47	1.54	2.64	0.80	455	286	642	4.3	2.6	10.3	3.9	13%	49	19	31	23%	81%	3%	0	16			0	0.83	11.8	142	184	$11
2nd Half	2	1	1	20	23	5.49	3.65	1.73	827	778	878	4.0	5.0	10.5	2.1	12%	54	21	25	38%	71%	21%	0	15			33	0.98	-3.9	86	111	-$6
14 Proj	**5**	**3**	**2**	**67**	**70**	**3.48**	**3.28**	**1.31**	**679**	**554**	**755**	**4.7**	**3.5**	**9.5**	**2.7**	**11%**	**46**	**20**	**34**	**32%**	**75%**	**9%**	**0**						**3.2**	**100**	**130**	**$3**

Chacin,Jhoulys

Age: 26 Th: R Role SP | Ht: 6' 3" Wt: 225 Type
Health F | PT/Exp A | Consist C
LIMA Plan C | Rand Var -1 | MM 3105

Came back strong after missing most of 2012 to pectoral injury... PRO: Posted career best Ctl by wide margin; just 2 of first 28 starts were PQS-DISasters before Sept fade; regained GB tilt; 2.86 career road ERA. CON: Dom well below '10-11 level, and LD% remains high. Not a ton of upside, but a decent mid-rotation arm.

Yr Tm	W	L	Sv	IP	K	ERA	xERA	WHIP	oOPS	vL	vR	BF/G	Ctl	Dom	Cmd	SwK	G	L	F	H%	S%	hr/f	GS	APC	DOM%	DIS%	Sv%	LI	RAR	BPV	BPX	R$
09 COL *	9	9	0	129	93	3.86	3.90	1.34	667	837	478	17.3	4.0	6.5	1.6	13%	48	9	43	27%	74%	10%	1	23	0%	100%	0	0.29	7.3	49	91	$6
10 COL *	12	13	0	173	166	2.92	3.05	1.26	650	705	612	20.2	4.0	8.6	2.2	11%	47	22	32	29%	78%	9%	21	82	57%	10%	0	0.70	24.8	90	146	$16
11 COL	11	14	0	194	150	3.62	3.86	1.31	707	759	654	26.7	4.0	7.0	1.7	9%	56	15	28	27%	75%	12%	31	101	52%	16%			7.7	50	76	$8
12 COL *	4	7	0	92	54	4.66	5.32	1.56	821	910	720	22.3	3.9	5.3	1.4	8%	39	24	37	31%	73%	12%	14	83	29%	50%			-7.3	21	27	-$8
13 COL	14	10	0	197	126	3.47	4.02	1.26	685	722	650	26.3	2.8	5.7	2.1	8%	47	25	29	29%	73%	6%	31	96	48%	13%			9.7	53	69	$10
1st Half	7	3	0	95	54	3.59	4.04	1.20	637	626	649	25.7	2.6	5.1	1.9	8%	48	24	28	28%	68%	2%	15	92	40%	13%			3.3	46	60	$11
2nd Half	7	7	0	102	72	3.35	4.01	1.32	727	819	650	26.9	2.9	6.4	2.2	8%	46	25	29	30%	77%	10%	16	99	56%	13%			6.5	59	77	$10
14 Proj	**12**	**13**	**0**	**196**	**132**	**3.76**	**3.98**	**1.34**	**722**	**786**	**661**	**23.9**	**3.2**	**6.1**	**1.9**	**8%**	**46**	**23**	**31**	**29%**	**74%**	**10%**	**34**						**2.6**	**46**	**60**	**$7**

Chamberlain,Joba

Age: 28 Th: R Role RP | Ht: 6' 2" Wt: 250 Type Pwr
Health F | PT/Exp D | Consist B
LIMA Plan D+ | Rand Var +2 | MM 3400

Strong finish to 2012 didn't carry over, as he struggled out of the gate, then suffered oblique injury. Returned with 10-game stretch where he posted 15:3 K:BB ratio, but then came 2H, where BPI, namely the sub-1.0 Cmd, were an absolute mess. At this point, looks like a ratio killer facing uphill battle for a high leverage role.

Yr Tm	W	L	Sv	IP	K	ERA	xERA	WHIP	oOPS	vL	vR	BF/G	Ctl	Dom	Cmd	SwK	G	L	F	H%	S%	hr/f	GS	APC	DOM%	DIS%	Sv%	LI	RAR	BPV	BPX	R$
09 NYY	9	6	0	157	133	4.75	4.46	1.54	802	796	808	22.2	4.3	7.6	1.8	8%	43	21	36	32%	72%	12%	31	85	39%	52%	0	0.75	-8.3	41	76	-$1
10 NYY	3	4	3	72	77	4.40	3.36	1.30	693	713	675	4.2	2.8	9.7	3.5	10%	46	17	37	34%	67%	8%	0	16			43	1.02	-2.8	123	200	$2
11 NYY	2	0	0	29	24	2.83	2.84	1.05	628	627	627	4.1	2.2	7.5	3.4	11%	60	16	25	26%	78%	16%	0	16			0	1.08	3.9	114	172	$1
12 NYY	1	0	0	21	22	4.35	3.64	1.55	835	609	962	4.3	2.6	9.6	3.7	12%	45	23	31	39%	76%	15%	0	16			0	1.12	-0.9	125	163	-$5
13 NYY	2	1	1	42	38	4.93	4.80	1.74	825	756	878	4.4	5.6	8.1	1.5	10%	42	25	34	33%	77%	18%	0	17			100	0.61	-5.5	16	21	-$7
1st Half	0	0	1	19	22	6.05	4.04	1.76	855	763	921	4.6	4.2	10.2	2.4	11%	35	32	33	39%	70%	20%	0	18			100	0.79	-5.2	84	109	-$8
2nd Half	2	1	0	23	16	3.97	5.53	1.72	798	750	836	4.2	6.8	6.4	0.9	9%	47	19	34	27%	83%	17%	0	17			0	0.47	-0.3	-43	-55	-$6
14 Proj	**2**	**2**	**0**	**44**	**41**	**4.45**	**3.93**	**1.48**	**742**	**719**	**761**	**4.7**	**4.5**	**8.5**	**1.9**	**9%**	**44**	**21**	**35**	**31%**	**74%**	**14%**	**0**						**-3.1**	**53**	**69**	**-$3**

Chapman,Aroldis

Age: 26 Th: L Role RP | Ht: 6' 4" Wt: 205 Type Pwr FB
Health B | PT/Exp B | Consist B
LIMA Plan C+ | Rand Var 0 | MM 5530

Couldn't maintain all of previous year's Ctl gains, but elite Dom more than makes up for the BBs and FBs. LH had no XBH, 29 K in 51 AB. Role for '14 is an open question—as closer, would remain an elite option; as SP, Dom would drop, but total Ks would increase substantially, and massive upside would remain intact.

Yr Tm	W	L	Sv	IP	K	ERA	xERA	WHIP	oOPS	vL	vR	BF/G	Ctl	Dom	Cmd	SwK	G	L	F	H%	S%	hr/f	GS	APC	DOM%	DIS%	Sv%	LI	RAR	BPV	BPX	R$
09 for	11	4	0	118	123	5.02	4.74	1.64				23.9	5.9	9.4	1.6					33%	70%								-10.2	67	125	-$2
10 CIN *	11	8	8	109	129	3.84	3.56	1.39	492	368	540	8.5	4.7	10.7	2.3	15%	73	12	15	33%	73%	0%	0	15			80	1.68	3.2	100	162	$9
11 CIN	4	1	1	50	71	3.60	3.17	1.30	534	392	598	3.8	7.4	12.8	1.7	14%	53	16	31	24%	71%	7%	0	16			33	1.13	2.1	62	93	$2
12 CIN	5	5	38	72	122	1.51	2.12	0.81	450	330	501	4.1	2.9	15.3	5.3	18%	37	20	43	28%	85%	7%	0	18			88	1.42	22.2	213	278	$32
13 CIN	4	5	38	64	112	2.54	2.30	1.04	544	379	592	3.8	4.1	15.8	3.9	17%	34	24	42	31%	81%	15%	0	16			88	1.38	10.4	186	243	$23
1st Half	3	3	20	34	57	2.65	2.67	1.15	582	369	652	3.8	4.5	15.1	3.4	15%	28	27	45	33%	81%	10%	0	16			87	1.43	5.1	156	202	$24
2nd Half	1	2	18	30	55	2.43	1.90	0.91	499	393	526	3.8	3.6	16.7	4.6	20%	41	20	39	28%	83%	21%	0	16			90	1.32	5.3	221	286	$22
14 Proj	**4**	**4**	**43**	**65**	**110**	**2.34**	**2.11**	**1.01**	**515**	**377**	**564**	**4.0**	**3.9**	**15.2**	**3.9**	**17%**	**39**	**21**	**40**	**30%**	**80%**	**10%**	**0**						**12.2**	**184**	**239**	**$27**

Chatwood,Tyler

Age: 24 Th: R Role SP | Ht: 6' 0" Wt: 185 Type xGB
Health C | PT/Exp D | Consist C
LIMA Plan B | Rand Var -2 | MM 3103

8-5, 3.15 ERA in 111 IP at COL. High GB% continued to trend up, and only allowed more than 2 ER in just two of first 14 starts. Spent August on DL with sore elbow, BPIs were weak in Sept, but all-in-all, a solid growth year. Low FB% minimizes downside, and given his age, 1st half may be for real.

Yr Tm	W	L	Sv	IP	K	ERA	xERA	WHIP	oOPS	vL	vR	BF/G	Ctl	Dom	Cmd	SwK	G	L	F	H%	S%	hr/f	GS	APC	DOM%	DIS%	Sv%	LI	RAR	BPV	BPX	R$
09																																
10 a/a	5	6	0	74	34	4.11	4.36	1.47				24.4	2.9	4.1	1.4					32%	71%								-0.3	38	62	-$2
11 LAA *	7	13	0	158	84	4.73	5.42	1.69	830	862	786	23.0	4.6	4.8	1.0	5%	47	22	31	32%	73%	10%	25	90	20%	44%	0	0.77	-15.4	20	30	-$12
12 COL *	6	9	1	126	83	5.80	5.84	1.72	836	890	774	17.9	4.3	5.9	1.4	6%	56	21	23	34%	67%	19%	12	61	8%	58%	100	0.62	-27.7	27	35	-$18
13 COL *	10	6	0	145	92	3.16	3.92	1.42	711	729	697	23.7	3.0	5.7	1.9	7%	59	21	21	33%	77%	7%	20	89	35%	30%			12.7	64	84	$4
1st Half	6	2	0	79	60	2.60	3.30	1.34	623	643	602	23.6	2.6	6.8	2.6	7%	59	18	22	34%	78%	0%	9	91	44%	22%			12.4	96	125	$10
2nd Half	4	4	0	66	32	3.83	4.67	1.52	779	808	759	23.9	3.4	4.4	1.3	7%	58	22	20	31%	76%	12%	11	88	27%	36%			0.3	30	39	-$3
14 Proj	**10**	**11**	**0**	**174**	**116**	**3.98**	**3.79**	**1.44**	**736**	**772**	**700**	**21.2**	**3.3**	**6.0**	**1.8**	**7%**	**56**	**21**	**23**	**32%**	**73%**	**10%**	**35**						**-2.4**	**54**	**70**	**$1**

Chavez,Jesse

Age: 30 Th: R Role RP | Ht: 6' 2" Wt: 160 Type Pwr FB
Health A | PT/Exp D | Consist C
LIMA Plan C | Rand Var 0 | MM 3300

2-4, 3.92 ERA in 57 IP at OAK. Entered season with 5.99 ERA in 156 appearances, but with new team came new approach. He threw very few fastballs, and a lot more cutters; seems to have worked. Skills history, low hr/f suggest it was a career year, but new pitch mix, 11.5 Dom in Aug-Sept say don't just dismiss it as a fluke.

Yr Tm	W	L	Sv	IP	K	ERA	xERA	WHIP	oOPS	vL	vR	BF/G	Ctl	Dom	Cmd	SwK	G	L	F	H%	S%	hr/f	GS	APC	DOM%	DIS%	Sv%	LI	RAR	BPV	BPX	R$
09 PIT	1	4	0	67	47	4.01	4.47	1.35	783	681	879	3.9	2.9	6.3	2.1	10%	39	20	41	29%	76%	13%	0	14			0	0.99	2.6	51	95	-$1
10 2 TM	5	5	0	63	45	5.89	4.86	1.47	834	884	798	5.5	3.3	6.5	2.0	9%	34	17	48	31%	63%	11%	0	21			0	0.81	-14.0	39	63	-$4
11 KC *	2	4	16	65	47	5.22	6.17	1.69	1112	924	1250	6.0	3.0	6.5	2.2	12%	54	19	27	37%	71%	43%	0	40			76	0.32	-10.3	38	57	-$2
12 2 AL *	9	6	2	130	101	5.37	4.97	1.44	983	1144	888	16.2	2.4	7.0	2.9	11%	36	29	35	34%	64%	26%	2	36	0%	50%	100	0.66	-21.7	65	85	-$6
13 OAK *	4	6	1	87	74	3.64	3.71	1.35	620	630	605	9.1	2.6	7.6	2.9	10%	43	17	39	34%	72%	5%	0	27			50	0.93	2.4	95	124	$0
1st Half	3	4	0	56	40	3.41	3.95	1.34	601	628	572	12.3	2.0	6.4	3.2	10%	38	17	45	34%	75%	6%	0	29			0	0.87	3.2	90	117	$2
2nd Half	1	2	1	31	34	4.06	3.56	1.35	635	632	638	6.5	3.8	9.9	2.6	10%	48	18	34	34%	68%	4%	0	26			50	0.97	-0.8	102	132	-$2
14 Proj	**3**	**4**	**0**	**61**	**52**	**3.92**	**3.78**	**1.30**	**723**	**715**	**730**	**7.6**	**2.9**	**7.6**	**2.6**	**10%**	**40**	**18**	**42**	**30%**	**73%**	**10%**	**0**						**-0.4**	**77**	**100**	**$0**

Chen,Bruce

Age: 37 Th: L Role SP | Ht: 6' 2" Wt: 215 Type xFB
Health C | PT/Exp A | Consist A
LIMA Plan C+ | Rand Var -4 | MM 1103

Began season in relief role, joined rotation in July, and reeled off six straight PQS-DOM outings. In nine starts the rest of the way, had 5.73 ERA and 1.6 Cmd. Despite impressive ERA for the year, skills show it's the same guy, with a little h% and hr/f fortune mixed in. Age, FB%, and xERA history all warn of significant downside.

Yr Tm	W	L	Sv	IP	K	ERA	xERA	WHIP	oOPS	vL	vR	BF/G	Ctl	Dom	Cmd	SwK	G	L	F	H%	S%	hr/f	GS	APC	DOM%	DIS%	Sv%	LI	RAR	BPV	BPX	R$
09 KC *	5	8	0	144	93	5.37	4.84	1.42	884	679	968	19.8	3.3	5.8	1.8	7%	31	17	51	29%	65%	12%	9	64	22%	33%	0	0.46	-18.7	31	59	-$4
10 KC *	12	8	1	161	112	3.85	3.96	1.34	735	756	727	18.6	3.5	6.3	1.8	7%	34	18	48	28%	74%	8%	23	73	35%	26%	100	0.87	4.5	51	83	$7
11 KC	12	8	0	155	97	3.77	4.57	1.30	727	678	747	26.2	2.9	5.6	1.9	7%	35	20	45	28%	74%	8%	25	101	56%	36%			3.2	36	54	$6
12 KC	11	14	0	192	140	5.07	4.59	1.37	813	852	800	24.3	2.2	6.6	3.0	8%	33	22	45	31%	67%	12%	34	94	44%	21%			-25.0	70	91	-$5
13 KC	9	4	0	121	78	3.27	4.73	1.18	675	755	634	14.6	2.7	5.8	2.2	8%	28	20	52	26%	76%	7%	15	58	53%	20%	0	0.87	8.8	28	50	$7
1st Half	3	0	0	28	20	2.22	5.09	1.41	724	819	664	7.5	3.5	6.4	1.8	8%	31	20	49	31%	87%	4%	0	30			0	1.02	5.7	29	37	$1
2nd Half	6	4	0	93	58	3.59	4.62	1.11	658	730	624	21.8	2.4	5.6	2.3	7%	27	21	53	25%	72%	7%	15	86	53%	20%	0	0.73	3.1	40	52	$10
14 Proj	**9**	**9**	**0**	**154**	**101**	**4.40**	**4.48**	**1.36**	**770**	**804**	**755**	**22.3**	**2.9**	**5.9**	**2.0**	**8%**	**31**	**21**	**49**	**29%**	**71%**	**9%**	**29**						**-10.2**	**36**	**46**	**$1**

BRIAN RUDD

Chen,Wei-Yin

Age: 28	Th: L	Role	SP	PT/Exp	A	Rand Var	0
Ht: 6' 0"	Wt: 195	Type	FB	Consist	B	MM	3203
				Health	C	LIMA Plan	B+

Oblique strain cost him two months, and may have had something to do with 1H Dom dip. ERA ballooned after he returned, but skills improved, as he had 5.12 Sept ERA despite 120 BPV. Overall line was very similar to 2012, and seems to be baseline expectation, though 2H Cmd improvement could push ERA below 4.00.

Yr	Tm	W	L	Sv	IP	K	ERA	xERA	WHIP	oOPS	vL	vR	BF/G	Ctl	Dom	Cmd	SwK	G	L	F	H%	S%	hr/f	GS	APC	DOM%	DIS%	Sv%	LI	RAR	BPV	BPX	R$
09	for	8	4	0	164	139	1.91	2.60	1.04				26.4	2.7	7.6	2.8					24%	88%								48.8	90	169	$26
10	for	13	10	0	188	145	3.57	4.46	1.27				26.5	2.9	6.9	2.4					27%	81%								11.9	47	75	$12
11	for	8	10	0	165	89	3.32	3.18	1.13				26.1	2.1	4.9	2.3					26%	73%								12.7	60	90	$11
12	BAL	12	11	0	193	154	4.02	4.33	1.26	729	682	747	25.6	2.7	7.2	2.7	10%	37	21	42	29%	73%	12%	32	98	56%	16%			-0.1	73	95	$8
13	BAL	7	7	0	137	104	4.07	4.19	1.32	761	689	783	24.9	2.6	6.8	2.7	8%	34	25	41	31%	73%	10%	23	95	35%	17%			-3.5	66	86	$1
1st Half		3	3	0	47	27	3.04	4.46	1.20	667	610	686	23.5	2.3	5.1	2.3	7%	31	24	45	28%	76%	5%	8	91	38%	13%			4.8	40	52	$4
2nd Half		4	4	0	90	77	4.62	4.04	1.38	807	734	828	25.6	2.7	7.7	2.9	9%	36	25	39	32%	71%	13%	15	98	33%	20%			-8.3	80	104	-$1
14	**Proj**	**10**	**9**	**0**	**174**	**135**	**3.88**	**3.89**	**1.27**	**725**	**665**	**745**	**25.0**	**2.6**	**7.0**	**2.6**	**9%**	**35**	**23**	**42**	**29%**	**73%**	**10%**	**28**						**-0.2**	**67**	**87**	**$7**

Cingrani,Tony

Age: 24	Th: L	Role	RP	PT/Exp	D	Rand Var	-2
Ht: 6' 4"	Wt: 215	Type	Pwr FB	Consist	C	MM	4503
				Health	B	LIMA Plan	C

7-4, 2.92 ERA in 105 IP at CIN. There's a lot to like in this skill set, as Dom had no problem translating to majors, and LH had no chance against him. Ctl still a work in progress, and FB% may lead to continued issues with long ball, but he still looks like a keeper. Don't count on a jump to 200 IP just yet, though.

Yr	Tm	W	L	Sv	IP	K	ERA	xERA	WHIP	oOPS	vL	vR	BF/G	Ctl	Dom	Cmd	SwK	G	L	F	H%	S%	hr/f	GS	APC	DOM%	DIS%	Sv%	LI	RAR	BPV	BPX	R$
09																																	
10																																	
11																																	
12	CIN *	5	3	0	94	96	2.81	3.47	1.26	623	533	700	20.3	4.1	9.2	2.2	13%	64	0	36	28%	83%	25%	0	34			0	0.86	14.0	81	105	$7
13	CIN *	10	4	0	136	161	2.60	2.47	1.06	649	533	693	18.2	3.6	10.7	3.0	11%	34	21	45	25%	81%	13%	18	79	61%	22%	0	0.93	21.2	113	147	$18
1st Half		6	0	0	79	98	2.67	2.52	1.04	714	589	770	16.9	3.3	11.3	3.4	10%	36	21	44	26%	81%	16%	7	70	86%	14%	0	1.09	11.6	124	160	$21
2nd Half		4	4	0	57	63	2.51	3.64	1.08	595	473	633	20.7	4.1	9.9	2.4	11%	33	21	46	23%	82%	10%	11	89	45%	27%			9.6	79	102	$14
14	**Proj**	**11**	**6**	**0**	**174**	**192**	**3.16**	**3.49**	**1.23**	**692**	**583**	**732**	**19.8**	**3.9**	**9.9**	**2.5**	**11%**	**34**	**21**	**45**	**29%**	**79%**	**10%**	**35**						**15.1**	**86**	**111**	**$16**

Cishek,Steve

Age: 28	Th: R	Role	RP	PT/Exp	C	Rand Var	-3
Ht: 6' 6"	Wt: 215	Type	Pwr GB	Consist	B	MM	5431
				Health	A	LIMA Plan	C

Got off to slow start, but Marlins stuck with him as closer, and were rewarded. From June 8 forward, he had a 10.4 Dom, 2.0 Ctl, no HR, and .486 OPS against. GB% and dominance of RH are impressive, and 2H skills surge has him looking like a potential upper echelon closer that won't cost as much as some of the bigger names.

Yr	Tm	W	L	Sv	IP	K	ERA	xERA	WHIP	oOPS	vL	vR	BF/G	Ctl	Dom	Cmd	SwK	G	L	F	H%	S%	hr/f	GS	APC	DOM%	DIS%	Sv%	LI	RAR	BPV	BPX	R$
09																																	
10	FLA *	3	1	2	36	33	4.76	3.33	1.37	276	167	333	6.0	3.0	8.4	2.8	10%	45	9	45	35%	61%	0%	0	21			67	0.14	-3.0	110	177	-$1
11	FLA *	3	2	3	78	70	2.57	2.66	1.23	591	661	545	5.2	3.6	8.2	2.3	9%	57	17	26	30%	78%	3%	0	20			100	0.86	13.2	100	150	$6
12	MIA	5	2	15	64	68	2.69	3.55	1.30	663	787	548	4.0	4.1	9.6	2.3	10%	52	16	31	31%	80%	6%	0	16			79	1.20	10.4	92	120	$10
13	MIA	4	6	34	70	74	2.33	2.96	1.08	568	664	459	4.1	2.8	9.6	3.4	10%	53	18	29	29%	79%	6%	0	16			94	1.23	13.2	126	165	$20
1st Half		2	4	14	34	32	3.15	3.37	1.05	576	691	388	4.0	3.1	8.4	2.7	10%	53	14	33	24%	73%	10%	0	16			88	1.29	3.0	97	126	$16
2nd Half		2	2	20	35	42	1.53	2.59	1.10	561	628	506	4.2	2.5	10.7	4.2	10%	53	21	26	33%	85%	0%	0	16			100	1.16	10.2	155	200	$24
14	**Proj**	**5**	**4**	**36**	**73**	**75**	**2.62**	**2.99**	**1.19**	**646**	**751**	**548**	**4.2**	**3.3**	**9.3**	**2.9**	**10%**	**53**	**17**	**29**	**30%**	**81%**	**10%**	**0**						**11.1**	**111**	**145**	**$21**

Cisnero,Jose

Age: 25	Th: R	Role	RP	PT/Exp	D	Rand Var	+3
Ht: 6' 3"	Wt: 230	Type	Pwr	Consist	F	MM	2400
				Health	A	LIMA Plan	D+

2-2, 4.12 ERA in 44 IP at HOU. Was impressive at times, including a 10-game stretch that featured no ER and 23:8 K:BB ratio in 19.1 IP. Rumored for save opps after trade deadline, but Ctl problems got him sent to Triple-A instead. Dom potential makes him worth watching, but other skills need a lot more refinement.

Yr	Tm	W	L	Sv	IP	K	ERA	xERA	WHIP	oOPS	vL	vR	BF/G	Ctl	Dom	Cmd	SwK	G	L	F	H%	S%	hr/f	GS	APC	DOM%	DIS%	Sv%	LI	RAR	BPV	BPX	R$
09																																	
10																																	
11																																	
12	a/a	13	7	0	148	129	3.79	4.01	1.45				22.6	3.7	7.8	2.1					34%	74%								4.1	79	103	$3
13	HOU *	3	3	0	61	61	5.76	6.03	1.83	826	871	784	7.1	5.1	9.0	1.8	12%	38	25	38	39%	69%	10%	0	28			0	1.10	-14.3	53	69	-$11
1st Half		3	2	0	43	39	3.98	4.75	1.59	698	752	658	9.5	4.0	8.1	2.0	12%	41	25	34	36%	75%	6%	0	35			0	1.06	-0.6	70	90	-$7
2nd Half		0	1	0	18	23	10.02	9.12	2.42	1244	1123	1479	4.7	8.0	11.3	1.4	12%	26	26	48	45%	60%	20%	0	18			0	1.16	-13.7	21	27	-$20
14	**Proj**	**3**	**2**	**0**	**48**	**49**	**4.49**	**4.04**	**1.52**	**687**	**761**	**631**	**7.5**	**5.3**	**9.2**	**1.7**	**12%**	**41**	**25**	**34**	**31%**	**73%**	**11%**	**0**						**-3.7**	**42**	**55**	**-$3**

Claiborne,Preston

Age: 26	Th: R	Role	RP	PT/Exp	D	Rand Var	+1
Ht: 6' 2"	Wt: 225	Type	Pwr	Consist	A	MM	3200
				Health	A	LIMA Plan	C

Great 1H (with an assist from S%), but he struggled down the stretch, surrendering 15 ER in last 15 IP (with an assist from S% regression). Platoon splits exaggerated by h% (21% vs RH, 41% vs LH). Decent bullpen arm, but LI underscores that he's a long way from being trusted in key spots.

Yr	Tm	W	L	Sv	IP	K	ERA	xERA	WHIP	oOPS	vL	vR	BF/G	Ctl	Dom	Cmd	SwK	G	L	F	H%	S%	hr/f	GS	APC	DOM%	DIS%	Sv%	LI	RAR	BPV	BPX	R$
09																																	
10																																	
11																																	
12	a/a	6	2	6	82	64	3.81	3.61	1.40				6.9	4.2	7.0	1.7					30%	72%								2.1	70	91	$2
13	NYY	0	2	0	50	42	4.11	3.86	1.29	734	823	653	4.9	2.5	7.5	3.0	11%	45	18	37	31%	72%	12%	0	19			0	0.78	-1.5	91	118	-$3
1st Half		0	1	0	25	20	1.46	3.26	0.93	554	660	441	4.6	1.5	7.3	5.0	11%	46	20	34	26%	90%	8%	0	17			0	0.67	7.3	116	151	$3
2nd Half		0	1	0	26	22	6.66	4.45	1.64	889	986	810	5.1	3.5	7.7	2.2	12%	43	17	40	35%	62%	15%	0	21			0	0.89	-8.9	66	85	-$9
14	**Proj**	**2**	**2**	**0**	**58**	**47**	**4.23**	**3.91**	**1.37**	**717**	**816**	**628**	**5.4**	**3.3**	**7.3**	**2.2**	**11%**	**42**	**20**	**38**	**31%**	**71%**	**9%**	**0**						**-2.6**	**64**	**83**	**-$2**

Clemens,Paul

Age: 26	Th: R	Role	RP	PT/Exp	D	Rand Var	+1
Ht: 6' 4"	Wt: 195	Type	xFB	Consist	D	MM	1101
				Health	A	LIMA Plan	D+

4-7, 5.40 ERA in 73 IP at HOU. FB tendencies and sub-par Cmd not a recipe for success. Future role remains unclear, though it probably shouldn't. He has a 6.22 ERA in 26 Triple-A starts past two years, and posted 1.2 Cmd in five late-season starts with HOU. No reason to call out his name on draft day.

Yr	Tm	W	L	Sv	IP	K	ERA	xERA	WHIP	oOPS	vL	vR	BF/G	Ctl	Dom	Cmd	SwK	G	L	F	H%	S%	hr/f	GS	APC	DOM%	DIS%	Sv%	LI	RAR	BPV	BPX	R$
09																																	
10																																	
11	a/a	8	7	0	144	108	4.19	4.09	1.41				23.4	3.7	6.7	1.8					30%	71%								-4.3	58	87	$0
12	a/a	11	10	0	143	90	6.04	6.55	1.70				24.0	2.6	5.6	2.2					36%	67%								-35.8	25	33	-$20
13	HOU *	7	9	0	103	62	5.34	5.11	1.46	865	871	859	10.8	3.2	5.4	1.7	8%	35	16	48	30%	67%	13%	5	33	40%	40%	0	0.90	-18.8	22	29	-$7
1st Half		5	3	0	45	33	4.69	4.98	1.31	810	869	769	7.4	2.8	6.5	2.3	9%	37	12	51	27%	73%	16%	0	27			0	0.89	-4.6	30	39	$0
2nd Half		2	6	0	58	30	5.84	5.22	1.57	926	871	1000	16.0	3.6	4.6	1.3	6%	33	21	46	31%	63%	11%	5	48	40%	40%	0	0.92	-14.2	18	24	-$13
14	**Proj**	**5**	**6**	**0**	**73**	**46**	**5.17**	**4.71**	**1.54**	**853**	**845**	**861**	**15.2**	**3.1**	**5.7**	**1.8**	**7%**	**35**	**17**	**48**	**32%**	**70%**	**10%**	**11**						**-11.6**	**32**	**41**	**-$6**

Clippard,Tyler

Age: 29	Th: R	Role	RP	PT/Exp	B	Rand Var	-5
Ht: 6' 3"	Wt: 200	Type	Pwr xFB	Consist	B	MM	4511
				Health	A	LIMA Plan	B

Signing of Rafael Soriano meant no more saves, so he was back near the top of Holds leaderboard. Long-favorable H% reached absurd levels, thanks in part to keeping LDs low, but that can't last. FB% leaves him at constant risk of HR, and Dom decline may be a concern. Still a nice LIMA play, with closer-worthy skills.

Yr	Tm	W	L	Sv	IP	K	ERA	xERA	WHIP	oOPS	vL	vR	BF/G	Ctl	Dom	Cmd	SwK	G	L	F	H%	S%	hr/f	GS	APC	DOM%	DIS%	Sv%	LI	RAR	BPV	BPX	R$
09	WAS *	8	3	1	99	101	2.10	2.45	1.09	633	443	860	6.0	4.3	9.1	2.1	14%	30	13	57	21%	88%	11%	0	24			50	0.71	27.2	88	165	$16
10	WAS	11	8	1	91	112	3.07	3.67	1.21	646	708	594	4.8	4.1	11.1	2.7	15%	28	17	56	30%	77%	7%	0	20			9	1.23	11.4	96	155	$10
11	WAS	3	0	0	88	104	1.83	3.20	0.84	535	549	522	4.6	2.6	10.6	4.0	17%	20	20	60	20%	89%	9%	0	19			0	1.49	23.0	117	176	$15
12	WAS	2	6	32	73	84	3.72	4.03	1.16	621	519	725	4.1	3.6	10.4	2.9	12%	30	14	57	28%	70%	7%	0	17			86	1.25	2.7	98	128	$16
13	WAS	6	3	0	71	73	2.41	3.68	0.86	517	507	527	3.8	3.0	9.3	3.0	15%	28	16	56	18%	81%	9%	0	16			0	1.10	12.8	90	118	$10
1st Half		6	1	0	34	34	2.41	4.08	1.01	534	503	573	4.0	4.0	9.1	2.3	15%	20	26	55	21%	81%	7%	0	18			0	1.03	6.1	53	68	$11
2nd Half		0	2	0	37	39	2.41	3.33	0.72	498	508	489	3.6	2.2	9.4	4.3	16%	36	8	57	15%	81%	12%	0	15			0	1.16	6.7	124	161	$10
14	**Proj**	**4**	**4**	**5**	**73**	**79**	**2.91**	**3.44**	**1.16**	**669**	**626**	**711**	**4.1**	**3.2**	**9.8**	**3.1**	**14%**	**30**	**18**	**52**	**28%**	**80%**	**9%**	**0**						**8.5**	**99**	**129**	**$8**

BRIAN RUDD

Cloyd,Tyler

Age: 27 Th: R Role SP
Ht: 6' 3" Wt: 210 Type Con FB

Health	A	LIMA Plan	C
PT/Exp	D	Rand Var	+1
Consist	C	MM	2101

2-7, 6.56 ERA in 60 IP at PHI. PRO: 5.4 career Cmd vs RH; history of stellar Ctl. CON: 1.2 career Cmd vs LH, ugly PQS-DOM/DIS mix, 26 ER in 15 IP in Sept. He's had some success at upper levels of minors, but Ctl is clearly his only above average skill. With low Dom and GB%, hitters may continue to tee off on him.

Yr	Tm	W	L	Sv	IP	K	ERA	xERA	WHIP	oOPS	vL	vR	BF/G	Ctl	Dom	Cmd	SwK	G	L	F	H%	S%	hr/f	GS	APC	DOM%	DIS%	Sv%	LI	RAR	BPV	BPX	R$
09																																	
10																																	
11	aa	6	3	0	107	83	3.17	3.64	1.21				23.9	1.3	7.0	5.6					33%	75%								10.2	140	211	$6
12	PHI *	17	3	0	200	123	3.17	3.71	1.18	797	985	665	25.0	2.3	5.5	2.4	9%	32	19	49	27%	79%	17%	6	88	50%	33%			20.9	55	72	$19
13	PHI *	7	16	0	173	116	5.99	6.33	1.64	927	879	968	24.1	2.7	6.0	2.2	7%	39	23	38	35%	67%	9%	11	82	9%	45%	0	0.84	-45.3	25	32	-$22
1st Half		3	9	0	89	59	7.07	7.39	1.82	791	814	764	25.7	3.3	6.0	1.8	6%	39	18	43	36%	65%	4%	6	97	17%	33%			-35.1	2	3	-$31
2nd Half		4	7	0	84	57	4.85	5.23	1.45	1076	959	1173	22.5	2.1	6.1	2.9	9%	40	28	32	33%	70%	16%	5	69	0%	60%	0	0.82	-10.3	54	70	-$11
14	**Proj**	**7**	**7**	**0**	**123**	**80**	**4.45**	**4.21**	**1.38**	**790**	**812**	**769**	**24.1**	**2.4**	**5.9**	**2.4**	**8%**	**37**	**22**	**42**	**31%**	**72%**	**10%**	**21**						**-8.8**	**55**	**72**	**-$1**

Cobb,Alex

Age: 26 Th: R Role SP
Ht: 6' 3" Wt: 190 Type Pwr xGB

Health	F	LIMA Plan	B
PT/Exp	C	Rand Var	0
Consist	B	MM	5303

Took line drive off his head in June, which resulted in mild concussion and two-month absence. Didn't seem to affect performance though, as 7 of his 9 starts after return were of the PQS-DOM variety. Magnitude of breakout was a bit surprising, but Dom/GB% combo says it's legit. UP: Same ERA, 20 Wins.

Yr	Tm	W	L	Sv	IP	K	ERA	xERA	WHIP	oOPS	vL	vR	BF/G	Ctl	Dom	Cmd	SwK	G	L	F	H%	S%	hr/f	GS	APC	DOM%	DIS%	Sv%	LI	RAR	BPV	BPX	R$
09																																	
10	aa	7	5	0	120	111	3.14	4.33	1.44				22.1	2.7	8.3	3.1					36%	79%								13.8	96	155	$5
11	TAM *	8	3	0	120	96	2.69	3.50	1.29	655	683	617	23.5	2.7	7.2	2.6	8%	54	20	26	31%	80%	7%	9	94	22%	22%			18.6	86	129	$9
12	TAM *	12	13	0	178	142	4.19	3.82	1.34	690	735	633	23.8	2.9	7.2	2.5	8%	59	20	21	32%	69%	13%	23	94	48%	26%			-3.8	79	103	$3
13	TAM	11	3	0	143	134	2.76	3.04	1.15	644	677	592	26.3	2.8	8.4	3.0	10%	56	22	23	28%	80%	15%	22	101	59%	14%			19.5	109	142	$15
1st Half		6	2	0	84	76	3.01	3.03	1.16	645	636	659	26.4	2.5	8.2	3.3	9%	57	21	21	29%	78%	18%	13	102	46%	23%			8.8	115	150	$16
2nd Half		5	1	0	60	58	2.41	3.06	1.14	643	734	487	26.1	3.3	8.7	2.6	11%	54	22	24	28%	81%	11%	9	100	78%	0%			10.7	99	129	$14
14	**Proj**	**14**	**6**	**0**	**160**	**141**	**3.10**	**3.10**	**1.25**	**678**	**722**	**615**	**24.6**	**2.9**	**8.0**	**2.7**	**9%**	**56**	**21**	**23**	**31%**	**77%**	**11%**	**26**						**15.1**	**99**	**129**	**$14**

Coke,Phil

Age: 31 Th: L Role RP
Ht: 6' 1" Wt: 210 Type Pwr

Health	C	LIMA Plan	D+
PT/Exp	C	Rand Var	+1
Consist	B	MM	2200

Ugly season turned even worse down the stretch, with late August demotion and 5 walks to 0 Ks in Sept. MRI revealed elbow inflammation, though he was able to make a post-season appearance. But even in 1H, didn't have the kind of ratios you want out of a short reliever. Window for save opps likely closed now.

Yr	Tm	W	L	Sv	IP	K	ERA	xERA	WHIP	oOPS	vL	vR	BF/G	Ctl	Dom	Cmd	SwK	G	L	F	H%	S%	hr/f	GS	APC	DOM%	DIS%	Sv%	LI	RAR	BPV	BPX	R$
09	NYY	4	3	2	60	49	4.50	4.03	1.07	668	584	778	3.3	3.0	7.4	2.5	11%	35	20	45	22%	63%	14%	0	13			29	1.42	-1.3	64	120	$3
10	DET	7	5	2	65	53	3.76	4.33	1.44	699	681	713	3.8	3.6	7.4	2.0	12%	35	21	43	33%	73%	2%	1	14	0%	100%	50	1.12	2.6	48	78	$2
11	DET	3	9	1	109	69	4.47	4.46	1.45	728	584	806	9.9	3.3	5.7	1.7	9%	43	22	35	32%	68%	4%	14	35	36%	43%	50	1.05	-7.1	34	52	-$4
12	DET	2	3	1	54	51	4.00	3.91	1.65	854	685	1050	3.7	3.0	8.5	2.8	13%	49	21	30	39%	77%	10%	0	14			33	1.25	0.1	99	129	-$5
13	DET	0	5	1	38	30	5.40	4.82	1.67	809	760	860	3.6	4.9	7.0	1.4	12%	45	21	34	34%	67%	7%	0	13			33	1.17	-7.3	17	22	-$8
1st Half		0	5	1	24	22	6.29	4.08	1.44	745	513	924	4.2	4.1	8.1	2.0	14%	43	24	34	33%	53%	4%	0	16			33	1.75	-7.3	57	74	-$7
2nd Half		0	0	0	14	8	3.86	6.27	2.07	900	1006	721	3.0	6.4	5.1	0.8	8%	49	17	34	35%	85%	11%	0	10			0	0.56	0.0	-54	-70	-$8
14	**Proj**	**1**	**4**	**0**	**36**	**28**	**4.57**	**4.34**	**1.53**	**762**	**615**	**883**	**4.6**	**4.2**	**6.9**	**1.6**	**12%**	**42**	**22**	**36**	**33%**	**70%**	**6%**	**0**						**-3.1**	**30**	**39**	**-$4**

Cole,Gerrit

Age: 23 Th: R Role SP
Ht: 6' 4" Wt: 240 Type

Health	A	LIMA Plan	C
PT/Exp	D	Rand Var	0
Consist	B	MM	4205

10-7, 3.22 ERA in 117 IP at PIT. Triple-A numbers were mediocre, but injuries to rotation resulted in June call-up, and he never looked back. Strong debut capped by 1.69 ERA and 11.0 Dom in Sept. Must improve SwK%, cut down on LD in order to reach ace level ceiling, but Cmd, GB tilt, prospect billing all point to big things ahead.

Yr	Tm	W	L	Sv	IP	K	ERA	xERA	WHIP	oOPS	vL	vR	BF/G	Ctl	Dom	Cmd	SwK	G	L	F	H%	S%	hr/f	GS	APC	DOM%	DIS%	Sv%	LI	RAR	BPV	BPX	R$
09																																	
10																																	
11																																	
12	a/a	4	6	0	65	55	3.58	3.68	1.39				21.0	3.1	7.6	2.4					34%	73%								3.5	90	117	-$1
13	PIT *	15	10	0	185	138	3.26	2.79	1.15	638	614	658	23.7	2.6	6.7	2.5	10%	49	25	26	28%	72%	8%	19	91	63%	0%			14.0	86	113	$16
1st Half		9	3	0	92	49	3.41	2.64	1.14	660	697	630	22.9	3.0	4.8	1.6	8%	50	22	28	25%	70%	4%	4	86	25%	0%			5.1	59	76	$16
2nd Half		6	7	0	93	89	3.10	3.00	1.15	632	590	665	24.5	2.3	8.6	3.7	10%	49	26	25	31%	74%	10%	15	92	73%	0%			8.8	119	154	$17
14	**Proj**	**16**	**11**	**0**	**195**	**157**	**3.38**	**3.40**	**1.25**	**639**	**633**	**644**	**22.6**	**2.8**	**7.3**	**2.6**	**9%**	**49**	**24**	**26**	**31%**	**73%**	**6%**	**35**						**11.7**	**82**	**106**	**$16**

Collins,Tim

Age: 24 Th: L Role RP
Ht: 5' 7" Wt: 165 Type Pwr FB

Health	A	LIMA Plan	D+
PT/Exp	C	Rand Var	-2
Consist	C	MM	3400

With Dom at 2012 level, can probably withstand the Ctl issues and relatively high FB%, but last year's rate left him skating on thin ice. Triple-digit BPV in April, May, Sept hint at upside, but 1.2 Cmd from June-August shows how inconsistent he is. Still young enough to work this out, but current skill set leaves him with minimal value.

Yr	Tm	W	L	Sv	IP	K	ERA	xERA	WHIP	oOPS	vL	vR	BF/G	Ctl	Dom	Cmd	SwK	G	L	F	H%	S%	hr/f	GS	APC	DOM%	DIS%	Sv%	LI	RAR	BPV	BPX	R$
09																																	
10	a/a	3	1	15	71	90	2.17	1.63	0.95				4.8	3.1	11.4	3.6					26%	80%								16.8	148	240	$16
11	KC	4	4	0	67	60	3.63	4.81	1.49	681	683	678	4.3	6.4	8.1	1.3	10%	41	17	42	27%	77%	7%	0	18			0	1.20	2.6	-10	-15	-$1
12	KC	5	4	0	70	93	3.36	3.40	1.28	692	769	626	4.1	4.4	12.0	2.7	13%	41	16	43	31%	78%	12%	0	17			0	1.09	5.6	117	152	$3
13	KC	3	6	0	53	52	3.54	4.36	1.44	677	638	715	3.5	4.7	8.8	1.9	10%	38	21	42	32%	76%	5%	0	15			0	1.22	2.1	46	60	-$2
1st Half		2	2	0	29	28	3.41	4.46	1.38	653	615	691	3.6	5.0	8.7	1.8	9%	36	18	46	29%	76%	5%	0	15			0	1.16	1.6	37	47	-$1
2nd Half		1	4	0	24	24	3.70	4.23	1.52	704	664	738	3.4	4.4	8.9	2.0	11%	39	24	37	35%	75%	4%	0	14			0	1.28	0.5	57	74	-$3
14	**Proj**	**4**	**6**	**0**	**66**	**66**	**3.80**	**3.89**	**1.37**	**670**	**675**	**666**	**3.7**	**4.7**	**9.1**	**1.9**	**11%**	**39**	**19**	**42**	**30%**	**73%**	**6%**	**0**						**0.5**	**54**	**70**	**$0**

Collmenter,Josh

Age: 28 Th: R Role RP
Ht: 6' 4" Wt: 235 Type Pwr xFB

Health	B	LIMA Plan	B+
PT/Exp	B	Rand Var	-2
Consist	A	MM	3301

Unorthodox delivery has helped him build respectable Dom despite 87 mph fastball, and SwK suggests he can maintain it. Multi-inning relief role makes him a speculative source for wins, but Ctl trending in wrong direction, and 1st half ERA was a product of low hr/f. Don't count on a repeat.

Yr	Tm	W	L	Sv	IP	K	ERA	xERA	WHIP	oOPS	vL	vR	BF/G	Ctl	Dom	Cmd	SwK	G	L	F	H%	S%	hr/f	GS	APC	DOM%	DIS%	Sv%	LI	RAR	BPV	BPX	R$
09																																	
10	a/a	12	6	0	137	91	4.01	4.15	1.38				26.2	3.1	6.0	1.9					31%	72%								1.1	55	88	$4
11	ARI	10	10	0	154	100	3.38	4.09	1.07	652	708	594	20.0	1.6	5.8	3.6	8%	33	20	47	26%	72%	8%	24	79	58%	21%	0	0.71	10.7	72	108	$13
12	ARI	5	3	0	90	80	3.69	3.97	1.26	742	806	677	13.4	2.2	8.0	3.6	9%	37	19	43	31%	76%	12%	11	54	36%	27%	0	0.66	3.7	99	130	$2
13	ARI	5	5	0	92	85	3.13	4.05	1.22	649	655	645	7.8	3.2	8.3	2.6	11%	33	21	47	29%	77%	7%	0	32			0	1.40	8.3	74	96	$5
1st Half		4	0	0	44	46	2.23	3.72	1.06	567	675	499	8.6	3.0	9.3	3.1	12%	30	20	50	28%	80%	4%	0	35			0	0.74	8.9	94	121	$11
2nd Half		1	5	0	48	39	3.97	4.37	1.36	723	638	778	7.3	3.4	7.4	2.2	11%	35	21	44	30%	75%	10%	0	29			0	1.90	-0.6	54	70	-$1
14	**Proj**	**6**	**4**	**0**	**73**	**66**	**3.47**	**3.67**	**1.23**	**687**	**723**	**659**	**10.3**	**2.7**	**8.2**	**3.0**	**10%**	**35**	**20**	**45**	**30%**	**75%**	**8%**	**1**						**3.6**	**86**	**111**	**$4**

Colon,Bartolo

Age: 41 Th: R Role SP
Ht: 5' 11" Wt: 265 Type Con

Health	D	LIMA Plan	D+
PT/Exp	A	Rand Var	-4
Consist	A	MM	3103

Nobody knew what to expect as he came off of 50-game PED suspension and approached his 40th birthday. Put up the lowest ERA of his career, but skills call it into question, as his lack of swing-and-miss stuff leaves very little margin for error. A little hr/f regression could quickly send ERA into recent xERA territory.

Yr	Tm	W	L	Sv	IP	K	ERA	xERA	WHIP	oOPS	vL	vR	BF/G	Ctl	Dom	Cmd	SwK	G	L	F	H%	S%	hr/f	GS	APC	DOM%	DIS%	Sv%	LI	RAR	BPV	BPX	R$
09	CHW	3	6	0	62	38	4.19	4.77	1.44	854	967	749	23.0	3.0	5.5	1.8	6%	44	16	40	29%	79%	16%	12	83	25%	25%			1.0	39	73	-$2
10																																	
11	NYY	8	10	0	164	135	4.00	3.70	1.29	751	880	621	23.9	2.2	7.4	3.4	6%	44	20	36	31%	73%	11%	26	88	50%	27%	0	0.77	-1.1	96	144	$5
12	OAK	10	9	0	152	91	3.43	4.23	1.21	692	782	587	26.5	1.4	5.4	4.0	5%	46	18	36	30%	75%	9%	24	89	50%	25%			11.1	84	110	$9
13	OAK	18	6	0	190	117	2.65	4.00	1.17	659	681	636	25.6	1.4	5.5	4.0	7%	42	21	38	30%	80%	6%	30	93	43%	13%			28.6	83	108	$21
1st Half		11	2	0	106	61	2.79	3.83	1.08	630	711	544	25.9	1.1	5.2	4.7	6%	45	18	37	28%	77%	6%	16	91	44%	13%			14.1	86	111	$25
2nd Half		7	4	0	84	56	2.46	4.20	1.27	693	645	747	25.3	1.7	6.0	3.5	7%	37	24	39	32%	83%	6%	14	95	43%	14%			14.5	77	100	$15
14	**Proj**	**12**	**9**	**0**	**168**	**105**	**3.71**	**3.82**	**1.24**	**706**	**758**	**650**	**24.6**	**1.7**	**5.6**	**3.3**	**6%**	**43**	**20**	**38**	**30%**	**73%**	**9%**	**28**						**3.3**	**76**	**98**	**$9**

BRIAN RUDD

Cook,Ryan

Age: 27	Th: R	Role RP	Health A	LIMA Plan A
Ht: 6' 2"	Wt: 215	Type Pwr	PT/Exp C	Rand Var -5
			Consist B	MM 4420

Another season of strong skills and good fortune on hr/f. An out pitch vs LH would be nice, as he has just 1.8 career Cmd against them, though continued dominance of RH means at worst, should provide nice ratios in middle relief. Had mixed results in closer role in 2012, but don't be surprised if he gets extended look now.

Yr Tm	W	L	Sv	IP	K	ERA	xERA	WHIP	oOPS	vL	vR	BF/G	Ctl	Dom	Cmd	SwK	G	L	F	H%	S%	hr/f	GS	APC	DOM%	DIS%	Sv%	LI	RAR	BPV	BPX	R$
09																																
10 a/a	1	1	0	24	14	5.15	4.04	1.43				25.1	4.4	5.4	1.2					28%	64%								-3.1	39	63	-$
11 ARI *	1	6	19	69	58	2.75	2.51	1.20	797	734	853	4.6	3.6	7.6	2.1	9%	46	19	35	28%	76%	0%	0	14			79	0.44	10.1	93	140	$1
12 OAK	6	2	14	73	80	2.09	3.23	0.94	517	568	473	4.1	3.3	9.8	3.0	12%	47	16	38	23%	80%	6%	0	16			67	1.40	17.4	112	146	$1
13 OAK	6	4	2	67	67	2.54	3.68	1.29	616	730	526	4.1	3.3	9.0	2.7	11%	47	19	34	33%	80%	3%	0	16			22	1.35	11.0	96	125	$
1st Half	1	1	1	35	35	2.80	3.44	1.08	561	695	460	4.1	2.3	8.9	3.9	12%	43	16	42	31%	71%	0%	0	16			25	1.07	4.6	119	154	$5
2nd Half	5	3	1	32	32	2.25	3.96	1.53	670	763	594	4.2	4.5	9.0	2.0	11%	51	22	27	35%	87%	7%	0	16			20	1.62	6.4	69	89	$5
14 Proj	**5**	**4**	**22**	**65**	**66**	**2.79**	**3.27**	**1.18**	**597**	**688**	**523**	**4.0**	**3.5**	**9.1**	**2.6**	**12%**	**47**	**18**	**35**	**29%**	**78%**	**6%**	**0**						**8.6**	**93**	**121**	**$14**

Corbin,Patrick

Age: 24	Th: L	Role SP	Health A	LIMA Plan C+
Ht: 6' 2"	Wt: 185	Type	PT/Exp B	Rand Var 0
			Consist B	MM 4305

ERA says it was a tale of two halves, but 2H slump actually masked some solid skill improvement. Twice had double digit streaks of PQS-DOM outings, which, combined with growth vs LH, hints at a little more upside. Stellar Cmd, good GB%, and positive Health grade all signal more good things to come. Invest.

Yr Tm	W	L	Sv	IP	K	ERA	xERA	WHIP	oOPS	vL	vR	BF/G	Ctl	Dom	Cmd	SwK	G	L	F	H%	S%	hr/f	GS	APC	DOM%	DIS%	Sv%	LI	RAR	BPV	BPX	R$
09																																
10																																
11 aa	9	8	0	160	121	4.65	4.63	1.40				26.0	2.1	6.8	3.3					34%	68%								-14.1	80	120	-$2
12 ARI *	11	10	1	186	154	3.90	4.26	1.34	783	780	784	22.1	2.2	7.4	3.3	9%	46	23	31	33%	73%	13%	17	73	47%	35%	100	0.77	2.6	88	114	$6
13 ARI	14	8	0	208	178	3.41	3.48	1.17	671	560	703	26.9	2.3	7.7	3.3	11%	47	22	31	29%	73%	10%	32	96	72%	6%			11.6	100	131	$16
1st Half	9	0	0	110	85	2.22	3.52	1.00	593	451	636	27.1	2.4	7.0	2.9	10%	47	21	33	25%	81%	7%	16	98	81%	0%			22.3	86	111	$30
2nd Half	5	8	0	99	93	4.74	3.44	1.35	750	684	767	26.7	2.3	8.5	3.7	12%	47	24	29	34%	67%	14%	16	95	63%	13%			-10.7	116	150	$1
14 Proj	**13**	**9**	**0**	**203**	**171**	**3.58**	**3.34**	**1.25**	**713**	**653**	**729**	**24.2**	**2.2**	**7.6**	**3.4**	**10%**	**46**	**23**	**31**	**31%**	**74%**	**11%**	**34**						**7.2**	**100**	**129**	**$14**

Correia,Kevin

Age: 33	Th: R	Role SP	Health C	LIMA Plan D+
Ht: 6' 3"	Wt: 200	Type Con	PT/Exp A	Rand Var 0
			Consist A	MM 2003

Was hot free agent pickup after 2.23 ERA in April, but soon numbers caught up to BPI. Skills don't get more consistent than this, as there's little variance in yearly xERA or BPV. Unfortunately, in his case, that's not a good thing. Pitch-to-contact approach minimizes value, and 2010 shows how thin margin for error is.

Yr Tm	W	L	Sv	IP	K	ERA	xERA	WHIP	oOPS	vL	vR	BF/G	Ctl	Dom	Cmd	SwK	G	L	F	H%	S%	hr/f	GS	APC	DOM%	DIS%	Sv%	LI	RAR	BPV	BPX	R$
09 SD	12	11	0	198	142	3.91	4.16	1.30	703	713	693	25.2	2.9	6.5	2.2	8%	45	19	36	30%	71%	8%	33	96	52%	15%			10.1	61	113	$12
10 SD	10	10	0	145	115	5.40	4.12	1.49	783	769	795	22.9	4.0	7.1	1.8	8%	49	21	30	31%	66%	15%	26	90	35%	19%	0	0.75	-23.6	48	78	-$5
11 PIT	12	11	0	154	77	4.79	4.47	1.39	791	745	826	24.4	2.3	4.5	2.0	6%	45	18	36	30%	69%	13%	26	87	27%	27%	0	0.73	-16.1	42	64	-$3
12 PIT	12	11	0	171	89	4.21	4.42	1.30	733	735	731	22.8	2.4	4.7	1.9	6%	51	20	29	28%	70%	12%	28	80	36%	18%	0	0.76	-4.1	48	63	$3
13 MIN	9	13	0	185	101	4.18	4.39	1.42	799	806	792	25.5	2.2	4.9	2.2	6%	44	24	32	32%	74%	12%	31	94	35%	16%			-7.1	51	67	-$3
1st Half	6	5	0	99	53	4.08	4.22	1.33	788	758	812	26.1	1.6	4.8	2.9	6%	45	21	34	30%	74%	13%	16	96	31%	13%			-2.6	65	85	$1
2nd Half	3	8	0	86	48	4.29	4.58	1.52	811	851	765	25.0	2.8	5.0	1.8	6%	43	26	31	33%	74%	10%	15	93	40%	20%			-4.5	35	45	-$8
14 Proj	**10**	**12**	**0**	**174**	**94**	**4.34**	**4.13**	**1.38**	**775**	**777**	**773**	**23.9**	**2.3**	**4.8**	**2.1**	**6%**	**46**	**22**	**32**	**30%**	**72%**	**11%**	**31**						**-10.2**	**49**	**63**	**$0**

Cosart,Jarred

Age: 24	Th: R	Role SP	Health A	LIMA Plan D
Ht: 6' 3"	Wt: 180	Type Pwr xGB	PT/Exp D	Rand Var -2
			Consist A	MM 1103

1-1, 1.95 ERA in 60 IP at HOU. Former prospect has seen his stock drop in recent years, and did nothing in 2013 to change that. Ctl continued to rise in minors, and behind shiny ERA in majors was a 0.9 Cmd. Extreme GB tendencies provide reason for cautious optimism, but he's a risky short-term investment... DN: 5.00 ERA.

Yr Tm	W	L	Sv	IP	K	ERA	xERA	WHIP	oOPS	vL	vR	BF/G	Ctl	Dom	Cmd	SwK	G	L	F	H%	S%	hr/f	GS	APC	DOM%	DIS%	Sv%	LI	RAR	BPV	BPX	R$
09																																
10																																
11 aa	1	2	0	36	20	4.91	3.91	1.29				21.3	3.0	4.8	1.6					27%	63%								-4.3	38	57	-$3
12 a/a	6	7	0	115	82	3.31	3.55	1.40				23.1	3.7	6.4	1.7					31%	75%								10.0	71	93	$2
13 HOU *	8	5	0	153	114	2.98	3.30	1.39	631	489	849	23.0	5.0	6.7	1.4	6%	55	21	24	27%	79%	7%	10	102	20%	10%			16.7	64	83	$6
1st Half	7	4	0	83	72	3.38	3.06	1.33				21.4	4.6	7.9	1.7					28%	75%	0%	0						5.0	80	103	$9
2nd Half	1	1	0	70	42	2.51	3.58	1.45	631	489	849	25.0	5.4	5.3	1.0	6%	55	21	24	26%	84%	7%	10	102	20%	10%			11.7	46	59	$2
14 Proj	**6**	**8**	**0**	**159**	**105**	**4.58**	**4.42**	**1.48**	**687**	**512**	**957**	**23.5**	**4.8**	**5.9**	**1.2**	**6%**	**52**	**21**	**27**	**29%**	**70%**	**9%**	**29**						**-14.1**	**7**	**8**	**-$5**

Cotts,Neal

Age: 34	Th: L	Role RP	Health F	LIMA Plan A
Ht: 6' 1"	Wt: 200	Type Pwr	PT/Exp F	Rand Var -5
			Consist F	MM 5500

8-3, 1.11 ERA in 57 IP at TEX. One of the unlikely success stories of 2013, after missing most of last three years due to injuries. BPV agrees with results, and he had shown similar skills (10.9 Dom) in '08, last healthy season. But prior skills were shaky, age and health history work against him, so expect some regression.

Yr Tm	W	L	Sv	IP	K	ERA	xERA	WHIP	oOPS	vL	vR	BF/G	Ctl	Dom	Cmd	SwK	G	L	F	H%	S%	hr/f	GS	APC	DOM%	DIS%	Sv%	LI	RAR	BPV	BPX	R$
09 CHC	0	2	0	11	9	7.36	5.29	2.09	1014	1255	776	2.9	7.4	7.4	1.0	10%	61	11	28	33%	70%	30%	0	12			0	0.99	-4.1	-27	-51	-$6
10																																
11																																
12 aaa	2	1	3	32	29	6.10	6.09	1.85				5.9	4.8	8.3	1.7					39%	67%								-8.1	54	70	-$7
13 TEX *	11	4	3	80	95	1.11	1.70	0.97	499	565	436	4.2	2.7	10.7	4.0	13%	44	22	34	28%	91%	4%	0	16			50	1.14	27.2	152	199	$18
1st Half	7	2	2	46	56	0.77	1.62	0.97	462	582	331	4.9	2.7	11.0	4.0	14%	49	21	30	29%	94%	0%	0	18			67	1.32	17.5	159	205	$22
2nd Half	4	2	1	34	39	1.57	2.97	0.96	523	549	497	3.5	2.6	10.2	3.9	12%	41	23	36	27%	87%	7%	0	15			33	1.05	9.7	132	171	$13
14 Proj	**5**	**2**	**0**	**45**	**48**	**3.13**	**3.19**	**1.22**	**642**	**747**	**542**	**4.5**	**3.5**	**9.6**	**2.7**	**13%**	**44**	**22**	**34**	**30%**	**75%**	**7%**	**0**						**4.1**	**100**	**130**	**$2**

Crain,Jesse

Age: 32	Th: R	Role RP	Health F	LIMA Plan A
Ht: 6' 1"	Wt: 215	Type Pwr FB	PT/Exp D	Rand Var -5
			Consist A	MM 4500

Career-best skills definitely played a role in stellar 1H, though high strand rate and no fly balls leaving the park sure helped. Traded to Tampa in July, but never pitched for them because of shoulder strain. Regression a no-brainer, and he has F Health grade for a reason, but still looks like an attractive LIMA target.

Yr Tm	W	L	Sv	IP	K	ERA	xERA	WHIP	oOPS	vL	vR	BF/G	Ctl	Dom	Cmd	SwK	G	L	F	H%	S%	hr/f	GS	APC	DOM%	DIS%	Sv%	LI	RAR	BPV	BPX	R$
09 MIN *	8	4	1	69	60	4.39	3.66	1.45	722	954	571	4.4	4.6	7.8	1.7	8%	43	16	41	31%	68%	5%	0	16			100	0.76	-0.6	75	141	$2
10 MIN	1	1	1	68	62	3.04	3.89	1.18	627	614	635	3.9	3.6	8.2	2.3	10%	39	17	44	27%	76%	6%	0	15			25	1.10	8.7	68	110	$4
11 CHW	8	3	1	65	70	2.62	3.85	1.24	655	506	744	4.0	4.3	9.6	2.3	14%	33	18	49	27%	84%	9%	0	17			14	1.71	10.7	69	104	$7
12 CHW	2	3	0	48	60	2.44	3.46	1.08	561	717	456	3.8	4.3	11.3	2.6	12%	37	19	44	24%	83%	11%	0	17			0	1.28	9.3	101	132	$4
13 TAM	2	3	0	37	46	0.74	3.12	1.15	562	675	447	4.0	2.7	11.3	4.2	11%	35	24	41	35%	93%	0%	0	18			0	1.77	14.2	143	187	$3
1st Half	2	3	0	37	46	0.74	3.12	1.15	562	675	447	4.0	2.7	11.3	4.2	11%	35	24	41	35%	93%	0%	0	18			0	1.77	14.2	143	185	$3
2nd Half																																
14 Proj	**4**	**3**	**0**	**53**	**59**	**2.77**	**3.36**	**1.19**	**641**	**692**	**603**	**3.9**	**3.7**	**10.1**	**2.7**	**12%**	**36**	**20**	**44**	**28%**	**81%**	**9%**	**0**						**7.2**	**94**	**123**	**$3**

Crow,Aaron

Age: 27	Th: R	Role RP	Health A	LIMA Plan B+
Ht: 6' 3"	Wt: 195	Type Pwr GB	PT/Exp C	Rand Var -1
			Consist A	MM 4400

Unable to sustain previous year's gains, as subpar Cmd and struggles vs LH resurfaced. Served up 6 BB, 4 HR in 6.1 IP span in mid-August, which may help explain why he was used sparingly down the stretch. Downside is limited by high number of strikeouts and grounders, but that doesn't mean he can't still hurt your WHIP.

Yr Tm	W	L	Sv	IP	K	ERA	xERA	WHIP	oOPS	vL	vR	BF/G	Ctl	Dom	Cmd	SwK	G	L	F	H%	S%	hr/f	GS	APC	DOM%	DIS%	Sv%	LI	RAR	BPV	BPX	R$
09																																
10 aa	7	7	0	119	72	6.33	5.56	1.70				24.5	4.3	5.4	1.3					34%	62%								-33.1	27	43	-$13
11 KC	4	4	0	62	65	2.76	3.44	1.39	711	919	537	4.7	4.5	9.4	2.1	12%	52	21	27	30%	86%	18%	0	18			0	1.30	9.1	78	118	$2
12 KC	3	1	2	65	65	3.48	3.22	1.18	601	556	626	3.6	3.1	9.0	3.0	13%	53	19	28	30%	71%	8%	0	13			25	1.09	4.3	111	145	$3
13 KC	7	5	1	48	44	3.38	3.91	1.48	776	846	712	3.7	4.1	8.3	2.0	11%	49	20	31	32%	82%	14%	0	14			25	1.78	2.9	64	84	$0
1st Half	5	3	1	24	19	3.70	4.05	1.40	698	623	761	3.5	3.7	7.0	1.9	10%	51	18	31	31%	75%	9%	0	14			33	1.92	0.5	56	72	$2
2nd Half	2	2	0	24	25	3.04	3.78	1.56	857	1046	655	3.9	4.6	9.5	2.1	11%	47	22	31	33%	88%	20%	0	14			0	1.62	2.4	73	94	-$2
14 Proj	**5**	**4**	**0**	**51**	**48**	**3.57**	**3.53**	**1.38**	**721**	**807**	**652**	**4.1**	**4.0**	**8.5**	**2.1**	**12%**	**51**	**20**	**30**	**31%**	**78%**	**13%**	**0**						**1.9**	**74**	**96**	**$0**

BRIAN RUDD

Cueto,Johnny

Age: 28	Th: R	Role SP	Health F	LIMA Plan B+
Ht: 5' 11"	Wt: 215	Type	PT/Exp A	Rand Var -1
			Consist A	MM 4203

Lat and shoulder issues forced him to the DL three separate times. When he did pitch, it was more of the same: Outpitched his xERA for the fourth straight year, while excellent GB% remained and Dom inched even higher. Health grade trumps consistency, though, so pay for 150 IP rather than 200.

Yr Tm	W	L	Sv	IP	K	ERA	xERA	WHIP	oOPS	vL	vR	BF/G	Ctl	Dom	Cmd	SwK	G	L	F	H%	S%	hr/f	GS	APC	DOM%	DIS%	Sv%	LI	RAR	BPV	BPX	R$
09 CIN	11	11	0	171	132	4.41	4.33	1.36	780	796	765	24.7	3.2	6.9	2.2	8%	42	18	41	30%	71%	11%	30	97	47%	17%			-1.9	58	109	$6
10 CIN	12	7	0	186	138	3.64	4.04	1.28	727	710	741	25.2	2.7	6.7	2.5	10%	42	19	39	30%	74%	9%	31	101	58%	13%			10.2	67	109	$11
11 CIN	9	5	0	156	104	2.31	3.64	1.09	593	588	598	26.3	2.7	6.0	2.2	8%	54	16	30	26%	80%	6%	24	100	54%	13%			31.5	67	100	$18
12 CIN	19	9	0	217	170	2.78	3.59	1.17	667	708	620	26.9	2.0	7.1	3.5	9%	49	22	29	30%	78%	8%	33	105	58%	12%			33.1	99	129	$26
13 CIN	5	2	0	61	51	2.82	3.27	1.05	607	561	644	22.0	2.7	7.6	2.8	11%	51	25	24	25%	79%	17%	11	87	64%	27%			7.8	93	121	$5
1st Half	4	2	0	49	41	3.33	3.24	1.07	623	557	674	21.7	2.6	7.6	2.9	10%	51	26	23	25%	74%	19%	9	86	56%	33%			3.2	96	124	$6
2nd Half	1	0	0	12	10	0.75	3.39	1.00	541	577	507	23.5	3.0	7.5	2.5	17%	50	22	28	23%	100%	11%	2	91	100%	0%			4.6	82	106	$0
14 Proj	**12**	**7**	**0**	**167**	**134**	**3.28**	**3.36**	**1.19**	**666**	**658**	**673**	**24.0**	**2.6**	**7.2**	**2.8**	**10%**	**50**	**22**	**29**	**29%**	**74%**	**9%**	**28**						**12.1**	**88**	**114**	**$14**

Danks,John

Age: 29	Th: L	Role SP	Health F	LIMA Plan B
Ht: 6' 1"	Wt: 215	Type	PT/Exp C	Rand Var +1
			Consist B	MM 2103

4-14, 4.75 ERA in 138 IP at CHW. Returned in mid-May from a year off (shoulder), but left his velocity on the DL. The result was a soft-tossing Dom that limits upside moving forward. Still owns excellent Ctl, and hr/f should regress, but poor health casts too dark a cloud to be drafted anywhere but in the end game.

Yr Tm	W	L	Sv	IP	K	ERA	xERA	WHIP	oOPS	vL	vR	BF/G	Ctl	Dom	Cmd	SwK	G	L	F	H%	S%	hr/f	GS	APC	DOM%	DIS%	Sv%	LI	RAR	BPV	BPX	R$
09 CHW	13	11	0	200	149	3.77	4.29	1.28	726	756	715	26.2	3.3	6.7	2.0	10%	44	15	41	27%	76%	11%	32	100	50%	13%			13.5	54	101	$14
10 CHW	15	11	0	213	162	3.72	3.95	1.22	657	694	640	27.4	3.0	6.8	2.3	9%	45	16	39	28%	71%	7%	32	106	63%	9%			9.5	66	107	$15
11 CHW	8	12	0	170	135	4.33	3.84	1.34	752	704	771	27.0	2.4	7.1	2.9	10%	44	20	36	32%	70%	10%	27	102	59%	19%			-8.2	85	127	$1
12 CHW	3	4	0	54	30	5.70	5.23	1.49	790	831	760	26.4	3.9	5.0	1.3	7%	41	22	37	29%	63%	11%	9	93	33%	33%			-11.2	5	7	-$8
13 CHW *	6	14	0	161	101	4.73	5.08	1.36	798	831	785	25.9	2.4	5.6	2.3	9%	41	22	37	29%	72%	17%	22	100	55%	14%			-17.1	29	38	-$6
1st Half	3	5	0	65	44	4.65	5.05	1.37	787	898	736	24.7	2.9	6.1	2.1	10%	42	19	39	28%	73%	19%	7	92	71%	29%			-6.3	27	35	-$4
2nd Half	3	9	0	96	57	4.78	4.39	1.35	803	796	805	27.4	2.2	5.3	2.5	9%	41	23	35	29%	71%	16%	15	104	47%	7%			-10.8	57	74	-$7
14 Proj	**8**	**13**	**0**	**174**	**113**	**4.41**	**4.09**	**1.36**	**768**	**798**	**754**	**25.8**	**2.7**	**5.8**	**2.2**	**9%**	**42**	**21**	**37**	**30%**	**71%**	**12%**	**28**						**-11.7**	**53**	**69**	**$0**

Darvish,Yu

Age: 27	Th: R	Role SP	Health B	LIMA Plan C
Ht: 6' 5"	Wt: 225	Type Pwr	PT/Exp A	Rand Var 0
			Consist B	MM 5505

Threw an Opening Night gem and never really looked back. Continued to rack up Ks in bunches, and is virtually unhittable against RH hitters. 2H Ctl fade might have been injury-related. If he regains 1H Ctl over a full season and hr/f regresses back to normal... UP: 2.50 ERA, 300 K

Yr Tm	W	L	Sv	IP	K	ERA	xERA	WHIP	oOPS	vL	vR	BF/G	Ctl	Dom	Cmd	SwK	G	L	F	H%	S%	hr/f	GS	APC	DOM%	DIS%	Sv%	LI	RAR	BPV	BPX	R$
09 for	15	5	0	182	158	2.15	2.22	1.00				30.2	2.8	7.8	2.8					24%	83%								48.8	100	187	$33
10 for	12	8	0	202	211	2.21	2.56	1.13				30.7	2.6	9.4	3.6					31%	81%								46.5	130	211	$27
11 for	18	6	0	232	262	1.78	1.65	0.91				30.9	1.7	10.2	5.9					29%	82%								61.8	189	283	$46
12 TEX	16	9	0	191	221	3.90	3.48	1.28	659	674	640	28.1	4.2	10.4	2.5	13%	46	22	32	31%	70%	9%	29	109	72%	3%			2.6	98	128	$13
13 TEX	13	9	0	210	277	2.83	2.86	1.07	611	655	543	26.3	3.4	11.9	3.5	13%	41	21	38	27%	80%	14%	32	108	84%	0%			26.7	140	183	$27
1st Half	8	3	0	113	151	2.78	2.67	1.01	598	636	538	26.8	2.9	12.0	4.1	14%	45	20	35	28%	79%	15%	17	109	88%	0%			15.2	159	206	$32
2nd Half	5	6	0	96	126	2.90	3.08	1.14	627	676	549	25.7	4.0	11.8	2.9	12%	37	22	41	27%	81%	14%	15	106	80%	0%			11.5	118	153	$22
14 Proj	**17**	**9**	**0**	**210**	**257**	**2.97**	**2.80**	**1.10**	**609**	**642**	**562**	**26.9**	**3.3**	**11.0**	**3.4**	**13%**	**42**	**22**	**36**	**29%**	**76%**	**11%**	**31**						**23.2**	**130**	**169**	**$28**

Davis,Wade

Age: 28	Th: R	Role RP	Health B	LIMA Plan C
Ht: 6' 5"	Wt: 225	Type Pwr	PT/Exp B	Rand Var +4
			Consist C	MM 3301

An unsuccessful transition back to the rotation after '12 skills breakout in the bullpen. Terrible H% luck said he wasn't quite THAT bad, but Dom plummeted, especially in 2H, and xERA fell back in line with baseline as a starter. Moved back to 'pen in Sept with limited success, leaving more questions than answers right now.

Yr Tm	W	L	Sv	IP	K	ERA	xERA	WHIP	oOPS	vL	vR	BF/G	Ctl	Dom	Cmd	SwK	G	L	F	H%	S%	hr/f	GS	APC	DOM%	DIS%	Sv%	LI	RAR	BPV	BPX	R$
09 TAM *	12	10	0	195	153	4.20	4.17	1.40	640	630	655	24.2	3.5	7.1	2.0	9%	39	25	36	31%	71%	6%	6	100	33%	17%			3.0	63	118	$7
10 TAM	12	10	0	168	113	4.07	4.59	1.35	756	776	732	24.9	3.3	6.1	1.8	7%	39	17	44	28%	74%	10%	29	96	31%	17%			0.2	36	59	$5
11 TAM	11	10	0	184	105	4.45	4.78	1.38	771	779	765	27.4	3.1	5.1	1.7	6%	36	21	43	29%	70%	9%	29	102	38%	21%			-11.5	23	35	-$1
12 TAM	3	0	0	70	87	2.43	3.31	1.09	570	464	654	5.3	3.7	11.1	3.0	13%	39	22	40	28%	81%	8%	0	23			0	0.85	13.7	117	153	$7
13 KC	8	11	0	135	114	5.32	4.38	1.68	822	910	721	19.9	3.9	7.6	2.0	8%	41	27	32	37%	69%	11%	24	80	38%	33%	0	0.85	-24.3	51	67	-$13
1st Half	4	6	0	83	73	5.55	4.41	1.81	877	933	815	24.1	4.0	7.9	2.0	8%	40	30	31	39%	71%	13%	16	97	50%	38%			-17.2	52	67	-$17
2nd Half	4	5	0	53	41	4.96	4.34	1.46	729	872	563	15.5	3.6	7.0	2.0	8%	42	24	34	33%	66%	7%	8	62	13%	25%	0	0.94	-7.1	49	64	-$7
14 Proj	**6**	**6**	**0**	**102**	**89**	**4.29**	**3.89**	**1.42**	**732**	**774**	**686**	**15.9**	**3.6**	**7.9**	**2.2**	**9%**	**40**	**24**	**37**	**32%**	**71%**	**9%**	**21**						**-5.3**	**62**	**81**	**-$1**

De Fratus,Justin

Age: 26	Th: R	Role RP	Health F	LIMA Plan B+
Ht: 6' 4"	Wt: 220	Type Pwr	PT/Exp D	Rand Var -1
			Consist C	MM 3300

3-3, 3.86 ERA in 47 IP at PHI. Called up in May after posting a 17/6 K/BB and 1.89 ERA at AAA, but that success didn't carry into the majors. Previously strong Ctl ballooned, resulting in an underwhelming Cmd that should restrict him to middle innings. And middle innings lead to fanalytic irrelevance.

Yr Tm	W	L	Sv	IP	K	ERA	xERA	WHIP	oOPS	vL	vR	BF/G	Ctl	Dom	Cmd	SwK	G	L	F	H%	S%	hr/f	GS	APC	DOM%	DIS%	Sv%	LI	RAR	BPV	BPX	R$
09																																
10 aa	1	0	6	25	23	2.41	2.27	0.95				4.7	1.7	8.6	4.9					27%	79%								5.1	145	234	$3
11 PHI *	7	3	15	79	86	3.52	3.36	1.29	396	700	125	5.8	3.2	9.7	3.0	9%	44	11	44	34%	73%	0%	0	12			88	0.69	4.1	112	168	$10
12 PHI *	0	1	3	32	26	3.32	2.55	1.04	478	646	361	4.2	2.3	7.2	3.2	12%	52	13	35	26%	70%	0%	0	14			100	0.59	2.8	100	131	$0
13 PHI *	6	3	0	66	56	3.40	3.95	1.49	738	684	759	4.0	4.3	7.6	1.8	12%	44	26	30	33%	77%	8%	0	14			0	1.21	3.8	73	95	-$1
1st Half	5	3	0	35	29	3.30	3.93	1.51	738	919	662	4.2	4.2	7.4	1.8	12%	40	29	31	34%	77%	7%	0	13			0	1.27	2.5	74	96	$1
2nd Half	1	0	0	31	27	3.52	4.03	1.47	737	539	808	3.9	4.4	7.9	1.8	12%	45	25	30	32%	77%	8%	0	16			0	1.16	1.3	47	61	-$3
14 Proj	**3**	**2**	**0**	**65**	**57**	**3.70**	**3.62**	**1.29**	**700**	**674**	**711**	**4.2**	**3.4**	**7.9**	**2.3**	**12%**	**43**	**24**	**33**	**30%**	**73%**	**9%**	**0**						**1.4**	**71**	**92**	**$1**

De La Rosa,Dane

Age: 31	Th: R	Role RP	Health A	LIMA Plan B
Ht: 6' 7"	Wt: 245	Type Pwr GB	PT/Exp D	Rand Var -2
			Consist C	MM 4311

Worked his way through bullpen ranks with strong Dom and GB%. Even held a share of the closer role in August. Skills dipped considerably in 2H despite strong finish (0.41 ERA in 22 IP after August 1). Fortunate hr/f certainly helped, and xERA says not to expect another sub-3.00 ERA, so chances of SV opps seem slim.

Yr Tm	W	L	Sv	IP	K	ERA	xERA	WHIP	oOPS	vL	vR	BF/G	Ctl	Dom	Cmd	SwK	G	L	F	H%	S%	hr/f	GS	APC	DOM%	DIS%	Sv%	LI	RAR	BPV	BPX	R$
09																																
10 aa	9	3	4	73	59	2.57	4.40	1.52				6.7	3.5	7.3	2.1					35%	84%								13.6	73	117	$6
11 TAM *	6	5	6	78	73	4.50	5.04	1.52	834	890	794	5.7	3.6	8.5	2.4	14%	52	30	17	35%	73%	25%	0	18			60	0.14	-5.4	65	98	$0
12 TAM *	0	4	20	73	71	4.11	3.00	1.37	1159	875	1345	5.2	5.9	8.8	1.5	7%	53	13	33	26%	70%	40%	0	19			87	0.03	-0.9	83	108	$5
13 LAA	6	1	2	72	65	2.86	3.43	1.16	571	475	668	3.9	3.5	8.1	2.3	12%	51	20	29	28%	75%	5%	0	16			40	0.97	9.0	81	105	$6
1st Half	3	1	0	37	35	3.16	3.31	1.16	563	527	593	4.3	2.9	8.5	2.9	13%	51	18	31	30%	71%	3%	0	17			0	0.82	3.2	104	135	$5
2nd Half	3	0	2	35	30	2.55	3.57	1.16	581	430	768	3.5	4.1	7.6	1.9	11%	51	23	26	25%	79%	8%	0	15			50	1.10	5.7	57	73	$7
14 Proj	**4**	**3**	**3**	**73**	**66**	**3.36**	**3.46**	**1.28**	**647**	**524**	**776**	**4.5**	**3.9**	**8.2**	**2.1**	**12%**	**51**	**21**	**28**	**29%**	**75%**	**10%**	**0**						**4.6**	**70**	**91**	**$4**

de la Rosa,Jorge

Age: 33	Th: L	Role SP	Health F	LIMA Plan C+
Ht: 6' 1"	Wt: 220	Type	PT/Exp C	Rand Var -1
			Consist F	MM 3203

Flashy Win total and ERA make this look like another post-TJ success story, but it came with warning signs: Dom fell way below career norms, pushing Cmd to lowest level since '07; xERA and hr/f didn't believe in a full rebound; and Sept. thumb injury reminded us of health history. BPX shows how far he is from average.

Yr Tm	W	L	Sv	IP	K	ERA	xERA	WHIP	oOPS	vL	vR	BF/G	Ctl	Dom	Cmd	SwK	G	L	F	H%	S%	hr/f	GS	APC	DOM%	DIS%	Sv%	LI	RAR	BPV	BPX	R$
09 COL	16	9	0	185	193	4.38	3.71	1.38	745	568	794	24.2	4.0	9.4	2.3	11%	45	21	34	32%	70%	12%	32	92	50%	19%	0	0.75	-1.3	83	155	$11
10 COL	8	7	0	122	113	4.22	3.56	1.32	737	671	755	25.6	4.1	8.4	2.1	12%	52	19	29	28%	71%	16%	20	101	60%	10%			-2.1	71	114	$4
11 COL	5	2	0	59	52	3.51	3.73	1.19	627	349	684	24.5	3.4	7.9	2.4	12%	43	20	38	28%	71%	7%	10	96	70%	20%			3.2	73	110	$3
12 COL	0	2	0	11	6	9.28	5.98	1.78	1065	250	1219	17.7	1.7	5.1	3.0	13%	34	14	52	33%	57%	22%	3	68	0%	100%			-6.9	58	75	-$8
13 COL	16	6	0	168	112	3.49	4.14	1.38	721	510	770	23.8	3.3	6.0	1.8	10%	47	25	28	31%	76%	8%	30	92	40%	17%			7.8	43	57	$7
1st Half	8	4	0	99	65	3.09	3.98	1.28	675	574	698	23.7	3.1	5.9	1.9	9%	46	25	28	29%	76%	6%	17	92	47%	18%			9.5	47	61	$11
2nd Half	8	2	0	69	47	4.06	4.37	1.53	781	433	870	23.9	3.7	6.2	1.7	10%	49	25	26	30%	75%	10%	13	93	31%	15%			-1.7	39	50	$0
14 Proj	**13**	**10**	**0**	**176**	**126**	**3.78**	**3.89**	**1.32**	**723**	**496**	**778**	**23.5**	**3.4**	**6.4**	**1.9**	**11%**	**47**	**22**	**31**	**29%**	**74%**	**11%**	**31**						**1.8**	**50**	**65**	**$8**

RYAN BLOOMFIELD

Deduno,Samuel

Age: 30	Th: R	Role SP	Health C	LIMA Plan D+	
Ht: 6' 3"	Wt: 190	Type Pwr xGB	PT/Exp D	Rand Var 0	
			Consist A	MM 2103	

8-8, 3.83 ERA in 108 IP at MIN. Kept inducing groundballs at a staggering rate, but there isn't much else here to like. Subpar Dom limits upside, and while Ctl made strides, his baseline says that can't be trusted. Struggles vs. RHB hurt chances as a SP, and ultimately cap fantasy value as he enters post-peak years.

Yr Tm	W	L	Sv	IP	K	ERA	xERA	WHIP	oOPS	vL	vR	BF/G	Ctl	Dom	Cmd	SwK	G	L	F	H%	S%	hr/f	GS	APC	DOM%	DIS%	Sv%	LI	RAR	BPV	BPX	R$
09 a/a	12	5	0	139	98	3.51	3.39	1.45				23.7	5.2	6.4	1.2					29%	75%								13.9	64	120	$7
10 COL *	3	1	0	33	24	3.29	3.78	1.35	879	400	1262	13.9	5.0	6.5	1.3	12%	38	25	38	24%	81%	33%	0	13			0	0.37	3.2	42	68	$0
11 SD *	4	6	0	108	72	3.32	3.79	1.53	899	929	875	11.2	4.8	6.0	1.2	12%	70	20	10	31%	77%	0%	0	35			0	0.16	8.3	61	92	-$1
12 MIN *	7	7	0	121	91	3.97	4.21	1.53	759	723	805	21.9	5.9	6.8	1.1	8%	58	21	20	27%	76%	21%	15	89	27%	47%			0.7	45	58	-$3
13 MIN *	8	8	0	125	79	3.78	3.85	1.41	714	584	884	25.1	3.8	5.7	1.5	8%	60	20	20	30%	73%	10%	18	97	50%	17%			1.3	52	68	$0
1st Half	4	2	0	60	36	3.36	3.72	1.40	654	555	745	25.3	3.8	5.5	1.4	7%	61	19	21	30%	76%	7%	7	98	57%	14%			3.7	52	68	$2
2nd Half	4	6	0	65	43	4.18	3.85	1.41	754	599	1015	25.2	3.8	6.0	1.6	9%	59	22	20	30%	71%	13%	11	96	45%	18%			-2.5	43	56	-$2
14 Proj	**8**	**9**	**0**	**139**	**94**	**3.99**	**4.01**	**1.48**	**735**	**651**	**845**	**20.9**	**4.6**	**6.1**	**1.3**	**8%**	**59**	**21**	**20**	**30%**	**73%**	**11%**	**30**						**-2.2**	**23**	**30**	**$0**

Delabar,Steve

Age: 30	Th: R	Role RP	Health B	LIMA Plan A	
Ht: 6' 4"	Wt: 230	Type Pwr xFB	PT/Exp D	Rand Var 0	
			Consist B	MM 5510	

First time All-Star's skills got better despite an ERA that almost quadrupled in the 2H. Missed plenty of bats, so electric Dom should stay intact. Wild hr/f swung too far in the 'lucky' category, putting a full repeat of '13 ERA in doubt. But if he can sustain 2H Ctl gains, there's profit, and Saves potential, waiting in the wings.

Yr Tm	W	L	Sv	IP	K	ERA	xERA	WHIP	oOPS	vL	vR	BF/G	Ctl	Dom	Cmd	SwK	G	L	F	H%	S%	hr/f	GS	APC	DOM%	DIS%	Sv%	LI	RAR	BPV	BPX	R$
09																																
10																																
11 SEA *	3	5	12	51	45	1.86	3.62	1.59	792	614	886	5.7	6.5	8.0	1.2	13%	31	25	44	30%	88%	14%	0	18			80	1.06	13.0	77	116	$6
12 2 AL	4	3	0	66	92	3.82	2.97	1.09	687	551	795	4.5	3.5	12.5	3.5	17%	43	16	42	27%	73%	20%	0	19			0	0.90	1.6	151	197	$4
13 TOR	5	5	1	59	82	3.22	3.44	1.35	680	712	654	4.6	4.4	12.6	2.8	15%	29	23	48	36%	77%	6%	0	18			17	1.20	4.7	113	148	$2
1st Half	5	1	0	39	54	1.62	3.55	1.28	572	604	543	4.9	5.1	12.5	2.5	16%	33	19	48	33%	88%	2%	0	20			0	1.02	10.8	98	127	$7
2nd Half	0	4	1	20	28	6.41	3.21	1.47	890	900	883	4.0	3.2	12.8	4.0	15%	23	30	47	41%	58%	14%	0	15			33	1.49	-6.2	146	188	-$7
14 Proj	**3**	**4**	**4**	**58**	**78**	**3.38**	**3.04**	**1.20**	**638**	**607**	**665**	**4.3**	**4.2**	**12.1**	**2.9**	**16%**	**33**	**21**	**45**	**31%**	**74%**	**8%**	**0**						**3.5**	**115**	**150**	**$5**

Delgado,Randall

Age: 24	Th: R	Role SP	Health A	LIMA Plan B+	
Ht: 6' 3"	Wt: 200	Type	PT/Exp C	Rand Var +2	
			Consist A	MM 3203	

5-7, 4.26 ERA in 116 IP at ARI. Mixed results for this former top prospect after June callup. Traded in Ks for more control, but the net gain was minimal, especially with higher FB% and a cruel hr/f. The flashes he's shown ('12 Dom and GB%, '13 2H Ctl) at this age are promising—though consolidation may take some time.

Yr Tm	W	L	Sv	IP	K	ERA	xERA	WHIP	oOPS	vL	vR	BF/G	Ctl	Dom	Cmd	SwK	G	L	F	H%	S%	hr/f	GS	APC	DOM%	DIS%	Sv%	LI	RAR	BPV	BPX	R$
09																																
10 aa	3	5	0	44	38	5.32	3.28	1.33				22.7	3.9	7.9	2.0					30%	58%								-6.7	83	135	-$2
11 ATL *	8	8	0	174	139	3.98	4.33	1.40	655	683	635	23.0	3.6	7.2	2.0	8%	38	20	42	31%	74%	11%	7	89	29%	14%			-0.9	58	87	$2
12 ATL *	8	12	0	137	121	4.40	4.47	1.48	727	744	711	22.6	4.1	8.0	2.0	9%	50	22	28	32%	72%	11%	17	90	35%	29%	0	0.80	-6.6	63	83	-$3
13 ARI *	7	12	0	180	127	4.74	4.75	1.33	793	765	819	22.7	2.7	6.4	2.4	9%	42	20	38	29%	70%	17%	19	91	47%	5%	0	0.75	-19.5	41	54	-$4
1st Half	2	7	0	84	64	5.26	5.34	1.56	953	1123	828	21.6	3.7	6.9	1.9	11%	52	18	29	33%	69%	21%	3	80	33%	0%	0	0.59	-14.4	38	50	-$13
2nd Half	5	5	0	96	63	4.30	4.02	1.13	758	696	816	24.2	1.8	5.9	3.3	9%	40	20	40	25%	71%	17%	16	93	50%	6%			-5.1	76	98	$3
14 Proj	**9**	**10**	**0**	**166**	**125**	**4.19**	**3.95**	**1.35**	**744**	**763**	**726**	**22.7**	**3.0**	**6.8**	**2.2**	**9%**	**41**	**22**	**37**	**30%**	**71%**	**10%**	**30**						**-6.7**	**58**	**76**	**$3**

Dempster,Ryan

Age: 37	Th: R	Role SP	Health B	LIMA Plan C	
Ht: 6' 2"	Wt: 215	Type Pwr	PT/Exp A	Rand Var +1	
			Consist A	MM 3303	

Looked like a steal in April (12.9 Dom, 137 BPV), then it all went downhill fast. Career-worst Ctl drove this decline, and 2H Dom didn't help matters, leading to a bullpen demotion in September. GB% and xERA both heading in the wrong direction, and offer little chance of a rebound at this age.

Yr Tm	W	L	Sv	IP	K	ERA	xERA	WHIP	oOPS	vL	vR	BF/G	Ctl	Dom	Cmd	SwK	G	L	F	H%	S%	hr/f	GS	APC	DOM%	DIS%	Sv%	LI	RAR	BPV	BPX	R$
09 CHC	11	9	0	200	172	3.65	3.77	1.31	731	803	665	27.2	2.9	7.7	2.6	11%	47	18	34	31%	75%	11%	31	102	65%	6%			16.7	85	160	$14
10 CHC	15	12	0	215	208	3.85	3.68	1.32	712	704	717	27.0	3.6	8.7	2.4	12%	47	16	37	30%	74%	11%	34	106	62%	15%			6.2	84	137	$12
11 CHC	10	14	0	202	191	4.80	3.81	1.45	788	861	729	25.9	3.6	8.5	2.3	10%	44	21	35	33%	69%	11%	34	103	62%	18%			-21.5	76	115	-$4
12 2 TM	12	8	0	173	153	3.38	3.82	1.20	677	618	742	25.6	2.7	8.0	2.9	11%	43	21	36	29%	76%	11%	28	98	68%	21%			13.5	91	119	$14
13 BOS	8	9	0	171	157	4.57	4.23	1.45	774	702	858	23.6	4.1	8.2	2.0	10%	41	22	38	31%	73%	14%	29	94	52%	14%	0	0.76	-14.9	55	72	-$5
1st Half	5	8	0	101	96	4.11	4.06	1.38	748	637	870	25.6	4.2	8.6	2.0	10%	44	18	38	29%	76%	16%	17	104	59%	18%			-3.1	63	81	$0
2nd Half	3	1	0	71	61	5.22	4.47	1.56	809	785	840	21.3	4.1	7.8	1.9	10%	37	26	37	33%	68%	11%	12	81	42%	8%	0	0.77	-11.8	44	58	-$12
14 Proj	**9**	**8**	**0**	**160**	**144**	**4.27**	**3.82**	**1.39**	**743**	**712**	**775**	**23.6**	**3.9**	**8.1**	**2.1**	**10%**	**42**	**23**	**35**	**30%**	**73%**	**13%**	**29**						**-8.0**	**61**	**80**	**$2**

Detwiler,Ross

Age: 28	Th: L	Role SP	Health F	LIMA Plan D+	
Ht: 6' 5"	Wt: 200	Type Con	PT/Exp C	Rand Var 0	
			Consist A	MM 2103	

Dealt with lingering back injury that eventually shelved him for the season in July. ERA predictably fell back, showing '12 numbers were way over his head. Soft-tossing Dom sunk even lower as righties continued to mash him. "A" consistency rating just means to expect more of the same mediocre results.

Yr Tm	W	L	Sv	IP	K	ERA	xERA	WHIP	oOPS	vL	vR	BF/G	Ctl	Dom	Cmd	SwK	G	L	F	H%	S%	hr/f	GS	APC	DOM%	DIS%	Sv%	LI	RAR	BPV	BPX	R$
09 WAS *	5	11	0	152	100	4.51	5.06	1.66	767	718	783	22.0	3.8	5.9	1.6	6%	43	25	32	35%	72%	4%	14	84	36%	29%	0	0.73	-3.6	49	91	-$6
10 WAS *	4	5	0	67	44	3.60	5.40	1.61	826	1024	780	18.6	3.0	5.9	2.0	6%	43	20	37	35%	80%	14%	5	62	0%	60%	0	0.53	4.0	44	72	-$2
11 WAS *	10	11	0	153	91	4.45	4.71	1.50	704	548	742	21.4	3.0	5.3	1.8	7%	43	24	33	33%	71%	11%	10	65	50%	10%	0	0.90	-9.6	45	68	-$4
12 WAS	10	8	0	164	105	3.40	4.24	1.22	681	513	734	20.8	2.8	5.8	2.0	8%	51	16	33	27%	75%	9%	27	77	33%	22%	0	0.83	12.6	56	73	$10
13 WAS	2	7	0	71	39	4.04	4.33	1.49	811	705	849	24.3	1.8	4.9	2.8	7%	46	23	31	35%	73%	6%	13	86	23%	15%			-1.5	65	85	-$5
1st Half	2	6	0	65	36	4.13	4.31	1.48	814	626	882	24.1	1.8	5.0	2.8	7%	46	22	31	35%	73%	7%	12	85	25%	17%			-2.2	65	84	-$5
2nd Half	0	1	0	6	3	3.00	4.51	1.50	786	1667	513	27.0	1.5	4.5	3.0	6%	37	32	32	36%	78%	0%	1	95	0%	0%			0.6	55	72	-$5
14 Proj	**7**	**9**	**0**	**130**	**79**	**4.16**	**4.11**	**1.43**	**769**	**618**	**815**	**20.3**	**2.6**	**5.4**	**2.1**	**7%**	**46**	**22**	**32**	**32%**	**71%**	**7%**	**27**						**-4.8**	**51**	**66**	**-$1**

Diamond,Scott

Age: 27	Th: L	Role SP	Health A	LIMA Plan D+	
Ht: 6' 3"	Wt: 220	Type Con	PT/Exp C	Rand Var 0	
			Consist D	MM 2001	

6-13, 5.43 ERA in 131 IP at MIN. This was a far cry from '12 career year, and the skills say it's a long road back. He posted the 2nd lowest Dom among all starters over 100 IP, while xERA and DOM%/DIS% suggested it could have been even worse. Should be barely a blip on your radar.

Yr Tm	W	L	Sv	IP	K	ERA	xERA	WHIP	oOPS	vL	vR	BF/G	Ctl	Dom	Cmd	SwK	G	L	F	H%	S%	hr/f	GS	APC	DOM%	DIS%	Sv%	LI	RAR	BPV	BPX	R$
09 aa	5	10	0	131	96	4.67	5.96	1.86				26.6	4.1	6.6	1.6					39%	74%								-5.6	50	93	-$10
10 a/a	8	7	0	159	103	4.17	4.73	1.57				25.8	3.2	5.9	1.8					35%	72%								-1.8	57	92	-$3
11 MIN *	5	19	0	162	91	6.28	6.28	1.79	821	996	777	24.9	3.0	5.1	1.7	7%	46	21	33	38%	64%	6%	7	91	14%	29%			-46.6	30	45	-$25
12 MIN *	16	10	0	208	110	3.53	4.09	1.28	731	792	709	25.8	1.7	4.8	2.8	7%	53	21	26	31%	75%	11%	27	93	52%	11%			12.5	64	83	$11
13 MIN *	10	13	0	172	67	4.83	5.16	1.44	851	911	829	24.4	2.4	3.5	1.5	6%	47	21	32	30%	70%	14%	24	92	17%	46%			-20.4	8	11	-$8
1st Half	5	7	0	77	36	5.40	4.49	1.50	856	937	832	23.4	1.9	4.2	2.3	7%	48	18	34	33%	66%	11%	14	92	29%	43%			-14.5	51	66	-$10
2nd Half	5	6	0	95	31	4.37	4.92	1.40	843	886	824	25.1	2.8	2.9	1.0	5%	46	25	29	27%	74%	18%	10	91	0%	50%			-5.9	-4	-6	-$7
14 Proj	**7**	**8**	**0**	**116**	**55**	**4.65**	**4.27**	**1.45**	**786**	**850**	**763**	**24.9**	**2.5**	**4.3**	**1.7**	**6%**	**49**	**22**	**29**	**31%**	**70%**	**11%**	**20**						**-11.2**	**38**	**49**	**-$4**

Dickey,R.A.

Age: 39	Th: R	Role SP	Health A	LIMA Plan B	
Ht: 6' 2"	Wt: 215	Type	PT/Exp A	Rand Var +1	
			Consist B	MM 4205	

2012 BPV now looks like a black swan. But don't give up on him altogether: 2H skill rebound was supposedly fueled by better health and the return of the "hard" knuckler. Health may be a dicey proposition as he approaches age 40, but there could still be value to be extracted here. Use 2H as your baseline.

Yr Tm	W	L	Sv	IP	K	ERA	xERA	WHIP	oOPS	vL	vR	BF/G	Ctl	Dom	Cmd	SwK	G	L	F	H%	S%	hr/f	GS	APC	DOM%	DIS%	Sv%	LI	RAR	BPV	BPX	R$
09 MIN *	3	2	0	98	55	5.51	5.71	1.70	826	747	891	11.0	3.7	5.1	1.4	7%	47	18	35	35%	68%	11%	1	32	0%	0%	0	0.70	-14.3	26	49	-$9
10 NYM *	15	11	0	235	131	2.79	3.44	1.21	660	614	693	27.0	1.9	5.0	2.6	9%	55	17	28	29%	79%	8%	26	97	50%	4%	0	0.78	37.2	69	112	$21
11 NYM	8	13	0	209	134	3.28	3.89	1.23	690	774	634	26.5	2.3	5.8	2.5	8%	51	16	33	29%	76%	8%	32	95	47%	9%	0	0.79	17.1	70	105	$12
12 NYM	20	6	0	234	230	2.73	3.22	1.05	640	682	605	27.3	2.1	8.9	4.3	13%	46	20	34	28%	79%	11%	33	99	70%	3%	0	0.76	36.9	127	166	$36
13 TOR	14	13	0	225	177	4.21	4.11	1.24	728	777	672	27.7	2.8	7.1	2.5	10%	40	19	40	27%	71%	13%	34	103	59%	15%			-9.4	69	90	$7
1st Half	7	8	0	109	78	4.72	4.37	1.31	742	798	685	27.1	3.4	6.5	1.9	10%	43	19	39	27%	68%	13%	17	103	53%	24%			-11.5	45	59	$2
2nd Half	7	5	0	116	99	3.72	3.88	1.17	714	758	658	28.4	2.3	7.7	3.3	10%	38	20	42	28%	75%	12%	17	104	65%	6%			2.0	91	118	$13
14 Proj	**13**	**9**	**0**	**203**	**165**	**3.65**	**3.55**	**1.21**	**704**	**747**	**664**	**24.7**	**2.5**	**7.3**	**2.9**	**10%**	**44**	**19**	**37**	**29%**	**74%**	**11%**	**33**						**5.3**	**86**	**111**	**$14**

RYAN BLOOMFIELD

Diekman,Jake

Age: 27	Th: L	Role RP	Health A	LIMA Plan C	
Ht: 6' 4"	Wt: 200	Type Pwr GB	PT/Exp D	Rand Var +1	
			Consist A	MM 4400	

1-4, 2.58 ERA in 38 IP at PHI. Called up in June with a 5.70 ERA in Triple-A, then mowed through MLB hitters. Continues to ride elite Dom and GB% combination, but Ctl issues have held him back despite HR stinginess. 2H Ctl is a start, but we'll need to see a longer run than that before speculating on a higher-leverage role.

Yr Tm	W	L	Sv	IP	K	ERA	xERA	WHIP	oOPS	vL	vR	BF/G	Ctl	Dom	Cmd	SwK	G	L	F	H%	S%	hr/f	GS	APC	DOM%	DIS%	Sv%	LI	RAR	BPV	BPX	R$
09																																
10																																
11 aa	0	1	3	65	70	3.47	3.47	1.49				5.3	6.0	9.6	1.6					31%	77%								3.8	88	132	-$1
12 PHI *	2	2	7	54	65	3.10	3.53	1.53	696	590	774	4.1	5.7	10.9	1.9	13%	52	25	23	35%	78%	6%	0	17			70	1.18	6.1	107	140	$1
13 PHI *	2	4	11	68	71	4.47	4.26	1.64	598	368	765	4.1	5.4	9.3	1.7	14%	51	29	20	36%	71%	5%	0	14			79	0.92	-5.1	85	110	-$2
1st Half	1	0	11	36	33	6.54	6.41	2.08	985	400	1304	4.6	6.6	8.2	1.2	12%	40	44	16	40%	67%	25%	0	15			85	0.88	-11.8	50	65	-$6
2nd Half	1	4	0	33	38	2.20	2.91	1.16	508	361	621	3.6	4.1	10.5	2.5	15%	55	24	21	30%	79%	0%	0	14			0	0.93	6.7	110	142	$2
14 Proj	2	3	0	65	68	3.88	3.60	1.35	578	437	687	4.0	5.0	9.4	1.9	15%	47	24	29	29%	72%	9%	0						-0.1	58	75	-$1

Doolittle,Sean

Age: 27	Th: L	Role RP	Health A	LIMA Plan B+	
Ht: 6' 3"	Wt: 210	Type Pwr xFB	PT/Exp D	Rand Var -3	
			Consist A	MM 4321	

Second tour against MLB hitters wasn't as dominant as the first, but this was still a solid repeat. Dom drop was the biggest concern, though SwK remained steady and velocity actually improved. Elite Ctl and high FB% make him a good bet even with the lower Dom. If he can overcome the southpaw bias... UP: 30 SV.

Yr Tm	W	L	Sv	IP	K	ERA	xERA	WHIP	oOPS	vL	vR	BF/G	Ctl	Dom	Cmd	SwK	G	L	F	H%	S%	hr/f	GS	APC	DOM%	DIS%	Sv%	LI	RAR	BPV	BPX	R$
09																																
10																																
11																																
12 OAK	2	1	1	47	60	3.04	3.17	1.08	611	794	509	4.3	2.1	11.4	5.5	13%	35	15	50	33%	73%	5%	0	18			50	1.38	5.7	162	211	$3
13 OAK	5	5	2	69	60	3.13	3.55	0.96	573	516	603	3.8	1.7	7.8	4.6	12%	33	20	47	27%	68%	5%	0	15			29	1.21	6.3	106	138	$7
1st Half	3	2	0	37	33	3.19	3.44	0.98	588	638	556	3.9	1.5	8.1	5.5	11%	37	20	43	28%	70%	7%	0	15			0	1.09	3.1	121	157	$7
2nd Half	2	3	2	32	27	3.06	3.67	0.93	555	323	652	3.7	1.9	7.5	3.9	13%	28	20	52	26%	66%	2%	0	14			50	1.35	3.2	88	114	$7
14 Proj	4	4	10	73	67	3.09	3.36	1.06	639	670	622	4.0	1.9	8.3	4.4	13%	33	18	49	29%	73%	6%	0						7.0	110	143	$10

Doubront,Felix

Age: 26	Th: L	Role SP	Health B	LIMA Plan C	
Ht: 6' 2"	Wt: 225	Type Pwr	PT/Exp B	Rand Var 0	
			Consist B	MM 3303	

Limped to the finish line (9.77 ERA in September) as 2H skills fell flat for 2nd straight season. The bigger red flag here was the Dom plunge, making already shaky Ctl an even bigger liability. Hard to say if it's just a stamina issue, but if these 2H skills stick... DN: 5.00 ERA, and a spot in the bullpen.

Yr Tm	W	L	Sv	IP	K	ERA	xERA	WHIP	oOPS	vL	vR	BF/G	Ctl	Dom	Cmd	SwK	G	L	F	H%	S%	hr/f	GS	APC	DOM%	DIS%	Sv%	LI	RAR	BPV	BPX	R$
09 aa	8	6	0	121	85	4.35	4.94	1.61				20.6	4.0	6.3	1.6					34%	73%								-0.4	47	89	-$2
10 BOS *	10	5	2	105	83	3.58	4.09	1.48	789	576	911	15.6	3.7	7.1	1.9	7%	47	10	42	34%	75%	9%	3	35	0%	67%	67	0.97	6.5	72	117	$4
11 BOS *	3	5	1	86	63	5.22	5.03	1.50	952	1347	632	12.3	3.6	6.7	1.8	6%	44	28	28	32%	68%	11%	0	16			100	0.33	-13.5	40	60	-$6
12 BOS	11	10	0	161	167	4.86	3.91	1.45	775	760	781	24.4	4.0	9.3	2.4	10%	44	23	33	32%	70%	16%	29	99	45%	24%			-16.8	83	108	-$3
13 BOS	11	6	0	162	139	4.32	4.13	1.43	729	648	760	24.3	3.9	7.7	2.0	8%	46	20	34	32%	70%	8%	27	98	52%	22%	0	0.75	-9.2	56	74	-$1
1st Half	4	3	0	85	82	4.22	3.87	1.48	735	750	731	25.1	4.1	8.6	2.1	9%	47	22	30	34%	72%	9%	14	101	50%	14%	0	0.78	-3.7	70	90	-$2
2nd Half	7	3	0	77	57	4.44	4.41	1.38	721	565	798	23.5	3.7	6.7	1.8	7%	44	17	39	30%	68%	7%	13	95	54%	31%	0	0.73	-5.5	41	53	$0
14 Proj	11	8	0	162	146	4.35	3.82	1.43	742	678	768	23.1	4.0	8.1	2.0	9%	45	21	34	32%	71%	10%	34						-9.7	62	80	$1

Downs,Scott

Age: 38	Th: L	Role RP	Health D	LIMA Plan C	
Ht: 6' 2"	Wt: 220	Type Pwr xGB	PT/Exp D	Rand Var -3	
			Consist B	MM 4200	

There's not much to get excited about despite another sub-3.00 ERA. While it remains nearly impossible to hit a HR off him, Cmd trend suggests his period of dominance is coming to an end. Steady IP decline reflects nagging injuries and move to situational lefty role, so don't expect much more than a pile of holds from here.

Yr Tm	W	L	Sv	IP	K	ERA	xERA	WHIP	oOPS	vL	vR	BF/G	Ctl	Dom	Cmd	SwK	G	L	F	H%	S%	hr/f	GS	APC	DOM%	DIS%	Sv%	LI	RAR	BPV	BPX	R$
09 TOR	1	3	9	47	43	3.09	3.25	1.26	688	786	643	4.2	2.5	8.3	3.3	11%	56	21	24	32%	78%	12%	0	15			69	1.35	7.1	116	216	$5
10 TOR	5	5	0	61	48	2.64	3.12	0.99	584	488	637	3.6	2.1	7.0	3.4	7%	58	13	29	26%	74%	6%	0	14			0	1.37	10.9	107	174	$7
11 LAA	6	3	1	54	35	1.34	3.37	1.01	539	483	581	3.6	2.5	5.9	2.3	8%	63	15	22	24%	90%	8%	0	13			25	1.77	17.2	79	118	$8
12 LAA	1	1	9	46	32	3.15	3.88	1.31	658	488	813	3.4	3.4	6.3	1.9	10%	60	18	22	29%	77%	10%	0	12			75	1.26	4.9	61	80	$2
13 2 TM	4	4	0	43	37	2.49	3.30	1.48	694	630	757	2.8	3.9	7.7	1.9	10%	64	23	13	34%	83%	6%	0	10			0	1.40	7.3	74	96	$0
1st Half	1	2	0	22	17	1.61	3.16	1.25	619	414	801	2.8	3.2	6.9	2.1	9%	63	26	11	30%	86%	0%	0	11			0	1.54	6.2	77	100	$1
2nd Half	3	2	0	21	20	3.43	3.44	1.71	770	828	708	2.8	4.7	8.6	1.8	12%	66	20	15	38%	80%	11%	0	10			0	1.27	1.1	71	91	-$2
14 Proj	3	3	0	44	35	3.45	3.30	1.36	666	599	725	3.0	3.5	7.2	2.0	10%	63	20	18	31%	74%	9%	0						2.2	75	97	$0

Drabek,Kyle

Age: 26	Th: R	Role RP	Health F	LIMA Plan D+	
Ht: 6' 1"	Wt: 230	Type GB	PT/Exp D	Rand Var +5	
			Consist B	MM 2101	

0-0, 7.71 ERA in 2 IP at TOR. Brief return from Tommy John surgery didn't tell us much. Improved Ctl is worth noting, but we'll need to see a much larger sample before buying in. His pedigree merits a speculative flyer, but for now, it's looking less and less likely he'll meet those first-round expectations.

Yr Tm	W	L	Sv	IP	K	ERA	xERA	WHIP	oOPS	vL	vR	BF/G	Ctl	Dom	Cmd	SwK	G	L	F	H%	S%	hr/f	GS	APC	DOM%	DIS%	Sv%	LI	RAR	BPV	BPX	R$
09 aa	8	2	0	96	66	4.42	4.57	1.41				27.2	2.9	6.2	2.2					32%	71%								-1.2	52	97	$1
10 TOR *	14	12	0	179	127	3.32	3.33	1.26	781	744	913	24.3	3.5	6.4	1.8	13%	62	12	26	27%	75%	15%	3	87	33%	0%			16.8	63	102	$13
11 TOR *	9	9	0	154	89	6.43	6.54	1.89	857	924	766	21.9	5.3	5.2	1.0	8%	45	24	31	34%	67%	13%	14	82	14%	50%	0	0.68	-47.1	7	11	-$25
12 TOR	4	7	0	71	47	4.67	5.12	1.60	811	652	988	24.4	5.9	5.9	1.0	9%	54	18	28	27%	74%	16%	13	100	23%	38%			-5.7	-21	-28	-$7
13 TOR *	1	3	0	25	15	4.89	4.72	1.26	1136	629	1571	11.2	1.9	5.4	2.9	10%	50	25	25	28%	67%	50%	0	21			0	0.23	-3.1	43	56	-$4
1st Half																																
2nd Half	1	3	0	25	15	4.89	4.72	1.26	1136	629	1571	11.2	1.9	5.4	2.9	10%	50	25	25	28%	67%	50%	0	21			0	0.23	-3.1	43	56	-$4
14 Proj	5	7	0	87	55	4.59	4.29	1.50	806	742	883	18.0	3.9	5.7	1.5	9%	50	20	29	30%	71%	12%	17						-7.8	26	34	-$4

Duensing,Brian

Age: 31	Th: L	Role RP	Health A	LIMA Plan C	
Ht: 6' 0"	Wt: 205	Type	PT/Exp B	Rand Var +1	
			Consist A	MM 3200	

Moved to the bullpen full-time and posted his best ERA since '09. Dom spike was validated by nice rise in SwK, and xERA supported the overall performance. But rising OPS trend vL continued, and his age and skill history suggest regression is more likely than further growth.

Yr Tm	W	L	Sv	IP	K	ERA	xERA	WHIP	oOPS	vL	vR	BF/G	Ctl	Dom	Cmd	SwK	G	L	F	H%	S%	hr/f	GS	APC	DOM%	DIS%	Sv%	LI	RAR	BPV	BPX	R$
09 MIN *	9	8	0	159	88	4.79	4.70	1.52	700	579	742	18.7	2.9	5.0	1.7	8%	45	15	40	34%	68%	7%	9	55	33%	33%	0	0.76	-9.3	46	86	-$3
10 MIN	10	3	0	131	78	2.62	3.89	1.20	666	457	751	10.1	2.4	5.4	2.2	8%	53	16	31	28%	82%	9%	13	36	54%	8%	0	0.82	23.6	63	101	$12
11 MIN	9	14	0	162	115	5.23	4.26	1.52	833	522	947	22.2	2.9	6.4	2.2	8%	43	21	36	34%	67%	11%	28	83	50%	32%	0	0.71	-25.7	58	87	-$9
12 MIN	4	12	0	109	69	5.12	4.37	1.40	759	678	808	8.6	2.2	5.7	2.6	8%	47	20	33	33%	64%	8%	11	31	27%	45%	0	1.00	-14.8	67	88	-$7
13 MIN	6	2	1	61	56	3.98	3.89	1.48	750	786	713	3.7	3.2	8.3	2.5	11%	41	27	32	36%	73%	7%	0	14			25	1.25	-0.9	80	104	-$1
1st Half	2	1	1	28	26	3.81	3.99	1.45	663	657	667	3.3	3.5	8.3	2.4	10%	40	27	33	35%	73%	4%	0	12			33	1.35	0.2	72	94	-$1
2nd Half	4	1	0	33	30	4.13	3.80	1.50	825	914	745	4.1	3.0	8.3	2.7	12%	42	27	32	36%	74%	10%	0	16			0	1.14	-1.1	87	112	-$2
14 Proj	4	4	0	58	45	4.13	3.75	1.35	717	682	741	5.4	2.9	7.0	2.5	10%	44	23	33	32%	70%	8%	0						-1.9	71	92	-$1

Duffy,Danny

Age: 25	Th: L	Role SP	Health F	LIMA Plan D+	
Ht: 6' 3"	Wt: 200	Type Pwr FB	PT/Exp D	Rand Var -1	
			Consist A	MM 2303	

2-0, 1.85 ERA in 24 IP at KC. Returned in late May from TJS, only to return to the DL in September (forearm). Poor Ctl continues to undermine elite Dom and good raw stuff, and xERA shows that walks and high FB% won't lead him to much success. More risk than reward here as the health issues pile up.

Yr Tm	W	L	Sv	IP	K	ERA	xERA	WHIP	oOPS	vL	vR	BF/G	Ctl	Dom	Cmd	SwK	G	L	F	H%	S%	hr/f	GS	APC	DOM%	DIS%	Sv%	LI	RAR	BPV	BPX	R$
09																																
10 aa	5	2	0	40	34	3.17	3.59	1.24				23.0	1.9	7.7	4.1					33%	76%								4.5	116	187	$2
11 KC *	7	9	0	147	126	5.09	4.90	1.49	864	811	882	22.7	3.7	7.7	2.1	8%	38	22	40	33%	68%	11%	20	98	20%	25%			-20.8	54	81	-$7
12 KC	2	2	0	28	28	3.90	4.80	1.59	771	491	859	20.2	5.9	9.1	1.6	10%	35	21	44	32%	76%	6%	6	88	17%	50%			0.4	19	25	-$4
13 KC *	5	2	0	93	91	4.22	4.44	1.53	608	692	571	19.4	4.4	8.7	2.0	11%	32	27	41	34%	73%	0%	5	94	20%	60%			-4.1	74	96	-$4
1st Half	2	2	0	36	33	6.51	5.37	1.67				18.1	4.6	8.2	1.8					35%	61%	0%	0						-11.9	52	67	-$11
2nd Half	3	0	0	57	57	2.77	3.85	1.45	608	692	571	20.3	4.2	9.1	2.1	11%	32	27	41	34%	82%	0%	5	94	20%	60%			7.7	88	114	$1
14 Proj	7	8	0	145	132	4.39	4.07	1.45	785	822	771	20.8	4.0	8.2	2.0	10%	34	25	41	32%	72%	9%	30						-9.4	52	67	-$1

RYAN BLOOMFIELD

Dunn,Mike

Age: 29	Th: L	Role RP	Health A	LIMA Plan B+
Ht: 6' 0"	Wt: 205	Type Pwr FB	PT/Exp D	Rand Var -4
			Consist C	MM 4510

Is sudden 2H Ctl growth real? Spent the previous 4.5 years having trouble preventing walks; then in 2H RHers hit only .231 with only 14 UIBB in 130 AB against him. The realistic play is to assume some regression as 32 IP doesn't erase a career-to-date... but if it's not a mirage, UP: Late LIMA play with possible Save opps.

Yr Tm	W	L	Sv	IP	K	ERA	xERA	WHIP	oOPS	vL	vR	BF/G	Ctl	Dom	Cmd	SwK	G	L	F	H%	S%	hr/f	GS	APC	DOM%	DIS%	Sv%	LI	RAR	BPV	BPX	R$
09 NYY *	4	3	2	77	87	4.82	4.89	1.74	800	500	879	8.4	6.8	10.1	1.5	10%	40	30	30	35%	73%	33%	0	20			50	0.05	-4.7	71	133	-$3
10 ATL *	4	0	7	66	80	1.88	3.09	1.43	659	581	742	4.5	5.9	10.9	1.8	12%	34	18	48	32%	87%	5%	0	15			78	1.04	18.0	107	173	$8
11 FLA	5	6	0	63	68	3.43	3.84	1.30	723	615	809	3.7	4.4	9.7	2.2	12%	39	16	46	28%	79%	12%	0	16			0	1.20	4.0	72	109	$2
12 MIA *	1	4	1	62	67	5.20	5.19	1.78	806	784	828	3.9	5.4	9.8	1.8	8%	34	28	38	39%	69%	6%	0	15			14	1.11	-9.0	79	103	-$10
13 MIA	3	4	2	68	72	2.66	3.73	1.20	604	549	655	3.8	3.7	9.6	2.6	12%	40	18	43	29%	80%	7%	0	16			40	1.26	10.1	90	117	$5
1st Half	2	2	1	36	34	2.75	4.29	1.39	636	609	664	3.8	4.8	8.5	1.8	12%	44	15	41	30%	81%	5%	0	16			50	1.31	5.0	47	61	$3
2nd Half	1	2	1	32	38	2.56	3.15	0.98	565	466	645	3.7	2.6	10.8	4.2	13%	34	21	45	27%	79%	9%	0	16			33	1.20	5.1	137	178	$6
14 Proj	**2**	**4**	**2**	**57**	**61**	**3.16**	**3.53**	**1.27**	**642**	**595**	**687**	**3.8**	**4.0**	**9.7**	**2.4**	**11%**	**36**	**21**	**42**	**30%**	**77%**	**7%**	**0**						**4.9**	**80**	**104**	**$3**

Eovaldi,Nathan

Age: 24	Th: R	Role SP	Health D	LIMA Plan B
Ht: 6' 2"	Wt: 210	Type	PT/Exp C	Rand Var -2
			Consist C	MM 3203

Nice results for a young pitcher, but run-of-the-mill skills set belies his surface stats. 1st half ERA driven by outlying hit/strand rates; 2nd half a better guideline. Young enough to get better, has huge fastball but not many Ks, so must keep whittling bb% to succeed. Heed xERA; for now he's a back-end SP.

Yr Tm	W	L	Sv	IP	K	ERA	xERA	WHIP	oOPS	vL	vR	BF/G	Ctl	Dom	Cmd	SwK	G	L	F	H%	S%	hr/f	GS	APC	DOM%	DIS%	Sv%	LI	RAR	BPV	BPX	R$
09																																
10																																
11 LA *	7	7	0	138	109	2.84	2.53	1.21	667	735	619	18.5	3.9	7.1	1.8	10%	41	26	34	27%	76%	6%	6	60	33%	17%	0	0.63	18.7	84	127	$11
12 2 NL *	6	15	0	154	104	4.11	4.40	1.46	771	845	665	21.3	3.5	6.1	1.7	8%	46	23	31	32%	73%	8%	22	94	32%	36%			-1.9	52	67	-$4
13 MIA	4	6	0	106	78	3.39	4.21	1.32	681	665	691	25.1	3.4	6.6	2.0	8%	44	22	34	30%	75%	6%	18	94	67%	17%			6.3	49	64	$2
1st Half	1	0	0	18	10	2.00	4.07	0.94	557	489	626	23.0	3.0	5.0	1.7	9%	45	22	33	18%	87%	12%	3	86	67%	0%			4.1	32	42	$2
2nd Half	3	6	0	88	68	3.67	4.23	1.39	703	706	700	25.5	3.5	6.9	2.0	8%	44	22	34	32%	74%	5%	15	96	67%	20%			2.2	53	68	$2
14 Proj	**7**	**10**	**0**	**161**	**116**	**3.82**	**3.95**	**1.30**	**689**	**717**	**660**	**22.0**	**3.5**	**6.5**	**1.9**	**9%**	**44**	**23**	**33**	**28%**	**72%**	**8%**	**30**						**1.0**	**46**	**59**	**$5**

Erlin,Robert

Age: 23	Th: L	Role SP	Health A	LIMA Plan B
Ht: 5' 11"	Wt: 190	Type Pwr	PT/Exp D	Rand Var 0
			Consist A	MM 3303

3-3, 4.23 ERA in 55 IP at SD. Showed why he has been a hot prospect with 114 BPV in Sept. Lefties hit him hard in SD; oddly, he had this reverse split was throughout minors too. Still, SP with 100+ BPVs don't grow on trees. Likely needs more seasoning, but could come quickly if he solves LH batters... UP: 12 Wins, 3.50 ERA.

Yr Tm	W	L	Sv	IP	K	ERA	xERA	WHIP	oOPS	vL	vR	BF/G	Ctl	Dom	Cmd	SwK	G	L	F	H%	S%	hr/f	GS	APC	DOM%	DIS%	Sv%	LI	RAR	BPV	BPX	R$
09																																
10																																
11 aa	6	2	0	93	84	3.23	3.69	1.17				21.8	1.0	8.2	8.3					34%	75%								8.1	199	300	$6
12 aa	3	1	0	52	65	2.76	3.77	1.26				19.4	2.2	11.1	5.1					37%	81%								8.1	152	198	$2
13 SD *	11	6	0	154	114	4.34	4.57	1.44	698	823	641	21.1	2.6	6.7	2.5	7%	37	25	37	34%	71%	10%	9	82	33%	22%	0	0.63	-9.1	65	85	-$2
1st Half	7	2	0	73	60	4.41	4.62	1.40	715	815	630	19.3	2.5	7.3	2.9	4%	30	36	34	33%	71%	13%	2	57	50%	0%	0	0.37	-4.9	71	92	$1
2nd Half	4	4	0	81	54	4.28	4.52	1.47	690	827	643	23.1	2.8	6.1	2.2	8%	40	21	39	34%	71%	9%	7	97	29%	29%			-4.1	61	79	-$4
14 Proj	**9**	**6**	**0**	**142**	**122**	**3.85**	**3.66**	**1.30**	**706**	**819**	**648**	**20.5**	**2.8**	**7.8**	**2.8**	**7%**	**38**	**24**	**38**	**31%**	**72%**	**9%**	**28**						**0.2**	**81**	**105**	**$6**

Estrada,Marco

Age: 30	Th: R	Role SP	Health F	LIMA Plan B+
Ht: 5' 11"	Wt: 200	Type Pwr xFB	PT/Exp B	Rand Var +1
			Consist A	MM 4403

Hamstring injury cost him a third of the season. When he returned, dominant 2H 2013 mirrored superb 2H 2012, so he's showed plus-plus ability twice. Flyball pitcher in a hitter's park led to ERA-damaging HR in 1H, but these BPIs command our full attention. On the cusp of the next level... UP: 15 wins, 3.25 ERA, 180 K.

Yr Tm	W	L	Sv	IP	K	ERA	xERA	WHIP	oOPS	vL	vR	BF/G	Ctl	Dom	Cmd	SwK	G	L	F	H%	S%	hr/f	GS	APC	DOM%	DIS%	Sv%	LI	RAR	BPV	BPX	R$
09 WAS *	9	6	0	144	85	5.01	4.93	1.49	741	1000	556	20.0	2.5	5.3	2.1	10%	37	5	58	33%	67%	9%	1	38	0%	100%	0	0.50	-12.2	46	87	-$3
10 MIL *	1	2	0	51	40	5.00	3.73	1.31	908	1348	571	15.2	3.1	7.0	2.2	12%	29	14	57	30%	62%	15%	1	34	0%	100%	0	0.60	-5.8	71	115	-$3
11 MIL	4	8	0	93	88	4.08	3.60	1.21	700	661	733	8.9	2.8	8.5	3.0	11%	40	18	43	29%	69%	10%	7	36	86%	0%	0	0.66	-1.6	96	144	$2
12 MIL	5	7	0	138	143	3.64	3.59	1.14	703	728	681	19.4	1.9	9.3	4.9	11%	34	20	45	31%	73%	10%	23	77	48%	26%	0	0.71	6.3	129	168	$9
13 MIL	7	4	0	128	118	3.87	3.60	1.08	670	651	687	24.4	2.0	8.3	4.1	11%	38	18	44	27%	70%	12%	21	95	62%	14%			0.0	110	144	$8
1st Half	4	4	0	69	62	5.32	3.94	1.36	817	717	905	24.9	2.3	8.0	3.4	11%	40	18	42	32%	66%	16%	12	95	42%	25%			-12.5	100	129	-$1
2nd Half	3	0	0	59	56	2.15	3.20	0.75	467	557	389	23.7	1.7	8.6	5.1	12%	34	18	48	20%	77%	7%	9	95	89%	0%			12.4	121	157	$18
14 Proj	**8**	**7**	**0**	**174**	**163**	**3.57**	**3.37**	**1.12**	**678**	**684**	**671**	**17.4**	**2.2**	**8.4**	**3.9**	**11%**	**36**	**19**	**45**	**29%**	**73%**	**10%**	**29**						**6.3**	**108**	**140**	**$14**

Familia,Jeurys

Age: 24	Th: R	Role RP	Health F	LIMA Plan C
Ht: 6' 4"	Wt: 230	Type Pwr	PT/Exp D	Rand Var -2
			Consist B	MM 3300

2011 MLEs show his potential, but 2012 was poor and 2013 was a lost year as he hurt his arm in May, had elbow surgery in July, and pitched just one inning in 2H. Rushed by the Mets (Rushed? By the Mets? Really?!), he needs more seasoning. Likely two years away from fanalytic value; sooner if he finds Ctl.

Yr Tm	W	L	Sv	IP	K	ERA	xERA	WHIP	oOPS	vL	vR	BF/G	Ctl	Dom	Cmd	SwK	G	L	F	H%	S%	hr/f	GS	APC	DOM%	DIS%	Sv%	LI	RAR	BPV	BPX	R$
09																																
10																																
11 aa	4	4	0	88	80	3.33	3.84	1.31				21.3	3.1	8.3	2.7					31%	77%								6.6	84	127	$3
12 NYM *	9	9	0	149	122	5.10	4.73	1.64	644	751	560	18.5	4.7	7.3	1.6	9%	48	18	33	35%	68%	0%	1	26	0%	100%	0	0.13	-19.9	61	79	-$12
13 NYM	0	0	1	11	8	4.22	5.79	1.97	908	889	918	5.8	7.6	6.8	0.9	7%	52	15	33	31%	84%	18%	0	22			100	0.69	-0.5	-54	-70	-$5
1st Half	0	0	1	10	7	3.48	5.17	1.65	852	779	892	5.9	6.1	6.1	1.0	7%	52	16	32	27%	87%	20%	0	22			100	0.76	0.5	-25	-33	-$5
2nd Half	0	0	0	0	1	27.00	109.22	12.00	1467	2000	1167	5.0	54.0	27.0	0.5	5%	50	0	50	103%	75%	0%	0	19			0	0.09	-1.0	-944	-1222	-$7
14 Proj	**2**	**2**	**0**	**44**	**37**	**4.39**	**3.92**	**1.51**				**19.5**	**4.0**	**7.7**	**1.9**	**0%**	**50**	**16**	**34**	**34%**	**71%**	**7%**	**9**						**-2.8**	**58**	**75**	**-$3**

Farquhar,Daniel

Age: 27	Th: R	Role RP	Health A	LIMA Plan B
Ht: 5' 10"	Wt: 180	Type Pwr	PT/Exp D	Rand Var +2
			Consist C	MM 5530

0-3, 4.20 ERA with 16 Sv in 55 IP at SEA. A younger Jason Grilli? Inherited the SEA closer role when everyone else stunk. Has the right profile with the big Dom and mastery of RH batters. Unlucky S% should regress, and xERA says he can get even better. If Dom sticks, only borderline Ctl keeps him from the top tier of closers.

Yr Tm	W	L	Sv	IP	K	ERA	xERA	WHIP	oOPS	vL	vR	BF/G	Ctl	Dom	Cmd	SwK	G	L	F	H%	S%	hr/f	GS	APC	DOM%	DIS%	Sv%	LI	RAR	BPV	BPX	R$
09 aa	1	4	15	46	47	3.25	3.43	1.53				5.4	6.4	9.2	1.4					31%	78%								6.1	88	164	$5
10 aa	4	3	17	77	69	3.79	2.95	1.24				5.9	4.7	8.1	1.7					24%	71%								2.7	74	120	$10
11 TOR *	4	5	15	62	45	4.05	4.79	1.55	1170	1750	829	4.7	3.0	6.6	2.2	5%	25	50	25	36%	74%	0%	0	14			83	0.01	-0.8	65	97	$3
12 a/a	3	3	9	68	60	2.85	2.42	1.11				6.1	2.8	7.9	2.8					28%	74%								9.7	107	140	$8
13 SEA *	0	4	22	76	104	3.70	2.55	1.17	586	485	695	4.9	3.1	12.4	4.0	14%	42	25	33	35%	67%	5%	0	20			81	1.18	1.6	158	206	$10
1st Half	0	1	6	39	53	4.14	3.22	1.21	673	494	844	5.9	2.5	12.1	4.8	14%	40	33	28	37%	66%	17%	0	28			67	1.12	-1.3	160	208	$5
2nd Half	0	3	16	36	51	3.22	2.78	1.13	540	480	608	4.4	3.7	12.6	3.4	14%	43	22	35	34%	68%	0%	0	18			89	1.20	2.9	148	192	$15
14 Proj	**2**	**4**	**30**	**65**	**73**	**3.48**	**3.06**	**1.23**	**645**	**529**	**767**	**5.1**	**3.3**	**10.1**	**3.0**	**14%**	**42**	**26**	**32**	**32%**	**73%**	**9%**	**0**						**3.1**	**112**	**145**	**$14**

Feldman,Scott

Age: 31	Th: R	Role SP	Health D	LIMA Plan B
Ht: 6' 7"	Wt: 230	Type	PT/Exp B	Rand Var 0
			Consist A	MM 3103

Shaved more than a run off 2012 ERA even as walk and strikeout rates both went in wrong direction. Thank you, hit/strand rate (over-)correction. He did keep ball on ground... except when it flew out of park. Free agent with little margin for error, he could use a home that suppresses HR. If he lands in hitter's park, avoid.

Yr Tm	W	L	Sv	IP	K	ERA	xERA	WHIP	oOPS	vL	vR	BF/G	Ctl	Dom	Cmd	SwK	G	L	F	H%	S%	hr/f	GS	APC	DOM%	DIS%	Sv%	LI	RAR	BPV	BPX	R$
09 TEX	17	8	0	190	113	4.08	4.33	1.28	693	660	733	23.3	3.1	5.4	1.7	7%	47	21	33	27%	70%	9%	31	94	35%	13%	0	0.76	5.6	38	72	$13
10 TEX	7	11	0	141	75	5.48	4.87	1.60	849	790	904	22.1	2.9	4.8	1.7	6%	43	20	37	34%	67%	10%	22	83	27%	36%	0	0.73	-24.4	30	48	-$10
11 TEX *	5	2	0	82	45	4.76	4.63	1.39	614	391	837	16.4	2.4	5.0	2.0	8%	62	13	25	31%	68%	13%	2	46	50%	0%	0	0.39	-8.2	40	60	-$3
12 TEX	6	11	0	124	96	5.09	4.12	1.38	745	752	736	18.5	2.3	7.0	3.0	8%	42	26	32	33%	64%	11%	21	73	38%	33%	0	0.71	-16.5	83	108	-$6
13 2 TM	12	12	0	182	132	3.86	3.85	1.18	671	672	670	25.3	2.8	6.5	2.4	8%	50	19	32	27%	70%	11%	30	100	50%	17%			0.0	71	92	$9
1st Half	7	6	0	91	67	3.46	3.75	1.14	656	611	699	25.1	2.5	6.6	2.7	7%	51	16	33	27%	73%	11%	15	101	53%	13%			4.5	81	105	$13
2nd Half	5	6	0	91	65	4.27	3.95	1.22	685	726	638	25.5	3.1	6.5	2.1	8%	49	21	30	27%	67%	11%	15	99	47%	20%			-4.5	60	77	$5
14 Proj	**10**	**11**	**0**	**174**	**121**	**4.28**	**3.82**	**1.30**	**723**	**694**	**756**	**24.2**	**2.8**	**6.3**	**2.3**	**8%**	**47**	**20**	**33**	**29%**	**69%**	**11%**	**30**						**-8.9**	**63**	**82**	**$4**

JOSH PALEY

Feliz,Neftali

Age: 26 Th: R Role RP	Health F	LIMA Plan C	
Ht: 6' 3" Wt: 225 Type Pwr xFB	PT/Exp C	Rand Var -5	
	Consist A	MM 3410	

Conventional wisdom is that a starter is more valuable than a reliever, due to higher IP totals. Superb as reliever, he blew out his elbow as as SP in 2012 and had Tommy John surgery. Assuming a relief role re-sets his Cmd to 2009-10 levels, he's a buy-low candidate. But that Health grade casts a large shadow.

Yr Tm	W	L	Sv	IP	K	ERA	xERA	WHIP	oOPS	vL	vR	BF/G	Ctl	Dom	Cmd	SwK	G	L	F	H%	S%	hr/f	GS	APC	DOM%	DIS%	Sv%	LI	RAR	BPV	BPX	R$
09 TEX *	5	6	2	108	104	3.72	2.89	1.23	416	533	274	9.7	3.2	8.7	2.7	11%	38	5	57	31%	69%	5%	0	25			67	1.50	8.1	105	197	$8
10 TEX	4	3	40	69	71	2.73	3.28	0.88	516	409	616	3.8	2.3	9.2	3.9	12%	37	15	48	23%	71%	6%	0	15			93	1.27	11.6	118	191	$25
11 TEX	2	3	32	62	54	2.74	4.16	1.16	598	561	644	3.9	4.3	7.8	1.8	12%	37	16	46	24%	78%	5%	0	17			84	1.10	9.2	38	58	$16
12 TEX	3	1	0	43	37	3.16	4.62	1.20	623	616	631	21.9	4.9	7.8	1.6	10%	37	15	48	22%	78%	9%	7	92	57%	14%	0	0.74	4.5	24	32	$1
13 TEX	0	0	0	5	4	0.00	4.72	1.50	659	629	665	3.5	3.9	7.7	2.0	9%	21	29	50	35%	100%	0%	0	18			0	0.75	2.2	34	44	-$4
1st Half																																
2nd Half	0	0	0	5	4	0.00	4.72	1.50	659	629	665	3.5	3.9	7.7	2.0	9%	21	29	50	35%	100%	0%	0	18			0	0.75	2.2	34	44	-$4
14 Proj	3	2	3	56	52	3.50	3.84	1.24	690	654	730	6.0	3.6	8.4	2.3	11%	37	14	49	28%	75%	7%	0						2.5	69	90	$2

Fernandez,Jose

Age: 21 Th: R Role SP	Health A	LIMA Plan C	
Ht: 6' 2" Wt: 240 Type Pwr	PT/Exp D	Rand Var -5	
	Consist F	MM 5505	

He is the very model of a modern Cuban pitcherman. xERA and RandVar point to regression, but even a flat-3.00 ERA would have been awesome. Dazzling across-the-board skills even got better in 2H. Has "multiple Cy Young awards" upside, but the lack of a pre-2013 track record is the one red flag here, and it's a biggie.

Yr Tm	W	L	Sv	IP	K	ERA	xERA	WHIP	oOPS	vL	vR	BF/G	Ctl	Dom	Cmd	SwK	G	L	F	H%	S%	hr/f	GS	APC	DOM%	DIS%	Sv%	LI	RAR	BPV	BPX	R$
09																																
10																																
11																																
12																																
13 MIA	12	6	0	173	187	2.19	3.06	0.98	522	546	494	24.3	3.0	9.7	3.2	11%	45	22	33	25%	80%	7%	28	93	75%	14%			35.7	117	152	$28
1st Half	4	4	0	85	84	2.98	3.50	1.12	571	593	537	23.1	3.4	8.9	2.6	9%	43	23	34	27%	75%	8%	15	88	60%	27%			9.3	90	116	$18
2nd Half	8	2	0	88	103	1.43	2.65	0.84	471	485	459	25.7	2.7	10.5	4.0	12%	47	20	32	23%	86%	6%	13	99	92%	0%			26.4	143	186	$38
14 Proj	16	9	0	193	204	3.07	2.95	1.08	592	616	564	24.5	3.0	9.5	3.2	11%	46	21	33	28%	73%	8%	31						18.9	115	150	$25

Fields,Joshua

Age: 28 Th: R Role RP	Health A	LIMA Plan D+	
Ht: 6' 0" Wt: 180 Type Pwr xFB	PT/Exp D	Rand Var +1	
	Consist B	MM 2420	

The formula for a stud power hitter is lots of HR and walks. The formula for making average hitters look like stud power hitters is FB pitcher whose wildness leads to grooving fat pitches. Nice Dom offers hope, and hr/f should normalize, but needs Ctl around 3.0—a neighborhood he has rarely visited—to emerge as an asset.

Yr Tm	W	L	Sv	IP	K	ERA	xERA	WHIP	oOPS	vL	vR	BF/G	Ctl	Dom	Cmd	SwK	G	L	F	H%	S%	hr/f	GS	APC	DOM%	DIS%	Sv%	LI	RAR	BPV	BPX	R$
09 aa	2	2	1	33	31	8.32	5.49	1.87				5.0	6.4	8.5	1.3					37%	52%								-16.4	57	107	-$8
10 aa	1	1	6	29	24	3.47	2.62	1.38				5.7	5.7	7.4	1.3					27%	72%								2.2	85	138	$1
11 a/a	4	2	4	56	50	4.81	4.16	1.63				6.6	7.1	8.0	1.1					28%	71%								-6.1	59	89	-$3
12 a/a	4	3	12	58	60	2.98	3.30	1.23				5.6	3.2	9.3	2.9					30%	79%								7.5	100	131	$8
13 HOU	1	3	5	38	40	4.97	4.11	1.29	783	884	706	3.9	4.3	9.5	2.2	10%	37	11	52	26%	68%	16%	0	16			83	1.11	-5.2	70	92	-$2
1st Half	0	0	0	10	7	4.35	3.93	0.97	694	455	784	3.4	0.9	6.1	7.0	8%	45	6	48	24%	63%	13%	0	12			0	0.46	-0.6	110	142	-$4
2nd Half	1	3	5	28	33	5.20	4.19	1.41	816	973	661	4.1	5.5	10.7	1.9	11%	33	14	53	26%	70%	17%	0	17			83	1.38	-4.6	55	72	-$1
14 Proj	3	4	13	51	51	4.37	4.25	1.42	710	838	585	5.1	4.9	9.1	1.9	11%	33	17	49	29%	72%	8%	0						-3.2	43	56	$3

Fien,Casey

Age: 30 Th: R Role RP	Health A	LIMA Plan A	
Ht: 6' 2" Wt: 205 Type Pwr xFB	PT/Exp D	Rand Var +3	
	Consist F	MM 4510	

Check out that out-of-nowhere Dom, SwK spike. Credit likely belongs to a new, nasty changeup. Unlucky 2H hr/f damaged his ERA, but everything else looks terrific. 2H GB% was new and pairs very nicely with suddenly-elite Cmd. Gopheritis and comparative struggles vR are concerns, but this version is potentially closer-worthy.

Yr Tm	W	L	Sv	IP	K	ERA	xERA	WHIP	oOPS	vL	vR	BF/G	Ctl	Dom	Cmd	SwK	G	L	F	H%	S%	hr/f	GS	APC	DOM%	DIS%	Sv%	LI	RAR	BPV	BPX	R$
09 DET *	2	2	14	69	60	5.43	4.99	1.48	914	771	996	5.8	3.0	7.8	2.6	6%	29	18	53	34%	65%	10%	0	23			74	0.47	-9.4	65	122	$2
10 DET *	3	3	8	65	33	3.70	4.98	1.32	1364	1400	1333	5.8	1.9	4.6	2.4	4%	36	18	45	29%	80%	40%	0	23			80	0.11	3.0	28	45	$3
11 aaa	2	2	3	24	19	6.01	8.36	1.78				5.3	3.2	6.9	2.1					34%	78%								-6.2	-19	-28	-$4
12 MIN *	4	6	9	81	63	4.40	3.86	1.27	578	491	638	4.9	2.9	7.0	2.4	10%	25	25	51	29%	68%	6%	0	17			75	0.98	-3.8	68	88	$2
13 MIN	5	2	0	62	73	3.92	2.93	1.02	627	750	545	3.3	1.7	10.6	6.1	15%	37	20	42	29%	67%	14%	0	13			0	1.25	-0.4	159	207	$3
1st Half	1	2	0	33	36	3.58	3.11	0.89	552	653	503	3.4	1.9	9.9	5.1	16%	32	21	47	24%	64%	11%	0	14			0	1.57	1.1	137	177	$4
2nd Half	4	0	0	29	37	4.30	2.72	1.16	704	817	601	3.3	1.5	11.4	7.4	14%	42	20	38	34%	69%	17%	0	13			0	0.92	-1.6	183	237	$3
14 Proj	4	3	5	65	68	3.25	3.27	1.16	677	722	645	4.0	2.4	9.4	3.9	13%	33	22	45	30%	77%	11%	0						4.9	115	149	$6

Fife,Stephen

Age: 27 Th: R Role SP	Health D	LIMA Plan D+	
Ht: 6' 3" Wt: 220 Type GB	PT/Exp D	Rand Var +2	
	Consist B	MM 2100	

4-4, 3.86 ERA in 58 IP at LA. On the plus side, he keeps the ball on the ground... and that's it for that side of the ledger. Subpar numbers abound, and marginal Dom with high hr/f spelled disaster. He's not young enough to be considered a prospect, and these skills can't keep him in the majors. Avoid.

Yr Tm	W	L	Sv	IP	K	ERA	xERA	WHIP	oOPS	vL	vR	BF/G	Ctl	Dom	Cmd	SwK	G	L	F	H%	S%	hr/f	GS	APC	DOM%	DIS%	Sv%	LI	RAR	BPV	BPX	R$
09																																
10 aa	8	6	0	136	67	5.45	4.93	1.53				22.8	3.0	4.4	1.5					32%	64%								-23.0	31	50	-$8
11 aa	14	4	0	137	77	3.96	4.55	1.50				23.7	3.2	5.1	1.6					33%	74%								-0.2	44	66	$1
12 LA *	11	9	0	162	95	3.99	4.68	1.48	695	660	731	23.2	2.9	5.3	1.8	8%	41	24	36	33%	74%	7%	5	84	40%	20%			0.4	45	58	-$2
13 LA *	6	8	0	96	71	4.74	5.61	1.69	815	831	795	19.6	3.8	6.7	1.7	7%	52	22	26	36%	73%	15%	10	80	30%	30%	0	0.74	-10.3	42	54	-$9
1st Half	4	3	0	55	46	3.33	4.47	1.37	730	668	816	23.1	2.3	7.5	3.3	7%	51	19	29	34%	79%	15%	7	87	43%	14%			3.6	83	108	$0
2nd Half	2	5	0	41	25	6.63	7.15	2.12	969	1158	758	16.7	5.9	5.5	0.9	6%	53	26	21	38%	68%	14%	3	69	0%	67%	0	0.69	-13.9	13	17	-$21
14 Proj	4	4	0	58	37	4.79	4.27	1.65	779	869	670	20.6	3.8	5.7	1.5	7%	52	24	24	34%	72%	11%	13						-6.6	31	40	-$6

Figaro,Alfredo

Age: 29 Th: R Role RP	Health C	LIMA Plan C	
Ht: 6' 0" Wt: 175 Type Con	PT/Exp C	Rand Var +3	
	Consist A	MM 3101	

Finesse pitcher has terrific control to produce groundballs and offset lack of Ks. Unlucky 1H hr/f had to come down and did; lucky 2H H% has to go up and will. Spent 2011/2012 in Japan, but nothing he did there suggested this Cmd. His ability to stay in the bigs depends on top-tier Ctl. Make him show it again.

Yr Tm	W	L	Sv	IP	K	ERA	xERA	WHIP	oOPS	vL	vR	BF/G	Ctl	Dom	Cmd	SwK	G	L	F	H%	S%	hr/f	GS	APC	DOM%	DIS%	Sv%	LI	RAR	BPV	BPX	R$
09 DET *	8	5	0	97	71	4.98	4.78	1.44	922	1301	705	19.7	3.2	6.6	2.1	9%	31	24	44	31%	68%	13%	3	63	33%	33%	0	0.53	-7.9	47	87	-$1
10 DET *	10	8	0	139	91	5.48	6.12	1.74	871	820	902	20.4	3.2	5.9	1.9	4%	36	26	38	37%	69%	5%	1	30	0%	100%	0	0.76	-24.0	37	59	-$11
11 for	8	6	0	124	85	4.24	4.51	1.45				22.1	3.2	6.2	1.9					32%	72%								-4.5	51	77	-$1
12 for	0	5	0	64	35	3.84	4.52	1.39				24.5	3.3	4.9	1.5					28%	76%								1.4	28	36	-$4
13 MIL	3	3	1	74	54	4.14	3.78	1.24	766	773	760	9.6	1.8	6.6	3.6	8%	49	19	32	29%	75%	20%	5	36	20%	40%	100	0.66	-2.5	96	125	-$1
1st Half	1	2	0	54	44	4.64	3.75	1.33	813	848	783	11.3	2.0	7.3	3.7	8%	48	19	33	30%	75%	23%	5	42	20%	40%	0	0.65	-5.2	104	134	-$2
2nd Half	2	1	1	20	10	2.75	3.87	1.02	626	584	678	6.6	1.4	4.6	3.3	8%	50	20	30	25%	78%	11%	0	25			100	0.67	2.7	73	95	$3
14 Proj	4	4	0	75	47	3.86	3.83	1.29	735	703	768	11.6	2.5	5.6	2.3	8%	49	20	31	29%	75%	14%	4						0.1	62	80	$0

Fister,Doug

Age: 30 Th: R Role SP	Health B	LIMA Plan B+	
Ht: 6' 8" Wt: 210 Type GB	PT/Exp A	Rand Var +1	
	Consist A	MM 4205	

13 HBP in 1H inflated his ERA. OK, maybe not, but they left plenty of bruises. Stopped hitting people in 2H, but experienced career-worst Ctl and suddenly had trouble with LH batters. Despite lofty BPV, pitch-to-contact profile is a risky way to roll. Split the 2012/2013 difference, but if 2H "wildness" persists... DN: 4.00+ ERA.

Yr Tm	W	L	Sv	IP	K	ERA	xERA	WHIP	oOPS	vL	vR	BF/G	Ctl	Dom	Cmd	SwK	G	L	F	H%	S%	hr/f	GS	APC	DOM%	DIS%	Sv%	LI	RAR	BPV	BPX	R$
09 SEA *	10	8	0	173	108	4.30	5.20	1.43	781	786	775	21.0	1.4	5.6	3.9	7%	41	20	39	34%	73%	14%	10	87	50%	20%	0	0.70	0.4	75	140	$3
10 SEA	6	14	0	171	93	4.11	4.13	1.28	698	710	685	25.7	1.7	4.9	2.9	5%	47	18	35	31%	68%	6%	28	96	39%	18%			-0.6	68	109	$4
11 2 AL	11	13	0	216	146	2.83	3.54	1.06	617	642	586	27.3	1.5	6.1	3.9	7%	48	20	32	28%	74%	5%	31	100	65%	3%	0	0.77	29.7	94	141	$23
12 DET	10	10	0	162	137	3.45	3.45	1.19	683	734	611	25.9	2.1	7.6	3.7	8%	51	22	27	31%	74%	12%	26	97	50%	23%			11.2	111	144	$12
13 DET	14	9	0	209	159	3.67	3.38	1.31	710	687	738	26.7	1.9	6.9	3.6	8%	54	21	24	33%	73%	9%	32	102	63%	13%	0	0.80	5.1	104	136	$8
1st Half	6	5	0	103	80	3.50	3.09	1.20	667	562	786	26.9	1.4	7.0	5.0	9%	57	22	22	33%	70%	6%	16	104	69%	25%			4.7	123	159	$12
2nd Half	8	4	0	106	79	3.83	3.68	1.41	750	796	687	26.5	2.4	6.7	2.8	8%	52	21	27	34%	75%	11%	16	100	56%	0%	0	0.82	0.4	87	112	$5
14 Proj	12	10	0	189	142	3.56	3.33	1.26	700	712	684	25.5	1.9	6.8	3.6	8%	51	21	28	32%	73%	9%	30						7.2	100	129	$11

JOSH PALEY

Floyd,Gavin

Age: 31	Th: R	Role SP	Health	F	LIMA Plan	C		
Ht: 6' 6"	Wt: 235	Type Pwr	PT/Exp	B	Rand Var	+5		
			Consist	A	MM	3301		

Already had a history of elbow injury from 2012, so Tommy John surgery in May was not a huge surprise. His command was good back when he was healthy, with xERAs in the 3.70 range and actual ERAs inflated by home park. Free agent; expect return around All-Star Break, but probably will spend 2H working off the rust.

Yr	Tm	W	L	Sv	IP	K	ERA	xERA	WHIP	oOPS	vL	vR	BF/G	Ctl	Dom	Cmd	SwK	G	L	F	H%	S%	hr/f	GS	APC	DOM%	DIS%	Sv%	LI	RAR	BPV	BPX	R$
09	CHW	11	11	0	193	163	4.06	3.73	1.23	680	680	679	26.6	2.8	7.6	2.8	10%	44	22	33	29%	69%	11%	30	99	53%	13%			6.3	85	158	$14
10	CHW	10	13	0	187	151	4.08	3.73	1.37	719	673	775	25.7	2.8	7.3	2.6	9%	50	18	32	33%	71%	8%	31	97	61%	10%			-0.1	83	135	$5
11	CHW	12	13	0	194	151	4.37	3.66	1.16	685	764	572	25.7	2.1	7.0	3.4	9%	44	19	37	29%	65%	10%	30	97	57%	13%	0	0.83	-10.2	92	138	$8
12	CHW	12	11	0	168	144	4.29	4.05	1.36	755	871	633	25.0	3.4	7.7	2.3	10%	47	18	35	30%	72%	13%	29	95	48%	24%			-5.6	73	95	$2
13	CHW	0	4	0	24	25	5.18	3.83	1.60	893	940	836	22.0	4.4	9.2	2.1	11%	50	21	29	35%	71%	20%	5	84	40%	40%			-3.9	75	97	-$6
1st Half		0	4	0	24	25	5.18	3.83	1.60	893	940	836	22.0	4.4	9.2	2.1	11%	50	21	29	35%	71%	20%	5	84	40%	40%			-3.9	75	97	-$6
2nd Half																																	
14	Proj	6	5	0	87	75	4.21	3.70	1.36	750	799	689	23.7	3.5	7.7	2.2	10%	47	20	33	30%	72%	13%	15						-3.7	69	89	$0

Francisco,Frank

Age: 34	Th: R	Role RP	Health	F	LIMA Plan	C		
Ht: 6' 2"	Wt: 250	Type Pwr FB	PT/Exp	C	Rand Var	0		
			Consist	B	MM	3500		

Had elbow problems most of the year, but doctors could not find structural damage. Cortisone injections didn't help him to return quickly. Still sports a high Dom when healthy, but he's an enormous injury risk whose Cmd trend is distinct, downward, and destructive. Fanalytically, he's high risk/low reward. Avoid.

Yr	Tm	W	L	Sv	IP	K	ERA	xERA	WHIP	oOPS	vL	vR	BF/G	Ctl	Dom	Cmd	SwK	G	L	F	H%	S%	hr/f	GS	APC	DOM%	DIS%	Sv%	LI	RAR	BPV	BPX	R$
09	TEX	2	3	25	49	57	3.83	3.56	1.11	639	637	643	4.0	2.7	10.4	3.8	11%	29	21	50	29%	69%	9%	0	16			86	1.07	3.0	120	225	$13
10	TEX	6	4	2	53	60	3.76	3.33	1.27	681	549	765	3.9	3.1	10.3	3.3	12%	39	20	40	33%	73%	9%	0	16			33	1.24	2.1	119	192	$3
11	TOR	1	4	17	51	53	3.55	3.62	1.32	721	819	568	4.0	3.2	9.4	2.9	12%	39	23	38	32%	78%	13%	0	16			81	1.04	2.4	100	151	$6
12	NYM	1	3	23	42	47	5.53	4.43	1.61	791	840	740	4.1	4.5	10.0	2.2	11%	33	28	39	37%	67%	10%	0	17			88	0.98	-7.9	70	92	$2
13	NYM	1	0	1	6	6	4.26	3.73	1.11	580	633	543	3.3	4.3	8.5	2.0	10%	44	19	38	25%	57%	0%	0	14			100	1.08	-0.3	60	79	-$3
1st Half																																	
2nd Half		1	0	1	6	6	4.26	3.73	1.11	580	633	543	3.3	4.3	8.5	2.0	10%	44	19	38	25%	57%	0%	0	14			100	1.08	-0.3	60	78	-$3
14	Proj	2	2	0	31	32	4.55	3.70	1.33	670	680	659	3.8	4.4	9.4	2.2	11%	36	23	41	29%	68%	11%	0						-2.6	66	86	-$2

Frasor,Jason

Age: 36	Th: R	Role RP	Health	D	LIMA Plan	B+		
Ht: 5' 9"	Wt: 180	Type Pwr	PT/Exp	D	Rand Var	-4		
			Consist	A	MM	4400		

First sub-3.00 ERA since 2009 but xERA tells a different story. Never been this good vL; thank a 22% H%. 1H was saved by S% spike, 2H by outlying hr/f and H% (traded ground balls for line drives and lowered his H%?). Maintains good Dom and iffy Ctl; the latter is why he hasn't been a closer for years—and won't be one now.

Yr	Tm	W	L	Sv	IP	K	ERA	xERA	WHIP	oOPS	vL	vR	BF/G	Ctl	Dom	Cmd	SwK	G	L	F	H%	S%	hr/f	GS	APC	DOM%	DIS%	Sv%	LI	RAR	BPV	BPX	R$
09	TOR	7	3	11	58	56	2.50	3.49	1.02	556	712	391	3.7	2.5	8.7	3.5	10%	38	18	43	27%	78%	6%	0	16			79	1.26	13.0	106	198	$13
10	TOR	3	4	4	64	65	3.68	3.67	1.38	691	718	671	4.0	3.8	9.2	2.4	9%	46	19	35	33%	74%	6%	0	16			50	1.00	3.2	86	140	$2
11	2 AL	3	3	0	60	57	3.60	4.04	1.40	770	841	706	4.1	3.9	8.6	2.2	9%	37	23	40	31%	78%	10%	0	18			0	1.19	2.5	64	96	$0
12	TOR	1	1	0	44	53	4.12	3.78	1.47	799	915	715	3.8	4.5	10.9	2.4	10%	38	23	38	34%	76%	14%	0	16			0	1.06	-0.6	90	118	-$4
13	TEX	4	3	0	49	48	2.57	3.62	1.14	598	427	699	3.3	3.7	8.8	2.4	10%	45	19	36	26%	81%	9%	0	14			0	1.20	7.8	83	108	$3
1st Half		0	1	0	21	24	2.95	3.48	1.31	712	448	844	3.1	3.8	10.1	2.7	11%	50	14	36	31%	84%	14%	0	13			0	1.09	2.4	108	139	-$1
2nd Half		4	2	0	28	24	2.28	3.72	1.01	501	412	562	3.5	3.6	7.8	2.2	8%	40	24	36	23%	78%	4%	0	15			0	1.29	5.4	62	81	$6
14	Proj	3	3	0	51	52	3.68	3.47	1.26	675	659	685	3.5	3.9	9.3	2.4	9%	41	21	38	29%	73%	10%	0						1.1	82	107	$1

Frieri,Ernesto

Age: 28	Th: R	Role RP	Health	A	LIMA Plan	C+		
Ht: 6' 2"	Wt: 200	Type Pwr xFB	PT/Exp	B	Rand Var	+1		
			Consist	B	MM	5530		

PRO: Undeniably awesome Dom remains closer-worthy; if 2H Ctl is real, he's a monster. CON: 2H says righties solved him; high hr/f plus general history of poor Ctl is a combustible combo that constantly threatens to cost him the closer role. VERDICT: Expect the roller-coaster ride to continue.

Yr	Tm	W	L	Sv	IP	K	ERA	xERA	WHIP	oOPS	vL	vR	BF/G	Ctl	Dom	Cmd	SwK	G	L	F	H%	S%	hr/f	GS	APC	DOM%	DIS%	Sv%	LI	RAR	BPV	BPX	R$
09	SD *	10	9	0	142	106	3.68	3.80	1.38	143	200	0	20.6	3.9	6.7	1.7	12%	0	25	75	30%	74%	0%	0	13			0	0.03	11.2	61	113	$8
10	SD *	4	2	17	69	83	1.58	1.33	0.99	553	731	469	3.9	4.6	10.7	2.4	14%	25	13	62	21%	87%	5%	0	18			89	0.62	21.4	126	203	$18
11	SD	1	2	0	63	76	2.71	3.98	1.35	692	823	596	4.7	4.9	10.9	2.2	11%	24	21	55	32%	80%	4%	0	19			0	0.60	9.5	66	100	$2
12	2 TM	5	2	23	66	98	2.32	3.12	0.98	556	373	706	4.0	4.1	13.4	3.3	15%	26	21	53	23%	86%	13%	0	18			88	1.03	13.8	134	175	$19
13	LAA	2	4	37	69	98	3.80	3.47	1.24	684	572	826	4.4	3.9	12.8	3.3	17%	24	17	59	32%	76%	12%	0	19			90	1.52	0.5	127	166	$16
1st Half		0	1	21	37	52	3.19	3.76	1.23	623	492	756	4.3	4.9	12.8	2.6	16%	25	11	64	28%	80%	10%	0	18			91	1.45	3.1	100	129	$19
2nd Half		2	3	16	32	46	4.50	3.17	1.25	750	642	926	4.4	2.8	12.9	4.6	18%	22	24	54	35%	71%	15%	0	19			89	1.60	-2.5	157	204	$12
14	Proj	3	3	33	65	89	3.24	3.19	1.19	657	588	726	4.3	4.0	12.3	3.1	15%	24	19	57	30%	78%	11%	0						5.1	115	150	$17

Fujikawa,Kyuji

Age: 33	Th: R	Role RP	Health	F	LIMA Plan	C+		
Ht: 6' 0"	Wt: 190	Type Pwr	PT/Exp	C	Rand Var	+5		
			Consist	B	MM	5510		

Earned an early look at the closer gig, and tiny-sample BPIs say he wasn't as horrible a failure in that role as ERA would indicate. Season derailed when he needed TJ surgery in June, and it's unclear whether/when he will be available in 2014. Skills are closer-worthy if intact; just don't expect to see them until 2015.

Yr	Tm	W	L	Sv	IP	K	ERA	xERA	WHIP	oOPS	vL	vR	BF/G	Ctl	Dom	Cmd	SwK	G	L	F	H%	S%	hr/f	GS	APC	DOM%	DIS%	Sv%	LI	RAR	BPV	BPX	R$
09	for	5	3	25	57	82	1.56	2.01	0.93				4.4	2.9	12.8	4.4					26%	93%								19.5	158	295	$21
10	for	3	4	28	62	77	2.52	3.91	1.21				4.3	3.6	11.1	3.1					28%	91%								12.0	92	148	$17
11	for	3	3	41	51	76	1.53	1.17	0.84				3.3	2.8	13.4	4.7					26%	86%								15.1	185	278	$25
12	for	2	2	24	47	55	1.66	2.43	1.17				3.9	3.6	10.5	3.0					31%	87%								13.7	127	166	$14
13	CHC	1	1	2	12	14	5.25	2.64	1.08	691	671	711	4.2	1.5	10.5	7.0	13%	50	19	31	34%	50%	10%	0	17			67	0.88	-2.0	177	230	-$3
1st Half		1	1	2	12	14	5.25	2.64	1.08	691	671	711	4.2	1.5	10.5	7.0	13%	50	19	31	34%	50%	10%	0	17			67	0.88	-2.0	177	229	-$3
2nd Half																																	
14	Proj	2	2	5	29	34	3.48	2.96	1.18				4.1	3.4	10.4	3.1	11%	44	22	34	31%	72%	9%	0						1.4	119	154	$1

Furbush,Charlie

Age: 28	Th: L	Role RP	Health	B	LIMA Plan	A		
Ht: 6' 5"	Wt: 215	Type Pwr	PT/Exp	D	Rand Var	0		
			Consist	B	MM	4510		

Stop us if you've heard this one before: Reliever with huge strikeout rate limited by lousy walk rate. Handling lefties with aplomb will keep him employed; comparative struggles vR and with Ctl preclude a shot at 9th inning. Classic LIMA reliever as long as Cmd holds up.

Yr	Tm	W	L	Sv	IP	K	ERA	xERA	WHIP	oOPS	vL	vR	BF/G	Ctl	Dom	Cmd	SwK	G	L	F	H%	S%	hr/f	GS	APC	DOM%	DIS%	Sv%	LI	RAR	BPV	BPX	R$
09																																	
10	a/a	4	4	0	82	60	6.11	6.21	1.59				25.9	2.8	6.5	2.3					34%	65%								-20.6	29	47	-$8
11	2 AL *	9	13	0	139	115	4.96	4.67	1.34	850	758	886	15.2	3.0	7.4	2.5	9%	42	19	39	29%	68%	15%	12	53	25%	42%	0	0.88	-17.5	52	78	-$2
12	SEA	5	2	0	46	53	2.72	3.13	0.95	529	404	637	3.8	3.1	10.3	3.3	12%	42	22	37	24%	73%	8%	0	16			0	1.16	7.4	121	158	$5
13	SEA	2	6	0	65	80	3.74	3.40	1.18	603	502	688	3.9	4.0	11.1	2.8	13%	40	22	38	29%	69%	8%	0	16			0	1.60	1.0	109	142	$1
1st Half		1	4	0	30	45	3.90	3.01	1.20	588	489	679	3.7	4.8	13.5	2.8	14%	43	17	40	30%	70%	12%	0	15			0	1.22	-0.1	134	174	$1
2nd Half		1	2	0	35	35	3.60	3.74	1.17	615	514	695	4.1	3.3	9.0	2.7	11%	38	25	37	29%	69%	6%	0	17			0	1.97	1.1	88	114	$1
14	Proj	4	5	3	65	71	3.49	3.23	1.19	651	517	753	4.7	3.5	9.7	2.8	12%	41	21	38	29%	74%	10%	0						3.1	100	130	$4

Gallardo,Yovani

Age: 28	Th: R	Role SP	Health	B	LIMA Plan	B+		
Ht: 6' 2"	Wt: 215	Type Pwr	PT/Exp	A	Rand Var	+1		
			Consist	A	MM	4305		

Erosion of Dom escalated into a freefall, moving him from star-potential power pitcher to groundball-inducing, innings-eating workhorse. Poor Ctl has long made him a WHIP-killer, now substandard Cmd says 4.00 ERA was mostly deserved. Even a mild rebound would only make him average. Don't overbid.

Yr	Tm	W	L	Sv	IP	K	ERA	xERA	WHIP	oOPS	vL	vR	BF/G	Ctl	Dom	Cmd	SwK	G	L	F	H%	S%	hr/f	GS	APC	DOM%	DIS%	Sv%	LI	RAR	BPV	BPX	R$
09	MIL	13	12	0	186	204	3.73	3.70	1.31	701	652	752	26.4	4.6	9.9	2.2	9%	45	19	36	29%	75%	12%	30	107	63%	3%			13.5	78	146	$15
10	MIL	14	7	0	185	200	3.84	3.50	1.37	693	781	620	25.9	3.6	9.7	2.7	9%	43	24	33	34%	72%	7%	31	103	81%	13%			5.4	98	158	$10
11	MIL	17	10	0	207	207	3.52	3.34	1.22	686	710	663	26.2	2.6	9.0	3.5	10%	47	17	36	31%	76%	13%	33	105	61%	15%			10.9	118	177	$17
12	MIL	16	9	0	204	204	3.66	3.67	1.30	706	759	654	26.1	3.6	9.0	2.5	8%	48	21	31	30%	76%	15%	33	105	64%	9%			8.9	92	119	$13
13	MIL	12	10	0	181	144	4.18	3.85	1.36	720	729	713	24.9	3.3	7.2	2.2	7%	49	23	28	31%	71%	12%	31	98	52%	19%			-7.1	67	88	$2
1st Half		6	7	0	99	80	4.20	3.81	1.39	733	712	754	25.1	3.3	7.3	2.2	7%	49	26	26	31%	72%	13%	17	99	47%	18%			-4.0	69	90	$2
2nd Half		6	3	0	82	64	4.17	3.90	1.33	705	755	669	24.8	3.3	7.0	2.1	7%	50	20	30	30%	70%	11%	14	98	57%	21%			-3.1	65	85	$2
14	Proj	14	9	0	189	168	3.91	3.53	1.33	709	738	683	24.9	3.4	8.0	2.3	8%	48	21	31	30%	73%	12%	31						-1.1	77	101	$9

JOSH PALEY

Garcia,Freddy

Age: 38	Th: R	Role SP	Health B	LIMA Plan D+
Ht: 6' 4"	Wt: 255	Type Con	PT/Exp B	Rand Var +2
			Consist B	MM 2001

4-7, 4.37 ERA in 80 IP at BAL and ATL. Insane hr/f crippled 1st half ERA. Punched up the Dom (by his standards) in 2nd half, and results went from poor to mediocre. Atlanta didn't have a better option for Game 4 of the NLDS; don't get caught in the same position.

Yr Tm	W	L	Sv	IP	K	ERA	xERA	WHIP	oOPS	vL	vR	BF/G	Ctl	Dom	Cmd	SwK	G	L	F	H%	S%	hr/f	GS	APC	DOM%	DIS%	Sv%	LI	RAR	BPV	BPX	R$
09 CHW *	3	7	0	73	48	5.73	4.85	1.41	690	576	795	25.7	2.3	5.9	2.6	11%	45	14	41	32%	60%	5%	9	92	67%	11%			-12.6	54	101	-$4
10 CHW	12	6	0	157	89	4.64	4.51	1.38	804	784	826	24.0	2.6	5.1	2.0	8%	41	21	38	29%	70%	12%	28	88	39%	25%			-10.9	41	67	$1
11 NYY	12	8	0	147	96	3.62	4.43	1.34	750	807	701	24.1	2.8	5.9	2.1	9%	36	22	41	30%	76%	8%	25	88	40%	20%	0	0.76	5.8	45	68	$6
12 NYY	7	6	0	107	89	5.20	4.16	1.37	784	822	739	15.4	2.9	7.5	2.5	9%	40	25	35	31%	66%	16%	17	59	24%	35%	0	0.71	-15.7	73	95	-$5
13 2 TM *	12	11	0	166	93	4.62	5.19	1.37	782	864	699	22.5	2.2	5.0	2.3	9%	43	24	33	29%	73%	21%	13	68	38%	31%	0	0.85	-15.4	26	34	-$3
1st Half	7	5	0	87	42	4.94	5.61	1.33	878	929	817	22.5	1.5	4.3	2.9	8%	40	24	36	28%	72%	25%	10	74	20%	40%	0	0.72	-11.5	19	25	-$2
2nd Half	5	6	0	80	51	4.26	4.74	1.42	578	684	500	22.5	2.9	5.8	2.0	11%	51	24	24	31%	73%	11%	3	58	100%	0%	0	1.09	-3.8	40	52	-$3
14 Proj	**6**	**5**	**0**	**84**	**50**	**4.64**	**4.12**	**1.37**	**792**	**856**	**731**	**20.3**	**2.6**	**5.4**	**2.1**	**9%**	**43**	**23**	**33**	**30%**	**71%**	**14%**	**17**						**-8.0**	**49**	**63**	**-$2**

Garcia,Jaime

Age: 27	Th: L	Role SP	Health F	LIMA Plan B+
Ht: 6' 2"	Wt: 215	Type GB	PT/Exp B	Rand Var +2
			Consist B	MM 4201

Torn labrum in May required surgery; expects to be ready for spring training. Home park appears to drive his value; road ERA two full runs above home for 2010-12. Dom trend is troubling, but hard to know how much of that is due to shoulder problems. Wait for some evidence of health before committing to him.

Yr Tm	W	L	Sv	IP	K	ERA	xERA	WHIP	oOPS	vL	vR	BF/G	Ctl	Dom	Cmd	SwK	G	L	F	H%	S%	hr/f	GS	APC	DOM%	DIS%	Sv%	LI	RAR	BPV	BPX	R$
09 aaa	2	0	0	21	18	4.49	4.87	1.34				21.8	3.8	7.8	2.1					26%	75%								-0.4	35	66	-$2
10 STL	13	8	0	163	132	2.70	3.64	1.32	638	550	660	24.8	3.5	7.3	2.1	11%	56	19	26	30%	81%	7%	28	93	61%	11%			27.8	70	113	$14
11 STL	13	7	0	195	156	3.56	3.47	1.32	711	770	697	25.8	2.3	7.2	3.1	11%	54	18	28	33%	74%	9%	32	93	47%	16%			9.2	99	149	$9
12 STL *	8	8	0	137	113	4.08	4.06	1.34	730	649	750	24.8	2.2	7.4	3.4	12%	54	20	26	34%	70%	7%	20	88	55%	20%			-1.1	96	125	$2
13 STL	5	2	0	55	43	3.58	3.35	1.30	725	905	666	26.0	2.4	7.0	2.9	12%	63	14	23	31%	76%	15%	9	92	44%	11%			2.0	101	132	$0
1st Half	5	2	0	55	43	3.58	3.35	1.30	725	905	666	26.0	2.4	7.0	2.9	12%	63	14	23	31%	76%	15%	9	92	44%	11%			2.0	101	131	$0
2nd Half																																
14 Proj	**7**	**4**	**0**	**101**	**79**	**3.81**	**3.36**	**1.30**	**695**	**750**	**681**	**24.9**	**2.6**	**7.0**	**2.7**	**11%**	**55**	**20**	**26**	**31%**	**72%**	**11%**	**17**						**0.7**	**89**	**116**	**$3**

Garza,Matt

Age: 30	Th: R	Role SP	Health D	LIMA Plan C+
Ht: 6' 4"	Wt: 215	Type Pwr	PT/Exp B	Rand Var 0
			Consist A	MM 4305

10-6, 3.82 ERA in 155 IP at CHC/TEX. Started season late as he recovered from 2012 elbow injury. Dom didn't come all the way back, leaving him as a serviceable starter, but with 2011 peak plainly in rear-view mirror. The question is whether elbow injury left him at this lower level permanently. If so... DN: 4.00+ ERA.

Yr Tm	W	L	Sv	IP	K	ERA	xERA	WHIP	oOPS	vL	vR	BF/G	Ctl	Dom	Cmd	SwK	G	L	F	H%	S%	hr/f	GS	APC	DOM%	DIS%	Sv%	LI	RAR	BPV	BPX	R$
09 TAM	8	12	0	203	189	3.95	4.03	1.26	695	608	787	26.9	3.5	8.4	2.4	8%	40	18	43	28%	72%	10%	32	107	50%	6%			9.4	74	139	$13
10 TAM	15	10	1	205	150	3.91	4.27	1.25	728	730	726	25.9	2.8	6.6	2.4	8%	36	19	45	28%	73%	10%	32	99	50%	16%	100	0.76	4.2	58	94	$12
11 CHC	10	10	0	198	197	3.32	3.36	1.26	654	634	672	27.1	2.9	9.0	3.1	12%	46	21	33	32%	75%	8%	31	103	68%	10%			15.2	108	162	$13
12 CHC	5	7	0	104	96	3.91	3.54	1.18	693	745	643	23.6	2.8	8.3	3.0	11%	47	19	33	28%	72%	16%	18	94	56%	22%			1.4	100	130	$4
13 2 TM *	11	7	0	171	144	3.62	3.75	1.23	712	733	687	24.7	2.5	7.6	3.1	10%	39	23	38	30%	74%	12%	24	101	58%	21%			5.1	83	108	$9
1st Half	4	2	0	65	55	3.30	3.09	1.16	689	704	673	21.4	2.7	7.7	2.8	11%	41	22	38	28%	74%	12%	8	96	63%	25%			4.5	88	114	$8
2nd Half	7	5	0	106	89	3.82	3.90	1.27	722	745	694	27.9	2.3	7.6	3.3	10%	38	24	38	31%	74%	11%	16	104	56%	19%			0.6	90	116	$9
14 Proj	**11**	**10**	**0**	**196**	**172**	**3.68**	**3.52**	**1.25**	**702**	**719**	**685**	**24.6**	**2.8**	**7.9**	**2.9**	**10%**	**42**	**21**	**37**	**30%**	**74%**	**11%**	**32**						**4.5**	**88**	**114**	**$12**

Gaudin,Chad

Age: 31	Th: R	Role RP	Health F	LIMA Plan B+
Ht: 5' 10"	Wt: 185	Type Pwr	PT/Exp C	Rand Var -2
			Consist C	MM 3301

xERA throws cold water on this ERA breakout. In fact that "breakout" didn't last all year: when the 1st half luck ran out, he returned to the realm of mortals, where yielding walks has consequences. He is what he has been for years: a professional replacement player. Look elsewhere for fanalytic profit.

Yr Tm	W	L	Sv	IP	K	ERA	xERA	WHIP	oOPS	vL	vR	BF/G	Ctl	Dom	Cmd	SwK	G	L	F	H%	S%	hr/f	GS	APC	DOM%	DIS%	Sv%	LI	RAR	BPV	BPX	R$
09 2 TM	6	10	0	147	139	4.64	4.31	1.51	747	823	673	21.4	4.6	8.5	1.8	9%	44	20	36	32%	70%	9%	25	83	40%	28%	0	0.79	-5.8	49	93	$0
10 2 AL	1	4	0	65	53	5.65	4.48	1.50	892	924	860	7.0	3.4	7.3	2.1	10%	39	15	46	30%	70%	17%	0	26			0	0.64	-12.6	55	90	-$6
11 TOR *	3	6	0	50	31	5.75	6.09	1.83	955	1127	839	10.6	3.5	5.6	1.6	7%	31	15	54	38%	67%	7%	0	20			0	0.94	-11.2	38	58	-$9
12 MIA	4	2	0	69	57	4.54	4.29	1.41	754	875	649	6.6	3.4	7.4	2.2	10%	41	24	35	32%	68%	8%	0	25			0	0.78	-4.5	61	80	-$4
13 SF	5	2	0	97	88	3.06	3.99	1.25	641	741	561	13.5	3.7	8.2	2.2	10%	38	23	38	29%	77%	6%	12	52	58%	33%	0	0.73	9.6	63	82	$5
1st Half	2	1	0	52	41	2.60	4.12	1.17	609	733	516	9.8	3.1	7.1	2.3	9%	39	21	40	27%	81%	7%	4	37	50%	50%	0	0.72	8.1	60	78	$7
2nd Half	3	1	0	45	47	3.60	3.85	1.33	679	751	616	23.9	4.4	9.4	2.1	10%	38	26	36	31%	72%	5%	8	93	63%	25%			1.5	66	86	$2
14 Proj	**5**	**4**	**0**	**89**	**76**	**4.11**	**3.93**	**1.37**	**712**	**806**	**631**	**11.8**	**3.7**	**7.7**	**2.1**	**10%**	**40**	**22**	**38**	**31%**	**71%**	**7%**	**6**						**-2.7**	**56**	**72**	**$0**

Gausman,Kevin John

Age: 23	Th: R	Role SP	Health A	LIMA Plan B+
Ht: 6' 3"	Wt: 190	Type Pwr	PT/Exp F	Rand Var +5
			Consist F	MM 5401

3-5, 5.66 ERA in 47 IP at BAL. Top-tier prospect had inauspicious MLB beginning, but there is a lot to like hiding behind ugly ERA. Small sample size, but unlucky 1st half LD% disappeared in 2nd half while Cmd arrived. Strikeout/groundball pitchers are a thing of beauty, and this will be the last year to get this one on the cheap.

Yr Tm	W	L	Sv	IP	K	ERA	xERA	WHIP	oOPS	vL	vR	BF/G	Ctl	Dom	Cmd	SwK	G	L	F	H%	S%	hr/f	GS	APC	DOM%	DIS%	Sv%	LI	RAR	BPV	BPX	R$
09																																
10																																
11																																
12																																
13 BAL *	6	11	0	130	119	4.73	4.14	1.30	792	811	772	14.8	1.9	8.3	4.4	10%	42	25	33	34%	65%	19%	5	40	20%	40%	0	0.80	-13.8	115	149	-$2
1st Half	3	8	0	81	69	5.36	4.97	1.36	903	908	897	22.6	1.3	7.7	5.8	8%	34	29	37	35%	63%	21%	5	81	20%	40%	0	0.83	-15.0	123	159	-$5
2nd Half	3	3	0	48	50	3.67	2.73	1.21	597	550	624	9.3	2.8	9.3	3.3	13%	59	17	24	33%	67%	10%	0	22			0	0.79	1.1	126	164	$3
14 Proj	**6**	**8**	**0**	**106**	**100**	**3.68**	**3.19**	**1.21**	**689**	**699**	**681**	**21.1**	**2.5**	**8.5**	**3.4**	**11%**	**46**	**22**	**32**	**31%**	**72%**	**11%**	**35**						**2.4**	**110**	**143**	**$5**

Gearrin,Cory

Age: 28	Th: R	Role RP	Health A	LIMA Plan C
Ht: 6' 3"	Wt: 200	Type Pwr GB	PT/Exp D	Rand Var 0
			Consist B	MM 4400

Through May 24, 21 IP, 0.86 ERA. Après ça, la déluge. Season ended with option to minors and shoulder tendinitis, which may explain Dom plummet. His big issue, other than the injury concern, is walks. It's hard to maintain sub-4.00 ERA with almost three baserunners per two innings. Heck, it's hard to keep a job that way.

Yr Tm	W	L	Sv	IP	K	ERA	xERA	WHIP	oOPS	vL	vR	BF/G	Ctl	Dom	Cmd	SwK	G	L	F	H%	S%	hr/f	GS	APC	DOM%	DIS%	Sv%	LI	RAR	BPV	BPX	R$
09 aa	1	2	2	25	17	3.79	3.55	1.26				5.2	3.2	6.1	1.9					28%	72%								1.7	59	110	-$1
10 aaa	3	5	0	80	56	4.06	4.30	1.45				6.6	3.7	6.3	1.7					31%	73%								0.2	52	85	-$1
11 ATL *	5	2	4	68	75	3.77	3.48	1.48	722	1157	427	5.5	4.4	9.9	2.3	8%	60	13	27	37%	72%	0%	0	17			57	1.11	1.4	110	165	$1
12 ATL *	3	4	9	75	74	2.50	2.92	1.28	642	992	411	5.0	3.4	8.9	2.7	13%	55	23	23	33%	79%	8%	0	13			82	0.88	13.9	112	146	$8
13 ATL	2	1	1	31	23	3.77	4.09	1.48	754	629	826	3.6	4.6	6.7	1.4	10%	51	25	24	30%	75%	10%	0	13			33	0.71	0.3	24	31	-$3
1st Half	2	1	1	30	23	3.30	3.95	1.43	733	643	786	3.5	4.5	6.9	1.5	11%	50	26	24	30%	78%	10%	0	13			33	0.73	2.1	31	40	-$3
2nd Half	0	0	0	1	0	18.00	9.43	3.00	1171	0	1417	7.0	9.0	0.0	0.0	0%	60	20	20	41%	33%	0%	0	16			0	0.26	-1.7	-205	-265	-$8
14 Proj	**3**	**2**	**0**	**56**	**52**	**3.76**	**3.57**	**1.39**	**665**	**584**	**714**	**4.7**	**4.3**	**8.4**	**2.0**	**11%**	**50**	**26**	**24**	**31%**	**74%**	**9%**	**0**						**0.7**	**64**	**84**	**-$1**

Gee,Dillon

Age: 28	Th: R	Role SP	Health D	LIMA Plan B
Ht: 6' 1"	Wt: 205	Type	PT/Exp A	Rand Var 0
			Consist B	MM 3203

A year ago, 2012 xERA looked like a breakout. Now it looks like an outlier. 2H was great on the surface, but high S% and low H% masked the Dom deficiency and home park saved his bacon by suppressing HR. This is the profile of an innate 4.00 ERA. Best use is now as a matchup/home park guy. Don't get sucked in for more.

Yr Tm	W	L	Sv	IP	K	ERA	xERA	WHIP	oOPS	vL	vR	BF/G	Ctl	Dom	Cmd	SwK	G	L	F	H%	S%	hr/f	GS	APC	DOM%	DIS%	Sv%	LI	RAR	BPV	BPX	R$
09 aaa	1	3	0	48	37	5.51	5.24	1.52				23.3	3.1	7.0	2.3					34%	65%								-7.1	50	94	-$5
10 NYM *	15	10	0	194	155	4.74	4.62	1.39	631	653	618	24.8	2.5	7.2	2.8	8%	47	10	43	33%	68%	5%	5	98	20%	0%			-15.9	69	112	$3
11 NYM	13	6	0	161	114	4.43	4.29	1.38	739	743	735	23.5	4.0	6.4	1.6	10%	47	19	34	28%	70%	11%	27	87	41%	22%	0	0.77	-9.6	33	49	$1
12 NYM	6	7	0	110	97	4.10	3.54	1.25	697	770	610	27.2	2.4	8.0	3.3	11%	50	20	30	31%	70%	13%	17	103	71%	0%			-1.2	107	140	$2
13 NYM	12	11	0	199	142	3.62	4.07	1.28	738	822	666	26.3	2.1	6.4	3.0	10%	43	20	38	31%	76%	10%	32	93	44%	16%			6.1	79	103	$8
1st Half	6	7	0	90	77	4.60	3.95	1.46	821	931	719	24.8	2.4	7.7	3.2	10%	43	21	37	34%	73%	13%	16	90	44%	25%			-8.2	94	122	-$1
2nd Half	6	4	0	109	65	2.81	4.15	1.14	664	717	621	27.8	1.9	5.4	2.8	10%	43	19	39	27%	79%	8%	16	97	44%	6%			14.2	66	85	$16
14 Proj	**11**	**9**	**0**	**174**	**131**	**3.97**	**3.71**	**1.30**	**736**	**800**	**678**	**25.1**	**2.5**	**6.8**	**2.7**	**10%**	**46**	**19**	**36**	**30%**	**72%**	**10%**	**29**						**-2.2**	**78**	**101**	**$6**

JOSH PALEY

Germen,Gonzalez

Age: 26 | Th: R | Role: RP | Health: A | LIMA Plan: C
Ht: 6' 2" | Wt: 200 | Type: Pwr xFB | PT/Exp: D | Rand Var: 0
Consist: B | MM: 3300

1-2, 3.93 ERA in 34 IP at NYM. 51K:11BB in AAA Vegas got him 2013 promotion. Handled RHB well, but lefties pound on him enough that he's probably best as a ROOGY, meaning he won't start and he won't get saves. When the fortunate hr/f regresses, the sub-4.00 ERA will disappear. Pass.

Yr	Tm	W	L	Sv	IP	K	ERA	xERA	WHIP	oOPS	vL	vR	BF/G	Ctl	Dom	Cmd	SwK	G	L	F	H%	S%	hr/f	GS	APC	DOM%	DIS%	Sv%	LI	RAR	BPV	BPX	R$
09																																	
10																																	
11																																	
12	a/a	9	12	0	127	84	5.18	4.88	1.47				25.9	2.4	5.9	2.4					34%	65%								-18.3	57	74	-$8
13	NYM *	4	5	5	78	75	4.51	4.00	1.35	676	720	646	5.1	3.0	8.6	2.9	15%	37	21	41	33%	67%	2%	0	20			56	0.95	-6.2	90	117	-$1
1st Half		3	3	3	43	39	5.11	4.67	1.34				5.2	1.9	8.3	4.4					34%	64%	0%	0						-6.6	103	133	$0
2nd Half		1	2	2	36	35	3.79	3.19	1.37	676	720	646	5.0	4.3	8.9	2.1	15%	37	21	41	32%	71%	2%	0	20			50	0.95	0.4	97	125	-$1
14	Proj	**3**	**4**	**0**	**58**	**49**	**4.67**	**3.95**	**1.35**	**683**	**783**	**617**	**7.4**	**2.9**	**7.5**	**2.6**	**15%**	**37**	**21**	**41**	**32%**	**66%**	**6%**	**0**						**-5.7**	**72**	**93**	**-$2**

Gibson,Kyle

Age: 26 | Th: R | Role: SP | Health: D | LIMA Plan: D+
Ht: 6' 6" | Wt: 210 | Type: GB | PT/Exp: D | Rand Var: +1
Consist: C | MM: 2103

2-4, 6.53 ERA in 51 IP at MIN. Nov 2011 TJS cost him all of 2012, returned in 2013 to decent 1H results that earned him a callup to MIN which had disastrous results. 2H shows the downside of a pitcher who doesn't miss bats and lacks pinpoint control. There's still promise in that 2010 stat line, but 2010 was a long time ago.

Yr	Tm	W	L	Sv	IP	K	ERA	xERA	WHIP	oOPS	vL	vR	BF/G	Ctl	Dom	Cmd	SwK	G	L	F	H%	S%	hr/f	GS	APC	DOM%	DIS%	Sv%	LI	RAR	BPV	BPX	R$
09																																	
10	a/a	7	5	0	109	70	3.73	3.52	1.29				23.5	2.2	5.8	2.6					32%	70%								4.7	80	129	$4
11	aaa	3	8	0	95	75	5.64	5.60	1.60				23.4	2.6	7.1	2.7					37%	65%								-20.0	62	93	-$10
12																																	
13	MIN *	9	9	0	153	97	4.48	4.44	1.47	874	875	869	24.2	3.2	5.7	1.8	8%	50	21	28	32%	70%	13%	10	90	20%	30%			-11.6	49	64	-$5
1st Half		8	5	0	99	67	3.53	3.47	1.31	746	818	690	25.5	2.7	6.1	2.3	11%	55	15	30	31%	72%	0%	1	91	100%	0%			4.1	76	98	$4
2nd Half		1	4	0	54	30	6.23	6.20	1.75	890	880	903	22.4	4.2	5.0	1.2	8%	50	22	28	33%	66%	15%	9	90	11%	33%			-15.7	8	10	-$21
14	Proj	**7**	**11**	**0**	**160**	**104**	**4.65**	**4.25**	**1.48**	**681**	**675**	**686**	**23.2**	**3.3**	**5.8**	**1.7**	**8%**	**47**	**22**	**31**	**32%**	**71%**	**10%**	**30**						**-15.5**	**40**	**52**	**-$5**

Gomez,Jeanmar

Age: 26 | Th: R | Role: RP | Health: B | LIMA Plan: B+
Ht: 6' 3" | Wt: 200 | Type: GB | PT/Exp: C | Rand Var: -2
Consist: B | MM: 3101

The bullpen seems to suit him well, but ground balls alone do not make a pitcher. 1H shows the effects of unsustainable H%/S% combination. 2H xERA shows value of keeping the ball in the park, but that hr/f will regress. This is simply not a long-term sustainable MLB skill set, pretty ERA or not.

Yr	Tm	W	L	Sv	IP	K	ERA	xERA	WHIP	oOPS	vL	vR	BF/G	Ctl	Dom	Cmd	SwK	G	L	F	H%	S%	hr/f	GS	APC	DOM%	DIS%	Sv%	LI	RAR	BPV	BPX	R$
09	aa	10	4	0	123	97	4.42	4.61	1.46				24.0	3.1	7.1	2.3					33%	71%								-1.6	63	117	$2
10	CLE *	12	13	0	174	101	5.17	5.36	1.56	841	752	961	24.6	3.2	5.3	1.6	6%	47	20	33	33%	68%	10%	11	91	18%	36%			-23.4	29	46	-$7
11	CLE *	15	10	0	196	122	3.31	4.07	1.38	804	855	756	25.7	2.8	5.6	2.0	6%	53	20	27	31%	77%	10%	10	87	20%	50%	0	0.83	15.3	56	85	$9
12	CLE *	11	13	0	160	92	5.53	4.92	1.44	810	822	800	22.0	2.8	5.2	1.8	8%	48	19	33	31%	63%	15%	17	73	12%	53%	0	0.68	-30.0	32	42	-$10
13	PIT	3	0	0	81	53	3.35	3.83	1.15	617	621	614	9.8	3.1	5.9	1.9	9%	55	19	26	25%	72%	10%	8	36	50%	50%	0	0.69	5.2	55	72	$2
1st Half		2	0	0	49	28	2.76	4.06	1.14	621	555	673	15.5	3.3	5.1	1.6	9%	55	18	27	23%	80%	13%	8	57	50%	50%	0	0.78	6.7	36	47	$5
2nd Half		1	0	0	32	25	4.26	3.48	1.17	612	724	530	6.3	2.8	7.1	2.5	10%	56	19	24	29%	61%	4%	0	24			0	0.64	-1.6	86	111	-$1
14	Proj	**4**	**2**	**0**	**73**	**48**	**4.31**	**3.81**	**1.34**	**716**	**741**	**696**	**12.1**	**3.0**	**5.9**	**2.0**	**8%**	**53**	**19**	**28**	**30%**	**68%**	**9%**	**5**						**-4.0**	**57**	**74**	**-$1**

Gonzalez,Gio

Age: 28 | Th: L | Role: SP | Health: A | LIMA Plan: C+
Ht: 6' 0" | Wt: 200 | Type: Pwr | PT/Exp: A | Rand Var: 0
Consist: A | MM: 4405

2012 Fun Fact: he went more than 7 IP only three times. In 2013, he reached that mark only twice. BPIs describe a borderline star, lacking the control and endurance to take the next step. He has been the same pitcher for three straight years and that's worth owning. Just not at a 21-win price.

Yr	Tm	W	L	Sv	IP	K	ERA	xERA	WHIP	oOPS	vL	vR	BF/G	Ctl	Dom	Cmd	SwK	G	L	F	H%	S%	hr/f	GS	APC	DOM%	DIS%	Sv%	LI	RAR	BPV	BPX	R$
09	OAK *	10	8	0	160	167	4.63	4.75	1.57	846	1095	767	21.9	5.1	9.4	1.9	10%	46	18	36	33%	73%	14%	17	91	41%	29%	0	0.80	-6.0	66	123	$1
10	OAK	15	9	0	201	171	3.23	3.98	1.31	644	615	653	25.8	4.1	7.7	1.9	9%	49	15	35	28%	77%	7%	33	102	58%	18%			21.0	54	87	$15
11	OAK	16	12	0	202	197	3.12	3.68	1.32	654	713	636	27.0	4.1	8.8	2.2	10%	47	18	34	30%	79%	9%	32	106	56%	13%			20.5	74	111	$16
12	WAS	21	8	0	199	207	2.89	3.40	1.13	582	659	561	25.7	3.4	9.3	2.7	10%	48	22	30	28%	75%	6%	32	100	78%	13%			27.7	102	132	$28
13	WAS	11	8	0	196	192	3.36	3.60	1.25	668	568	696	25.6	3.5	8.8	2.5	10%	44	23	33	30%	75%	10%	32	104	69%	22%			12.3	87	113	$12
1st Half		5	3	0	105	104	3.09	3.58	1.14	607	455	655	25.4	3.8	8.9	2.4	10%	46	19	35	26%	76%	9%	17	105	71%	24%			10.1	82	107	$17
2nd Half		6	5	0	91	88	3.67	3.63	1.38	735	715	740	25.8	3.2	8.7	2.8	10%	42	26	32	34%	75%	10%	15	102	67%	20%			2.2	91	118	$7
14	Proj	**15**	**9**	**0**	**203**	**201**	**3.30**	**3.40**	**1.27**	**658**	**659**	**657**	**24.9**	**3.6**	**8.9**	**2.5**	**10%**	**45**	**22**	**34**	**30%**	**76%**	**9%**	**33**						**14.1**	**85**	**110**	**$17**

Gonzalez,Michael

Age: 36 | Th: L | Role: RP | Health: D | LIMA Plan: C
Ht: 6' 2" | Wt: 200 | Type: Pwr FB | PT/Exp: D | Rand Var: +5
Consist: A | MM: 3510

In 2004, 55 K vs. 6 BB hinted at a future closer. Dom has always been plenty good to hold a job, but pitchers who walk four guys per nine innings don't get save chances unless they play for the Cubs. Classic LOOGY (increasingly awful vR), but 2013 vL and age suggest his long career may be coming to an end.

Yr	Tm	W	L	Sv	IP	K	ERA	xERA	WHIP	oOPS	vL	vR	BF/G	Ctl	Dom	Cmd	SwK	G	L	F	H%	S%	hr/f	GS	APC	DOM%	DIS%	Sv%	LI	RAR	BPV	BPX	R$
09	ATL	5	4	10	74	90	2.42	3.47	1.20	658	581	699	3.9	4.0	10.9	2.7	11%	38	18	44	29%	84%	9%	0	16			59	1.18	17.4	104	195	$13
10	BAL	1	3	1	25	31	4.01	3.72	1.30	629	849	495	3.7	5.1	11.3	2.2	13%	33	22	45	31%	68%	4%	0	14			33	1.71	0.2	77	124	-$1
11	2 AL	2	2	1	53	51	4.39	3.79	1.35	738	574	900	4.1	3.5	8.6	2.4	11%	41	23	36	31%	71%	13%	0	17			50	0.88	-2.9	78	118	-$2
12	WAS	0	0	0	36	39	3.03	3.81	1.32	692	525	863	3.2	4.0	9.8	2.4	10%	40	23	38	32%	78%	6%	0	13			0	0.90	4.3	86	112	-$2
13	MIL	0	3	0	50	60	4.68	4.09	1.66	853	780	929	3.1	4.5	10.8	2.4	12%	33	25	42	37%	78%	17%	0	13			0	1.07	-5.0	84	109	-$7
1st Half		0	3	0	29	39	3.41	3.73	1.48	744	740	748	3.1	5.0	12.1	2.4	13%	31	27	42	35%	82%	13%	0	13			0	1.28	1.6	93	120	-$4
2nd Half		0	0	0	21	21	6.43	4.60	1.90	989	829	1156	3.1	3.9	9.0	2.3	10%	35	23	42	40%	74%	21%	0	12			0	0.80	-6.6	71	92	-$11
14	Proj	**1**	**2**	**3**	**51**	**54**	**4.27**	**3.78**	**1.52**	**804**	**684**	**920**	**3.2**	**4.1**	**9.6**	**2.3**	**11%**	**37**	**23**	**40**	**34%**	**77%**	**14%**	**0**						**-2.5**	**77**	**100**	**-$3**

Gonzalez,Miguel M

Age: 30 | Th: R | Role: RP | Health: B | LIMA Plan: C+
Ht: 6' 1" | Wt: 170 | Type: FB | PT/Exp: C | Rand Var: -1
Consist: F | MM: 2203

11-8, 3.78 ERA in 171 IP at BAL. Not a young prospect, TJS in 2009 ate up two years of his career. Earned a promotion with a 1.61 ERA in AAA in 2012, but MLB is another matter. xERA reflects pedestrian skills; doesn't miss enough bats or get enough GBs to keep the ball in the park. Take this projection seriously.

Yr	Tm	W	L	Sv	IP	K	ERA	xERA	WHIP	oOPS	vL	vR	BF/G	Ctl	Dom	Cmd	SwK	G	L	F	H%	S%	hr/f	GS	APC	DOM%	DIS%	Sv%	LI	RAR	BPV	BPX	R$
09																																	
10																																	
11	a/a	0	6	0	52	38	7.70	6.47	1.84				15.0	4.0	6.7	1.7					38%	57%								-23.9	34	51	-$13
12	BAL *	12	6	1	150	117	3.03	3.02	1.13	694	701	685	18.5	2.8	7.0	2.5	9%	35	22	43	26%	77%	10%	15	94	47%	20%	100	0.69	18.2	78	102	$17
13	BAL	11	8	0	171	120	3.78	4.28	1.23	713	689	736	23.7	2.8	6.3	2.3	9%	39	21	40	27%	74%	11%	28	90	54%	14%	0	0.75	1.8	55	72	$7
1st Half		6	3	0	88	68	3.77	4.03	1.19	704	614	802	25.7	2.8	6.9	2.5	9%	41	17	41	26%	74%	12%	14	98	57%	7%			1.0	70	90	$10
2nd Half		5	5	0	83	52	3.80	4.55	1.27	723	774	676	22.0	2.8	5.6	2.0	8%	37	24	39	27%	74%	11%	14	84	50%	21%	0	0.74	0.7	40	52	$5
14	Proj	**8**	**8**	**0**	**138**	**100**	**4.09**	**4.09**	**1.32**	**745**	**746**	**744**	**19.7**	**3.0**	**6.5**	**2.2**	**9%**	**37**	**22**	**41**	**29%**	**72%**	**10%**	**28**						**-3.8**	**52**	**68**	**$3**

Gonzalez,Miguel A

Age: 27 | Th: R | Role: SP | Health: A | LIMA Plan: B+
Ht: 6' 2" | Wt: 185 | Type: | PT/Exp: D | Rand Var: 0
Consist: F | MM: 2101

Suspended after trying to defect from Cuba in 2012. Made it to El Salvador in 2013. PHI signed him to a 3-year, $12M contract but questions remain. Dom shows he isn't the second coming of Aroldis Chapman. We have learned how good Cuban players can be, but his MLEs are a warning, not a recommendation.

Yr	Tm	W	L	Sv	IP	K	ERA	xERA	WHIP	oOPS	vL	vR	BF/G	Ctl	Dom	Cmd	SwK	G	L	F	H%	S%	hr/f	GS	APC	DOM%	DIS%	Sv%	LI	RAR	BPV	BPX	R$
09	for	8	4	0	126	96	3.55	4.51	1.42				29.7	2.7	6.8	2.6					33%	77%								12.0	68	128	$5
10	for	6	6	0	100	73	3.70	3.65	1.19				25.0	1.8	6.6	3.7					30%	71%								4.7	93	150	$5
11	for	8	5	0	113	70	3.96	4.55	1.37				29.6	2.9	5.6	1.9					30%	75%								-0.2	39	59	$1
12																																	
13																																	
1st Half																																	
2nd Half																																	
14	Proj	**7**	**5**	**0**	**102**	**72**	**3.92**	**4.04**	**1.30**				**28.0**	**2.5**	**6.3**	**2.5**	**0%**				**30%**	**73%**		**15**						**-0.7**	**63**	**82**	**$2**

JOSH PALEY

Gorzelanny,Tom

Age: 31	Th: L	Role RP	Health	D	LIMA Plan	B+
Ht: 6' 2"	Wt: 210	Type Pwr	PT/Exp	C	Rand Var	+1
			Consist	A	MM	3301

Skills-wise, this was his best year in majors, fueled by jump in Dom. Lucky H%/S% combo led to low 1H ERA, but the baseball gods reversed that in 2H. The nutshell is .776 OPS as starter, .574 as reliever and 9 HR at home, 2 on the road. It is really hard to milk a middle reliever's road games for fanalytic value.

Yr Tm	W	L	Sv	IP	K	ERA	xERA	WHIP	oOPS	vL	vR	BF/G	Ctl	Dom	Cmd	SwK	G	L	F	H%	S%	hr/f	GS	APC	DOM%	DIS%	Sv%	LI	RAR	BPV	BPX	R$
09 2 NL *	11	6	0	134	110	4.09	3.98	1.39	708	563	751	15.2	3.3	7.4	2.2	10%	41	21	38	32%	71%	12%	7	35	43%	29%	0	1.16	3.8	74	139	$6
10 CHC	7	9	1	136	119	4.09	4.42	1.50	742	823	716	20.8	4.5	7.9	1.8	10%	41	19	40	32%	74%	7%	23	80	48%	17%	100	0.77	-0.2	39	63	$1
11 WAS	4	6	0	105	95	4.03	3.96	1.29	753	497	826	14.9	2.8	8.1	2.9	11%	36	17	47	30%	73%	11%	15	57	40%	27%	0	0.88	-1.1	84	127	$2
12 WAS	4	2	1	72	62	2.88	4.20	1.32	718	687	740	6.8	3.8	7.8	2.1	11%	43	21	36	29%	82%	9%	1	26	0%	100%	100	0.93	10.1	59	77	$3
13 MIL	3	6	0	85	83	3.90	3.64	1.27	697	600	741	8.3	3.3	8.8	2.7	11%	44	19	36	30%	73%	13%	10	31	40%	40%	0	0.62	-0.4	91	119	$0
1st Half	1	0	0	37	36	2.43	3.58	1.11	611	754	505	4.8	4.1	8.8	2.1	11%	46	18	36	22%	86%	15%	1	19	0%	100%	0	0.59	6.5	70	90	$5
2nd Half	2	6	0	48	47	5.03	3.68	1.39	756	406	861	17.3	2.6	8.8	3.4	11%	43	20	37	34%	66%	11%	9	64	44%	33%	0	0.70	-6.9	108	140	-$3
14 Proj	**4**	**5**	**0**	**87**	**80**	**3.73**	**3.63**	**1.30**	**716**	**620**	**760**	**8.9**	**3.4**	**8.3**	**2.5**	**11%**	**42**	**20**	**38**	**30%**	**75%**	**11%**	**0**						**1.5**	**79**	**102**	**$2**

Gray,Sonny

Age: 24	Th: R	Role SP	Health	A	LIMA Plan	C+
Ht: 5' 11"	Wt: 200	Type Pwr xGB	PT/Exp	D	Rand Var	0
			Consist	D	MM	4205

5-3, 2.67 ERA in 64 IP at OAK. MLEs didn't suggest this level of performance, but who's quibbling? 2H skills were strong across the board, where BPV says he was a star, if not yet an All-Star. He's young, he's good, and his ERA was fully supported by xERA. Strikeout/ground ball combo a real plus. UP: 3.00 ERA.

Yr Tm	W	L	Sv	IP	K	ERA	xERA	WHIP	oOPS	vL	vR	BF/G	Ctl	Dom	Cmd	SwK	G	L	F	H%	S%	hr/f	GS	APC	DOM%	DIS%	Sv%	LI	RAR	BPV	BPX	R$
09																																
10																																
11 aa	1	0	0	20	16	0.44	1.87	1.05				15.5	2.5	7.1	2.9					28%	95%								8.6	115	173	$1
12 a/a	6	9	0	152	84	4.43	4.26	1.48				24.2	3.3	5.0	1.5					32%	69%								-7.8	48	62	-$7
13 OAK *	15	10	0	182	165	3.20	3.29	1.28	570	622	499	23.4	2.8	8.1	2.9	10%	53	20	28	32%	75%	8%	10	83	80%	10%	0	0.66	15.1	101	131	$13
1st Half	7	6	0	95	81	3.26	3.57	1.36				24.9	3.1	7.7	2.5					33%	75%	0%	0						7.1	91	117	$10
2nd Half	8	4	0	87	84	3.12	3.00	1.19	570	622	499	21.8	2.6	8.6	3.4	10%	53	20	28	31%	74%	8%	10	83	80%	10%	0	0.66	8.0	114	148	$16
14 Proj	**13**	**8**	**0**	**181**	**148**	**3.59**	**3.48**	**1.29**	**603**	**656**	**530**	**23.1**	**3.0**	**7.3**	**2.4**	**10%**	**53**	**20**	**28**	**31%**	**73%**	**8%**	**32**						**6.2**	**82**	**106**	**$11**

Gregerson,Luke

Age: 30	Th: R	Role RP	Health	B	LIMA Plan	B+
Ht: 6' 3"	Wt: 200	Type Pwr	PT/Exp	C	Rand Var	-2
			Consist	A	MM	5410

His skills are precisely what one wants in a pitcher: combines ground balls with strikeouts without walking lots of guys or yielding homers. SD didn't trust him to close after 2011 and signed Huston Street. While he rebounded, he's not the dominant force of his youth. Perpetual closer-in-waiting. Given a chance... UP: 35 Sv.

Yr Tm	W	L	Sv	IP	K	ERA	xERA	WHIP	oOPS	vL	vR	BF/G	Ctl	Dom	Cmd	SwK	G	L	F	H%	S%	hr/f	GS	APC	DOM%	DIS%	Sv%	LI	RAR	BPV	BPX	R$
09 SD	2	4	1	75	93	3.24	3.14	1.24	613	789	443	4.4	3.7	11.2	3.0	16%	46	21	33	33%	73%	5%	0	16			14	1.28	10.0	124	233	$5
10 SD	4	7	2	78	89	3.22	2.66	0.83	524	540	511	3.7	2.1	10.2	4.9	16%	48	15	37	23%	65%	12%	0	14			29	1.34	8.3	154	250	$11
11 SD	3	3	0	56	34	2.75	4.18	1.37	681	770	622	4.0	3.1	5.5	1.8	12%	49	22	29	31%	80%	4%	0	14			0	1.15	8.2	43	65	$1
12 SD	2	0	9	72	72	2.39	3.30	1.09	612	663	578	3.8	2.6	9.0	3.4	16%	50	18	32	28%	83%	11%	0	14			69	1.19	14.4	120	156	$10
13 SD	6	8	4	66	64	2.71	3.27	1.01	572	624	521	3.7	2.4	8.7	3.6	14%	45	20	35	27%	73%	5%	0	13			44	1.26	9.4	113	148	$8
1st Half	4	3	3	35	30	2.60	3.23	1.01	568	708	458	3.7	2.1	7.8	3.8	13%	51	21	29	27%	76%	7%	0	13			43	1.27	5.4	113	146	$10
2nd Half	2	5	1	32	34	2.84	3.30	1.01	577	550	608	3.7	2.8	9.7	3.4	16%	39	19	42	28%	71%	3%	0	14			50	1.26	4.0	114	148	$6
14 Proj	**4**	**5**	**6**	**65**	**62**	**2.70**	**3.15**	**1.13**	**636**	**680**	**599**	**3.6**	**2.7**	**8.6**	**3.2**	**15%**	**46**	**19**	**34**	**29%**	**79%**	**8%**	**0**						**9.4**	**107**	**139**	**$8**

Gregg,Kevin

Age: 36	Th: R	Role RP	Health	A	LIMA Plan	C
Ht: 6' 6"	Wt: 245	Type Pwr	PT/Exp	C	Rand Var	-2
			Consist	A	MM	2320

1H ERA came from 5-year high in Dom, which not only couldn't repeat, but cratered like the Grand Canyon in 2H. BPV splits were freakish, but his corpus of work for the year was par for the course for a Cubs closer: lots of saves and lots of ninth inning excitement. And pain. Will be sold off into middle relief for a bag of chips.

Yr Tm	W	L	Sv	IP	K	ERA	xERA	WHIP	oOPS	vL	vR	BF/G	Ctl	Dom	Cmd	SwK	G	L	F	H%	S%	hr/f	GS	APC	DOM%	DIS%	Sv%	LI	RAR	BPV	BPX	R$
09 CHC	5	6	23	69	71	4.72	4.06	1.31	740	592	860	4.1	3.9	9.3	2.4	10%	38	18	44	28%	70%	15%	0	18			77	1.21	-3.4	77	145	$11
10 TOR	2	6	37	59	58	3.51	4.06	1.39	712	732	692	4.0	4.6	8.8	1.9	9%	42	17	40	31%	76%	6%	0	17			86	1.29	4.2	56	90	$15
11 BAL	0	3	22	60	53	4.37	4.88	1.64	773	855	684	4.4	6.0	8.0	1.3	7%	42	18	41	31%	76%	10%	0	19			76	0.98	-3.2	1	1	$3
12 FAA	3	2	0	44	37	4.95	4.72	1.69	838	911	778	5.0	4.9	7.6	1.5	8%	48	18	34	34%	74%	13%	0	20			0	0.46	-5.0	30	39	-$7
13 CHC	2	6	33	62	56	3.48	4.41	1.37	695	518	843	4.3	4.6	8.1	1.8	7%	37	23	40	28%	77%	9%	0	18			87	1.53	2.9	36	47	$12
1st Half	2	1	13	27	29	1.65	3.13	0.99	551	416	689	3.9	2.6	9.5	3.6	9%	39	25	36	26%	88%	8%	0	17			93	1.67	7.5	118	152	$17
2nd Half	0	5	20	35	27	4.93	5.57	1.67	794	598	936	4.7	6.2	7.0	1.1	6%	35	22	43	30%	72%	9%	0	19			83	1.41	-4.6	-29	-37	$8
14 Proj	**2**	**5**	**10**	**65**	**58**	**4.11**	**4.27**	**1.50**	**752**	**693**	**803**	**4.4**	**5.0**	**8.0**	**1.6**	**8%**	**41**	**21**	**39**	**30%**	**75%**	**10%**	**0**						**-2.0**	**29**	**38**	**$1**

Greinke,Zack

Age: 30	Th: R	Role SP	Health	D	LIMA Plan	C
Ht: 6' 2"	Wt: 195	Type Pwr	PT/Exp	A	Rand Var	-2
			Consist	A	MM	5305

Here's the theory: if you are a matador, it is best to come with the red cape and dodge the bull lest you get gored or wind up with a broken collabone. xERA and Dom say that he is a star, not a superstar. 2H ERA was awesome, fueled by abnormally good H%/S% combination which won't repeat. Split 2012/2013 difference.

Yr Tm	W	L	Sv	IP	K	ERA	xERA	WHIP	oOPS	vL	vR	BF/G	Ctl	Dom	Cmd	SwK	G	L	F	H%	S%	hr/f	GS	APC	DOM%	DIS%	Sv%	LI	RAR	BPV	BPX	R$
09 KC	16	8	0	229	242	2.16	3.20	1.07	611	651	574	27.7	2.0	9.5	4.7	10%	40	19	41	31%	81%	5%	33	105	88%	0%			61.2	135	253	$39
10 KC	10	14	0	220	181	4.17	3.65	1.25	696	774	601	27.8	2.3	7.4	3.3	8%	46	18	36	31%	67%	8%	33	104	55%	9%			-2.5	97	156	$9
11 MIL	16	6	0	172	201	3.83	2.82	1.20	708	738	679	25.5	2.4	10.5	4.5	11%	47	22	31	33%	71%	14%	28	101	71%	11%			2.4	151	227	$14
12 2 TM	15	5	0	212	200	3.48	3.34	1.20	663	691	635	25.5	2.3	8.5	3.7	9%	49	22	29	31%	73%	10%	34	100	65%	12%			14.1	118	154	$18
13 LA	15	4	0	178	148	2.63	3.43	1.11	647	733	568	25.6	2.3	7.5	3.2	11%	46	24	31	28%	79%	9%	28	101	64%	11%			27.0	96	125	$21
1st Half	5	2	0	64	48	3.94	3.95	1.36	781	857	707	24.8	2.4	6.8	2.8	9%	40	27	33	33%	73%	9%	11	97	55%	27%			-0.6	75	97	$1
2nd Half	10	2	0	114	100	1.90	3.15	0.98	566	654	488	26.1	2.3	7.9	3.4	12%	49	22	29	25%	84%	8%	17	103	71%	0%			27.6	108	139	$33
14 Proj	**16**	**6**	**0**	**203**	**187**	**3.12**	**3.12**	**1.16**	**665**	**725**	**608**	**25.1**	**2.3**	**8.3**	**3.6**	**10%**	**46**	**22**	**31**	**30%**	**75%**	**9%**	**32**						**18.8**	**111**	**144**	**$22**

Griffin,A.J.

Age: 26	Th: R	Role SP	Health	B	LIMA Plan	C+
Ht: 6' 5"	Wt: 230	Type xFB	PT/Exp	C	Rand Var	-1
			Consist	D	MM	3205

ERA paints a picture of a 2H fade, but xERA says 1H wasn't as good as it looked. Low H% points to ERA regression, and all the FB are dangerous. But there are raw elements of success: 1H Ctl and hr/f combined with 2H Dom would be interesting. It's speculative, but... UP: 3.50 ERA, 180 K.

Yr Tm	W	L	Sv	IP	K	ERA	xERA	WHIP	oOPS	vL	vR	BF/G	Ctl	Dom	Cmd	SwK	G	L	F	H%	S%	hr/f	GS	APC	DOM%	DIS%	Sv%	LI	RAR	BPV	BPX	R$
09																																
10																																
11 a/a	2	4	0	38	24	5.91	5.70	1.56				23.8	2.9	5.7	2.0					33%	64%								-9.2	29	43	-$6
12 OAK *	14	4	0	184	139	3.03	2.92	1.07	630	629	631	22.4	1.8	6.8	3.8	9%	37	24	39	27%	75%	10%	15	95	53%	27%			22.5	105	137	$22
13 OAK	14	10	0	200	171	3.83	4.10	1.13	688	666	713	25.7	2.4	7.7	3.2	9%	32	18	49	26%	74%	13%	32	100	56%	3%			1.0	83	108	$14
1st Half	6	6	0	104	81	3.56	4.13	1.09	657	602	721	26.3	2.2	7.0	3.2	9%	33	19	49	26%	73%	10%	16	101	56%	6%			3.9	79	102	$16
2nd Half	8	4	0	96	90	4.11	4.05	1.16	720	731	704	25.1	2.7	8.4	3.1	9%	32	18	51	25%	75%	15%	16	99	56%	0%			-2.9	88	114	$12
14 Proj	**13**	**9**	**0**	**189**	**153**	**3.89**	**3.79**	**1.22**	**699**	**692**	**705**	**23.9**	**2.4**	**7.3**	**3.0**	**9%**	**34**	**20**	**45**	**29%**	**73%**	**11%**	**32**						**-0.6**	**79**	**102**	**$12**

Grilli,Jason

Age: 37	Th: R	Role RP	Health	D	LIMA Plan	C+
Ht: 6' 4"	Wt: 225	Type Pwr FB	PT/Exp	C	Rand Var	+1
			Consist	A	MM	5530

He's like a luxury sports car with limited resale value... perhaps a 14-year-old Maserati salvage vehicle? As long as it runs, it's super-fun and top performance. When rear axle falls off and car crashes into a buffalo, it's a depressing bummer. Elite skills; he could repeat 1H, but age/health will always temper expectations.

Yr Tm	W	L	Sv	IP	K	ERA	xERA	WHIP	oOPS	vL	vR	BF/G	Ctl	Dom	Cmd	SwK	G	L	F	H%	S%	hr/f	GS	APC	DOM%	DIS%	Sv%	LI	RAR	BPV	BPX	R$
09 2 TM	2	3	1	46	49	5.32	4.68	1.69	813	833	795	4.1	5.3	9.7	1.8	11%	34	21	46	37%	68%	7%	0	17			100	0.85	-5.6	42	79	-$4
10																																
11 PIT *	6	2	4	65	69	2.63	3.55	1.35	601	766	508	4.9	4.0	9.5	2.4	13%	45	22	33	32%	83%	7%	0	19			100	1.41	10.6	94	141	$6
12 PIT	1	6	2	59	90	2.91	2.88	1.14	635	485	767	3.8	3.4	13.8	4.1	15%	31	24	45	33%	80%	12%	0	16			40	1.20	8.0	166	217	$5
13 PIT	0	2	33	50	74	2.70	2.57	1.06	595	707	496	3.7	2.3	13.3	5.7	15%	33	25	42	35%	78%	9%	0	16			94	1.17	7.2	188	244	$16
1st Half	0	1	27	37	59	1.72	2.21	0.85	464	529	400	3.7	1.7	14.5	8.4	16%	31	23	46	34%	80%	3%	0	15			96	1.28	9.7	223	289	$24
2nd Half	0	1	6	13	15	5.40	3.77	1.65	920	1242	700	3.9	4.1	10.1	2.5	12%	37	29	34	37%	74%	23%	0	16			86	0.88	-2.5	88	114	-$8
14 Proj	**2**	**3**	**33**	**57**	**71**	**3.13**	**3.01**	**1.15**	**604**	**643**	**573**	**3.9**	**3.5**	**11.1**	**3.1**	**14%**	**36**	**23**	**41**	**30%**	**75%**	**7%**	**0**						**5.2**	**118**	**154**	**$17**

JOSH PALEY

Grimm,Justin

Age: 25 Th: R Role RP | Health A | LIMA Plan D+
Ht: 6' 3" Wt: 200 Type | PT/Exp D | Rand Var +4
Consist C | MM 2100

7-9, 5.97 ERA in 98 IP at TEX and CHC. Tried a bunch of different roles/environments: first in Texas as SP, then as RP. Dealt to Cubs in July, worked in AAA-Iowa as SP, then Chicago as RP. In none of those situations did he demonstrate anything resembling rosterable skill. H%, S%, hr/f all hurt; at 25, maybe one more chance.

Yr Tm	W	L	Sv	IP	K	ERA	xERA	WHIP	oOPS	vL	vR	BF/G	Ctl	Dom	Cmd	SwK	G	L	F	H%	S%	hr/f	GS	APC	DOM%	DIS%	Sv%	LI	RAR	BPV	BPX	R$
09																																
10																																
11																																
12 TEX *	12	7	0	149	96	4.06	4.07	1.36	935	1006	855	20.7	2.1	5.8	2.8	8%	44	29	27	33%	69%	8%	2	50	50%	50%	0	0.33	-0.8	78	102	$2
13 2 TM *	10	12	0	146	113	5.73	5.34	1.60	846	860	830	17.9	3.3	7.0	2.1	8%	43	21	36	35%	65%	13%	17	61	29%	35%	0	0.80	-33.5	50	65	-$14
1st Half	8	5	0	83	65	5.31	5.13	1.50	822	821	822	24.0	2.9	7.1	2.4	8%	43	22	35	34%	66%	12%	14	92	36%	21%			-14.9	53	69	-$8
2nd Half	2	7	0	63	48	6.27	5.61	1.73	937	1018	857	13.6	3.9	6.8	1.8	7%	42	21	37	37%	63%	15%	3	27	0%	100%	0	0.83	-18.6	48	62	-$21
14 Proj	**3**	**3**	**0**	**44**	**29**	**4.74**	**4.23**	**1.43**	**739**	**760**	**717**	**17.5**	**3.3**	**6.1**	**1.8**	**7%**	**43**	**21**	**36**	**31%**	**68%**	**9%**	**8**						**-4.7**	**40**	**52**	**-$3**

Guerrier,Matt

Age: 35 Th: R Role RP | Health F | LIMA Plan D+
Ht: 6' 3" Wt: 195 Type | PT/Exp D | Rand Var -1
Consist A | MM 2100

Dealt to the Cubs in July, he put in a good month's work there before getting shut down with elbow injury. Eventually had flexor tendon surgery, which casts doubt on his spring availability. Given ERA/xERA gap of that small-sample 2H stretch in Chicago, best course might be to just leave on that high note.

Yr Tm	W	L	Sv	IP	K	ERA	xERA	WHIP	oOPS	vL	vR	BF/G	Ctl	Dom	Cmd	SwK	G	L	F	H%	S%	hr/f	GS	APC	DOM%	DIS%	Sv%	LI	RAR	BPV	BPX	R$
09 MIN	5	1	1	76	47	2.36	4.04	0.97	598	525	645	3.8	1.9	5.5	2.9	9%	42	18	40	22%	84%	11%	0	14			25	1.31	18.5	69	129	$10
10 MIN	5	7	1	71	42	3.17	4.14	1.10	625	649	611	3.9	2.8	5.3	1.9	11%	47	15	38	24%	75%	9%	0	14			14	1.32	8.0	46	74	$5
11 LA	4	3	1	66	50	4.07	4.35	1.27	633	631	634	4.0	3.4	6.8	2.0	12%	40	17	43	29%	68%	5%	0	15			25	1.11	-1.0	49	73	$1
12 LA	0	2	0	14	9	3.86	4.87	1.07	682	1119	373	3.5	4.5	5.8	1.3	13%	41	11	49	14%	75%	17%	0	14			0	1.17	0.3	2	2	-$3
13 2 NL	4	4	0	43	30	4.01	4.40	1.41	737	604	818	3.7	3.6	6.3	1.8	11%	43	21	37	31%	72%	6%	0	14			0	1.01	-0.7	38	50	-$2
1st Half	2	3	0	30	21	4.80	4.57	1.47	776	660	836	3.8	3.6	6.3	1.8	11%	43	18	39	31%	68%	8%	0	14			0	0.80	-3.5	37	48	-$3
2nd Half	2	1	0	13	9	2.13	4.02	1.26	640	507	763	3.4	3.6	6.4	1.8	9%	43	27	30	29%	81%	0%	0	13			0	1.50	2.7	40	52	$0
14 Proj	**2**	**2**	**0**	**29**	**19**	**4.03**	**4.19**	**1.36**	**740**	**692**	**768**	**3.9**	**3.0**	**5.9**	**2.0**	**11%**	**43**	**17**	**40**	**30%**	**72%**	**8%**	**0**						**-0.6**	**47**	**61**	**-$2**

Guthrie,Jeremy

Age: 35 Th: R Role SP | Health B | LIMA Plan B
Ht: 6' 1" Wt: 205 Type Con | PT/Exp A | Rand Var 0
Consist A | MM 2005

Another 200+ IP of few walks or Ks. You can see from ERA and H% history that only good fortune (2010) can nudge his ERA under 4.00. Two things he excels at: eating innings and generating work for defenders behind him. Would love to see pedometer readings on his defense compared to a Shields or Santana start.

Yr Tm	W	L	Sv	IP	K	ERA	xERA	WHIP	oOPS	vL	vR	BF/G	Ctl	Dom	Cmd	SwK	G	L	F	H%	S%	hr/f	GS	APC	DOM%	DIS%	Sv%	LI	RAR	BPV	BPX	R$
09 BAL	10	17	0	200	110	5.04	5.09	1.42	828	886	772	26.5	2.7	5.0	1.8	6%	35	19	47	29%	69%	11%	33	102	27%	21%			-17.7	29	55	-$1
10 BAL	11	14	0	209	119	3.83	4.36	1.16	714	783	643	27.3	2.1	5.1	2.4	6%	42	14	43	26%	71%	9%	32	104	56%	13%			6.5	54	87	$12
11 BAL	9	17	0	208	130	4.33	4.43	1.34	770	767	773	26.1	2.9	5.6	2.0	7%	40	21	40	29%	71%	10%	32	98	38%	13%	0	0.73	-9.9	42	63	$1
12 2 TM	8	12	0	182	101	4.76	4.76	1.41	822	868	775	23.9	2.5	5.0	2.0	7%	41	23	36	30%	71%	14%	29	89	34%	21%	0	0.74	-16.6	42	55	-$7
13 KC	15	12	0	212	111	4.04	4.55	1.39	784	905	623	27.4	2.5	4.7	1.9	6%	43	22	35	30%	75%	12%	33	102	39%	12%			-4.5	38	50	$1
1st Half	7	6	0	101	49	4.11	4.91	1.40	805	903	705	27.1	3.2	4.4	1.4	5%	43	20	38	27%	78%	15%	16	101	44%	25%			-3.1	13	16	$0
2nd Half	8	6	0	111	62	3.97	4.24	1.39	765	907	527	27.8	1.9	5.0	2.7	6%	43	25	32	32%	73%	9%	17	104	35%	0%			-1.5	61	80	$2
14 Proj	**12**	**13**	**0**	**203**	**112**	**4.30**	**4.28**	**1.38**	**789**	**870**	**690**	**25.7**	**2.5**	**5.0**	**2.0**	**6%**	**41**	**22**	**37**	**30%**	**73%**	**12%**	**33**						**-10.8**	**42**	**54**	**$1**

Gutierrez,Juan

Age: 30 Th: R Role RP | Health D | LIMA Plan C
Ht: 6' 3" Wt: 245 Type Pwr FB | PT/Exp D | Rand Var 0
Consist F | MM 2300

Actually put together one of the better stretches of his career in 1H (albeit not supported by the skills), and still got released in July. LAA claimed him and got stuck with the correction. Goes to show you that even MLB GMs can get sucked into a trendy pickup and having the grenade go off on their roster. Comforting, isn't it?

Yr Tm	W	L	Sv	IP	K	ERA	xERA	WHIP	oOPS	vL	vR	BF/G	Ctl	Dom	Cmd	SwK	G	L	F	H%	S%	hr/f	GS	APC	DOM%	DIS%	Sv%	LI	RAR	BPV	BPX	R$
09 ARI	4	3	9	71	66	4.06	4.11	1.37	660	762	559	4.7	3.8	8.4	2.2	10%	40	20	39	33%	68%	3%	0	18			90	0.98	2.3	66	123	$5
10 ARI	0	6	15	57	47	5.08	4.52	1.38	806	927	715	4.3	3.7	7.5	2.0	11%	35	14	51	27%	71%	15%	0	16			88	1.15	-7.0	49	79	$2
11 ARI	0	0	0	18	23	5.40	3.67	1.69	793	1009	608	4.5	4.4	11.3	2.6	13%	46	23	32	40%	71%	17%	0	17			0	0.56	-3.3	108	162	-$5
12 a/a	0	1	3	16	9	10.61	8.87	1.99				5.1	3.1	4.9	1.6					38%	47%								-13.0	-28	-37	-$9
13 2 AL	1	5	0	55	45	4.23	4.12	1.37	697	779	609	4.5	3.3	7.3	2.3	10%	43	21	37	31%	70%	8%	0	17			0	0.72	-2.5	65	85	-$4
1st Half	0	1	0	25	17	2.92	3.79	1.22	669	863	495	4.6	2.6	6.2	2.4	9%	47	21	33	29%	79%	8%	0	18			0	0.50	2.9	67	87	-$1
2nd Half	1	4	0	31	28	5.28	4.37	1.50	718	727	704	4.3	3.8	8.2	2.2	10%	40	21	40	34%	65%	8%	0	16			0	0.87	-5.4	62	81	-$6
14 Proj	**1**	**4**	**0**	**44**	**37**	**4.35**	**4.01**	**1.38**	**731**	**820**	**647**	**4.3**	**3.5**	**7.6**	**2.2**	**10%**	**40**	**18**	**42**	**30%**	**72%**	**10%**	**0**						**-2.6**	**59**	**77**	**-$3**

Hagadone,Nick

Age: 28 Th: L Role RP | Health A | LIMA Plan D+
Ht: 6' 5" Wt: 230 Type Pwr xFB | PT/Exp D | Rand Var +1
Consist C | MM 2400

0-1, 5.46 ERA in 31 IP at CLE. Talk about the AAA shuttle: actually made TEN trips between Columbus and Cleveland this year. The two cities are 143 miles apart; by season's end, he was likely making a game of it, trying to make it in under 2 hours. Until he improves Ctl, he'll get more chances to break his record time.

Yr Tm	W	L	Sv	IP	K	ERA	xERA	WHIP	oOPS	vL	vR	BF/G	Ctl	Dom	Cmd	SwK	G	L	F	H%	S%	hr/f	GS	APC	DOM%	DIS%	Sv%	LI	RAR	BPV	BPX	R$
09																																
10 aa	2	2	1	48	36	5.02	5.09	1.73				11.5	6.4	6.8	1.1					31%	72%								-5.5	39	64	-$5
11 CLE *	7	4	4	82	74	3.45	2.96	1.20	380	248	470	6.0	3.1	8.1	2.6	11%	33	8	58	29%	72%	0%	0	21			67	0.62	4.9	94	142	$7
12 CLE	1	0	1	25	26	6.39	4.84	1.62	778	605	919	4.3	5.3	9.2	1.7	10%	34	22	44	33%	62%	13%	0	17			50	0.93	-7.4	34	45	-$7
13 CLE *	2	4	7	64	66	4.41	3.80	1.48	710	679	744	4.3	5.6	9.3	1.7	10%	38	18	44	30%	71%	11%	0	15			78	0.77	-4.3	77	101	-$2
1st Half	1	2	0	34	36	4.69	3.41	1.45	691	591	798	4.3	6.6	9.6	1.5	9%	36	22	42	26%	68%	11%	0	15			0	0.71	-3.4	79	102	-$4
2nd Half	1	2	7	30	30	4.09	4.26	1.51	775	971	558	4.4	4.5	9.1	2.0	15%	47	0	53	34%	74%	13%	0	13			88	0.96	-0.8	79	102	$1
14 Proj	**2**	**2**	**0**	**44**	**44**	**4.09**	**4.05**	**1.42**	**695**	**609**	**786**	**5.4**	**4.7**	**9.1**	**1.9**	**9%**	**36**	**22**	**42**	**31%**	**73%**	**8%**	**0**						**-1.2**	**50**	**66**	**-$2**

Halladay,Roy

Age: 37 Th: R Role SP | Health F | LIMA Plan D+
Ht: 6' 6" Wt: 225 Type Pwr | PT/Exp A | Rand Var +5
Consist B | MM 2203

Had a lousy spring and awful April before finally owning up to sore shoulder that required May surgery. Got some Aug/Sept work before being shut down again due to arm fatigue. Clearly never healthy in 2013, no reason to look at those BPIs. But we can't assume he gets back to anything resembling prior form, either.

Yr Tm	W	L	Sv	IP	K	ERA	xERA	WHIP	oOPS	vL	vR	BF/G	Ctl	Dom	Cmd	SwK	G	L	F	H%	S%	hr/f	GS	APC	DOM%	DIS%	Sv%	LI	RAR	BPV	BPX	R$
09 TOR	17	10	0	239	208	2.79	3.14	1.13	667	647	694	30.1	1.3	7.8	5.9	10%	50	20	29	31%	79%	11%	32	106	78%	6%			45.3	133	250	$32
10 PHI	21	10	0	251	219	2.44	2.93	1.04	645	682	610	30.1	1.1	7.9	7.3	10%	51	19	30	30%	81%	11%	33	108	70%	3%			50.6	141	229	$37
11 PHI	19	6	0	234	220	2.35	2.88	1.04	582	659	511	29.2	1.3	8.5	6.3	12%	51	19	31	31%	78%	5%	32	108	84%	3%			45.9	145	218	$35
12 PHI	11	8	0	156	132	4.49	3.66	1.22	713	738	683	25.8	2.1	7.6	3.7	11%	45	23	32	31%	65%	12%	25	96	60%	12%			-9.2	104	135	$5
13 PHI	4	5	0	62	51	6.82	4.69	1.47	812	861	770	21.7	5.2	7.4	1.4	10%	41	21	38	26%	56%	18%	13	86	31%	54%			-22.6	11	15	-$9
1st Half	2	4	0	34	35	8.65	3.94	1.46	853	764	934	22.1	4.5	9.2	2.1	11%	44	23	33	28%	41%	28%	7	89	43%	57%			-20.3	67	86	-$12
2nd Half	2	1	0	28	16	4.55	5.69	1.48	757	996	572	21.2	6.2	5.2	0.8	8%	37	20	43	23%	71%	9%	6	81	17%	50%			-2.3	-58	-75	-$6
14 Proj	**9**	**8**	**0**	**140**	**109**	**4.45**	**4.02**	**1.34**	**750**	**814**	**689**	**23.2**	**3.6**	**7.0**	**1.9**	**10%**	**42**	**21**	**37**	**28%**	**70%**	**12%**	**25**						**-10.1**	**48**	**63**	**$1**

Hamels,Cole

Age: 30 Th: L Role SP | Health A | LIMA Plan B
Ht: 6' 3" Wt: 195 Type Pwr | PT/Exp A | Rand Var 0
Consist A | MM 5405

Rough start to 2013, captured by 1H ERA, set the narrative for the whole year. Skills tell a different story, though: They remain remarkably consistent and elite, touching new highs in 2H. Poor support ruined W-L, but he's sufficiently skilled to overcome that in 2014. Remains a top-shelf pitcher at a second-tier price. Invest.

Yr Tm	W	L	Sv	IP	K	ERA	xERA	WHIP	oOPS	vL	vR	BF/G	Ctl	Dom	Cmd	SwK	G	L	F	H%	S%	hr/f	GS	APC	DOM%	DIS%	Sv%	LI	RAR	BPV	BPX	R$
09 PHI	10	11	0	194	168	4.32	3.76	1.29	755	711	767	25.4	2.0	7.8	3.9	12%	40	21	39	32%	68%	11%	32	97	53%	25%			0.0	105	196	$10
10 PHI	12	11	0	209	211	3.06	3.29	1.18	692	645	703	25.9	2.6	9.1	3.5	13%	45	17	38	30%	80%	12%	33	102	61%	12%			26.2	116	187	$21
11 PHI	14	9	0	216	194	2.79	3.02	0.99	596	662	577	26.6	1.8	8.1	4.4	12%	52	15	33	27%	75%	10%	31	98	77%	10%	0	0.76	30.7	126	189	$29
12 PHI	17	6	0	215	216	3.05	3.32	1.12	661	629	673	28.0	2.2	9.0	4.2	14%	43	22	35	30%	78%	12%	31	107	77%	0%			25.6	125	163	$27
13 PHI	8	14	0	220	202	3.60	3.46	1.16	699	712	695	27.4	2.0	8.3	4.0	13%	43	21	37	31%	71%	9%	33	104	76%	3%			7.2	115	149	$13
1st Half	2	11	0	106	99	4.58	3.72	1.30	771	723	787	26.6	2.8	8.4	3.0	13%	42	21	37	32%	67%	12%	17	103	65%	6%			-9.4	95	124	$1
2nd Half	6	3	0	114	103	2.68	3.22	1.03	630	699	613	28.3	1.3	8.1	6.1	12%	44	20	37	30%	76%	7%	16	104	88%	0%			16.6	132	171	$25
14 Proj	**15**	**9**	**0**	**218**	**204**	**3.27**	**3.10**	**1.12**	**671**	**678**	**670**	**26.5**	**2.0**	**8.4**	**4.2**	**13%**	**44**	**20**	**36**	**30%**	**74%**	**10%**	**32**						**15.9**	**120**	**156**	**$23**

RAY MURPHY

Hammel,Jason

Age: 31	Th: R	Role SP	Health F	LIMA Plan C	
Ht: 6' 6"	Wt: 225	Type	PT/Exp A	Rand Var +1	
			Consist C	MM 3203	

If you evaluate in terms of ERA, 2012 now looks like a blind squirrel finding a nut. But if you look at BPV, 2012 gets validation from 2009-10. So what happened in 2013? May have just never been healthy: pre-season knee surgery, illness in June, DL stint for arm problems in 2H. If we give him a pass, then... UP: sub-4.00 ERA.

Yr	Tm	W	L	Sv	IP	K	ERA	xERA	WHIP	oOPS	vL	vR	BF/G	Ctl	Dom	Cmd	SwK	G	L	F	H%	S%	hr/f	GS	APC	DOM%	DIS%	Sv%	LI	RAR	BPV	BPX	R$
09	COL	10	8	0	177	133	4.33	3.91	1.39	775	785	763	22.7	2.1	6.8	3.2	10%	46	23	31	34%	70%	10%	30	82	50%	23%	0	0.73	-0.2	88	165	$5
10	COL	10	9	0	178	141	4.81	3.80	1.40	755	761	750	25.7	2.4	7.1	3.0	8%	47	20	33	34%	67%	10%	30	95	47%	20%			-16.1	89	144	$0
11	COL	7	13	1	170	94	4.76	4.66	1.43	778	808	752	23.1	3.6	5.0	1.4	7%	44	21	35	29%	69%	11%	27	85	41%	26%	100	0.78	-17.1	14	22	-$5
12	BAL	8	6	0	118	113	3.43	3.48	1.24	637	586	692	24.7	3.2	8.6	2.7	11%	53	19	28	30%	74%	10%	20	97	50%	15%			8.5	100	130	$7
13	BAL	7	8	1	139	96	4.97	4.52	1.46	813	881	716	23.5	3.1	6.2	2.0	8%	40	22	38	31%	70%	13%	23	89	22%	17%	100	0.77	-19.0	46	60	-$7
1st Half		7	4	0	94	66	5.09	4.41	1.40	802	818	777	25.5	3.1	6.3	2.1	8%	42	20	38	30%	68%	14%	16	98	31%	19%			-14.2	51	67	-$6
2nd Half		0	4	1	46	30	4.73	4.74	1.58	835	1015	605	20.3	3.2	5.9	1.9	8%	36	27	38	34%	73%	10%	7	74	0%	14%	100	0.74	-4.9	35	45	-$11
14	Proj	9	9	0	160	118	4.13	3.95	1.38	746	803	681	22.3	3.1	6.6	2.1	9%	44	22	34	30%	73%	11%	30						-5.1	57	74	$2

Hand,Donovan

Age: 28	Th: R	Role RP	Health A	LIMA Plan D+	
Ht: 6' 3"	Wt: 210	Type Con	PT/Exp D	Rand Var 0	
			Consist B	MM 2000	

1-5, 3.69 ERA in 68 IP at MIL. Soft-tosser started year in Triple-A and actually broke a few panes of glass down there (more than 1 K/IP), but newfound strikeout ability didn't translate to the bigs. Without pinpoint control or a huge GB tilt (or better yet, both) to mitigate poor Dom, there's little here to hold our attention.

Yr	Tm	W	L	Sv	IP	K	ERA	xERA	WHIP	oOPS	vL	vR	BF/G	Ctl	Dom	Cmd	SwK	G	L	F	H%	S%	hr/f	GS	APC	DOM%	DIS%	Sv%	LI	RAR	BPV	BPX	R$
09	aa	8	5	1	99	45	4.19	4.99	1.40				15.4	2.0	4.1	2.1					31%	74%								1.5	28	52	$2
10	a/a	4	1	2	76	42	3.85	4.70	1.45				6.7	1.6	5.0	3.2					35%	73%								2.1	75	122	$0
11	a/a	2	6	2	66	37	3.77	6.08	1.73				6.3	3.0	5.0	1.7					36%	80%								1.4	27	41	-$5
12	aaa	3	3	0	80	44	5.18	6.25	1.68				8.1	2.3	5.0	2.2					36%	71%								-11.5	30	39	-$11
13	MIL *	4	6	0	104	67	3.78	4.73	1.39	785	878	694	8.6	2.9	5.8	2.0	7%	47	20	33	30%	78%	14%	7	33	0%	29%	0	0.68	1.1	39	50	-$2
1st Half		2	2	0	52	40	3.28	3.95	1.26	666	748	576	7.9	2.2	6.8	3.1	9%	57	11	32	31%	78%	8%	2	30	0%	50%	0	0.28	3.8	78	101	$2
2nd Half		2	4	0	52	28	4.29	5.52	1.53	846	948	750	9.4	3.5	4.8	1.4	7%	42	25	34	30%	78%	16%	5	35	0%	20%	0	0.91	-2.7	7	9	-$6
14	Proj	2	3	0	58	34	4.23	4.25	1.53	871	960	782	8.1	2.7	5.3	2.0	7%	48	19	33	33%	76%	11%	0						-2.6	49	63	-$4

Hanrahan,Joel

Age: 32	Th: R	Role RP	Health F	LIMA Plan C+	
Ht: 6' 4"	Wt: 250	Type Pwr	PT/Exp B	Rand Var +5	
			Consist D	MM 5510	

Opened season as BOS closer; got knocked around for a few weeks before getting shut down with elbow problems that led to Tommy John surgery in May. Not expected to be ready at start of 2014, and is a free agent. Even the best crystal ball would have a hard time forseeing how this one plays out. Keep expectations low.

Yr	Tm	W	L	Sv	IP	K	ERA	xERA	WHIP	oOPS	vL	vR	BF/G	Ctl	Dom	Cmd	SwK	G	L	F	H%	S%	hr/f	GS	APC	DOM%	DIS%	Sv%	LI	RAR	BPV	BPX	R$
09	2 NL	1	4	5	64	72	4.78	4.24	1.67	780	795	766	4.4	4.8	10.1	2.1	13%	36	25	39	39%	70%	4%	0	18			50	0.96	-3.6	67	126	-$3
10	PIT	4	1	6	70	100	3.62	2.77	1.21	649	750	589	4.1	3.4	12.9	3.8	14%	42	18	40	35%	72%	9%	0	16			60	0.84	4.0	162	262	$7
11	PIT	1	4	40	69	61	1.83	3.05	1.05	543	528	555	3.9	2.1	8.0	3.8	11%	52	19	29	29%	82%	2%	0	15			91	1.27	17.8	117	176	$23
12	PIT	5	2	36	60	67	2.72	4.20	1.27	648	525	763	4.0	5.4	10.1	1.9	13%	39	16	45	24%	85%	13%	0	16			90	1.17	9.6	52	68	$18
13	BOS	0	1	4	7	5	9.82	7.01	2.18	1211	762	1793	4.1	7.4	6.1	0.8	9%	36	8	56	28%	67%	29%	0	18			67	0.96	-5.4	-74	-97	-$5
1st Half		0	1	4	7	5	9.82	7.01	2.18	1211	762	1793	4.1	7.4	6.1	0.8	9%	36	8	56	28%	67%	29%	0	18			67	0.96	-5.4	-74	-96	-$5
2nd Half																																	
14	Proj	1	1	5	26	30	3.52	3.19	1.26	650	641	656	3.9	3.9	10.7	2.7	13%	42	19	39	31%	74%	8%	0						1.1	106	138	$1

Hanson,Tommy

Age: 27	Th: R	Role SP	Health D	LIMA Plan C	
Ht: 6' 6"	Wt: 220	Type Pwr FB	PT/Exp B	Rand Var 0	
			Consist D	MM 2203	

Latest example of the axiom "If the Braves offer to trade you a pitcher, assume they know something that you don't." Dom took another huge step back, and seemed to leave him without answers. 2H forearm strain was latest concern re: health of his arm. Only good news: he's young enough to rebound. But don't bet on that.

Yr	Tm	W	L	Sv	IP	K	ERA	xERA	WHIP	oOPS	vL	vR	BF/G	Ctl	Dom	Cmd	SwK	G	L	F	H%	S%	hr/f	GS	APC	DOM%	DIS%	Sv%	LI	RAR	BPV	BPX	R$
09	ATL *	14	7	0	194	194	2.52	2.67	1.11	660	743	566	23.8	3.0	9.0	3.0	10%	40	18	42	28%	81%	7%	21	95	57%	10%			43.2	108	202	$29
10	ATL	10	11	0	203	173	3.33	3.75	1.17	648	606	685	24.9	2.5	7.7	3.1	9%	42	17	42	30%	73%	6%	34	96	65%	12%			18.7	91	147	$16
11	ATL	11	7	0	130	142	3.60	3.38	1.17	680	783	593	24.5	3.2	9.8	3.1	11%	39	20	40	28%	74%	13%	22	99	73%	14%			5.5	108	162	$11
12	ATL	13	10	0	175	161	4.48	4.27	1.45	808	889	719	24.5	3.7	8.3	2.3	10%	40	21	39	32%	74%	14%	31	94	45%	16%			-10.1	69	89	-$1
13	LAA *	4	5	0	93	68	5.34	5.32	1.54	813	866	745	21.2	3.4	6.6	1.9	8%	33	23	45	33%	68%	10%	13	84	31%	46%	0	0.69	-16.8	37	48	-$9
1st Half		4	2	0	48	33	5.10	4.93	1.55	859	923	780	23.9	3.2	6.2	1.9	8%	36	19	44	32%	72%	13%	9	91	33%	33%			-7.2	40	52	-$7
2nd Half		0	3	0	45	35	5.59	4.80	1.52	720	755	673	19.5	3.7	7.0	1.9	8%	25	30	45	33%	63%	3%	4	73	25%	75%	0	0.57	-9.6	52	67	-$12
14	Proj	7	7	0	135	111	4.45	4.09	1.39	768	833	693	22.0	3.4	7.4	2.2	9%	35	23	43	30%	71%	11%	26						-9.7	54	70	$0

Happ,J.A.

Age: 31	Th: L	Role SP	Health F	LIMA Plan D+	
Ht: 6' 6"	Wt: 195	Type Pwr FB	PT/Exp B	Rand Var -1	
			Consist B	MM 2301	

His first half was ended by a line drive to the head, as if there wasn't enough evidence that he was getting hit hard. PQS DOM%/DIS% splits nicely summarize the feast-or-famine nature of his season. As a flyball pitcher with shaky control, it's hard to see the disasters suddenly stopping. Best to stay clear.

Yr	Tm	W	L	Sv	IP	K	ERA	xERA	WHIP	oOPS	vL	vR	BF/G	Ctl	Dom	Cmd	SwK	G	L	F	H%	S%	hr/f	GS	APC	DOM%	DIS%	Sv%	LI	RAR	BPV	BPX	R$
09	PHI	12	4	0	166	119	2.93	4.33	1.23	710	643	732	19.6	3.0	6.5	2.1	8%	38	19	43	27%	82%	10%	23	76	43%	17%	0	0.71	28.5	50	94	$17
10	2 NL *	7	5	0	122	94	4.68	5.12	1.61	688	551	724	22.5	5.0	6.9	1.4	9%	39	18	43	31%	74%	7%	16	99	56%	19%			-9.0	37	60	-$5
11	HOU *	7	15	0	174	146	5.00	4.60	1.51	806	751	819	24.4	4.8	7.5	1.6	8%	33	23	44	30%	69%	10%	28	106	29%	21%			-22.7	49	74	-$8
12	2 TM	10	11	0	145	144	4.79	3.98	1.40	787	730	807	22.4	3.5	9.0	2.6	10%	44	17	39	33%	68%	12%	24	91	54%	17%	0	0.73	-13.8	89	116	-$2
13	TOR	5	7	0	93	77	4.56	4.83	1.47	734	802	708	23.1	4.4	7.5	1.7	8%	36	18	46	31%	71%	8%	18	96	39%	44%			-8.0	31	40	-$5
1st Half		2	2	0	33	26	4.91	5.46	1.55	753	670	789	21.4	5.2	7.1	1.4	7%	29	18	53	30%	69%	6%	7	93	43%	43%			-4.2	-6	-7	-$6
2nd Half		3	5	0	60	51	4.37	4.48	1.42	724	885	665	24.1	3.9	7.7	2.0	9%	41	18	41	31%	72%	9%	11	98	36%	45%			-3.7	51	66	-$4
14	Proj	7	9	0	122	105	4.62	4.24	1.46	759	761	758	23.1	4.2	7.8	1.8	9%	38	18	44	31%	70%	9%	19						-11.3	42	55	-$2

Harang,Aaron

Age: 36	Th: R	Role SP	Health D	LIMA Plan D+	
Ht: 6' 7"	Wt: 260	Type FB	PT/Exp A	Rand Var +3	
			Consist B	MM 2201	

Released by Seattle in August after an absolutely brutal run (5-11, 5.76 in 120 IP), got picked up by the Mets and did some competent work for them in September. Skills were reasonably in line with prior years that delivered better results, but don't get sucked in. "Competent" is the upside; "season-killer" is the downside.

Yr	Tm	W	L	Sv	IP	K	ERA	xERA	WHIP	oOPS	vL	vR	BF/G	Ctl	Dom	Cmd	SwK	G	L	F	H%	S%	hr/f	GS	APC	DOM%	DIS%	Sv%	LI	RAR	BPV	BPX	R$
09	CIN	6	14	0	162	142	4.21	4.07	1.41	797	772	822	27.0	2.4	7.9	3.3	9%	35	24	41	34%	75%	12%	26	103	58%	19%			2.2	90	169	$3
10	CIN	6	7	0	112	82	5.32	4.60	1.59	841	800	873	22.9	3.1	6.6	2.2	8%	37	22	41	35%	69%	10%	20	94	40%	45%	0	0.70	-17.1	51	83	-$7
11	SD	14	7	0	171	124	3.64	4.22	1.37	758	787	732	25.7	3.1	6.5	2.1	9%	41	18	41	30%	77%	9%	28	98	46%	18%			6.4	54	81	$7
12	LA	10	10	0	180	131	3.61	4.96	1.40	711	761	662	25.4	4.3	6.6	1.5	8%	39	20	41	29%	76%	6%	31	100	32%	23%			9.0	20	26	$4
13	2 TM	5	12	0	143	113	5.40	4.37	1.35	795	800	789	24.1	2.5	7.1	2.8	8%	36	20	44	30%	64%	13%	26	94	46%	27%			-27.1	74	96	-$8
1st Half		3	7	0	73	60	5.08	4.00	1.24	766	791	742	24.0	1.4	7.4	5.5	9%	36	20	44	32%	63%	11%	13	92	46%	31%			-10.9	111	143	-$3
2nd Half		2	5	0	71	53	5.73	4.78	1.46	824	807	848	24.2	3.7	6.8	1.8	8%	36	19	44	29%	65%	14%	13	96	46%	23%			-16.3	36	47	-$12
14	Proj	5	7	0	101	74	4.48	4.31	1.41	778	792	763	24.0	3.4	6.6	2.0	8%	36	20	44	30%	72%	11%	18						-7.7	42	55	-$2

Haren,Dan

Age: 33	Th: R	Role SP	Health C	LIMA Plan A	
Ht: 6' 5"	Wt: 215	Type FB	PT/Exp A	Rand Var +2	
			Consist B	MM 4303	

In terms of results, as stark a contrast between halves as you'll ever see, sandwiched around July DL stint for shoulder soreness. Our trusty skill gauges are unmoved, arguing that 1H wasn't bad and 2H only marginally better. 2H reminds us what he can do when healthy, though that's an elusive concept... UP: 15 Wins, 3.25 ERA.

Yr	Tm	W	L	Sv	IP	K	ERA	xERA	WHIP	oOPS	vL	vR	BF/G	Ctl	Dom	Cmd	SwK	G	L	F	H%	S%	hr/f	GS	APC	DOM%	DIS%	Sv%	LI	RAR	BPV	BPX	R$
09	ARI	14	10	0	229	223	3.14	3.15	1.00	635	679	586	27.5	1.5	8.8	5.9	11%	43	20	37	28%	74%	12%	33	105	79%	0%			33.4	138	259	$33
10	2 TM	12	12	0	235	216	3.91	3.66	1.27	736	761	715	28.4	2.1	8.3	4.0	11%	40	19	41	32%	74%	11%	35	107	60%	6%			5.0	111	180	$13
11	LAA	16	10	0	238	192	3.17	3.39	1.02	630	617	648	27.2	1.2	7.3	5.8	10%	43	20	38	28%	71%	8%	34	108	71%	9%	0	0.82	22.6	118	177	$27
12	LAA	12	13	0	177	142	4.33	4.08	1.29	775	731	825	24.9	1.9	7.2	3.7	9%	40	21	40	31%	72%	13%	30	95	53%	17%			-6.9	96	125	$4
13	WAS	10	14	1	170	151	4.67	3.75	1.24	760	722	792	23.1	1.6	8.0	4.9	10%	36	22	42	32%	67%	13%	30	90	40%	20%	100	0.83	-16.8	114	148	$2
1st Half		4	9	0	82	67	6.15	4.17	1.44	888	806	960	24.4	1.4	7.4	5.2	9%	35	21	44	34%	63%	16%	15	92	27%	27%			-23.1	107	138	-$11
2nd Half		6	5	1	88	84	3.29	3.37	1.05	626	627	625	21.9	1.8	8.6	4.7	10%	37	23	39	28%	72%	9%	15	87	53%	13%	100	0.87	6.3	121	156	$14
14	Proj	10	11	0	160	138	3.96	3.42	1.20	717	690	743	23.6	1.9	7.8	4.1	10%	40	20	40	30%	71%	11%	27						-1.8	106	138	$9

RAY MURPHY

Harrell,Lucas

Age: 29	Th: R	Role RP	Health	A	LIMA Plan	D
Ht: 6' 2"	Wt: 210	Type Pwr GB	PT/Exp	B	Rand Var	+2
			Consist	B	MM	1001

There's no split or combination that makes his 2013 look good. Sure, the hr/f cost him a few points of ERA, but that's merely a quibble. Even a move to the bullpen didn't help—he had a 5.49 ERA and 0.6 Cmd in 39 IP there. Fact is, skills were barely average in 2011-12, so even a large regression won't leave him much value.

Yr Tm	W	L	Sv	IP	K	ERA	xERA	WHIP	oOPS	vL	vR	BF/G	Ctl	Dom	Cmd	SwK	G	L	F	H%	S%	hr/f	GS	APC	DOM%	DIS%	Sv%	LI	RAR	BPV	BPX	R$
09 a/a	12	4	0	146	79	4.58	5.17	1.70				26.4	4.8	4.8	1.0					33%	73%								-4.7	28	52	-$4
10 CHW *	11	10	0	162	85	5.65	5.94	1.79	898	1047	727	21.9	4.8	4.7	1.0	7%	51	28	22	34%	69%	11%	3	60	0%	33%	0	0.43	-31.3	15	24	-$15
11 2 TM *	12	7	0	145	91	3.31	4.06	1.46	710	897	647	20.0	3.7	5.7	1.5	7%	55	15	30	31%	77%	0%	2	40	50%	50%	0	0.71	11.3	54	81	$4
12 HOU	11	11	0	194	140	3.76	3.99	1.36	685	713	663	25.8	3.6	6.5	1.8	7%	57	20	22	30%	73%	10%	32	100	41%	13%			6.0	54	71	$5
13 HOU	6	17	0	154	89	5.86	5.08	1.70	836	776	905	19.6	5.2	5.2	1.0	5%	51	21	27	31%	67%	14%	22	79	27%	41%	0	0.79	-37.7	-16	-21	-$21
1st Half	5	8	0	100	64	4.59	4.47	1.56	794	713	889	24.7	4.2	5.8	1.4	6%	53	21	26	31%	73%	14%	18	101	33%	33%			-8.9	20	26	-$14
2nd Half	1	9	0	54	25	8.22	6.33	1.98	911	891	933	14.6	6.9	4.2	0.6	5%	49	21	30	31%	58%	14%	4	58	0%	75%	0	0.84	-28.8	-83	-107	-$34
14 Proj	**5**	**9**	**0**	**101**	**60**	**5.33**	**4.63**	**1.64**	**798**	**785**	**811**	**19.5**	**4.9**	**5.4**	**1.1**	**6%**	**53**	**21**	**26**	**31%**	**68%**	**12%**	**22**						**-18.2**	**-3**	**-4**	**-$10**

Harris,Will

Age: 29	Th: R	Role RP	Health	A	LIMA Plan	A
Ht: 6' 4"	Wt: 225	Type Pwr	PT/Exp	D	Rand Var	-1
			Consist	B	MM	5400

Solid skills posted in his first full season, with fortunate hr/f offset by a bit of misfortune with H%. Skills dipped a bit overall in 2nd half, but the improved Cmd was a welcome development. Has a pretty significant reverse platoon split; that and lack of high-leverage usage make any real save totals unlikely.

Yr Tm	W	L	Sv	IP	K	ERA	xERA	WHIP	oOPS	vL	vR	BF/G	Ctl	Dom	Cmd	SwK	G	L	F	H%	S%	hr/f	GS	APC	DOM%	DIS%	Sv%	LI	RAR	BPV	BPX	R$
09																																
10																																
11																																
12 COL *	5	2	1	70	66	4.34	4.17	1.36	922	724	1073	4.6	2.7	8.5	3.2	12%	37	23	40	34%	69%	13%	0	17			50	0.65	-2.8	94	122	-$1
13 ARI	4	1	0	53	53	2.91	3.18	1.23	661	509	759	3.6	2.6	9.1	3.5	11%	47	23	29	33%	77%	7%	0	14			0	1.01	6.2	119	155	$2
1st Half	1	0	0	18	22	2.00	2.89	1.28	625	452	761	3.6	3.5	11.0	3.1	13%	47	29	24	34%	86%	9%	0	13			0	0.99	4.1	128	166	$1
2nd Half	3	1	0	35	31	3.38	3.33	1.21	679	544	756	3.6	2.1	8.0	3.9	11%	48	21	32	32%	73%	6%	0	15			0	1.02	2.1	114	148	$2
14 Proj	**3**	**2**	**0**	**57**	**56**	**3.44**	**3.07**	**1.20**	**647**	**485**	**752**	**3.8**	**2.7**	**8.8**	**3.3**	**11%**	**47**	**24**	**29**	**31%**	**72%**	**9%**	**0**						**3.0**	**111**	**145**	**$2**

Harrison,Matt

Age: 28	Th: L	Role SP	Health	F	LIMA Plan	D+
Ht: 6' 4"	Wt: 240	Type	PT/Exp	B	Rand Var	+5
			Consist	A	MM	2103

Missed most of the season following back surgery. Ignore his 2013—it's small sample noise—and realize that his 2011-2012 ERAs were much lower than xERAs. Expected to be ready to start 2014, but a return to "form" would be closer to his recent xERA, and he's still a health risk. That's not something you go out on a limb for.

Yr Tm	W	L	Sv	IP	K	ERA	xERA	WHIP	oOPS	vL	vR	BF/G	Ctl	Dom	Cmd	SwK	G	L	F	H%	S%	hr/f	GS	APC	DOM%	DIS%	Sv%	LI	RAR	BPV	BPX	R$
09 TEX	4	5	0	63	34	6.11	4.79	1.64	876	564	974	25.7	3.3	4.8	1.5	6%	47	23	31	33%	64%	13%	11	97	27%	45%			-14.0	24	44	-$7
10 TEX	3	2	2	78	46	4.71	4.97	1.52	757	723	770	9.6	4.5	5.3	1.2	8%	47	21	33	29%	72%	12%	6	38	33%	17%	67	0.89	-6.1	-1	-1	-$3
11 TEX	14	9	0	186	126	3.39	3.92	1.28	685	729	667	24.9	2.8	6.1	2.2	8%	47	20	32	30%	75%	7%	30	97	43%	13%	0	0.75	12.6	60	91	$11
12 TEX	18	11	0	213	133	3.29	4.15	1.26	714	571	764	27.4	2.5	5.6	2.3	8%	49	20	31	29%	77%	11%	32	101	50%	13%			19.1	61	79	$16
13 TEX	0	2	0	11	12	8.44	4.34	1.97	970	432	1149	25.5	5.9	10.1	1.7	14%	45	23	32	40%	58%	20%	2	98	0%	50%			-6.0	46	60	-$7
1st Half	0	2	0	11	12	8.44	4.34	1.97	970	432	1149	25.5	5.9	10.1	1.7	14%	45	23	32	40%	58%	20%	2	98	0%	50%			-6.0	46	59	-$7
2nd Half																																
14 Proj	**10**	**7**	**0**	**162**	**103**	**4.12**	**4.02**	**1.36**	**741**	**652**	**774**	**22.5**	**2.9**	**5.7**	**2.0**	**8%**	**48**	**21**	**32**	**30%**	**72%**	**11%**	**44**						**-5.1**	**49**	**64**	**$3**

Harvey,Matt

Age: 25	Th: R	Role RP	Health	C	LIMA Plan	
Ht: 6' 4"	Wt: 225	Type ###	PT/Exp	C	Rand Var	
			Consist	A	MM	

Missed the last five weeks with a torn UCL and will miss 2014 with Tommy John surgery. A shame, because with only 59 MLB innings coming in, this was a jump all the way into the elite. Should be fully recovered by 2015, and showed more than enough to be worth the wait in keeper formats.

Yr Tm	W	L	Sv	IP	K	ERA	xERA	WHIP	oOPS	vL	vR	BF/G	Ctl	Dom	Cmd	SwK	G	L	F	H%	S%	hr/f	GS	APC	DOM%	DIS%	Sv%	LI	RAR	BPV	BPX	R$
09																																
10																																
11 aa	5	3	0	60	54	4.33	3.57	1.32				20.6	2.9	8.1	2.7					33%	66%								-2.9	94	141	-$1
12 NYM *	10	10	0	169	168	3.50	3.41	1.29	631	662	592	23.2	3.8	8.9	2.4	13%	38	24	37	30%	75%	10%	10	98	70%	0%			10.8	89	115	$10
13 NYM	9	5	0	178	191	2.27	2.73	0.93	530	456	603	26.5	1.6	9.6	6.2	13%	48	20	33	29%	76%	5%	26	104	85%	0%			35.1	157	205	$28
1st Half	7	1	0	117	132	2.00	2.68	0.85	489	465	515	26.1	1.8	10.2	5.5	13%	46	19	35	26%	78%	5%	17	103	88%	0%			26.9	156	203	$37
2nd Half	2	4	0	61	59	2.79	2.82	1.08	602	438	740	27.4	1.0	8.7	8.4	13%	51	21	28	33%	73%	4%	9	105	78%	0%			8.2	157	204	$10
14 Proj																																

Hawkins,LaTroy

Age: 41	Th: R	Role RP	Health	F	LIMA Plan	B
Ht: 6' 5"	Wt: 220	Type Con GB	PT/Exp	C	Rand Var	-1
			Consist	B	MM	4110

Discovered fountain of youth and showed his best skills in 10 years. Perhaps pressure situations agree with him; LI was up as well. Has displayed all of these skills before, though age and health history warn against a repeat. Don't expect many saves, he's a competent stopgap in the 9th but unlikely to be The Guy.

Yr Tm	W	L	Sv	IP	K	ERA	xERA	WHIP	oOPS	vL	vR	BF/G	Ctl	Dom	Cmd	SwK	G	L	F	H%	S%	hr/f	GS	APC	DOM%	DIS%	Sv%	LI	RAR	BPV	BPX	R$
09 HOU	1	4	11	63	45	2.13	3.79	1.20	679	529	828	4.0	2.3	6.4	2.8	8%	45	24	31	28%	88%	12%	0	16			73	1.08	17.1	77	144	$9
10 MIL	0	3	0	16	18	8.44	3.45	1.69	890	783	957	4.1	3.4	10.1	3.0	10%	47	21	32	41%	48%	13%	0	18			0	0.84	-8.6	116	188	-$5
11 MIL	3	1	0	48	28	2.42	3.55	1.24	627	584	661	3.9	1.9	5.2	2.8	6%	62	16	22	31%	80%	3%	0	14			0	0.81	9.1	84	126	$2
12 LAA	2	3	1	42	23	3.64	4.27	1.38	735	576	906	3.7	2.8	4.9	1.8	6%	57	17	26	30%	77%	14%	0	15			25	0.80	1.9	49	63	-$3
13 NYM	3	2	13	71	55	2.93	3.31	1.15	656	670	646	4.0	1.3	7.0	5.5	9%	48	24	28	31%	77%	10%	0	14			81	1.11	8.2	118	153	$8
1st Half	3	1	0	33	28	3.24	3.37	1.41	754	745	761	4.3	1.9	7.6	4.0	9%	55	21	25	35%	81%	15%	0	15			0	1.08	2.6	118	152	$1
2nd Half	0	1	13	37	27	2.65	3.24	0.91	557	591	536	3.8	0.7	6.5	9.0	9%	42	27	31	27%	72%	6%	0	13			93	1.14	5.6	118	153	$15
14 Proj	**3**	**3**	**8**	**68**	**46**	**3.20**	**3.39**	**1.21**	**666**	**609**	**713**	**3.8**	**1.8**	**6.1**	**3.4**	**8%**	**52**	**21**	**27**	**30%**	**76%**	**10%**	**0**						**5.6**	**91**	**118**	**$5**

Hefner,Jeremy

Age: 28	Th: R	Role SP	Health	D	LIMA Plan	C
Ht: 6' 4"	Wt: 215	Type	PT/Exp	C	Rand Var	+1
			Consist	A	MM	3100

Missed the last two months with Tommy John surgery. BPX says he's an average arm—though with good Cmd now in two straight seasons—but ERA and value haven't cooperated thus far. He'll miss most of the season, and his mediocre skills really aren't worth the keeper-league DL stash maneuver.

Yr Tm	W	L	Sv	IP	K	ERA	xERA	WHIP	oOPS	vL	vR	BF/G	Ctl	Dom	Cmd	SwK	G	L	F	H%	S%	hr/f	GS	APC	DOM%	DIS%	Sv%	LI	RAR	BPV	BPX	R$
09																																
10 aa	11	8	0	168	100	3.37	3.96	1.37				25.1	2.9	5.4	1.9					31%	76%								14.8	56	90	$7
11 aaa	9	7	0	157	102	3.95	4.36	1.42				23.8	3.1	5.9	1.9					31%	74%								-0.1	51	77	$1
12 NYM *	9	9	0	155	92	4.32	4.15	1.30	768	828	704	17.8	1.6	5.3	3.3	8%	44	20	37	32%	67%	8%	13	58	54%	23%	0	0.62	-5.8	76	100	$1
13 NYM	4	8	0	131	99	4.34	4.03	1.29	756	846	687	23.2	2.5	6.8	2.7	9%	45	19	37	29%	71%	13%	23	89	48%	26%	0	0.71	-7.6	77	100	-$2
1st Half	2	6	0	87	65	3.72	4.01	1.29	734	899	584	23.0	2.6	6.7	2.6	9%	46	18	36	29%	76%	12%	15	87	47%	20%	0	0.69	1.5	75	97	$1
2nd Half	2	2	0	44	34	5.56	4.06	1.31	799	709	851	23.5	2.5	7.0	2.8	8%	43	20	37	29%	61%	15%	8	93	50%	38%			-9.2	80	104	-$7
14 Proj	**1**	**1**	**0**	**15**	**10**	**4.43**	**3.89**	**1.32**	**752**	**791**	**719**	**21.5**	**2.4**	**6.2**	**2.6**	**8%**	**44**	**19**	**37**	**30%**	**69%**	**11%**	**3**						**-1.0**	**68**	**88**	**-$3**

Hellickson,Jeremy

Age: 27	Th: R	Role SP	Health	A	LIMA Plan	C
Ht: 6' 1"	Wt: 190	Type FB	PT/Exp	A	Rand Var	+3
			Consist	A	MM	3205

Karma caught to him, after three years of outperforming xERA with favorable H%/S%. This time, S% swung the other way. It obscured a nice increase in overall skills, though he's just now approaching league average. Set expectations against a 4.00 ERA and hope for continued skills consolidation to carry him lower.

Yr Tm	W	L	Sv	IP	K	ERA	xERA	WHIP	oOPS	vL	vR	BF/G	Ctl	Dom	Cmd	SwK	G	L	F	H%	S%	hr/f	GS	APC	DOM%	DIS%	Sv%	LI	RAR	BPV	BPX	R$
09 a/a	9	2	0	114	115	3.05	2.22	0.99				21.7	2.3	9.1	4.0					27%	71%								17.9	131	244	$16
10 TAM *	16	3	0	154	139	2.90	3.30	1.22	666	906	391	20.1	2.5	8.1	3.3	13%	37	13	50	32%	78%	10%	4	59	100%	0%	0	0.86	22.4	105	170	$16
11 TAM	13	10	0	189	117	2.95	4.58	1.15	660	726	585	26.7	3.4	5.6	1.6	10%	35	20	45	23%	79%	8%	29	102	45%	7%			23.1	21	31	$17
12 TAM	10	11	0	177	124	3.10	4.39	1.25	710	703	717	23.9	3.0	6.3	2.1	9%	42	21	37	27%	82%	12%	31	97	42%	23%			19.9	52	68	$12
13 TAM	12	10	0	174	135	5.17	4.16	1.35	775	785	763	23.0	2.6	7.0	2.7	10%	40	20	40	31%	64%	11%	31	90	35%	26%	0	1.04	-28.0	74	96	-$4
1st Half	7	3	0	105	80	4.90	3.97	1.23	745	782	698	25.2	2.2	6.9	3.1	10%	40	19	41	29%	63%	11%	17	98	47%	6%			-13.4	81	105	$0
2nd Half	5	7	0	69	55	5.58	4.44	1.53	817	788	850	20.6	3.1	7.1	2.3	10%	39	21	40	34%	66%	11%	14	81	21%	50%	0	1.30	-14.7	62	80	-$11
14 Proj	**13**	**10**	**0**	**185**	**140**	**4.08**	**3.94**	**1.29**	**731**	**759**	**696**	**22.5**	**2.8**	**6.8**	**2.4**	**10%**	**39**	**20**	**41**	**29%**	**72%**	**10%**	**34**						**-4.8**	**64**	**83**	**$7**

MATT CEDERHOLM

Henderson,Jim

Age:	31	Th:	R	Role	RP	Health	B	LIMA Plan	C
Ht:	6' 5"	Wt:	220	Type	Pwr FB	PT/Exp	D	Rand Var	-2
						Consist	B	MM	4530

Missed three weeks with a strained hamstring and had to work his way back as closer. A bit of his old Ctl issues crept back in 2H, but when paired with that Dom, it's not so bad. However, there is risk, most notably his high LD% and FB%. Closers can see their first success in their 30s but the window is small.

Yr Tm	W	L	Sv	IP	K	ERA	xERA	WHIP	oOPS	vL	vR	BF/G	Ctl	Dom	Cmd	SwK	G	L	F	H%	S%	hr/f	GS	APC	DOM%	DIS%	Sv%	LI	RAR	BPV	BPX	R$
09																																
10 aa	4	5	7	61	48	6.73	5.21	1.62				6.0	5.7	7.1	1.2					29%	60%								-20.0	30	49	-$5
11 a/a	7	2	5	61	53	5.20	4.59	1.47				6.2	5.0	7.8	1.5					28%	68%								-9.5	44	66	-$1
12 MIL *	5	6	18	79	87	2.88	3.80	1.46	609	734	497	4.7	4.6	10.0	2.2	16%	42	23	35	35%	81%	4%	0	15			78	1.13	11.1	96	126	$9
13 MIL	5	5	28	60	75	2.70	3.37	1.13	625	786	475	4.0	3.6	11.3	3.1	14%	28	28	44	28%	83%	13%	0	17			88	1.23	8.6	111	145	$16
1st Half	2	2	10	30	31	2.12	3.34	1.01	539	648	452	3.9	2.7	9.4	3.4	12%	36	24	41	27%	82%	6%	0	17			77	1.03	6.4	109	141	$14
2nd Half	3	3	18	30	44	3.26	3.38	1.25	706	897	500	4.2	4.5	13.1	2.9	16%	19	33	48	29%	84%	18%	0	18			95	1.44	2.3	112	145	$18
14 Proj	**5**	**4**	**35**	**69**	**77**	**3.57**	**3.57**	**1.33**	**688**	**857**	**532**	**4.5**	**4.4**	**10.2**	**2.3**	**15%**	**32**	**27**	**41**	**30%**	**77%**	**12%**	**0**						**2.5**	**76**	**98**	**$16**

Hernandez,David

Age:	29	Th:	R	Role	RP	Health	A	LIMA Plan	A
Ht:	6' 3"	Wt:	230	Type	Pwr xFB	PT/Exp	C	Rand Var	0
						Consist	B	MM	4510

He didn't come close to duplicating his fine 2012, but this wasn't quite as bad it appears to be. Earned an August demotion to Triple-A, but came back strong and posted a 124 BPV and 4.0 Cmd in September. Sudden struggles against lefties are a concern, but he's still a sound skills play with some saves upside.

Yr Tm	W	L	Sv	IP	K	ERA	xERA	WHIP	oOPS	vL	vR	BF/G	Ctl	Dom	Cmd	SwK	G	L	F	H%	S%	hr/f	GS	APC	DOM%	DIS%	Sv%	LI	RAR	BPV	BPX	R$
09 BAL *	7	12	0	163	134	5.21	5.57	1.49	912	912	913	21.9	3.7	7.4	2.0	8%	29	18	53	30%	71%	15%	19	96	26%	42%	0	0.75	-17.8	29	54	-$3
10 BAL	8	8	2	79	72	4.31	4.72	1.44	731	743	723	8.5	4.8	8.2	1.7	11%	28	21	51	29%	72%	8%	8	35	13%	25%	33	1.13	-2.3	24	39	$2
11 ARI	5	3	11	69	77	3.38	3.69	1.14	561	462	641	3.9	3.9	10.0	2.6	12%	31	23	46	28%	71%	5%	0	16			79	1.17	4.9	84	126	$9
12 ARI	2	3	4	68	98	2.50	2.94	1.02	544	683	415	3.9	2.9	12.9	4.5	15%	31	22	46	32%	77%	6%	0	15			40	1.04	12.7	163	213	$10
13 ARI	5	6	2	62	66	4.48	3.85	1.19	702	847	578	4.2	3.5	9.5	2.8	13%	32	21	47	27%	67%	13%	0	17			25	1.14	-4.7	88	115	$1
1st Half	4	5	1	35	37	4.58	3.81	1.19	705	748	666	4.4	3.1	9.4	3.1	13%	27	25	47	28%	67%	13%	0	17			17	1.29	-3.1	92	120	$2
2nd Half	1	1	1	27	29	4.33	3.89	1.19	698	989	468	4.1	4.0	9.7	2.4	14%	37	16	47	25%	68%	12%	0	17			50	0.96	-1.6	81	105	-$1
14 Proj	**3**	**4**	**3**	**58**	**66**	**3.82**	**3.33**	**1.17**	**650**	**763**	**552**	**4.1**	**3.5**	**10.3**	**2.9**	**13%**	**32**	**21**	**47**	**28%**	**71%**	**10%**	**0**						**0.3**	**100**	**129**	**$3**

Hernandez,Felix

Age:	28	Th:	R	Role	SP	Health	A	LIMA Plan	C
Ht:	6' 3"	Wt:	230	Type	Pwr GB	PT/Exp	A	Rand Var	0
						Consist	A	MM	5405

Missed some starts in Sept with a back issue that affected him over the last six weeks or so. That explains the IP drop, which is the only stain on his best skills season. Maintained a nice jump in Dom all year and Ctl held up until the injury surfaced. For the risk averse, note all the innings and think twice about bidding to the limit.

Yr Tm	W	L	Sv	IP	K	ERA	xERA	WHIP	oOPS	vL	vR	BF/G	Ctl	Dom	Cmd	SwK	G	L	F	H%	S%	hr/f	GS	APC	DOM%	DIS%	Sv%	LI	RAR	BPV	BPX	R$
09 SEA	19	5	0	239	217	2.49	3.33	1.14	605	625	582	28.7	2.7	8.2	3.1	11%	53	17	30	29%	80%	8%	34	107	74%	9%			54.0	106	198	$36
10 SEA	13	12	0	250	232	2.27	3.09	1.06	585	593	576	29.4	2.5	8.4	3.3	10%	54	16	30	27%	81%	8%	34	110	76%	6%			55.7	114	185	$35
11 SEA	14	14	0	234	222	3.47	3.20	1.22	660	662	656	29.2	2.6	8.6	3.3	10%	50	19	31	31%	73%	10%	33	109	70%	6%			13.7	112	169	$17
12 SEA	13	9	0	232	223	3.06	3.19	1.14	629	643	608	28.5	2.2	8.7	4.0	11%	49	22	29	31%	74%	8%	33	104	70%	9%			27.2	124	162	$25
13 SEA	12	10	0	204	216	3.04	2.83	1.13	643	671	610	26.5	2.0	9.5	4.7	11%	51	21	27	32%	75%	10%	31	102	74%	10%			20.8	146	190	$20
1st Half	8	4	0	117	123	2.70	2.70	1.10	652	673	629	27.1	1.7	9.5	5.6	12%	52	22	26	32%	78%	11%	17	104	76%	6%			16.8	155	200	$27
2nd Half	4	6	0	88	93	3.49	3.00	1.17	632	669	581	25.9	2.5	9.5	3.9	11%	51	21	29	32%	71%	9%	14	101	71%	14%			4.1	134	174	$12
14 Proj	**12**	**10**	**0**	**212**	**211**	**3.24**	**2.87**	**1.15**	**636**	**656**	**610**	**26.9**	**2.3**	**8.9**	**3.9**	**11%**	**51**	**21**	**29**	**31%**	**73%**	**9%**	**31**						**16.4**	**129**	**167**	**$21**

Hernandez,Pedro

Age:	25	Th:	L	Role	SP	Health	A	LIMA Plan	D+
Ht:	5' 10"	Wt:	210	Type	Con	PT/Exp	D	Rand Var	+1
						Consist	C	MM	1000

3-3, 6.83 ERA in 57 IP at MIN. Staring at these numbers doesn't make them any better—really, don't even try it. The one number that could play is his OPS vs. lefties. That relative success relegates him to a specialist role, and that's probably his best bet as a major leaguer. Stop looking before you hurt your eyes.

Yr Tm	W	L	Sv	IP	K	ERA	xERA	WHIP	oOPS	vL	vR	BF/G	Ctl	Dom	Cmd	SwK	G	L	F	H%	S%	hr/f	GS	APC	DOM%	DIS%	Sv%	LI	RAR	BPV	BPX	R$
09																																
10																																
11 a/a	5	3	0	59	45	3.52	3.97	1.30				18.8	2.1	6.9	3.2					32%	75%								3.1	87	131	$1
12 MIN *	8	5	0	107	56	4.56	5.44	1.53	1437	1778	1238	23.3	2.0	4.7	2.4	7%	41	14	45	35%	72%	30%	1	87	0%	100%			-7.2	42	55	-$6
13 MIN *	6	5	0	114	61	5.56	6.12	1.66	949	705	1031	21.2	3.0	4.8	1.6	6%	40	22	38	34%	69%	13%	12	73	17%	58%	0	0.82	-23.8	12	16	-$14
1st Half	4	3	0	71	40	4.90	5.78	1.60	889	548	1037	21.0	3.0	5.0	1.6	7%	40	23	37	33%	73%	12%	7	75	14%	43%	0	0.84	-9.1	17	22	-$12
2nd Half	2	2	0	42	21	6.66	6.69	1.75	1053	1200	1023	21.5	3.0	4.6	1.5	4%	40	19	40	35%	64%	13%	5	69	20%	80%			-14.6	4	5	-$17
14 Proj	**3**	**4**	**0**	**56**	**31**	**5.07**	**4.55**	**1.58**	**931**	**853**	**953**	**21.5**	**2.5**	**5.0**	**2.0**	**5%**	**40**	**21**	**39**	**34%**	**70%**	**9%**	**11**						**-8.3**	**40**	**52**	**-$6**

Hernandez,Roberto

Age:	33	Th:	R	Role	SP	Health	B	LIMA Plan	C
Ht:	6' 4"	Wt:	230	Type	GB	PT/Exp	B	Rand Var	+5
						Consist	D	MM	3103

New name, new skills? Posted his best Dom since his Fausto days and best Cmd of his career. He perhaps deserved better, as he completely outpitched his ERA; blame it on the horrific hr/f. Drop in 2H skills, struggles vs. lefties, and DOM/DIS hint that this may be the pinnacle. He's worth a bit of speculation, but just a bit.

Yr Tm	W	L	Sv	IP	K	ERA	xERA	WHIP	oOPS	vL	vR	BF/G	Ctl	Dom	Cmd	SwK	G	L	F	H%	S%	hr/f	GS	APC	DOM%	DIS%	Sv%	LI	RAR	BPV	BPX	R$
09 CLE *	7	15	0	165	105	5.80	5.64	1.65	852	964	696	24.6	4.2	5.7	1.4	7%	55	18	27	32%	66%	14%	24	94	17%	25%			-30.2	22	41	-$12
10 CLE	13	14	0	210	124	3.77	4.07	1.31	703	722	681	26.7	3.1	5.3	1.7	7%	56	14	31	28%	72%	8%	33	100	39%	15%			8.1	46	75	$9
11 CLE	7	15	0	189	109	5.25	4.10	1.40	776	801	748	26.0	2.9	5.2	1.8	8%	55	19	27	30%	64%	13%	32	94	34%	22%			-30.4	49	74	-$9
12 CLE	0	3	0	14	2	7.53	5.33	1.40	964	1072	805	20.7	1.9	1.3	0.7	3%	51	18	31	25%	50%	24%	3	77	0%	67%			-6.2	1	1	-$7
13 TAM	6	13	1	151	113	4.89	3.53	1.34	797	905	668	20.1	2.3	6.7	3.0	8%	53	22	24	31%	67%	21%	24	75	46%	25%	100	0.84	-19.0	91	119	-$4
1st Half	4	9	0	90	74	4.98	3.45	1.33	782	858	677	26.0	2.1	7.4	3.5	9%	51	24	25	32%	67%	21%	15	97	47%	13%			-12.4	106	137	-$4
2nd Half	2	4	1	61	39	4.75	3.65	1.35	819	993	656	14.9	2.5	5.8	2.3	8%	56	21	23	30%	68%	20%	9	55	44%	44%	100	0.89	-6.6	70	91	-$5
14 Proj	**7**	**11**	**0**	**145**	**95**	**4.57**	**3.75**	**1.38**	**786**	**869**	**690**	**20.9**	**2.8**	**5.9**	**2.1**	**8%**	**55**	**19**	**26**	**30%**	**70%**	**16%**	**29**						**-12.6**	**64**	**83**	**-$2**

Herrera,Kelvin

Age:	24	Th:	R	Role	RP	Health	A	LIMA Plan	B+
Ht:	5' 10"	Wt:	200	Type	Pwr GB	PT/Exp	D	Rand Var	+3
						Consist	B	MM	5510

5-7 with 3.86 ERA in 58 IP at KC. Poor Ctl and hr/f in 1st half explain why he was sent to the minors twice. Returned in July and was lights-out the rest of the way. Issues vs. LHP may preclude save chances, but if he can come close to replicating those eye-popping 2nd half skills, that won't matter.

Yr Tm	W	L	Sv	IP	K	ERA	xERA	WHIP	oOPS	vL	vR	BF/G	Ctl	Dom	Cmd	SwK	G	L	F	H%	S%	hr/f	GS	APC	DOM%	DIS%	Sv%	LI	RAR	BPV	BPX	R$
09																																
10																																
11 KC *	5	1	13	55	49	2.38	2.09	0.91	1232	2500	733	5.3	2.0	7.9	4.0	0%	29	14	57	24%	79%	25%	0	16			81	1.25	10.6	122	184	$12
12 KC	4	3	3	84	77	2.35	3.16	1.19	643	742	580	4.5	2.2	8.2	3.7	12%	56	20	25	32%	81%	7%	0	17			75	1.20	17.3	121	158	$9
13 KC *	5	8	4	76	96	3.23	2.90	1.09	701	738	661	4.2	3.2	11.3	3.6	15%	48	18	34	28%	76%	18%	0	17			67	1.19	6.0	121	158	$8
1st Half	3	6	3	36	40	4.56	5.06	1.40	856	809	910	4.3	4.7	10.0	2.1	14%	46	18	36	27%	78%	30%	0	18			75	1.08	-3.1	45	58	$2
2nd Half	2	2	1	40	56	2.03	0.94	0.80	553	666	438	4.1	1.8	12.5	7.0	16%	49	19	32	29%	74%	4%	0	17			50	1.30	9.1	235	304	$13
14 Proj	**4**	**4**	**3**	**58**	**63**	**2.69**	**2.70**	**1.07**	**613**	**676**	**558**	**4.4**	**2.6**	**9.8**	**3.8**	**14%**	**51**	**19**	**30**	**29%**	**79%**	**12%**	**0**						**8.4**	**137**	**178**	**$6**

Hochevar,Luke

Age:	30	Th:	R	Role	RP	Health	C	LIMA Plan	B
Ht:	6' 5"	Wt:	215	Type	Pwr FB	PT/Exp	A	Rand Var	-5
						Consist	B	MM	5411

First Pitch Forum attendees had this one tucked away. Blossomed in relief and got stronger as the season went on. FB tilt leaves him vulnerable to the long ball, but high Dom should keep that in check. H%/S% muted ERA, but xERA was still excellent. These are closer-worthy skills—it's the opportunity he lacks.

Yr Tm	W	L	Sv	IP	K	ERA	xERA	WHIP	oOPS	vL	vR	BF/G	Ctl	Dom	Cmd	SwK	G	L	F	H%	S%	hr/f	GS	APC	DOM%	DIS%	Sv%	LI	RAR	BPV	BPX	R$
09 KC *	12	14	0	191	133	5.42	5.01	1.46	852	902	804	24.8	2.8	6.3	2.2	9%	47	18	36	32%	65%	14%	25	94	36%	32%			-25.9	46	86	-$3
10 KC	6	6	0	103	76	4.81	4.16	1.43	754	796	712	25.0	3.2	6.6	2.1	10%	46	21	33	32%	67%	8%	17	91	41%	18%	0	0.73	-9.2	56	91	-$2
11 KC	11	11	0	198	128	4.68	4.00	1.28	742	766	714	26.9	2.8	5.8	2.1	8%	50	18	32	28%	65%	12%	31	101	45%	16%			-18.1	57	85	$1
12 KC	8	16	0	185	144	5.73	4.23	1.42	818	877	749	25.0	3.0	7.0	2.4	9%	43	22	35	32%	61%	14%	32	94	44%	31%			-39.2	67	87	-$13
13 KC	5	2	2	70	82	1.92	2.89	0.82	533	607	452	4.5	2.2	10.5	4.8	14%	35	19	46	22%	86%	11%	0	18			40	0.92	16.9	143	187	$12
1st Half	1	1	1	30	30	2.37	3.39	0.89	593	688	495	5.0	2.4	8.9	3.8	13%	36	17	47	21%	83%	11%	0	20			33	0.75	5.6	110	142	$7
2nd Half	4	1	1	40	52	1.58	2.54	0.78	486	546	416	4.2	2.0	11.7	5.8	15%	35	21	44	23%	89%	11%	0	17			50	1.02	11.3	168	218	$16
14 Proj	**4**	**4**	**3**	**73**	**74**	**3.59**	**3.11**	**1.07**	**663**	**722**	**598**	**4.6**	**2.3**	**9.2**	**4.0**	**12%**	**38**	**20**	**42**	**28%**	**71%**	**11%**	**0**						**2.4**	**120**	**155**	**$6**

MATT CEDERHOLM

Holland,Derek

Age: 27 Th: L Role SP	Health B	LIMA Plan C+
Ht: 6' 2" Wt: 210 Type Pwr	PT/Exp A	Rand Var 0
	Consist A	MM 3305

Was this a big step up? Naw, it was really only one great month, with a 72 BPV and 4.09 xERA outside of May. BPV was consistent otherwise, though, and recent history suggests that he does have occasional good months. Uptick in SwK% held for full season—which hints at a touch of upside—but use 2H skills as your guide.

Yr Tm	W	L	Sv	IP	K	ERA	xERA	WHIP	oOPS	vL	vR	BF/G	Ctl	Dom	Cmd	SwK	G	L	F	H%	S%	hr/f	GS	APC	DOM%	DIS%	Sv%	LI	RAR	BPV	BPX	R$
09 TEX	8	13	0	138	107	6.12	4.42	1.50	856	809	870	18.5	3.1	7.0	2.3	8%	41	19	39	32%	62%	15%	21	68	19%	33%	0	0.95	-30.6	62	116	-$7
10 TEX *	9	6	0	120	95	3.12	3.78	1.30	727	362	818	19.8	3.2	7.2	2.2	9%	42	15	43	29%	79%	8%	10	76	40%	50%	0	0.74	14.2	68	110	$8
11 TEX	16	5	0	198	162	3.95	3.80	1.35	724	601	765	26.3	3.0	7.4	2.4	8%	46	20	34	31%	74%	11%	32	100	47%	22%			-0.3	74	112	$7
12 TEX	12	7	0	175	145	4.67	4.08	1.22	745	656	770	25.2	2.7	7.4	2.8	8%	43	17	40	27%	68%	15%	27	95	63%	15%	0	0.81	-14.2	83	108	$4
13 TEX	10	9	0	213	189	3.42	3.78	1.29	711	671	722	27.1	2.7	8.0	3.0	10%	41	23	36	32%	76%	9%	33	99	58%	15%			11.6	90	117	$10
1st Half	6	4	0	106	97	3.14	3.51	1.22	675	724	663	27.1	2.3	8.2	3.6	10%	42	23	35	32%	75%	6%	16	102	50%	13%			9.5	106	137	$15
2nd Half	4	5	0	107	92	3.70	4.06	1.36	746	625	780	27.1	3.1	7.7	2.5	10%	40	22	38	31%	77%	12%	17	97	65%	18%			2.2	73	95	$5
14 Proj	12	9	0	203	173	3.79	3.62	1.29	727	640	751	24.8	2.7	7.7	2.8	9%	42	20	37	30%	74%	11%	34						2.0	85	110	$10

Holland,Greg

Age: 28 Th: R Role RP	Health B	LIMA Plan C
Ht: 5' 10" Wt: 200 Type Pwr	PT/Exp B	Rand Var -5
	Consist C	MM 5530

Some nit-picking: ridiculous 2nd half S% and hr/f artificially lowered ERA; size of Ctl drop was driven by 2nd half, and that's a small sample; drop in GB%. Who cares, really? If he regresses all the way to 2012 BPV (unlikely), he's still solid. Closers are inherently unsafe, but he's as good a bet as you'll find.

Yr Tm	W	L	Sv	IP	K	ERA	xERA	WHIP	oOPS	vL	vR	BF/G	Ctl	Dom	Cmd	SwK	G	L	F	H%	S%	hr/f	GS	APC	DOM%	DIS%	Sv%	LI	RAR	BPV	BPX	R$
09 a/a	4	3	10	54	39	4.75	5.51	1.73				7.1	4.2	6.5	1.6					36%	73%								-2.9	45	84	$0
10 KC *	3	4	3	75	70	5.03	3.85	1.42	835	838	832	6.3	4.5	8.3	1.8	12%	35	24	42	31%	64%	13%	0	21			60	0.68	-8.8	73	119	-$1
11 KC *	7	1	6	82	95	1.96	1.77	1.01	521	522	519	5.3	3.3	10.4	3.1	17%	45	16	39	26%	82%	6%	0	21			67	1.38	20.0	133	201	$15
12 KC	7	4	16	67	91	2.96	3.31	1.37	653	577	712	4.3	4.6	12.2	2.7	13%	45	18	36	36%	78%	3%	0	17			80	1.41	8.8	120	156	$10
13 KC	2	1	47	67	103	1.21	2.10	0.87	479	512	439	3.8	2.4	13.8	5.7	17%	39	27	33	30%	89%	7%	0	16			94	1.34	22.0	201	262	$31
1st Half	2	1	17	30	50	2.10	2.06	1.00	542	621	465	3.8	3.3	15.0	4.5	17%	41	27	32	33%	82%	11%	0	16			89	1.23	6.5	200	259	$22
2nd Half	0	0	30	37	53	0.49	2.13	0.76	428	438	412	3.7	1.7	12.9	7.6	18%	38	28	34	28%	96%	4%	0	15			97	1.43	15.4	202	262	$38
14 Proj	4	2	45	68	93	2.36	2.49	1.03	554	534	574	4.1	3.2	12.2	3.8	16%	42	22	35	30%	79%	8%	0						12.7	153	199	$27

Holmberg,David

Age: 22 Th: L Role SP	Health A	LIMA Plan D+
Ht: 6' 3" Wt: 225 Type	PT/Exp D	Rand Var -3
	Consist B	MM 2100

0-0 with 7.36 ERA in 4 IP at ARI. Promising lefty got a demitasse of coffee in the bigs, which is all of his experience above Double-A. Middling Dom makes him a risk despite a GB scouting profile, and lack of upper-level experience makes him riskier still. Modest upside and enhanced risk, at least for the short-term.

Yr Tm	W	L	Sv	IP	K	ERA	xERA	WHIP	oOPS	vL	vR	BF/G	Ctl	Dom	Cmd	SwK	G	L	F	H%	S%	hr/f	GS	APC	DOM%	DIS%	Sv%	LI	RAR	BPV	BPX	R$
09																																
10																																
11																																
12 aa	5	5	0	95	58	4.34	5.03	1.47				27.2	2.1	5.5	2.6					34%	72%								-3.8	56	74	-$5
13 ARI *	5	8	0	161	100	3.77	4.33	1.41	950	1100	900	25.2	3.0	5.6	1.9	5%	25	25	50	31%	75%	0%	1	80	0%	100%			1.8	47	61	-$1
1st Half	4	4	0	103	62	3.30	3.97	1.27				26.2	2.3	5.5	2.3					29%	78%	0%	0						7.2	54	70	$5
2nd Half	1	4	0	58	38	4.61	4.97	1.65	950	1100	900	23.7	4.2	5.9	1.4	5%	25	25	50	34%	72%	0%	1	80	0%	100%			-5.3	43	55	-$12
14 Proj	1	2	0	29	18	4.20	4.16	1.39				25.0	2.9	5.6	1.9	7%	45	20	35	31%	71%	8%	5						-1.2	45	58	-$3

Hoover,J.J.

Age: 26 Th: R Role RP	Health A	LIMA Plan B
Ht: 6' 3" Wt: 225 Type Pwr xFB	PT/Exp D	Rand Var -4
	Consist F	MM 4510

Why he's not (yet) a good option for saves speculation: BPV and xERA not elite; FB tilt spells possible danger; SwK% very average; doesn't dominate RHB. Did have nice improvement in Ctl and Cmd in 2H, and drop in FB% is progress. Another step forward would make him interesting, but for now he's a solid LIMA play.

Yr Tm	W	L	Sv	IP	K	ERA	xERA	WHIP	oOPS	vL	vR	BF/G	Ctl	Dom	Cmd	SwK	G	L	F	H%	S%	hr/f	GS	APC	DOM%	DIS%	Sv%	LI	RAR	BPV	BPX	R$
09																																
10 aa	3	1	0	21	29	4.11	3.67	1.56				22.6	6.6	12.8	1.9					36%	73%								-0.1	113	184	-$1
11 a/a	3	6	2	106	100	3.06	2.82	1.21				9.9	3.4	8.5	2.5					29%	75%								11.5	99	149	$7
12 CIN *	5	0	14	68	77	1.75	1.16	0.89	512	427	589	4.3	3.4	10.2	3.0	11%	24	20	57	22%	83%	5%	0	19			88	0.70	18.9	135	176	$18
13 CIN	5	5	3	66	67	2.86	3.86	1.11	627	477	722	3.9	3.5	9.1	2.6	10%	31	21	48	26%	78%	7%	0	17			60	1.29	8.2	78	101	$6
1st Half	1	5	3	34	37	4.24	4.14	1.32	729	617	798	4.2	4.2	9.8	2.3	10%	31	21	48	30%	71%	9%	0	18			100	1.28	-1.6	71	92	$2
2nd Half	4	0	0	32	30	1.41	3.56	0.88	503	313	628	3.6	2.8	8.4	3.0	10%	31	22	47	21%	88%	5%	0	15			0	1.30	9.7	85	110	$11
14 Proj	5	2	3	65	70	3.02	3.44	1.16	661	507	774	4.5	3.4	9.6	2.9	11%	32	21	47	28%	77%	8%	0						6.8	92	120	$6

Howell,J.P.

Age: 31 Th: L Role RP	Health F	LIMA Plan B
Ht: 6' 0" Wt: 185 Type Pwr GB	PT/Exp D	Rand Var -5
	Consist A	MM 4310

A jump in skills this big—driven by improved Ctl and GB rate—is more than just a league change. Was über lucky, with H%, S%, and hr/f all swinging his way, but xERA is all the way back to 2009 levels. Re-mastery of RH batters supports an expanded role. He's hardly elite, but has re-established fantasy relevance.

Yr Tm	W	L	Sv	IP	K	ERA	xERA	WHIP	oOPS	vL	vR	BF/G	Ctl	Dom	Cmd	SwK	G	L	F	H%	S%	hr/f	GS	APC	DOM%	DIS%	Sv%	LI	RAR	BPV	BPX	R$
09 TAM	7	5	17	67	79	2.84	3.31	1.20	627	772	561	4.0	4.5	10.7	2.4	12%	49	16	35	27%	81%	13%	0	16			68	1.56	12.2	99	185	$15
10																																
11 TAM	2	3	1	31	26	6.16	4.22	1.57	770	581	978	3.0	5.3	7.6	1.4	8%	53	19	29	29%	63%	19%	0	12			50	1.04	-8.4	26	39	-$5
12 TAM	1	0	0	50	42	3.04	3.84	1.21	706	612	795	3.7	3.9	7.5	1.9	8%	49	20	31	24%	81%	17%	0	15			0	0.71	6.1	56	73	$0
13 LA	4	1	0	62	54	2.18	3.31	1.05	531	452	608	3.7	3.3	7.8	2.3	10%	57	15	28	25%	79%	4%	0	14			0	0.93	12.9	86	112	$6
1st Half	2	0	0	33	28	2.70	3.54	1.14	565	436	666	4.3	3.2	7.6	2.3	10%	57	15	28	27%	76%	4%	0	17			0	0.95	4.8	83	108	$5
2nd Half	2	1	0	29	26	1.57	3.05	0.94	486	468	511	3.1	3.5	8.2	2.4	11%	58	14	28	21%	85%	5%	0	12			0	0.91	8.1	90	116	$7
14 Proj	4	2	2	65	58	3.12	3.41	1.28	686	600	769	3.5	3.6	8.0	2.2	10%	54	17	29	29%	78%	10%	0						6.0	79	102	$3

Hudson,Daniel

Age: 27 Th: R Role SP	Health F	LIMA Plan B+
Ht: 6' 3" Wt: 225 Type Pwr FB	PT/Exp C	Rand Var 0
	Consist B	MM 3300

Missed the first two months rehabbing from Tommy John surgery, and was then diagnosed with another UCL tear. He underwent a second TJS in June and will miss most of 2014. He showed great promise early in his career, but the track record of pitchers after two Tommy Johns is not good. Consider him to be a long shot.

Yr Tm	W	L	Sv	IP	K	ERA	xERA	WHIP	oOPS	vL	vR	BF/G	Ctl	Dom	Cmd	SwK	G	L	F	H%	S%	hr/f	GS	APC	DOM%	DIS%	Sv%	LI	RAR	BPV	BPX	R$
09 CHW *	10	1	0	99	91	2.84	2.95	1.18	711	596	830	19.8	2.7	8.2	3.1	9%	30	12	58	30%	77%	9%	2	53	50%	0%	0	0.29	18.1	105	197	$12
10 2 TM *	19	6	0	189	178	3.32	3.50	1.18	579	571	586	24.3	2.9	8.5	2.9	13%	35	19	45	28%	77%	7%	14	103	79%	7%			17.6	86	139	$20
11 ARI	16	12	0	222	169	3.49	3.80	1.20	694	698	691	27.9	2.0	6.9	3.4	10%	42	19	39	30%	72%	6%	33	104	67%	6%			12.5	89	133	$16
12 ARI	3	2	0	45	37	7.35	4.34	1.63	910	994	807	22.4	2.4	7.3	3.1	10%	37	27	36	37%	57%	17%	9	89	22%	44%			-18.6	83	108	-$11
13																																
1st Half																																
2nd Half																																
14 Proj	5	2	0	57	49	4.02	3.64	1.27	731	780	685	23.1	2.5	7.8	3.1	11%	38	22	41	30%	72%	11%	10						-1.1	87	113	$1

Hudson,Tim

Age: 38 Th: R Role SP	Health F	LIMA Plan B+
Ht: 6' 1" Wt: 175 Type xGB	PT/Exp A	Rand Var 0
	Consist B	MM 4101

Missed the last two months with a broken ankle. Up to that point, he was defying the aging curve yet again, even reversing 2012's Dom and Cmd declines. Concerns at this point center on his age and Health grade, but a broken ankle does not presage a physical demise. There's some innings upside in this projection.

Yr Tm	W	L	Sv	IP	K	ERA	xERA	WHIP	oOPS	vL	vR	BF/G	Ctl	Dom	Cmd	SwK	G	L	F	H%	S%	hr/f	GS	APC	DOM%	DIS%	Sv%	LI	RAR	BPV	BPX	R$
09 ATL *	3	1	0	61	38	3.94	5.23	1.58	768	833	721	24.4	2.3	5.6	2.5	10%	62	18	20	36%	75%	15%	7	86	29%	29%			2.9	59	111	-$3
10 ATL	17	9	0	229	139	2.83	3.49	1.15	641	667	616	27.1	2.9	5.5	1.9	8%	64	14	22	25%	79%	13%	34	98	50%	9%			35.1	62	100	$24
11 ATL	16	10	0	215	158	3.22	3.32	1.14	627	692	571	26.8	2.3	6.6	2.8	10%	57	19	25	28%	73%	9%	33	97	55%	9%			19.1	91	136	$20
12 ATL	16	7	0	179	102	3.62	4.03	1.21	666	668	663	26.8	2.4	5.1	2.1	8%	55	19	25	28%	71%	8%	28	94	39%	11%			8.7	60	78	$12
13 ATL	8	7	0	131	95	3.97	3.52	1.19	662	661	662	25.4	2.5	6.5	2.6	10%	56	18	27	29%	67%	10%	21	96	57%	19%			-1.8	85	110	$4
1st Half	4	7	0	102	73	4.22	3.70	1.21	685	668	702	24.9	2.6	6.4	2.5	10%	54	17	29	28%	67%	11%	17	94	53%	24%			-4.5	79	102	$5
2nd Half	4	0	0	29	22	3.10	2.90	1.10	575	631	526	27.8	2.2	6.8	3.1	8%	61	21	18	29%	69%	0%	4	102	75%	0%			2.7	103	134	$3
14 Proj	9	6	0	123	84	3.87	3.48	1.24	679	709	649	26.5	2.6	6.2	2.4	9%	56	19	25	29%	69%	9%	19						-0.1	75	97	$5

MATT CEDERHOLM

Hughes,Phil

Age: 28	Th: R	Role SP	Health D	LIMA Plan C
Ht: 6' 6"	Wt: 240	Type xFB	PT/Exp B	Rand Var +3
			Consist A	MM 2203

All things considered, this debacle was not all that statistically different from 2010 or 2012. xERAs were less than half a run apart. Ctl was a bit better in '12 but Dom/Ctl not significantly different. H%/S% inflated ERA and 2H consistency took a dive but this is the same pitcher. When looking for growth, that's not a good thing.

Yr	Tm	W	L	Sv	IP	K	ERA	xERA	WHIP	oOPS	vL	vR	BF/G	Ctl	Dom	Cmd	SwK	G	L	F	H%	S%	hr/f	GS	APC	DOM%	DIS%	Sv%	LI	RAR	BPV	BPX	R$
09	NYY *	11	3	3	105	112	2.95	3.12	1.14	635	740	546	7.7	2.7	9.6	3.6	11%	34	22	44	30%	78%	8%	7	29	43%	43%	50	1.14	17.9	114	213	$15
10	NYY	18	8	0	176	146	4.19	4.16	1.25	702	728	674	23.5	3.0	7.5	2.5	9%	36	16	47	28%	71%	10%	29	97	55%	14%	0	0.89	-2.3	68	110	$11
11	NYY	5	5	0	75	47	5.79	4.93	1.49	799	841	729	19.6	3.3	5.7	1.7	7%	32	23	45	31%	62%	8%	14	76	29%	43%	0	0.86	-17.0	24	36	-$7
12	NYY	16	13	0	191	165	4.23	4.30	1.26	765	610	928	25.5	2.2	7.8	3.6	9%	32	20	48	30%	73%	12%	32	101	53%	22%			-5.2	91	119	$8
13	NYY	4	14	0	146	121	5.19	4.44	1.46	832	863	793	21.4	2.6	7.5	2.9	9%	31	23	46	34%	68%	11%	29	85	38%	52%	0	0.76	-23.8	74	96	-$10
1st Half		3	7	0	84	73	4.82	4.29	1.36	799	922	652	23.9	2.5	7.8	3.2	9%	29	20	51	32%	69%	11%	15	96	53%	40%			-9.9	81	105	-$6
2nd Half		1	7	0	62	48	5.69	4.67	1.59	874	792	984	18.9	2.8	7.0	2.5	9%	33	26	41	35%	67%	11%	14	74	21%	64%	0	0.74	-13.9	62	80	-$16
14	Proj	**9**	**11**	**0**	**161**	**130**	**4.45**	**4.02**	**1.36**	**780**	**758**	**808**	**22.1**	**2.7**	**7.3**	**2.7**	**9%**	**32**	**22**	**46**	**31%**	**72%**	**11%**	**35**						**-11.5**	**69**	**90**	**$1**

Hunter,Tommy

Age: 27	Th: R	Role RP	Health D	LIMA Plan C+
Ht: 6' 3"	Wt: 250	Type Con	PT/Exp C	Rand Var -3
			Consist C	MM 3111

Move to bullpen was obviously a winner; he shattered previous BPI bests across the board. It remains to be seen which gains were skill based vs. role dependent. Dom, Cmd hikes were sure encouraging, but that 1H H% reached deal-with-devil depths. As new baseline forms, it's reasonable to expect some regression.

Yr	Tm	W	L	Sv	IP	K	ERA	xERA	WHIP	oOPS	vL	vR	BF/G	Ctl	Dom	Cmd	SwK	G	L	F	H%	S%	hr/f	GS	APC	DOM%	DIS%	Sv%	LI	RAR	BPV	BPX	R$
09	TEX *	13	8	0	183	107	4.59	4.85	1.45	736	869	595	24.4	2.6	5.3	2.0	7%	38	20	42	32%	70%	8%	19	91	37%	21%			-6.0	40	75	$2
10	TEX *	14	6	0	155	79	3.92	4.50	1.31	739	763	708	22.0	2.6	4.6	1.8	6%	42	18	40	27%	75%	12%	22	83	18%	23%	0	0.77	3.0	26	42	$7
11	2 AL *	6	6	1	115	61	5.01	5.34	1.44	782	864	686	16.9	1.5	4.8	3.2	6%	41	21	38	33%	68%	11%	11	65	18%	18%	50	0.95	-15.2	52	78	-$5
12	BAL *	10	9	1	163	93	5.24	5.58	1.37	864	840	891	18.0	1.9	5.1	2.7	7%	45	20	35	30%	68%	20%	20	63	25%	25%	50	0.87	-24.6	27	35	-$7
13	BAL	6	5	4	86	68	2.81	3.55	0.98	617	857	344	4.9	1.5	7.1	4.9	11%	39	21	40	25%	78%	11%	0	19			67	1.09	11.2	105	137	$10
1st Half		3	1	2	45	37	2.00	3.44	0.84	541	763	298	5.4	1.6	7.4	4.6	10%	41	17	42	21%	88%	11%	0	20			67	0.87	10.4	109	141	$14
2nd Half		3	4	2	41	31	3.70	3.67	1.14	696	952	394	4.6	1.3	6.8	5.2	12%	37	25	38	30%	71%	10%	0	17			67	1.29	0.8	102	131	$6
14	Proj	**6**	**5**	**3**	**87**	**58**	**3.79**	**3.73**	**1.21**	**730**	**860**	**579**	**5.0**	**1.7**	**6.0**	**3.6**	**9%**	**41**	**21**	**38**	**29%**	**74%**	**12%**	**0**						**0.8**	**82**	**106**	**$4**

Iwakuma,Hisashi

Age: 33	Th: R	Role SP	Health A	LIMA Plan C
Ht: 6' 3"	Wt: 210	Type GB	PT/Exp A	Rand Var -3
			Consist A	MM 4205

GB arm built on last year's 2H gains to finish in AL's Top Three in ERA/WHIP. 1H featured airtight Ctl and superb Cmd that he couldn't quite sustain. Even so, take that 2H and throw in equal success vL/vR and home/ road. At 33, tough to dub him an ace and expect him to maintain, but you won't pay an ace price, either.

Yr	Tm	W	L	Sv	IP	K	ERA	xERA	WHIP	oOPS	vL	vR	BF/G	Ctl	Dom	Cmd	SwK	G	L	F	H%	S%	hr/f	GS	APC	DOM%	DIS%	Sv%	LI	RAR	BPV	BPX	R$
09	for	13	6	0	169	115	4.03	5.09	1.45				30.1	2.8	6.1	2.1					32%	77%								6.0	40	74	$6
10	for	10	9	0	201	145	3.50	3.59	1.20				28.9	2.0	6.5	3.2					30%	73%								14.3	86	139	$13
11	for	6	7	0	119	85	3.03	3.35	1.16				27.9	1.8	6.4	3.5					29%	77%								13.5	95	142	$9
12	SEA	9	5	2	125	101	3.16	3.74	1.28	718	716	720	17.3	3.1	7.3	2.3	10%	52	20	27	28%	81%	17%	16	64	44%	13%	100	0.59	13.2	77	101	$9
13	SEA	14	6	0	220	185	2.66	3.29	1.01	630	599	667	26.2	1.7	7.6	4.4	11%	49	18	34	26%	80%	12%	33	94	58%	3%			32.6	117	152	$29
1st Half		7	3	0	115	101	2.42	3.12	0.88	603	611	593	25.6	1.3	7.9	5.9	12%	46	16	38	24%	81%	13%	17	94	65%	0%			20.6	130	168	$36
2nd Half		7	3	0	104	84	2.93	3.48	1.15	657	586	742	26.9	2.2	7.2	3.4	10%	52	19	30	29%	78%	11%	16	94	50%	6%			12.0	102	132	$22
14	Proj	**13**	**7**	**0**	**202**	**160**	**3.21**	**3.30**	**1.17**	**688**	**660**	**718**	**23.4**	**2.2**	**7.2**	**3.3**	**10%**	**50**	**19**	**31**	**29%**	**77%**	**12%**	**34**						**16.4**	**98**	**127**	**$18**

Jackson,Edwin

Age: 30	Th: R	Role SP	Health A	LIMA Plan C
Ht: 6' 3"	Wt: 210	Type	PT/Exp A	Rand Var +3
			Consist A	MM 3205

Eight MLB teams in eleven years. Why he's often in demand: High IP totals; health grade; solid hr/9. Why he's often deemed expendable: ERA swings; .467 lifetime win%; game-to-game volatility. Be it MLB or fantasy, it's difficult to trust the ball with someone whose DOM%/DIS% have been on a three-year collision course.

Yr	Tm	W	L	Sv	IP	K	ERA	xERA	WHIP	oOPS	vL	vR	BF/G	Ctl	Dom	Cmd	SwK	G	L	F	H%	S%	hr/f	GS	APC	DOM%	DIS%	Sv%	LI	RAR	BPV	BPX	R$
09	DET	13	9	0	214	161	3.62	4.28	1.26	726	688	774	27.0	2.9	6.8	2.3	10%	39	18	42	28%	76%	10%	33	105	52%	12%			18.6	59	111	$17
10	2 TM	10	12	0	209	181	4.47	3.77	1.39	735	742	725	28.2	3.4	7.8	2.3	11%	49	19	32	32%	69%	11%	32	105	53%	9%			-10.1	77	124	$2
11	2 TM	12	9	0	200	148	3.79	3.96	1.44	768	800	736	26.9	2.8	6.7	2.4	10%	44	25	31	33%	75%	8%	31	101	52%	10%	0	0.76	3.8	67	100	$3
12	WAS	10	11	0	190	168	4.03	3.80	1.22	719	758	677	25.5	2.8	8.0	2.9	13%	47	17	36	29%	70%	12%	31	96	48%	16%			-0.4	94	123	$9
13	CHC	8	18	0	175	135	4.98	3.98	1.46	775	816	741	25.1	3.0	6.9	2.3	9%	51	20	28	33%	66%	10%	31	95	42%	26%			-24.1	72	94	-$9
1st Half		4	10	0	88	79	5.75	3.86	1.54	784	783	784	25.0	3.5	8.1	2.3	10%	51	21	28	36%	62%	11%	16	94	44%	25%			-20.4	81	105	-$13
2nd Half		4	8	0	88	56	4.21	4.10	1.38	766	854	701	25.1	2.6	5.7	2.2	8%	52	19	29	32%	71%	9%	15	95	40%	27%			-3.7	64	83	-$4
14	Proj	**10**	**14**	**0**	**189**	**148**	**4.39**	**3.73**	**1.39**	**758**	**794**	**725**	**25.1**	**3.0**	**7.1**	**2.3**	**10%**	**49**	**20**	**32**	**32%**	**70%**	**10%**	**32**						**-12.3**	**72**	**93**	**$1**

Jansen,Kenley

Age: 26	Th: R	Role RP	Health B	LIMA Plan C+
Ht: 6' 5"	Wt: 260	Type Pwr FB	PT/Exp B	Rand Var -3
			Consist A	MM 5531

After his terrific 2H in 2012, it's hard to fathom how LA waited until mid-June to plug him back into closer role. Check out that incredible alliance of Dom and Cmd, not to mention two straight years of lopping off a walk every nine IP. FB%/GB% are trending nicely. He's got sick skills, as the kids would say.

Yr	Tm	W	L	Sv	IP	K	ERA	xERA	WHIP	oOPS	vL	vR	BF/G	Ctl	Dom	Cmd	SwK	G	L	F	H%	S%	hr/f	GS	APC	DOM%	DIS%	Sv%	LI	RAR	BPV	BPX	R$
09																																	
10	LA *	5	0	12	54	84	1.18	1.06	1.05	422	586	273	4.4	5.0	14.0	2.8	15%	34	16	50	28%	88%	0%	0	19			100	0.83	19.3	168	272	$14
11	LA	2	1	5	54	96	2.85	2.38	1.04	494	494	493	4.3	4.4	16.1	3.7	17%	27	24	49	33%	74%	7%	0	19			83	0.88	7.2	177	266	$7
12	LA	5	3	25	65	99	2.35	2.63	0.85	504	518	490	3.9	3.0	13.7	4.5	15%	33	19	48	24%	78%	10%	0	16			78	1.31	13.3	175	229	$22
13	LA	4	3	28	77	111	1.88	2.29	0.86	509	531	494	3.9	2.1	13.0	6.2	16%	37	24	39	29%	83%	10%	0	17			88	1.33	18.8	192	251	$24
1st Half		2	3	7	41	59	2.41	2.31	0.95	620	668	585	3.9	1.3	13.0	9.8	16%	34	25	41	33%	82%	14%	0	16			70	1.37	7.3	210	271	$18
2nd Half		2	0	21	36	52	1.26	2.26	0.76	371	352	384	3.9	3.0	13.1	4.3	15%	42	22	36	22%	85%	4%	0	17			95	1.28	11.5	174	226	$31
14	Proj	**4**	**2**	**48**	**73**	**111**	**2.12**	**2.12**	**0.86**	**479**	**492**	**469**	**3.8**	**2.8**	**13.8**	**4.8**	**15%**	**37**	**22**	**41**	**27%**	**79%**	**8%**	**0**						**15.6**	**186**	**242**	**$32**

Janssen,Casey

Age: 32	Th: R	Role RP	Health C	LIMA Plan C+
Ht: 6' 3"	Wt: 225	Type Pwr	PT/Exp B	Rand Var -2
			Consist A	MM 5430

Maybe it's the exchange rate from playing home games in Canada, but he's all about economy. Took him only 53 IP to rack up those saves; only two other opps were squandered. Walked a mere 13. WHIP almost an even one. Dom and Cmd were marked down a bit, but competitive. Good value whatever the currency.

Yr	Tm	W	L	Sv	IP	K	ERA	xERA	WHIP	oOPS	vL	vR	BF/G	Ctl	Dom	Cmd	SwK	G	L	F	H%	S%	hr/f	GS	APC	DOM%	DIS%	Sv%	LI	RAR	BPV	BPX	R$
09	TOR *	3	4	1	62	39	5.36	5.38	1.63	930	921	938	8.1	3.0	5.7	1.9	8%	50	24	26	36%	67%	13%	5	34	0%	40%	100	0.67	-7.9	44	83	-$5
10	TOR	5	2	0	69	63	3.67	3.57	1.38	748	798	709	5.3	2.8	8.3	3.0	9%	47	22	31	34%	77%	12%	0	21			0	0.48	3.5	99	161	$1
11	TOR	6	0	2	56	53	2.26	3.08	1.10	594	539	659	4.1	2.3	8.6	3.8	9%	47	21	31	30%	80%	4%	0	16			50	0.85	11.5	118	178	$7
12	TOR	1	1	22	64	67	2.54	2.92	0.86	564	467	666	3.9	1.6	9.5	6.1	10%	43	21	36	25%	77%	12%	0	15			88	1.03	11.5	149	195	$17
13	TOR	4	1	34	53	50	2.56	3.10	0.99	558	619	458	3.8	2.2	8.5	3.8	8%	48	23	30	27%	76%	7%	0	15			94	1.39	8.5	120	156	$18
1st Half		2	0	17	27	24	2.03	2.85	0.71	441	353	568	3.5	1.4	8.1	6.0	9%	46	22	32	21%	72%	5%	0	13			94	1.52	6.1	134	173	$21
2nd Half		2	1	17	26	26	3.12	3.35	1.27	663	842	342	4.0	3.1	9.0	2.9	8%	49	23	27	32%	77%	10%	0	16			94	1.26	2.4	105	136	$15
14	Proj	**4**	**2**	**38**	**58**	**56**	**2.92**	**2.93**	**1.05**	**601**	**619**	**579**	**3.9**	**2.2**	**8.7**	**3.9**	**9%**	**47**	**22**	**31**	**28%**	**74%**	**9%**	**0**						**6.7**	**121**	**157**	**$20**

Jennings,Dan

Age: 27	Th: L	Role RP	Health A	LIMA Plan D+
Ht: 6' 3"	Wt: 210	Type Pwr GB	PT/Exp D	Rand Var -2
			Consist B	MM 2300

2-4, 3.76 in 41 IP at MIA. Had a bit more success in his second MLB trial with Ctl drop to 3.5 and corresponding Dom boost. Still, 27 walks in 60 career MLB IP underscores the root concern, and he's been strangely ineffective against LHB. A penchant for inducing GB isn't enough to create much buzz about him at this point.

Yr	Tm	W	L	Sv	IP	K	ERA	xERA	WHIP	oOPS	vL	vR	BF/G	Ctl	Dom	Cmd	SwK	G	L	F	H%	S%	hr/f	GS	APC	DOM%	DIS%	Sv%	LI	RAR	BPV	BPX	R$
09																																	
10	aa	4	2	0	53	40	3.16	4.13	1.62				6.3	4.8	6.8	1.4					34%	78%								6.0	70	113	-$1
11	a/a	5	4	4	56	46	5.50	4.89	1.65				5.6	4.5	7.4	1.7					35%	65%								-10.8	60	90	-$4
12	MIA *	2	3	2	71	50	3.34	4.23	1.47	771	788	753	4.7	3.7	6.3	1.7	7%	45	20	35	32%	78%	9%	0	15			50	0.62	5.9	58	76	-$1
13	MIA *	6	6	1	66	59	3.26	3.49	1.40	714	745	675	4.3	4.0	8.1	2.0	11%	49	20	32	33%	76%	3%	0	14			25	1.24	4.9	87	113	$1
1st Half		4	2	1	39	35	2.28	3.25	1.40	613	439	784	4.9	4.7	8.2	1.8	10%	52	6	42	31%	84%	0%	0	14			50	2.00	7.5	85	110	$4
2nd Half		2	4	0	27	24	4.67	3.69	1.41	759	865	616	3.7	3.0	8.0	2.7	11%	48	25	27	35%	65%	4%	0	15			0	0.88	-2.7	89	115	-$4
14	Proj	**2**	**3**	**0**	**35**	**29**	**4.07**	**4.02**	**1.48**	**710**	**779**	**616**	**4.6**	**4.4**	**7.4**	**1.7**	**11%**	**48**	**25**	**27**	**32%**	**73%**	**7%**	**0**						**-0.9**	**40**	**52**	**-$3**

ROB CARROLL

Jepsen,Kevin

Age: 29 Th: R Role RP | Ht: 6' 3" Wt: 235 Type Pwr
Health D | PT/Exp D | Consist F
LIMA Plan C | Rand Var +2 | MM 3300

This five-year ledger is a mosaic of inconsistencies. 9.3 Dom one year, 4.7 the next. 1.82 WHIP one year, 1.14 in other. xERAs from 2.72 to 6.33. And on and on. Missed 82 games with tricep tightness and appendictis, so now health grade is in the mix. Just two things you can count on: he throws hard and walks too many.

Yr	Tm	W	L	Sv	IP	K	ERA	xERA	WHIP	oOPS	vL	vR	BF/G	Ctl	Dom	Cmd	SwK	G	L	F	H%	S%	hr/f	GS	APC	DOM%	DIS%	Sv%	LI	RAR	BPV	BPX	R$
09	LAA *	7	4	3	73	64	6.27	6.02	1.82	693	881	497	5.0	4.3	7.9	1.8	12%	57	16	27	39%	65%	4%	0	17			43	1.09	-17.5	53	100	-$
10	LAA	2	4	0	59	61	3.97	3.36	1.41	665	669	661	3.7	4.4	9.3	2.1	11%	56	18	26	33%	70%	5%	0	15			0	1.22	0.8	82	133	-$
11	LAA *	2	5	7	41	22	5.42	6.33	1.75	981	894	1068	4.7	3.6	4.7	1.3	7%	55	16	29	35%	71%	13%	0	14			64	1.32	-7.6	10	14	-$4
12	LAA *	5	4	4	70	65	3.08	2.72	1.14	647	744	552	3.8	2.6	8.4	3.2	9%	35	23	42	30%	73%	6%	0	14			67	1.16	8.0	112	146	$7
13	LAA	1	3	0	36	36	4.50	4.10	1.53	769	865	679	3.6	3.5	9.0	2.6	9%	40	20	39	37%	71%	7%	0	15			0	1.12	-2.8	86	111	-$5
1st Half		1	2	0	20	20	4.12	4.02	1.22	658	793	535	3.7	3.7	9.2	2.5	8%	37	17	46	28%	68%	8%	0	15			0	1.51	-0.6	81	105	-$3
2nd Half		0	1	0	16	16	4.96	4.19	1.90	884	938	831	3.6	3.3	8.8	2.7	10%	44	24	33	44%	73%	6%	0	15			0	0.72	-2.2	91	118	-$8
14	**Proj**	**2**	**4**	**0**	**54**	**48**	**4.08**	**3.66**	**1.35**	**695**	**784**	**607**	**3.6**	**3.4**	**8.2**	**2.4**	**10%**	**43**	**20**	**36**	**32%**	**71%**	**8%**	**0**						**-1.4**	**77**	**100**	**-$2**

Jimenez,Ubaldo

Age: 30 Th: R Role SP | Ht: 6' 5" Wt: 210 Type Pwr
Health A | PT/Exp A | Consist C
LIMA Plan C+ | Rand Var -1 | MM 4405

On Aug 22, he was 9-7 with a 4.00 ERA. He then knocked out eight straight PQS-5 starts with a 71/10 K/BB ratio, insisting he did so by finally reconciling his velocity drop and adopting a new pitch mix. Long-inconsistent mechanics call into question whether he can bring these gains back next spring. If so... UP: 16 Wins, 3.00 ERA.

Yr	Tm	W	L	Sv	IP	K	ERA	xERA	WHIP	oOPS	vL	vR	BF/G	Ctl	Dom	Cmd	SwK	G	L	F	H%	S%	hr/f	GS	APC	DOM%	DIS%	Sv%	LI	RAR	BPV	BPX	R$
09	COL	15	12	0	218	198	3.47	3.53	1.23	635	681	585	27.7	3.5	8.2	2.3	10%	53	20	28	29%	72%	8%	33	108	79%	12%			23.0	83	156	$22
10	COL	19	8	0	222	214	2.88	3.42	1.15	610	582	638	27.1	3.7	8.7	2.3	10%	49	16	35	27%	75%	5%	33	109	82%	6%			32.7	83	134	$26
11	2 TM	10	13	0	188	180	4.68	3.72	1.40	752	710	791	25.7	3.7	8.6	2.3	8%	47	20	33	32%	67%	9%	32	102	44%	22%			-17.2	79	119	-$1
12	CLE	9	17	0	177	143	5.40	5.03	1.61	817	854	778	26.0	4.8	7.3	1.5	8%	38	23	38	32%	69%	12%	31	101	35%	19%			-30.2	16	21	-$16
13	CLE	13	9	0	183	194	3.30	3.66	1.33	684	661	708	24.3	3.9	9.6	2.4	9%	44	20	36	31%	78%	9%	32	99	56%	19%			12.7	88	114	$11
1st Half		6	4	0	84	85	4.63	3.99	1.46	751	728	776	22.7	4.7	9.1	1.9	9%	45	19	36	30%	72%	15%	16	96	44%	25%			-7.8	60	77	$0
2nd Half		7	5	0	99	109	2.18	3.39	1.22	626	598	654	25.9	3.3	9.9	3.0	10%	43	20	37	32%	83%	4%	16	102	69%	13%			20.6	111	144	$20
14	**Proj**	**13**	**10**	**0**	**194**	**192**	**3.72**	**3.59**	**1.34**	**700**	**693**	**707**	**24.3**	**4.0**	**8.9**	**2.3**	**9%**	**44**	**20**	**36**	**31%**	**75%**	**10%**	**33**						**3.6**	**75**	**98**	**$10**

Johnson,Jim

Age: 31 Th: R Role RP | Ht: 6' 6" Wt: 240 Type xGB
Health A | PT/Exp A | Consist A
LIMA Plan C | Rand Var 0 | MM 5231

Ignoring the Sv column yields an undistinguished five-year history. 2013 skills gains, headlined by Dom gain, offset by drop in saves conversion rate. Calling-card GB% remains premium. So what if he's not a sexy fireballer; he has back-to-back 50-save seasons. In this case, the best ability is dependability.

Yr	Tm	W	L	Sv	IP	K	ERA	xERA	WHIP	oOPS	vL	vR	BF/G	Ctl	Dom	Cmd	SwK	G	L	F	H%	S%	hr/f	GS	APC	DOM%	DIS%	Sv%	LI	RAR	BPV	BPX	R$
09	BAL	4	6	10	70	49	4.11	4.03	1.37	747	746	747	4.7	3.0	6.3	2.1	10%	52	18	30	30%	73%	12%	0	18			63	1.00	1.8	64	119	$4
10	BAL	1	1	1	26	22	3.42	3.40	1.41	722	668	773	4.5	1.7	7.5	4.4	10%	51	24	24	36%	77%	10%	0	16			17	1.53	2.1	118	191	-$1
11	BAL	6	5	9	91	58	2.67	3.32	1.11	628	567	690	5.3	2.1	5.7	2.8	10%	61	15	24	27%	77%	8%	0	18			64	1.11	14.3	86	130	$12
12	BAL	2	1	51	69	41	2.49	3.41	1.02	556	581	526	3.8	2.0	5.4	2.7	7%	62	16	21	25%	76%	7%	0	14			94	1.29	12.9	84	109	$27
13	BAL	3	8	50	70	56	2.94	3.17	1.28	699	740	653	3.9	2.3	7.2	3.1	9%	58	20	21	32%	79%	11%	0	15			85	1.39	8.0	103	134	$22
1st Half		2	6	28	39	31	3.92	3.40	1.21	682	741	605	3.9	2.8	7.2	2.6	8%	54	19	27	29%	68%	10%	0	15			85	1.44	-0.3	86	112	$24
2nd Half		1	2	22	31	25	1.72	2.89	1.37	721	739	703	4.0	1.7	7.2	4.2	9%	62	23	15	36%	90%	14%	0	15			85	1.32	8.3	123	159	$19
14	**Proj**	**3**	**5**	**42**	**73**	**52**	**3.11**	**3.19**	**1.21**	**662**	**675**	**648**	**4.1**	**2.2**	**6.4**	**3.0**	**9%**	**60**	**19**	**22**	**30%**	**76%**	**10%**	**0**						**6.8**	**95**	**123**	**$20**

Johnson,Josh

Age: 30 Th: R Role SP | Ht: 6' 7" Wt: 250 Type Pwr
Health F | PT/Exp B | Consist A
LIMA Plan C | Rand Var +5 | MM 3303

Two extensive DL stints sandwiched two victories, and then came post-season elbow surgery. Cmd and xERA would say he didn't stray far from last year. But H%, S% and hr/f indicate many early exits, and RHB had their way with him. Precious little good news here; significant repairs needed for a return of prior utility.

Yr	Tm	W	L	Sv	IP	K	ERA	xERA	WHIP	oOPS	vL	vR	BF/G	Ctl	Dom	Cmd	SwK	G	L	F	H%	S%	hr/f	GS	APC	DOM%	DIS%	Sv%	LI	RAR	BPV	BPX	R$
09	FLA	15	5	0	209	191	3.23	3.37	1.16	629	611	649	25.9	2.5	8.2	3.3	10%	50	18	32	30%	73%	8%	33	100	70%	15%			28.2	109	203	$25
10	FLA	11	6	0	184	186	2.30	3.11	1.11	607	612	602	26.6	2.4	9.1	3.9	12%	46	21	34	31%	80%	4%	28	107	71%	4%			40.2	125	202	$24
11	FLA	3	1	0	60	56	1.64	3.18	0.98	509	579	422	26.0	3.0	8.4	2.8	9%	51	15	34	24%	84%	4%	9	104	67%	0%			17.1	99	149	$8
12	MIA	8	14	0	191	165	3.81	3.79	1.28	678	691	661	25.7	3.1	7.8	2.5	10%	46	24	30	31%	71%	8%	31	101	65%	13%			4.8	81	106	$7
13	TOR	2	8	0	81	83	6.20	3.89	1.66	852	727	1032	24.0	3.3	9.2	2.8	10%	45	24	31	38%	66%	19%	16	92	44%	25%			-23.4	99	129	-$13
1st Half		1	2	0	48	49	5.21	3.90	1.59	811	688	988	24.9	3.4	9.1	2.7	12%	44	24	32	38%	69%	12%	9	94	56%	22%			-8.0	96	125	-$11
2nd Half		1	6	0	33	34	7.64	3.89	1.76	909	783	1094	22.9	3.3	9.3	2.8	8%	46	25	29	39%	61%	28%	7	89	29%	29%			-15.3	102	133	-$16
14	**Proj**	**8**	**12**	**0**	**160**	**144**	**4.36**	**3.60**	**1.39**	**709**	**667**	**766**	**23.5**	**3.3**	**8.1**	**2.5**	**10%**	**45**	**23**	**32**	**33%**	**71%**	**11%**	**29**						**-9.7**	**80**	**104**	**$1**

Jones,Nate

Age: 28 Th: R Role RP | Ht: 6' 5" Wt: 210 Type Pwr
Health A | PT/Exp D | Consist B
LIMA Plan A | Rand Var +2 | MM 5511

Skills-wise, a strong follow up to "Who's He?" 2012. S% inflated ERA, although difficulties with LH batters are a concern. But improved command and a Dom-fueled, groundball-filled 2H led to more significant innings and some closer-like numbers. If setup guys have value in your league, here's a viable option.

Yr	Tm	W	L	Sv	IP	K	ERA	xERA	WHIP	oOPS	vL	vR	BF/G	Ctl	Dom	Cmd	SwK	G	L	F	H%	S%	hr/f	GS	APC	DOM%	DIS%	Sv%	LI	RAR	BPV	BPX	R$
09																																	
10																																	
11	aa	2	3	12	63	57	4.33	4.83	1.63				6.7	4.6	8.0	1.8					36%	74%								-3.0	65	98	$0
12	CHW	8	0	0	72	65	2.39	4.00	1.38	686	528	774	4.6	4.0	8.2	2.0	11%	46	23	32	31%	84%	6%	0	18			0	1.19	14.4	62	81	$5
13	CHW	4	5	0	78	89	4.15	2.87	1.22	659	710	621	4.5	3.0	10.3	3.4	14%	51	21	28	33%	66%	9%	0	18			0	1.36	-2.8	133	173	$1
1st Half		3	4	0	41	41	4.35	3.31	1.23	649	642	654	4.9	3.0	8.9	2.9	12%	47	21	32	32%	63%	6%	0	19			0	1.10	-2.5	104	134	$1
2nd Half		1	1	0	37	48	3.93	2.40	1.20	670	773	580	4.1	2.9	11.8	4.0	17%	55	22	23	34%	68%	15%	0	16			0	1.61	-0.3	165	214	$1
14	**Proj**	**5**	**3**	**2**	**73**	**78**	**3.52**	**3.01**	**1.22**	**644**	**631**	**654**	**4.6**	**3.3**	**9.6**	**2.9**	**13%**	**49**	**22**	**29**	**31%**	**72%**	**8%**	**0**						**3.1**	**111**	**144**	**$4**

Jordan,Taylor

Age: 25 Th: R Role SP | Ht: 6' 3" Wt: 190 Type Con xGB
Health C | PT/Exp F | Consist F
LIMA Plan B+ | Rand Var -2 | MM 3001

1-3 with 3.66 ERA in 52 IP at WAS. Made favorable impression in jump from Double-A before lower-back strain ended season in mid-Aug. Showed nice Ctl and heavy sinker that induced many GB outs, much needed in light of meager Dom. Pitch-to-contact style has smaller margin of error. Expect some clunkers along the way.

Yr	Tm	W	L	Sv	IP	K	ERA	xERA	WHIP	oOPS	vL	vR	BF/G	Ctl	Dom	Cmd	SwK	G	L	F	H%	S%	hr/f	GS	APC	DOM%	DIS%	Sv%	LI	RAR	BPV	BPX	R$
09																																	
10																																	
11																																	
12																																	
13	WAS *	8	3	0	106	64	2.31	2.88	1.16	704	761	658	23.3	1.7	5.4	3.2	11%	57	20	23	30%	80%	8%	9	86	22%	11%			20.3	96	126	$10
1st Half		7	1	0	58	36	1.10	1.92	1.01	598	600	585	22.4	1.6	5.5	3.3	10%	58	16	26	27%	88%	0%	1	84	0%	100%			19.9	112	146	$19
2nd Half		1	2	0	47	28	3.80	3.58	1.33	716	781	664	24.6	1.7	5.3	3.1	11%	57	20	23	33%	72%	9%	8	86	25%	0%			0.4	85	110	-$1
14	**Proj**	**7**	**4**	**0**	**111**	**65**	**3.77**	**3.63**	**1.30**	**648**	**711**	**598**	**24.3**	**1.8**	**5.3**	**2.9**	**11%**	**54**	**22**	**24**	**32%**	**72%**	**8%**	**19**						**1.3**	**78**	**101**	**$3**

Karns,Nathan

Age: 26 Th: R Role SP | Ht: 6' 3" Wt: 230 Type Pwr FB
Health A | PT/Exp F | Consist F
LIMA Plan C | Rand Var +5 | MM 2300

0-1 with 7.50 ERA in 12 IP at WAS. Coughing up five HR in those 12 innings (three starts) earned him a quick return to AA-Harrisburg. High-90s fastball has harvested double-digit Dom at each rung of the minors, while 3.5+ Ctl has plagued him. Early-career injury has forced him to play catch-up; may need to wait a while longer.

Yr	Tm	W	L	Sv	IP	K	ERA	xERA	WHIP	oOPS	vL	vR	BF/G	Ctl	Dom	Cmd	SwK	G	L	F	H%	S%	hr/f	GS	APC	DOM%	DIS%	Sv%	LI	RAR	BPV	BPX	R$
09																																	
10																																	
11																																	
12																																	
13	WAS *	10	7	0	145	130	4.44	4.70	1.42	1060	1266	845	23.6	3.4	8.1	2.4	10%	36	31	33	32%	73%	36%	3	82	0%	100%			-10.2	60	78	-$1
1st Half		5	4	0	68	63	5.55	5.70	1.58	1060	1266	845	21.4	3.7	8.3	2.2	10%	36	31	33	34%	69%	36%		82	0%	100%			-14.1	45	58	-$8
2nd Half		5	3	0	77	68	3.45	3.82	1.27				26.1	3.1	8.0	2.6					29%	77%	0%							3.9	74	96	$5
14	**Proj**	**4**	**3**	**0**	**54**	**47**	**4.27**	**4.06**	**1.43**				**24.1**	**3.6**	**7.8**	**2.1**	**10%**	**36**	**22**	**42**	**31%**	**74%**	**11%**	**10**						**-2.7**	**56**	**72**	**-$2**

ROB CARROLL

Kazmir,Scott

Age: 30	Th: L	Role SP	Health F
Ht: 6' 0"	Wt: 185	Type Pwr FB	PT/Exp D
			Consist F
LIMA Plan A	Rand Var +2	MM 4403	

Adrift for most of 2011 and a Sugar Land Skeeter in 2012, he finished 2013 with the best Ctl and Cmd of MLB career. Crediting slider and changeup, made sweeping strides in 2H. Repeat hinges on mitigating damage of BBs and righties. If he does, the sequel to the comeback could surpass the original with... UP: 200 IP, 200 Ks.

Yr	Tm	W	L	Sv	IP	K	ERA	xERA	WHIP	oOPS	vL	vR	BF/G	Ctl	Dom	Cmd	SwK	G	L	F	H%	S%	hr/f	GS	APC	DOM%	DIS%	Sv%	LI	RAR	BPV	BPX	R$
09	2 AL	10	9	0	147	117	4.89	4.77	1.42	743	785	730	24.9	3.7	7.1	2.0	9%	34	19	48	31%	67%	7%	26	101	62%	23%			-10.3	42	78	$2
10	LAA	9	15	0	150	93	5.94	5.30	1.58	841	790	855	24.4	4.7	5.6	1.2	8%	39	17	44	29%	65%	12%	28	98	18%	46%			-34.4	-11	-17	-$11
11	LAA *	0	5	0	17	11	17.90	9.61	2.94	1643	2667	1214	16.3	11.1	5.8	0.5	3%	30	10	60	43%	33%	17%	1	63	0%	100%			-29.3	9	14	-$16
12																																	
13	CLE	10	9	0	158	162	4.04	3.53	1.32	735	573	794	23.2	2.7	9.2	3.4	11%	41	23	36	34%	73%	12%	29	95	52%	21%			-3.5	113	147	$4
1st Half		4	4	0	69	66	4.83	3.94	1.42	831	526	954	23.0	3.1	8.6	2.8	10%	41	19	40	32%	72%	16%	13	93	62%	31%			-8.2	89	115	-$3
2nd Half		6	5	0	89	96	3.44	3.22	1.25	659	615	674	23.3	2.3	9.7	4.2	11%	41	26	33	35%	73%	7%	16	96	44%	13%			4.7	131	170	$9
14	**Proj**	**13**	**8**	**0**	**174**	**168**	**3.77**	**3.51**	**1.28**	**708**	**619**	**737**	**22.4**	**3.0**	**8.7**	**2.9**	**9%**	**39**	**20**	**40**	**31%**	**74%**	**10%**	**32**						**2.0**	**94**	**122**	**$11**

Kelley,Shawn

Age: 30	Th: R	Role RP	Health F
Ht: 6' 2"	Wt: 220	Type Pwr xFB	PT/Exp D
			Consist A
LIMA Plan C+	Rand Var +2	MM 4500	

Dom explosion confirms arm is fully sound after missing most of 2011. Command/control need stabilizing and hr/f may need watching, but xERA, BPV suggest a nice collection of skills that haven't quite consolidated yet. Even if he doesn't break out of his 0-for-career save streak, he'll provide decent value at a low price.

Yr	Tm	W	L	Sv	IP	K	ERA	xERA	WHIP	oOPS	vL	vR	BF/G	Ctl	Dom	Cmd	SwK	G	L	F	H%	S%	hr/f	GS	APC	DOM%	DIS%	Sv%	LI	RAR	BPV	BPX	R$
09	SEA	5	4	0	46	41	4.50	3.96	1.17	742	555	920	4.7	1.8	8.0	4.6	10%	31	17	51	29%	69%	13%	0	18			0	1.32	-1.0	106	198	$1
10	SEA	3	1	0	25	26	3.96	4.63	1.52	841	696	968	5.1	4.3	9.4	2.2	12%	23	16	61	32%	82%	12%	0	20			0	0.88	0.4	53	85	-$2
11	SEA *	1	1	0	30	25	0.92	2.69	1.08	417	683	226	4.7	2.7	7.3	2.7	12%	38	6	56	26%	99%	0%	0	17			0	0.56	11.3	89	134	$2
12	SEA *	4	4	6	64	65	2.52	2.83	1.12	717	747	701	4.2	2.7	9.1	3.4	12%	29	20	51	29%	81%	8%	0	16			67	1.00	11.8	115	150	$8
13	NYY	4	2	0	53	71	4.39	3.42	1.31	729	760	707	4.0	3.9	12.0	3.1	12%	33	21	46	33%	71%	13%	0	17			0	1.33	-3.4	122	159	-$1
1st Half		3	0	0	30	44	4.20	3.01	1.20	705	713	699	4.3	3.9	13.2	3.4	12%	39	16	45	31%	71%	16%	0	18			0	1.25	-1.2	149	193	$1
2nd Half		1	2	0	23	27	4.63	3.95	1.46	759	832	715	3.6	3.9	10.4	2.7	11%	27	27	47	35%	71%	10%	0	16			0	1.41	-2.2	88	114	-$4
14	**Proj**	**4**	**3**	**0**	**58**	**64**	**3.44**	**3.44**	**1.24**	**686**	**685**	**685**	**4.0**	**3.2**	**10.0**	**3.1**	**12%**	**31**	**21**	**49**	**31%**	**77%**	**10%**	**0**						**3.0**	**102**	**132**	**$2**

Kelly,Joe

Age: 26	Th: R	Role SP	Health A
Ht: 6' 1"	Wt: 175	Type GB	PT/Exp C
			Consist A
LIMA Plan C+	Rand Var -4	MM 3103	

ERA and win-loss record might presume growth year, but Cmd, Dom, and Ctl all lost ground from 2012. S% was greatest ally to ERA; was also the beneficiary of 6+ run support. He throws in the mid-90s without getting many punchouts, which is a skill in itself. It's just not a skill that you want your fantasy pitcher to have.

Yr	Tm	W	L	Sv	IP	K	ERA	xERA	WHIP	oOPS	vL	vR	BF/G	Ctl	Dom	Cmd	SwK	G	L	F	H%	S%	hr/f	GS	APC	DOM%	DIS%	Sv%	LI	RAR	BPV	BPX	R$
09																																	
10																																	
11	aa	6	4	0	59	43	4.33	4.78	1.53				23.4	3.4	6.5	1.9					34%	72%								-2.9	54	81	-$2
12	STL *	7	12	0	179	112	3.35	4.17	1.40	740	917	607	21.0	2.8	5.6	2.0	8%	52	21	27	32%	77%	11%	16	71	44%	6%	0	0.78	14.6	57	74	$3
13	STL	10	5	0	124	79	2.69	4.17	1.35	694	691	696	14.4	3.2	5.7	1.8	8%	51	21	28	30%	83%	9%	15	53	33%	13%	0	0.87	18.1	46	60	$7
1st Half		0	3	0	37	30	3.86	3.82	1.45	771	700	840	7.4	2.7	7.2	2.7	11%	47	24	29	34%	78%	14%	1	27	0%	0%	0	0.94	0.0	84	108	-$6
2nd Half		10	2	0	87	49	2.18	4.33	1.32	659	686	639	24.7	3.4	5.1	1.5	6%	53	19	28	28%	85%	6%	14	92	36%	14%	0	0.77	18.0	30	39	$13
14	**Proj**	**9**	**8**	**0**	**146**	**96**	**3.70**	**3.97**	**1.42**	**729**	**787**	**683**	**21.8**	**3.2**	**5.9**	**1.8**	**8%**	**51**	**21**	**28**	**31%**	**75%**	**9%**	**39**						**3.1**	**48**	**62**	**$3**

Kendrick,Kyle

Age: 29	Th: R	Role SP	Health A
Ht: 6' 3"	Wt: 210	Type Con	PT/Exp A
			Consist A
LIMA Plan C	Rand Var 0	MM 2003	

Cited as "breakout candidate" in this space last year, he made us look good through June. But being blasted for 21 ER in the next 26 IP blew that away, and shoulder woes shelved him later. He has nice Ctl and OK GB% but with chronically subpar Dom he's very hittable. Loss of 2012 SwK gain closes the door on that breakout.

Yr	Tm	W	L	Sv	IP	K	ERA	xERA	WHIP	oOPS	vL	vR	BF/G	Ctl	Dom	Cmd	SwK	G	L	F	H%	S%	hr/f	GS	APC	DOM%	DIS%	Sv%	LI	RAR	BPV	BPX	R$
09	PHI *	12	8	0	169	66	4.32	4.41	1.41	636	704	576	21.7	2.5	3.5	1.4	6%	56	22	22	30%	70%	5%	2	44	50%	50%	0	0.72	0.0	28	52	$3
10	PHI	11	10	0	181	84	4.73	4.68	1.37	807	902	713	23.4	2.4	4.2	1.7	5%	45	17	38	29%	69%	11%	31	86	32%	32%	0	0.74	-14.6	32	52	-$1
11	PHI	8	6	0	115	59	3.22	4.27	1.22	734	766	708	14.1	2.4	4.6	2.0	6%	45	19	36	27%	79%	11%	15	51	47%	40%	0	0.87	10.2	43	64	$6
12	PHI	11	12	0	159	116	3.90	4.21	1.27	731	701	760	18.2	2.8	6.6	2.4	10%	47	18	36	29%	73%	11%	25	68	52%	28%	0	1.06	2.3	68	89	$6
13	PHI	10	13	0	182	110	4.70	4.24	1.40	751	679	812	26.7	2.3	5.4	2.3	7%	49	20	31	32%	67%	10%	30	96	47%	23%			-18.7	62	81	-$5
1st Half		7	5	0	113	70	3.59	4.03	1.22	678	649	706	27.9	2.2	5.6	2.6	7%	51	17	33	29%	73%	8%	17	98	59%	18%			3.8	71	92	$5
2nd Half		3	8	0	69	40	6.49	4.59	1.67	859	728	955	25.1	2.6	5.2	2.0	7%	48	24	28	36%	61%	11%	13	93	31%	31%			-22.4	49	63	-$22
14	**Proj**	**9**	**11**	**0**	**145**	**87**	**4.26**	**4.05**	**1.39**	**773**	**731**	**808**	**20.2**	**2.5**	**5.4**	**2.2**	**7%**	**47**	**19**	**33**	**31%**	**72%**	**11%**	**30**						**-7.1**	**55**	**71**	**$0**

Kennedy,Ian

Age: 29	Th: R	Role SP	Health A
Ht: 6' 0"	Wt: 190	Type Pwr	PT/Exp A
			Consist A
LIMA Plan C	Rand Var +2	MM 3305	

The impulse might be to look at 2011 as the outlier here, but his skills maintained into 2012. That makes 2013 look like an outlier, or at least a throwback to 2010. The changes? Wildness returned, gopheritis ticked up despite drop in FB% and ERA was hurt by S%. Most of this is fixable, especially if he's in PETCO.

Yr	Tm	W	L	Sv	IP	K	ERA	xERA	WHIP	oOPS	vL	vR	BF/G	Ctl	Dom	Cmd	SwK	G	L	F	H%	S%	hr/f	GS	APC	DOM%	DIS%	Sv%	LI	RAR	BPV	BPX	R$
09	NYY *	1	0	0	24	21	2.18	3.28	1.41	500	500	500	20.0	3.9	8.1	2.1	11%	0	50	50	34%	83%	0%	0	28			0	1.86	6.3	96	179	-$1
10	ARI	9	10	0	194	168	3.80	4.01	1.20	696	674	716	25.3	3.2	7.8	2.4	9%	37	19	44	27%	73%	11%	32	99	63%	13%			6.6	68	109	$12
11	ARI	21	4	0	222	198	2.88	3.50	1.09	641	656	626	27.3	2.2	8.0	3.6	9%	39	22	40	28%	77%	8%	33	104	70%	6%			29.1	101	152	$28
12	ARI	15	12	0	208	187	4.02	4.06	1.30	775	790	759	27.2	2.4	8.1	3.4	11%	37	21	42	32%	73%	11%	33	102	58%	9%			-0.1	96	126	$9
13	2 NL	7	10	0	181	163	4.91	4.14	1.40	781	828	736	25.6	3.6	8.1	2.2	10%	38	23	39	31%	68%	13%	31	100	48%	19%			-23.4	64	83	-$6
1st Half		3	4	0	89	77	5.36	4.21	1.35	798	869	724	25.9	3.3	7.8	2.3	11%	35	23	42	29%	64%	14%	15	101	60%	13%			-16.4	63	82	-$7
2nd Half		4	6	0	92	86	4.48	4.07	1.44	766	787	747	25.4	3.9	8.4	2.2	10%	41	24	35	32%	72%	13%	16	99	38%	25%			-7.0	65	84	-$5
14	**Proj**	**12**	**11**	**0**	**195**	**175**	**3.91**	**3.63**	**1.28**	**734**	**755**	**713**	**26.7**	**2.9**	**8.1**	**2.8**	**10%**	**38**	**22**	**40**	**31%**	**73%**	**10%**	**30**						**-1.1**	**84**	**110**	**$10**

Kershaw,Clayton

Age: 26	Th: L	Role SP	Health A
Ht: 6' 3"	Wt: 220	Type Pwr	PT/Exp A
			Consist A
LIMA Plan D+	Rand Var -5	MM 5405	

That he lost nine games underscores how silly W-L records can be. DOM%/DIS% are the very definition of "ace". Already fine Ctl and Cmd were ridiculous in 2H. Just one note of caution from xERA: he's long outpitched xERA, but the gap is getting absurd. Invest with confidence, just don't pay for a sub-2.00 repeat.

Yr	Tm	W	L	Sv	IP	K	ERA	xERA	WHIP	oOPS	vL	vR	BF/G	Ctl	Dom	Cmd	SwK	G	L	F	H%	S%	hr/f	GS	APC	DOM%	DIS%	Sv%	LI	RAR	BPV	BPX	R$
09	LA	8	8	0	171	185	2.79	3.82	1.23	588	489	616	22.6	4.8	9.7	2.0	10%	39	19	42	27%	77%	4%	30	98	50%	23%	0	0.76	32.3	63	118	$19
10	LA	13	10	0	204	212	2.91	3.61	1.18	615	673	599	26.5	3.6	9.3	2.6	11%	40	18	42	29%	77%	6%	32	106	81%	13%			29.5	90	145	$22
11	LA	21	5	0	233	248	2.28	2.95	0.98	554	512	563	27.6	2.1	9.6	4.6	12%	43	18	39	28%	79%	7%	33	105	88%	3%			48.0	137	206	$40
12	LA	14	9	0	228	229	2.53	3.23	1.02	593	570	599	27.3	2.5	9.1	3.6	11%	47	19	34	27%	78%	8%	33	105	82%	6%			41.7	121	157	$36
13	LA	16	9	0	236	232	1.83	2.93	0.92	521	477	532	27.5	2.0	8.8	4.5	12%	46	23	31	26%	82%	6%	33	104	88%	3%			59.2	130	169	$44
1st Half		6	5	0	121	118	2.08	3.15	0.96	533	360	575	27.8	2.4	8.8	3.6	11%	46	21	34	26%	81%	7%	17	108	88%	6%			26.8	115	149	$40
2nd Half		10	4	0	115	114	1.57	2.70	0.86	509	613	486	27.2	1.5	8.9	6.0	13%	47	25	28	27%	83%	5%	16	100	88%	0%			32.5	145	188	$49
14	**Proj**	**18**	**6**	**0**	**232**	**231**	**2.42**	**2.89**	**1.00**	**571**	**550**	**576**	**26.5**	**2.3**	**9.0**	**3.9**	**12%**	**45**	**21**	**34**	**28%**	**78%**	**7%**	**33**						**41.5**	**123**	**160**	**$38**

Keuchel,Dallas

Age: 26	Th: L	Role SP	Health A
Ht: 6' 3"	Wt: 200	Type GB	PT/Exp C
			Consist A
LIMA Plan C	Rand Var +5	MM 3103	

Improved major-league GB%, Ctl, and Dom (+3) but remained stuck in same statistical quagmire. Hit rate did him no favors as ERA took a beating, and that's with his GB bent limiting damage of high hr/f. But skills do say he's improved some, as does xERA. If the Dom sticks and he gets Ctl back under 3.0... UP: sub-4.00 ERA

Yr	Tm	W	L	Sv	IP	K	ERA	xERA	WHIP	oOPS	vL	vR	BF/G	Ctl	Dom	Cmd	SwK	G	L	F	H%	S%	hr/f	GS	APC	DOM%	DIS%	Sv%	LI	RAR	BPV	BPX	R$
09																																	
10	aa	2	6	0	54	32	5.97	4.77	1.50				25.7	1.9	5.3	2.8					36%	57%								-12.5	72	116	-$6
11	a/a	10	7	0	164	79	4.53	4.37	1.36				25.3	2.1	4.3	2.1					31%	67%								-11.8	43	65	-$1
12	HOU *	9	12	0	178	81	4.56	4.48	1.40	823	750	844	23.4	2.9	4.1	1.4	6%	52	17	31	29%	69%	16%	16	87	19%	38%			-12.0	25	33	-$5
13	HOU	6	10	0	154	123	5.15	3.72	1.54	812	750	832	22.0	3.0	7.2	2.4	9%	56	21	23	35%	69%	17%	22	81	36%	18%	0	0.90	-24.4	81	106	-$11
1st Half		4	4	0	75	58	4.34	3.75	1.46	809	854	794	20.4	2.7	7.0	2.6	9%	55	18	27	33%	75%	18%	9	72	44%	11%	0	0.87	-4.4	87	113	-$5
2nd Half		2	6	0	79	65	5.92	3.69	1.61	816	642	867	23.7	3.4	7.4	2.2	10%	57	24	20	36%	63%	18%	13	90	31%	23%	0	0.93	-20.1	76	98	-$18
14	**Proj**	**7**	**11**	**0**	**160**	**113**	**4.33**	**3.74**	**1.42**	**740**	**668**	**761**	**22.8**	**3.1**	**6.4**	**2.0**	**9%**	**54**	**20**	**26**	**32%**	**71%**	**12%**	**30**						**-9.2**	**63**	**82**	**-$1**

ROB CARROLL

Kimbrel,Craig

Age: 26 Th: R Role RP	Health A	LIMA Plan C
Ht: 5' 11" Wt: 205 Type Pwr	PT/Exp A	Rand Var -5
	Consist B	MM 5530

Elite bullpen aces will have BPVs in excess of 100. Last year, his BPV was 84 less than in 2012, losing almost an elite closer's worth of value in his "plunge" to 189. Meanwhile, he twice went two months without giving up an ER, saving 50 games with still-inhuman Dom. And he got back on track in the 2H. More excellence awaits.

Yr	Tm	W	L	Sv	IP	K	ERA	xERA	WHIP	oOPS	vL	vR	BF/G	Ctl	Dom	Cmd	SwK	G	L	F	H%	S%	hr/f	GS	APC	DOM%	DIS%	Sv%	LI	RAR	BPV	BPX	R$
09																																	
10	ATL *	7	2	24	76	113	1.48	1.85	1.19	437	523	361	4.4	6.0	13.3	2.2	14%	28	22	50	27%	89%	0%	0	18			89	0.53	24.4	139	226	$21
11	ATL	4	3	46	77	127	2.10	2.21	1.04	499	442	549	3.9	3.7	14.8	4.0	16%	45	15	40	33%	81%	5%	0	17			85	1.32	17.5	189	284	$29
12	ATL	3	1	42	63	116	1.01	1.43	0.65	358	331	387	3.7	2.0	16.7	8.3	20%	49	19	32	28%	89%	10%	0	15			93	1.29	23.3	273	356	$34
13	ATL	4	3	50	67	98	1.21	2.12	0.88	487	574	393	3.8	2.7	13.2	4.9	14%	47	24	29	28%	91%	10%	0	15			93	1.30	22.0	189	247	$32
1st Half		2	1	23	30	43	1.48	2.42	1.02	604	649	542	3.8	3.0	12.8	4.3	15%	44	21	35	30%	93%	14%	0	15			88	1.30	8.9	171	222	$28
2nd Half		2	2	27	37	55	0.98	1.88	0.76	388	496	293	3.8	2.5	13.5	5.5	14%	51	26	23	26%	89%	6%	0	15			96	1.30	13.0	205	266	$36
14	Proj	**4**	**2**	**48**	**68**	**107**	**1.98**	**1.78**	**0.84**	**447**	**474**	**418**	**3.7**	**2.7**	**14.3**	**5.3**	**17%**	**48**	**21**	**31**	**29%**	**79%**	**9%**	**0**						**15.7**	**210**	**273**	**$32**

Kintzler,Brandon

Age: 29 Th: R Role RP	Health F	LIMA Plan B
Ht: 5' 10" Wt: 185 Type xGB	PT/Exp D	Rand Var -1
	Consist D	MM 5210

Became a reliable option in his first full year by minimizing walks and HR. Kept his infielders busy, even more so in 2H when he traded Dom for GB. He was rewarded with more late-inning work; Holds leagues will want to take notice of his 14 in Aug-Sept. Major-league xERAs are stable. A nice get at the back of the draft.

Yr	Tm	W	L	Sv	IP	K	ERA	xERA	WHIP	oOPS	vL	vR	BF/G	Ctl	Dom	Cmd	SwK	G	L	F	H%	S%	hr/f	GS	APC	DOM%	DIS%	Sv%	LI	RAR	BPV	BPX	R$
09	aa	1	2	0	36	27	5.58	6.30	1.64				17.7	2.5	6.9	2.8					37%	69%								-5.6	46	85	-$5
10	MIL *	4	1	16	56	45	2.45	2.28	1.00	1045	964	1087	4.4	1.8	7.2	4.0	17%	68	11	21	27%	77%	50%	0	18			80	0.54	11.3	123	199	$13
11	MIL	1	1	0	15	15	3.68	2.86	1.16	725	678	742	6.8	1.8	9.2	5.0	9%	60	9	30	29%	79%	23%	0	25			0	0.57	0.5	154	231	-$2
12	MIL *	3	3	9	64	38	3.94	4.46	1.53	732	744	717	5.3	3.3	5.4	1.6	10%	51	27	22	34%	73%	9%	0	21			90	0.64	0.6	53	69	-$1
13	MIL	3	3	0	77	58	2.69	3.03	1.06	567	540	586	4.3	1.9	6.8	3.6	9%	57	24	18	29%	74%	5%	0	15			0	1.05	11.2	107	139	$5
1st Half		2	0	0	35	32	3.34	3.03	1.09	558	507	586	4.2	2.6	8.2	3.2	11%	53	25	22	29%	68%	5%	0	16			0	0.84	2.3	109	142	$4
2nd Half		1	3	0	42	26	2.14	3.03	1.05	573	559	586	4.3	1.3	5.6	4.3	7%	61	23	16	29%	79%	5%	0	15			0	1.23	8.9	105	135	$6
14	Proj	**3**	**3**	**3**	**65**	**46**	**3.21**	**3.18**	**1.23**	**653**	**625**	**674**	**4.9**	**2.3**	**6.4**	**2.8**	**9%**	**58**	**24**	**18**	**31%**	**74%**	**8%**	**0**						**5.3**	**90**	**117**	**$3**

Kluber,Corey

Age: 28 Th: R Role SP	Health C	LIMA Plan B
Ht: 6' 4" Wt: 215 Type Pwr	PT/Exp C	Rand Var +3
	Consist C	MM 4305

His BPIs are on positive trends, and so is his rosterability. Dom, Cmd, GB% are up; Ctl is down, and xERA says more growth ahead. He did skirt some LD danger and his past includes ample base runners, but 2H DOM%-DIS% says he was grooving despite losing time to a strained finger. Keeper material.

Yr	Tm	W	L	Sv	IP	K	ERA	xERA	WHIP	oOPS	vL	vR	BF/G	Ctl	Dom	Cmd	SwK	G	L	F	H%	S%	hr/f	GS	APC	DOM%	DIS%	Sv%	LI	RAR	BPV	BPX	R$
09	aa	2	4	0	45	31	4.69	5.23	1.78				23.0	6.5	6.3	1.0					31%	74%								-2.0	34	64	-$5
10	a/a	9	9	0	160	137	3.84	4.51	1.52				24.0	3.1	7.7	2.5					36%	74%								4.8	82	132	$2
11	CLE *	7	11	0	155	121	6.46	5.45	1.64	740	900	286	23.1	4.2	7.0	1.7	12%	27	47	27	34%	61%	0%	0	30			0	0.15	-48.0	41	61	-$19
12	CLE *	13	12	0	188	157	4.53	4.91	1.52	834	860	801	24.7	3.2	7.5	2.3	12%	45	22	33	35%	71%	13%	12	90	33%	25%			-12.1	64	84	-$5
13	CLE	11	5	0	147	136	3.85	3.25	1.26	729	751	704	23.4	2.0	8.3	4.1	11%	46	26	29	33%	72%	12%	24	88	42%	17%	0	0.73	0.3	119	155	$6
1st Half		6	5	0	76	73	4.16	3.12	1.30	772	764	782	22.5	1.7	8.7	5.2	12%	45	27	28	35%	71%	15%	12	85	33%	25%	0	0.70	-2.8	134	174	$5
2nd Half		5	0	0	72	63	3.52	3.39	1.23	682	735	628	24.4	2.4	7.9	3.3	10%	46	25	29	31%	73%	10%	12	91	50%	8%			3.1	102	132	$7
14	Proj	**12**	**9**	**0**	**189**	**164**	**3.74**	**3.47**	**1.33**	**723**	**754**	**686**	**23.2**	**2.8**	**7.8**	**2.8**	**11%**	**45**	**24**	**30**	**32%**	**74%**	**10%**	**34**						**2.9**	**89**	**116**	**$9**

Koehler,Tom

Age: 28 Th: R Role SP	Health A	LIMA Plan D+
Ht: 6' 3" Wt: 235 Type	PT/Exp D	Rand Var 0
	Consist C	MM 2103

5-10, 4.41 ERA in 143 IP at MIA. The setup—unheralded rookie reliever being thrust into starting rotation for lousy team—spelled disaster. There were some of those, and a few gems. Mostly, though, it was a lot of very low-grade pitching and substandard BPIs. There's simply not much to hitch the wagon to here.

Yr	Tm	W	L	Sv	IP	K	ERA	xERA	WHIP	oOPS	vL	vR	BF/G	Ctl	Dom	Cmd	SwK	G	L	F	H%	S%	hr/f	GS	APC	DOM%	DIS%	Sv%	LI	RAR	BPV	BPX	R$
09																																	
10	aa	16	2	0	159	129	3.28	4.05	1.37				23.7	2.9	7.3	2.5					33%	78%								15.5	77	125	$11
11	aaa	12	7	0	150	94	5.09	4.72	1.56				23.5	4.7	5.6	1.2					30%	68%								-21.4	33	50	-$8
12	MIA *	12	12	0	164	130	5.28	5.74	1.67	896	818	941	19.9	4.0	7.1	1.8	5%	24	27	49	35%	70%	20%	1	26	0%	0%	0	0.70	-25.6	41	53	-$15
13	MIA *	5	12	0	166	107	4.32	4.03	1.38	754	706	796	21.1	3.7	5.8	1.6	8%	48	22	30	29%	70%	10%	23	78	39%	30%	0	0.72	-9.4	45	58	-$4
1st Half		1	6	0	81	49	4.09	3.26	1.24	699	789	605	18.3	3.9	5.4	1.4	7%	53	19	28	24%	69%	13%	9	66	44%	33%	0	0.65	-2.2	45	58	-$1
2nd Half		4	6	0	85	58	4.55	4.77	1.52	795	633	923	24.6	3.5	6.2	1.7	9%	44	24	32	33%	71%	9%	14	91	36%	29%			-7.2	46	59	-$7
14	Proj	**7**	**8**	**0**	**131**	**91**	**4.59**	**4.18**	**1.49**	**809**	**746**	**864**	**21.6**	**3.8**	**6.3**	**1.6**	**8%**	**47**	**22**	**31**	**31%**	**71%**	**11%**	**26**						**-11.7**	**36**	**46**	**-$4**

Kohn,Michael

Age: 28 Th: R Role RP	Health F	LIMA Plan D+
Ht: 6' 2" Wt: 200 Type Pwr xFB	PT/Exp D	Rand Var -3
	Consist A	MM 2400

First-half H% and S% were apparitions, fading into darkness in 2H along with ERA, again laying bare his inability to retire RHB. Having TJS in 2012 didn't help him subdue his other bogeyman, wildness. With Ctl near 5.0, he's constantly pitching in the arrears. It's a scary neighborhood he's living in. Best to mosey on by.

Yr	Tm	W	L	Sv	IP	K	ERA	xERA	WHIP	oOPS	vL	vR	BF/G	Ctl	Dom	Cmd	SwK	G	L	F	H%	S%	hr/f	GS	APC	DOM%	DIS%	Sv%	LI	RAR	BPV	BPX	R$
09																																	
10	LAA *	7	4	12	67	67	2.25	2.66	1.29	623	776	454	4.3	5.2	8.9	1.7	12%	40	9	51	27%	83%	0%	0	17			75	0.84	15.2	92	150	$11
11	LAA *	1	4	13	61	61	4.59	5.08	1.49	1080	1089	1072	4.4	4.0	9.0	2.2	9%	24	7	68	32%	74%	21%	0	17			68	1.28	-4.8	57	86	$1
12																																	
13	LAA	1	4	0	53	52	3.74	4.70	1.32	711	589	847	3.7	4.8	8.8	1.9	12%	23	22	54	26%	76%	9%	0	15			0	1.14	0.8	32	41	-$2
1st Half		1	0	0	23	23	1.96	4.20	1.00	581	515	617	3.4	4.3	9.0	2.1	12%	23	21	56	19%	86%	6%	0	15			0	1.02	5.4	47	60	$3
2nd Half		0	4	0	30	29	5.10	5.10	1.57	800	616	1127	3.8	5.1	8.7	1.7	12%	23	23	53	31%	71%	10%	0	16			0	1.23	-4.6	20	26	-$6
14	Proj	**2**	**4**	**0**	**58**	**57**	**4.49**	**4.32**	**1.43**	**771**	**631**	**933**	**3.9**	**4.6**	**8.9**	**1.9**	**12%**	**23**	**22**	**54**	**30%**	**72%**	**9%**	**0**						**-4.5**	**38**	**50**	**-$3**

Kontos,George

Age: 29 Th: R Role RP	Health A	LIMA Plan B+
Ht: 6' 3" Wt: 215 Type	PT/Exp D	Rand Var 0
	Consist F	MM 4201

2-2, 4.39 ERA in 55 IP at SF. Wasn't quite as steadfast as last year, the biggest difference being a tanked GB rate and sudden helplessness against lefties (.747 OPS vL lifetime). Both rebounded in 2H, where xERA said he has enough Cmd and Ctl to succeed. Harmless, but lacking upward role mobility.

Yr	Tm	W	L	Sv	IP	K	ERA	xERA	WHIP	oOPS	vL	vR	BF/G	Ctl	Dom	Cmd	SwK	G	L	F	H%	S%	hr/f	GS	APC	DOM%	DIS%	Sv%	LI	RAR	BPV	BPX	R$
09	a/a	4	5	0	71	52	4.49	5.22	1.60				24.3	4.4	6.6	1.5					32%	75%								-1.4	36	67	-$3
10	a/a	0	3	0	35	24	5.14	5.60	1.62				8.1	3.4	6.3	1.8					35%	70%								-4.6	37	60	-$5
11	NYY *	4	4	2	95	78	3.74	5.06	1.37	625	400	691	8.5	3.1	7.3	2.3	18%	20	7	73	29%	82%	9%	0	13			67	0.37	2.4	40	60	$1
12	SF *	4	1	1	75	64	2.14	2.33	1.04	591	468	653	4.3	2.2	7.7	3.5	13%	51	15	34	28%	81%	8%	0	15			50	0.62	17.4	116	152	$9
13	SF *	5	4	4	79	67	4.34	4.10	1.29	788	1024	689	4.6	2.4	7.6	3.2	11%	38	25	37	32%	69%	11%	0	17			67	1.01	-4.6	83	108	$1
1st Half		4	2	1	40	38	5.00	4.36	1.40	811	1327	587	4.4	2.9	8.5	2.9	12%	31	23	46	34%	65%	9%	0	16			50	0.88	-5.5	85	110	-$1
2nd Half		1	2	3	39	29	3.67	3.84	1.18	756	566	831	4.9	1.8	6.7	3.7	11%	48	27	25	29%	74%	17%	0	19			75	1.24	0.9	85	110	$2
14	Proj	**4**	**3**	**0**	**73**	**58**	**3.81**	**3.59**	**1.28**	**727**	**741**	**720**	**5.3**	**2.7**	**7.2**	**2.7**	**12%**	**45**	**21**	**34**	**30%**	**73%**	**11%**	**0**						**0.5**	**81**	**105**	**$1**

Krol,Ian

Age: 23 Th: L Role RP	Health A	LIMA Plan C
Ht: 6' 1" Wt: 210 Type Pwr FB	PT/Exp F	Rand Var -2
	Consist F	MM 3300

2-1, 3.95 ERA in 27 IP at WAS. 2013 was first year as full-time RP and he responded with 10.9 Dom and 0.81 WHIP at two minor-league stops. In small-sample shot in the bigs, he showed that nice Dom with average Ctl and Cmd, but was clearly taken to task by RHB. Expect more bumps, but young lefties have that allure.

Yr	Tm	W	L	Sv	IP	K	ERA	xERA	WHIP	oOPS	vL	vR	BF/G	Ctl	Dom	Cmd	SwK	G	L	F	H%	S%	hr/f	GS	APC	DOM%	DIS%	Sv%	LI	RAR	BPV	BPX	R$
09																																	
10																																	
11																																	
12																																	
13	WAS *	3	2	1	57	52	2.60	2.84	1.07	785	593	957	3.8	2.4	8.2	3.4	7%	39	20	41	27%	81%	14%	0	15			20	1.18	8.9	103	135	$4
1st Half		0	0	1	38	37	1.04	0.96	0.75	396	325	455	4.3	1.8	8.9	5.0	9%	30	22	48	21%	91%	8%	0	16			33	1.65	13.1	165	214	$10
2nd Half		3	2	0	19	15	5.70	6.64	1.71	1012	740	1268	3.2	3.7	6.9	1.9	6%	43	19	38	35%	72%	18%	0	14			0	0.96	-4.4	17	22	-$6
14	Proj	**3**	**2**	**0**	**29**	**25**	**3.73**	**3.74**	**1.32**	**648**	**469**	**817**	**3.5**	**2.9**	**7.7**	**2.7**	**6%**	**43**	**19**	**38**	**30%**	**77%**	**12%**	**0**						**0.5**	**82**	**106**	**-$1**

ROB CARROLL

Kuroda,Hiroki

Age: 39	Th: R	Role SP	Health B	LIMA Plan C+	
Ht: 6' 1"	Wt: 205	Type	PT/Exp A	Rand Var 0	
			Consist A	MM 4205	

Seems he's been pitching forever. Age hasn't eroded his remarkably stable skill set; let your eyes wander down any BPI column and you'll see little variance. Sure, Dom may be leaking slightly, but Cmd has tightened. No discernable vL/vR splits. He avoids DISasters. With him, the past is prologue; pick a year and go with it.

Yr Tm	W	L	Sv	IP	K	ERA	xERA	WHIP	oOPS	vL	vR	BF/G	Ctl	Dom	Cmd	SwK	G	L	F	H%	S%	hr/f	GS	APC	DOM%	DIS%	Sv%	LI	RAR	BPV	BPX	R$
09 LA	8	7	0	117	87	3.76	3.71	1.14	676	712	643	23.1	1.8	6.7	3.6	10%	49	17	33	29%	70%	10%	20	86	55%	15%	0	0.77	8.2	97	182	$9
10 LA	11	13	0	196	159	3.39	3.47	1.16	642	664	623	26.1	2.2	7.3	3.3	11%	51	17	32	29%	72%	8%	31	98	68%	13%			16.6	101	163	$16
11 LA	13	16	0	202	161	3.07	3.65	1.21	716	767	667	26.2	2.2	7.2	3.3	11%	43	22	35	30%	80%	11%	32	100	56%	13%			21.6	91	137	$17
12 NYY	16	11	0	220	167	3.32	3.59	1.17	705	734	665	27.0	2.1	6.8	3.3	10%	52	18	30	28%	76%	13%	33	101	61%	9%			18.9	97	126	$20
13 NYY	11	13	0	201	150	3.31	3.64	1.16	683	742	602	25.8	1.9	6.7	3.5	10%	47	22	31	29%	75%	10%	32	100	50%	6%			13.9	94	122	$14
1st Half	7	6	0	107	75	2.95	3.69	1.06	638	707	550	25.1	1.8	6.3	3.6	10%	45	21	34	26%	77%	11%	17	98	47%	12%			12.0	89	116	$21
2nd Half	4	7	0	95	75	3.71	3.57	1.28	732	778	662	26.5	2.1	7.1	3.4	11%	48	23	29	32%	73%	10%	15	102	53%	0%			1.8	98	127	$7
14 Proj	**11**	**12**	**0**	**189**	**139**	**3.59**	**3.42**	**1.18**	**697**	**744**	**639**	**25.4**	**2.0**	**6.7**	**3.3**	**10%**	**48**	**21**	**31**	**29%**	**73%**	**11%**	**30**						**6.4**	**91**	**118**	**$13**

Lackey,John

Age: 35	Th: R	Role SP	Health F	LIMA Plan C+	
Ht: 6' 6"	Wt: 235	Type	PT/Exp B	Rand Var +1	
			Consist C	MM 3205	

Shed extra pounds and distractions in driven return from TJS, cajoling strongest skills in years. Ks and GBs were plentiful in the 1H; 69%-0% DOM%-DIS% brought him home in the 2H. Constants were career-best Ctl and Cmd, plus he approached 200 IP. With a clean arm and a clear head, stands a fair chance of repeating.

Yr Tm	W	L	Sv	IP	K	ERA	xERA	WHIP	oOPS	vL	vR	BF/G	Ctl	Dom	Cmd	SwK	G	L	F	H%	S%	hr/f	GS	APC	DOM%	DIS%	Sv%	LI	RAR	BPV	BPX	R$
09 LAA	11	8	0	176	139	3.83	3.87	1.27	718	756	666	27.7	2.4	7.1	3.0	9%	45	20	35	31%	72%	9%	27	102	59%	22%			10.7	86	161	$12
10 BOS	14	11	0	215	156	4.35	4.16	1.42	765	802	719	28.2	3.0	6.5	2.2	7%	46	18	36	32%	70%	7%	33	109	55%	12%			-7.3	60	97	$3
11 BOS	12	12	0	160	108	6.41	4.63	1.62	852	915	778	26.5	3.2	6.1	1.9	7%	40	22	37	35%	61%	10%	28	102	29%	32%			-48.7	42	64	-$17
12																																
13 BOS	10	13	0	189	161	3.52	3.50	1.16	703	657	760	26.8	1.9	7.7	4.0	10%	47	18	35	29%	75%	13%	29	99	66%	10%			8.1	111	145	$12
1st Half	5	5	0	78	73	2.99	3.27	1.20	691	594	820	25.2	2.0	8.4	4.3	9%	50	19	31	31%	81%	14%	13	95	62%	23%			8.5	126	163	$13
2nd Half	5	8	0	111	88	3.89	3.66	1.13	711	705	718	28.1	1.9	7.1	3.8	11%	45	17	38	28%	71%	13%	16	103	69%	0%			-0.4	101	130	$12
14 Proj	**15**	**12**	**0**	**189**	**151**	**3.83**	**3.61**	**1.29**	**736**	**739**	**733**	**25.9**	**2.4**	**7.2**	**3.0**	**9%**	**45**	**19**	**36**	**31%**	**74%**	**11%**	**30**						**0.8**	**86**	**112**	**$10**

Lannan,John

Age: 29	Th: L	Role SP	Health F	LIMA Plan D+	
Ht: 6' 4"	Wt: 235	Type Con GB	PT/Exp B	Rand Var +1	
			Consist C	MM 1000	

That's some painfully low Dom for a major-league pitcher. Add to that below-average Ctl, and you get tons of baserunners with nowhere to go but home. Thank goodness for that GB tilt. He does get a bit of a pass for missing 100 games with quad and knee injuries, but even at his best (2011), those BPVs ain't much.

Yr Tm	W	L	Sv	IP	K	ERA	xERA	WHIP	oOPS	vL	vR	BF/G	Ctl	Dom	Cmd	SwK	G	L	F	H%	S%	hr/f	GS	APC	DOM%	DIS%	Sv%	LI	RAR	BPV	BPX	R$
09 WAS	9	13	0	206	89	3.88	4.63	1.35	750	873	711	26.5	3.0	3.9	1.3	5%	52	18	30	28%	74%	11%	33	95	27%	18%			11.2	20	37	$7
10 WAS *	9	12	0	184	93	4.89	5.50	1.61	799	747	817	25.5	2.9	4.5	1.6	6%	51	21	27	34%	71%	10%	25	94	32%	28%			-18.4	26	42	-$9
11 WAS	10	13	0	185	106	3.70	4.26	1.46	736	589	788	24.5	3.7	5.2	1.4	8%	54	21	25	30%	76%	10%	33	89	30%	21%			5.4	25	38	$1
12 WAS *	13	12	0	181	80	5.34	5.89	1.69	720	674	737	27.3	3.3	4.0	1.2	6%	57	22	22	34%	69%	0%	6	85	17%	33%			-29.6	12	16	-$20
13 PHI	3	6	0	74	38	5.33	4.65	1.52	801	833	792	23.7	3.3	4.6	1.4	7%	52	17	30	31%	64%	8%	14	88	36%	36%			-13.4	25	32	-$9
1st Half	1	2	0	32	16	4.83	4.00	1.33	778	397	870	22.5	2.0	4.5	2.3	8%	52	22	26	32%	61%	4%	6	89	50%	17%			-3.8	59	76	-$5
2nd Half	2	4	0	43	22	5.70	5.16	1.66	817	1089	732	24.6	4.2	4.6	1.1	7%	52	14	33	32%	67%	10%	8	88	25%	50%			-9.6	0	0	-$11
14 Proj	**3**	**4**	**0**	**58**	**29**	**5.01**	**4.41**	**1.55**	**829**	**824**	**830**	**24.4**	**3.3**	**4.5**	**1.3**	**7%**	**54**	**19**	**27**	**32%**	**68%**	**9%**	**10**						**-8.2**	**23**	**29**	**-$6**

Latos,Mat

Age: 26	Th: R	Role SP	Health A	LIMA Plan C+	
Ht: 6' 6"	Wt: 245	Type Pwr	PT/Exp A	Rand Var -1	
			Consist A	MM 4305	

A repeat of 2012 with some Ctl and Cmd gains solidify his stature as a near-elite fantasy SP. Consistently outpitches xERA, equally adept vL/vR. Even during 2H struggles past two years, no glaring weaknesses exposed. If he recaptures a bit of lost Dom and strings two good halves together...UP: 18 wins, 3.00 ERA.

Yr Tm	W	L	Sv	IP	K	ERA	xERA	WHIP	oOPS	vL	vR	BF/G	Ctl	Dom	Cmd	SwK	G	L	F	H%	S%	hr/f	GS	APC	DOM%	DIS%	Sv%	LI	RAR	BPV	BPX	R$
09 SD *	9	6	0	98	81	3.32	2.61	1.10	689	800	589	20.2	2.9	7.5	2.6	10%	36	19	45	26%	71%	11%	10	87	30%	50%			12.1	91	171	$11
10 SD	14	10	0	185	189	2.92	3.29	1.08	601	580	623	24.1	2.4	9.2	3.8	12%	45	15	40	29%	76%	8%	31	96	65%	13%			26.3	123	199	$23
11 SD	9	14	0	194	185	3.47	3.57	1.18	655	697	607	25.8	2.9	8.6	3.0	11%	43	16	41	30%	72%	7%	31	102	71%	3%			11.2	98	147	$14
12 CIN	14	4	0	209	185	3.48	3.75	1.16	681	753	608	26.0	2.8	8.0	2.9	11%	46	18	36	28%	74%	12%	33	99	52%	12%			13.7	93	121	$19
13 CIN	14	7	0	211	187	3.16	3.56	1.21	668	699	642	27.5	2.5	8.0	3.2	11%	45	21	34	31%	75%	7%	32	101	66%	6%			18.3	100	130	$17
1st Half	7	2	0	110	109	3.03	3.37	1.20	673	730	626	26.9	2.5	8.9	3.6	12%	44	22	34	32%	77%	8%	17	100	76%	0%			11.4	117	151	$19
2nd Half	7	5	0	101	78	3.31	3.78	1.22	663	667	660	28.2	2.5	7.0	2.8	9%	46	21	33	30%	74%	6%	15	103	53%	13%			6.9	82	106	$14
14 Proj	**15**	**8**	**0**	**203**	**180**	**3.30**	**3.38**	**1.18**	**661**	**702**	**622**	**25.5**	**2.6**	**8.0**	**3.0**	**11%**	**45**	**19**	**36**	**30%**	**74%**	**8%**	**32**						**14.1**	**95**	**124**	**$19**

League,Brandon

Age: 31	Th: R	Role RP	Health A	LIMA Plan C	
Ht: 6' 2"	Wt: 215	Type xGB	PT/Exp B	Rand Var +4	
			Consist B	MM 4100	

Not sure where that 2009 Dom came from, but it got a lot of hopes up for 9th inning work. Then came the glorious 2011 with its harmonic convergence of Ctl, Cmd and saves. In 2013, he contracted gopheritis and went Dom-less though he still threw a lot of GBs. One thing's obvious amid the noise: Saves ain't coming back.

Yr Tm	W	L	Sv	IP	K	ERA	xERA	WHIP	oOPS	vL	vR	BF/G	Ctl	Dom	Cmd	SwK	G	L	F	H%	S%	hr/f	GS	APC	DOM%	DIS%	Sv%	LI	RAR	BPV	BPX	R$
09 TOR	3	6	0	75	76	4.58	2.99	1.25	735	788	682	4.7	2.5	9.2	3.6	14%	56	18	26	32%	65%	15%	0	17			0	0.79	-2.4	131	244	$1
10 SEA	9	7	6	79	56	3.42	3.40	1.19	630	714	556	4.7	3.1	6.4	2.1	11%	63	16	21	26%	74%	14%	0	16			50	1.37	6.4	73	118	$8
11 SEA	1	5	37	61	45	2.79	3.14	1.08	601	658	543	3.8	1.5	6.6	4.5	11%	57	19	24	29%	75%	7%	0	14			88	1.20	8.7	114	172	$18
12 2 TM	2	6	15	72	54	3.13	4.08	1.36	628	755	519	4.1	4.1	6.8	1.6	11%	50	27	23	30%	75%	2%	0	15			71	1.09	7.9	38	50	$6
13 LA	6	4	14	54	28	5.30	4.21	1.55	818	905	758	4.3	2.5	4.6	1.9	10%	60	19	21	33%	68%	19%	0	16			74	0.88	-9.6	54	71	$0
1st Half	3	3	14	29	13	5.83	4.39	1.53	833	823	841	4.3	2.5	4.0	1.6	9%	59	18	23	32%	63%	16%	0	16			78	1.22	-7.1	42	55	$4
2nd Half	3	1	0	25	15	4.68	4.00	1.56	802	1035	686	4.3	2.5	5.4	2.1	10%	61	21	18	34%	74%	24%	0	15			0	0.49	-2.5	68	88	-$5
14 Proj	**4**	**4**	**0**	**51**	**33**	**3.99**	**3.59**	**1.34**	**685**	**771**	**619**	**4.0**	**2.8**	**5.9**	**2.1**	**11%**	**57**	**21**	**22**	**31%**	**71%**	**11%**	**0**						**-0.8**	**66**	**85**	**-$1**

Leake,Mike

Age: 26	Th: R	Role SP	Health A	LIMA Plan C+	
Ht: 5' 10"	Wt: 185	Type Con	PT/Exp A	Rand Var 0	
			Consist A	MM 3105	

It's been deviations in search of a mean for this control specialist. Base proficiencies—Ctl, Dom, Cmd, GB%—have taken root, but low Dom means more situation dependence (and luck), leading to W-L and ERA swings. Be mindful of uneven results, but 2012-13 xERA consistency sets a clear mid-line expectation.

Yr Tm	W	L	Sv	IP	K	ERA	xERA	WHIP	oOPS	vL	vR	BF/G	Ctl	Dom	Cmd	SwK	G	L	F	H%	S%	hr/f	GS	APC	DOM%	DIS%	Sv%	LI	RAR	BPV	BPX	R$
09																																
10 CIN	8	4	0	138	91	4.23	4.24	1.50	804	832	779	25.2	3.2	5.9	1.9	8%	50	18	32	32%	76%	13%	22	89	41%	14%	0	0.75	-2.6	48	78	-$1
11 CIN	12	9	0	168	118	3.86	3.64	1.17	714	743	688	23.9	2.0	6.3	3.1	8%	48	21	32	28%	72%	14%	26	88	50%	12%	0	0.81	1.6	85	128	$10
12 CIN	8	9	0	179	116	4.58	4.00	1.35	805	806	803	25.2	2.1	5.8	2.8	7%	49	25	27	31%	70%	17%	30	90	40%	27%			-12.4	76	100	-$3
13 CIN	14	7	0	192	122	3.37	3.93	1.25	719	717	721	25.8	2.2	5.7	2.5	7%	49	21	30	29%	77%	12%	31	94	42%	10%			11.8	69	90	$11
1st Half	7	3	0	104	67	2.52	3.67	1.13	649	683	610	26.4	1.8	5.8	3.2	8%	52	18	30	28%	81%	8%	16	95	56%	6%			17.2	85	110	$20
2nd Half	7	4	0	89	55	4.36	4.23	1.40	797	758	833	25.3	2.7	5.6	2.0	6%	45	25	29	30%	73%	15%	15	93	27%	13%			-5.5	50	65	$1
14 Proj	**13**	**9**	**0**	**203**	**132**	**3.96**	**3.75**	**1.31**	**759**	**761**	**757**	**24.8**	**2.3**	**5.8**	**2.5**	**7%**	**48**	**22**	**29**	**30%**	**74%**	**14%**	**34**						**-2.3**	**69**	**89**	**$7**

Lecure,Sam

Age: 30	Th: R	Role RP	Health B	LIMA Plan A	
Ht: 6' 0"	Wt: 205	Type Pwr	PT/Exp C	Rand Var -3	
			Consist A	MM 5400	

Can you find a more anonymous RP with a better three-year run? Sure, he has one career save and his Ctl can be iffy, but his Dom is just short of double digits and he's becoming nails against LHB. More valuable in real baseball, those skills are still worth a buck as your draft winds down. If you can flash on his name.

Yr Tm	W	L	Sv	IP	K	ERA	xERA	WHIP	oOPS	vL	vR	BF/G	Ctl	Dom	Cmd	SwK	G	L	F	H%	S%	hr/f	GS	APC	DOM%	DIS%	Sv%	LI	RAR	BPV	BPX	R$
09 aaa	10	8	0	143	104	6.07	5.88	1.59				25.3	3.1	6.5	2.1					34%	64%								-30.8	32	60	-$8
10 CIN *	10	8	0	146	108	4.55	4.93	1.49	800	928	720	21.0	3.1	6.6	2.2	7%	46	20	34	33%	71%	12%	6	57	17%	17%	0	0.68	-8.5	53	85	-$1
11 CIN	2	1	0	78	73	3.71	3.25	1.00	645	661	635	7.1	2.4	8.5	3.5	9%	46	14	40	24%	68%	13%	4	28	50%	50%	0	0.83	2.2	111	166	$4
12 CIN	3	3	0	57	61	3.14	3.44	1.20	627	613	640	4.9	3.6	9.6	2.7	9%	48	21	31	30%	74%	7%	0	20			0	1.09	6.2	101	132	$2
13 CIN	2	1	1	61	66	2.66	3.37	1.21	624	446	756	4.0	3.5	9.7	2.8	11%	43	23	34	30%	80%	7%	0	16			33	1.32	9.1	101	131	$3
1st Half	1	1	0	31	30	2.32	3.84	1.16	579	462	685	4.2	3.8	8.7	2.3	10%	38	19	43	27%	82%	6%	0	17			0	1.30	5.9	71	92	$3
2nd Half	1	0	1	30	36	3.00	2.89	1.27	669	427	813	3.8	3.3	10.8	3.3	11%	48	27	25	34%	78%	11%	0	15			100	1.34	3.2	131	170	$2
14 Proj	**2**	**2**	**0**	**58**	**60**	**3.24**	**3.20**	**1.22**	**658**	**569**	**721**	**4.8**	**3.3**	**9.3**	**2.8**	**9%**	**45**	**21**	**33**	**30%**	**75%**	**9%**	**0**						**4.5**	**101**	**131**	**$2**

ROB CARROLL

Lee,Cliff

Age: 35 Th: L Role SP	Health A	LIMA Plan C+
Ht: 6' 3" Wt: 205 Type Pwr	PT/Exp A	Rand Var 0
	Consist A	MM 5405

Vintage again and showing little decline. Missed some 2H starts with minor issues, like neck stiffness, the All-Star break, trade talk caution and a team going nowhere. But his only blemish was that 2H win total, the result of hr/f luck and poor run support. Velocity downtick and age will eventually factor in. But we'll take him.

Yr	Tm	W	L	Sv	IP	K	ERA	xERA	WHIP	oOPS	vL	vR	BF/G	Ctl	Dom	Cmd	SwK	G	L	F	H%	S%	hr/f	GS	APC	DOM%	DIS%	Sv%	LI	RAR	BPV	BPX	R$
09	2 TM	14	13	0	232	181	3.22	3.80	1.24	696	583	734	28.5	1.7	7.0	4.2	8%	41	22	36	33%	76%	7%	34	104	59%	9%			31.4	100	188	$22
10	2 AL	12	9	0	212	185	3.18	3.26	1.00	618	706	591	30.1	0.8	7.8	10.3	9%	42	18	40	30%	70%	6%	28	106	64%	4%			23.6	141	227	$25
11	PHI	17	8	0	233	238	2.40	2.83	1.03	607	518	634	28.8	1.6	9.2	5.7	10%	46	21	32	30%	80%	9%	32	106	81%	9%			44.3	146	219	$35
12	PHI	6	9	0	211	207	3.16	3.23	1.11	690	626	707	28.2	1.2	8.8	7.4	9%	45	18	37	32%	77%	12%	30	103	80%	3%			22.3	150	195	$20
13	PHI	14	8	0	223	222	2.87	2.94	1.01	631	537	659	28.3	1.3	9.0	6.9	10%	44	22	33	30%	76%	11%	31	105	77%	0%			27.4	149	194	$29
1st Half		9	2	0	125	115	2.59	3.12	0.97	570	662	539	28.6	1.5	8.3	5.5	9%	44	22	34	28%	75%	7%	17	108	88%	0%			19.8	130	168	$35
2nd Half		5	6	0	97	107	3.24	2.71	1.07	707	363	804	27.9	1.0	9.9	9.7	10%	45	23	32	32%	77%	17%	14	101	64%	0%			7.6	174	225	$20
14	**Proj**	**13**	**9**	**0**	**203**	**202**	**3.09**	**2.78**	**1.06**	**656**	**542**	**690**	**27.6**	**1.3**	**9.0**	**7.0**	**10%**	**45**	**21**	**34**	**31%**	**75%**	**11%**	**28**						**19.4**	**149**	**194**	**$25**

Lee,Zach

Age: 22 Th: R Role SP	Health A	LIMA Plan B+
Ht: 6' 4" Wt: 190 Type	PT/Exp F	Rand Var 0
	Consist B	MM 3200

LA's 1st-rd pick from 2010 draft, struggled with 2H GB consistency, still finished with career-best numbers (3.22 ERA, 131/35 K/BB in 143 IP) at Double-A. Doesn't possess a single knockout pitch, but broad repertoire gives him mid-rotation upside. Growing pains are likely, but solid Ctl has him knocking at the door in 2014.

Yr	Tm	W	L	Sv	IP	K	ERA	xERA	WHIP	oOPS	vL	vR	BF/G	Ctl	Dom	Cmd	SwK	G	L	F	H%	S%	hr/f	GS	APC	DOM%	DIS%	Sv%	LI	RAR	BPV	BPX	R$
09																																	
10																																	
11																																	
12	aa	4	3	0	66	45	4.74	4.75	1.47				21.7	2.9	6.2	2.1					33%	69%								-5.9	53	69	-$5
13	aa	10	10	0	143	114	3.94	4.14	1.31				21.1	2.2	7.2	3.2					32%	72%								-1.3	83	108	$3
1st Half		6	5	0	88	70	3.62	3.63	1.29				21.4	2.5	7.1	2.9					32%	72%								2.7	87	113	$6
2nd Half		4	5	0	54	44	4.46	4.97	1.35				20.6	1.9	7.4	4.0					33%	72%								-4.0	80	104	-$2
14	**Proj**	**3**	**3**	**0**	**44**	**33**	**4.19**	**3.81**	**1.35**				**21.1**	**2.8**	**6.8**	**2.4**	**0%**	**44**	**22**	**34**	**31%**	**71%**	**11%**	**9**						**-1.8**	**68**	**89**	**-$2**

Lester,Jon

Age: 30 Th: L Role SP	Health A	LIMA Plan B
Ht: 6' 4" Wt: 240 Type Pwr	PT/Exp A	Rand Var 0
	Consist A	MM 4305

Turned year around with S% regression, improved 2H Ctl and hr/f luck. 1H/2H xERA didn't budge. In fact, most of his other skills were near-identical to 2012 "disaster." Dom slide says his previous upside is gone, and GB deterioration is a concern. He's above-average and highly reliable, just not an ace.

Yr	Tm	W	L	Sv	IP	K	ERA	xERA	WHIP	oOPS	vL	vR	BF/G	Ctl	Dom	Cmd	SwK	G	L	F	H%	S%	hr/f	GS	APC	DOM%	DIS%	Sv%	LI	RAR	BPV	BPX	R$
09	BOS	15	8	0	203	225	3.41	3.20	1.23	667	717	649	26.3	2.8	10.0	3.5	11%	48	18	35	32%	75%	11%	32	106	69%	13%			22.9	129	241	$22
10	BOS	19	9	0	208	225	3.25	3.08	1.20	628	651	620	26.9	3.6	9.7	2.7	11%	54	17	30	30%	74%	9%	32	105	69%	6%			21.4	110	178	$22
11	BOS	15	9	0	192	182	3.47	3.46	1.26	690	580	728	25.8	3.5	8.5	2.4	9%	50	16	34	29%	76%	11%	31	103	61%	16%			11.1	87	130	$14
12	BOS	9	14	0	205	166	4.82	3.92	1.38	773	738	785	26.5	3.0	7.3	2.4	9%	49	22	29	32%	67%	14%	33	104	52%	18%			-20.4	77	101	-$4
13	BOS	15	8	0	213	177	3.75	3.88	1.29	702	670	711	27.4	2.8	7.5	2.6	9%	45	20	35	31%	73%	8%	33	108	61%	9%			2.9	81	106	$9
1st Half		8	4	0	107	88	4.61	3.86	1.35	742	896	706	26.9	3.3	7.4	2.3	8%	50	18	32	30%	68%	13%	17	107	65%	12%			-9.9	73	94	$3
2nd Half		7	4	0	106	89	2.89	3.90	1.24	663	510	717	27.8	2.4	7.6	3.2	9%	40	21	39	32%	78%	5%	16	109	56%	6%			12.8	90	116	$15
14	**Proj**	**13**	**10**	**0**	**203**	**177**	**3.85**	**3.51**	**1.30**	**709**	**659**	**725**	**26.2**	**3.0**	**7.8**	**2.6**	**9%**	**47**	**20**	**34**	**31%**	**72%**	**10%**	**32**						**0.5**	**86**	**112**	**$10**

Lincecum,Tim

Age: 30 Th: R Role SP	Health A	LIMA Plan B+
Ht: 5' 11" Wt: 170 Type Pwr	PT/Exp A	Rand Var +1
	Consist A	MM 4405

Stabilized velocity looks fine, as does SwK. Improved Ctl drove 2H, pointing the way to rebound hopes. Walks and elevated hr/f are the difference between now and the glory days. Slow GB% decay accompanied by first ever sub-9.0 Dom, but those are still good enough. With some hr/f and S% normalization...UP: 3.50 ERA.

Yr	Tm	W	L	Sv	IP	K	ERA	xERA	WHIP	oOPS	vL	vR	BF/G	Ctl	Dom	Cmd	SwK	G	L	F	H%	S%	hr/f	GS	APC	DOM%	DIS%	Sv%	LI	RAR	BPV	BPX	R$
09	SF	15	7	0	225	261	2.48	2.91	1.05	561	583	532	28.3	2.7	10.4	3.8	11%	48	19	33	30%	77%	5%	32	107	81%	6%			51.3	140	263	$38
10	SF	15	10	0	206	224	3.53	3.22	1.28	681	736	616	27.3	3.2	9.8	3.0	12%	49	19	32	32%	74%	10%	32	104	63%	19%			13.9	116	187	$16
11	SF	13	14	0	217	220	2.74	3.35	1.21	646	628	663	27.3	3.6	9.1	2.6	12%	48	19	33	29%	79%	8%	33	109	73%	6%			32.3	94	141	$22
12	SF	10	15	0	186	190	5.18	3.97	1.47	767	722	813	25.0	4.4	9.2	2.1	12%	46	24	30	32%	66%	15%	33	100	48%	24%			-26.7	72	94	-$8
13	SF	10	14	0	198	193	4.37	3.60	1.32	711	664	755	26.3	3.5	8.8	2.5	12%	45	23	32	31%	69%	12%	32	103	56%	13%			-12.3	88	114	$2
1st Half		4	8	0	95	93	4.64	3.69	1.43	721	695	749	25.9	3.9	8.8	2.3	11%	46	27	27	33%	69%	12%	16	99	50%	13%			-9.1	78	101	-$3
2nd Half		6	6	0	103	100	4.12	3.52	1.21	701	629	760	26.7	3.1	8.8	2.9	12%	44	20	36	29%	69%	12%	16	106	63%	13%			-3.2	97	126	$7
14	**Proj**	**13**	**13**	**0**	**203**	**203**	**4.04**	**3.46**	**1.32**	**708**	**673**	**743**	**25.5**	**3.7**	**9.0**	**2.4**	**12%**	**45**	**21**	**34**	**31%**	**72%**	**11%**	**33**						**-4.3**	**85**	**110**	**$9**

Lincoln,Brad

Age: 29 Th: R Role RP	Health A	LIMA Plan C
Ht: 6' 0" Wt: 225 Type Pwr	PT/Exp D	Rand Var -3
	Consist B	MM 2200

1-2, 3.98 ERA in 32 IP with TOR. What happened to "closer-in-waiting" from 2012? Dom fell back to earth, while Ctl soared. Unstable GB% is now trending in the wrong direction. Only 2H H%/S% luck along with a career-low hr/f saved his ERA. Still has time for a career, but inconsistency says to avoid until further notice.

Yr	Tm	W	L	Sv	IP	K	ERA	xERA	WHIP	oOPS	vL	vR	BF/G	Ctl	Dom	Cmd	SwK	G	L	F	H%	S%	hr/f	GS	APC	DOM%	DIS%	Sv%	LI	RAR	BPV	BPX	R$
09	a/a	7	7	0	136	85	4.15	4.46	1.37				22.9	1.8	5.6	3.0					33%	71%								2.9	71	132	$3
10	PIT *	8	9	0	147	90	5.43	4.59	1.36	893	922	870	21.9	2.4	5.5	2.3	6%	37	19	44	31%	61%	11%	9	78	11%	44%	0	0.64	-24.5	48	77	-$4
11	PIT *	9	11	0	159	99	5.01	4.54	1.44	773	878	689	21.9	2.1	5.6	2.7	8%	52	23	26	34%	64%	10%	8	63	38%	25%	0	0.64	-20.9	67	101	-$6
12	2 TM	5	2	1	88	88	3.68	3.60	1.18	727	621	816	7.0	2.5	9.0	3.7	9%	40	22	38	29%	76%	15%	5	25	40%	60%	50	0.84	3.6	114	148	$5
13	TOR *	4	4	5	58	47	3.44	4.47	1.50	757	806	711	5.6	4.8	7.3	1.5	8%	37	12	51	30%	81%	8%	0	26			63	1.45	3.0	49	63	$0
1st Half		1	3	3	38	32	4.35	5.33	1.61	760	722	796	6.4	4.7	7.6	1.6	9%	39	11	50	32%	77%	10%	0	29			50	1.52	-2.2	39	50	-$2
2nd Half		3	1	2	20	15	1.77	2.88	1.31	751	990	533	4.4	5.0	6.7	1.4	7%	34	13	53	26%	88%	6%	0	22			100	1.34	5.3	68	88	$4
14	**Proj**	**3**	**2**	**0**	**42**	**33**	**3.97**	**4.02**	**1.40**	**771**	**778**	**764**	**6.9**	**3.6**	**7.2**	**2.0**	**8%**	**43**	**19**	**38**	**30%**	**76%**	**11%**	**0**						**-0.6**	**54**	**70**	**-$2**

Lindstrom,Matt

Age: 34 Th: R Role RP	Health D	LIMA Plan C
Ht: 6' 3" Wt: 220 Type GB	PT/Exp D	Rand Var -2
	Consist A	MM 4210

Serviceable RP, successfully battled through 1H Ctl and vL issues, delivered nice year-long GB spike in HR venue. Cmd improvement drove broad 2H skills surge that was marred only by inflated h%. Doesn't have enough Dom to close again, other than on an interim basis. But there are worse deep-league RP options.

Yr	Tm	W	L	Sv	IP	K	ERA	xERA	WHIP	oOPS	vL	vR	BF/G	Ctl	Dom	Cmd	SwK	G	L	F	H%	S%	hr/f	GS	APC	DOM%	DIS%	Sv%	LI	RAR	BPV	BPX	R$
09	FLA	2	1	15	47	39	5.89	4.70	1.65	804	850	757	4.1	4.6	7.4	1.6	11%	45	20	35	34%	64%	9%	0	15			88	0.84	-9.2	33	62	$0
10	HOU	2	5	23	53	43	4.39	4.20	1.65	792	769	809	4.2	3.4	7.3	2.2	10%	49	19	32	37%	75%	9%	0	16			79	0.97	-2.0	66	108	$5
11	COL	2	2	2	54	36	3.00	3.82	1.22	661	698	636	3.6	2.3	6.0	2.6	9%	47	21	31	30%	76%	6%	0	13			40	1.23	6.3	70	105	$2
12	2 TM	1	0	0	47	40	2.68	3.61	1.26	642	737	573	4.3	2.7	7.7	2.9	10%	51	22	27	32%	79%	5%	0	17			0	0.77	7.7	94	123	$0
13	CHW	2	4	0	61	46	3.12	3.87	1.43	683	778	629	3.4	3.4	6.8	2.0	10%	56	17	27	33%	78%	4%	0	12			0	1.27	5.6	65	84	-$2
1st Half		2	2	0	32	23	2.78	4.28	1.45	650	894	516	3.5	4.5	6.4	1.4	9%	53	17	31	31%	79%	0%	0	13			0	1.24	4.3	26	33	$0
2nd Half		0	2	0	28	23	3.49	3.45	1.41	716	659	749	3.4	2.2	7.3	3.3	12%	59	17	24	35%	76%	9%	0	12			0	1.31	1.3	108	140	-$3
14	**Proj**	**2**	**3**	**3**	**65**	**51**	**3.38**	**3.59**	**1.38**	**686**	**746**	**647**	**3.6**	**3.0**	**7.0**	**2.4**	**10%**	**53**	**19**	**28**	**33%**	**75%**	**6%**	**0**						**3.9**	**77**	**100**	**$1**

Liriano,Francisco

Age: 30 Th: L Role SP	Health D	LIMA Plan C+
Ht: 6' 2" Wt: 215 Type Pwr	PT/Exp B	Rand Var 0
	Consist B	MM 4405

16-8, 3.02 ERA in 161 IP at PIT. Winter (non-throwing) arm injury delayed his debut until May, but he was worth the wait. Rendered LH batters helpless, conquered gopheritis and notched career-best SwK. History says it all; terrific Dom, but volatile Ctl, GB%, hr/f are key. Can he repeat? Don't bet the house.

Yr	Tm	W	L	Sv	IP	K	ERA	xERA	WHIP	oOPS	vL	vR	BF/G	Ctl	Dom	Cmd	SwK	G	L	F	H%	S%	hr/f	GS	APC	DOM%	DIS%	Sv%	LI	RAR	BPV	BPX	R$
09	MIN	5	13	0	137	122	5.80	4.49	1.55	830	631	899	21.0	4.3	8.0	1.9	12%	40	19	41	32%	65%	13%	24	80	38%	33%	0	0.73	-24.8	47	88	-$7
10	MIN	14	10	0	192	201	3.62	2.99	1.26	670	517	713	26.0	2.7	9.4	3.5	13%	54	19	27	34%	71%	6%	31	97	65%	13%			11.0	128	208	$14
11	MIN	9	10	0	134	112	5.09	4.35	1.49	726	669	744	22.7	5.0	7.5	1.5	12%	49	15	36	29%	67%	10%	24	88	46%	29%	0	0.75	-19.0	26	40	-$5
12	2 AL	6	12	0	157	167	5.34	4.12	1.47	741	603	784	20.4	5.0	9.6	1.9	13%	44	21	35	31%	65%	13%	28	80	50%	32%	0	0.83	-25.7	60	78	-$9
13	PIT *	18	9	0	180	182	3.36	3.15	1.26	611	321	689	24.4	3.4	9.1	2.7	14%	50	24	25	31%	74%	8%	26	96	65%	15%			11.3	102	133	$15
1st Half		9	4	0	79	86	3.18	3.59	1.35	606	325	683	23.6	3.1	9.7	3.1	15%	49	26	25	35%	77%	5%	10	95	60%	0%			6.8	113	146	$13
2nd Half		9	5	0	100	96	3.50	3.32	1.19	614	319	693	25.5	3.6	8.6	2.4	13%	51	23	25	28%	71%	10%	16	97	69%	25%			4.5	88	113	$16
14	**Proj**	**14.**	**12**	**0**	**193**	**190**	**3.70**	**3.38**	**1.30**	**667**	**474**	**723**	**22.3**	**3.8**	**8.8**	**2.3**	**13%**	**48**	**22**	**30**	**30%**	**73%**	**10%**	**36**						**4.1**	**84**	**109**	**$12**

JOCK THOMPSON

Lo,Chia-Jen

Age: 28	Th: R	Role: RP	Health: F	LIMA Plan: D
			PT/Exp: F	Rand Var: -3
Ht: 5' 11"	Wt: 190	Type: Pwr FB	Consist: F	MM: 1310

2011 Tommy John surgery held Taiwanese import to 47 IP over 2010-2012. Made July MLB debut after starting 2013 on DL. Parlayed mid-90s velocity, 9.9 career minor league Dom into brief HOU closer shot, but poor Ctl says he's a work-in-progress. May need a little AAA time, still has a chance for a career if health cooperates.

Yr	Tm	W	L	Sv	IP	K	ERA	xERA	WHIP	oOPS	vL	vR	BF/G	Ctl	Dom	Cmd	SwK	G	L	F	H%	S%	hr/f	GS	APC	DOM%	DIS%	Sv%	LI	RAR	BPV	BPX	R$
09	aa	0	2	2	39	34	2.70	3.18	1.38				5.5	4.5	7.8	1.7					30%	80%								7.8	83	156	$0
10	aa	0	1	0	15	11	2.39	2.74	1.44				9.1	6.3	6.6	1.0					26%	82%								3.1	75	122	-$2
11																																	
12																																	
13	HOU	0	3	2	19	16	4.19	4.95	1.40	615	482	789	4.4	6.1	7.4	1.2	8%	38	23	40	24%	72%	10%	0	18			40	1.13	-0.8	-13	-17	-$3
1st Half																																	
2nd Half		0	3	2	19	16	4.19	4.95	1.40	615	482	789	4.4	6.1	7.4	1.2	8%	38	23	40	24%	72%	10%	0	18			40	1.13	-0.8	-14	-18	-$3
14	**Proj**	**1**	**4**	**4**	**47**	**40**	**4.58**	**4.64**	**1.52**	**651**	**494**	**855**	**4.8**	**5.5**	**7.6**	**1.4**	**8%**	**38**	**23**	**40**	**29%**	**72%**	**9%**	**0**						**-4.1**	**5**	**6**	**-$3**

Locke,Jeff

Age: 26	Th: L	Role: SP	Health: A	LIMA Plan: B
			PT/Exp: B	Rand Var: -1
Ht: 6' 0"	Wt: 185	Type: Pwr GB	Consist: A	MM: 3203

Held solid GB gains and controlled gopheritis all season, while hiking 2H Dom to career best. But 1H H%/S% luck turned bad after June and walks were a problem from the get-go. Horrid stretch run—10%/50% DOM%/DIS%—in final 10 games jeopardizes SP status. Not worth your attention unless Ctl comes around.

Yr	Tm	W	L	Sv	IP	K	ERA	xERA	WHIP	oOPS	vL	vR	BF/G	Ctl	Dom	Cmd	SwK	G	L	F	H%	S%	hr/f	GS	APC	DOM%	DIS%	Sv%	LI	RAR	BPV	BPX	R$
09																																	
10	aa	3	2	0	58	45	4.22	4.26	1.33				23.9	1.8	7.0	3.8					34%	69%								-1.0	97	157	-$1
11	PIT *	8	13	0	170	113	4.62	4.46	1.47	954	917	961	22.8	3.4	6.0	1.8	6%	34	28	38	32%	69%	14%	4	74	0%	75%			-14.2	51	77	-$5
12	PIT *	11	8	0	176	135	3.60	4.22	1.38	749	836	716	23.1	2.8	6.9	2.5	9%	49	15	36	32%	76%	17%	6	70	33%	33%	0	0.64	9.1	70	92	$5
13	PIT	10	7	0	166	125	3.52	4.11	1.38	686	748	667	23.7	4.5	6.8	1.5	9%	53	21	26	28%	75%	9%	30	91	30%	23%			7.2	30	39	$4
1st Half		7	1	0	96	67	2.06	3.84	1.11	598	611	593	24.0	3.8	6.3	1.6	8%	53	20	27	23%	84%	8%	16	93	44%	6%			21.5	40	52	$19
2nd Half		3	6	0	70	58	5.53	4.48	1.76	791	931	751	23.4	5.5	7.5	1.3	10%	53	23	24	35%	68%	10%	14	87	14%	43%			-14.4	16	21	-$16
14	**Proj**	**7**	**7**	**0**	**131**	**99**	**4.28**	**3.93**	**1.45**	**716**	**809**	**685**	**23.2**	**3.8**	**6.8**	**1.8**	**9%**	**52**	**19**	**30**	**32%**	**71%**	**8%**	**24**						**-6.7**	**49**	**64**	**-$1**

Lohse,Kyle

Age: 35	Th: R	Role: SP	Health: D	LIMA Plan: C+
			PT/Exp: A	Rand Var: 0
Ht: 6' 2"	Wt: 210	Type: Con	Consist: A	MM: 3105

Continues to outpitch BPIs. Exquisite Ctl still leads the way, offsetting that mild hr/f spike. Solid Cmd sets a nice floor. Stable H% and vL/vR history says that he's still keeping hitters on both sides off balance, even without a killer Dom or GB%. The profile still points to some risk, but his 3-yr consistency isn't debatable.

Yr	Tm	W	L	Sv	IP	K	ERA	xERA	WHIP	oOPS	vL	vR	BF/G	Ctl	Dom	Cmd	SwK	G	L	F	H%	S%	hr/f	GS	APC	DOM%	DIS%	Sv%	LI	RAR	BPV	BPX	R$
09	STL	6	10	0	118	77	4.74	4.43	1.37	772	739	800	22.3	2.8	5.9	2.1	7%	45	20	36	30%	68%	12%	22	85	45%	41%	0	0.74	-6.1	55	102	$0
10	STL *	5	9	0	111	67	6.40	6.17	1.73	905	985	846	23.0	3.0	5.4	1.8	5%	43	19	38	37%	63%	7%	18	90	22%	39%			-31.7	30	49	-$14
11	STL	14	8	0	188	111	3.39	4.09	1.17	680	696	667	25.8	2.0	5.3	2.6	6%	41	22	37	28%	73%	7%	30	93	47%	10%			12.8	60	91	$14
12	STL	16	3	0	211	143	2.86	4.02	1.09	642	664	623	26.2	1.6	6.1	3.8	7%	41	24	36	28%	77%	8%	33	95	67%	0%			30.1	85	111	$26
13	MIL	11	10	0	199	125	3.35	4.03	1.17	700	727	676	25.2	1.6	5.7	3.5	8%	40	21	38	28%	77%	11%	32	94	53%	6%			12.6	76	99	$13
1st Half		3	6	0	94	59	3.63	4.06	1.21	739	661	814	24.1	1.5	5.6	3.7	8%	38	24	38	29%	76%	12%	16	89	50%	13%			2.8	77	99	$8
2nd Half		8	4	0	104	66	3.11	4.01	1.13	664	791	557	26.3	1.7	5.7	3.3	7%	42	19	39	27%	77%	9%	16	99	56%	0%			9.8	76	98	$18
14	**Proj**	**13**	**8**	**0**	**196**	**123**	**3.53**	**3.85**	**1.20**	**706**	**737**	**679**	**24.7**	**1.9**	**5.7**	**3.0**	**7%**	**41**	**21**	**38**	**29%**	**75%**	**10%**	**32**						**8.1**	**70**	**90**	**$13**

Lopez,Javier

Age: 36	Th: L	Role: RP	Health: A	LIMA Plan: B+
			PT/Exp: D	Rand Var: -5
Ht: 6' 5"	Wt: 220	Type: Pwr xGB	Consist: A	MM: 4210

Lefty specialist rode lucky H%/S% combo to career-best ERA and WHIP. But even with reversal of small-sample abysmal 2012 vR luck, his opportunities aren't expanding. Solid GB profile and nice Dom-and-Ctl trends, but age warns against expecting a repeat. Limited IP say he's relevant only in the deepest of leagues.

Yr	Tm	W	L	Sv	IP	K	ERA	xERA	WHIP	oOPS	vL	vR	BF/G	Ctl	Dom	Cmd	SwK	G	L	F	H%	S%	hr/f	GS	APC	DOM%	DIS%	Sv%	LI	RAR	BPV	BPX	R$
09	BOS *	1	3	0	51	21	6.61	6.58	1.94	1080	1110	1059	4.7	4.6	3.7	0.8	7%	49	26	26	36%	65%	8%	0	18			0	0.53	-14.5	5	10	-$11
10	2 NL	4	2	0	58	38	2.34	3.53	1.21	636	492	766	3.1	3.1	5.9	1.9	9%	62	16	23	28%	81%	5%	0	11			0	0.94	12.4	62	101	$4
11	SF	5	2	1	53	40	2.72	3.63	1.28	603	430	761	3.2	4.4	6.8	1.5	11%	63	15	22	28%	76%	0%	0	12			33	1.52	8.0	44	66	$3
12	SF	3	0	7	36	28	2.50	3.74	1.42	700	543	979	2.2	3.5	7.0	2.0	11%	60	19	21	33%	82%	4%	0	8			78	1.85	6.7	70	91	$2
13	SF	4	2	1	39	37	1.83	2.99	1.07	573	431	805	2.3	2.7	8.5	3.1	12%	61	16	23	28%	83%	4%	0	9			100	1.71	9.9	117	153	$4
1st Half		1	0	0	18	22	1.47	2.39	1.15	597	501	804	2.3	2.9	10.8	3.7	15%	65	20	15	34%	86%	0%	0	10			0	1.18	5.4	158	205	$3
2nd Half		3	2	1	21	15	2.14	3.51	1.00	552	356	806	2.3	2.6	6.4	2.5	10%	58	14	29	24%	80%	6%	0	9			100	1.61	4.5	82	106	$5
14	**Proj**	**3**	**3**	**3**	**40**	**33**	**2.87**	**3.23**	**1.23**	**653**	**490**	**884**	**2.4**	**3.3**	**7.3**	**2.2**	**11%**	**61**	**17**	**23**	**29%**	**77%**	**8%**	**0**						**4.9**	**82**	**107**	**$2**

Lopez,Wilton

Age: 30	Th: R	Role: RP	Health: C	LIMA Plan: C
			PT/Exp: C	Rand Var: +1
Ht: 6' 0"	Wt: 205	Type: GB	Consist: B	MM: 4101

Not surprisingly, his numbers took a big across-the-board hit with the move to Coors Field, apart from the GB%. But his splits weren't far apart, and his road ERA (4.31) was actually worse than at home. With Ctl intact, he should rebound a tad. Still wracking up the IP, but the shine of future-closer label looks tarnished.

Yr	Tm	W	L	Sv	IP	K	ERA	xERA	WHIP	oOPS	vL	vR	BF/G	Ctl	Dom	Cmd	SwK	G	L	F	H%	S%	hr/f	GS	APC	DOM%	DIS%	Sv%	LI	RAR	BPV	BPX	R$
09	HOU *	4	7	0	130	65	6.27	6.18	1.65	1039	1028	1057	15.7	1.5	4.5	3.0	6%	58	17	25	37%	62%	21%	2	42	0%	100%	0	0.51	-31.1	49	92	-$14
10	HOU	5	2	1	67	50	2.96	2.99	1.06	653	694	624	3.9	0.7	6.7	10.0	11%	56	16	28	31%	73%	7%	0	14			33	0.87	9.3	137	221	$6
11	HOU	2	6	0	71	56	2.79	3.36	1.27	686	804	619	4.1	2.3	7.1	3.1	10%	56	17	27	31%	81%	10%	0	15			0	1.06	10.1	100	151	$3
12	HOU	6	3	10	66	54	2.17	2.92	1.04	626	540	677	4.1	1.1	7.3	6.8	10%	55	24	21	30%	82%	10%	0	15			77	1.23	15.1	136	177	$12
13	COL	3	4	0	75	48	4.06	3.90	1.41	754	693	803	4.3	2.2	5.7	2.7	10%	50	25	26	33%	72%	9%	0	15			0	0.88	-1.8	73	95	-$3
1st Half		1	3	0	41	24	3.95	4.11	1.44	758	690	814	4.3	2.2	5.3	2.4	9%	48	26	26	33%	73%	8%	0	15			0	0.81	-0.4	61	80	-$4
2nd Half		2	1	0	34	24	4.19	3.64	1.37	750	696	791	4.3	2.1	6.3	3.0	12%	52	24	25	33%	70%	11%	0	16			0	0.95	-1.4	86	112	-$3
14	**Proj**	**4**	**4**	**0**	**73**	**52**	**3.72**	**3.41**	**1.31**	**723**	**695**	**743**	**4.3**	**2.0**	**6.4**	**3.1**	**11%**	**53**	**22**	**25**	**32%**	**73%**	**10%**	**0**						**1.3**	**91**	**118**	**$1**

Loup,Aaron

Age: 26	Th: L	Role: RP	Health: A	LIMA Plan: B+
			PT/Exp: D	Rand Var: -2
Ht: 6' 0"	Wt: 210	Type: xGB	Consist: B	MM: 5211

Nice followup to 2012 debut for xGB lefty, as Dom and GB% climbed all season. RHBs touched him up as Ctl wavered in smaller sample 2H. Low-90s velocity and heavy reliance on moving fastball point to a continuing bullpen roll, and suggest more confirmation may be necessary. But he could be moderately helpful again.

Yr	Tm	W	L	Sv	IP	K	ERA	xERA	WHIP	oOPS	vL	vR	BF/G	Ctl	Dom	Cmd	SwK	G	L	F	H%	S%	hr/f	GS	APC	DOM%	DIS%	Sv%	LI	RAR	BPV	BPX	R$
09																																	
10																																	
11																																	
12	TOR *	0	5	3	76	56	3.26	3.94	1.31	547	462	638	4.5	2.0	6.6	3.4	6%	55	17	27	33%	76%	0%	0	13			60	1.16	7.1	91	119	$1
13	TOR	4	6	2	69	53	2.47	3.06	1.14	670	506	777	4.4	1.7	6.9	4.1	9%	60	17	23	30%	81%	11%	0	16			67	0.96	12.0	116	152	$6
1st Half		3	3	2	40	29	1.79	3.02	0.99	630	574	659	4.8	1.1	6.5	5.8	8%	56	19	24	27%	86%	10%	0	18			67	0.84	10.4	121	156	$10
2nd Half		1	3	0	29	24	3.41	3.11	1.34	724	420	934	3.9	2.5	7.4	3.0	11%	65	15	20	33%	76%	11%	0	14			0	1.10	1.6	110	142	-$1
14	**Proj**	**2**	**6**	**3**	**73**	**55**	**2.92**	**3.16**	**1.20**	**705**	**507**	**864**	**4.2**	**2.0**	**6.9**	**3.5**	**8%**	**56**	**19**	**25**	**31%**	**78%**	**11%**	**0**						**8.5**	**105**	**136**	**$4**

Luebke,Cory

Age: 29	Th: L	Role: RP	Health: F	LIMA Plan: B+
			PT/Exp: D	Rand Var: 0
Ht: 6' 4"	Wt: 200	Type:	Consist: B	MM: 3201

One of several 2013 reminders that a 12-mo TJS recovery isn't a sure thing. Following May '12 surgery, he was shut down three times during rehab and never made it out of the gate. 2011 breakout remains impressive, but that and the 9.9 Dom outlier are now two years in the rear view mirror. Has to prove he's healthy.

Yr	Tm	W	L	Sv	IP	K	ERA	xERA	WHIP	oOPS	vL	vR	BF/G	Ctl	Dom	Cmd	SwK	G	L	F	H%	S%	hr/f	GS	APC	DOM%	DIS%	Sv%	LI	RAR	BPV	BPX	R$
09	aa	3	2	0	41	28	3.85	3.71	1.35				19.1	3.2	6.1	1.9					30%	71%								2.4	64	120	-$1
10	SD *	11	2	0	132	93	3.08	2.83	1.11	751	867	719	22.5	2.5	6.4	2.6	11%	50	14	36	26%	74%	17%	3	76	33%	33%	0	0.61	16.2	81	131	$13
11	SD	6	10	0	140	154	3.29	3.12	1.07	608	422	680	12.1	2.8	9.9	3.5	11%	39	22	39	28%	72%	9%	17	51	71%	12%	0	0.91	11.3	119	179	$13
12	SD	3	1	0	31	23	2.61	4.01	1.16	615	681	595	26.0	2.3	6.7	2.9	7%	48	19	33	30%	77%	3%	5	102	40%	20%			5.4	83	109	$0
13																																	
1st Half																																	
2nd Half																																	
14	**Proj**	**7**	**3**	**0**	**87**	**69**	**3.42**	**3.65**	**1.23**	**681**	**612**	**704**	**19.5**	**2.8**	**7.1**	**2.5**	**9%**	**44**	**20**	**36**	**29%**	**74%**	**8%**	**17**						**4.8**	**74**	**97**	**$5**

JOCK THOMPSON

Lyles,Jordan

Age: 23 Th: R Role SP	Health A	LIMA Plan D+
Ht: 6' 4" Wt: 215 Type	PT/Exp C	Rand Var +4
	Consist A	MM 2103

7-9, 5.59 ERA in 142 IP at HOU. Horrid March led to AAA demotion; May return brought little improvement. Only June (3.53/3.63 ERA/xERA) hinted at upside. 2H disaster fueled by Ctl and hr/f spikes, vanishing Dom and S%. Lacks plus offerings, he must be fine to succeed. Age helps, but he has work to do before he's rosterable.

Yr Tm	W	L	Sv	IP	K	ERA	xERA	WHIP	oOPS	vL	vR	BF/G	Ctl	Dom	Cmd	SwK	G	L	F	H%	S%	hr/f	GS	APC	DOM%	DIS%	Sv%	LI	RAR	BPV	BPX	R$
09																																
10 a/a	7	12	0	159	124	4.03	4.97	1.51				25.5	2.5	7.1	2.9					36%	74%								0.9	75	121	$0
11 HOU *	5	11	0	156	104	4.79	4.66	1.39	817	795	834	20.6	2.4	6.0	2.5	9%	41	21	38	32%	67%	12%	15	79	40%	13%	0	0.80	-16.4	55	82	-$5
12 HOU *	10	12	0	182	128	4.72	4.60	1.37	772	886	683	23.9	2.4	6.3	2.6	7%	54	17	29	32%	68%	15%	25	95	36%	32%			-15.8	59	77	-$3
13 HOU *	9	11	1	165	103	5.63	5.10	1.53	801	751	859	21.8	3.0	5.6	1.9	7%	48	21	30	33%	64%	12%	25	91	36%	28%	50	1.01	-36.1	39	50	-$14
1st Half	6	5	0	91	60	4.48	4.46	1.45	749	710	781	21.6	2.5	5.9	2.4	7%	52	20	28	34%	69%	8%	12	95	50%	17%			-7.0	64	83	-$7
2nd Half	3	6	1	74	43	7.05	4.95	1.64	848	778	953	22.9	3.6	5.2	1.4	7%	45	23	32	32%	58%	14%	13	87	23%	38%	100	1.19	-29.1	19	24	-$24
14 Proj	**7**	**10**	**0**	**140**	**92**	**4.67**	**4.07**	**1.43**	**758**	**763**	**752**	**22.1**	**3.0**	**5.9**	**2.0**	**8%**	**47**	**20**	**33**	**31%**	**69%**	**11%**	**27**						**-13.9**	**51**	**66**	**-$3**

Lynn,Lance

Age: 27 Th: R Role SP	Health C	LIMA Plan B
Ht: 6' 5" Wt: 240 Type Pwr	PT/Exp A	Rand Var 0
	Consist A	MM 4405

Another solid 1H, more late-season volatility. 2H SwK and GB% actually improved, but he was victimized by H% luck, hr/f regression. Uninspiring Ctl is neutralized by terrific Dom and his ability to control the HR ball, at least most of the time. The upside of this mid-rotation workhorse depends on more consistency, fewer walks.

Yr Tm	W	L	Sv	IP	K	ERA	xERA	WHIP	oOPS	vL	vR	BF/G	Ctl	Dom	Cmd	SwK	G	L	F	H%	S%	hr/f	GS	APC	DOM%	DIS%	Sv%	LI	RAR	BPV	BPX	R$
09 a/a	11	4	0	133	91	3.23	3.63	1.39				24.3	3.5	6.1	1.8					31%	76%								17.9	67	126	$9
10 aaa	13	10	0	164	118	4.75	4.39	1.40				23.9	3.2	6.5	2.0					31%	67%								-13.6	54	87	$1
11 STL *	8	4	1	110	93	3.67	3.51	1.32	591	723	504	15.1	2.9	7.6	2.6	10%	57	11	32	33%	71%	12%	2	31	50%	0%	50	0.94	3.7	92	138	$4
12 STL	18	7	0	176	180	3.78	3.58	1.32	728	841	624	21.3	3.3	9.2	2.8	10%	44	24	32	32%	73%	10%	29	86	59%	14%	0	0.83	5.0	99	130	$11
13 STL	15	10	0	202	198	3.97	3.63	1.31	701	765	652	25.9	3.4	8.8	2.6	10%	43	23	34	32%	70%	7%	33	102	64%	15%			-2.6	88	115	$8
1st Half	10	2	0	100	98	3.52	3.68	1.16	635	746	541	25.8	3.4	8.8	2.6	9%	38	23	39	29%	69%	5%	16	101	63%	6%			4.2	83	108	$17
2nd Half	5	8	0	102	100	4.41	3.58	1.46	763	784	748	26.1	3.4	8.8	2.6	11%	47	22	30	35%	71%	10%	17	102	65%	24%			-6.9	94	121	-$1
14 Proj	**16**	**10**	**0**	**203**	**195**	**3.80**	**3.38**	**1.28**	**690**	**777**	**621**	**25.5**	**3.3**	**8.6**	**2.6**	**10%**	**46**	**21**	**33**	**31%**	**71%**	**8%**	**39**						**1.8**	**91**	**118**	**$13**

Lyons,Tyler

Age: 26 Th: L Role SP	Health A	LIMA Plan B+
Ht: 6' 4" Wt: 200 Type	PT/Exp D	Rand Var +2
	Consist C	MM 3200

2-4, 4.75 ERA in 53 IP at STL. Strike-thrower without world-beater stuff had fine AAA year—3.32 ERA, 86/19 K/BB in 100 IP. Recorded 4 PQS-DOMs in 8 STL starts, but a 62% S% drove a 5.56 ERA. Fared better in relief (9 IP, one run, 10/1 K/BB). Projected swing-man will need injuries or a trade to get an extended rotation shot.

Yr Tm	W	L	Sv	IP	K	ERA	xERA	WHIP	oOPS	vL	vR	BF/G	Ctl	Dom	Cmd	SwK	G	L	F	H%	S%	hr/f	GS	APC	DOM%	DIS%	Sv%	LI	RAR	BPV	BPX	R$
09																																
10																																
11																																
12 a/a	9	13	0	153	117	4.50	4.45	1.38				23.7	2.2	6.9	3.2					34%	68%								-9.2	82	107	-$2
13 STL *	9	6	0	153	112	4.10	3.24	1.18	725	630	762	21.2	2.1	6.6	3.2	9%	47	19	33	30%	65%	10%	8	66	50%	25%	0	0.97	-4.5	92	119	$5
1st Half	5	4	0	86	55	4.82	4.09	1.35	730	884	677	23.9	2.1	5.7	2.7	9%	49	18	33	32%	64%	9%	6	77	33%	33%			-10.1	71	92	-$1
2nd Half	4	2	0	67	57	3.19	2.16	0.97	717	305	911	18.2	2.0	7.7	3.8	10%	45	21	34	25%	68%	11%	2	55	100%	0%	0	1.15	5.6	119	154	$13
14 Proj	**3**	**3**	**0**	**58**	**42**	**3.81**	**3.62**	**1.23**	**744**	**528**	**834**	**21.6**	**2.1**	**6.6**	**3.1**	**10%**	**45**	**20**	**36**	**30%**	**70%**	**7%**	**11**						**0.4**	**84**	**109**	**$0**

Machi,Jean

Age: 32 Th: R Role RP	Health A	LIMA Plan B+
Ht: 6' 0" Wt: 260 Type xGB	PT/Exp F	Rand Var -3
	Consist F	MM 4200

3-1, 2.38 ERA in 53 IP at SF. Late-blooming journeyman turned heads in first extended MLB role. Picked up steam in 2H, partially due to H% but also SwK that dominated LHB and RHB alike. Historical strength has been ability to induce GBs; Dom spike, Ctl gains need confirmation before we believe. Some regression guaranteed.

Yr Tm	W	L	Sv	IP	K	ERA	xERA	WHIP	oOPS	vL	vR	BF/G	Ctl	Dom	Cmd	SwK	G	L	F	H%	S%	hr/f	GS	APC	DOM%	DIS%	Sv%	LI	RAR	BPV	BPX	R$
09 a/a	3	4	12	52	28	2.69	3.13	1.24				5.1	3.5	4.9	1.4					26%	80%								10.4	50	94	$8
10 aaa	5	5	23	60	43	4.72	4.77	1.58				4.5	5.0	6.5	1.3					30%	72%								-4.7	40	64	$6
11																																
12 SF *	2	1	15	63	37	4.40	5.79	1.61	804	286	1352	4.6	2.5	5.2	2.0	13%	41	14	45	35%	75%	20%	0	13			83	0.39	-3.0	33	43	-$1
13 SF *	6	2	2	71	65	2.03	2.32	1.06	586	642	552	4.1	1.9	8.2	4.3	11%	54	20	26	30%	81%	5%	0	15			50	1.16	16.2	141	184	$9
1st Half	4	1	1	36	29	3.04	4.02	1.36	736	908	626	4.5	2.0	7.4	3.7	9%	52	19	30	35%	78%	8%	0	15			50	1.19	3.6	104	135	$5
2nd Half	2	1	1	36	36	1.02	0.62	0.77	426	336	476	3.8	1.8	9.0	5.1	14%	58	21	21	24%	85%	0%	0	14			50	1.14	12.5	182	236	$13
14 Proj	**4**	**2**	**0**	**58**	**45**	**3.13**	**3.34**	**1.27**	**677**	**688**	**671**	**4.4**	**2.7**	**7.0**	**2.6**	**12%**	**55**	**20**	**25**	**31%**	**76%**	**9%**	**0**						**5.3**	**87**	**112**	**$2**

Maholm,Paul

Age: 32 Th: L Role SP	Health D	LIMA Plan C
Ht: 6' 2" Wt: 220 Type	PT/Exp A	Rand Var +2
	Consist A	MM 3103

Sailed through 1H despite inability to reverse 2012 hr/f spike. July wrist injury launched 2H slide, shelving him for a month; Sept elbow soreness didn't help. That 2H hr/f and accompanying loss of Cmd drove ERA way up. Better health could yield better numbers, but his Dom and Ctl are walking a fine line.

Yr Tm	W	L	Sv	IP	K	ERA	xERA	WHIP	oOPS	vL	vR	BF/G	Ctl	Dom	Cmd	SwK	G	L	F	H%	S%	hr/f	GS	APC	DOM%	DIS%	Sv%	LI	RAR	BPV	BPX	R$
09 PIT	8	9	0	195	119	4.44	4.21	1.44	773	510	836	27.0	2.8	5.5	2.0	7%	52	18	30	32%	69%	7%	31	98	29%	13%			-2.8	54	101	$1
10 PIT	9	15	0	185	102	5.10	4.52	1.56	812	645	842	26.3	3.0	5.0	1.6	6%	51	19	30	34%	67%	8%	32	96	34%	31%			-23.3	37	60	-$9
11 PIT	6	14	0	162	97	3.66	4.00	1.29	711	697	714	26.4	2.8	5.4	1.9	6%	50	22	28	29%	72%	8%	26	94	35%	23%			5.7	50	75	$4
12 2 NL	13	11	0	189	140	3.67	3.76	1.22	714	703	718	24.6	2.5	6.7	2.6	8%	51	21	27	29%	73%	13%	31	93	65%	19%	0	0.77	8.1	81	105	$12
13 ATL	10	11	0	153	105	4.41	3.93	1.41	773	559	845	25.8	2.8	6.2	2.2	7%	51	24	25	32%	71%	14%	26	96	35%	19%			-10.3	66	85	-$3
1st Half	9	6	0	105	75	3.69	3.64	1.29	710	456	795	26.2	2.5	6.4	2.6	7%	52	24	24	30%	74%	13%	17	98	47%	12%			2.3	79	102	$5
2nd Half	1	5	0	48	30	6.00	4.58	1.69	898	754	948	24.9	3.4	5.6	1.7	7%	50	24	27	35%	66%	16%	9	93	11%	33%			-12.6	38	49	-$18
14 Proj	**11**	**11**	**0**	**174**	**115**	**3.96**	**3.88**	**1.41**	**775**	**657**	**811**	**24.7**	**2.8**	**6.0**	**2.1**	**7%**	**50**	**22**	**28**	**32%**	**74%**	**11%**	**30**						**-2.1**	**58**	**76**	**$2**

Maness,Seth

Age: 25 Th: R Role RP	Health A	LIMA Plan A
Ht: 6' 0" Wt: 190 Type Con xGB	PT/Exp D	Rand Var 0
	Consist A	MM 4001

5-2, 2.32 ERA in 63 IP at STL. A starter in the minors, this soft-tossing GBer thrived in 66 appearances in STL out of the bullpen. Relies on exquisite command and movement; sub-par Dom will likely keep him in the pen and limit his upside. Hard to foresee a path to measurable fantasy value.

Yr Tm	W	L	Sv	IP	K	ERA	xERA	WHIP	oOPS	vL	vR	BF/G	Ctl	Dom	Cmd	SwK	G	L	F	H%	S%	hr/f	GS	APC	DOM%	DIS%	Sv%	LI	RAR	BPV	BPX	R$
09																																
10																																
11																																
12 aa	11	3	0	124	68	3.62	3.91	1.17				24.7	0.7	5.0	7.6					31%	72%								6.0	162	211	$7
13 STL *	7	4	1	87	49	3.06	4.36	1.38	725	726	724	5.2	1.7	5.1	3.1	7%	68	19	12	33%	79%	17%	0	13			33	1.16	8.6	73	95	$2
1st Half	6	3	0	52	27	3.76	5.22	1.51	773	847	725	7.5	1.2	4.8	3.9	7%	72	19	9	36%	76%	25%	0	14			0	0.97	0.7	80	103	$1
2nd Half	1	1	1	35	22	2.04	3.18	1.19	687	581	724	3.5	2.3	5.6	2.4	7%	65	19	15	29%	85%	13%	0	13			50	1.28	8.0	82	107	$4
14 Proj	**4**	**3**	**0**	**73**	**41**	**3.13**	**3.22**	**1.26**	**760**	**757**	**761**	**6.7**	**1.4**	**5.1**	**3.7**	**7%**	**63**	**19**	**18**	**31%**	**77%**	**13%**	**0**						**6.6**	**96**	**125**	**$2**

Marcum,Shaun

Age: 32 Th: R Role SP	Health F	LIMA Plan C
Ht: 6' 0" Wt: 195 Type FB	PT/Exp B	Rand Var +3
	Consist A	MM 3301

Shoulder impingement delayed his debut until late April. Struggled with back woes and a poor S% until surgery for thoracic outlet syndrome ended his season in July. Through all of the injuries, his BPIs continue to suggest a useful mid-rotation profile. It's all about health, but those problems seem to be snowballing.

Yr Tm	W	L	Sv	IP	K	ERA	xERA	WHIP	oOPS	vL	vR	BF/G	Ctl	Dom	Cmd	SwK	G	L	F	H%	S%	hr/f	GS	APC	DOM%	DIS%	Sv%	LI	RAR	BPV	BPX	R$
09																																
10 TOR	13	8	0	195	165	3.64	3.74	1.15	691	532	859	25.8	2.0	7.6	3.8	11%	38	18	43	29%	73%	10%	31	98	61%	13%			10.6	99	161	$16
11 MIL	13	7	0	201	158	3.54	3.95	1.16	655	749	564	24.9	2.6	7.1	2.8	11%	37	20	43	27%	73%	9%	33	96	61%	12%			9.9	74	111	$15
12 MIL	7	4	0	124	109	3.70	4.21	1.27	720	792	648	25.1	3.0	7.9	2.7	11%	35	23	41	29%	75%	11%	21	99	57%	14%			4.8	75	98	$5
13 NYM	1	10	0	78	60	5.29	4.20	1.35	753	838	690	23.9	2.4	6.9	2.9	10%	35	24	41	33%	61%	7%	12	88	25%	33%	0	0.98	-13.7	72	94	-$7
1st Half	1	9	0	67	55	5.08	4.02	1.26	710	879	587	23.3	2.3	7.4	3.2	11%	33	23	44	32%	59%	6%	10	88	30%	40%	0	1.01	-10.1	82	106	-$6
2nd Half	0	1	0	11	5	6.55	5.41	1.91	988	634	1283	27.0	3.3	4.1	1.3	8%	43	26	31	37%	68%	15%	2	92	0%	0%			-3.6	6	8	-$11
14 Proj	**4**	**5**	**0**	**73**	**60**	**4.05**	**3.71**	**1.21**	**691**	**758**	**629**	**23.9**	**2.5**	**7.4**	**3.0**	**11%**	**36**	**21**	**43**	**29%**	**69%**	**8%**	**12**						**-1.6**	**81**	**105**	**$1**

JOCK THOMPSON

Marmol,Carlos

Age: 31	Th: R	Role RP	Health B	LIMA Plan D+	
Ht: 6' 2"	Wt: 215	Type Pwr	PT/Exp B	Rand Var +1	
			Consist A	MM 3510	

Lost closer role after 3 appearances (1.2 IP, 5 runs) and never regained it. Dom says he's still untouchable when he throws strikes; Ctl says the strike zone is pretty much untouchable too. 2nd half ERA/xERA hint at a possible rebound, but the saves that once drove his value aren't likely to return.

Yr	Tm	W	L	Sv	IP	K	ERA	xERA	WHIP	oOPS	vL	vR	BF/G	Ctl	Dom	Cmd	SwK	G	L	F	H%	S%	hr/f	GS	APC	DOM%	DIS%	Sv%	LI	RAR	BPV	BPX	R$
09	CHC	2	4	15	74	93	3.41	4.59	1.46	612	549	664	4.2	7.9	11.3	1.4	10%	36	16	48	26%	75%	3%	0	19			79	1.25	8.4	4	8	$8
10	CHC	2	3	38	78	138	2.55	2.71	1.18	500	490	508	4.3	6.0	16.0	2.7	15%	35	17	48	32%	77%	2%	0	18			88	1.45	14.7	138	224	$23
11	CHC	2	6	34	74	99	4.01	3.52	1.38	643	561	710	4.4	5.8	12.0	2.1	12%	39	20	40	31%	71%	7%	0	19			77	1.40	-0.6	76	114	$13
12	CHC	3	3	20	55	72	3.42	4.32	1.54	662	703	618	4.0	7.3	11.7	1.6	9%	41	20	40	30%	79%	8%	0	18			87	0.80	4.1	32	42	$7
13	2 NL	2	4	2	49	59	4.41	4.45	1.63	763	566	891	4.3	7.3	10.8	1.5	11%	38	26	37	29%	77%	16%	0	18			40	0.67	-3.3	13	17	-$4
1st Half		2	4	2	28	32	5.86	4.63	1.70	876	469	1153	4.2	6.8	10.4	1.5	11%	35	21	44	30%	71%	20%	0	17			40	0.94	-6.8	16	21	-$5
2nd Half		0	0	0	21	27	2.53	4.21	1.55	608	706	546	4.6	8.0	11.4	1.4	12%	41	33	27	28%	84%	8%	0	19			0	0.28	3.5	7	10	-$3
14	**Proj**	**2**	**3**	**2**	**51**	**65**	**4.39**	**3.93**	**1.53**	**677**	**619**	**723**	**4.1**	**7.2**	**11.6**	**1.6**	**11%**	**39**	**23**	**38**	**30%**	**72%**	**10%**	**0**						**-3.3**	**32**	**42**	**-$2**

Marquis,Jason

Age: 35	Th: R	Role SP	Health F	LIMA Plan D	
Ht: 6' 1"	Wt: 220	Type GB	PT/Exp B	Rand Var 0	
			Consist B	MM 1000	

Wrung the max out of fortunate 1H H%, tip-toeing around Ctl spike and more HR woes. Put up surprisingly effective innings-eater performance for team going nowhere, until Tommy John surgery ended season in July. Won't return until late 2014 at best, if at all. Not that it matters, as recent R$ history speaks to his upside.

Yr	Tm	W	L	Sv	IP	K	ERA	xERA	WHIP	oOPS	vL	vR	BF/G	Ctl	Dom	Cmd	SwK	G	L	F	H%	S%	hr/f	GS	APC	DOM%	DIS%	Sv%	LI	RAR	BPV	BPX	R$
09	COL	15	13	0	216	115	4.04	4.37	1.38	724	747	702	27.9	3.3	4.8	1.4	7%	56	17	27	29%	71%	8%	33	98	36%	21%			7.5	30	57	$9
10	WAS	2	9	0	59	31	6.60	4.74	1.70	877	977	783	21.2	3.7	4.8	1.3	7%	53	18	29	33%	63%	15%	13	79	23%	54%			-18.2	17	28	-$9
11	2 NL	8	6	0	132	76	4.43	4.12	1.49	779	840	729	25.5	2.9	5.2	1.8	7%	55	20	25	33%	71%	10%	23	89	26%	26%			-8.0	47	71	-$4
12	2 TM *	10	11	0	149	103	4.75	5.09	1.41	843	943	748	25.2	2.7	6.2	2.3	8%	53	21	27	31%	71%	21%	22	93	41%	18%			-13.5	41	54	-$4
13	SD	9	5	0	118	72	4.05	4.79	1.52	785	868	720	25.9	5.2	5.5	1.1	8%	52	21	27	26%	78%	18%	20	96	25%	35%			-2.7	-11	-15	-$3
1st Half		9	3	0	95	62	3.99	4.52	1.44	765	827	712	25.6	5.0	5.9	1.2	8%	55	18	27	25%	78%	21%	16	96	31%	31%			-1.5	3	4	-$1
2nd Half		0	2	0	23	10	4.30	5.96	1.87	862	1082	747	27.0	5.9	3.9	0.7	6%	44	28	28	32%	78%	9%	4	96	0%	50%			-1.2	-66	-86	-$13
14	**Proj**	**1**	**1**	**0**	**22**	**12**	**4.47**	**4.53**	**1.58**	**813**	**917**	**732**	**25.4**	**4.2**	**5.2**	**1.2**	**7%**	**51**	**22**	**27**	**31%**	**74%**	**14%**	**4**						**-1.6**	**8**	**10**	**-$4**

Marshall,Sean

Age: 31	Th: L	Role RP	Health F	LIMA Plan C+	
Ht: 6' 7"	Wt: 225	Type Pwr GB	PT/Exp C	Rand Var -5	
			Consist A	MM 5510	

Recurring shoulder inflammation resulted in a lost season. Velocity was down in uneventful Sept small-sample return. Consistent track record says GB-Ctl specialist should rebound somewhere near his past prominence, but his health will likely make that call. Even with a sound shoulder, expect his IP to decline a tad.

Yr	Tm	W	L	Sv	IP	K	ERA	xERA	WHIP	oOPS	vL	vR	BF/G	Ctl	Dom	Cmd	SwK	G	L	F	H%	S%	hr/f	GS	APC	DOM%	DIS%	Sv%	LI	RAR	BPV	BPX	R$
09	CHC	3	7	0	85	68	4.32	4.00	1.44	776	708	808	6.8	3.4	7.2	2.1	8%	49	23	28	32%	73%	14%	9	26	33%	22%	0	1.23	0.0	65	122	-$1
10	CHC	7	5	1	75	90	2.65	2.66	1.11	569	539	585	3.8	3.0	10.8	3.6	11%	52	23	25	31%	76%	7%	0	15			33	1.16	13.1	144	233	$9
11	CHC	6	6	5	76	79	2.26	2.64	1.10	566	503	599	3.9	2.0	9.4	4.6	12%	58	18	25	33%	78%	2%	0	15			56	1.36	15.7	150	225	$11
12	CIN	5	5	9	61	74	2.51	2.66	1.16	597	410	725	3.5	2.4	10.9	4.6	13%	56	20	24	35%	79%	8%	0	14			69	1.20	11.3	167	218	$9
13	CIN	0	1	0	10	10	1.74	2.37	0.58	307	451	71	2.3	1.7	8.7	5.0	10%	58	17	25	17%	67%	0%	0	10			0	1.28	2.7	146	190	-$2
1st Half		0	1	0	7	7	2.57	2.74	0.86	382	513	111	2.5	2.6	9.0	3.5	11%	56	22	22	24%	67%	0%	0	10			0	1.47	1.1	126	163	-$2
2nd Half		0	0	0	3	3	0.00	1.59	0.00	100	200	0	2.0	0.0	8.1	0.0	9%	67	0	33	0%	0%	0%	0	9			0	0.87	1.6	190	247	-$2
14	**Proj**	**4**	**4**	**2**	**53**	**56**	**2.78**	**2.73**	**1.15**	**599**	**503**	**655**	**3.8**	**2.7**	**9.5**	**3.6**	**12%**	**54**	**21**	**25**	**31%**	**76%**	**8%**	**0**						**7.1**	**131**	**170**	**$5**

Martinez,Carlos

Age: 22	Th: R	Role RP	Health A	LIMA Plan B+	
Ht: 6' 0"	Wt: 185	Type GB	PT/Exp D	Rand Var -1	
			Consist A	MM 3201	

2-1, 5.08 ERA in 28 IP at STL. Precocious youngster peaked in Sept, parlaying 3.48/3.13 ERA/xERA, 5.0 Cmd over 9 appearances into post-season roster spot. Despite the slight build, SP role is still in his future, which BPIs suggest is bright. Short-term role is a little murkier, but this blue-chipper is worth an extra dollar.

Yr	Tm	W	L	Sv	IP	K	ERA	xERA	WHIP	oOPS	vL	vR	BF/G	Ctl	Dom	Cmd	SwK	G	L	F	H%	S%	hr/f	GS	APC	DOM%	DIS%	Sv%	LI	RAR	BPV	BPX	R$
09																																	
10																																	
11																																	
12	aa	4	3	0	71	50	3.05	3.32	1.21				19.2	2.6	6.3	2.4					29%	77%								8.5	74	97	$3
13	STL *	8	4	1	108	86	3.26	3.13	1.26	704	764	661	11.9	3.0	7.1	2.4	10%	52	19	29	30%	74%	4%	1	23	0%	100%	100	0.75	8.1	87	114	$6
1st Half		3	2	0	55	46	2.53	2.80	1.21	733	829	650	13.1	2.5	7.4	3.0	11%	62	29	10	31%	78%	0%	0	20			0	0.35	9.1	108	140	$8
2nd Half		5	2	1	53	40	4.03	3.47	1.31	692	736	662	10.9	3.5	6.8	2.0	9%	49	15	35	29%	70%	4%	1	24	0%	100%	100	0.94	-1.0	69	89	$4
14	**Proj**	**6**	**3**	**0**	**87**	**66**	**3.50**	**3.75**	**1.25**	**604**	**606**	**602**	**13.8**	**2.9**	**6.8**	**2.4**	**9%**	**49**	**15**	**35**	**29%**	**74%**	**8%**	**10**						**3.9**	**72**	**94**	**$4**

Masterson,Justin

Age: 29	Th: R	Role SP	Health A	LIMA Plan C+	
Ht: 6' 6"	Wt: 250	Type Pwr xGB	PT/Exp A	Rand Var 0	
			Consist B	MM 4305	

His GB-inducing ways continue to be a given. Skills surged to peak levels, led by a huge, season-long Dom spike and significant improvement (finally!) vs. LH hitters. Ctl became a 2H issue, and oblique strain effectively shelved him in Sept. His stock is up, but the Cmd remains at risk. Don't pay for a full repeat.

Yr	Tm	W	L	Sv	IP	K	ERA	xERA	WHIP	oOPS	vL	vR	BF/G	Ctl	Dom	Cmd	SwK	G	L	F	H%	S%	hr/f	GS	APC	DOM%	DIS%	Sv%	LI	RAR	BPV	BPX	R$
09	2 AL	4	10	0	129	119	4.52	3.87	1.45	740	877	591	13.5	4.2	8.3	2.0	9%	54	15	31	32%	70%	10%	16	52	38%	25%	0	0.78	-3.2	68	128	$0
10	CLE	6	13	0	180	140	4.70	3.78	1.50	738	784	681	23.6	3.7	7.0	1.9	9%	60	15	25	33%	69%	10%	29	91	41%	28%	0	0.85	-13.8	65	106	-$4
11	CLE	12	10	0	216	158	3.21	3.56	1.28	667	746	560	26.7	2.7	6.6	2.4	8%	55	18	27	31%	75%	6%	33	102	55%	12%	0	0.75	19.6	78	118	$14
12	CLE	11	15	0	206	159	4.93	4.08	1.45	736	825	613	26.6	3.8	6.9	1.8	9%	56	19	25	31%	66%	11%	34	101	47%	26%			-23.3	55	72	-$7
13	CLE	14	10	0	193	195	3.45	3.08	1.20	624	698	507	25.1	3.5	9.1	2.6	10%	58	18	24	29%	72%	11%	29	94	79%	10%	0	0.72	9.9	104	136	$15
1st Half		10	6	0	124	125	3.48	3.10	1.18	627	708	494	28.4	3.3	9.1	2.8	10%	56	16	27	29%	72%	11%	18	104	83%	0%			5.8	110	142	$20
2nd Half		4	4	0	69	70	3.39	3.04	1.25	617	677	528	20.9	4.0	9.1	2.3	9%	61	21	18	29%	72%	9%	11	82	73%	27%	0	0.66	4.0	94	122	$6
14	**Proj**	**12**	**12**	**0**	**203**	**181**	**3.71**	**3.29**	**1.31**	**670**	**746**	**561**	**22.9**	**3.6**	**8.0**	**2.2**	**9%**	**57**	**19**	**24**	**30%**	**72%**	**10%**	**37**						**3.9**	**82**	**107**	**$10**

Matsuzaka,Daisuke

Age: 33	Th: R	Role SP	Health F	LIMA Plan D	
Ht: 6' 0"	Wt: 185	Type Pwr xFB	PT/Exp D	Rand Var 0	
			Consist B	MM 0201	

3-3, 4.42 ERA in 39 IP with NYM. Made seven late-season starts after Aug release by CLE. PRO: 7.7 Dom; best MLB Cmd since '07; PQS-DOMs in final four starts. CON: Velocity now sub-90 mph 2+ years after TJS; 2.1 Cmd, Ctl still woefully sub-par, scary FB%, history. Even if he's a tad improved post-surgery, history says avoid.

Yr	Tm	W	L	Sv	IP	K	ERA	xERA	WHIP	oOPS	vL	vR	BF/G	Ctl	Dom	Cmd	SwK	G	L	F	H%	S%	hr/f	GS	APC	DOM%	DIS%	Sv%	LI	RAR	BPV	BPX	R$
09	BOS *	4	8	0	77	68	6.15	7.12	1.90	935	975	876	21.5	4.8	7.9	1.6	9%	34	23	43	38%	71%	12%	12	92	25%	33%			-17.4	22	41	-$10
10	BOS *	11	6	0	170	142	4.46	3.61	1.33	706	770	626	25.3	4.0	7.5	1.9	8%	33	22	45	29%	67%	7%	25	105	48%	16%			-8.0	69	112	$4
11	BOS	3	3	0	37	26	5.30	5.62	1.47	664	777	491	20.9	5.5	6.3	1.1	7%	32	13	56	26%	65%	6%	7	82	43%	57%	0	0.90	-6.3	-27	-40	-$4
12	BOS *	2	10	0	101	76	6.38	6.08	1.63	938	1056	815	19.6	3.8	6.7	1.8	8%	40	18	42	33%	64%	17%	11	77	27%	45%			-29.6	21	28	-$17
13	NYM *	8	11	0	142	103	5.29	5.03	1.54	689	679	700	23.8	3.9	6.6	1.7	8%	28	23	49	32%	67%	8%	7	95	57%	29%			-25.0	39	51	-$11
1st Half		1	4	0	38	30	6.51	5.57	1.81				19.4	6.9	7.3	1.1					31%	65%	0%	0						-12.3	30	39	-$16
2nd Half		7	7	0	104	73	4.85	4.83	1.44	689	679	700	26.2	2.8	6.3	2.3	8%	28	23	49	32%	69%	8%	7	95	57%	29%			-12.7	50	64	-$9
14	**Proj**	**3**	**6**	**0**	**73**	**54**	**4.92**	**4.83**	**1.58**	**819**	**885**	**735**	**21.5**	**4.4**	**6.7**	**1.5**	**8%**	**33**	**19**	**48**	**31%**	**72%**	**9%**	**15**						**-9.4**	**12**	**15**	**-$6**

Matusz,Brian

Age: 27	Th: L	Role RP	Health C	LIMA Plan B+	
Ht: 6' 4"	Wt: 200	Type Pwr FB	PT/Exp D	Rand Var -1	
			Consist D	MM 4400	

Built on strong 2012 bullpen debut and then some, adding more Dom as he got more concentrated vL work. Numbers vR weren't hopeless in small sample 86 AB (1 HR, 17 K). But 2H use says more LOOGY work is in his future. Still an outside chance for another rotation shot; he offers little fantasy upside unless that happens.

Yr	Tm	W	L	Sv	IP	K	ERA	xERA	WHIP	oOPS	vL	vR	BF/G	Ctl	Dom	Cmd	SwK	G	L	F	H%	S%	hr/f	GS	APC	DOM%	DIS%	Sv%	LI	RAR	BPV	BPX	R$
09	BAL *	12	2	0	91	76	3.48	3.93	1.29	823	708	850	23.4	2.6	7.5	2.9	10%	31	21	48	31%	76%	9%	8	93	25%	13%			9.5	82	154	$8
10	BAL	10	12	0	176	143	4.30	4.33	1.34	718	581	755	23.8	3.2	7.3	2.3	8%	36	19	45	30%	70%	8%	32	94	44%	25%			-4.9	59	95	$4
11	BAL *	3	12	0	110	72	7.02	6.81	1.73	1121	1058	1141	22.8	3.6	5.9	1.6	6%	28	22	50	34%	62%	20%	12	79	0%	75%			-41.8	4	6	-$19
12	BAL *	8	11	1	145	107	5.28	5.24	1.56	818	528	933	14.4	3.6	6.6	1.8	8%	41	20	40	33%	68%	12%	16	50	19%	38%	50	1.34	-22.7	42	54	-$11
13	BAL	2	1	0	51	50	3.53	3.54	1.16	616	502	747	3.2	2.8	8.8	3.1	13%	39	21	40	30%	70%	6%	0	13			0	1.04	2.1	100	130	$0
1st Half		2	1	0	32	27	3.90	3.75	1.08	604	440	796	3.5	2.5	7.5	3.0	12%	40	18	42	26%	66%	8%	0	15			0	0.97	-0.1	86	111	$1
2nd Half		0	0	0	19	23	2.89	3.17	1.29	635	607	667	2.8	3.4	11.1	3.3	15%	37	26	37	36%	75%	0%	0	11			0	1.15	2.2	123	160	-$2
14	**Proj**	**2**	**2**	**0**	**54**	**52**	**3.73**	**3.53**	**1.25**	**663**	**517**	**757**	**5.1**	**3.1**	**8.8**	**2.8**	**11%**	**37**	**22**	**41**	**31%**	**72%**	**8%**	**0**						**0.9**	**90**	**117**	**$0**

JOCK THOMPSON

Maurer,Brandon

Age: 23	Th: R	Role RP		Health	C	LIMA Plan	B+
Ht: 6' 5"	Wt: 215	Type Pwr		PT/Exp	D	Rand Var	+5
				Consist	C	MM	3201

5-8, 4.34 ERA in 90 IP with SEA. Shoulder/elbow injuries, conditioning slowed 2010-11 development. Rushed to SEA after a fine March, he skipped Triple-A with predictable results—a May demotion. August return points to potential: 3.8 Cmd, 3.78 xERA, 47% GB% in final 41 IP. Legit prospect, but a work-in-progress flyer now.

Yr	Tm	W	L	Sv	IP	K	ERA	xERA	WHIP	oOPS	vL	vR	BF/G	Ctl	Dom	Cmd	SwK	G	L	F	H%	S%	hr/f	GS	APC	DOM%	DIS%	Sv%	LI	RAR	BPV	BPX	R$
09																																	
10																																	
11																																	
12	aa	9	2	0	138	106	3.71	3.89	1.43				24.4	3.2	6.9	2.2					34%	73%								5.2	80	104	$1
13	SEA *	8	12	0	137	112	5.84	5.33	1.57	883	919	835	18.7	3.4	7.4	2.2	10%	44	19	37	35%	64%	15%	14	70	29%	36%	0	0.74	-33.4	51	66	-$14
1st Half		4	9	0	78	60	5.79	5.60	1.59	964	1038	869	21.6	3.4	6.9	2.0	9%	42	20	38	34%	66%	16%	10	82	30%	40%			-18.6	39	50	-$15
2nd Half		4	3	0	58	51	5.92	4.97	1.54	786	780	792	15.9	3.3	7.9	2.4	11%	47	18	35	36%	61%	13%	4	60	25%	25%	0	0.73	-14.8	67	87	-$12
14	**Proj**	**6**	**5**	**0**	**98**	**79**	**4.06**	**3.82**	**1.34**	**684**	**698**	**663**	**19.2**	**3.3**	**7.2**	**2.2**	**10%**	**45**	**19**	**36**	**31%**	**71%**	**8%**	**20**						**-2.3**	**66**	**85**	**$1**

Mazzaro,Vin

Age: 27	Th: R	Role RP		Health	A	LIMA Plan	C+
Ht: 6' 2"	Wt: 220	Type		PT/Exp	C	Rand Var	-3
				Consist	B	MM	3101

Failed SP found Ctl, GB pitch and profitability in the bullpen. Despite the improvements, this is as good as it gets. So-so Dom kept Cmd sub-par as career-best H%/S% fueled ERA, WHIP gains. Win total was the cherry on his 2013 sundae. RandVar and R$ history speak to his downside and unlikeliness of repeat.

Yr	Tm	W	L	Sv	IP	K	ERA	xERA	WHIP	oOPS	vL	vR	BF/G	Ctl	Dom	Cmd	SwK	G	L	F	H%	S%	hr/f	GS	APC	DOM%	DIS%	Sv%	LI	RAR	BPV	BPX	R$
09	OAK *	6	11	0	148	95	4.29	4.73	1.50	873	899	836	23.7	3.4	5.8	1.7	7%	39	21	40	32%	73%	10%	17	98	29%	47%			0.6	44	82	$0
10	OAK *	9	9	0	160	111	4.00	4.63	1.44	765	797	733	21.9	3.7	6.2	1.7	8%	43	21	37	30%	76%	13%	18	86	56%	22%	0	0.64	1.6	40	64	$2
11	KC *	8	3	0	152	93	5.48	5.84	1.80	989	1178	825	24.2	4.4	5.5	1.2	6%	43	15	42	36%	69%	9%	4	71	0%	25%	0	0.68	-28.7	30	44	-$17
12	KC *	6	5	5	111	74	4.72	4.84	1.56	795	908	714	12.1	3.1	6.0	1.9	7%	46	27	27	35%	69%	8%	6	40	17%	33%	83	0.70	-9.6	54	71	-$6
13	PIT	8	2	1	74	46	2.81	3.90	1.21	628	616	637	5.3	2.6	5.6	2.2	8%	52	19	29	29%	77%	5%	0	21			33	1.04	9.6	62	81	$5
1st Half		4	2	0	39	23	2.52	3.86	1.17	657	589	702	5.8	2.1	5.3	2.6	9%	52	16	33	28%	81%	8%	0	22			0	0.97	6.5	69	89	$6
2nd Half		4	0	1	34	23	3.15	3.93	1.25	596	641	561	4.9	3.1	6.0	1.9	7%	53	23	24	30%	72%	0%	0	20			50	1.09	3.0	54	70	$4
14	**Proj**	**5**	**3**	**0**	**73**	**48**	**3.85**	**3.92**	**1.33**	**678**	**723**	**642**	**5.1**	**3.0**	**5.9**	**1.9**	**8%**	**48**	**22**	**30**	**30%**	**72%**	**7%**	**0**						**0.1**	**50**	**65**	**$0**

McAllister,Zach

Age: 26	Th: R	Role SP		Health	D	LIMA Plan	B+
Ht: 6' 6"	Wt: 240	Type FB		PT/Exp	C	Rand Var	-1
				Consist	A	MM	2203

Fast start derailed by mid-season finger injury, but xERA wasn't buying that 1H ERA anyway. Ctl and Cmd are going the wrong way; GB% is stagnant at best. 2H DOM%/DIS% says he was a crap-shoot whenever he took the ball. Age, Some level of rebound is possible, but durability issues add to less-than-optimistic outlook.

Yr	Tm	W	L	Sv	IP	K	ERA	xERA	WHIP	oOPS	vL	vR	BF/G	Ctl	Dom	Cmd	SwK	G	L	F	H%	S%	hr/f	GS	APC	DOM%	DIS%	Sv%	LI	RAR	BPV	BPX	R$
09	aa	7	5	0	121	83	3.09	3.47	1.30				22.6	2.8	6.2	2.2					31%	76%								18.3	74	139	$8
10	aaa	9	12	0	150	84	5.82	5.94	1.63				24.7	2.6	5.0	1.9					35%	65%								-32.1	28	45	-$12
11	CLE *	12	4	0	172	120	3.99	4.31	1.38	860	1069	659	25.0	1.9	6.3	3.2	7%	43	27	30	34%	71%	5%	4	85	0%	50%			-0.9	84	126	$3
12	CLE *	11	10	0	189	153	3.97	4.53	1.37	767	724	820	23.9	2.7	7.3	2.7	9%	41	19	40	32%	75%	12%	22	96	50%	18%			1.1	66	86	$4
13	CLE	9	9	0	134	101	3.75	4.46	1.36	739	737	741	24.1	3.3	6.8	2.1	7%	37	22	41	30%	75%	8%	24	96	38%	25%			1.9	48	63	$2
1st Half		4	5	0	66	45	3.43	4.53	1.37	738	802	658	25.8	3.0	6.2	2.0	7%	38	21	40	30%	78%	8%	11	103	27%	9%			3.6	46	60	$3
2nd Half		5	4	0	69	56	4.06	4.40	1.35	740	670	818	22.7	3.5	7.3	2.1	8%	36	22	43	30%	71%	7%	13	89	46%	38%			-1.7	50	65	$2
14	**Proj**	**9**	**10**	**0**	**154**	**116**	**4.05**	**4.03**	**1.34**	**733**	**712**	**758**	**23.5**	**2.9**	**6.8**	**2.3**	**8%**	**38**	**21**	**41**	**31%**	**72%**	**8%**	**27**						**-3.6**	**60**	**78**	**$3**

McCarthy,Brandon

Age: 30	Th: R	Role SP		Health	F	LIMA Plan	C
Ht: 6' 7"	Wt: 200	Type Con		PT/Exp	B	Rand Var	+1
				Consist	B	MM	3103

Move from OAK—where he posted a 2.74 ERA in 2011-12—didn't help hr/f or H%. Health woes (shoulder inflammation, seizure) are ongoing, and chipping away at his Dom. GB% rebounded and Ctl remains elite, but his inability to remain whole casts a dark shadow. This projection may be best case scenario.

Yr	Tm	W	L	Sv	IP	K	ERA	xERA	WHIP	oOPS	vL	vR	BF/G	Ctl	Dom	Cmd	SwK	G	L	F	H%	S%	hr/f	GS	APC	DOM%	DIS%	Sv%	LI	RAR	BPV	BPX	R$
09	TEX *	7	5	0	119	82	4.85	4.47	1.41	739	795	679	22.9	3.5	6.2	1.8	7%	39	19	42	30%	68%	10%	17	93	29%	29%			-7.8	44	82	$0
10	aaa	4	2	0	56	34	4.29	5.06	1.33				21.3	1.9	5.4	2.8					30%	74%								-1.4	40	65	-$1
11	OAK	9	9	0	171	123	3.32	3.47	1.13	659	675	640	27.6	1.3	6.5	4.9	8%	47	21	32	30%	71%	6%	25	100	64%	4%			13.1	106	160	$13
12	OAK	8	6	0	111	73	3.24	4.23	1.25	706	769	636	26.1	1.9	5.9	3.0	7%	41	24	35	30%	77%	8%	18	92	39%	17%			10.6	73	95	$6
13	ARI	5	11	0	135	76	4.53	3.95	1.35	759	716	807	26.2	1.4	5.1	3.6	6%	48	25	27	33%	67%	10%	22	91	32%	18%			-11.1	79	103	-$4
1st Half		2	4	0	67	39	5.00	4.17	1.43	797	781	818	26.4	1.4	5.3	3.9	6%	43	26	31	34%	66%	10%	11	93	27%	18%			-9.3	79	102	-$8
2nd Half		3	7	0	68	37	4.08	3.72	1.27	722	638	797	26.1	1.4	4.9	3.4	6%	54	24	23	31%	69%	11%	11	90	36%	18%			-1.8	80	104	-$1
14	**Proj**	**8**	**9**	**0**	**145**	**89**	**3.99**	**3.71**	**1.29**	**730**	**728**	**732**	**25.2**	**1.7**	**5.5**	**3.3**	**7%**	**46**	**23**	**31**	**31%**	**71%**	**9%**	**24**						**-2.2**	**79**	**102**	**$4**

McDonald,James

Age: 29	Th: R	Role RP		Health	F	LIMA Plan	D+
Ht: 6' 4"	Wt: 205	Type Pwr FB		PT/Exp	B	Rand Var	+3
				Consist	B	MM	1201

2-2, 5.76 ERA in 30 IP at PIT. Struggled with velocity, then shoulder discomfort before hitting the DL in May. Triple-A rehab was even less impressive, leading to his 2H release. Ctl was his big hurdle; now it's even worse, accompanied by health questions and a Dom plunge. He should be off your radar until further notice.

Yr	Tm	W	L	Sv	IP	K	ERA	xERA	WHIP	oOPS	vL	vR	BF/G	Ctl	Dom	Cmd	SwK	G	L	F	H%	S%	hr/f	GS	APC	DOM%	DIS%	Sv%	LI	RAR	BPV	BPX	R$
09	LA *	6	5	0	93	88	3.83	3.75	1.39	725	590	815	7.7	4.5	8.5	1.9	9%	44	17	39	30%	74%	8%	4	25	0%	75%	0	0.91	5.6	74	139	$3
10	2 NL *	10	7	0	135	114	3.89	3.65	1.35	712	732	689	20.9	3.3	7.6	2.3	9%	30	23	46	32%	71%	4%	12	81	42%	17%	0	0.86	3.1	84	135	$5
11	PIT	9	9	0	171	142	4.21	4.43	1.49	780	875	716	24.3	4.1	7.5	1.8	9%	39	19	42	31%	76%	11%	31	94	39%	26%			-5.7	41	61	-$1
12	PIT	12	8	0	171	151	4.21	4.16	1.26	715	653	780	23.8	3.6	7.9	2.2	9%	39	21	39	28%	70%	11%	29	93	52%	34%	0	0.75	-4.1	62	81	$6
13	FAN *	3	6	0	55	35	6.89	5.68	1.85	768	703	826	21.4	5.7	5.7	1.0	8%	42	17	41	34%	61%	3%	6	86	33%	17%			-20.5	30	39	-$13
1st Half		3	6	0	55	35	6.89	5.68	1.85	768	703	826	21.4	5.7	5.7	1.0	8%	42	17	41	34%	61%	3%	6	86	33%	17%			-20.5	30	38	-$13
2nd Half																																	
14	**Proj**	**7**	**8**	**0**	**116**	**92**	**4.77**	**4.45**	**1.52**	**801**	**776**	**823**	**18.8**	**4.4**	**7.2**	**1.6**	**9%**	**39**	**19**	**42**	**31%**	**71%**	**9%**	**24**						**-12.9**	**27**	**35**	**-$4**

McFarland,T.J.

Age: 25	Th: L	Role RP		Health	A	LIMA Plan	D+
Ht: 6' 3"	Wt: 220	Type xGB		PT/Exp	D	Rand Var	+2
				Consist	B	MM	3100

Rule 5 pick spent MLB debut as a long man out of the pen after minor league career as an SP. Showed volatile BPIs all year... except for that GB%, which barely kept his head above water. Career 3.83 ERA, 2.2 Cmd (618 IP) in the minors hardly suggest value in the making. Barring unforeseen improvements, nothing to see here.

Yr	Tm	W	L	Sv	IP	K	ERA	xERA	WHIP	oOPS	vL	vR	BF/G	Ctl	Dom	Cmd	SwK	G	L	F	H%	S%	hr/f	GS	APC	DOM%	DIS%	Sv%	LI	RAR	BPV	BPX	R$
09																																	
10																																	
11	aa	9	9	0	137	89	4.57	4.59	1.51				23.8	3.2	5.8	1.8					33%	69%								-10.7	52	78	-$4
12	a/a	16	8	0	163	82	4.89	4.81	1.50				26.1	2.5	4.5	1.8					33%	67%								-17.5	42	55	-$7
13	BAL	4	1	0	75	58	4.22	3.85	1.49	737	761	718	8.7	3.4	7.0	2.1	9%	58	18	24	33%	73%	12%	1	32	0%	100%	0	0.81	-3.3	71	92	-$4
1st Half		1	0	0	44	40	4.50	3.75	1.50	747	781	722	10.5	3.1	8.2	2.7	10%	54	18	28	36%	71%	10%	1	38	0%	100%	0	0.65	-3.4	96	125	-$5
2nd Half		3	1	0	31	18	3.82	4.00	1.47	722	733	711	6.9	3.8	5.3	1.4	9%	64	18	19	30%	76%	17%	0	26			0	0.97	0.2	34	44	-$3
14	**Proj**	**4**	**2**	**0**	**53**	**33**	**4.43**	**3.85**	**1.42**	**706**	**727**	**688**	**7.7**	**3.1**	**5.7**	**1.8**	**9%**	**56**	**20**	**25**	**31%**	**69%**	**10%**	**0**						**-3.7**	**52**	**68**	**-$2**

McGee,Jake

Age: 27	Th: L	Role RP		Health	A	LIMA Plan	A
Ht: 6' 3"	Wt: 230	Type Pwr		PT/Exp	D	Rand Var	+2
				Consist	C	MM	5510

1st half Ctl woes were accompanied by new hr/f, H% and S% issues. All returned to health during 2nd half rebound, as xERA shows the full-year skill consistency. Even with a little less Dom and a little less success vR, it seems like he has closer caliber skills. But teams prefer to entrust 9th innings to strand rates over 80%.

Yr	Tm	W	L	Sv	IP	K	ERA	xERA	WHIP	oOPS	vL	vR	BF/G	Ctl	Dom	Cmd	SwK	G	L	F	H%	S%	hr/f	GS	APC	DOM%	DIS%	Sv%	LI	RAR	BPV	BPX	R$
09																																	
10	TAM *	4	8	1	111	113	3.52	3.22	1.31	426	697	111	12.0	3.2	9.2	2.9	10%	55	18	27	34%	72%	0%	0	10			100	0.31	7.6	112	182	$5
11	TAM *	9	4	9	61	58	3.75	4.67	1.38	801	510	1143	4.2	2.9	8.6	2.9	10%	33	18	49	33%	78%	13%	0	14			90	1.10	1.5	74	111	$5
12	TAM	5	2	0	55	73	1.95	2.49	0.80	452	665	291	3.1	1.8	11.9	6.6	14%	44	19	37	27%	78%	7%	0	13			0	1.39	14.1	187	244	$10
13	TAM	5	3	1	63	75	4.02	3.20	1.18	659	678	648	3.7	3.2	10.8	3.4	12%	43	19	39	30%	70%	13%	0	16			20	1.16	-1.2	130	169	$2
1st Half		2	2	0	32	40	4.83	3.20	1.26	655	663	650	3.7	3.7	11.4	3.1	11%	41	26	33	32%	64%	15%	0	16			0	1.15	-3.8	124	161	-$1
2nd Half		3	1	1	31	35	3.19	3.20	1.10	663	697	647	3.6	2.6	10.2	3.9	13%	44	12	45	29%	77%	11%	0	16			100	1.18	2.6	134	173	$5
14	**Proj**	**5**	**3**	**3**	**58**	**68**	**3.33**	**2.87**	**1.12**	**628**	**733**	**565**	**3.7**	**2.7**	**10.5**	**3.8**	**13%**	**43**	**18**	**39**	**30%**	**74%**	**11%**	**0**						**3.8**	**136**	**177**	**$5**

JOCK THOMPSON

Medina,Yoervis

Age: 25	Th: R	Role RP	Health A	LIMA Plan B+	
Ht: 6' 3"	Wt: 245	Type Pwr GB	PT/Exp D	Rand Var -3	
			Consist B	MM 4410	

Power stuff and GB-generating ways elevated him to a setup role in his MLB debut, and make him a viable pen commodity in the MLB game. Too many walks will impede a role upgrade and make him less valuable in ours. Minor league track record says that Ctl is a recent problem; age says he has time. But avoid until he fixes it.

Yr	Tm	W	L	Sv	IP	K	ERA	xERA	WHIP	oOPS	vL	vR	BF/G	Ctl	Dom	Cmd	SwK	G	L	F	H%	S%	hr/f	GS	APC	DOM%	DIS%	Sv%	LI	RAR	BPV	BPX	R$
09																																	
10																																	
11	aa	0	1	0	25	15	5.17	4.94	1.37				26.2	3.2	5.4	1.7					27%	67%								-3.8	19	28	-$4
12	aa	5	5	5	69	67	3.92	4.57	1.59				6.6	4.8	8.7	1.8					35%	76%								0.8	72	94	-$1
13	SEA	4	6	1	68	71	2.91	3.63	1.31	629	644	617	4.6	5.3	9.4	1.8	10%	54	19	27	27%	80%	11%	0	18			25	1.57	8.0	58	76	$3
1st Half		3	2	1	29	29	2.76	3.61	1.36	544	604	501	4.5	5.5	8.9	1.6	10%	62	16	22	29%	78%	0%	0	17			100	1.40	4.0	51	67	$3
2nd Half		1	4	0	39	42	3.03	3.64	1.27	695	664	725	4.7	5.1	9.8	1.9	11%	47	22	31	25%	82%	17%	0	19			0	1.71	4.0	63	81	$2
14	**Proj**	**4**	**5**	**3**	**65**	**66**	**3.31**	**3.58**	**1.42**	**697**	**703**	**692**	**5.2**	**5.1**	**9.1**	**1.8**	**10%**	**53**	**19**	**28**	**30%**	**78%**	**10%**	**0**						**4.5**	**58**	**75**	**$2**

Medlen,Kris

Age: 28	Th: R	Role SP	Health C	LIMA Plan C+	
Ht: 5' 10"	Wt: 190	Type	PT/Exp B	Rand Var -1	
			Consist A	MM 5305	

2013 Forecaster said "Some regression is inevitable"; the 3.17/3.42 ERA/xERA was almost dead on. The 1H H% regression and Cmd drop were tempered by a favorable S%. Best news is that his BPIs—Dom, Ctl, GB%, xERA—all took a 2H step forward almost en masse. With TJS and health issues now 2+ years away, pay up.

Yr	Tm	W	L	Sv	IP	K	ERA	xERA	WHIP	oOPS	vL	vR	BF/G	Ctl	Dom	Cmd	SwK	G	L	F	H%	S%	hr/f	GS	APC	DOM%	DIS%	Sv%	LI	RAR	BPV	BPX	R$
09	ATL *	8	5	0	105	109	3.26	2.86	1.23	731	568	894	9.5	3.5	9.3	2.7	10%	41	24	36	31%	73%	8%	4	30	25%	50%	0	0.70	13.8	108	203	$10
10	ATL	6	2	0	108	83	3.68	3.57	1.20	725	765	693	14.1	1.8	6.9	4.0	10%	43	22	35	30%	73%	12%	14	51	50%	21%	0	0.84	5.3	98	159	$6
11	ATL	0	0	0	2	2	0.00	2.87	0.43	250	0	500	4.0	0.0	7.7	0.0	4%	33	17	50	18%	0%	0%	0	12			0	3.05	1.1	150	225	-$3
12	ATL	10	1	1	138	120	1.57	2.97	0.91	529	519	539	10.4	1.5	7.8	5.2	10%	53	19	28	26%	85%	6%	12	38	92%	0%	50	0.81	41.7	131	171	$29
13	ATL	15	12	0	197	157	3.11	3.60	1.22	706	730	680	25.6	2.1	7.2	3.3	11%	45	24	31	31%	78%	10%	31	95	71%	13%	0	0.82	18.4	94	123	$16
1st Half		5	7	0	98	76	3.02	3.91	1.26	714	725	700	26.4	2.4	7.0	2.9	10%	44	22	34	30%	80%	10%	16	98	69%	19%			10.3	83	107	$13
2nd Half		10	5	0	99	81	3.19	3.30	1.19	697	734	661	24.9	1.9	7.4	3.9	13%	47	26	27	31%	75%	10%	15	92	73%	7%	0	0.85	8.2	106	137	$18
14	**Proj**	**15**	**8**	**0**	**196**	**164**	**2.83**	**3.20**	**1.14**	**659**	**659**	**659**	**25.5**	**2.0**	**7.5**	**3.7**	**11%**	**47**	**23**	**31**	**30%**	**78%**	**9%**	**30**						**25.0**	**105**	**137**	**$23**

Mejia,Jenrry

Age: 24	Th: R	Role SP	Health F	LIMA Plan C	
Ht: 6' 0"	Wt: 205	Type Pwr GB	PT/Exp D	Rand Var 0	
			Consist F	MM 4301	

TJS in 2011, forearm tendinitis in May, bone spur surgery (pitching elbow) in Aug. Has yet to throw 95 IP in a professional season. The stunner of this profile is his 2H pre-surgery effectiveness, with reduced low-90s velocity. Power stuff with big potential, but health will determine his ceiling and perhaps his role.

Yr	Tm	W	L	Sv	IP	K	ERA	xERA	WHIP	oOPS	vL	vR	BF/G	Ctl	Dom	Cmd	SwK	G	L	F	H%	S%	hr/f	GS	APC	DOM%	DIS%	Sv%	LI	RAR	BPV	BPX	R$
09	aa	0	5	0	44	44	4.81	4.16	1.52				19.2	4.2	8.9	2.1					36%	67%								-2.6	86	162	-$4
10	NYM *	2	4	0	74	53	3.01	3.66	1.40	770	590	877	7.8	4.1	6.4	1.6	8%	61	13	26	30%	79%	8%	3	22	0%	100%	0	0.79	9.8	62	100	$1
11	aaa	1	2	0	28	18	2.90	1.62	1.03				21.8	4.0	5.6	1.4					20%	71%								3.6	75	112	$0
12	NYM *	4	6	0	98	49	4.29	4.74	1.52	897	822	964	12.8	3.2	4.5	1.4	7%	67	11	22	32%	72%	17%	3	60	33%	33%	0	0.57	-3.4	34	44	-$6
13	NYM	1	2	0	27	27	2.30	2.65	1.17	641	683	609	22.4	1.3	8.9	6.8	13%	58	22	20	34%	83%	13%	5	87	80%	20%			5.3	160	209	-$1
1st Half																																	
2nd Half		1	2	0	27	27	2.30	2.65	1.17	642	683	609	22.4	1.3	8.9	6.8	13%	58	22	20	34%	83%	13%	5	87	80%	20%			5.3	160	208	-$1
14	**Proj**	**3**	**7**	**0**	**102**	**87**	**3.70**	**3.44**	**1.31**	**642**	**608**	**666**	**21.0**	**3.5**	**7.7**	**2.2**	**11%**	**53**	**21**	**26**	**30%**	**73%**	**11%**	**35**						**2.0**	**76**	**99**	**$2**

Melancon,Mark

Age: 29	Th: R	Role RP	Health A	LIMA Plan C+	
Ht: 6' 2"	Wt: 215	Type Pwr xGB	PT/Exp C	Rand Var -5	
			Consist C	MM 5321	

A career year usually demands skill and luck. He doubled both Ctl and Cmd effectiveness as Dom, GB% also spiked. Add a difficult-to-repeat S%, a next-to-perfect hr/f and voila! Injuries put him in 2H closer role, which he ran with despite rocky, H%-fueled Sept. Even with likely regression, he looks very closer-worthy again.

Yr	Tm	W	L	Sv	IP	K	ERA	xERA	WHIP	oOPS	vL	vR	BF/G	Ctl	Dom	Cmd	SwK	G	L	F	H%	S%	hr/f	GS	APC	DOM%	DIS%	Sv%	LI	RAR	BPV	BPX	R$
09	NYY *	4	1	3	69	55	4.00	2.95	1.18	665	831	511	6.2	2.9	7.1	2.4	6%	62	14	24	28%	66%	0%	0	20			60	0.60	2.8	85	159	$4
10	2 TM *	9	1	7	82	72	3.97	5.26	1.66	674	457	805	5.7	4.4	7.9	1.8	12%	46	17	37	36%	78%	9%	0	16			70	1.17	1.1	57	92	$2
11	HOU	8	4	20	74	66	2.78	3.16	1.22	631	704	581	4.4	3.1	8.0	2.5	10%	57	22	21	29%	79%	11%	0	16			80	1.12	10.6	94	141	$14
12	BOS *	0	2	12	67	62	4.59	3.82	1.21	754	875	655	4.3	2.1	8.3	4.0	10%	50	24	26	31%	64%	22%	0	18			92	0.62	-4.7	105	137	$2
13	PIT	3	2	16	71	70	1.39	2.33	0.96	511	357	638	3.9	1.0	8.9	8.8	12%	60	24	16	31%	85%	3%	0	14			76	1.31	21.6	170	222	$16
1st Half		2	1	2	40	43	0.89	2.22	0.84	481	389	557	3.8	0.9	9.6	10.8	13%	60	22	18	29%	91%	5%	0	14			67	1.36	14.8	186	241	$16
2nd Half		1	1	14	31	27	2.05	2.50	1.11	550	315	742	3.9	1.2	7.9	6.8	12%	61	27	12	34%	79%	0%	0	13			78	1.25	6.9	150	194	$17
14	**Proj**	**3**	**2**	**13**	**73**	**67**	**2.76**	**2.68**	**1.13**	**601**	**558**	**635**	**4.1**	**1.9**	**8.3**	**4.4**	**11%**	**56**	**24**	**20**	**31%**	**76%**	**9%**	**0**						**9.9**	**134**	**174**	**$11**

Mendoza,Luis

Age: 30	Th: R	Role RP	Health A	LIMA Plan D+	
Ht: 6' 3"	Wt: 245	Type GB	PT/Exp B	Rand Var +1	
			Consist B	MM 2000	

Lost his rotation spot in early July; BPI history and 5.01 ERA as SP—4.98 career—says he never should have had it in the first place. Stagnant Dom and Ctl collapsed in small sample 2H bullpen effort. GB% is the only bright spot. He seems unlikely to hold onto any role or value for too long. That 2011 looks like a huge outlier.

Yr	Tm	W	L	Sv	IP	K	ERA	xERA	WHIP	oOPS	vL	vR	BF/G	Ctl	Dom	Cmd	SwK	G	L	F	H%	S%	hr/f	GS	APC	DOM%	DIS%	Sv%	LI	RAR	BPV	BPX	R$
09	TEX *	6	7	0	112	62	6.68	6.78	2.02	1571	3500	400	20.9	4.6	5.0	1.1	0%	0	40	60	39%	65%	33%	0	22			0	0.10	-32.7	22	41	-$19
10	KC *	10	10	0	136	45	5.53	6.04	1.63	1656	1357	1796	21.6	2.4	3.0	1.2	3%	35	20	45	33%	68%	44%	0	24			0	1.13	-24.3	0	0	-$10
11	KC *	14	5	2	159	66	2.50	3.74	1.42	550	550	550	19.2	3.5	3.7	1.1	5%	44	24	31	29%	82%	0%	2	101	50%	0%			28.3	38	57	$11
12	KC	8	10	0	166	104	4.23	4.26	1.42	759	790	725	23.6	3.2	5.6	1.8	7%	52	21	27	31%	71%	11%	25	84	44%	24%	0	0.79	-4.4	45	59	-$2
13	KC	2	6	0	94	54	5.36	4.78	1.59	820	877	749	19.0	4.1	5.2	1.3	7%	50	20	30	31%	67%	11%	15	72	33%	40%	0	0.80	-17.3	10	13	-$12
1st Half		2	4	0	76	49	4.16	4.40	1.40	761	815	700	23.4	3.6	5.8	1.6	8%	48	21	31	29%	72%	11%	13	88	38%	31%	0	0.82	-2.8	35	45	-$9
2nd Half		0	2	0	18	5	10.31	6.58	2.35	1036	1074	975	11.4	6.4	2.5	0.4	5%	56	18	26	37%	54%	11%	2	44	0%	100%	0	0.77	-14.6	-95	-122	-$23
14	**Proj**	**2**	**3**	**0**	**44**	**26**	**4.52**	**4.23**	**1.50**	**779**	**823**	**723**	**16.1**	**3.5**	**5.3**	**1.5**	**7%**	**52**	**20**	**28**	**32%**	**71%**	**10%**	**7**						**-3.5**	**32**	**42**	**-$4**

Mijares,Jose

Age: 29	Th: L	Role RP	Health C	LIMA Plan C	
Ht: 5' 11"	Wt: 265	Type Pwr FB	PT/Exp D	Rand Var +3	
			Consist C	MM 3400	

Terrific 1H, as Ctl gains and fortunate S% trumped unlucky H%. Craptastic 2H caused by the disappearance of his Ctl, as S% followed suit and H% turned disastrous. He confirmed the 2012 Dom spike, but RHBs strafed him all season. It's volatile picture at best. It's also why he's in the pen—and why you should stay away.

Yr	Tm	W	L	Sv	IP	K	ERA	xERA	WHIP	oOPS	vL	vR	BF/G	Ctl	Dom	Cmd	SwK	G	L	F	H%	S%	hr/f	GS	APC	DOM%	DIS%	Sv%	LI	RAR	BPV	BPX	R$
09	MIN	2	2	0	62	55	2.34	4.17	1.18	649	480	791	3.6	3.4	8.0	2.4	9%	38	12	51	27%	86%	8%	0	14			0	1.25	15.1	70	131	$5
10	MIN	1	1	0	33	28	3.31	4.30	1.32	768	776	761	3.0	2.5	7.7	3.1	9%	31	14	55	32%	79%	7%	0	13			0	1.21	3.1	81	131	-$1
11	MIN	0	2	0	49	30	4.59	5.81	1.69	797	698	874	3.9	5.5	5.5	1.0	6%	31	22	47	31%	73%	5%	0	16			0	1.14	-3.9	-41	-61	-$7
12	2 TM	3	2	0	56	57	2.56	3.94	1.26	672	586	789	3.1	3.4	9.1	2.7	9%	35	26	39	32%	81%	5%	0	12			0	0.87	10.1	86	113	$3
13	SF	0	3	0	49	54	4.22	4.17	1.78	847	710	966	3.9	3.7	9.9	2.7	10%	35	27	39	43%	76%	5%	0	14			0	0.91	-2.2	92	120	-$7
1st Half		0	1	0	28	26	2.60	4.20	1.52	789	561	950	4.3	2.6	8.5	3.3	11%	35	23	42	37%	87%	8%	0	15			0	0.71	4.3	95	123	-$4
2nd Half		0	2	0	21	28	6.33	4.11	2.11	915	851	988	3.6	5.1	11.8	2.3	9%	34	32	34	51%	67%	0%	0	14			0	1.12	-6.5	88	114	-$12
14	**Proj**	**1**	**3**	**0**	**58**	**59**	**4.03**	**3.79**	**1.35**	**693**	**591**	**794**	**3.2**	**4.0**	**9.1**	**2.3**	**9%**	**33**	**24**	**43**	**31%**	**72%**	**8%**	**0**						**-1.2**	**67**	**87**	**-$2**

Miley,Wade

Age: 27	Th: L	Role SP	Health A	LIMA Plan B	
Ht: 6' 0"	Wt: 220	Type	PT/Exp A	Rand Var 0	
			Consist A	MM 3205	

A mixed bag. 1H Ctl, hr/f spikes wrecked encore until 2H H%/S% luck salvaged season. PRO: Confirmed Dom gains, displayed GB mastery, held both all season. CON: Exquisite 2012 Ctl looks flukish; ditto the Cmd. Strengths make for a decent floor and a serviceable SP. But with a limited ceiling and volatile / win-reliant R$.

Yr	Tm	W	L	Sv	IP	K	ERA	xERA	WHIP	oOPS	vL	vR	BF/G	Ctl	Dom	Cmd	SwK	G	L	F	H%	S%	hr/f	GS	APC	DOM%	DIS%	Sv%	LI	RAR	BPV	BPX	R$
09																																	
10	aa	5	2	0	73	51	2.72	4.26	1.43				23.8	3.7	6.3	1.7					31%	84%								12.2	52	84	$3
11	ARI *	12	5	0	170	107	4.42	4.47	1.44	873	808	885	24.1	3.1	5.7	1.8	9%	46	24	30	31%	70%	15%	7	82	43%	29%	0	0.73	-9.9	47	71	-$1
12	ARI	16	11	0	195	144	3.33	3.89	1.18	685	544	723	25.2	1.7	6.7	3.9	9%	43	23	34	31%	73%	7%	29	94	59%	14%	0	0.82	16.5	95	123	$17
13	ARI	10	10	0	203	147	3.55	3.79	1.32	727	704	732	25.7	2.9	6.5	2.2	8%	52	21	27	30%	76%	13%	33	98	52%	18%			7.8	68	89	$7
1st Half		4	7	0	95	69	4.55	3.93	1.43	797	800	796	25.4	3.0	6.5	2.2	8%	52	19	29	31%	72%	15%	16	95	56%	25%			-8.0	66	85	-$3
2nd Half		6	3	0	108	78	2.67	3.66	1.22	662	586	678	25.9	2.8	6.5	2.3	9%	52	22	26	28%	80%	10%	17	101	47%	12%			15.8	71	91	$15
14	**Proj**	**12**	**9**	**0**	**189**	**134**	**3.62**	**3.70**	**1.30**	**719**	**639**	**738**	**24.8**	**2.7**	**6.4**	**2.4**	**9%**	**48**	**22**	**30**	**30%**	**74%**	**10%**	**31**						**5.7**	**68**	**88**	**$9**

JOCK THOMPSON

Miller,Andrew

Age: 29	Th: L	Role RP	Health F	LIMA Plan C	
Ht: 6' 7"	Wt: 210	Type Pwr	PT/Exp D	Rand Var +2	
			Consist C	MM 4500	

The "finally found his place" stories are nice, but a huge Dom and GB% covered up a recurring thesis: gobs and gobs of walks. Foot surgery wiped out his second half, and though he's likely to be ready by spring, that Ctl trend isn't improving. Too many possible negative outcomes.

Yr Tm	W	L	Sv	IP	K	ERA	xERA	WHIP	oOPS	vL	vR	BF/G	Ctl	Dom	Cmd	SwK	G	L	F	H%	S%	hr/f	GS	APC	DOM%	DIS%	Sv%	LI	RAR	BPV	BPX	R
09 FLA *	4	7	0	98	77	5.26	4.70	1.65	792	865	765	18.2	5.5	7.1	1.3	7%	48	22	30	32%	68%	9%	14	69	29%	36%	0	0.64	-11.3	52	97	-$
10 FLA *	2	13	0	118	85	7.95	7.59	2.24	1054	1262	975	22.1	7.2	6.5	0.9	6%	38	28	34	39%	64%	16%	7	72	0%	71%	0	0.60	-56.4	16	26	-$3
11 BOS *	9	6	0	131	98	4.52	4.59	1.62	857	812	874	19.3	5.5	6.7	1.2	8%	45	23	31	31%	72%	12%	12	72	17%	42%	0	0.61	-9.4	47	71	-$
12 BOS	3	2	0	40	51	3.35	3.32	1.19	588	429	829	3.2	4.5	11.4	2.6	10%	43	23	34	28%	73%	9%	0	13			0	1.17	3.3	105	137	$
13 BOS	1	2	0	31	48	2.64	2.47	1.37	624	725	526	3.6	5.0	14.1	2.8	14%	56	21	23	36%	85%	20%	0	15			0	0.81	4.6	153	199	-$
1st Half	1	2	0	31	48	2.64	2.46	1.34	613	703	526	3.7	5.0	14.1	2.8	13%	55	22	23	35%	84%	20%		15	0%	0%			4.6	152	197	-$
2nd Half	0	0	0	0	0	0.00	0.00	0.00				1.0	0.0	0.0	0.0					0%	0%	0%			0%	0%			0.0	78	101	-$
14 Proj	**3**	**4**	**0**	**56**	**61**	**4.15**	**3.52**	**1.46**	**687**	**648**	**712**	**5.8**	**4.9**	**9.9**	**2.0**	**10%**	**47**	**23**	**30**	**32%**	**73%**	**11%**	**0**						**-2.0**	**70**	**91**	**-$**

Miller,Shelby

Age: 23	Th: R	Role SP	Health A	LIMA Plan C	
Ht: 6' 3"	Wt: 215	Type Pwr FB	PT/Exp C	Rand Var -2	
			Consist D	MM 4405	

Ho-hum—another stud rookie Cardinals pitcher. An in-season look, though, reveals some cracks (Ctl almost doubled and Dom/Cmd dove in 2H, Sept BPV was -6) that make STL's no-October policy less perplexing. With his pre-2H skills, he's still a horse long-term, but consistency will need to precede stardom.

Yr Tm	W	L	Sv	IP	K	ERA	xERA	WHIP	oOPS	vL	vR	BF/G	Ctl	Dom	Cmd	SwK	G	L	F	H%	S%	hr/f	GS	APC	DOM%	DIS%	Sv%	LI	RAR	BPV	BPX	R
09																																
10																																
11 aa	9	3	0	87	77	2.27	2.19	1.12				21.3	3.0	8.0	2.7					29%	79%								17.9	112	168	$1
12 STL *	12	10	0	150	153	4.58	4.54	1.37	463	485	445	19.1	3.1	9.1	3.0	13%	42	15	42	33%	70%	0%	1	33	100%	0%	0	0.88	-10.5	81	106	$
13 STL	15	9	0	173	169	3.06	3.73	1.21	670	761	588	23.3	3.0	8.8	3.0	10%	38	20	41	29%	79%	10%	31	96	55%	13%			17.2	94	123	$1
1st Half	8	6	0	94	101	2.79	3.22	1.07	616	661	569	23.4	2.1	9.7	4.6	10%	37	21	42	30%	77%	8%	16	98	63%	6%			12.5	133	172	$2
2nd Half	7	3	0	80	68	3.39	4.38	1.37	732	894	607	23.1	4.0	7.7	1.9	10%	40	19	41	28%	81%	13%	15	93	47%	20%			4.7	49	64	$
14 Proj	**16**	**10**	**0**	**189**	**181**	**3.53**	**3.56**	**1.27**	**692**	**799**	**599**	**21.0**	**3.1**	**8.7**	**2.8**	**10%**	**39**	**20**	**41**	**30%**	**76%**	**10%**	**37**						**7.8**	**88**	**115**	**$1**

Milone,Tommy

Age: 27	Th: L	Role SP	Health A	LIMA Plan B+	
Ht: 6' 0"	Wt: 205	Type FB	PT/Exp B	Rand Var 0	
			Consist A	MM 3203	

As none of his pitches top 90 mph, he relies on location and pitch mix. ERA indicates he took a step back, though BPV barely moved and 2013 ERA matched 2012 xERA. Lots can go wrong with all those FB and LD. Without much upside, continue to expect replacement-level performance.

Yr Tm	W	L	Sv	IP	K	ERA	xERA	WHIP	oOPS	vL	vR	BF/G	Ctl	Dom	Cmd	SwK	G	L	F	H%	S%	hr/f	GS	APC	DOM%	DIS%	Sv%	LI	RAR	BPV	BPX	R
09																																
10 aa	12	5	0	158	129	3.65	4.42	1.36				24.5	1.3	7.3	5.5					36%	74%								8.3	135	218	$
11 WAS *	13	6	0	174	140	3.84	3.57	1.18	742	1164	695	24.1	1.0	7.2	7.2	8%	31	20	49	33%	68%	5%	5	82	20%	40%			2.1	176	264	$1
12 OAK	13	10	0	190	137	3.74	4.10	1.28	738	749	734	25.5	1.7	6.5	3.8	9%	38	25	37	31%	75%	11%	31	98	52%	16%			6.4	87	113	$
13 OAK	12	9	0	156	126	4.14	4.22	1.27	738	790	724	23.8	2.2	7.3	3.2	9%	35	20	45	30%	73%	11%	26	93	46%	23%	0	0.75	-5.4	83	108	$
1st Half	7	7	0	106	81	4.17	4.39	1.26	753	789	743	26.4	2.2	6.9	3.1	9%	33	18	48	29%	74%	12%	17	102	47%	18%			-4.0	76	98	$
2nd Half	5	2	0	51	45	4.09	3.84	1.30	709	791	681	19.8	2.3	8.0	3.5	10%	39	24	37	32%	72%	10%	9	78	44%	33%	0	0.65	-1.4	99	128	$
14 Proj	**13**	**8**	**0**	**174**	**140**	**3.93**	**3.71**	**1.28**	**716**	**757**	**703**	**22.8**	**2.1**	**7.2**	**3.4**	**9%**	**36**	**23**	**41**	**31%**	**73%**	**10%**	**31**						**-1.4**	**88**	**114**	**$**

Minor,Mike

Age: 26	Th: L	Role SP	Health A	LIMA Plan C	
Ht: 6' 4"	Wt: 205	Type Pwr FB	PT/Exp A	Rand Var -1	
			Consist A	MM 4305	

He built on 2012's 93-BPV second half and zoomed into near-elite status. Ctl and Dom each took steps up, he broke the 200-IP barrier for the first time, and reined in the HR without the benefit of a lucky hr/f. Confidence in four pitches and perfect reliability make him a low-risk, high-reward investment.

Yr Tm	W	L	Sv	IP	K	ERA	xERA	WHIP	oOPS	vL	vR	BF/G	Ctl	Dom	Cmd	SwK	G	L	F	H%	S%	hr/f	GS	APC	DOM%	DIS%	Sv%	LI	RAR	BPV	BPX	R
09																																
10 ATL *	9	9	0	161	169	4.55	3.97	1.34	880	795	907	22.3	3.2	9.4	2.9	12%	35	17	48	33%	67%	10%	8	85	50%	25%	0	0.71	-9.3	96	155	$
11 ATL *	9	8	0	183	162	3.99	4.60	1.42	785	835	774	25.1	2.9	7.9	2.8	9%	37	27	35	34%	75%	10%	15	92	27%	20%			-1.1	75	113	$
12 ATL	11	10	0	179	145	4.12	4.18	1.15	702	724	694	24.3	2.8	7.3	2.6	8%	35	21	44	26%	69%	12%	30	95	50%	17%			-2.2	68	89	$1
13 ATL	13	9	0	205	181	3.21	3.68	1.09	657	583	680	25.6	2.0	8.0	3.9	10%	35	22	43	28%	75%	9%	32	98	75%	3%			16.6	102	132	$2
1st Half	8	3	0	103	95	2.98	3.55	1.05	672	539	715	25.5	1.8	8.3	4.8	11%	36	20	45	28%	78%	10%	16	99	81%	0%			11.2	116	150	$2
2nd Half	5	6	0	102	86	3.44	3.82	1.13	642	631	645	25.8	2.3	7.6	3.3	9%	34	25	41	28%	72%	7%	16	97	69%	6%			5.3	87	113	$1
14 Proj	**15**	**8**	**0**	**196**	**172**	**3.71**	**3.57**	**1.18**	**692**	**661**	**702**	**24.4**	**2.5**	**7.9**	**3.2**	**10%**	**35**	**22**	**42**	**29%**	**72%**	**9%**	**32**						**3.9**	**88**	**115**	**$1**

Moore,Matt

Age: 25	Th: L	Role SP	Health C	LIMA Plan C+	
Ht: 6' 3"	Wt: 210	Type Pwr FB	PT/Exp B	Rand Var -2	
			Consist C	MM 3403	

Missed August with a sore elbow, and Sept was a disaster once you get past the 2.79 ERA (1.4 Cmd, 5.07 xERA, 9 BPV). Inconsistency was a problem despite those 17 wins; still walks too many and recent xERA is decidedly mediocre. Has the skills, but let's be frank: he's still in the adjustment phase.

Yr Tm	W	L	Sv	IP	K	ERA	xERA	WHIP	oOPS	vL	vR	BF/G	Ctl	Dom	Cmd	SwK	G	L	F	H%	S%	hr/f	GS	APC	DOM%	DIS%	Sv%	LI	RAR	BPV	BPX	R
09																																
10																																
11 TAM *	13	3	0	164	200	2.05	2.05	0.98	651	697	633	20.8	2.5	11.0	4.4	16%	43	19	38	29%	83%	13%	1	56	100%	0%	0	0.79	38.3	155	233	$2
12 TAM	11	11	0	177	175	3.81	4.24	1.35	706	685	712	24.5	4.1	8.9	2.2	12%	37	20	43	30%	74%	9%	31	98	45%	23%			4.6	64	83	$
13 TAM	17	4	0	150	143	3.29	4.23	1.30	655	617	672	23.8	4.5	8.6	1.9	10%	39	18	42	27%	77%	8%	27	97	41%	22%			10.6	48	63	$1
1st Half	10	3	0	87	83	3.95	4.45	1.40	705	689	712	23.8	5.0	8.6	1.7	10%	37	20	43	29%	73%	8%	16	97	44%	25%			-0.9	36	46	$
2nd Half	7	1	0	64	60	2.40	3.93	1.16	586	510	618	23.8	4.0	8.5	2.1	10%	43	15	42	25%	84%	8%	11	97	36%	18%			11.5	66	86	$1
14 Proj	**12**	**7**	**0**	**174**	**170**	**3.92**	**3.86**	**1.33**	**676**	**634**	**692**	**23.4**	**4.3**	**8.8**	**2.0**	**11%**	**38**	**18**	**44**	**29%**	**72%**	**8%**	**31**						**-1.2**	**59**	**76**	**$**

Morales,Franklin

Age: 28	Th: L	Role RP	Health F	LIMA Plan D+	
Ht: 6' 1"	Wt: 210	Type Pwr xFB	PT/Exp D	Rand Var 0	
			Consist A	MM 2300	

Posted his best skills in 2012, but a late-season shoulder injury bled into 2013, leaving additional health issues in its wake (back, chest, shoulder again). Last six weeks were impressive (his 2H line), but it was a tiny sample. Young enough to rebound, but only draftable if he proves he can stay off the DL.

Yr Tm	W	L	Sv	IP	K	ERA	xERA	WHIP	oOPS	vL	vR	BF/G	Ctl	Dom	Cmd	SwK	G	L	F	H%	S%	hr/f	GS	APC	DOM%	DIS%	Sv%	LI	RAR	BPV	BPX	R
09 COL *	5	4	7	81	70	4.17	4.44	1.50	701	593	738	7.3	4.5	7.8	1.7	9%	27	23	50	31%	74%	7%	2	18	50%	50%	88	1.55	1.6	58	109	$
10 COL *	3	4	4	59	53	4.49	4.48	1.55	823	652	900	4.4	6.3	8.2	1.3	7%	39	14	47	27%	74%	13%	0	16			44	0.91	-3.0	47	77	-$
11 2 TM	1	2	0	46	42	3.69	4.22	1.27	757	789	725	3.9	3.7	8.2	2.2	10%	30	16	54	28%	75%	9%	0	15			0	0.94	1.4	55	83	-$
12 BOS	3	4	1	76	76	3.77	3.98	1.23	685	490	788	8.8	3.5	9.0	2.5	11%	40	19	41	28%	75%	13%	9	36	44%	33%	100	1.14	2.3	84	109	$
13 BOS *	3	3	0	45	36	4.53	4.34	1.43	737	446	925	6.8	4.1	7.2	1.7	10%	39	24	38	29%	71%	7%	1	22	0%	0%	0	1.12	-3.7	50	65	-$
1st Half	3	1	0	26	20	6.20	6.30	1.71	893	494	1069	11.9	5.0	6.9	1.4	10%	38	30	32	32%	68%	17%	1	39	0%	0%	0	0.99	-7.6	10	14	-$
2nd Half	0	2	0	18	15	2.14	1.51	1.01	573	414	718	3.9	2.9	7.6	2.6	11%	40	17	43	26%	77%	0%	0	15			0	1.17	3.9	115	149	$
14 Proj	**2**	**4**	**0**	**58**	**50**	**4.06**	**4.18**	**1.36**	**716**	**633**	**761**	**5.7**	**3.9**	**7.8**	**2.0**	**10%**	**32**	**20**	**48**	**30%**	**73%**	**8%**	**0**						**-1.4**	**46**	**60**	**-$**

Morris,Bryan

Age: 27	Th: R	Role RP	Health A	LIMA Plan B	
Ht: 6' 3"	Wt: 225	Type GB	PT/Exp D	Rand Var -1	
			Consist A	MM 2001	

Spent the first two months on the AAA/PIT seesaw, but then settled into middle relief role. Lots of grounders is the allure, but inconsistent Ctl and poor Dom led to second-half slide. 2012's success was mostly in the minors; no one will blame you if you pick up your ball and head home.

Yr Tm	W	L	Sv	IP	K	ERA	xERA	WHIP	oOPS	vL	vR	BF/G	Ctl	Dom	Cmd	SwK	G	L	F	H%	S%	hr/f	GS	APC	DOM%	DIS%	Sv%	LI	RAR	BPV	BPX	R
09																																
10 aa	6	4	0	89	68	5.00	4.66	1.45				20.0	3.1	6.8	2.2					33%	66%								-10.1	59	95	-$
11 aa	3	4	3	78	50	4.07	4.04	1.50				9.6	3.8	5.8	1.5					33%	71%								-1.2	59	89	-$
12 PIT *	2	2	5	86	67	3.28	4.18	1.31	375	125	533	7.0	2.0	7.0	3.5	20%	73	0	27	33%	78%	0%	0	15			83	0.16	7.8	89	116	$
13 PIT	5	7	0	65	37	3.46	4.18	1.31	705	745	674	4.9	3.9	5.1	1.3	12%	58	18	25	25%	78%	16%	0	17			0	1.18	3.2	23	29	$
1st Half	4	2	0	35	23	2.83	3.69	1.00	597	722	501	5.9	4.1	5.9	1.4	12%	65	8	28	16%	80%	19%	0	21			0	0.91	4.5	38	49	$
2nd Half	1	5	0	30	14	4.20	4.73	1.67	814	766	849	4.2	3.6	4.2	1.2	12%	51	26	22	33%	77%	13%	0	15			0	1.36	-1.2	8	10	-$
14 Proj	**4**	**6**	**0**	**73**	**43**	**4.36**	**4.17**	**1.44**	**744**	**760**	**731**	**6.2**	**3.6**	**5.4**	**1.5**	**12%**	**54**	**19**	**28**	**30%**	**71%**	**11%**	**0**						**-4.4**	**30**	**39**	**-$**

BRENT HERSHEY

Morrow,Brandon

Morrow,Brandon	Health	F	LIMA Plan	C
Age: 29 Th: R Role SP	PT/Exp	B	Rand Var	+3
Ht: 6' 3" Wt: 200 Type Pwr FB	Consist	B	MM	3403

An entrapped radial nerve in his right forearm cut loose two-thirds of his season and put an end to 2013's misery. Trouble with strand rate has haunted most of his recent seasons, and now a steep Dom dive and injury questions are piling on. Seems he'll be ready for spring, but durability is a question mark.

Yr	Tm	W	L	Sv	IP	K	ERA	xERA	WHIP	oOPS	vL	vR	BF/G	Ctl	Dom	Cmd	SwK	G	L	F	H%	S%	hr/f	GS	APC	DOM%	DIS%	Sv%	LI	RAR	BPV	BPX	R$
09	SEA *	7	7	6	125	97	4.19	4.39	1.52	755	854	628	15.0	4.9	7.0	1.4	10%	37	20	43	30%	74%	11%	10	48	20%	40%	75	0.95	2.1	50	94	$3
10	TOR	10	7	0	146	178	4.49	3.44	1.38	725	739	704	24.2	4.1	10.9	2.7	11%	40	18	42	35%	68%	7%	26	97	58%	23%			-7.4	105	171	$4
11	TOR	11	11	0	179	203	4.72	3.55	1.29	705	641	790	25.9	3.5	10.2	2.9	12%	36	22	42	32%	65%	10%	30	104	67%	23%			-17.1	104	156	$4
12	TOR	10	7	0	125	108	2.96	3.94	1.11	635	561	724	24.0	3.0	7.8	2.6	9%	41	19	40	26%	77%	9%	21	94	48%	29%			16.2	79	104	$14
13	TOR	2	3	0	54	42	5.63	4.58	1.49	880	1014	706	24.2	3.0	7.0	2.3	9%	37	20	43	31%	68%	16%	10	91	30%	30%			-11.8	60	78	-$7
1st Half		2	3	0	54	42	5.63	4.58	1.49	880	1014	706	24.2	3.0	7.0	2.3	9%	37	20	43	31%	68%	16%	10	91	30%	30%			-11.8	60	77	-$7
2nd Half																																	
14	Proj	8	8	0	139	132	3.91	3.74	1.35	751	775	720	24.4	3.4	8.5	2.5	10%	38	20	42	31%	75%	11%	26						-0.7	77	100	$4

Morton,Charlie

Morton,Charlie	Health	D	LIMA Plan	B+
Age: 30 Th: R Role SP	PT/Exp	C	Rand Var	0
Ht: 6' 5" Wt: 235 Type xGB	Consist	B	MM	3105

7-4, 3.26 ERA in 116 IP at PIT. A Tommy John success story, as his 2H was impressive (see DOM/DIS). He'll need to prove his 2H Dom bump is for real, and even then his Cmd may be a little short. But as long as those grounders are converted into outs at an efficient pace, he deserves to be considered again.

Yr	Tm	W	L	Sv	IP	K	ERA	xERA	WHIP	oOPS	vL	vR	BF/G	Ctl	Dom	Cmd	SwK	G	L	F	H%	S%	hr/f	GS	APC	DOM%	DIS%	Sv%	LI	RAR	BPV	BPX	R$
09	PIT *	12	11	0	169	109	3.86	3.81	1.36	761	923	594	24.3	3.1	5.8	1.9	8%	49	18	33	30%	72%	7%	18	89	39%	28%			9.5	60	112	$9
10	PIT *	6	16	0	160	98	6.08	6.08	1.68	908	936	887	23.2	3.2	5.5	1.7	8%	47	24	29	35%	65%	18%	17	84	41%	41%			-39.4	25	40	-$16
11	PIT	10	10	0	172	110	3.83	4.02	1.53	737	960	567	26.5	4.0	5.8	1.4	8%	59	23	19	32%	74%	6%	29	94	31%	24%			2.4	32	48	-$1
12	PIT	2	6	0	50	25	4.65	4.25	1.45	812	740	886	24.8	2.0	4.5	2.3	7%	57	21	23	33%	69%	13%	9	88	33%	22%			-3.9	61	80	-$6
13	PIT *	8	6	0	154	101	3.45	3.45	1.30	683	848	550	22.6	3.1	5.9	1.9	9%	63	18	19	29%	74%	9%	20	86	50%	15%			7.9	64	83	$5
1st Half		2	3	0	56	28	3.54	3.28	1.31	580	692	488	19.1	3.8	4.5	1.2	8%	66	14	21	26%	73%	0%	4	67	0%	25%			2.2	44	58	$0
2nd Half		6	3	0	98	73	3.40	3.26	1.30	703	875	562	25.7	2.8	6.7	2.4	9%	62	19	18	31%	74%	11%	16	90	63%	13%			5.7	87	112	$8
14	Proj	11	11	0	189	114	3.96	3.72	1.39	730	827	647	23.3	3.0	5.5	1.8	8%	60	19	21	31%	72%	10%	34						-2.3	55	72	$3

Motte,Jason

Motte,Jason	Health	F	LIMA Plan	A
Age: 32 Th: R Role RP	PT/Exp	C	Rand Var	0
Ht: 6' 0" Wt: 205 Type Pwr FB	Consist	A	MM	5510

Tommy John surgery in May makes Opening Day 2014 a possibility but not a certainty. Had made important, consistent steps in Cmd and SwK before the injury, but will return into an entirely different context. Despite history of success, still likely only to be an end-game flyer due to the wide range of unknowns.

Yr	Tm	W	L	Sv	IP	K	ERA	xERA	WHIP	oOPS	vL	vR	BF/G	Ctl	Dom	Cmd	SwK	G	L	F	H%	S%	hr/f	GS	APC	DOM%	DIS%	Sv%	LI	RAR	BPV	BPX	R$
09	STL	4	4	0	57	54	4.76	4.17	1.41	804	987	686	3.5	3.7	8.6	2.3	9%	38	17	45	31%	71%	14%	0	14			0	0.96	-3.1	72	134	-$1
10	STL	4	2	2	52	54	2.24	3.50	1.13	618	789	531	3.7	3.1	9.3	3.0	12%	40	13	47	28%	85%	8%	0	15			67	1.20	11.9	102	164	$6
11	STL	5	2	9	68	63	2.25	3.21	0.96	558	738	454	3.4	2.1	8.3	3.9	12%	44	18	39	27%	76%	3%	0	14			69	1.35	14.2	115	173	$12
12	STL	4	5	42	72	86	2.75	2.91	0.92	576	381	756	4.2	2.1	10.8	5.1	14%	41	20	40	25%	77%	13%	0	17			86	1.43	11.2	155	202	$27
13																																	
1st Half																																	
2nd Half																																	
14	Proj	3	2	5	44	46	3.39	3.17	1.12	648	690	621	3.7	2.7	9.4	3.5	12%	41	17	43	29%	73%	9%	0						2.5	116	150	$4

Mujica,Edward

Mujica,Edward	Health	A	LIMA Plan	C+
Age: 30 Th: R Role RP	PT/Exp	C	Rand Var	-2
Ht: 6' 3" Wt: 225 Type Con	Consist	A	MM	4230

Composite of a first-time closer looks great on the surface, but move the split date to Aug 1. Before: 45 IP, 38:2 K:BB, 30 Sv. After: 20 IP, 8:3 K:BB, 7 Sv. Fatigue and then shoulder problems reported in mid-August, though workload in line with history. May get a saves shot somewhere, but far from a sure thing.

Yr	Tm	W	L	Sv	IP	K	ERA	xERA	WHIP	oOPS	vL	vR	BF/G	Ctl	Dom	Cmd	SwK	G	L	F	H%	S%	hr/f	GS	APC	DOM%	DIS%	Sv%	LI	RAR	BPV	BPX	R$
09	SD	3	5	2	94	76	3.94	4.01	1.28	748	815	685	5.9	1.8	7.3	4.0	10%	39	17	44	32%	75%	11%	4	22	0%	75%	67	0.84	4.4	99	186	$4
10	SD	2	1	0	70	72	3.62	2.86	0.93	684	625	727	4.5	0.8	9.3	12.0	14%	45	13	42	27%	73%	18%	0	17			0	0.66	4.0	169	274	$6
11	FLA	9	6	0	76	63	2.96	3.16	1.03	638	570	700	4.4	1.7	7.5	4.5	11%	48	18	34	27%	75%	10%	0	17			0	1.12	9.2	116	174	$9
12	2 NL	0	3	2	65	47	3.03	3.62	1.04	643	669	620	3.7	1.7	6.5	3.9	11%	51	16	33	26%	75%	11%	0	13			25	1.21	7.9	101	132	$4
13	STL	2	1	37	65	46	2.78	3.52	1.01	674	659	687	3.9	0.7	6.4	9.2	13%	45	16	39	27%	80%	12%	0	14			90	1.29	8.6	119	156	$19
1st Half		0	0	21	33	28	2.20	3.09	0.73	512	408	606	3.8	0.6	7.7	14.0	13%	43	15	42	22%	80%	11%	0	13			100	1.48	6.7	145	188	$24
2nd Half		2	1	16	32	18	3.38	4.00	1.28	825	911	756	4.1	0.8	5.1	6.0	13%	47	17	36	31%	81%	13%	0	15			80	1.10	1.9	94	121	$13
14	Proj	3	2	25	65	48	3.03	3.26	1.06	682	681	682	3.9	1.2	6.6	5.7	12%	47	16	37	28%	78%	12%	0						6.7	113	147	$14

Nathan,Joe

Nathan,Joe	Health	B	LIMA Plan	C
Age: 39 Th: R Role RP	PT/Exp	B	Rand Var	-5
Ht: 6' 4" Wt: 230 Type Pwr FB	Consist	B	MM	5530

Sparkling Ctl from 2012 proved unrepeatable, but just about every other BPI hung tight. So when the luck gods smiled (H%/S%/hr/f), the results were fantastic. SwK says he still has the gas even at 38, but if he lands in a bandbox, be aware of the risk of mid-40s FB% and hr/f regression. Should still be money, though.

Yr	Tm	W	L	Sv	IP	K	ERA	xERA	WHIP	oOPS	vL	vR	BF/G	Ctl	Dom	Cmd	SwK	G	L	F	H%	S%	hr/f	GS	APC	DOM%	DIS%	Sv%	LI	RAR	BPV	BPX	R$
09	MIN	2	2	47	69	89	2.10	2.95	0.93	549	548	551	3.9	2.9	11.7	4.0	15%	41	12	47	25%	84%	10%	0	16			90	1.14	18.8	151	283	$30
10																																	
11	MIN	2	1	14	45	43	4.84	3.88	1.16	705	620	791	4.0	2.8	8.7	3.1	9%	35	18	47	27%	62%	11%	0	17			82	1.14	-4.9	93	140	$4
12	TEX	3	5	37	64	78	2.80	2.76	1.06	631	617	650	3.9	1.8	10.9	6.0	13%	45	21	33	32%	79%	13%	0	16			93	1.10	9.7	170	222	$21
13	TEX	6	2	43	65	73	1.39	3.25	0.90	464	515	407	3.7	3.1	10.2	3.3	12%	32	23	45	24%	86%	3%	0	15			93	1.43	19.7	110	144	$29
1st Half		1	0	27	36	35	1.51	3.49	0.81	464	543	382	3.6	2.5	8.8	3.5	12%	27	24	49	21%	85%	5%	0	14			96	1.39	10.3	96	124	$33
2nd Half		5	2	16	29	38	1.24	2.93	1.00	465	484	440	3.8	3.7	11.8	3.2	12%	39	23	39	28%	86%	0%	0	16			89	1.47	9.4	128	166	$24
14	Proj	5	3	35	65	76	3.00	3.06	1.10	632	638	625	3.8	2.9	10.5	3.6	12%	34	22	44	29%	77%	10%	0						7.0	122	158	$20

Nelson,Jimmy

Nelson,Jimmy	Health	A	LIMA Plan	D
Age: 25 Th: R Role SP	PT/Exp	D	Rand Var	-3
Ht: 6' 5" Wt: 245 Type Pwr	Consist	A	MM	1300

0-0, 0.90 ERA in 10 IP at MIL. With a good fastball/slider combination, he started the season in Double-A and ended it in the majors. Strikeouts have been plentiful at each stop, but a high-effort delivery has led to control problems and lots of baserunners at every level. Best watched from afar for now.

Yr	Tm	W	L	Sv	IP	K	ERA	xERA	WHIP	oOPS	vL	vR	BF/G	Ctl	Dom	Cmd	SwK	G	L	F	H%	S%	hr/f	GS	APC	DOM%	DIS%	Sv%	LI	RAR	BPV	BPX	R$
09																																	
10																																	
11																																	
12	aa	2	4	0	46	37	4.88	4.28	1.72				20.9	7.6	7.2	0.9					29%	71%								-4.9	55	72	-$8
13	MIL *	10	10	0	162	147	3.74	3.87	1.45	286	473	63	22.3	4.1	8.2	2.0	11%	42	33	25	33%	74%	0%	1	36	0%	0%	0	0.28	2.5	79	103	$2
1st Half		5	6	0	89	78	3.29	4.14	1.42				23.7	3.2	7.8	2.5					34%	78%	0%	0						6.4	80	103	$5
2nd Half		5	4	0	73	69	4.29	3.54	1.48	286	473	63	20.9	5.1	8.6	1.7	11%	42	33	25	32%	69%	0%	1	36	0%	0%	0	0.28	-3.9	83	108	-$2
14	Proj	2	3	0	44	38	4.50	4.54	1.56				21.5	5.7	7.8	1.4	10%	41	21	38	31%	71%	5%	9						-3.4	7	9	-$4

Nicasio,Juan

Nicasio,Juan	Health	F	LIMA Plan	C
Age: 27 Th: R Role SP	PT/Exp	C	Rand Var	+1
Ht: 6' 3" Wt: 230 Type Pwr	Consist	A	MM	3303

Finally put together a full season, but the results were less than expected. Strikeouts were down, especially in 1H, and Cmd never passed the 2.0 mark. Continued GB bent, unfortunate S%, and 2H Dom tick provide some hope, though at 27 the first step is simply replacement level. End-gamer, but not worth reaching for.

Yr	Tm	W	L	Sv	IP	K	ERA	xERA	WHIP	oOPS	vL	vR	BF/G	Ctl	Dom	Cmd	SwK	G	L	F	H%	S%	hr/f	GS	APC	DOM%	DIS%	Sv%	LI	RAR	BPV	BPX	R$
09																																	
10																																	
11	COL *	9	5	0	128	106	3.53	3.75	1.24	735	859	595	23.7	2.0	7.4	3.7	9%	46	22	32	32%	74%	11%	13	89	38%	23%			6.5	100	151	$7
12	COL	2	3	0	58	54	5.28	4.19	1.62	861	902	825	23.4	3.4	8.4	2.5	8%	40	25	36	37%	69%	11%	11	93	45%	27%			-9.0	77	100	-$8
13	COL	9	9	0	158	119	5.14	4.41	1.47	785	737	827	22.7	3.7	6.8	1.9	8%	45	21	34	32%	66%	10%	31	92	29%	26%			-24.7	47	61	-$9
1st Half		4	4	0	81	56	5.31	4.45	1.46	785	737	830	22.8	3.3	6.2	1.9	7%	48	20	32	31%	65%	11%	16	91	25%	19%			-14.5	48	62	-$10
2nd Half		5	5	0	76	63	4.95	4.37	1.48	785	738	823	22.6	4.0	7.4	1.9	9%	42	23	35	32%	67%	9%	15	94	33%	33%			-10.2	46	59	-$8
14	Proj	9	9	0	174	145	4.30	3.81	1.39	751	763	741	22.1	3.4	7.5	2.2	8%	43	23	34	31%	71%	11%	33						-9.3	66	85	$2

BRENT HERSHEY

Niemann,Jeff

Age: 31	Th: R	Role	RP	Health	F	LIMA Plan	B+
Ht: 6' 9"	Wt: 285	Type		PT/Exp	D	Rand Var	0
				Consist	A	MM	3201

A shoulder injury from Sept 2012 seemed to have affected his velocity in spring training; he was shut down in April before making an appearance and quickly went under the knife. When healthy, showed solid Cmd and league-average ERA—but those days are almost two years out. At this point, just not a good gamble.

Yr	Tm	W	L	Sv	IP	K	ERA	xERA	WHIP	oOPS	vL	vR	BF/G	Ctl	Dom	Cmd	SwK	G	L	F	H%	S%	hr/f	GS	APC	DOM%	DIS%	Sv%	LI	RAR	BPV	BPX	R$
09	TAM	13	6	0	181	125	3.94	4.40	1.35	728	753	701	24.8	2.9	6.2	2.1	7%	41	20	39	30%	73%	8%	30	93	40%	30%	0	0.76	8.6	52	97	$10
10	TAM	12	8	0	174	131	4.39	4.10	1.26	724	749	698	24.4	3.1	6.8	2.1	9%	44	16	39	27%	69%	12%	29	88	34%	14%	0	0.84	-6.7	59	95	$6
11	TAM	11	7	0	135	105	4.06	3.77	1.24	729	726	732	24.9	2.5	7.0	2.8	7%	46	20	34	29%	71%	13%	23	93	61%	30%			-1.9	83	125	$6
12	TAM	2	3	0	38	34	3.08	3.52	1.11	594	732	407	19.5	2.8	8.1	2.8	10%	51	19	30	28%	73%	6%	8	81	38%	25%			4.4	97	127	$0
13																																	
1st Half																																	
2nd Half																																	
14	**Proj**	**5**	**4**	**0**	**73**	**55**	**3.99**	**3.90**	**1.31**	**720**	**775**	**656**	**18.4**	**3.1**	**6.9**	**2.2**	**9%**	**43**	**19**	**38**	**29%**	**72%**	**9%**	**15**						**-1.1**	**60**	**78**	**$1**

Niese,Jon

Age: 27	Th: L	Role	SP	Health	D	LIMA Plan	C
Ht: 6' 4"	Wt: 215	Type		PT/Exp	A	Rand Var	0
				Consist	A	MM	4203

From the Massive Anomaly Dept: Diagnosed with a partially torn rotator cuff, took six weeks off to rest/rehab, then returned in 2H to put together a career-best run. The injury risk is reflected in his Health grade, but his solid Cmd, strong GB tilt and consistent history presents potential reward, too. Roster only at a discount.

Yr	Tm	W	L	Sv	IP	K	ERA	xERA	WHIP	oOPS	vL	vR	BF/G	Ctl	Dom	Cmd	SwK	G	L	F	H%	S%	hr/f	GS	APC	DOM%	DIS%	Sv%	LI	RAR	BPV	BPX	R$
09	NYM *	6	7	0	120	91	4.93	4.73	1.48	731	813	685	24.6	2.6	6.8	2.6	8%	48	19	33	35%	67%	4%	5	80	20%	40%			-9.1	69	130	-$2
10	NYM	9	10	0	174	148	4.20	3.88	1.46	783	831	772	25.7	3.2	7.7	2.4	9%	48	21	32	33%	74%	12%	30	98	40%	23%			-2.5	77	125	$1
11	NYM	11	11	0	157	138	4.40	3.49	1.41	754	664	781	25.7	2.5	7.9	3.1	9%	51	21	28	35%	70%	10%	26	92	42%	15%	0	0.76	-9.0	103	155	$1
12	NYM	13	9	0	190	155	3.40	3.70	1.17	663	665	663	26.3	2.3	7.3	3.2	8%	48	21	31	28%	75%	13%	30	101	70%	7%			14.3	95	124	$16
13	NYM	8	8	0	143	105	3.71	3.93	1.44	739	660	765	25.9	3.0	6.6	2.2	8%	52	21	27	33%	75%	8%	24	98	50%	17%			2.7	67	88	$0
1st Half		3	6	0	77	49	4.32	4.44	1.61	769	735	782	24.9	3.9	5.7	1.5	8%	55	20	25	34%	73%	8%	14	95	29%	29%			-4.4	32	41	-$7
2nd Half		5	2	0	66	56	3.00	3.39	1.24	701	545	745	27.2	2.0	7.6	3.7	8%	47	23	29	32%	78%	9%	10	101	80%	0%			7.0	108	139	$8
14	**Proj**	**10**	**9**	**0**	**164**	**131**	**3.73**	**3.48**	**1.31**	**705**	**646**	**722**	**25.1**	**2.6**	**7.2**	**2.7**	**8%**	**50**	**21**	**29**	**31%**	**73%**	**10%**	**27**						**2.7**	**86**	**111**	**$7**

Noesi,Hector

Age: 27	Th: R	Role	RP	Health	A	LIMA Plan	D+
Ht: 6' 3"	Wt: 200	Type		PT/Exp	D	Rand Var	+2
				Consist	B	MM	2100

0-1, 6.59 ERA in 21 IP at SEA. Spread out those 21 IP over five of the six months of the season, but the abuse he took at Tacoma (5.83 ERA) indicates that his promotions were not merit-based. We've seen worse base skills, but needs some extra fastball juice or a more of a GB lean to take the next step. We're not optimistic.

Yr	Tm	W	L	Sv	IP	K	ERA	xERA	WHIP	oOPS	vL	vR	BF/G	Ctl	Dom	Cmd	SwK	G	L	F	H%	S%	hr/f	GS	APC	DOM%	DIS%	Sv%	LI	RAR	BPV	BPX	R$
09																																	
10	a/a	9	5	0	117	84	4.28	4.34	1.33				24.4	1.8	6.4	3.6					33%	69%								-2.9	87	141	$3
11	NYY *	3	3	0	81	59	4.50	5.05	1.60	785	806	766	10.0	3.6	6.6	1.8	10%	41	26	34	35%	72%	10%	2	32	0%	100%	0	0.80	-5.6	53	80	-$6
12	SEA *	4	18	0	171	115	5.70	5.16	1.47	826	865	782	22.2	3.1	6.0	1.9	10%	37	18	45	31%	63%	14%	18	78	39%	33%	0	0.64	-35.5	33	43	-$15
13	SEA *	4	4	0	105	72	6.02	6.05	1.64	935	938	931	16.1	2.6	6.2	2.4	9%	36	27	36	36%	65%	8%	1	41	0%	100%	0	0.40	-27.8	39	51	-$15
1st Half		2	2	0	54	40	5.77	6.33	1.64	824	692	934	16.0	2.4	6.7	2.8	9%	36	27	37	37%	68%	4%	1	48	0%	100%	0	0.41	-12.6	43	56	-$13
2nd Half		2	2	0	51	32	6.28	5.76	1.63	1179	1379	921	16.2	2.7	5.6	2.0	10%	38	28	34	35%	62%	18%	0	31			0	0.40	-15.2	36	46	-$16
14	**Proj**	**2**	**2**	**0**	**44**	**30**	**4.75**	**4.24**	**1.49**	**806**	**778**	**833**	**16.0**	**2.8**	**6.2**	**2.2**	**10%**	**38**	**24**	**38**	**33%**	**71%**	**10%**	**7**						**-4.8**	**51**	**67**	**-$4**

Nolasco,Ricky

Age: 31	Th: R	Role	SP	Health	B	LIMA Plan	B
Ht: 6' 2"	Wt: 235	Type		PT/Exp	A	Rand Var	0
				Consist	B	MM	4205

Reversed the Dom skid that jeopardized his fanalytic relevance, and seemed energized by mid-season trade to LA. Batters still see him well (LD%), which makes his WHIP not-so-outstanding. But with consistent Ctl, above-average SwK and beginnings of a ground-ball lean, the prospects are positive for a similar follow-up.

Yr	Tm	W	L	Sv	IP	K	ERA	xERA	WHIP	oOPS	vL	vR	BF/G	Ctl	Dom	Cmd	SwK	G	L	F	H%	S%	hr/f	GS	APC	DOM%	DIS%	Sv%	LI	RAR	BPV	BPX	R$
09	FLA *	14	10	0	200	205	4.91	3.96	1.25	734	725	744	24.7	2.1	9.2	4.3	10%	38	22	40	33%	62%	11%	31	98	58%	19%			-14.6	117	219	$11
10	FLA	14	9	0	158	147	4.51	3.60	1.28	766	758	772	25.6	1.9	8.4	4.5	11%	40	19	41	33%	69%	12%	26	95	54%	23%			-8.4	118	191	$7
11	FLA	10	12	0	206	148	4.67	3.82	1.40	770	835	708	27.0	1.9	6.5	3.4	9%	45	24	31	34%	68%	10%	33	97	48%	15%			-18.6	87	132	-$3
12	MIA	12	13	0	191	125	4.48	4.27	1.37	755	809	696	26.8	2.2	5.9	2.7	9%	47	22	32	32%	68%	9%	31	96	39%	23%			-10.9	71	93	-$1
13	2 NL	13	11	0	199	165	3.70	3.62	1.21	693	721	660	24.5	2.1	7.4	3.6	11%	43	24	33	31%	71%	9%	33	94	42%	12%	0	0.75	4.0	99	129	$11
1st Half		4	8	0	105	83	3.93	3.79	1.24	720	761	665	25.9	2.1	7.1	3.3	10%	41	24	34	31%	70%	9%	17	101	41%	12%			-0.8	89	116	$7
2nd Half		9	3	0	94	82	3.45	3.43	1.17	663	671	655	23.1	2.0	7.9	3.9	12%	45	24	31	31%	72%	8%	16	86	44%	13%	0	0.74	4.9	110	142	$15
14	**Proj**	**14**	**10**	**0**	**196**	**154**	**3.84**	**3.47**	**1.25**	**707**	**740**	**671**	**24.3**	**2.1**	**7.1**	**3.4**	**10%**	**44**	**23**	**33**	**31%**	**71%**	**9%**	**33**						**0.7**	**94**	**122**	**$11**

Norris,Bud

Age: 29	Th: R	Role	SP	Health	B	LIMA Plan	C
Ht: 6' 0"	Wt: 220	Type	Pwr	PT/Exp	A	Rand Var	0
				Consist	A	MM	3303

Sure seems as if Ctl is keeping him from taking the next step. When it improved in the 1H, Dom declined; when he just chucked it as hard as he could in the 2H (a new boss to impress?), Ctl also rose. DIS outings on the increase, and reports of Sept elbow discomfort aren't consoling, either. Ks are useful, but come at a cost.

Yr	Tm	W	L	Sv	IP	K	ERA	xERA	WHIP	oOPS	vL	vR	BF/G	Ctl	Dom	Cmd	SwK	G	L	F	H%	S%	hr/f	GS	APC	DOM%	DIS%	Sv%	LI	RAR	BPV	BPX	R$
09	HOU *	10	12	0	176	150	3.87	4.65	1.53	798	600	940	25.5	4.2	7.7	1.8	11%	37	20	43	33%	77%	13%	10	87	50%	10%	0	0.67	9.8	59	110	$4
10	HOU	9	10	0	154	158	4.92	4.00	1.48	758	799	721	25.3	4.5	9.3	2.1	11%	43	18	39	33%	69%	11%	27	101	52%	30%			-15.9	66	106	-$2
11	HOU	6	11	0	186	176	3.77	3.81	1.33	732	811	650	25.6	3.4	8.5	2.5	11%	40	21	39	31%	76%	12%	31	102	55%	13%			3.9	80	120	$6
12	HOU	7	13	0	168	165	4.65	4.10	1.37	751	782	720	25.3	3.5	8.8	2.5	11%	39	21	40	31%	69%	12%	29	97	59%	21%			-13.2	81	105	-$2
13	2 AL	10	12	0	177	147	4.18	4.27	1.49	779	889	629	24.2	3.4	7.5	2.2	10%	40	21	38	34%	74%	8%	30	94	47%	27%	0	0.88	-6.8	61	79	-$3
1st Half		5	7	0	102	71	3.35	4.30	1.37	725	838	595	25.4	2.8	6.3	2.2	10%	41	21	38	32%	77%	6%	17	95	53%	18%			6.5	56	72	$3
2nd Half		5	5	0	75	76	5.30	4.23	1.65	848	947	682	22.8	4.2	9.2	2.2	10%	39	22	39	37%	70%	11%	13	93	38%	38%	0	1.01	-13.2	68	88	-$11
14	**Proj**	**9**	**12**	**0**	**174**	**161**	**4.22**	**3.85**	**1.43**	**760**	**832**	**674**	**24.8**	**3.7**	**8.3**	**2.3**	**11%**	**40**	**21**	**39**	**32%**	**73%**	**10%**	**31**						**-7.7**	**69**	**89**	**$1**

Nova,Ivan

Age: 27	Th: R	Role	SP	Health	C	LIMA Plan	B
Ht: 6' 5"	Wt: 225	Type	GB	PT/Exp	B	Rand Var	-1
				Consist	A	MM	4203

9-6, 3.10 ERA in 139 IP at NYY. A skills near-repeat of 2012, but an oblique and recurring triceps injury limited his IP. Most encouraging was his GB spike in 2H and ability to maintain his above-average Dom. He's not without health risk, but he's at the age for the next step. UP: 200 IP, 180 K.

Yr	Tm	W	L	Sv	IP	K	ERA	xERA	WHIP	oOPS	vL	vR	BF/G	Ctl	Dom	Cmd	SwK	G	L	F	H%	S%	hr/f	GS	APC	DOM%	DIS%	Sv%	LI	RAR	BPV	BPX	R$
09	a/a	6	8	0	139	78	5.03	5.15	1.67				26.0	4.3	5.0	1.2					33%	69%								-12.1	31	59	-$8
10	NYY *	13	5	0	187	122	3.93	4.64	1.47	729	747	703	24.3	3.3	5.9	1.8	7%	51	18	30	32%	75%	10%	7	67	43%	43%	0	0.91	3.5	46	74	$3
11	NYY *	17	6	0	181	113	3.79	4.03	1.34	706	681	730	24.3	2.9	5.6	1.9	7%	53	18	29	29%	74%	8%	27	92	37%	19%	0	0.82	3.5	50	75	$8
12	NYY	12	8	0	170	153	5.02	3.95	1.47	860	848	872	26.7	3.0	8.1	2.7	9%	45	22	32	34%	70%	17%	28	96	46%	21%			-21.1	89	116	-$6
13	NYY *	11	6	0	157	129	3.08	3.57	1.29	678	676	680	24.8	2.8	7.4	2.7	10%	54	20	26	31%	78%	8%	20	91	50%	20%	0	0.77	15.1	86	112	$9
1st Half		4	2	0	53	50	4.07	4.66	1.52	788	696	883	20.8	3.0	8.6	2.9	11%	51	22	27	38%	74%	7%	5	76	20%	40%	0	0.78	-1.3	90	116	-$3
2nd Half		7	4	0	104	79	2.59	3.48	1.18	639	670	602	28.5	2.7	6.8	2.5	9%	54	20	26	28%	80%	9%	15	99	60%	13%			16.4	83	107	$16
14	**Proj**	**13**	**7**	**0**	**174**	**138**	**3.76**	**3.57**	**1.35**	**735**	**718**	**753**	**24.7**	**3.0**	**7.2**	**2.4**	**9%**	**51**	**20**	**29**	**31%**	**75%**	**11%**	**29**						**2.2**	**77**	**101**	**$7**

O Day,Darren

Age: 31	Th: R	Role	RP	Health	D	LIMA Plan	B+
Ht: 6' 4"	Wt: 220	Type	Pwr FB	PT/Exp	D	Rand Var	-5
				Consist	C	MM	5410

Underrated relief arm that limits runners, notches almost a K per IP, and has proven he can pitch in tight spots. Was about to take a bigger role in Sept when finger injury limited him to 6 IP. Serves up too many LD/FB and problems vLHB will push ERA back up. He's a premium set-up arm but not likely to close.

Yr	Tm	W	L	Sv	IP	K	ERA	xERA	WHIP	oOPS	vL	vR	BF/G	Ctl	Dom	Cmd	SwK	G	L	F	H%	S%	hr/f	GS	APC	DOM%	DIS%	Sv%	LI	RAR	BPV	BPX	R$
09	2 TM	2	1	2	59	56	1.84	3.50	1.01	543	666	484	3.4	2.8	8.6	3.1	12%	41	17	42	26%	84%	5%	0	14			100	1.21	18.0	99	185	$8
10	TEX	6	2	0	62	45	2.03	3.62	0.89	548	561	542	3.3	1.7	6.5	3.8	10%	37	21	42	23%	82%	7%	0	12			0	1.15	15.7	86	138	$9
11	TEX *	1	1	1	38	37	4.21	5.50	1.27	929	900	938	4.6	2.3	8.8	3.9	11%	35	17	48	28%	82%	30%	0	17			100	0.47	-1.3	59	88	-$2
12	BAL	7	1	0	67	69	2.28	3.34	0.94	613	664	584	3.8	1.9	9.3	4.9	12%	34	23	43	26%	81%	8%	0	15			0	1.10	14.3	128	167	$10
13	BAL	5	3	2	62	59	2.18	3.38	1.00	617	922	443	3.6	2.2	8.6	3.9	12%	37	22	41	26%	85%	10%	0	14			33	1.22	12.9	110	144	$8
1st Half		3	0	1	36	38	2.25	3.36	1.08	648	936	462	3.9	2.8	9.5	3.5	12%	37	22	41	27%	86%	11%	0	16			33	1.18	7.2	112	145	$9
2nd Half		2	3	1	26	21	2.08	3.41	0.88	570	890	418	3.2	1.4	7.3	5.3	13%	36	22	42	23%	85%	10%	0	13			33	1.27	5.7	108	139	$7
14	**Proj**	**4**	**3**	**3**	**58**	**55**	**2.94**	**3.16**	**1.01**	**647**	**867**	**531**	**3.6**	**2.0**	**8.5**	**4.2**	**12%**	**36**	**22**	**42**	**26%**	**77%**	**12%**	**0**						**6.6**	**112**	**146**	**$6**

BRENT HERSHEY

Oberholtzer,Brett

Age: 25	Th: L	Role SP	Health A	LIMA Plan B+
Ht: 6' 1"	Wt: 235	Type xFB	PT/Exp D	Rand Var 0
			Consist C	MM 2103

4-5, 2.76 ERA in 72 IP at HOU. Considered a fringe prospect, he was a fixture in the rotation in Aug and Sept. He features a 90-mph fastball along with a curve and change. 2H repeat unlikely even with very good Ctl, as hr/f will normalize and ERA will correct. Has value, but pedestrian Dom should temper our expectations.

Yr Tm	W	L	Sv	IP	K	ERA	xERA	WHIP	oOPS	vL	vR	BF/G	Ctl	Dom	Cmd	SwK	G	L	F	H%	S%	hr/f	GS	APC	DOM%	DIS%	Sv%	LI	RAR	BPV	BPX	R$
09																																
10																																
11 aa	11	12	0	155	107	4.22	3.69	1.32				23.8	2.8	6.2	2.2					31%	68%								-5.3	70	105	$3
12 a/a	10	10	0	167	119	4.48	5.10	1.42				25.2	2.0	6.4	3.1					33%	72%								-9.6	63	82	-$3
13 HOU *	10	11	0	152	106	3.91	3.89	1.26	654	745	617	21.4	2.3	6.3	2.8	9%	36	22	42	30%	72%	7%	10	85	70%	10%	0	0.69	-0.9	70	91	$4
1st Half	5	6	0	76	54	5.30	5.22	1.48	1444	0	1857	20.5	2.8	6.3	2.2	0%	22	11	67	32%	67%	33%	0	38			0	0.93	-13.5	41	53	-$6
2nd Half	5	5	0	76	53	2.51	2.56	1.03	628	763	571	22.4	1.7	6.3	3.8	9%	36	22	42	27%	78%	5%	10	89	70%	10%	0	0.67	12.6	108	139	$15
14 Proj	9	10	0	145	99	4.01	4.15	1.32	701	851	639	23.2	2.4	6.2	2.6	9%	36	22	42	30%	73%	9%	26						-2.7	60	78	$4

Odorizzi,Jake

Age: 24	Th: R	Role SP	Health A	LIMA Plan B+
Ht: 6' 2"	Wt: 185	Type xFB	PT/Exp D	Rand Var 0
			Consist B	MM 2201

0-1, 3.94 ERA in 30 IP at TAM. Looks ready for the Show but beware... Has a history of Dom dropping on first exposure at each level before a recovery (Double-A 7.1 then 11.1; Triple-A 7.4 then 8.9). Has four-pitch arsenal with a 91-mph fastball and his BPV is trending up, but expect an adjustment period.

Yr Tm	W	L	Sv	IP	K	ERA	xERA	WHIP	oOPS	vL	vR	BF/G	Ctl	Dom	Cmd	SwK	G	L	F	H%	S%	hr/f	GS	APC	DOM%	DIS%	Sv%	LI	RAR	BPV	BPX	R$
09																																
10																																
11 aa	5	3	0	69	45	4.97	4.56	1.32				23.7	2.7	5.9	2.2					28%	66%								-8.7	41	61	-$2
12 KC *	15	6	0	153	117	3.36	3.89	1.32	820	899	400	22.6	3.0	6.9	2.3	7%	27	27	46	30%	77%	8%	2	76	0%	50%			12.3	69	89	$10
13 TAM *	9	7	1	154	129	3.76	3.39	1.21	744	846	627	21.4	2.7	7.5	2.8	8%	32	26	42	29%	71%	8%	4	76	25%	25%	100	0.80	2.0	84	110	$8
1st Half	6	1	0	88	77	4.10	3.87	1.23	873	906	829	22.2	2.6	7.9	3.1	7%	25	25	51	30%	71%	10%	3	89	33%	33%	0	0.61	-2.5	81	104	$7
2nd Half	3	6	1	66	52	3.32	2.76	1.18	487	703	293	20.4	2.9	7.1	2.4	11%	48	28	24	29%	71%	0%	1	60	0%	0%	100	1.05	4.5	90	117	$8
14 Proj	7	5	0	95	73	3.82	4.10	1.26	678	694	657	22.0	2.8	7.0	2.5	7%	32	22	46	29%	74%	8%	18						0.6	60	78	$3

Ogando,Alexi

Age: 30	Th: R	Role SP	Health F	LIMA Plan B
Ht: 6' 4"	Wt: 200	Type FB	PT/Exp C	Rand Var -3
			Consist A	MM 3201

7-4, 3.11 ERA in 104 IP at TEX. First bicep, then shoulder woes cost him 12 weeks. Frequent injuries, changing roles make inconsistent Dom and Ctl difficult to baseline. A consistently low H% helps maintain ERA, but can it continue? Potential to excel when healthy, but can't contribute from the disabled list.

Yr Tm	W	L	Sv	IP	K	ERA	xERA	WHIP	oOPS	vL	vR	BF/G	Ctl	Dom	Cmd	SwK	G	L	F	H%	S%	hr/f	GS	APC	DOM%	DIS%	Sv%	LI	RAR	BPV	BPX	R$
09																																
10 TEX *	4	1	1	72	71	1.93	2.02	1.07	554	678	492	4.5	3.5	8.8	2.5	11%	44	18	38	25%	84%	5%	0	16			20	1.02	19.2	109	177	$9
11 TEX	13	8	0	169	126	3.51	3.90	1.14	649	709	560	22.4	2.3	6.7	2.9	10%	36	24	40	28%	72%	8%	29	88	62%	21%	0	0.74	8.9	73	110	$14
12 TEX	2	0	3	66	66	3.27	3.52	1.00	615	637	598	4.5	2.3	9.0	3.9	14%	38	21	41	25%	74%	12%	1	18	0%	100%	50	1.20	6.0	115	151	$6
13 TEX *	8	5	0	123	78	3.63	3.96	1.26	678	620	753	18.6	3.3	5.7	1.7	8%	41	18	41	25%	77%	9%	18	74	50%	17%	0	0.73	3.6	35	46	$4
1st Half	5	2	0	61	46	2.64	3.47	1.20	678	575	813	22.4	3.2	6.7	2.1	9%	38	20	42	26%	84%	9%	10	93	60%	10%			9.3	59	77	$10
2nd Half	3	3	0	62	32	4.61	4.48	1.31	678	673	685	16.0	3.5	4.6	1.3	7%	44	16	40	25%	71%	9%	8	60	38%	25%	0	0.70	-5.7	12	15	-$2
14 Proj	8	6	0	130	99	3.59	3.90	1.26	729	735	722	22.1	3.0	6.9	2.3	10%	40	19	41	28%	76%	11%	58						4.4	62	80	$7

Ohlendorf,Ross

Age: 31	Th: R	Role RP	Health F	LIMA Plan D+
Ht: 6' 4"	Wt: 240	Type FB	PT/Exp D	Rand Var 0
			Consist C	MM 2101

4-1, 3.28 ERA in 60 IP at WAS. Redid repertoire by throwing more fastballs (all four-seamers) and fewer sliders with mixed results. His improved 2H Ctl and Dom (and high S%) lowered his ERA, but xERA still mediocre. With a history of arm woes (lost 3 weeks to a sore shoulder), any tangible improvement could be fleeting.

Yr Tm	W	L	Sv	IP	K	ERA	xERA	WHIP	oOPS	vL	vR	BF/G	Ctl	Dom	Cmd	SwK	G	L	F	H%	S%	hr/f	GS	APC	DOM%	DIS%	Sv%	LI	RAR	BPV	BPX	R$
09 PIT	11	10	0	177	109	3.92	4.42	1.23	761	818	697	25.0	2.7	5.6	2.1	8%	41	17	42	26%	73%	11%	29	93	38%	10%			8.7	46	86	$11
10 PIT	1	11	0	108	79	4.07	4.74	1.38	773	833	730	22.6	3.7	6.6	1.8	9%	31	22	46	29%	73%	8%	21	84	33%	29%			0.1	28	46	-$1
11 PIT *	2	4	0	68	37	6.61	6.93	1.77	1047	1110	1015	22.2	3.3	5.0	1.5	10%	36	22	41	35%	65%	16%	9	74	22%	44%			-22.2	1	1	-$13
12 SD *	9	8	0	118	80	5.78	5.38	1.59	885	861	906	20.1	3.2	6.1	1.9	9%	29	24	47	35%	64%	9%	9	70	44%	56%	0	0.65	-25.7	42	55	-$13
13 WAS *	8	7	0	135	96	4.42	4.16	1.36	703	771	653	18.8	3.0	6.4	2.1	10%	39	20	41	30%	69%	11%	7	61	43%	29%	0	0.63	-9.3	56	74	-$2
1st Half	5	5	0	84	55	4.92	3.93	1.40	577	401	738	22.3	3.6	5.8	1.6	9%	26	16	58	30%	64%	5%	1	66	0%	0%	0	0.63	-11.0	54	69	-$3
2nd Half	3	2	0	51	41	3.60	4.53	1.29	734	878	634	14.9	2.1	7.3	3.4	10%	43	21	36	31%	79%	14%	6	60	50%	33%	0	0.63	1.7	72	93	$2
14 Proj	5	5	0	87	60	4.68	4.33	1.46	813	862	779	19.0	3.0	6.2	2.1	10%	36	22	42	32%	71%	10%	18						-8.8	47	60	-$4

Oliver,Darren

Age: 43	Th: L	Role RP	Health C	LIMA Plan D
Ht: 6' 3"	Wt: 250	Type	PT/Exp D	Rand Var +1
			Consist A	MM 0000

His 20-year major league career included 766 appearances, 229 as a starter. He hurled 1915.2 innings, gave up 2037 hits, struck out 1259 while walking 720 (1.7 Cmd). He pitched for nine different teams, including TEX three times. And he didn't have a sub-4.00 ERA until his 13th season after which he never touched 4.00 again.

Yr Tm	W	L	Sv	IP	K	ERA	xERA	WHIP	oOPS	vL	vR	BF/G	Ctl	Dom	Cmd	SwK	G	L	F	H%	S%	hr/f	GS	APC	DOM%	DIS%	Sv%	LI	RAR	BPV	BPX	R$
09 LAA	5	1	0	73	65	2.71	3.61	1.14	651	707	605	4.7	2.7	8.0	3.0	10%	44	14	41	28%	78%	6%	1	18	0%	100%	0	1.30	14.5	93	174	$7
10 TEX	1	2	1	62	65	2.48	2.83	1.10	654	529	765	3.8	2.2	9.5	4.3	10%	48	20	32	31%	80%	8%	0	15			25	1.23	12.2	138	223	$5
11 TEX	5	5	2	51	44	2.29	3.53	1.14	591	587	594	3.5	1.9	7.8	4.0	7%	38	29	33	31%	82%	6%	0	14			33	1.28	10.4	103	155	$5
12 TOR	3	4	2	57	52	2.06	3.33	1.02	575	644	514	3.6	2.4	8.3	3.5	9%	44	22	34	27%	82%	6%	0	14			50	0.95	13.6	106	139	$7
13 TOR	3	4	0	49	40	3.86	3.70	1.27	745	932	619	4.1	2.8	7.3	2.7	8%	47	19	33	29%	73%	13%	0	14			0	0.79	0.1	83	108	-$1
1st Half	3	1	0	23	16	3.52	4.06	1.39	784	1166	514	4.1	3.1	6.3	2.0	7%	51	20	29	30%	79%	15%	0	14			0	0.99	1.0	57	74	$0
2nd Half	0	3	0	26	24	4.15	3.40	1.15	708	696	713	4.0	2.4	8.3	3.4	9%	44	19	37	29%	67%	12%	0	15			0	0.61	-0.9	106	138	-$2
14 Proj																																

Ondrusek,Logan

Age: 29	Th: R	Role RP	Health A	LIMA Plan C
Ht: 6' 8"	Wt: 230	Type Pwr	PT/Exp D	Rand Var +2
			Consist C	MM 3200

After two straight seasons of a respectable ERA despite poor BPIs, the reverse occurred. He markedly improved his skills (especially in 2H) only to sport a career-worst ERA. BPV jump intriguing, but with more reliable fish in the reliever sea, it's not worth casting a line in his direction unless Dom increase persists.

Yr Tm	W	L	Sv	IP	K	ERA	xERA	WHIP	oOPS	vL	vR	BF/G	Ctl	Dom	Cmd	SwK	G	L	F	H%	S%	hr/f	GS	APC	DOM%	DIS%	Sv%	LI	RAR	BPV	BPX	R$
09 a/a	2	1	19	53	30	2.23	2.50	1.13				4.9	2.6	5.0	1.9					27%	80%								13.7	73	136	$12
10 CIN *	5	1	1	78	51	4.02	3.56	1.24	669	561	725	4.3	2.7	5.8	2.2	11%	48	14	38	28%	69%	10%	0	15			25	1.06	0.6	62	100	$2
11 CIN	5	5	0	61	41	3.23	4.45	1.35	676	635	698	4.1	4.1	6.0	1.5	9%	49	17	34	27%	79%	9%	0	15			0	1.26	5.4	24	37	$1
12 CIN	5	2	2	55	39	3.46	5.22	1.50	752	643	828	3.9	5.1	6.4	1.3	10%	43	15	42	27%	82%	12%	0	15			50	1.46	3.8	-1	-2	-$1
13 CIN	3	1	0	55	53	4.09	3.55	1.25	730	854	633	4.5	2.6	8.7	3.3	12%	46	19	36	31%	72%	14%	0	17			0	0.72	-1.5	109	143	-$1
1st Half	2	0	0	22	18	5.64	4.23	1.30	794	848	752	4.5	3.2	7.3	2.3	13%	41	17	42	27%	60%	14%	0	17			0	0.64	-4.9	62	81	-$4
2nd Half	1	1	0	33	35	3.03	3.10	1.22	687	858	551	4.5	2.2	9.6	4.4	12%	49	20	31	33%	81%	14%	0	17			0	0.77	3.4	141	182	$1
14 Proj	3	1	0	44	36	3.70	3.82	1.32	719	746	700	4.1	3.5	7.4	2.1	11%	46	17	37	29%	76%	12%	0						0.9	64	83	-$1

Ortiz,Joseph

Age: 23	Th: L	Role RP	Health A	LIMA Plan C
Ht: 5' 7"	Wt: 175	Type	PT/Exp F	Rand Var 0
			Consist A	MM 3100

2-2, 4.23 ERA in 45 IP at TEX. Diminutive southpaw features a 90-mph fastball and relies on location to get ground balls. 2H ERA drop more a result of low H% and nary a HR more than improved skills. Dom best suited for low leverage bullpen work, though a LOOGY role is not out of the question if results vL improve.

Yr Tm	W	L	Sv	IP	K	ERA	xERA	WHIP	oOPS	vL	vR	BF/G	Ctl	Dom	Cmd	SwK	G	L	F	H%	S%	hr/f	GS	APC	DOM%	DIS%	Sv%	LI	RAR	BPV	BPX	R$
09																																
10																																
11																																
12 a/a	2	3	6	63	44	2.61	4.29	1.18				4.9	1.3	6.3	4.9					29%	87%								10.8	98	128	$5
13 TEX *	4	3	2	71	51	4.09	4.09	1.30	747	684	791	5.7	2.3	6.4	2.8	11%	39	31	29	31%	71%	12%	0	22			67	0.74	-2.0	70	91	-$1
1st Half	3	2	0	40	31	5.33	5.78	1.50	834	778	872	5.9	2.5	7.1	2.8	11%	40	29	32	34%	69%	16%	0	22			0	0.73	-7.2	44	57	-$4
2nd Half	1	1	2	31	20	2.51	1.95	1.04	576	500	629	5.5	2.0	5.7	2.8	10%	39	37	24	27%	73%	0%	0	21			100	0.77	5.2	102	132	$4
14 Proj	2	2	0	42	29	4.16	3.88	1.29	751	675	803	5.5	2.5	6.3	2.5	11%	39	25	35	30%	70%	10%	0						-1.5	63	82	-$2

TODD ZOLA

Otero,Dan

Age: 29 | Th: R | Role: RP | Ht: 6' 3" | Wt: 215 | Type: Con xGB
Health: A | PT/Exp: D | Consist: D
LIMA Plan: A | Rand Var: -5 | MM: 4100

2-0, 1.38 ERA in 39 IP at OAK. Perfect HR avoidance in MLB drives high S%, which produces a better ERA than xERA despite sub-par Dom and dwindling SwK. He'll eventually give up some HR, but elite GB and excellent Ctl should limit frequency and damage. Still, that low Dom increases risk of a blow-up.

Yr	Tm	W	L	Sv	IP	K	ERA	xERA	WHIP	oOPS	vL	vR	BF/G	Ctl	Dom	Cmd	SwK	G	L	F	H%	S%	hr/f	GS	APC	DOM%	DIS%	Sv%	LI	RAR	BPV	BPX	R$
09	aa	0	3	19	39	25	1.56	4.39	1.53				4.4	2.4	5.8	2.4					37%	89%								13.3	79	147	$7
10																																	
11	a/a	4	4	13	74	61	2.52	3.63	1.24				5.4	1.3	7.4	5.8					35%	81%								12.9	151	227	$10
12	SF *	5	5	0	74	43	3.35	4.47	1.41	894	950	864	5.2	1.2	5.2	4.6	8%	67	22	11	36%	76%	0%	0	16			0	0.29	6.1	109	142	-$1
13	OAK *	3	0	15	66	44	1.27	1.97	0.99	613	613	613	4.5	1.0	5.9	6.2	6%	56	20	24	29%	86%	0%	0	18			94	0.75	21.3	173	226	$15
1st Half		1	0	15	34	23	1.66	1.21	0.80	700	667	733	4.1	0.3	6.0	21.6	6%	58	25	17	26%	77%	0%	0	18			100	0.46	9.3	502	650	$22
2nd Half		2	0	0	32	21	0.84	3.48	1.19	592	600	583	5.0	1.7	5.9	3.5	6%	55	19	26	32%	92%	0%	0	18			0	0.83	11.9	94	122	$7
14	**Proj**	**2**	**2**	**0**	**48**	**32**	**3.10**	**3.25**	**1.16**	**587**	**592**	**581**	**4.8**	**1.3**	**6.0**	**4.6**	**6%**	**55**	**19**	**26**	**31%**	**74%**	**7%**	**0**						**4.5**	**106**	**138**	**$1**

Ottavino,Adam

Age: 28 | Th: R | Role: RP | Ht: 6' 5" | Wt: 230 | Type: Pwr
Health: A | PT/Exp: D | Consist: B
LIMA Plan: B+ | Rand Var: -4 | MM: 3301

2012 conversion to relief has worked, with Dom jumping 50%. 1st half S% skewed final ERA mark; though 1H/2H BPIs remained the same. Far more effective against RHP; high GB is nice but he's still owed a few more HR. Bullpen punchouts always welcome, but fantasy impact negated by impending ERA correction.

Yr	Tm	W	L	Sv	IP	K	ERA	xERA	WHIP	oOPS	vL	vR	BF/G	Ctl	Dom	Cmd	SwK	G	L	F	H%	S%	hr/f	GS	APC	DOM%	DIS%	Sv%	LI	RAR	BPV	BPX	R$
09	aaa	7	12	0	144	97	5.64	5.15	1.70				24.1	5.1	6.0	1.2					33%	66%								-23.4	37	69	-$10
10	STL *	5	5	0	70	47	5.50	5.27	1.49	1072	1213	973	21.6	2.7	6.0	2.3	6%	36	32	32	33%	65%	18%	3	84	0%	33%	0	0.53	-12.3	42	69	-$4
11	aaa	7	8	0	141	94	5.18	5.52	1.73				24.7	4.6	6.0	1.3					35%	70%								-21.5	35	52	-$13
12	COL *	5	1	0	99	99	4.43	4.60	1.46	717	745	698	6.4	3.8	9.1	2.4	12%	48	26	26	34%	72%	16%	0	25			0	0.64	-5.0	74	97	-$4
13	COL	1	3	0	78	78	2.64	3.62	1.33	672	853	544	6.6	3.6	9.0	2.5	12%	46	22	33	32%	82%	7%	0	25			0	1.01	11.8	89	116	$2
1st Half		0	1	0	42	43	1.94	3.59	1.22	636	838	463	7.4	3.5	9.3	2.7	11%	41	23	35	30%	88%	8%	0	30			0	0.89	9.9	93	121	$4
2nd Half		1	2	0	37	35	3.44	3.65	1.45	712	873	620	5.8	3.7	8.6	2.3	14%	50	20	30	34%	76%	6%	0	21			0	1.12	1.9	83	108	-$1
14	**Proj**	**2**	**3**	**0**	**73**	**66**	**3.37**	**3.60**	**1.38**	**698**	**814**	**620**	**7.6**	**3.8**	**8.2**	**2.2**	**12%**	**47**	**23**	**30**	**31%**	**78%**	**10%**	**0**						**4.4**	**70**	**90**	**$1**

Outman,Josh

Age: 29 | Th: L | Role: RP | Ht: 6' 1" | Wt: 205 | Type: Pwr
Health: B | PT/Exp: D | Consist: C
LIMA Plan: C | Rand Var: +2 | MM: 3300

After struggling as a starter, he's taken to relief (evidenced by career best xERA). Uniform should say "Hitman vR" (career .343 BAA). Unless he faces strictly LHB (career .195 BAA), his value will be limited as poor Ctl will keep WHIP in no-trespassing zone.

Yr	Tm	W	L	Sv	IP	K	ERA	xERA	WHIP	oOPS	vL	vR	BF/G	Ctl	Dom	Cmd	SwK	G	L	F	H%	S%	hr/f	GS	APC	DOM%	DIS%	Sv%	LI	RAR	BPV	BPX	R$
09	OAK	4	1	0	67	53	3.48	4.28	1.16	640	373	717	19.7	3.3	7.1	2.1	9%	38	19	43	24%	75%	11%	12	79	50%	33%	0	0.84	7.0	53	100	$4
10																																	
11	OAK *	11	8	0	137	92	3.99	4.77	1.61	737	508	821	20.2	4.7	6.1	1.3	8%	40	17	44	32%	76%	5%	9	74	33%	22%	0	0.82	-0.8	43	64	-$3
12	COL *	3	8	0	112	91	6.27	5.63	1.68	866	623	1006	11.7	4.4	7.3	1.7	13%	47	20	33	35%	63%	18%	7	28	0%	86%	0	1.17	-31.2	42	55	-$18
13	COL	3	0	0	54	53	4.33	3.62	1.46	700	539	883	3.9	3.8	8.8	2.3	14%	51	21	28	35%	70%	7%	0	15			0	0.88	-3.1	85	110	-$4
1st Half		2	0	0	30	32	4.45	3.36	1.38	664	526	785	5.0	3.0	9.5	3.2	13%	49	21	29	37%	66%	4%	0	18			0	0.69	-2.2	118	153	-$3
2nd Half		1	0	0	24	21	4.18	3.98	1.56	747	551	1063	3.1	4.9	8.0	1.6	14%	54	20	26	32%	74%	12%	0	12			0	1.03	-0.9	42	55	-$5
14	**Proj**	**2**	**1**	**0**	**44**	**40**	**4.25**	**3.73**	**1.46**	**723**	**531**	**869**	**5.6**	**4.0**	**8.4**	**2.1**	**12%**	**48**	**20**	**33**	**33%**	**72%**	**9%**	**0**						**-2.1**	**68**	**88**	**-$3**

Papelbon,Jonathan

Age: 33 | Th: R | Role: RP | Ht: 6' 4" | Wt: 225 | Type: Pwr FB
Health: A | PT/Exp: A | Consist: B
LIMA Plan: C+ | Rand Var: -2 | MM: 5431

With a pronounced drop in velocity (-2 mph fastball, -4 mph slider) at his age, it's fair to question how much returns. With closers, it's all about "can he do the job?" and Sv% says that's waning. Leverage index says management is losing confidence too. Skills are still closer-worthy but time is running out.

Yr	Tm	W	L	Sv	IP	K	ERA	xERA	WHIP	oOPS	vL	vR	BF/G	Ctl	Dom	Cmd	SwK	G	L	F	H%	S%	hr/f	GS	APC	DOM%	DIS%	Sv%	LI	RAR	BPV	BPX	R$
09	BOS	1	1	38	68	76	1.85	3.83	1.15	600	570	633	4.3	3.2	10.1	3.2	11%	27	21	52	30%	88%	5%	0	18			93	1.38	20.7	100	188	$23
10	BOS	5	7	37	67	76	3.90	3.63	1.27	674	717	619	4.4	3.8	10.2	2.7	13%	38	18	44	31%	72%	9%	0	18			82	1.37	1.5	98	159	$18
11	BOS	4	1	31	64	87	2.94	2.47	0.93	546	428	663	4.0	1.4	12.2	8.7	18%	38	21	41	33%	68%	5%	0	16			91	1.27	8.0	197	297	$20
12	PHI	5	6	38	70	92	2.44	2.84	1.06	621	627	616	4.1	2.3	11.8	5.1	13%	41	18	40	31%	83%	12%	0	16			90	1.24	13.6	169	221	$24
13	PHI	5	1	29	62	57	2.92	3.58	1.14	631	644	618	4.2	1.6	8.3	5.2	11%	40	17	43	31%	78%	8%	0	16			81	1.18	7.2	124	162	$15
1st Half		2	0	15	31	27	2.05	3.51	0.88	580	688	448	3.9	1.5	7.9	5.4	12%	37	14	49	23%	87%	10%	0	14			79	1.12	6.9	118	153	$19
2nd Half		3	1	14	31	30	3.77	3.65	1.39	676	596	736	4.4	1.7	8.7	5.0	10%	42	20	37	38%	73%	5%	0	18			82	1.24	0.3	130	169	$12
14	**Proj**	**5**	**3**	**35**	**73**	**76**	**3.01**	**3.08**	**1.14**	**635**	**617**	**653**	**4.0**	**2.0**	**9.4**	**4.8**	**13%**	**39**	**19**	**42**	**32%**	**77%**	**8%**	**0**						**7.7**	**133**	**173**	**$20**

Parker,Blake

Age: 29 | Th: R | Role: RP | Ht: 6' 3" | Wt: 225 | Type: Pwr xFB
Health: D | PT/Exp: F | Consist: D
LIMA Plan: B+ | Rand Var: -2 | MM: 3400

1-2, 2.72 ERA in 46 IP at CHC. Triple-A closer, promoted in June and quickly worked his way into late-inning duties. Success largely a result of Dom bump, which SwK validates. 2nd half Ctl gains somewhat sketchier due to sample size. Low reliability is signal not to overreact to 2013's luster.

Yr	Tm	W	L	Sv	IP	K	ERA	xERA	WHIP	oOPS	vL	vR	BF/G	Ctl	Dom	Cmd	SwK	G	L	F	H%	S%	hr/f	GS	APC	DOM%	DIS%	Sv%	LI	RAR	BPV	BPX	R$
09	a/a	2	3	25	63	64	3.61	3.59	1.45				4.9	5.4	9.1	1.7					30%	76%								5.5	82	153	$11
10	a/a	1	5	7	66	54	4.89	5.45	1.62				6.1	4.7	7.3	1.6					32%	73%								-6.6	34	56	-$3
11	a/a	4	5	7	75	64	3.51	3.62	1.39				6.0	4.8	7.6	1.6					28%	76%								4.0	65	98	$4
12	CHC *	1	1	6	30	23	4.49	5.04	1.37	1155	1026	1200	4.4	3.5	7.1	2.0	9%	38	33	29	27%	75%	50%	0	19			86	0.25	-1.7	31	41	-$2
13	CHC *	1	3	8	64	75	2.70	2.80	1.18	626	572	661	3.9	3.7	10.5	2.8	12%	29	22	49	29%	80%	7%	0	17			89	0.70	9.2	113	148	$6
1st Half		0	2	8	30	35	2.45	1.87	1.08	429	587	170	4.3	4.9	10.5	2.1	13%	38	14	48	22%	80%	7%	0	18			89	0.89	5.2	111	144	$10
2nd Half		1	1	0	34	40	2.91	3.64	1.26	692	564	755	3.8	2.6	10.6	4.0	11%	26	25	49	35%	80%	7%	0	16			0	0.64	4.0	123	159	$2
14	**Proj**	**2**	**3**	**0**	**58**	**59**	**3.62**	**3.84**	**1.26**	**629**	**508**	**687**	**4.6**	**3.6**	**9.2**	**2.6**	**11%**	**26**	**25**	**49**	**29%**	**75%**	**9%**	**0**						**1.8**	**73**	**95**	**$0**

Parker,Jarrod

Age: 25 | Th: R | Role: SP | Ht: 6' 1" | Wt: 195 | Type:
Health: A | PT/Exp: B | Consist: A
LIMA Plan: B | Rand Var: -1 | MM: 3205

First glance implies sophomore season was a step back, but 2.81 ERA/1.03 WHIP from May through Aug intriguing. One culprit? 1.6 HR/9 in Apr/Sep, 1.0 the rest. At 25, reliability already a plus and still time for Dom to approach minor league's 8.6. Lots to like here; not yet finished product. UP: 3.20 ERA with 175 K.

Yr	Tm	W	L	Sv	IP	K	ERA	xERA	WHIP	oOPS	vL	vR	BF/G	Ctl	Dom	Cmd	SwK	G	L	F	H%	S%	hr/f	GS	APC	DOM%	DIS%	Sv%	LI	RAR	BPV	BPX	R$
09	aa	4	6	0	78	63	4.96	4.96	1.69				22.1	4.0	7.2	1.8					37%	69%								-6.2	66	124	-$5
10																																	
11	ARI *	11	8	0	136	95	4.10	3.50	1.33	513	286	641	21.0	3.5	6.3	1.8	7%	35	6	59	30%	69%	0%	1	73	0%	0%			-2.6	65	98	$3
12	OAK *	14	8	0	202	157	3.35	3.43	1.28	670	685	654	25.1	3.1	7.0	2.3	10%	44	26	30	30%	75%	7%	29	98	62%	10%			16.6	78	102	$13
13	OAK	12	8	0	197	134	3.97	4.28	1.22	695	725	654	25.6	2.9	6.1	2.1	10%	41	19	40	27%	71%	10%	32	94	56%	16%			-2.6	51	67	$7
1st Half		6	6	0	101	70	4.11	4.30	1.24	730	747	710	24.5	3.1	6.3	2.0	11%	42	17	41	26%	72%	12%	17	91	59%	18%			-3.1	48	62	$7
2nd Half		6	2	0	96	64	3.83	4.27	1.20	659	705	588	26.8	2.6	6.0	2.3	9%	40	22	38	27%	71%	9%	15	96	53%	13%			0.4	55	72	$8
14	**Proj**	**13**	**9**	**0**	**196**	**140**	**3.73**	**3.93**	**1.30**	**702**	**729**	**667**	**24.0**	**3.0**	**6.5**	**2.1**	**10%**	**42**	**22**	**36**	**29%**	**73%**	**8%**	**34**						**3.3**	**55**	**72**	**$9**

Parnell,Bobby

Age: 29 | Th: R | Role: RP | Ht: 6' 4" | Wt: 200 | Type: Pwr GB
Health: D | PT/Exp: C | Consist: A
LIMA Plan: B | Rand Var: -3 | MM: 5330

Was reiterating that saves can come from bad teams before neck woes ended season prematurely. Elite GB% helps keeps ball in yard, but won't repeat allowing just 1 HR. Improving Ctl and H% correction bodes well for more cheap saves, if healthy. Full recovery expected after off-season surgery; spring workload will be telling.

Yr	Tm	W	L	Sv	IP	K	ERA	xERA	WHIP	oOPS	vL	vR	BF/G	Ctl	Dom	Cmd	SwK	G	L	F	H%	S%	hr/f	GS	APC	DOM%	DIS%	Sv%	LI	RAR	BPV	BPX	R$
09	NYM	4	8	1	88	74	5.30	4.75	1.66	769	762	775	6.1	4.7	7.5	1.6	9%	47	16	37	35%	68%	8%	8	24	25%	50%	20	0.92	-10.6	34	64	-$6
10	NYM *	1	2	4	76	67	3.78	3.99	1.41	686	806	614	5.0	3.0	7.9	2.6	11%	56	26	18	34%	73%	5%	0	14			50	0.69	2.8	89	144	$1
11	NYM	4	6	6	59	64	3.64	3.57	1.47	679	685	672	4.5	4.1	9.7	2.4	11%	51	17	32	35%	76%	8%	0	18			50	1.10	2.2	93	140	$2
12	NYM	5	4	7	69	61	2.49	3.23	1.24	648	626	666	3.9	2.6	8.0	3.1	10%	62	17	22	32%	81%	9%	0	15			58	1.13	12.9	113	148	$8
13	NYM	5	5	22	50	44	2.16	3.09	1.00	555	606	519	4.0	2.2	7.9	3.7	10%	52	22	26	28%	78%	3%	0	16			85	1.66	10.5	114	149	$14
1st Half		5	4	14	35	30	2.83	3.01	0.97	552	503	590	3.9	2.1	7.7	3.8	9%	54	21	25	27%	68%	0%	0	16			82	1.86	4.5	115	150	$18
2nd Half		0	1	8	15	14	0.60	3.26	1.07	561	929	395	4.4	2.4	8.4	3.5	12%	47	26	28	28%	100%	8%	0	18			89	1.18	6.0	111	144	$6
14	**Proj**	**3**	**5**	**35**	**58**	**53**	**2.68**	**2.99**	**1.16**	**625**	**714**	**566**	**4.1**	**2.5**	**8.3**	**3.4**	**11%**	**53**	**21**	**26**	**30%**	**79%**	**9%**	**0**						**8.5**	**113**	**147**	**$18**

TODD ZOLA

Parra,Manny

Age: 31	Th: L	Role: RP	Health: F	LIMA Plan: A
Ht: 6' 3"	Wt: 205	Type: Pwr	PT/Exp: D	Rand Var: +1
			Consist: C	MM: 4500

Adding 5 mph to Uncle Charlie and increasing its frequency nudged Dom up and improved Ctl markedly. However, frequent arm issues means a repeat is not assured. Historically high H% hasn't regressed yet but it's coming. At 31, there's a better chance for a return to WHIP-killer than trusted fantasy asset.

Yr Tm	W	L	Sv	IP	K	ERA	xERA	WHIP	oOPS	vL	vR	BF/G	Ctl	Dom	Cmd	SwK	G	L	F	H%	S%	hr/f	GS	APC	DOM%	DIS%	Sv%	LI	RAR	BPV	BPX	R$
09 MIL *	12	13	0	165	132	5.95	5.78	1.76	865	778	887	24.3	5.0	7.2	1.4	9%	48	18	34	35%	67%	12%	27	95	30%	30%			-33.1	37	70	-$12
10 MIL	3	10	0	122	129	5.02	3.96	1.62	816	983	752	13.3	4.6	9.5	2.0	12%	47	18	34	35%	72%	15%	16	51	19%	19%	0	0.60	-14.1	71	115	-$7
11																																
12 MIL	2	3	0	59	61	5.06	4.22	1.65	738	635	827	4.4	5.4	9.4	1.7	10%	49	24	27	36%	68%	7%	0	17			0	0.79	-7.6	50	66	-$8
13 CIN	2	3	0	46	56	3.33	2.93	1.20	684	475	893	3.3	2.9	11.0	3.7	15%	44	22	34	32%	76%	13%	0	13			0	1.06	3.1	140	182	$0
1st Half	1	1	0	19	24	4.74	3.57	1.68	907	486	1201	4.0	3.3	11.4	3.4	15%	42	19	39	42%	79%	18%	0	16			0	0.82	-2.0	135	175	-$5
2nd Half	1	2	0	27	32	2.33	2.48	0.85	477	467	491	2.9	2.7	10.7	4.0	14%	45	25	29	24%	73%	6%	0	12			0	1.21	5.1	143	186	$4
14 Proj	**2**	**4**	**0**	**55**	**60**	**3.93**	**3.27**	**1.35**	**695**	**555**	**798**	**4.4**	**4.0**	**10.0**	**2.5**	**12%**	**46**	**22**	**32**	**32%**	**73%**	**12%**	**0**						**-0.4**	**95**	**124**	**-$1**

Patton,Troy

Age: 28	Th: L	Role: RP	Health: C	LIMA Plan: C
Ht: 6' 1"	Wt: 180	Type:	PT/Exp: D	Rand Var: 0
			Consist: A	MM: 3200

On the surface it appears that he gave his 2012 gains back. But his ERA outside of May was 2.64, in line with previous two seasons, and his 2nd half BPV mirrored 2012. Even so, his value is limited with moderate Dom and relatively few IP. Won't hurt—but won't help, either.

Yr Tm	W	L	Sv	IP	K	ERA	xERA	WHIP	oOPS	vL	vR	BF/G	Ctl	Dom	Cmd	SwK	G	L	F	H%	S%	hr/f	GS	APC	DOM%	DIS%	Sv%	LI	RAR	BPV	BPX	R$
09 a/a	7	5	0	108	58	5.77	6.90	1.68				24.3	2.9	4.8	1.6					33%	71%								-19.3	-7	-13	-$9
10 BAL *	8	11	0	137	72	5.60	5.85	1.61	1167	1000	1000	23.3	3.0	4.7	1.6	13%	50	0	50	33%	67%	0%	0	16			0	0.02	-25.6	16	26	-$10
11 BAL *	6	2	0	74	45	2.62	3.52	1.30	567	550	582	8.3	2.1	5.5	2.6	10%	39	13	48	32%	79%	5%	0	23			0	0.87	12.1	80	120	$4
12 BAL	1	0	0	56	49	2.43	3.34	1.02	598	554	650	4.1	1.9	7.9	4.1	11%	50	19	31	27%	81%	10%	0	15			0	1.03	10.9	118	154	$4
13 BAL	2	0	0	56	42	3.70	3.97	1.30	757	798	723	4.2	2.6	6.8	2.6	11%	45	18	37	30%	77%	13%	0	15			0	0.87	1.2	75	98	-$2
1st Half	1	0	0	36	24	3.79	4.27	1.43	770	831	728	4.7	3.3	6.1	1.8	10%	48	17	36	31%	77%	10%	0	17			0	0.81	0.4	46	60	-$3
2nd Half	1	0	0	20	18	3.54	3.50	1.08	734	758	699	3.5	1.3	8.0	6.0	14%	41	20	39	28%	78%	17%	0	13			0	0.95	0.8	127	164	$0
14 Proj	**3**	**1**	**0**	**58**	**44**	**3.55**	**3.63**	**1.24**	**722**	**719**	**726**	**4.7**	**2.3**	**6.9**	**3.0**	**12%**	**45**	**18**	**37**	**30%**	**76%**	**11%**	**0**						**2.3**	**85**	**110**	**$1**

Paxton,James

Age: 25	Th: L	Role: SP	Health: A	LIMA Plan: B
Ht: 6' 4"	Wt: 220	Type: Pwr xGB	PT/Exp: D	Rand Var: +1
			Consist: C	MM: 3203

3-0, 1.50 ERA in 24 IP at SEA. Impressed during Sept callup, but 3.12 xERA starts to ground expectations. Features mid-90s heater, a changeup he'll use anytime and a curve as his out pitch. Erosion of Cmd on the way up the ladder is a concern, but as 25-year-old groundballer with three plus pitches, there's still time.

Yr Tm	W	L	Sv	IP	K	ERA	xERA	WHIP	oOPS	vL	vR	BF/G	Ctl	Dom	Cmd	SwK	G	L	F	H%	S%	hr/f	GS	APC	DOM%	DIS%	Sv%	LI	RAR	BPV	BPX	R$
09																																
10																																
11 aa	3	0	0	39	45	2.04	2.47	1.12				22.0	3.0	10.5	3.5					31%	83%								9.1	134	202	$3
12 aa	9	4	0	106	96	3.68	4.34	1.58				22.3	4.8	8.1	1.7					34%	76%								4.4	72	95	-$2
13 SEA *	11	11	0	170	133	4.01	4.20	1.45	533	790	475	22.7	3.3	7.0	2.1	10%	59	17	24	33%	72%	13%	4	96	75%	0%			-3.0	69	90	-$1
1st Half	4	6	0	77	69	5.21	5.38	1.68				21.8	3.7	8.0	2.2					38%	69%	0%	0						-12.8	66	85	-$12
2nd Half	7	5	0	92	64	3.01	3.21	1.26	533	790	475	23.6	3.0	6.2	2.0	10%	59	17	24	29%	77%	13%	4	96	75%	0%			9.8	72	94	$9
14 Proj	**11**	**9**	**0**	**174**	**142**	**3.80**	**3.65**	**1.40**	**685**	**1069**	**599**	**22.3**	**3.6**	**7.4**	**2.0**	**10%**	**55**	**18**	**27**	**31%**	**74%**	**9%**	**33**						**1.5**	**68**	**88**	**$5**

Peacock,Brad

Age: 26	Th: R	Role: SP	Health: A	LIMA Plan: B+
Ht: 6' 1"	Wt: 175	Type: Pwr FB	PT/Exp: D	Rand Var: +1
			Consist: D	MM: 2303

5-6, 5.18 ERA in 83 IP at HOU. Began year in rotation but demoted after allowing 7 HR in April. Earned second chance and rewarded with 3.65 ERA. With an 8.9 Dom and 3.3 Ctl in Aug/Sept, there's a chance the switch went on in 2nd half and the cost to find out will be minimal... UP: 3.50 ERA with 160 K.

Yr Tm	W	L	Sv	IP	K	ERA	xERA	WHIP	oOPS	vL	vR	BF/G	Ctl	Dom	Cmd	SwK	G	L	F	H%	S%	hr/f	GS	APC	DOM%	DIS%	Sv%	LI	RAR	BPV	BPX	R$
09																																
10 aa	2	2	0	39	25	5.85	4.99	1.56				24.2	5.1	5.9	1.2					28%	64%								-8.4	24	38	-$5
11 WAS *	17	3	0	159	149	2.68	2.35	1.07	438	355	568	22.0	2.9	8.5	2.9	5%	32	8	61	27%	77%	0%	2	67	0%	0%	0	1.30	24.7	109	164	$22
12 aaa	12	9	0	135	115	6.17	5.28	1.65				21.5	4.3	7.7	1.8					35%	62%								-35.7	54	70	-$16
13 HOU *	11	8	0	162	141	4.20	4.21	1.31	779	919	594	20.9	3.3	7.8	2.4	8%	37	19	45	29%	73%	14%	14	83	43%	36%	0	0.79	-6.7	60	78	$3
1st Half	4	5	0	76	61	5.27	5.05	1.48	998	1237	734	19.2	4.1	7.3	1.8	6%	28	25	47	30%	69%	18%	5	64	0%	80%	0	0.78	-13.1	35	46	-$7
2nd Half	7	3	0	86	79	3.26	3.47	1.16	650	755	497	22.9	2.6	8.2	3.1	9%	42	15	43	28%	78%	11%	9	101	67%	11%			6.5	88	114	$12
14 Proj	**10**	**11**	**0**	**160**	**138**	**4.14**	**4.00**	**1.36**	**744**	**886**	**560**	**21.6**	**3.5**	**7.8**	**2.2**	**8%**	**37**	**19**	**45**	**30%**	**73%**	**9%**	**31**						**-5.3**	**61**	**79**	**$4**

Peavy,Jake

Age: 33	Th: R	Role: SP	Health: F	LIMA Plan: B
Ht: 6' 1"	Wt: 195	Type: FB	PT/Exp: B	Rand Var: 0
			Consist: A	MM: 3303

Returned to the DL for six weeks after making 56 starts since last visit in 2011. However, it was due to a fractured rib, not arm. 2nd half Dom dip not a concern as SwK stable, but dropping BPV and rising FB warn that ERA could continue to rise. Injuries hijacked former stud status, but still gets an "A" for Consistency.

Yr Tm	W	L	Sv	IP	K	ERA	xERA	WHIP	oOPS	vL	vR	BF/G	Ctl	Dom	Cmd	SwK	G	L	F	H%	S%	hr/f	GS	APC	DOM%	DIS%	Sv%	LI	RAR	BPV	BPX	R$
09 2TM *	10	7	0	117	123	3.60	3.07	1.18	615	708	503	23.4	3.0	9.5	3.2	10%	42	18	40	30%	71%	8%	16	98	75%	6%			10.4	110	205	$12
10 CHW	7	6	0	107	93	4.63	3.87	1.23	696	729	663	26.4	2.9	7.8	2.7	9%	41	18	42	29%	65%	10%	17	101	59%	18%			-7.2	83	134	$3
11 CHW *	8	8	0	141	118	5.12	4.32	1.31	701	669	740	23.2	1.7	7.5	4.4	10%	39	23	39	34%	62%	8%	18	98	67%	17%	0	0.81	-20.4	108	163	-$2
12 CHW	11	12	0	219	194	3.37	3.82	1.10	671	714	614	27.6	2.0	8.0	4.0	10%	37	19	45	28%	74%	10%	32	109	75%	0%			17.4	104	136	$22
13 2AL	12	5	0	145	121	4.17	4.00	1.15	697	731	659	25.7	2.2	7.5	3.4	9%	33	21	47	28%	68%	10%	23	103	74%	13%			-5.4	86	112	$7
1st Half	6	4	0	67	66	4.30	3.57	1.16	718	810	597	24.8	2.0	8.9	4.4	9%	37	18	45	30%	68%	12%	11	99	73%	18%			-3.6	120	155	$7
2nd Half	6	1	0	78	55	4.06	4.39	1.13	679	652	705	26.4	2.4	6.4	2.6	8%	30	23	48	26%	68%	9%	12	106	75%	8%			-1.8	57	73	$8
14 Proj	**11**	**7**	**0**	**160**	**136**	**3.93**	**3.61**	**1.20**	**701**	**726**	**671**	**25.3**	**2.2**	**7.7**	**3.5**	**9%**	**35**	**20**	**44**	**30%**	**70%**	**9%**	**25**						**-1.2**	**92**	**120**	**$10**

Pelfrey,Mike

Age: 30	Th: R	Role: SP	Health: F	LIMA Plan: D+
Ht: 6' 7"	Wt: 250	Type:	PT/Exp: B	Rand Var: +1
			Consist: B	MM: 2101

Returned from TJS and showed 2012 was a sample size tease. BPIs same as pre-surgery—and that's not a good thing. He doesn't miss bats and too many batted balls miss gloves. For that matter, 2010 wasn't real either; the quest to reclaim that season is what is keeping him employed. Don't be taken in.

Yr Tm	W	L	Sv	IP	K	ERA	xERA	WHIP	oOPS	vL	vR	BF/G	Ctl	Dom	Cmd	SwK	G	L	F	H%	S%	hr/f	GS	APC	DOM%	DIS%	Sv%	LI	RAR	BPV	BPX	R$
09 NYM	10	12	0	184	107	5.03	4.57	1.51	779	787	768	26.6	3.2	5.2	1.6	6%	51	19	30	32%	67%	10%	31	102	35%	26%			-16.1	36	67	-$4
10 NYM	15	9	1	204	113	3.66	4.34	1.38	735	776	690	25.6	3.0	5.0	1.7	6%	48	20	32	30%	74%	6%	33	100	45%	24%	100	0.82	10.5	35	56	$8
11 NYM	7	13	0	194	105	4.74	4.63	1.47	777	776	778	25.3	3.0	4.9	1.6	6%	46	20	35	31%	69%	9%	33	95	30%	24%	0	0.75	-19.1	30	46	-$8
12 NYM	0	0	0	20	13	2.29	3.77	1.42	683	672	697	28.3	1.8	5.9	3.3	9%	53	27	20	36%	82%	0%	3	102	33%	0%			4.2	89	116	-$3
13 MIN	5	13	0	153	101	5.19	4.59	1.55	789	762	821	23.4	3.1	6.0	1.9	6%	43	21	36	34%	67%	7%	29	94	21%	34%			-24.9	44	57	-$13
1st Half	3	6	0	71	38	6.11	4.85	1.63	853	857	850	22.6	2.7	4.8	1.8	6%	45	18	37	35%	62%	7%	14	91	14%	50%			-19.6	38	49	-$18
2nd Half	2	7	0	82	63	4.39	4.37	1.49	730	683	791	24.2	3.5	6.9	2.0	6%	41	24	35	33%	71%	7%	15	97	27%	20%			-5.3	49	63	-$9
14 Proj	**5**	**9**	**0**	**129**	**79**	**4.78**	**4.30**	**1.47**	**774**	**769**	**779**	**23.8**	**3.1**	**5.5**	**1.8**	**6%**	**45**	**21**	**34**	**32%**	**69%**	**9%**	**23**						**-14.4**	**39**	**50**	**-$6**

Peralta,Joel

Age: 38	Th: R	Role: RP	Health: A	LIMA Plan: B+
Ht: 5' 11"	Wt: 205	Type: Pwr xFB	PT/Exp: C	Rand Var: -4
			Consist: B	MM: 3511

Leads MLB in appearances since 2011 with 228. While that may have contributed to his BPI slide, his velocity did not change. His main issue was a spike in Ctl, especially in 2H. A low H% and hr/f, especially in light of his extreme FB nature, rescued his ERA. Reliability and whiffs have value, but threat of HR elevates the risk.

Yr Tm	W	L	Sv	IP	K	ERA	xERA	WHIP	oOPS	vL	vR	BF/G	Ctl	Dom	Cmd	SwK	G	L	F	H%	S%	hr/f	GS	APC	DOM%	DIS%	Sv%	LI	RAR	BPV	BPX	R$
09 COL *	6	3	4	61	44	4.36	4.68	1.47	877	1128	646	4.5	3.5	6.5	1.8	10%	25	26	49	32%	72%	8%	0	17			80	0.96	-0.3	47	89	$1
10 WAS *	3	0	20	82	76	1.83	2.25	0.97	521	596	474	4.7	1.9	8.3	4.5	12%	26	18	56	27%	86%	7%	0	19			91	0.85	22.8	136	219	$19
11 TAM	3	4	6	68	61	2.93	3.73	0.92	586	435	718	3.6	2.4	8.1	3.4	11%	27	16	57	22%	73%	7%	0	15			75	1.20	8.5	86	130	$9
12 TAM	2	6	2	67	84	3.63	3.23	0.99	629	556	708	3.4	2.3	11.3	4.9	13%	30	18	52	28%	68%	11%	0	14			40	1.15	3.2	149	195	$6
13 TAM	3	8	1	71	74	3.41	4.16	1.14	586	556	627	3.6	4.3	9.3	2.2	11%	27	19	54	24%	73%	7%	0	15			25	1.38	4.0	57	75	$3
1st Half	1	4	1	36	35	2.97	4.12	1.07	556	520	605	3.5	4.0	8.7	2.2	12%	30	18	52	23%	75%	6%	0	14			100	1.25	4.0	57	74	$5
2nd Half	2	4	0	35	39	3.86	4.20	1.20	617	593	650	3.8	4.6	10.0	2.2	10%	23	21	56	25%	71%	8%	0	15			0	1.51	0.0	57	74	$2
14 Proj	**3**	**7**	**5**	**73**	**77**	**3.53**	**3.65**	**1.12**	**643**	**593**	**699**	**3.6**	**3.8**	**9.5**	**2.5**	**12%**	**27**	**19**	**54**	**24%**	**74%**	**10%**	**0**						**3.0**	**75**	**98**	**$6**

TODD ZOLA

Peralta,Wily

Age: 25	Th: R	Role SP	Health A
Ht: 6' 1"	Wt: 245	Type Pwr GB	PT/Exp C
			Consist C
LIMA Plan D+	Rand Var 0	MM 3205	

On surface, Ctl gains offset by Dom loss, leaving him as an end-gamer again. But late K surge, 95-mph four-seamer give hope for much more, especially with that consistent 50% groundball rate. RH bats absolutely hammered his change-up; a simple repertoire tweak could make a huge difference. UP: 3.50 ERA, 200 K

Yr	Tm	W	L	Sv	IP	K	ERA	xERA	WHIP	oOPS	vL	vR	BF/G	Ctl	Dom	Cmd	SwK	G	L	F	H%	S%	hr/f	GS	APC	DOM%	DIS%	Sv%	LI	RAR	BPV	BPX	R$
09																																	
10	aa	2	3	0	42	26	3.88	5.24	1.64				23.6	4.9	5.6	1.1					31%	80%								1.0	24	39	-$3
11	a/a	11	7	0	151	140	3.31	3.23	1.27				23.7	3.3	8.3	2.5					31%	75%								11.8	93	140	$10
12	MIL *	9	12	0	176	146	5.34	5.17	1.71	601	639	564	23.4	4.8	7.5	1.6	9%	55	21	24	36%	68%	0%	5	76	60%	20%	0	0.66	-28.7	56	72	-$18
13	MIL	11	15	0	183	129	4.37	4.17	1.42	722	753	692	25.1	3.6	6.3	1.8	9%	51	21	28	30%	71%	12%	32	93	41%	22%			-11.4	46	60	-$2
1st Half		5	9	0	92	51	5.58	4.66	1.61	776	846	711	24.9	3.6	5.0	1.4	9%	53	23	24	33%	66%	13%	17	91	24%	29%			-19.4	23	30	-$14
2nd Half		6	6	0	91	78	3.15	3.72	1.23	661	654	668	25.2	3.5	7.7	2.2	9%	49	19	33	27%	78%	11%	15	97	60%	13%			8.0	69	90	$10
14	Proj	11	13	0	189	148	4.08	3.85	1.41	705	727	684	23.6	3.8	7.1	1.8	9%	50	21	29	31%	72%	10%	34						-4.9	52	68	$3

Perez,Chris

Age: 29	Th: R	Role RP	Health C
Ht: 6' 4"	Wt: 230	Type Pwr	PT/Exp B
			Consist B
LIMA Plan B	Rand Var +3	MM 3420	

Talky closer with a balky shoulder has nine lives, but he's nearly used all of them up. With continued mediocre xERAs for a closer, you still can't bank on him as your #1 stopper. Raw stuff an issue too. Four-seamer dipped 1.3 mph to 93 mph and batters smoked it; health another big red flag. DN: total loss of Save opps.

Yr	Tm	W	L	Sv	IP	K	ERA	xERA	WHIP	oOPS	vL	vR	BF/G	Ctl	Dom	Cmd	SwK	G	L	F	H%	S%	hr/f	GS	APC	DOM%	DIS%	Sv%	LI	RAR	BPV	BPX	R$
09	2 TM	1	2	2	57	68	4.26	3.63	1.19	667	679	661	3.9	4.3	10.7	2.5	10%	35	18	47	26%	68%	13%	0	16			40	1.02	0.4	91	171	$2
10	CLE	2	2	23	63	61	1.71	3.90	1.08	583	752	445	4.1	4.0	8.7	2.2	8%	34	20	46	24%	88%	5%	0	17			85	1.53	18.4	61	98	$16
11	CLE	4	7	36	60	39	3.32	4.80	1.21	648	598	702	3.9	3.9	5.9	1.5	6%	28	21	50	24%	75%	6%	0	15			90	1.68	4.6	6	9	$15
12	CLE	0	4	39	58	59	3.59	3.67	1.13	652	538	780	4.0	2.5	9.2	3.7	10%	41	19	40	29%	71%	9%	0	16			91	1.23	3.0	117	153	$17
13	CLE	5	3	25	54	54	4.33	3.86	1.43	847	916	765	4.5	3.5	9.0	2.6	8%	42	23	35	31%	77%	20%	0	17			83	1.24	-3.1	88	114	$8
1st Half		2	1	7	19	19	3.86	4.12	1.34	776	737	800	4.4	4.8	9.2	1.9	8%	42	21	37	25%	81%	21%	0	18			78	1.25	0.0	55	71	$3
2nd Half		3	2	18	35	35	4.58	3.73	1.47	884	993	736	4.5	2.8	8.9	3.2	9%	42	24	34	34%	76%	19%	0	16			86	1.24	-3.1	105	136	$10
14	Proj	3	4	10	58	56	3.84	3.60	1.29	747	755	738	4.0	3.4	8.7	2.5	8%	39	21	40	29%	76%	14%	0						0.2	80	104	$4

Perez,Martin

Age: 23	Th: L	Role SP	Health C
Ht: 6' 0"	Wt: 190	Type	PT/Exp D
			Consist A
LIMA Plan B	Rand Var 0	MM 3105	

10-6, 3.62 ERA in 124 IP at TEX. Former top prospect finally flashed upside, but he's still a work in progress. PROs: SwK spike says his K ceiling is higher than what it appears; still very young. CONs: xERA doesn't give him support for a sub-4 mark; history of marginal Cmd. As likely to take step back as another step forward.

Yr	Tm	W	L	Sv	IP	K	ERA	xERA	WHIP	oOPS	vL	vR	BF/G	Ctl	Dom	Cmd	SwK	G	L	F	H%	S%	hr/f	GS	APC	DOM%	DIS%	Sv%	LI	RAR	BPV	BPX	R$
09	aa	1	3	0	21	13	6.13	6.01	1.65				18.8	1.9	5.7	2.9					38%	63%								-4.7	56	104	-$5
10	aa	5	8	0	100	90	7.35	6.52	1.82				19.3	4.5	8.1	1.8					38%	60%								-40.2	38	61	-$16
11	a/a	8	6	0	137	102	4.69	4.93	1.56				22.3	3.5	6.7	1.9					35%	70%								-12.6	55	83	-$6
12	TEX *	8	10	0	165	83	4.95	4.68	1.51	819	596	924	21.0	3.7	4.5	1.2	7%	49	21	30	30%	68%	8%	6	55	0%	50%	0	0.75	-19.0	28	36	-$11
13	TEX *	15	8	0	168	109	3.80	4.30	1.35	728	759	718	25.0	2.5	5.9	2.3	10%	48	21	31	31%	75%	12%	20	93	55%	25%			1.4	55	72	$5
1st Half		7	3	0	62	33	3.72	4.11	1.37	664	571	700	23.7	2.1	4.8	2.3	11%	46	32	22	32%	73%	7%	3	85	67%	33%			1.1	59	77	$3
2nd Half		8	5	0	105	76	3.84	4.07	1.35	739	799	720	26.5	2.8	6.5	2.3	10%	49	18	33	30%	76%	13%	17	94	53%	24%			0.3	67	87	$6
14	Proj	13	10	0	181	120	4.34	3.96	1.41	745	636	788	22.4	3.0	5.9	2.0	9%	48	23	29	31%	71%	11%	34						-10.5	52	68	$1

Perez,Oliver

Age: 32	Th: L	Role RP	Health D
Ht: 6' 3"	Wt: 220	Type Pwr xFB	PT/Exp D
			Consist D
LIMA Plan C	Rand Var +2	MM 3510	

Sexy start to year before H%/S% gods intervened late. Truth be told, role expansion wasn't in the cards anyway, for batters hit for plenty of power against his hard stuff. As a flyball pitcher with a hittable fastball and chronic wildness, his dominant slider can only cover up so much. Not likely to maintain LIMA gains.

Yr	Tm	W	L	Sv	IP	K	ERA	xERA	WHIP	oOPS	vL	vR	BF/G	Ctl	Dom	Cmd	SwK	G	L	F	H%	S%	hr/f	GS	APC	DOM%	DIS%	Sv%	LI	RAR	BPV	BPX	R$
09	NYM	3	4	0	66	62	6.82	6.19	1.92	897	590	1029	23.1	7.9	8.5	1.1	8%	28	20	52	31%	67%	12%	14	94	21%	36%			-20.3	-55	-104	-$11
10	NYM	0	5	0	46	37	6.80	6.44	2.07	935	863	956	13.8	8.2	7.2	0.9	7%	35	19	46	32%	70%	13%	7	56	14%	43%	0	0.96	-15.5	-78	-126	-$11
11	aa	3	5	0	76	41	4.27	6.66	1.76				21.7	3.5	4.9	1.4					34%	81%								-3.1	3	5	-$7
12	SEA *	3	5	1	61	56	3.55	4.59	1.57	628	679	575	4.8	4.4	8.4	1.9	11%	33	23	44	35%	78%	3%	0	14			25	1.24	3.5	70	91	-$3
13	SEA	3	3	2	53	74	3.74	3.47	1.43	731	645	786	3.8	4.4	12.6	2.8	13%	31	20	49	37%	77%	10%	0	16			67	1.50	0.8	116	151	-$1
1st Half		2	2	1	30	43	1.52	3.22	1.28	630	628	634	3.8	4.2	13.0	3.1	15%	27	22	51	34%	94%	9%	0	16			100	1.45	8.6	125	162	$5
2nd Half		1	1	1	23	31	6.56	3.81	1.63	850	675	921	3.7	4.6	12.0	2.6	11%	34	18	48	40%	60%	10%	0	16			50	1.56	-7.7	103	133	-$7
14	Proj	3	4	3	58	67	3.86	3.75	1.41	720	589	780	4.8	4.5	10.4	2.3	10%	32	20	48	32%	76%	10%	0						0.0	75	98	$0

Perkins,Glen

Age: 31	Th: L	Role RP	Health B
Ht: 6' 0"	Wt: 205	Type Pwr	PT/Exp B
			Consist A
LIMA Plan C	Rand Var -1	MM 5530	

Teams prefer to reserve lefty relievers for situational work because there are far more righties available to close. But sometimes a skill set is too good to hold back. Hefty skills are backed by a 95-mph four-seamer. Big gains vs. RH bats in '13 cement his status as a premium stopper.

Yr	Tm	W	L	Sv	IP	K	ERA	xERA	WHIP	oOPS	vL	vR	BF/G	Ctl	Dom	Cmd	SwK	G	L	F	H%	S%	hr/f	GS	APC	DOM%	DIS%	Sv%	LI	RAR	BPV	BPX	R$
09	MIN	6	7	0	96	45	5.89	4.86	1.48	802	873	781	23.5	2.1	4.2	2.0	6%	47	14	39	32%	62%	10%	17	82	35%	24%	0	0.74	-18.6	43	80	-$6
10	MIN *	5	10	0	146	87	6.78	6.71	1.82	938	657	1080	17.3	2.7	5.4	2.0	8%	50	22	28	39%	62%	14%	1	26	0%	100%	0	0.64	-48.5	30	48	-$22
11	MIN	4	4	2	62	65	2.48	3.04	1.23	644	589	681	3.9	3.1	9.5	3.1	12%	50	21	29	33%	80%	4%	0	14			40	1.22	11.1	116	174	$5
12	MIN	3	1	16	70	78	2.56	3.12	1.04	631	488	721	4.0	2.0	10.0	4.9	14%	42	19	39	29%	82%	12%	0	15			80	0.92	12.6	144	188	$14
13	MIN	2	0	36	63	77	2.30	2.67	0.93	562	544	568	3.9	2.2	11.1	5.1	14%	36	26	38	28%	79%	9%	0	15			90	1.16	12.1	155	202	$21
1st Half		1	0	20	31	43	2.05	2.36	0.82	495	544	478	3.7	2.1	12.6	6.1	15%	35	26	38	27%	78%	8%	0	15			91	1.14	6.9	185	240	$25
2nd Half		1	0	16	32	34	2.53	2.99	1.03	626	545	652	4.1	2.3	9.6	4.3	13%	37	26	37	28%	80%	11%	0	16			89	1.18	5.3	126	163	$18
14	Proj	3	1	40	65	71	2.82	2.89	1.08	632	570	658	4.3	2.3	9.8	4.3	13%	41	22	37	30%	77%	9%	0						8.4	133	173	$21

Pestano,Vinnie

Age: 29	Th: R	Role RP	Health B
Ht: 6' 0"	Wt: 200	Type Pwr FB	PT/Exp C
			Consist B
LIMA Plan C	Rand Var 0	MM 3500	

Chronic sore elbow likely to blame for this control collapse. With steady fastball decline last two years and absence of out pitch vs. lefties, he was already a risky closer-in-waiting. Even with regression of H%, soaring xERA trend gives him more risk than reward. Pass until health, velocity align again.

Yr	Tm	W	L	Sv	IP	K	ERA	xERA	WHIP	oOPS	vL	vR	BF/G	Ctl	Dom	Cmd	SwK	G	L	F	H%	S%	hr/f	GS	APC	DOM%	DIS%	Sv%	LI	RAR	BPV	BPX	R$
09	aa	2	3	24	35	26	3.88	4.31	1.49				4.4	3.8	6.8	1.8					33%	74%								1.9	61	114	$8
10	CLE *	2	3	18	65	71	2.15	2.80	1.22	614	875	408	4.2	3.0	9.8	3.3	18%	30	20	50	33%	82%	0%	0	20			90	0.39	15.4	128	207	$13
11	CLE	1	2	2	62	84	2.32	2.82	1.05	577	812	410	3.7	3.5	12.2	3.5	17%	39	19	42	28%	82%	9%	0	15			33	1.22	12.4	142	214	$7
12	CLE	3	3	2	70	76	2.57	3.55	1.10	631	752	487	4.1	3.1	9.8	3.2	11%	41	17	43	27%	81%	9%	0	17			40	1.54	12.5	112	146	$7
13	CLE	1	2	6	35	37	4.08	4.53	1.64	838	878	792	4.3	5.3	9.4	1.8	12%	35	21	44	33%	81%	14%	0	18			67	0.81	-0.9	38	50	-$3
1st Half		1	2	6	26	28	3.81	4.16	1.38	784	856	678	4.3	4.5	9.7	2.2	11%	27	27	46	28%	81%	16%	0	18			75	0.97	0.2	58	75	$0
2nd Half		0	0	0	9	9	4.82	5.57	2.36	968	958	975	4.3	7.7	8.7	1.1	12%	53	7	40	43%	81%	8%	0	17			0	0.44	-1.1	-21	-27	-$10
14	Proj	2	3	0	58	63	3.25	3.69	1.36	726	886	560	4.1	4.3	9.8	2.3	13%	35	21	43	31%	80%	9%	0						4.4	74	96	$0

Petit,Yusmeiro

Age: 29	Th: R	Role RP	Health A
Ht: 6' 1"	Wt: 255	Type xFB	PT/Exp D
			Consist A
LIMA Plan B+	Rand Var 0	MM 3203	

4-1, 3.56 ERA in 48 IP at SF. Late surge puts this '04 top prospect back on map. 104 BPV in Sept shows it was legit, especially w/steady Ctl gains and elite SwK. Wipeout curve makes up for 88-mph FB, but as a soft-tossing flyball pitcher, he's got a thin margin of error. There's profit here, but only under $5.

Yr	Tm	W	L	Sv	IP	K	ERA	xERA	WHIP	oOPS	vL	vR	BF/G	Ctl	Dom	Cmd	SwK	G	L	F	H%	S%	hr/f	GS	APC	DOM%	DIS%	Sv%	LI	RAR	BPV	BPX	R$
09	ARI *	3	11	0	105	84	6.09	6.13	1.56	837	851	820	16.5	3.3	7.2	2.2	9%	31	20	49	32%	66%	13%	17	66	29%	47%	0	0.75	-22.9	25	46	-$8
10	aaa	4	2	0	59	45	5.35	4.40	1.31				10.2	2.5	6.9	2.8					30%	61%								-9.3	64	103	-$2
11	for	2	1	0	37	27	5.14	3.68	1.12				20.9	1.5	6.5	4.3					28%	56%								-5.4	97	145	-$2
12	SF *	7	7	0	171	118	3.48	4.47	1.42	936	885	1100	25.0	2.0	6.2	3.1	2%	38	25	38	35%	76%	0%	1	94	0%	100%			11.3	80	105	$2
13	SF *	9	7	0	136	115	4.26	4.34	1.28	660	562	717	24.2	1.6	7.6	4.8	13%	30	26	44	33%	70%	7%	7	91	57%	14%	0	0.73	-6.7	113	147	$2
1st Half		2	3	0	41	36	7.29	7.64	1.86				23.8	2.4	8.0	3.3					42%	63%	0%	0						-17.2	48	63	-$21
2nd Half		7	4	0	95	79	2.97	2.93	1.04	660	562	717	24.4	1.2	7.5	6.1	13%	30	26	44	29%	75%	7%	7	91	57%	14%	0	0.73	10.5	155	201	$12
14	Proj	7	7	0	131	103	4.06	3.86	1.32	750	720	774	19.1	1.9	7.1	3.7	11%	32	22	46	32%	73%	9%	26						-3.1	87	113	$3

STEPHEN NICKRAND

Pettibone,Jonathan

Age: 23 Th: R Role SP	Health D	LIMA Plan D+	
Ht: 6' 6" Wt: 225 Type GB	PT/Exp D	Rand Var 0	
	Consist B	MM 3101	

5-4, 4.04 ERA in 100 IP at PHI. On surface, solid debut before shoulder strain sidelined him for final two months. Before you go all-in, as a GBer with a low strikeout rate and very few swinging strikes, his success is dependent upon his defense. Without the skills to control his own fate, he's mediocre end-rotation fodder.

Yr Tm	W	L	Sv	IP	K	ERA	xERA	WHIP	oOPS	vL	vR	BF/G	Ctl	Dom	Cmd	SwK	G	L	F	H%	S%	hr/f	GS	APC	DOM%	DIS%	Sv%	LI	RAR	BPV	BPX	R$
09																																
10																																
11																																
12 a/a	13	8	0	160	99	3.64	3.82	1.33				25.5	2.7	5.6	2.0					30%	73%								7.5	60	79	$6
13 PHI *	5	6	0	123	78	4.60	4.77	1.52	781	825	735	23.2	3.2	5.7	1.8	6%	49	21	30	33%	70%	10%	18	93	39%	17%			-11.1	46	60	-$8
1st Half	3	4	0	85	51	4.82	4.92	1.50	790	850	723	22.8	3.0	5.4	1.8	6%	45	22	34	32%	69%	10%	13	94	31%	15%			-9.9	38	49	-$8
2nd Half	2	2	0	38	27	4.18	4.48	1.59	757	751	762	24.0	3.8	6.5	1.7	7%	63	18	19	35%	72%	7%	5	91	60%	20%			-1.5	64	83	-$7
14 Proj	**5**	**4**	**0**	**79**	**51**	**4.50**	**3.99**	**1.47**	**787**	**814**	**760**	**24.3**	**3.2**	**5.8**	**1.8**	**7%**	**52**	**21**	**27**	**32%**	**70%**	**8%**	**14**						**-6.1**	**49**	**64**	**-$3**

Pettitte,Andy

Age: 42 Th: L Role RP	Health F	LIMA Plan C+	
Ht: 6' 5" Wt: 225 Type ###	PT/Exp C	Rand Var 0	
	Consist B	MM 0000	

Will go down as the epitome of a winner and workhorse. From '95 to '13, had most wins (255) and IP (3,300) of any SP, and those don't include his post-season heroics. For reference, guy with next-most regular season wins over same period was Maddux at *224*. PED use clouds legacy, but results and durability were remarkable.

Yr Tm	W	L	Sv	IP	K	ERA	xERA	WHIP	oOPS	vL	vR	BF/G	Ctl	Dom	Cmd	SwK	G	L	F	H%	S%	hr/f	GS	APC	DOM%	DIS%	Sv%	LI	RAR	BPV	BPX	R$
09 NYY	14	8	0	195	148	4.16	4.35	1.38	721	730	717	26.1	3.5	6.8	1.9	8%	43	19	38	30%	72%	9%	32	103	47%	16%			3.9	49	92	$9
10 NYY	11	3	0	129	101	3.28	3.90	1.27	701	482	780	25.5	2.9	7.0	2.5	8%	44	18	38	30%	77%	9%	21	95	57%	24%			12.7	72	116	$9
11																																
12 NYY	5	4	0	75	69	2.87	3.27	1.14	632	516	681	25.3	2.5	8.2	3.3	10%	56	15	29	28%	79%	13%	12	94	50%	17%			10.7	115	150	$6
13 NYY	11	11	0	185	128	3.74	3.97	1.33	731	566	781	26.1	2.3	6.2	2.7	9%	46	23	31	31%	74%	9%	30	97	40%	27%			2.9	73	95	$5
1st Half	5	6	0	81	64	4.22	3.72	1.32	735	419	832	26.5	2.4	7.1	2.9	9%	49	20	31	32%	69%	9%	13	94	54%	31%			-3.6	89	116	$2
2nd Half	6	5	0	104	64	3.36	4.17	1.33	728	682	742	25.8	2.2	5.5	2.5	8%	44	24	32	31%	78%	9%	17	98	29%	24%			6.5	60	78	$6
14 Proj																																

Phelps,David

Age: 27 Th: R Role RP	Health D	LIMA Plan C	
Ht: 6' 2" Wt: 200 Type Pwr	PT/Exp C	Rand Var +2	
	Consist C	MM 3201	

Starter or reliever? Last two years, you decide... As SP: 4.42 ERA, 1.36 WHIP, 7.9 Dom. As RP: 3.57 ERA, 1.25 WHIP, 9.7 Dom. Even out of bullpen, upside really limited by lack of dominant pitch; fastball barely hits 90 mph. Low SwK suggests strikeouts will come down, and with eroding control, that's a recipe for failure.

Yr Tm	W	L	Sv	IP	K	ERA	xERA	WHIP	oOPS	vL	vR	BF/G	Ctl	Dom	Cmd	SwK	G	L	F	H%	S%	hr/f	GS	APC	DOM%	DIS%	Sv%	LI	RAR	BPV	BPX	R$
09																																
10 a/a	10	2	0	159	117	3.23	3.70	1.30				25.1	2.2	6.6	3.0					33%	75%								16.7	89	145	$10
11 aaa	6	6	0	107	72	4.51	6.23	1.64				26.6	2.5	6.1	2.4					36%	77%								-7.6	36	55	-$7
12 NYY	4	4	0	100	96	3.34	3.82	1.19	682	786	597	12.5	3.4	8.7	2.5	7%	43	19	38	27%	78%	14%	11	51	45%	45%	0	0.83	8.3	84	110	$6
13 NYY	6	5	0	87	79	4.98	3.97	1.42	749	756	738	17.1	3.6	8.2	2.3	7%	42	22	36	33%	65%	9%	12	68	58%	17%	0	0.92	-12.0	70	91	-$4
1st Half	5	5	0	76	70	4.95	3.98	1.44	760	773	742	19.5	3.8	8.3	2.2	7%	43	22	35	33%	66%	9%	11	77	55%	18%	0	0.94	-10.2	68	88	-$4
2nd Half	1	0	0	10	9	5.23	3.87	1.26	668	657	685	8.8	2.6	7.8	3.0	5%	39	23	39	31%	58%	8%	1	37	100%	0%	0	0.84	-1.7	87	113	-$5
14 Proj	**7**	**6**	**0**	**115**	**94**	**4.38**	**3.89**	**1.44**	**808**	**853**	**757**	**19.7**	**3.0**	**7.3**	**2.4**	**7%**	**43**	**20**	**37**	**33%**	**72%**	**10%**	**24**						**-7.3**	**71**	**92**	**-$2**

Porcello,Rick

Age: 25 Th: R Role SP	Health A	LIMA Plan A	
Ht: 6' 5" Wt: 200 Type GB	PT/Exp A	Rand Var +3	
	Consist A	MM 4205	

The power of pitch mix. Substituting dominant curveball for blah slider turned his skills from average to elite. Dom/BPV/SwK growth all aligning together, so immediate next step is 2nd half x 2. As a GB artist, his fate will be tied closely to infield defense. This is your last chance to buy him cheap... UP: 3.25 ERA, 180 K.

Yr Tm	W	L	Sv	IP	K	ERA	xERA	WHIP	oOPS	vL	vR	BF/G	Ctl	Dom	Cmd	SwK	G	L	F	H%	S%	hr/f	GS	APC	DOM%	DIS%	Sv%	LI	RAR	BPV	BPX	R$
09 DET	14	9	0	171	89	3.96	4.28	1.34	738	753	719	23.2	2.7	4.7	1.7	7%	54	17	29	28%	75%	14%	31	88	39%	32%			7.7	42	79	$9
10 DET *	11	14	0	191	100	4.76	4.47	1.38	752	784	717	25.8	2.2	4.7	2.1	6%	50	18	32	31%	66%	10%	27	96	30%	19%			-16.0	45	72	-$1
11 DET	14	9	0	182	104	4.75	4.05	1.41	774	857	650	25.3	2.3	5.1	2.3	7%	51	19	30	32%	67%	10%	31	92	29%	23%			-18.1	60	90	-$2
12 DET	10	12	0	176	107	4.59	4.15	1.53	808	883	725	25.3	2.2	5.5	2.4	8%	53	24	23	35%	71%	12%	31	91	32%	26%			-12.6	69	90	-$9
13 DET	13	8	0	177	142	4.32	3.32	1.28	709	808	602	23.0	2.1	7.2	3.4	9%	55	21	24	32%	68%	14%	29	89	48%	17%	0	0.84	-10.0	105	137	$4
1st Half	4	6	0	86	68	5.21	3.24	1.29	720	771	656	22.6	1.8	7.1	4.0	8%	57	20	23	32%	60%	16%	15	90	53%	20%	0	0.72	-14.3	115	149	-$3
2nd Half	9	2	0	91	74	3.47	3.39	1.28	698	851	554	23.4	2.5	7.3	3.0	9%	53	22	25	31%	75%	12%	14	87	43%	14%	0	0.96	4.4	96	125	$10
14 Proj	**15**	**10**	**0**	**189**	**146**	**3.67**	**3.31**	**1.29**	**695**	**777**	**603**	**23.3**	**2.3**	**6.9**	**3.1**	**8%**	**54**	**21**	**25**	**32%**	**73%**	**11%**	**33**						**4.6**	**96**	**124**	**$11**

Pressly,Ryan

Age: 25 Th: R Role RP	Health A	LIMA Plan D+	
Ht: 6' 3" Wt: 205 Type	PT/Exp D	Rand Var -1	
	Consist A	MM 2100	

Rule 5 pick with nice MLB debut on surface. Closer look suggests that a sprinkle of H% and hr/f help was the only thing standing between him and a mid-4 ERA. With middling command, average stuff, and no strikeout pitch, there's no chance he'll have sustained success late in games. Ignore without hesitation.

Yr Tm	W	L	Sv	IP	K	ERA	xERA	WHIP	oOPS	vL	vR	BF/G	Ctl	Dom	Cmd	SwK	G	L	F	H%	S%	hr/f	GS	APC	DOM%	DIS%	Sv%	LI	RAR	BPV	BPX	R$
09																																
10																																
11																																
12 aa	2	2	0	28	17	4.04	4.27	1.43				8.4	3.5	5.6	1.6					30%	73%								-0.1	45	59	-$4
13 MIN	3	3	0	77	49	3.87	4.29	1.28	677	746	614	6.4	3.2	5.8	1.8	8%	44	21	35	28%	70%	6%	0	24			0	0.70	-0.1	40	52	-$1
1st Half	2	0	0	38	25	2.63	4.71	1.35	670	701	647	6.4	3.6	6.0	1.7	7%	36	23	42	30%	80%	2%	0	24			0	0.48	5.7	24	32	$1
2nd Half	1	3	0	39	24	5.08	3.86	1.21	684	779	569	6.5	2.8	5.5	2.0	9%	52	20	28	27%	58%	12%	0	25			0	0.92	-5.8	55	71	-$4
14 Proj	**2**	**3**	**0**	**65**	**41**	**4.24**	**4.02**	**1.26**	**678**	**753**	**607**	**6.4**	**3.1**	**5.7**	**1.8**	**8%**	**46**	**21**	**34**	**28%**	**67%**	**7%**	**0**						**-3.0**	**43**	**56**	**-$1**

Price,David

Age: 28 Th: L Role SP	Health B	LIMA Plan C+	
Ht: 6' 6" Wt: 220 Type	PT/Exp A	Rand Var 0	
	Consist A	MM 5305	

A touch of bad H%/S% luck and gopheritis infected his 1st half before a triceps strain shelved him for six weeks. BPIs remained strong, however, and were vintage upon his return. With rising Cmd and low-3 xERAs, he's a better offense and bullpen away from consistently duplicating his 2012 line. Bid with confidence.

Yr Tm	W	L	Sv	IP	K	ERA	xERA	WHIP	oOPS	vL	vR	BF/G	Ctl	Dom	Cmd	SwK	G	L	F	H%	S%	hr/f	GS	APC	DOM%	DIS%	Sv%	LI	RAR	BPV	BPX	R$
09 TAM *	11	11	0	163	131	4.54	4.31	1.38	716	642	738	22.1	4.0	7.3	1.8	8%	41	19	39	28%	71%	11%	23	99	39%	26%			-4.3	49	92	$5
10 TAM	19	6	0	209	188	2.72	3.78	1.19	637	569	656	26.9	3.4	8.1	2.4	10%	44	17	40	28%	79%	7%	31	105	68%	3%	0	0.77	35.0	76	123	$24
11 TAM	12	13	0	224	218	3.49	3.32	1.14	659	508	709	27.0	2.5	8.7	3.5	9%	44	19	37	29%	72%	10%	34	109	62%	12%			12.5	111	167	$19
12 TAM	20	5	0	211	205	2.56	3.10	1.10	602	520	626	27.0	2.5	8.7	3.5	9%	53	20	27	29%	80%	11%	31	107	74%	13%			37.9	120	157	$32
13 TAM	10	8	0	187	151	3.33	3.34	1.10	661	489	712	27.4	1.3	7.3	5.6	8%	45	22	33	30%	72%	9%	27	100	78%	7%			12.4	119	155	$15
1st Half	1	4	0	55	49	5.24	3.57	1.44	811	709	847	26.4	2.3	8.0	3.5	9%	49	20	31	35%	66%	15%	9	98	67%	22%			-9.3	109	142	-$12
2nd Half	9	4	0	132	102	2.53	3.23	0.96	591	369	654	27.9	0.9	7.0	7.8	8%	43	22	35	28%	75%	6%	18	101	83%	0%			21.7	123	159	$26
14 Proj	**17**	**8**	**0**	**203**	**180**	**3.11**	**3.16**	**1.15**	**661**	**531**	**701**	**26.4**	**2.1**	**8.0**	**3.8**	**9%**	**47**	**20**	**33**	**30%**	**76%**	**10%**	**31**						**18.9**	**111**	**145**	**$22**

Pryor,Stephen

Age: 24 Th: R Role RP	Health F	LIMA Plan C	
Ht: 6' 4" Wt: 250 Type Pwr	PT/Exp F	Rand Var -5	
	Consist C	MM 4510	

High-octane bullpen arm derailed by lingering oblique problem before torn lat put him on shelf for good. With consistent 96-mph fastball and improving slider, he's got the tools to become a dominant late-inning reliever. Just 50 IP in high minors, so he needs more seasoning. A great $1 stash in deep keeper leagues.

Yr Tm	W	L	Sv	IP	K	ERA	xERA	WHIP	oOPS	vL	vR	BF/G	Ctl	Dom	Cmd	SwK	G	L	F	H%	S%	hr/f	GS	APC	DOM%	DIS%	Sv%	LI	RAR	BPV	BPX	R$
09																																
10																																
11 aa	2	1	6	23	24	1.29	0.11	0.73				4.7	2.7	9.7	3.6					20%	80%								7.4	162	244	$5
12 SEA *	4	1	10	59	66	1.84	2.69	1.18	849	750	921	4.5	4.3	10.1	2.3	13%	37	18	45	27%	89%	18%	0	17			100	1.07	15.8	102	133	$10
13 SEA	0	0	0	7	7	0.00	2.82	0.55	274	0	358	3.7	1.2	8.6	7.0	6%	39	22	39	18%	100%	0%	0	17			0	2.13	3.5	139	180	-$2
1st Half	0	0	0	7	7	0.00	2.82	0.55	274	0	358	3.7	1.2	8.6	7.0	6%	39	22	39	18%	100%	0%	0	17			0	2.13	3.5	138	179	-$2
2nd Half																																
14 Proj	**4**	**1**	**2**	**49**	**55**	**2.93**	**3.47**	**1.31**				**4.2**	**4.3**	**10.2**	**2.3**	**12%**	**39**	**21**	**40**	**30%**	**81%**	**9%**	**0**						**5.6**	**83**	**108**	**$3**

STEPHEN NICKRAND

Putz,J.J.

Age: 37	Th: R	Role RP	Health F	LIMA Plan A
Ht: 6' 5"	Wt: 250	Type Pwr	PT/Exp B	Rand Var -4
			Consist A	MM 5510

Elbow shelved him again, and with inability to reach 60 IP in a season, even desperate teams will be hesitant to throw him into closer mix. Small sample 2-ish ERA was fueled by friendly H% and S%, so it's headed way north, even with hr/f correction. Mid-90s heat is gone too; fastball sits at 92 mph. More risk than reward now.

Yr Tm	W	L	Sv	IP	K	ERA	xERA	WHIP	oOPS	vL	vR	BF/G	Ctl	Dom	Cmd	SwK	G	L	F	H%	S%	hr/f	GS	APC	DOM%	DIS%	Sv%	LI	RAR	BPV	BPX	R$
09 NYM	1	4	2	29	19	5.22	5.42	1.64	739	887	588	4.7	5.8	5.8	1.0	8%	47	19	34	31%	66%	3%	0	18			50	1.16	-3.2	-27	-51	-$4
10 CHW	7	5	3	54	65	2.83	2.86	1.04	575	721	454	3.7	2.5	10.8	4.3	13%	49	13	39	30%	75%	8%	0	13			43	1.27	8.3	155	250	$8
11 ARI	2	2	45	58	61	2.17	3.09	0.91	566	509	629	3.8	1.9	9.5	5.1	13%	42	13	44	27%	80%	6%	0	14			92	1.37	12.7	140	211	$25
12 ARI	1	5	32	54	65	2.82	2.80	1.03	600	592	609	3.8	1.8	10.8	5.9	13%	46	21	33	32%	75%	9%	0	14			86	1.07	8.0	169	220	$17
13 ARI	3	1	6	34	38	2.36	3.34	1.25	665	621	695	3.5	4.5	10.0	2.2	13%	51	18	32	27%	87%	15%	0	13			55	1.29	6.4	88	115	$3
1st Half	2	1	5	13	17	4.15	3.51	1.62	827	901	780	3.9	5.5	11.8	2.1	14%	53	15	32	34%	83%	27%	0	15			56	1.54	-0.5	93	121	$2
2nd Half	1	0	1	21	21	1.27	3.22	1.03	549	438	630	3.2	3.8	8.9	2.3	12%	49	20	31	23%	90%	6%	0	12			50	1.14	6.8	84	109	$4
14 Proj	**2**	**2**	**8**	**44**	**47**	**3.16**	**3.06**	**1.17**	**671**	**635**	**704**	**3.7**	**2.9**	**9.7**	**3.3**	**13%**	**46**	**17**	**37**	**30%**	**76%**	**9%**	**0**						**3.8**	**120**	**156**	**$4**

Qualls,Chad

Age: 35	Th: R	Role RP	Health B	LIMA Plan B+
Ht: 6' 4"	Wt: 240	Type xGB	PT/Exp C	Rand Var -1
			Consist B	MM 4100

Halted steep skill decline by finding strikeouts and solution vs. LH bats. Tightened slider responsible for both gains, but now in mid-30s and with seven teams in four years, he's safely typecast as a middle-man. Skill foundation is strong enough for LIMA bullpen filler. That's the only way he'll provide value to you now.

Yr Tm	W	L	Sv	IP	K	ERA	xERA	WHIP	oOPS	vL	vR	BF/G	Ctl	Dom	Cmd	SwK	G	L	F	H%	S%	hr/f	GS	APC	DOM%	DIS%	Sv%	LI	RAR	BPV	BPX	R$
09 ARI	2	2	24	52	45	3.63	3.00	1.15	683	728	638	4.3	1.2	7.8	6.4	10%	57	20	23	32%	71%	14%	0	15			83	1.24	4.4	142	267	$12
10 2 TM	3	4	12	59	49	7.32	4.04	1.80	894	1031	766	4.0	3.2	7.5	2.3	9%	55	17	28	40%	59%	12%	0	15			63	1.01	-23.6	81	131	-$5
11 SD	6	8	0	74	43	3.51	3.76	1.25	689	881	537	4.0	2.4	5.2	2.2	9%	57	17	26	28%	74%	11%	0	14			0	1.22	4.0	63	95	$2
12 3 TM	2	1	0	52	27	5.33	4.44	1.47	809	988	679	3.9	2.4	4.6	1.9	8%	55	19	26	32%	66%	15%	0	14			0	0.81	-8.5	52	67	-$7
13 MIA	5	2	0	62	49	2.61	3.14	1.23	658	600	698	3.8	2.8	7.1	2.6	11%	63	17	20	30%	81%	11%	0	13			0	1.41	9.6	95	123	$3
1st Half	2	1	0	31	23	3.45	3.12	1.18	686	551	779	3.9	2.3	6.6	2.9	10%	64	15	21	28%	76%	21%	0	13			0	1.45	1.6	99	128	$2
2nd Half	3	1	0	31	26	1.76	3.17	1.27	630	651	615	3.7	3.2	7.6	2.4	12%	62	19	19	32%	85%	0%	0	13			0	1.36	8.0	91	117	$5
14 Proj	**3**	**2**	**0**	**51**	**36**	**3.62**	**3.42**	**1.32**	**714**	**785**	**662**	**3.8**	**2.6**	**6.3**	**2.4**	**10%**	**59**	**18**	**23**	**31%**	**74%**	**12%**	**0**						**1.5**	**81**	**105**	**$0**

Quintana,Jose

Age: 25	Th: L	Role SP	Health A	LIMA Plan C+
Ht: 6' 1"	Wt: 215	Type	PT/Exp C	Rand Var 0
			Consist A	MM 3205

A $10 season that flew under the radar. Lack of dominant offering offset by four-pitch mix, strong command vs. both LH and RH bats. With second half surge to elite levels during his first full season around the league, he's got the ingredients for a repeat—and even more if that 2H Cmd holds... UP: 15 wins, 3.00 ERA, 180 K.

Yr Tm	W	L	Sv	IP	K	ERA	xERA	WHIP	oOPS	vL	vR	BF/G	Ctl	Dom	Cmd	SwK	G	L	F	H%	S%	hr/f	GS	APC	DOM%	DIS%	Sv%	LI	RAR	BPV	BPX	R$
09																																
10																																
11																																
12 CHW *	7	9	0	185	117	3.68	4.06	1.35	754	700	775	22.7	2.8	5.7	2.0	8%	47	22	31	30%	74%	11%	22	87	32%	32%	0	0.73	7.6	55	72	$3
13 CHW	9	7	0	200	164	3.51	3.85	1.22	695	717	687	25.2	2.5	7.4	2.9	9%	43	20	37	29%	75%	10%	33	101	55%	12%			8.8	86	112	$10
1st Half	3	2	0	93	67	3.97	4.21	1.26	702	753	684	24.7	2.8	6.5	2.3	9%	45	18	37	28%	72%	10%	16	101	44%	19%			-1.2	64	83	$4
2nd Half	6	5	0	107	97	3.11	3.56	1.19	690	687	691	25.7	2.3	8.2	3.6	10%	40	22	38	30%	78%	10%	17	101	65%	6%			9.9	104	134	$16
14 Proj	**9**	**8**	**0**	**203**	**152**	**3.56**	**3.72**	**1.27**	**711**	**701**	**715**	**23.8**	**2.6**	**6.8**	**2.6**	**9%**	**44**	**21**	**35**	**30%**	**75%**	**10%**	**35**						**7.7**	**73**	**95**	**$10**

Ramirez,Erasmo

Age: 24	Th: R	Role SP	Health D	LIMA Plan B
Ht: 5' 11"	Wt: 200	Type	PT/Exp D	Rand Var 0
			Consist C	MM 3203

5-3, 4.98 ERA in 72 IP at SEA. Spring triceps issue lingered, ending possible breakout season before it could begin. Showed in five August starts w/SEA what could've been (3.90 ERA, 1.11 WHIP, 116 BPV). He still owns those '11-'12 skills, so with good health, there's still plenty of profit here... UP: 3.50 ERA

Yr Tm	W	L	Sv	IP	K	ERA	xERA	WHIP	oOPS	vL	vR	BF/G	Ctl	Dom	Cmd	SwK	G	L	F	H%	S%	hr/f	GS	APC	DOM%	DIS%	Sv%	LI	RAR	BPV	BPX	R$
09																																
10																																
11 a/a	10	8	0	153	106	4.45	4.24	1.34				24.4	1.7	6.3	3.7					34%	67%								-9.6	93	140	$0
12 SEA *	7	6	0	136	101	3.35	3.11	1.14	616	612	622	17.4	1.8	6.6	3.6	12%	40	24	36	29%	72%	10%	8	55	50%	25%	0	0.76	11.1	102	133	$10
13 SEA *	8	6	0	121	97	4.27	4.64	1.42	772	791	742	23.3	3.1	7.2	2.3	9%	42	21	36	32%	73%	14%	13	91	54%	31%	0	0.74	-6.1	57	74	-$2
1st Half	2	3	0	43	36	2.95	3.55	1.21				25.0	2.1	7.6	3.7					31%	79%	0%	0						4.9	102	133	$4
2nd Half	6	3	0	78	61	5.01	5.24	1.53	772	791	742	22.5	3.7	7.0	1.9	9%	42	21	36	32%	71%	14%	13	91	54%	31%	0	0.74	-11.0	39	50	-$5
14 Proj	**9**	**7**	**0**	**152**	**117**	**3.81**	**3.67**	**1.28**	**706**	**722**	**682**	**21.0**	**2.3**	**6.9**	**3.1**	**10%**	**42**	**22**	**36**	**31%**	**73%**	**9%**	**30**						**1.1**	**83**	**107**	**$6**

Ramos,A.J.

Age: 27	Th: R	Role RP	Health A	LIMA Plan B+
Ht: 5' 10"	Wt: 210	Type Pwr FB	PT/Exp D	Rand Var -2
			Consist D	MM 3511

Had no idea where ball was going for most of year, especially in that wild second half. With 93-mph fastball and wipeout slider, he's got the stuff to stick as a setup guy. That said, all those walks make a 4-ish ERA much more likely than another 3-ish one, and he'll never be trusted late in games until he can find the plate.

Yr Tm	W	L	Sv	IP	K	ERA	xERA	WHIP	oOPS	vL	vR	BF/G	Ctl	Dom	Cmd	SwK	G	L	F	H%	S%	hr/f	GS	APC	DOM%	DIS%	Sv%	LI	RAR	BPV	BPX	R$
09																																
10																																
11																																
12 MIA *	3	3	21	78	89	2.11	2.13	1.04	754	436	1056	4.6	3.3	10.2	3.1	18%	32	23	45	26%	83%	20%	0	14			81	0.94	18.3	124	162	$19
13 MIA	3	4	0	80	86	3.15	3.97	1.26	603	740	484	5.0	4.8	9.7	2.0	12%	39	19	43	28%	75%	5%	0	20			0	0.98	7.1	61	79	$3
1st Half	2	2	0	41	37	4.17	4.21	1.29	695	858	509	5.5	4.0	8.1	2.1	10%	39	18	43	28%	69%	8%	0	21			0	0.93	-1.5	57	74	$0
2nd Half	1	2	0	39	49	2.08	3.73	1.23	498	548	463	4.5	5.8	11.3	2.0	14%	38	20	43	27%	81%	0%	0	19			0	1.02	8.6	64	82	$5
14 Proj	**3**	**3**	**5**	**73**	**81**	**3.97**	**3.63**	**1.32**	**643**	**796**	**519**	**4.8**	**4.8**	**10.1**	**2.1**	**13%**	**38**	**19**	**43**	**30%**	**70%**	**6%**	**0**						**-0.9**	**69**	**89**	**$3**

Ramos,Cesar

Age: 30	Th: L	Role RP	Health A	LIMA Plan C
Ht: 6' 2"	Wt: 205	Type	PT/Exp D	Rand Var 0
			Consist A	MM 3200

Lefty specialist was overexposed vs. RH bats late. With a marginal 2.1 Cmd against them and a 91-mph fastball that righties torched, he just doesn't have the goods to sustain a sub-4.00 ERA in an expanded role. Dangerous to even roster him as a LOOGY when his real-life skipper thinks he is something more.

Yr Tm	W	L	Sv	IP	K	ERA	xERA	WHIP	oOPS	vL	vR	BF/G	Ctl	Dom	Cmd	SwK	G	L	F	H%	S%	hr/f	GS	APC	DOM%	DIS%	Sv%	LI	RAR	BPV	BPX	R$
09 SD *	5	7	0	91	49	4.20	5.18	1.63	750	235	954	20.3	3.5	4.8	1.4	11%	52	17	30	34%	74%	0%	2	48	0%	50%	0	1.01	1.3	33	62	-$4
10 SD *	6	8	0	104	62	4.12	4.77	1.59	1049	697	1330	10.5	4.2	5.3	1.3	13%	44	21	35	32%	74%	8%	0	14			0	0.71	-0.5	38	62	-$3
11 TAM	0	1	0	44	31	3.92	4.62	1.40	670	639	705	3.3	5.2	6.4	1.2	9%	49	16	35	26%	74%	9%	0	12			0	0.82	0.1	3	4	-$3
12 TAM *	6	5	1	92	65	3.79	4.13	1.27	490	510	470	9.0	2.6	6.3	2.4	10%	54	20	25	28%	75%	10%	1	25	0%	100%	33	0.26	2.6	55	72	$2
13 TAM	2	2	1	67	53	4.14	4.09	1.31	687	693	682	6.0	2.9	7.1	2.4	10%	41	24	35	30%	70%	8%	0	21			100	0.84	-2.3	67	87	-$2
1st Half	1	2	1	36	27	4.25	4.17	1.36	686	869	584	5.7	3.0	6.8	2.3	10%	41	23	35	32%	68%	5%	0	21			100	1.01	-1.7	60	78	-$2
2nd Half	1	0	0	31	26	4.02	3.99	1.24	687	532	811	6.3	2.9	7.5	2.6	10%	40	25	35	29%	71%	12%	0	22			0	0.62	-0.6	75	97	-$2
14 Proj	**2**	**2**	**0**	**58**	**43**	**4.02**	**3.85**	**1.33**	**703**	**681**	**722**	**5.9**	**3.3**	**6.6**	**2.0**	**10%**	**47**	**22**	**32**	**29%**	**72%**	**11%**	**0**						**-1.1**	**56**	**73**	**-$1**

Redmond,Todd

Age: 29	Th: R	Role SP	Health A	LIMA Plan B+
Ht: 6' 3"	Wt: 235	Type xFB	PT/Exp D	Rand Var +2
			Consist C	MM 2201

4-3, 4.32 ERA in 77 IP at TOR. Career minor leaguer finally got extended taste of MLB, posting skills never seen by him before. Dominated RH bats (11.0 Dom, 2.0 Ctl) with newfound plus-slider. Problem is, they mashed his 90-mph fastball. Can't bank on repeat as a one-trick pony, so don't fall in love with his 2nd half.

Yr Tm	W	L	Sv	IP	K	ERA	xERA	WHIP	oOPS	vL	vR	BF/G	Ctl	Dom	Cmd	SwK	G	L	F	H%	S%	hr/f	GS	APC	DOM%	DIS%	Sv%	LI	RAR	BPV	BPX	R$
09 aaa	9	6	0	145	90	5.40	5.76	1.58				23.6	3.1	5.6	1.8					33%	69%								-19.4	22	42	-$6
10 aaa	9	10	0	163	118	5.25	5.00	1.42				24.7	2.6	6.5	2.5					32%	66%								-23.5	52	83	-$4
11 aaa	10	8	0	170	116	3.77	4.66	1.40				25.6	2.7	6.2	2.3					31%	77%								3.7	51	76	$3
12 CIN *	8	12	0	152	110	4.82	5.99	1.58	1193	1199	1167	24.8	2.8	6.5	2.3	14%	33	27	40	35%	74%	17%	1	91	0%	100%			-15.1	35	46	-$10
13 TOR *	7	4	0	104	98	4.99	4.45	1.31	757	724	794	18.6	2.5	8.5	3.4	11%	30	19	50	32%	65%	12%	14	76	36%	36%	0	0.80	-14.4	84	109	-$2
1st Half	3	2	0	31	24	6.75	5.57	1.56	728	222	1100	17.2	2.2	6.9	3.2	5%	47	13	40	37%	56%	17%	0	38			0	1.25	-11.1	68	88	-$10
2nd Half	4	2	0	72	74	4.23	3.87	1.20	759	748	771	20.3	2.6	9.2	3.5	11%	29	20	51	29%	71%	12%	14	81	36%	36%	0	0.74	-3.3	102	132	$1
14 Proj	**6**	**5**	**0**	**102**	**82**	**4.44**	**4.20**	**1.34**	**756**	**737**	**778**	**20.8**	**2.6**	**7.3**	**2.8**	**11%**	**29**	**20**	**51**	**31%**	**71%**	**9%**	**20**						**-7.2**	**69**	**90**	**$0**

STEPHEN NICKRAND

Reed,Addison

Age: 25	Th: R	Role	RP	Health	A	LIMA Plan	C+
Ht: 6' 4"	Wt: 220	Type	Pwr FB	PT/Exp	B	Rand Var	0
				Consist	C	MM	4430

Significant hit rate regression turned this seemingly shaky near-5 ERA closer into a much safer play. xERA says this is closer to true skill level, as does lack of LH/RH splits. Stamina is the next hurdle. BPV by month, last four months: 152, 141, 85, -53. Until that improves, you can't bank on him as your #1 stopper.

Yr Tm	W	L	Sv	IP	K	ERA	xERA	WHIP	oOPS	vL	vR	BF/G	Ctl	Dom	Cmd	SwK	G	L	F	H%	S%	hr/f	GS	APC	DOM%	DIS%	Sv%	LI	RAR	BPV	BPX	R$
09																																
10																																
11 CHW *	0	1	4	49	66	1.70	1.59	0.86	802	875	728	6.1	2.0	12.0	5.8	18%	20	35	45	27%	85%	11%	0	23			67	0.13	13.6	193	290	$8
12 CHW	3	2	29	55	54	4.75	4.13	1.36	753	773	737	3.8	2.9	8.8	3.0	10%	33	24	43	34%	67%	9%	0	15			88	1.53	-5.0	91	118	$8
13 CHW	5	4	40	71	72	3.79	3.75	1.11	603	608	597	4.3	2.9	9.1	3.1	12%	33	22	45	28%	67%	7%	0	17			83	1.19	0.7	96	125	$19
1st Half	3	1	21	36	39	4.00	3.55	1.06	580	578	582	4.4	2.3	9.8	4.3	13%	29	23	47	29%	63%	6%	0	17			84	1.10	-0.6	122	158	$21
2nd Half	2	3	19	35	33	3.57	3.97	1.16	628	642	611	4.3	3.6	8.4	2.4	10%	37	20	43	26%	71%	7%	0	17			83	1.28	1.3	70	90	$17
14 Proj	**3**	**3**	**40**	**65**	**66**	**3.78**	**3.40**	**1.16**	**646**	**651**	**640**	**4.1**	**2.9**	**9.1**	**3.2**	**11%**	**33**	**23**	**44**	**29%**	**69%**	**8%**	**0**						**0.7**	**98**	**127**	**$18**

Richard,Clayton

Age: 30	Th: L	Role	SP	Health	F	LIMA Plan	D+
Ht: 6' 5"	Wt: 245	Type	Con GB	PT/Exp	B	Rand Var	+5
				Consist	B	MM	2001

Another shoulder surgery stopped season early, and this one was in the same area as his initial procedure. Sliding Dom probably should've told us he hasn't been healthy for a few years. Guys with chronically bad shoulders don't suddenly get healthy, and there hasn't been much positive to chase here anyway. Stay away.

Yr Tm	W	L	Sv	IP	K	ERA	xERA	WHIP	oOPS	vL	vR	BF/G	Ctl	Dom	Cmd	SwK	G	L	F	H%	S%	hr/f	GS	APC	DOM%	DIS%	Sv%	LI	RAR	BPV	BPX	R$
09 2 TM	9	5	0	153	114	4.41	4.41	1.47	756	645	788	17.4	4.2	6.7	1.6	7%	48	18	34	30%	72%	11%	26	69	31%	38%	0	0.74	-1.7	34	64	$2
10 SD	14	9	0	202	153	3.75	4.09	1.41	718	574	770	26.1	3.5	6.8	2.0	8%	46	20	34	31%	75%	8%	33	97	52%	15%			8.2	53	86	$7
11 SD	5	9	0	100	53	3.88	4.48	1.42	741	639	773	23.7	3.4	4.8	1.4	7%	50	18	32	30%	74%	8%	18	91	22%	33%			0.7	21	32	-$1
12 SD	14	14	0	219	107	3.99	4.17	1.23	739	591	784	27.6	1.7	4.4	2.5	7%	54	18	28	28%	72%	15%	33	96	42%	15%			0.6	65	84	$8
13 SD	2	5	0	53	24	7.01	4.94	1.63	947	639	1050	19.9	3.6	4.1	1.1	6%	52	21	27	29%	62%	25%	11	71	18%	55%	0	0.89	-20.4	7	9	-$12
1st Half	2	5	0	53	24	7.01	4.94	1.63	947	639	1050	19.9	3.6	4.1	1.1	6%	52	21	27	29%	62%	25%	11	71	18%	55%	0	0.89	-20.4	7	9	-$12
2nd Half																																
14 Proj	**5**	**7**	**0**	**93**	**51**	**4.87**	**4.27**	**1.45**	**803**	**620**	**862**	**22.1**	**3.2**	**5.0**	**1.6**	**7%**	**51**	**19**	**30**	**30%**	**70%**	**14%**	**18**						**-11.5**	**32**	**41**	**-$5**

Richards,Garrett

Age: 26	Th: R	Role	RP	Health	A	LIMA Plan	C
Ht: 6' 3"	Wt: 215	Type	GB	PT/Exp	C	Rand Var	+1
				Consist	B	MM	3103

4 reasons why a 3.50 ERA breakout is around the corner... 1) Surging GB rate raises floor and gives him unique skill; 2) 95-mph fastball, solid SwK lay foundation for more strikeouts; 3) SP/RP skills nearly identical; 4) high PQS-DOM% confirms he's very close to taking a big step forward. A premium target for your end game.

Yr Tm	W	L	Sv	IP	K	ERA	xERA	WHIP	oOPS	vL	vR	BF/G	Ctl	Dom	Cmd	SwK	G	L	F	H%	S%	hr/f	GS	APC	DOM%	DIS%	Sv%	LI	RAR	BPV	BPX	R$
09																																
10																																
11 LAA *	12	4	0	157	96	3.94	3.89	1.30	989	1140	813	22.3	2.7	5.5	2.1	9%	43	28	28	29%	71%	31%	3	36	0%	67%	0	0.64	0.1	54	81	$5
12 LAA *	11	6	1	148	102	4.23	4.65	1.54	793	900	682	14.7	3.9	6.2	1.6	11%	45	22	33	33%	73%	9%	9	40	22%	22%	33	0.95	-3.9	50	65	-$4
13 LAA	7	8	1	145	101	4.16	3.70	1.34	699	751	626	13.2	2.7	6.3	2.3	9%	58	19	23	31%	70%	11%	17	50	59%	18%	50	0.78	-5.2	75	98	$0
1st Half	2	4	1	56	37	5.30	3.91	1.36	690	657	724	8.7	2.4	5.9	2.5	10%	55	19	26	32%	60%	8%	4	34	50%	0%	50	0.84	-9.9	75	97	-$6
2nd Half	5	4	0	89	64	3.44	3.57	1.34	704	802	540	19.8	2.9	6.5	2.2	9%	60	19	21	30%	77%	14%	13	74	62%	23%	0	0.69	4.7	75	98	$3
14 Proj	**11**	**8**	**0**	**174**	**122**	**3.87**	**3.68**	**1.35**	**709**	**774**	**631**	**14.1**	**2.9**	**6.3**	**2.2**	**10%**	**53**	**20**	**27**	**31%**	**73%**	**10%**	**21**						**0.0**	**67**	**88**	**$5**

Rienzo,Andre

Age: 26	Th: R	Role	SP	Health	A	LIMA Plan	D+
Ht: 6' 3"	Wt: 190	Type	Pwr GB	PT/Exp	D	Rand Var	+3
				Consist	C	MM	2200

2-3, 4.82 ERA in 56 IP at CHW. Brazilian import wasn't able to miss MLB bats like he did in minors. Curveball is a legit strikeout pitch, but lack of other dominant pitches and little FB velocity don't bode well for return to '12 Dom. Chronic wildness seals his fate.

Yr Tm	W	L	Sv	IP	K	ERA	xERA	WHIP	oOPS	vL	vR	BF/G	Ctl	Dom	Cmd	SwK	G	L	F	H%	S%	hr/f	GS	APC	DOM%	DIS%	Sv%	LI	RAR	BPV	BPX	R$
09																																
10																																
11																																
12 a/a	4	3	0	78	70	4.05	3.81	1.50				24.2	4.8	8.0	1.7					32%	72%								-0.4	77	101	-$3
13 CHW *	10	9	0	169	132	5.22	5.08	1.59	794	780	821	24.8	4.4	7.1	1.6	7%	48	19	33	32%	69%	18%	10	94	50%	30%			-28.3	41	54	-$12
1st Half	5	6	0	84	73	6.75	6.44	1.89				24.6	4.5	7.8	1.7					40%	64%	0%	0						-29.8	45	58	-$25
2nd Half	5	3	0	85	60	3.73	3.75	1.29	794	780	821	25.0	4.3	6.3	1.4	7%	48	19	33	24%	76%	18%	10	94	50%	30%			1.5	40	51	$0
14 Proj	**3**	**3**	**0**	**58**	**48**	**4.59**	**4.22**	**1.52**	**671**	**650**	**711**	**24.6**	**4.6**	**7.4**	**1.6**	**7%**	**48**	**19**	**33**	**32%**	**71%**	**8%**	**10**						**-5.2**	**35**	**46**	**-$4**

Rivera,Mariano

Age: 44	Th: R	Role	RP	Health	F	LIMA Plan	F
Ht: 6' 2"	Wt: 195	Type	###	PT/Exp	B	Rand Var	-4
				Consist	A	MM	0000

All-time Sv leader ended career in typical Mariano fashion. Had a 100+ BPV every year from 2001 through this finale. Just 22 guys had 200+ saves during his career, and only THREE managed 400+. Rivera had 652, and he was a horse—had 244 more IP than any other reliever—not even counting Oct/Nov heroics.

Yr Tm	W	L	Sv	IP	K	ERA	xERA	WHIP	oOPS	vL	vR	BF/G	Ctl	Dom	Cmd	SwK	G	L	F	H%	S%	hr/f	GS	APC	DOM%	DIS%	Sv%	LI	RAR	BPV	BPX	R$
09 NYY	3	3	44	66	72	1.76	2.60	0.90	549	511	586	3.9	1.6	9.8	6.0	8%	51	22	27	26%	89%	15%	0	16			96	1.35	20.9	161	301	$29
10 NYY	3	3	33	60	45	1.80	3.19	0.83	493	565	426	3.8	1.7	6.8	4.1	9%	51	15	33	23%	79%	4%	0	15			87	1.40	16.9	106	171	$22
11 NYY	1	2	44	61	60	1.91	2.71	0.90	534	595	480	3.6	1.2	8.8	7.5	9%	47	20	33	28%	81%	6%	0	14			90	1.44	15.4	152	228	$25
12 NYY	1	1	5	8	8	2.16	3.37	0.96	550	522	572	3.6	2.2	8.6	4.0	13%	45	14	41	28%	75%	0%	0	14			83	1.48	1.9	120	157	-$1
13 NYY	6	2	44	64	54	2.11	3.23	1.05	615	568	673	4.0	1.3	7.6	6.0	10%	46	23	31	29%	85%	10%	0	15			86	1.41	13.9	127	165	$25
1st Half	1	1	26	29	27	1.55	3.35	1.24	630	637	624	3.8	1.9	8.4	4.5	11%	43	26	31	35%	89%	4%	0	14			96	1.37	8.3	121	157	$26
2nd Half	5	1	18	35	27	2.57	3.12	0.89	601	516	727	4.2	0.8	6.9	9.0	9%	49	20	31	24%	81%	16%	0	15			75	1.44	5.6	131	170	$24
14 Proj																																

Roark,Tanner

Age: 27	Th: R	Role	RP	Health	A	LIMA Plan	B+
Ht: 6' 2"	Wt: 220	Type	Con GB	PT/Exp	D	Rand Var	-1
				Consist	D	MM	3101

7-1, 1.51 ERA in 54 IP at WAS. A sterling debut from former 25th round pick as he bounced between rotation and pen. RH bats couldn't even manage ONE hit against his slider the 141 times he threw it. Excellent Cmd as SP, so don't worry about him sticking in that role. With sustained control, a $1 bid could net you $10 profit.

Yr Tm	W	L	Sv	IP	K	ERA	xERA	WHIP	oOPS	vL	vR	BF/G	Ctl	Dom	Cmd	SwK	G	L	F	H%	S%	hr/f	GS	APC	DOM%	DIS%	Sv%	LI	RAR	BPV	BPX	R$
09 aa	1	1	0	18	8	5.66	4.59	1.53				15.4	3.6	3.9	1.1					31%	62%								-2.9	25	48	-$4
10 aa	11	6	0	141	88	4.93	5.47	1.58				22.2	2.8	5.6	2.0					35%	70%								-14.8	40	64	-$5
11 aa	9	9	0	117	72	5.87	5.47	1.61				24.7	3.0	5.6	1.9					35%	63%								-27.7	39	58	-$11
12 aaa	6	17	0	148	100	5.47	5.74	1.63				23.5	2.8	6.1	2.1					36%	67%								-26.5	43	57	-$17
13 WAS *	16	4	2	159	103	3.01	2.59	1.07	476	634	358	13.2	1.7	5.8	3.4	7%	50	24	26	28%	72%	3%	5	54	80%	0%	100	0.95	16.8	100	131	$19
1st Half	5	3	2	67	43	4.02	2.74	1.15				9.8	2.1	5.8	2.7					29%	63%	0%	0						-1.3	89	115	$8
2nd Half	11	1	0	92	60	2.28	2.47	1.01	476	634	358	17.7	1.5	5.9	4.0	7%	50	24	26	27%	80%	3%	5	54	80%	0%	0	0.95	18.1	113	146	$26
14 Proj	**8**	**6**	**0**	**102**	**66**	**3.86**	**3.67**	**1.28**	**640**	**890**	**454**	**17.1**	**2.3**	**5.8**	**2.5**	**7%**	**50**	**24**	**26**	**30%**	**70%**	**8%**	**17**						**0.0**	**70**	**91**	**$3**

Robertson,David

Age: 29	Th: R	Role	RP	Health	B	LIMA Plan	A
Ht: 5' 11"	Wt: 195	Type	Pwr	PT/Exp	C	Rand Var	-3
				Consist	A	MM	5530

Mariano's heir-apparent continues to show that he's ready to take over. With three straight years of elite skills under his belt, he's got all the tools to run with the role. Steady Ctl gains suggest he hasn't hit his ceiling yet, and 4.0+ Cmd against both LH and RH bats says he won't be overexposed. UP: 50 SV.

Yr Tm	W	L	Sv	IP	K	ERA	xERA	WHIP	oOPS	vL	vR	BF/G	Ctl	Dom	Cmd	SwK	G	L	F	H%	S%	hr/f	GS	APC	DOM%	DIS%	Sv%	LI	RAR	BPV	BPX	R$
09 NYY	2	1	1	44	63	3.30	3.33	1.35	685	601	751	4.2	4.7	13.0	2.7	10%	36	23	41	35%	78%	9%	0	19			100	0.67	5.5	120	224	$1
10 NYY	4	5	1	61	71	3.82	3.74	1.50	724	759	697	4.3	4.8	10.4	2.2	8%	40	25	36	35%	76%	9%	0	18			33	1.12	2.0	75	121	$0
11 NYY	4	0	1	67	100	1.08	2.57	1.13	506	466	549	3.9	4.7	13.5	2.9	11%	46	22	32	31%	91%	2%	0	17			25	1.38	23.5	139	210	$11
12 NYY	2	7	2	61	81	2.67	2.84	1.17	638	575	710	3.8	2.8	12.0	4.3	10%	45	20	35	34%	80%	5%	0	15			40	1.15	10.1	163	213	$5
13 NYY	5	1	3	66	77	2.04	2.66	1.04	584	484	695	3.7	2.4	10.4	4.3	10%	51	20	29	29%	84%	11%	0	15			60	1.19	15.0	151	197	$9
1st Half	4	1	0	31	39	2.59	2.96	1.05	573	444	707	3.7	3.4	11.2	3.3	12%	42	21	37	27%	80%	12%	0	15			0	1.27	4.9	129	167	$8
2nd Half	1	0	3	35	38	1.54	2.41	1.03	592	515	684	3.8	1.5	9.8	6.3	8%	58	19	23	32%	88%	10%	0	15			75	1.12	10.0	170	220	$10
14 Proj	**4**	**3**	**42**	**68**	**86**	**2.30**	**2.59**	**1.12**	**600**	**525**	**680**	**3.7**	**3.0**	**11.4**	**3.7**	**10%**	**48**	**20**	**32**	**32%**	**82%**	**9%**	**0**						**13.2**	**148**	**192**	**$25**

STEPHEN NICKRAND

Rodney,Fernando

Age: 37 Th: R Role RP	Health C	LIMA Plan C	
Ht: 5' 11" Wt: 220 Type Pwr GB	PT/Exp B	Rand Var 0	
	Consist C	MM 4530	

We all knew H%/S% would regress and make insane 2012 a one-shot deal, but this wasn't bad. In some ways, it validates 2012 as being somewhat less insane. But the reversion to previous levels of wildness is confounding. Dom is for real and 2nd half lends hope that he can milk another year out of this skill set.

Yr Tm	W	L	Sv	IP	K	ERA	xERA	WHIP	oOPS	vL	vR	BF/G	Ctl	Dom	Cmd	SwK	G	L	F	H%	S%	hr/f	GS	APC	DOM%	DIS%	Sv%	LI	RAR	BPV	BPX	R$
09 DET	2	5	37	76	61	4.40	4.22	1.47	731	727	737	4.5	4.9	7.3	1.5	9%	58	11	31	29%	72%	12%	0	19			97	1.08	-0.7	35	65	$14
10 LAA	4	3	14	68	53	4.24	4.32	1.54	739	728	750	4.3	4.6	7.0	1.5	10%	50	20	30	32%	72%	6%	0	18			67	1.10	-1.3	29	47	$3
11 LAA	3	5	3	32	26	4.50	4.87	1.69	672	766	588	3.8	7.9	7.3	0.9	9%	58	19	22	28%	72%	5%	0	16			43	1.69	-2.2	-45	-68	-$3
12 TAM	2	2	48	75	76	0.60	2.58	0.78	417	435	394	3.7	1.8	9.2	5.1	13%	58	17	25	23%	95%	4%	0	15			96	1.24	31.4	152	198	$37
13 TAM	5	4	37	67	82	3.38	3.24	1.34	634	716	538	4.3	4.9	11.1	2.3	13%	51	25	25	32%	74%	7%	0	18			82	1.34	4.0	97	126	$17
1st Half	3	2	17	35	47	4.41	3.23	1.41	675	734	604	4.4	6.0	12.2	2.0	14%	52	23	25	31%	70%	15%	0	18			77	1.28	-2.3	88	114	$14
2nd Half	2	2	20	32	35	2.25	3.26	1.25	590	696	472	4.2	3.7	9.8	2.7	12%	49	26	25	33%	80%	0%	0	17			87	1.41	6.4	106	137	$19
14 Proj	4	4	35	61	64	3.26	3.29	1.30	605	663	539	3.9	4.8	9.5	2.0	12%	54	21	25	29%	74%	6%	0						4.6	72	94	$16

Rodriguez,Francisco

Age: 32 Th: R Role RP	Health B	LIMA Plan B+	
Ht: 6' 0" Wt: 195 Type Pwr	PT/Exp C	Rand Var -2	
	Consist B	MM 5410	

It's easy to dismiss his prospects of being a viable closer again given lack of chances last two seasons in multiple uniforms. Elite skills, sub-2.75 ERA in three of last four indicate otherwise. Don't be worried about funky LH/RH oOPS splits; they were H%-induced. Stash as a LIMA reliever and hope he gets another shot.

Yr Tm	W	L	Sv	IP	K	ERA	xERA	WHIP	oOPS	vL	vR	BF/G	Ctl	Dom	Cmd	SwK	G	L	F	H%	S%	hr/f	GS	APC	DOM%	DIS%	Sv%	LI	RAR	BPV	BPX	R$
09 NYM	3	6	35	68	73	3.71	4.27	1.31	644	541	750	4.2	5.0	9.7	1.9	13%	35	19	46	27%	74%	9%	0	18			83	1.01	5.2	51	96	$17
10 NYM	4	2	25	57	67	2.20	3.19	1.15	597	680	531	4.5	3.3	10.5	3.2	12%	42	19	39	31%	83%	5%	0	18			83	1.22	13.3	120	195	$16
11 2 NL	6	2	23	72	79	2.64	3.17	1.30	663	776	515	4.2	3.3	9.9	3.0	13%	52	17	31	34%	81%	6%	0	16			79	1.37	11.5	120	181	$14
12 MIL	2	7	3	72	72	4.38	3.87	1.33	708	723	684	3.9	3.9	9.0	2.3	8%	42	26	33	30%	69%	12%	0	16			30	1.15	-3.2	77	101	-$1
13 2 TM	3	2	10	47	54	2.70	3.22	1.20	734	513	1003	4.0	2.7	10.4	3.9	11%	36	25	39	31%	86%	15%	0	16			100	0.91	6.7	129	168	$6
1st Half	1	1	6	18	17	1.02	3.55	0.96	524	455	625	3.7	3.1	8.7	2.8	11%	35	19	47	23%	94%	5%	0	15			100	1.03	6.2	86	112	$8
2nd Half	2	1	4	29	37	3.72	3.02	1.34	844	547	1169	4.2	2.5	11.5	4.6	11%	37	28	35	36%	82%	23%	0	16			100	0.84	0.5	155	201	$4
14 Proj	3	3	5	58	64	3.11	3.19	1.25	702	615	805	3.9	3.2	9.9	3.1	11%	40	23	37	31%	80%	12%	0						5.4	110	142	$5

Rodriguez,Paco

Age: 23 Th: L Role RP	Health A	LIMA Plan B+	
Ht: 6' 3" Wt: 220 Type Pwr	PT/Exp D	Rand Var -4	
	Consist B	MM 5510	

Lefty w/dominant slider took elite 1H skills to a whole new level in 2H. Overall SwK was second among NL RP behind only Chapman, so Dom surge may not be over yet. Middling 1.9 Cmd vs. RH shows that he has work to do before role expansion is in the cards, and H% regression will send ERA north. Still, a premium LIMA target.

Yr Tm	W	L	Sv	IP	K	ERA	xERA	WHIP	oOPS	vL	vR	BF/G	Ctl	Dom	Cmd	SwK	G	L	F	H%	S%	hr/f	GS	APC	DOM%	DIS%	Sv%	LI	RAR	BPV	BPX	R$
09																																
10																																
11																																
12 LA	0	1	0	7	6	1.35	3.78	1.05	406	343	489	2.4	5.4	8.1	1.5	13%	47	33	20	19%	86%	0%	0	10			0	0.98	2.2	25	33	-$3
13 LA	3	4	2	54	63	2.32	2.81	0.90	511	400	641	2.7	3.1	10.4	3.3	16%	47	19	35	22%	80%	12%	0	11			40	1.67	10.4	128	167	$7
1st Half	2	2	1	28	30	2.86	2.98	0.88	443	385	507	2.7	3.5	9.5	2.7	16%	49	15	36	21%	67%	5%	0	11			33	1.49	3.5	104	135	$7
2nd Half	1	2	1	26	33	1.73	2.63	0.92	580	414	783	2.8	2.8	11.4	4.1	17%	44	23	33	23%	95%	21%	0	11			50	1.88	6.8	153	198	$7
14 Proj	3	4	3	58	69	2.96	2.91	1.17	637	496	805	2.9	3.5	10.7	3.0	16%	46	20	34	30%	78%	11%	0						6.5	121	157	$5

Rodriguez,Wandy

Age: 35 Th: L Role SP	Health F	LIMA Plan B+	
Ht: 5' 10" Wt: 195 Type	PT/Exp A	Rand Var 0	
	Consist A	MM 3103	

Strained flexor tendon ended his season at halfway point. Prior to that, he was on his way to his usual mid-3 ERA, solid WHIP line. Steady Dom decline offset by improving control, but his margin for error is getting smaller, even with good health. Last two xERAs tell you to use a 3.90ish ERA as your new baseline.

Yr Tm	W	L	Sv	IP	K	ERA	xERA	WHIP	oOPS	vL	vR	BF/G	Ctl	Dom	Cmd	SwK	G	L	F	H%	S%	hr/f	GS	APC	DOM%	DIS%	Sv%	LI	RAR	BPV	BPX	R$
09 HOU	14	12	0	206	193	3.02	3.59	1.24	695	502	742	25.7	2.8	8.4	3.1	9%	45	18	37	31%	79%	10%	33	102	67%	18%			33.0	101	188	$23
10 HOU	11	12	0	195	178	3.60	3.53	1.29	700	642	715	25.7	3.1	8.2	2.6	9%	48	20	32	31%	74%	9%	32	100	66%	16%			11.5	89	144	$12
11 HOU	11	11	0	191	166	3.49	3.75	1.31	739	628	768	26.9	3.3	7.8	2.4	9%	45	20	35	30%	78%	13%	30	105	57%	7%			10.7	76	114	$10
12 2 NL	12	13	0	206	139	3.76	4.19	1.27	695	689	697	25.7	2.5	6.1	2.5	8%	48	20	32	29%	73%	10%	33	94	52%	15%	0	0.83	6.4	69	90	$9
13 PIT	6	4	0	63	46	3.59	3.87	1.12	707	785	681	21.7	1.7	6.6	3.8	7%	42	19	39	27%	75%	13%	12	86	50%	25%			2.1	92	120	$3
1st Half	6	4	0	63	46	3.59	3.87	1.12	707	785	681	21.7	1.7	6.6	3.8	7%	42	19	39	27%	75%	13%	12	86	50%	25%			2.1	93	120	$3
2nd Half																																
14 Proj	10	8	0	139	96	3.93	3.90	1.26	714	687	722	23.9	2.8	6.3	2.3	8%	43	20	37	28%	72%	11%	24						-1.2	59	77	$6

Roenicke,Josh

Age: 31 Th: R Role RP	Health A	LIMA Plan D	
Ht: 6' 3" Wt: 200 Type Pwr	PT/Exp C	Rand Var -2	
	Consist A	MM 1100	

When MLB clubs keep giving guys like this chances, it makes us fanalytic types wonder why we can't be the GMs. After all, we know that he's a WHIP killer, hasn't posted a rosterable Cmd in four years, and his skills have fallen off a cliff during that period. BPV column tells the story; it's not that hard to figure out.

Yr Tm	W	L	Sv	IP	K	ERA	xERA	WHIP	oOPS	vL	vR	BF/G	Ctl	Dom	Cmd	SwK	G	L	F	H%	S%	hr/f	GS	APC	DOM%	DIS%	Sv%	LI	RAR	BPV	BPX	R$
09 2 TM *	1	0	12	59	58	4.48	4.65	1.60	705	923	499	5.1	3.5	8.9	2.5	10%	49	22	30	39%	70%	8%	0	23			80	0.46	-1.2	93	173	$1
10 TOR *	10	1	1	78	60	3.96	4.64	1.53	718	592	809	6.6	4.2	6.9	1.6	10%	51	14	35	32%	76%	5%	0	22			33	0.48	1.1	51	83	$1
11 COL *	1	4	0	70	41	4.32	4.63	1.48	657	501	728	5.2	3.6	5.3	1.5	10%	45	19	36	30%	72%	6%	0	15			0	0.80	-3.3	35	53	-$4
12 COL	4	2	1	89	54	3.25	4.73	1.44	753	646	824	6.1	4.4	5.5	1.3	9%	50	22	28	28%	81%	12%	0	23			33	0.70	8.4	9	11	$0
13 MIN	3	1	1	62	45	4.35	5.30	1.60	773	937	664	4.5	5.2	6.5	1.3	8%	41	15	44	31%	74%	7%	0	18			33	0.88	-3.7	-5	-6	-$5
1st Half	2	1	0	35	22	3.38	5.29	1.41	748	933	633	4.7	4.7	5.7	1.2	8%	38	13	49	26%	82%	10%	0	18			0	0.88	2.1	-7	-9	-$2
2nd Half	1	0	1	27	23	5.60	5.29	1.83	801	940	702	4.3	5.9	7.6	1.3	8%	44	17	39	36%	67%	3%	0	18			50	0.89	-5.8	-1	-2	-$9
14 Proj	2	1	0	50	36	4.76	4.58	1.57	770	852	712	4.9	4.7	6.4	1.3	9%	46	18	36	31%	70%	8%	0						-5.5	11	14	-$5

Rogers,Esmil

Age: 28 Th: R Role RP	Health D	LIMA Plan D+	
Ht: 6' 1" Wt: 190 Type Pwr	PT/Exp C	Rand Var +3	
	Consist D	MM 2201	

So much for that '12 skill spike. The '13 version looked very similar to his pre-'12 mediocrity, save for an unlucky hr/f that sabotaged him in 2H. Good Cmd, GB rate as a starter suggest some upside in that role, but he still hasn't solved lefties, so we can't really trust him there, either.

Yr Tm	W	L	Sv	IP	K	ERA	xERA	WHIP	oOPS	vL	vR	BF/G	Ctl	Dom	Cmd	SwK	G	L	F	H%	S%	hr/f	GS	APC	DOM%	DIS%	Sv%	LI	RAR	BPV	BPX	R$
09 COL *	11	7	0	159	104	5.49	5.15	1.59	543	472	629	25.0	3.2	5.9	1.8	4%	55	27	18	35%	65%	0%	1	80	0%	100%			-22.9	45	85	-$6
10 COL *	5	6	0	133	106	6.14	5.08	1.55	835	919	772	14.5	3.0	7.2	2.4	10%	52	21	27	36%	59%	8%	8	45	13%	50%	0	0.85	-33.9	65	105	-$11
11 COL *	7	9	0	110	76	6.80	7.13	1.90	919	991	860	21.6	4.3	6.2	1.4	8%	42	22	35	37%	66%	14%	13	84	46%	38%	0	0.63	-38.8	10	15	-$20
12 2 TM	3	3	0	79	83	4.69	3.63	1.44	749	676	817	5.2	3.4	9.5	2.8	10%	47	23	30	35%	68%	10%	0	22			0	0.77	-6.6	103	135	-$4
13 TOR	5	9	0	138	96	4.77	4.12	1.42	799	854	731	13.6	2.9	6.3	2.2	7%	47	23	30	31%	70%	16%	20	51	35%	35%	0	0.67	-15.4	60	79	-$7
1st Half	3	3	0	61	38	3.12	4.07	1.25	702	765	641	8.6	2.7	5.6	2.1	8%	45	24	31	28%	79%	10%	6	33	33%	50%	0	0.63	5.6	52	67	$4
2nd Half	2	6	0	77	58	6.08	4.15	1.56	869	905	814	23.2	3.0	6.8	2.2	7%	49	23	28	33%	65%	20%	14	87	36%	29%	0	0.74	-21.0	67	87	-$15
14 Proj	5	7	0	116	90	4.68	4.05	1.55	819	847	790	10.3	3.6	7.0	1.9	8%	46	23	31	33%	73%	13%	2						-11.6	53	69	-$6

Romo,Sergio

Age: 31 Th: R Role RP	Health B	LIMA Plan C+	
Ht: 5' 10" Wt: 185 Type Pwr	PT/Exp C	Rand Var -3	
	Consist B	MM 5530	

PROs: Consistently elite skills, RH bats still have no chance against his slider. CONs: Second half fade reminds us about stamina worries and elbow concerns, two years of big Dom erosion became even worse late in '13. He remains an elite closer and near-40 Sv lock for now, but he's more risky than his stats and skills show.

Yr Tm	W	L	Sv	IP	K	ERA	xERA	WHIP	oOPS	vL	vR	BF/G	Ctl	Dom	Cmd	SwK	G	L	F	H%	S%	hr/f	GS	APC	DOM%	DIS%	Sv%	LI	RAR	BPV	BPX	R$
09 SF	5	2	2	34	41	3.97	3.61	1.21	631	542	684	3.2	2.9	10.9	3.7	10%	32	15	53	35%	65%	2%	0	13			100	1.20	1.5	127	237	$2
10 SF	5	3	0	62	70	2.18	3.20	0.97	599	652	570	3.6	2.0	10.2	5.0	14%	35	14	51	28%	83%	8%	0	13			0	1.28	14.5	141	228	$9
11 SF	3	1	1	48	70	1.50	2.03	0.71	458	599	402	2.7	0.9	13.1	14.0	17%	34	24	42	29%	81%	5%	0	10			50	1.39	14.5	223	335	$10
12 SF	4	2	14	55	63	1.79	2.64	0.85	525	491	537	3.1	1.6	10.2	6.3	16%	49	21	30	26%	86%	12%	0	12			93	1.43	15.2	168	219	$15
13 SF	5	8	38	60	58	2.54	3.39	1.08	614	745	511	3.8	1.8	8.7	4.8	14%	41	24	36	30%	80%	8%	0	15			88	1.58	9.9	126	165	$21
1st Half	3	3	19	31	34	2.32	3.05	1.00	584	636	540	3.7	1.5	9.9	6.8	12%	37	26	37	31%	79%	6%	0	14			86	1.57	5.9	154	199	$23
2nd Half	2	5	19	29	24	2.76	3.77	1.16	644	860	483	4.0	2.1	7.4	3.4	15%	44	22	34	29%	81%	10%	0	16			90	1.58	4.0	97	125	$18
14 Proj	5	5	35	58	63	2.74	2.79	1.04	605	721	537	3.3	1.9	9.8	5.2	15%	41	22	37	30%	77%	8%	0						8.1	144	187	$20

STEPHEN NICKRAND

Rondon,Bruce

Age: 23	Th: R	Role RP	Health A	LIMA Plan A	
Ht: 6' 3"	Wt: 275	Type Pwr xGB	PT/Exp F	Rand Var -1	
			Consist A	MM 5510	

1-2, 3.45 ERA, 1 Sv in 29 IP at DET. Spring "closer" noise faded, but in 2H he showed why the noise started in the first place. A "whoa" stat: threw over 100 pitches at 100 mph-plus. Now the bad: Sept. right elbow flexor strain. Should be ready in March, but that's a scary caveat. If healthy, though, it gets noisy again. UP: 35 Sv.

Yr Tm	W	L	Sv	IP	K	ERA	xERA	WHIP	oOPS	vL	vR	BF/G	Ctl	Dom	Cmd	SwK	G	L	F	H%	S%	hr/f	GS	APC	DOM%	DIS%	Sv%	LI	RAR	BPV	BPX	R$
09																																
10																																
11																																
12 a/a	1	1	14	30	26	1.45	3.03	1.28				4.1	4.6	8.0	1.7					26%	93%								9.4	77	100	$6
13 DET *	2	3	15	58	62	2.67	2.55	1.17	720	873	608	3.9	3.7	9.6	2.6	15%	47	24	29	29%	78%	9%	0	15			79	0.93	8.6	110	144	$9
1st Half	1	2	14	34	35	2.75	2.28	1.17	1034	1000	1045	3.8	4.0	9.4	2.4	15%	24	41	35	28%	76%	0%	0	14			82	0.97	4.6	111	144	$14
2nd Half	1	1	1	25	27	2.55	2.98	1.18	653	829	532	4.0	3.3	9.9	3.0	15%	53	19	27	30%	81%	12%	0	15			50	0.93	4.0	120	155	$2
14 Proj	2	3	4	58	62	2.91	3.06	1.17	573	733	462	3.9	3.6	9.7	2.7	15%	51	19	30	29%	76%	7%	0						6.8	106	137	$5

Rondon,Hector

Age: 26	Th: R	Role RP	Health F	LIMA Plan D+	
Ht: 6' 3"	Wt: 180	Type Pwr	PT/Exp F	Rand Var 0	
			Consist F	MM 3300	

One-time top CLE prospect returned from TJ surgery and showed the Ctl problems typical of a first season back, but found his stride and finished strong in Sept (9 IP, 4.0 Cmd, 2.85 xERA). By year's end, was being mentioned as a 2014 setup candidate, and 2009 BPV shows he owns the skills to succeed.

Yr Tm	W	L	Sv	IP	K	ERA	xERA	WHIP	oOPS	vL	vR	BF/G	Ctl	Dom	Cmd	SwK	G	L	F	H%	S%	hr/f	GS	APC	DOM%	DIS%	Sv%	LI	RAR	BPV	BPX	R$
09 a/a	11	10	0	146	122	4.10	4.07	1.31				22.4	1.8	7.5	4.1					34%	69%								4.0	109	204	$8
10 aaa	1	3	0	32	29	8.88	9.02	1.91				21.4	2.7	8.1	3.0					40%	58%								-18.8	6	10	-$9
11																																
12																																
13 CHC	2	1	0	55	44	4.77	4.39	1.41	737	546	908	5.4	4.1	7.2	1.8	11%	43	22	35	29%	68%	10%	0	21			0	0.65	-6.1	40	52	-$5
1st Half	1	0	0	27	21	6.08	4.70	1.46	816	693	931	5.3	4.1	7.1	1.8	10%	39	20	40	29%	62%	15%	0	21			0	0.82	-7.3	36	46	-$7
2nd Half	1	1	0	28	23	3.54	4.08	1.36	659	393	885	5.5	4.2	7.4	1.8	11%	48	23	29	30%	73%	4%	0	21			0	0.47	1.1	46	59	-$3
14 Proj	2	3	0	59	50	4.14	3.95	1.44	753	541	942	8.3	4.0	7.6	1.9	11%	44	22	34	31%	73%	10%	0						-2.0	52	67	-$2

Rosario,Sandy

Age: 28	Th: R	Role RP	Health D	LIMA Plan D+	
Ht: 6' 1"	Wt: 210	Type	PT/Exp D	Rand Var -3	
			Consist B	MM 3100	

3-2, 3.02 ERA in 42 IP at SF. What an ego booster: Waived or DFA'ed FIVE TIMES last offseason. Then showed 'em with great 1H, but 2H Cmd isn't a misprint. Reported hip/back pain in Sept; we'll bet it started in July. You'd hide it too, if you had an employment trend like his. Some skills, but Health/Rand Var say don't bother.

Yr Tm	W	L	Sv	IP	K	ERA	xERA	WHIP	oOPS	vL	vR	BF/G	Ctl	Dom	Cmd	SwK	G	L	F	H%	S%	hr/f	GS	APC	DOM%	DIS%	Sv%	LI	RAR	BPV	BPX	R$
09																																
10 FLA	0	0	0	1	0	54.00	18.34	10.00	2288	2233	2333	6.0	9.0	0.0	0.0	2%	45	18	36	71%	50%	50%	0	21			0	0.14	-6.2	-220	-356	-$6
11 FLA *	3	3	27	58	42	4.38	4.96	1.62	826	606	1300	4.5	3.9	6.5	1.7	9%	57	29	14	35%	73%	0%	0	16			82	0.20	-3.1	53	80	$6
12 MIA *	0	2	17	31	25	3.26	3.93	1.30	1059	800	1429	4.1	1.0	7.3	7.1	15%	67	20	13	36%	74%	0%	0	15			100	0.16	2.9	179	234	$4
13 SF *	4	3	4	74	51	2.93	3.34	1.36	644	597	667	4.8	3.6	6.2	1.7	8%	45	27	29	31%	78%	3%	0	16			100	0.99	8.6	71	92	$3
1st Half	3	1	4	47	43	2.86	3.50	1.35	691	726	675	6.0	3.2	8.2	2.6	13%	43	28	30	33%	79%	8%	0	20			100	0.96	5.9	96	124	$6
2nd Half	1	2	0	27	8	3.04	5.49	1.39	618	546	661	3.7	4.4	2.7	0.6	5%	46	26	28	26%	76%	0%	0	14			0	1.01	2.7	-46	-60	-$3
14 Proj	1	2	0	27	18	3.93	3.97	1.39	702	634	736	4.3	3.0	6.0	2.0	8%	44	27	29	32%	70%	3%	0						-0.2	50	65	-$3

Rosenberg,B.J.

Age: 28	Th: R	Role RP	Health A	LIMA Plan C	
Ht: 6' 3"	Wt: 220	Type xFB	PT/Exp D	Rand Var 0	
			Consist C	MM 2200	

2-0, 4.58 ERA, 1 Sv in 20 IP at PHI. After another failed 1st half try as a starter at Triple-A, this hard thrower settled in with much better skills in his more accustomed relief role. Has generally fared better in shorter outings in the minors, so these 2nd half skills appear to be a reasonable upside.

Yr Tm	W	L	Sv	IP	K	ERA	xERA	WHIP	oOPS	vL	vR	BF/G	Ctl	Dom	Cmd	SwK	G	L	F	H%	S%	hr/f	GS	APC	DOM%	DIS%	Sv%	LI	RAR	BPV	BPX	R$
09																																
10																																
11 aa	5	7	2	109	83	5.09	5.38	1.59				12.4	3.2	6.8	2.1					35%	69%								-15.4	49	74	-$7
12 PHI *	6	4	3	87	81	3.51	4.23	1.37	725	703	719	7.8	3.5	8.4	2.4	13%	39	23	38	31%	78%	17%	1	19	0%	100%	60	0.91	5.4	73	95	$3
13 PHI *	5	6	3	95	64	5.47	5.37	1.74	683	823	613	8.7	4.4	6.1	1.4	11%	37	18	46	36%	68%	0%	0	16			100	0.88	-18.8	42	55	-$12
1st Half	2	5	0	56	31	6.92	6.53	1.97	1071	1125	1000	19.2	5.8	5.0	0.9	9%	33	33	33	35%	64%	0%	0	18			0	0.20	-21.1	10	13	-$21
2nd Half	3	1	3	39	33	3.39	3.72	1.41	595	679	554	4.6	2.4	7.6	3.2	11%	38	13	49	37%	73%	0%	0	16			100	0.98	2.3	110	143	$1
14 Proj	4	3	0	58	45	4.10	4.08	1.27	646	760	600	5.0	2.8	6.9	2.5	11%	40	13	47	30%	68%	5%	0						-1.7	67	87	$0

Rosenthal,Trevor

Age: 24	Th: R	Role RP	Health A	LIMA Plan A	
Ht: 6' 2"	Wt: 220	Type Pwr	PT/Exp D	Rand Var +1	
			Consist A	MM 5531	

Former starter screwed up in reverse, becoming such a dominant reliever that he may never start again. It might just work out for him, though; was closing by (and dominating in) the post-season, and he owns the skills to keep the gig for a long time. And make no mistake, these are Eck/Kimbrel-level skills.

Yr Tm	W	L	Sv	IP	K	ERA	xERA	WHIP	oOPS	vL	vR	BF/G	Ctl	Dom	Cmd	SwK	G	L	F	H%	S%	hr/f	GS	APC	DOM%	DIS%	Sv%	LI	RAR	BPV	BPX	R$
09																																
10																																
11																																
12 STL *	8	8	0	132	114	3.06	2.40	1.09	513	395	597	13.2	3.2	7.8	2.4	13%	54	13	33	26%	73%	11%	0	19			0	0.63	15.6	94	123	$14
13 STL	2	4	3	75	108	2.63	2.47	1.10	608	586	626	4.2	2.4	12.9	5.4	15%	44	19	36	36%	77%	6%	0	17			38	1.21	11.5	190	247	$7
1st Half	1	1	0	39	56	2.08	2.35	1.08	609	452	760	4.4	1.8	12.9	7.0	15%	45	18	36	36%	85%	9%	0	18			0	1.22	8.6	206	267	$8
2nd Half	1	3	3	36	52	3.22	2.61	1.13	607	763	503	4.1	3.0	12.9	4.3	15%	43	20	36	36%	70%	3%	0	17			50	1.21	2.9	173	224	$7
14 Proj	3	4	43	73	87	2.75	2.69	1.05	571	573	570	5.4	2.8	10.9	3.9	15%	44	20	36	30%	75%	6%	0						10.0	142	185	$25

Ross,Robbie

Age: 25	Th: L	Role SP	Health B	LIMA Plan B+	
Ht: 5' 11"	Wt: 215	Type GB	PT/Exp D	Rand Var 0	
			Consist A	MM 4201	

That's two years of 2H ERA spikes after a heavy 1H relief workload, but xERA shows it's less a bad 2H than a S% lucky 1H. Given neutral-to-reverse splits, TEX sent him to winter ball to re-convert to starting. Solid skills, and clearly would be far more valuable as a starter than a middle reliever, so monitor his role this spring.

Yr Tm	W	L	Sv	IP	K	ERA	xERA	WHIP	oOPS	vL	vR	BF/G	Ctl	Dom	Cmd	SwK	G	L	F	H%	S%	hr/f	GS	APC	DOM%	DIS%	Sv%	LI	RAR	BPV	BPX	R$
09																																
10																																
11 aa	1	1	0	38	30	3.14	4.01	1.12				25.0	1.2	7.1	5.9					29%	81%								3.8	125	189	$0
12 TEX	6	0	0	65	47	2.22	3.52	1.20	624	613	632	4.6	3.2	6.5	2.0	8%	62	18	20	28%	83%	8%	0	18			0	0.97	14.4	71	93	$6
13 TEX	4	2	0	62	58	3.03	3.43	1.32	684	950	523	4.1	2.7	8.4	3.1	11%	45	28	26	33%	78%	8%	0	15			0	1.18	6.4	100	130	$1
1st Half	4	1	0	39	39	1.86	3.26	1.24	616	766	535	4.3	3.0	9.1	3.0	10%	47	25	27	33%	85%	3%	0	16			0	1.37	9.6	107	138	$6
2nd Half	0	1	0	24	19	4.94	3.70	1.44	788	1195	500	3.8	2.3	7.2	3.2	12%	43	32	25	34%	68%	16%	0	14			0	0.90	-3.1	89	116	-$6
14 Proj	5	4	0	88	72	3.40	3.27	1.27	690	879	562	23.7	2.6	7.3	2.8	10%	52	25	23	31%	75%	12%	15						5.1	92	119	$4

Ross,Tyson

Age: 27	Th: R	Role RP	Health D	LIMA Plan B	
Ht: 6' 6"	Wt: 230	Type Pwr GB	PT/Exp C	Rand Var 0	
			Consist C	MM 4303	

Huge breakout, masked only by a poor team and IP lost to left (non-throwing) shoulder injury. Found command of a beastly slider and became one of the toughest SP to hit in the NL, with a GB lean to boot. 2nd half was the really big jump, but is this his new level? So many strong signs... UP: 15 Wins, 3.00 ERA.

Yr Tm	W	L	Sv	IP	K	ERA	xERA	WHIP	oOPS	vL	vR	BF/G	Ctl	Dom	Cmd	SwK	G	L	F	H%	S%	hr/f	GS	APC	DOM%	DIS%	Sv%	LI	RAR	BPV	BPX	R$
09 aa	5	4	0	50	26	3.88	2.79	1.19				22.3	3.3	4.7	1.4					25%	67%								2.7	55	102	$2
10 OAK *	3	5	1	65	58	4.69	3.97	1.44	754	674	819	8.6	4.4	8.0	1.8	10%	53	18	29	31%	67%	12%	2	27	0%	100%	50	0.58	-4.9	71	114	-$2
11 OAK *	6	5	0	73	53	5.23	5.24	1.68	617	617	616	18.2	4.2	6.5	1.6	8%	48	22	30	35%	68%	3%	6	60	50%	33%	0	0.76	-11.6	47	71	-$7
12 OAK *	8	13	0	152	98	4.76	4.73	1.56	870	974	759	20.2	3.9	5.8	1.5	7%	50	23	27	33%	69%	10%	13	72	23%	38%	0	0.97	-13.9	45	59	-$10
13 SD	3	8	0	125	119	3.17	3.20	1.15	627	709	548	14.4	3.2	8.6	2.7	12%	55	15	30	28%	74%	8%	16	57	81%	19%	0	1.09	10.8	102	133	$7
1st Half	0	4	0	42	32	3.24	4.16	1.30	653	701	605	8.7	4.3	6.9	1.6	8%	51	14	35	26%	78%	10%	3	34	33%	67%	0	1.30	3.2	37	47	-$1
2nd Half	3	4	0	83	87	3.13	2.76	1.08	614	713	519	22.1	2.6	9.4	3.6	14%	57	16	27	30%	71%	7%	13	86	92%	8%	0	0.82	7.5	134	174	$12
14 Proj	12	8	0	162	143	3.71	3.48	1.34	693	752	633	15.1	3.5	7.9	2.3	10%	52	19	29	31%	73%	8%	23						3.1	79	103	$8

ROD TRUESDELL

Rusin,Chris

Age: 27	Th: L	Role: SP	Health	A	LIMA Plan	D+
Ht: 6' 2"	Wt: 195	Type: Con GB	PT/Exp	C	Rand Var	0
			Consist	C	MM	2001

2-6, 3.93 in 66 IP at CHC. Finesse lefty gets some GB, but not enough to offset chronic lack of a strikeout pitch, a deficiency that is trending in the wrong direction. And when he does get a pitch up? That hr/f tells the story. Until or unless his Dom improves, he's safe to ignore.

Yr	Tm	W	L	Sv	IP	K	ERA	xERA	WHIP	oOPS	vL	vR	BF/G	Ctl	Dom	Cmd	SwK	G	L	F	H%	S%	hr/f	GS	APC	DOM%	DIS%	Sv%	LI	RAR	BPV	BPX	R$
09																																	
10	aa	2	1	0	19	12	2.22	4.28	1.48				20.4	1.9	5.8	3.1					37%	83%								4.4	92	149	-$1
11	a/a	8	4	0	139	77	4.22	4.70	1.41				22.6	1.9	5.0	2.6					33%	71%								-4.7	55	83	-$1
12	CHC *	10	12	0	173	97	5.62	5.70	1.63	881	678	955	23.3	3.6	5.1	1.4	10%	45	25	30	33%	67%	14%	7	72	43%	43%			-34.2	19	24	-$19
13	CHC *	10	13	0	187	90	4.13	4.33	1.38	750	521	819	24.6	2.6	4.3	1.7	8%	48	23	29	30%	72%	13%	13	79	31%	38%			-6.2	35	46	-$2
1st Half		7	7	0	110	49	4.15	4.08	1.33				26.9	2.0	4.0	2.0					30%	69%	0%	0						-3.8	46	59	$1
2nd Half		3	6	0	77	41	4.11	4.69	1.46	750	521	819	22.1	3.4	4.7	1.4	8%	48	23	29	29%	75%	13%	13	79	31%	38%			-2.4	25	33	-$5
14	Proj	**5**	**6**	**0**	**86**	**45**	**4.66**	**4.37**	**1.48**	**751**	**537**	**816**	**23.4**	**3.0**	**4.7**	**1.6**	**8%**	**48**	**23**	**29**	**31%**	**70%**	**10%**	**16**						**-8.4**	**31**	**41**	**-$5**

Russell,James

Age: 28	Th: L	Role: RP	Health	A	LIMA Plan	D+
Ht: 6' 4"	Wt: 200	Type: xFB	PT/Exp	C	Rand Var	-3
			Consist	B	MM	1100

At least he took it up a notch vs. LH hitters. That said, only fortune, in the form of 1st half hr/f and strand rate, and 2nd half hit rate, kept this from being as mediocre-to-poor as xERA says it should've been. Cmd tailspin continues, and that 2nd half number is a real eye-opener. There's nothing to recommend here.

Yr	Tm	W	L	Sv	IP	K	ERA	xERA	WHIP	oOPS	vL	vR	BF/G	Ctl	Dom	Cmd	SwK	G	L	F	H%	S%	hr/f	GS	APC	DOM%	DIS%	Sv%	LI	RAR	BPV	BPX	R$
09	a/a	5	6	0	103	61	5.29	6.10	1.65				12.4	2.6	5.3	2.0					35%	70%								-12.2	28	52	-$7
10	CHC	1	1	0	49	42	4.96	4.27	1.35	822	726	887	3.8	2.0	7.7	3.8	12%	31	20	49	31%	71%	14%	0	15			0	0.94	-5.3	93	151	-$3
11	CHC	1	6	0	68	43	4.12	4.50	1.33	812	685	902	4.6	1.9	5.7	3.1	10%	38	14	48	30%	76%	11%	5	17	0%	100%	0	0.89	-1.5	69	103	-$2
12	CHC	7	1	2	69	55	3.25	4.36	1.30	732	727	735	3.8	3.0	7.1	2.4	10%	37	21	41	31%	76%	6%	0	15			40	0.98	6.6	63	82	$3
13	CHC	1	6	0	53	37	3.59	4.54	1.22	746	543	1033	2.9	3.1	6.3	2.1	10%	33	16	51	26%	75%	9%	0	11			0	1.38	1.8	42	54	-$1
1st Half		1	1	0	32	27	2.53	3.85	1.19	686	509	885	3.3	2.5	7.6	3.0	10%	37	20	43	31%	78%	3%	0	13			0	1.34	5.3	83	107	$1
2nd Half		0	5	0	21	10	5.23	5.67	1.26	839	585	1365	2.4	3.9	4.4	1.1	9%	29	11	61	19%	70%	15%	0	10			0	1.42	-3.5	-21	-27	-$6
14	Proj	**2**	**4**	**1**	**65**	**44**	**4.15**	**4.41**	**1.37**	**818**	**657**	**981**	**3.4**	**2.9**	**6.1**	**2.1**	**10%**	**34**	**17**	**49**	**29%**	**75%**	**10%**	**0**						**-2.3**	**43**	**56**	**-$2**

Ryu,Hyun-Jin

Age: 27	Th: L	Role: SP	Health	A	LIMA Plan	C+
Ht: 6' 2"	Wt: 255	Type: Pwr GB	PT/Exp	A	Rand Var	-1
			Consist	B	MM	5305

Not only a terrific debut, but great signs going forward. 2H skills gains across the board bode well, as does just 2 PQS-DIS all season. GB lean helps keep the ball in the yard, and he performed even better on the road. With his body type, fitness may be an issue at some point, but he finished strong in the playoffs. Invest.

Yr	Tm	W	L	Sv	IP	K	ERA	xERA	WHIP	oOPS	vL	vR	BF/G	Ctl	Dom	Cmd	SwK	G	L	F	H%	S%	hr/f	GS	APC	DOM%	DIS%	Sv%	LI	RAR	BPV	BPX	R$
09	for	13	12	0	189	178	4.44	4.95	1.46				28.9	4.0	8.5	2.1					31%	75%								-2.7	53	99	$6
10	for	16	4	0	193	177	2.26	2.97	1.12				30.4	2.6	8.3	3.2					28%	85%								43.3	100	162	$27
11	for	11	7	0	126	121	4.17	3.88	1.23				21.3	3.4	8.7	2.6					27%	72%								-3.5	72	108	$6
12	for	9	9	0	183	199	3.30	2.96	1.21				27.3	2.8	9.8	3.5					33%	72%								16.2	127	165	$15
13	LA	14	8	0	192	154	3.00	3.51	1.20	660	738	633	26.1	2.3	7.2	3.1	9%	51	19	31	30%	77%	9%	30	102	60%	7%			20.5	97	126	$16
1st Half		6	3	0	105	87	2.83	3.66	1.24	658	849	589	27.0	2.9	7.5	2.6	8%	50	18	32	29%	80%	9%	16	104	63%	0%			13.4	83	108	$17
2nd Half		8	5	0	87	67	3.21	3.34	1.16	662	592	684	25.1	1.6	6.9	4.5	9%	52	20	29	31%	74%	8%	14	101	57%	14%			7.1	112	146	$16
14	Proj	**14**	**9**	**0**	**196**	**177**	**3.31**	**3.18**	**1.21**	**660**	**701**	**646**	**25.5**	**2.6**	**8.2**	**3.2**	**9%**	**51**	**19**	**30**	**30%**	**75%**	**10%**	**31**						**13.5**	**106**	**137**	**$17**

Rzepczynski,Marc

Age: 28	Th: L	Role: RP	Health	B	LIMA Plan	C
Ht: 6' 1"	Wt: 215	Type: Pwr xGB	PT/Exp	D	Rand Var	-1
			Consist	B	MM	4200

0-0, 3.23 ERA in 31 IP at STL and CLE. Found Ctl and looked like a different pitcher in 20 IP down the stretch (0.89 ERA, 20 K, 2 BB), devastating LH hitters. History shows he can lose that Ctl without warning, and as a situational lefty, he isn't going to provide much more than holds. So value remains limited regardless.

Yr	Tm	W	L	Sv	IP	K	ERA	xERA	WHIP	oOPS	vL	vR	BF/G	Ctl	Dom	Cmd	SwK	G	L	F	H%	S%	hr/f	GS	APC	DOM%	DIS%	Sv%	LI	RAR	BPV	BPX	R$
09	TOR *	11	9	0	149	151	3.43	4.12	1.50	682	651	691	23.9	4.3	9.1	2.1	8%	51	20	28	35%	77%	15%	11	99	73%	18%			16.4	86	161	$8
10	TOR *	9	9	0	131	108	5.13	5.34	1.59	840	671	895	22.1	3.7	7.4	2.0	10%	51	16	32	34%	70%	13%	12	77	33%	42%	0	0.83	-16.9	49	80	-$5
11	2 TM	2	6	0	62	61	3.34	2.90	1.23	623	478	748	3.6	3.8	8.9	2.3	12%	65	15	20	29%	73%	9%	0	13			0	1.28	4.6	100	151	$2
12	STL	1	3	0	47	33	4.24	3.78	1.35	729	682	781	2.8	3.3	6.4	1.9	10%	59	22	19	28%	73%	25%	0	11			0	1.31	-1.3	63	82	-$4
13	2 TM *	1	2	0	75	52	3.51	4.07	1.48	674	480	859	4.6	3.6	6.3	1.8	13%	56	17	27	33%	76%	9%	0	12			0	0.71	3.2	64	83	-$4
1st Half		0	2	0	42	30	4.09	5.40	1.76	915	819	966	5.7	4.1	6.4	1.5	9%	55	17	28	37%	76%	13%	0	16			0	0.40	-1.2	50	64	-$8
2nd Half		1	0	0	33	23	2.77	2.35	1.12	562	378	787	3.6	2.8	6.2	2.2	15%	56	16	27	27%	74%	7%	0	11			0	0.80	4.4	86	111	$2
14	Proj	**1**	**2**	**0**	**51**	**39**	**3.63**	**3.55**	**1.35**	**727**	**570**	**851**	**3.9**	**3.4**	**6.9**	**2.0**	**12%**	**58**	**18**	**25**	**31%**	**74%**	**10%**	**0**						**1.5**	**68**	**88**	**-$1**

Sabathia,CC

Age: 33	Th: L	Role: SP	Health	A	LIMA Plan	C
Ht: 6' 8"	Wt: 290	Type: Pwr	PT/Exp	A	Rand Var	+2
			Consist	A	MM	4305

ERA was about a run higher than it should have been; otherwise - ouch. Lost another mph off his fastball, and 2H is a major red flag, as everything trended badly. RHBs killed him, and most troubling is that 2H Ctl, so far out of his usual range that a hidden injury seems possible. Young enough to rebound, but far from a lock.

Yr	Tm	W	L	Sv	IP	K	ERA	xERA	WHIP	oOPS	vL	vR	BF/G	Ctl	Dom	Cmd	SwK	G	L	F	H%	S%	hr/f	GS	APC	DOM%	DIS%	Sv%	LI	RAR	BPV	BPX	R$
09	NYY	19	8	0	230	197	3.37	3.71	1.15	653	560	681	27.6	2.6	7.7	2.9	11%	43	20	37	28%	72%	7%	34	106	59%	9%			27.1	89	167	$28
10	NYY	21	7	0	238	197	3.18	3.55	1.19	656	678	649	28.5	2.8	7.5	2.7	10%	51	15	34	29%	76%	9%	34	106	56%	3%			26.3	88	142	$24
11	NYY	19	8	0	237	230	3.00	3.17	1.23	666	554	709	29.8	2.3	8.7	3.8	12%	47	23	30	33%	77%	8%	33	109	79%	0%			27.7	120	180	$23
12	NYY	15	6	0	200	197	3.38	3.29	1.14	666	667	665	29.8	2.0	8.9	4.5	12%	48	21	31	31%	74%	13%	28	108	75%	4%			15.8	132	172	$21
13	NYY	14	13	0	211	175	4.78	3.89	1.37	770	662	804	28.4	2.8	7.5	2.7	10%	45	22	33	32%	68%	13%	32	104	44%	6%			-23.7	83	108	-$2
1st Half		8	6	0	117	97	4.15	3.54	1.20	726	616	754	28.4	1.8	7.5	4.2	11%	46	20	34	30%	70%	14%	17	104	53%	6%			-4.2	110	143	$8
2nd Half		6	7	0	94	78	5.55	4.36	1.59	823	703	867	28.4	4.0	7.5	1.9	8%	43	25	32	34%	66%	12%	15	105	33%	7%			-19.6	47	61	-$14
14	Proj	**11**	**12**	**0**	**199**	**169**	**3.94**	**3.58**	**1.32**	**725**	**648**	**750**	**28.1**	**2.9**	**7.7**	**2.7**	**10%**	**45**	**21**	**34**	**31%**	**73%**	**10%**	**29**						**-1.7**	**84**	**109**	**$8**

Salas,Fernando

Age: 29	Th: R	Role: RP	Health	C	LIMA Plan	C
Ht: 6' 2"	Wt: 210	Type: Pwr xFB	PT/Exp	C	Rand Var	0
			Consist	B	MM	3300

0-1, 4.50 ERA in 28 IP at STL. A riddle wrapped in a mystery inside an enigma. Continues to flash closer-worthy skills at times, then goes a month with a 4.8 Dom (May) or 4.2 Ctl (July). Overall K/9 slide is notable as he lost a mph off heater. And those 12 saves? Did you no good, unless you're in a AAA fantasy league.

Yr	Tm	W	L	Sv	IP	K	ERA	xERA	WHIP	oOPS	vL	vR	BF/G	Ctl	Dom	Cmd	SwK	G	L	F	H%	S%	hr/f	GS	APC	DOM%	DIS%	Sv%	LI	RAR	BPV	BPX	R$
09	a/a	4	2	0	38	25	4.07	3.71	1.26				4.6	2.8	5.9	2.1					28%	70%								1.2	58	108	$0
10	STL *	1	0	19	66	64	3.74	3.19	1.21	748	866	665	4.4	3.2	8.7	2.7	12%	33	18	48	29%	71%	10%	0	21			95	0.48	2.8	95	153	$9
11	STL	5	6	24	75	75	2.28	3.52	0.95	566	649	502	4.3	2.5	9.0	3.6	11%	34	14	52	24%	81%	7%	0	17			80	1.45	15.4	106	159	$20
12	STL	1	4	0	59	60	4.30	4.13	1.41	720	681	747	3.9	4.1	9.2	2.2	13%	38	24	38	33%	71%	8%	0	16			0	1.18	-2.0	70	91	-$4
13	STL *	1	5	12	52	38	3.49	2.90	1.10	715	829	645	4.1	2.0	6.6	3.3	10%	32	15	53	28%	70%	7%	0	17			80	1.05	2.4	95	124	$5
1st Half		1	2	0	22	18	2.82	2.84	1.02	703	1010	544	4.3	1.2	7.3	6.0	11%	37	10	53	28%	76%	7%	0	18			0	1.15	2.9	153	198	$1
2nd Half		0	3	12	29	20	4.00	2.94	1.15	732	636	810	4.0	2.6	6.1	2.3	9%	25	22	53	27%	65%	5%	0	15			92	0.92	-0.5	75	97	$8
14	Proj	**1**	**3**	**0**	**44**	**37**	**3.77**	**3.80**	**1.21**	**683**	**802**	**606**	**4.1**	**2.7**	**7.7**	**2.8**	**12%**	**36**	**15**	**49**	**30%**	**70%**	**6%**	**0**						**0.5**	**79**	**103**	**-$1**

Salazar,Danny

Age: 24	Th: R	Role: RP	Health	A	LIMA Plan	C
Ht: 6' 0"	Wt: 190	Type: Pwr FB	PT/Exp	D	Rand Var	+1
			Consist	A	MM	5503

2-3, 3.12 ERA in 52 IP at CLE. Blazing, malevolent stuff: averages (that's *averages*) 96 mph on a fastball with sinister movement, mixes in a nasty splitter. Works up in zone, so hitters will occasionally run into a long one, and he's had issues lasting deep into games. But BPV shows he's the real deal. UP: sub-3.00 ERA, 200 K.

Yr	Tm	W	L	Sv	IP	K	ERA	xERA	WHIP	oOPS	vL	vR	BF/G	Ctl	Dom	Cmd	SwK	G	L	F	H%	S%	hr/f	GS	APC	DOM%	DIS%	Sv%	LI	RAR	BPV	BPX	R$
09																																	
10																																	
11																																	
12	aa	4	0	0	34	20	2.44	2.62	1.12				22.3	2.2	5.3	2.5					27%	78%								6.6	82	107	$1
13	CLE *	8	8	1	145	175	3.10	2.88	1.12	655	588	733	18.4	2.4	10.9	4.6	15%	34	26	40	32%	75%	14%	10	82	50%	40%			13.6	148	193	$14
1st Half		3	5	0	66	77	4.05	3.53	1.31				18.2	2.9	10.5	3.6					36%	69%	0%	0						-1.5	126	163	$4
2nd Half		5	3	1	79	98	2.31	2.34	0.96	655	588	733	18.6	1.9	11.2	5.8	15%	34	26	40	29%	82%	14%	10	82	50%	40%			15.1	175	227	$23
14	Proj	**14**	**6**	**0**	**175**	**188**	**3.13**	**3.11**	**1.10**	**563**	**523**	**610**	**19.8**	**2.4**	**9.7**	**4.0**	**15%**	**34**	**26**	**40**	**30%**	**75%**	**9%**	**34**						**15.8**	**122**	**158**	**$21**

ROD TRUESDELL

Sale,Chris

Age: 25 Th: L Role SP	Health A	LIMA Plan C	
Ht: 6' 6" Wt: 180 Type Pwr	PT/Exp A	Rand Var +1	
	Consist A	MM 5405	

While W/L doesn't don't show it, this was another step up. DOM/DIS% highlights reliability—only one PQS DISaster all year, way back in April. In 2012, his one flaw was a 2nd half fade; not this time. Now, there's scarcely a blemish to find, other than pitching for a poor team. A Cy Young candidate.

Yr	Tm	W	L	Sv	IP	K	ERA	xERA	WHIP	oOPS	vL	vR	BF/G	Ctl	Dom	Cmd	SwK	G	L	F	H%	S%	hr/f	GS	APC	DOM%	DIS%	Sv%	LI	RAR	BPV	BPX	R$
09																																	
10	CHW	2	1	4	23	32	1.93	2.61	1.07	546	694	454	4.4	3.9	12.3	3.2	10%	51	12	37	28%	87%	11%	0	19			100	1.65	6.2	147	238	$3
11	CHW	2	2	8	71	79	2.79	3.00	1.11	612	558	660	5.0	3.4	10.0	2.9	12%	50	18	32	28%	78%	11%	0	19			80	1.25	10.1	116	174	$9
12	CHW	17	8	0	192	192	3.05	3.27	1.14	660	601	682	25.7	2.4	9.0	3.8	11%	45	23	32	30%	77%	12%	29	101	72%	7%	0	0.87	22.9	120	157	$24
13	CHW	11	14	0	214	226	3.07	2.94	1.07	636	360	699	28.9	1.9	9.5	4.9	11%	47	21	32	30%	76%	13%	30	108	77%	3%			21.2	144	187	$23
1st Half		5	7	0	106	114	2.79	2.90	0.96	563	280	631	27.9	2.0	9.6	4.8	11%	45	21	34	27%	74%	10%	15	108	87%	7%			14.1	142	183	$27
2nd Half		6	7	0	108	112	3.33	2.99	1.19	705	443	762	29.8	1.8	9.3	5.1	11%	48	21	30	32%	77%	15%	15	109	67%	0%			7.1	145	187	$18
14	Proj	**14**	**11**	**0**	**208**	**215**	**2.96**	**2.91**	**1.11**	**648**	**508**	**696**	**27.9**	**2.3**	**9.3**	**4.0**	**11%**	**46**	**21**	**33**	**30%**	**78%**	**12%**	**51**						**23.3**	**129**	**167**	**$25**

Samardzija,Jeff

Age: 29 Th: R Role RP	Health A	LIMA Plan A	
Ht: 6' 5" Wt: 225 Type Pwr	PT/Exp A	Rand Var +2	
	Consist A	MM 4405	

May have lost some steam after that heavy 1H workload, but xERA confirms his 2H fade wasn't as bad as ERA suggests. Bad home stats (4.76 ERA at Wrigley, 3.91 road) were the reverse of 2012, and shouldn't repeat. Mostly kept Ctl gains. In short, this is two straight years of excellent skills. UP: sub-3.50 ERA.

Yr	Tm	W	L	Sv	IP	K	ERA	xERA	WHIP	oOPS	vL	vR	BF/G	Ctl	Dom	Cmd	SwK	G	L	F	H%	S%	hr/f	GS	APC	DOM%	DIS%	Sv%	LI	RAR	BPV	BPX	R$
09	CHC *	7	9	0	124	80	6.21	6.50	1.69	981	1164	837	14.7	3.2	5.8	1.8	8%	41	18	40	35%	66%	15%	2	30	0%	50%	0	0.58	-28.8	15	28	-$11
10	CHC *	13	5	0	131	91	5.45	4.47	1.57	930	470	1202	13.7	6.0	6.3	1.0	6%	30	17	52	27%	66%	11%	3	53	0%	67%	0	0.57	-22.0	37	60	-$5
11	CHC	8	4	0	88	87	2.97	4.11	1.30	613	660	581	5.1	5.1	8.9	1.7	11%	41	18	41	27%	78%	5%	0	20			0	0.85	10.6	41	62	$6
12	CHC	9	13	0	175	180	3.81	3.45	1.22	698	759	636	25.8	2.9	9.3	3.2	13%	45	22	33	30%	72%	13%	28	99	64%	11%			4.4	112	146	$10
13	CHC	8	13	0	214	214	4.34	3.49	1.35	736	783	695	27.7	3.3	9.0	2.7	11%	48	20	31	32%	70%	13%	33	105	70%	9%			-12.5	100	130	$1
1st Half		5	7	0	113	120	3.34	3.16	1.20	654	701	613	27.5	2.9	9.5	3.2	12%	48	22	30	31%	75%	11%	17	105	82%	0%			7.4	118	153	$13
2nd Half		3	6	0	100	94	5.47	3.88	1.51	825	865	788	27.9	3.7	8.4	2.3	11%	48	19	33	34%	66%	15%	16	105	56%	19%			-19.9	79	102	-$13
14	Proj	**11**	**13**	**0**	**210**	**210**	**3.65**	**3.37**	**1.30**	**710**	**773**	**656**	**14.8**	**3.4**	**9.0**	**2.6**	**11%**	**46**	**20**	**34**	**31%**	**75%**	**12%**	**28**						**5.7**	**93**	**121**	**$12**

Sanabia,Alex

Age: 25 Th: R Role SP	Health F	LIMA Plan D+	
Ht: 6' 2" Wt: 210 Type FB	PT/Exp D	Rand Var 0	
	Consist B	MM 1000	

Apparently sufferered the worst strained groin of all time: went on DL at the end of May, and missed the rest of the season. Shaky Dom now pairs with increasingly bad Ctl. To top it off, he's a contact flyballer, thus risking a badly strained neck from all that sudden head-turning. Heck, it probably keeps him out all year.

Yr	Tm	W	L	Sv	IP	K	ERA	xERA	WHIP	oOPS	vL	vR	BF/G	Ctl	Dom	Cmd	SwK	G	L	F	H%	S%	hr/f	GS	APC	DOM%	DIS%	Sv%	LI	RAR	BPV	BPX	R$
09																																	
10	FLA *	11	4	0	171	112	2.84	2.63	1.08	686	576	791	21.5	1.9	5.9	3.1	8%	36	19	45	28%	74%	6%	12	75	25%	25%	0	0.76	26.1	96	156	$18
11	FLA *	0	3	0	33	19	6.25	6.82	1.69	911	511	1405	21.1	1.6	5.2	3.2	7%	32	16	51	38%	65%	11%	2	59	50%	50%	0	0.57	-9.3	41	62	-$8
12	aaa	6	7	0	89	56	4.91	5.34	1.51				22.6	2.7	5.7	2.1					33%	70%								-9.8	38	49	-$6
13	MIA	3	7	0	55	31	4.88	5.25	1.70	935	1170	683	25.1	4.1	5.0	1.2	10%	39	22	39	32%	76%	14%	10	91	10%	40%			-6.9	-2	-3	-$8
1st Half		3	7	0	55	31	4.88	5.25	1.70	935	1170	683	25.1	4.1	5.0	1.2	10%	39	22	39	32%	76%	14%	10	91	10%	40%			-6.9	-2	-3	-$8
2nd Half																																	
14	Proj	**2**	**5**	**0**	**55**	**33**	**5.08**	**4.62**	**1.49**	**822**	**929**	**713**	**22.1**	**3.3**	**5.4**	**1.6**	**9%**	**38**	**21**	**41**	**31%**	**69%**	**10%**	**11**						**-8.2**	**24**	**31**	**-$5**

Sanchez,Anibal

Age: 30 Th: R Role SP	Health C	LIMA Plan C	
Ht: 6' 0" Wt: 205 Type Pwr	PT/Exp A	Rand Var -2	
	Consist A	MM 5405	

Right up front: Yes, this was a fine skills step up. However, regression analysis and that 2H xERA both say not to expect another sub-3 ERA. He also missed more time with injury, and now at age 30, that elusive 200 IP season is looking more and more unlikely. So let someone else take the bidding over $20. DN: see 2010-12.

Yr	Tm	W	L	Sv	IP	K	ERA	xERA	WHIP	oOPS	vL	vR	BF/G	Ctl	Dom	Cmd	SwK	G	L	F	H%	S%	hr/f	GS	APC	DOM%	DIS%	Sv%	LI	RAR	BPV	BPX	R$
09	FLA	4	8	0	86	71	3.87	4.70	1.51	756	701	814	23.9	4.8	7.4	1.5	9%	42	20	38	30%	78%	10%	16	92	44%	31%			4.8	24	44	$0
10	FLA	13	12	0	195	157	3.55	4.06	1.34	680	686	674	26.3	3.2	7.2	2.2	10%	45	17	38	32%	73%	5%	32	101	59%	16%			12.6	66	107	$10
11	FLA	8	9	0	196	202	3.67	3.38	1.28	711	671	751	25.9	2.9	9.3	3.2	12%	44	20	36	32%	74%	10%	32	101	66%	16%			6.7	109	165	$10
12	2 TM	9	13	0	196	167	3.86	3.70	1.27	716	645	797	26.5	2.2	7.7	3.5	10%	46	21	32	32%	72%	11%	31	99	68%	13%			3.6	103	134	$8
13	DET	14	8	0	182	202	2.57	3.08	1.15	616	673	548	25.7	2.7	10.0	3.7	13%	45	22	33	32%	79%	6%	29	103	72%	7%			29.1	131	170	$22
1st Half		6	5	0	82	101	2.76	2.83	1.15	622	698	541	25.5	2.5	11.1	4.4	13%	42	25	33	34%	77%	6%	13	102	69%	15%			11.2	152	196	$19
2nd Half		8	3	0	100	101	2.42	3.29	1.16	611	654	554	25.9	2.8	9.1	3.3	13%	48	20	32	31%	80%	6%	16	103	75%	0%			17.9	114	148	$25
14	Proj	**12**	**10**	**0**	**189**	**188**	**3.16**	**3.17**	**1.23**	**666**	**666**	**665**	**25.1**	**2.7**	**9.0**	**3.3**	**12%**	**45**	**21**	**33**	**32%**	**76%**	**8%**	**30**						**16.3**	**111**	**144**	**$17**

Santana,Ervin

Age: 31 Th: R Role SP	Health B	LIMA Plan C	
Ht: 6' 2" Wt: 185 Type	PT/Exp A	Rand Var 0	
	Consist B	MM 3205	

Per ERA, he's the Jekyll and Hyde of pitchers. But toss out what looks like an aberrant 1st half, and skills are actually very consistent. Why is 1H the outlier? Ctl has never been that good, and had already started to regress by June. So base your bid on the 3.90-4.30 xERA skills foundation, not the dart throw of ERA.

Yr	Tm	W	L	Sv	IP	K	ERA	xERA	WHIP	oOPS	vL	vR	BF/G	Ctl	Dom	Cmd	SwK	G	L	F	H%	S%	hr/f	GS	APC	DOM%	DIS%	Sv%	LI	RAR	BPV	BPX	R$
09	LAA	8	8	0	140	107	5.03	4.47	1.47	833	911	746	25.6	3.0	6.9	2.3	9%	38	20	42	32%	70%	13%	23	96	48%	22%	0	0.78	-12.1	58	109	-$2
10	LAA	17	10	0	223	169	3.92	4.29	1.32	744	793	687	28.9	3.0	6.8	2.3	9%	35	22	43	30%	74%	9%	33	108	55%	6%			4.3	56	91	$11
11	LAA	11	12	0	229	178	3.38	3.87	1.22	693	703	681	28.8	2.8	7.0	2.5	9%	44	19	38	28%	76%	10%	33	105	58%	6%			15.7	72	108	$15
12	LAA	9	13	0	178	133	5.16	4.38	1.27	774	867	664	25.5	3.1	6.7	2.2	9%	43	20	37	25%	66%	19%	30	95	47%	23%			-25.1	59	77	-$2
13	KC	9	10	0	211	161	3.24	3.66	1.14	668	675	659	26.8	2.2	6.9	3.2	10%	46	21	33	27%	77%	12%	32	100	66%	6%			16.2	89	116	$15
1st Half		5	5	0	111	89	2.84	3.41	1.04	641	613	675	27.6	1.8	7.2	4.0	10%	48	18	34	26%	80%	14%	16	103	75%	0%			14.1	108	139	$22
2nd Half		4	5	0	100	72	3.69	3.96	1.26	698	741	641	26.1	2.6	6.5	2.5	10%	44	23	32	29%	74%	11%	16	97	56%	13%			2.2	69	89	$8
14	Proj	**10**	**11**	**0**	**203**	**154**	**3.92**	**3.75**	**1.24**	**717**	**756**	**670**	**25.9**	**2.8**	**6.8**	**2.5**	**10%**	**43**	**21**	**37**	**28%**	**74%**	**13%**	**32**						**-1.3**	**69**	**89**	**$9**

Santana,Johan

Age: 35 Th: L Role SP	Health F	LIMA Plan D+	
Ht: 6' 0" Wt: 210 Type Pwr xFB	PT/Exp D	Rand Var 0	
	Consist F	MM 2201	

Yet another surgery to repair the capsule in the front of his left shoulder. Says he'll be ready for spring training, but consider: he'll be 35; he's pitched 2/3 of a season in three years; and xERA shows that he's been merely average since age 31. Past dominance breeds long memories but it's time to move on.

Yr	Tm	W	L	Sv	IP	K	ERA	xERA	WHIP	oOPS	vL	vR	BF/G	Ctl	Dom	Cmd	SwK	G	L	F	H%	S%	hr/f	GS	APC	DOM%	DIS%	Sv%	LI	RAR	BPV	BPX	R$
09	NYM	13	9	0	167	146	3.13	4.09	1.21	692	814	644	28.0	2.5	7.9	3.2	11%	36	17	48	30%	79%	9%	25	103	56%	4%			24.5	89	166	$18
10	NYM	11	9	0	199	144	2.98	4.18	1.18	648	706	627	28.2	2.5	6.5	2.6	10%	35	20	45	28%	77%	6%	29	104	62%	3%			26.9	63	102	$18
11																																	
12	NYM	6	9	0	117	111	4.85	4.16	1.33	750	796	735	23.8	3.0	8.5	2.8	12%	33	24	43	31%	67%	12%	21	92	57%	19%			-12.0	84	109	-$2
13																																	
1st Half																																	
2nd Half																																	
14	Proj	**3**	**5**	**0**	**73**	**57**	**4.32**	**4.09**	**1.30**	**711**	**789**	**682**	**25.9**	**3.2**	**7.0**	**2.2**	**11%**	**34**	**20**	**45**	**29%**	**69%**	**9%**	**12**						**-4.0**	**54**	**70**	**-$1**

Santiago,Hector

Age: 26 Th: L Role RP	Health A	LIMA Plan B	
Ht: 6' 0" Wt: 210 Type Pwr FB	PT/Exp C	Rand Var -2	
	Consist A	MM 2403	

PRO: Fine Dom; 3.30 career ERA and 2.0 Cmd as a SP; swing role has kept IP managed. CON: Chronically shaky Ctl and high FB rate give him a high blow-up risk; fastball speed has declined three straight years. xERA shows his true level. Still some upside here, but until his Cmd touches 2.5, he's a high risk.

Yr	Tm	W	L	Sv	IP	K	ERA	xERA	WHIP	oOPS	vL	vR	BF/G	Ctl	Dom	Cmd	SwK	G	L	F	H%	S%	hr/f	GS	APC	DOM%	DIS%	Sv%	LI	RAR	BPV	BPX	R$
09																																	
10																																	
11	CHW *	7	5	0	89	66	4.34	4.06	1.50	170	0	311	22.5	4.7	6.7	1.4	6%	60	13	27	31%	71%	0%	0	33			0	0.43	-4.4	57	86	-$2
12	CHW	4	1	4	70	79	3.33	4.11	1.34	680	592	744	7.3	5.1	10.1	2.0	9%	38	20	42	27%	81%	14%	4	32	50%	50%	67	0.83	6.0	60	78	$3
13	CHW	4	9	0	149	137	3.56	4.38	1.40	739	686	762	19.3	4.3	8.3	1.9	9%	36	20	44	30%	78%	9%	23	79	52%	17%	0	0.88	5.5	46	59	$1
1st Half		3	5	0	68	70	3.59	3.91	1.34	716	819	675	14.6	4.5	9.3	2.1	10%	39	23	39	29%	76%	10%	9	61	67%	22%	0	0.97	2.3	62	80	$3
2nd Half		1	4	0	81	67	3.54	4.78	1.45	758	595	835	26.1	4.2	7.4	1.8	8%	35	18	47	30%	80%	9%	14	105	43%	14%			3.3	33	42	-$1
14	Proj	**7**	**9**	**0**	**179**	**168**	**4.10**	**4.01**	**1.36**	**713**	**637**	**753**	**12.0**	**4.4**	**8.5**	**1.9**	**9%**	**37**	**19**	**44**	**29%**	**73%**	**10%**	**12**						**-5.2**	**50**	**65**	**$3**

ROD TRUESDELL

Santos,Sergio				
Age: 30	Th: R	Role RP	Health F	LIMA Plan A
Ht: 6' 3"	Wt: 240	Type Pwr	PT/Exp D	Rand Var -5
			Consist F	MM 5500

Considering the time lost to 2012 shoulder surgery AND a 2013 elbow clean-up, this performance was simply amazing. Of course, the "oops" is that he had those injuries to begin with. So what's the draft-day balance between the superb skills and that flunking Health grade? Your risk aversion. UP: 2011+. DN: 2012-.

Yr	Tm	W	L	Sv	IP	K	ERA	xERA	WHIP	oOPS	vL	vR	BF/G	Ctl	Dom	Cmd	SwK	G	L	F	H%	S%	hr/f	GS	APC	DOM%	DIS%	Sv%	LI	RAR	BPV	BPX	R$
09																																	
10	CHW	2	2	1	52	56	2.96	3.89	1.53	692	513	812	4.2	4.5	9.8	2.2	11%	43	21	36	36%	81%	4%	0	16			33	1.03	7.1	74	120	$0
11	CHW	4	5	30	63	92	3.55	2.72	1.11	596	723	472	4.1	4.1	13.1	3.2	14%	43	18	39	29%	70%	11%	0	16			83	1.31	3.0	145	218	$16
12	TOR	0	1	2	5	4	9.00	5.51	2.00	996	740	1350	4.0	7.2	7.2	1.0	7%	50	25	25	33%	56%	25%	0	17			50	1.52	-3.1	-37	-48	-$5
13	TOR	1	1	1	26	28	1.75	2.51	0.58	393	312	449	3.1	1.4	9.8	7.0	18%	50	9	41	18%	71%	4%	0	11			33	1.23	6.7	167	217	$3
1st Half		0	1	0	4	6	2.08	2.99	0.92	673	500	773	3.4	2.1	12.5	6.0	17%	30	10	60	24%	100%	17%	0	13			0	0.90	1.0	176	228	-$5
2nd Half		1	0	1	21	22	1.69	2.41	0.52	327	272	367	3.0	1.3	9.3	7.3	19%	54	8	38	17%	64%	0%	0	10			33	1.29	5.7	165	214	$4
14	Proj	**3**	**2**	**0**	**58**	**65**	**3.13**	**2.97**	**1.10**	**604**	**540**	**652**	**3.6**	**3.3**	**10.1**	**3.1**	**14%**	**47**	**16**	**37**	**28%**	**73%**	**8%**	**0**						**5.3**	**118**	**153**	**$4**

Saunders,Joe				
Age: 33	Th: L	Role SP	Health B	LIMA Plan D+
Ht: 6' 3"	Wt: 215	Type Con	PT/Exp A	Rand Var +4
			Consist A	MM 2003

Ludicrous streak of stats-exceeding-skills finally ended at six years. Signs of decline and change, as he evolves into even more of a soft-tosser. Overall, these are consistent skills, but also rather paltry ones: No, he's not a 5-ERA or a 3-ERA pitcher, but BPX, RAR should tell you he's not a winning fantasy piece, either.

Yr	Tm	W	L	Sv	IP	K	ERA	xERA	WHIP	oOPS	vL	vR	BF/G	Ctl	Dom	Cmd	SwK	G	L	F	H%	S%	hr/f	GS	APC	DOM%	DIS%	Sv%	LI	RAR	BPV	BPX	R$
09	LAA	16	7	0	186	101	4.60	4.73	1.43	794	696	829	26.0	3.1	4.9	1.6	6%	47	17	36	29%	72%	13%	31	97	23%	23%			-6.3	29	55	$4
10	2 TM	9	17	0	203	114	4.47	4.58	1.46	801	715	829	26.7	2.8	5.0	1.8	6%	44	19	37	31%	72%	10%	33	100	42%	24%			-9.8	36	59	-$2
11	ARI	12	13	0	212	108	3.69	4.37	1.31	762	581	810	26.5	2.8	4.6	1.6	6%	44	21	35	27%	77%	12%	33	97	24%	3%			6.5	28	42	$7
12	2 TM	9	13	0	175	112	4.07	4.37	1.34	755	451	849	26.6	2.0	5.8	2.9	7%	43	21	36	31%	73%	10%	28	97	54%	11%			-1.2	71	92	$2
13	SEA	11	16	0	183	107	5.26	4.42	1.60	872	566	953	25.6	3.0	5.3	1.8	6%	51	22	27	34%	69%	15%	32	97	31%	41%			-31.5	43	56	-$15
1st Half		5	8	0	94	49	4.98	4.52	1.45	836	497	926	25.4	2.9	4.7	1.6	7%	49	21	30	30%	68%	13%	16	94	38%	38%			-12.9	34	44	-$10
2nd Half		6	8	0	89	58	5.56	4.31	1.76	907	632	979	25.8	3.1	5.9	1.9	6%	54	23	24	37%	70%	16%	16	100	25%	44%			-18.6	52	68	-$21
14	Proj	**8**	**13**	**0**	**171**	**101**	**4.69**	**4.25**	**1.51**	**826**	**562**	**901**	**25.8**	**2.8**	**5.3**	**1.9**	**7%**	**47**	**21**	**32**	**32%**	**72%**	**12%**	**29**						**-17.4**	**44**	**57**	**-$6**

Scheppers,Tanner				
Age: 27	Th: R	Role RP	Health A	LIMA Plan B+
Ht: 6' 4"	Wt: 200	Type Pwr	PT/Exp D	Rand Var -5
			Consist D	MM 4320

Got by in 1H with a LOT of help from his friends (the ones with gloves). But he began to earn it via a strong finish, with BPVs well over 100 in Aug and Sept. Won't repeat sub-2 ERA, but upper-90s heater and 2H growth say he'll be good enough. The more pertinent issue now is opportunity. UP: 40 saves. DN: setting up again.

Yr	Tm	W	L	Sv	IP	K	ERA	xERA	WHIP	oOPS	vL	vR	BF/G	Ctl	Dom	Cmd	SwK	G	L	F	H%	S%	hr/f	GS	APC	DOM%	DIS%	Sv%	LI	RAR	BPV	BPX	R$
09																																	
10	a/a	1	3	6	80	75	6.01	5.36	1.63				9.9	3.5	8.4	2.4					38%	63%								-19.1	70	113	-$6
11	a/a	4	1	2	44	35	4.31	4.17	1.56				6.8	4.4	7.2	1.7					34%	71%								-2.0	70	106	-$2
12	TEX *	2	3	12	63	54	4.34	5.57	1.51	908	949	881	4.2	1.9	7.7	4.2	9%	43	20	37	37%	75%	15%	0	14			80	0.95	-2.6	89	116	$0
13	TEX	6	2	1	77	59	1.88	3.48	1.07	605	599	610	4.0	2.8	6.9	2.5	10%	50	19	31	25%	87%	9%	0	14			33	1.26	18.8	77	100	$10
1st Half		5	1	0	41	27	1.55	3.80	1.01	549	624	484	4.1	3.5	6.0	1.7	9%	52	18	30	20%	89%	9%	0	15			0	1.36	11.6	42	54	$12
2nd Half		1	1	1	36	32	2.25	3.15	1.14	664	573	758	3.9	2.0	8.0	4.0	12%	49	19	32	30%	84%	10%	0	14			33	1.15	7.2	117	151	$6
14	Proj	**4**	**2**	**17**	**65**	**56**	**3.06**	**3.34**	**1.22**	**662**	**643**	**677**	**4.5**	**2.5**	**7.7**	**3.1**	**10%**	**48**	**19**	**32**	**30%**	**78%**	**9%**	**0**						**6.5**	**98**	**127**	**$10**

Scherzer,Max				
Age: 29	Th: R	Role SP	Health A	LIMA Plan D+
Ht: 6' 3"	Wt: 220	Type Pwr FB	PT/Exp A	Rand Var -2
			Consist A	MM 5505

Main difference between this season and last? A league-leading 6.80 in average run support. Now, before you go all Leyland on us, this was a great and even more consistent year (note IP, DOM/DIS%). But you can see the BPV similarity to '12. You can also see that history and 2H xERA imply a small regression is in the offing.

Yr	Tm	W	L	Sv	IP	K	ERA	xERA	WHIP	oOPS	vL	vR	BF/G	Ctl	Dom	Cmd	SwK	G	L	F	H%	S%	hr/f	GS	APC	DOM%	DIS%	Sv%	LI	RAR	BPV	BPX	R$
09	ARI	9	11	0	170	174	4.12	3.81	1.34	751	793	702	24.7	3.3	9.2	2.8	11%	42	18	40	32%	72%	10%	30	102	50%	20%			4.2	96	179	$9
10	DET *	14	11	0	211	197	3.30	3.22	1.19	700	666	737	25.6	3.1	8.4	2.7	10%	40	20	40	29%	75%	10%	31	106	65%	13%			20.2	91	147	$19
11	DET	15	9	0	195	174	4.43	3.78	1.35	780	840	706	25.2	2.6	8.0	3.1	10%	40	20	39	32%	71%	13%	33	101	52%	9%			-11.7	93	139	$4
12	DET	16	7	0	188	231	3.74	3.35	1.27	721	831	588	24.6	2.9	11.1	3.9	13%	36	22	41	34%	75%	12%	32	102	63%	19%			6.3	136	177	$14
13	DET	21	3	0	214	240	2.90	3.16	0.97	583	645	494	26.1	2.4	10.1	4.3	13%	36	19	45	27%	73%	8%	32	106	88%	3%			25.6	132	172	$33
1st Half		12	0	0	110	131	3.10	2.81	0.90	570	593	530	26.3	2.0	10.7	5.2	13%	39	19	42	26%	69%	10%	16	105	94%	0%			10.4	155	200	$37
2nd Half		9	3	0	104	109	2.68	3.53	1.05	596	707	465	26.0	2.7	9.4	3.5	13%	34	19	47	28%	76%	5%	16	106	81%	6%			15.2	109	141	$30
14	Proj	**17**	**7**	**0**	**203**	**222**	**3.40**	**3.16**	**1.14**	**664**	**735**	**573**	**24.8**	**2.6**	**9.8**	**3.7**	**12%**	**36**	**20**	**44**	**30%**	**74%**	**9%**	**32**						**11.8**	**120**	**155**	**$22**

Shaw,Bryan				
Age: 26	Th: R	Role RP	Health A	LIMA Plan B
Ht: 6' 1"	Wt: 210	Type Pwr	PT/Exp D	Rand Var -1
			Consist B	MM 4310

Cutter specialist mixed in a few more solid sliders, and this Dom spike was a result. Chances for increased role? Has some closing experience, and ended '12 on a club with a shaky stopper. But '13 2H notwithstanding, struggles vs LHB are holding him back. Monitor spring outlook for opportunity, OPS vL for ability to stick there.

Yr	Tm	W	L	Sv	IP	K	ERA	xERA	WHIP	oOPS	vL	vR	BF/G	Ctl	Dom	Cmd	SwK	G	L	F	H%	S%	hr/f	GS	APC	DOM%	DIS%	Sv%	LI	RAR	BPV	BPX	R$
09																																	
10	aa	4	9	2	101	62	5.72	5.06	1.67				13.8	4.0	5.5	1.4					35%	64%								-20.6	43	70	-$9
11	ARI *	5	1	16	67	49	2.56	3.44	1.19	699	587	776	4.2	2.5	6.6	2.6	11%	60	22	18	28%	83%	13%	0	15			94	0.58	11.3	73	110	$11
12	ARI	1	6	2	59	41	3.49	4.03	1.42	747	863	630	3.9	3.6	6.2	1.7	9%	56	21	23	31%	76%	10%	0	15			50	0.78	3.9	48	62	-$2
13	CLE	7	3	1	75	73	3.24	3.58	1.17	586	678	506	4.5	3.4	8.8	2.6	11%	43	25	33	29%	73%	6%	0	18			20	0.99	5.8	88	115	$5
1st Half		0	1	0	38	34	3.79	4.10	1.29	651	803	503	4.9	3.6	8.1	2.3	10%	36	24	39	30%	72%	7%	0	19			0	0.77	0.4	63	82	-$1
2nd Half		7	2	1	37	39	2.68	3.04	1.05	519	532	509	4.1	3.2	9.5	3.0	12%	49	25	26	28%	74%	4%	0	16			33	1.19	5.4	113	146	$11
14	Proj	**4**	**3**	**4**	**58**	**52**	**3.39**	**3.40**	**1.27**	**660**	**762**	**567**	**4.5**	**3.4**	**8.0**	**2.4**	**10%**	**49**	**23**	**28**	**30%**	**74%**	**8%**	**0**						**3.4**	**81**	**105**	**$3**

Shields,James				
Age: 32	Th: R	Role SP	Health A	LIMA Plan C+
Ht: 6' 4"	Wt: 215	Type Pwr	PT/Exp A	Rand Var -1
			Consist A	MM 4305

Some skills erosion, notably Dom and GB rate, both of which deteriorated further in 2H. Regression analysis says to expect a partial skills rebound. But check xERAs: even a return all the way to '11-'12 levels—which may well be his peak—nets worse stats in a luck-neutral season. So base your bid on 2012 ERA, '13 wins.

Yr	Tm	W	L	Sv	IP	K	ERA	xERA	WHIP	oOPS	vL	vR	BF/G	Ctl	Dom	Cmd	SwK	G	L	F	H%	S%	hr/f	GS	APC	DOM%	DIS%	Sv%	LI	RAR	BPV	BPX	R$
09	TAM	11	12	0	220	167	4.14	4.03	1.32	768	779	756	28.2	2.1	6.8	3.2	10%	42	20	37	32%	73%	11%	33	101	55%	6%			5.0	86	160	$10
10	TAM	13	15	0	203	187	5.18	3.81	1.46	828	796	866	26.4	2.3	8.3	3.7	10%	41	20	38	35%	68%	14%	33	99	48%	18%		0.81	-27.6	107	173	-$2
11	TAM	16	12	0	249	225	2.82	3.21	1.04	623	602	648	29.5	2.3	8.1	3.5	11%	46	18	35	26%	78%	11%	33	108	67%	9%			34.7	107	161	$32
12	TAM	15	10	0	228	223	3.52	3.23	1.17	678	706	645	28.6	2.3	8.8	3.8	11%	52	19	29	30%	73%	13%	33	110	70%	6%			13.9	127	165	$21
13	KC	13	9	0	229	196	3.15	3.72	1.24	678	614	753	27.8	2.7	7.7	2.9	10%	42	23	35	30%	77%	9%	34	108	71%	9%			20.2	87	113	$16
1st Half		3	6	0	117	104	2.99	3.48	1.17	660	585	746	28.0	2.5	8.0	3.2	10%	44	23	33	29%	78%	10%	17	108	82%	0%			12.7	97	126	$17
2nd Half		10	3	0	111	92	3.31	3.98	1.31	697	643	761	27.6	2.8	7.4	2.6	11%	39	24	37	31%	77%	7%	17	107	59%	18%			7.6	75	97	$15
14	Proj	**14**	**9**	**0**	**220**	**195**	**3.36**	**3.34**	**1.21**	**685**	**657**	**718**	**27.5**	**2.5**	**8.0**	**3.2**	**11%**	**45**	**21**	**34**	**30%**	**76%**	**10%**	**32**						**13.7**	**99**	**129**	**$18**

Siegrist,Kevin				
Age: 24	Th: L	Role RP	Health A	LIMA Plan B+
Ht: 6' 5"	Wt: 215	Type Pwr FB	PT/Exp F	Rand Var -5
			Consist F	MM 5500

3-1, 0.45 ERA in 40 IP at STL. In 2012 he was throwing 88-92 as a starter, and by the end of 2013 he was pumping 98-mph gas out of the pen. (Aside: What's STL feeding these guys?) Too inexperienced and too left-handed to have much chance at the 9th inning for now, but this is a LIMA skills set to own.

Yr	Tm	W	L	Sv	IP	K	ERA	xERA	WHIP	oOPS	vL	vR	BF/G	Ctl	Dom	Cmd	SwK	G	L	F	H%	S%	hr/f	GS	APC	DOM%	DIS%	Sv%	LI	RAR	BPV	BPX	R$
09																																	
10																																	
11																																	
12	aa	1	2	0	32	23	3.92	3.37	1.15				16.0	2.4	6.3	2.6					26%	69%								0.4	69	90	-$2
13	STL *	5	2	1	67	86	1.14	0.76	0.85	432	388	479	3.9	3.7	11.5	3.1	10%	39	24	37	20%	89%	3%	0	15			100	0.84	22.6	151	196	$13
1st Half		2	1	1	38	49	1.57	0.34	0.72	205	311	67	4.8	3.1	11.7	3.8	8%	37	26	37	18%	81%	0%	0	15			100	0.33	10.7	168	218	$15
2nd Half		3	1	0	30	37	0.61	3.13	1.01	503	414	590	3.3	4.6	11.2	2.5	10%	40	24	37	23%	97%	4%	0	15			0	0.98	11.9	97	125	$11
14	Proj	**4**	**3**	**0**	**65**	**72**	**2.74**	**3.18**	**1.16**	**617**	**469**	**763**	**5.7**	**3.4**	**10.0**	**3.0**	**10%**	**40**	**24**	**37**	**29%**	**79%**	**7%**	**0**						**9.0**	**106**	**138**	**$5**

ROD TRUESDELL

Simon,Alfredo

Age: 33 | Th: R | Role: RP | Ht: 6' 6" | Wt: 265 | Type:
Health: D | PT/Exp: C | Consist: B
LIMA Plan: B | Rand Var: -4 | MM: 3201

Limped to the finish, with stats buoyed by an unrepeatable 2H hit rate. Second straight year he's managed a sub-3 ERA on barely average skills, but you only have to go back to 2011 to see he doesn't posess any magical ability to out-pitch his talent. Heed RandVar and xERA. The smart money says bet on skills, not stats.

Yr Tm	W	L	Sv	IP	K	ERA	xERA	WHIP	oOPS	vL	vR	BF/G	Ctl	Dom	Cmd	SwK	G	L	F	H%	S%	hr/f	GS	APC	DOM%	DIS%	Sv%	LI	RAR	BPV	BPX	R$
09 BAL	0	1	0	6	3	9.95	5.99	1.58	1242	1308	1152	14.0	2.8	4.3	1.5	8%	22	17	61	17%	60%	36%	2	58	0%	50%			-4.4	0	0	-$5
10 BAL *	5	3	17	66	47	4.23	5.45	1.53	825	684	953	5.4	3.7	6.4	1.7	11%	47	19	34	31%	78%	18%	0	17			81	1.16	-1.2	26	43	$5
11 BAL *	5	9	0	134	97	4.85	4.86	1.47	834	808	862	21.2	3.2	6.6	2.1	9%	43	20	37	32%	69%	11%	16	83	44%	38%	0	0.84	-15.0	48	72	-$6
12 CIN	3	2	1	61	52	2.66	3.77	1.43	747	745	748	7.5	3.2	7.7	2.4	9%	54	21	25	34%	81%	4%	0	28			100	0.61	10.2	82	108	$1
13 CIN	6	4	1	88	63	2.87	3.90	1.07	625	729	543	5.7	2.7	6.5	2.4	10%	45	18	36	25%	77%	9%	0	21			33	0.73	10.7	67	88	$8
1st Half	5	3	1	44	38	3.07	3.70	1.11	621	705	549	5.9	2.5	7.8	3.2	12%	44	17	39	28%	74%	6%	0	23			50	0.72	4.3	95	124	$9
2nd Half	1	1	0	44	25	2.68	4.11	1.03	629	759	538	5.5	2.9	5.2	1.8	8%	47	20	34	21%	80%	12%	0	19			0	0.74	6.4	40	51	$6
14 Proj	4	3	0	73	53	3.85	3.89	1.34	750	784	719	6.7	3.0	6.6	2.2	10%	45	19	35	31%	73%	8%	0						0.1	61	80	$0

Sipp,Tony

Age: 30 | Th: L | Role: RP | Ht: 6' 0" | Wt: 190 | Type: Pwr xFB
Health: A | PT/Exp: D | Consist: A
LIMA Plan: D+ | Rand Var: 0 | MM: 2400

A sure sign things aren't going well: designated for assignment in August, and the league collectively yawned and let him pass right through. Really, with his extreme flyball ways (career 1.5 hr/9) and a return of that unruly Ctl, it's not that surprising. xERA should tell you everything you need to know—pass.

Yr Tm	W	L	Sv	IP	K	ERA	xERA	WHIP	oOPS	vL	vR	BF/G	Ctl	Dom	Cmd	SwK	G	L	F	H%	S%	hr/f	GS	APC	DOM%	DIS%	Sv%	LI	RAR	BPV	BPX	R$
09 CLE *	3	0	1	57	66	3.44	3.75	1.39	682	685	677	4.1	5.0	10.4	2.1	12%	35	14	51	30%	79%	11%	0	16			100	1.03	6.2	87	162	$2
10 CLE	2	2	1	63	69	4.14	4.32	1.38	770	805	742	3.8	5.6	9.9	1.8	12%	31	14	55	25%	77%	14%	0	16			33	1.15	-0.5	36	58	$0
11 CLE	6	3	0	62	57	3.03	4.24	1.11	664	664	665	3.6	3.5	8.2	2.4	13%	26	14	60	23%	81%	10%	0	15			0	1.25	7.0	59	88	$5
12 CLE	1	2	1	55	51	4.42	4.29	1.27	739	663	823	3.7	3.8	8.3	2.2	10%	33	25	42	27%	70%	14%	0	15			50	0.91	-2.7	60	78	-$2
13 ARI	3	2	0	38	42	4.78	4.80	1.51	780	859	701	3.1	5.3	10.0	1.9	12%	26	16	58	31%	73%	10%	0	13			0	1.00	-4.2	43	56	-$4
1st Half	3	1	0	24	22	4.56	5.06	1.44	742	833	639	3.1	4.2	8.4	2.0	11%	21	17	61	32%	69%	5%	0	12			0	0.98	-2.0	37	48	-$3
2nd Half	0	1	0	14	20	5.14	4.32	1.64	845	907	791	3.2	7.1	12.9	1.8	14%	35	15	50	29%	79%	24%	0	14			0	1.02	-2.2	54	70	-$6
14 Proj	2	1	0	29	28	4.60	4.35	1.45	785	810	760	3.5	4.5	8.8	1.9	11%	28	17	55	30%	71%	9%	0						-2.6	41	53	-$3

Skaggs,Tyler

Age: 22 | Th: L | Role: SP | Ht: 6' 5" | Wt: 215 | Type: Pwr
Health: A | PT/Exp: D | Consist: B
LIMA Plan: B+ | Rand Var: +4 | MM: 3301

2-3, 5.12 ERA in 39 IP at ARI. Let's hope frequent flyer account was in good standing, as he made no less than five round trips from ARI to exotic minor league destinations. Showed flashes of brilliance, but DOM% / DIS% highlight current feast-or-famine ways. Still just 22, still a bright future, still very much a work in progress.

Yr Tm	W	L	Sv	IP	K	ERA	xERA	WHIP	oOPS	vL	vR	BF/G	Ctl	Dom	Cmd	SwK	G	L	F	H%	S%	hr/f	GS	APC	DOM%	DIS%	Sv%	LI	RAR	BPV	BPX	R$
09																																
10																																
11 aa	4	1	0	58	64	2.68	2.59	1.06				22.4	2.1	10.0	4.8					31%	77%								9.0	151	227	$5
12 ARI *	10	9	0	152	122	3.53	3.99	1.28	785	333	863	22.2	2.7	7.3	2.7	10%	34	18	48	30%	76%	13%	6	87	33%	50%			9.0	71	93	$8
13 ARI *	8	13	0	143	128	4.51	4.18	1.41	780	710	799	23.2	3.0	8.1	2.7	9%	45	20	35	34%	68%	17%	7	94	29%	43%			-11.4	83	108	-$3
1st Half	7	7	0	93	92	4.24	3.83	1.33	833	753	852	24.0	2.9	8.9	3.1	9%	37	24	39	34%	69%	20%	3	98	33%	33%			-4.3	99	128	$2
2nd Half	1	6	0	50	36	5.02	4.84	1.55	738	683	755	21.9	3.3	6.5	2.0	10%	51	17	32	35%	67%	14%	4	91	25%	50%			-7.1	56	72	-$11
14 Proj	6	9	0	116	98	4.01	3.75	1.36	725	683	736	22.6	3.1	7.6	2.5	9%	43	20	37	32%	72%	8%	21						-2.1	75	98	$2

Slowey,Kevin

Age: 30 | Th: R | Role: SP | Ht: 6' 2" | Wt: 210 | Type: Con xFB
Health: F | PT/Exp: D | Consist: C
LIMA Plan: C | Rand Var: +1 | MM: 2101

Right forearm strain shut him down in July. Otherwise, a return step in the right direction, with Dom and SwK back to '09 levels. Extreme LD/FB lean still there, though; with all those strikes that means lots of hits, many leaving the yard. Hard to find a friendlier home park, unlikely to get healthy. So this may be as good as it gets.

Yr Tm	W	L	Sv	IP	K	ERA	xERA	WHIP	oOPS	vL	vR	BF/G	Ctl	Dom	Cmd	SwK	G	L	F	H%	S%	hr/f	GS	APC	DOM%	DIS%	Sv%	LI	RAR	BPV	BPX	R$
09 MIN	10	3	0	91	75	4.86	4.21	1.41	843	946	746	24.6	1.5	7.4	5.0	8%	32	20	48	35%	70%	11%	16	89	44%	31%			-6.1	104	194	$1
10 MIN	13	6	0	156	116	4.45	4.34	1.29	770	734	807	22.1	1.7	6.7	4.0	7%	28	21	51	32%	69%	8%	28	86	39%	36%	0	0.74	-7.2	81	132	$5
11 MIN *	1	10	0	97	56	5.80	5.59	1.46	868	963	785	19.8	1.0	5.2	5.4	5%	31	23	46	35%	62%	10%	8	65	25%	38%	0	0.68	-22.3	99	149	-$10
12 aaa	3	3	0	49	26	6.33	5.99	1.58				27.0	2.5	4.8	1.9					33%	62%								-14.0	18	24	-$10
13 MIA	3	6	0	92	76	4.11	4.10	1.35	807	828	787	19.8	1.8	7.4	4.2	8%	29	27	44	34%	73%	9%	14	73	43%	21%	0	0.68	-2.8	93	122	-$2
1st Half	3	6	0	83	67	3.90	4.07	1.31	804	833	772	22.1	1.6	7.3	4.5	7%	29	28	44	33%	75%	11%	13	82	38%	23%	0	0.79	-0.4	94	121	-$1
2nd Half	0	0	0	9	9	6.00	4.41	1.67	840	748	876	10.3	3.0	9.0	3.0	12%	29	21	50	42%	60%	0%	1	39	100%	0%	0	0.28	-2.4	88	113	-$10
14 Proj	5	6	0	92	63	4.34	4.10	1.35	806	835	777	21.8	1.6	6.2	3.8	7%	30	23	47	32%	72%	9%	17						-5.4	75	97	-$1

Smith,Burch

Age: 24 | Th: R | Role: SP | Ht: 6' 4" | Wt: 215 | Type: Pwr xFB
Health: A | PT/Exp: F | Consist: F
LIMA Plan: A | Rand Var: +3 | MM: 3501

1-3, 6.44 ERA in 36 IP at SD. Took his lumps in first call-up, but fared much better in longer Sept look; overall, not bad at all for his first high-minors year. Another extreme FBer, but elite SwK, 1+ Ks per inning helps. Solid prospect who may see a more prominent role next year. Trivia: first "Burch" in MLB history.

Yr Tm	W	L	Sv	IP	K	ERA	xERA	WHIP	oOPS	vL	vR	BF/G	Ctl	Dom	Cmd	SwK	G	L	F	H%	S%	hr/f	GS	APC	DOM%	DIS%	Sv%	LI	RAR	BPV	BPX	R$
09																																
10																																
11																																
12																																
13 SD *	7	6	0	129	136	3.68	3.43	1.22	899	977	828	18.6	3.0	9.5	3.2	13%	27	23	49	31%	73%	18%	7	64	29%	29%	0	0.58	3.0	103	135	$6
1st Half	4	4	0	69	67	3.51	3.39	1.21	1221	1165	1329	18.4	2.6	8.8	3.4	16%	19	38	44	31%	73%	29%	3	50	0%	67%	0	0.63	3.0	104	135	$7
2nd Half	3	2	0	60	68	3.86	3.48	1.24	759	840	704	18.8	3.4	10.2	3.0	12%	31	16	52	31%	72%	14%	4	74	50%	0%	0	0.55	0.0	103	134	$4
14 Proj	4	3	0	73	78	3.76	3.61	1.22	646	720	597	22.6	3.0	9.6	3.2	12%	31	16	52	31%	72%	7%	16						1.0	101	131	$3

Smith,Joe

Age: 30 | Th: R | Role: RP | Ht: 6' 2" | Wt: 205 | Type: Pwr GB
Health: B | PT/Exp: C | Consist: A
LIMA Plan: B | Rand Var: -5 | MM: 4210

PRO: Another sub-3 ERA; Dom rate continued upward; managed to grab a few Saves; four-leaf clover intact.
CON: Again posted mid-3 xERA, riding that four-leaf clover to lucky S%, 1st half H%; GB% dipped sharply.
Despite what ERA says, skills continue to be pretty average. NEXT year that ERA will finally spike—surely.

Yr Tm	W	L	Sv	IP	K	ERA	xERA	WHIP	oOPS	vL	vR	BF/G	Ctl	Dom	Cmd	SwK	G	L	F	H%	S%	hr/f	GS	APC	DOM%	DIS%	Sv%	LI	RAR	BPV	BPX	R$
09 CLE	0	0	0	34	30	3.44	3.57	1.26	707	992	615	3.8	3.4	7.9	2.3	10%	55	17	28	28%	77%	15%	0	15			0	1.20	3.7	83	155	-$1
10 CLE *	4	3	2	63	47	3.24	3.16	1.33	659	979	538	3.6	4.9	6.7	1.4	8%	56	16	28	26%	77%	13%	0	12			50	1.13	6.5	63	103	$3
11 CLE	3	3	0	67	45	2.01	3.44	1.09	541	460	582	3.8	2.8	6.0	2.1	6%	57	20	23	26%	81%	2%	0	14			0	1.05	15.9	68	102	$6
12 CLE	7	4	0	67	53	2.96	3.68	1.16	594	585	600	3.9	3.4	7.1	2.1	9%	58	17	25	26%	76%	8%	0	15			0	1.22	8.8	73	96	$5
13 CLE	6	2	3	63	54	2.29	3.59	1.22	643	698	592	3.7	3.3	7.7	2.3	9%	49	21	30	28%	85%	10%	0	14			38	1.37	12.3	77	101	$6
1st Half	4	0	1	30	29	2.08	3.15	1.02	613	722	504	3.6	3.0	8.6	2.9	10%	52	17	31	24%	86%	13%	0	14			25	1.20	6.7	105	136	$9
2nd Half	2	2	2	33	25	2.48	4.01	1.41	668	674	662	3.8	3.6	6.9	1.9	9%	47	24	29	32%	84%	7%	0	14			50	1.53	5.6	52	68	$4
14 Proj	5	3	5	65	52	3.23	3.52	1.27	665	705	637	3.7	3.3	7.2	2.2	9%	53	19	27	29%	77%	10%	0						5.1	70	91	$5

Smyly,Drew

Age: 25 | Th: L | Role: RP | Ht: 6' 3" | Wt: 190 | Type: Pwr FB
Health: B | PT/Exp: D | Consist: D
LIMA Plan: B+ | Rand Var: -3 | MM: 4411

Another erstwhile LH starter moved to pen to get his arm in play, and it worked out well for DET. 2H IP dip not injury related; he moved into a LOOGY role. So with a new Mgr, what will his role be in '14? Owns the skills, effectiveness vs. RH to start. Ready for a big step up if he gets the chance. UP: 180 IP, $20 value, 10+ Wins.

Yr Tm	W	L	Sv	IP	K	ERA	xERA	WHIP	oOPS	vL	vR	BF/G	Ctl	Dom	Cmd	SwK	G	L	F	H%	S%	hr/f	GS	APC	DOM%	DIS%	Sv%	LI	RAR	BPV	BPX	R$
09																																
10																																
11 aa	4	3	0	46	44	1.35	2.00	1.06				22.2	2.8	8.7	3.1					28%	88%								14.6	124	187	$6
12 DET *	4	5	0	117	114	4.51	4.39	1.36	732	671	759	16.3	3.1	8.8	2.8	9%	40	19	41	32%	70%	10%	18	76	56%	33%	0	0.83	-7.2	78	102	-$3
13 DET	6	0	2	76	81	2.37	3.06	1.04	601	471	699	4.8	2.0	9.6	4.8	11%	43	18	39	30%	79%	5%	0	20			33	1.12	14.0	139	182	$10
1st Half	3	0	2	49	51	2.20	3.11	1.02	556	327	687	6.7	2.6	9.4	3.6	11%	45	17	38	29%	78%	2%	0	29			67	0.95	10.0	122	158	$12
2nd Half	3	0	0	27	30	2.67	2.98	1.07	676	635	724	3.2	1.0	10.0	10.0	11%	41	19	41	33%	81%	10%	0	13			0	1.27	4.0	172	222	$5
14 Proj	8	3	3	109	104	3.37	3.28	1.16	672	582	733	6.5	2.3	8.6	3.7	10%	41	18	40	30%	73%	8%	0						6.7	111	144	$10

ROD TRUESDELL

Soria,Joakim

Age: 30	Th: R	Role: RP	Health: F	LIMA Plan: C+
Ht: 6' 3"	Wt: 200	Type: Pwr	PT/Exp: D	Rand Var: +1
			Consist: A	MM: 5510

Control is usually the last piece to return on path back from TJ surgery, and that's the case here. Still, plenty of Ks and he even sprinkled in a GB tilt we haven't seen in a while, albeit in tiny sample. Prior elite BPVs confirm that he was a top-tier closer pre-surgery. Ignore role; these skills will play in back-end again.

Yr Tm	W	L	Sv	IP	K	ERA	xERA	WHIP	oOPS	vL	vR	BF/G	Ctl	Dom	Cmd	SwK	G	L	F	H%	S%	hr/f	GS	APC	DOM%	DIS%	Sv%	LI	RAR	BPV	BPX	R$
09 KC	3	2	30	53	69	2.21	3.05	1.13	614	560	674	4.7	2.7	11.7	4.3	13%	40	18	42	33%	85%	9%	0	19			91	1.52	13.8	156	291	$1
10 KC	1	2	43	66	71	1.78	2.99	1.05	568	587	541	4.1	2.2	9.7	4.4	10%	48	17	35	30%	86%	7%	0	17			93	1.28	18.6	142	230	$25
11 KC	5	5	28	60	60	4.03	3.51	1.28	709	631	793	4.3	2.5	9.0	3.5	10%	40	21	39	32%	71%	10%	0	17			80	1.32	-0.6	111	166	$12
12																																
13 TEX	1	0	0	24	28	3.80	3.43	1.35	624	316	943	3.9	5.3	10.6	2.0	10%	52	18	30	29%	73%	12%	0	17			0	1.04	0.2	78	102	-$3
1st Half																																
2nd Half	1	0	0	24	28	3.80	3.43	1.35	624	316	943	3.9	5.3	10.6	2.0	10%	52	18	30	29%	73%	12%	0	17			0	1.04	0.2	78	101	-$3
14 Proj	**2**	**2**	**8**	**58**	**65**	**2.90**	**3.02**	**1.20**	**621**	**516**	**744**	**4.0**	**3.3**	**10.1**	**3.1**	**10%**	**46**	**18**	**35**	**31%**	**79%**	**9%**	**0**						**6.9**	**119**	**154**	**$6**

Soriano,Rafael

Age: 34	Th: R	Role: RP	Health: D	LIMA Plan: C
Ht: 6' 1"	Wt: 210	Type: Pwr FB	PT/Exp: B	Rand Var: -2
			Consist: C	MM: 3330

40 saves in 3 of 4 years will keep him one of the first closers to go off the board in many leagues, but not so fast. Early shoulder problems, four years of FB velocity loss, and steep Dom reduction are all warning signs, as are two 4+ xERAs in last three years. Don't roster him as your top stopper without a backup plan. DN: 2011.

Yr Tm	W	L	Sv	IP	K	ERA	xERA	WHIP	oOPS	vL	vR	BF/G	Ctl	Dom	Cmd	SwK	G	L	F	H%	S%	hr/f	GS	APC	DOM%	DIS%	Sv%	LI	RAR	BPV	BPX	R$
09 ATL	1	6	27	76	102	2.97	3.11	1.06	586	746	445	4.0	3.2	12.1	3.8	13%	31	21	48	30%	74%	7%	0	16			87	1.16	12.6	141	263	$19
10 TAM	3	2	45	62	57	1.73	3.51	0.80	509	590	431	3.7	2.0	8.2	4.1	12%	33	16	52	21%	83%	5%	0	14			94	1.44	18.0	105	169	$28
11 NYY	2	3	2	39	36	4.12	4.10	1.30	645	850	477	3.9	4.1	8.2	2.0	12%	35	20	44	28%	70%	8%	0	16			40	1.14	-0.9	50	75	-$1
12 NYY	2	1	42	68	69	2.26	3.78	1.17	639	713	549	4.0	3.2	9.2	2.9	12%	36	24	40	29%	85%	8%	0	16			91	1.27	14.6	93	121	$23
13 WAS	3	3	43	67	51	3.11	4.15	1.23	668	785	584	4.1	2.3	6.9	3.0	9%	34	25	42	30%	79%	8%	0	17			88	1.27	6.3	73	95	$19
1st Half	1	1	21	34	27	2.38	3.98	1.21	643	768	552	4.1	1.9	7.1	3.9	9%	32	26	42	32%	82%	5%	0	17			88	1.19	6.2	89	115	$20
2nd Half	2	2	22	33	24	3.86	4.33	1.26	693	804	617	4.0	2.8	6.6	2.4	9%	35	24	42	28%	75%	12%	0	16			88	1.35	0.0	57	74	$17
14 Proj	**3**	**3**	**37**	**60**	**53**	**3.51**	**3.66**	**1.20**	**649**	**764**	**552**	**3.9**	**2.9**	**8.0**	**2.8**	**10%**	**34**	**23**	**42**	**29%**	**74%**	**9%**	**0**						**2.6**	**78**	**101**	**$16**

Stammen,Craig

Age: 30	Th: R	Role: RP	Health: A	LIMA Plan: B+
Ht: 6' 3"	Wt: 215	Type: Pwr GB	PT/Exp: C	Rand Var: -2
			Consist: C	MM: 4301

Looked like he might finally get another rotation shot in mid-season, just as skills were spiking. Didn't happen, but great GB rate, two years of high Dom/SwK suggest he has the tools for it, and new Mgr might have new outlook on his role. A premium hidden arm to stash on your staff for a few bucks. UP: 3.00 ERA, 180 K

Yr Tm	W	L	Sv	IP	K	ERA	xERA	WHIP	oOPS	vL	vR	BF/G	Ctl	Dom	Cmd	SwK	G	L	F	H%	S%	hr/f	GS	APC	DOM%	DIS%	Sv%	LI	RAR	BPV	BPX	R$
09 WAS *	8	9	0	146	59	4.37	4.28	1.27	774	789	757	22.9	2.0	3.6	1.8	6%	47	21	32	28%	69%	12%	19	83	32%	32%			-0.8	26	49	$4
10 WAS *	6	4	0	148	93	4.85	4.89	1.47	814	742	871	16.7	2.7	5.6	2.1	10%	51	23	26	33%	68%	12%	19	60	37%	32%	0	0.59	-14.0	46	75	-$4
11 WAS *	11	8	0	152	108	5.72	6.05	1.64	272	192	333	21.2	2.7	6.4	2.4	15%	52	14	33	36%	67%	0%	0	21			0	1.55	-33.4	41	62	-$13
12 WAS	6	1	1	88	87	2.34	3.80	1.20	636	605	655	6.3	3.7	8.9	2.4	14%	45	20	35	28%	84%	8%	0	23			50	0.92	18.2	84	109	$9
13 WAS	7	6	0	82	79	2.76	3.07	1.29	684	761	634	6.2	3.0	8.7	2.9	13%	60	16	24	33%	79%	7%	0	23			0	0.95	11.2	114	149	$5
1st Half	4	3	0	43	41	3.16	3.09	1.29	707	865	591	7.3	2.7	8.6	3.2	13%	55	21	24	34%	75%	7%	0	27			0	0.91	3.7	114	148	$5
2nd Half	3	3	0	39	38	2.31	3.04	1.28	661	635	676	5.3	3.2	8.8	2.7	14%	65	10	25	32%	83%	8%	0	20			0	0.98	7.5	114	147	$5
14 Proj	**7**	**5**	**0**	**98**	**87**	**3.23**	**3.29**	**1.29**	**696**	**709**	**687**	**7.2**	**3.1**	**8.0**	**2.6**	**12%**	**54**	**18**	**28**	**31%**	**77%**	**10%**	**0**						**7.6**	**93**	**121**	**$6**

Stauffer,Tim

Age: 32	Th: R	Role: RP	Health: F	LIMA Plan: B+
Ht: 6' 1"	Wt: 215	Type: GB	PT/Exp: C	Rand Var: 0
			Consist: B	MM: 4201

3-1, 3.75 ERA in 70 IP at SD. An end-gamer every year because he just doesn't have the durability to throw more than 120 IP (see health grade). xERA supports his solid sub-4 ERA consistency, especially with continued high GB rate. In deep leagues, spending a buck on a guy like this can help you win a tight ERA race.

Yr Tm	W	L	Sv	IP	K	ERA	xERA	WHIP	oOPS	vL	vR	BF/G	Ctl	Dom	Cmd	SwK	G	L	F	H%	S%	hr/f	GS	APC	DOM%	DIS%	Sv%	LI	RAR	BPV	BPX	R$
09 SD *	7	8	1	115	76	3.16	3.54	1.28	755	672	840	15.7	3.3	6.0	1.8	8%	44	20	36	28%	78%	10%	14	90	36%	36%			16.5	57	106	$9
10 SD *	6	5	0	100	67	2.41	3.01	1.24	591	529	641	10.7	2.8	6.0	2.1	7%	55	15	31	29%	80%	4%	7	38	57%	29%	0	0.74	20.6	79	127	$8
11 SD	9	12	0	186	128	3.73	3.69	1.25	729	774	683	25.1	2.6	6.2	2.4	7%	52	20	28	29%	73%	13%	31	97	45%	16%			4.8	72	109	$8
12 SD	0	0	0	5	5	5.40	4.40	2.00	893	833	984	24.0	5.4	9.0	1.7	10%	53	20	27	40%	78%	25%	1	91	0%	0%			-0.9	47	62	-$5
13 SD *	5	3	0	112	93	3.54	3.85	1.35	644	529	748	9.2	2.8	7.5	2.6	9%	51	23	26	33%	75%	14%	0	26			0	0.84	4.5	83	108	$1
1st Half	3	2	0	71	53	3.34	4.42	1.46	663	575	731	12.6	2.8	6.8	2.4	10%	45	24	32	34%	78%	17%	0	26			0	0.93	4.6	69	89	$1
2nd Half	2	1	0	42	40	3.89	3.05	1.15	632	503	760	6.4	2.8	8.6	3.1	9%	54	23	22	29%	67%	12%	0	26			0	0.78	-0.1	112	145	$2
14 Proj	**4**	**3**	**0**	**73**	**56**	**3.44**	**3.49**	**1.27**	**694**	**635**	**748**	**10.6**	**2.8**	**7.0**	**2.5**	**8%**	**51**	**21**	**28**	**30%**	**74%**	**9%**	**2**						**3.8**	**79**	**103**	**$2**

Storen,Drew

Age: 26	Th: R	Role: RP	Health: C	LIMA Plan: C+
Ht: 6' 1"	Wt: 225	Type: Pwr	PT/Exp: C	Rand Var: +2
			Consist: A	MM: 4311

On surface, a lost season that saw him fall out of closer talk. High hit rate got him in 1H; depressed strand rate doomed him after break. No reason for panic as other skills were fine, and GB% should bounce back given pre-'13 trend. 100+ BPV in 3 of 6 months confirms he's still an elite plan B. Now's the time to buy low.

Yr Tm	W	L	Sv	IP	K	ERA	xERA	WHIP	oOPS	vL	vR	BF/G	Ctl	Dom	Cmd	SwK	G	L	F	H%	S%	hr/f	GS	APC	DOM%	DIS%	Sv%	LI	RAR	BPV	BPX	R$
09																																
10 WAS *	4	4	9	72	64	3.07	2.99	1.21	655	624	674	4.3	3.1	8.1	2.6	10%	40	20	40	30%	75%	5%	0	17			82	1.25	9.0	95	154	$8
11 WAS	6	3	43	75	74	2.75	3.16	1.02	599	541	643	4.2	2.4	8.8	3.7	9%	47	17	35	26%	78%	11%	0	15			90	1.42	11.1	120	180	$25
12 WAS	3	1	4	30	24	2.37	3.31	0.99	496	635	418	3.1	2.4	7.1	3.0	14%	54	18	28	26%	73%	0%	0	11			80	1.21	6.1	96	125	$3
13 WAS	4	2	3	62	58	4.52	3.85	1.36	729	816	668	3.9	2.8	8.5	3.1	10%	41	20	39	33%	69%	10%	0	14			38	1.09	-5.0	96	126	-$2
1st Half	2	1	2	33	34	3.86	3.28	1.38	755	955	584	4.1	2.5	9.4	3.8	11%	54	14	32	36%	76%	13%	0	14			40	1.18	0.0	133	173	$0
2nd Half	2	1	1	29	24	5.28	4.47	1.34	701	618	749	3.8	3.1	7.4	2.4	8%	27	26	47	31%	61%	7%	0	14			33	1.01	-5.0	56	72	-$4
14 Proj	**5**	**3**	**6**	**73**	**68**	**3.55**	**3.34**	**1.20**	**644**	**691**	**613**	**3.7**	**2.7**	**8.4**	**3.1**	**10%**	**43**	**20**	**37**	**30%**	**72%**	**8%**	**0**						**2.8**	**100**	**129**	**$6**

Straily,Dan

Age: 25	Th: R	Role: SP	Health: A	LIMA Plan: C+
Ht: 6' 2"	Wt: 215	Type: Pwr xFB	PT/Exp: D	Rand Var: 0
			Consist: A	MM: 3303

10-8, 3.96 ERA in 152 IP at OAK. Filthy slider makes up for modest fastball, and with top-tier SwK and prior profile as minors K leader, more strikeouts are coming. Mediocre PQS results reflect stamina issues; reached 7 IP in just one of 27 starts. If he can pitch deeper into games and tweak vs. LHB... UP: 3.00 ERA, 200 K

Yr Tm	W	L	Sv	IP	K	ERA	xERA	WHIP	oOPS	vL	vR	BF/G	Ctl	Dom	Cmd	SwK	G	L	F	H%	S%	hr/f	GS	APC	DOM%	DIS%	Sv%	LI	RAR	BPV	BPX	R$
09																																
10																																
11																																
12 OAK *	11	8	0	191	190	3.15	2.94	1.11	803	1047	640	23.5	2.7	8.9	3.3	10%	30	15	55	28%	75%	17%	7	96	29%	43%			20.5	107	139	$21
13 OAK *	13	9	0	184	151	3.48	3.26	1.22	666	711	617	23.2	3.2	7.4	2.3	12%	36	20	44	28%	74%	8%	27	91	37%	30%			8.7	76	99	$12
1st Half	7	3	0	91	74	4.06	3.20	1.20	665	724	608	23.0	2.6	7.3	2.8	12%	36	21	43	29%	67%	7%	12	88	33%	33%			-2.1	88	114	$10
2nd Half	6	6	0	93	77	2.91	3.31	1.23	667	702	625	23.5	3.8	7.4	2.0	11%	37	19	44	26%	81%	9%	15	94	40%	27%			10.9	67	87	$14
14 Proj	**11**	**8**	**0**	**177**	**157**	**3.44**	**3.80**	**1.21**	**648**	**730**	**574**	**23.5**	**3.1**	**8.0**	**2.6**	**11%**	**34**	**18**	**48**	**28%**	**75%**	**8%**	**30**						**9.2**	**73**	**95**	**$14**

Strasburg,Stephen

Age: 25	Th: R	Role: SP	Health: C	LIMA Plan: C+
Ht: 6' 4"	Wt: 220	Type: Pwr	PT/Exp: B	Rand Var: 0
			Consist: A	MM: 5505

W-L record doesn't show it, but this remains one of the best young arms in the game; reference PQS DOM%. Addition of a big groundball tilt a reflection thrower-to-pitcher maturation. Remaining hurdle is 200 IP. With it will come the $25-30 breakout we're still waiting for... UP: 2.50 ERA, 250 K, Cy Young.

Yr Tm	W	L	Sv	IP	K	ERA	xERA	WHIP	oOPS	vL	vR	BF/G	Ctl	Dom	Cmd	SwK	G	L	F	H%	S%	hr/f	GS	APC	DOM%	DIS%	Sv%	LI	RAR	BPV	BPX	R$
09																																
10 WAS *	12	5	0	123	147	2.33	2.02	0.99	596	680	533	20.4	2.2	10.7	4.9	13%	48	21	32	30%	78%	10%	12	89	58%	17%			26.6	167	271	$20
11 WAS	1	1	0	24	24	1.50	2.68	0.71	398	296	489	17.6	0.8	9.0	12.0	12%	38	25	38	26%	76%	0%	5	66	60%	40%			7.2	158	237	$2
12 WAS	15	6	0	159	197	3.16	2.96	1.15	649	714	578	23.3	2.7	11.1	4.1	12%	44	23	33	32%	76%	11%	28	93	71%	14%			16.7	149	194	$19
13 WAS	8	9	0	183	191	3.00	2.98	1.05	587	629	550	24.4	2.8	9.4	3.4	11%	52	17	31	27%	74%	11%	30	95	77%	13%			19.5	125	163	$19
1st Half	4	6	0	93	90	2.41	3.11	1.04	587	622	555	24.7	2.6	8.7	3.3	11%	52	16	33	27%	80%	9%	15	98	73%	7%			16.8	116	150	$22
2nd Half	4	3	0	90	101	3.61	2.84	1.06	588	636	546	24.1	2.9	10.1	3.5	11%	51	19	29	27%	69%	14%	15	92	80%	20%			2.8	133	173	$16
14 Proj	**16**	**7**	**0**	**199**	**220**	**2.98**	**2.76**	**1.08**	**602**	**660**	**548**	**22.7**	**2.7**	**10.0**	**3.7**	**12%**	**48**	**20**	**32**	**29%**	**75%**	**11%**	**34**						**21.8**	**134**	**174**	**$27**

STEPHEN NICKRAND

Street,Huston

Age: 30	Th: R	Role RP	Health F	LIMA Plan C+	
Ht: 6' 0"	Wt: 195	Type Pwr FB	PT/Exp B	Rand Var -5	
			Consist B	MM 4430	

Why does a guy with F health keep getting full-time closer work every year? It's easy: a 91% Sv conversion rate since '09. Elite Cmd limits blow-up risk, and that Dom dip might have been caused by early calf strain, so don't panic. Just use his '10-'11 ERA as your baseline, as friendly H% and S% drove his sub-3 marks in '12-'13.

Yr	Tm	W	L	Sv	IP	K	ERA	xERA	WHIP	oOPS	vL	vR	BF/G	Ctl	Dom	Cmd	SwK	G	L	F	H%	S%	hr/f	GS	APC	DOM%	DIS%	Sv%	LI	RAR	BPV	BPX	R$
09	COL	4	1	35	62	70	3.06	3.03	0.91	561	492	619	3.8	1.9	10.2	5.4	15%	38	19	43	26%	71%	11%	0	14			95	1.04	9.6	149	278	$23
10	COL	4	4	20	47	45	3.61	3.48	1.06	648	575	700	4.3	2.1	8.6	4.1	14%	37	16	48	28%	69%	8%	0	16			80	1.22	2.7	113	182	$11
11	COL	1	4	29	58	55	3.86	3.38	1.22	781	811	760	3.9	1.4	8.5	6.1	13%	35	24	41	32%	75%	14%	0	15			88	1.18	0.6	128	193	$11
12	SD	2	1	23	39	47	1.85	2.76	0.72	425	384	461	3.6	2.5	10.8	4.3	14%	42	20	38	19%	77%	6%	0	15			96	1.19	10.4	147	191	$15
13	SD	2	5	33	57	46	2.70	3.93	1.02	691	689	693	3.8	2.2	7.3	3.3	12%	30	22	48	22%	89%	16%	0	15			94	1.22	8.1	79	104	$17
1st Half		0	4	15	27	15	4.61	4.83	1.32	916	886	945	4.1	2.6	4.9	1.9	8%	33	22	45	22%	85%	25%	0	16			94	1.18	-2.5	28	37	$9
2nd Half		2	1	18	29	31	0.92	3.18	0.75	459	467	451	3.6	1.8	9.5	5.2	16%	27	21	51	21%	95%	6%	0	14			95	1.25	10.7	127	164	$24
14	Proj	2	3	31	51	49	3.28	3.28	1.11	700	679	718	3.8	2.1	8.8	4.1	13%	34	21	45	28%	77%	12%	0						3.7	113	146	$15

Strop,Pedro

Age: 29	Th: R	Role RP	Health B	LIMA Plan C	
Ht: 6' 0"	Wt: 215	Type Pwr GB	PT/Exp D	Rand Var +4	
			Consist B	MM 5420	

Has long had the talent to assume a late-inning role given mid-90s fastball, filthy slider, and high GB rate. Chronically bad control has been his tormentor. That all changed in the 2H, just as he was starting to get end-game work. Small sample size or real step forward? We don't know yet, but w/sustained 2H Ctl... UP: 40 Sv.

Yr	Tm	W	L	Sv	IP	K	ERA	xERA	WHIP	oOPS	vL	vR	BF/G	Ctl	Dom	Cmd	SwK	G	L	F	H%	S%	hr/f	GS	APC	DOM%	DIS%	Sv%	LI	RAR	BPV	BPX	R$
09	TEX *	6	6	5	71	60	6.73	4.82	1.68	679	462	855	5.9	4.9	7.6	1.5	16%	41	35	24	35%	57%	0%	0	18			50	0.11	-21.1	61	114	-$5
10	TEX *	1	2	13	53	56	3.91	4.25	1.52	1109	1132	1093	4.3	4.4	9.6	2.2	12%	31	28	42	36%	74%	13%	0	16			76	1.22	1.1	88	143	$3
11	2 AL *	6	5	11	70	63	3.42	4.33	1.58	519	515	521	4.9	4.4	8.1	1.8	10%	56	20	24	36%	78%	0%	0	16			73	1.12	4.5	77	116	$4
12	BAL	5	2	3	66	58	2.44	3.72	1.34	613	674	556	4.0	5.0	7.9	1.6	11%	64	16	20	28%	82%	6%	0	16			30	1.25	12.9	48	63	$5
13	2 TM	2	5	1	57	66	4.55	3.24	1.24	663	653	671	3.8	4.1	10.4	2.5	13%	49	26	26	29%	64%	14%	0	15			25	1.25	-4.9	103	135	-$2
1st Half		0	3	0	22	24	7.25	4.26	1.70	861	913	821	3.8	6.0	9.7	1.6	10%	48	28	23	33%	59%	27%	0	15			0	1.29	-9.3	37	48	-$11
2nd Half		2	2	1	35	42	2.83	2.67	0.94	520	461	564	3.9	2.8	10.8	3.8	15%	49	24	28	27%	69%	5%	0	15			100	1.21	4.5	145	187	$4
14	Proj	4	4	20	65	67	3.53	3.14	1.28	652	675	633	3.9	4.2	9.2	2.2	12%	55	22	23	30%	73%	10%	0						2.7	86	112	$10

Stults,Eric

Age: 34	Th: L	Role RP	Health D	LIMA Plan B	
Ht: 6' 0"	Wt: 230	Type Con	PT/Exp C	Rand Var -1	
			Consist D	MM 2105	

The epitome of a lefty soft-tosser. Four-pitch mix makes up for 87-mph fastball, but it's pinpoint control that makes him (barely) rosterable. That and risk management: in 48 games started last two years, only FIVE have been PQS disasters. As SP filler in deep leagues, he's got a purpose. Just don't bank on him.

Yr	Tm	W	L	Sv	IP	K	ERA	xERA	WHIP	oOPS	vL	vR	BF/G	Ctl	Dom	Cmd	SwK	G	L	F	H%	S%	hr/f	GS	APC	DOM%	DIS%	Sv%	LI	RAR	BPV	BPX	R$
09	LA *	9	7	0	114	64	5.58	6.01	1.81	789	797	787	24.0	4.0	5.0	1.3	8%	35	17	48	36%	69%	4%	10	88	50%	30%			-17.7	26	50	-$10
10																																	
11	COL *	4	4	1	80	55	4.81	5.63	1.45	802	589	943	5.9	2.2	6.1	2.8	9%	28	15	58	32%	73%	17%	0	32			20	0.39	-8.5	39	59	-$4
12	2 TM *	9	4	0	134	82	2.86	3.31	1.25	667	482	728	20.3	2.7	5.5	2.0	7%	40	26	34	29%	78%	6%	15	76	60%	0%	0	0.67	19.2	66	86	$10
13	SD	11	13	0	204	131	3.93	4.22	1.27	729	557	779	26.0	1.8	5.8	3.3	8%	40	21	39	31%	71%	7%	33	98	45%	15%			-1.7	74	97	$5
1st Half		6	6	0	108	69	3.51	4.09	1.13	652	598	671	25.6	1.8	5.8	3.1	7%	41	18	41	28%	70%	5%	17	94	41%	12%			4.7	73	95	$12
2nd Half		5	7	0	96	62	4.41	4.36	1.43	806	502	880	26.4	1.7	5.8	3.4	8%	40	23	37	34%	71%	9%	16	102	50%	19%			-6.4	77	99	-$3
14	Proj	10	11	0	189	119	4.03	4.11	1.37	773	598	826	16.1	2.3	5.7	2.5	8%	40	22	38	32%	72%	8%	30						-3.8	58	76	$3

Swarzak,Anthony

Age: 28	Th: R	Role RP	Health C	LIMA Plan B+	
Ht: 6' 4"	Wt: 210	Type	PT/Exp C	Rand Var -2	
			Consist A	MM 3101	

There can be nice value in rostering skilled long men, since you can get them cheap and they'll give you 100 IP of solid stats. This one would seem to fit the bill given solid Cmd, but he's never shown it before, and xERA history sure ain't pretty. Save this one for only the deepest of leagues and don't expect another sub-4 mark.

Yr	Tm	W	L	Sv	IP	K	ERA	xERA	WHIP	oOPS	vL	vR	BF/G	Ctl	Dom	Cmd	SwK	G	L	F	H%	S%	hr/f	GS	APC	DOM%	DIS%	Sv%	LI	RAR	BPV	BPX	R$
09	MIN *	7	12	0	139	72	5.01	5.26	1.52	879	956	799	24.1	2.7	4.7	1.7	4%	36	19	45	32%	69%	13%	12	88	8%	50%			-11.8	27	51	-$4
10	aaa	5	12	0	112	54	7.11	6.62	1.82				23.6	3.2	4.3	1.4					37%	60%								-41.8	12	19	-$18
11	MIN *	6	8	0	134	75	4.43	4.45	1.39	724	690	766	17.1	2.2	5.0	2.2	6%	38	20	42	32%	69%	6%	11	62	64%	27%	0	0.69	-8.1	50	76	-$2
12	MIN	3	6	0	97	62	5.03	4.58	1.42	798	771	821	9.4	2.9	5.8	2.0	8%	43	21	35	30%	68%	13%	5	33	0%	40%	0	0.77	-12.1	47	61	-$7
13	MIN	3	2	0	96	69	2.91	3.79	1.16	649	772	540	8.1	2.1	6.5	3.1	8%	45	19	36	29%	77%	7%	0	31			0	0.78	11.4	84	109	$5
1st Half		1	2	0	53	36	3.08	3.80	1.18	684	898	490	9.1	1.7	6.2	3.6	9%	42	22	36	30%	76%	7%	0	35			0	0.78	5.1	85	110	$4
2nd Half		2	0	0	43	33	2.70	3.78	1.13	607	617	599	7.1	2.5	6.9	2.8	7%	49	16	36	28%	78%	7%	0	28			0	0.78	6.2	83	107	$6
14	Proj	3	4	0	90	59	4.15	3.96	1.30	717	755	682	9.6	2.4	5.9	2.4	7%	43	19	37	30%	70%	8%	0						-3.1	62	81	-$1

Taillon,Jameson

Age: 22	Th: R	Role SP	Health A	LIMA Plan C	
Ht: 6' 6"	Wt: 225	Type	PT/Exp F	Rand Var +1	
			Consist F	MM 3200	

No. 2 overall pick (PIT) in 2010 draft has drawn comparisons to a young Josh Beckett. Skills so far in minors don't reflect that upside, but that's a product of him learning how to pitch, not an erosion of talent. One K per inning in late stint at Triple-A confirms that he's close. A keeper league gem with potential for late '14 impact.

Yr	Tm	W	L	Sv	IP	K	ERA	xERA	WHIP	oOPS	vL	vR	BF/G	Ctl	Dom	Cmd	SwK	G	L	F	H%	S%	hr/f	GS	APC	DOM%	DIS%	Sv%	LI	RAR	BPV	BPX	R$
09																																	
10																																	
11																																	
12	aa	3	0	0	17	15	1.83	1.00	0.77				20.4	0.5	7.9	16.0					27%	74%								4.6	398	519	$1
13	a/a	5	10	0	147	117	4.12	3.89	1.38				23.8	2.9	7.2	2.5					33%	70%								-4.5	80	105	-$2
1st Half		3	5	0	84	66	3.18	3.87	1.39				23.5	3.0	7.1	2.3					33%	78%								7.1	79	102	$2
2nd Half		2	5	0	64	51	5.31	3.87	1.37				24.2	2.7	7.2	2.6					33%	59%								-11.3	84	108	-$8
14	Proj	3	4	0	58	46	4.05	3.70	1.29				23.4	2.8	7.2	2.5	9%	44	20	36	31%	68%	5%	10						-1.3	75	97	-$1

Tanaka,Masahiro

Age: 25	Th: R	Role SP	Health A	LIMA Plan D+	
Ht: 6' 2"	Wt: 205	Type Pwr	PT/Exp A	Rand Var -5	
			Consist B	MM 4303	

Japan ace pitched like it again, and unlike some who came before him, he's still young enough to experience a growth curve in MLB. Arrival date in USA remains up in air, as it's based on when he will get posted. Elite command, age all support a successful transition to the big leagues once opportunity comes.

Yr	Tm	W	L	Sv	IP	K	ERA	xERA	WHIP	oOPS	vL	vR	BF/G	Ctl	Dom	Cmd	SwK	G	L	F	H%	S%	hr/f	GS	APC	DOM%	DIS%	Sv%	LI	RAR	BPV	BPX	R$
09	for	15	6	1	189	162	2.90	3.83	1.25				30.8	2.5	7.7	3.0					30%	82%								33.2	83	156	$22
10	for	11	6	0	155	113	3.10	4.34	1.36				32.4	2.3	6.6	2.8					32%	80%								18.7	72	116	$9
11	for	19	5	0	226	229	1.58	2.21	0.96				31.6	1.3	9.1	6.8					29%	87%								65.8	192	289	$44
12	for	10	4	0	173	160	2.33	2.97	1.13				31.1	1.2	8.3	6.8					34%	80%								36.0	185	242	$23
13	for	22	0	1	199	164	1.52	2.41	1.03				29.5	1.7	7.4	4.4					29%	88%								57.7	132	173	$38
1st Half																																	
2nd Half																																	
14	Proj	11	5	0	160	138	3.38	3.49	1.22				27.8	2.4	7.8	3.2	9%	41	21	38	31%	75%	8%	20						9.6	94	122	$12

Tazawa,Junichi

Age: 28	Th: R	Role RP	Health F	LIMA Plan A	
Ht: 5' 11"	Wt: 200	Type Pwr	PT/Exp D	Rand Var 0	
			Consist B	MM 5411	

Already-elite skills got even better in '13 due to filthy FB/splitter combo, making him an even more premium plan B closer. Has top-tier command vs. LH and RH bats, so there aren't any platoon chinks. Only thing he needs now is opportunity. A LIMA relief gem with... UP: 40 Saves.

Yr	Tm	W	L	Sv	IP	K	ERA	xERA	WHIP	oOPS	vL	vR	BF/G	Ctl	Dom	Cmd	SwK	G	L	F	H%	S%	hr/f	GS	APC	DOM%	DIS%	Sv%	LI	RAR	BPV	BPX	R$
09	BOS *	11	10	0	135	90	4.40	4.65	1.42	997	770	1291	22.0	2.6	6.0	2.3	5%	25	23	53	32%	71%	7%	4	83	25%	50%	0	0.94	-1.3	55	102	$3
10																																	
11	BOS *	4	3	0	40	41	5.02	4.68	1.38	974	1500	722	8.9	2.5	9.1	3.6	9%	13	0	88	35%	66%	14%	0	18			0	0.21	-5.4	93	139	-$2
12	BOS *	4	3	5	86	89	2.56	3.10	1.23	558	519	583	5.6	2.5	9.3	3.7	15%	49	24	27	34%	79%	3%	0	18			63	0.82	15.5	126	165	$9
13	BOS	5	4	0	68	72	3.16	3.31	1.20	744	796	700	4.0	1.6	9.5	6.0	13%	34	27	39	34%	79%	12%	0	15			0	1.09	5.9	140	182	$3
1st Half		4	3	0	37	40	2.92	3.15	1.14	770	727	821	4.0	1.0	9.7	10.0	13%	31	28	41	33%	83%	14%	0	14			0	1.02	4.3	158	205	$6
2nd Half		1	1	0	31	32	3.45	3.52	1.28	713	913	598	4.0	2.3	9.2	4.0	13%	37	27	37	34%	76%	9%	0	16			0	1.18	1.6	118	153	$0
14	Proj	5	4	7	73	72	3.23	3.03	1.14	670	716	636	5.0	2.1	9.0	4.2	14%	40	26	34	31%	75%	11%	0						5.7	122	159	$8

STEPHEN NICKRAND

Teheran,Julio

Age: 23	Th: R	Role SP	Health A	LIMA Plan C
Ht: 6' 2"	Wt: 175	Type Pwr FB	PT/Exp B	Rand Var -1
			Consist D	MM 3303

A case study in why post-hype targets can be profit centers. This former top prospect's K surge came with full SwK support, and three years of improving Ctl tells us he hasn't reached ceiling yet, even if xERA points towards some minor regression. A strikeout pitch vs. LH bats brings the next step... UP: sub-3.00 ERA, 200 K

Yr	Tm	W	L	Sv	IP	K	ERA	xERA	WHIP	oOPS	vL	vR	BF/G	Ctl	Dom	Cmd	SwK	G	L	F	H%	S%	hr/f	GS	APC	DOM%	DIS%	Sv%	LI	RAR	BPV	BPX	R$
09																																	
10	aa	3	2	0	40	35	3.71	2.57	1.17				22.8	3.6	7.9	2.2					27%	68%								1.8	92	150	$1
11	ATL *	16	4	0	164	122	3.19	3.39	1.28	828	968	598	22.5	3.0	6.7	2.2	7%	30	24	46	30%	76%	13%	3	70	0%	67%	0	0.72	15.2	76	115	$13
12	ATL *	7	9	0	137	92	5.55	5.16	1.49	467	250	579	21.1	2.7	6.0	2.2	8%	22	33	44	33%	64%	0%	1	50	0%	100%	0	0.71	-26.0	44	58	-$12
13	ATL	14	8	0	186	170	3.20	3.67	1.17	700	823	580	25.8	2.2	8.2	3.8	11%	38	21	41	30%	78%	10%	30	96	60%	10%			15.3	105	137	$16
1st Half		6	4	0	95	81	3.12	3.51	1.19	722	760	679	26.3	1.6	7.6	4.8	11%	42	22	36	31%	78%	11%	15	96	60%	13%			8.8	114	148	$16
2nd Half		8	4	0	90	89	3.29	3.84	1.16	677	901	493	25.3	2.8	8.9	3.2	12%	33	21	46	28%	77%	9%	15	96	60%	7%			6.4	95	123	$17
14	**Proj**	**13**	**8**	**0**	**174**	**153**	**3.65**	**3.63**	**1.25**	**716**	**862**	**579**	**25.0**	**2.5**	**7.9**	**3.2**	**11%**	**37**	**21**	**42**	**31%**	**74%**	**8%**	**31**						**4.5**	**89**	**116**	**$11**

Tepesch,Nicholas

Age: 25	Th: R	Role SP	Health D	LIMA Plan C
Ht: 6' 4"	Wt: 225	Type GB	PT/Exp D	Rand Var +2
			Consist F	MM 3101

Non-roster invitee made club out of spring training and managed 17 starts in MLB debut. While near-5 ERA will keep many away, you'll look at improving Dom, sustained control, and GB tilt and see profit potential that others will miss. If second half elbow inflammation doesn't linger, there's sneaky sub-4.00 ERA potential here.

Yr	Tm	W	L	Sv	IP	K	ERA	xERA	WHIP	oOPS	vL	vR	BF/G	Ctl	Dom	Cmd	SwK	G	L	F	H%	S%	hr/f	GS	APC	DOM%	DIS%	Sv%	LI	RAR	BPV	BPX	R$
09																																	
10																																	
11																																	
12	aa	6	3	0	90	55	5.78	6.13	1.63				25.1	2.8	5.4	2.0					35%	67%								-19.7	24	31	-$12
13	TEX	4	6	0	93	76	4.84	3.81	1.37	757	841	646	21.4	2.6	7.4	2.8	9%	47	22	30	32%	67%	13%	17	81	29%	35%	0	0.83	-11.2	87	113	-$5
1st Half		3	6	0	80	61	4.71	3.78	1.33	747	873	569	23.3	2.5	6.8	2.8	8%	51	21	28	31%	68%	15%	15	87	33%	33%			-8.3	86	111	-$4
2nd Half		1	0	0	13	15	5.68	3.92	1.58	819	593	1022	14.3	3.6	10.7	3.0	12%	19	36	44	40%	63%	6%	2	58	0%	50%	0	0.98	-2.8	93	121	-$7
14	**Proj**	**5**	**6**	**0**	**95**	**66**	**4.28**	**3.82**	**1.38**	**692**	**806**	**533**	**22.9**	**2.6**	**6.3**	**2.4**	**8%**	**49**	**21**	**30**	**31%**	**72%**	**12%**	**17**						**-4.8**	**71**	**92**	**-$1**

Thatcher,Joe

Age: 32	Th: L	Role RP	Health F	LIMA Plan C+
Ht: 6' 2"	Wt: 230	Type Pwr	PT/Exp D	Rand Var -1
			Consist B	MM 4500

You won't find many guys with an 86-mph fastball who can consistently post an 8.0+ Dom, but this is one. That said, since he's used mostly as a LOOGY and has flunking health, he'll never pitch enough innings to really make a difference with your pitching categories. All the while, he collects an MLB paycheck. Nice gig.

Yr	Tm	W	L	Sv	IP	K	ERA	xERA	WHIP	oOPS	vL	vR	BF/G	Ctl	Dom	Cmd	SwK	G	L	F	H%	S%	hr/f	GS	APC	DOM%	DIS%	Sv%	LI	RAR	BPV	BPX	R$
09	SD *	2	2	1	64	73	2.63	3.19	1.28	628	513	730	3.7	3.3	10.2	3.1	10%	44	18	38	34%	80%	5%	0	16			33	0.95	13.3	120	225	$4
10	SD	1	0	0	35	45	1.29	2.50	0.86	465	527	395	2.1	1.8	11.6	6.4	12%	41	21	38	29%	86%	3%	0	9			0	1.08	12.1	179	289	$5
11	SD	0	0	0	10	9	4.50	4.78	1.50	665	431	909	2.4	6.3	8.1	1.3	10%	38	19	42	27%	71%	9%	0	10			0	1.07	-0.7	-8	-12	-$4
12	SD	1	4	1	32	39	3.41	3.57	1.39	680	509	862	2.6	4.0	11.1	2.8	12%	43	19	38	36%	76%	6%	0	10			100	1.39	2.4	113	148	-$2
13	2 NL	3	2	0	39	36	3.20	3.67	1.27	693	632	768	2.3	2.3	8.2	3.6	11%	36	26	38	32%	78%	9%	0	9			0	1.50	3.2	100	131	-$1
1st Half		3	1	0	22	20	2.45	3.21	1.18	664	543	821	2.4	0.8	8.2	10.0	9%	45	22	33	34%	83%	9%	0	10			0	1.44	3.8	148	192	$2
2nd Half		0	1	0	17	16	4.15	4.31	1.38	732	754	693	2.1	4.2	8.3	2.0	12%	24	30	46	30%	73%	10%	0	9			0	1.58	-0.6	39	51	-$4
14	**Proj**	**2**	**3**	**0**	**46**	**49**	**3.44**	**3.27**	**1.26**	**661**	**599**	**734**	**2.3**	**3.0**	**9.7**	**3.2**	**11%**	**38**	**23**	**39**	**33%**	**74%**	**7%**	**0**						**2.4**	**108**	**141**	**$0**

Thayer,Dale

Age: 33	Th: R	Role RP	Health A	LIMA Plan A
Ht: 6' 0"	Wt: 215	Type Pwr	PT/Exp D	Rand Var 0
			Consist A	MM 4310

Career minor league closer has never been able to get extended MLB look as stopper. Steady strikeouts surge shows potential, as does two straight years of near-elite skills. Main concern is high 4.5 Ctl vs. LH bats; he's lethal vs. righties. As it stands, a solid LIMA target. With tweak vs. LHBs... UP: Some 9th inning work

Yr	Tm	W	L	Sv	IP	K	ERA	xERA	WHIP	oOPS	vL	vR	BF/G	Ctl	Dom	Cmd	SwK	G	L	F	H%	S%	hr/f	GS	APC	DOM%	DIS%	Sv%	LI	RAR	BPV	BPX	R$
09	TAM *	2	5	18	77	41	3.46	5.01	1.49	822	573	1000	5.4	2.1	4.8	2.2	5%	30	16	54	34%	79%	11%	0	21			75	0.17	8.2	46	85	$6
10	TAM *	4	1	3	62	43	5.15	6.76	1.97	1385	1000	1556	6.3	4.1	6.3	1.5	6%	50	30	20	40%	74%	50%	0	53			75	0.37	-8.2	36	58	-$7
11	NYM *	4	6	21	81	52	3.22	3.56	1.16	729	1295	474	5.0	1.7	5.8	3.3	6%	44	28	28	28%	76%	0%	0	14			81	0.59	7.3	79	119	$13
12	SD	2	2	7	58	47	3.43	3.82	1.13	627	654	607	3.7	1.9	7.3	3.9	10%	41	21	38	30%	70%	6%	0	15			70	1.15	4.1	100	131	$4
13	SD	3	5	1	65	64	3.32	3.57	1.25	691	770	622	3.9	3.0	8.9	2.9	9%	41	22	37	30%	78%	12%	0	16			25	1.00	4.4	96	125	$1
1st Half		0	3	1	37	35	3.44	3.57	0.98	596	667	535	3.8	2.5	8.6	3.5	9%	37	16	47	23%	71%	11%	0	16			25	1.14	1.9	103	134	$3
2nd Half		3	2	0	28	29	3.18	3.57	1.59	800	883	723	4.1	3.8	9.2	2.4	10%	46	29	24	37%	83%	15%	0	17			0	0.84	2.4	87	113	-$1
14	**Proj**	**3**	**4**	**4**	**65**	**59**	**3.41**	**3.44**	**1.26**	**688**	**750**	**636**	**4.0**	**2.7**	**8.1**	**3.0**	**10%**	**42**	**22**	**36**	**31%**	**76%**	**10%**	**0**						**3.7**	**94**	**122**	**$4**

Thielbar,Caleb

Age: 27	Th: L	Role RP	Health A	LIMA Plan B+
Ht: 6' 0"	Wt: 195	Type xFB	PT/Exp F	Rand Var -2
			Consist F	MM 3300

3-2, 1.76 ERA in 46 IP at MIN. Devastating stuff vs. same-sided bats, including 9.1 Dom and 5.8 Cmd. Lack of Cmd against RHers restricts him to LOOGY-only value, as he'll get exposed if given more work. Tiny ERA w/MIN was driven by similarly tiny hit rate, so it's not coming back. In deeeeep leagues, pay a buck and stash in pen.

Yr	Tm	W	L	Sv	IP	K	ERA	xERA	WHIP	oOPS	vL	vR	BF/G	Ctl	Dom	Cmd	SwK	G	L	F	H%	S%	hr/f	GS	APC	DOM%	DIS%	Sv%	LI	RAR	BPV	BPX	R$
09																																	
10																																	
11																																	
12	a/a	5	1	5	65	47	3.67	4.54	1.42				6.8	2.8	6.4	2.3					32%	77%								2.8	59	76	$1
13	MIN *	4	3	1	72	66	2.74	2.49	1.08	530	482	575	4.3	2.8	8.2	2.9	12%	27	19	54	27%	77%	6%	0	13			100	0.72	10.1	104	136	$6
1st Half		2	1	1	42	40	2.79	2.78	1.24	357	132	525	5.5	3.3	8.5	2.6	13%	39	17	44	31%	77%	0%	0	16			100	0.25	5.6	107	138	$6
2nd Half		2	2	0	30	26	2.67	3.94	0.86	609	620	598	3.3	2.1	7.7	3.7	11%	21	20	59	20%	77%	9%	0	12			0	0.90	4.5	82	106	$6
14	**Proj**	**3**	**2**	**0**	**47**	**39**	**3.12**	**3.94**	**1.17**	**733**	**658**	**803**	**4.8**	**2.6**	**7.4**	**2.8**	**12%**	**28**	**19**	**53**	**28%**	**76%**	**6%**	**0**						**4.3**	**69**	**90**	**$2**

Thornburg,Tyler

Age: 25	Th: R	Role RP	Health A	LIMA Plan B+
Ht: 5' 11"	Wt: 190	Type Pwr FB	PT/Exp D	Rand Var -1
			Consist A	MM 2301

3-1, 2.03 ERA in 67 IP at MIL. Tale of two halves for solid SP prospect. Upside didn't come out until until string of four PQS-4/5s in Sept. Wasn't enough to push the needle on continued marginal xERAs, so don't invest on tiny 2H ERA. Age, filthy curveball, 1H Dom are nice building blocks, but you can't take this risk w/o a bench.

Yr	Tm	W	L	Sv	IP	K	ERA	xERA	WHIP	oOPS	vL	vR	BF/G	Ctl	Dom	Cmd	SwK	G	L	F	H%	S%	hr/f	GS	APC	DOM%	DIS%	Sv%	LI	RAR	BPV	BPX	R$
09																																	
10																																	
11																																	
12	MIL *	10	4	0	135	116	4.17	4.45	1.37	922	757	1071	19.5	3.1	7.8	2.5	8%	42	20	38	31%	73%	32%	3	48	0%	100%	0	0.42	-2.5	66	86	$1
13	MIL *	3	10	0	141	121	4.49	4.71	1.51	575	479	684	18.5	3.6	7.7	2.2	7%	36	24	39	34%	72%	1%	7	59	86%	0%	0	0.52	-11.0	63	82	-$8
1st Half		1	9	0	84	79	5.98	6.23	1.70	530	462	573	21.0	3.3	8.5	2.5	6%	31	35	35	38%	67%	0%	0	45			0	0.40	-21.8	52	68	-$17
2nd Half		2	1	0	58	42	2.34	4.36	1.23	582	480	707	15.7	3.9	6.6	1.7	8%	37	23	40	27%	80%	2%	7	62	86%	0%	0	0.55	10.8	28	36	$6
14	**Proj**	**5**	**5**	**0**	**116**	**97**	**3.98**	**4.09**	**1.40**	**697**	**522**	**911**	**18.3**	**3.5**	**7.5**	**2.2**	**8%**	**37**	**23**	**40**	**32%**	**73%**	**7%**	**22**						**-1.7**	**57**	**74**	**$0**

Thornton,Matt

Age: 37	Th: L	Role RP	Health C	LIMA Plan C
Ht: 6' 6"	Wt: 235	Type GB	PT/Exp C	Rand Var 0
			Consist A	MM 3200

Dom erosions don't get any more steep. Even FB velo has dropped two mph since '10. That, combined with steep SwK slide, wipes out hope for Dom resurrection. oOPS vR heading in wrong direction too, so he'll be a LH specialist soon. After long elite run, time to hedge your bullpen speculation bets elsewhere.

Yr	Tm	W	L	Sv	IP	K	ERA	xERA	WHIP	oOPS	vL	vR	BF/G	Ctl	Dom	Cmd	SwK	G	L	F	H%	S%	hr/f	GS	APC	DOM%	DIS%	Sv%	LI	RAR	BPV	BPX	R$
09	CHW	6	3	4	72	87	2.74	2.89	1.08	599	596	601	4.2	2.5	10.8	4.4	13%	46	17	36	31%	77%	8%	0	17			44	1.46	14.1	152	284	$11
10	CHW	5	4	8	61	81	2.67	2.64	1.01	547	500	584	3.9	3.0	12.0	4.1	16%	40	23	37	30%	74%	6%	0	16			80	1.38	10.5	154	249	$11
11	CHW	2	5	3	60	63	3.32	3.28	1.36	649	619	672	4.2	3.2	9.5	3.0	11%	49	24	27	35%	76%	7%	0	17			43	1.28	4.6	113	169	$2
12	CHW	4	10	3	65	53	3.46	3.42	1.23	685	660	709	3.6	2.4	7.3	3.1	9%	54	20	26	31%	72%	8%	0	14			43	1.43	4.4	101	131	$3
13	2 AL	0	4	0	43	30	3.74	4.09	1.43	738	638	827	3.1	3.1	6.2	2.0	8%	51	19	30	32%	76%	10%	0	12			0	1.33	0.7	57	74	-$4
1st Half		0	2	0	26	20	3.16	3.87	1.21	712	556	868	2.9	3.2	7.0	2.2	9%	47	15	38	26%	81%	15%	0	12			0	1.50	2.2	66	86	-$2
2nd Half		0	2	0	18	10	4.58	4.44	1.75	771	755	781	3.4	3.1	5.1	1.7	8%	55	23	22	39%	71%	0%	0	12			0	1.07	-1.6	42	54	-$7
14	**Proj**	**1**	**4**	**0**	**49**	**35**	**4.01**	**3.80**	**1.40**	**705**	**655**	**747**	**3.4**	**3.1**	**6.4**	**2.1**	**9%**	**51**	**21**	**28**	**32%**	**71%**	**7%**	**0**						**-0.9**	**61**	**80**	**-$3**

STEPHEN NICKRAND

Tillman,Chris

Age: 26 Th: R Role SP	Health A	LIMA Plan C+	
Ht: 6' 5" Wt: 210 Type Pwr FB	PT/Exp B	Rand Var +1	
	Consist C	MM 3305	

A fine follow-up to surprising '12, and this may just be the start. So many encouraging nuggets in the rather gaudy across-the-board 2H skills growth—GB, Dom and SwK all up, better Ctl. Of course, doing it over a full season is another challenge, but age & this growth suggest far more upside than down... UP: sub-3.50 ERA.

Yr Tm	W	L	Sv	IP	K	ERA	xERA	WHIP	oOPS	vL	vR	BF/G	Ctl	Dom	Cmd	SwK	G	L	F	H%	S%	hr/f	GS	APC	DOM%	DIS%	Sv%	LI	RAR	BPV	BPX	R$
09 BAL *	10	11	0	162	122	4.37	4.85	1.42	890	811	972	22.9	2.8	6.8	2.4	7%	37	18	45	32%	73%	15%	12	97	0%	33%			-1.1	53	99	$3
10 BAL *	13	12	0	175	111	4.56	4.61	1.41	828	930	733	23.1	3.1	5.7	1.8	7%	43	22	36	30%	70%	15%	11	87	18%	55%			-10.4	40	65	$1
11 BAL *	6	11	0	138	91	5.94	6.08	1.65	812	797	833	22.1	4.1	5.9	1.4	6%	37	18	45	32%	68%	5%	13	90	31%	54%			-34.1	12	18	-$15
12 BAL *	17	12	0	179	143	4.02	3.95	1.31	639	601	701	23.0	2.9	7.2	2.4	9%	35	21	44	30%	72%	11%	15	96	60%	20%			-0.1	70	91	$8
13 BAL	16	7	0	206	179	3.71	3.87	1.22	730	744	711	25.6	3.0	7.8	2.6	9%	39	22	40	27%	76%	14%	33	105	52%	15%			4.0	77	101	$13
1st Half	10	2	0	100	81	3.68	4.18	1.30	748	726	780	24.5	3.4	7.3	2.1	7%	37	22	41	27%	79%	15%	17	103	41%	18%			2.3	54	70	$12
2nd Half	6	5	0	106	98	3.74	3.59	1.15	712	762	647	26.8	2.5	8.3	3.3	10%	40	21	39	28%	73%	13%	16	108	63%	13%			1.7	99	128	$13
14 Proj	15	10	0	189	157	3.87	3.84	1.31	756	752	763	24.9	3.0	7.5	2.5	9%	38	21	42	30%	75%	12%	33						0.0	71	92	$10

Torres,Alexander

Age: 26 Th: L Role RP	Health A	LIMA Plan B+	
Ht: 5' 10" Wt: 175 Type Pwr	PT/Exp D	Rand Var -1	
	Consist F	MM 4501	

4-2, 1.71 ERA in 58 IP at TAM. Sessions with a former pitching coach helped him simplify mechanics & find the plate, and that's all it took to revive his career. Generates elite SwK from mix of FB and a filthy change. Lack of third pitch may limit him as a SP, but oOPS splits show he's no LOOGY. Big upside for this smallish pitcher.

Yr Tm	W	L	Sv	IP	K	ERA	xERA	WHIP	oOPS	vL	vR	BF/G	Ctl	Dom	Cmd	SwK	G	L	F	H%	S%	hr/f	GS	APC	DOM%	DIS%	Sv%	LI	RAR	BPV	BPX	R$
09 aa	3	3	0	35	28	3.65	4.32	1.66				22.2	5.8	7.2	1.2					33%	77%								2.9	63	118	-$2
10 aa	11	6	0	143	129	4.14	4.64	1.59				23.3	4.5	8.2	1.8					35%	74%								-1.1	69	111	$0
11 TAM *	10	8	0	154	141	3.47	4.31	1.60	701	450	897	22.0	5.1	8.2	1.6	7%	59	23	18	34%	78%	0%	0	40			0	0.71	8.9	72	108	$1
12 aaa	3	7	0	69	75	8.35	6.18	2.07				13.0	8.2	9.8	1.2					38%	58%								-36.9	58	76	-$23
13 TAM *	6	4	0	104	111	2.81	1.96	1.09	468	466	470	8.5	3.6	9.6	2.7	13%	42	20	38	28%	73%	2%	0	23			0	1.03	13.6	122	159	$10
1st Half	4	2	0	69	80	2.92	1.86	1.08	265	299	244	12.8	3.7	10.5	2.8	17%	57	5	39	28%	72%	0%	0	26			0	0.49	8.0	131	169	$13
2nd Half	2	2	0	35	31	2.57	3.80	1.11	587	560	606	5.3	3.3	8.0	2.4	11%	35	27	38	27%	76%	3%	0	22			0	1.28	5.6	66	86	$4
14 Proj	4	5	0	72	75	3.60	3.39	1.23	649	632	660	9.3	3.8	9.4	2.5	13%	44	18	38	30%	70%	5%	0						2.4	88	115	$3

Torres,Carlos

Age: 31 Th: R Role RP	Health A	LIMA Plan B+	
Ht: 6' 1" Wt: 185 Type	PT/Exp D	Rand Var +1	
	Consist B	MM 3201	

4-6, 3.44 ERA in 86 IP at NYM. Another who reigned in control, he found a solid niche for NYM as a swingman in 2nd half. Excellent Dom, Cmd as a starter gives hope that he'll stick if stretched out. Age, skill history not on his side, but if this shiny new command sticks, he's a solid end-rotation stash. Monitor Ctl to find out.

Yr Tm	W	L	Sv	IP	K	ERA	xERA	WHIP	oOPS	vL	vR	BF/G	Ctl	Dom	Cmd	SwK	G	L	F	H%	S%	hr/f	GS	APC	DOM%	DIS%	Sv%	LI	RAR	BPV	BPX	R$
09 CHW *	11	6	1	156	125	4.09	4.44	1.57	862	819	906	22.1	4.9	7.2	1.5	8%	38	18	45	32%	74%	13%	5	61	40%	40%	100	0.54	4.5	56	105	$3
10 CHW *	9	10	0	174	123	4.93	5.02	1.60	1041	1039	1041	24.0	4.9	6.3	1.3	9%	29	35	37	31%	71%	11%	1	54	0%	0%	0	0.24	-18.3	34	55	-$7
11																																
12 COL *	10	7	0	114	83	5.20	4.97	1.59	723	660	768	11.2	4.2	6.5	1.5	8%	44	27	29	33%	68%	5%	0	29			0	0.60	-16.6	45	58	-$9
13 NYM *	10	9	0	158	126	3.60	4.01	1.22	701	678	716	14.2	2.0	7.2	3.6	11%	44	20	37	30%	76%	16%	9	40	78%	22%	0	1.04	5.3	84	109	$8
1st Half	6	4	0	81	60	3.47	3.87	1.28	440	277	556	18.4	2.3	6.7	2.9	10%	50	14	36	31%	75%	13%	0	21			0	1.34	3.9	78	101	$8
2nd Half	4	5	0	77	66	3.72	3.54	1.16	729	725	731	11.8	1.7	7.7	4.4	11%	43	20	37	29%	76%	17%	9	44	78%	22%	0	0.97	1.4	112	145	$8
14 Proj	8	7	0	125	96	4.04	3.82	1.37	770	745	786	14.2	3.0	7.0	2.4	10%	43	23	34	31%	73%	11%	15						-2.7	67	87	$2

Turner,Jacob

Age: 23 Th: R Role SP	Health A	LIMA Plan D+	
Ht: 6' 5" Wt: 215 Type	PT/Exp C	Rand Var 0	
	Consist A	MM 2103	

3-8, 3.74 ERA in 118 IP at MIA. Looked like he was taking a step up, but hit a wall in 2H, losing FB velocity and command. Low K rate vs LHB (29 K in 239 PA) a lingering issue. Still very young, w/1st-round pedigree; that and some 1H success (see DOM/DIS%, high SwK) keep us hoping. But nothing here says 2014 is the year.

Yr Tm	W	L	Sv	IP	K	ERA	xERA	WHIP	oOPS	vL	vR	BF/G	Ctl	Dom	Cmd	SwK	G	L	F	H%	S%	hr/f	GS	APC	DOM%	DIS%	Sv%	LI	RAR	BPV	BPX	R$
09																																
10																																
11 DET *	4	6	0	144	102	4.34	3.82	1.27	904	903	910	25.5	2.3	6.4	2.8	8%	41	20	39	30%	67%	17%	3	80	33%	67%			-7.1	74	112	$1
12 2 TM *	8	7	0	145	88	3.68	3.80	1.32	716	548	853	24.0	3.3	5.5	1.6	10%	45	19	36	28%	74%	14%	10	90	40%	10%			6.1	48	62	$4
13 MIA *	6	12	0	174	109	4.34	4.53	1.46	746	716	770	24.9	3.6	5.6	1.6	9%	46	19	35	30%	72%	9%	20	93	40%	20%			-10.2	38	50	-$6
1st Half	5	4	0	97	59	3.98	4.02	1.32	606	518	691	25.2	2.5	5.5	2.2	11%	51	18	31	30%	71%	3%	6	94	83%	0%			-1.4	55	71	$0
2nd Half	1	8	0	77	50	4.79	5.20	1.62	811	818	805	25.2	4.9	5.8	1.2	8%	43	20	37	30%	73%	11%	14	92	21%	29%			-8.8	-6	-8	-$14
14 Proj	7	11	0	174	110	4.16	4.27	1.41	754	665	828	24.6	3.5	5.7	1.6	9%	46	19	35	30%	72%	9%	30						-6.4	33	42	-$1

Uehara,Koji

Age: 39 Th: R Role RP	Health F	LIMA Plan C+	
Ht: 6' 2" Wt: 195 Type Pwr xFB	PT/Exp C	Rand Var -5	
	Consist A	MM 5530	

In short, the best relief season since Eck's vintage 1990. Threw splitter more than ever, and SwK on it was over 25%! Pure brilliance. That said... the same red flag he had entering 2013 is still there: the health risk. (And now he's 39.) Skills are not in question, but can you spend top dollar on the age and health risk?

Yr Tm	W	L	Sv	IP	K	ERA	xERA	WHIP	oOPS	vL	vR	BF/G	Ctl	Dom	Cmd	SwK	G	L	F	H%	S%	hr/f	GS	APC	DOM%	DIS%	Sv%	LI	RAR	BPV	BPX	R$
09 BAL	2	4	0	67	48	4.05	4.49	1.25	743	743	744	23.3	1.6	6.5	4.0	12%	30	17	53	31%	70%	6%	12	88	33%	17%			2.2	81	151	$1
10 BAL	1	2	13	44	55	2.86	3.06	0.95	598	747	474	4.1	1.0	11.3	11.0	13%	24	18	58	32%	76%	8%	0	16			87	1.23	6.6	177	286	$9
11 2 AL	2	3	0	65	85	2.35	2.61	0.72	535	472	597	3.7	1.2	11.8	9.4	17%	32	14	53	22%	83%	14%	0	14			0	1.06	12.7	188	283	$10
12 TEX	0	0	1	36	43	1.75	2.74	0.64	466	545	369	3.5	0.8	10.8	14.3	19%	33	17	51	21%	84%	10%	0	14			100	0.66	10.1	184	240	$5
13 BOS	4	1	21	74	101	1.09	2.24	0.57	400	338	466	3.6	1.1	12.2	11.2	20%	40	11	48	20%	89%	7%	0	14			88	1.34	25.5	209	272	$27
1st Half	1	0	4	34	49	2.12	2.64	0.82	576	407	776	3.6	1.9	13.0	7.0	16%	34	10	56	25%	87%	12%	0	15			67	1.34	7.3	196	253	$14
2nd Half	3	1	17	40	52	0.22	1.90	0.35	234	264	206	3.6	0.4	11.6	26.0	24%	46	13	41	16%	93%	0%	0	14			94	1.34	18.1	221	286	$37
14 Proj	3	2	33	68	83	2.03	2.45	0.78	523	517	528	3.8	1.3	11.0	8.6	19%	36	14	50	25%	81%	8%	0						15.3	178	231	$25

Valverde,Jose

Age: 36 Th: R Role RP	Health B	LIMA Plan C	
Ht: 6' 4" Wt: 255 Type Pwr FB	PT/Exp B	Rand Var +5	
	Consist B	MM 3310	

BPV column shows the tragi-comedy here: was arguably better than in the 49-save season two years ago, and clearly much better than the 35-save guy from last year. But teams flinch when you give up six HR in really bad late-inning spots. At this point, his reputation far exceeds any possibility that 2013's BPIs were for real.

Yr Tm	W	L	Sv	IP	K	ERA	xERA	WHIP	oOPS	vL	vR	BF/G	Ctl	Dom	Cmd	SwK	G	L	F	H%	S%	hr/f	GS	APC	DOM%	DIS%	Sv%	LI	RAR	BPV	BPX	R$
09 HOU	4	2	25	54	56	2.33	3.69	1.13	626	772	500	4.2	3.5	9.3	2.7	14%	41	13	46	27%	84%	8%	0	17			86	1.06	13.2	93	173	$16
10 DET	2	4	26	63	63	3.00	3.47	1.16	585	662	502	4.3	4.6	9.0	2.0	11%	55	13	32	24%	76%	10%	0	17			90	0.95	8.4	72	116	$14
11 DET	2	4	49	72	69	2.24	3.84	1.19	580	687	432	4.0	4.2	8.6	2.0	11%	43	16	41	26%	84%	6%	0	16			100	1.10	15.2	61	92	$25
12 DET	3	4	35	69	48	3.78	4.83	1.25	647	754	510	4.1	3.5	6.3	1.8	8%	34	22	44	28%	69%	3%	0	16			88	0.98	2.0	30	39	$14
13 DET	0	1	9	19	19	5.59	3.85	1.24	796	912	644	4.2	2.8	8.8	3.2	9%	40	16	44	25%	67%	24%	0	17			75	1.08	-4.1	102	133	-$1
1st Half	0	1	9	19	19	5.59	3.85	1.24	796	912	644	4.2	2.8	8.8	3.2	9%	40	16	44	25%	67%	24%	0	17			75	1.08	-4.1	102	132	-$1
2nd Half																																
14 Proj	1	1	1	28	25	4.00	3.79	1.35	741	862	592	4.1	3.6	8.3	2.3	10%	42	16	42	30%	75%	12%	0						-0.5	72	93	-$2

Vargas,Jason

Age: 31 Th: L Role SP	Health D	LIMA Plan B+	
Ht: 6' 0" Wt: 215 Type FB	PT/Exp A	Rand Var 0	
	Consist A	MM 2105	

Consistency grade, xERA show his steadiness. Sure, some things are up (overall BPV, Cmd) and some are down (DOM%, notably), but it all comes out in the wash. Lost time last year to a blood clot, but otherwise he's good for 200 fair-to-middling, blandly consumed IP.... Umm, are you yawning? Good, glad it's not just me.

Yr Tm	W	L	Sv	IP	K	ERA	xERA	WHIP	oOPS	vL	vR	BF/G	Ctl	Dom	Cmd	SwK	G	L	F	H%	S%	hr/f	GS	APC	DOM%	DIS%	Sv%	LI	RAR	BPV	BPX	R$
09 SEA *	7	9	0	143	92	4.40	4.51	1.34	803	841	786	18.6	2.5	5.8	2.3	9%	37	21	42	30%	71%	13%	14	64	14%	43%	0	0.86	-1.4	48	91	$3
10 SEA	9	12	0	193	116	3.78	4.64	1.25	699	550	747	26.2	2.5	5.4	2.1	8%	36	17	47	28%	72%	6%	31	97	39%	13%			7.0	43	70	$9
11 SEA	10	13	0	201	131	4.25	4.48	1.31	712	720	709	26.8	2.6	5.9	2.2	8%	36	20	44	30%	70%	8%	32	102	50%	22%			-7.7	48	73	$3
12 SEA	14	11	0	217	141	3.85	4.37	1.18	714	705	717	26.9	2.3	5.8	2.6	9%	40	19	40	26%	74%	13%	33	102	48%	21%			4.4	62	80	$13
13 LAA	9	8	0	150	109	4.02	4.30	1.39	758	789	747	26.8	2.8	6.5	2.4	9%	40	21	38	32%	74%	9%	24	99	38%	21%			-2.9	61	80	$0
1st Half	6	4	0	91	62	3.65	4.44	1.36	735	735	736	27.9	3.0	6.1	2.1	9%	42	19	39	30%	76%	8%	14	102	36%	7%			2.5	50	65	$3
2nd Half	3	4	0	59	47	4.60	4.07	1.43	793	913	762	25.3	2.5	7.2	2.9	9%	37	25	38	34%	71%	11%	10	97	40%	40%			-5.3	78	101	-$5
14 Proj	11	11	0	189	132	4.12	4.03	1.32	744	767	736	25.4	2.5	6.3	2.5	9%	39	21	40	30%	72%	10%	31						-5.9	61	79	$5

ROD TRUESDELL

Varvaro,Anthony

Age: 29 Th: R Role RP | Ht: 6' 0" Wt: 195 Type Pwr
Health A | PT/Exp D | Consist B
LIMA Plan B | Rand Var -4 | MM 2200

Seemingly tried to reinvent himself in 2013, throwing fewer curves and more changeups. Despite flashy ERA, Cmd and BPV say net effect was not positive, moving from a "throws hard with no idea where it's going" to a "pitch to contact, get GBs" profile. Unless he somehow marries 2013 Ctl with 2012 Dom, he's safe to ignore.

Yr Tm	W	L	Sv	IP	K	ERA	xERA	WHIP	oOPS	vL	vR	BF/G	Ctl	Dom	Cmd	SwK	G	L	F	H%	S%	hr/f	GS	APC	DOM%	DIS%	Sv%	LI	RAR	BPV	BPX	R$
09 aa	4	3	8	54	54	3.69	3.08	1.57				6.6	8.1	8.9	1.1					26%	75%								4.2	87	163	$3
10 SEA *	1	4	9	69	64	4.87	4.10	1.54	1167	1300	1115	5.6	5.4	8.4	1.5	5%	46	31	23	31%	68%	67%	0	24			69	0.35	-6.7	69	112	-$1
11 ATL *	2	10	1	83	78	3.48	3.16	1.34	594	627	566	6.2	5.4	8.5	1.6	11%	33	20	47	26%	76%	11%	0	22			33	0.69	4.8	76	114	$1
12 ATL *	1	3	6	61	58	3.51	4.50	1.63	766	869	656	6.0	5.2	8.5	1.7	11%	42	16	42	35%	79%	11%	0	27			75	0.48	3.8	73	95	-$2
13 ATL	3	1	1	73	43	2.82	4.24	1.27	644	548	717	4.9	3.1	5.3	1.7	8%	47	24	29	28%	78%	4%	0	18			33	0.57	9.4	37	48	$2
1st Half	3	1	0	39	24	3.03	3.99	1.16	618	469	771	4.8	2.6	5.6	2.2	9%	48	23	29	27%	74%	6%	0	18			0	0.72	4.0	57	74	$4
2nd Half	0	0	1	35	19	2.60	4.53	1.38	672	672	671	5.1	3.6	4.9	1.4	7%	46	26	28	30%	81%	3%	0	18			100	0.40	5.4	15	20	$0
14 Proj	1	2	0	44	33	4.04	4.06	1.41	672	594	727	5.4	4.4	6.9	1.6	8%	47	25	28	30%	71%	6%	0						-0.9	30	39	-$3

Venters,Jonny

Age: 29 Th: L Role RP | Ht: 6' 3" Wt: 195 Type Pwr xGB
Health F | PT/Exp D | Consist B
LIMA Plan C+ | Rand Var 0 | MM 5400

Balky elbow in March led to Tommy John surgery (his second) in May. The usual TJS timetable from that surgery date would put him on track for a summer return, barring complications. This skill set remains terrific, but even assuming a full recovery, don't expect to see him at full strength again until 2015.

Yr Tm	W	L	Sv	IP	K	ERA	xERA	WHIP	oOPS	vL	vR	BF/G	Ctl	Dom	Cmd	SwK	G	L	F	H%	S%	hr/f	GS	APC	DOM%	DIS%	Sv%	LI	RAR	BPV	BPX	R$
09 a/a	8	11	0	157	83	5.71	5.59	1.80				24.9	4.9	4.8	1.0					34%	67%								-26.7	25	46	-$14
10 ATL	4	4	1	83	93	1.95	2.64	1.20	552	570	543	4.4	4.2	10.1	2.4	15%	68	15	17	30%	83%	3%	0	17			20	1.05	21.8	113	183	$9
11 ATL	6	2	5	88	96	1.84	2.49	1.09	508	402	545	4.2	4.4	9.8	2.2	16%	73	14	14	25%	83%	7%	0	16			56	1.28	22.8	109	164	$14
12 ATL	5	4	0	59	69	3.22	2.98	1.52	739	653	786	4.0	4.3	10.6	2.5	15%	63	21	16	36%	82%	24%	0	15			0	0.97	5.7	116	151	-$1
13																																
1st Half																																
2nd Half																																
14 Proj	2	1	0	28	29	3.20	2.84	1.33	631	591	650	4.7	4.4	9.4	2.1	15%	68	17	16	31%	76%	12%	0						2.3	96	125	-$1

Ventura,Yordano

Age: 23 Th: R Role SP | Ht: 5' 11" Wt: 140 Type Pwr GB
Health A | PT/Exp D | Consist B
LIMA Plan B+ | Rand Var +2 | MM 3301

0-1, 3.52 ERA in 15 IP at KC. Little guy with a big arm (fastball touches 100 mph) and secondary offerings that are still something of a work-in-progress. Has top-of-rotation potential, and if he really is figuring out Ctl as quickly as MLE suggests, he could get there quickly... UP: 14 Wins, 3.25 ERA, 180 K.

Yr Tm	W	L	Sv	IP	K	ERA	xERA	WHIP	oOPS	vL	vR	BF/G	Ctl	Dom	Cmd	SwK	G	L	F	H%	S%	hr/f	GS	APC	DOM%	DIS%	Sv%	LI	RAR	BPV	BPX	R$
09																																
10																																
11																																
12 aa	1	2	0	29	21	5.20	2.98	1.28				20.1	3.8	6.5	1.7					28%	56%								-4.3	74	97	-$4
13 KC *	8	7	0	150	141	3.68	3.72	1.37	693	670	737	21.6	3.5	8.5	2.4	8%	49	15	36	33%	74%	18%	3	81	33%	33%			3.5	87	114	$3
1st Half	5	3	0	81	80	3.65	3.21	1.29				20.9	3.8	8.8	2.3					31%	72%	0%	0						2.2	93	120	$7
2nd Half	3	4	0	69	61	3.72	4.33	1.45	693	670	737	22.6	3.1	8.0	2.6	8%	49	15	36	35%	75%	18%	3	81	33%	33%			1.3	82	106	-$1
14 Proj	5	5	0	93	86	3.95	3.64	1.37	622	593	678	21.8	3.4	8.3	2.5	8%	49	15	36	32%	73%	8%	18						-1.0	85	111	$1

Veras,Jose

Age: 33 Th: R Role RP | Ht: 6' 6" Wt: 240 Type Pwr FB
Health A | PT/Exp C | Consist A
LIMA Plan C+ | Rand Var -3 | MM 3410

Case study in how modern closer role isn't that difficult: BPX shows a multi-year track record of skills that are just a tick above average, but that skill set was sufficient to convert 19 of 22 save opps in HOU. Doesn't necessarily mean you want to bet on him to be a top closer in 2014, but it does show that Opportunity is king.

Yr Tm	W	L	Sv	IP	K	ERA	xERA	WHIP	oOPS	vL	vR	BF/G	Ctl	Dom	Cmd	SwK	G	L	F	H%	S%	hr/f	GS	APC	DOM%	DIS%	Sv%	LI	RAR	BPV	BPX	R$
09 2 AL	4	3	0	50	40	5.19	5.01	1.39	756	850	684	4.8	5.0	7.2	1.4	7%	36	16	47	25%	66%	12%	0	19			0	0.70	-5.4	8	14	-$2
10 FLA *	4	4	2	77	83	4.53	4.47	1.57	622	555	686	4.7	5.4	9.7	1.8	10%	40	23	37	33%	72%	12%	0	17			50	1.22	-4.3	74	120	-$2
11 PIT	2	4	1	71	79	3.80	3.78	1.24	636	690	600	3.9	4.3	10.0	2.3	9%	37	18	45	28%	71%	7%	0	16			13	1.26	1.2	79	119	$2
12 MIL	5	4	1	67	79	3.63	3.94	1.51	694	724	665	4.2	5.4	10.6	2.0	9%	44	25	31	34%	77%	9%	0	18			50	0.91	3.2	68	89	-$1
13 2 AL	0	5	21	63	60	3.02	3.67	1.07	605	684	520	3.8	3.2	8.6	2.7	10%	42	15	44	25%	75%	8%	0	15			84	1.15	6.6	90	117	$11
1st Half	0	4	16	35	38	3.60	3.35	1.11	650	684	618	4.0	3.6	9.8	2.7	10%	43	17	40	26%	71%	12%	0	16			84	1.24	1.1	100	129	$14
2nd Half	0	1	5	28	22	2.28	4.07	1.01	550	682	380	3.5	2.6	7.2	2.8	9%	41	12	47	24%	81%	5%	0	15			83	1.06	5.4	77	100	$6
14 Proj	2	4	5	58	59	3.52	3.63	1.29	667	733	604	3.8	4.0	9.1	2.3	9%	41	18	41	29%	75%	8%	0						2.5	75	97	$2

Verlander,Justin

Age: 31 Th: R Role SP | Ht: 6' 5" Wt: 225 Type Pwr
Health A | PT/Exp A | Consist A
LIMA Plan B | Rand Var -1 | MM 4405

Much was made of his diminished velocity; he blames mechanics and says he fixed them in-season. Monthly SwK numbers (11%-14%-9%-9%-11%-13%) back that up, as does his dominant postseason work. If there's a perception that he's past peak entering 2014, use that to buy at a discount... UP: 20 Wins, 2.75 ERA.

Yr Tm	W	L	Sv	IP	K	ERA	xERA	WHIP	oOPS	vL	vR	BF/G	Ctl	Dom	Cmd	SwK	G	L	F	H%	S%	hr/f	GS	APC	DOM%	DIS%	Sv%	LI	RAR	BPV	BPX	R$
09 DET	19	9	0	240	269	3.45	3.33	1.18	665	684	640	28.1	2.4	10.1	4.3	11%	36	21	43	33%	73%	7%	35	112	77%	6%			25.8	132	247	$29
10 DET	18	9	0	224	219	3.37	3.55	1.16	630	635	622	28.0	2.8	8.8	3.1	10%	41	19	40	30%	72%	6%	33	114	70%	3%			19.6	100	162	$23
11 DET	24	5	0	251	250	2.40	3.14	0.92	555	504	617	28.5	2.0	9.0	4.4	11%	40	18	42	25%	79%	9%	34	116	88%	0%			47.7	124	187	$45
12 DET	17	8	0	238	239	2.64	3.35	1.06	601	608	593	29.0	2.3	9.0	4.0	12%	42	22	36	29%	78%	8%	33	114	79%	3%			40.3	121	158	$36
13 DET	13	12	0	218	217	3.46	3.75	1.31	691	658	739	27.2	3.1	8.9	2.9	11%	38	23	39	33%	76%	8%	34	109	65%	9%			10.9	94	122	$11
1st Half	8	5	0	105	114	3.77	3.52	1.40	716	672	784	26.7	3.3	9.8	2.9	11%	43	23	34	35%	74%	8%	17	108	53%	12%			1.2	107	138	$9
2nd Half	5	7	0	113	103	3.18	3.96	1.24	667	643	699	27.7	2.9	8.2	2.9	11%	34	22	44	30%	78%	8%	17	109	76%	6%			9.6	82	106	$14
14 Proj	17	9	0	225	224	3.07	3.27	1.17	643	624	670	27.1	2.7	9.0	3.4	11%	39	22	39	30%	76%	8%	33						22.1	107	138	$25

Villanueva,Carlos

Age: 30 Th: R Role RP | Ht: 6' 2" Wt: 215 Type Pwr FB
Health B | PT/Exp B | Consist A
LIMA Plan B+ | Rand Var 0 | MM 3301

He's a rare breed these days: a true swingman. Splits say he's much more effective as an RP (8.8 Dom, 3.8 Cmd, 3.03 ERA in 2013), if only his manager would leave him in pen. Even as an RP, multi-inning utility makes him a prime target for vulture wins (6 wins out of pen in just 32 relief appearances). Sneaky value here.

Yr Tm	W	L	Sv	IP	K	ERA	xERA	WHIP	oOPS	vL	vR	BF/G	Ctl	Dom	Cmd	SwK	G	L	F	H%	S%	hr/f	GS	APC	DOM%	DIS%	Sv%	LI	RAR	BPV	BPX	R$
09 MIL	4	10	3	96	83	5.34	4.19	1.43	776	765	786	6.6	3.3	7.8	2.4	12%	40	23	37	32%	65%	12%	6	25	17%	50%	38	0.80	-12.1	69	130	-$2
10 MIL	2	0	1	53	67	4.61	3.35	1.33	702	768	637	4.6	3.8	11.4	3.0	13%	34	27	39	33%	68%	13%	0	18			25	0.98	-3.5	117	189	$0
11 TOR	6	4	0	107	68	4.04	4.46	1.26	696	713	677	13.8	2.7	5.7	2.1	8%	36	22	43	28%	70%	8%	13	53	46%	23%	0	0.75	-1.3	44	67	$2
12 TOR	7	7	0	125	122	4.16	4.02	1.27	758	816	703	13.7	3.3	8.8	2.7	11%	37	19	44	28%	74%	15%	16	53	63%	19%	0	0.79	-2.3	84	109	$3
13 CHC	7	8	0	129	103	4.06	3.91	1.22	726	731	721	11.1	2.8	7.2	2.6	11%	40	21	39	28%	69%	10%	15	42	60%	20%	0	0.85	-3.0	72	94	$3
1st Half	2	4	0	68	51	3.59	3.65	1.17	707	697	715	11.8	2.4	6.8	2.8	11%	44	24	33	27%	73%	13%	8	43	63%	13%	0	0.86	2.3	79	102	$5
2nd Half	5	4	0	61	52	4.57	4.19	1.28	745	776	726	10.5	3.2	7.7	2.4	11%	36	19	45	29%	65%	8%	7	42	57%	29%	0	0.84	-5.3	65	84	$1
14 Proj	7	4	0	86	76	3.92	3.70	1.26	733	759	711	10.5	3.0	8.0	2.6	10%	38	21	41	29%	73%	11%	2						-0.6	78	101	$3

Vincent,Nick

Age: 27 Th: R Role RP | Ht: 6' 0" Wt: 185 Type Pwr FB
Health A | PT/Exp D | Consist B
LIMA Plan A | Rand Var -3 | MM 4400

6-3, 2.14 ERA in 46 IP at SD. They really do grow relievers on trees in SD. This one barely breaks 90 on radar gun, but followed up a terrific MLB debut from 2012 (1.71 ERA, 123 BPV in 26 IP) with a full repeat. Relative success of LHBs against him is an obstacle to higher-leverage work, but he's a nice LIMA/holds play at least.

Yr Tm	W	L	Sv	IP	K	ERA	xERA	WHIP	oOPS	vL	vR	BF/G	Ctl	Dom	Cmd	SwK	G	L	F	H%	S%	hr/f	GS	APC	DOM%	DIS%	Sv%	LI	RAR	BPV	BPX	R$
09																																
10																																
11 aa	8	2	3	79	76	2.25	2.06	0.98				4.6	2.2	8.6	3.8					26%	79%								16.5	129	195	$13
12 SD *	4	1	2	58	56	3.17	3.09	1.20	551	475	598	3.9	2.7	8.8	3.2	13%	37	24	39	31%	75%	8%	0	17			40	1.03	6.0	110	144	$3
13 SD *	10	6	1	72	68	2.59	2.81	1.16	525	781	313	4.1	2.8	8.6	3.0	12%	43	23	34	30%	79%	3%	0	16			50	1.08	11.3	108	141	$8
1st Half	6	3	1	36	28	2.37	3.80	1.33	431	701	200	4.4	3.4	7.0	2.1	11%	59	22	19	30%	86%	0%	0	16			50	1.08	6.7	66	86	$8
2nd Half	4	3	0	35	40	2.80	3.01	0.99	552	804	344	4.0	2.3	10.2	4.4	12%	38	24	39	30%	71%	3%	0	16			0	1.08	4.6	137	178	$8
14 Proj	6	3	0	58	57	3.08	3.35	1.14	590	874	356	4.1	2.7	8.8	3.3	12%	38	24	39	30%	74%	5%	0						5.6	101	131	$5

RAY MURPHY

Vogelsong,Ryan

Age: 36	Th: R	Role SP	Health F	LIMA Plan D+	
Ht: 6' 4"	Wt: 215	Type	PT/Exp A	Rand Var +3	
			Consist A	MM 2103	

Got lit up in 1H before getting shelved for three months (broken pitching hand). Upon return, 2H results were much better but skills actually worse. Had been significantly outpitching his skills during 2011-12 resurgence; a return to relevance hinges on him rediscovering that secret sauce. Rostering him is a dart throw.

Yr	Tm	W	L	Sv	IP	K	ERA	xERA	WHIP	oOPS	vL	vR	BF/G	Ctl	Dom	Cmd	SwK	G	L	F	H%	S%	hr/f	GS	APC	DOM%	DIS%	Sv%	LI	RAR	BPV	BPX	R$
09																																	
10	aaa	3	8	1	95	80	5.41	6.48	1.99				13.9	5.9	7.5	1.3					39%	73%								-15.7	40	64	-$12
11	SF	13	7	0	180	139	2.71	3.85	1.25	671	727	626	25.1	3.1	7.0	2.3	8%	46	20	34	29%	81%	8%	28	98	61%	7%	0	0.75	27.4	67	100	$16
12	SF	14	9	0	190	158	3.37	4.02	1.23	688	722	653	25.4	2.9	7.5	2.5	8%	44	18	38	29%	75%	8%	31	99	61%	13%			15.1	78	101	$15
13	SF	4	6	0	104	67	5.73	4.62	1.56	840	736	928	24.6	3.3	5.8	1.8	6%	41	27	32	33%	65%	13%	19	92	26%	32%			-23.8	35	45	-$12
1st Half		2	4	0	46	40	7.19	4.48	1.73	931	883	980	24.2	3.5	7.8	2.2	7%	40	24	36	36%	62%	20%	9	93	22%	33%			-19.0	63	82	-$17
2nd Half		2	2	0	57	27	4.55	4.74	1.43	759	578	889	24.9	3.1	4.2	1.4	5%	42	29	29	30%	68%	7%	10	91	30%	30%			-4.9	11	15	-$9
14	Proj	7	7	0	131	92	4.45	4.24	1.47	786	748	819	22.4	3.4	6.4	1.9	7%	42	22	36	32%	72%	10%	25						-9.4	42	54	-$3

Volquez,Edinson

Age: 30	Th: R	Role SP	Health D	LIMA Plan D+	
Ht: 6' 0"	Wt: 225	Type Pwr	PT/Exp A	Rand Var +5	
			Consist A	MM 2203	

PRO: He actually scraped 2.0 Cmd in 2H, for first time since 2008 breakout. CON: Those Cmd gains came amid a 2nd-half laser show where batters were unloading on him. And unfortunately for him, 2.0 Cmd is no longer the gold standard. We've moved the clip level up to 2.5, and it's unlikely we'll ever see Edinson there. Pass.

Yr	Tm	W	L	Sv	IP	K	ERA	xERA	WHIP	oOPS	vL	vR	BF/G	Ctl	Dom	Cmd	SwK	G	L	F	H%	S%	hr/f	GS	APC	DOM%	DIS%	Sv%	LI	RAR	BPV	BPX	R$
09	CIN	4	2	0	50	47	4.35	4.32	1.33	683	644	715	24.2	5.8	8.5	1.5	10%	45	21	34	23%	70%	14%	9	94	44%	33%			-0.2	20	37	$0
10	CIN *	7	3	0	86	84	3.82	3.55	1.36	739	691	776	22.4	4.6	8.8	1.9	14%	54	15	31	29%	73%	12%	12	92	50%	33%			2.7	79	127	$3
11	CIN *	9	9	0	196	168	4.49	4.64	1.49	833	862	811	25.6	4.4	7.7	1.7	12%	52	18	30	31%	73%	21%	20	98	35%	20%			-13.2	51	77	-$3
12	SD	11	11	0	183	174	4.14	4.14	1.45	706	700	711	25.1	5.2	8.6	1.7	11%	51	21	28	30%	72%	10%	32	101	44%	25%			-2.8	44	57	$1
13	2 NL	9	12	0	170	142	5.71	4.28	1.59	804	836	771	23.5	4.1	7.5	1.8	9%	48	23	30	34%	65%	12%	32	91	25%	28%	0	0.77	-38.7	51	67	-$16
1st Half		6	6	0	93	79	5.50	4.29	1.59	793	866	712	24.9	4.3	7.6	1.8	9%	48	23	29	34%	65%	9%	17	94	24%	24%			-18.8	46	59	-$14
2nd Half		3	6	0	77	63	5.96	4.29	1.58	818	800	835	22.1	3.7	7.4	2.0	9%	47	23	30	34%	64%	15%	15	88	27%	33%	0	0.77	-19.9	57	74	-$18
14	Proj	8	11	0	159	131	4.72	4.20	1.52	746	761	733	23.3	4.7	7.4	1.6	10%	47	20	33	31%	70%	9%	25						-16.8	30	39	-$5

Wacha,Michael

Age: 23	Th: R	Role SP	Health A	LIMA Plan B	
Ht: 6' 6"	Wt: 210	Type Pwr	PT/Exp F	Rand Var -2	
			Consist F	MM 4303	

4-1, 2.78 ERA in 65 IP at STL. 2012 1st-rounder made it to majors in under 12 months, with a big splash. 2nd half Dom gains are backed by big SwK. The big negative in this box is the white space: no track record. He might really be this good, but it's a leap of faith to assume that this is his true skill level.

Yr	Tm	W	L	Sv	IP	K	ERA	xERA	WHIP	oOPS	vL	vR	BF/G	Ctl	Dom	Cmd	SwK	G	L	F	H%	S%	hr/f	GS	APC	DOM%	DIS%	Sv%	LI	RAR	BPV	BPX	R$
09																																	
10																																	
11																																	
12																																	
13	STL *	9	4	0	150	127	2.80	2.71	1.06	603	493	710	19.4	2.2	7.7	3.4	12%	44	17	39	27%	77%	7%	9	69	33%	22%	0	0.66	19.6	104	136	$16
1st Half		5	1	0	75	48	2.98	2.93	1.08	685	518	944	22.6	2.2	5.8	2.6	10%	47	15	38	25%	76%	10%	3	95	67%	33%			8.2	72	94	$14
2nd Half		4	3	0	74	79	2.62	2.48	1.04	571	478	644	16.9	2.3	9.6	4.2	13%	43	18	40	29%	78%	6%	6	63	17%	17%	0	0.64	11.4	136	177	$17
14	Proj	10	6	0	160	147	3.30	3.27	1.15	644	522	773	22.2	2.4	8.3	3.5	12%	45	16	39	30%	74%	8%	33						11.1	109	141	$15

Wainwright,Adam

Age: 32	Th: R	Role SP	Health B	LIMA Plan C	
Ht: 6' 7"	Wt: 235	Type GB	PT/Exp A	Rand Var 0	
			Consist A	MM 5305	

Now here is a track record you can invest in. Put 2011's TJS another year further into his rear-view mirror, with rock-solid skills that are a virtual mirror-image from before and after surgery. 1H Ctl/Cmd likely won't return, but 2H skills are still plenty good. The words "safe" and "starting pitcher" rarely intersect, but they do here.

Yr	Tm	W	L	Sv	IP	K	ERA	xERA	WHIP	oOPS	vL	vR	BF/G	Ctl	Dom	Cmd	SwK	G	L	F	H%	S%	hr/f	GS	APC	DOM%	DIS%	Sv%	LI	RAR	BPV	BPX	R$
09	STL	19	8	0	233	212	2.63	3.43	1.21	646	764	545	28.5	2.5	8.2	3.2	9%	51	19	30	31%	81%	8%	34	106	65%	0%			48.7	108	201	$31
10	STL	20	11	0	230	213	2.42	3.04	1.05	604	575	627	27.6	2.2	8.3	3.8	10%	52	18	31	28%	79%	8%	33	102	82%	3%			47.1	121	195	$34
11																																	
12	STL	14	13	0	199	184	3.94	3.36	1.25	701	724	681	26.0	2.4	8.3	3.5	9%	51	23	26	32%	69%	10%	32	97	69%	13%			1.8	115	151	$11
13	STL	19	9	0	242	219	2.94	2.94	1.07	636	631	639	28.1	1.3	8.2	6.3	10%	49	23	28	31%	74%	8%	34	104	82%	6%			27.5	139	181	$29
1st Half		11	5	0	126	114	2.22	2.80	0.99	601	588	615	28.7	0.9	8.2	9.5	11%	48	25	27	31%	78%	4%	17	104	76%	0%			25.5	150	194	$39
2nd Half		8	4	0	116	105	3.72	3.09	1.15	672	682	663	27.5	1.8	8.1	4.6	9%	50	22	28	31%	70%	12%	17	104	88%	12%			2.0	127	164	$19
14	Proj	16	9	0	203	186	3.17	2.90	1.10	638	651	626	26.6	1.9	8.2	4.4	10%	50	22	28	30%	73%	9%	30						17.4	126	163	$23

Walden,Jordan

Age: 26	Th: R	Role RP	Health D	LIMA Plan A	
Ht: 6' 5"	Wt: 235	Type Pwr FB	PT/Exp C	Rand Var -1	
			Consist A	MM 4511	

Looked like he had taken a leap forward in 1H, but reverted to his "too many walks and fly balls" pitfalls in 2H. Was handled very gently after May DL stint for sore shoulder, it's possible he was never back to 100%. He remains a very live arm that carries some volatility, which he's still young enough to overcome.

Yr	Tm	W	L	Sv	IP	K	ERA	xERA	WHIP	oOPS	vL	vR	BF/G	Ctl	Dom	Cmd	SwK	G	L	F	H%	S%	hr/f	GS	APC	DOM%	DIS%	Sv%	LI	RAR	BPV	BPX	R$
09	aa	1	5	0	60	48	7.00	6.55	1.94				22.0	4.5	7.2	1.6					40%	62%								-19.8	42	79	-$12
10	LAA *	1	2	9	65	57	3.33	4.16	1.50	670	527	803	4.7	4.0	7.9	2.0	14%	60	23	17	34%	78%	17%	0	17			64	1.00	6.0	78	126	$3
11	LAA	5	5	32	60	67	2.98	3.38	1.24	642	650	631	4.1	3.9	10.0	2.6	13%	45	18	37	31%	76%	5%	0	18			76	1.70	7.1	98	148	$17
12	LAA	3	2	1	39	48	3.46	3.68	1.36	674	606	743	3.8	4.2	11.1	2.7	14%	40	25	36	34%	76%	8%	0	16			50	0.61	2.7	105	137	-$1
13	ATL	4	3	1	47	54	3.45	3.53	1.13	620	542	690	3.9	2.7	10.3	3.9	15%	31	18	51	31%	71%	6%	0	16			33	1.23	2.4	123	160	$2
1st Half		3	1	0	27	30	2.63	3.21	0.99	548	471	639	3.9	1.6	9.9	6.0	15%	37	16	47	31%	73%	3%	0	15			0	1.23	4.2	148	192	$5
2nd Half		1	2	1	20	24	4.58	3.99	1.32	719	680	742	3.8	4.1	11.0	2.7	15%	22	20	57	31%	70%	11%	0	16			33	1.22	-1.7	87	113	-$2
14	Proj	5	5	3	73	83	3.48	3.35	1.24	647	592	698	3.9	3.6	10.3	2.9	14%	35	21	45	31%	74%	8%	0						3.4	101	131	$5

Walker,Taijuan

Age: 21	Th: R	Role SP	Health A	LIMA Plan B	
Ht: 6' 4"	Wt: 210	Type Pwr FB	PT/Exp D	Rand Var -2	
			Consist C	MM 3403	

1-0, 3.60 ERA in 15 IP at SEA. Top-10 prospect earned late-season callup after splitting 2013 between Double-A and Triple-A. Brings upper-90s heat and a power curve from his big frame. Still awfully young and the usual perils apply (inconsistency, monitored workloads), but this is a potential gem that's close to being ready.

Yr	Tm	W	L	Sv	IP	K	ERA	xERA	WHIP	oOPS	vL	vR	BF/G	Ctl	Dom	Cmd	SwK	G	L	F	H%	S%	hr/f	GS	APC	DOM%	DIS%	Sv%	LI	RAR	BPV	BPX	R$
09																																	
10																																	
11																																	
12	aa	7	10	0	127	110	5.27	4.37	1.45				21.6	3.5	7.8	2.3					33%	63%								-19.7	71	93	-$7
13	SEA *	10	10	0	156	159	3.15	2.92	1.21	546	536	563	22.5	3.4	9.1	2.7	10%	38	21	40	30%	75%	0%	3	78	33%	0%			13.8	103	135	$12
1st Half		5	7	0	90	92	2.44	2.23	1.06				23.3	3.1	9.2	3.0					27%	79%	0%	0						15.9	115	149	$20
2nd Half		5	3	0	66	67	4.12	3.85	1.41	546	536	563	21.6	3.8	9.1	2.4	10%	38	21	40	34%	71%	0%	3	78	33%	0%			-2.1	89	116	$2
14	Proj	10	11	0	160	159	3.96	3.66	1.30	671	642	727	21.8	3.5	8.9	2.6	10%	38	21	40	31%	70%	6%	30						-1.8	83	107	$7

Warren,Adam

Age: 26	Th: R	Role RP	Health A	LIMA Plan D+	
Ht: 6' 2"	Wt: 200	Type	PT/Exp C	Rand Var -1	
			Consist C	MM 2201	

After rising through minors as a starter, transitioned to bullpen with good effect: punched up his Dom and Cmd, even got more GBs. Those gains were undermined in 2nd half by significant Ctl problems, which temper future optimism, at least for now. But if the guy from the first half re-appears, he's worth owning.

Yr	Tm	W	L	Sv	IP	K	ERA	xERA	WHIP	oOPS	vL	vR	BF/G	Ctl	Dom	Cmd	SwK	G	L	F	H%	S%	hr/f	GS	APC	DOM%	DIS%	Sv%	LI	RAR	BPV	BPX	R$
09																																	
10	aa	4	2	0	54	49	3.84	3.74	1.35				22.7	2.7	8.2	3.0					34%	71%								1.6	100	162	$0
11	aaa	6	8	0	152	91	5.00	5.36	1.58				24.8	3.5	5.4	1.5					32%	70%								-19.8	27	40	-$10
12	NYY *	7	8	0	155	87	5.19	6.13	1.71	1588	1500	1636	26.0	3.0	5.1	1.7	5%	29	29	43	36%	71%	33%	1	77	0%	100%			-22.5	25	33	-$18
13	NYY	3	2	1	77	64	3.39	4.02	1.43	766	896	625	9.7	3.5	7.5	2.1	11%	45	22	32	31%	81%	13%	2	38	50%	50%	100	0.58	4.5	63	82	-$1
1st Half		1	0	1	38	28	3.11	3.55	1.22	701	856	539	11.8	2.2	6.7	3.1	10%	50	23	28	29%	80%	16%	0	47			100	0.64	3.5	90	116	$2
2nd Half		2	2	0	39	36	3.66	4.49	1.63	825	931	704	8.4	4.8	8.2	1.7	12%	41	22	37	34%	81%	11%	2	33	50%	50%	0	0.54	1.0	38	49	-$3
14	Proj	3	3	0	73	54	3.90	4.02	1.42	759	880	626	9.4	3.4	6.7	1.9	12%	45	22	33	31%	76%	11%	0						-0.3	50	65	-$1

RAY MURPHY

Watson,Tony

Age: 29	Th: L	Role	RP	Health	A	LIMA Plan	B
Ht: 6' 4"	Wt: 210	Type		PT/Exp	D	Rand Var	-4
				Consist	A	MM	4201

Got off to slow start, but from mid-June on, allowed just 3 ER, .373 oOPS in 41 IP. Previous year's Dom may not be matched again, but that'll be just fine if Ctl, GB% gains stick. Improvement vs RH a little exaggerated (21% H%), but should continue to rack up holds, and perhaps the occasional save.

Yr Tm	W	L	Sv	IP	K	ERA	xERA	WHIP	oOPS	vL	vR	BF/G	Ctl	Dom	Cmd	SwK	G	L	F	H%	S%	hr/f	GS	APC	DOM%	DIS%	Sv%	LI	RAR	BPV	BPX	R$
09 aa	0	3	0	15	11	10.01	8.83	2.39				16.0	6.4	6.5	1.0					42%	57%								-10.8	3	6	-$
10 aa	6	4	2	111	81	3.27	3.14	1.09				12.8	2.0	6.5	3.3					27%	74%								11.1	88	143	$1
11 PIT *	5	5	0	75	63	3.47	3.42	1.25	711	708	713	4.4	3.7	7.5	2.0	9%	32	24	44	27%	76%	13%	0	15			0	1.28	4.4	68	102	$
12 PIT	5	2	0	53	53	3.38	3.86	1.13	623	554	691	3.2	3.9	8.9	2.3	12%	40	18	42	25%	73%	9%	0	13			0	1.21	4.2	74	97	$
13 PIT	3	1	2	72	54	2.39	3.44	0.88	544	483	582	4.2	1.5	6.8	4.5	12%	44	19	37	24%	76%	7%	0	16			50	1.14	13.1	103	135	$
1st Half	2	1	2	40	33	3.57	3.71	0.97	620	543	662	4.7	2.2	7.4	3.3	12%	38	18	44	24%	66%	8%	0	18			67	1.01	1.5	88	115	$
2nd Half	1	0	0	31	21	0.86	3.10	0.77	444	420	462	3.7	0.6	6.0	10.5	12%	51	20	30	24%	91%	4%	0	14			0	1.28	11.6	122	157	$1
14 Proj	**4**	**2**	**0**	**74**	**60**	**3.15**	**3.43**	**1.12**	**649**	**605**	**682**	**4.1**	**2.3**	**7.3**	**3.1**	**12%**	**44**	**19**	**37**	**28%**	**74%**	**8%**	**0**						**6.5**	**90**	**117**	**$**

Weaver,Jered

Age: 31	Th: R	Role	SP	Health	C	LIMA Plan	C+
Ht: 6' 7"	Wt: 210	Type	xFB	PT/Exp	A	Rand Var	-1
				Consist	A	MM	3205

Broken bone in left elbow cost him better part of first two months. Upon return, had just one PQS-DIS in 22 starts, and once again bested xERA by wide margin, as H%, hr/f continued to cooperate. Fastball velocity has dipped three straight years though, and may start affecting his ability to outpitch these skills.

Yr Tm	W	L	Sv	IP	K	ERA	xERA	WHIP	oOPS	vL	vR	BF/G	Ctl	Dom	Cmd	SwK	G	L	F	H%	S%	hr/f	GS	APC	DOM%	DIS%	Sv%	LI	RAR	BPV	BPX	R$
09 LAA	16	8	0	211	174	3.75	4.38	1.24	723	812	615	26.7	2.8	7.4	2.6	10%	31	19	50	29%	74%	8%	33	103	58%	15%			14.8	67	125	$1
10 LAA	13	12	0	224	233	3.01	3.46	1.07	622	593	653	26.6	2.2	9.3	4.3	12%	36	16	48	29%	76%	8%	34	109	79%	6%			29.6	124	200	$2
11 LAA	18	8	0	236	198	2.41	3.75	1.01	598	578	621	28.1	2.1	7.6	3.5	10%	32	19	49	26%	80%	6%	33	114	79%	6%			44.7	88	133	$3
12 LAA	20	5	0	189	142	2.81	4.01	1.02	605	541	690	24.6	2.1	6.8	3.2	9%	36	21	43	25%	77%	9%	30	95	60%	17%			27.9	78	102	$2
13 LAA	11	8	0	154	117	3.27	4.17	1.14	671	638	725	26.4	2.2	6.8	3.2	10%	31	22	47	28%	75%	8%	24	100	63%	8%			11.4	74	96	$1
1st Half	1	4	0	48	36	4.15	4.43	1.26	738	784	686	25.0	2.6	6.8	2.6	12%	29	22	49	29%	70%	8%	8	95	50%	13%			-1.7	58	75	-$
2nd Half	10	4	0	107	81	2.87	4.06	1.09	641	584	750	27.1	1.9	6.8	3.5	10%	32	23	46	27%	78%	8%	16	102	69%	6%			13.1	80	104	$1
14 Proj	**15**	**8**	**0**	**189**	**143**	**3.43**	**3.81**	**1.14**	**671**	**643**	**709**	**25.6**	**2.2**	**6.8**	**3.1**	**10%**	**33**	**21**	**46**	**28%**	**74%**	**8%**	**29**						**10.2**	**74**	**96**	**$1**

Webb,Ryan

Age: 28	Th: R	Role	RP	Health	C	LIMA Plan	B+
Ht: 6' 6"	Wt: 245	Type	GB	PT/Exp	C	Rand Var	-2
				Consist	A	MM	3100

Struggled out of the gate, but closed out season with 25:5 K:BB ratio over final 34.1 IP. Hard sinker has made the long ball a non-issue, and he's been pretty effective against RH bats. But with a history of subpar Cmd and no out pitch vs LH (1.5 career Cmd), it's doubtful that saves or fantasy relevance are in his future.

Yr Tm	W	L	Sv	IP	K	ERA	xERA	WHIP	oOPS	vL	vR	BF/G	Ctl	Dom	Cmd	SwK	G	L	F	H%	S%	hr/f	GS	APC	DOM%	DIS%	Sv%	LI	RAR	BPV	BPX	R$
09 SD *	9	2	2	75	56	4.23	4.99	1.57	771	889	662	5.3	3.2	6.7	2.1	9%	57	18	25	36%	74%	14%	0	16			50	0.88	0.8	59	110	$
10 SD *	4	1	1	80	64	2.37	3.11	1.26	680	846	566	4.6	2.7	7.2	2.7	9%	62	21	17	32%	81%	3%	0	18			33	0.80	16.8	97	158	$6
11 FLA	2	4	0	51	31	3.20	3.81	1.34	693	771	627	4.0	3.6	5.5	1.6	8%	61	17	22	29%	76%	6%	0	14			0	1.15	4.7	42	63	$0
12 MIA	4	3	0	60	44	4.03	4.03	1.52	749	809	706	4.2	3.0	6.6	2.2	7%	52	27	21	36%	72%	5%	0	16			0	1.03	-0.1	68	88	-$4
13 MIA	2	6	0	80	54	2.91	3.74	1.21	695	714	681	5.0	3.0	6.0	2.0	9%	56	19	25	27%	77%	8%	0	18			0	1.20	9.4	61	80	$2
1st Half	1	3	0	36	22	3.22	4.44	1.35	725	830	627	4.6	4.2	5.4	1.3	9%	50	22	29	28%	75%	3%	0	17			0	1.24	2.9	12	15	$0
2nd Half	1	3	0	44	32	2.66	3.20	1.09	671	598	717	5.5	2.0	6.5	3.2	10%	62	17	21	27%	80%	14%	0	20			0	1.15	6.5	102	133	$5
14 Proj	**3**	**4**	**0**	**69**	**47**	**3.52**	**3.65**	**1.32**	**710**	**758**	**674**	**4.5**	**3.0**	**6.2**	**2.1**	**8%**	**54**	**22**	**25**	**30%**	**73%**	**7%**	**0**						**3.0**	**62**	**80**	**$0**

Webster,Allen

Age: 24	Th: R	Role	SP	Health	A	LIMA Plan	D+
Ht: 6' 2"	Wt: 190	Type	Pwr FB	PT/Exp	D	Rand Var	+5
				Consist	B	MM	2300

1-2, 8.60 ERA in 30 IP at BOS. Ctl has been an issue in upper level of minors, and was too much to overcome in first taste of majors. LH crushed him: he allowed seven HR while striking out just eight. Long-term future still bright, but more minor league seasoning may be in order.

Yr Tm	W	L	Sv	IP	K	ERA	xERA	WHIP	oOPS	vL	vR	BF/G	Ctl	Dom	Cmd	SwK	G	L	F	H%	S%	hr/f	GS	APC	DOM%	DIS%	Sv%	LI	RAR	BPV	BPX	R$
09																																
10																																
11 aa	6	3	0	91	64	4.96	4.50	1.48				21.7	3.1	6.3	2.0					34%	66%								-11.4	60	90	-$4
12 aa	6	9	0	131	110	5.11	4.85	1.70				20.4	4.4	7.6	1.7					38%	67%								-17.7	72	94	-$14
13 BOS *	9	6	0	135	120	5.43	3.93	1.35	926	1253	550	19.4	4.1	8.0	1.9	13%	43	21	36	28%	61%	19%	7	67	29%	57%	0	0.71	-26.1	62	81	-$5
1st Half	5	3	0	71	65	5.09	4.11	1.30	998	1278	695	19.6	3.8	8.2	2.1	14%	50	13	37	27%	65%	22%	4	80	25%	50%			-10.7	58	75	-$2
2nd Half	4	3	0	64	55	5.82	3.74	1.39	815	1207	304	19.3	4.4	7.7	1.8	11%	33	33	35	29%	57%	14%	3	54	33%	67%	0	0.62	-15.4	67	87	-$8
14 Proj	**3**	**3**	**0**	**58**	**49**	**4.64**	**4.32**	**1.53**	**698**	**854**	**529**	**20.2**	**4.4**	**7.6**	**1.7**	**14%**	**43**	**18**	**39**	**31%**	**74%**	**12%**	**12**						**-5.6**	**39**	**51**	**-$4**

Westbrook,Jake

Age: 36	Th: R	Role	SP	Health	D	LIMA Plan	D+
Ht: 6' 3"	Wt: 210	Type	Con xGB	PT/Exp	A	Rand Var	-1
				Consist	B	MM	2001

Extreme groundballer has had some past success despite low Dom, but not this low. Somehow posted 1.76 ERA in first eight starts, but then it got ugly. Similar skills the rest of the way led to 6.85 ERA. August back strain may have played role in 2H collapse, but even so, probably best to wait and see if Dom can rebound.

Yr Tm	W	L	Sv	IP	K	ERA	xERA	WHIP	oOPS	vL	vR	BF/G	Ctl	Dom	Cmd	SwK	G	L	F	H%	S%	hr/f	GS	APC	DOM%	DIS%	Sv%	LI	RAR	BPV	BPX	R$
09																																
10 2 TM	10	11	0	203	128	4.22	3.90	1.34	727	767	694	26.1	3.0	5.7	1.9	8%	56	17	26	29%	70%	12%	33	101	36%	18%			-3.5	55	89	$4
11 STL	12	9	0	183	104	4.66	4.17	1.53	789	734	838	24.5	3.6	5.1	1.4	7%	59	18	23	32%	70%	11%	33	93	27%	36%			-16.3	32	48	-$6
12 STL	13	11	0	175	106	3.97	3.97	1.39	729	780	683	26.8	2.7	5.5	2.0	8%	58	21	21	32%	72%	10%	28	96	39%	21%			1.0	62	81	$2
13 STL	7	8	0	117	44	4.63	4.87	1.56	774	884	680	24.9	3.9	3.4	0.9	6%	56	20	23	30%	70%	7%	19	89	11%	26%	0	0.80	-11.0	-9	-12	-$8
1st Half	4	3	0	61	27	2.95	4.39	1.46	745	936	575	26.2	3.8	4.0	1.0	6%	60	20	20	30%	79%	5%	10	95	20%	30%			6.9	6	8	$0
2nd Half	3	5	0	56	17	6.47	5.40	1.67	804	830	781	23.7	3.9	2.7	0.7	5%	52	21	26	31%	60%	9%	9	83	0%	22%	0	0.79	-17.9	-25	-32	-$17
14 Proj	**6**	**7**	**0**	**102**	**49**	**4.64**	**4.30**	**1.50**	**764**	**818**	**718**	**24.7**	**3.4**	**4.3**	**1.3**	**7%**	**57**	**20**	**23**	**31%**	**69%**	**9%**	**18**						**-9.7**	**20**	**26**	**-$5**

Wheeler,Zack

Age: 24	Th: R	Role	SP	Health	A	LIMA Plan	C+
Ht: 6' 4"	Wt: 185	Type	Pwr	PT/Exp	D	Rand Var	0
				Consist	C	MM	3305

7-5, 3.42 ERA in 100 IP at NYM. An up-and-down first month in majors was followed by eight PQS-DOM scores in 10-start span. Ctl is a work in progress, and he needs out-pitch vs LH, against whom he had a 1.2 Cmd. That said, future #1 starter could make strides quickly... UP: 16 Wins, 3.00 ERA.

Yr Tm	W	L	Sv	IP	K	ERA	xERA	WHIP	oOPS	vL	vR	BF/G	Ctl	Dom	Cmd	SwK	G	L	F	H%	S%	hr/f	GS	APC	DOM%	DIS%	Sv%	LI	RAR	BPV	BPX	R$
09																																
10																																
11																																
12 a/a	12	8	0	149	132	3.44	2.58	1.19				23.9	3.3	8.0	2.4					29%	69%								10.5	101	132	$12
13 NYM *	11	7	0	169	148	3.38	3.58	1.29	696	766	639	23.1	3.7	7.9	2.2	9%	43	23	33	29%	77%	10%	17	102	59%	12%			10.2	72	94	$9
1st Half	5	3	0	85	77	3.64	3.56	1.24	797	847	766	21.5	3.5	8.1	2.4	8%	38	21	42	28%	75%	15%	3	100	33%	33%			2.3	74	96	$9
2nd Half	6	4	0	84	71	3.11	4.02	1.33	677	753	611	25.6	3.9	7.6	2.0	9%	44	24	32	29%	79%	9%	14	102	64%	7%			7.9	55	71	$9
14 Proj	**13**	**8**	**0**	**181**	**159**	**3.52**	**3.68**	**1.26**	**661**	**714**	**622**	**23.6**	**3.6**	**7.9**	**2.2**	**9%**	**42**	**23**	**36**	**29%**	**74%**	**9%**	**31**						**7.8**	**66**	**85**	**$13**

White,Alex

Age: 25	Th: R	Role	SP	Health	F	LIMA Plan	D+
Ht: 6' 3"	Wt: 215	Type		PT/Exp	D	Rand Var	0
				Consist	A	MM	1100

Underwent TJ surgery in April, putting 2014 status in doubt. Progress of former first round pick may be worth monitoring as a potential end-game flyer, but "skills" when we last saw him leave a lot to be desired. Escaping Coors Field may not cure all ills, either, as he has a 6.15 career ERA and 1.2 Cmd on the road.

Yr Tm	W	L	Sv	IP	K	ERA	xERA	WHIP	oOPS	vL	vR	BF/G	Ctl	Dom	Cmd	SwK	G	L	F	H%	S%	hr/f	GS	APC	DOM%	DIS%	Sv%	LI	RAR	BPV	BPX	R$
09																																
10 aa	8	7	0	107	66	2.44	3.10	1.16				23.6	2.2	5.5	2.5					28%	81%								21.6	74	120	$11
11 2 TM *	5	5	0	91	67	4.73	4.83	1.35	988	1036	954	21.1	3.0	6.6	2.2	9%	46	14	40	28%	71%	22%	10	91	20%	50%			-8.9	38	57	-$2
12 COL *	5	13	0	159	99	5.02	4.97	1.57	854	833	880	20.5	4.2	5.6	1.4	8%	54	21	24	31%	69%	16%	20	78	10%	70%	0	0.72	-19.7	32	42	-$13
13																																
1st Half																																
2nd Half																																
14 Proj	**2**	**3**	**0**	**44**	**28**	**4.76**	**4.49**	**1.55**	**821**	**822**	**820**	**22.8**	**3.9**	**5.8**	**1.5**	**9%**	**45**	**20**	**35**	**31%**	**72%**	**12%**	**8**						**-4.8**	**23**	**30**	**-$5**

BRIAN RUDD

Wilhelmsen,Tom

Age: 30	Th: R	Role RP	Health	A	LIMA Plan C+
Ht: 6' 6"	Wt: 220	Type Pwr	PT/Exp	B	Rand Var -3
			Consist	C	MM 3310

Don't just look at the saves column; it tells a deceptive tale. Skills have been sliding since 1H of 2012, when he posted a 4.5 Cmd and 155 BPV. Steadily rising Ctl and erratic Dom have led to his downfall. Still has some useful skills—like the ability to get out RH hitters—but there are too many issues to reclaim a bigger role.

Yr Tm	W	L	Sv	IP	K	ERA	xERA	WHIP	oOPS	vL	vR	BF/G	Ctl	Dom	Cmd	SwK	G	L	F	H%	S%	hr/f	GS	APC	DOM%	DIS%	Sv%	LI	RAR	BPV	BPX	R$
09																																
10																																
11 SEA *	6	5	0	93	62	5.55	5.13	1.58	580	508	651	10.5	4.0	6.0	1.5	12%	34	21	45	32%	66%	5%	0	20			0	0.59	-18.5	34	51	-$8
12 SEA	4	3	29	79	87	2.50	3.37	1.11	578	637	519	4.5	3.3	9.9	3.0	12%	48	16	35	28%	80%	7%	0	17			85	1.38	14.9	115	150	$20
13 SEA	0	3	24	59	45	4.12	4.54	1.32	603	743	468	4.3	5.0	6.9	1.4	11%	43	23	34	26%	67%	4%	0	17			83	1.13	-1.8	9	11	$6
1st Half	0	2	16	35	27	3.89	4.25	1.13	541	635	446	4.2	4.4	7.0	1.6	10%	44	20	36	22%	65%	6%	0	16			76	1.04	-0.1	29	38	$11
2nd Half	0	1	8	24	18	4.44	4.98	1.60	685	895	497	4.4	5.9	6.7	1.1	12%	42	27	31	31%	69%	0%	0	18			100	1.25	-1.7	-20	-25	-$1
14 Proj	2	3	3	58	50	3.82	3.95	1.33	669	759	581	4.7	4.4	7.8	1.8	12%	44	21	36	28%	73%	8%	0						0.3	42	54	$0

Williams,Jerome

Age: 32	Th: R	Role SP	Health	C	LIMA Plan D+
Ht: 6' 3"	Wt: 240	Type	PT/Exp	B	Rand Var +1
			Consist	B	MM 2101

2nd half DOM/DIS shows that he's not succeeding as SP, and the splits back that up. As Starter: 139 IP, 5.06 ERA, 1.48 WHIP, 1.8 Cmd. As Reliever: 31 IP, 2.35 ERA, 0.98 WHIP, 2.8 Cmd. Similar results in 2012. GB% remains a plus, but hr/f remains stubbornly high. The odds of a step forward at this age are minimal.

Yr Tm	W	L	Sv	IP	K	ERA	xERA	WHIP	oOPS	vL	vR	BF/G	Ctl	Dom	Cmd	SwK	G	L	F	H%	S%	hr/f	GS	APC	DOM%	DIS%	Sv%	LI	RAR	BPV	BPX	R$
09 aaa	5	6	0	102	39	6.83	6.87	1.83				17.5	3.9	3.4	0.9					34%	64%								-31.5	-15	-28	-$16
10																																
11 LAA *	11	2	0	118	72	3.95	4.87	1.40	769	628	911	23.7	2.3	5.5	2.4	11%	50	16	34	32%	76%	13%	6	68	50%	17%	0	0.82	-0.1	45	68	$2
12 LAA	6	8	1	138	98	4.58	3.79	1.26	743	747	738	17.9	2.3	6.4	2.8	10%	54	18	28	30%	66%	14%	15	64	40%	20%	100	0.67	-9.5	86	112	$0
13 LAA	9	10	0	169	107	4.57	4.30	1.39	772	818	716	19.7	2.9	5.7	1.9	10%	47	21	32	30%	70%	13%	25	71	28%	32%	0	0.74	-14.7	48	63	-$4
1st Half	5	3	0	84	53	3.21	4.06	1.19	693	717	670	17.2	2.5	5.7	2.3	11%	45	21	33	27%	78%	11%	9	61	44%	22%	0	0.71	6.7	59	77	$8
2nd Half	4	7	0	85	54	5.91	4.53	1.59	845	892	771	22.6	3.4	5.7	1.7	9%	49	21	30	33%	65%	15%	16	83	19%	38%	0	0.76	-21.5	38	49	-$16
14 Proj	7	7	0	125	78	4.55	4.22	1.45	803	812	793	22.5	3.0	5.6	1.9	10%	46	19	35	31%	72%	12%	27						-10.5	43	56	-$3

Wilson,C.J.

Age: 33	Th: L	Role SP	Health	A	LIMA Plan C+
Ht: 6' 1"	Wt: 210	Type Pwr	PT/Exp	A	Rand Var -1
			Consist	A	MM 3305

Off-season elbow surgery could have caused early bout of wildness (5.3 Ctl in five April starts). 2nd half ERA looks nice, but xERA shows there really wasn't major skills improvement. While he keeps the ball on the ground and dominates lefties, marginal Dom limits his upside. He's reliable, but very average.

Yr Tm	W	L	Sv	IP	K	ERA	xERA	WHIP	oOPS	vL	vR	BF/G	Ctl	Dom	Cmd	SwK	G	L	F	H%	S%	hr/f	GS	APC	DOM%	DIS%	Sv%	LI	RAR	BPV	BPX	R$
09 TEX	5	6	14	74	84	2.81	3.15	1.33	651	556	701	4.4	3.9	10.3	2.6	11%	55	20	25	34%	79%	6%	0	18			78	1.12	13.7	112	210	$12
10 TEX	15	8	0	204	170	3.35	3.88	1.25	622	400	679	25.8	4.1	7.5	1.8	7%	49	17	34	27%	73%	5%	33	104	45%	12%			18.3	51	83	$16
11 TEX	16	7	0	223	206	2.94	3.34	1.19	651	658	650	26.9	3.0	8.3	2.8	9%	49	19	32	29%	77%	8%	34	106	59%	15%			27.6	96	144	$23
12 LAA	13	10	0	202	173	3.83	4.07	1.34	684	590	713	25.4	4.0	7.7	1.9	8%	50	20	30	29%	74%	11%	34	101	47%	12%			4.7	57	75	$8
13 LAA	17	7	0	212	188	3.39	3.94	1.34	684	485	741	27.7	3.6	8.0	2.2	9%	44	22	33	31%	76%	7%	33	111	48%	9%			12.4	68	89	$12
1st Half	8	5	0	107	99	3.63	3.82	1.35	693	639	706	27.2	3.8	8.4	2.2	10%	48	21	31	31%	75%	9%	17	108	41%	6%			3.1	74	95	$11
2nd Half	9	2	0	106	89	3.15	4.05	1.33	674	358	778	28.2	3.4	7.6	2.2	8%	41	24	35	31%	77%	5%	16	113	56%	13%			9.3	64	82	$13
14 Proj	15	8	0	203	178	3.60	3.71	1.34	692	537	740	26.8	3.6	7.9	2.2	8%	45	21	34	31%	75%	8%	32						6.7	67	87	$11

Wilson,Justin

Age: 26	Th: L	Role RP	Health	A	LIMA Plan B
Ht: 6' 2"	Wt: 195	Type Pwr GB	PT/Exp	D	Rand Var -5
			Consist	B	MM 3201

With a 95 mph fastball and a GB bent, there's something here. xERA says it's not a 2.00 ERA-something; that was thanks to H% and S%. Continued success will depend on whether he's put his history of wildness behind him. But with good results vs LH hitters, he's carved out a niche.

Yr Tm	W	L	Sv	IP	K	ERA	xERA	WHIP	oOPS	vL	vR	BF/G	Ctl	Dom	Cmd	SwK	G	L	F	H%	S%	hr/f	GS	APC	DOM%	DIS%	Sv%	LI	RAR	BPV	BPX	R$
09																																
10 aa	11	8	0	143	108	3.64	3.14	1.36				22.1	4.4	6.8	1.6					29%	72%								7.8	74	119	$6
11 aaa	10	8	3	124	73	4.84	5.10	1.64				18.5	4.7	5.3	1.1					31%	71%								-13.7	28	41	-$6
12 PIT *	9	6	0	140	113	4.69	3.58	1.35	1111	1053	1161	15.8	4.5	7.3	1.6	10%	20	53	27	28%	66%	0%	0	13			0	0.43	-11.7	63	82	-$1
13 PIT	6	1	0	74	59	2.08	3.59	1.06	543	501	563	5.1	3.4	7.2	2.1	10%	53	17	30	24%	82%	7%	0	21			0	1.11	16.3	68	89	$8
1st Half	5	1	0	45	39	2.18	3.36	1.04	548	622	517	6.0	3.8	7.7	2.1	10%	57	17	27	22%	82%	10%	0	24			0	1.21	9.4	72	93	$11
2nd Half	1	0	0	28	20	1.91	3.94	1.09	535	361	641	4.1	2.9	6.4	2.2	9%	48	18	34	26%	83%	3%	0	16			0	1.00	6.8	63	82	$4
14 Proj	5	2	0	73	56	3.64	3.74	1.30	656	550	711	7.5	3.6	7.0	1.9	10%	52	17	31	29%	72%	7%	0						2.0	57	75	$2

Withrow,Chris

Age: 25	Th: R	Role RP	Health	B	LIMA Plan B+
Ht: 6' 4"	Wt: 215	Type Pwr xFB	PT/Exp	D	Rand Var -2
			Consist	C	MM 3400

3-0, 2.60 ERA in 35 IP at LA. Wasn't doing much as a starter, and was stuck at AA for four years; the light bulb came on when he was switched to the pen. Apparently 96 mph gas works better in limited quantities, especially when combined with high SwK. Be careful, though—S% and past results scream regression.

Yr Tm	W	L	Sv	IP	K	ERA	xERA	WHIP	oOPS	vL	vR	BF/G	Ctl	Dom	Cmd	SwK	G	L	F	H%	S%	hr/f	GS	APC	DOM%	DIS%	Sv%	LI	RAR	BPV	BPX	R$
09 aa	2	2	0	27	24	4.52	3.77	1.36				19.0	3.6	7.9	2.2					31%	67%								-0.7	78	145	-$2
10 aa	4	9	0	130	107	5.86	5.02	1.61				21.3	4.1	7.4	1.8					35%	63%								-28.4	56	91	-$10
11 aa	6	6	0	129	112	4.17	3.53	1.41				21.7	4.6	7.9	1.7					30%	70%								-3.6	75	113	$0
12 aa	3	3	2	60	55	5.35	4.17	1.57				12.0	5.4	8.2	1.5					33%	64%								-9.9	71	92	-$7
13 LA *	7	0	1	61	71	2.20	2.77	1.17	536	533	538	4.8	3.7	10.4	2.8	12%	36	21	44	29%	85%	15%	0	23			33	1.51	12.5	112	146	$7
1st Half	4	0	0	29	31	2.44	3.94	1.55	733	667	788	4.6	4.0	9.4	2.3	2%	29	43	29	38%	83%	0%	0	20			0	0.69	5.2	105	135	$3
2nd Half	3	0	1	32	40	1.99	1.68	0.82	501	501	501	5.0	3.4	11.3	3.3	14%	38	16	47	15%	90%	17%	0	24			100	1.66	7.3	123	160	$11
14 Proj	5	2	0	58	60	3.65	3.88	1.32	608	713	551	5.7	4.3	9.3	2.2	13%	37	16	47	30%	74%	6%	0						1.5	67	88	$1

Wolf,Ross

Age: 31	Th: R	Role RP	Health	A	LIMA Plan D+
Ht: 6' 0"	Wt: 180	Type Con	PT/Exp	D	Rand Var -1
			Consist	B	MM 2000

1-3, 4.15 ERA in 48 IP at TEX. Pulled a neat trick in 1st half in majors: 1.27 ERA despite a single-digit BPV. (Thanks, 88% S%). Looking under the hood, the issues are obvious. Low Dom; LD% and OPS vLHB say that he was whacked around like a pinata. Age and a lack of a successful track record say it's best to stay away.

Yr Tm	W	L	Sv	IP	K	ERA	xERA	WHIP	oOPS	vL	vR	BF/G	Ctl	Dom	Cmd	SwK	G	L	F	H%	S%	hr/f	GS	APC	DOM%	DIS%	Sv%	LI	RAR	BPV	BPX	R$
09 aaa	4	2	1	82	54	6.05	5.13	1.62				7.7	4.2	6.0	1.4					33%	62%								-17.5	37	70	-$7
10 OAK *	0	3	3	61	37	3.30	3.73	1.39	741	945	569	5.6	3.6	5.5	1.6	7%	54	13	33	30%	76%	8%	0	20			50	0.36	5.8	56	91	$0
11 aaa	4	3	3	74	42	6.09	6.16	1.83				6.1	3.7	5.1	1.4					38%	65%								-19.5	30	44	-$11
12 a/a	3	1	10	62	41	4.53	5.61	1.58				5.5	2.5	6.0	2.4					35%	74%								-4.0	46	59	-$2
13 TEX *	2	5	0	85	40	3.62	4.69	1.49	797	920	637	12.2	2.9	4.3	1.5	6%	47	27	26	32%	77%	11%	3	31	0%	33%	0	0.69	2.5	32	42	-$4
1st Half	2	3	0	57	25	2.40	3.66	1.36	575	535	610	14.9	2.7	3.9	1.5	5%	50	26	24	30%	82%	0%	1	31	0%	0%	0	1.09	10.3	46	60	$0
2nd Half	0	2	0	28	16	6.11	6.77	1.76	959	1155	663	9.2	3.3	5.1	1.5	7%	45	27	27	35%	68%	19%	2	31	0%	50%	0	0.41	-7.7	3	4	-$13
14 Proj	1	1	0	22	12	4.81	4.23	1.52	784	913	614	7.4	3.1	5.2	1.7	6%	47	27	26	32%	70%	12%	0						-2.5	36	46	-$4

Wood,Alex

Age: 23	Th: L	Role SP	Health	A	LIMA Plan B
Ht: 6' 4"	Wt: 215	Type Pwr GB	PT/Exp	F	Rand Var -3
			Consist	F	MM 4403

3-3, 3.13 ERA in 78 IP at ATL. 2012 second rounder flew through minors and dominated early, with four PQS-DOM outings in four starts in August. But the workload caught up with him as he was cuffed around in September. With high GB% and solid Cmd, the foundation is here for sustained success. Invest.

Yr Tm	W	L	Sv	IP	K	ERA	xERA	WHIP	oOPS	vL	vR	BF/G	Ctl	Dom	Cmd	SwK	G	L	F	H%	S%	hr/f	GS	APC	DOM%	DIS%	Sv%	LI	RAR	BPV	BPX	R$
09																																
10																																
11																																
12																																
13 ATL *	8	5	0	140	132	2.44	2.84	1.22	670	622	690	13.4	2.8	8.5	3.0	10%	49	24	27	32%	80%	5%	11	42	36%	45%	0	0.60	24.6	113	147	$13
1st Half	4	4	0	71	70	1.92	2.36	1.15	628	556	669	13.4	2.8	8.9	3.1	15%	60	23	17	31%	83%	0%	1	23	0%	100%	0	0.41	16.9	124	161	$17
2nd Half	4	1	0	69	62	3.03	3.43	1.31	679	639	694	13.6	2.9	8.1	2.8	9%	47	24	29	33%	77%	6%	10	53	40%	40%	0	0.71	7.1	100	129	$9
14 Proj	9	5	0	157	147	3.37	3.24	1.22	587	533	609	22.4	2.8	8.4	3.0	9%	47	24	29	31%	73%	8%	27						9.7	100	130	$12

DAVE ADLER

Wood,Travis

Age: 27	Th: L	Role SP	Health A
Ht: 5' 11"	Wt: 175	Type FB	PT/Exp B
			Consist B
LIMA Plan D+	Rand Var -4	MM 2205	

Falling ERA and nice DOM/DIS scores—signs of a young pitcher figuring it out, right? Maybe—but H%, S%, and hr/f sure helped. Cmd and G/L/F have been the same for three years; BPV over that span shows this isn't a special skill set. While others bid him up, keep regression in mind; set expectations to his 2012/13 xERA.

Yr	Tm	W	L	Sv	IP	K	ERA	xERA	WHIP	oOPS	vL	vR	BF/G	Ctl	Dom	Cmd	SwK	G	L	F	H%	S%	hr/f	GS	APC	DOM%	DIS%	Sv%	LI	RAR	BPV	BPX	R$
09	a/a	13	5	0	168	119	2.25	2.77	1.18				24.8	3.0	6.4	2.1					27%	82%								42.8	80	149	$23
10	CIN *	10	10	0	203	171	3.54	3.27	1.15	616	446	651	24.4	2.2	7.6	3.4	8%	31	21	48	29%	72%	6%	17	95	59%	12%			13.4	98	158	$16
11	CIN *	8	9	0	158	116	5.26	5.21	1.56	813	807	815	21.7	3.2	6.6	2.0	7%	32	22	45	34%	67%	7%	18	81	33%	22%	0	0.79	-25.7	49	73	-$10
12	CHC *	9	16	0	197	151	4.47	4.25	1.28	745	614	779	24.5	3.0	6.9	2.3	7%	34	22	44	28%	70%	13%	26	96	46%	15%			-11.2	53	69	$2
13	CHC	9	12	0	200	144	3.11	4.34	1.15	643	599	656	25.7	3.0	6.5	2.2	8%	33	22	44	26%	76%	7%	32	97	66%	16%			18.8	47	62	$15
1st Half		5	6	0	104	75	2.85	4.14	1.00	567	396	622	25.7	2.8	6.5	2.3	9%	34	20	45	23%	74%	6%	16	97	75%	0%			13.1	54	70	$22
2nd Half		4	6	0	96	69	3.39	4.56	1.31	719	815	690	25.6	3.2	6.5	2.0	8%	32	24	44	29%	77%	8%	16	96	56%	31%			5.7	41	53	$8
14	**Proj**	**9**	**13**	**0**	**195**	**144**	**3.96**	**4.15**	**1.30**	**742**	**686**	**758**	**25.4**	**3.0**	**6.7**	**2.2**	**8%**	**33**	**22**	**45**	**29%**	**72%**	**8%**	**29**						**-2.3**	**50**	**65**	**$6**

Worley,Vance

Age: 26	Th: R	Role SP	Health C
Ht: 6' 2"	Wt: 230	Type Con	PT/Exp C
			Consist D
LIMA Plan D+	Rand Var +3	MM 2003	

1-5, 7.21 ERA in 49 IP at MIN. 2011's success seems long ago. Bone spurs hurt his 2012 results, but don't explain the 2013 debacle. See that 2011/12 Dom spike? SwK said it wasn't going to last, and it didn't. His luck will turn around as H% and hr/f regress, but when you start this low, even that won't make him rosterable.

Yr	Tm	W	L	Sv	IP	K	ERA	xERA	WHIP	oOPS	vL	vR	BF/G	Ctl	Dom	Cmd	SwK	G	L	F	H%	S%	hr/f	GS	APC	DOM%	DIS%	Sv%	LI	RAR	BPV	BPX	R$
09	aa	7	12	0	153	87	6.48	5.39	1.53				24.7	2.9	5.1	1.8					33%	58%								-40.9	28	52	-$12
10	PHI *	11	8	0	171	112	3.79	4.40	1.41	512	500	520	22.6	2.6	5.9	2.3	7%	45	15	39	32%	74%	8%	2	41	0%	0%	0	0.40	6.1	58	94	$5
11	PHI *	16	5	0	182	161	2.99	3.39	1.23	673	570	775	21.7	2.9	7.9	2.7	6%	39	24	37	30%	79%	7%	21	87	71%	14%	0	0.80	21.5	88	133	$17
12	PHI	6	9	0	133	107	4.20	4.16	1.51	806	847	764	25.7	3.2	7.2	2.3	6%	46	24	30	35%	74%	10%	23	95	39%	22%			-3.0	68	89	-$5
13	MIN *	7	8	0	107	52	5.78	6.56	1.79	1004	1013	994	25.9	2.8	4.4	1.6	4%	47	22	31	37%	68%	16%	10	92	10%	40%			-25.2	15	19	-$17
1st Half		5	8	0	95	47	5.69	6.60	1.77	1004	1013	994	25.7	2.3	4.4	1.9	4%	47	22	31	38%	69%	16%		92	10%	40%			-21.5	21	27	-$18
2nd Half		2	0	0	11	5	6.57	6.21	1.99				27.2	6.7	3.7	0.6					33%	66%	0%							-3.8	4	6	-$6
14	**Proj**	**8**	**8**	**0**	**131**	**77**	**4.51**	**4.35**	**1.53**	**803**	**784**	**823**	**24.1**	**2.9**	**5.3**	**1.8**	**5%**	**44**	**23**	**33**	**33%**	**72%**	**9%**	**24**						**-10.3**	**39**	**50**	**-$5**

Wright,Jamey

Age: 39	Th: R	Role RP	Health A
Ht: 6' 6"	Wt: 235	Type Pwr xGB	PT/Exp C
			Consist A
LIMA Plan B+	Rand Var -1	MM 4301	

With the best Cmd of his career, has this (very) old dog learned new tricks? He basically abandoned the fastball and used his cutter a lot more. Seemed to work—surge in Dom supported by SwK, Ctl has never been this good, and dominated RH hitters. Even a drop in GB% didn't hurt. Shame he didn't learn this ten years ago.

Yr	Tm	W	L	Sv	IP	K	ERA	xERA	WHIP	oOPS	vL	vR	BF/G	Ctl	Dom	Cmd	SwK	G	L	F	H%	S%	hr/f	GS	APC	DOM%	DIS%	Sv%	LI	RAR	BPV	BPX	R$
09	KC	3	5	0	79	60	4.33	4.19	1.48	726	634	800	5.4	5.0	6.8	1.4	7%	59	17	24	29%	72%	14%	0	21			0	0.98	-0.1	25	46	-$2
10	2 AL	1	3	0	58	28	4.17	4.31	1.37	705	641	758	5.4	3.9	4.3	1.1	5%	61	14	25	28%	69%	6%	0	20			0	1.02	-0.6	13	20	-$2
11	SEA	2	3	1	68	48	3.16	3.74	1.33	713	700	725	4.8	4.0	6.3	1.6	7%	58	17	24	28%	79%	13%	0	18			20	1.02	6.6	43	65	$1
12	LA	5	3	0	68	54	3.72	3.59	1.51	678	643	703	4.6	4.0	7.2	1.8	10%	67	21	12	34%	74%	8%	0	17			0	0.75	2.4	67	87	-$2
13	TAM	2	2	0	70	65	3.09	3.32	1.20	647	665	620	4.4	3.0	8.4	2.8	10%	51	20	29	30%	75%	7%	1	17	0%	100%	0	0.60	6.7	100	130	$2
1st Half		1	1	0	39	37	3.03	3.29	1.06	548	505	605	4.4	3.3	8.6	2.6	10%	51	18	30	26%	72%	6%	0	17			0	0.40	4.0	96	125	$4
2nd Half		1	1	0	31	28	3.16	3.36	1.37	765	836	640	4.4	2.6	8.0	3.1	9%	50	22	28	35%	78%	8%	1	17	0%	100%	0	0.84	2.7	103	133	-$1
14	**Proj**	**3**	**3**	**0**	**73**	**60**	**3.51**	**3.42**	**1.34**	**687**	**691**	**683**	**4.5**	**3.5**	**7.4**	**2.1**	**9%**	**57**	**20**	**24**	**31%**	**74%**	**8%**	**0**						**3.2**	**75**	**98**	**$1**

Wright,Wesley

Age: 29	Th: L	Role RP	Health A
Ht: 5' 11"	Wt: 185	Type Pwr	PT/Exp D
			Consist A
LIMA Plan C+	Rand Var +2	MM 4400	

Don't get too wrapped up in the 1H/2H splits; H%, S% deviations caused the ERA swing. Wasn't as dominant vs LH hitters, but since he keeps the ball on the ground and has high Dom, it still works. Occasional bouts of wildness creep in now and then, though. That plus southpaw-disease will keep his role from expanding.

Yr	Tm	W	L	Sv	IP	K	ERA	xERA	WHIP	oOPS	vL	vR	BF/G	Ctl	Dom	Cmd	SwK	G	L	F	H%	S%	hr/f	GS	APC	DOM%	DIS%	Sv%	LI	RAR	BPV	BPX	R$
09	HOU *	5	5	0	64	62	5.16	5.37	1.65	880	924	853	4.6	5.0	8.8	1.7	10%	43	23	34	34%	71%	20%	0	17			0	0.71	-6.6	51	95	-$4
10	HOU *	5	3	0	103	63	5.44	5.77	1.65	890	678	967	15.8	4.0	5.5	1.4	10%	44	20	37	33%	69%	16%	4	40	25%	50%	0	0.31	-17.2	19	30	-$8
11	HOU *	3	1	2	77	53	2.32	3.01	1.20	583	205	1352	5.2	3.4	6.2	1.8	8%	57	11	32	26%	84%	11%	0	8			67	1.96	15.5	66	99	$6
12	HOU	2	2	1	52	54	3.27	3.13	1.18	638	538	790	2.9	2.9	9.3	3.2	10%	55	22	24	30%	74%	12%	0	11			50	1.10	4.8	121	158	$1
13	2 AL	0	4	0	54	55	3.69	3.35	1.36	769	753	786	3.3	3.2	9.2	2.9	8%	50	22	28	33%	77%	16%	0	13			0	1.05	1.2	108	141	-$3
1st Half		0	2	0	29	24	4.40	3.66	1.53	809	781	832	3.4	2.5	7.5	3.0	7%	49	27	24	37%	71%	9%	0	13			0	0.91	-1.9	95	123	-$5
2nd Half		0	2	0	25	31	2.88	3.03	1.16	718	722	712	3.1	4.0	11.2	2.8	9%	52	13	35	25%	88%	24%	0	13			0	1.21	3.0	124	160	$0
14	**Proj**	**1**	**3**	**0**	**58**	**59**	**3.44**	**3.21**	**1.30**	**705**	**648**	**761**	**3.4**	**3.4**	**9.1**	**2.7**	**9%**	**50**	**20**	**30**	**31%**	**77%**	**12%**	**0**						**3.0**	**101**	**131**	**$0**

Ziegler,Brad

Age: 34	Th: R	Role RP	Health A
Ht: 6' 4"	Wt: 210	Type xGB	PT/Exp C
			Consist A
LIMA Plan C+	Rand Var -3	MM 5121	

Surprisingly successful run as closer in 2H, despite low Dom. What he does—better than anyone else—is keep the ball on the ground. Has always dominated righties, now making progress vL, which gives him at least a shot to hold the 9th inning gig. But don't be surprised if he loses job to a "proven" closer with bigger Dom.

Yr	Tm	W	L	Sv	IP	K	ERA	xERA	WHIP	oOPS	vL	vR	BF/G	Ctl	Dom	Cmd	SwK	G	L	F	H%	S%	hr/f	GS	APC	DOM%	DIS%	Sv%	LI	RAR	BPV	BPX	R$
09	OAK	2	4	7	73	54	3.07	3.64	1.50	734	912	616	4.5	3.4	6.6	1.9	8%	62	18	20	34%	79%	4%	0	17			70	0.88	11.3	67	124	$3
10	OAK	3	7	0	61	41	3.26	4.08	1.35	694	1034	560	4.0	4.2	6.1	1.5	8%	54	19	27	28%	77%	8%	0	14			0	1.14	6.1	29	47	$1
11	2 TM	3	2	1	58	44	2.16	2.96	1.23	598	889	464	3.6	2.9	6.8	2.3	8%	69	18	13	31%	81%	0%	0	13			50	0.96	12.8	90	135	$4
12	ARI	6	1	0	69	42	2.49	2.92	1.09	578	749	501	3.4	2.8	5.5	2.0	10%	76	17	8	26%	77%	13%	0	12			0	0.93	12.9	79	103	$7
13	ARI	8	1	13	73	44	2.22	3.16	1.14	594	647	550	3.8	2.7	5.4	2.0	10%	70	19	11	26%	81%	13%	0	13			87	1.50	14.8	72	94	$13
1st Half		4	1	0	38	22	1.88	2.77	0.94	548	618	512	3.4	2.3	5.2	2.2	10%	76	17	7	22%	82%	25%	0	11			0	1.57	9.4	83	108	$11
2nd Half		4	0	13	35	22	2.60	3.59	1.36	638	664	604	4.3	3.1	5.7	1.8	10%	65	21	14	31%	80%	6%	0	15			87	1.40	5.4	62	80	$15
14	**Proj**	**6**	**2**	**22**	**73**	**47**	**2.79**	**3.15**	**1.25**	**649**	**765**	**572**	**3.8**	**2.9**	**5.8**	**2.0**	**9%**	**70**	**18**	**12**	**29%**	**78%**	**12%**	**0**						**9.6**	**73**	**95**	**$13**

Zimmermann,Jordan

Age: 28	Th: R	Role SP	Health D
Ht: 6' 2"	Wt: 220	Type	PT/Exp A
			Consist A
LIMA Plan C	Rand Var 0	MM 4205	

Combine fine Ctl with low H% as in the first half, and you have great results. Second half paled in comparison, but xERA shows that the skills weren't that different. Split the difference, and you have a low ERA with excellent Cmd and rising GB%. Dom is pedestrian, holding 2H gains there will be key to an ERA repeat.

Yr	Tm	W	L	Sv	IP	K	ERA	xERA	WHIP	oOPS	vL	vR	BF/G	Ctl	Dom	Cmd	SwK	G	L	F	H%	S%	hr/f	GS	APC	DOM%	DIS%	Sv%	LI	RAR	BPV	BPX	R$
09	WAS	3	5	0	91	92	4.63	3.49	1.36	760	773	744	24.4	2.9	9.1	3.2	9%	44	24	32	34%	68%	12%	16	98	56%	6%			-3.5	108	202	$0
10	WAS *	2	2	0	53	39	3.13	3.30	1.08	817	812	819	17.1	2.6	6.7	2.6	6%	49	13	38	24%	79%	22%	7	79	43%	57%			6.2	64	104	$3
11	WAS	8	11	0	161	124	3.18	3.75	1.15	671	703	643	25.5	1.7	6.9	4.0	8%	39	19	42	30%	74%	6%	26	95	62%	8%			15.2	95	143	$13
12	WAS	12	8	0	196	153	2.94	3.78	1.17	686	650	723	25.2	2.0	7.0	3.6	9%	43	23	33	30%	78%	9%	32	97	56%	6%			25.9	94	123	$20
13	WAS	19	9	0	213	161	3.25	3.50	1.09	654	702	601	27.0	1.7	6.8	4.0	9%	48	21	31	28%	73%	10%	32	96	66%	6%			16.2	103	134	$22
1st Half		11	3	0	115	80	2.28	3.35	0.92	558	597	506	27.9	1.3	6.3	4.7	9%	49	22	30	25%	78%	8%	16	97	69%	0%			22.5	104	134	$35
2nd Half		8	6	0	99	81	4.38	3.67	1.29	759	840	685	26.2	2.1	7.4	3.5	9%	46	21	33	32%	68%	11%	16	95	63%	13%			-6.2	101	130	$8
14	**Proj**	**14**	**9**	**0**	**189**	**148**	**3.37**	**3.37**	**1.16**	**682**	**706**	**659**	**24.6**	**1.9**	**7.1**	**3.7**	**9%**	**45**	**21**	**34**	**29%**	**74%**	**9%**	**30**						**11.6**	**98**	**127**	**$17**

Zito,Barry

Age: 36	Th: L	Role RP	Health D
Ht: 6' 2"	Wt: 205	Type FB	PT/Exp B
			Consist A
LIMA Plan D	Rand Var +3	MM 1103	

Strong finish to 2012 gave a glimmer of hope, but it faded out quickly. H% and 2H hr/f certainly hurt, but between marginal Cmd and a ton of line drives, he didn't exactly do a lot to help himself. Five of his last six starts were PQS-0, which is the fitting end to his disastrous 7-year deal. No reason to consider him.

Yr	Tm	W	L	Sv	IP	K	ERA	xERA	WHIP	oOPS	vL	vR	BF/G	Ctl	Dom	Cmd	SwK	G	L	F	H%	S%	hr/f	GS	APC	DOM%	DIS%	Sv%	LI	RAR	BPV	BPX	R$
09	SF	10	13	0	192	154	4.03	4.37	1.35	720	640	745	24.8	3.8	7.2	1.9	8%	38	22	40	29%	73%	9%	33	97	48%	24%			6.9	43	81	$9
10	SF	9	14	0	199	150	4.15	4.52	1.34	726	718	728	24.9	3.8	6.8	1.8	8%	36	19	45	28%	71%	7%	33	96	42%	33%	0	0.82	-1.8	34	54	$5
11	SF *	5	4	0	71	45	5.07	4.01	1.28	816	978	781	18.3	3.6	5.6	1.5	7%	40	22	38	25%	64%	16%	9	67	22%	33%	0	0.54	-9.9	33	49	-$2
12	SF	15	8	0	184	114	4.15	4.92	1.39	758	559	823	25.0	3.4	5.6	1.6	7%	40	20	40	29%	72%	9%	32	96	34%	28%			-3.1	26	34	$2
13	SF	5	11	0	133	86	5.74	5.00	1.70	874	938	857	20.3	3.6	5.8	1.6	8%	36	26	38	35%	68%	11%	25	79	20%	52%	0	0.67	-30.8	20	26	-$18
1st Half		4	6	0	91	59	4.53	4.76	1.60	801	998	762	25.3	3.4	5.8	1.7	8%	37	26	36	35%	72%	6%	16	98	31%	38%			-7.5	30	38	-$14
2nd Half		1	5	0	42	27	8.36	5.54	1.93	1025	873	1095	14.5	4.3	5.8	1.4	6%	34	26	40	35%	61%	20%	9	56	0%	78%	0	0.56	-23.3	1	1	-$27
14	**Proj**	**7**	**10**	**0**	**136**	**86**	**4.95**	**4.76**	**1.60**	**861**	**809**	**877**	**19.3**	**3.7**	**5.7**	**1.5**	**7%**	**36**	**24**	**40**	**32%**	**73%**	**12%**	**29**						**-18.2**	**15**	**20**	**-$9**

DAVE ADLER

FIVE-YEAR INJURY LOG

Batters	Yr	Days	Injury
Kubel,Jason	11	52	Strained L. foot
	13	15	Strained Lt. quad
Laird,Gerald	11	45	R. index finger fracture
	13	16	Kidney stone
LaRoche,Adam	11	130	Torn labrum in L. shoulder
Lawrie,Brett	11	8	Fractured R. middle finger
	12	34	Strained R. oblique
	13	61	Sprained Lt. ankle; Lt. ribcage
Lee,Carlos	12	15	Stained L. hamstring
Lee,Derrek	11	18	Strained L. oblique muscle
Lewis,Fred	10	11	Strain intercostal muscle - L. side
	11	35	Strained R. oblique
Lillibridge,Brent	11	20	Fract. metacarpal bone in R. hand
Lind,Adam	11	27	Soreness - lower back
	12	31	Strained mid-back
Lobaton,Jose	11	46	Sprained L. knee
	12	45	Sore R. shoulder
Longoria,Evan	11	30	Strained L. oblique muscle
	12	98	Torn L. hamstring
Lowrie,Jed	09	119	Fractured and strained L. wrist
	10	108	Mononucleosis
	11	52	Sore L. shoulder
	12	66	R. ankle + R. thumb sprains
Lucroy,Jonathan	11	12	Fractured R. pinkie finger
	12	58	R. hand fracture
Ludwick,Ryan	09	15	Strained R. hamstring
	10	28	Strained L. calf muscle
	11	15	Mid-back muscle spasms
	13	132	Torn cartilage in Rt. shoulder
Machado,Manny	13	5	Torn ligament - Lt. knee
Mahoney,Joseph	13	59	Hammy strain; intercostal strain
Maldonado,Carlos	12	127	Strained lower back
Markakis,Nick	12	40	Fractured R. hand
Marrero,Chris	12	184	Torn L. hamstring
Marson,Lou	13	173	Neck strain; Sore Rt. shoulder
Marte,Starling	12	19	Strained R. oblique
	13	19	Rt. hand contusion
Martin,Russell	10	60	Torn labrum – R. hip
Martinez,Fernando	09	93	Inflam behind R. knee
	12	9	Concussion
	13	21	Strained Lt. oblique
Martinez,J.D.	13	65	Sprnd Rt. knee; Sprained Lt. wrist
Martinez,Michael	12	65	R. foot fracture
Martinez,Victor	10	28	Fractured L. thumb
	11	15	Strained R. groin
	12	183	Recovery from surgery - L. knee
Mastroianni,Darin	13	121	Stress reaction in Lt. ankle
Mathis,Jeff	10	58	Fractured R. wrist
	13	44	Broken Rt. collarbone
Mauer,Joe	09	26	Inflamed R. sacroiliac joint
	11	79	Bilateral leg weakness; Pneumonia
	13	41	Concussion
Maxwell,Justin	11	28	Recovery from TJS
	12	17	Loose bodies in L. ankle
	13	69	Fractured Lt. hand; Concussion
Maybin,Cameron	11	16	R. knee Inflam
	13	163	Strained Lt. knee; Sore Rt. wrist

FIVE-YEAR INJURY LOG

Batters	Yr	Days	Injury
McCann,Brian	09	15	L. eye infection
	11	19	Strained L. oblique
	13	36	Recovery from Rt. shoulder surgery
McDonald,Darnell	11	19	Strained L. quad muscle
	12	24	Strained R. oblique
McDonald,John	11	21	Strained R. hamstring
	12	29	Strained L. oblique
	13	26	Lower back discomfort
McKenry,Michael	13	64	Lt. knee surgery
McLouth,Nate	09	19	Strained-L. hamstring
	10	41	Post concussion syndrome
	11	89	L. oblique strain
Mesoraco,Devin	12	8	Concussion
Middlebrooks,Will	12	54	Fractured R. wrist
	13	17	Low back strain
Miller,Corky	13	25	Rt. quad contusion
Molina,Jose	09	61	Strained L. hamstring
Molina,Yadier	13	15	Sprained Rt. knee
Montero,Miguel	10	62	Torn meniscus - R. knee
	13	28	Lower back strain
Moore,Adam	10	40	Sublexed L. fibula
	11	175	Surgery to repair R. meniscus
Moore,Jeremy	12	182	Recovering from L. hip surgery
Morales,Kendrys	11	183	Recovery from surgeries - L. ankle
Morel,Brent	12	75	Strained back
Moreland,Mitch	12	40	Strained L. hamstring
	13	15	Strained Rt. hamstring
Morgan,Nyjer	09	38	Fractured L. hand
	10	15	Strained R. hip flexor
	11	36	Deep thigh bruise
Morneau,Justin	10	87	Concussion
	11	80	Strain L. wrist; Post conc. synd.
	12	15	Sore R. wrist
Morrison,Logan	11	22	L. foot strain
	12	67	R. knee Inflam
	13	70	Recovery from Rt. knee surgery
Morse,Michael	10	35	Strained L. calf
	12	58	Strained R. lat
	13	38	Strained Rt. quad
Murphy,Daniel	10	50	Sprained R. knee
	11	52	Torn ligament in L. knee
Murphy,Donnie	10	31	Dislocated R. wrist
	11	128	R. wrist Inflam
	12	15	L. hamstring strain
Nady,Xavier	09	172	Torn ligament - R. elbow
	11	47	Fractured L. hand
	12	69	R. wrist tendonitis
Nakajima,Hiroyuki	13	53	Strained Lt. hamstring
Napoli,Mike	11	22	Strained L. oblique muscle
	12	35	Strained L. quadriceps
Nava,Daniel	12	40	Sprained L. wristx2
Navarro,Dioner	11	26	R. oblique strain
Neal,Thomas	13	53	Dislocated Rt. shoulder
Negron,Kristopher	12	34	R. knee injury
Nelson,Chris	09	27	Torn ligament – R. wrist
	12	37	Irreg. heaR.beat+ L. wrist Inflam
	13	19	Strained Rt. hamstring
Nieves,Wil	12	31	Turf toe in R. foot
Nishioka,Tsuyoshi	11	85	Fract. L. fibula; Strain R. oblique

FIVE-YEAR INJURY LOG

Batters	Yr	Days	Injury
Nix,Jayson	09	26	Strained R. quad muscle
	11	23	Contusion - L. shin
	13	65	fX Lt. hand; Strained rt hammy
Nix,Laynce	09	15	Herniated disc-cervical spine
	10	23	Sprained R. ankle
	12	73	Strained R. elbow
Norris,Derek	13	15	Fractured big toe, Lt. foot
Nunez,Eduardo	13	61	Lt. ribcage strain
Olivo,Miguel	12	23	Strained R. groin
Ortiz,David	12	78	Strained R. achilles tendonx2
	13	20	Rt. Achilles tendon soreness
Ozuna,Marcell	13	69	Torn Lt. thumb ligament
Pagan,Angel	09	80	Strained R. groin; R. elbow surgery
	11	35	Pulled L. oblique
	13	125	Strained Rt. hamstring
Parrino,Andy	12	24	Injured R. hand
Pastornicky,Tyler	13	46	Torn Lt. ACL
Paul,Xavier	09	137	Skin infection - L. leg
Paulino,Ronny	11	19	Anemia
Pearce,Steve	10	131	Sprained R. ankle
	11	91	R. calf strain
	13	61	Lt. wrist tendinitis x2
Pedroia,Dustin	10	97	Fx L. navicular bone; sore L. foot
	12	15	Sprained R. thumb
Pena,Carlos	09	27	Fractured L. index and ring finger
	10	15	Plantar Fasciitis - R. foot
	13	13	Appendectomy
Pena,Ramiro	11	50	Appendicitis
	13	105	Rt. shoulder impingement
Pennington,Cliff	12	18	Tendinitis in L. elbow
Perez,Salvador	12	78	Surgery for torn L. meniscus
	13	7	Concussion
Phelps,Cord	13	33	Rt. wrist inflammation
Pie,Felix	10	81	Strained L. shoulder
Pierzynski,A.J.	11	20	Bruised L. wrist
	13	15	Strained Rt. oblique
Pill,Brett	13	15	Recovery from minor knee surgery
Pina,Manuel	12	149	Surgery on R. knee
Plouffe,Trevor	12	23	Bruised R. thumb
	13	23	Concussion; Strained Lt. calf
Polanco,Placido	10	21	Bone spur –R. elbow
	11	40	Lower back Inflam
	12	57	Lower back Inflamx2
	13	8	Concussion
Posada,Jorge	09	24	Strained R. hamstring
	10	16	Stress fracture – R. foot
Posey,Buster	11	126	Fract. L. fibula and torn ankle lig.
Prado,Martin	10	17	Fractured R. pinky finger
	11	37	Staph infection in R. calf
Presley,Alex	11	33	L. hand contusion
	12	12	Concussion
Pujols,Albert	11	15	Fractured L. forearm
	13	65	Plantar fasciitis
Punto,Nick	09	15	Strained R. groin
	11	99	SpoR.s hernia surgery
Quentin,Carlos	09	55	Plantar Fasciitis – L. foot
	11	22	Sprained L. shoulder
	12	54	R. knee surgery
	13	61	Rt. knee strain

FIVE-YEAR INJURY LOG

Batters	Yr	Days	Injury
Quintero,Humberto	09	17	Strained R. shoulder
	11	39	High R. ankle sprain
Raburn,Ryan	12	52	Sprain R. thumb; Strain R. quad
	13	15	Strained Lt. Achilles
Ramirez,Aramis	09	58	Dislocated L. shoulder
	13	64	Sprained Lt. knee x 2
Ramirez,Hanley	11	72	L. back strain
	13	60	Str Lt. hamMY; Rt. thumb ligament
Ramirez,Wilkin	13	109	Head Injury; Fractured Lt. tibia
Ramos,Wilson	12	144	Torn R. knee ligament
	13	64	Strained Lt. hamstring x 2
Ransom,Cody	09	60	Strained R. quad muscle
Rasmus,Colby	11	23	Jammed R. wrist
	13	41	Lt. oblique str; contusion - Lt. eye
Reddick,Josh	13	39	Sprained Rt. wrist x 2
Reimold,Nolan	09	17	Tendinitis – L. Achilles tendon
	12	156	Surgery for herniated disk
	13	129	Str rt hammy; Nerve inflam neck
Renteria,Edgar	10	57	Strained R. groin; hammy; biceps
Repko,Jason	11	36	Strain R. quad; Bursitis-L. should.
	12	62	Separation of R. shoulder
Revere,Ben	13	78	Broken Rt. foot
Reyes,Jose	09	137	Tendinitis R. calf
	10	6	Recovery from hypeR.hyroidism
	11	37	L. hamstring strain
	13	74	Sprained Lt. ankle
Reynolds,Mark	12	17	Strained L. oblique
Rivera,Juan	12	148	Torn L. hamstring
Roberts,Brian	10	104	Strained ab muscle; sore back
	11	135	Concussion
	12	162	Surg.-torn R. hip labrum+concuss.
	13	86	Ruptured tendon, Rt. knee
Robinson,Shane	13	15	Strained Rt. shoulder
Rodriguez,Alex	09	33	Surg. to repair torn labrum - R. hip
	10	15	Strained L. calf
	11	44	Torn meniscus in R. knee
	12	40	Broken L. hand
	13	127	Lt. hip surgery
Rodriguez,Luis	09	28	Sprained L. ankle
Rodriguez,Sean	12	15	Fractured R. hand
Rohlinger,Ryan	10	30	Strained L. hamstring
Rollins,Jimmy	10	65	Strained R. calf x 2
	11	17	R. groin strain
Romine,Austin	12	182	Strained lower back
Rosales,Adam	10	29	Stress fracture – R. ankle
	11	67	Fractured R. foot
	13	25	Strained Lt. intercostal
Ross,Cody	11	21	R. calf strain
	12	31	Fractured bone in L. foot
	13	62	Lt. calf strain; Dislocated Rt. hip
Ross,David	09	12	Strained L. groin
	13	77	Concussion x 2
Rowand,Aaron	10	15	Fractured check bone
Ruggiano,Justin	11	22	Bursitis in L. knee
Ruiz,Carlos	09	21	Strained R. oblique
	10	21	Concussion
	11	15	Lower back Inflam
	12	35	Plantar fasciitis in L. foot
	13	29	Strained Rt. hamstring

FIVE-YEAR INJURY LOG

Batters	Yr	Days	Injury
Ryan,Brendan	09	15	Strained L. hamstring
	11	15	Sprained L. shoulder
Saltalamacchia,Jar.	09	18	Numbness, fatigue-R. arm
	10	35	Strained upper back; infected leg
Sanchez,Angel	13	45	Lower back strain
Sanchez,Freddy	09	20	Strained L. shoulder
	10	45	Recov. from surgery - L. shoulder
	12	182	Recov. from surgery - R. shoulder
Sanchez,Hector	12	15	L. knee sprain
	13	15	Strained Rt. shoulder
Sandoval,Pablo	11	45	Broken hamate bone in R. hand
	12	56	Strained L. hamstring+ Fx R. hand
	13	15	Strained Lt. foot
Santana,Carlos	12	10	Concussion
Saunders,Michael	13	18	Sprained Rt. shoulder
Schafer,Jordan	09	30	Rehab from surgery – R. wrist
	10	43	Recovery from surgery - L. wrist
	11	26	Chip fracture in L. middle finger
	12	25	Shoulder
	13	37	Rt. ankle contusion
Schierholtz,Nate	09	16	Strained L. hip
	11	38	Hairline fracture in R. foot
	12	19	Fractured R. great toe
Schneider,Brian	09	42	Strained back muscle
	10	15	Strained R. Achilles
	11	43	Straing L. hamstring
	12	77	Strain L. hamstring+ spr R. Ankle
Schumaker,Skip	11	37	R. triceps strain
	12	36	R. hammy strain+torn R. oblique
Scott,Luke	09	16	Strained L. shoulder
	10	18	Strained L. hamstring
	11	86	Bruise-R. knee; Strain R. should.
	12	50	Str R. oblique+back spasms
	13	46	Back spasms; Strained Rt. calf
Scutaro,Marco	11	30	Strained L. oblique muscle
Sellers,Justin	12	134	Bulging disc in lower back
Shoppach,Kelly	10	54	Sprained R. knee
Silverio,Alfredo	13	183	Sprained Rt. elbow
Simmons,Andrelton	12	63	Non-displaced fract. R. hand
Sizemore,Grady	09	54	Inflamed L. elbow; torn ab. wall
	10	139	Bone brse–L. knee;microfrac surg.
	11	77	Recv. L. knee surg.; Bruise R. Knee
	12	183	Recovery from back surgery
Sizemore,Scott	12	182	Recovery from torn ACL surgery
	13	173	Torn Lt. ACL
Smith,Seth	12	18	Strained L. hamstring
Smoak,Justin	11	20	Fracture of the nose
	13	19	Rt. oblique strain
Snider,Travis	10	63	Sprained R. wrist
	13	35	Lt. big toe discomfort
Snyder,Brandon	13	24	Ulnar neuritis, Rt. elbow
Snyder,Chris	09	81	Strained lower back x 2
	11	126	Sore lower back
Sogard,Eric	12	58	Strained back/sprained ankle
Solano,Donovan	13	34	Strained Lt. intercostal muscle
Solano,Jhonatan	12	78	L. oblique strain
Soriano,Alfonso	09	31	Surgery – L. knee
	11	15	L. quadriceps strain

FIVE-YEAR INJURY LOG

Batters	Yr	Days	Injury
Soto,Geovany	09	90	Strained L. oblique
	10	30	Sprain R. shoulder; Shoulder Surg.
	11	18	L. groin strain
	12	30	Torn L. meniscus
Span,Denard	09	15	R. ear infection
	11	91	Concussion; Migraine headaches
	12	15	Strained R. sternoclavicular joint
Spilborghs,Ryan	11	45	Plantar fascitis in R. foot
Stairs,Matt	10	24	Sore R. knee
Stanton,Giancarlo	12	30	AR.hroscopic R. knee surgery
	13	41	Strained Rt. hamstring
Stassi,Max	13	32	Concussion
Stewart,Ian	10	28	Strained R. oblique
	12	113	Sore L. wrist
	13	33	Strained Lt. quad
Stubbs,Drew	12	19	Strained L. oblique
Sucre,Jesus	13	72	Lt. wrist sprain
Suzuki,Ichiro	09	10	Bleeding ulcer
Suzuki,Kurt	10	22	Intercostal strain
Sweeney,Ryan	09	15	Sprained L. knee
	10	83	Pending surg. for patella tendinitis
	12	93	Concussion+toe+fx L. hand
	13	63	Fractured Lt. rib
Tabata,Jose	11	50	R. hand contusion
	13	39	Strained Lt. oblique
Teagarden,Taylor	12	100	Strained back
	13	37	Dislocated Lt. thumb
Teahen,Mark	10	73	Fractured R. middle finger
	11	24	Strained R. oblique muscle
Teixeira,Mark	13	167	Rt wrist surgery; Strained rt wrist
Tejada,Miguel	11	28	Lower abdominal strain
	13	50	Strained Rt. calf
Tejada,Ruben	12	48	Strained R. quadriceps
	13	37	Rt. quad strain
Thames,Marcus	09	46	Strained R. oblique
	10	21	Strained R. hamstring
	11	34	R. quad strain
Theriot,Ryan	12	15	R. elbow Inflam
Thole,Josh	12	24	Concussion
Thomas,Brad	11	141	R. elbow surgery
Thome,Jim	11	45	Strain L. oblique; Strain L. quad
	12	92	Strained lower back, Back spasms
Tolbert,Matt	10	45	Sprained R. middle finger
Torrealba,Yorvit	13	8	Concussion
Torres,Andres	09	59	Strained L. hamstring x 2
	11	45	Strained L. Achilles Tendon
	12	24	L. calf strain
	13	39	Surgery, Lt. Achilles
Tracy,Chad	12	65	R. adductor strain
Treanor,Matt	09	166	Torn labrum - R. hip
	10	30	Sprained R. knee
	11	32	Concussion
Tuiasosopo,Matt	13	15	Strained Lt. intercostal
Tulowitzki,Troy	10	39	Fractured L. wrist
	12	126	Strained L. groin muscle
	13	27	Fractured rib, Rt. ribcage
Turner,Justin	12	18	Sprained R. ankle
	13	35	Intercostal strain
Uggla,Dan	13	15	Eye surgery

FIVE-YEAR INJURY LOG

Batters	Yr	Days	Injury
Upton,B.J.	09	8	Recov. Fr. labrum surg. - R. should.
	12	15	Soreness in lower back
	13	21	Rt. adductor strain
Upton,Justin	09	20	Strained R. oblique
Uribe,Juan	11	83	L. hip flexor muscle strain
	12	28	L. wrist injury
Utley,Chase	10	49	Sprained R. thumb
	11	53	R. knee tendinitis
	12	84	Worn caR.ilage behind L. kneecap
	13	31	Strained Rt. oblique
Valaika,Chris	13	76	Fractured Lt. wrist
Valbuena,Luis	13	29	Rt. oblique strain
Van Slyke,Scott	13	17	Lt. shoulder bursitis
Velez,Eugenio	10	18	Concussion
Venable,Will	10	19	Lower back pain
Viciedo,Dayan	11	6	Fractured R. thumb
	13	21	Strained Lt. oblique
Victorino,Shane	10	15	Strained L. abdominal muscle
	11	30	R. hamstring strain
	13	18	Lt. hamstring strain
Votto,Joey	09	24	Stress-related issue
	12	50	Torn medial meniscus in L. knee
Walker,Neil	13	32	Strained Rt. oblique; Rt. finger cut
Weeks,Rickie	09	140	Torn sheath L. wrist.
	11	42	Sprained L. ankle
	13	53	Lt. hamstring surgery
Wells,Casper	13	32	Vision complications
Wells,Vernon	11	28	Strained R. groin
	12	67	Torn ligament in R. thumb
Werth,Jayson	12	87	Broken L. wrist
	13	32	Strained Rt. hamstring
Whiteside,Eli	11	7	Concussion
Wieters,Matt	10	15	Strained R. hamstring
Wigginton,Ty	11	16	L. oblique strain
Willingham,Josh	10	48	Surgery – L. knee
	11	19	Strained L. achilles tendon
	13	39	Medial meniscus tear, Lt. knee
Willits,Reggie	10	10	Strained R. hamstring
	11	13	Strained L. calf
Wilson,Bobby	10	22	Bruised ankle; concussion
	12	13	Concussion
Wilson,Jack	09	17	Sprained L. index finger
	10	101	Fract R. hand; Strain R. hamstring
	11	15	Bruised L. heel
	12	82	Dislocated R. pinky finger
Wise,DeWayne	09	61	Sep. R. shoulder; strained A/C joint
	13	65	Strained Rt. hamstring
Wood,Brandon	10	22	R. Hip flexor strain
Worth,Danny	13	3	Dislocated Lt. shoulder
Wright,David	09	15	Concussion
	11	67	Lower back stress fracture
	13	48	Strained Rt. hamstring
Youkilis,Kevin	09	15	Strained L. oblique
	10	61	Sprained R. thumb
	11	16	Sore back; Bursitis R. hip
	12	23	Strained lower back
	13	141	Strained lower back x 2
Young,Chris	12	30	R. shoulder contusion

FIVE-YEAR INJURY LOG

Batters	Yr	Days	Injury
Young,Delmon	09	10	Recovery from elbow surgery
	11	39	Strain L. oblique; Sprain R. ankle
	13	30	Recovery from Rt. ankle surgery
Young,Eric	10	77	Stress Fracture; R. tibia
	12	45	L. intercostal muscle strain
Zimmerman,Ryan	11	65	L. abdominal strain
	12	17	Sore R. shoulder
	13	15	Strained Lt. hamstring
Zunino,Mike	13	38	Fractured Lt. hamate bone

FIVE-YEAR INJURY LOG

Pitchers	Yr	Days	Injury
Aardsma,David	11	182	Recov. from surgery-L. hip; TJS
Abad,Fernando	11	88	L. shoulder tendinitis
	12	20	R. intercostal strain
Aceves,Alfredo	10	147	Herniated disk in lower back
Adams,Mike	09	90	Labrum surg-R. should+strain
	10	26	Strained L. oblique
	13	117	Back Strain; Rt. biceps tend.
Affeldt,Jeremy	10	28	Torn L. oblique muscle
	12	15	Sprained R. knee
	13	71	Strained Lt. groin; Rt. oblique
Albers,Matt	11	15	Sore R. lat muscle
Alburquerque,Al	11	39	Inflam - R. elbow; Concussion
	12	141	Recov. fr. surg. - R. elbow
Alvarez,Henderson	13	95	Mild Rt. shoulder inflammation
Anderson,Brett	10	90	L. elbow Inflam x 2
	11	115	Soreness in L. elbow
	12	137	Recovery from TJS
	13	119	Rt. foot stress fracture
Arredondo,Jose	11	60	R. shoulder Inflam
Arrieta,Jake	11	59	Bone spur in R. elbow
Atchison,Scott	12	60	Tightness In R. forearm
	13	60	Rt. groin strain; Rt. elbow
Ayala,Luis	11	28	Strained lat muscle
	13	71	Anxiety disorder
Badenhop,Burke	09	30	Strained R. trapezius muscle
Bailey,Andrew	10	32	R. intercostal strain
	11	59	Strained R. forearm
	12	132	R. thumb surgery
	13	100	Rt biceps soreness; Rt shoulder str
Bailey,Homer	10	83	Inflam – R. shoulder
	11	66	R. shoulder impingement
Baker,Scott	09	10	Stiffness - R. shoulder
	11	58	Strained R. flexor muscle
	12	182	TJS - R. elbow
	13	161	Strained Rt. elbow
Balfour,Grant	10	34	Strained intercostal muscle
	11	15	Strained R. oblique muscle
Barnes,Scott	13	32	Sprained Lt. wrist
Bass,Anthony	12	72	R. shoulder Inflam
Bastardo,Antonio	09	69	Strained R. shoulder
	10	29	Ulnar Neuritis – L. elbow
Batista,Miguel	12	16	Lower back strain
Beachy,Brandon	11	39	L. oblique strain
	12	109	TJS
	13	160	Rt. elbow inflam; Rt. elbow surgery
Beato,Pedro	11	15	R. elbow tendinitis
	12	92	R. shoulder stiffness
Beckett,Josh	10	65	Strained lower back
	12	18	Inflam in R. shoulder
	13	139	Neck & shoulder surgery
Bedard,Erik	09	100	Inflamed L. shoulder x 2
	10	182	Recov. fr. surg. on L. shoulder
	11	31	Sprained L. knee
Beimel,Joe	09	15	Strained L. hip flexor
	11	48	Sore L. elbow
Betances,Dellin	12	15	R. shoulder Inflam
Betancourt,Rafael	09	38	Strained R. groin
	10	15	Strained R. groin
	13	98	Strained Rt. groin; Rt. elbow; Appx

FIVE-YEAR INJURY LOG

Pitchers	Yr	Days	Injury
Billingsley,Chad	10	16	Strained R. groin
	12	46	R. elbow pain
	13	177	Rt. elbow surgery; finger bruise
Blackburn,Nick	11	38	Strained R. forearm
	12	18	Strained L. quad
Blackley,Travis	13	15	Lt. shoulder strain
Blanton,Joe	10	29	Strained L. oblique
	11	127	Impingement in R. elbow
Braden,Dallas	09	65	Infection - L. foot
	10	27	Sore L. elbow
	11	165	Surg. - torn capsule in L. shoulder
	12	182	Recov. fr. surg. - L. shoulder
Bray,Bill	12	78	Lumbar strain+ L. groin str
Breslow,Craig	13	36	Lt. shoulder tendinitis
Britton,Zach	11	17	Strained L. shoulder
	12	62	L. shoulder impingement
Broxton,Jonathan	11	148	Sore R. elbow
	13	108	Rt. flexor strain x 2
Buchholz,Clay	10	24	Strained L. hamstring
	11	103	Strained lower back
	12	24	Gastro-intestinal problem
	13	93	Neck strain
Buchholz,Taylor	09	183	Sprained UCL - R. elbow
	10	129	Sore back; R. elbow
	11	122	R. shoulder fatigue
Burgos,Hiram	13	37	Rt. shoulder impingement
Burnett,A.J.	12	17	Fractured R. orbital bone
	13	28	Strained Rt. calf
Burnett,Sean	13	150	Sore Lt. forearm; Lt. elbow surgery
Burton,Jared	09	16	Fatigue – R. shoulder
	11	135	AR.hroscopic surg-R. shoulder
Bush,Dave	09	106	Fatigue – R. arm
Byrdak,Tim	10	20	Strained R. hamstring
	12	62	L. shoulder soreness
Cabral,Cesar	12	182	Fractured L. elbow
	13	75	Lt. elbow pain
Cabrera,Edwar	13	183	Lt. shoulder impingement
Cahill,Trevor	10	16	Stress reaction - L. scapula
	13	47	Rt. hip contusion
Cain,Matt	13	15	Rt. forearm contusion
Camp,Shawn	13	24	Sprained Rt. big toe
Capps,Matt	12	88	Irritation of R. rotator cuff
Capuano,Chris	13	39	Lt. lat strain; Strained Lt. calf
Carignan,Andrew	12	120	TJS - R. elbow
Carlson,Jesse	11	182	Surgery - torn L. rotator cuff
Carlyle,Buddy	09	73	Strained upper back
Carpenter,Chris	09	35	Strained L. ribcage muscle
	12	171	Nerve irritation in R. shoulder
	12	182	Recov. fr. surg.-bone spur R. elbow
	13	183	Nerve irritation, Rt. shoulder
Carrasco,Carlos	11	16	Inflam - R. elbow
	12	183	Recovery from TJS
Cashner,Andrew	11	150	R. rotator cuff strain
	12	59	Strained R. latissimus dorsi
Casilla,Santiago	09	15	Sprain R. lat. collateral ligament
	11	57	Sore R. elbow
	13	53	Cyst on Rt. knee
Cassevah,Bobby	12	22	Inflam in R. shoulder
Castillo,Alberto	11	33	L. shoulder tendinitis

FIVE-YEAR INJURY LOG

Pitchers	Yr	Days	Injury
Castillo,Lendy	12	87	L. groin strain
Cecil,Brett	13	13	Lt. elbow soreness
Ceda,Jose	12	184	TJS
	13	183	Recovery from Rt. elbow surgery
Chacin,Jhoulys	12	111	R. shoulder Inflam
	13	15	Lt. lower back strain
Chamberlain,Joba	11	115	TJS
	12	117	Dislocated R. ankle
	13	30	Strained Rt. oblique
Chapman,Aroldis	11	39	L. shoulder Inflam
Chatwood,Tyler	13	31	Rt. elbow inflammation
Chen,Bruce	09	17	Torn L. oblique muscle
	11	49	Strained L. lat muscle
Chen,Wei-Yin	13	58	Strained Rt. oblique
Choate,Randy	11	44	L. elbow Inflam
Cingrani,Tony	13	15	Strained lower back
Cobb,Alex	11	53	Surgery - rib cage
	13	60	Concussion
Coello,Robert	12	101	Strained R. elbow
	13	98	Rt. shoulder inflammation
Coffey,Todd	10	21	Bruised R. thumb
	11	15	L. calf strain
	12	109	R. knee Inflam+TJS
Coke,Phil	11	15	Bone bruise in R. foot
	13	15	Lt. groin strain
Collmenter,Josh	12	22	Ulcers
Colome,Alexander	13	94	Strained Rt. elbow
Colon,Bartolo	09	99	Inflamed R. knee; R. elbow
	11	20	Strained L. hamstring
	12	15	Strained R. oblique
	13	15	Lt. groin strain
Contreras,Jose	11	135	R. elbow strain
	12	136	R. elbow strain
	13	16	Lower back inflammation
Cook,Aaron	09	34	Strained R. shoulder
	10	54	Turf toe; Fx R. fibula
	11	69	Broken finger on R. hand
	12	49	Laceration of L. knee
Cordero,Francisco	12	63	R. foot sesamoiditis
Cortes,Dan	11	15	Bruised L. ankle
Crain,Jesse	09	16	Inflamed R. shoulder
	12	51	Strained R. shoulder+ L. oblique
	13	85	Sprained Rt. shoulder
Crotta,Michael	11	141	R. posterior elbow Inflam
Cruz,Juan	09	48	Strained R. shoulder
	11	15	Strained R. groin
	12	22	R. shoulder Inflam
Cruz,Rhiner	12	15	Sprained R. ankle
Cueto,Johnny	09	15	Inflam R. shoulder
	11	39	R. biceps/triceps irritation
	13	130	Strained Rt. lat x 2; Rt. shoulder
Daley,Matt	09	18	Sprained L. foot
	10	87	Inflam – R. shoulder
	11	120	R. shoulder Inflam
Danks,John	11	24	Strained R. oblique muscle
	12	137	Surgery - strained L. shoulder
	13	54	Recovery from Lt. shoulder surgery
Darvish,Yu	13	15	Upper back strain
Davies,Kyle	11	111	Inflam R/C; Impingement R. should.

FIVE-YEAR INJURY LOG

Pitchers	Yr	Days	Injury
Davis,Wade	10	18	Strained R. shoulder
	11	15	Strained R. forearm
De Fratus,Justin	12	152	R. elbow sprain
De La Rosa,Jorge	10	74	Torn tendon – L. middle finger
	11	127	TJS
	12	168	TJS
De La Rosa,Rubby	11	59	TJS
De Vries,Cole	12	20	Fractured Rib
	13	48	Rt. forearm strain
Deduno,Samuel	13	31	Rt. shoulder soreness
Del Rosario,Enerio	11	27	Strained R. shoulder
Delabar,Steve	13	29	Rt. shoulder inflammation
Demel,Sam	11	38	R. shoulder tendinitis
Dempster,Ryan	09	25	Fractured R. big toe
	12	37	R. quad strain, Tight R. lat.
Detwiler,Ross	10	110	R. hip strain; hip caR.ilage
	13	116	Back strain; x 2
Devine,Joey	09	183	Sprained R. elbow
	10	182	Recov. fr. surg. - R. elbow
	11	2	Strained rhomboid- R. shoulder
	12	182	TJS - R. elbow
Diamond,Scott	13	13	Recovery from Lt. elbow surgery
Dolis,Rafael	13	126	Strained Rt. forearm
Dominguez,Jose	13	69	Lt. quad strain
Dotel,Octavio	11	8	Sore L. hamstring
	12	16	Inflam in R. elbow
	13	163	Rt. elbow inflammation
Doubront,Felix	11	8	Inflam - L. forearm
	12	15	Contusion in R. knee
Downs,Darin	13	28	Lt. rotator cuff tendinitis
Downs,Scott	09	43	Bruised L. toe; sprained L. toe
	11	27	Fx L. big toe; Gastrointestinal virus
	12	21	Strained L. shoulder
Drabek,Kyle	12	112	TJS
	13	95	Recovery from Rt. elbow surgery
Drake,Oliver	12	8	Tendinitis in R. shoulder
Duchscherer,Justin	09	183	Recov. fr. surg. on R. elbow
	10	156	L. Hip Inflam x 2
	11	182	Strained L. hip
Duffy,Danny	12	143	TJS
	13	99	Recov lt elbow surg; lt flexor strain
Duke,Zach	10	25	Strained L. elbow
	11	58	Broken L. hand
Edgin,Josh	13	62	Ribcage stress fracture
Elbert,Scott	12	62	L. elbow Inflamx2
	13	183	Recovery from Lt. elbow surgery
Eovaldi,Nathan	13	79	Mild Rt. shoulder inflammation
Escalona,Edgmer	11	20	R. rotator cuff strain
	12	27	R. elbow Inflam
	13	22	Rt. elbow inflammation
Escalona,Sergio	11	33	L. elbow tendinitis
	12	183	TJS
Estrada,Marco	10	124	R. shoulder fatigue
	12	33	R. quadriceps strain
	13	64	Strained Lt. hamstring
Familia,Jeurys	13	128	Rt. elbow surgery
Farina,Alan	12	183	Recovery from TJS
Farnsworth,Kyle	12	86	Strained R. elbow

FIVE-YEAR INJURY LOG

Pitchers	Yr	Days	Injury
Feldman,Scott	10	16	Bone bruise – R. knee
	11	105	Recov. fr. surg. - R. knee
Feliciano,Pedro	11	183	Strained L. rotator cuff
	12	182	Recov. fr. surg. - R. shoulder
Feliz,Neftali	11	15	Inflam - R. shoulder
	12	136	TJS - R. elbow
	13	155	Recovery from Rt. elbow surgery
Fife,Stephen	13	66	Rt. shoulder bursitis x 2
Figaro,Alfredo	13	30	Strained Rt. oblique
Fish,Robert	12	183	L. elbow tendinitis
Fister,Doug	10	24	R. shoulder fatigue
	12	47	Strained L. side
Floyd,Gavin	12	31	Strain R. elbow flex+ tend R. Elbow
	13	155	Rt. elbow surgery
Francis,Jeff	09	183	Recov. fr. labrum surg. - L. shoulder
	10	73	Soreness – L. shoulder x 2
	13	24	Lt. groin strain
Francisco,Frank	09	53	Tendntis R. should. x 2; pneumonia
	10	36	Strained R. lat muscle
	11	19	Sore R. pectoral
	12	42	L. oblique strain
	13	160	Rt. elbow inflammation
Frasor,Jason	12	48	Tightness In R. forearm
Friedrich,Christian	12	67	Stress fract-R. side of lower spine
	13	53	Lower back inflammation
Frieri,Ernesto	11	15	Back problem
Fuentes,Brian	10	178	Mid-back strain
Fujikawa,Kyuji	13	153	Rt. elbow strain; Rt. forearm
Fulchino,Jeff	10	34	Tendinitis - R. elbow
Furbush,Charlie	12	30	Strained L. triceps muscle
Gallardo,Yovani	10	17	Strained oblique muscle
	13	17	Strained Lt. hamstring
Garcia,Christian	13	183	Strained Rt. forearm tendon
Garcia,Freddy	11	20	Lacerated R. index finger
Garcia,Jaime	09	137	Sore L. elbow
	12	74	L. shoulder strain
	13	135	Lt. shoulder strain
Garland,Jon	11	133	L. oblique strain
Garza,Matt	11	13	R. elbow bone contusion
	12	68	R. elbow stress reaction
	13	51	Strained Lt. lat
Gast,John	13	127	Lt. shoulder tightness
Gaudin,Chad	11	156	R. shoulder Inflam
	13	60	Rt. elbow bruise; sore wrist
Gee,Dillon	12	88	Damaged aR.ery in R. shoulder
Gomes,Brandon	13	146	Strained Rt. lat
Gomez,Jeanmar	13	23	Rt. forearm tightness
Gonzalez,Edgar	13	104	Strained Rt. shoulder
Gonzalez,Miguel	13	17	Rt. thumb blister
Gonzalez,Mike	10	102	Strained L. shoulder
Gorzelanny,Tom	11	26	L. elbow Inflam
	13	16	Lt. shoulder tendinitis
Green,Sean	10	126	Strained R. ribcage
Gregerson,Luke	09	28	Strained R. shoulder
	11	28	L. oblique strain
Greinke,Zack	11	35	Fractured L. rib
	13	33	Broken Lt. collarbone
Griffin,AJ	12	27	Strained R. shoulder

FIVE-YEAR INJURY LOG

Pitchers	Yr	Days	Injury
Grilli,Jason	09	20	Inflam-R. elbow
	13	42	Strained Rt. forearm
Guerra,Javy	12	63	Strained L. oblique+ R. knee Inflam
Guerrier,Matt	12	133	R. elbow tendinitis
	13	53	Rt. elbow soreness
Guthrie,Jeremy	12	22	R. shoulder sprain
Gutierrez,Juan	10	15	Inflam – R. shoulder
	11	127	R. shoulder Inflam
Halladay,Roy	09	15	R. groin strain
	12	50	R. back strain
	13	111	Rt. shoulder surgery
Hamels,Cole	11	16	L. shoulder Inflam
Hammel,Jason	10	18	Strained R. groin
	12	54	Injured R. knee
	13	38	Rt. forearm tenderness
Hanrahan,Joel	10	8	Strained flexor tendon - R. forearm
	13	162	Rt elbow surgery; Sore rt hamstring
Hanson,Tommy	11	68	R. shoulder tendinitis
	12	17	Lower back strain
	13	32	Strained Rt. forearm
Happ,J.A.	10	81	Strained L. forearm
	12	30	Fractured R. foot
	13	89	Head contusion
Harang,Aaron	09	45	Appendectomy
	10	61	Lower back spasms
	11	29	Sore R. foot
Harden,Rich	09	26	Strained lower back
	10	64	Tendinitis R. should.; Strain L. glut.
	11	92	Strained R. shoulder
Haren,Dan	12	18	Stiff lower back
	13	15	Rt. shoulder inflammation
Harrison,Matt	09	125	Inflamed L. elbow; shoulder
	10	22	L. biceps tendinitis
	13	177	Inflamed nerve in lower back
Harvey,Matt	13	34	Torn Rt. UCL
Hawkins,LaTroy	09	16	Shingles
	10	136	R. shoulder weakness x 2
	11	22	R. shoulder surgery
	12	33	Fractured R. pinkie finger
Hawksworth,Blake	11	26	Strained R. groin
	12	183	R. elbow surgery
Hefner,Jeremy	13	51	Partially torn ligament, Rt. elbow
Heilman,Aaron	11	20	R. shoulder tendinitis
Hellickson,Jeremy	12	15	Fatigued R. shoulder
Henderson,Jim	13	15	Strained Rt. hamstring
Hensley,Clay	10	20	Strained L. neck muscle
	11	62	L. rib contusion
	12	15	R. groin strain
Hernandez,David	10	33	Sprained L. ankle
Hernandez,Roberto	11	15	Strained R. quad muscle
Herndon,David	12	157	TJS
Herrmann,Frank	13	182	Rt. elbow surgery
Hill,Rich	09	110	Inflamed R. shoulder; L. elbow
	11	119	Sprained L. elbow
	12	107	TJS recov.+Soreness in L. forearm
Hochevar,Luke	10	83	Strained R. elbow
Holland,Derek	10	62	L. rotator cuff Inflam
	12	31	Fatigued L. shoulder
Holland,Greg	12	21	Stress reaction in L. ribs

FIVE-YEAR INJURY LOG

Pitchers	Yr	Days	Injury
Horst,Jeremy	13	106	Strained Lt. elbow
Howell,J.P.	10	182	Strained L. shoulder
	11	50	Recov. fr. surg. - L. labrum
Hudson,Daniel	12	137	R. shoulder impingement +TJS
	13	183	Recovery from Rt. elbow surgery
Hudson,Tim	09	150	Recovery from TJS
	12	25	Recovering from back surgery
	13	67	Fractured Rt. ankle
Huff,David	12	18	Strained R. hamstring
Hughes,Jared	13	57	Rt. shoulder inflammation
Hughes,Phil	11	82	Tired arm
	13	6	Rt. upper back thoracic injury
Humber,Philip	11	15	Facial Contusion
	12	30	Strained R. elbow
Hunter,Tommy	10	24	Strained L. oblique
	11	92	Stained R. groin
Hutchison,Drew	12	110	TJS - R. elbow
	13	131	Recovery from Rt. elbow surgery
Igarashi,Ryota	10	32	Strained L. hamstring
Irwin,Phillip	13	119	Rt. arm fatigue
Jakubauskas,Chris	10	115	Concussion
Jansen,Kenley	11	49	R. shoulder Inflam
Janssen,Casey	09	66	Sore R. shoulder x 2
	11	34	Sore R. forearm
Jenks,Bobby	11	132	Strain R. biceps; Tightness in back
	12	183	Recov. fr. surg. - back
Jepsen,Kevin	09	15	Lower back spasms
	13	82	Rt tricep tightness; Appendectomy
Jimenez,Cesar	09	183	Tendinitis L. biceps tendon
Jimenez,Ubaldo	11	17	Cuticle cut on R. thumb
Johnson,Jim	10	91	Small tear in R. elbow
Johnson,Josh	11	135	R. shoulder Inflam
	13	90	Strnd rt forearm; Strnd rt triceps
Johnson,Steve	13	86	Strained lt oblique; Strained rt lat
Jordan,Taylor	13	44	Lower back strain
Jurrjens,Jair	10	61	Strained L. hamstring
	11	28	Sore R. torso
	12	64	Strained R. groin
Karstens,Jeff	09	22	Strained lower back
	12	68	Sore R. shoulder
	13	183	Rt. shoulder inflammation
Kazmir,Scott	09	37	Strained R. quadriceps
	10	36	Strain R. hammy;Fatigue L. should.
	11	178	Lower back stiffness
	13	18	Strained Rt. rib cage
Kelley,Shawn	09	58	Strained L. oblique
	10	109	R. elbow Inflam
	11	132	Recov. fr. surg. - R. elbow
Kelly,Casey	13	183	Rt. elbow surgery
Kendrick,Kyle	13	8	Inflammation - Rt. shoulder
Kimball,Cole	11	111	R. shoulder Inflam
	12	184	Rehab from R. shoulder surgery
Kinney,Josh	13	89	Stress reaction, Lt. shoulder
Kintzler,Brandon	11	147	R. triceps tendonitis
	12	151	Sore R. forearm
Kirkman,Michael	13	86	Cutaneous lymphoma in Rt. triceps
Kluber,Corey	13	32	Sprained finger, Rt. hand
Kohn,Michael	12	182	R. forearm strain

FIVE-YEAR INJURY LOG

Pitchers	Yr	Days	Injury
Kuo,Hong-Chih	09	85	Sore L. elbow
	10	18	Sore L. shoulder
	11	56	L. low back strain
Kuroda,Hiroki	09	72	Strained L. oblique; concussion
Lackey,John	09	41	Inflam - R. elbow
	11	24	Strained R. elbow
	12	182	TJS - R. elbow
	13	176	Rt. biceps strain
Laffey,Aaron	09	46	Strained R. oblique
	10	42	Fatigued – L. shoulder
Lannan,John	13	106	Strained Lt. quad; Lt. knee tend.
Latos,Mat	10	15	Strained L. oblique
	11	11	Strained R. shoulder
Leake,Mike	10	15	Fatigue – R. shoulder
LeCure,Sam	11	30	R. forearm strain
Lee,Cliff	10	26	Strained R. abdominal muscle
	12	20	L. oblique strain
Leroux,Chris	09	22	Inflamed R. shoulder
	10	30	Strained R. elbow
	11	25	Strained L. calf
	12	151	Strained R. pectoral muscle
Lester,Jon	11	19	Strained lower L. lat muscle
Lewis,Colby	12	101	Surg. torn tendon R. elbow
	13	185	Recovery from Rt. elbow surgery
Lidge,Brad	09	19	Sprained R. knee
	10	47	Inflam R. elbow;R knee; elbow surg.
	11	113	R. posterior rotator cuff strain
	12	46	Abdominal wall strain
Lilly,Ted	09	27	Inflam L. shoulder; surgery L. knee
	10	20	Recov. fr. surg. - L. shoulder
	12	143	L. shoulder inflam.; str neck
	13	85	Neck sprain; Rt. ribcage strain
Lincoln,Brad	11	11	Bruised R. arm
Lindstrom,Matt	09	37	Strained R. elbow
	10	15	Back spasms
	11	16	Nerve injury in upper R. arm
	12	47	Torn ligament in R. middle finger
Liriano,Francisco	09	22	L. arm fatigue
	09	174	Strained R. forearm
	11	36	Inflam L. should.; Strain L. should.
	13	41	Fractured Rt. forearm
Litsch,Jesse	10	128	TJS recovery; Torn labrum R. hip
	11	60	Impingement in R. shoulder
	12	183	Surgery to repair R. biceps tendon
Lohse,Kyle	09	54	Strained R. forearm; L. groin
	10	84	Exertional compart,R. forearm
Lopez,Wilton	11	19	Irritation-ulnar nerve R. elbow
	12	28	Sprained R. elbow
Loux,Shane	12	62	Neck strain
Lowe,Mark	10	148	Herniated lumbar disc
	12	45	Strained R. intercostal muscle
	13	16	Neck stiffness
Luebke,Cory	12	159	TJS
	13	183	Recovery from Lt. elbow surgery
Lynn,Lance	11	50	L. oblique strain
Lyon,Brandon	11	142	PaR.ially rotator cuff tear

FIVE-YEAR INJURY LOG

Pitchers	Yr	Days	Injury
Madson,Ryan	10	70	Fractured R. toe + surgery
	11	26	R. hand contusion
	12	183	TJS
	13	127	Recovery from Rt. elbow surgery
Maholm,Paul	11	42	L. shoulder strain
	13	32	Bruised Lt. wrist
Maloney,Matt	11	87	L. oblique strain
Marcum,Shaun	09	183	Recovery from TJS 9/08
	10	16	Inflam – R. elbow
	12	70	R. elbow tightness
	13	41	Neck Strain; TOS
Marmol,Carlos	12	16	Strained R. hamstring
Marquis,Jason	10	111	Debris in R. elbow
	11	44	Fractured R. fibula
	12	43	Fractured L. wrist
	13	72	Strained Rt. elbow
Marshall,Sean	13	131	Sprained Lt. shoulder; Tendinitis
Marte,Luis	12	51	Strained L. hamstring
	13	61	Recovery from Rt. shoulder surgery
Martinez,Cristhian	13	176	Rt. shoulder strain
Masset,Nick	09	15	Strained L. oblique
	12	182	Sore R. shoulder
	13	183	Recovery from Rt. shoulder surgery
Mateo,Marcos	11	86	R. elbow soreness
	12	183	Sore R. elbow
Matsuzaka,Daisuke	09	124	Weak and strained R. shoulder
	10	44	Strained neck; R. forearm
	11	135	Sprained R. elbow
	12	121	TJS recovery+trained R. upper trap
Mattheus,Ryan	11	25	R. shoulder strain
	12	27	Plantar fascia strain in L. foot
	13	67	Fractured Rt. hand
Matusz,Brian	11	59	Strained L. intecostal muscle
Mazzaro,Vin	09	27	Tendinitis – R. shoulder
McAllister,Zach	13	50	Sprained Rt. middle finger
McCarthy,Brandon	09	88	Stress fracture – R. scapula
	10	66	Recovery from shoulder surgery
	11	45	Stress reaction in R. scapula
	12	95	Strained R. shoulderx2 + skull Fx
	13	65	Rt. shoulder inflammation
McClellan,Kyle	11	15	L. hip flexor strain
	12	139	R. elbow strain
McDonald,James	13	129	Rt. shoulder discomfort
McGowan,Dustin	09	183	Recov. Fr. labrum surg.-R. shoulder
	10	182	Sore R. shoulder
	11	158	Recov. fr. surg. - R. shoulder
	12	183	R. Plant. Fasciitis+R. should. surg.
	13	101	Strnd rt oblique; Sore rt shoulder
McPherson,Kyle	13	34	Recovery from Rt. elbow surgery
Medlen,Kris	10	59	PaR.ial tear of UCL- R. elbow
	11	178	Recovery from TJS
Meek,Evan	09	54	Strained L. oblique
	11	116	R. shoulder tendinitis
Mejia,Jenry	13	160	Rt. elbow inflamon; discomfort
Mickolio,Kam	09	28	Inflam R. shoulder
Mijares,Jose	10	58	Strained L. knee; blured vision
	11	15	Strained L. elbow

FIVE-YEAR INJURY LOG

Pitchers	Yr	Days	Injury
Miller,Andrew	09	25	Strained R. oblique
	12	32	Strained L. hamstring
	13	85	Lt. foot surgery
Miller,Justin	13	62	Recovery from Rt. elbow surgery
Millwood,Kevin	10	16	Strained R. forearm
Moore,Matt	13	36	Lt. elbow soreness
Morales,Franklin	09	51	Strained L. shoulder
	10	27	L. shoulder weakness
	11	33	Strained L. forearm
	12	41	Fatigue in L. shoulder
	13	106	Strained lower back; Lt. pectoral
Morrow,Brandon	09	15	Tendinitis – R. triceps
	11	21	Inflam - R. forearm
	12	74	Strained L. oblique
	13	121	Rt. forearm strain
Mortensen,Clayton	13	15	Rt. hip impingement
Morton,Charlie	09	7	Strained L. oblique
	10	35	R. shoulder weakness
	12	137	Recovering from R. hip surgery+TJS
	13	74	Recovery from Rt. elbow surgery
Moscoso,Guillermo	10	4	Blister - R. index finger
Moseley,Dustin	09	170	Irritation - R. elbow
	11	60	L. shoulder strain
	12	179	Strained R. shoulder
Mota,Guillermo	09	15	Ingrown toenail
	10	15	IT band syndrome
Motte,Jason	10	27	Sprained R. shoulder
	13	183	Rt. elbow surgery
Moylan,Peter	11	143	Back surgery
Mujica,Edward	12	18	Fractured R. pinky toe
Myers,Brett	09	98	Torn and frayed labrum - R. hip
	13	131	Rt. elbow inflammation
Narveson,Chris	11	15	L. thumb laceration
	12	171	L. rotator cuff tear
	13	74	Sprained middle finger
Nathan,Joe	10	182	TJS - R. elbow
	11	31	Strained R. flexor muscle
Neshek,Pat	09	185	Recovery from TJS
	10	37	Inflamed R. middle finger
Nicasio,Juan	11	54	Neck surgery
	12	123	Strained L. knee
Niemann,Jeff	10	21	Strained R. shoulder
	11	45	Stiff back
	12	109	Fractured R. fibula
	13	183	Rt. shoulder surgery
Niese,Jonathon	09	60	Torn R. hamstring tendon
	10	19	Strained R. hamstring
	11	36	Intercostal strain of the R. side
	13	51	Partially torn Lt. rotator cuff
Nolasco,Ricky	10	35	Torn meniscus – R. knee
Norberto,Jordan	12	68	Str + tendinitis in L. shoulder
Norris,Bud	10	35	Biceps tendinitis – R. shoulder
	12	16	L. knee sprain
Nova,Ivan	12	17	Inflam in R. rotator cuff
	13	27	Rt. triceps inflammation
Nuno,Vidal	13	23	Strained Lt. groin
O'Day,Darren	11	85	Torn labrm R. hip+Inflam R. should.
O'Flaherty,Eric	10	41	Viral infection
	13	135	Lt. elbow surgery

FIVE-YEAR INJURY LOG

Pitchers	Yr	Days	Injury
Ogando,Alexi	12	35	Strained R. groin
	13	87	Rt. shoulder inflam x 2; Rt. biceps
Ohlendorf,Ross	10	68	Strained R. lat; sore back
	11	136	R. shoulder strain
	13	20	Rt. shoulder inflammation
Ohman,Will	09	130	Inflam – L. shoulder
Okajima,Hideki	10	22	Strained R. hamstring
Oliver,Darren	09	11	Strained L. triceps
	13	22	Lt. shoulder strain
Olsen,Scott	09	129	Tendinitis/torn labrum R. shoulder
	10	68	Tightness L. shoulder
	11	182	L. shoulder Inflam
Ondrusek,Logan	11	18	Strained R. forearm
Ortiz,Ramon	13	119	Rt. elbow strain
Oswalt,Roy	09	19	Lower back pain
	11	63	Lower back Inflam
	13	60	Strained Lt. hamstring
Outman,Josh	09	107	Sprained L. elbow
	10	182	Recov. fr. surg. - L. elbow
	12	37	Strained oblique
Oviedo,Juan Carlos	12	73	TJS
	13	183	Recovery from Rt. elbow surgery
Owings,Micah	09	24	Tightness - R. shoulder
	12	161	R. elbow surgery
Padilla,Vicente	09	16	Strained deLoid - R. shoulder
	10	75	Sore R. foreram; herniated disc
	11	161	R. elbow surgery
	12	15	Strained R. bicep
Parker,Blake	12	112	R. elbow stress react+bone bruise
Parnell,Bobby	11	40	Circulatory issues R. middle finger
	13	61	Neck stiffness
Parra,Manny	11	183	Facet joint injury in R. back
	13	30	Strained Lt. pectoral muscle
Patton,Troy	12	39	Sprained R. ankle
Paulino,Felipe	09	19	Strained R. groin
	10	83	R. shoulder tendinitis
	12	149	TJS - L. elbow
	13	183	Recovery from Rt. elbow surgery
Peavy,Jake	09	101	Strained tendon - R. ankle
	10	88	Detached lat in R. shoulder
	11	57	Recov.,R. should, Str adductor
	13	44	Fractured rib
Pelfrey,Mike	12	165	TJS
	13	15	Back strain
Pena,Tony	11	124	Tendinitis In R. elbow
Perez,Chris	13	31	Rt. shoulder soreness
Perez,Juan	13	51	Torn UCL ligament, Lt. elbow
Perez,Luis	12	87	TJS - L. elbow
	13	155	Recovery from Lt. elbow surgery
Perez,Martin	13	43	Cracked ulna bone, Lt. forearm
Perez,Rafael	12	161	Strained L. lat/ankle injury
Perkins,Glen	09	52	Inflam L. shoulder; elbow
	11	26	Strained R. oblique muscle
Perry,Ryan	10	26	Tendinitis upper R. biceps
	11	15	Infected eye
Pestano,Vinnie	13	16	Rt. elbow tendinitis
Pettibone,Jonathan	13	63	Strained Rt. shoulder
Pettitte,Andy	12	83	Fractured fibula in L. ankle
	13	17	Strained Lt. trapezius muscle

FIVE-YEAR INJURY LOG

Pitchers	Yr	Days	Injury
Phelps,David	13	71	Rt. forearm strain
Pineda,Michael	12	182	Surgery torn labrum R. shoulder
	13	98	Recovery from Rt. shoulder surgery
Pomeranz,Drew	13	45	Lt. bicep tendinitis
Pomeranz,Stuart	12	131	Strained L. oblique
Price,David	13	47	Lt. triceps strain
Pryor,Stephen	13	168	Torn Rt. lat muscle
Purcey,David	10	19	Strained ligaments – R. foot
Putnam,Zach	13	110	Rt. elbow soreness
Putz,J.J.	09	122	Bone chips - R. elbow
	10	15	Tendinitis – R. knee
	11	27	R. elbow tendinitis
	13	75	Strnd Rt. elbow; dislocated finger
Qualls,Chad	09	35	Dislocated kneecap - L. leg
	12	15	Irritation of L. toe
Ramirez,Erasmo	12	62	Strained R. elbow flexor
Ramirez,Ramon	12	24	Hamstring strain
Rauch,Jon	11	33	Appendicitis; Torn caR.ilge R. knee
Ray,Chris	09	25	Biceps tendinitis - R. arm
	10	16	Strained R. ribcage muscle
	11	61	Strained R. shoulder
Resop,Chris	10	49	Strained L. oblique
Reyes,Jo-Jo	09	56	Strained L. hamstring
	10	33	Strained R. knee
Reynolds,Greg	09	34	Sore R. shoulder
	10	70	Bruised R. elbow
Reynolds,Matt	13	112	Strained Lt. elbow
Rice,Scott	13	21	Sports hernia
Richard,Clayton	11	86	Strained L. shoulder
	13	122	Lt. shoulder surgery; stomach virus
Richards,Garrett	11	21	R. adductor strain
Richmond,Scott	09	28	Tendinitis – R. shoulder
	10	78	Impingement - R. shoulder
Rivera,Mariano	12	153	Torn ACL in R. knee
Robertson,David	12	33	Strained L. oblique
Robles,Maricio	11	74	Recov. fr. surg. - L. shoulder
Rodney,Fernando	11	39	Strained upper back
Rodriguez,Fernando	13	183	Rt. elbow surgery
Rodriguez,Francisco	11	142	Inflam - R. shoulder
Rodriguez,Henry	11	28	R. arm injury
	12	91	Low back strain+ R. index finger
Rodriguez,Wandy	11	21	Fluid in L. elbow
	13	116	Lt. forearm tightness
Rogers,Esmil	11	84	R. lat strain
Rogers,Mark	13	152	Rt. shoulder instability
Romero,J.C.	09	70	Strained L. forearm
	10	18	Recov. fr. surg. on L. elbow
	11	15	R. calf strain
Romero,Ricky	09	22	Strained L. oblique
Romo,Sergio	09	54	Sprained R. elbow
	11	18	R. elbow Inflam
Rosario,Sandy	12	110	R. quad strain
Ross,Robbie	12	20	Sore L. forearm
Ross,Tyson	11	66	Strained L. oblique muscle
	13	17	Lt. shoulder subluxation
Runzler,Dan	10	54	Dislocated L. knee
	12	153	Strained lat muscle
Rzepczynski,Marc	10	45	Fractured middle finger - L. hand

FIVE-YEAR INJURY LOG

Pitchers	Yr	Days	Injury
Sabathia,C.C.	12	15	Sore L. elbow+ strain abductor
	13	5	Strained Lt. hamstring
Saito,Takashi	10	18	L. hamstring strain
	11	88	L. hamstring strain
	12	126	Strained L. hamstring+ calf str
Salas,Fernando	13	36	Rt. shoulder irritation
Sanabia,Alex	13	126	Rt. groin discomfort
Sanches,Brian	10	22	Strained R. hamstring
	11	26	R. elbow strain
Sanchez,Anibal	09	104	Sprained R. shoulder x 2
	13	20	Strained Rt. shoulder
Sanchez,Eduardo	11	92	R. shoulder strain
Sanchez,Jonathan	11	80	L. biceps tendinitis
	12	61	L. bicep tendinitis
	12	36	Tendinitis in L. bicep
Santana,Ervin	09	60	Spr MCL R. elbow+inflam triceps
Santana,Johan	09	45	Bone spurs-L. elbow
	11	182	L. sholder surgery
	12	70	Inflam of lower back+ spr R. ankle
	13	183	Lt. shoulder surgery
Santos,Sergio	12	166	Surgery torn labrum in R. shoulder
	13	109	Rt. triceps strain
Saunders,Joe	09	18	Tightness - L. shoulder
	12	15	L. shoulder strain
Savery,Joe	13	45	Lt. elbow stiffness
Scherzer,Max	09	9	Sore R. shoulder
Schlereth,Daniel	12	166	Tendinitis in L. shoulder
Schwimer,Michael	13	39	Rt. shoulder strain
Scribner,Evan	11	27	R. shoulder strain
Septimo,Leyson	12	18	Inflam in L. biceps
	13	72	Lt. shoulder strain
Sheets,Ben	12	25	R. shoulder Inflam
Sherrill,George	10	15	Back tightness
	11	30	L. elbow Inflam
	12	177	TJS - L. elbow
Simon,Alfredo	09	173	Soreness R. elbow
	10	21	Strained L. hamstring
	11	16	Strained R. hamstring
Slaten,Doug	11	89	L. elbow ulnar neuritis
Slowey,Kevin	09	95	Strained R. wrist
	10	15	Strained R. triceps
	11	94	Sore R. biceps; Abdominal strain
	13	66	Rt. forearm discomfort
Smith,Joe	09	66	Sprained L. knee; sore R. R/C
	11	15	Abdominal strain
Smith,Jordan	12	182	Sore R. elbow
Smyly,Drew	12	37	Strain R. intercostal+ fing. blister
Sonnanstine,Andy	10	16	Strained L. hamstring
Soria,Joakim	09	25	Strained rotator cuff – R. shoulder
	12	182	Recovering from TJS
	13	99	Recovery from Rt. elbow surgery
Soriano,Rafael	11	76	Inflam - R. elbow
Sosa,Henry	09	61	Torn muscle-R. shoulder
Stauffer,Tim	10	52	Appendectomy
	12	182	R. elbow sprain
Stetter,Mitch	11	137	L. hip injury
Storen,Drew	12	106	Elbow injury

FIVE-YEAR INJURY LOG

Pitchers	Yr	Days	Injury
Strasburg,Stephen	10	61	Stiff R. shoulder; TJS surgery 9/10
	11	160	Recovery from TJS
	13	15	Strained Rt. latissimus dorsi
Street,Huston	10	79	Strained R. shoulder
	11	17	R. triceps strain
	12	72	Strained L. calf+ L. lat str
	13	15	Strained Lt. calf
Strop,Pedro	13	15	Lower back strain
Stults,Eric	09	31	Sprained L. thumb
	12	48	Strained L. latissimus dorsi
Stutes,Michael	12	26	R. shoulder Inflam
	13	89	Rt. biceps tendinitis
Surkamp,Eric	12	182	TJS
	13	88	Recovery from Lt. elbow surgery
Swarzak,Anthony	12	33	Strained R. rotator cuff
	13	7	Fractured ribs
Talbot,Mitch	10	15	Strained back
	11	125	Strain R. elbow; Strain lower back
	11	56	Strained R. intercostal muscle
Taylor,Andrew	13	183	Lt. labrum tear
Tazawa,Junichi	09	14	Strained L. groin
	10	182	TJS out for 2010
	11	88	Recovery from TJS
Teaford,Everett	12	25	Strained lower abdominal
Tejeda,Robinson	09	30	Tendinitis – R. rotator cuff
	10	30	Tendinitis – R. biceps
	11	36	Inflam - R. shoulder
Tepesch,Nicholas	13	57	Rt. elbow inflammation
Texeira,Kanekoa	10	27	Strained R. elbow
Thatcher,Joe	10	18	STrained L. shoulder
	11	125	L. shoulder surgery
	12	37	Mid-back strain
Thompson,Rich	10	20	Inflam – R. shoulder
Thornton,Matt	10	16	Inflam L. forearm
	13	20	Strained Rt. oblique
Tillman,Chris	13	5	Strained Lt. abdominal
Tobin,Mason	11	162	TJS
Tolleson,Shawn	13	170	Strained lower back
Tomlin,Josh	11	35	Soreness in R. elbow
	12	72	Inflam in R. elbow+R. wrist
	13	146	Recovery from Rt. elbow surgery
Troncoso,Ramon	13	21	Pericarditis
Uehara,Koji	09	121	Tndntis R. elbow+strain L. hammy
	10	70	Strained L. hammy; R. elbow
	12	77	Strained R. lat
Valdes,Raul	12	62	Torn meniscus r. knee+Str R. hip
Valverde,Jose	09	47	Strained R. calf
Vargas,Jason	13	56	Blood clot, Lt. arm
Venters,Jonny	12	16	L. elbow impingement
	13	183	Sprained Lt. elbow
Villanueva,Carlos	11	27	Strained R. forearm
Vizcaino,Arodys	12	183	TJS
	13	183	Recovery from Rt. elbow surgery
Vogelsong,Ryan	12	10	Strained lower back
	13	80	Fractured Rt. hand
Volquez,Edinson	09	140	Inflam nerve R. elb.; back spasms
	10	104	Recovery from TJS 8/09
Wada,Tsuyoshi	12	182	TJS - R. elbow
	13	74	Recovery from Lt. elbow surgery

FIVE-YEAR INJURY LOG

Pitchers	Yr	Days	Injury
Wade,Cory	09	40	Strained & bursitis - R. shoulder
	10	88	Surg.-frayed labrum, R/C
Wainwright,Adam	11	182	TJS
Walden,Jordan	12	41	Strained R. bicep
	13	17	Rt. shoulder inflammation
Walters,PJ	12	79	Inflam in R. shoulder
Wang,Chien-Ming	09	125	Strain R. shoulder; weak hip
	10	182	Recov. fr. surg. - R. shoulder
	11	121	Recovery from R. shoulder surgery
	12	113	Strained L. hamstring+R. hip str
Weaver,Jered	12	22	Strained lower back
	13	51	Fractured Lt. elbow
Webb,Brandon	09	176	Bursitis - R. shoulder
	10	182	Recovery from 8/09 shoulder surg.
	11	183	Recov. fr. surg. - R. shoulder
Webb,Ryan	11	51	R. shoulder Inflam
Weiland,Kyle	12	162	R. shoulder bursitis
Wells,Randy	11	50	R. forearm strain
Westbrook,Jake	09	183	Recovery from TJ Surgery
	13	51	Sore back; Rt. elbow inflammation
Wheeler,Dan	11	15	Strained L. calf
White,Alex	11	94	Soreness in R. middle finger
	13	184	Rt. elbow strain
Wieland,Joe	12	150	TJS
	13	183	Recovery from Rt. elbow surgery
Williams,Jerome	12	35	Respir. infection+str L. hamstring
Wilson,Alex	13	83	Sprained Rt. thumb
Wilson,Brian	11	35	L. oblique strain
	12	174	TJS
	13	20	Recovery from Rt. elbow surgery
Withrow,Chris	12	32	R. shoulder strain
Wolf,Randy	12	11	TJS 10/2012
Wood,Blake	12	182	TJS - R. elbow
	13	103	Recovery from Rt. elbow surgery
Wood,Kerry	10	52	Strained back; R. index finger
	11	22	Blister on R. index finger
	12	19	R. shoulder fatigue
Wood,Tim	13	150	Rt. rotator cuff strain
Worley,Vance	12	54	Loose bodies in R. elbow+ Inflam
Worrell,Mark	09	183	TJS 3/09
Wright,Wesley	09	20	Strained L. shoulder
Wuertz,Michael	10	29	Tendinitis - R. shoulder
	11	53	Strain L. hammy; Tndnts R. thumb
Young,Chris	09	112	Inflam R. shoulder
	10	164	Inflam - R. shoulder
	11	165	R. biceps tendinitis
	13	18	Strained Lt. quad
Zagurski,Mike	09	183	Recovery from TJ Surgery
Zambrano,Carlos	09	42	Strain L. hamstring; strained back
	11	15	Lower back soreness
Zimmermann,Jord.	09	78	R. elbow soreness
	10	119	Recovery from TJS
Zito,Barry	11	110	R. foot sprain
Zumaya,Joel	09	96	Sore R. shoulder x 2
	10	96	Fract. olecranon process-R. elbow
	11	183	Recov. fr. surg. - R. elbow
	12	173	Recovery from TJS

Top 100 Impact Prospects for 2014

by Rob Gordon and Jeremy Deloney

The following minor league prospects are expected to be the ones who will have the most impact during the 2014 season.

Jose Abreu (1B, CHW) agreed to a huge MLB deal (6 years/ $68M), and much will be expected. He'll be 27 at the start of 2014, and projects to hit for middle-of-the-order power. He lacks secondary skills, but the offensive production is too good to ignore.

Javier Baez (SS, CHC) has become one of the most exciting prospects in baseball. He smacked 37 HR in 2013 and has tremendous raw power. Logically, the Cubs will give the 21-year-old time to dominate at AAA, but the retooling organization might be tempted to bring him to MLB by mid-season.

Matt Barnes (RHP, BOS) performed inconsistently in AA, but still posted an 11.3 Dom. At times inefficient and overly aggressive, his plus fastball and solid-average secondary pitches give him upside. If his fastball location returns, he could become a #3-type starter.

Trevor Bauer (RHP, CLE) has been seemingly forgotten after a mediocre 2013 AAA campaign (5.4 Ctl, 7.9 Dom). The 22-year-old still owns excellent, natural stuff, and adds a hint of deception to keep hitters off guard. His turnaround will depend on his ability to command the fastball.

Tim Beckham (INF, TAM) hasn't lived up to #1 overall (2008) expectations, but the 23-year-old has plentiful tools. He profiles as an offensive-oriented second baseman, though he mostly played shortstop in 2013.

Engel Beltre (OF, TEX) is all about speed and defense, and will likely be on the MLB/AAA shuttle this season. The 24-year-old has tantalized for years with his offensive upside, but appears to have settled in as a guy who can hit .280 with 10 HR and 20+ SB.

Christian Bethancourt (C, ATL) is a defensive whiz with a strong throwing arm. He's struggled offensively in the past, but hit .277 with 12 HR in 2013. He won't provide a ton of offense, but his receiving skills could give him a shot at starting if the Braves are unable to re-sign Brian McCann.

Chad Bettis (RHP, COL) has a good mid-90s heater and plus slider, and looked fully recovered from a shoulder injury last year. His 5.64 ERA in 44.2 IP in MLB was mostly due to walks (4.0 Ctl), but he showed better skills in the minors (2.0 Ctl). Some scouts see him as a setup guy or future closer.

Xander Bogaerts (INF, BOS) is an impact bat, as evidenced by his .297/.388/.477 line with 15 HR between AA and AAA, but he also stands out with his glove. He was impressive enough to find a spot on the Red Sox playoff roster, and at only 20 years old, could earn an everyday job in 2014.

Archie Bradley (RHP, ARI) might be the best pitching prospect in baseball, and simply overpowered hitters at High-A and AA with his plus 93-96 mph fastball. In 26 starts, he was 14-5 with a 1.84 ERA and 9.6 Dom. He'll likely start the year at AAA, but could push for a rotation spot by mid-season.

Jackie Bradley (OF, BOS) began 2013 in the Opening Day lineup, but faltered. However, he should still have significant future value as a top-of-the-order hitter and stellar defender. With a patient approach, good pop, and average speed, he can contribute in a number of ways.

Gary Brown (OF, SF) has steadily regressed since his breakout season in 2011, and hit just .231 in the PCL as his strike zone judgment completely collapsed (33 BB/135 K). He still has fantasy potential for speed, and with a 40-man roster question looming, the Giants could use him as a 4th or 5th OF in 2014.

Kris Bryant (3B, CHC) had an outstanding pro debut. The 2013 2nd overall pick hit .336/.390/.688 across three different levels. He was the MVP of the Arizona Fall League (.364 BA, 6 HR), and could be ready sooner than anticipated.

Dylan Bundy (RHP, BAL) missed the entire 2013 season after having Tommy John surgery in June. The Orioles are likely to bring him back slowly, but given his athleticism, feel, and exquisite pitch mix, it wouldn't be surprising to see him start a handful of games in late 2014 and post solid results.

Nick Castellanos (OF, DET) stands a good chance at earning significant time in the majors given the Tigers uncertain outfield. Now that he has a few years of outfield play under his belt, he can be expected to increase his offensive production.

Kevin Chapman (LHP, HOU) continues to impress, with a loose, strong arm that can register 95 mph on the gun. He was excellent in AAA to begin the season, and was even better in 20.1 IP with the Astros. He may not project as a closer, but could work his way into setup innings and earn a handful of saves.

Michael Choice (OF, OAK) has advanced a level per year since being a first-rounder in 2010, and while he hasn't managed to repeat his 30 HR output from 2011, he did hit .302/.390/.445 with 14 HR in AAA last year. He draws walks and has improved his ct%, all while playing solid defense at all three OF positions.

Alex Colome (RHP, TAM) saw his season end in June thanks to an elbow strain, though he's expected to be healthy for spring training. He offers both velocity and movement, and his two breaking balls can give hitters fits. He should have a key role in 2014.

Daniel Corcino (RHP, CIN) got a lot of buzz last year as the next Johnny Cueto, but this was due more to his size than his stuff. He took a huge step back, going 7-14 with a 5.86 ERA at AAA, mostly because of walks (5.1 Ctl). He should get another shot in 2014, but is a risky play until he can throw more strikes.

C.J. Cron (1B, LAA) spent the entire season at AA and hit .274/.310/.428 with 36 doubles and 14 HR. He get criticized for his lack of walks, but he puts bat to ball easily and has plus-plus long ball pop. Albert Pujols is ensconced at 1B, but Cron could work his way into the DH mix.

Travis D'Arnaud (C, NYM) looked overmatched in his debut (.202 BA, 1 HR), but has a solid track record in the minors (.286/.347/.476). Catchers can take longer to develop, so you may have to be patient, but long-term, he has strong fantasy potential.

Matt Davidson (3B, ARI) is likely to challenge for the 3B job in the spring. He needs to make more consistent contact (72% career) to improve upon his .237 BA, but he has a good glove, the potential to hit 20+ HR, and is worth a flyer.

Chris Dwyer (LHP, KC) regressed in 2011-12, and many pundits dropped him from top prospect lists. But he rebounded in AAA in 2013 (3.55 ERA), and earned a late-season call-up. He still struggles to throw strikes (1.6 Cmd in AAA), though he has a strong arm and can be tough to make hard contact against.

Wilmer Flores (2B/3B, NYM) had an impressive breakout, hitting .321 with 15 HR at AAA. He failed to duplicate those results when filling in for David Wright, and has been slow to adjust in the past. He can be overly aggressive at times, but has good power and should see plenty of action in 2014.

Brian Flynn (LHP, MIA) lacks an overpowering fastball, but makes up for it by throwing two breaking balls and a good change-up. He got rocked in four September starts (8.50 ERA), but posted an impressive 2.63 ERA and 3.4 Cmd in 161 AA/AAA IP. He should get a shot at the back end of the Marlins rotation.

Maikel Franco (3B/1B, PHI) had a monster breakout in 2013, a combined .320 BA/36 doubles/31 HR. He can be overly aggressive at the plate, but his contact rate continues to improve (89% at AA). He's an average defender at 3B, but did see action at 1B also. Franco will likely start 2014 in AAA, waiting for an opportunity.

Reymond Fuentes (OF, SD) had a breakout season in 2013, hitting .330 with 35 SB between AA/AAA, but struggled when called up. He has plus speed and defense, but does not have much power. If Carlos Quentin is slow to recover from off-season knee surgery, Fuentes could earn early playing time.

Leury Garcia (INF, CHW) is mostly known for his defense, and his versatility could give him an opportunity in 2014. A switch-hitter, he has a fluid swing from both sides (though he won't hit for much power), and has plus speed to be effective on the basepaths.

Kevin Gausman (RHP, BAL) wasn't particularly effective in his 47.2 MLB IP in 2013. He reached the majors quickly (2012 first-rounder), and has the plus fastball and change-up to eventually become a #2-type starter.

Sean Gilmartin (LHP, ATL) had a horrible spring, and it carried over to the regular season. International League hitters teed off to the tune of a .304 BAA and a 5.74 ERA. A shoulder injury caused him to miss eight weeks of action, but he should be ready to compete for a rotation spot again in 2014.

Brian Goodwin (OF, WAS) has all the tools to be a superstar. He's athletic, runs well, and has good power. While he drew 66 walks in 2013, he also struck out 121 times, which resulted in only a .252 BA at AA. It will likely take an injury or trade of Denard Span to create an opportunity.

Alex Guerrero (SS/2B, LA) hit .290/.402/.576 with 21 HR in 328 in AB his last season in Cuba. He has good power for his size and decent plate discipline, but there are concerns about his ability to hit quality breaking balls. A good defender, Guerrero could contend for the starting 2B job.

David Hale (RHP, ATL) has a 92-94 mph fastball and good feel for his change-up. He doesn't rack up a ton of Ks, but induces weak contact. He impressed in two starts with the Braves (0.82 ERA), and should be in contention for a starting role.

Billy Hamilton (OF, CIN) remains the fastest player in baseball, and will give MLB catchers nightmares. Was used mostly as a pinch-runner in September, and compiled 13 SB and 9 runs in 13 games. He'll likely make the Reds 2014 roster, and could push for the starting CF job.

Andrew Heaney (LHP, MIA) has a good-but-not-overpowering fastball, and complements it with a nice slider and average change-up. He throws all three for strikes, and was 9-3 with a 1.60 ERA and just 26 walks in 95 IP between High-A and AA last year. He should reach MLB at some point in 2014.

Johnny Hellweg (RHP, MIL) was surprisingly effective at AAA (12-5, 3.15 ERA) before getting raked in MLB. He walked 81 batters in AAA, and had even more difficulty finding the strike zone after his call-up (7.6 Ctl, 0.4 Cmd). He still has potential, but tread carefully, as he could be a WHIP killer.

Heath Hembree (RHP, SF) made his MLB debut after spending two full-seasons at AAA. The 25-year-old reliever has a fastball the reaches the upper-90s, and backs it up with a plus slider. He has the dominating stuff to be a closer in the majors.

David Holmberg (RHP, ARI) was impressive in 2013, going 5-8 with a 2.75 ERA at AA. Not overpowering, he instead relies on excellent control and a good four-pitch mix. He made one start for the Diamondbacks, and could see sporadic action in 2014.

Bryan Holaday (C, DET) isn't known for his offensive skills, and doesn't profile as an everyday backstop. That doesn't mean he won't have value—the 25-year-old should win the backup job in Detroit, and get plenty of opportunities to contribute his average power behind the mediocre Alex Avila.

Luis Jimenez (3B, ANA) should compete for the Angels' starting 3B job, especially after hitting .260 in 104 AB in 2013. He lacks the plus power usually required for the position, but is a sound all-around hitter with decent defensive skills. His plate patience leaves lots to be desired, however.

Erik Johnson (RHP, CHW) had an incredible AA/AAA season (1.96 ERA, 2.5 Ctl, 8.3 Dom), and earned five late-season MLB starts. He has a strong, durable build, and a frame that allows him to keep the ball low in the zone. His velocity is much more consistent, and his hard slider is a legitimate strikeout pitch.

Nate Karns (RHP, WAS) struggled in three MLB starts, but put together a solid campaign at AA, going 10-6 with a 3.26 ERA and 155 Ks in 132.2 IP. He has two plus offerings in his 92-94 mph fastball and good power curve, and should compete for the 5th spot in the Nationals rotation.

Casey Kelly (RHP, SD) had Tommy John surgery in 2013, but has already started a throwing program. Prior to the injury, he came after hitters with a good low-90s sinking fastball and power curveball. The Padres will probably proceed cautiously, but he could be ready to return to the majors by mid-season.

Kevin Kiermaier (OF, TAM) offers outstanding speed and defense, and also finished second in BA in the AA Southern League. With keen instincts and above average wheels, he could be a solid contributor off the bench and a cheap source of SB.

Jeff Kobernus (2B, WAS) was taken by the Tigers in the Rule V draft in 2012, but failed to make their roster and was returned to the Nationals. He has a nice approach at the plate, and stole 40+ in each of the past three seasons. He projects as a utility player who can fill in at 2B/3B and all three OF spots.

Tommy La Stella (2B, ATL) might be the best pure hitter in the Braves system. The 24-year-old has a short, quick stroke, makes consistent contact, and now has a career line of .327/.422/.473 over three seasons. He's a solid defender, and could get a chance to replace Dan Uggla.

C.C. Lee (RHP, CLE) missed most of 2012 after Tommy John surgery, but returned with aplomb. He pitched on four levels, including eight games with the Indians. He throws from a deceptive, low ¾ slot, and possesses a quality, lively sinker and wipeout slider. He could be a speculative source of saves.

Zach Lee (RHP, LA) had his best season as a pro, going 10-10 with a 3.22 ERA, walking just 35 while striking out 131. The 22-year-old uses a solid four-pitch mix to keep hitters off balance. He'll likely start at AAA, but is the Dodgers most advanced pitching prospect, and should be in MLB by mid-season.

Chia-Jen Lo (RHP, HOU) has missed a lot of time over the past three seasons due to elbow injuries, but he could factor into the closer mix for the Astros in 2014. He pitched 19 games with Houston and notched two saves. He has a heavy fastball and a solid-average curveball that give him strikeout ability.

Taylor Lindsey (2B, LAA) stood out among a number of disappointing Angels prospects, and is on the cusp of an MLB role. He hit a career-high 17 HR in AA last year, and batted .274/.339/.441. One of the knocks against the 21-year-old is his defense, but he's shown marked improvement with his footwork and range at 2B.

Francisco Lindor (SS, CLE) is a Top 10 player in virtually every prospect list, and his time to shine will likely come in 2015. However, he has the fundamentals and approach to be successful in MLB right now. The only thing currently lacking is over-the-fence power, and even that could evolve to 15+ HR someday.

Matt Magill (RHP, LA) is an unconventional prospect (former 31st rounder) who has added life and velocity to his fastball. His bread-and-butter offering is a wipe-out slider that led to a 10.6 Dom in AAA last year, but control issues caught up to him in six MLB starts (9.1 Ctl, 6.51 ERA). He could see additional starts in 2014, but keep expectations realistic.

Jake Marisnick (OF, MIA) was horrible after his call-up, hitting .183 with 27 whiffs in 109 AB. A torn meniscus in his left knee required off-season surgery, but he should be ready to go by spring training, and will compete for a starting role. He's a plus defender with a great arm and above-average speed, but will need to prove he can hit in the majors.

Nick Maronde (LHP, LAA) has been utilized as a lefty specialist in MLB, but his talent warrants a shot at higher leverage innings, and that should come in 2014. With a mid-90s fastball and plus slider, he could eventually slide into a setup role.

Cody Martin (RHP, ATL) has an outside chance to win a spot in the Braves rotation. The 23-year-old utilizes an effective four-pitch mix to keep hitters off balance, and was 6-7 with a 3.16 ERA between AA and AAA last year. He started his career as a reliever, and could make the roster as a swingman in 2014.

Ethan Martin (RHP, PHI) is strong-armed but has struggled with control in the past, and that hurt him in his first MLB stint (6.08 ERA, 26 BB and 42 hits in 40 IP). If he can improve his command, he has good long-term potential.

Carlos Martinez (RHP, STL) has one of the better fastballs in the NL, hitting 100 mph during the World Series. He shuttled between Memphis and St. Louis for most of 2013, logging only 79.2 IP in the minors, going 6-3 with a 2.49 ERA. He was very effective in relief, but his role (SP/RP) is still up in the air.

Alex Meyer (RHP, MIN) missed time in 2013 due to shoulder soreness, but returned in August and pitched well. The 6'9" former Nationals prospect has high strikeout ability and should play a prominent role in 2014.

Rafael Montero (RHP, NYM) continues to make strong progress despite having less than overpowering stuff. His best asset is pinpoint control, as he walked 35 batters and struck out 150 in AA/AAA. With all of the injuries to the Mets rotation, he'll be given a shot to win a starting role.

Mark Montgomery (RHP, NYY) expected to see bullpen action in 2013 based on his deceptive delivery and knockout slider, but that never materialized. His control went backwards (5.6 Ctl in AAA), but his swing-and-miss stuff could work well in late innings.

Adam Morgan (LHP, PHI) was on the verge of making his MLB debut last May, but a shoulder injury cost him eight weeks. He was only marginally effective afterwards, going 2-8 with a 3.91 ERA. When healthy, he does a great job of throwing strikes and could develop into a nice back-end starter.

Hunter Morris (1B, MIL) has been on the verge of being a useful fantasy option, but failed to secure a starting role last spring, and then regressed at AAA. He has plus power (24 HR last year), but was overly aggressive, striking out 122 times and hitting just .247. He should get another shot at the starting 1B job.

J.R. Murphy (C, NYY) could benefit from an uncertain Yankees catching situation, though he'll need to show more than the .154 BA he posted in MLB in 2013. He doesn't profile as a superstar, but his line drive approach gets him to double-digit HR on an annual basis. His defense continues to improve as well.

Jimmy Nelson (RHP, MIL) has a fastball that sits in the 92-94 mph range, and he backs that up with a good hard slider. 2013 was his most consistent season as a pro, as he was 10-10 with a 3.25 ERA, and struck out 163 batters in 152.1 IP. He should contend for a spot at the back-end of the Brewers rotation in 2014, but could also be effective in relief.

Sean Nolin (LHP, TOR) earned a spot start for the Blue Jays in May, and his numbers appear better than what his stuff should indicate. He has a big body, but possesses outstanding command and control of four offerings. He posted a 2.77 ERA and 9.5 Dom between AA and AAA.

Jake Odorizzi (RHP, TAM) finished third in the International League in strikeouts, and is among the most steady and consistent pitchers in the high minors. The 23-year-old may not have a true out pitch, but he sequences his offerings very well, and can add and subtract effectively.

Mike Olt (3B, CHC) had a disastrous season, hitting .201/.303./.381 with 132 punch-outs. He suffered a concussion the previous winter and had lingering vision problems. The Cubs hope he can rediscover the stroke that saw him hit .288 with 28 HR in 2012. He should be have a shot at a starting job in March.

Chris Owings (SS, ARI) followed his breakout 2012 season with an even more impressive campaign, hitting .330 with 12 HR and 20 SB. The 22-year-old also looked good in his MLB debut. His range and arm are below average, but his offense more than makes up for it. He will likely push Didi Gregorius for the starting SS job in the spring.

Kyle Parker (OF/1B, COL) might have the best raw power in the Rockies system. He swings and misses too often to hit for a high BA, but has the tools to develop into a solid corner OF. He'll likely start 2014 at AAA, and could challenge for playing time later in the year. He also saw action at 1B in the AFL.

James Paxton (LHP, SEA) did not fare particularly well at AAA in 2013 (4.45 ERA, 3.6 Ctl, 8.1 Dom), but he impressed the organization with four September MLB starts. He's long struggled with his fastball command, but his pitch mix and tenacity have always given him upside.

Joc Pederson (OF, LA) hit .278/.381/.497 with 22 HR and 31 SB. He has a nice left-handed bat, and one of the best power/speed mixes in the minors. He'll probably spend most of 2014 at AAA, and wait for an opening.

Jake Petricka (RHP, CHW) moved to the bullpen in 2013 and had his best season as a pro. He can reach the mid-to-high 90s and effectively pitches low in the zone due to his height and arm slot. He could see high leverage innings if he can clean up his control and find consistency with his erratic curveball.

Kevin Pillar (OF, TOR) is by no means a toolsy prospect, but he's a consistent and steady performer who maximizes his abilities. The natural hitter batted .307/.353/.471 across AA and AAA, makes easy contact with a simple stroke, and has the speed to steal bags and range well at all three OF positions.

Josmil Pinto (C, MIN) could be the main benefactor of the Twins decision to move Joe Mauer to 1B. The 24-year-old backstop vastly exceeded expectations by hitting .309/.400/.482 between AA and AAA, with 32 doubles and 15 HR. He'll need polish behind the plate, but the offensive production is there for a prominent role.

Anthony Ranaudo (RHP, BOS) has the pitch mix and tenacity to work his way into the rotation mix. He rebounded to appear in the Futures Game after a miserable 2012 campaign. With improving fastball command and the ability to induce weak contact, the 23-year-old is back on the prospect map.

Enny Romero (LHP, TAM) has a plus fastball, and leveraged his success in AA to reach the majors for a spot start in September. His 7.1 Dom may not be eye-popping, but that should increase once he learns to command his secondary offerings and throw more consistent strikes.

Keyvius Sampson (RHP, SD) got off to a slow start at AAA and was demoted after only four starts. The 22-year-old corrected the problem and posted a 2.26 ERA in AA. He'll likely contend with Robbie Erlin, Joe Wieland, and others for the 4th and 5th spots in the Padres rotation, and is worth an endgame look.

Tony Sanchez (C, PIT), the 4th overall pick in the 2009 draft, has been a huge disappointment, but he did show some growth at the plate last year, and had a career high 10 HR to go along with a

.288 average in AAA. He's improved defensively and could see an expanded role as the season progresses.

Miguel Sano (3B, MIN) is a long shot to win the Twins starting 3B job in spring training, but he'll certanly be available for an early promotion. His winter league was cut short by an elbow strain, though he'll be healthy by spring. He blasted 35 HR between High-A and AA, and has a mature approach. There are some wrinkles to iron out, but the near-term and long-term benefits are immense.

Jonathan Schoop (INF, BAL) is a versatile infielder who continues to evolve with both the bat and glove. He's finally tapping into his above average power potential while maintaining his natural feel for hitting. There is certainly room for improvement in his plate discipline, but he reached the majors at age 21, and should be a nifty infield option.

Marcus Semien (INF, CHW) had a breakout season that culminated in a September call-up. The extremely athletic 22-year-old can play all infield positions but 1B, and should be able to carve out a role. Not the most polished defender, he's evolving into a potent offensive contributor with average pop and solid speed.

Jonathan Singleton (1B, HOU) began 2013 serving a 50-game drug suspension. He returned in late May and didn't have a standout campaign, hitting .220/.340/.347 in 245 AB in AAA. With plus bat speed and a discerning eye at the plate, he offers significant offensive value.

Matt Skole (1B, WAS) missed all of 2013 following wrist and elbow surgery, but was back in action in the AFL. In 2012, he hit .291 with 27 HR, 11 SB, and 99 BB. He has some nice offensive potential, and could be in line for significant playing time if Adam LaRoche gets off to another slow start.

Carson Smith (RHP, SEA) is not a household name, not even among prospect pundits. An 8th round pick in 2011, he throws from a low ¾ slot and uses a mid-90s fastball that rarely gets hit into the air. He can also wipe hitters out with a plus, hard slider. And after posting a 1.80 ERA, 3.1 Ctl, and 12.8 Dom along with 15 saves in AA last year, he's a terrific sleeper for saves.

Max Stassi (C, HOU) doesn't have a ton of offensive upside, though he hit .277/.333/.529 with 17 HR prior in AA prior to a September call-up last year. He's a solid receiver with a strong, accurate arm and starting potential.

George Springer (OF, HOU) finished 3 HR shy of posting a 40 HR/40 SB between AA and AAA. There is still quite a bit of swing-and-miss in his game, though he works counts and gets on base consistently. He should be patrolling CF for the Astros at some point in 2014, and could be a viable Rookie of the Year candidate if given an opportunity.

Zeke Spruill (RHP, ARI) came over in the Martin Prado trade and made six appearances with the Diamondbacks, posting a 5.56 ERA. The 23-year-old has decent stuff, but the lack of a true out pitch could leave him a bit short as a starter. Still, he could be a stop-gap option until top prospect Archie Bradley is ready.

Robert Stephenson (RHP, CIN) has one of the better power arsenals in the minors. The 20-year-old overpowered hitters at three levels, going 7-7 with a 2.99 ERA with 136 K's in 114.1 IP.

He's only made four starts at AA, but if he pitches like he did in 2013, the Reds may have to find a spot for him by July.

Marcus Stroman (RHP, TOR) has long been considered a future reliever due to his 5'9" frame, but the Jays still see him as a starter. After serving a 50-game drug suspension, he was dominant in AA, posting a 3.30 ERA, 2.2 Ctl, and 10.4 Dom. He owns explosive stuff, highlighted by an incredible slider.

Jameson Taillon (RHP, PIT) gives the Pirates another power arm. The 22-year-old has a good mid-90s fastball, an improved change-up, and a plus curve ball. He'll likely start the season at AAA, where he'll work on improving his control, but could be an MLB rotation option by mid-season.

Oscar Taveras (OF, STL) has as much offensive upside as any prospect in the NL. He missed out on a September call-up due to an ankle injury that required surgery, but hit .306/.341/.462 at AAA for the year. It isn't clear how he'll fit into the Cardinals plans, but he has the talent for full-time AB.

Henry Urrutia (OF, BAL) was among the minor league leaders in BA in 2013, and earned a late-season stint with the Orioles. The LHH can be menacing to RHP with his natural hitting ability and average long ball pop. At 26, he doesn't have a high ceiling, but he has a high likelihood of success in the right role.

Yordano Ventura (RHP, KC) was a September call-up and could leverage his three-start audition into an Opening Day rotation slot. With a big fastball and swing-and-miss curveball, the 22-year-old has the aggressiveness and stuff to become a #2 starter in the near-term. He should be a good source of strikeouts, as he posted an 11.5 Dom in AAA and a 9.5 Dom in AAA.

Arodys Vizcaino (RHP, CHC) has had a slow recovery from Tommy John surgery that cost him all of 2012-13. He pitched in instructional ball in August, where his fastball was already in the mid-90s. He's a wild-card for 2014, but the Cubs can use all the power arms they can get, so he might be worth a flyer.

Taijuan Walker (RHP, SEA) had one of the most impressive seasons of any top pitching prospect in 2013. Between AA and AAA, the 21-year-old had a 2.93 ERA, 3.6 Ctl, and 10.2 Dom before starting three games with the Mariners. Given his youth, he is quite advanced. Big league hitters won't be looking forward to his plus-plus fastball.

Allen Webster (RHP, BOS) wasn't at his best when he got lit up for an 8.60 ERA and 5.3 Ctl in seven MLB starts. His impressive arsenal consists of a few plus pitches, including a 91-97 mph fastball with excellent, late movement. He has youth on his side, and should rebound to become a mid-rotation stalwart.

Tim Wheeler (OF, COL) has had a two-year power outage that saw his HR production drop from 33 in 2011 to 7 in 2013. He's continued to hit for BA, but will likely be limited to LF in MLB, and his future is clouded by the emergence of Kyle Parker. He could make the club as a 4th/5th OF, which still has some value.

Joe Wieland (RHP, SD) has been slow to recover from Tommy John surgery, but is finally back on track. Prior to the injury, he relied on his ability to throw strikes and set up hitters with his good breaking ball and plus change-up. He has a career 1.8 Ctl, and should contend for a back-end rotation spot.

Kolten Wong (2B, STL) had a forgettable World Series, and was just 9-for-59 in limited action for the Cardinals, but has developed into the top 2B prospect in baseball. 2013 was his best season as a pro, as he hit .303 with a .466 SLG% and 20 SB at AAA. He isn't going to take Matt Carpenter's spot in the lineup, but if the STL moves Carpenter to 3B, it could be the opening for Wong.

Kyle Zimmer (RHP, KC) began very slowly in High-A before turning it around late in the season. He was promoted to AA in July, and showed off his strikeout ability and relative polish. He has a deep repertoire and can throw all of his pitches for strikes, and should front the top of the rotation for years to come.

• • •

The chart on the following page ranks the Top 100 Impact Prospects for 2014, along with BaseballHQ.com's rating system grade and projected Mayberry Scores. The rating system grade consists of two parts:

Player Potential Rating (1-10) representing a player's upside potential

    10 - Hall of Fame-type player
    9 - Elite player
    8 - Solid regular
    7 - Average regular
    6 - Platoon player
    5 - Major League reserve player
    4 - Top minor league player
    3 - Average minor league player
    2 - Minor league reserve player
    1 - Minor league roster filler

Probability Rating (A-E) representing the player's realistic chances of achieving their potential

    A - 90% probability of reaching potential
    B - 70% probability of reaching potential
    C - 50% probability of reaching potential
    D - 30% probability of reaching potential
    E - 10% probability of reaching potential

This grading system is used thoughout BaseballHQ.com in our daily minor-league coverage and offseason organizational reports.

The Mayberry Scores are explained on page 56, and these projected scores reflect 2014 only, not a player's potential long-term impact. For complete prospect and minors coverage, turn to the Baseball Forecaster's *minors companion, the* Minor League Baseball Analyst. *For more information, visit:*

www.baseballhq.com/content/minor-league-baseball-analyst-2014

Top 100 Impact Prospects for 2014

RANK/BATTER/POS, TM	RATING	POWER	SPEED	BATAVG	PT '13	RANK/BATTER/POS, TM	RATING	POWER	SPEED	BATAVG	PT '13
RANK/PITCHER/POS, TM	RATING	ERA	DOM	SAVES	PT '13	RANK/PITCHER/POS, TM	RATING	ERA	DOM	SAVES	PT '13
1 Jose Abreu (1B, CHW)	8B	3	0	3	5	51 Tony Sanchez (C, PIT)	7D	1	0	2	3
2 Xander Bogaerts (INF, BOS)	9B	2	2	3	3	52 David Hale (RHP, ATL)	7C	2	2	0	3
3 Carlos Martinez (RHP, STL)	9C	4	5	1	3	53 Kevin Chapman (LHP, HOU)	6A	2	3	1	0
4 Billy Hamilton (OF, CIN)	9D	1	4	2	3	54 Tim Beckham (INF, TAM)	7C	1	3	2	1
5 Oscar Taveras (OF, STL)	9B	2	1	4	3	55 Luis Jimenez (3B, ANA)	7C	1	0	2	1
6 Travis D'Arnaud (C, NYM)	8A	2	0	2	5	56 Alex Colome (RHP, TAM)	8C	2	3	0	1
7 Yordano Ventura (RHP, KC)	9C	3	3	0	3	57 Kris Bryant (3B, CHC)	9B	2	0	3	0
8 Jonathan Singleton (1B, HOU)	9C	2	1	2	3	58 Joc Pederson (OF, LA)	9D	1	2	2	1
9 Nick Castellanos (OF, DET)	9C	2	0	4	3	59 Brian Flynn (LHP, MIA)	7B	2	2	0	3
10 Matt Davidson (3B, ARI)	8C	2	0	2	3	60 Sean Gilmartin (LHP, ATL)	8C	1	3	0	3
11 Trevor Bauer (RHP, CLE)	8C	2	3	0	3	61 Nate Karns (RHP, WAS)	7C	2	2	0	3
12 George Springer (OF, HOU)	8A	2	2	2	3	62 C.J. Cron (1B, LAA)	8C	1	0	2	1
13 Taijuan Walker (RHP, SEA)	9B	3	4	0	3	63 Jonathan Schoop (INF, BAL)	8C	1	1	2	3
14 Kevin Gausman (RHP, BAL)	9C	3	3	0	3	64 David Holmberg (RHP, ARI)	8C	1	2	0	1
15 Marcus Semien (INF, CHW)	8C	1	2	3	3	65 Raymond Fuentes (OF, SD)	8C	1	2	3	3
16 Jake Marisnick (OF, MIA)	9D	2	1	2	5	66 Mark Montgomery (RHP, NYY)	7A	2	3	1	0
17 Archie Bradley (RHP, ARI)	9B	3	5	0	1	67 Sean Nolin (LHP, TOR)	7C	2	2	0	1
18 Michael Choice (OF, OAK)	8C	1	1	3	3	68 Leury Garcia (INF, CHW)	7B	0	2	2	3
19 Jake Odorizzi (RHP, TAM)	8C	3	2	0	1	69 Miguel Sano (3B, MIN)	9B	1	0	2	1
20 Rafael Montero (RHP, NYM)	8C	2	3	0	3	70 Matt Skole (1B, WAS)	8D	2	1	2	1
21 Chris Owings (SS, ARI)	8C	1	2	3	3	71 Adam Morgan (LHP, PHI)	8C	2	2	0	1
22 Jimmy Nelson (RHP, MIL)	8D	2	3	0	3	72 Daniel Corcino (RHP, CIN)	8C	2	3	0	1
23 Jameson Taillon (RHP, PIT)	9C	2	4	0	1	73 Nick Maronde (LHP, ANA)	8D	1	3	1	0
24 Kyle Zimmer (RHP, KC)	9B	2	3	0	1	74 Casey Kelly (RHP, SD)	8C	2	3	0	3
25 Erik Johnson (RHP, CHW)	8C	2	3	0	1	75 Arodys Vizcaino (RHP, CHC)	9D	3	3	1	3
26 Ethan Martin (RHP, PHI)	8D	2	3	1	3	76 Matt Barnes (RHP, BOS)	8C	1	3	0	1
27 Kolten Wong (2B, STL)	8B	1	1	3	3	77 Brian Goodwin (OF, WAS)	9D	1	2	2	1
28 Mike Olt (3B, CHC)	9D	3	0	1	3	78 Bryan Holaday (C, DET)	6A	0	0	1	3
29 Max Stassi (C, HOU)	8C	1	0	2	1	79 Kyle Parker (OF/1B, COL)	8C	1	0	3	3
30 Marcus Stroman (RHP, TOR)	8B	2	3	1	1	80 C.C. Lee (RHP, CLE)	7A	3	2	1	0
31 Jackie Bradley (OF, BOS)	8B	1	2	3	3	81 Alex Guerrero (2B/SS, LA)	8C	2	1	3	3
32 Christian Bethancourt (C, ATL)	8D	1	0	2	3	82 Maikel Franco (3B, PHI)	9C	3	0	3	1
33 Andrew Heaney (LHP, MIA)	8C	3	2	0	3	83 Hunter Morris (1B, MIL)	7C	2	0	2	3
34 Henry Urrutia (OF, BAL)	7C	1	0	4	3	84 Jake Petricka (RHP, CHW)	8D	1	3	1	0
35 Alex Meyer (RHP, MIN)	9C	2	4	1	1	85 Zeke Spruill (RHP, ARI)	7C	1	1	0	1
36 James Paxton (LHP, SEA)	8C	2	4	0	1	86 Carson Smith (RHP, SEA)	7A	3	3	1	0
37 Wilmer Flores (2B/3B, NYM)	9D	2	0	3	3	87 Tim Wheeler (OF, COL)	8D	1	0	3	3
38 Chi-Jen Lo (RHP, HOU)	7A	2	3	1	0	88 Engel Beltre (OF, TEX)	7C	0	1	2	1
39 Javier Baez (SS, CHC)	9B	2	0	3	1	89 Matt Magill (RHP, LA)	7C	2	4	0	1
40 Josmil Pinto (C, MIN)	7C	1	0	2	3	90 Kevin Kiermaier (OF, TAM)	6A	0	1	2	1
41 Allen Webster (RHP, BOS)	9D	2	4	1	0	91 Cody Martin (RHP, ATL)	7C	2	3	0	3
42 Joe Wieland (RHP, SD)	8B	3	2	0	5	92 Francisco Lindor (SS, CLE)	9B	0	1	3	1
43 Zach Lee (RHP, LA)	9D	3	2	0	3	93 Johnny Hellweg (RHP, MIL)	7C	1	3	1	1
44 Anthony Ranaudo (RHP, BOS)	8C	2	3	0	1	94 Taylor Lindsey (2B, LAA)	7A	0	1	3	1
45 Enny Romero (LHP, TAM)	8C	2	2	0	1	95 Gary Brown (OF, SF)	8D	1	2	1	3
46 Robert Stephenson (RHP, CIN)	9D	3	4	0	1	96 Dylan Bundy (RHP, BAL)	9A	3	3	0	1
47 Chad Bettis (RHP, COL)	8D	1	4	1	3	97 Keyvius Sampson (RHP, SD)	8D	1	3	0	1
48 Chris Dwyer (LHP, KC)	7B	2	3	1	0	98 Jeff Kobernus (2B, WAS)	7D	1	2	2	1
49 Tommy La Stella (2B, ATL)	7B	1	1	4	3	99 Heath Hembree (RHP, SF)	8C	2	4	1	0
50 Kevin Pillar (OF, TOR)	6A	1	1	2	3	100 J.R. Murphy (C, NYY)	7C	1	0	2	1

Top Japanese Players for 2014 and Beyond

by Tom Mulhall

The 2012 season may be the high-water mark for Japanese players joining MLB in both quantity and quality. No one in 2013 came anywhere near the talent or impact of Darvish, Iwakuma, or Aoki. However, there are rumors the restrictive posting system may finally be fracturing. If you have a large reserve or farm roster, consider stashing more Japanese prospects than usual on the chance that the posting rules will be eased.

Yoshio Itoi (OF, Orix Buffaloes) is a good defender with a decent BA, speed and power. Itoi is somewhat reminiscent of Kosuke Fukudome in that he doesn't do anything great but he does everything well. Considered something of an eccentric, he is famous for his odd comments and malaprops in the Yogi Berra vein. He wants to be posted, but at age 32, his window of opportunity is closing fast. Itoi could be a capable fourth outfielder but you probably stopped reading at "somewhat reminiscent of Kosuke Fukudome."
Possible ETA: 2014.

Chihiro Kaneko (RHP, Orix Buffaloes) isn't getting the publicity of other Japanese players but actually has a better K/IP rate than heralded pitchers like Masahiro Tanaka. At age 30, he is nearing the point where he could be posted. While nowhere near the talent of Darvish or Tanaka, he is still an interesting player who could make a passable 4th SP.
Possible ETA: 2015.

Dae-Ho Lee (1B/OF Orix Buffaloes) joined the Japanese major leagues after dominating the Korean league for almost 11 years, where he won almost every hitting award. He had no trouble making the transition, hitting 24 HR with a .286 BA and beating Vladimir Balentien in their Home Run Derby. In 2013, he hit 24 HR again and improved his BA to .303. Lee has an solid batting eye and is a good defender. His two year contract with Orix is up, so the question is whether he wants to move up another league.
Possible ETA: 2014.

Kenta Maeda (RHP, Hiroshima Toyo Carp) is a control-pitcher with a decent but not overpowering fastball. In 2010 he became the youngest pitcher in the history of Japanese baseball to win the pitching Triple Crown. He ended the 2013 season with an ERA right at 2.10, leading the Central League. Maeda had minor injury issues and may not want to make the transition in the same year as Masahiro Tanaka. He will be 26 years old next season and projects as a decent 4th SP or better if he ends up in the right situation.
Probable ETA: 2015.

Takeya Nakamura (3B, Seibu Lions) is possibly the premier power hitter in Japan. The four-time Pacific League HR King had surgery in 2013 on his left knee which limited him to 24 games. He still managed to hit a dramatic 9th inning HR to put his team into the playoffs. But his BA is a major concern. When he looks in a mirror, Dave Kingman stares back.
Possible ETA: 2015.

Toshiya Sugiuchi (LHP, Yomiuri Giants) has exceptional command of his pitches and has more international experience than almost any player from any country. After two sub-2.0 ERA seasons in a row, he was something of a disappointment in 2013

with an ERA "only" in the low 3s. That and his age may lead his team to decide now is the time to get what they can for him. The former MVP and Sawamura Award winner could be a capable MLB pitcher, but at age 33, this may be his last chance.
Possible ETA: 2014.

Masahiro Tanaka (RHP, Rakuten Eagles) could now be the best starting pitcher in Japan. Last year his team stated they had no intention of posting him and, in fact, were looking to build around him. In a surprising turnaround, they now say, "We're in no position to stop someone from pursuing his dreams and ambitions." Translation: "Make us an offer." If Tanaka joins MLB, at age 26 he could have a major impact, perhaps almost as much as Darvish. His 2013 record was 23-0 (as in 23 wins and no losses) with an ERA of 1.27. This is the guy you want.
Probable ETA: 2014.

Takashi Toritani (SS, Hanshin Tigers) has always been rumored to be interested in MLB. Unfortunately, after several strong years, he struggled offensively the past two seasons. Toritani is a solid defender but will almost certainly have to move to 2B or accept a utility role. At age 33 he would be a gamble for any MLB team or yours. Repeat after me: "I will not draft Japanese middle infielders. I will not draft Japanese middle infielders. I will not draft..."
Probable ETA: 2014.

Hideaki Wakui (RHP, Seibu Lions) wants to play in MLB and at age 30, the former Sawamura Award winner is nearing the time when he might be posted. After a rare win in arbitration, an embarrassing magazine article about his private life further irritated team owners. They responded with the "Uehara" treatment, which is to change his role so often it destroys his value. His transition to the majors could be tough since he possesses only an average fastball, although it is complemented by an array of solid off-pitches and good control. He may be worth a gamble with a low reserve selection.
Possible ETA: 2014.

Young and talented: Unless the posting system completely collapses, these players are years away, but remember the names of **Shintaro Fujinami** (RHP, age 20), **Hideto Asamura** (1B/2B, age 24), **Sho Nakata** (1B, age 25) and especially **Hayato Sakamoto** (SS, age 26), **Shohei Otani** (RHP, age 20) and **Yusei Kikuchi** (LHP, age 22).

Caveat about pitching stats: Japan instituted a new ball in 2011 with lower-elasticity rubber surrounding the cork. The new design limited offense and inflated pitching stats. A more hitter-friendly ball was used in 2013 and home runs were back up to pre-2011 levels. But continue to exercise a little skepticism when analyzing pitching stats and look for possible signs of optimism in hitting stats other than the power categories.

MAJOR LEAGUE EQUIVALENTS

In his 1985 *Baseball Abstract*, Bill James introduced the concept of major league equivalencies. His assertion was that, with the proper adjustments, a minor leaguer's statistics could be converted to an equivalent major league level performance with a great deal of accuracy.

Because of wide variations in the level of play among different minor leagues, it is difficult to get a true reading on a player's potential. For instance, a .300 batting average achieved in the high-offense Pacific Coast League is not nearly as much of an accomplishment as a similar level in the Eastern League. MLEs normalize these types of variances, for all statistical categories.

The actual MLEs are not projections. They represent how a player's previous performance might look at the major league level. However, the MLE stat line can be used in forecasting future performance in just the same way as a major league stat line would.

The model we use contains a few variations to James' version and updates all of the minor league and ballpark factors. In addition, we designed a module to convert pitching statistics, which is something James did not originally do.

Players are listed if they spent at least part of 2012 or 2013 in Triple-A or Double-A and had at least 100 AB or 30 IP within those two levels (players who split a season at both levels are indicated as a/a). Major league and Single-A (and lower) stats are excluded. Each player is listed in the organization with which they finished the season.

These charts also provide the unique perspective of looking at two years' worth of data. These are only short-term trends, for sure. But even here we can find small indications of players improving their skills, or struggling, as they rise through more difficult levels of competition. Since players—especially those with any modicum of talent—are promoted rapidly through major league systems, a two-year scan is often all we get to spot any trends. Five-year trends do appear in the *Minor League Baseball Analyst*.

Used correctly, MLEs are excellent indicators of potential. But, just like we cannot take traditional major league statistics at face value, the same goes for MLEs. The underlying measures of base skill—contact rates, pitching command ratios, BPV, etc.—are far more accurate in evaluating future talent than raw home runs, batting averages or ERAs. This year's chart format focuses more on those underlying gauges.

Here are some things to look for as you scan these charts:

Target players who...

- had a full season's worth of playing time in AA and then another full year in AAA
- had consistent playing time from one year to the next
- improved their base skills as they were promoted

Raise the warning flag for players who...

- were stuck at the same level both years, or regressed
- displayed marked changes in playing time from one year to the next
- showed large drops in BPIs from one year to the next

BATTER	yr	b	age	pos	lvl	org	ab	hr	sb	ba	bb%	ct%	px	sx	bpv
Abraham,Adam	12	R	25	1B	aa	CLE	379	11	2	230	9	76	117	59	34
	13	R	26	1B	a/a	CLE	182	1	0	201	7	66	58	41	-63
Acosta,Mayobanex	12	R	25	C	a/a	TAM	112	4	0	204	9	77	106	26	20
	13	R	26	C	aa	TAM	234	5	0	157	6	69	67	13	-54
Adames,Cristhian	13	B	22	SS	aa	COL	389	3	10	259	6	80	63	86	11
Adams,David	12	R	25	2B	aa	NYY	327	7	2	263	8	81	87	42	26
	13	R	26	3B	aaa	NYY	220	5	0	232	10	77	84	48	12
Adams,Lane	13	R	24	RF	aa	KC	156	4	12	211	8	68	95	151	13
Adduci,James	12	L	27	DH	a/a	CHC	399	5	13	240	8	73	69	94	-6
	13	L	28	RF	aaa	TEX	473	12	22	243	8	73	96	101	18
Adrianza,Ehire	12	B	23	SS	aa	SF	451	2	14	200	7	78	59	116	11
	13	B	24	SS	a/a	SF	395	1	12	217	9	78	54	107	5
Aguilar,Jesus	12	R	22	1B	aa	CLE	72	3	0	277	14	64	169	26	29
	13	R	23	1B	aa	CLE	499	12	0	233	8	76	91	24	-1
Ahmed,Nick	13	R	23	SS	aa	ARI	487	4	22	223	5	84	59	134	36
Ahrens,Kevin	13	R	24	1B	aa	TOR	238	3	0	188	6	74	84	30	-13
Alberto,Hanser	13	R	21	SS	aa	TEX	356	4	11	208	4	88	40	115	29
Albitz,Vance	12	R	24	2B	a/a	STL	99	1	1	158	8	88	31	34	2
	13	R	25	2B	a/a	STL	226	2	4	209	2	86	36	74	0
Alcantara,Arismendy	13	B	22	SS	aa	CHC	494	12	25	243	9	72	120	116	40
Aliotti,Anthony	12	L	25	1B	aa	OAK	455	7	0	237	10	66	86	37	-32
	13	L	26	1B	a/a	OAK	494	9	2	256	11	69	95	41	-14
Allen,Brandon	12	L	26	1B	aaa	TAM	122	3	0	212	2	68	114	62	-11
	13	L	27	1B	aaa	SD	423	10	4	201	8	73	97	100	19
Almanzar,Michael	13	R	23	3B	aa	BOS	507	12	10	245	6	79	99	91	34
Almonte,Abraham	12	B	23	DH	aa	NYY	319	4	10	233	9	80	69	130	32
	13	B	24	CF	a/a	SEA	440	11	20	255	11	74	98	124	36
Almonte,Denny	12	B	24	DH	aa	SEA	434	9	22	214	10	63	97	113	-15
	13	B	25	CF	a/a	SEA	332	6	10	142	6	49	112	113	-65
Almonte,Zoilo	12	B	23	DH	aa	NYY	419	19	12	249	5	73	129	88	33
	13	B	24	LF	aaa	NYY	259	6	3	269	9	80	79	58	20
Anderson,Bryan	12	L	26	C	aaa	STL	347	4	0	177	7	70	51	30	-56
	13	L	27	C	aaa	CHW	210	6	1	186	8	65	127	61	-2
Anderson,Lars	12	L	25	1B	aaa	CLE	396	7	1	206	11	68	96	49	-12
	13	L	26	1B	aaa	CHW	227	2	1	162	11	62	49	31	-81
Anderson,Leslie	12	L	30	DH	aaa	TAM	444	9	0	232	4	83	63	28	2
	13	L	31	1B	aaa	TAM	431	9	1	220	8	82	82	34	22
Andino,Robert	13	R	29	SS	aaa	PIT	249	2	1	198	4	72	61	51	-37
Andreoli,John	13	R	23	LF	aa	CHC	201	2	13	255	8	79	72	132	29
Angelini,Carmen	13	R	25	SS	aa	NYY	236	4	6	190	7	75	74	76	-3
Angle,Matt	12	L	27	C	aaa	LA	393	3	8	219	6	73	51	86	-27
	13	L	28	CF	aaa	LA	400	5	14	208	7	67	77	123	-18
Anna,Dean	12	L	26	2B	aa	SD	425	6	4	214	10	78	58	75	2
	13	L	27	2B	aaa	SD	498	5	2	252	7	83	76	62	28
Arcia,Oswaldo	12	L	21	DH	aa	MIN	262	8	2	305	8	75	136	108	58
	13	L	22	DH	aaa	MIN	128	7	2	276	12	68	157	48	39
Asche,Cody	12	L	22	3B	aa	PHI	263	8	1	269	6	76	126	70	42
	13	L	23	3B	aaa	PHI	404	12	9	257	6	73	117	90	29
Asencio,Yeison	13	R	24	RF	aa	SD	291	2	2	230	4	88	54	71	27
Ashley,Nevin	12	R	28	C	aaa	TAM	110	3	1	189	9	71	105	75	11
	13	R	29	C	aaa	CIN	238	5	3	188	9	68	92	68	-13
Austin,Tyler	13	R	22	RF	aa	NYY	319	6	3	237	10	73	85	70	4
Avery,Xavier	12	L	22	C	aaa	BAL	390	8	20	226	11	71	79	123	9
	13	L	23	CF	a/a	SEA	467	3	24	230	9	70	63	125	-11
Baez,Javier	13	R	21	SS	aa	CHC	218	16	6	266	7	65	223	74	77
Baker,Aaron	13	L	26	1B	aa	BAL	215	4	1	207	8	72	92	57	-3
Baker,John	13	L	32	C	aaa	LA	146	2	0	145	8	66	39	28	-79
Bandy,Jett	13	R	23	C	aa	LAA	245	3	0	210	4	82	81	56	20
Bantz,Brandon	12	R	25	C	aaa	SEA	109	1	1	174	3	68	72	49	-47
	13	R	26	C	a/a	SEA	192	2	1	177	6	69	46	52	-59
Barden,Brian	13	R	32	3B	aaa	LA	415	3	1	197	6	79	51	46	-17
Barfield,Jeremy	12	R	24	C	aa	OAK	482	9	1	224	5	80	73	46	6
	13	R	25	RF	a/a	OAK	216	8	1	166	9	74	85	45	-3
Barnhart,Tucker	12	B	21	C	aa	CIN	130	2	1	190	7	82	56	60	6
	13	B	22	C	aa	CIN	339	3	1	244	11	82	65	40	13
Barton,Daric	12	L	27	1B	aaa	OAK	259	5	5	192	15	75	78	92	20
	13	L	28	1B	aaa	OAK	391	4	1	219	13	81	69	41	21
Baxter,Mike	12	L	28	DH	a/a	NYM	34	0	0	273	6	65	24	13	-102
	13	L	29	LF	aaa	NYM	187	4	2	196	7	80	86	99	35
Beckham,Tim	12	R	22	SS	aaa	TAM	285	5	5	225	8	72	62	87	-18
	13	R	23	SS	aaa	TAM	460	3	14	242	7	73	74	127	7
Bell,Josh	12	B	26	3B	aaa	ARI	360	8	2	225	6	74	100	53	4
	13	B	27	3B	aaa	NYY	177	4	0	192	11	70	89	28	-16
Belnome,Vince	12	L	24	DH	aaa	SD	258	3	3	216	10	66	62	58	-46
	13	L	25	1B	aaa	TAM	444	6	0	250	13	71	101	55	8
Beltre,Engel	12	L	23	DH	aa	TEX	564	12	28	243	3	78	84	147	32
	13	L	24	CF	aaa	TEX	394	6	11	259	5	77	71	79	-1
Benson,Joe	12	R	24	DH	a/a	MIN	236	4	6	161	8	67	78	107	-19
	13	R	25	CF	a/a	TEX	283	5	5	176	6	63	97	128	-16
Beresford,James	12	L	23	SS	aa	MIN	369	0	2	238	7	84	32	62	-2
	13	L	24	2B	a/a	MIN	356	0	7	263	6	84	29	87	-2
Bermudez,Ronald	12	R	24	DH	a/a	BOS	201	2	4	236	3	78	67	84	0
	13	R	25	CF	a/a	BOS	234	1	1	230	4	78	52	65	-17
Bernier,Douglas	12	B	32	SS	aaa	NYY	174	0	1	154	10	65	45	28	-76
	13	B	33	SS	aaa	MIN	302	2	3	225	6	69	67	96	-28
Berry,Quintin	12	L	28	C	aaa	DET	159	0	14	218	9	66	44	91	-54
	13	L	29	CF	aaa	BOS	319	2	20	153	9	69	44	107	-37

BATTER	yr	b	age	pos	lvl	org	ab	hr	sb	ba	bb%	ct%	px	sx	bpv
Bethancourt,Christian	13	R	22	C	aa	ATL	358	10	10	259	4	82	98	69	38
Bianucci,Michael	12	R	26	1B	aaa	TEX	325	11	1	221	3	72	94	37	-17
	13	R	27	DH	aaa	TEX	196	9	0	235	7	74	147	27	39
Bigley,Evan	12	R	25	DH	a/a	MIN	487	11	3	216	4	71	93	62	-11
	13	R	26	RF	a/a	MIN	256	3	1	194	5	67	71	59	-45
Bixler,Brian	12	R	30	SS	aaa	HOU	249	2	7	193	6	68	54	91	-43
	13	R	31	CF	aaa	NYM	309	3	4	172	4	60	65	72	-74
Black,Daniel	12	L	24	SS	aa	MIA	34	0	2	230	7	61	94	82	-41
	13	L	25	SS	aa	MIA	315	2	6	173	9	71	34	118	-33
Black,Daniel	13	B	26	1B	aa	CHW	449	15	5	250	15	74	119	54	37
Blackmon,Charlie	12	L	26	DH	aaa	COL	228	4	6	248	7	79	96	128	48
	13	L	27	CF	aaa	COL	257	2	4	226	7	82	70	112	32
Blackwood,Jacob	12	R	27	3B	aa	SD	283	3	4	168	3	70	51	76	-49
	13	R	28	3B	aa	SD	478	5	1	208	3	79	57	48	-15
Blanke,Michael	13	R	25	C	aa	CHW	332	6	2	197	9	73	78	40	-13
Bloxom,Justin	12	B	24	1B	aa	WAS	243	7	0	221	6	71	98	36	-14
	13	B	25	1B	aa	WAS	460	6	4	216	10	73	70	57	-14
Bocock,Brian	12	R	27	2B	a/a	TOR	346	1	12	190	5	81	58	99	11
	13	R	28	SS	aaa	PIT	143	2	2	136	5	76	64	54	-18
Bogaerts,Xander	12	R	20	SS	aa	BOS	92	4	1	326	1	77	187	44	73
	13	R	21	SS	a/a	BOS	444	11	6	281	10	77	107	92	45
Boggs,Brandon	12	B	29	DH	aaa	PIT	409	6	4	205	10	65	93	85	-19
	13	B	30	RF	aaa	ATL	411	5	3	182	9	60	78	65	-57
Bogusevic,Brian	13	L	29	RF	aaa	CHC	265	7	11	246	10	72	99	117	23
Bonilla,Leury	12	R	27	3B	a/a	SEA	257	1	3	201	5	70	46	87	-45
	13	R	28	3B	a/a	SEA	228	1	4	191	8	71	32	52	-55
Bortnick,Tyler	12	R	25	2B	a/a	ARI	480	4	18	200	7	79	67	119	22
	13	R	26	2B	aaa	ARI	251	2	11	226	8	74	61	138	4
Boscan,J.C.	12	R	33	C	aaa	ATL	222	2	1	142	5	65	63	41	-64
	13	R	34	C	aaa	CHC	233	0	1	175	6	76	30	29	-51
Bour,Justin	12	L	24	1B	aa	CHC	506	13	3	245	9	74	106	42	13
	13	L	25	1B	aa	CHC	317	13	0	198	8	77	117	30	28
Bourgeois,Jason	12	R	30	DH	aaa	KC	222	2	4	178	5	86	34	94	14
	13	R	31	LF	aaa	TAM	348	1	16	220	6	86	40	115	23
Bowe,Theodis	13	L	23	LF	aa	CIN	238	4	11	192	6	75	64	110	-2
Bradley,Jackie	12	L	22	DH	aa	BOS	229	5	7	262	11	77	110	94	51
	13	L	23	CF	aaa	BOS	320	7	5	254	9	75	131	89	50
Brentz,Bryce	12	R	24	DH	a/a	BOS	473	13	6	269	7	68	123	57	4
	13	R	25	RF	aaa	BOS	326	12	1	231	4	70	124	38	1
Brewer,Daniel	12	R	25	DH	aa	NYY	104	1	2	188	5	73	47	38	-49
	13	R	26	LF	aa	ATL	345	2	19	228	9	79	61	124	23
Brignac,Reid	12	L	26	SS	aaa	TAM	346	6	2	186	9	72	66	64	-19
	13	L	27	3B	aaa	COL	165	1	1	177	6	77	51	51	-21
Britton,Buck	12	L	26	2B	a/a	BAL	387	8	4	249	7	81	79	51	19
	13	L	27	2B	a/a	BAL	467	10	4	225	5	83	74	70	25
Brown,Andrew	12	R	28	DH	aaa	COL	390	16	2	242	5	70	152	74	35
	13	R	29	RF	aaa	NYM	153	4	0	238	8	69	142	91	35
Brown,Corey	12	L	27	DH	aaa	WAS	484	19	13	235	8	66	128	116	20
	13	L	28	CF	aaa	WAS	389	13	8	199	6	59	144	80	-10
Brown,Gary	12	R	24	DH	aa	SF	538	5	29	247	6	82	68	100	25
	13	R	25	CF	aaa	SF	558	7	11	179	4	71	75	106	-14
Brown,Jordan	12	L	29	1B	aaa	MIL	359	7	1	243	4	82	74	42	11
	13	L	30	1B	aaa	MIA	291	1	0	226	6	84	63	25	8
Broxton,Keon	13	R	23	CF	aa	ARI	334	7	5	217	7	62	103	108	-20
Buchholz,Alexander	12	R	25	3B	aa	TEX	301	6	3	218	5	80	69	81	10
	13	R	26	3B	a/a	TEX	469	14	2	237	5	85	99	49	47
Buck,Travis	12	L	29	DH	a/a	HOU	85	1	0	227	6	73	67	25	-31
	13	L	30	LF	aaa	SD	125	3	0	179	3	78	97	35	9
Burgess,Michael	12	L	24	DH	aa	CHC	332	8	0	224	10	78	94	29	19
	13	L	25	LF	aa	HOU	320	9	0	169	7	65	119	20	-21
Burns,Andrew	13	R	23	3B	aa	TOR	265	6	9	224	6	77	106	111	40
Burriss,Emmanuel	12	B	27	2B	aaa	SF	106	0	3	207	6	86	52	100	29
	13	B	28	SS	aaa	CIN	369	1	13	196	4	86	15	73	-11
Buschini,Adam	13	R	26	2B	aa	SD	285	6	10	200	5	78	69	120	14
Buss,Nicholas	12	L	26	C	aa	LA	492	6	14	223	6	83	64	109	28
	13	L	27	RF	aaa	LA	459	11	14	229	5	75	102	130	35
Butler,Daniel	12	R	26	C	a/a	BOS	320	7	0	220	9	78	93	38	17
	13	R	27	C	aaa	BOS	282	10	1	221	8	75	122	24	23
Butler,Joey	12	R	26	DH	aaa	TEX	493	15	4	241	10	70	107	51	2
	13	R	27	RF	aaa	TEX	426	9	1	242	10	67	102	31	-18
Cabrera,Ramon	12	B	23	C	a/a	PIT	389	2	0	250	7	88	58	41	28
	13	B	24	DH	a/a	DET	461	1	3	251	9	87	59	71	37
Calhoun,Kole	12	L	25	1B	aaa	LAA	410	8	8	227	6	74	98	112	21
	13	L	26	CF	aaa	LAA	240	7	6	264	7	83	98	112	60
Calixte,Orlando	13	R	21	SS	aa	KC	484	6	11	229	7	72	82	97	-3
Campana,Tony	12	L	26	C	aaa	CHC	143	1	12	226	6	71	25	122	-45
	13	L	27	CF	aaa	ARI	351	1	18	223	5	73	41	139	-23
Campbell,Eric	12	R	25	1B	aa	NYM	394	7	8	243	10	77	80	69	13
	13	R	26	RF	aaa	NYM	341	5	7	229	10	77	79	78	18
Canha,Mark	13	R	24	1B	aa	MIA	425	10	5	242	10	71	123	78	28
Canham,Mitchell	12	L	28	C	aaa	STL	48	0	0	93	1	72	0	52	-91
	13	L	29	C	a/a	KC	306	1	8	209	10	76	75	100	18
Canzler,Russ	12	R	26	1B	aaa	CLE	487	16	1	214	6	68	129	48	5
	13	R	27	DH	aaa	PIT	452	8	1	202	9	74	65	46	-18
Carrera,Ezequiel	12	L	25	DH	aaa	CLE	394	4	19	244	5	82	62	126	27
	13	L	26	CF	aaa	CLE	416	4	35	208	7	75	59	145	7
Carrithers,Alden	12	L	28	2B	aa	ATL	165	0	7	259	14	84	27	67	7
	13	L	29	3B	a/a	ATL	278	2	12	226	9	85	51	87	26

BATTER	yr	b	age	pos	lvl	org	ab	hr	sb	ba	bb%	ct%	px	sx	bpv
Carroll,Brett	12	R	30	DH	aaa	WAS	364	7	5	194	7	67	93	73	-19
	13	R	31	LF	aaa	PIT	275	8	5	166	9	67	89	81	-16
Carson,Matt	12	R	31	DH	aaa	MIN	422	10	7	223	6	68	103	83	-5
	13	R	32	RF	aaa	CLE	436	10	10	196	6	65	86	92	-30
Cartwright,Albert	13	R	26	2B	aa	PHI	489	5	18	202	4	73	54	124	-19
Castellanos,Alex	12	R	26	2B	aaa	LA	344	10	10	245	7	69	121	104	20
	13	R	27	RF	aaa	LA	385	12	12	193	6	64	106	119	-10
Castellanos,Nick	12	R	20	3B	aa	DET	322	6	4	245	3	76	71	67	-9
	13	R	21	LF	aaa	DET	533	15	3	257	8	81	108	68	48
Castillo,Ali	13	R	24	SS	aa	NYY	156	0	3	191	6	79	34	104	-11
Castillo,Luis	13	B	24	RF	aa	DET	293	2	0	211	8	79	62	64	4
Castro,Erik	13	L	26	1B	aa	HOU	410	14	1	231	9	69	128	32	7
Castro,Leandro	12	R	23	DH	aa	PHI	478	8	10	250	3	83	84	75	31
	13	R	24	RF	aaa	PHI	438	6	15	217	3	80	69	90	8
Catricala,Vincent	12	R	24	3B	aaa	SEA	463	6	3	177	5	77	59	58	-15
	13	R	25	3B	aa	OAK	405	5	4	190	5	73	56	56	-36
Cavazos-Galvez,Bria	12	R	25	1B	a/a	LA	256	8	4	236	3	81	91	92	31
	13	R	26	LF	aa	LA	377	6	12	223	3	84	58	82	14
Cecchini,Garin	13	L	22	3B	aa	BOS	240	2	6	278	14	77	79	93	29
Ceciliani,Darrell	13	L	23	CF	aa	NYM	418	5	24	224	5	71	66	137	-11
Centeno,Juan	12	L	23	C	aa	NYM	281	0	1	242	6	82	35	48	-15
	13	L	24	C	a/a	NYM	236	0	1	237	3	85	38	67	-1
Cervenak,Mike	12	R	36	1B	aaa	MIA	371	9	1	260	8	82	78	30	16
	13	R	37	3B	aaa	DET	323	4	2	229	4	86	53	46	9
Chambers,Adron	12	L	26	DH	aaa	STL	357	2	9	256	9	73	51	83	-21
	13	L	27	RF	aaa	STL	333	5	11	198	8	73	68	121	-1
Chang,Ray	12	R	29	3B	aaa	MIN	266	0	2	192	5	82	22	47	-28
	13	R	30	2B	a/a	CIN	261	3	0	213	7	78	48	29	-27
Chavez,Ozzie	13	B	30	SS	a/a	MIL	171	0	1	158	3	66	21	37	-99
Chen,Chun-Hsiu	12	R	24	1B	aa	CLE	399	4	5	281	11	71	94	68	5
	13	R	25	1B	a/a	CLE	487	11	10	211	8	65	99	88	-16
Chiang,Chih-Hsien	12	L	24	DH	a/a	SEA	449	5	2	204	4	79	60	52	-11
	13	L	25	RF	aa	TEX	476	10	0	238	4	80	105	48	26
Chirinos,Robinson	13	R	29	C	aaa	TEX	265	6	1	204	9	75	76	60	-3
Choi,Ji-Man	13	L	22	1B	a/a	SEA	243	8	2	231	11	83	101	64	57
Choice,Michael	12	R	23	DH	aa	OAK	359	7	4	241	7	72	73	84	-12
	13	R	24	LF	aaa	OAK	510	9	1	244	9	74	80	41	-10
Christian,Justin	12	R	32	C	aaa	SF	303	4	7	247	5	86	70	91	39
	13	R	33	LF	aaa	STL	374	2	9	201	5	85	41	85	11
Ciriaco,Audy	12	R	25	3B	aaa	DET	348	9	13	191	3	77	80	89	7
	13	R	26	SS	a/a	MIA	260	5	5	191	7	78	58	97	4
Ciriaco,Juan	12	R	29	SS	a/a	SF	243	3	7	179	7	78	51	94	-4
	13	R	30	SS	a/a	SF	144	1	2	173	4	79	36	49	-30
Ciriaco,Pedro	12	R	27	SS	aaa	BOS	276	3	11	263	2	79	64	105	5
	13	R	28	SS	aaa	KC	160	1	3	227	3	84	49	88	7
Clark,Andrew	13	L	26	1B	aa	NYY	141	3	0	235	6	74	107	29	6
Clark,Cody	12	R	31	C	aaa	KC	205	2	0	130	5	76	39	32	-42
	13	R	32	C	a/a	HOU	151	1	0	158	3	72	35	36	-65
Cleary,Delta	13	B	24	CF	aa	COL	397	2	14	192	6	76	37	108	-22
Clement,Jeff	12	L	29	1B	aaa	PIT	416	11	1	219	7	71	121	53	11
	13	L	30	DH	aaa	MIN	446	10	1	163	6	70	89	37	-24
Clevlen,Brent	12	R	29	DH	a/a	ARI	300	8	4	221	7	62	130	111	3
	13	R	30	RF	a/a	ARI	161	4	1	164	5	66	87	72	-33
Colabello,Chris	12	R	29	1B	aa	MIN	496	12	0	221	6	76	99	35	9
	13	R	30	1B	aaa	MIN	338	15	1	267	8	66	154	34	15
Coleman,Dustin	12	R	25	SS	aa	OAK	427	10	6	161	7	50	110	92	-67
	13	R	26	SS	a/a	OAK	505	2	12	202	7	62	92	123	-25
Collier,Zachary	13	L	23	CF	aa	PHI	446	6	13	188	7	67	73	126	-18
Collins,Tyler	13	L	23	LF	aa	DET	466	16	3	212	8	72	121	47	18
Colon,Christian	12	R	23	SS	a/a	KC	290	4	9	258	8	89	50	79	39
	13	R	24	2B	aaa	KC	512	9	12	240	6	88	49	99	34
Colvin,Tyler	13	L	28	CF	aaa	COL	229	6	3	213	8	68	98	109	1
Constanza,Jose	12	L	29	DH	aaa	ATL	344	1	9	242	7	84	29	93	0
	13	L	30	LF	aaa	ATL	341	0	14	213	6	81	20	98	-17
Corona,Reegie	13	B	27	3B	a/a	NYY	335	4	5	199	6	75	64	75	-14
Costanzo,Mike	12	L	29	3B	a/a	CIN	343	10	0	213	10	66	107	30	-18
	13	L	30	1B	a/a	CIN	382	12	2	193	10	62	131	64	-7
Court,Ryan	13	R	25	3B	aa	ARI	178	1	2	232	13	64	97	38	-27
Cousins,Scott	12	L	27	C	aaa	MIA	233	5	10	239	7	68	95	105	-6
	13	L	28	CF	aaa	LAA	193	1	4	162	4	69	28	119	-55
Cowart,Kaleb	13	B	21	3B	aa	LAA	498	5	12	199	6	73	56	81	-26
Cowgill,Collin	12	R	26	DH	aaa	OAK	260	2	5	195	5	77	65	80	-5
	13	R	27	LF	aaa	LAA	138	4	3	218	7	74	86	70	0
Cox,Zack	12	L	23	3B	a/a	MIA	394	8	1	223	5	73	102	43	-3
	13	L	24	3B	a/a	MIA	288	2	2	234	11	72	71	62	-15
Cron,C.J.	13	R	23	1B	aa	LAA	519	11	7	240	4	82	91	66	29
Crowe,Trevor	12	B	29	DH	a/a	LAA	310	2	12	207	7	78	58	105	5
	13	B	30	LF	aaa	HOU	237	2	11	229	6	81	41	107	2
Crumbliss,Conner	12	L	25	2B	aa	OAK	470	7	17	209	16	76	67	111	23
	13	L	26	LF	a/a	OAK	406	8	9	202	12	77	79	94	28
Culberson,Charlie	12	R	23	2B	aaa	COL	476	9	9	228	3	79	82	104	21
	13	R	24	SS	aaa	COL	397	10	8	261	2	80	110	104	45
Cunningham,Aaron	12	R	26	C	aaa	CLE	74	1	0	162	7	66	86	12	-47
	13	R	27	LF	aaa	TEX	421	8	8	205	8	77	97	90	29
Cunningham,Jarek	12	R	23	2B	aa	PIT	359	4	2	194	8	68	83	74	-24
	13	R	24	2B	aa	PIT	468	13	9	182	5	71	95	97	-1
Cunningham,Todd	12	B	23	DH	aa	ATL	466	2	20	283	6	88	54	120	44
	13	B	24	CF	aaa	ATL	427	2	16	231	7	83	38	111	12
Curtis,Jermaine	12	R	25	3B	a/a	STL	397	1	4	255	9	84	40	67	8
	13	R	26	3B	aaa	STL	370	3	7	206	9	83	50	70	14
Cuthbert,Cheslor	13	R	21	3B	aa	KC	237	5	4	194	6	78	93	63	18
Cutler,Charles	12	L	26	C	aa	PIT	152	1	1	250	9	87	59	86	43
	13	L	27	DH	aa	PIT	255	2	2	241	10	83	68	73	30
D Arnaud,Chase	12	R	25	SS	aaa	PIT	381	4	28	218	7	73	84	148	21
	13	R	26	SS	a/a	PIT	254	3	13	187	5	81	53	140	19
Danks,Jordan	12	L	26	C	aaa	CHW	218	8	5	281	16	64	154	66	31
	13	L	27	CF	aaa	CHW	208	5	2	232	9	66	99	81	-12
Davidson,Matthew	12	R	21	3B	aa	ARI	486	19	2	244	10	72	130	59	33
	13	R	22	3B	aaa	ARI	443	11	1	235	6	66	129	51	-3
Davis,Blake	12	L	29	SS	aaa	BAL	355	3	5	206	5	79	55	85	-3
	13	L	30	SS	aaa	MIL	332	1	3	190	4	72	57	82	-35
Davis,Kentrail	12	L	24	DH	aa	MIL	438	6	15	242	9	68	91	108	-3
	13	L	25	RF	a/a	MIL	500	6	19	226	9	70	81	117	1
Davis,Khristopher	12	R	25	DH	a/a	MIL	241	11	2	305	12	70	160	43	47
	13	R	26	LF	aaa	MIL	243	10	4	208	8	70	124	65	18
Davis,Lars	12	L	27	C	aa	COL	307	9	1	259	5	73	84	28	-19
	13	L	28	C	aaa	COL	298	2	1	193	4	66	68	51	-55
De Jesus,Ivan	12	R	25	2B	aaa	BOS	250	2	2	278	5	75	75	80	-5
	13	R	26	2B	aaa	PIT	304	2	4	267	6	76	97	77	19
Decker,Cody	12	R	25	DH	a/a	SD	453	18	1	194	9	65	128	34	-5
	13	R	26	1B	a/a	SD	359	12	0	209	8	61	153	63	3
Decker,Jaff	12	L	22	DH	aa	SD	147	2	5	157	18	72	55	116	3
	13	L	23	CF	aaa	SD	350	6	3	233	10	68	97	56	-12
Delarosa,Anderson	12	R	28	C	aa	MIL	224	5	0	184	4	70	80	36	-34
	13	R	29	C	a/a	MIL	242	2	2	209	4	71	77	47	-30
Den Dekker,Matthew	12	L	25	DH	a/a	NYM	533	13	16	223	5	65	109	119	-6
	13	L	26	CF	aaa	NYM	179	4	5	216	6	67	88	121	-11
Dent,Ryan	12	R	23	2B	a/a	BOS	280	2	3	222	8	75	40	63	-30
	13	R	24	2B	a/a	BOS	219	2	8	216	6	73	50	82	-29
Diaz,Argenis	12	R	25	SS	aaa	DET	356	0	9	217	5	80	26	61	-27
	13	R	26	SS	aaa	DET	471	2	3	217	6	73	67	72	-18
Diaz,Jonathan	12	B	27	2B	a/a	TOR	457	3	12	177	10	78	35	94	-11
	13	B	28	2B	aaa	BOS	332	1	7	208	9	76	41	82	-21
Diaz,Juan	12	B	24	SS	a/a	CLE	443	10	1	233	5	71	106	55	-3
	13	B	25	SS	aaa	CLE	442	6	2	208	8	66	83	38	-40
Diaz,Robinzon	12	R	29	C	aaa	TEX	183	3	1	224	2	93	64	69	51
	13	R	30	C	a/a	MIL	351	5	1	231	3	89	66	42	29
Dickerson,Alex	13	L	23	RF	aa	PIT	451	12	8	252	4	79	120	84	48
Dickerson,Chris	12	L	30	DH	aaa	NYY	266	6	12	247	12	65	130	123	26
	13	L	31	RF	aaa	BAL	136	2	1	190	10	68	78	91	-18
Dickerson,Corey	12	L	23	C	aa	COL	266	13	6	274	5	81	143	99	80
	13	L	24	LF	aaa	COL	315	8	4	319	5	83	121	92	67
Dietrich,Derek	12	L	23	2B	aa	TAM	133	3	0	233	4	69	95	76	-15
	13	L	24	2B	aa	MIA	218	9	2	240	11	67	154	98	43
Dinkelman,Brian	12	L	29	DH	aaa	MIN	246	3	4	203	7	77	68	89	5
	13	L	30	RF	aaa	MIN	237	4	4	161	8	79	62	101	13
Dominguez,Chris	12	R	26	3B	a/a	SF	362	3	3	188	2	68	64	52	-56
	13	R	27	3B	aaa	SF	466	8	3	221	3	70	83	66	-27
Donald,Jason	12	R	28	SS	aaa	CLE	256	4	3	215	7	71	96	88	6
	13	R	29	2B	aaa	CIN	251	2	1	173	4	64	75	74	-49
Dorn,Daniel	12	L	28	1B	aaa	DET	393	10	4	202	8	68	106	67	-6
	13	L	29	RF	aaa	DET	496	18	6	205	8	68	110	72	1
Douglas,Brandon	12	R	27	2B	aa	DET	471	2	10	217	6	82	47	89	6
	13	R	28	2B	a/a	DET	354	4	9	227	5	80	60	101	8
Downs,Matt	12	R	28	1B	aaa	HOU	90	2	2	198	5	71	55	63	-40
	13	R	29	2B	aaa	MIA	270	6	0	169	7	73	77	46	-17
Dugan,Kelly	13	L	23	RF	aa	PHI	212	8	0	226	2	71	124	44	2
Duncan,Shelley	13	R	34	DH	aaa	TAM	335	7	0	160	6	68	97	34	-25
Duran,Edgar	13	B	22	SS	aa	PHI	405	3	9	194	4	75	59	81	-18
Durango,Luis	12	B	26	C	aaa	ATL	499	0	33	238	7	78	27	113	-18
	13	B	27	LF	a/a	CIN	196	0	9	201	9	78	20	75	-30
Duvall,Adam	13	R	25	3B	aa	SF	385	10	1	200	6	78	100	79	29
Dykstra,Allan	12	L	25	1B	aa	NYM	191	6	1	214	17	59	107	38	-32
	13	L	26	1B	aa	NYM	372	16	0	217	16	59	151	13	-5
Earley,Michael	13	R	25	LF	a/a	CHW	319	4	3	226	6	79	74	71	10
Easley,Edward	12	R	27	C	aa	ARI	204	2	1	218	10	82	37	24	-13
	13	R	28	C	aaa	ARI	293	4	1	249	5	78	79	41	0
Eibner,Brett	13	R	25	CF	aa	KC	441	13	5	209	8	62	128	118	5
Elmore,Jake	12	R	25	SS	aaa	ARI	419	1	19	275	9	84	66	129	50
	13	R	26	2B	aaa	HOU	268	4	12	245	8	83	69	117	40
Erickson,Gorman	12	B	24	C	aa	LA	274	2	1	199	11	77	60	34	-11
	13	B	25	C	aa	LA	181	8	0	171	13	67	140	35	17
Escobar,Eduardo	12	B	23	3B	aaa	MIN	138	1	3	201	5	80	46	127	5
	13	B	24	SS	aaa	MIN	166	3	4	264	7	75	125	100	45
Espinosa,Danny	13	B	26	2B	aaa	WAS	283	1	5	175	4	59	59	92	-78
Estrada,Robi	13	B	25	SS	aa	TAM	215	2	2	203	7	84	60	57	18
Evans,Nick	12	R	26	1B	aaa	PIT	71	1	0	165	7	78	67	29	-9
	13	R	27	1B	aa	ARI	454	16	2	230	10	71	117	47	13
Exposito,Luis	12	R	25	C	aaa	BAL	215	6	0	240	7	81	94	43	27
	13	R	26	C	aaa	BAL	206	3	0	189	6	71	87	27	-23
Falu,Irving	12	B	29	3B	aaa	KC	365	4	13	248	5	86	61	105	35
	13	B	30	3B	aaa	KC	508	1	14	201	6	88	38	95	23
Farris,Eric	12	R	26	2B	aaa	MIL	483	6	27	241	4	86	52	94	24
	13	R	27	2B	a/a	MIN	406	2	16	199	5	84	34	99	6
Fedroff,Tim	12	L	25	DH	a/a	CLE	468	10	11	271	9	80	84	108	42
	13	L	26	CF	aaa	CLE	513	5	18	203	10	73	41	80	-31

BATTER	yr	b	age	pos	lvl	org	ab	hr	sb	ba	bb%	ct%	px	sx	bpv
Fellhauer,Joshua	12	L	24	DH	aa	CIN	338	4	5	284	12	82	69	70	29
	13	L	25	RF	a/a	CIN	270	4	2	234	10	72	69	48	-20
Field,Tommy	12	R	25	SS	aaa	COL	435	6	2	202	5	81	83	90	29
	13	R	26	SS	aaa	LAA	314	6	4	222	8	73	87	74	-1
Fields,Daniel	12	L	21	DH	aa	DET	106	2	7	243	9	80	55	83	8
	13	L	22	CF	aa	DET	457	8	19	261	7	71	103	137	22
Fields,Josh	12	R	30	3B	aaa	LA	490	7	5	223	6	68	80	75	-28
	13	R	31	DH	aaa	PHI	377	3	7	218	5	62	88	84	-45
Fields,Matthew	13	R	28	1B	aa	KC	454	20	4	174	8	52	161	63	-24
Figueroa,Cole	12	L	25	3B	a/a	TAM	397	4	3	243	8	91	59	70	48
	13	L	26	3B	aaa	TAM	461	2	8	235	8	92	41	92	47
Fisher,Ryan	13	L	25	3B	aa	MIA	145	4	2	190	9	62	125	63	-14
Fletcher,Scott	12	R	24	DH	aa	KC	254	7	5	220	4	58	117	95	-34
	13	R	25	LF	a/a	KC	315	12	5	249	4	73	113	88	21
Flores,Jesus	13	R	29	C	aaa	TAM	253	1	0	130	3	70	45	16	-73
Flores,Luis	12	R	26	C	aa	CHC	72	1	0	136	14	79	48	3	-15
	13	R	27	C	aaa	CHC	191	4	0	162	8	80	63	14	-9
Flores,Ramon	13	L	21	LF	aa	NYY	534	6	6	242	11	81	66	80	23
Flores,Wilmer	12	R	21	3B	aa	NYM	251	7	0	274	6	86	95	47	50
	13	R	22	2B	aaa	NYM	424	10	1	255	4	82	103	55	38
Fontenot,Mike	12	L	32	2B	aaa	PHI	52	1	0	243	7	73	120	14	7
	13	L	33	2B	aaa	TAM	417	3	4	198	6	73	75	82	-11
Ford,Darren	12	R	27	C	aaa	SEA	304	2	17	201	5	74	56	106	-17
	13	R	28	LF	aaa	PIT	239	1	21	181	7	73	41	135	-20
Forsythe,Blake	13	R	24	C	aa	NYM	307	8	2	155	7	61	114	78	-24
Francisco,Ben	12	R	31	DH	aa	TOR	36	0	0	175	5	86	57	11	5
	13	R	32	LF	aaa	SD	187	1	3	170	5	72	40	78	-42
Franco,Angel	13	B	23	2B	aa	KC	282	3	6	264	5	84	63	78	23
Franco,Maikel	13	R	21	3B	aa	PHI	277	12	1	303	3	88	108	60	62
Franklin,Nick	12	B	21	SS	a/a	SEA	472	8	10	239	8	74	98	109	25
	13	B	22	2B	aaa	SEA	142	3	5	274	14	83	78	75	47
Freeman,Michael	13	L	26	2B	aa	ARI	454	1	23	216	10	78	42	89	-4
Freitas,David	12	R	23	C	aa	OAK	63	1	0	284	7	73	120	36	14
	13	R	24	C	a/a	OAK	321	6	0	186	7	81	66	36	3
Frey,Evan	12	L	26	C	a/a	ARI	464	1	22	202	9	81	36	108	5
	13	L	27	CF	a/a	TAM	293	0	13	201	10	76	29	104	-21
Fryer,Eric	12	R	27	C	aaa	PIT	162	0	1	168	4	73	37	45	-53
	13	R	28	C	aaa	MIN	200	3	5	167	11	71	83	114	9
Fuentes,Reymond	12	L	21	C	aa	SD	473	3	28	189	8	68	58	123	-25
	13	L	22	RF	a/a	SD	400	4	27	290	9	77	77	111	21
Gale,Rocky	12	R	24	C	a/a	SD	128	0	0	135	3	79	34	38	-38
	13	R	25	C	a/a	SD	227	1	0	197	3	89	23	22	-12
Gallagher,Jim	12	L	27	1B	a/a	CHW	320	2	5	195	9	76	54	73	-11
	13	L	28	RF	aaa	CHW	282	3	2	197	8	55	81	74	-76
Galloway,Isaac	13	R	24	CF	aa	MIA	139	2	4	152	4	59	75	98	-65
Galvez,Jonathan	12	R	21	2B	aa	SD	312	4	10	255	8	74	84	103	13
	13	R	22	2B	aaa	SD	410	4	15	232	6	70	72	100	-17
Galvis,Freddy	13	B	24	SS	aaa	PHI	241	2	2	207	3	76	74	78	-6
Garcia,Adonis	12	R	27	C	aa	NYY	118	3	1	237	3	82	118	60	47
	13	R	28	CF	aaa	NYY	199	3	3	212	4	87	55	58	21
Garcia,Avisail	12	R	21	DH	aa	DET	215	5	7	291	3	82	81	114	34
	13	R	22	CF	aaa	CHW	174	6	3	348	6	77	103	86	29
Garcia,Drew	12	B	26	2B	a/a	CHW	498	5	4	218	6	75	73	70	-6
	13	B	27	2B	aaa	COL	216	1	2	178	3	66	76	67	-47
Garcia,Greg	12	L	23	SS	aa	STL	412	7	8	243	13	78	72	84	21
	13	L	24	SS	aaa	STL	354	2	10	228	10	78	71	107	20
Garcia,Jonathan	13	R	22	RF	aa	LA	185	1	1	152	5	65	58	81	-57
Garcia,Leury	12	B	21	2B	aa	TEX	377	2	25	280	5	78	60	149	17
	13	B	22	SS	aaa	CHW	223	4	12	243	6	69	88	146	6
Garcia,Rene	12	R	22	C	aa	HOU	27	0	0	293	6	87	28	30	-7
	13	R	23	C	a/a	HOU	368	4	2	256	5	84	63	48	13
Garneau,Dustin	13	R	26	C	aa	COL	326	12	3	212	5	81	104	53	36
Garner,Cole	12	R	28	DH	aaa	NYY	236	5	2	208	5	61	99	63	-45
	13	R	29	RF	aaa	MIL	214	6	1	144	5	46	134	54	-81
Gartrell,Maurice	12	R	28	DH	aaa	ATL	418	13	7	196	8	62	115	86	-16
	13	R	29	DH	aaa	ATL	255	6	1	208	7	55	114	43	-61
Gaynor,Wade	12	R	24	3B	aa	DET	35	2	1	198	11	76	97	93	32
	13	R	25	3B	aa	DET	477	9	9	192	5	65	106	106	-11
Gennett,Scooter	12	L	22	2B	aa	MIL	533	5	9	267	4	85	61	74	22
	13	L	23	2B	aaa	MIL	321	3	7	241	5	79	50	105	-2
Giansanti,Anthony	13	R	25	RF	a/a	CHC	130	0	1	227	3	76	71	87	-6
Giavotella,Johnny	12	R	25	2B	aaa	KC	362	6	5	265	8	87	68	79	45
	13	R	26	2B	aaa	KC	370	5	6	240	9	82	73	55	22
Gibson,Derrik	12	R	23	SS	aa	BOS	405	0	12	212	8	75	38	90	-23
	13	R	24	2B	aa	BOS	260	1	9	225	10	74	74	89	3
Gillespie,Cole	12	R	28	DH	aaa	ARI	441	8	6	228	7	77	91	78	19
	13	R	29	LF	aaa	SF	235	5	4	197	8	71	79	88	-10
Gillies,Tyson	12	L	24	DH	aa	PHI	276	3	6	261	5	78	76	134	25
	13	L	25	CF	a/a	PHI	390	8	12	198	6	72	81	124	2
Gimenez,Chris	12	R	30	C	aaa	TAM	261	7	0	233	8	71	90	26	-19
	13	R	31	C	aaa	TAM	308	2	1	167	12	73	52	41	-28
Gindl,Caleb	12	L	24	C	aaa	MIL	452	11	3	232	6	75	101	77	18
	13	L	25	CF	aaa	MIL	312	9	1	245	6	72	118	45	11
Glaesmann,Todd	13	R	23	LF	aa	TAM	487	8	5	206	4	74	86	83	1
Glenn,Brad	12	R	25	DH	aa	TOR	423	16	6	209	5	67	135	56	5
	13	R	26	RF	a/a	TOR	485	17	1	220	7	72	123	51	16
Goebbert,Jacob	12	L	25	DH	a/a	HOU	398	6	3	237	10	80	80	86	33
	13	L	26	LF	a/a	OAK	466	14	4	204	9	74	100	81	21

BATTER	yr	b	age	pos	lvl	org	ab	hr	sb	ba	bb%	ct%	px	sx	bpv
Goedert,Jared	12	R	27	3B	a/a	CLE	450	14	0	256	8	75	105	34	11
	13	R	28	3B	aaa	PIT	464	7	3	190	7	72	91	72	-1
Goins,Ryan	12	L	24	SS	aa	TOR	546	6	12	260	6	84	70	84	31
	13	L	25	SS	aaa	TOR	377	5	2	222	5	74	78	50	-14
Golson,Greg	12	R	27	DH	aaa	CHW	449	6	16	238	3	69	95	144	3
	13	R	28	CF	a/a	ATL	240	4	14	203	6	64	77	150	-26
Gomez,Hector	13	R	25	SS	aa	MIL	368	2	5	167	4	75	41	60	-38
Gomez,Mauro	12	R	28	1B	aaa	BOS	387	17	1	265	6	73	162	47	49
	13	R	29	1B	aaa	TOR	405	22	1	199	7	59	174	42	5
Gomez,Raywilly	13	B	23	C	aa	ARI	224	0	1	255	10	88	49	28	23
Gomez,Rolando	13	L	24	SS	aa	LAA	345	3	12	218	5	70	52	113	-30
Gonzalez,Alberto	12	R	29	SS	aaa	TEX	51	1	0	243	0	73	79	9	-39
	13	R	30	SS	aaa	NYY	224	1	0	159	6	79	23	21	-44
Gonzalez,Jose	12	R	25	C	aa	COL	174	1	1	216	5	76	47	47	-33
	13	R	26	C	a/a	COL	221	3	1	158	6	67	57	55	-58
Gonzalez,Marwin	12	B	23	SS	aaa	HOU	39	1	0	280	5	79	111	-3	15
	13	B	24	SS	aaa	HOU	172	1	3	222	3	84	57	75	14
Gonzalez,Miguel	12	R	22	C	aa	CHW	70	0	0	192	8	75	13	15	-69
	13	R	23	C	a/a	CHW	169	2	2	230	8	76	67	64	-6
Goodwin,Brian	12	L	22	C	aa	WAS	166	4	2	204	8	69	98	65	-11
	13	L	23	CF	aa	WAS	457	8	15	228	10	72	92	137	23
Gordon,Dee	12	L	24	SS	aaa	LA	30	0	1	203	4	88	12	103	3
	13	L	25	SS	aaa	LA	374	0	33	234	8	77	46	145	9
Gose,Anthony	12	L	22	C	aaa	TOR	420	4	24	250	7	73	78	148	17
	13	L	23	CF	aaa	TOR	393	3	17	217	7	66	75	143	-17
Gosewisch,Tuffy	12	R	29	C	aaa	TOR	296	3	0	159	3	75	72	41	-23
	13	R	30	C	aaa	ARI	250	4	1	203	3	79	86	41	6
Gosselin,Phil	12	R	24	2B	aa	ATL	484	2	10	216	7	79	52	88	-1
	13	R	25	2B	a/a	ATL	425	2	5	220	4	81	40	78	-11
Gotay,Ruben	12	B	30	3B	aaa	ATL	259	3	3	208	10	67	62	69	-41
	13	B	31	3B	aa	STL	498	10	10	205	9	75	81	63	5
Graterol,Juan	13	R	24	C	aa	KC	182	2	2	248	2	87	44	51	4
Green,Grant	12	R	25	SS	aaa	OAK	524	9	9	235	4	83	71	82	24
	13	R	26	2B	aaa	LAA	402	6	2	241	4	76	81	67	-3
Green,Nick	12	R	34	2B	aaa	MIA	212	8	1	264	5	76	122	68	35
	13	R	35	SS	aaa	MIA	318	8	1	166	4	65	88	55	-43
Greene,Brodie	12	R	25	2B	aa	CIN	435	3	10	214	8	81	54	87	11
	13	R	26	2B	aa	CIN	304	3	3	197	6	85	42	55	4
Greene,Justin	12	R	27	DH	a/a	CHW	320	7	20	216	9	67	97	124	4
	13	R	28	LF	aa	ARI	380	1	24	264	8	76	69	156	25
Greene,Tyler	13	R	30	RF	aaa	ATL	250	3	7	197	5	62	84	106	-43
Grice,Cody	13	R	23	CF	a/a	NYY	164	3	7	194	7	60	62	137	-54
Grichuk,Randal	13	R	22	RF	aa	LAA	500	17	8	228	4	80	114	124	58
Griffin,Jonathan	13	R	24	1B	aa	ARI	220	3	0	213	5	65	65	51	-62
Grossman,Robert	12	B	23	C	aa	HOU	485	8	10	228	11	71	89	93	7
	13	B	24	CF	aaa	HOU	253	2	11	239	13	69	60	100	-18
Guez,Ben	12	R	25	DH	a/a	DET	370	7	12	251	10	72	102	118	28
	13	R	26	RF	aaa	DET	425	14	6	206	10	64	115	79	-5
Gutierrez,Chris	12	R	28	SS	a/a	MIA	430	3	4	192	8	73	60	49	-26
	13	R	29	SS	a/a	MIA	274	2	1	194	9	75	58	50	-19
Gutierrez,Franklin	12	R	29	DH	aaa	SEA	62	1	0	179	8	71	88	54	-11
	13	R	30	RF	aaa	SEA	194	2	2	147	5	58	94	76	-60
Guyer,Brandon	12	R	26	DH	aaa	TAM	85	2	2	240	6	78	76	73	10
	13	R	27	RF	aaa	TAM	356	5	17	242	6	78	86	159	43
Gwynn,Tony	12	L	30	DH	aaa	LA	68	0	2	233	6	76	44	87	-21
	13	L	31	CF	aaa	LA	333	1	7	215	8	79	37	85	-10
Ha,Jae-Hoon	12	R	22	DH	a/a	CHC	465	5	9	247	8	77	74	83	12
	13	R	23	CF	a/a	CHC	323	5	12	221	6	77	73	88	8
Hague,Matt	12	R	27	3B	aaa	PIT	367	3	2	235	5	84	38	46	-6
	13	R	28	1B	aaa	PIT	536	5	3	227	8	79	74	50	8
Hague,Rick	13	R	25	2B	aaa	WAS	437	6	2	212	5	74	71	76	-11
Halton,Sean	12	R	25	1B	aaa	MIL	358	15	0	240	9	73	135	42	33
	13	R	26	RF	aaa	MIL	352	9	4	221	7	68	127	78	11
Hamilton,Billy	12	B	22	SS	a/a	CIN	175	1	45	271	15	73	56	175	22
	13	B	23	CF	aaa	CIN	504	6	63	233	6	77	57	159	16
Hamilton,Mark	12	L	28	DH	aaa	STL	303	9	1	173	10	66	93	32	-31
	13	L	29	DH	aaa	BOS	283	8	1	211	10	62	139	40	-8
Hankerd,Kevin	13	R	28	LF	aa	LAA	127	4	0	204	5	65	95	50	-37
Hanson,Alen	13	B	21	SS	aa	PIT	137	1	5	232	4	81	61	123	19
Hanson,Nate	12	R	25	2B	aa	MIN	351	5	2	236	3	87	56	50	15
	13	R	26	3B	a/a	MIN	431	6	1	197	7	80	71	58	10
Hanzawa,Troy	12	R	27	SS	aa	PHI	413	0	3	198	5	80	41	83	-12
	13	R	28	SS	a/a	PHI	253	1	1	226	2	82	59	65	1
Harbin,Taylor	12	R	26	2B	aaa	ARI	478	3	10	238	2	87	73	98	41
	13	R	27	2B	aaa	ARI	364	3	3	174	2	82	53	87	3
Harris,Alonzo	13	R	24	CF	aa	NYM	355	3	19	175	7	70	58	108	-24
Harrison,Josh	13	R	26	2B	aaa	PIT	268	3	14	266	5	84	114	147	82
Hassan,Alexander	12	R	24	DH	aaa	BOS	312	6	1	238	13	75	71	29	-6
	13	R	25	RF	aaa	BOS	187	3	0	285	12	70	108	21	-2
Hawpe,Brad	12	L	33	DH	aa	TEX	123	2	0	208	12	61	87	19	-54
	13	L	34	DH	aaa	LAA	131	3	1	207	8	58	106	37	-54
Hayes,Brett	12	R	28	C	aaa	MIA	59	2	0	283	4	70	121	22	-6
	13	R	29	C	aaa	KC	275	11	1	180	4	72	125	71	18
Hazelbaker,Jeremy	12	L	25	DH	a/a	BOS	466	15	29	247	6	71	119	137	32
	13	L	26	LF	aaa	BOS	428	8	27	220	6	64	74	119	-34
Head,Jerad	12	R	30	DH	aaa	DET	295	8	6	207	6	74	94	81	8
	13	R	31	LF	a/a	WAS	405	9	1	193	4	75	82	42	-14

BATTER	yr	b	age	pos	lvl	org	ab	hr	sb	ba	bb%	ct%	px	sx	bpv
Head,Miles	13	R	22	3B	aa	OAK	148	1	0	168	6	69	43	32	-65
Heathcott,Zachary	13	L	23	CF	aa	NYY	399	8	12	235	7	71	101	122	16
Hefflinger,Robby	13	R	23	LF	aa	ATL	188	5	2	155	6	62	117	77	-21
Heid,Andrew	12	L	25	DH	a/a	LAA	118	1	4	169	8	82	26	73	-12
	13	L	26	LF	a/a	LAA	347	4	5	238	9	70	82	79	-11
Henry,Justin	12	L	27	3B	aaa	DET	476	1	16	251	7	84	31	100	9
	13	L	28	2B	aaa	BOS	357	1	6	174	7	81	50	81	4
Henson,Bobby	12	R	25	2B	a/a	LA	156	3	1	213	10	59	106	57	-38
Henson,Tyler	13	R	26	3B	a/a	PHI	353	6	9	225	7	60	120	99	-18
Hermida,Jeremy	12	L	28	DH	aaa	SD	151	2	1	179	6	62	61	44	-75
	13	L	29	DH	aaa	CLE	474	13	1	194	12	60	113	44	-30
Hernandez,Cesar	12	B	22	2B	a/a	PHI	532	2	18	264	5	84	65	116	33
	13	B	23	2B	a/a	PHI	401	2	25	272	7	77	51	141	7
Hernandez,Enrique	12	R	21	2B	aa	HOU	81	1	2	216	4	88	33	50	1
	13	R	22	2B	aa	HOU	437	11	4	209	6	82	77	69	24
Hernandez,Gorkys	12	R	25	C	aaa	PIT	237	1	11	223	10	70	61	113	-13
	13	R	26	CF	aaa	KC	430	4	19	223	5	67	70	130	-26
Hernandez,Luis	12	B	28	SS	aaa	TEX	519	6	6	207	4	81	56	81	4
	13	B	29	2B	aaa	CLE	131	1	2	180	6	84	32	60	-8
Hernandez,Roman	13	R	25	LF	aa	KC	271	1	4	224	6	73	52	64	-34
Herrera,Elian	12	B	27	SS	aaa	LA	273	2	6	248	4	78	75	114	14
	13	B	28	2B	aaa	LA	408	4	10	209	7	76	43	86	-20
Herrera,Javier	13	R	28	LF	aa	SF	480	9	15	223	7	69	107	95	6
Herrera,Odubel	13	L	22	2B	aa	TEX	389	2	13	248	4	82	51	123	16
Herrmann,Chris	12	L	25	C	aa	MIN	490	7	2	235	8	79	65	59	5
	13	L	26	C	aaa	MIN	247	1	2	186	7	71	52	91	-31
Hessman,Mike	12	R	34	1B	aaa	HOU	441	21	0	165	5	59	143	29	-29
	13	R	35	1B	aaa	CIN	420	21	0	192	8	59	187	21	10
Hester,John	12	R	29	C	aaa	LAA	126	2	0	158	5	58	100	67	-56
	13	R	30	C	aaa	LAA	253	4	2	157	5	60	80	69	-63
Hewitt,Anthony	13	R	24	RF	aa	PHI	386	12	15	203	5	60	123	114	-16
Hicks,Brandon	12	R	27	SS	aaa	OAK	328	11	3	182	9	57	156	88	-2
	13	R	28	SS	aaa	NYM	318	7	5	197	5	53	94	104	-68
Hicks,John	13	R	24	C	aa	SEA	296	3	12	212	6	75	64	108	0
Hill,Koyie	12	B	33	C	a/a	TEX	200	3	1	147	5	68	48	44	-64
	13	B	34	C	aaa	MIA	190	1	0	185	6	73	68	24	-34
Hissey,Peter	12	L	22	DH	aa	BOS	236	1	13	242	6	79	66	93	10
	13	L	23	RF	aa	BOS	262	2	13	238	6	74	80	113	7
Hoes,LJ	12	R	22	DH	a/a	BAL	513	5	17	267	10	84	59	100	35
	13	R	23	RF	aaa	BAL	365	3	6	276	11	83	71	60	32
Hoffmann,Jamie	12	R	28	DH	aaa	BAL	366	10	7	215	11	76	90	76	21
	13	R	29	LF	aaa	NYM	365	5	4	186	3	78	75	71	1
Holaday,Bryan	12	R	25	C	aaa	DET	250	2	2	206	6	81	49	49	-7
	13	R	26	C	aaa	DET	288	3	0	221	4	78	72	41	-8
Holt,Brock	12	L	24	SS	a/a	PIT	477	2	13	306	8	86	66	87	42
	13	L	25	2B	aaa	BOS	291	2	6	225	7	79	31	62	-25
Holt,Tyler	12	R	23	C	aa	CLE	216	0	12	230	9	79	27	115	-8
	13	R	24	CF	aa	CLE	521	1	20	221	7	80	52	128	16
Hood,Destin	12	R	22	DH	aa	WAS	355	3	5	225	5	74	70	96	-8
	13	R	23	RF	aa	WAS	392	3	4	202	5	68	73	91	-29
Horton,Joshua	12	L	26	2B	a/a	OAK	471	6	3	220	7	70	76	62	-23
	13	L	27	2B	a/a	BAL	318	3	2	235	4	77	77	73	2
Howard,Justin	13	L	26	1B	aa	PIT	283	5	5	259	9	75	82	61	4
Howell,Jeffery	12	R	29	C	a/a	WAS	101	0	0	179	3	77	22	34	-56
	13	R	30	C	a/a	WAS	139	4	0	199	2	70	104	57	-15
Hoying,Jared	12	L	23	DH	aa	TEX	247	4	7	255	5	78	58	109	6
	13	L	24	RF	a/a	TEX	341	11	5	234	4	67	131	118	17
Hudson,Kyle	12	L	25	C	aaa	PHI	406	0	18	227	8	79	14	90	-29
	13	L	26	LF	aa	BAL	353	0	19	241	10	81	17	97	-10
Huffman,Chad	12	R	27	DH	aaa	CLE	234	4	1	224	6	69	114	42	-4
	13	R	28	LF	aaa	STL	309	8	1	216	10	72	100	55	5
Hughes,Rhyne	12	L	29	1B	aa	BAL	266	10	3	219	10	65	137	65	11
	13	L	30	1B	aa	NYM	162	3	1	202	8	49	140	71	-53
Hunter,Cedric	12	L	24	C	aaa	STL	355	3	5	222	8	86	55	62	26
	13	L	25	LF	a/a	CLE	330	11	3	236	5	82	119	75	60
Ibarra,Walter	12	B	25	SS	aa	NYY	156	1	2	234	2	80	91	79	24
	13	B	26	SS	a/a	NYY	199	3	2	237	4	63	68	75	-61
Inciarte,Ender David	13	L	23	CF	aa	ARI	473	4	37	264	5	89	49	136	48
Iribarren,Hernan	12	L	28	2B	aaa	COL	381	1	11	234	6	82	42	101	4
	13	L	29	2B	aaa	COL	253	1	5	234	5	79	50	80	-8
Ishikawa,Travis	13	L	30	1B	aaa	CHW	297	7	1	228	10	67	116	56	1
Jackson,Brett	12	L	24	C	aaa	CHC	407	11	19	217	8	55	149	142	1
	13	L	25	CF	a/a	CHC	310	4	7	182	8	57	89	111	-49
Jackson,Ryan	12	R	24	SS	aaa	STL	445	7	1	225	7	81	64	49	4
	13	R	25	SS	aaa	STL	442	2	7	229	8	76	45	71	-20
Jacobs,Brandon	13	R	23	LF	aa	CHW	164	2	2	221	6	64	89	63	-40
Jacobs,Mike	12	L	32	1B	aaa	ARI	333	10	1	197	6	67	93	35	-32
	13	L	33	1B	aaa	ARI	329	10	0	217	5	73	97	21	-14
Janish,Paul	12	R	30	SS	aaa	CIN	169	3	0	179	7	80	80	58	18
	13	R	31	SS	aaa	ATL	135	0	0	159	6	69	32	22	-78
Jaramillo,Jason	12	B	30	C	a/a	OAK	292	1	1	159	7	76	37	33	-41
	13	B	31	C	aaa	SEA	205	1	0	150	6	71	59	28	-48
Jensen,Kyle	12	R	24	DH	aa	MIA	445	18	1	201	12	56	151	53	-14
	13	R	25	RF	a/a	MIA	447	22	5	202	9	60	184	64	28
Jeroloman,Brian	12	L	27	C	aa	TOR	113	0	2	161	9	74	0	42	-74
	13	L	28	C	a/a	WAS	179	0	0	182	9	65	41	46	-74
Jimenez,Antonio	12	R	22	C	aa	TOR	105	2	2	240	4	86	64	92	31
	13	R	23	C	a/a	TOR	233	2	1	241	5	81	76	38	10
Jimenez,Luis	12	L	30	DH	aaa	SEA	471	11	2	216	8	71	92	48	-10
	13	L	31	DH	aaa	TOR	354	13	2	225	7	77	105	67	26
Jimenez,Luis	12	R	24	3B	aaa	LAA	485	10	11	242	2	83	86	86	32
	13	R	25	3B	aaa	LAA	197	2	7	213	3	84	53	102	17
Johnson,Dan	12	L	33	1B	aaa	CHW	476	25	1	221	14	75	126	31	39
	13	L	34	1B	aaa	BAL	472	16	1	197	12	77	101	23	24
Johnson,Jamie	12	L	25	DH	a/a	DET	463	2	11	237	9	88	35	79	23
	13	L	26	RF	aa	DET	406	1	20	230	15	80	43	107	17
Johnson,Joshua	12	B	26	SS	a/a	WAS	272	1	6	214	9	85	41	73	17
	13	B	27	SS	a/a	WAS	249	6	7	240	10	81	84	99	41
Johnson,Rob	12	R	30	C	aaa	NYM	164	3	2	150	3	79	57	83	-5
	13	R	31	C	aaa	STL	195	4	0	173	8	72	75	50	-18
Jones,James	13	L	25	RF	a/a	SEA	378	4	21	231	8	76	71	136	19
Jones,Mycal	12	R	25	C	aa	ATL	85	0	6	122	8	66	0	111	-87
	13	R	26	CF	aa	ATL	345	3	23	225	8	78	60	107	10
Joseph,Caleb	12	R	26	C	a/a	BAL	347	10	2	224	8	77	102	55	22
	13	R	27	C	aa	BAL	518	17	3	244	5	79	105	53	26
Joseph,Corban	12	L	24	2B	a/a	NYY	413	13	0	243	11	81	109	35	47
	13	L	25	2B	aaa	NYY	188	6	2	212	8	77	93	62	18
Jurica,Carter	13	R	25	SS	aaa	SF	359	1	2	194	6	72	44	54	-45
Ka aihue,Kila	12	L	28	DH	aaa	OAK	254	9	1	186	10	70	109	37	1
	13	L	29	1B	aaa	ARI	192	9	0	227	10	72	129	38	24
Kang,Kyeong	12	L	24	DH	aa	TAM	345	10	3	204	10	54	140	96	-19
	13	L	25	LF	aa	TAM	346	11	2	209	11	65	130	104	18
Kazmar,Sean	12	R	28	SS	a/a	NYM	224	3	0	168	4	79	55	57	-13
	13	R	29	SS	aaa	ATL	272	1	6	177	4	81	53	78	0
Kelly,Tyler	12	B	24	3B	a/a	BAL	208	2	2	272	9	83	65	69	26
	13	B	25	2B	a/a	SEA	480	3	5	248	14	77	59	61	4
Kiermaier,Kevin	13	L	23	CF	a/a	TAM	508	5	17	260	7	80	72	139	36
Kieschnick,Roger	12	L	25	DH	aaa	SF	222	8	0	239	7	63	145	88	9
	13	L	26	RF	aaa	SF	374	7	3	209	6	67	119	100	6
Kirby-Jones,A.J.	13	R	25	DH	aa	SD	168	4	1	202	7	61	111	38	-41
Kjeldgaard,Riley	12	R	26	DH	aa	MIL	158	7	1	199	12	67	134	34	12
	13	R	27	LF	aa	MIL	446	20	0	186	10	58	134	38	-25
Kleinknecht,Barrett	12	R	24	SS	aa	ATL	128	0	2	195	8	79	72	58	11
	13	R	25	1B	aa	ATL	235	6	0	209	6	78	79	34	1
Kobernus,Jeff	12	R	24	2B	aa	WAS	330	1	33	250	4	81	32	121	-4
	13	R	25	LF	aaa	WAS	371	1	31	269	5	82	47	124	14
Kouzmanoff,Kevin	12	R	31	3B	a/a	KC	330	1	1	208	3	78	64	54	-14
	13	R	32	3B	aaa	MIA	218	4	1	230	5	83	78	36	17
Krauss,Marc	12	L	25	1B	a/a	HOU	432	14	5	217	12	67	129	71	21
	13	L	26	LF	aaa	HOU	253	7	2	230	13	75	111	62	35
Krill,Brett	13	R	24	RF	aa	SF	225	1	2	212	3	72	50	60	-47
Kuhn,Tyler	12	L	26	2B	aaa	ARI	489	4	4	209	3	81	62	81	5
	13	L	27	RF	a/a	COL	350	1	7	195	6	82	56	111	21
La Stella,Tommy	13	L	24	2B	aa	ATL	283	3	6	311	10	86	83	77	56
Ladendorf,Tyler	12	R	24	2B	aa	OAK	416	6	5	197	7	75	64	71	-9
	13	R	25	3B	a/a	OAK	294	4	1	198	7	81	67	54	9
Laird,Brandon	12	R	25	3B	aaa	NYY	503	13	1	219	5	77	96	40	7
	13	R	26	3B	aaa	HOU	470	12	1	225	4	77	101	49	15
Lake,Junior	12	R	22	SS	aa	CHC	405	8	17	253	7	71	102	101	13
	13	R	23	3B	aaa	CHC	156	3	11	260	5	76	101	148	41
Lalli,Blake	12	L	29	1B	aaa	OAK	316	4	0	183	4	77	66	26	-20
	13	L	30	C	aaa	MIL	284	8	0	211	5	68	96	19	-34
LaMarre,Ryan	12	R	24	C	aa	CIN	482	5	26	238	10	72	64	108	-8
	13	R	25	CF	a/a	CIN	462	10	20	216	7	76	77	108	16
Lambo,Andrew	12	L	24	C	aa	PIT	92	3	0	216	11	78	87	62	23
	13	L	25	LF	a/a	PIT	444	22	5	234	7	68	158	92	42
Landry,Leon	13	L	24	LF	aa	SEA	422	5	19	193	5	80	52	111	9
Langerhans,Ryan	12	L	32	DH	aaa	LAA	336	6	3	170	9	55	107	90	-48
	13	L	33	LF	aaa	TOR	208	7	1	174	11	58	117	65	-31
Langfels,Jayson	13	R	25	3B	aa	COL	376	13	10	199	6	63	106	67	-29
LaPorta,Matt	12	R	27	1B	aaa	CLE	375	13	0	209	8	73	104	30	3
	13	R	28	1B	aaa	CLE	164	8	0	192	7	77	123	20	30
LaRoche,Andy	12	R	29	3B	aaa	BOS	327	8	1	209	8	81	91	31	22
	13	R	30	3B	aaa	TOR	365	9	3	213	6	81	85	49	21
Lasater,Ben	12	R	28	1B	a/a	MIA	209	3	1	231	7	67	85	34	-39
	13	R	29	1B	aaa	MIA	175	3	0	170	7	59	64	31	-85
Latimore,Quincy	12	R	23	DH	aa	PIT	413	11	8	224	7	73	106	84	19
	13	R	24	LF	aa	CLE	295	4	4	190	6	74	75	67	-9
Lavarnway,Ryan	12	R	25	C	aaa	BOS	319	6	1	269	9	78	95	42	22
	13	R	26	C	aaa	BOS	180	2	0	215	9	84	61	24	12
Lawson,Matthew	12	R	27	2B	aa	CLE	196	1	6	279	9	81	85	84	39
	13	R	28	2B	a/a	CLE	343	3	9	186	9	70	56	96	-28
LeMahieu,DJ	12	R	24	2B	aaa	COL	255	1	8	266	5	88	48	79	25
	13	R	25	SS	aaa	COL	143	1	5	303	4	85	72	134	48
Lemmerman,Jacob	12	R	23	SS	aa	LA	373	6	6	203	10	72	98	90	15
	13	R	24	SS	aa	STL	308	5	8	189	12	67	86	88	-10
Lemon,Marcus	13	L	25	2B	aa	DET	294	1	2	211	6	77	48	105	-10
Lennerton,Jordan	12	L	26	1B	aa	DET	495	16	2	224	10	68	121	39	3
	13	L	27	1B	aaa	DET	514	13	0	231	11	70	91	26	-14
Leon,Sandy	12	B	23	C	a/a	WAS	187	2	1	290	8	84	92	34	37
	13	B	24	C	aa	WAS	310	2	0	155	10	80	47	40	-8
Leonard,Joe	12	R	24	3B	aa	ATL	426	7	5	235	9	76	78	76	9
	13	R	25	3B	aaa	ATL	418	0	1	195	4	74	52	51	-37
Lerud,Steven	12	L	28	C	aa	PHI	102	0	0	182	8	57	70	22	-91
	13	L	29	C	aaa	PHI	180	2	1	164	12	65	65	32	-55

BATTER	yr	b	age	pos	lvl	org	ab	hr	sb	ba	bb%	ct%	px	sx	bpv
Liddi,Alex	13	R	25	3B	aaa	BAL	425	13	8	213	5	62	125	121	-5
Lillibridge,Brent	13	R	30	2B	aaa	NYY	310	10	13	223	5	67	113	97	1
Limonta,Johan	12	L	29	DH	aaa	SEA	147	2	1	196	4	73	62	54	-32
	13	L	30	1B	aa	SD	247	3	0	197	10	70	60	26	-41
Lin,Che-Hsuan	12	R	24	DH	aaa	BOS	396	2	12	230	8	82	40	100	8
	13	R	25	CF	aaa	HOU	350	2	14	194	11	81	44	95	12
Linares,J.C.	12	R	28	DH	a/a	BOS	412	11	0	269	5	81	104	39	30
	13	R	29	RF	a/a	BOS	346	5	0	215	6	70	107	46	-7
Linden,Todd	12	B	32	1B	aaa	SF	425	6	2	198	7	69	81	68	-23
	13	B	33	1B	aaa	SF	137	0	0	143	4	54	73	43	-101
Lindsey,Taylor	13	L	22	2B	aa	LAA	508	13	3	245	7	80	88	78	30
Loewen,Adam	12	L	28	1B	aaa	NYM	207	6	3	171	9	66	91	60	-26
	13	L	29	CF	a/a	TOR	435	11	7	210	8	64	106	79	-19
Lohman,Devin	13	R	24	SS	aa	CIN	484	8	14	213	6	80	65	65	6
Lollis,Ryan	12	L	26	C	aaa	SF	175	2	1	239	8	82	57	65	11
	13	L	27	CF	aa	SF	469	5	4	205	7	84	54	62	13
Loman,Seth	12	L	27	DH	a/a	CHW	424	14	0	234	8	73	105	38	5
	13	L	28	1B	a/a	BAL	316	11	0	199	7	59	139	29	-28
Long,Matt	12	L	25	2B	a/a	LAA	444	8	17	227	7	76	87	121	25
	13	L	26	LF	a/a	LAA	488	9	14	227	8	71	91	124	14
Lopez,Rafael	13	L	26	C	aa	CHC	316	6	0	202	10	75	91	28	2
Lopez,Roberto	12	R	27	1B	aa	LAA	524	12	4	211	5	84	84	48	30
	13	R	28	LF	aaa	LAA	432	5	6	203	4	77	66	82	-3
Lough,David	12	L	26	DH	aaa	KC	491	6	17	223	3	85	62	139	38
	13	L	27	LF	aaa	KC	154	2	4	283	5	84	67	118	37
Lowery,Jake	13	L	23	C	aa	CLE	236	4	0	234	9	68	126	21	0
Lozada,Jose	12	B	27	SS	aa	WAS	286	4	1	199	6	77	54	53	-18
	13	B	28	SS	aa	WAS	201	1	2	164	5	69	33	53	-70
Lucas,Edward	12	R	30	SS	aaa	LAA	412	6	3	180	4	73	61	63	-30
	13	R	31	2B	aaa	MIA	181	4	1	238	5	72	92	52	-11
Lucas,Richard	13	R	25	3B	aa	NYM	345	6	4	164	4	64	69	77	-55
Luna,Omar	12	R	26	3B	aa	TAM	470	2	14	256	6	89	38	87	26
	13	R	27	2B	aa	ATL	226	1	2	209	4	86	42	55	4
Lutz,Donald	12	L	23	1B	aa	CIN	149	5	1	225	7	76	90	56	9
	13	L	24	LF	aa	CIN	229	7	3	224	7	72	119	120	35
Lutz,Zach	12	R	26	3B	aaa	NYM	244	8	0	238	11	62	125	31	-20
	13	R	27	3B	aaa	NYM	399	8	0	208	7	67	97	45	-26
Maggi,Andrew	12	R	23	SS	aa	PIT	179	0	4	194	7	76	28	113	-23
	13	R	24	SS	aa	PIT	264	1	14	218	7	80	55	117	15
Mahoney,Joseph	12	L	25	1B	aaa	BAL	491	9	3	239	6	78	82	51	7
	13	L	26	1B	aaa	MIA	195	2	1	159	1	58	64	30	-104
Mahoney,Kevin	12	L	25	3B	aa	NYY	318	10	3	213	8	74	97	78	14
	13	L	26	3B	a/a	NYY	139	1	2	177	9	58	54	59	-86
Mahtook,Mikie	12	R	23	DH	aa	TAM	153	3	3	212	5	77	90	79	16
	13	R	24	RF	aa	TAM	511	5	20	216	6	77	79	136	26
Main,Michael	13	R	25	RF	aa	MIA	206	0	2	193	6	77	25	60	-38
Manzella,Tommy	12	R	29	SS	a/a	CHW	299	1	2	175	8	60	42	38	-96
	13	R	30	SS	a/a	CHW	207	0	1	150	5	50	74	74	-105
Marder,Jack	13	R	23	2B	aa	SEA	275	3	7	199	7	75	60	97	-5
Marisnick,Jake	12	R	21	C	aa	TOR	223	2	12	221	4	79	69	133	19
	13	R	22	CF	aa	MIA	265	10	9	272	6	70	131	118	34
Marrero,Chris	12	R	24	1B	a/a	WAS	149	1	0	218	7	77	58	41	-16
	13	R	25	1B	aaa	WAS	408	8	0	226	6	81	68	38	5
Marrero,Christian	12	L	26	1B	a/a	PIT	259	5	5	201	10	75	84	68	12
	13	L	27	1B	aa	ATL	399	6	5	194	14	78	81	75	29
Marte,Alfredo	12	R	23	DH	aa	ARI	398	16	5	268	6	80	125	77	57
	13	R	24	RF	aaa	ARI	311	4	1	225	4	76	91	46	2
Marte,Jefry	12	R	21	3B	aa	NYM	462	8	7	220	7	82	62	78	15
	13	R	22	3B	aa	OAK	245	1	6	242	8	78	72	93	14
Martin,Dustin	12	L	28	C	a/a	NYM	315	5	8	212	8	68	87	106	-9
	13	L	29	RF	aa	ARI	217	6	9	246	9	71	125	132	45
Martinez,Fernando	12	L	24	DH	aaa	HOU	341	9	1	257	5	70	111	54	-4
	13	L	25	RF	aaa	NYY	188	7	1	236	7	74	123	48	25
Martinez,Francisco	12	R	22	3B	aa	SEA	352	2	25	204	10	72	50	122	-11
	13	R	23	CF	aa	SEA	126	0	6	188	4	61	52	86	-79
Martinez,Jose	12	R	26	2B	a/a	HOU	498	9	3	228	5	88	62	77	36
	13	R	27	2B	a/a	HOU	338	4	3	240	4	88	63	56	31
Martinez,Jose	12	R	24	C	aa	CHW	436	4	5	215	7	77	47	58	-21
	13	R	25	RF	aa	ATL	431	5	5	252	7	83	54	40	1
Martinez,Luis	12	R	27	C	aaa	TEX	215	1	0	218	7	75	73	46	-10
	13	R	28	C	a/a	BAL	214	1	0	205	6	76	67	29	-20
Martinez,Michael	12	B	30	SS	aaa	PHI	107	2	2	213	7	86	58	89	31
	13	B	31	SS	aaa	PHI	243	2	4	227	5	80	55	86	2
Martinez,Osvaldo	12	R	24	SS	aaa	LA	316	0	2	152	3	82	27	49	-27
	13	R	25	3B	a/a	LA	296	3	4	202	6	84	55	53	9
Martinez,Teodoro	13	R	21	LF	aa	TEX	443	15	18	242	3	84	76	92	34
Martinson,Jason	13	R	25	SS	aa	WAS	173	3	2	159	8	64	70	99	-40
Maruszak,Addison	12	R	26	SS	aa	NYY	416	14	4	233	6	78	101	47	21
	13	R	27	SS	aaa	NYY	299	4	0	214	8	77	81	48	5
Mateo,Luis	13	R	23	SS	a/a	STL	360	4	11	202	4	82	44	90	1
Mattair,Travis	13	R	25	1B	aa	CIN	475	13	2	217	7	74	79	51	-10
Matthes,Kent	12	R	25	DH	aa	COL	336	17	5	206	5	75	139	87	50
	13	R	26	RF	a/a	COL	431	15	11	238	4	73	132	86	33
Mattison,Kevin	12	L	27	C	aaa	MIA	482	9	19	193	7	61	95	125	-27
	13	L	28	CF	aaa	MIA	334	5	13	174	8	46	133	150	-47
May,Lucas	12	R	28	C	aaa	NYM	256	2	1	159	3	63	86	83	-48
	13	R	29	C	aaa	PIT	186	2	1	172	4	72	36	56	-55

BATTER	yr	b	age	pos	lvl	org	ab	hr	sb	ba	bb%	ct%	px	sx	bpv
Maysonet,Edwin	13	R	32	SS	aaa	CHC	219	4	1	183	3	74	89	53	-8
McBride,Matt	12	R	27	1B	aaa	COL	439	7	0	276	2	88	95	56	50
	13	R	28	C	aaa	COL	180	10	0	255	3	86	151	27	82
McCann,James	12	R	22	C	aa	DET	220	2	2	180	3	79	56	43	-17
	13	R	23	C	aa	DET	441	6	2	246	5	80	82	51	11
McClure,Alex	12	R	23	SS	aa	KC	193	1	5	188	3	67	43	93	-63
	13	B	24	SS	aa	MIA	175	0	3	176	4	73	38	61	-47
McCoy,Mike	12	R	31	2B	aaa	TOR	278	2	12	192	11	76	50	82	-7
	13	R	32	2B	aaa	TOR	355	3	20	191	10	76	51	100	-5
McDade,Michael	12	B	23	1B	a/a	TOR	449	14	1	251	7	76	88	34	2
	13	B	24	DH	aaa	CHW	428	9	1	221	7	67	94	26	-31
McDonald,Darnell	12	R	34	DH	aaa	NYY	129	2	1	150	8	66	62	60	-51
	13	R	35	LF	aaa	CHC	263	3	5	178	7	75	61	88	-8
McGuiness,Christoph	12	L	24	1B	aa	TEX	456	20	0	243	10	75	124	17	25
	13	L	25	1B	aaa	TEX	362	9	1	213	12	74	120	43	29
Medchill,Neil	12	L	25	DH	aa	NYY	58	4	0	241	4	51	248	-7	10
	13	L	26	RF	a/a	NYY	222	5	2	208	8	58	96	48	-57
Medica,Thomas	13	R	25	1B	aa	SD	280	13	3	254	8	71	164	94	61
Mejia,Ernesto	12	R	27	1B	aaa	ATL	514	16	7	237	4	68	116	62	-7
	13	R	28	1B	aaa	ATL	489	19	6	198	7	60	162	63	5
Melker,Adam	12	L	24	1B	aa	STL	352	7	4	233	7	76	67	64	-8
	13	L	25	RF	aa	STL	318	5	5	209	6	73	80	73	-10
Mendonca,Thomas	12	L	24	3B	a/a	TEX	332	10	0	201	4	60	95	24	-66
	13	L	25	3B	aa	PHI	136	1	0	210	4	70	74	59	-32
Meneses,Heiker	12	R	21	2B	aa	BOS	127	1	1	189	8	73	26	65	-50
	13	R	22	SS	a/a	BOS	376	2	10	237	5	73	64	108	-13
Merchan,Jesus	12	R	31	3B	aaa	SD	145	2	1	261	3	92	50	67	37
	13	R	32	3B	aaa	SD	181	0	1	180	3	83	35	56	-14
Merrifield,Whit	12	R	23	2B	aa	KC	96	1	2	231	6	79	39	95	-12
	13	R	24	LF	aa	KC	322	2	13	238	5	81	77	121	32
Mesa,Melky	12	R	25	DH	a/a	NYY	458	20	17	229	6	71	131	109	33
	13	R	26	CF	aaa	NYY	314	12	11	228	3	59	147	119	-4
Meyer,Jonathan	13	R	23	3B	aa	HOU	484	12	2	227	6	74	90	41	-5
Miclat,Gregory	12	B	25	SS	aaa	TEX	109	1	4	232	7	71	93	76	-3
	13	B	26	2B	a/a	TEX	290	0	7	201	8	78	32	63	-24
Middlebrooks,Will	12	R	24	3B	aaa	BOS	93	7	2	306	6	79	163	91	85
	13	R	25	3B	aaa	BOS	179	7	1	233	6	76	97	37	6
Mier,Jiovanni	13	R	23	SS	aa	HOU	355	4	7	167	9	69	49	64	-46
Miller,Bradley	12	L	23	SS	aa	SEA	147	3	4	284	12	79	82	86	35
	13	L	24	SS	a/a	SEA	257	9	5	272	10	77	102	86	39
Miller,Corky	12	R	36	C	aaa	CIN	243	5	1	179	13	75	61	19	-15
	13	R	37	C	aaa	CIN	135	3	0	158	8	78	75	1	-10
Minicozzi,Mark	12	R	29	1B	aa	SF	282	5	1	226	8	71	90	32	-16
	13	R	30	3B	aa	SF	443	5	2	227	8	63	87	48	-45
Mitchell,Derrick	12	R	25	DH	aaa	PHI	238	6	7	189	6	74	83	66	-2
	13	R	26	LF	a/a	PHI	329	10	9	196	7	69	120	90	14
Mitchell,Jared	12	L	24	DH	a/a	CHW	455	10	17	213	13	55	143	126	0
	13	L	25	CF	a/a	CHW	300	5	13	144	13	52	79	99	-72
Mitchell,Jermaine	12	L	28	DH	aaa	OAK	409	3	10	188	8	68	64	126	-21
	13	L	29	CF	aaa	MIN	340	4	13	207	7	61	91	144	-24
Moncrief,Carlos	13	L	25	RF	aa	CLE	489	12	11	231	7	76	96	100	28
Monell,Johnny	12	L	26	C	aa	SF	323	8	2	218	10	69	124	47	11
	13	L	27	C	aaa	SF	415	11	4	204	8	68	109	70	-1
Moore,Adam	12	R	28	C	aaa	KC	201	4	1	195	6	77	76	48	-4
	13	R	29	C	aaa	KC	131	5	0	146	8	52	138	34	-54
Moore,Jeremy	13	L	26	LF	a/a	LA	240	5	4	166	7	59	96	71	-52
Moore,Scott	12	L	29	3B	aaa	HOU	245	6	2	234	8	72	128	56	25
	13	L	30	3B	aaa	SD	424	8	0	191	7	65	100	30	-34
Moore,Tyler	12	R	25	1B	aaa	WAS	101	7	1	265	8	71	183	57	65
	13	R	26	LF	aaa	WAS	173	7	1	263	8	74	148	47	46
Morales,Angel	13	R	24	CF	aa	MIN	166	3	2	141	5	58	94	100	-52
Morban,Julio	13	L	21	RF	aa	SEA	295	6	7	279	8	64	134	128	20
Morel,Brent	12	R	25	3B	aaa	CHW	124	1	0	173	6	74	43	30	-49
	13	R	26	3B	aaa	CHW	395	5	11	225	9	68	104	97	5
Morla,Ramon	13	R	24	3B	aa	SEA	246	7	4	218	6	58	137	108	-10
Morris,Hunter	12	L	24	1B	aa	MIL	522	25	2	270	6	74	159	69	57
	13	L	25	1B	aaa	MIL	497	19	2	205	6	71	123	57	12
Mota,Jonathan	12	R	25	3B	a/a	CHC	75	3	0	235	6	70	139	57	22
	13	R	26	1B	aa	CHC	301	5	1	228	7	76	76	62	-2
Muncy,Max	13	L	23	1B	aa	OAK	172	3	0	213	10	78	94	61	27
Muno,Daniel	13	B	24	2B	aa	NYM	449	7	11	203	13	74	78	82	13
Muren,Andrew	12	L	24	C	aa	HOU	110	1	4	246	5	81	65	119	22
	13	L	25	CF	aa	HOU	282	1	4	199	6	72	74	120	-4
Murphy,Donnie	12	R	29	2B	aaa	MIA	106	9	1	231	9	64	214	35	57
	13	R	30	SS	aaa	CHC	302	8	3	201	6	68	108	62	-10
Murphy,James	13	R	28	1B	aa	PHI	505	16	1	210	7	70	103	33	-10
Murphy,John	12	B	24	C	aa	TOR	24	2	0	301	9	67	177	26	37
	13	B	25	C	a/a	TOR	205	2	0	187	5	78	73	41	-5
Murphy,John	12	R	21	C	aa	NYY	147	4	0	212	8	77	116	55	35
	13	R	22	C	a/a	NYY	413	12	1	251	9	81	107	39	42
Mustelier,Ronnier	12	R	28	3B	a/a	NYY	449	12	7	254	5	81	90	71	32
	13	R	29	3B	aaa	NYY	334	6	3	220	5	84	74	47	20
Myers,D'Arby	12	R	24	DH	aa	PHI	121	2	5	261	4	81	64	88	10
	13	R	25	CF	aa	OAK	485	3	15	234	2	83	60	114	21
Myers,Wil	12	R	22	DH	a/a	KC	522	26	5	278	8	71	147	90	48
	13	R	23	RF	aaa	TAM	252	11	6	249	9	68	142	108	36
Nady,Xavier	12	R	34	1B	aaa	SF	89	3	0	187	4	70	104	23	-19
	13	R	35	LF	aaa	COL	443	9	2	218	5	75	82	46	-11

BATTER	yr	b	age	pos	lvl	org	ab	hr	sb	ba	bb%	ct%	px	sx	bpv
Nakajima,Hiroyuki	13	R	31	3B	aaa	OAK	346	2	2	202	4	68	51	45	-62
Nanita,Ricardo	12	L	31	DH	aaa	TOR	333	8	2	226	4	85	68	38	14
	13	L	32	DH	a/a	TOR	271	4	2	199	5	81	64	60	5
Navarro Jr,Efren	12	L	26	1B	aaa	LAA	528	4	2	220	4	83	55	51	3
	13	L	27	1B	aaa	LAA	513	4	5	236	7	75	71	64	-9
Navarro,Reynaldo	12	B	23	2B	a/a	KC	460	3	7	222	6	89	40	83	25
	13	B	24	3B	aa	KC	446	9	5	247	3	87	74	82	39
Navarro,Yamaico	12	R	25	3B	aaa	PIT	222	6	7	241	10	80	109	113	62
	13	R	26	SS	aaa	BAL	390	10	7	227	9	78	90	72	27
Neal,Thomas	12	R	25	DH	aa	CLE	405	10	11	279	9	80	92	80	36
	13	R	26	RF	aaa	NYY	265	2	2	281	7	77	67	47	-10
Negron,Kristopher	12	R	26	SS	aaa	CIN	284	5	12	179	5	67	80	111	-21
	13	R	27	SS	aaa	CIN	334	5	9	187	6	66	68	81	-44
Negrych,James	12	L	27	2B	a/a	WAS	281	6	1	223	10	83	63	34	14
	13	L	28	2B	aaa	TOR	382	2	4	231	7	80	68	66	10
Nelson,Brad	12	L	30	DH	aaa	TEX	502	17	1	214	8	69	112	40	-3
	13	L	31	1B	aaa	CHC	428	13	1	206	7	73	98	45	-1
Nelson,Chris	12	R	27	3B	aaa	COL	51	0	1	235	2	73	77	127	-2
	13	R	28	3B	aaa	LAA	134	3	2	232	3	77	97	60	12
Ngoepe,Gift	13	B	23	SS	aa	PIT	220	2	8	154	9	61	80	124	-35
Nicholas,Brett	13	L	25	1B	aa	TEX	506	19	2	263	7	73	120	58	22
Nickeas,Mike	12	R	29	C	aaa	NYM	66	1	0	272	6	82	75	26	8
	13	R	30	C	aaa	TOR	175	1	0	128	6	71	66	29	-40
Nicol,Sean	12	R	26	3B	aa	WAS	242	2	2	217	5	74	60	66	-24
	13	R	27	3B	aa	WAS	277	2	4	209	9	83	46	69	8
Nieuwenhuis,Kirk	13	L	26	CF	aaa	NYM	282	9	4	179	8	65	108	89	-9
Nina,Angelys	12	R	24	2B	aa	COL	412	6	8	260	5	83	66	77	21
	13	R	25	2B	aa	COL	446	9	14	257	5	86	80	98	51
Noel,Rico	13	B	24	CF	aa	SD	496	0	48	234	8	72	52	144	-10
Nolan,Kevin	13	R	26	SS	aa	TOR	451	7	4	217	6	83	70	68	23
Noonan,Nick	12	L	23	SS	aaa	SF	490	5	5	243	5	80	61	66	2
	13	L	24	2B	aaa	SF	165	0	1	204	6	69	75	59	-32
Noriega,Gabriel	12	B	22	SS	aa	SEA	269	0	2	187	6	74	13	48	-66
	13	B	23	SS	aa	SEA	371	2	6	235	3	78	51	100	-10
Nunez,Gustavo	12	B	24	SS	aa	PIT	22	0	1	199	7	81	38	67	-12
	13	B	25	2B	aaa	DET	186	0	5	167	5	74	19	58	-61
Nunez,Luis	12	R	26	2B	aa	LA	405	9	16	210	7	84	78	110	48
	13	R	27	SS	a/a	ATL	232	2	5	167	2	87	45	100	20
O Neill,Mike	12	L	24	C	aa	STL	32	0	2	496	17	93	109	64	112
	13	L	25	LF	a/a	STL	471	1	14	259	13	91	30	87	40
Oberacker,Chad	13	L	24	RF	aa	OAK	448	4	13	200	7	74	87	143	25
Ochinko,Sean	12	R	25	C	aa	TOR	216	7	0	232	3	79	96	38	11
	13	R	26	C	a/a	TOR	294	4	1	192	7	75	76	20	-16
Odor,Rougned	13	L	19	2B	aa	TEX	134	6	4	313	6	82	143	110	90
Oeltjen,Trent	12	L	29	DH	aaa	LA	402	7	8	202	5	65	87	95	-32
	13	L	30	RF	aaa	LAA	333	7	12	169	6	55	136	111	-24
Olmedo,Ray	12	B	31	SS	aaa	CHW	275	0	7	221	8	80	43	67	-7
	13	B	32	3B	aaa	MIN	312	1	7	176	7	81	36	86	-6
Olt,Mike	12	R	24	3B	aa	TEX	354	25	3	263	12	69	176	57	60
	13	R	25	3B	a/a	CHC	373	11	0	167	10	59	127	34	-31
O'Malley,Shawn	12	B	25	SS	a/a	TAM	337	1	14	199	7	74	35	138	-17
	13	B	26	SS	aa	TAM	321	2	18	214	7	77	55	159	17
Orlando,Paulo	12	R	27	DH	aa	KC	420	4	15	226	5	84	48	94	14
	13	R	28	CF	aaa	KC	293	3	6	224	5	77	53	101	-6
Orloff,Ben	12	R	25	SS	aa	HOU	122	0	2	243	5	94	31	79	36
	13	R	26	SS	aa	HOU	131	0	4	244	7	92	26	73	28
Oropesa,Ricky	13	L	24	1B	aa	SF	241	4	0	167	4	65	55	17	-82
Ortega,Rafael	13	L	22	CF	aa	COL	158	1	7	222	9	84	43	119	24
Ortiz,Danny	13	L	23	LF	aa	MIN	484	8	1	225	4	80	82	62	14
Overbeck,Cody	12	R	26	1B	aaa	PHI	458	12	0	212	6	71	102	41	-8
	13	R	27	1B	aaa	PHI	440	14	1	203	4	61	136	35	-26
Owings,Christopher	12	R	21	SS	aa	ARI	297	5	3	246	3	75	70	87	-10
	13	R	22	SS	aaa	ARI	546	8	13	280	2	80	83	117	26
Owings,Micah	13	R	31	LF	a/a	MIL	241	7	1	195	4	52	145	89	-41
Panik,Joe	13	L	23	2B	aa	SF	522	2	7	216	8	85	52	80	23
Paredes,Jimmy	12	B	24	2B	aaa	HOU	507	9	25	261	3	76	83	128	17
	13	B	25	RF	aaa	HOU	327	6	12	241	6	75	101	123	33
Parker,Jarrett	13	L	24	RF	aa	SF	444	11	9	199	9	58	111	103	-29
Parker,Kyle	13	R	24	LF	aa	COL	480	21	5	270	6	79	124	67	47
Parker,Stephen	12	L	25	3B	aaa	OAK	328	4	3	203	6	67	71	95	-34
	13	L	26	3B	aaa	MIL	399	6	2	174	8	68	78	53	-34
Parmelee,Chris	12	L	24	1B	aaa	MIN	228	13	1	301	16	74	169	51	82
	13	L	25	1B	aaa	MIN	173	2	1	192	9	79	85	65	22
Parraz,Jordan	12	R	28	DH	a/a	ATL	142	1	4	220	7	71	63	83	-23
	13	R	29	RF	a/a	MIN	319	9	6	174	7	69	90	72	-14
Parrino,Andy	12	B	27	SS	aaa	SD	235	1	3	246	7	73	87	97	4
	13	B	28	SS	aaa	OAK	367	2	2	153	7	65	56	75	-56
Pastornicky,Tyler	12	R	23	SS	aaa	ATL	153	1	2	235	5	84	87	64	38
	13	R	24	2B	aaa	ATL	288	3	7	255	7	81	60	96	16
Patterson,Corey	12	L	33	DH	aaa	MIL	363	8	13	197	3	72	91	120	4
	13	L	34	CF	aaa	NYY	272	6	4	159	3	73	71	85	-16
Paulino,Carlos	13	R	24	C	a/a	PIT	334	0	4	190	6	84	30	77	-2
Paulsen,Benjamin	12	L	25	1B	aa	COL	436	13	1	240	6	73	97	54	0
	13	L	26	1B	aaa	COL	459	12	1	236	4	69	130	78	12
Pederson,Joc	13	L	21	CF	aa	LA	439	20	28	260	13	72	142	119	64
Pedroza,Jaime	12	B	26	SS	aa	ATL	109	3	1	163	7	61	115	64	-26
	13	B	27	SS	aa	ATL	370	3	5	238	7	78	50	72	-9

BATTER	yr	b	age	pos	lvl	org	ab	hr	sb	ba	bb%	ct%	px	sx	bpv
Peguero,Carlos	13	L	26	RF	aaa	SEA	454	12	7	199	6	56	128	76	-36
Peguero,Francisco	12	R	24	C	aaa	SF	449	3	1	219	2	79	57	73	-12
	13	R	25	RF	aaa	SF	272	2	2	251	3	77	50	76	-20
Pena,Francisco	12	R	23	C	aa	NYM	126	2	1	166	9	77	74	42	1
	13	R	24	C	a/a	NYM	287	6	1	198	4	82	88	37	17
Perez,Audry	12	R	24	C	aa	STL	312	3	0	220	1	79	46	31	-33
	13	R	25	C	a/a	STL	305	4	0	169	1	82	59	27	-14
Perez,Carlos	13	R	23	C	a/a	HOU	317	2	1	236	7	82	59	34	0
Perez,Darwin	12	B	23	SS	aa	LAA	407	5	13	191	8	73	56	101	-14
	13	B	24	SS	aa	OAK	393	2	14	198	9	70	64	126	-11
Perez,Eury	12	R	22	C	a/a	WAS	510	0	38	286	2	84	32	107	-1
	13	R	23	CF	aaa	WAS	403	5	17	264	2	83	65	120	25
Perez,Felix	12	L	28	DH	aaa	CIN	392	3	4	237	4	80	59	48	-11
	13	L	29	LF	aaa	CIN	462	9	3	209	5	75	75	55	-13
Perez,Hernan	13	R	22	2B	a/a	DET	429	3	24	277	3	87	73	110	46
Perez,Juan	12	R	26	DH	aa	SF	483	8	15	259	4	79	75	98	15
	13	R	27	RF	aaa	SF	382	5	12	219	2	75	88	114	12
Perez,Roberto	12	R	24	C	aa	CLE	283	1	0	192	13	73	63	46	-14
	13	R	25	C	a/a	CLE	280	1	1	166	13	65	72	27	-47
Perez,Rossmel	12	L	23	C	aa	ARI	263	0	3	243	9	92	28	42	23
	13	L	24	C	aa	ARI	237	2	3	223	7	92	24	35	16
Perio,Noah	13	L	22	2B	aa	MIA	177	1	2	213	8	82	42	56	-3
Pertusati,Daniel	12	R	22	2B	aa	MIA	120	3	1	272	9	79	98	85	38
	13	R	23	LF	aa	MIA	252	5	2	189	6	79	76	79	14
Petersen,Bryan	12	L	26	DH	aaa	MIA	243	2	6	266	6	77	46	88	-13
	13	L	27	RF	aaa	MIA	506	6	9	228	10	70	90	86	-1
Peterson,Brock	12	R	29	1B	aaa	STL	72	3	0	184	7	70	117	63	8
	13	R	30	1B	aaa	STL	456	16	1	220	6	68	124	38	-4
Peterson,Shane	12	L	24	DH	a/a	OAK	288	6	9	270	15	68	104	107	20
	13	L	25	CF	aaa	OAK	463	7	12	195	10	68	80	90	-16
Petit,Gregorio	12	R	28	SS	aaa	CLE	377	7	1	201	5	75	80	38	-13
	13	R	29	SS	aaa	SD	503	2	3	211	5	80	46	54	-17
Pettit,Chris	12	R	28	DH	a/a	COL	291	5	5	234	6	67	112	101	2
	13	R	29	CF	aa	BAL	126	1	1	96	7	70	57	85	-34
Pham,Thomas	12	R	24	DH	aa	STL	39	1	0	125	7	46	116	16	-104
	13	R	25	CF	a/a	STL	269	5	6	235	7	71	90	109	4
Phegley,Joshua	12	R	24	C	aaa	CHW	394	6	3	245	5	83	71	59	16
	13	R	25	C	aaa	CHW	231	14	1	279	5	80	163	52	80
Phelps,Cord	12	B	25	2B	aaa	CLE	503	12	7	229	9	78	95	74	30
	13	B	26	2B	aaa	CLE	255	7	3	225	8	77	104	57	26
Phipps,Denis	12	R	27	DH	aaa	CIN	357	12	3	179	6	65	114	51	-21
	13	R	28	RF	aaa	CIN	423	8	11	202	8	71	92	87	0
Pie,Felix	12	L	27	DH	aaa	ATL	333	4	11	230	5	83	87	125	49
	13	L	28	LF	aaa	PIT	354	5	27	198	7	72	76	143	9
Pill,Brett	12	R	28	1B	aaa	SF	246	6	0	207	3	81	88	37	14
	13	R	29	1B	aaa	SF	276	9	1	248	3	81	114	56	39
Pillar,Kevin	13	R	24	CF	a/a	TOR	505	7	17	271	4	84	94	109	56
Pina,Manny	12	R	25	C	aa	KC	131	3	0	217	12	79	60	0	-9
	13	R	26	C	a/a	KC	298	5	1	189	4	85	71	33	15
Pinto,Josmil	12	R	23	DH	aa	MIN	47	1	0	267	7	77	143	81	60
	13	R	24	C	a/a	MIN	456	10	0	264	10	79	98	30	26
Pirela,Jose	12	R	23	2B	aa	NYY	317	7	7	263	6	83	87	97	46
	13	R	24	2B	a/a	NYY	482	9	16	245	9	85	81	116	61
Piscotty,Stephen	13	R	22	RF	aa	STL	184	4	5	259	7	89	71	50	43
Polanco,Gregory	13	L	22	CF	a/a	PIT	252	4	11	234	10	85	75	100	53
Poythress,Richard	12	R	25	1B	aa	SEA	303	5	3	258	13	87	72	56	49
	13	R	26	1B	a/a	SEA	379	11	2	203	9	74	104	55	17
Prades,Yem	12	R	24	DH	aa	KC	495	6	11	232	2	75	77	102	-4
	13	R	25	RF	aa	KC	306	4	5	162	3	74	53	98	-24
Presley,Alex	12	L	27	C	aaa	PIT	153	3	5	255	11	80	69	116	35
	13	L	28	CF	aaa	PIT	342	3	12	237	7	81	66	120	28
Price,Robby	13	L	25	2B	aa	TAM	420	4	2	186	8	88	30	31	3
Pridie,Jason	12	L	29	DH	aaa	PHI	178	4	3	238	6	73	82	86	-3
	13	L	30	CF	aaa	BAL	479	12	6	212	6	68	98	89	-7
Prince,Joshua	12	R	24	3B	aa	MIL	505	6	32	220	11	75	73	107	15
	13	R	25	CF	aaa	MIL	418	9	17	195	9	70	82	103	-3
Profar,Jurickson	12	B	19	SS	aa	TEX	480	13	14	280	10	84	101	112	72
	13	B	20	SS	aaa	TEX	144	4	5	266	10	83	94	115	64
Proscia,Steven	12	R	22	1B	aa	SEA	76	3	0	186	5	76	93	58	7
	13	R	23	1B	aa	SEA	314	9	10	183	6	66	86	106	-21
Puckett,Cody	12	R	25	2B	a/a	CIN	433	15	7	203	8	68	99	81	-8
	13	R	26	3B	a/a	CHW	367	15	5	216	5	83	99	52	41
Puello,Cesar	13	R	22	RF	aa	NYM	331	13	19	283	6	71	133	114	41
Puig,Yasiel	13	R	23	RF	aa	LA	147	7	11	283	8	78	167	140	106
Quintanilla,Omar	12	L	31	SS	aaa	NYM	156	4	1	206	6	77	98	58	16
	13	L	32	SS	aaa	NYM	126	1	1	226	8	72	73	75	-12
Rahl,Christopher	12	R	29	DH	aa	WAS	330	9	19	231	4	69	99	125	1
	13	R	30	RF	aaa	WAS	399	5	9	223	2	70	77	106	-23
Ramirez,Carlos	12	R	24	C	aa	LAA	275	2	3	178	9	77	47	73	-12
	13	R	25	C	aa	LAA	155	4	1	170	7	75	115	44	22
Ramirez,Jose	13	B	21	2B	aa	CLE	482	2	29	237	6	91	39	129	46
Ramirez,Max	12	R	28	DH	aaa	KC	387	10	0	227	7	74	77	21	-20
	13	R	29	DH	aaa	KC	411	6	0	205	7	69	68	18	-47
Ramsey,James	13	L	24	CF	a/a	STL	350	10	6	206	10	65	96	87	-16
Realmuto,Jacob	13	R	22	C	aa	MIA	368	4	8	221	8	79	77	99	25
Rendon,Anthony	12	R	22	3B	aa	WAS	68	2	0	148	11	76	111	92	43
	13	R	23	3B	a/a	WAS	127	5	1	274	16	76	161	71	88

BATTER	yr	b	age	pos	lvl	org	ab	hr	sb	ba	bb%	ct%	px	sx	bpv
Retherford,Chris	13	R	28	3B	aa	LA	146	3	0	176	5	76	105	67	20
Rhymes,Will	12	L	29	2B	aaa	TAM	172	3	1	195	7	86	52	74	22
	13	L	30	2B	aaa	WAS	453	2	5	208	8	92	33	63	31
Richardson,Antoan	12	B	29	DH	a/a	BAL	315	1	20	216	14	74	22	132	-18
	13	B	30	CF	a/a	MIN	421	0	26	219	11	71	54	150	-4
Rivera,Juan	13	R	35	LF	aaa	ARI	359	6	1	217	2	89	55	40	19
Rivera,Rene	12	R	29	C	aaa	MIN	288	7	0	179	7	73	83	38	-12
	13	R	30	C	aaa	SD	251	3	0	246	4	77	70	28	-19
Rivero,Carlos	12	R	24	3B	aaa	WAS	455	8	5	267	5	79	80	50	7
	13	R	25	3B	a/a	WAS	396	4	1	206	5	73	60	29	-37
Robbins,James	13	L	23	1B	aa	DET	468	5	2	198	3	62	84	47	-65
Robertson,Daniel	12	R	27	DH	aaa	SD	490	1	11	225	6	85	45	85	14
	13	R	28	RF	aaa	SD	484	1	14	212	7	83	48	123	23
Robinson,Christophe	12	R	28	C	aaa	BAL	177	0	0	194	6	82	50	59	-1
	13	R	29	C	aaa	SD	241	0	1	203	2	76	26	48	-54
Robinson,Clint	12	L	27	1B	aaa	KC	487	8	1	227	10	84	78	35	30
	13	L	28	1B	a/a	TOR	397	10	1	204	9	74	96	44	7
Robinson,Trayvon	12	B	25	DH	aaa	SEA	340	5	13	203	7	69	75	99	-21
	13	B	26	CF	a/a	BAL	376	9	15	207	8	64	104	102	-10
Rodriguez,Eddy	12	R	27	C	aaa	SD	50	1	0	128	2	67	83	13	-55
	13	R	28	C	a/a	SD	281	4	0	175	4	61	98	45	-54
Rodriguez,Guilder	12	B	29	2B	a/a	TEX	265	0	9	170	7	84	5	69	-21
	13	B	30	3B	a/a	TEX	348	1	12	196	8	85	22	83	1
Rodriguez,Henry	12	B	22	3B	a/a	CIN	345	5	7	261	3	83	57	64	6
	13	B	23	2B	aaa	CIN	478	4	5	249	5	84	41	46	-7
Rodriguez,Josh	12	R	28	SS	a/a	NYM	471	10	6	210	7	71	85	65	-11
	13	R	29	3B	aa	NYM	441	4	3	199	10	72	71	67	-16
Rodriguez,Luis	12	B	32	2B	aaa	SEA	361	7	3	207	8	84	58	45	15
	13	B	33	2B	aaa	LAA	439	5	1	179	5	85	59	46	13
Rodriguez,Reynaldo	12	R	26	1B	a/a	BOS	370	12	5	222	8	71	144	85	43
	13	R	27	1B	aa	MIN	415	13	3	183	7	69	142	94	33
Rodriguez,Ronny	13	R	21	SS	aa	CLE	468	4	9	231	3	82	65	111	21
Rodriguez,Starlin	13	B	24	2B	aa	STL	248	4	6	210	4	72	79	87	-14
Rodriguez,Yorman	13	R	21	RF	aa	CIN	262	4	4	255	8	69	97	86	-5
Rogers,Jason	13	R	25	1B	aa	MIL	481	20	5	236	9	79	115	69	48
Rohlfing,Danny	12	R	23	C	aa	MIN	163	0	0	225	3	75	69	53	-20
	13	R	24	C	a/a	MIN	375	2	0	228	9	71	52	47	-40
Rohlinger,Ryan	12	R	29	3B	a/a	CLE	366	6	1	185	9	79	54	38	-8
	13	R	30	3B	aaa	CLE	319	4	2	208	8	72	66	52	-26
Rojas Jr.,Mel	13	B	23	CF	aa	PIT	446	3	11	241	6	76	86	117	23
Rojas,Miguel	12	R	23	SS	a/a	CIN	272	1	2	177	6	86	16	39	-15
	13	R	24	SS	aa	LA	420	4	9	206	8	87	40	78	20
Roling,Kiel	12	R	25	1B	aa	COL	268	13	1	248	6	70	142	35	17
	13	R	26	1B	aa	COL	410	21	0	235	6	72	156	14	30
Roller,Kyle	13	L	25	1B	aa	NYY	443	15	0	220	9	63	129	32	-15
Romak,Jamie	12	R	27	1B	a/a	STL	389	6	4	204	7	73	75	81	-6
	13	R	28	RF	aaa	STL	458	14	4	184	7	69	120	69	8
Romero,Deibinson	12	R	26	3B	aa	MIN	469	13	2	221	9	76	88	48	10
	13	R	27	3B	a/a	MIN	335	8	3	219	10	70	94	60	-3
Romero,Niuman	12	B	27	SS	aa	DET	523	7	14	247	7	86	61	97	36
	13	B	28	SS	a/a	BAL	419	3	6	214	10	80	54	61	2
Romero,Stefen	12	R	24	2B	aa	SEA	216	9	5	301	6	79	137	111	73
	13	R	25	LF	aaa	SEA	375	7	5	218	5	71	91	85	-6
Romine,Andrew	12	L	27	SS	aaa	LAA	351	2	14	209	4	83	38	116	8
	13	L	28	SS	aaa	LAA	363	2	9	201	6	75	47	99	-17
Rosa,Garabez	13	R	24	RF	aa	BAL	460	5	6	238	1	81	56	82	-2
Rosario,Alberto	12	R	25	C	a/a	LAA	240	1	4	176	3	76	41	56	-40
	13	R	26	C	a/a	BOS	126	1	0	182	5	76	41	35	-39
Rosario,Eddie	13	L	22	2B	aa	MIN	289	3	5	254	5	75	87	97	11
Ruf,Darin	12	R	26	1B	aa	PHI	489	29	1	262	9	75	156	45	57
	13	R	27	LF	aaa	PHI	305	5	1	212	8	65	104	38	-30
Rupp,Cameron	13	R	25	C	a/a	PHI	325	11	1	213	5	67	112	28	-22
Russell,Kyle	12	L	26	DH	a/a	LA	247	7	3	194	10	64	125	61	-3
	13	L	27	LF	aa	ATL	170	3	2	188	10	54	92	85	-62
Russo,Kevin	12	R	28	3B	aaa	NYY	402	0	11	227	8	78	43	93	-8
	13	R	29	3B	aaa	DET	376	2	7	167	3	72	69	67	-29
Rutledge,Josh	12	R	23	SS	aa	COL	356	13	12	304	3	81	135	113	72
	13	R	24	SS	aaa	COL	143	3	1	313	5	84	129	55	66
Ryal,Rusty	12	R	29	2B	aaa	ATL	292	4	5	196	2	67	77	81	-38
	13	R	30	1B	aaa	LAA	375	2	0	180	3	71	48	49	-55
Saladino,Tyler	12	R	23	SS	a/a	CHW	467	4	32	214	13	74	53	126	5
	13	R	24	SS	aa	CHW	424	5	22	203	10	77	58	102	5
Salcedo,Edward	13	R	22	3B	aa	ATL	468	10	17	224	8	74	89	91	11
Sams,Kalian	12	R	26	DH	aa	SEA	256	8	11	198	7	61	121	137	-3
	13	R	27	RF	a/a	TEX	207	12	7	207	11	64	173	73	39
Sanchez,Angel	12	R	29	SS	aaa	HOU	344	3	4	234	7	90	37	52	22
	13	R	30	3B	aaa	CHW	148	1	0	146	6	78	35	52	-31
Sanchez,Carlos	12	B	20	SS	a/a	CHW	158	0	6	328	6	81	66	86	15
	13	B	21	2B	aaa	CHW	432	0	13	221	6	81	44	97	0
Sanchez,Jorge Tony	12	R	24	C	a/a	PIT	347	6	1	220	9	76	97	46	13
	13	R	25	C	a/a	PIT	277	7	0	237	7	75	131	24	27
Sands,Jerry	12	R	25	1B	aaa	LA	452	16	1	225	7	71	95	49	-7
	13	R	26	RF	aaa	PIT	343	5	0	170	9	66	81	46	-37
Sano,Miguel	13	R	20	3B	aa	MIN	233	14	2	213	11	63	210	85	72
Santana,Daniel	13	B	23	SS	aa	MIN	539	1	23	263	3	81	53	129	13
Santana,Domingo	13	R	21	RF	aa	HOU	416	21	10	228	8	63	170	97	35
Santos,Adalberto	12	R	25	DH	aa	PIT	238	1	14	295	9	82	56	95	22
	13	R	26	3B	aa	PIT	409	4	16	231	9	81	63	85	19

BATTER	yr	b	age	pos	lvl	org	ab	hr	sb	ba	bb%	ct%	px	sx	bpv
Santos,Omir	12	R	31	C	aaa	COL	203	1	0	233	1	79	68	35	-13
	13	R	32	C	aaa	CLE	206	2	0	193	3	71	64	39	-46
Sappelt,Dave	12	R	25	C	aaa	CHC	500	5	11	219	5	83	58	78	13
	13	R	26	LF	aaa	CHC	321	4	3	207	6	86	58	72	25
Sardinas,Luis	13	B	20	SS	aa	TEX	135	1	4	256	3	84	39	67	-4
Satin,Josh	12	R	28	1B	aaa	NYM	441	10	2	217	11	68	88	41	-22
	13	R	29	1B	aaa	NYM	220	5	0	208	10	72	87	34	-11
Savastano,Scott	12	R	26	1B	aaa	SEA	224	1	1	194	6	67	68	72	-41
	13	R	27	1B	aaa	SEA	183	2	3	177	5	71	42	72	-48
Schimpf,Ryan	12	L	24	3B	aa	TOR	111	7	2	251	14	68	186	53	65
	13	L	25	3B	aa	TOR	442	18	2	179	11	64	137	64	9
Schlehuber,Braeden	13	R	25	C	aa	ATL	176	3	2	174	4	78	51	62	-18
Schoop,Jonathan	12	R	21	2B	aa	BAL	485	12	4	226	8	77	86	56	13
	13	R	22	2B	aaa	BAL	270	8	1	237	4	78	88	33	3
Scruggs,Xavier	12	R	25	1B	aa	STL	452	15	6	190	9	62	125	65	-15
	13	R	26	1B	aa	STL	448	19	8	195	12	53	153	59	-22
Seitzer,Cameron	13	L	23	1B	aa	TAM	489	5	1	231	12	77	61	34	-7
Selen,Alejandro	13	R	24	DH	aa	TEX	189	3	1	205	1	69	77	82	-34
Sellers,Justin	13	R	27	SS	aaa	LA	326	4	3	202	5	79	82	75	16
Semien,Marcus	13	R	23	SS	a/a	CHW	518	18	19	259	15	80	120	120	84
Seratelli,Anthony	12	B	29	3B	aaa	KC	384	10	9	224	7	70	88	93	-7
	13	B	30	RF	aaa	KC	400	7	17	212	12	75	72	115	17
Shaw,Nicholas	13	L	25	2B	aa	MIL	450	2	6	217	10	81	28	67	-10
Shaw,Travis	12	L	22	1B	aa	BOS	110	2	1	223	14	68	174	36	50
	13	L	23	1B	aa	BOS	444	12	5	201	12	71	106	76	19
Shepherd,Jaron	13	L	25	LF	a/a	COL	230	0	6	192	6	74	38	85	-34
Short,Brandon	12	R	24	C	a/a	CHW	48	0	1	203	4	81	34	59	-23
	13	R	25	LF	a/a	CIN	257	2	3	184	8	75	63	89	-5
Sierra,Moises	12	R	24	DH	aaa	TOR	377	12	5	241	6	74	93	58	1
	13	R	25	RF	aaa	TOR	379	9	9	228	3	68	106	127	2
Silva,Rubi	12	L	23	C	aa	CHC	80	2	2	237	2	76	63	110	-5
	13	L	24	RF	aa	CHC	468	11	10	246	3	76	114	112	35
Simunic,Andrew	12	R	27	3B	a/a	HOU	400	1	10	224	5	78	27	80	-31
	13	R	28	RF	aaa	HOU	144	0	6	215	7	75	17	87	-45
Singleton,Jonathan	12	L	21	1B	aa	HOU	461	17	5	252	13	68	131	90	32
	13	L	22	1B	a/a	HOU	283	6	1	200	13	58	117	48	-29
Skipworth,Kyle	12	L	22	C	aa	MIA	420	16	1	191	7	61	129	60	-21
	13	L	23	C	aaa	MIA	239	9	0	168	4	60	153	49	-13
Smith,Blake	12	L	25	DH	aa	LA	461	10	11	224	10	66	106	87	-4
	13	L	26	RF	aa	LA	240	5	2	197	8	69	96	66	-7
Smith,Bryson	12	R	24	C	aa	CIN	153	1	3	280	2	83	59	111	17
	13	R	25	RF	aa	CIN	207	5	2	246	7	81	81	67	28
Smith,Curt	12	R	26	1B	aa	MIA	268	7	2	217	6	72	103	75	7
	13	R	27	DH	aa	MIN	147	3	0	183	5	63	89	26	-55
Smolinski,Jacob	12	R	23	DH	aa	MIA	408	5	7	228	14	78	76	82	29
	13	R	24	LF	a/a	MIA	370	7	7	219	11	77	74	82	15
Snyder,Brad	12	L	30	DH	aaa	HOU	362	12	10	221	6	60	136	88	-12
	13	L	31	CF	aaa	ARI	411	7	4	224	5	62	109	86	-27
Snyder,Brandon	12	R	26	3B	aaa	TEX	87	2	0	208	3	60	117	31	-48
	13	R	27	1B	aaa	BOS	249	7	2	220	5	67	124	72	2
Snyder,Chris	13	R	32	C	aaa	BAL	259	10	0	217	6	67	125	17	-13
Sobolewski,Mark	12	R	26	3B	a/a	TOR	454	15	2	205	3	74	95	61	1
	13	R	27	3B	a/a	MIN	165	2	0	133	5	63	54	27	-86
Solano,Jhonatan	12	R	27	C	a/a	WAS	93	1	0	185	2	77	38	43	-40
	13	R	28	C	aaa	WAS	140	0	0	167	2	85	39	34	-10
Solarte,Yangervis	12	B	25	2B	aaa	TEX	518	9	2	244	5	90	60	40	34
	13	B	26	2B	aaa	TEX	526	10	2	234	5	85	74	47	25
Songco,Angelo	13	L	25	1B	aa	LA	210	5	1	184	7	76	96	60	15
Sosa,Ruben	13	B	23	LF	aaa	HOU	125	1	6	237	7	68	65	133	-21
Soto,Neftali	12	R	23	1B	aaa	CIN	465	13	2	215	6	72	103	37	-5
	13	R	24	3B	aaa	CIN	461	14	2	243	4	74	95	45	-2
Souza,Steven	13	R	24	RF	aa	WAS	273	12	16	266	10	69	170	111	69
Spangenberg,Cory	13	L	22	2B	aa	SD	287	2	16	266	5	76	51	116	-9
Spears,Nate	12	L	27	3B	aaa	BOS	346	7	2	209	9	71	92	74	-1
	13	L	28	2B	a/a	CLE	214	3	4	171	10	69	65	87	-23
Spring,Matthew	12	R	28	C	a/a	BOS	207	5	1	171	8	55	109	24	-69
	13	R	29	C	aa	BOS	185	6	0	177	3	57	156	20	-31
Springer,George	12	R	23	C	aa	HOU	73	2	3	186	6	61	86	71	-54
	13	R	24	CF	a/a	HOU	492	29	34	261	12	61	194	133	66
Stang,Chadwin	13	R	24	CF	aa	MIL	218	1	5	201	7	60	50	95	-76
Stanley,Cody	13	L	25	C	aa	STL	272	3	3	202	4	77	51	61	-23
Stassi,Max	13	R	22	C	aa	HOU	289	14	1	248	5	73	155	50	45
Statia,Hainley	12	B	26	SS	a/a	MIL	342	0	5	215	7	80	34	55	-18
	13	B	27	2B	aaa	MIL	291	4	4	188	11	80	47	48	-4
Stevenson,Casey	13	L	25	3B	a/a	NYY	214	5	2	209	8	76	82	41	-2
Stewart,Ian	13	L	28	3B	aaa	LA	199	4	0	123	10	49	129	52	-64
Stovall,Ryan	13	R	27	RF	a/a	ARI	130	3	0	184	4	54	106	62	-73
Strausborger,Ryan	12	R	24	2B	aa	TEX	433	5	20	225	6	75	72	156	17
	13	R	25	CF	aa	TEX	461	9	22	197	6	76	83	121	20
Suarez,Eugenio	13	R	22	SS	aa	DET	442	7	7	231	7	77	84	82	17
Susac,Andrew	13	R	23	C	aa	SF	262	7	1	211	11	70	114	30	5
Susdorf,Stephen	12	L	26	DH	a/a	PHI	377	2	5	239	7	82	63	56	10
	13	L	27	RF	aaa	PHI	310	2	8	251	8	79	61	72	5
Sutton,Drew	12	B	29	2B	aaa	PIT	158	0	2	192	10	77	63	85	4
	13	B	30	1B	aaa	BOS	359	1	3	196	10	73	64	64	-17
Swauger,Christopher	12	L	26	1B	a/a	STL	357	9	1	231	5	75	72	52	-14
	13	L	27	RF	a/a	STL	390	6	5	195	4	71	69	69	-31

BATTER	yr	b	age	pos	lvl	org	ab	hr	sb	ba	bb%	ct%	px	sx	bpv
Swift,James	13	R	26	SS	a/a	LAA	406	4	4	209	3	70	70	69	-38
Szczur,Matthew	12	R	23	DH	aa	CHC	143	2	3	188	7	77	80	134	31
	13	R	24	CF	aa	CHC	512	2	17	243	7	83	55	100	23
Taijeron,Travis	13	R	24	RF	aa	NYM	232	11	0	201	7	61	177	23	7
Tanaka,Kensuke	13	L	32	2B	aaa	SF	343	1	13	238	7	86	33	94	14
Tartamella,Travis	12	R	25	C	aa	STL	132	1	0	128	2	68	49	23	-75
	13	R	26	C	a/a	STL	199	2	0	179	5	64	44	17	-90
Taveras,Oscar	12	L	20	DH	aa	STL	477	17	8	290	7	87	120	103	92
	13	L	21	CF	aaa	STL	173	4	4	271	4	86	88	72	47
Taveras,Willy	13	R	32	RF	aaa	KC	247	1	8	189	5	80	52	146	17
Taylor,Beau	12	L	22	C	aa	OAK	120	0	0	200	7	67	39	28	-77
	13	L	23	C	aa	OAK	267	2	1	160	9	70	52	31	-48
Taylor,Chris	13	R	23	SS	aa	SEA	256	1	16	270	13	75	60	143	19
Taylor,Michael	12	R	27	DH	aaa	OAK	449	7	12	217	12	71	83	80	-1
	13	R	28	RF	aaa	OAK	420	10	3	206	7	73	91	53	-2
Tejada,Ruben	12	R	23	SS	aaa	NYM	20	0	0	165	4	83	35	59	-14
	13	R	24	SS	aaa	NYM	240	1	1	217	3	85	48	60	4
Tejeda,Oscar	12	R	23	DH	aa	PIT	400	6	4	225	5	78	80	66	8
	13	R	24	2B	a/a	PIT	131	1	2	168	6	74	47	55	-36
Tekotte,Blake	12	L	25	DH	aaa	SD	321	5	6	185	4	65	90	82	-36
	13	L	26	CF	aaa	CHW	296	4	9	200	8	70	114	97	17
Telis,Tomas	13	B	22	C	aa	TEX	348	4	7	254	2	86	64	66	23
Tenbrink,Nathaniel	12	L	26	3B	aa	SEA	152	6	4	233	12	54	176	121	18
	13	L	27	3B	aaa	SEA	430	9	8	201	9	59	106	91	-32
Terdoslavich,Joseph	12	B	24	1B	a/a	ATL	492	7	5	229	7	73	82	90	2
	13	B	25	RF	aaa	ATL	321	13	2	272	5	76	141	49	43
Thames,Eric	12	L	26	DH	aaa	TOR	197	4	1	267	8	74	109	71	22
	13	L	27	RF	aaa	BAL	352	8	4	232	8	68	103	71	-7
Thole,Josh	13	L	27	C	aaa	TOR	149	5	0	269	6	80	94	39	20
Thomas,Anthony	12	R	26	2B	aaa	BOS	223	8	9	214	7	67	119	122	16
	13	R	27	LF	a/a	BOS	478	7	13	193	5	68	107	135	10
Thomas,Clete	12	L	29	DH	aaa	MIN	393	8	11	185	5	66	102	120	-8
	13	L	30	CF	aaa	MIN	125	6	4	221	9	64	150	54	12
Thomas,Mark	12	R	24	C	aa	TAM	311	4	3	213	7	71	81	88	-10
	13	R	25	C	aa	TAM	186	3	1	123	3	64	78	101	-42
Thompson,Rich	12	L	33	DH	aaa	TAM	339	1	20	235	6	79	54	136	14
	13	L	34	CF	aaa	TAM	189	0	16	189	6	74	36	172	-12
Thompson,Trayce	12	R	21	C	a/a	CHW	68	3	3	238	12	65	146	104	33
	13	R	22	CF	aa	CHW	507	15	21	213	10	70	111	122	26
Tolisano,John	12	B	24	2B	aa	TOR	436	10	16	224	9	79	96	97	41
	13	B	25	2B	aa	TOR	222	4	2	206	6	71	103	63	-1
Tolleson,Steve	12	R	29	SS	aaa	BAL	162	1	2	229	10	76	48	39	-25
	13	R	30	2B	aaa	CHW	392	7	10	226	10	69	95	67	-3
Toole,Justin	12	R	26	1B	a/a	CLE	43	0	0	154	0	86	17	19	-34
	13	R	27	2B	a/a	CLE	177	0	1	231	5	86	29	43	-8
Torres,Tim	12	B	29	2B	aa	COL	292	3	10	193	10	66	75	104	-23
	13	B	30	1B	a/a	CHC	202	3	5	177	5	60	91	108	-43
Torreyes,Ronald	13	R	21	2B	aa	HOU	375	2	4	243	6	91	58	103	56
Torrez,Riccio	13	R	24	3B	aa	TAM	299	4	2	209	4	78	70	76	2
Tosoni,Rene	12	L	26	DH	a/a	MIN	289	2	3	183	7	78	45	41	-23
	13	L	27	CF	aa	MIL	446	9	4	197	6	77	71	56	-4
Tovar,Wilfredo	12	R	21	SS	aa	NYM	193	0	2	220	4	87	45	71	17
	13	R	22	SS	aa	NYM	441	3	9	225	5	87	38	101	23
Tracy,Chad	12	R	27	1B	aaa	COL	454	8	1	212	4	72	100	26	-15
	13	R	28	1B	aaa	KC	139	3	0	147	9	68	50	17	-61
Triunfel,Carlos	12	R	22	SS	aaa	SEA	496	6	2	211	3	79	69	68	0
	13	R	23	SS	aaa	SEA	383	3	4	232	3	76	65	83	-10
Tucker,Preston	13	L	23	LF	aa	HOU	237	8	0	229	8	78	112	47	33
Urrutia,Henry	13	L	26	RF	a/a	BAL	314	7	1	294	7	81	94	43	28
Urshela,Giovanny	13	R	22	3B	aa	CLE	445	6	1	233	2	88	63	41	21
Valaika,Chris	12	R	27	2B	aaa	CIN	291	5	1	179	3	73	71	61	-22
	13	R	28	2B	aaa	MIA	130	2	1	198	6	75	69	51	-17
Valdez,Jeudy	12	R	23	SS	aa	SD	462	8	10	187	3	68	83	94	-24
	13	R	24	SS	aa	SD	443	8	13	219	5	72	102	105	12
Valencia,Danny	12	R	28	3B	aaa	BOS	317	6	1	221	4	80	84	39	11
	13	R	29	3B	aaa	BAL	262	11	1	229	4	77	134	50	42
Valle,Sebastian	12	R	22	C	a/a	PHI	388	15	0	229	3	68	111	26	-25
	13	R	23	C	aa	PHI	354	9	1	172	4	72	90	55	-13
Van Kirk,Brian	12	R	27	DH	aa	TOR	399	6	9	229	7	79	78	58	12
	13	R	28	LF	aa	TOR	234	1	2	220	13	79	47	61	-1
Van Ostrand,James	12	R	28	DH	aa	WAS	271	7	0	252	4	85	71	24	15
	13	R	29	DH	a/a	WAS	325	7	0	203	5	84	86	32	27
Van Slyke,Scott	12	R	26	1B	aaa	LA	358	11	3	244	7	77	117	51	35
	13	R	27	1B	aaa	LA	204	8	5	267	14	62	166	98	39
Vasquez,Andy	13	B	26	LF	aa	PIT	262	3	9	203	4	69	49	115	-39
Vaughn,Cory	13	R	24	LF	aa	NYM	262	8	7	220	6	65	95	91	-23
Vazquez,Christian	12	R	22	C	aa	BOS	73	0	0	199	8	87	48	43	18
	13	R	23	C	a/a	BOS	345	4	5	264	10	86	67	62	38
Vazquez,Jan	13	B	22	C	aa	LA	126	5	2	176	9	64	97	48	-32
Velazquez,Gil	12	R	33	SS	aaa	MIA	398	3	4	238	8	83	38	41	-8
	13	R	34	SS	aaa	MIA	331	0	2	198	11	74	20	30	-57
Velez,Eugenio	12	B	30	3B	aaa	STL	457	7	24	206	7	72	88	116	9
	13	B	31	2B	aaa	MIL	373	7	19	236	9	77	80	113	26
Vidal,David	12	R	23	3B	aa	CIN	335	11	0	213	7	70	120	40	4
	13	R	24	3B	aa	CIN	131	1	0	186	9	65	31	14	-90
Villalona,Angel	13	R	23	1B	aa	SF	196	5	0	193	3	65	107	30	-37
Villanueva,Christian	13	R	22	3B	aa	CHC	490	15	4	233	5	74	136	59	34

BATTER	yr	b	age	pos	lvl	org	ab	hr	sb	ba	bb%	ct%	px	sx	bpv
Villar,Jonathan	13	B	22	SS	aaa	HOU	339	6	24	248	7	69	104	151	21
Vitek,Kolbrin	12	R	23	3B	aa	BOS	186	1	0	231	4	73	83	36	-21
	13	R	24	LF	aa	BOS	201	0	4	183	5	67	48	70	-61
Vogt,Stephen	12	L	28	C	aaa	TAM	349	6	1	212	8	78	74	67	8
	13	L	29	C	aaa	OAK	296	7	0	236	8	80	96	58	32
Vucinich,Shea	13	R	25	3B	aa	MIL	222	2	3	169	13	64	67	54	-45
Wagner,Daniel	12	L	24	2B	aa	CHW	63	0	3	234	6	87	44	96	27
	13	L	25	3B	aa	CHW	296	1	18	237	5	87	28	90	9
Wagner,Mark	13	R	29	C	a/a	SF	125	1	1	119	7	65	42	27	-81
Walker,Keenyn	13	B	23	RF	aa	CHW	462	3	31	181	12	63	61	138	-33
Walker,Mike	13	L	25	3B	aa	MIL	368	11	2	193	10	65	102	43	-23
Wallace,Brett	12	L	26	3B	aaa	HOU	310	11	0	235	5	65	114	31	-27
	13	L	27	1B	aaa	HOU	233	8	1	263	7	63	149	66	5
Wallace,Christopher	12	R	24	C	a/a	HOU	236	4	2	209	7	65	97	51	-30
	13	R	25	C	a/a	CLE	170	2	0	242	5	62	91	28	-59
Wallach,Matthew	12	L	26	C	aa	LA	168	3	2	191	10	75	45	46	-28
	13	L	27	C	a/a	LA	233	3	0	179	9	66	47	19	-72
Walters,Zachary	12	B	23	SS	a/a	WAS	262	6	1	237	4	73	100	80	6
	13	B	24	SS	aaa	WAS	487	22	3	216	3	70	153	83	33
Ward,Brian	12	R	27	C	aa	BAL	161	1	3	177	10	82	30	57	-8
	13	R	28	C	a/a	BAL	154	2	1	208	7	78	63	52	-7
Waring,Brandon	12	R	26	3B	a/a	BAL	419	21	2	226	9	61	173	62	19
	13	R	27	3B	a/a	BAL	383	20	0	177	9	54	170	12	-23
Wates,Austin	12	R	24	DH	aa	HOU	359	5	12	256	6	76	69	102	6
	13	R	25	LF	a/a	HOU	136	1	11	260	8	81	54	143	30
Watkins,Logan	12	L	23	2B	aa	CHC	488	7	22	251	11	78	76	140	38
	13	L	24	2B	aaa	CHC	412	6	8	209	9	73	80	100	5
Watts,Kristopher	12	L	28	C	a/a	WAS	133	1	0	138	9	77	49	13	-30
	13	L	29	C	a/a	WAS	147	2	0	174	9	76	67	21	-17
Weber,Garrett	13	R	24	3B	aa	ARI	320	4	4	259	6	78	79	71	12
Weeks,Jemile	12	B	25	2B	aaa	OAK	45	0	1	267	9	79	66	37	-2
	13	B	26	2B	aaa	OAK	520	2	11	211	10	77	49	128	7
Weisenburger,Adam	12	R	24	C	aa	MIL	139	2	0	162	8	70	43	31	-57
	13	R	25	C	aa	MIL	175	4	0	218	10	68	100	45	-14
Wheeler,Ryan	12	L	24	3B	aaa	ARI	362	10	2	286	4	78	109	66	29
	13	L	25	3B	aaa	COL	438	8	2	250	4	77	90	64	8
Wheeler,Timothy	12	L	24	DH	aaa	COL	379	1	4	257	4	80	69	78	11
	13	L	25	RF	aaa	COL	397	3	7	212	4	76	54	82	-18
Wheeler,Zelous	12	R	25	3B	a/a	BAL	386	12	4	238	8	79	96	65	31
	13	R	26	3B	a/a	BAL	408	9	4	231	8	80	81	54	18
Whitaker,Josh	13	R	24	RF	aa	OAK	125	2	2	199	6	68	128	104	20
Widlansky,Robert	12	L	28	DH	aa	BAL	469	6	8	254	9	81	77	64	23
	13	L	29	DH	a/a	LAA	363	6	3	199	6	76	57	56	-22
Wilkerson,Shannon	12	R	24	DH	aa	BOS	91	0	2	245	4	81	50	58	-9
	13	R	25	CF	aa	BOS	465	3	17	208	8	75	67	119	8
Wilkins,Andrew	12	L	24	1B	aa	CHW	435	15	5	210	11	75	115	54	32
	13	L	25	1B	a/a	CHW	458	16	4	243	9	72	121	49	18
Williams,Everett	13	L	23	LF	aa	SD	331	2	8	230	7	72	42	80	-40
Williams,Jackson	12	R	26	C	aaa	SF	295	6	0	187	3	74	76	34	-24
	13	R	27	C	aaa	SF	261	3	0	171	5	77	62	48	-16
Wilson,Josh	12	R	31	SS	aaa	ATL	407	3	5	182	5	69	72	73	-34
	13	R	32	2B	aaa	ARI	192	2	1	153	3	70	55	33	-57
Wilson,Kenneth	13	R	23	CF	aa	TOR	216	2	12	229	6	71	87	115	3
Wilson,Mike	12	R	29	DH	aaa	SEA	230	7	1	165	9	63	102	57	-29
	13	R	30	LF	aaa	SD	220	4	1	207	5	61	94	54	-54
Wimberly,Corey	12	B	29	DH	aaa	NYM	133	1	5	224	7	85	29	110	12
	13	B	30	2B	a/a	CIN	254	1	7	199	4	85	40	89	7
Wise,Jeremy	12	R	26	1B	aa	LA	418	7	1	228	10	64	125	41	-9
	13	R	27	1B	aa	LA	278	7	0	203	10	62	123	20	-27
Witherspoon,Travis	12	R	23	C	aa	LAA	208	5	8	179	9	71	88	116	9
	13	R	24	CF	aa	LAA	448	8	25	183	9	70	77	119	-4
Wong,Joey	13	L	25	SS	aa	COL	279	2	2	218	5	79	68	52	-3
Wong,Kolten	12	L	22	2B	aa	STL	523	7	16	251	6	85	59	100	30
	13	L	23	2B	aaa	STL	412	7	15	261	7	84	80	138	57
Wood,Brandon	12	R	27	3B	aaa	COL	401	7	1	205	4	73	88	51	-15
	13	R	28	SS	aaa	BAL	234	3	0	183	4	77	61	22	-28
Worth,Danny	12	R	27	2B	aaa	DET	216	4	7	218	9	69	98	97	5
	13	R	28	2B	aaa	DET	305	1	7	181	8	65	69	92	-39
Wright,Ty	12	R	27	DH	a/a	CHC	244	4	2	236	5	77	91	51	9
	13	R	28	LF	a/a	CHC	390	6	3	212	6	82	69	48	13
Yelich,Christian	13	L	22	CF	aa	MIA	193	6	4	260	11	69	156	115	59
Yepez,Jose	12	R	31	C	aaa	ATL	254	2	1	200	6	81	58	40	-4
	13	R	32	C	aaa	ATL	192	0	0	168	3	85	29	22	-23
Ynoa,Rafael	12	B	25	SS	aa	LA	421	0	18	233	10	80	46	97	9
	13	B	26	2B	aa	LA	484	5	13	226	8	83	65	70	23
Young,Matt	12	L	30	2B	aaa	STL	336	1	12	177	12	70	30	104	-40
	13	L	31	CF	aaa	LAA	130	1	6	138	7	83	34	101	4
Zaneski,Zach	12	R	26	C	aa	TEX	209	3	0	245	7	78	85	39	9
	13	R	27	C	a/a	TEX	186	5	0	164	6	68	88	27	-35
Zarraga,Shawn	13	B	24	C	aa	MIL	168	1	0	256	6	79	55	22	-18
Zazueta,Amadeo	12	B	26	SS	aaa	SD	115	0	0	136	1	79	29	53	-40
	13	B	27	2B	aa	TOR	155	1	0	170	1	87	44	28	-6
Zunino,Mike	12	R	21	C	aa	SEA	51	2	0	303	9	84	134	12	67

PITCHER	yr	t	age	lvl	org	ip	era	whip	bf/g	ctl	dom	cmd	hr/9	h%	s%	bpv
Achter,A.J.	13	R	25	a/a	MIN	60	2.94	1.42	6.2	5.1	6.7	1.3	1.0	26	84	46
Adam,Jason	13	R	22	aa	KC	144	6.04	1.55	24.2	3.3	6.6	2.0	0.7	35	60	55
Adams,Austin	13	R	27	aa	CLE	55	3.02	1.47	5.2	4.8	9.8	2.0	0.5	34	80	91
Adcock,Nathan	12	R	24	aaa	KC	99	5.92	1.57	22.9	2.6	4.4	1.7	0.4	35	60	42
	13	R	25	aaa	ARI	113	6.63	1.71	19.7	3.6	4.4	1.2	1.1	34	61	10
Additon,Nicholas	12	L	25	aaa	STL	87	5.01	1.66	24.4	4.3	6.7	1.6	1.0	34	71	40
	13	L	26	aaa	STL	132	4.75	1.34	22.8	2.7	6.3	2.3	1.0	30	66	58
Aguasviva,Geisor	12	L	25	aa	LA	64	3.04	1.22	5.2	4.1	4.6	1.1	0.5	24	76	49
	13	L	26	a/a	LA	51	5.78	1.96	6.9	4.8	3.6	0.7	1.1	35	72	-10
Alaniz,Ruben	13	R	22	aa	HOU	113	5.01	1.72	19.0	3.6	4.6	1.3	0.7	35	71	23
Albaladejo,Jonath	12	R	30	aaa	ARI	57	3.97	1.36	4.8	3.6	7.0	1.9	1.3	28	76	48
	13	R	31	aaa	MIA	73	5.61	1.95	6.1	3.6	6.9	1.9	0.8	42	71	42
Albers,Andrew	12	L	27	aa	MIN	98	4.81	1.53	22.5	1.2	5.1	4.2	0.7	37	69	88
	13	L	28	aaa	MIN	132	3.53	1.42	25.5	2.4	5.9	2.5	1.0	33	78	55
Alderson,Tim	12	R	24	a/a	PIT	89	5.22	1.55	13.9	2.8	5.3	1.9	0.8	34	66	41
	13	R	25	a/a	BAL	89	4.89	1.39	8.5	2.4	6.6	2.8	1.2	32	67	60
Alexander,Scott	13	L	24	aa	KC	33	6.28	1.90	6.5	5.0	8.8	1.8	0.0	42	63	80
Almarante,Jose	13	R	25	a/a	STL	41	2.97	1.16	5.8	2.5	5.7	2.3	0.2	28	73	83
Alvarez,Jose	12	L	23	aa	MIA	136	5.15	1.40	23.0	1.9	4.2	2.2	0.6	32	62	51
	13	L	24	aaa	DET	129	3.60	1.26	25.0	1.8	6.3	3.6	0.9	31	74	87
Ames,Steven	12	R	24	aa	LA	63	1.84	1.15	4.7	1.9	8.6	4.6	0.3	33	85	143
	13	R	25	aaa	MIA	46	4.92	2.00	5.7	3.9	5.7	1.5	1.4	39	79	8
Anderson,Chase	12	R	25	aa	ARI	104	3.70	1.31	20.5	2.2	6.8	3.0	1.0	32	75	76
	13	R	26	aaa	ARI	88	5.82	1.67	15.2	3.1	6.5	2.1	1.1	37	66	41
Andriese,Matt	13	R	24	a/a	SD	135	3.29	1.27	20.4	1.9	6.1	3.3	0.3	32	73	96
Antigua,Jeffry	12	L	22	aa	CHC	40	4.51	1.49	8.6	3.0	7.9	2.6	1.4	34	74	56
	13	L	23	a/a	CHC	53	5.32	1.47	10.9	3.6	6.1	1.7	1.1	31	65	39
Antolin,Dustin	13	R	24	aa	TOR	32	13.45	2.41	6.5	7.6	7.2	0.9	1.3	41	40	8
Archer,Chris	12	R	24	aaa	TAM	128	4.09	1.34	21.3	4.2	8.3	2.0	0.4	30	68	86
	13	R	25	aaa	TAM	50	4.61	1.62	22.2	4.1	7.8	1.9	1.1	35	74	50
Arguelles,Noel	12	L	22	aa	KC	119	7.31	1.89	22.5	4.8	3.7	0.8	0.9	34	60	3
	13	L	23	aa	KC	71	7.04	1.91	13.5	6.6	4.6	0.7	0.8	32	62	15
Arias,Jonathan	12	R	24	aa	SEA	33	3.58	1.23	6.1	5.4	5.4	1.0	1.3	18	77	33
	13	R	25	a/a	SEA	80	6.02	1.59	8.0	4.2	8.8	2.1	1.4	34	65	52
Armstrong,Shawn	12	R	22	aa	CLE	20	1.16	1.31	4.9	5.4	8.5	1.6	0.0	27	90	99
	13	R	23	aa	CLE	33	4.33	1.64	4.9	5.3	10.0	1.9	0.5	37	73	85
Arredondo,Jose	13	R	29	aaa	CIN	54	8.73	1.95	6.0	7.7	7.9	1.0	0.8	34	53	44
Arrieta,Jake	12	R	26	aaa	BAL	56	6.00	1.67	25.2	5.3	6.8	1.3	0.7	33	63	46
	13	R	27	aaa	CHC	79	5.17	1.62	22.0	3.8	6.9	1.8	0.8	35	68	51
Arroyo,Spencer	12	L	24	aa	CHW	69	5.82	1.85	26.7	4.7	4.0	0.9	1.2	33	70	-4
	13	L	25	a/a	CHW	149	4.73	1.55	24.2	3.3	4.8	1.5	0.8	32	70	32
Asencio,Jairo	13	R	29	aaa	BAL	51	3.83	1.26	4.4	3.0	7.3	2.5	1.3	28	75	63
Atkins,Mitch	12	R	27	aaa	WAS	118	6.20	1.72	19.2	3.0	5.2	1.7	1.1	36	64	24
	13	R	28	aa	ATL	96	4.98	1.76	25.9	3.8	5.6	1.5	0.7	36	72	33
Aumont,Phillippe	12	R	23	aaa	PHI	44	5.40	1.71	4.9	7.2	10.2	1.4	0.7	33	68	76
	13	R	24	aaa	PHI	36	4.67	2.00	5.4	9.7	8.9	0.9	0.0	34	74	78
Baker,Nathaniel	12	L	25	aa	PIT	107	6.05	1.67	14.5	4.9	5.1	1.0	0.8	32	63	27
	13	L	26	aa	PIT	80	7.19	1.91	10.0	5.0	5.8	1.1	0.9	37	61	23
Banwart,Travis	12	R	26	aaa	OAK	129	4.12	1.44	17.1	2.6	5.5	2.1	0.9	32	73	47
	13	R	27	aaa	OAK	131	4.99	1.69	20.4	3.8	6.7	1.8	1.2	35	73	34
Barnes,Matt	13	R	23	a/a	BOS	113	5.15	1.62	20.1	3.9	9.4	2.4	1.0	38	69	75
Barrett,Aaron	13	R	25	aa	WAS	50	2.68	1.25	4.0	2.6	9.7	3.7	0.4	34	79	128
Bascom,Timothy	12	R	27	a/a	BAL	135	6.14	1.72	22.7	4.3	5.1	1.2	1.0	34	64	21
	13	R	28	aa	BAL	58	4.87	1.77	11.1	5.9	5.6	0.9	0.4	33	71	40
Bass,Anthony	13	R	26	aaa	SD	79	5.11	1.63	23.5	1.8	5.6	3.1	1.0	38	70	57
Bassitt,Chris	13	R	24	aa	CHW	48	3.04	1.33	24.7	3.8	6.0	1.6	0.5	28	78	59
Batista,Frank	12	R	23	a/a	CHC	60	3.09	1.30	5.1	3.8	5.6	1.5	1.1	26	81	40
	13	R	24	aa	CHC	62	3.11	1.49	5.6	4.2	6.3	1.5	0.3	32	79	61
Batista,Lay	13	R	24	aa	LAA	123	4.00	1.33	23.1	3.1	5.5	1.8	0.6	30	70	57
Battisto,A.J.	13	R	30	aaa	MIA	38	11.27	2.60	12.0	7.4	4.5	0.6	2.2	40	57	-48
Bauer,Trevor	12	R	21	a/a	ARI	130	2.51	1.28	24.3	3.8	9.5	2.5	0.6	31	83	99
	13	R	22	aaa	CLE	121	5.06	1.72	25.0	5.3	6.9	1.3	1.1	33	73	32
Baumann,George	12	L	25	aa	KC	59	5.00	1.51	8.0	5.1	7.0	1.4	1.1	29	69	42
	13	L	26	a/a	KC	53	3.26	1.66	7.4	4.5	9.4	2.1	0.9	37	83	70
Bawcom,Logan	12	R	24	aa	SEA	49	2.88	1.52	5.5	6.0	8.2	1.4	0.4	30	81	75
	13	R	25	aaa	SEA	65	2.89	1.28	5.2	3.2	7.6	2.4	0.5	30	78	86
Baxendale,D.J.	13	R	23	aa	MIN	93	6.27	1.55	25.3	2.1	5.2	2.5	1.2	35	60	39
Beachy,Brandon	13	R	27	a/a	ATL	35	4.49	1.65	19.6	5.4	6.2	1.1	1.2	30	76	25
Beato,Pedro	12	R	26	aaa	BOS	42	5.33	1.43	6.4	3.6	5.7	1.6	1.9	27	69	11
	13	R	27	aaa	BOS	51	4.07	1.66	6.8	4.7	6.1	1.3	1.5	31	81	17
Beavan,Blake	12	R	23	aaa	SEA	38	2.39	1.25	25.8	1.9	3.2	1.6	0.5	28	83	39
	13	R	24	aaa	SEA	94	5.41	1.57	25.8	2.1	3.9	1.9	1.2	33	67	17
Beeler,Dallas	12	R	23	aa	CHC	136	5.10	1.77	23.1	3.3	4.0	1.2	0.8	36	72	14
	13	R	24	aa	CHC	55	3.74	1.24	24.6	2.9	4.8	1.6	0.5	27	70	54
Belfiore,Michael	12	L	24	aa	BAL	47	3.54	1.54	7.36	4.2	7.8	1.9	0.5	34	77	72
	13	L	25	aaa	BAL	76	4.19	1.72	9.36	3.7	7.8	2.1	1.3	37	79	45
Beliveau,Jeff	12	L	25	aaa	CHC	44	4.46	1.57	5.22	3.8	8.7	2.3	0.9	36	73	72
	13	L	26	a/a	TAM	49	2.84	1.50	5.12	4.3	12.1	2.8	0.2	40	80	128
Bell,Trevor	12	R	26	aaa	LAA	37	7.80	2.34	19.1	5.2	3.7	0.7	1.3	40	67	-24
	13	R	27	a/a	CIN	35	2.62	1.28	4.78	2.6	8.0	3.0	0.8	32	83	90
Below,Duane	12	L	27	aaa	DET	17	8.30	2.48	23	6.6	2.7	0.4	1.9	38	69	-53
	13	L	28	aaa	MIA	100	3.47	1.53	25.5	2.8	5.0	1.8	0.5	34	77	48
Berg,Jeremy	12	R	26	a/a	LAA	74	4.11	1.37	6.49	2.2	7.3	3.3	0.9	34	72	85
	13	R	27	a/a	LAA	78	3.04	1.27	5.82	2.1	6.6	3.2	0.6	32	77	89
Berger,Eric	12	L	26	a/a	CLE	111	6.81	1.62	15.9	3.2	6.4	2.0	1.8	34	61	21
	13	L	27	a/a	HOU	75	3.80	1.55	7.13	4.5	5.5	1.2	0.8	30	77	34
Bergman,Christiai	13	R	25	aa	COL	171	5.11	1.40	26.7	1.4	4.5	3.3	2.2	30	72	23
Berken,Jason	13	R	30	aaa	CHW	161	5.61	1.83	27.8	3.4	4.9	1.4	1.3	37	72	7
Betances,Dellin	12	R	24	a/a	NYY	131	8.28	2.11	24.0	7.1	7.0	1.0	1.2	37	60	18
	13	R	25	aaa	NYY	84	3.80	1.35	9.2	5.0	9.3	1.8	0.3	30	70	96
Bettis,Chad	13	R	24	aa	COL	63	5.52	1.46	22.5	2.1	7.6	3.7	2.1	34	69	54
Bibens-Dirkx,Aust	12	R	27	a/a	COL	70	9.18	2.08	8.8	4.3	5.9	1.4	1.4	40	55	4
	13	R	28	aa	TOR	66	2.47	1.17	21.9	2.5	5.9	2.4	0.5	28	81	77
Biddle,Jesse	13	L	22	aa	PHI	138	3.86	1.36	21.4	5.0	8.7	1.7	0.7	28	72	80
Billings,Bruce	12	R	27	a/a	OAK	139	4.47	1.41	21.8	2.9	6.0	2.1	0.9	32	70	52
	13	R	28	aaa	OAK	148	4.78	1.46	22.7	3.3	6.2	1.9	0.9	32	69	49
Bischoff,Matthew	13	R	26	aa	BAL	51	5.52	1.58	9.0	4.2	6.9	1.7	1.1	33	66	41
Bisenius,Joe	13	R	31	a/a	ATL	54	8.29	2.44	20.3	4.3	4.9	1.1	1.0	45	65	-5
Black,Sean	13	R	25	aa	NYY	32	5.70	1.74	24.3	3.4	3.4	1.0	1.6	33	71	-16
Black,Victor	12	R	24	aa	PIT	60	2.00	1.25	4.8	4.3	10.0	2.4	0.3	30	84	113
	13	R	25	aaa	PIT	47	2.97	1.14	4.9	4.0	9.4	2.4	0.4	27	74	110
Blair,Seth	13	R	24	aa	STL	130	5.47	1.63	24.0	3.3	6.7	2.0	1.1	35	68	41
Blazek,Michael	12	R	23	a/a	STL	83	4.73	1.29	8.2	3.8	7.6	2.0	1.2	27	66	60
	13	R	24	a/a	STL	46	2.16	1.24	5.2	5.1	8.4	1.7	0.2	26	82	96
Bleich,Jeremy	13	L	26	aa	NYY	65	3.80	1.77	11.1	6.0	6.2	1.0	0.2	34	77	51
Bleier,Richard	12	L	25	aa	TEX	32	5.43	1.57	6.4	2.1	3.8	1.8	1.2	33	67	14
	13	L	26	a/a	TEX	81	4.68	1.60	8.6	2.5	4.2	1.7	1.0	34	72	23
Bochy,Brett	12	R	25	aa	SF	53	3.18	1.00	5.0	3.2	9.5	3.0	0.5	25	68	124
	13	R	26	aaa	SF	56	3.84	1.22	5.1	2.4	7.3	3.1	0.2	32	67	106
Boggs,Mitchell	13	R	29	a/a	COL	46	8.51	2.42	7.1	4.9	3.3	0.7	1.2	41	64	-27
Bolsinger,Michael	12	R	24	aa	ARI	78	4.85	1.76	23.7	4.5	6.1	1.4	0.7	36	73	38
	13	R	25	a/a	ARI	144	4.77	1.59	24.4	3.3	6.5	2.0	0.8	35	71	50
Bonderman,Jeren	13	R	31	aaa	DET	73	5.70	1.76	18.7	2.5	3.3	1.3	1.1	36	69	-1
Bonilla,Lisalberto	12	R	22	aa	PHI	33	1.82	1.23	6.4	4.5	10.9	2.4	0.3	30	86	122
	13	R	23	a/a	TEX	73	6.34	1.59	6.9	4.2	10.7	2.5	1.3	37	61	75
Bonine,Eddie	13	R	32	a/a	SD	98	5.85	1.77	20.4	3.0	1.8	0.6	1.0	34	67	-19
Boone,Randy	13	R	29	aa	TOR	62	4.56	1.66	8.5	2.5	5.3	2.1	0.9	36	74	37
Boscan,Wilfredo	12	R	23	aa	TEX	98	4.96	1.43	12.3	2.7	6.7	2.5	1.2	32	68	53
	13	R	24	a/a	SD	62	5.97	1.67	14.6	2.4	4.1	1.7	1.5	34	67	6
Boshers,Jeffrey	12	L	24	aa	LAA	24	4.68	1.59	5.6	1.9	8.6	4.6	1.1	40	73	103
	13	L	25	a/a	LAA	48	3.40	1.32	4.5	4.2	9.4	2.2	0.3	31	73	103
Bowlin,Drew	13	R	27	a/a	SF	46	5.43	1.49	6.0	5.1	5.3	1.0	0.8	27	63	36
Bowman,Joshua	13	R	25	aa	OAK	40	5.20	1.73	22.6	4.9	3.3	0.7	1.1	30	71	-2
Boxberger,Brad	12	R	24	aaa	SD	43	2.32	1.23	4.7	3.5	11.1	3.2	0.0	35	79	143
	13	R	25	aaa	SD	57	3.31	1.20	5.5	2.8	11.8	4.3	0.4	36	72	156
Brach,Brad	13	R	27	aaa	SD	44	2.72	1.34	5.6	2.7	7.2	2.6	0.8	32	83	75
Brach,Brett	12	R	24	aa	CLE	94	5.00	1.80	22.8	3.6	3.9	1.1	0.9	35	73	7
	13	R	25	a/a	CLE	142	5.44	1.46	20.9	2.4	4.3	1.8	0.9	32	63	32
Bradley,Archie	13	R	21	aa	ARI	123	2.62	1.38	24.7	4.4	7.6	1.7	0.5	30	82	75
Bradley,Ryan	13	L	25	aa	SF	65	6.46	2.15	14.0	4.4	4.2	1.0	0.8	40	69	4
Brady,Michael	13	R	26	aa	MIA	53	2.10	1.21	4.4	1.8	7.9	4.3	0.4	33	84	129
Bramhall,Bobby	12	L	27	a/a	MIA	62	4.37	1.43	9.1	3.4	7.4	2.1	0.7	33	70	70
	13	L	28	a/a	PHI	72	5.36	1.74	10.6	4.2	4.7	1.1	1.6	32	73	-4
Branham,Matthew	13	R	26	a/a	SD	34	3.88	1.38	6.2	4.5	8.3	1.8	0.7	30	73	75
Brasier,Ryan	12	R	25	aaa	LAA	60	4.04	1.49	4.7	3.1	6.7	2.2	0.1	35	70	80
	13	R	26	aaa	LAA	57	3.69	1.49	6.4	2.2	7.3	3.4	0.7	37	76	87
Brewer,Charles	12	R	24	a/a	ARI	151	6.32	1.66	25.1	2.0	5.8	2.9	1.7	36	65	30
	13	R	25	aaa	ARI	140	4.87	1.49	24.1	2.5	5.6	2.2	0.8	34	68	52
Brigham,Jacob	12	R	24	aa	CHC	128	5.81	1.64	24.8	3.7	7.0	1.9	1.6	34	68	29
	13	R	25	a/a	TEX	127	5.56	1.74	17.6	4.1	5.3	1.3	0.7	35	67	30
Britton,Drake	12	L	23	aa	BOS	85	5.03	1.71	24.0	4.3	6.8	1.6	0.4	37	69	57
	13	L	24	a/a	BOS	103	4.80	1.59	25.1	3.4	6.1	1.8	0.5	35	69	55
Britton,Zach	12	L	25	a/a	BAL	63	5.59	1.52	25.0	3.6	5.5	1.5	1.0	31	64	34
	13	L	26	aaa	BAL	103	5.73	1.85	25.4	4.4	5.1	1.2	0.6	37	68	27
Broadway,Michae	12	R	25	aa	SD	40	6.37	1.70	5.4	2.9	8.6	3.0	0.7	41	61	83
	13	R	26	a/a	WAS	40	3.00	1.30	5.5	2.6	6.9	2.6	0.8	31	80	76
Broderick,Brian	12	R	26	a/a	WAS	108	8.09	2.09	18.9	3.1	4.4	1.4	1.6	40	62	-12
	13	R	27	aa	WAS	38	6.81	1.80	25.1	2.0	5.4	2.7	2.0	38	66	13
Bromberg,David	12	R	25	a/a	MIN	92	4.48	1.65	12.4	4.8	6.6	1.4	0.5	34	72	52
	13	R	26	a/a	PIT	147	4.20	1.44	22.3	3.4	6.3	1.9	0.7	32	71	57
Brooks,Aaron	13	R	23	aa	KC	104	4.95	1.35	27.0	0.9	4.8	5.0	1.1	33	65	94
Brown,Brooks	12	R	27	aaa	DET	112	6.53	1.96	18.5	4.9	4.8	1.0	1.1	36	67	6
	13	R	28	aaa	PIT	91	6.01	1.58	10.8	2.5	4.9	2.0	1.1	34	63	30
Brummett,Tyson	12	R	28	a/a	PHI	90	4.27	1.42	8.7	3.3	6.4	1.9	0.5	32	69	65
	13	R	29	a/a	TOR	88	7.79	1.81	11.9	3.9	5.9	1.5	1.1	37	56	24
Bryson,Robert	12	R	25	a/a	CLE	65	3.66	1.59	6.7	6.4	8.6	1.3	0.7	30	78	67
	13	R	26	a/a	CLE	34	11.61	2.40	6.1	9.2	8.7	0.9	3.2	36	54	-33
Buchanan,David	12	R	23	aa	PHI	72	4.38	1.44	25.7	2.8	4.3	1.5	0.9	30	71	27
	13	R	24	a/a	PHI	170	4.97	1.49	26.1	2.8	4.8	1.7	1.0	32	68	32
Buchanan,Jake	12	R	23	a/a	HOU	142	5.70	1.66	21.2	2.3	4.9	2.1	0.7	37	65	41
	13	R	24	a/a	HOU	158	3.38	1.23	21.4	1.3	4.8	3.8	0.6	31	73	90
Buchter,Ryan	12	L	25	a/a	ATL	49	3.39	1.58	4.94	6.9	8.4	1.2	0.4	29	78	74
	13	L	26	aaa	ATL	62	3.47	1.58	5.35	7.9	12.2	1.6	0.8	30	80	97
Buckner,Billy	12	R	29	a/a	BOS	153	5.66	1.68	25.5	3.8	4.8	1.3	1.4	32	69	5
	13	R	30	aaa	LAA	94	4.70	1.68	23.6	4.4	5.5	1.2	0.5	34	71	39
Bueno,Francisley	12	L	31	aaa	KC	56	3.32	1.25	6.47	2.6	6.2	2.4	0.8	29	76	67
	13	L	32	aaa	KC	68	3.72	1.67	8.44	3.7	5.3	1.4	0.8	34	79	32
Burawa,Daniel	13	R	25	aa	NYY	66	3.50	1.58	6.31	6.2	7.2	1.2	0.2	30	76	69
Burgoon,Tyler	13	R	24	a/a	SEA	54	4.49	1.47	6.06	4.2	9.9	2.3	1.0	34	71	82
Burgos,Hiram	12	R	25	a/a	MIL	130	3.00	1.38	25.9	3.3	6.5	2.0	0.7	31	80	63
	13	R	26	aaa	MIL	31	4.51	1.38	18.4	3.7	5.8	1.5	2.2	25	77	6
Burke,Greg	12	R	30	a/a	BAL	65	2.30	1.26	6	2.5	5.1	2.0	0.2	30	81	69
	13	R	31	aaa	NYM	32	4.42	1.46	4.37	2.7	7.3	2.7	0.8	35	71	73
Burns,Cory	12	R	25	aaa	SD	66	2.75	0.98	4.64	2.1	9.0	4.3	0.1	29	69	154
	13	R	26	aaa	TEX	38	2.87	1.73	4.51	3.9	8.8	2.3	0.0	41	82	93

PITCHER	yr	t	age	lvl	org	ip	era	whip	bf/g	ctl	dom	cmd	hr/9	h%	s%	bpv
Buschmann,Matth	12	R	28	a/a	TAM	151	4.83	1.57	25.6	3.3	5.5	1.7	0.9	33	70	35
	13	R	29	a/a	TAM	161	3.60	1.54	24.2	4.1	7.1	1.7	0.6	33	77	60
Butler,Keith	12	R	23	aa	STL	59	2.96	1.35	4.58	3.4	7.5	2.2	0.7	31	80	74
	13	R	24	a/a	STL	41	2.88	1.05	4.81	2.4	9.0	3.8	0.8	28	76	120
Byrd,Darren	12	R	26	aa	MIL	73	3.44	1.55	6.38	5.0	7.2	1.4	0.3	32	77	66
	13	R	27	a/a	OAK	41	5.70	1.71	7.21	5.5	6.6	1.2	0.6	33	66	45
Cabrera,Alberto	12	R	24	a/a	CHC	55	3.65	1.50	6.59	2.4	10.1	4.3	1.0	40	79	113
	13	R	25	a/a	CHC	133	4.61	1.55	17.6	3.7	7.0	1.9	1.0	33	72	48
Cabrera,Fernando	12	R	31	aaa	NYM	68	5.03	1.84	5.56	5.0	6.0	1.2	1.4	34	76	12
	13	R	32	aaa	LAA	73	3.35	1.53	5.85	4.0	6.6	1.6	1.0	32	81	44
Caminero,Arquim	12	R	25	aa	MIA	18	3.88	1.74	6.71	5.8	7.5	1.3	0.0	36	75	71
	13	R	26	a/a	MIA	54	4.76	1.26	5.15	4.2	9.7	2.3	0.8	29	62	94
Campos,Leonel	13	R	26	aa	SD	31	1.04	1.09	4.61	5.0	10.4	2.1	0.0	24	89	129
Cargill,Collin	13	R	26	aa	MIA	56	2.21	0.98	5.6	2.9	3.7	1.3	0.4	20	78	54
Carl,Edwin	13	R	25	aa	KC	35	6.94	1.82	6.56	3.9	6.2	1.6	1.9	36	65	4
Carpenter,Chris	12	R	27	a/a	BOS	18	2.27	1.20	4.18	4.7	7.8	1.7	0.7	24	84	78
	13	R	28	aaa	BOS	45	6.93	2.17	7.54	6.5	7.2	1.1	0.7	40	67	32
Carpenter,David	12	R	25	aaa	LAA	20	2.53	0.88	4.84	3.2	5.3	1.7	0.7	17	74	70
	13	R	26	a/a	LAA	61	6.77	1.66	5.13	4.8	6.3	1.3	0.6	33	57	44
Carpenter,Drew	12	R	27	a/a	NYM	84	3.63	1.55	11.9	2.3	6.2	2.7	1.3	35	82	46
	13	R	28	a/a	OAK	127	5.79	1.63	23.5	2.8	4.0	1.4	1.3	33	66	8
Carrasco,Carlos	13	R	26	aaa	CLE	72	4.16	1.34	18.6	2.8	8.0	2.8	0.9	32	71	82
Carraway,Andrew	12	R	26	a/a	SEA	150	4.56	1.40	23.4	2.3	5.1	2.2	0.9	32	68	49
	13	R	27	aaa	SEA	119	5.83	1.77	24.8	4.2	5.2	1.2	1.2	34	69	12
Carreno,Joel	12	R	25	a/a	TOR	90	7.01	1.71	15.1	4.6	7.1	1.6	1.3	34	59	32
	13	R	26	a/a	TOR	67	3.08	1.09	5.21	3.4	9.7	2.9	0.8	26	75	108
Carson,Robert	12	L	23	a/a	NYM	51	3.96	1.66	5.61	3.5	7.9	2.3	0.5	39	76	72
	13	L	24	aaa	NYM	44	3.49	1.43	4.38	3.3	6.2	1.9	0.5	32	76	63
Carter,Anthony	12	R	26	aaa	CHW	63	6.99	1.97	7.69	4.1	6.3	1.5	1.4	39	66	14
	13	R	27	aaa	BOS	62	4.73	1.56	5.25	3.7	8.8	2.4	1.0	36	72	69
Castillo,Fabio	12	R	23	a/a	TEX	56	4.38	1.41	6.76	4.2	5.4	1.3	0.6	28	69	46
	13	R	24	a/a	SF	89	5.11	1.59	10.7	3.9	8.0	2.1	0.5	36	67	73
Castillo,Richard	12	R	23	aa	STL	110	4.07	1.53	25.2	2.6	4.5	1.7	0.6	34	74	39
	13	R	24	a/a	STL	148	4.47	1.44	24.2	3.2	4.4	1.4	1.0	29	71	23
Castillo,Yeiper	13	R	25	aa	CHC	62	4.64	1.50	12.7	4.8	6.3	1.3	0.6	30	69	50
Castro,Angel	13	R	31	aaa	LA	116	3.88	1.59	20.5	3.0	5.2	1.7	0.6	35	76	44
Castro,Simon	12	R	24	a/a	CHW	115	5.20	1.58	25.3	2.5	5.9	2.3	0.7	36	67	56
	13	R	25	aaa	CHW	93	7.78	1.74	15.6	3.9	6.7	1.7	1.9	34	57	10
Cedeno,Juan	12	L	29	aaa	NYY	64	4.07	1.78	5.55	3.5	5.9	1.7	1.1	37	80	28
	13	L	30	aaa	ATL	61	5.02	1.71	5.88	5.1	4.2	0.8	0.2	32	68	35
Cedeno,Xavier	12	L	26	aaa	HOU	28	2.38	1.40	5.31	2.9	6.7	2.3	0.0	34	81	88
	13	L	27	aaa	WAS	34	1.57	1.26	3.59	4.1	8.9	2.2	0.6	29	91	92
Celestino,Miguel	13	R	24	aa	BOS	72	7.76	1.86	8.64	4.7	7.2	1.5	1.4	37	58	25
Cervenka,Hunter	13	L	23	aa	CHC	38	3.58	1.39	5.38	4.8	6.6	1.4	0.3	29	73	69
Chaffee,Ryan	12	R	24	aa	LAA	43	3.39	1.29	4.77	5.6	9.9	1.8	0.6	26	75	94
	13	R	25	aa	LAA	62	3.53	1.35	5.46	5.1	8.8	1.7	0.4	29	73	88
Chafin,Andrew	13	L	23	aa	ARI	126	3.91	1.49	25.9	3.0	5.2	1.7	0.5	33	73	51
Chapman,Kevin	12	L	24	aa	HOU	58	2.89	1.48	5.09	4.9	7.8	1.6	0.3	32	80	76
	13	L	25	aaa	HOU	51	3.69	1.68	5.07	6.6	9.1	1.4	0.4	33	78	76
Chatwood,Tyler	12	R	23	a/a	COL	61	6.19	1.79	21.8	3.9	6.2	1.6	0.8	37	65	35
	13	R	24	aaa	COL	34	3.17	1.40	23.9	1.8	6.8	3.9	0.0	37	75	117
Chavez,Jesse	12	R	29	aaa	OAK	105	4.32	1.34	20.8	2.0	6.0	3.0	0.8	32	69	73
	13	R	30	aaa	OAK	30	3.10	1.59	26.5	1.6	5.7	3.5	0.3	39	80	88
Christiani,Nick	12	R	25	aaa	CIN	73	4.13	1.79	6.2	3.7	3.6	1.0	0.6	35	77	12
	13	R	26	aaa	CIN	56	5.36	1.45	4.88	3.0	6.4	2.1	1.4	31	66	38
Church,John	13	R	27	a/a	NYM	65	3.39	1.36	4.91	3.5	7.6	2.2	0.5	32	76	79
Cingrani,Tony	12	L	23	aa	CIN	89	2.87	1.27	22.8	4.2	8.8	2.1	1.0	27	82	77
	13	L	24	aaa	CIN	31	1.53	0.92	19.5	3.3	11.9	3.6	0.4	25	86	156
Cisco,Michael	12	R	25	a/a	PHI	75	2.25	1.42	7.95	3.3	5.7	1.7	0.9	30	88	46
	13	R	26	aa	LAA	59	4.93	1.46	5.46	3.7	5.1	1.4	0.5	31	65	46
Clark,Tyler	13	R	24	aa	DET	33	4.39	1.96	7.1	5.7	7.2	1.3	0.3	39	76	51
Clark,Zachary	12	R	29	a/a	BAL	168	4.14	1.61	26.5	3.5	3.9	1.1	0.7	32	75	19
	13	R	30	a/a	BAL	50	9.15	2.31	23.1	5.8	4.9	0.8	0.8	41	58	5
Claudio,Alexande	13	L	21	aa	TEX	32	3.88	1.43	6.41	3.3	7.0	2.1	0.8	32	75	63
Clay,Caleb	12	R	24	aa	BOS	66	6.37	1.74	8.89	2.8	6.8	2.4	2.0	37	68	21
	13	R	25	a/a	WAS	158	3.54	1.17	23.4	1.7	4.9	2.9	0.7	28	71	73
Clemens,Paul	12	R	24	a/a	HOU	143	6.04	1.70	24	2.6	5.6	2.2	1.4	36	67	25
	13	R	25	aaa	HOU	30	5.20	1.41	21.2	3.4	4.0	1.2	0.3	30	61	40
Cleto,Maikel	12	R	23	aaa	STL	54	5.67	1.42	5.06	3.6	9.3	2.6	0.6	35	58	94
	13	R	24	aaa	KC	91	6.84	1.91	12.4	7.5	7.1	0.9	0.5	34	62	46
Clinard,Will	13	R	24	aa	DET	34	6.75	1.84	7.27	5.2	5.4	1.0	1.7	33	66	-5
Cloyd,Tyler	12	R	25	a/a	PHI	167	2.82	1.17	25.6	2.3	5.0	2.1	1.0	26	80	52
	13	R	26	aaa	PHI	113	5.68	1.56	26	2.2	6.0	2.7	1.9	34	69	27
Cochran,Thomas	12	L	30	aaa	PHI	127	5.78	1.81	23.6	6.0	5.6	0.9	1.0	32	69	21
	13	L	31	a/a	PHI	102	6.97	2.09	22.8	5.4	4.6	0.9	1.2	37	67	-4
Cofield,Kyle	12	R	25	aa	PIT	15	6.53	1.27	5.7	2.3	6.8	2.9	1.8	28	51	51
	13	R	26	a/a	LA	33	4.39	1.47	7.52	5.0	6.3	1.3	1.2	27	73	35
Cohoon,Mark	12	L	25	a/a	NYM	155	4.70	1.41	26.1	1.9	4.2	2.2	0.9	32	67	42
	13	L	26	aa	NYM	120	4.44	1.63	21.3	2.1	5.5	2.6	0.7	37	73	55
Cole,A.J.	13	R	21	aa	WAS	45	2.54	0.96	24.5	1.8	8.2	4.5	0.6	27	76	138
Cole,Gerrit	12	R	22	a/a	PIT	65	3.58	1.39	21	3.1	7.6	2.4	0.3	34	73	90
	13	R	23	aaa	PIT	68	3.31	1.11	22.3	3.5	5.0	1.4	0.5	23	70	60
Coleman,Casey	12	R	25	aaa	CHC	58	4.99	1.49	19.2	4.0	6.6	1.6	0.6	32	66	56
	13	R	26	aaa	CHC	88	3.91	1.49	9.29	4.0	5.4	1.4	0.8	30	75	37
Coleman,Louis	12	R	26	aaa	KC	20	3.58	1.16	7.12	3.6	9.2	2.5	0.4	28	69	108
	13	R	27	aaa	KC	45	2.13	1.43	7.91	3.7	7.9	2.1	0.2	34	85	87
Colla,Michael	12	R	26	aa	PIT	96	4.73	1.50	11.2	2.6	5.3	2.1	1.0	33	70	38
	13	R	27	aa	TAM	75	4.43	1.44	22.9	2.4	4.6	2.0	1.2	31	73	29

PITCHER	yr	t	age	lvl	org	ip	era	whip	bf/g	ctl	dom	cmd	hr/9	h%	s%	bpv
Colome,Alexande	12	R	23	a/a	TAM	92	3.74	1.41	22.8	4.0	7.6	1.9	0.3	32	72	81
	13	R	24	aaa	TAM	70	3.50	1.42	21.3	3.6	7.8	2.1	0.6	33	76	75
Colvin,Brody	12	R	22	aa	PHI	33	12.26	2.12	23.1	6.1	3.8	0.6	1.7	34	39	-29
	13	R	23	aa	PHI	77	6.92	1.79	17	6.1	3.6	0.6	1.1	29	61	0
Conley,Adam	13	L	23	aa	MIA	139	4.19	1.38	22.4	2.7	7.6	2.8	0.5	34	69	89
Contreras,Carlos	13	R	22	aa	CIN	42	3.71	1.54	23.1	4.7	4.9	1.0	0.6	30	77	35
Contreras,Jose	13	R	42	a/a	BOS	31	3.76	1.37	5	3.7	8.4	2.3	1.1	31	76	70
Cook,Aaron	12	R	33	aaa	BOS	37	3.82	1.65	27.8	3.6	2.8	0.8	0.3	33	76	17
	13	R	34	aaa	COL	35	10.03	2.31	22.7	3.0	3.9	1.3	1.4	43	55	-18
Cook,Cole	12	R	24	a/a	CLE	16	0.68	1.25	9.49	2.8	6.5	2.3	0.0	31	94	92
	13	R	25	a/a	CLE	59	9.09	1.92	9.65	4.3	6.0	1.4	1.5	37	52	9
Cooney,Tim	13	L	23	aa	STL	118	4.02	1.35	24.7	1.3	8.0	6.0	0.5	37	70	153
Cooper,Jordan	13	R	24	aa	CLE	72	3.36	1.21	16.2	3.8	5.9	1.6	0.7	25	74	58
Cooper,Matthew	13	R	25	aa	ARI	43	4.19	1.48	4.74	5.0	5.1	1.0	0.3	28	70	49
Cooper,Patrick	12	R	23	aa	DET	109	6.19	1.57	20.9	2.8	4.8	1.7	1.1	33	61	26
	13	R	24	aa	DET	86	7.16	1.96	24.3	3.6	4.3	1.2	1.3	38	64	-4
Corcino,Daniel	12	R	22	aa	CIN	143	4.00	1.40	23.2	4.2	7.0	1.6	0.8	29	73	58
	13	R	23	aaa	CIN	129	7.65	1.90	21.7	5.3	5.4	1.0	1.6	34	61	-4
Cordero,Chad	13	R	31	aaa	LAA	50	5.25	1.63	4.25	1.9	5.3	2.9	0.7	38	68	58
Cordier,Erik	12	R	26	a/a	ATL	29	8.35	2.46	11.6	8.7	5.4	0.6	0.4	39	63	21
	13	R	27	aaa	PIT	53	5.68	1.71	5.46	4.9	8.2	1.7	0.5	37	65	65
Cornelius,Jonatha	13	L	25	aa	STL	79	4.92	1.57	19.2	3.3	6.1	1.8	1.0	34	70	41
Corpas,Manuel	12	R	30	aaa	CHC	34	5.09	1.44	7.54	2.8	3.8	1.4	1.2	29	67	12
	13	R	31	aaa	COL	41	6.75	1.76	8.95	3.5	5.3	1.5	1.5	35	63	9
Correa,Manuarys	13	R	24	aa	LAA	133	6.67	1.70	23.1	1.5	4.4	2.9	1.1	38	61	41
Cosart,Jarred	12	R	22	a/a	HOU	115	3.31	1.40	23.1	3.7	6.4	1.7	0.2	31	75	71
	13	R	23	aaa	HOU	93	3.64	1.41	21.8	4.8	7.8	1.6	0.5	30	74	74
Cotham,Caleb	13	R	26	a/a	NYY	124	7.17	1.90	20.9	3.8	4.9	1.3	1.3	37	63	4
Couch,Keith	13	R	24	a/a	BOS	131	4.65	1.59	19.2	3.2	5.4	1.7	0.8	34	72	36
Crabbe,Timothy	12	R	24	aa	CIN	86	6.77	1.99	23.1	7.4	8.2	1.1	1.4	35	67	28
	13	R	25	a/a	CIN	153	4.26	1.56	24.8	2.8	5.3	1.9	1.0	34	75	34
Crawford,Evan	12	L	26	a/a	TOR	32	7.25	1.99	5.26	4.0	5.6	1.4	0.7	40	62	27
	13	L	27	aa	TOR	38	7.14	2.07	5.81	4.7	6.1	1.3	0.3	41	63	39
Crosby,Casey	12	L	24	aaa	DET	126	5.01	1.57	25.1	4.6	6.3	1.4	1.0	31	69	38
	13	L	25	aaa	DET	58	6.35	1.89	20.9	6.4	7.3	1.1	0.6	36	65	48
Crotta,Michael	13	R	29	aaa	WAS	58	4.47	1.72	5.16	4.0	4.9	1.2	0.0	36	71	48
Crouse,Matt	13	L	23	aa	DET	145	5.37	1.45	20	2.5	5.6	2.3	1.4	32	66	35
Cruz,Rhiner	13	R	27	aaa	HOU	42	5.73	1.81	5.21	7.4	6.6	0.9	1.5	28	71	17
Cumpton,Brandor	12	R	24	aa	PIT	152	4.64	1.44	24	2.7	4.1	1.5	0.5	31	67	39
	13	R	25	a/a	PIT	132	4.26	1.47	24.6	3.3	5.1	1.6	0.4	32	70	50
Daley,Matt	13	R	31	a/a	NYY	48	3.44	1.21	4.84	2.3	8.7	3.8	0.9	32	75	110
Darnell,Logan	12	L	23	aa	MIN	156	5.97	1.71	25.3	2.8	4.7	1.7	1.2	36	67	15
	13	L	24	a/a	MIN	154	3.66	1.46	24.4	2.7	5.8	2.2	0.5	34	75	62
Davis,Erik	12	R	26	a/a	WAS	73	3.42	1.46	6.5	2.5	7.0	2.9	0.9	35	79	72
	13	R	27	aaa	WAS	52	3.71	1.64	5.18	3.4	7.0	2.1	0.8	37	79	56
Dayton,Grant	13	L	26	aa	MIA	38	3.26	1.48	5.45	3.4	11.3	3.3	1.1	38	83	101
de la Cruz,Frankie	12	R	28	aaa	CHC	95	4.66	1.86	16.4	6.1	4.2	0.7	0.6	32	75	16
	13	R	29	a/a	MIL	88	8.79	2.21	12.3	6.9	5.1	0.7	1.6	36	61	-14
De La Cruz,Kelvir	12	L	24	aa	DET	115	6.08	1.61	17	3.9	5.7	1.5	1.4	32	64	19
	13	L	25	a/a	LA	67	3.04	1.64	6.01	4.7	9.2	1.9	0.4	37	82	82
De la Rosa,Eury	12	L	22	aa	ARI	63	3.46	1.11	4.7	2.3	8.3	3.6	0.5	30	69	119
	13	L	23	aaa	ARI	50	5.01	1.55	4.93	4.3	7.5	1.8	1.0	33	69	52
De La Rosa,Rubb	13	R	24	aaa	BOS	80	5.45	1.59	14.8	5.6	7.0	1.3	1.1	29	67	38
De La Rosa,Wilki	12	L	27	aa	CIN	43	3.68	1.82	4.37	6.5	6.8	1.0	1.0	32	82	32
	13	L	28	a/a	CIN	38	8.39	2.14	5.94	6.9	5.5	0.8	1.9	35	62	-17
De La Torre,Jose	12	R	27	a/a	BOS	74	4.15	1.40	6.79	3.4	6.9	2.1	0.3	33	69	77
	13	R	28	aaa	BOS	52	3.84	1.46	6.59	5.3	7.6	1.5	0.4	30	73	71
De Leon,Jorge	13	R	26	a/a	HOU	68	4.12	1.14	6.53	2.4	5.2	2.2	1.0	25	67	54
De los Santos,Fra	12	L	25	a/a	TAM	81	2.40	1.39	6.69	2.7	4.7	1.7	0.3	31	83	54
	13	L	26	aaa	TAM	32	6.36	1.81	5.7	4.0	4.8	1.2	0.9	36	64	18
De Paula,Jose	13	L	23	aa	SD	75	4.29	1.39	22.5	1.3	6.0	4.6	0.3	36	68	116
Dean,Pat	13	L	24	a/a	MIN	165	4.58	1.43	25	1.2	3.7	3.1	0.6	34	68	60
Degrom,Jacob	13	R	25	a/a	NYM	136	4.52	1.51	24.5	2.7	5.9	2.2	0.6	35	70	59
Delcarmen,Manny	12	R	30	aaa	NYY	57	6.48	2.24	7.39	6.8	6.8	1.0	1.2	39	72	12
	13	R	31	aaa	BAL	54	4.12	1.60	4.97	4.4	5.6	1.3	0.7	32	75	37
Delgado,Ramon	13	R	27	a/a	STL	31	3.69	1.23	6.34	1.5	6.0	3.9	0.6	32	70	102
Delgado,Randall	12	R	22	aaa	ATL	44	4.47	1.61	24.5	4.1	9.2	2.3	1.2	36	75	64
	13	R	23	aaa	ARI	64	5.63	1.58	21.7	4.3	6.8	1.6	1.1	32	66	38
DeMark,Mike	12	R	29	aaa	ARI	69	4.50	1.64	5.78	2.6	6.1	2.4	0.7	37	73	57
	13	R	30	aa	OAK	39	7.09	1.97	5.97	5.3	5.6	1.1	1.0	37	63	17
Demel,Sam	12	R	27	aaa	ARI	66	4.17	1.31	4.9	2.8	7.9	2.8	1.5	30	74	66
	13	R	28	aaa	NYY	52	2.61	1.51	6.48	4.7	8.4	1.8	0.8	32	86	67
Demny,Paul	12	R	23	aa	WAS	124	6.53	1.75	20.2	4.2	5.8	1.4	1.0	35	63	25
	13	R	24	a/a	WAS	89	6.18	1.55	20.4	3.4	7.5	2.2	1.2	34	61	51
Dennick,Ryan	12	L	25	aa	KC	74	5.61	1.45	10.5	3.7	6.9	1.8	1.1	31	62	48
	13	L	26	a/a	CIN	123	5.43	1.60	20.1	2.9	4.6	1.6	1.1	34	68	21
DeSclafani,Anthoi	13	R	23	aa	MIA	75	4.34	1.39	24.3	1.9	6.7	3.6	1.0	34	71	83
DeVries,Cole	12	R	27	aaa	MIN	70	5.99	1.54	25.4	1.5	4.9	3.4	1.0	36	61	59
	13	R	28	a/a	MIN	66	7.09	1.91	24	2.2	3.6	1.6	1.3	39	63	-2
Diamond,Scott	12	L	26	aaa	MIN	35	3.48	1.49	24.9	2.0	5.3	2.6	0.3	36	76	71
	13	L	27	aaa	MIN	41	2.92	1.20	27.5	2.1	3.2	1.5	0.9	26	80	28
Diaz,Jose	12	R	28	aaa	PIT	45	4.87	1.69	4.95	4.1	5.3	1.3	0.7	34	71	34
	13	R	29	aaa	CIN	54	2.46	1.34	5.13	4.1	7.5	1.8	1.3	27	89	52
Diekman,Jake	12	L	25	aaa	PHI	27	2.23	1.41	4.51	4.8	10.2	2.1	0.0	34	82	114
	13	L	26	aaa	PHI	30	6.87	2.07	4.89	7.6	8.9	1.2	0.3	39	64	62
Dillard,Tim	12	R	29	a/a	MIL	19	12.00	2.85	6.45	5.1	6.1	1.2	2.8	48	60	-56
	13	R	30	aaa	MIL	47	5.64	1.78	5.69	5.5	4.2	0.8	0.5	32	67	22

PITCHER	yr	t	age	lvl	org	ip	era	whip	bf/g	ctl	dom	cmd	hr/9	h%	s%	bpv
Doran,Robert	13	R	24	a/a	HOU	138	4.01	1.35	18.6	2.5	5.1	2.0	1.0	30	73	41
Dott,Aaron	13	L	25	aa	NYY	46	6.30	1.83	5.98	3.4	8.6	2.5	0.8	42	65	67
Doyle,John	12	R	27	aaa	CHW	76	4.40	1.26	26	2.8	6.7	2.4	1.0	29	67	66
	13	R	28	a/a	BOS	149	6.80	1.76	23.6	3.8	5.1	1.3	1.2	35	62	14
Drake,Oliver	12	R	25	aa	BAL	18	1.90	0.77	21.6	2.1	6.0	2.8	0.6	18	80	99
	13	R	26	aa	BAL	31	2.18	1.19	6.55	4.0	8.7	2.1	0.4	27	83	99
Duffy,Danny	13	L	25	a/a	KC	69	5.06	1.60	19.1	4.1	8.9	2.2	1.0	36	69	68
Dunning,Jake	12	R	24	aa	SF	68	5.05	1.61	6.84	3.0	5.9	2.0	0.2	37	66	62
	13	R	25	aaa	SF	48	1.40	1.27	5.82	2.3	6.7	2.9	0.4	32	91	91
Dwyer,Christophe	12	L	24	a/a	KC	136	6.64	1.74	23.9	4.4	5.5	1.3	1.4	33	64	10
	13	L	25	aaa	KC	160	4.50	1.53	23.9	4.2	5.0	1.2	0.9	30	72	28
Dyson,Sam	12	R	24	aa	TOR	45	3.08	1.35	5.73	3.0	3.6	1.2	0.5	28	78	34
	13	R	25	a/a	MIA	106	3.51	1.49	21.8	3.5	4.2	1.2	0.1	32	74	46
Edlefsen,Steve	12	R	27	aaa	SF	38	3.72	1.39	4.57	4.0	5.4	1.3	0.5	28	73	50
	13	R	28	aaa	SF	53	6.32	1.99	5.42	7.4	5.5	0.7	0.4	34	66	33
Egan,Patrick	12	R	28	a/a	BAL	67	2.53	1.40	7.25	2.1	5.4	2.6	0.2	34	81	77
	13	R	29	a/a	ATL	73	4.14	1.55	5.94	2.6	5.3	2.0	0.6	35	74	49
Eitel,Derek	12	R	25	aa	ARI	150	5.66	1.71	25.2	3.2	4.4	1.4	1.3	34	69	8
	13	R	26	aa	ARI	68	5.00	1.28	6.67	4.0	6.3	1.6	1.3	25	64	42
Ekstrom,Mike	12	R	29	aaa	COL	57	3.22	1.38	5.57	3.1	6.3	2.0	0.0	33	74	82
	13	R	30	aaa	LAA	56	4.97	1.70	6.66	3.0	5.9	2.0	0.6	37	70	48
Elias,Roenis	13	L	25	aa	SEA	130	4.24	1.49	25.5	3.9	7.1	1.9	0.7	33	72	60
Ellis,Shaun	13	R	27	aa	CIN	60	6.45	1.85	10.8	4.3	4.1	1.0	1.2	34	66	-1
Enright,Barry	12	R	26	aaa	LAA	163	4.58	1.41	23.8	3.4	4.6	1.3	0.9	29	69	29
	13	R	27	aaa	LAA	116	6.49	1.74	22.1	3.3	4.8	1.5	1.7	34	66	-3
Eppley,Cody	13	R	28	aaa	MIN	43	8.02	2.23	5.3	6.4	6.1	1.0	0.2	41	61	35
Erlin,Robert	12	L	22	aa	SD	52	2.76	1.26	19.4	2.2	11.1	5.1	0.8	37	81	152
	13	L	23	aaa	SD	99	4.47	1.54	21.7	2.7	6.7	2.5	0.7	36	72	63
Escobar,Edwin	13	L	21	aa	SF	54	2.52	1.03	20.8	1.9	7.8	4.1	0.2	29	75	136
Espino,Paolo	12	R	25	a/a	CLE	123	4.16	1.55	22.4	2.9	6.7	2.3	0.7	36	74	61
	13	R	26	a/a	CLE	141	5.75	1.64	19.7	2.9	7.2	2.5	1.1	37	66	54
Evans,Bryan	12	R	25	aa	MIA	135	5.92	1.69	21.1	4.7	5.6	1.2	1.0	33	65	26
	13	R	26	aa	MIA	79	4.56	1.32	15.5	1.0	7.9	8.2	1.2	36	69	177
Faulk,Kenny	12	L	25	aa	DET	58	5.72	1.77	6.62	5.1	8.2	1.6	0.9	37	68	52
	13	L	26	aaa	DET	44	4.90	1.47	5.95	6.6	8.0	1.2	0.7	25	67	65
Feierabend,Ryan	12	L	27	aaa	CIN	35	8.71	2.14	24.6	4.8	5.1	1.1	3.9	34	69	-81
	13	L	28	a/a	TEX	148	5.46	1.74	23.3	2.7	4.5	1.7	1.3	36	71	11
Ferguson,Andrew	13	R	25	aa	KC	96	6.38	1.58	12.4	3.6	6.2	1.7	1.1	33	60	37
Fernandez,Anthoı	12	L	22	aa	SEA	76	3.84	1.41	24.7	2.9	5.9	2.1	0.7	32	74	58
	13	L	23	aa	SEA	120	5.65	1.51	23.6	3.2	4.9	1.5	1.1	31	64	26
Ferrara,Anthony	13	L	24	aa	STL	99	6.30	1.59	18.9	4.8	6.4	1.3	1.3	30	62	26
Fick,Chuckie	12	R	27	aaa	HOU	46	5.43	1.61	4.33	3.0	3.6	1.2	1.2	32	68	5
	13	R	28	aaa	COL	32	7.10	2.22	7.25	5.9	3.5	0.6	0.7	38	67	-6
Fife,Stephen	12	R	26	aaa	LA	135	4.25	1.50	23.4	2.7	5.0	1.9	0.7	33	72	42
	13	R	27	aaa	LA	37	6.35	1.94	17.8	5.0	6.2	1.2	0.7	38	66	31
Figueroa,Eduardc	13	R	25	aa	CHC	34	2.91	1.26	23.1	2.3	3.7	1.6	0.9	27	81	32
Figueroa,Pedro	12	L	27	aaa	OAK	45	2.86	1.31	5.77	3.7	6.3	1.7	0.2	29	77	74
	13	L	28	aaa	OAK	59	4.54	1.70	5.84	5.3	5.6	1.1	1.2	31	77	18
Fisher,Carlos	12	R	29	aaa	CIN	66	6.23	2.09	6.26	8.7	6.6	0.8	1.2	32	71	19
	13	R	30	aa	TAM	57	5.02	1.85	6.3	7.0	9.3	1.3	0.9	35	74	58
Fitzgerald,Justin	12	R	26	aa	SF	165	4.14	1.39	24.7	3.5	5.7	1.6	0.4	30	69	58
	13	R	27	a/a	SF	110	4.34	1.53	23.9	3.2	6.8	2.1	0.9	34	73	55
Flande,Yohan	12	L	26	aaa	ATL	148	5.04	1.61	22.6	3.5	5.3	1.5	0.7	34	69	37
	13	L	27	a/a	ATL	136	5.86	1.80	19.6	3.5	5.0	1.4	0.7	37	67	27
Fleet,Austin	12	R	25	aa	SF	56	4.82	1.92	6.52	3.5	7.1	2.0	0.0	43	72	70
	13	R	26	aaa	SF	61	3.39	1.28	19.3	2.3	5.5	2.4	1.2	29	79	50
Fleming,Marquis	12	R	26	a/a	TAM	76	5.20	1.59	7.01	5.2	7.5	1.4	0.9	31	68	49
	13	R	27	aa	TAM	92	6.20	1.74	10.2	3.4	6.9	2.0	1.0	38	64	43
Floethe,Jake	13	R	24	aa	TAM	51	6.57	1.96	24.2	4.7	4.8	1.0	0.7	37	65	17
Flores,Jose	13	R	24	aa	CLE	66	2.93	1.28	4.61	3.3	9.9	3.0	0.1	34	75	124
Flynn,Brian	12	L	22	aa	MIA	50	5.16	1.59	24.5	2.9	5.8	2.0	0.8	35	68	47
	13	L	23	a/a	MIA	161	3.38	1.37	25	2.7	7.5	2.8	0.6	34	76	86
Foltynewicz,Mike	13	R	22	aa	HOU	103	3.18	1.28	18.4	4.4	7.4	1.7	0.7	26	77	69
Font,Wilmer	12	R	22	aa	TEX	15	3.89	1.19	6.01	4.3	14.6	3.4	0.8	34	69	149
	13	R	23	a/a	TEX	52	1.38	1.19	4.97	6.2	10.1	1.6	0.5	21	91	105
Fornataro,Eric	12	R	24	aa	STL	68	2.65	1.16	4.72	2.2	4.5	2.0	0.1	28	75	71
	13	R	25	aaa	STL	55	6.82	1.76	6.85	3.8	5.1	1.3	0.8	36	60	26
Fox,Matt	12	R	30	a/a	SEA	20	6.33	1.71	18.4	3.4	4.1	1.2	0.4	35	61	28
	13	R	31	aaa	NYM	112	4.46	1.56	24.4	2.1	4.6	2.2	0.8	35	72	41
Francescon,P.J.	13	R	24	aa	CHC	30	5.03	1.52	8.14	5.0	5.3	1.1	0.7	29	67	38
Francis,Jeff	12	L	31	aaa	CIN	77	5.09	1.70	29.1	2.4	5.7	2.4	1.0	38	71	41
	13	L	32	aaa	COL	37	5.34	1.66	15.2	2.3	5.5	2.4	0.3	38	66	61
Fraser,Ryan	12	R	24	aa	NYM	34	3.87	1.34	5.38	3.4	5.7	1.7	0.3	30	69	65
	13	R	25	aa	NYM	38	6.14	2.15	7.05	5.9	4.9	0.8	1.0	38	72	4
Frazier,Parker	12	R	24	aa	COL	167	6.26	1.75	28.3	2.5	3.9	1.6	1.8	35	68	-12
	13	R	25	a/a	CIN	73	5.52	1.86	8.95	4.2	5.6	1.3	0.7	37	70	29
Freeman,Sam	12	L	25	a/a	STL	48	2.10	1.22	4.58	3.1	5.9	1.9	0.7	27	86	62
	13	L	26	aaa	STL	70	3.44	1.36	5.94	3.6	6.7	1.8	0.5	30	75	68
Friend,Justin	12	R	26	a/a	PHI	54	1.70	1.36	4.51	3.2	7.2	2.2	0.2	33	88	87
	13	R	27	a/a	PHI	73	5.17	1.76	7	6.1	5.7	0.9	1.1	30	73	19
Froneberger,Isaia	13	L	24	aa	COL	37	5.78	2.06	5.47	7.5	7.6	1.0	1.2	36	74	26
Gagnon,Drew	13	R	23	aa	MIL	84	7.05	1.85	24.5	4.8	5.4	1.1	1.7	34	64	-3
Gailey,Frank	12	L	27	a/a	PHI	30	5.93	2.05	5.35	4.0	6.2	1.5	0.8	42	71	30
	13	L	28	aa	OAK	62	3.20	1.34	6.62	1.8	6.0	3.4	0.4	34	76	91
Galarraga,Armanı	12	R	30	aaa	HOU	44	4.66	1.46	20.7	4.0	4.8	1.2	1.5	27	73	11
	13	R	31	aaa	COL	121	4.49	1.65	23.5	3.7	4.3	1.2	1.2	32	76	8
Gallagher,Sean	12	R	27	aaa	CIN	139	6.35	1.78	24.6	5.2	4.3	0.8	1.6	30	67	-9
	13	R	28	a/a	COL	114	5.41	1.69	27.1	4.0	4.5	1.1	1.7	31	72	-6

PITCHER	yr	t	age	lvl	org	ip	era	whip	bf/g	ctl	dom	cmd	hr/9	h%	s%	bpv
Gamboa,Eduardo	12	R	28	a/a	BAL	109	5.64	1.75	18.4	2.1	5.0	2.3	1.0	38	68	35
	13	R	29	a/a	BAL	142	6.14	1.62	25.3	4.3	5.3	1.2	0.7	32	61	34
Garcia,Freddy	13	R	37	aaa	ATL	86	4.85	1.49	26.5	2.4	4.9	2.0	1.4	32	71	25
Garcia,Onelki	13	L	24	a/a	LA	62	3.23	1.39	7.45	5.0	8.1	1.6	0.4	29	77	79
Garcia,Ramon	12	L	28	a/a	DET	159	6.44	1.73	25	2.4	4.2	1.7	1.4	35	65	4
	13	L	29	a/a	DET	138	8.04	1.78	25.4	2.0	4.4	2.2	1.7	37	56	4
Garcia,Yimi	13	R	23	aa	LA	60	3.17	0.92	4.61	2.2	10.8	5.0	1.6	24	76	140
Gardner,Joe	12	R	24	aa	COL	138	6.50	1.59	21.8	3.0	5.0	1.7	1.5	33	61	13
	13	R	25	aa	COL	55	8.39	1.61	7	3.3	7.4	2.2	1.6	35	47	37
Garrido,Santiago	13	R	24	a/a	KC	63	3.87	1.63	6.96	5.7	5.8	1.0	0.7	29	77	37
Garrison,Steve	12	L	26	a/a	SEA	125	5.65	1.60	23	1.8	3.5	2.0	1.2	34	66	14
	13	L	27	aa	ARI	44	4.92	1.59	4.1	3.3	7.8	2.4	1.8	35	75	39
Gast,John	12	L	23	a/a	STL	161	4.37	1.43	24.4	3.0	6.0	2.0	0.8	32	70	54
	13	L	24	aaa	STL	39	1.29	1.14	21.9	3.0	6.7	2.2	0.0	28	87	97
Gausman,Kevin J	13	R	22	a/a	BAL	82	4.19	1.28	21	1.5	7.7	5.0	0.5	35	67	134
Geer,Josh	12	R	29	a/a	SD	160	5.41	1.68	25.7	2.1	4.5	2.2	0.7	37	68	38
	13	R	30	a/a	SD	104	4.01	1.64	13.3	2.4	5.3	2.2	0.9	36	78	40
Geltz,Steve	12	R	25	a/a	LAA	59	3.27	1.10	5.03	2.8	8.8	3.1	0.5	28	71	114
	13	R	26	aaa	TAM	67	3.36	0.98	6.22	3.3	8.7	2.6	1.1	21	71	94
Germano,Justin	12	R	30	aaa	BOS	105	3.80	1.26	25.2	1.4	4.5	3.3	1.8	28	79	41
	13	R	31	aaa	TOR	151	6.32	1.84	28.1	1.8	4.5	2.5	1.0	40	66	31
Germen,Gonzalez	12	R	25	a/a	NYM	127	5.18	1.47	25.9	2.4	5.9	2.4	0.8	34	65	57
	13	R	26	aaa	NYM	44	4.96	1.32	5.2	2.0	8.5	4.3	1.2	34	65	103
Gibson,Kyle	13	R	26	aaa	MIN	102	3.45	1.33	24.8	3.1	6.1	2.0	0.4	30	74	68
Gil,Jerry	12	0	30	aaa	TOR	64	5.88	1.63	4.92	2.9	5.3	1.8	1.3	34	66	21
	13	0	31	aaa	CLE	48	5.95	1.82	7.13	5.9	5.7	1.0	0.7	33	67	30
Gillheeney,James	12	L	25	aa	SEA	28	4.70	1.76	25.9	4.1	7.3	1.8	0.9	37	75	45
	13	L	26	a/a	SEA	136	4.86	1.47	22.4	3.4	4.9	1.5	1.2	30	70	22
Gilliam,Robert	12	R	25	aa	WAS	85	7.96	1.76	19.4	3.9	6.3	1.6	1.1	36	53	30
	13	R	26	aa	WAS	90	5.62	1.55	20.7	3.8	5.9	1.6	1.1	32	65	34
Gilmartin,Sean	12	L	22	a/a	ATL	157	4.48	1.33	24.1	2.2	5.7	2.6	0.9	31	68	61
	13	L	23	aaa	ATL	91	6.78	1.77	24.5	3.3	5.6	1.7	1.2	37	62	21
Gloor,Christopher	12	L	25	aa	SF	106	3.53	1.40	13.9	2.6	5.2	2.0	0.6	32	75	54
	13	L	26	aa	SF	156	4.18	1.40	25.4	2.3	5.6	2.5	0.7	33	71	61
Godfrey,Graham	12	R	28	aaa	OAK	104	3.68	1.37	21.8	2.4	3.9	1.7	0.6	30	74	38
	13	R	29	aaa	PIT	119	5.10	1.57	16.3	2.7	4.0	1.5	1.3	32	70	10
Goeddel,Erik	13	R	25	aa	NYM	134	4.76	1.55	23.4	3.8	7.0	1.9	1.0	33	71	50
Goforth,David	13	R	25	aa	MIL	47	4.33	1.27	9.55	3.9	5.8	1.5	0.3	27	64	67
Gomez,Leuris	13	R	27	aa	COL	42	2.02	1.33	7.02	4.0	8.7	2.2	0.0	32	83	105
Gonzalez,Jose	12	L	22	aa	MIN	16	3.89	1.13	4.86	4.5	8.2	1.8	0.5	23	65	90
	13	L	23	aa	MIN	40	6.82	1.89	6.03	4.7	6.7	1.4	0.8	38	63	34
Gonzalez,Juan	13	R	23	aa	COL	46	3.11	1.33	4.94	1.7	5.3	3.1	1.2	31	83	57
Gorgen,Matthew	12	R	25	a/a	ARI	62	3.24	1.37	5.42	3.5	8.4	2.4	0.6	33	78	85
	13	R	26	a/a	ARI	58	6.17	1.69	5.66	3.8	6.4	1.7	1.4	35	66	25
Gorski,Darin	12	L	25	aa	NYM	140	4.54	1.40	23.6	3.2	6.4	2.0	1.4	30	72	39
	13	L	26	a/a	NYM	92	2.52	1.05	19.9	2.8	5.9	2.1	0.2	25	75	87
Gould,Garrett	13	R	22	aa	LA	41	7.20	1.54	16.4	3.3	8.5	2.6	1.2	36	53	65
Grace,Matt	13	L	25	aa	WAS	38	4.74	1.51	5.87	1.6	5.8	3.5	0.5	37	68	84
Gracey,Scott	12	R	26	aa	TOR	26	5.14	1.83	10.1	5.2	5.0	1.0	0.5	35	71	29
	13	R	27	a/a	TOR	36	3.56	1.55	5.82	4.0	7.8	2.0	0.0	36	74	86
Graham,Caleb	12	R	25	a/a	LAA	59	3.12	1.12	4.71	2.6	8.5	3.3	0.7	29	74	110
	13	R	26	aa	LAA	45	4.73	1.56	4.25	4.1	6.2	1.5	0.8	32	70	43
Graham,J.R.	12	R	22	aa	ATL	45	3.93	1.27	20.6	3.4	7.4	2.2	0.4	30	68	84
	13	R	23	aa	ATL	36	5.20	1.59	19.7	2.6	6.2	2.3	0.0	38	64	78
Granier,Drew	13	R	25	aa	OAK	72	5.99	1.90	24.4	5.4	5.7	1.0	1.0	35	69	16
Gray,Sonny	12	R	23	aa	OAK	152	4.43	1.48	24.2	3.3	5.0	1.5	0.4	32	69	48
	13	R	24	aaa	OAK	118	3.48	1.37	24.8	2.9	7.4	2.6	0.3	34	74	90
Greene,Shane	13	R	25	a/a	NYY	79	4.29	1.72	25.7	2.5	6.2	2.5	1.0	39	77	49
Greenwood,Nick	12	L	25	aaa	STL	78	4.85	1.56	6.94	2.7	4.4	1.6	0.7	34	69	34
	13	L	26	a/a	STL	95	5.63	1.73	13.1	2.9	3.4	1.2	1.1	34	69	1
Grimm,Justin	12	R	24	a/a	TEX	135	3.55	1.32	22.3	2.1	5.5	2.7	0.4	32	73	76
	13	R	25	aaa	CHC	48	5.23	1.65	23.8	3.8	6.9	1.8	0.2	37	66	68
Guerra,Javy	13	R	28	aaa	LA	39	3.94	1.71	6.59	3.3	6.3	1.9	1.4	36	82	28
Guilmet,Preston	12	R	25	aa	CLE	53	3.35	1.25	4.29	2.4	7.1	3.0	0.9	31	76	83
	13	R	26	aaa	CLE	64	2.22	1.07	5.1	2.1	8.1	3.9	0.7	28	82	119
Gurka,Jason	12	L	24	a/a	BAL	20	4.46	1.75	7.61	5.6	8.1	1.4	1.7	33	80	26
	13	L	25	aa	BAL	40	3.61	1.52	8.61	4.3	8.4	2.0	0.6	34	77	75
Gustafson,Timoth	12	R	28	a/a	CIN	132	7.58	1.97	19.8	4.5	4.9	1.1	1.7	36	63	-14
	13	R	29	aa	COL	146	8.97	2.04	26.4	4.0	4.5	1.1	1.7	38	56	-17
Haeger,Charlie	13	R	30	a/a	BOS	142	6.02	2.00	27.4	6.2	5.3	0.9	1.4	34	72	-2
Hagadone,Nick	13	L	27	aaa	CLE	32	3.39	1.52	5.2	5.2	10.1	1.9	0.3	35	77	96
Hagens,Bradin	13	R	24	aa	ARI	148	4.85	1.72	25.8	4.3	4.7	1.1	0.8	33	72	21
Hale,David	12	R	25	aa	ATL	146	4.96	1.52	23.4	4.5	6.4	1.4	0.8	31	68	47
	13	R	26	aaa	ATL	115	4.05	1.64	23.2	3.0	4.9	1.6	0.7	35	76	35
Haley,Trey	12	R	22	aa	CLE	15	2.32	1.51	7.38	6.6	11.8	1.8	0.0	34	83	120
	13	R	23	aa	CLE	44	4.98	1.73	5.13	7.4	8.0	1.1	0.0	32	68	77
Hall,Brooks	13	R	23	aa	MIL	61	5.07	1.67	16	3.6	5.0	1.4	1.6	33	74	6
Hallock,Kyle	13	L	25	a/a	HOU	49	8.36	1.77	11.2	5.7	3.7	0.6	1.8	28	53	-21
Hamren,Erik	12	R	26	a/a	SD	62	3.61	1.51	4.63	4.7	9.0	1.9	0.4	34	76	84
	13	R	27	aa	TAM	64	3.68	1.67	6.42	4.5	8.4	1.9	0.4	37	78	73
Hand,Brad	12	L	22	aaa	MIA	148	4.65	1.51	23.8	4.8	7.9	1.6	0.9	31	71	58
	13	L	23	aaa	MIA	82	4.37	1.62	24.2	5.6	8.1	1.5	0.9	32	74	56
Hand,Donovan	12	R	26	aaa	MIL	80	5.18	1.68	8.14	2.3	5.0	2.2	1.1	36	71	30
	13	R	27	aaa	MIL	36	3.97	1.48	7.67	3.0	7.7	2.5	1.3	34	78	59
Hankins,Derek	12	R	29	aaa	TEX	83	6.61	1.96	11.3	3.5	3.9	1.1	1.6	37	69	-19
	13	R	30	a/a	DET	104	4.31	1.58	26.8	2.5	3.3	1.3	1.3	32	77	0
Hardy,Blaine	12	L	25	a/a	KC	75	3.99	1.72	8.55	3.7	5.5	1.5	1.0	35	80	24
	13	L	26	a/a	DET	92	2.19	1.19	12.3	3.2	5.9	1.8	0.9	25	87	55

PITCHER	yr	t	age	lvl	org	ip	era	whip	bf/g	ctl	dom	cmd	hr/9	h%	s%	bpv
Harper,Ryne	13	R	24	aa	ATL	55	2.35	1.38	5.67	3.1	7.5	2.4	0.6	33	85	80
Hatcher,Chris	12	R	27	aaa	MIA	47	0.99	1.25	5.17	3.4	7.2	2.1	0.2	30	93	89
	13	R	28	aaa	MIA	67	5.14	1.87	5.27	4.7	7.1	1.5	1.3	37	76	24
Hatley,Marcus	12	R	24	a/a	CHC	60	5.43	1.47	6.47	4.6	8.0	1.7	0.5	32	61	74
	13	R	25	a/a	CHC	61	4.70	1.65	5.53	5.5	9.0	1.6	0.5	35	71	75
Hauser,Matthew	12	R	24	aa	MIN	16	4.05	1.57	7.02	2.3	3.7	1.6	1.7	32	81	-4
	13	R	25	aa	MIN	39	6.97	1.56	6.57	2.9	6.5	2.3	1.3	34	56	40
Hayes,Andrew	12	R	25	aa	CIN	63	4.82	1.73	5.14	6.0	7.5	1.3	0.6	33	72	53
Hayes,Drew	13	R	26	aa	CIN	63	7.92	2.11	6.09	5.3	7.1	1.3	1.5	40	63	9
Heaney,Andrew	13	L	22	aa	MIA	34	3.72	1.37	23.5	2.7	5.7	2.1	0.6	32	73	61
Heath,Deunte	12	R	27	aaa	CHW	67	2.30	1.35	7.77	3.6	8.0	2.2	0.9	31	88	72
	13	R	28	aaa	CHW	45	3.14	1.46	6.42	3.6	5.6	1.6	0.3	32	78	58
Heckathorn,Kyle	12	R	24	aa	MIL	119	6.05	1.62	15.1	3.1	5.7	1.9	0.7	35	61	45
	13	R	25	aaa	MIL	65	4.17	1.38	5.69	4.5	5.3	1.2	0.8	26	71	39
Heidenreich,Matt	12	R	21	aa	HOU	53	4.80	1.53	20.9	1.9	5.4	2.8	0.5	36	68	67
	13	R	22	aa	HOU	55	9.12	1.94	10.4	2.6	5.0	1.9	1.7	39	53	0
Hellweg,John	12	R	24	aa	MIL	140	4.19	1.62	22.1	5.2	5.8	1.1	0.7	31	75	39
	13	R	25	aaa	MIL	126	3.65	1.61	24.2	6.0	5.3	0.9	0.5	28	78	40
Hembree,Heath	12	R	23	aaa	SF	38	4.27	1.21	3.93	4.1	7.3	1.8	0.3	26	63	84
	13	R	24	aaa	SF	55	3.75	1.25	4.17	2.3	8.6	3.7	0.8	33	72	109
Hendricks,Kyle	13	R	24	a/a	CHC	166	2.39	1.20	24.8	1.9	5.8	3.0	0.3	31	80	93
Hendriks,Liam	12	R	23	aaa	MIN	106	2.77	1.12	26.2	2.5	5.8	2.3	0.4	27	76	80
	13	R	24	aaa	MIN	98	5.29	1.47	26.4	1.4	4.7	3.4	0.8	35	64	67
Henn,Sean	12	L	31	aaa	SEA	30	3.86	1.79	9.13	3.5	6.8	1.9	0.3	40	77	62
	13	L	32	aaa	NYM	58	2.73	1.69	5	4.8	5.8	1.2	0.0	35	82	57
Henry,Randy	13	R	23	aa	TEX	51	1.50	0.93	6.14	1.3	5.8	4.4	0.3	26	85	130
Hensley,Steven	12	R	26	a/a	SEA	71	5.33	1.51	6.96	5.1	6.2	1.2	0.9	28	65	40
	13	R	27	a/a	COL	51	5.68	1.94	5.92	5.6	6.6	1.2	2.1	34	77	-7
Hermsen,BJ	12	R	23	aa	MIN	140	3.79	1.36	26.6	1.6	4.0	2.5	0.8	32	74	49
	13	R	24	aa	MIN	86	5.47	1.87	13.4	3.0	3.0	1.0	0.6	37	70	6
Hernandez,Carlos	12	L	25	a/a	OAK	102	5.53	1.61	14.6	2.7	5.8	2.2	1.2	35	67	37
	13	L	26	a/a	OAK	152	2.97	1.35	21.8	2.5	5.0	2.0	0.3	31	78	62
Hernandez,Chris	12	L	24	a/a	BOS	146	4.53	1.61	24.9	3.5	4.5	1.3	0.8	33	73	24
	13	L	25	aaa	BOS	135	6.14	1.89	22	4.2	4.3	1.0	0.9	36	67	8
Hernandez,Moise	12	R	28	aa	SEA	50	8.77	2.31	8.02	6.4	2.4	0.4	1.0	37	61	-23
	13	R	29	aa	SEA	47	7.25	1.73	9.31	4.0	3.0	0.8	1.2	32	58	-10
Hernandez,Pedro	12	L	23	a/a	MIN	103	4.04	1.47	23.2	2.0	4.8	2.4	0.7	34	73	51
	13	L	24	a/a	MIN	57	4.30	1.49	24.6	2.4	5.1	2.1	1.2	33	75	33
Herron,Tyler	13	R	27	aa	WAS	46	4.06	1.68	6.32	4.2	8.5	2.0	0.5	38	76	74
Heston,Chris	12	R	24	aa	SF	149	2.75	1.25	24.2	2.5	6.8	2.8	0.1	32	76	99
	13	R	25	aaa	SF	109	5.46	1.61	25.4	3.4	6.6	1.9	0.8	35	66	49
Hill,Nicholas	13	L	28	a/a	SEA	53	2.70	1.57	5.25	4.5	6.5	1.4	0.0	34	81	70
Hill,Shawn	12	R	31	aaa	TOR	90	5.40	1.84	27.8	2.3	3.8	1.7	1.2	38	72	6
	13	R	32	aaa	DET	150	8.00	2.08	28.3	3.2	3.5	1.1	1.3	39	62	-17
Hill,Taylor	13	R	24	a/a	WAS	80	3.41	1.43	26.2	1.9	4.5	2.4	0.8	33	79	46
Hoffman,Matthew	12	L	24	aaa	DET	46	4.61	1.75	4.92	3.1	4.9	1.6	0.9	37	75	25
	13	L	25	aaa	DET	35	2.70	1.59	3.86	4.2	6.9	1.6	0.6	34	85	56
Holland,Neil	13	R	25	aa	WAS	51	3.56	1.35	5.15	1.9	8.8	4.6	0.6	37	74	128
Hollands,Mario	12	L	24	a/a	PHI	60	6.96	1.93	23.8	4.2	4.8	1.1	1.4	36	65	-3
	13	L	25	aa	PHI	63	4.85	1.59	21.3	2.9	6.2	2.2	0.9	35	71	48
Holle,Gregory	13	R	25	a/a	MIL	66	4.73	1.59	5.46	3.7	6.0	1.6	0.4	35	69	55
Hollingsworth,Eth	12	R	25	a/a	KC	103	5.55	1.69	13.6	2.6	4.6	1.7	0.7	36	67	32
	13	R	26	a/a	PIT	94	4.38	1.30	14.8	2.0	3.8	1.9	1.1	28	69	30
Holmberg,David	12	L	21	aa	ARI	95	4.34	1.47	27.2	2.1	5.5	2.6	0.9	34	72	56
	13	L	22	aa	ARI	157	3.69	1.38	25.4	2.9	5.7	2.0	0.9	31	76	50
Hooker,James	12	R	23	aa	STL	48	4.67	1.53	5.64	3.1	6.8	2.2	0.9	34	70	56
	13	R	24	a/a	STL	68	4.51	1.21	5.05	2.4	8.2	3.5	0.7	31	63	104
Hottovy,Tommy	12	L	31	aaa	KC	50	3.05	1.38	5.13	3.1	7.8	2.5	1.1	32	83	68
	13	L	32	a/a	TOR	43	5.74	1.85	4.79	4.0	6.5	1.6	1.1	38	70	27
House,T.J.	12	L	23	aa	CLE	124	5.34	1.48	23.3	3.3	5.6	1.7	0.6	32	63	49
	13	L	24	a/a	CLE	164	4.87	1.62	26	3.1	6.3	2.0	0.7	36	70	53
Houston,Daniel	12	R	26	aa	COL	161	6.38	1.81	27.7	2.6	4.0	1.6	1.7	36	68	-9
	13	R	27	a/a	COL	105	4.58	1.56	14	3.1	4.5	1.5	0.9	33	72	26
Hoyt,James	13	R	27	aa	ATL	33	3.48	1.13	5.86	4.1	7.3	1.8	0.3	24	68	87
Hubbard,Austin	13	R	25	a/a	TAM	32	10.28	2.12	5.51	6.9	4.6	0.7	2.2	32	52	-34
Huchingson,Chas	13	L	24	aa	NYM	67	1.72	1.31	6.15	3.7	7.8	2.1	0.5	30	90	81
Huff,David	12	L	28	a/a	CLE	138	6.52	1.73	25.1	2.5	4.1	1.6	2.1	34	67	-18
	13	L	29	aaa	NYY	92	6.05	1.76	19.2	2.6	6.6	2.5	1.3	39	67	41
Hultzen,Danny	12	L	23	a/a	SEA	124	3.15	1.33	20.6	5.2	8.8	1.7	0.2	28	75	94
	13	L	24	aaa	SEA	31	2.00	0.86	18.8	1.9	8.7	4.5	0.2	25	77	156
Humber,Philip	13	R	31	aaa	HOU	50	5.98	1.86	11.7	3.7	5.2	1.4	1.5	36	71	2
Hunter,Brett	12	R	25	aa	OAK	56	5.06	1.64	5.95	5.1	7.8	1.5	1.0	33	71	48
	13	R	26	aa	OAK	32	3.96	1.21	5.61	5.6	9.4	1.7	0.3	24	65	104
Hunter,Kyle	13	L	24	aa	SEA	58	1.83	1.29	6.97	2.7	5.8	2.1	0.4	30	87	73
Huntzinger,Brock	12	R	24	a/a	BOS	74	5.58	1.45	7.89	3.3	5.9	1.8	0.6	32	60	55
	13	R	25	a/a	BOS	69	2.39	1.34	5.83	3.9	6.5	1.7	0.4	29	83	67
Hyde,Lee	12	L	27	a/a	NYY	44	5.33	1.69	4.05	5.5	6.9	1.3	0.6	33	68	50
	13	L	28	a/a	CIN	55	2.94	1.37	4.17	3.5	4.8	1.4	0.3	30	78	54
Hynes,Colt	12	L	27	aaa	SD	127	5.27	1.79	19.5	1.9	4.3	2.2	0.6	39	70	38
	13	L	28	a/a	SD	47	1.67	1.10	4.52	0.4	8.7	21.9	0.2	36	85	509
Hynick,Brandon	12	R	27	a/a	COL	102	4.56	1.56	26.3	2.4	4.2	1.8	1.1	33	73	21
	13	R	28	aa	LAA	142	3.61	1.27	24.1	2.3	4.8	2.1	1.1	28	75	43
Ibarra,Edgar	12	L	23	aa	MIN	34	7.23	1.80	6.49	4.1	6.3	1.5	1.6	36	61	13
	13	L	24	a/a	MIN	61	2.19	1.25	5.25	4.3	6.6	1.5	0.4	26	84	71
Ibarra,Jeffrey	12	L	25	aa	SD	24	0.75	1.18	4.81	1.8	7.6	4.2	0.0	33	93	137
	13	L	26	a/a	SD	54	7.28	1.62	4.09	2.3	7.4	3.2	0.9	39	53	75
Infante,Gregory	12	R	25	a/a	CHW	33	4.91	1.74	7.17	5.3	4.8	0.9	0.4	32	70	33
	13	R	26	a/a	LA	40	4.48	1.76	6.49	6.6	6.9	1.1	0.5	32	74	51

PITCHER	yr	t	age	lvl	org	ip	era	whip	bf/g	ctl	dom	cmd	hr/9	h%	s%	bpv
Inman,Will	12	R	25	aaa	BOS	48	3.20	1.71	6.25	7.0	9.0	1.3	0.7	32	83	65
	13	R	26	aaa	TAM	32	7.70	1.82	7.08	7.8	5.7	0.7	1.1	28	57	19
Jackson,Jay	12	R	25	aaa	CHC	86	7.54	1.91	11	4.6	6.5	1.4	1.5	37	62	12
	13	R	26	a/a	MIA	105	4.82	1.44	21.2	3.4	6.8	2.0	0.9	32	68	55
Jackson,Zach	12	L	29	aaa	TEX	158	6.86	1.96	28	3.9	3.1	0.8	1.4	36	66	-22
	13	L	30	a/a	KC	41	1.82	1.26	4.78	1.8	2.8	1.6	0.8	28	90	27
Jaime,Juan Jose	13	R	26	aa	ATL	42	5.59	1.65	5.36	6.7	12.3	1.8	0.3	38	63	111
Javier,Omar	13	R	26	aa	SF	50	5.78	1.75	8.46	4.8	6.5	1.3	1.0	34	68	32
Jenkins,Chad	12	R	25	aa	TOR	114	6.55	1.84	26.7	2.6	3.6	1.4	1.7	36	68	-16
	13	R	26	a/a	TOR	37	6.22	1.63	18.1	1.5	3.3	2.2	1.8	34	66	-2
Jimenez,Cesar	12	L	28	aaa	SEA	40	5.94	1.92	8.31	4.3	6.6	1.5	0.6	40	68	43
	13	L	29	aaa	PHI	66	4.03	1.61	8.16	4.0	6.5	1.6	0.5	35	75	55
Johnson,Blake	12	R	27	a/a	LA	72	5.10	1.50	7.37	3.5	5.3	1.5	1.0	31	67	32
	13	R	28	aaa	LA	94	5.14	1.55	18.8	2.8	6.0	2.1	0.8	35	67	52
Johnson,Cole	13	R	25	aa	MIN	39	5.09	1.43	5.92	3.6	8.9	2.5	1.3	33	68	67
Johnson,Erik	13	R	24	a/a	CHW	142	2.60	1.19	23.7	3.0	7.1	2.4	0.6	28	80	82
Johnson,Jay	12	L	23	aa	PHI	29	5.70	1.91	4.84	5.6	8.1	1.4	1.0	38	71	40
	13	L	24	a/a	PHI	55	3.51	1.64	4.46	7.2	9.3	1.3	0.4	31	78	82
Johnson,Kevin	12	R	24	a/a	LAA	63	3.87	1.46	4.85	2.1	3.7	1.8	0.9	32	75	29
	13	R	25	a/a	LAA	63	4.08	1.52	5.23	3.0	3.8	1.3	0.5	32	73	31
Johnson,Kristofer	12	L	28	a/a	PIT	102	4.26	1.60	12.8	4.0	4.8	1.2	1.0	32	75	22
	13	L	29	aaa	PIT	136	3.10	1.43	22.2	3.1	4.4	1.4	0.4	31	78	43
Johnson,Steve	12	R	25	aaa	BAL	91	4.17	1.32	19.9	3.5	6.8	1.9	1.0	28	71	56
	13	R	26	aaa	BAL	46	5.52	1.50	19.9	3.7	8.0	2.2	1.1	34	64	61
Jokisch,Eric	12	L	23	aa	CHC	105	3.51	1.27	23.9	2.9	4.6	1.6	0.7	27	74	46
	13	L	24	aa	CHC	161	4.09	1.39	25.1	3.2	6.4	2.0	0.9	31	72	57
Jones,Chris	12	L	24	aa	ATL	60	5.02	1.72	6.05	3.0	7.8	2.6	0.2	41	68	86
	13	L	25	a/a	BAL	79	3.61	1.74	10	4.4	4.9	1.1	0.4	35	79	34
Jones,Devin	13	R	23	aa	BAL	123	6.86	1.74	23.4	3.5	6.6	1.9	1.5	36	62	25
Jordan,Taylor	13	R	24	aa	WAS	54	1.02	0.96	22.7	1.4	5.8	4.0	0.0	27	88	129
Joseph,Don	12	L	25	a/a	KC	70	2.68	1.35	5.28	3.9	8.9	2.3	0.3	33	80	99
	13	L	26	aaa	KC	55	5.11	1.66	5.21	7.0	10.7	1.5	0.9	32	70	76
Judy,Josh	12	R	26	aaa	CIN	57	8.82	2.02	6.85	5.0	7.2	1.4	1.3	40	55	22
	13	R	27	a/a	LAA	35	7.15	2.03	5.1	3.7	6.0	1.6	2.0	39	69	-9
Jungmann,Taylor	13	R	24	aa	MIL	139	5.59	1.58	23.6	5.1	4.5	0.9	1.0	28	65	19
Jurrjens,Jair	12	R	26	aaa	ATL	72	5.96	1.52	22.4	2.1	4.0	1.9	1.3	33	63	17
	13	R	27	aaa	DET	134	6.26	1.71	26.4	2.7	3.8	1.4	0.7	36	62	20
Kahnle,Thomas	13	R	24	aa	NYY	60	3.77	1.57	5.73	7.2	9.1	1.3	0.8	27	78	69
Karns,Nathan	13	R	26	aa	WAS	133	4.16	1.37	24.2	3.3	8.1	2.5	1.1	31	73	69
Kasparek,Kenn	13	R	28	aa	PIT	61	4.06	1.54	6.95	2.5	4.7	1.9	0.4	35	73	48
Keck,Jonathon	12	L	24	aa	KC	42	4.80	1.70	6.84	5.7	7.2	1.2	0.4	33	71	57
	13	L	25	aa	KC	52	4.71	1.53	5.03	7.0	6.8	1.0	0.9	24	70	47
Keeling,Thomas	13	L	25	aa	ATL	42	6.28	2.15	4.57	8.8	6.4	0.7	1.5	32	73	4
Kehrt,Jeremy	12	R	27	a/a	BOS	113	6.36	1.88	19.7	2.9	4.2	1.4	1.1	38	67	6
	13	R	28	a/a	BOS	86	6.54	2.03	15.5	3.4	5.2	1.5	0.9	41	68	17
Kelly,Kenneth	12	R	24	aa	TAM	88	3.72	1.35	11.5	2.8	5.3	1.9	0.4	31	72	61
Kelly,Merrill	13	R	25	a/a	TAM	158	4.20	1.34	23.5	3.7	5.2	1.4	0.4	28	67	55
Kelly,Ryan	12	R	25	a/a	SD	55	3.06	1.31	5.04	2.6	7.0	2.7	0.2	33	76	94
	13	R	26	a/a	SD	67	4.90	1.60	5.83	3.9	6.1	1.6	1.1	33	71	34
Kensing,Logan	12	R	30	a/a	PIT	29	6.08	1.63	5.54	3.8	5.3	1.4	0.7	33	61	35
	13	R	31	aaa	COL	44	3.75	1.58	4.43	4.8	5.7	1.2	1.4	29	81	20
Kickham,Mike	12	L	24	aa	SF	151	3.75	1.44	22.9	4.6	6.9	1.5	0.4	30	74	65
	13	L	25	aaa	SF	111	4.06	1.38	23.3	3.6	6.0	1.7	0.5	30	70	59
Kingham,Nicholas	13	R	22	aa	PIT	73	2.95	1.41	22.2	3.4	6.9	2.1	0.1	33	77	83
Kirk,Austin	12	L	22	aa	CHC	23	3.64	1.39	19.7	4.7	4.4	0.9	1.2	24	79	16
	13	L	23	aa	CHC	42	8.23	1.95	22.4	5.0	5.5	1.1	0.7	37	55	24
Kittredge,Andrew	13	R	23	a/a	SEA	39	7.31	2.30	7.4	4.8	7.2	1.5	0.7	46	67	33
Klein,Phil	13	R	24	aa	TEX	54	3.61	1.97	8.86	8.1	10.0	1.2	0.7	36	83	64
Kloess,Brandon	12	R	28	a/a	CHW	74	3.98	1.67	8.93	4.8	6.7	1.4	0.2	35	74	61
	13	R	29	aaa	SD	101	5.01	1.72	11.2	3.5	6.7	1.9	0.8	38	71	48
Knigge,Tyler	12	R	24	aa	PHI	25	3.38	1.65	5.25	4.4	7.6	1.7	0.4	36	79	67
	13	R	25	aa	PHI	66	4.79	1.50	5.91	4.1	6.2	1.5	1.2	30	71	34
Kohlscheen,Steph	13	R	25	aa	SEA	67	3.06	1.29	6.68	3.8	9.8	2.6	0.9	31	80	93
Kolarek,Adam	13	L	24	a/a	NYM	67	2.18	1.14	5.76	3.0	7.3	2.4	0.4	28	82	95
Kopp,David	12	R	27	a/a	DET	32	8.08	2.16	9.48	4.4	4.9	1.1	1.6	40	64	-16
	13	R	28	aa	DET	48	7.28	2.02	8.6	5.6	4.5	0.8	1.3	35	65	-8
Kroenke,Zach	12	L	28	aaa	ARI	119	5.95	1.72	16.9	2.6	3.4	1.3	0.9	35	65	8
	13	L	29	aaa	MIL	130	5.71	1.73	18.4	3.9	4.7	1.2	0.9	34	67	18
Kussmaul,Ryan	12	R	26	a/a	CHW	58	1.98	1.27	6.25	4.7	7.7	1.7	0.7	26	88	73
	13	R	27	aa	CHW	33	3.48	1.21	5.84	2.4	7.8	3.2	0.8	30	74	95
Laffey,Aaron	12	L	27	aaa	TOR	64	5.10	1.72	26.3	2.8	4.2	1.5	0.9	36	71	17
	13	L	28	aaa	MIL	111	7.85	1.97	23	3.7	3.5	0.9	1.8	36	62	-29
LaFromboise,Rob	12	L	26	a/a	SEA	66	1.49	1.10	5.53	2.9	7.9	2.7	0.1	28	86	113
	13	L	27	aaa	SEA	61	3.52	1.50	5.86	2.7	7.6	2.8	0.7	36	78	80
Lamm,Mark	12	R	24	aa	ATL	60	5.05	1.64	5.33	3.2	6.8	2.1	0.5	37	68	63
	13	R	25	a/a	ATL	68	3.74	1.65	5.74	5.1	7.7	1.5	0.3	35	76	69
Langwell,Matt	12	R	26	a/a	CLE	69	3.54	1.47	7.04	3.7	8.5	2.3	0.0	36	73	99
	13	R	27	aaa	CLE	60	3.03	1.48	6.18	3.1	6.1	2.0	0.2	34	78	70
Lanigan,Robert	12	R	25	a/a	MIN	71	5.49	1.62	7.13	2.9	5.0	1.7	0.8	35	66	34
	13	R	26	a/a	BOS	48	7.02	1.94	7.09	3.1	4.8	1.6	1.3	39	65	4
Lara,Braulio	13	L	25	a/a	TAM	75	4.85	1.63	7.25	5.3	5.6	1.1	0.7	30	70	35
Larez,Victor	13	R	26	aa	DET	137	5.90	1.54	21.3	2.0	4.5	2.3	1.9	32	66	9
Latimer,William	12	L	27	a/a	BOS	59	7.51	1.91	10.3	3.7	5.1	1.4	1.8	37	63	-9
	13	L	28	a/a	BOS	41	4.92	2.16	8.8	5.3	6.3	1.2	0.3	42	76	39
Layne,Tom	12	L	28	a/a	SD	78	6.37	1.78	8.51	4.6	6.3	1.4	0.9	36	64	32
	13	L	29	aaa	SD	46	4.51	1.79	4.33	5.3	6.2	1.2	0.2	36	73	52
Leathersich,John	13	L	23	a/a	NYM	58	4.32	1.56	4.92	6.1	13.7	2.2	0.4	39	71	124

PITCHER	yr	t	age	lvl	org	ip	era	whip	bf/g	ctl	dom	cmd	hr/9	h%	s%	bpv
LeBlanc,Wade	13	L	29	aaa	HOU	50	5.95	1.76	12	3.3	6.5	2.0	1.1	38	67	38
Lee,Michael	13	R	27	a/a	ATL	134	5.06	1.79	23.7	1.6	4.3	2.7	0.8	39	72	42
Lee,Zach	12	R	21	aa	LA	66	4.74	1.47	21.7	2.9	6.2	2.1	0.9	33	69	53
	13	R	22	aa	LA	143	3.94	1.31	21.1	2.2	7.2	3.2	0.9	32	72	83
Leesman,Charles	12	L	25	aaa	CHW	135	3.67	1.74	23.7	4.4	5.7	1.3	0.8	35	81	30
	13	L	26	aaa	CHW	88	5.28	1.86	25.8	5.1	6.5	1.3	1.6	35	76	9
Leon,Arcenio	12	R	26	aa	HOU	64	5.00	1.63	6.43	4.8	6.7	1.4	0.9	32	70	42
	13	R	27	aa	MIL	71	7.83	2.02	9.87	8.5	4.1	0.5	1.4	28	62	-9
Leon,Arnold	12	R	24	a/a	OAK	51	2.05	1.26	6.54	3.1	7.1	2.3	0.6	29	87	79
	13	R	25	a/a	OAK	144	4.50	1.47	24.7	1.5	4.9	3.3	0.7	35	70	68
Leverton,James	12	L	26	aa	MIA	56	4.36	1.49	10.5	3.7	7.2	1.9	0.7	33	71	62
	13	L	27	a/a	MIA	71	4.99	1.33	7.16	3.6	7.1	2.0	1.1	29	64	56
Lewis,Frederick	13	L	27	a/a	NYY	45	3.20	1.90	10	4.9	6.4	1.3	0.9	37	86	28
Liberatore,Adam	12	L	25	a/a	TAM	73	2.80	1.49	6.42	3.4	4.9	1.4	0.5	32	82	44
	13	L	26	a/a	TAM	62	4.09	1.37	5.94	3.7	8.4	2.3	0.1	33	68	98
Lindblom,Josh	13	R	26	aaa	TEX	108	4.11	1.31	22.3	2.8	5.1	1.8	1.4	27	74	30
Link,Jon	12	R	28	a/a	MIA	36	3.72	1.63	4.96	4.0	5.7	1.4	0.6	34	78	43
	13	R	29	a/a	DET	83	4.84	1.48	22.4	1.7	3.0	1.8	0.9	32	68	20
Lively,Mitchell	12	R	27	aaa	SF	78	2.93	1.18	6.66	2.5	6.2	2.5	0.4	29	75	84
	13	R	28	aaa	SF	124	4.74	1.42	17.5	3.8	5.5	1.4	0.8	29	67	41
Lobstein,Kyle	12	L	23	aa	TAM	144	4.40	1.51	23.1	4.1	7.0	1.7	0.7	32	71	57
	13	L	24	a/a	DET	168	4.11	1.48	25.7	2.8	6.3	2.2	0.5	34	72	67
Loe,Kameron	13	R	32	aaa	ATL	76	4.17	1.57	12.4	2.3	3.3	1.4	0.4	34	73	29
Lollis,Matthew	12	R	22	a/a	SD	42	5.47	1.54	6.78	3.4	8.1	2.4	0.9	36	65	68
	13	R	23	a/a	SD	43	6.17	2.01	5.94	5.5	5.9	1.1	1.0	37	70	15
Long,Nathan	13	R	27	aa	OAK	63	4.62	1.62	8.74	3.1	6.3	2.1	0.3	37	70	65
Loomis,Andrew	12	L	27	a/a	BAL	26	6.46	2.00	7.73	2.0	6.5	3.2	1.5	43	70	39
	13	L	28	a/a	BAL	48	5.80	1.77	8.54	4.7	5.5	1.2	0.8	35	67	28
Loosen,Matthew	13	R	24	aa	CHC	66	7.34	1.83	19.2	6.8	6.9	1.0	2.2	29	64	-5
Lorin,Brett	12	R	25	aa	ARI	103	8.28	1.86	16.6	3.2	5.0	1.6	1.3	38	55	9
	13	R	26	a/a	ARI	52	3.55	1.38	6.58	3.2	5.3	1.7	1.0	29	78	38
Loux,Barret	12	R	23	aa	TEX	127	4.59	1.48	21.8	3.0	5.8	1.9	1.0	32	71	44
	13	R	24	aaa	CHC	80	5.74	1.83	19.6	5.4	7.2	1.3	0.5	37	67	51
Loux,Shane	12	R	33	aaa	SF	32	1.46	0.98	5.29	1.4	4.6	3.3	0.0	26	83	106
	13	R	34	aaa	SF	51	4.25	1.31	23.2	3.2	2.2	0.7	0.8	25	69	7
Lowe,Johnnie	12	R	27	a/a	MIL	86	6.30	1.97	13.7	6.2	5.0	0.8	1.6	33	71	-9
	13	R	28	aaa	MIL	79	4.37	1.76	9.78	2.7	5.5	2.1	1.0	38	77	33
Lueke,Josh	12	R	28	aaa	TAM	68	6.82	1.80	7.45	2.4	7.3	3.1	0.8	42	61	67
	13	R	29	aaa	TAM	57	0.80	1.19	5.75	2.6	9.6	3.7	0.2	34	94	138
Luetge,Lucas	13	L	26	aaa	SEA	31	4.42	1.49	6.08	4.6	10.9	2.4	1.0	35	73	88
Lyons,Tyler	12	L	24	a/a	STL	153	4.50	1.38	23.7	2.2	6.9	3.2	0.8	34	68	82
	13	L	25	aaa	STL	100	3.76	1.16	23.5	1.7	6.2	3.6	0.5	30	67	101
Maday,Daryl	12	R	27	aa	SF	84	4.08	1.42	8.27	1.9	6.1	3.3	0.8	34	72	79
	13	R	28	a/a	SF	50	4.35	1.53	5.4	3.6	5.4	1.5	0.3	33	70	53
Madrigal,Warner	13	R	29	aaa	ARI	36	2.99	1.07	6.36	3.5	7.6	2.2	0.5	24	73	92
Magill,Matthew	12	R	23	aa	LA	146	4.32	1.39	23.7	3.7	8.8	2.4	0.5	33	68	90
	13	R	24	aaa	LA	86	3.42	1.43	20.2	4.9	8.9	1.8	0.7	31	77	78
Mandel,Jeff	12	R	27	a/a	WAS	149	4.50	1.50	21.5	2.2	3.9	1.8	0.7	33	70	32
	13	R	28	aaa	WAS	107	5.65	1.71	13.5	2.3	4.9	2.2	1.0	37	68	31
Manno,Chris	12	L	24	aa	CIN	50	6.22	1.75	4.57	4.3	7.8	1.8	1.3	36	66	38
	13	L	25	aa	CIN	62	5.63	1.67	6.6	4.2	7.1	1.7	1.8	33	71	21
Manship,Jeff	12	R	27	aaa	MIN	80	3.99	1.76	16.7	4.5	4.5	1.0	0.6	34	78	22
	13	R	28	aaa	COL	104	5.76	1.64	19.3	2.9	4.4	1.5	0.9	34	65	23
Marbry,Michael	12	R	28	aa	COL	65	7.17	1.80	6.13	3.5	3.5	1.0	2.7	31	67	-52
	13	R	29	aa	COL	38	5.84	1.81	5.92	3.8	3.6	1.0	3.0	30	79	-59
Marimon,Sugar	12	R	24	aa	KC	67	5.45	1.58	24.4	3.9	3.9	1.0	1.2	30	67	5
	13	R	25	aa	KC	148	5.33	1.59	24.2	2.8	5.7	2.0	1.7	33	71	20
Mariot,Michael	12	R	24	a/a	KC	122	3.75	1.35	15.4	2.4	5.0	2.1	0.8	30	74	48
	13	R	25	aaa	KC	61	4.51	1.60	5.71	3.9	7.7	2.0	0.6	36	72	65
Marks,Justin	12	L	24	a/a	KC	87	5.24	1.57	21.2	4.1	6.1	1.5	0.8	32	67	42
	13	L	25	a/a	KC	141	5.43	1.72	24.6	4.4	6.5	1.5	0.5	36	67	48
Maronde,Nick	12	L	23	aa	LAA	32	4.08	1.49	19.9	0.8	5.0	6.2	0.3	38	71	141
	13	L	24	aa	LAA	56	4.16	1.48	5.9	5.7	8.5	1.5	0.6	29	72	73
Marshall,Brett	12	R	22	aa	NYY	158	4.31	1.43	24.9	3.0	5.8	1.9	1.1	31	73	42
	13	R	23	aaa	NYY	139	6.98	1.80	25.6	4.7	6.5	1.4	1.6	34	63	14
Marshall,Evan	12	R	22	aa	ARI	49	4.27	1.61	5.14	2.9	4.3	1.5	0.4	35	73	37
	13	R	23	aaa	ARI	58	4.14	1.77	4.94	4.1	7.7	1.9	0.3	40	75	69
Marte,Victor	13	R	33	aaa	STL	55	6.19	1.99	5.84	5.0	6.6	1.3	0.4	40	67	44
Martin,Blake	12	L	26	aa	MIN	77	5.86	1.63	8.78	4.4	6.7	1.5	0.9	33	64	44
	13	L	27	a/a	MIN	57	6.69	2.07	7.54	7.6	6.3	0.8	1.8	33	71	-3
Martin,Christophe	12	R	26	aa	BOS	76	6.45	1.68	14.9	2.4	6.0	2.5	0.6	39	60	60
	13	R	27	a/a	BOS	72	3.06	1.31	7.08	2.2	7.1	3.2	0.4	33	77	97
Martin,Cody	13	R	24	a/a	ATL	137	3.98	1.50	20.4	4.0	7.7	1.9	0.7	33	74	67
Martin,Ethan	12	R	23	aa	PHI	158	3.95	1.33	24.2	4.5	7.2	1.6	0.5	28	70	71
	13	R	24	aaa	PHI	116	4.77	1.51	23.8	5.3	7.0	1.3	0.9	29	70	47
Martin,J.D.	12	R	29	aaa	MIA	130	8.04	1.84	20.9	1.4	4.9	3.4	1.5	40	57	36
	13	R	30	aaa	TAM	160	3.54	1.52	25.8	1.6	4.9	3.0	0.9	35	80	55
Martinez,Carlos	12	R	21	aa	STL	71	3.05	1.21	19.2	2.6	6.3	2.4	0.7	29	77	74
	13	R	22	a/a	STL	80	2.61	1.20	20	3.0	7.0	2.3	0.4	29	79	86
Martinez,David	13	R	26	a/a	HOU	140	3.06	1.28	19.8	2.1	5.0	2.4	0.8	30	79	58
Martinez,Joe	12	R	29	aaa	ARI	155	5.78	1.85	26.9	2.8	4.3	1.5	0.9	38	69	15
	13	R	30	aaa	CLE	130	7.54	1.93	25.7	2.2	4.6	2.1	1.7	39	63	2
Martinez,Nicholas	13	R	23	aa	TEX	32	1.58	0.66	22.3	2.1	5.3	2.5	0.4	15	79	101
Martis,Shairon	12	R	25	a/a	MIN	139	6.55	1.56	21	3.1	4.5	1.4	1.4	31	59	9
	13	R	26	aaa	MIN	80	5.03	1.40	8.08	3.7	5.7	1.6	0.9	29	65	44
Marzec,Eric	13	R	25	aa	MIL	54	2.62	1.52	5.48	3.7	7.1	1.9	0.5	34	84	68
Mateo,Victor	13	R	24	aa	TAM	153	4.41	1.23	23	3.1	4.7	1.5	1.0	25	66	38

PITCHER	yr	t	age	lvl	org	ip	era	whip	bf/g	ctl	dom	cmd	hr/9	h%	s%	bpv
Mathis,Doug	13	R	30	aaa	PIT	121	5.28	1.74	21.2	4.3	4.6	1.1	0.9	33	70	15
Matzek,Tyler	13	L	23	aa	COL	142	5.52	1.89	25.8	5.2	4.8	0.9	1.3	34	73	0
Maurer,Brandon	12	R	22	aa	SEA	138	3.71	1.43	24.4	3.2	6.9	2.2	0.2	34	73	80
	13	R	23	aaa	SEA	47	4.97	1.57	20.5	4.6	8.1	1.7	0.3	35	66	76
Mavare,Jose	13	R	23	a/a	TEX	72	6.92	1.61	11.1	4.2	7.2	1.7	2.0	31	61	15
May,Trevor	12	R	23	aa	PHI	150	5.53	1.55	23.4	4.6	7.8	1.7	1.4	31	67	40
	13	R	24	aa	MIN	152	5.13	1.56	24.6	4.0	7.7	1.9	0.8	34	67	62
Maya,Yunesky	12	R	31	aaa	WAS	167	5.24	1.50	25.7	2.3	3.4	1.5	1.3	31	68	5
	13	R	32	aaa	WAS	146	4.91	1.58	26.8	2.0	4.3	2.2	0.7	35	69	40
Mazzoni,Cory	12	R	23	aa	NYM	81	4.87	1.46	24.6	2.1	5.4	2.6	1.0	33	68	50
	13	R	24	aa	NYM	66	4.66	1.43	21.6	2.5	8.6	3.5	0.6	37	67	105
McBride,Nicholas	13	R	22	a/a	TEX	60	8.42	2.17	21.3	3.9	4.2	1.1	0.6	42	59	8
McBryde,Jeremy	12	R	25	aa	SD	53	3.58	1.18	4.33	2.6	9.3	3.5	0.4	32	69	125
	13	R	26	aa	SD	61	2.78	1.05	3.89	2.3	8.9	3.8	0.9	27	78	117
McCarthy,Michael	13	R	26	aa	BOS	37	7.96	1.76	17.1	2.3	3.6	1.5	1.1	36	53	6
McClellan,Kyle	13	R	29	a/a	TEX	34	4.79	1.78	6.25	2.5	6.9	2.7	1.2	40	76	47
McClendon,Mike	12	R	27	aaa	MIL	43	5.77	1.68	5.86	4.4	4.5	1.0	0.6	33	64	26
	13	R	28	aaa	COL	72	4.78	1.80	7.36	4.6	5.3	1.2	0.3	36	72	38
McCormick,Phil	13	L	25	aa	SF	57	4.03	1.49	4.21	5.0	7.4	1.5	0.4	31	72	70
McCoy,Patrick	12	L	24	aa	WAS	58	4.52	1.60	5.16	2.7	7.4	2.8	1.6	36	77	48
	13	L	25	a/a	WAS	48	6.06	1.75	4.76	2.5	5.8	2.3	1.4	37	68	26
McCray,Stephen	13	R	26	a/a	CHW	132	5.17	1.74	21.5	4.7	4.5	1.0	0.9	32	71	15
McCully,Nicholas	12	R	24	aa	CHW	55	6.03	1.74	15.7	5.9	5.9	1.0	1.1	31	66	22
	13	R	25	a/a	CHW	120	5.36	1.47	18.4	3.8	4.5	1.2	1.5	27	67	7
McCurry,Cole	12	L	27	a/a	ATL	80	7.40	1.81	12	4.9	4.5	0.9	0.8	34	57	16
	13	L	28	a/a	ATL	41	7.23	2.14	8.47	4.7	5.5	1.2	1.6	39	68	-8
McCutchen,Danie	12	R	30	aaa	PIT	63	4.18	1.38	7.4	2.2	5.5	2.4	0.5	33	69	67
	13	R	31	a/a	BAL	60	4.81	1.53	10.5	2.6	5.9	2.2	1.5	33	73	31
McGough,Scott	13	R	24	a/a	MIA	67	3.70	1.36	7.36	3.1	7.0	2.3	0.8	31	74	69
McGregor,Scott	12	R	26	aa	STL	59	7.91	1.77	22.6	2.9	3.6	1.3	1.6	35	56	-14
	13	R	27	a/a	STL	149	4.73	1.50	24.7	2.6	5.4	2.1	0.9	33	70	44
McGuire,Deck	12	R	23	aa	TOR	144	7.44	1.76	23.6	3.9	5.1	1.3	1.7	34	59	-2
	13	R	24	aa	TOR	157	5.73	1.45	24.9	3.3	6.8	2.1	0.8	32	60	60
McHugh,Collin	12	R	25	a/a	NYM	148	3.27	1.25	24.1	2.7	6.8	2.5	0.8	29	76	75
	13	R	26	a/a	COL	113	4.49	1.55	24.7	2.3	5.9	2.6	0.7	36	71	62
McNutt,Kenneth	12	R	23	aa	CHC	95	5.13	1.62	12.4	4.4	5.3	1.2	1.2	31	71	18
	13	R	24	aa	CHC	31	5.50	1.50	5.02	4.2	5.5	1.3	0.9	30	64	34
Medlen,Casey	13	R	24	aa	MIL	60	4.87	1.69	5.61	5.6	6.1	1.1	1.0	31	73	29
Meek,Evan	12	R	29	aaa	PIT	46	3.79	1.57	5.61	5.6	5.7	1.0	0.7	28	77	40
	13	R	30	aaa	TEX	108	6.50	1.94	15.6	4.5	4.7	1.1	1.1	36	67	5
Meo,Anthony	13	R	23	aa	ARI	35	8.73	1.82	20.5	6.6	3.7	0.6	2.0	26	53	-26
Meyer,Alex	13	R	23	aa	MIN	70	3.58	1.36	22.5	3.7	9.0	2.5	0.4	33	73	100
Mikolas,Miles	12	R	24	a/a	SD	32	2.83	1.46	4.72	2.8	6.8	2.4	0.2	35	80	82
	13	R	25	aaa	SD	61	2.98	1.30	4.66	2.3	5.0	2.1	0.7	30	79	55
Miller,Jim	12	R	30	aaa	OAK	19	3.23	1.17	4.82	2.0	7.2	3.5	0.0	32	69	122
	13	R	31	aaa	NYY	63	5.58	1.71	6.68	4.4	9.5	2.2	1.9	37	73	41
Miller,Quinton	13	R	24	aa	PIT	58	4.27	1.55	8.14	5.3	5.5	1.0	0.4	29	72	46
Miller,Trevor	13	R	22	aa	SEA	47	6.04	1.61	25.9	4.4	4.9	1.1	1.0	31	63	19
Mills,Brad	12	L	27	aaa	LAA	109	5.65	1.64	23.2	3.0	4.4	1.5	0.8	34	66	23
	13	L	28	aaa	TEX	98	5.40	1.57	23.8	3.0	5.0	1.6	1.2	33	67	23
Miner,Zach	12	R	30	a/a	DET	38	3.99	1.60	6.99	5.8	2.8	0.5	0.9	25	77	5
	13	R	31	aaa	PHI	85	5.09	1.73	14.4	3.4	4.2	1.3	0.7	35	70	22
Misch,Pat	12	L	31	aaa	PHI	112	7.27	1.92	25.3	2.8	4.8	1.7	1.8	38	64	-6
	13	L	32	aaa	DET	71	7.36	2.07	26.7	2.3	4.5	1.9	1.8	41	67	-10
Mitchell,D.J.	12	R	25	aaa	SEA	134	4.11	1.32	24.2	3.0	6.0	2.0	0.6	30	69	62
	13	R	26	aaa	NYM	86	6.88	1.99	11.8	5.0	5.7	1.1	1.1	37	65	13
Mock,Garrett	12	R	29	aaa	HOU	62	4.24	1.71	5.94	4.3	7.6	1.8	0.9	36	77	49
	13	R	30	aaa	ARI	75	7.39	1.99	10.9	4.6	4.8	1.0	1.4	37	64	-5
Molina,Nestor	12	R	23	a/a	CHW	127	6.04	1.83	25.6	2.3	5.5	2.4	0.9	40	67	40
	13	R	24	aa	CHW	36	6.32	1.85	9.98	3.3	6.1	1.9	0.7	40	65	41
Montero,Rafael	13	R	23	a/a	NYM	155	2.60	1.09	22.5	1.8	7.6	4.3	0.3	30	76	133
Montgomery,Mark	12	R	22	aa	NYY	24	2.29	0.83	5.83	2.3	12.2	5.4	0.5	26	74	193
	13	R	23	aaa	NYY	40	4.60	1.77	7.35	6.0	9.2	1.5	1.3	35	77	48
Montgomery,Mich	12	L	23	a/a	KC	150	6.70	1.73	25.2	3.7	5.5	1.5	1.3	35	62	15
	13	L	24	aaa	TAM	109	5.38	1.59	24	3.9	5.4	1.4	0.7	33	66	36
Moran,Brian	12	L	24	a/a	SEA	69	2.77	1.10	5.72	2.3	9.4	4.0	0.8	30	78	127
	13	L	25	aaa	SEA	63	3.43	1.50	5.64	2.8	10.4	3.8	0.5	41	77	122
Moran,Gary	12	R	27	aa	ATL	161	4.00	1.52	24	2.6	5.2	2.0	0.5	34	73	53
	13	R	28	aa	ATL	49	4.74	1.77	14	3.0	3.6	1.2	0.5	36	72	20
Morey,Robert	13	R	25	a/a	MIA	113	6.91	1.91	23.3	4.6	5.0	1.1	1.2	36	64	5
Morgan,Adam	12	L	22	aa	PHI	36	3.93	1.34	24.7	2.7	6.4	2.4	0.5	32	71	73
	13	L	23	aaa	PHI	71	4.57	1.67	20	3.2	5.3	1.6	1.4	34	77	17
Morin,Michael	13	R	22	aa	LAA	31	2.31	1.08	4.65	1.4	8.4	6.2	0.5	32	81	171
Morris,AJ	13	R	27	aa	CHC	72	6.06	1.81	10.8	4.9	5.2	1.1	0.6	35	65	29
Morrison,Michael	12	R	25	aa	DET	63	3.97	1.52	6.84	5.8	7.9	1.4	1.0	28	76	55
	13	R	26	a/a	DET	43	9.52	2.18	6.98	6.7	5.0	0.7	0.5	38	53	19
Mortensen,Clayto	12	R	27	a/a	BOS	39	3.45	1.31	6.38	4.3	6.4	1.5	0.9	26	77	53
	13	R	28	aaa	KC	50	3.68	1.55	14.5	4.6	5.5	1.2	1.0	29	80	28
Morton,Charlie	13	R	30	a/a	PIT	38	4.04	1.34	19.6	4.1	3.8	0.9	0.7	25	71	27
Moscoso,Guillerm	12	R	29	aaa	COL	98	7.81	1.92	25.9	2.6	5.4	2.1	1.8	39	61	5
	13	R	30	aaa	CHC	94	5.27	1.63	24.6	5.3	6.7	1.3	1.6	29	72	19
Moscot,Jon	13	R	22	aa	CIN	31	4.29	1.72	23.5	3.6	7.2	2.0	1.2	37	79	38
Moye,Andrew	13	R	26	aa	MIL	127	5.73	1.49	21.1	3.3	5.1	1.5	1.8	29	66	7
Mueller,Josh	13	R	24	aa	COL	37	5.47	1.59	7.02	3.8	4.6	1.2	0.8	32	65	26
Munson,Kevin	12	R	23	aa	ARI	53	7.80	1.72	5.47	4.6	9.2	2.0	0.6	39	52	74
	13	R	24	aa	ARI	55	4.73	1.26	4.21	3.5	9.0	2.6	1.1	29	64	84
Murata,Toru	12	R	27	a/a	CLE	73	3.89	1.46	12.1	2.8	6.2	2.2	0.3	34	72	72
	13	R	28	a/a	CLE	158	5.66	1.62	25.1	1.8	5.2	2.9	1.6	36	69	32

PITCHER	yr	t	age	lvl	org	ip	era	whip	bf/g	ctl	dom	cmd	hr/9	h%	s%	bpv
Murphy,Sean	13	R	25	aa	OAK	137	4.68	1.53	23.8	3.4	6.5	1.9	0.6	34	69	59
Narveson,Chris	13	L	32	aaa	MIL	77	6.59	1.77	23.5	3.2	5.2	1.6	1.4	36	64	12
Navarro,Eliecer	13	L	26	aa	PIT	76	5.37	1.64	22.5	4.1	4.9	1.2	0.9	32	68	23
Neal,Zachary	12	R	24	aa	MIA	69	4.73	1.52	14.2	1.8	5.2	3.0	0.6	36	68	68
	13	R	25	aa	OAK	166	4.98	1.42	25.1	2.0	4.2	2.1	0.9	32	66	38
Negrin,Yoannis	12	R	28	a/a	CHC	20	3.46	1.60	22.1	2.5	4.5	1.8	0.5	35	79	40
	13	R	29	aaa	CHC	108	5.52	1.84	14.8	3.0	7.4	2.5	0.6	42	69	63
Neil,Matthew	12	R	26	aa	MIA	92	6.20	1.63	21.6	1.9	5.5	2.8	1.2	37	63	44
	13	R	27	a/a	MIA	109	5.18	1.70	19.8	3.1	6.6	2.1	0.9	37	70	47
Nelo,Hector	12	R	26	aa	WAS	53	3.48	1.57	4.92	5.0	8.3	1.7	0.8	33	80	62
	13	R	27	aa	LA	61	3.63	1.61	5.98	4.9	5.8	1.2	0.4	32	77	49
Nelson,Jimmy	12	R	23	aa	MIL	46	4.88	1.72	20.9	7.6	7.2	0.9	0.5	29	71	55
	13	R	24	a/a	MIL	152	3.93	1.50	24.4	4.0	8.2	2.0	0.5	34	74	77
Neris,Hector	13	R	24	aa	PHI	97	5.02	1.42	8.94	3.6	7.2	2.0	1.4	30	68	47
Nesseth,Michael	13	R	25	a/a	PHI	51	1.63	1.22	5.43	2.7	3.8	1.4	0.4	27	88	46
Newby,Kyler	12	R	27	a/a	BAL	56	3.39	1.35	5.47	4.0	9.1	2.2	0.2	33	73	101
	13	R	28	a/a	OAK	60	3.14	1.48	5.48	3.1	6.7	2.2	0.4	34	79	71
Nicolino,Justin	13	L	22	aa	MIA	45	6.28	1.92	23.9	2.6	5.7	2.2	0.4	42	65	48
Nieve,Fernando	12	R	30	aaa	LA	119	5.89	1.84	22.2	2.8	6.0	2.1	1.3	39	70	26
	13	R	31	aaa	OAK	57	2.17	1.18	7.86	2.4	7.4	3.1	0.7	29	85	93
Nix,Michael	13	R	30	a/a	CHW	58	8.41	1.92	24.9	4.4	5.2	1.2	1.2	37	55	6
Noesi,Hector	12	R	25	aaa	SEA	64	5.49	1.63	26	2.9	6.6	2.3	0.8	37	66	56
	13	R	26	a/a	SEA	77	5.82	1.52	19.7	2.1	5.9	2.8	1.4	34	64	45
Nolin,Sean	12	L	23	aa	TOR	15	1.52	1.11	19.6	3.6	9.1	2.5	0.0	28	85	123
	13	L	24	a/a	TOR	110	3.37	1.39	23.2	2.8	7.8	2.8	0.7	34	77	85
Northcraft,Aaron	13	R	23	aa	ATL	137	4.40	1.47	22.6	3.5	6.9	2.0	0.5	33	69	67
Nuding,Zachary	13	R	23	a/a	NYY	134	5.62	1.81	19.4	4.3	6.0	1.4	0.9	36	69	28
O Sullivan,Sean	12	R	25	aaa	TOR	143	4.57	1.50	19.9	2.7	3.6	1.3	0.7	31	70	22
	13	R	26	aaa	SD	115	3.60	1.44	24.5	2.3	6.4	2.8	0.4	35	75	80
Oberholtzer,Brett	12	L	23	a/a	HOU	167	4.48	1.42	25.2	2.0	6.4	3.1	1.2	33	72	63
	13	L	24	aaa	HOU	80	4.94	1.39	21.2	2.8	6.9	2.4	1.1	32	66	60
Obispo,Wirfin	12	R	28	a/a	CIN	96	4.22	1.34	11.4	4.6	6.6	1.4	1.1	25	72	46
	13	R	29	aaa	ATL	64	4.76	1.56	5.17	5.6	7.6	1.3	0.5	31	69	64
O'Brien,Michael	12	R	22	aa	NYY	105	5.14	1.58	23.1	3.4	5.3	1.6	0.8	33	67	37
	13	R	23	aa	NYY	107	5.34	1.62	22.6	3.9	6.3	1.6	1.1	34	69	34
Odorizzi,Jake	12	R	22	a/a	KC	145	3.28	1.30	23	2.9	7.0	2.4	0.8	30	77	72
	13	R	23	aaa	TAM	124	3.72	1.21	22.8	2.8	7.7	2.8	0.8	29	71	87
Ohlendorf,Ross	12	R	30	aaa	SD	70	4.38	1.47	23	2.3	5.3	2.3	0.7	34	71	54
	13	R	31	aaa	WAS	75	5.35	1.52	23.2	3.8	6.1	1.6	0.7	32	64	48
Okajima,Hideki	13	L	38	aaa	OAK	43	4.84	1.36	4.82	2.1	7.0	3.4	1.0	33	66	81
Oliver,Andrew	12	L	25	aaa	DET	118	6.23	1.81	19.5	6.8	6.6	1.0	0.6	32	64	42
	13	L	26	aaa	PIT	124	4.91	1.85	20	8.1	7.5	0.9	0.4	31	72	57
Olmos,Edgar	12	L	22	aa	MIA	17	0.65	1.58	8.14	9.3	6.5	0.7	0.0	21	95	76
	13	L	23	aa	MIA	50	3.23	1.72	6.01	5.4	6.6	1.2	0.2	34	80	58
Olmsted,Michael	12	R	25	aa	BOS	20	0.00	1.09	5.58	3.5	11.2	3.2	0.0	31	100	150
	13	R	26	a/a	MIL	60	7.42	1.93	5.15	7.1	7.4	1.0	1.2	34	62	28
Oramas,Juan	12	L	22	aa	SD	35	6.00	1.52	19.2	3.7	7.5	2.0	1.0	34	60	58
	13	L	23	aa	SD	56	3.42	1.32	19.2	2.6	9.1	3.5	0.6	35	75	112
Ortega,Anthony	13	R	28	aaa	LA	62	5.16	1.62	7.07	4.3	5.5	1.3	1.3	31	71	18
Ortega,Jose	12	R	24	aaa	DET	63	7.18	2.25	7.06	7.3	7.7	1.1	0.6	41	67	37
	13	R	25	aaa	DET	48	2.45	1.42	5.12	6.3	8.0	1.3	0.4	26	84	76
Oswalt,Roy	12	R	35	a/a	TEX	15	8.38	2.06	18.7	2.7	5.4	2.0	0.9	43	57	27
	13	R	36	aa	COL	33	3.62	1.31	27.6	2.4	4.7	2.0	2.5	25	88	-4
Owens,Henry	13	L	21	aa	BOS	30	2.14	1.16	20.1	4.4	11.8	2.7	0.9	27	87	116
Oye,Matthew	12	R	26	aa	LAA	112	5.01	1.61	14.6	3.3	4.9	1.5	0.9	33	70	28
	13	R	27	aa	LAA	112	6.07	1.71	22.1	2.8	4.6	1.6	1.7	34	68	-2
Packer,Matt	12	L	25	a/a	CLE	53	5.58	1.77	27	2.6	4.9	1.9	1.5	36	72	8
	13	L	26	aa	CLE	154	3.69	1.57	24.1	2.5	5.6	2.2	0.5	36	76	58
Paduch,Jim	12	R	30	a/a	TAM	120	6.97	1.85	19.3	3.5	4.2	1.2	1.1	36	62	5
	13	R	31	aaa	TAM	37	9.71	2.27	15.7	4.6	4.2	0.9	2.7	38	60	-58
Palmer,Matt	12	R	33	aaa	SD	99	5.48	1.77	21.6	3.8	4.5	1.2	0.2	36	67	35
	13	R	34	aaa	LA	134	4.28	1.58	23.5	4.0	6.5	1.6	1.0	33	75	40
Paredes,Willy	13	R	24	a/a	ARI	45	3.22	1.22	5.35	3.3	6.5	2.0	0.7	27	75	69
Partch,Curtis	12	R	25	aa	CIN	70	6.68	1.87	7.34	4.7	6.8	1.5	1.3	37	66	21
	13	R	26	a/a	CIN	37	5.24	1.59	5.05	3.8	9.0	2.3	0.7	37	67	77
Paterson,Joe	12	L	26	aaa	ARI	43	4.17	1.37	3.78	3.1	6.6	2.2	1.4	29	75	45
	13	L	27	aaa	ARI	52	1.96	1.12	4.3	2.4	7.1	2.9	0.3	29	83	102
Patterson,James	13	L	24	aa	TAM	41	4.67	1.31	9.96	1.9	5.0	2.6	0.8	31	65	59
Patterson,John	12	R	25	aa	LA	70	3.68	1.64	6.67	4.2	7.4	1.8	0.3	36	77	69
Patterson,Red	13	R	26	aaa	LA	107	3.12	1.46	11.7	4.0	7.4	1.8	1.1	31	83	51
Paxton,James	12	L	24	aa	SEA	106	3.68	1.58	22.3	4.8	8.1	1.7	0.4	34	76	72
	13	L	25	aaa	SEA	146	4.42	1.54	22.7	3.5	6.9	2.0	0.5	35	71	64
Peacock,Brad	12	R	24	aaa	OAK	135	6.17	1.65	21.5	4.3	7.7	1.8	0.9	35	62	54
	13	R	25	aaa	HOU	79	3.16	1.23	22.9	2.6	7.2	2.8	1.1	29	79	74
Peavey,Greg	12	R	24	aa	NYM	144	5.64	1.56	25.2	2.2	4.5	2.0	1.2	34	65	25
	13	R	25	a/a	NYM	96	4.67	1.40	8.98	3.3	5.1	1.6	0.7	30	67	44
Pena,Ariel	12	R	23	aa	MIL	147	4.90	1.54	24.6	4.2	7.5	1.8	1.5	31	73	37
	13	R	24	aa	MIL	142	4.82	1.58	23.2	5.4	7.1	1.3	1.4	29	74	30
Pena,Tony	12	R	31	aaa	BOS	91	7.51	2.09	14	3.6	4.5	1.2	1.5	39	65	-12
	13	R	32	aaa	CHW	86	5.72	2.02	12.6	4.3	5.7	1.3	0.7	40	71	26
Perdomo,Luis	12	R	28	a/a	MIN	73	3.52	1.31	6.66	3.1	6.3	2.0	0.6	30	74	68
	13	R	29	aaa	MIN	65	7.53	2.04	7.02	6.7	6.0	0.9	1.3	35	64	7
Perez,Kelvin	12	R	27	a/a	NYY	86	2.16	1.45	7.62	4.7	6.5	1.4	0.4	30	86	60
	13	R	28	a/a	DET	76	8.63	2.05	13.7	4.1	5.0	1.2	1.2	39	57	3
Perez,Martin	12	L	21	aaa	TEX	127	4.80	1.47	24.8	3.8	4.1	1.1	0.8	29	68	24
	13	L	22	a/a	TEX	43	4.31	1.41	22.9	2.1	5.2	2.5	0.6	33	69	62
Perez,Rafael	13	L	31	a/a	BOS	35	3.73	1.40	5.04	2.4	6.0	2.5	1.3	31	78	47

PITCHER	yr	t	age	lvl	org	ip	era	whip	bf/g	ctl	dom	cmd	hr/9	h%	s%	bpv
Perry,Ryan	13	R	26	a/a	WAS	64	8.21	1.82	9.94	5.0	5.3	1.1	1.9	32	56	-10
Petit,Yusmeiro	12	R	28	aaa	SF	167	3.47	1.39	25.1	1.9	6.3	3.4	0.6	35	76	88
	13	R	29	aaa	SF	88	4.65	1.34	24.3	1.3	7.0	5.3	1.3	34	69	111
Petrick,Zachary	13	R	24	aa	STL	47	4.31	1.34	21.9	2.8	6.9	2.4	0.5	32	67	79
Petricka,Jacob	12	R	24	aa	CHW	58	6.94	2.01	27.8	6.3	3.6	0.6	1.5	32	67	-19
	13	R	25	a/a	CHW	55	2.45	1.58	7.76	5.0	8.0	1.6	0.2	34	84	76
Petrini,Christophe	12	L	25	aa	BAL	69	3.32	1.38	12	3.1	7.1	2.3	0.2	33	74	87
	13	L	26	aa	BAL	67	3.89	1.60	7.76	4.8	6.3	1.3	0.5	32	76	50
Pettit,Jacob	12	L	26	aa	BAL	124	4.99	1.34	21.4	1.9	4.9	2.6	1.5	30	67	36
	13	L	27	a/a	BAL	148	5.88	1.60	25.1	3.2	5.1	1.6	1.1	33	64	23
Phillips,Zach	12	L	26	aaa	BAL	54	4.73	1.85	6	4.3	5.9	1.4	0.3	38	73	46
	13	L	27	aaa	MIA	59	3.40	1.57	5.18	4.5	9.4	2.1	0.6	36	79	83
Piazza,Michael	12	R	26	aa	LAA	107	4.60	1.41	11.6	3.1	6.1	2.0	0.6	32	67	60
	13	R	27	aa	LAA	89	3.97	1.53	18.4	3.9	7.0	1.8	0.7	33	75	57
Pimentel,Carlos	12	R	23	aa	TEX	88	3.37	1.41	10.7	5.5	7.7	1.4	0.6	27	77	70
	13	R	24	a/a	TEX	128	5.23	1.43	19.4	3.3	7.5	2.3	1.7	31	68	43
Pimentel,Stolmy	12	R	22	aa	BOS	116	6.08	1.56	23.1	3.4	5.7	1.7	0.8	33	60	41
	13	R	23	a/a	PIT	169	3.77	1.30	25.8	2.8	5.3	1.9	0.7	29	72	54
Pineda,Michael	13	R	24	a/a	NYY	32	5.28	1.32	16.7	3.6	7.8	2.2	1.6	27	64	51
Pino,Yohan	12	R	29	a/a	TOR	143	6.20	1.59	22.6	2.2	5.5	2.5	1.4	35	63	34
	13	R	30	a/a	CIN	132	4.61	1.51	16.4	2.5	6.0	2.4	0.8	35	70	58
Pomeranz,Drew	12	L	24	a/a	COL	51	3.11	1.80	23.4	3.9	6.9	1.8	0.5	39	83	53
	13	L	25	a/a	COL	91	5.97	1.63	25.3	3.5	7.6	2.2	1.1	36	64	52
Pounders,Brooks	13	R	23	aa	KC	116	5.34	1.41	18.2	3.2	6.4	2.0	0.9	31	63	52
Poveda,Omar	12	R	25	a/a	MIA	131	6.01	1.85	23.6	4.4	6.8	1.5	1.2	37	69	26
	13	R	26	aaa	ATL	164	4.56	1.52	26.4	3.4	6.0	1.7	0.7	33	71	48
Price,Bryan	12	R	26	a/a	CLE	70	5.17	1.62	7.73	3.3	6.5	2.0	1.2	35	70	39
	13	R	27	a/a	CLE	75	2.54	1.15	6.34	2.0	8.7	4.3	0.7	32	81	128
Pucetas,Kevin	12	R	28	a/a	WAS	105	4.87	1.44	15.4	1.9	4.6	2.4	1.0	32	68	41
	13	R	29	aa	TEX	118	7.48	1.92	25.3	3.4	3.5	1.0	1.4	36	62	-14
Pugh,Bruce	12	R	24	aa	MIN	42	1.80	1.29	5.56	5.1	8.4	1.7	0.4	26	88	87
	13	R	25	a/a	MIN	30	11.35	2.34	6.8	7.0	4.8	0.7	1.4	38	49	-16
Purcey,David	12	L	30	aaa	PHI	58	6.38	2.03	5.96	6.2	7.3	1.2	0.4	39	67	46
	13	L	31	aaa	CHW	39	4.47	1.47	6.39	3.7	7.6	2.0	0.7	33	70	66
Putkonen,Luke	12	R	26	aaa	DET	57	6.42	1.83	11	3.1	5.5	1.8	0.6	39	63	39
	13	R	27	aaa	DET	38	2.62	1.22	7.61	3.3	6.7	2.0	0.0	29	76	91
Quackenbush,Ke\	13	R	25	a/a	SD	65	1.70	1.25	4.65	3.9	9.8	2.5	0.1	32	86	118
Quevedo,Carlos	13	R	24	aa	HOU	82	4.07	1.35	9.46	2.2	5.6	2.5	1.7	29	77	34
Quirarte,Edwin	12	R	26	aa	SF	45	4.08	1.44	4.95	3.0	3.8	1.3	0.2	31	70	43
	13	R	27	aa	SF	72	2.77	1.41	5.46	3.4	4.3	1.3	0.2	30	79	48
Raley,Brooks	12	L	24	a/a	CHC	131	4.20	1.49	25.6	2.9	5.7	2.0	0.7	34	72	52
	13	L	25	aaa	CHC	141	5.41	1.52	22.7	3.0	5.0	1.6	0.9	32	65	32
Ramirez,Elvin	12	R	25	a/a	NYM	55	2.39	1.25	5.46	5.2	7.8	1.5	0.3	25	81	84
	13	R	26	a/a	LAA	61	5.66	1.77	5.71	6.1	5.9	1.0	0.1	33	65	51
Ramirez,Erasmo	12	R	22	aaa	SEA	77	3.35	1.24	20.9	1.9	6.1	3.3	0.4	32	73	95
	13	R	23	a/a	SEA	49	3.23	1.36	25.4	2.9	7.4	2.5	0.7	32	78	78
Ramirez,J.C.	12	R	24	a/a	PHI	67	4.90	1.45	6.39	4.3	5.8	1.4	0.9	29	67	39
	13	R	25	a/a	PHI	49	4.66	1.55	6.3	4.7	6.6	1.4	0.4	32	69	59
Ramirez,Jose	13	R	23	a/a	NYY	74	4.87	1.45	18.5	4.7	8.0	1.7	1.7	28	72	39
Ramirez,Neil	12	R	23	a/a	TEX	123	7.77	1.57	19.3	3.5	6.5	1.9	1.7	32	51	24
	13	R	24	aa	CHC	108	4.40	1.27	20	3.8	9.2	2.4	0.7	30	66	93
Ramos,Jhonathar	12	L	23	aa	PIT	21	3.10	1.33	6.59	2.5	4.9	2.0	0.8	30	80	46
	13	L	24	aa	PIT	48	5.38	1.48	5.69	2.0	6.2	3.2	0.7	36	63	76
Ranaudo,Anthony	12	R	23	aa	BOS	38	9.05	2.09	20.5	6.8	5.4	0.8	1.1	35	55	6
	13	R	24	a/a	BOS	140	3.77	1.30	23.1	3.1	6.7	2.1	0.7	30	72	68
Rasmus,Cory	12	R	25	aa	ATL	59	4.84	1.53	5.1	5.3	8.0	1.5	0.5	31	67	68
	13	R	26	aaa	LAA	46	1.73	1.07	3.92	4.5	8.8	2.0	0.3	23	85	107
Rasmussen,Robe	12	L	23	aa	HOU	54	5.15	1.48	21.2	2.9	6.4	2.2	1.0	33	66	51
	13	L	24	a/a	LA	136	4.58	1.46	20.7	3.9	6.3	1.6	1.0	30	71	42
Ravin,Joshua	12	R	24	aa	CIN	24	6.74	2.09	5.9	8.1	7.0	0.9	1.6	33	70	6
	13	R	25	a/a	CIN	51	8.12	2.20	5.34	7.3	7.0	1.0	1.3	38	63	12
Ray,Robbie	13	L	22	aa	WAS	58	4.38	1.42	22.4	3.0	7.8	2.6	0.7	34	69	80
Rearick,Christoph	12	L	25	aa	TAM	25	4.94	1.34	6.83	2.9	7.9	2.7	1.4	31	67	64
	13	L	26	aa	SD	38	2.25	1.24	4.41	2.5	8.2	3.3	0.2	33	82	115
Reed,Chris	12	L	22	aa	LA	35	5.46	1.52	12.8	5.0	6.4	1.3	0.5	30	63	54
	13	L	23	aa	LA	138	4.82	1.57	20.8	4.3	5.9	1.4	0.7	32	69	43
Reed,Evan	12	R	26	a/a	MIA	67	5.99	1.68	6.06	4.2	8.0	1.9	0.5	38	62	69
	13	R	27	aaa	DET	50	3.48	1.41	6.57	3.9	6.6	1.7	0.2	31	74	71
Reid,Ryan	12	R	27	aaa	TAM	79	4.20	1.50	7.44	3.3	7.1	2.2	0.9	34	74	58
	13	R	28	aaa	PIT	59	3.46	1.42	6.98	3.5	6.1	1.8	0.6	31	77	57
Reifer,Adam	12	R	26	aaa	STL	64	5.51	1.46	4.75	2.9	4.8	1.7	1.5	30	65	18
	13	R	27	aaa	MIA	41	1.83	1.34	6.1	6.7	6.8	1.0	0.5	21	89	66
Reineke,Chad	12	R	30	aaa	CIN	152	6.24	1.85	26.2	3.0	4.8	1.6	1.4	37	68	6
	13	R	31	aaa	CIN	130	6.15	1.81	22.3	2.7	4.3	1.6	2.1	35	72	-19
Remenowsky,Dar	12	R	26	a/a	CHW	67	3.80	1.41	7.87	4.5	8.2	1.8	0.8	30	75	70
	13	R	27	a/a	CHW	45	6.26	1.71	6.98	3.1	6.6	2.2	2.1	35	69	11
Renken,Daniel	13	R	24	aa	CIN	142	5.58	1.60	23.2	4.1	6.3	1.5	1.2	32	67	30
Resop,Chris	13	R	31	aaa	OAK	36	7.82	2.02	6.64	3.6	5.4	1.5	1.2	40	61	10
Reyes,James	13	L	24	aa	TEX	67	3.86	1.39	6.41	3.0	6.2	2.1	1.0	31	75	51
Reyes,Jorge	12	R	25	aaa	SD	152	4.46	1.55	19.5	2.4	4.9	2.1	0.6	35	71	47
	13	R	26	aaa	SD	75	4.95	1.64	7.96	4.3	7.1	1.7	0.5	35	69	60
Reynolds,Greg	12	R	27	aaa	TEX	163	6.71	1.87	28.3	2.7	2.9	1.1	1.6	36	66	-25
	13	R	28	aaa	CIN	156	3.51	1.38	28.5	1.7	4.3	2.5	0.5	33	75	58
Rhee,Dae-Eun	12	R	23	aa	CHC	142	5.79	1.73	24	3.3	4.2	1.3	1.2	34	68	4
	13	R	24	aa	CHC	59	3.99	1.25	22	3.2	4.4	1.4	1.0	25	71	33
Rhoderick,Kevin	12	R	24	aa	CHC	58	6.14	1.86	6.14	7.8	6.9	0.9	0.9	31	67	37
	13	R	25	aa	CHC	43	6.91	2.17	6.5	9.4	4.5	0.5	0.2	32	65	28
Richardson,Dustir	13	L	29	aaa	LAA	56	6.17	1.73	12.7	4.8	6.1	1.3	0.4	35	62	48

PITCHER	yr	t	age	lvl	org	ip	era	whip	bf/g	ctl	dom	cmd	hr/9	h%	s%	bpv
Riefenhauser,Cha	12	L	22	aa	TAM	18	3.65	1.28	8.35	3.6	6.5	1.8	1.8	24	81	30
	13	L	23	a/a	TAM	74	1.35	0.88	5.34	2.2	7.4	3.3	0.6	22	89	115
Rienzo,Andre	12	R	24	a/a	CHW	78	4.05	1.50	24.2	4.8	8.0	1.7	0.3	32	72	77
	13	R	25	aaa	CHW	113	5.42	1.64	25.2	4.4	7.5	1.7	0.8	35	67	54
Riordan,Cory	12	R	26	a/a	COL	95	6.14	1.57	12.6	1.8	4.7	2.6	1.3	35	62	34
	13	R	27	a/a	COL	89	8.27	2.14	13.8	2.9	4.8	1.7	1.9	41	63	-17
Roach,Donn	12	R	23	aa	SD	17	1.53	0.98	16.2	3.9	2.3	0.6	0.0	18	83	49
	13	R	24	aa	SD	143	4.01	1.38	21.4	2.6	4.2	1.6	0.4	31	70	46
Roark,Tanner	12	R	26	aaa	WAS	148	5.47	1.63	23.5	2.8	6.1	2.1	1.0	36	67	43
	13	R	27	aaa	WAS	106	3.77	1.15	12.7	1.7	5.4	3.2	0.6	29	67	87
Roberts,Will	13	R	23	aa	CLE	134	4.83	1.41	24.6	2.0	5.2	2.6	0.8	33	66	57
Robertson,Tyler	12	L	25	aaa	MIN	29	4.95	1.61	3.85	4.5	8.3	1.9	0.7	35	69	67
	13	L	26	aaa	WAS	47	3.56	1.85	4.7	4.4	6.4	1.5	0.4	38	81	47
Robinson,James	13	R	25	aa	HOU	49	3.87	1.40	5.48	2.7	5.6	2.1	1.2	31	77	41
Robles,Mauricio	12	L	23	a/a	SEA	72	5.97	1.71	7.55	7.6	7.7	1.0	0.5	29	63	60
	13	L	24	a/a	PHI	64	2.22	1.30	5.17	6.2	7.4	1.2	0.2	23	82	84
Robowski,Ryan	12	L	24	a/a	DET	55	4.50	1.29	7.01	2.6	6.1	2.3	0.9	29	66	61
	13	L	25	aa	DET	50	3.61	1.36	6.14	3.8	4.0	1.1	1.0	26	77	21
Rodebaugh,Ryan	12	R	23	aa	TEX	52	3.22	1.25	5.69	1.8	8.9	4.9	1.0	34	78	128
	13	R	24	a/a	TEX	64	4.40	1.26	6.19	4.2	7.3	1.7	1.2	25	68	55
Rodriguez,Arman	12	R	24	a/a	NYM	77	3.47	1.17	8.77	2.6	7.9	3.0	1.6	27	79	71
	13	R	25	a/a	NYM	64	4.68	1.67	5.72	4.3	7.2	1.7	1.3	34	75	35
Rodriguez,Daniel	13	L	29	aaa	ATL	53	7.77	2.02	21.4	7.3	7.1	1.0	0.6	36	59	40
Rodriguez,Eduarc	13	L	20	aa	BAL	60	4.72	1.35	22.6	3.5	7.8	2.3	0.9	31	66	73
Rodriguez,Santos	12	L	24	a/a	CHW	71	3.94	1.28	6.97	5.3	7.4	1.4	1.1	22	73	57
	13	L	25	a/a	CHW	48	6.64	1.93	6.86	9.4	9.6	1.0	1.1	30	66	54
Rogers,Chad	12	R	23	aa	CIN	32	2.69	1.24	21.4	1.8	5.6	3.1	1.2	29	85	64
	13	R	24	a/a	CIN	140	4.39	1.34	23.3	3.1	5.6	1.8	1.3	28	71	35
Rogers,Jared	13	R	25	aaa	MIA	85	5.67	1.63	22.2	2.7	5.7	2.1	1.4	35	68	28
Rogers,Taylor	13	R	26	aa	SF	104	5.63	1.65	18	4.6	4.8	1.0	0.3	33	64	38
Rollins,David	13	L	24	a/a	HOU	39	4.22	1.48	23.9	2.6	7.9	3.1	1.0	36	74	78
Romanski,Joshua	12	L	26	aa	NYY	29	6.61	1.89	11.4	3.1	4.9	1.6	0.9	39	64	21
	13	L	27	a/a	CHW	33	8.86	2.31	7.69	5.2	7.2	1.4	1.6	43	62	2
Romero,Enny Mai	13	L	22	a/a	TAM	148	2.83	1.31	21.9	4.3	6.0	1.4	0.5	26	79	60
Romero,Ricky	13	L	29	aaa	TOR	114	8.08	2.21	26	5.6	4.8	0.8	1.2	39	63	-6
Rondon,Franciscc	12	L	24	a/a	NYY	66	5.44	1.73	7.15	5.7	8.1	1.4	1.1	34	70	44
	13	L	25	a/a	NYY	83	5.43	1.67	11.2	6.5	7.4	1.1	1.1	29	69	41
Rondon,Jorge	12	R	24	a/a	STL	49	3.81	1.41	4.51	4.4	7.5	1.7	0.3	31	72	77
	13	R	25	aaa	STL	68	3.47	1.77	6.09	5.0	4.5	0.9	0.8	33	82	18
Rosario,Sandy	12	R	27	a/a	MIA	28	1.68	1.16	4.12	1.1	7.5	6.6	0.4	33	87	173
	13	R	28	aaa	SF	32	2.80	1.33	6.39	2.7	7.5	2.8	0.2	34	78	99
Rosenbaum,Danie	12	L	25	aa	WAS	155	4.91	1.51	25.9	2.2	4.5	2.0	0.5	34	66	47
	13	L	26	aaa	WAS	158	4.53	1.64	25.2	3.7	4.5	1.2	0.6	33	72	28
Rosenberg,B.J.	12	R	27	a/a	PHI	62	2.46	1.41	10.5	2.9	8.3	2.9	0.9	34	87	83
	13	R	28	aaa	PHI	76	5.70	1.81	12.5	4.4	5.4	1.2	0.7	36	68	28
Rosin,Seth	13	R	25	aa	PHI	127	4.88	1.35	20.3	2.5	5.6	2.2	1.0	31	65	51
Rosscup,Zachary	12	L	24	aa	CHC	22	5.94	1.64	9.05	8.1	9.8	1.2	0.5	28	62	84
	13	L	25	a/a	CHC	51	2.58	1.36	4.63	4.7	12.0	2.6	0.4	35	81	123
Roth,Michael	13	L	23	aa	LAA	79	4.87	1.53	20.3	3.9	5.0	1.3	0.9	31	69	30
Rowen,Benjamin	13	R	25	a/a	TEX	66	0.95	1.07	5.01	2.5	6.3	2.5	0.2	26	92	95
Rowland-Smith,R	12	L	29	aaa	CHC	78	4.94	1.81	12	5.4	5.4	1.0	0.8	34	73	25
	13	L	30	aaa	BOS	52	2.24	1.29	5.82	3.0	5.6	1.9	0.7	29	86	58
Ruffin,Chance	12	R	24	aaa	SEA	71	5.61	1.55	6.17	4.1	6.0	1.5	0.8	32	63	43
	13	R	25	a/a	SEA	113	4.46	1.38	15.3	2.4	5.6	2.3	1.1	31	70	48
Ruiz,Pete	13	R	26	aa	BOS	53	6.91	1.71	8.06	4.9	9.2	1.9	0.8	37	58	67
Runion,Sam	12	R	24	aa	KC	16	2.73	1.21	6.32	2.3	5.1	2.2	0.0	30	75	81
	13	R	25	a/a	KC	58	5.21	1.46	6.57	2.2	5.5	2.4	0.7	34	64	59
Runzler,Dan	12	L	27	aaa	SF	27	5.89	1.93	4.43	4.4	8.6	2.0	0.5	43	68	65
	13	L	28	aaa	SF	52	5.71	1.91	4.85	6.1	6.6	1.1	0.7	36	69	37
Rusin,Chris	12	L	26	a/a	CHC	143	5.46	1.62	24.5	3.6	4.8	1.3	1.2	32	68	16
	13	L	27	aaa	CHC	121	4.24	1.40	26.9	2.2	4.0	1.8	0.7	31	70	39
Russell,Adam	12	R	29	a/a	LAA	50	8.21	2.29	5.81	6.2	6.7	1.1	0.3	43	61	35
	13	R	30	aaa	BAL	61	3.45	1.82	6.7	5.9	6.4	1.1	0.4	35	81	44
Russell,Andrew	12	R	28	a/a	ATL	64	2.79	1.44	5.05	4.4	4.8	1.1	0.3	29	81	47
	13	R	29	a/a	ATL	76	4.14	1.78	6.26	5.3	5.5	1.0	0.6	34	77	33
Rzepczynski,Marc	13	L	28	aaa	STL	44	3.71	1.66	6.16	4.0	4.8	1.2	0.2	34	76	42
Sadler,Casey	13	R	23	a/a	PIT	136	3.79	1.30	23.4	2.7	3.8	1.4	0.7	28	72	34
Salazar,Danny	12	R	22	aa	CLE	34	2.44	1.12	22.3	2.2	5.3	2.5	0.3	27	78	82
	13	R	23	a/a	CLE	93	3.10	1.10	17.4	2.2	10.7	4.8	0.5	33	72	158
Sampson,Keyvius	12	R	21	aa	SD	122	4.67	1.30	19.4	3.8	8.1	2.2	0.6	30	63	83
	13	R	22	a/a	SD	141	3.44	1.25	20.6	3.6	7.7	2.1	0.7	28	74	78
Sanches,Brian	12	R	34	aaa	HOU	52	3.92	1.52	6.1	1.9	5.4	2.9	0.9	35	76	57
	13	R	35	aaa	KC	101	4.48	1.59	16.6	2.2	3.9	1.8	0.3	36	70	41
Sanchez,Eduardo	12	R	23	aaa	STL	28	6.19	1.78	4.25	6.6	7.1	1.1	0.9	32	65	40
	13	R	24	aaa	CHC	40	4.01	1.49	5.23	5.4	6.6	1.2	0.7	28	74	50
Sanchez,Jesus	12	R	25	a/a	MIL	72	2.14	1.31	5.7	3.1	6.7	2.2	0.3	31	84	80
	13	R	26	aaa	MIL	70	3.35	1.43	6.2	2.5	5.3	2.1	0.8	32	79	49
Sanchez,Jonathai	13	L	31	aaa	LA	67	5.72	1.95	22.7	6.0	7.9	1.3	1.7	36	74	17
Sanchez,Salvado	12	R	27	aa	CHW	23	5.75	1.83	6.78	8.1	3.7	0.5	1.1	25	70	4
	13	R	28	aa	CHW	43	4.02	1.28	6.48	2.7	7.6	2.8	0.3	32	67	97
Santiago,Andres	12	R	23	aa	LA	26	3.19	1.41	18.3	4.5	7.7	1.7	0.4	31	77	77
	13	R	24	aa	LA	134	6.34	1.62	19.8	5.3	6.1	1.2	0.7	31	59	41
Sanz,Luis	13	R	26	aa	PIT	62	5.87	1.72	5.99	5.0	6.7	1.3	1.1	33	67	31
Saupold,Warwick	13	R	23	aa	DET	129	3.94	1.49	25.3	3.4	4.6	1.3	0.9	30	76	27
Scahill,Rob	12	R	25	aaa	COL	152	6.63	1.76	24	4.3	7.2	1.7	0.8	37	61	45
	13	R	26	aaa	COL	46	5.12	1.57	8.77	2.1	6.6	3.1	1.5	36	71	51
Schenk,Neil	12	L	26	aa	TAM	61	3.25	1.50	6.24	3.0	5.0	1.7	1.0	32	82	31
	13	L	27	aa	TAM	40	8.40	2.15	6.16	4.9	4.9	1.0	0.9	40	59	4

PITCHER	yr	t	age	lvl	org	ip	era	whip	bf/g	ctl	dom	cmd	hr/9	h%	s%	bpv
Schlitter,Brian	12	R	27	aa	CHC	42	3.93	1.58	6.37	2.7	7.4	2.8	0.5	38	75	80
	13	R	28	a/a	CHC	63	3.14	1.51	5.07	2.4	6.3	2.6	0.7	35	81	67
Schlosser,Gus	13	R	25	aa	ATL	135	3.22	1.44	23	3.2	5.6	1.8	0.4	32	77	58
Schmidt,Nick	12	L	27	a/a	COL	147	6.24	1.73	25.7	3.2	5.4	1.7	1.3	36	66	17
	13	L	28	aaa	COL	92	5.60	1.84	11.5	3.9	5.1	1.3	1.3	36	72	8
Schrader,Clayton	12	R	22	aa	BAL	23	3.26	1.78	5.57	9.4	5.7	0.6	0.5	24	82	46
	13	R	23	aa	BAL	56	5.10	1.64	7.14	5.7	8.3	1.5	1.1	32	71	49
Schugel,Andrew	12	R	23	aa	LAA	140	3.53	1.35	21.7	3.4	6.0	1.8	0.6	30	74	60
	13	R	24	aaa	LAA	89	6.03	1.63	20.9	2.7	6.5	2.4	0.8	37	63	54
Schultz,Bo	12	R	27	aa	ARI	21	2.85	1.55	5.48	3.2	4.3	1.3	0.0	34	80	49
	13	R	28	a/a	ARI	105	4.20	1.44	12	3.3	4.9	1.5	0.7	30	72	39
Schwinden,Chris	12	R	26	aaa	NYM	129	4.11	1.49	21.4	2.6	5.8	2.2	0.9	33	74	49
	13	R	27	aaa	NYM	146	5.30	1.63	22.4	2.5	4.4	1.7	1.2	34	70	16
Scribner,Evan	12	R	27	aaa	OAK	36	3.31	1.12	5.41	2.6	7.5	2.9	0.9	27	74	87
	13	R	28	aaa	OAK	45	2.46	1.05	5.57	1.9	8.9	4.7	0.4	30	77	150
Seaton,Ross	12	R	23	a/a	HOU	169	4.03	1.34	24.3	1.9	5.4	2.8	1.0	31	72	61
	13	R	24	a/a	HOU	123	7.08	1.73	22.4	2.9	4.5	1.6	1.6	35	60	1
Seidel,RJ	12	R	25	aa	MIL	67	4.35	1.63	7.69	4.6	5.9	1.3	1.1	32	76	28
	13	R	26	a/a	MIL	89	5.89	1.67	15.3	3.9	7.8	2.0	1.9	34	69	27
Septimo,Leyson	12	L	27	aaa	CHW	34	2.04	1.41	6.05	7.0	9.0	1.3	0.4	24	87	87
	13	L	28	aaa	CHW	39	6.31	2.09	6.78	9.9	6.9	0.7	0.7	31	69	38
Serrano,Mark	12	R	27	aa	CIN	93	5.83	1.65	10.2	3.3	7.3	2.2	1.7	35	68	32
	13	R	28	a/a	ARI	57	3.78	1.42	13.3	2.3	5.3	2.3	0.8	33	75	54
Severino,Atahual	12	L	28	aaa	WAS	48	3.67	1.75	4.77	7.0	5.9	0.8	1.1	28	83	23
	13	L	29	aaa	PIT	55	4.67	1.62	6.26	3.3	6.7	2.0	1.2	35	74	40
Sexton,Timothy	12	R	25	a/a	COL	35	6.71	1.57	6.41	2.2	6.7	3.0	1.2	37	57	59
	13	R	26	aa	SD	50	3.84	1.50	7.46	2.3	4.2	1.8	0.9	33	77	30
Shankin,Brett	13	R	24	aa	SEA	42	5.27	1.92	25.1	4.6	4.1	0.9	1.0	35	74	3
Shoemaker,Matth	12	R	26	aaa	LAA	177	5.43	1.59	26.9	2.0	5.1	2.5	1.0	36	67	44
	13	R	27	aaa	LAA	184	4.23	1.34	26.4	1.2	6.2	5.0	1.0	34	71	107
Shreve,Chasen	12	L	22	aa	ATL	18	4.86	1.95	7.96	7.9	7.0	0.9	0.5	33	75	44
	13	L	23	aa	ATL	43	5.71	1.74	5.4	4.8	5.1	1.1	0.2	34	64	41
Simon,Kyle	12	R	22	aa	PHI	25	1.58	0.71	6.88	1.7	6.5	3.8	0.0	20	75	142
	13	R	23	aa	PHI	57	4.81	1.49	5.43	3.4	4.5	1.3	0.7	31	67	34
Skaggs,Tyler	12	L	21	a/a	ARI	122	2.98	1.23	22.5	2.4	7.4	3.1	0.9	30	79	87
	13	L	22	aaa	ARI	104	4.29	1.42	23.2	2.9	8.0	2.8	0.4	35	69	94
Smith,Burch	13	R	23	a/a	SD	92	2.59	1.06	19.9	2.1	8.8	4.2	0.4	30	76	138
Smith,Carson	13	R	24	aa	SEA	50	2.35	1.17	4.53	3.3	11.1	3.3	0.2	33	79	141
Smith,Eric	12	R	24	aa	ARI	42	5.43	1.75	6.4	6.1	4.1	0.7	0.3	31	67	31
	13	R	25	aa	ARI	38	10.16	1.88	5.41	5.4	5.2	1.0	1.6	33	44	-4
Smith,Greg	12	L	29	a/a	LAA	173	4.74	1.52	26.9	2.4	4.2	1.8	1.1	32	71	21
	13	L	30	a/a	PHI	116	4.25	1.58	19.6	2.0	3.3	1.6	0.8	34	74	21
Smith,Jordan	12	R	26	aaa	CIN	57	6.02	1.74	5.06	2.7	4.6	1.7	0.4	38	63	39
	13	R	27	aaa	MIA	44	7.35	2.13	7.57	3.7	4.2	1.1	1.5	40	67	-16
Smith,Josh	13	R	26	aa	CIN	160	4.76	1.56	25.1	3.2	6.3	2.0	1.4	33	73	33
Smith,Murphy	12	R	25	aa	OAK	140	5.42	1.80	24	3.8	4.3	1.2	0.5	36	69	25
	13	R	26	aa	OAK	150	4.08	1.55	25.2	2.9	4.7	1.6	0.8	33	75	32
Smith,Steve	13	R	27	a/a	LA	73	5.44	1.72	10.3	3.9	5.9	1.5	0.8	36	68	35
Smith,Will	12	L	23	aaa	KC	90	3.79	1.47	25.7	2.1	6.1	3.0	0.7	35	75	71
	13	L	24	aaa	KC	89	3.76	1.35	13.3	2.5	8.1	3.3	0.7	34	74	95
Smyth,Paul	12	R	25	aa	OAK	69	4.52	1.53	6.86	3.2	5.6	1.8	0.9	33	72	38
	13	R	26	a/a	OAK	60	2.86	1.30	5.47	3.1	6.6	2.1	0.5	30	79	72
Snodgrass,Jack	13	L	26	aa	SF	141	3.84	1.25	23	2.4	4.1	1.7	0.5	28	69	50
Snodgress,Scott	13	L	24	aa	CHW	144	6.31	1.74	25.2	4.4	4.8	1.1	0.8	34	63	21
Snow,Forrest	12	R	24	a/a	SEA	118	6.70	1.76	16.8	5.0	6.6	1.3	0.6	35	60	43
	13	R	25	a/a	SEA	82	3.37	1.20	7.85	3.2	7.9	2.5	0.8	28	74	85
Sogard,Alexander	12	L	25	aa	HOU	54	4.31	1.74	7.41	4.2	4.9	1.2	0.5	35	75	31
	13	L	26	a/a	HOU	48	7.15	2.02	6.11	5.7	5.7	1.0	0.8	37	64	19
Solbach,Michael	13	R	28	a/a	COL	54	11.04	2.46	7.09	6.7	5.5	0.8	1.3	42	53	-8
Sosa,Juan	13	R	24	aa	PHI	71	6.15	1.79	9.35	5.1	5.9	1.2	0.9	34	66	27
Souza,Justin	12	R	27	aaa	OAK	58	7.51	2.03	7.77	2.9	3.2	1.1	1.7	38	65	-29
	13	R	28	a/a	DET	55	6.28	1.57	4.83	3.6	5.2	1.5	1.4	31	62	16
Spence,Josh	12	L	24	aaa	SD	49	3.60	1.31	6.58	3.2	5.7	1.8	0.5	29	73	60
	13	L	25	aaa	NYY	43	5.65	1.93	6.18	4.0	6.9	1.7	0.0	42	67	64
Spoone,Chorye	12	R	27	a/a	TOR	64	4.21	1.77	6.96	7.2	4.6	0.6	0.7	28	77	24
	13	R	28	aa	TOR	50	5.12	1.83	8.24	6.0	8.0	1.3	0.5	37	71	59
Spruill,Ezekiel	12	R	23	aa	ATL	162	4.64	1.45	25.5	2.6	5.1	1.9	0.5	33	67	54
	13	R	24	a/a	ARI	124	4.01	1.47	25.3	3.2	4.1	1.3	0.6	31	73	31
Stange,Daniel	12	R	27	a/a	SD	58	4.12	1.45	4.82	3.0	8.5	2.8	0.4	36	70	97
	13	R	28	aaa	LAA	66	4.22	1.56	5.54	4.6	7.8	1.7	0.6	34	73	64
Startup,Will	13	L	29	aa	DET	58	4.67	1.46	7.52	2.7	3.7	1.4	1.7	29	74	-3
Stauffer,Tim	13	R	31	aaa	SD	43	3.21	1.69	24.1	3.2	6.1	1.9	0.2	38	80	62
Stewart,Zach	12	R	26	aaa	BOS	59	5.77	1.55	23.6	2.4	5.0	2.1	1.2	34	64	31
	13	R	27	aaa	CHW	167	5.92	1.72	27.1	2.5	5.3	2.1	1.3	37	67	24
Stilson,John	12	R	22	aa	TOR	50	6.26	1.70	13.3	4.1	6.8	1.7	1.3	35	65	31
	13	R	23	a/a	TOR	50	2.59	1.19	5.69	2.6	8.1	3.1	0.6	30	81	101
Stinson,Josh	12	R	24	aa	MIL	145	4.02	1.90	23.7	4.7	4.8	1.0	0.6	36	79	22
	13	R	25	aaa	BAL	131	4.97	1.63	25.3	4.0	4.8	1.2	1.0	32	71	20
Stites,Matthew	13	R	23	aa	SD	52	2.31	0.94	4.25	1.4	7.8	5.6	1.0	26	82	147
Stoffel,Jason	12	R	24	aa	HOU	58	2.55	1.06	4.02	2.5	7.6	3.1	0.5	27	77	107
	13	R	25	a/a	HOU	70	3.77	1.41	5.78	4.0	6.3	1.6	0.3	30	72	66
Stohr,Tyler	12	R	26	aa	DET	25	2.83	1.90	5.07	9.1	5.5	0.6	0.4	28	86	40
	13	R	27	aa	DET	48	6.92	1.78	6.09	6.6	4.5	0.7	0.4	30	58	28
Stoneburner,Grah	12	R	25	aa	NYY	38	6.53	1.75	8.6	2.3	5.4	2.3	1.9	37	67	9
	13	R	26	a/a	NYY	90	6.08	1.70	13.6	3.0	3.3	1.1	1.2	33	65	-3
Stoppelman,Lee	13	L	23	a/a	STL	42	1.61	0.99	4	3.3	9.3	2.8	0.6	24	88	116
Storey,Mickey	12	R	26	aaa	HOU	65	3.18	1.27	6.99	1.9	8.2	4.3	1.1	33	80	106
	13	R	27	aaa	TOR	60	3.43	1.20	6.66	2.6	8.2	3.2	1.0	30	75	92

PITCHER	yr	t	age	lvl	org	ip	era	whip	bf/g	ctl	dom	cmd	hr/9	h%	s%	bpv
Stowell,Bryce	12	R	26	aa	CLE	29	5.32	1.37	4.86	3.1	11.0	3.5	2.0	33	68	82
	13	R	27	aa	CLE	45	2.97	1.32	5.22	4.2	9.7	2.3	0.4	32	78	102
Straily,Dan	12	R	24	a/a	OAK	152	2.95	1.06	23.6	2.4	9.3	3.8	0.5	29	72	134
	13	R	25	aaa	OAK	32	1.18	1.11	24.9	2.5	7.6	3.0	0.2	29	90	112
Stripling,Ross	13	R	24	aa	LA	94	3.54	1.37	18.8	1.9	6.7	3.5	0.5	35	74	96
Stroman,Marcus	13	R	22	aa	TOR	112	3.74	1.21	22.5	2.0	9.0	4.4	1.2	32	73	115
Struck,Nicholas	12	R	23	aa	CHC	156	3.83	1.33	23.1	2.6	6.1	2.3	0.9	30	73	60
	13	R	24	a/a	CHC	137	6.83	1.91	24	4.9	3.7	0.8	1.4	33	66	-15
Stuifbergen,Tom	13	R	25	aa	MIN	31	7.16	1.58	16.9	2.7	4.7	1.7	1.4	33	55	15
Sulbaran,Juan	12	R	23	aa	KC	131	5.53	1.72	23.7	5.1	7.6	1.5	1.6	33	72	25
	13	R	24	aa	KC	46	8.47	1.79	8.55	5.5	4.1	0.7	1.8	29	53	-18
Surkamp,Eric	13	L	26	aaa	SF	71	2.67	1.09	25.4	2.3	5.5	2.4	0.4	26	76	81
Swynenberg,Matt	13	R	24	aa	WAS	74	3.87	1.44	8.75	3.5	5.7	1.6	0.8	30	75	44
Syndergaard,Noa	13	R	21	aa	NYM	54	3.04	1.09	19.2	1.8	10.3	5.7	1.3	31	79	151
Taillon,Jameson	12	R	21	aa	PIT	17	1.83	0.77	20.4	0.5	7.9	16.0	0.0	27	74	398
	13	R	22	a/a	PIT	147	4.12	1.38	23.8	2.9	7.2	2.5	0.5	33	70	80
Takahashi,Hisanc	13	L	38	aaa	COL	53	5.23	1.69	6.3	4.0	7.1	1.8	1.1	36	71	40
Tanaka,Masahiro	12	R	0	for	JPN	173	2.33	1.13	31.1	1.2	8.3	6.8	0.3	34	80	185
	13	R	0	for	JPN	199	1.52	1.03	29.5	1.7	7.4	4.4	0.4	29	88	132
Tateyama,Yoshin	12	R	37	aaa	TEX	40	1.52	1.15	4.93	1.8	7.3	4.0	0.6	31	91	114
	13	R	38	aaa	NYY	76	4.44	1.60	7.66	2.0	7.4	3.6	1.3	38	76	69
Tatusko,Ryan	12	R	27	aa	WAS	82	4.56	1.51	13.2	3.9	6.4	1.6	0.5	33	69	57
	13	R	28	a/a	WAS	128	5.22	1.81	20.4	5.9	5.4	0.9	0.6	33	70	31
Teaford,Everett	12	L	28	aaa	KC	33	1.27	1.12	18.6	2.3	5.0	2.2	0.5	26	92	68
	13	L	29	aaa	KC	95	4.83	1.74	14	4.2	6.7	1.6	0.8	36	73	44
Tejeda,Enosil	13	R	24	aa	CLE	41	0.96	0.93	4.62	2.7	6.7	2.5	0.0	23	89	110
Teller,Carlos	13	L	27	a/a	SF	50	5.32	1.81	17.8	6.7	4.9	0.7	1.1	29	72	12
Tepera,Dennis	12	R	25	aa	TOR	74	6.40	1.88	21.8	4.7	5.6	1.2	0.6	37	65	30
	13	R	26	aa	TOR	116	5.53	1.62	15.6	4.4	6.5	1.5	1.0	33	67	37
Thomas,Ian	13	L	26	aa	ATL	104	3.79	1.27	10.9	3.5	8.7	2.5	0.7	30	71	89
Thomas,Justin	12	L	28	aaa	NYY	63	4.88	1.50	7.97	3.3	5.8	1.8	0.6	33	67	51
	13	L	29	aaa	OAK	84	5.09	1.73	24	3.9	5.4	1.4	0.8	35	71	30
Thomas,Kevin	12	R	26	aa	STL	73	4.95	1.36	6.81	2.8	7.0	2.5	1.2	31	66	60
	13	R	27	a/a	STL	63	3.50	1.32	5.21	2.7	8.8	3.2	0.7	34	75	102
Thomas,Michael	13	L	24	aa	LA	47	4.13	1.61	6.16	4.2	8.1	1.9	0.5	36	74	73
Thompson,Aaron	12	L	25	aa	MIN	86	6.42	1.86	18.3	2.4	3.8	1.6	1.0	38	65	9
	13	L	26	a/a	MIN	59	3.27	1.49	6.02	2.6	6.4	2.5	0.5	35	78	72
Thompson,Jacob	12	R	23	aa	TAM	125	6.02	1.84	23.3	3.8	5.6	1.5	0.8	38	67	28
	13	R	24	aa	TAM	149	4.68	1.51	23.8	3.5	5.2	1.5	0.8	32	69	38
Thompson,Taylor	13	R	26	a/a	CHW	66	4.88	1.41	6.38	2.7	6.9	2.6	0.4	34	64	82
Thornburg,Tyler	12	R	24	a/a	MIL	113	4.10	1.37	22.5	3.2	7.7	2.4	0.7	32	71	77
	13	R	25	aaa	MIL	75	6.70	1.79	23	3.6	8.8	2.4	1.6	40	65	44
Thornton,Zachary	13	R	25	a/a	PIT	61	3.28	1.05	7.41	1.6	8.6	5.5	0.6	30	69	157
Tobin,Mason	13	R	26	aaa	SF	34	5.04	1.57	4.86	4.1	4.8	1.2	0.6	31	67	35
Todd,Jess	12	R	26	aaa	STL	66	4.89	1.71	6.39	2.9	7.8	2.7	0.8	40	72	68
	13	R	27	aaa	DET	63	2.96	1.27	6.56	4.0	6.9	1.7	0.5	27	78	71
Tonkin,Michael	13	R	24	a/a	MIN	57	3.94	1.35	4.57	2.5	8.6	3.4	0.4	35	70	108
Torres,Alexander	12	L	25	aaa	TAM	69	8.35	2.07	13	8.2	9.8	1.2	0.8	35	58	58
	13	L	26	aaa	TAM	46	4.19	1.34	21.3	4.2	9.7	2.3	0.4	32	68	102
Torres,Carlos	12	R	30	aaa	COL	61	5.14	1.75	19.9	4.0	6.0	1.5	1.3	35	73	22
	13	R	31	aaa	NYM	72	3.78	1.36	24.9	2.3	6.4	2.8	0.8	32	74	71
Townsend,Jason	13	R	25	aa	PIT	54	7.81	2.02	7.21	4.4	4.9	1.1	1.1	38	61	5
Tracy,Matthew	13	L	25	aa	NYY	64	7.45	1.94	21.7	5.7	6.8	1.2	1.2	36	62	22
Treinen,Blake	13	R	25	aa	WAS	119	4.55	1.54	24.6	2.5	5.1	2.1	0.8	34	71	44
Tropeano,Nichola	13	R	23	aa	HOU	134	4.64	1.46	20.4	2.6	7.6	2.9	1.1	35	70	71
Tufts,Tyler	12	R	26	a/a	TEX	30	7.43	1.77	7.32	2.2	3.4	1.5	1.6	35	59	-11
	13	R	27	aa	TEX	100	5.12	1.69	16.6	2.2	2.7	1.2	1.6	33	74	-18
Turley,Nikolas	13	L	24	a/a	NYY	145	5.13	1.60	22.9	5.1	7.2	1.4	1.0	31	69	45
Turner,Jacob	12	R	21	aaa	MIA	90	3.22	1.39	25.3	3.8	5.2	1.4	0.4	29	77	52
	13	R	22	aaa	MIA	56	5.60	1.49	24.3	2.5	5.2	2.1	1.2	32	64	33
Turpen,Daniel	12	R	26	aa	MIN	72	5.67	1.74	7.15	5.2	7.3	1.4	0.7	35	67	49
	13	R	27	a/a	MIN	65	6.03	1.94	6.58	6.0	5.2	0.9	1.3	34	71	4
Urckfitz,Patrick	13	L	25	a/a	HOU	67	3.43	1.56	5.89	3.0	4.0	1.3	0.3	33	77	38
Urlaub,Jeffrey	13	L	26	aa	OAK	47	4.52	1.53	5.07	2.6	6.1	2.3	0.4	36	69	69
Valdes,Raul	12	L	35	aaa	PHI	30	3.94	1.26	7.65	0.7	9.1	12.6	1.2	37	73	279
	13	L	36	aaa	PHI	79	3.73	1.41	23.8	2.9	5.6	2.0	0.7	32	75	52
Valdez,Jose	13	R	25	aa	SF	56	5.54	2.03	7.15	7.2	7.0	1.0	0.2	37	71	49
	12	R	29	aaa	HOU	44	5.53	1.73	4.32	2.6	9.3	3.6	1.1	42	69	86
Valdez,Jose	13	R	30	aaa	HOU	39	7.31	1.97	5.38	5.5	5.7	1.0	1.1	36	63	13
Van Mil,Loek	12	R	28	a/a	CLE	65	4.32	1.55	6.89	3.5	5.2	1.5	0.7	33	72	39
	13	R	29	a/a	CIN	64	5.36	1.86	5.87	5.1	3.6	0.7	1.4	32	74	-12
Vance,Kevin	13	R	23	aa	CHW	69	5.15	1.57	7.57	5.5	9.6	1.7	0.7	33	67	76
Vargas,Claudio	12	R	34	aaa	MIL	110	5.39	1.75	25	3.2	5.2	1.6	1.4	36	72	13
	13	R	35	aaa	TOR	83	8.28	2.06	20.2	4.4	4.4	1.0	1.5	37	60	-14
Varner,Rett	13	R	25	a/a	MIA	73	4.29	1.64	8.14	3.9	7.0	1.8	1.3	34	78	35
Vasquez,Anthony	12	L	26	aaa	SEA	61	6.39	1.73	25.1	3.0	3.8	1.3	0.5	36	61	25
	13	L	27	aa	SEA	70	5.93	1.54	25.3	2.9	3.3	1.1	2.0	29	67	-23
Vasquez,Luis	12	R	26	a/a	LA	53	7.82	2.02	5.97	6.2	5.3	0.9	0.3	37	58	31
	13	R	27	a/a	LA	36	3.00	1.73	6.49	7.5	9.1	1.2	0.3	33	82	78
Vasquez,Virgil	13	R	31	a/a	MIN	136	5.08	1.55	19.9	2.0	4.5	2.2	1.1	34	69	31
Ventura,Yordano	12	R	21	aa	KC	29	5.20	1.28	20.1	3.8	6.5	1.7	0.3	28	56	74
	13	R	22	a/a	KC	135	3.70	1.38	21.8	3.5	8.7	2.5	0.5	34	73	94
Verdugo,Ryan	12	L	25	aaa	KC	137	4.11	1.41	21.4	4.3	6.1	1.4	1.2	27	74	37
	13	L	26	a/a	KC	70	5.76	1.76	18.9	4.2	5.1	1.2	1.4	34	70	6
Verhagen,Drew	13	R	23	aa	DET	60	3.60	1.29	20.5	2.5	4.8	2.0	0.5	30	72	58
Verrett,Logan	13	R	23	aa	NYM	146	4.45	1.20	24.4	1.8	7.1	4.0	1.3	30	67	91
Vessella,Thomas	12	L	27	aa	SF	53	5.38	1.72	5.69	5.2	6.0	1.2	0.3	34	67	48
	13	L	28	a/a	SF	48	5.63	1.98	6.82	4.6	4.3	0.9	0.6	38	71	14

PITCHER	yr	t	age	lvl	org	ip	era	whip	bf/g	ctl	dom	cmd	hr/9	h%	s%	bpv
Villanueva,Elih	12	R	26	aaa	MIA	113	4.93	1.74	16.1	4.0	5.6	1.4	1.0	35	73	26
	13	R	27	aaa	MIA	46	4.87	1.43	24.6	2.6	5.0	1.9	1.2	31	69	32
Villarreal,Brayan	13	R	26	aaa	BOS	40	3.94	1.74	5.48	7.4	8.4	1.1	0.0	33	75	80
Villarreal,Pedro	12	R	25	a/a	CIN	149	5.74	1.60	25.2	2.5	5.4	2.2	0.9	35	64	41
	13	R	26	aaa	CIN	110	6.16	1.62	14.8	2.5	5.6	2.2	2.1	34	67	9
Volstad,Chris	12	R	26	aaa	CHC	71	6.06	1.69	26.8	2.5	5.3	2.1	0.9	37	64	35
	13	R	27	aaa	COL	128	5.33	1.79	25.6	3.1	2.9	0.9	1.1	35	72	-8
Von Schamann,D	13	R	22	aa	LA	67	6.12	1.72	18.9	2.7	5.9	2.1	1.1	37	65	36
Wacha,Michael	13	R	22	aaa	STL	85	2.82	1.03	21.8	1.9	6.6	3.4	0.9	26	77	96
Wade,Cory	12	R	29	aaa	NYY	32	3.29	1.27	7.62	3.0	4.2	1.4	1.3	25	80	21
	13	R	30	aaa	NYM	68	3.75	1.48	6.93	2.7	5.1	1.9	0.9	33	77	41
Walczak,Jamie	13	R	26	aa	CIN	33	5.57	1.73	6.26	5.3	9.5	1.8	0.4	38	66	79
Walden,Marcus	13	R	25	aa	TOR	162	4.47	1.64	27.8	2.8	4.0	1.4	0.6	35	73	27
Walker,Taijuan	12	R	20	aa	SEA	127	5.27	1.45	21.6	3.5	7.8	2.3	0.8	33	63	71
	13	R	21	a/a	SEA	141	3.10	1.23	22.9	3.5	9.3	2.7	0.6	30	76	102
Wall,Josh	12	R	25	aaa	LA	54	4.05	1.28	4	3.0	7.2	2.4	1.0	29	71	69
	13	R	26	aaa	MIA	49	6.21	1.86	5.13	5.2	7.1	1.4	0.7	37	66	44
Walters,Jeffrey	13	R	26	aa	NYM	56	2.33	1.22	4.27	2.5	7.9	3.1	0.3	32	81	107
Walters,P.J.	12	R	27	aaa	MIN	58	5.50	1.77	19.1	2.6	5.6	2.1	1.2	38	71	27
	13	R	28	aaa	MIN	103	5.17	1.80	25.1	4.4	5.4	1.2	0.5	36	70	36
Wang,Chien-Minc	12	R	32	a/a	WAS	66	8.18	1.92	26.1	2.1	4.0	1.9	1.4	39	57	3
	13	R	33	aaa	TOR	110	4.06	1.49	26.2	2.1	3.3	1.6	0.6	33	73	30
Watts,Dakota	12	R	25	aa	MIN	34	3.28	1.60	6.19	4.5	5.8	1.3	0.3	33	79	53
	13	R	26	aa	MIN	36	0.88	1.30	5.34	2.6	6.0	2.3	0.0	32	92	87
Webb,Daniel	13	R	24	a/a	CHW	48	3.25	1.44	5.98	4.9	9.5	1.9	0.3	33	77	96
Webb,Travis	12	L	28	aaa	CIN	58	6.35	1.68	4.83	5.8	8.1	1.4	1.5	31	64	33
	13	L	29	aaa	MIL	55	8.91	2.35	5.08	8.0	8.4	1.0	1.7	40	63	7
Weber,Thad	12	R	28	aaa	SD	147	3.96	1.28	24.1	2.0	5.4	2.7	0.8	30	70	66
	13	R	29	aaa	TOR	134	4.12	1.48	24.1	1.9	5.7	3.0	0.5	36	72	76
Webster,Allen	12	R	22	aa	BOS	131	5.11	1.70	20.4	4.4	7.6	1.7	0.2	38	67	72
	13	R	23	aaa	BOS	105	4.51	1.21	20.2	3.8	8.3	2.2	0.8	27	64	82
Weinhardt,Robbie	12	R	27	aa	DET	66	3.60	1.50	6.48	3.7	5.6	1.5	1.0	31	79	36
	13	R	28	a/a	DET	69	4.29	1.87	9.81	3.8	4.3	1.1	1.3	36	81	-1
Welker,Duke	12	R	26	a/a	PIT	55	2.93	1.40	5.66	4.2	6.1	1.4	0.2	30	78	67
	13	R	27	aaa	PIT	63	4.42	1.53	5.71	4.5	6.9	1.5	0.4	32	70	62
Werner,Andrew	12	L	25	a/a	SD	126	3.47	1.32	23.8	2.1	6.6	3.2	0.4	33	73	94
	13	L	26	aaa	OAK	165	6.13	1.60	27	2.1	4.8	2.3	0.9	36	61	39
Westcott,Craig	12	R	26	aa	SF	165	5.25	1.71	26.7	3.3	2.9	0.9	0.3	34	67	17
	13	R	27	aa	SF	144	4.44	1.62	23.7	3.4	4.5	1.3	0.6	34	73	31
Wheeler,Zack	12	R	22	a/a	NYM	149	3.44	1.19	23.9	3.3	8.0	2.4	0.2	29	69	101
	13	R	23	aaa	NYM	69	3.31	1.18	21.1	3.0	8.3	2.8	0.9	28	76	89
Whelan,Kevin	12	R	28	aaa	NYY	25	5.03	1.92	5.01	6.6	9.6	1.5	1.0	38	76	53
	13	R	29	aaa	CIN	51	7.40	1.93	5.12	6.9	9.8	1.4	2.2	34	66	18
White,Cole	13	R	25	aa	COL	48	6.01	2.00	5.11	7.1	6.1	0.9	0.6	35	69	30
White,Sean	12	R	31	aaa	LAA	38	8.29	2.18	6.5	5.5	3.8	0.7	0.4	39	59	8
	13	R	32	aaa	LA	74	3.92	1.76	10	5.5	3.9	0.7	0.6	31	78	16
Whiting,Boone	13	R	24	a/a	STL	136	4.19	1.44	21.5	3.1	7.2	2.3	0.8	33	72	68
Whitley,Chase	12	R	23	a/a	NYY	84	3.90	1.20	7.88	3.0	6.5	2.2	1.0	27	70	64
	13	R	24	aaa	NYY	68	4.25	1.47	10	3.1	6.8	2.2	0.6	34	71	68
Williams,Alan	13	L	23	aa	MIL	30	3.80	1.41	9.77	3.5	8.4	2.4	0.8	33	75	78
Williams,Mark	13	R	24	aa	MIL	30	6.98	1.96	9.56	7.2	7.2	1.0	2.8	30	72	-24
Wilson,Tyler	13	R	24	aa	BAL	89	4.59	1.36	23.3	2.3	5.8	2.5	1.6	30	72	39
Wisler,Matthew	13	R	21	aa	SD	105	3.24	1.12	20.7	2.2	8.0	3.6	0.5	30	72	115
Wojciechowski,As	12	R	24	aa	HOU	44	2.48	1.08	21.3	2.9	6.0	2.1	0.0	26	74	92
	13	R	25	a/a	HOU	160	3.87	1.29	23.5	3.0	6.2	2.1	0.7	29	71	65
Wolf,Ross	12	R	30	a/a	TEX	62	4.53	1.58	5.48	2.5	6.0	2.4	1.1	35	74	46
	13	R	31	aaa	TEX	37	2.95	1.44	19.9	2.9	4.6	1.6	0.4	32	80	48
Wood,Alex	13	L	22	a/a	ATL	62	1.58	1.08	22	2.5	8.0	3.2	0.2	29	85	122
Woodall,Bryan	12	R	26	a/a	ARI	67	7.20	1.85	6.52	3.3	6.7	2.0	0.9	40	60	43
	13	R	27	a/a	ARI	62	4.45	1.54	5.01	3.1	7.7	2.4	1.4	35	75	52
Woods,Coty	12	R	24	a/a	COL	56	4.30	1.67	4.14	3.2	5.9	1.8	1.2	35	77	30
	13	R	25	aaa	COL	39	7.96	2.17	5.89	5.1	3.7	0.7	1.4	37	64	-22
Wooten,Robert	12	R	27	a/a	MIL	73	4.54	1.53	5.6	3.3	6.9	2.1	0.9	34	72	56
	13	R	28	aaa	MIL	52	3.64	1.20	5.23	2.3	6.1	2.6	0.9	28	72	70
Workman,Brando	12	R	24	aa	BOS	25	5.47	1.36	20.9	1.9	6.8	3.5	0.9	34	60	85
	13	R	25	a/a	BOS	101	4.17	1.40	25.1	2.8	7.7	2.7	1.2	33	74	67
Worley,Vance	13	R	26	aaa	MIN	58	4.59	1.63	28.7	2.8	4.1	1.5	0.5	35	71	34
Wright,Austin	13	L	24	aa	PHI	94	6.53	1.69	15.8	5.5	6.2	1.1	1.3	30	62	21
Wright,Justin	12	L	23	aa	STL	61	4.82	1.48	5.21	3.9	8.0	2.0	0.8	33	68	67
	13	L	24	aa	STL	59	5.76	1.74	5.38	3.8	8.0	2.1	0.8	39	67	59
Wright,Matthew	12	L	25	aa	TOR	52	5.22	1.28	7.94	3.2	8.1	2.5	2.0	27	66	47
	13	L	26	aa	TOR	63	8.08	1.90	10.3	3.9	6.1	1.6	2.4	36	61	-16
Wright,Mike	12	R	22	aa	BAL	62	5.84	1.56	22.8	2.5	5.6	2.3	1.2	34	64	36
	13	R	23	a/a	BAL	150	3.79	1.48	24	2.4	6.9	2.9	0.7	36	75	77
Wright,Steven	12	R	28	a/a	BOS	142	4.05	1.63	25.2	5.2	5.7	1.1	0.8	31	76	35
	13	R	29	aaa	BOS	135	4.94	1.84	26.3	5.0	4.8	1.0	0.8	34	74	17
Wyatt,Heath	13	R	25	aa	STL	47	3.59	1.31	5.4	1.9	5.8	3.0	0.9	32	75	71
Yan,Johan	12	R	24	a/a	TEX	52	5.03	1.70	5.22	5.0	5.0	1.0	1.1	31	72	14
	13	R	25	aaa	TEX	58	6.11	1.72	5.95	3.5	6.5	1.9	0.8	37	64	44
Yates,Kirby	12	R	25	aa	TAM	68	2.99	1.37	5.7	5.1	10.3	2.0	0.5	31	79	100
	13	R	26	aaa	TAM	62	2.26	1.11	4.75	3.4	11.0	3.2	0.3	30	80	138
Young,Chris	13	R	34	aaa	WAS	32	9.98	2.44	24	4.1	3.2	0.8	3.0	40	63	-81
Zagurski,Mike	13	L	30	aaa	OAK	53	3.49	1.49	5.1	4.4	10.3	2.3	0.6	36	78	95
Zeid,Joshua	12	R	25	aa	HOU	56	6.25	1.50	5.18	3.2	8.8	2.7	1.0	36	58	77
	13	R	26	aaa	HOU	44	4.13	1.62	4.51	5.8	8.9	1.5	0.7	33	75	69
Zinicola,Zechry	12	R	27	aa	WAS	27	3.00	1.20	5.23	1.4	6.7	5.0	0.8	32	78	121
	13	R	28	aa	BAL	65	3.82	1.48	6.04	3.4	6.1	1.8	0.6	33	74	56

This section provides rankings of projected skills indicators for 2014. Rather than take shots in the dark predicting league leaders in the exact number of home runs, or stolen bases, or strikeouts, the Forecaster's Leaderboards focus on the component elements of each skill.

For batters, we've ranked the top players in terms of pure power, speed, and batting average skill, breaking each down in a number of different ways to provide more insight. For pitchers, we rank some of the key base skills, differentiating between starters and relievers, and provide a few interesting cuts that might uncover some late round sleepers.

These are clearly not exhaustive lists of sorts and filters. If there is another cut you'd like to see, drop us a note and I'll consider it for next year's book. Also note that the database at BaseballHQ.com allows you to construct your own custom sorts and filters. Finally, remember that these are just tools. Some players will appear on multiple lists—even mutually exclusive lists—so you have to assess what makes most sense and make decisions for your specific application.

Power

Top PX, 400+ AB: Top power skills among projected full-time players.

Top PX, –300 AB: Top power skills among projected part-time players. Possible end-game options are here.

Position Scarcity: A quick scan to see which positions have deeper power options than others.

Top PX, ct% over 85%: Top power skills among the top contact hitters. Best pure power options here.

Top PX, ct% under 75%: Top power skills among the worst contact hitters. These are free-swingers who might be prone to streakiness or lower batting averages.

Top PX, FB% over 40%: Top power skills among the most extreme fly ball hitters. Most likely to convert their power into home runs.

Top PX, FB% under 35%: Top power skills among those with lesser fly ball tendencies. There may be more downside to their home run potential.

Speed

Top Spd, 400+ AB: Top speed skills among projected full-time players.

Top Spd, -300 AB: Top speed skills among projected part-time players. Possible end-game options here.

Position Scarcity: A quick scan to see which positions have deeper speed options than others.

Top Spd, OB% .340 and above: Top speed skills among those who get on base most often. Best opportunities for stolen bases here.

Top Spd, OB% under .300: Top speed skills among those who have trouble getting on base. These names may bear watching if they can improve their on base ability.

Top Spd, SBO% over 20%: Top speed skills among those who get the green light most often. Most likely to convert their speed into stolen bases.

Top Spd, SBO% under 15%: Top speed skills among those who are currently not getting the green light. There may be sleeper SBs here if given more opportunities to run.

Batting Average

Top ct%, 400+ AB: Top contact skills among projected full-time players. Contact does not always convert to higher BAs, but is still strongly correlated.

Top ct%, -300 AB: Top contact skills among projected part-time players. Possible end-gamers here.

Low ct%, 400+ AB: The poorest contact skills among projected full-time players. Potential BA killers.

Top ct%, bb% over 10%: Top contact skills among the most patient hitters. Best batting average upside here.

Top ct%, bb% under 6%: Top contact skills among the least patient hitters. These are free-swingers who might be prone to streakiness or lower batting averages.

Top ct%, GB% over 50%: Top contact skills among the most extreme ground ball hitters. A ground ball has a higher chance of becoming a hit than a non-HR fly ball so there may be some batting average upside here.

Top ct%, GB% under 40%: Top contact skills from those with lesser ground ball tendencies. These players make contact but hit more fly balls, which tend to convert to hits at a lower rate than GB.

Pitching Skills

Top Command: Leaders in projected K/BB rates.

Top Control: Leaders in fewest projected walks allowed.

Top Dominance: Leaders in projected strikeout rate.

Top Ground Ball Rate: GB pitchers tend to have lower ERAs (and higher WHIP) than fly ball pitchers.

Top Fly Ball Rate: FB pitchers tend to have higher ERAs (and lower WHIP) than ground ball pitchers.

High GB, Low Dom: GB pitchers tend to have lower K rates, but these are the most extreme examples.

High GB, High Dom: The best at dominating hitters and keeping the ball down. These are the pitchers who keep runners off the bases and batted balls in the park, a skills combination that is the most valuable a pitcher can own.

Lowest xERA: Leaders in projected skills-based ERA.

Top BPV: Two lists of top skilled pitchers. For starters, those projected to be rotation regulars (180+ IP) and fringe starters with skill (<150 IP). For relievers, those projected to be frontline closers (10+ saves) and high-skilled bullpen fillers (<9 saves).

Risk Management

These lists include players who've accumulated the most days on the disabled list over the past five years (Grade "F" in Health) and whose performance was the most consistent over the past three years. Also listed are the most reliable batters and pitchers overall, with a focus on positional and skills reliability. As a reminder, reliability in this context is not tied to skill level; it is a gauge of which players manage to accumulate playing time and post consistent output from year to year, whether that output is good or bad.

LIMA Plan

These are the players ranked as B or better for those employing the LIMA Plan, set up in a grid by position. A full description of this plan appears in the Encyclopedia.

Portfolio3 Plan

Players are sorted and ranked based on how they fit into the three draft tiers of the Portfolio3 Plan. A full description of this plan appears in the Encyclopedia.

Random Variance

These charts list +/– 3, 4 and 5 Rand Var scores for players with a minimum of 300 AB or 100 IP. The scores identify players who, in 2013, posted outlying levels that are prone to regression. A full description appears in the Batters and Pitchers introductory pages.

BATTER SKILLS RANKING - POWER

TOP PX, 400+ AB

NAME	POS	PX
Davis,Chris	3	204
Stanton,Giancarlo	9	202
Napoli,Mike	3	195
Moss,Brandon	3 9	189
Carter,Chris	0 3 7	185
Goldschmidt,Paul	3	177
Dunn,Adam	0 3	171
Kemp,Matt	8	166
Ortiz,David	0	166
Alvarez,Pedro	5	165
Saltalamacchia,Jarrod	2	165
Bruce,Jay	9	163
Gonzalez,Carlos	7	162
Howard,Ryan	3	160
Encarnacion,Edwin	0 3	158
Longoria,Evan	5	157
Votto,Joey	3	155
Braun,Ryan	7	154
Granderson,Curtis	8	154
Cabrera,Miguel	5	153
Bautista,Jose	9	152
Hart,Corey	3	151
Rasmus,Colby	8	151
Upton,Justin	7 9	150
Willingham,Josh	0 7	149
Soriano,Alfonso	7	148
Belt,Brandon	3	147
Trout,Mike	7 8	147
Puig,Yasiel	9	145
Arcia,Oswaldo	7 9	144
Hamilton,Josh	0 9	144
Middlebrooks,Will	5	144
Adams,Matt	3	143
Myers,Wil	9	143
Trumbo,Mark	3	143
Gomez,Carlos	8	142
Jones,Adam	8	141
Teixeira,Mark	3	141
Tulowitzki,Troy	6	141
Davis,Ike	3	140

TOP PX, 300 or fewer AB

NAME	POS	PX
Soto,Geovany	2	155
Carp,Mike	3 7	154
Kottaras,George	2	152
Maxwell,Justin	8 9	152
Flowers,Tyler	2	150
Raburn,Ryan	9	149
Van Slyke,Scott	7	147
Moore,Tyler	7	142
Ross,David	2	140
Hairston,Scott	9	139
Brown,Andrew	9	135
Dietrich,Derek	4	134
Scott,Luke	0	132
Murphy,Donnie	5	131
Davidson,Matthew	5	130
Norris,Derek	2	130
Shoppach,Kelly	2	130
Recker,Anthony	2	129
Gindl,Caleb	7	128
Pena,Carlos	0 3	128
Betemit,Wilson	0	127
Sanchez,Jorge Tony	2	127
Kratz,Erik	2	126

POSITIONAL SCARCITY

NAME	POS	PX
Carter,Chris	DH	185
Dunn,Adam	2	171
Ortiz,David	3	166
Encarnacion,Edwin	4	158
Willingham,Josh	5	149
Hamilton,Josh	6	144
Saltalamacchia,Jarrod	CA	165
Soto,Geovany	2	155
Kottaras,George	3	152
Flowers,Tyler	4	150
Gattis,Evan	5	150
Ross,David	6	140
Rosario,Wilin	7	139
Gomes,Yan	8	138
Davis,Chris	1B	204
Napoli,Mike	2	195
Moss,Brandon	3	189
Carter,Chris	4	185
Goldschmidt,Paul	5	177
Dunn,Adam	6	171
Ruf,Darin	7	164
Howard,Ryan	8	160
Encarnacion,Edwin	9	158
Francisco,Juan	10	158
Cano,Robinson	2B	136
Uggla,Dan	2	135
Dietrich,Derek	3	134
Gyorko,Jedd	4	134
Espinosa,Danny	5	125
Lowrie,Jed	6	125
Weeks,Rickie	7	122
Sizemore,Scott	8	121
Alvarez,Pedro	3B	165
Francisco,Juan	2	158
Longoria,Evan	3	157
Reynolds,Mark	4	156
Cabrera,Miguel	5	153
Middlebrooks,Will	6	144
Bogaerts,Xander	7	137
Wright,David	8	134
Frazier,Todd	9	133
Murphy,Donnie	10	131
Tulowitzki,Troy	SS	141
Ramirez,Hanley	2	138
Lowrie,Jed	3	125
Desmond,Ian	4	124
Drew,Stephen	5	122
Cabrera,Asdrubal	6	110
Zobrist,Ben	7	109
Peralta,Jhonny	8	107
Stanton,Giancarlo	OF	202
Moss,Brandon	2	189
Carter,Chris	3	185
Kemp,Matt	4	166
Ruf,Darin	5	164
Bruce,Jay	6	163
Gonzalez,Carlos	7	162
Braun,Ryan	8	154
Carp,Mike	9	154
Granderson,Curtis	10	154
Bautista,Jose	11	152
Maxwell,Justin	12	152
Quentin,Carlos	13	152
Rasmus,Colby	14	151
Gattis,Evan	15	150
Upton,Justin	16	150

TOP PX, Ct% over 85%

NAME	Ct%	PX
Encarnacion,Edwin	86	158
Cano,Robinson	86	136
Beltre,Adrian	87	125
Pujols,Albert	87	121
Hill,Aaron	86	120
Taveras,Oscar	87	110
Molina,Yadier	89	103
Arenado,Nolan	87	102
Hardy,J.J.	86	101
Kinsler,Ian	88	99
Pedroia,Dustin	89	99
Harrison,Josh	87	96
Martinez,Victor	90	95
Victorino,Shane	86	95
Pierzynski,A.J.	86	94
Crisp,Coco	87	93
Perez,Salvador	89	91
Ruiz,Carlos	87	91
Reyes,Jose	89	90
Cabrera,Melky	86	89
Murphy,Daniel	86	89
Pagan,Angel	86	89
Prado,Martin	90	88
Simmons,Andrelton	90	86
Rollins,Jimmy	86	84
Infante,Omar	89	80
Aybar,Erick	88	79
Furcal,Rafael	86	78
Loney,James	87	78
Young,Michael	86	78
Aviles,Mike	87	77
Markakis,Nick	88	74
Brantley,Michael	88	73
Suzuki,Kurt	87	73
Pacheco,Jordan	87	72
Escobar,Yunel	86	71
Ramirez,Alexei	88	71
Callaspo,Alberto	89	70
Sogard,Eric	86	69
Pena,Brayan	88	67

TOP PX, Ct% under 75%

NAME	Ct%	PX
Davis,Chris	66	204
Stanton,Giancarlo	67	202
Napoli,Mike	64	195
Moss,Brandon	69	189
Carter,Chris	61	185
Dunn,Adam	62	171
Kemp,Matt	74	166
Alvarez,Pedro	67	165
Saltalamacchia,Jarrod	68	165
Ruf,Darin	68	164
Bruce,Jay	72	163
Gonzalez,Carlos	74	162
Howard,Ryan	67	160
Francisco,Juan	64	158
Reynolds,Mark	65	156
Soto,Geovany	69	155
Carp,Mike	71	154
Granderson,Curtis	71	154
Kottaras,George	66	152
Maxwell,Justin	62	152
Rasmus,Colby	72	151
Flowers,Tyler	59	150
Raburn,Ryan	73	149

Top PX, FB% over 40%

NAME	FB%	PX
Davis,Chris	42	204
Napoli,Mike	41	195
Moss,Brandon	48	189
Carter,Chris	46	185
Dunn,Adam	44	171
Saltalamacchia,Jarrod	42	165
Ruf,Darin	41	164
Bruce,Jay	43	163
Encarnacion,Edwin	45	158
Longoria,Evan	43	157
Reynolds,Mark	44	156
Soto,Geovany	42	155
Granderson,Curtis	44	154
Bautista,Jose	46	152
Quentin,Carlos	46	152
Hart,Corey	41	151
Rasmus,Colby	44	151
Gattis,Evan	45	150
Raburn,Ryan	41	149
Willingham,Josh	45	149
Soriano,Alfonso	42	148
Belt,Brandon	41	147
Van Slyke,Scott	42	147
Gomes,Jonny	49	143
Teixeira,Mark	45	141
Ross,David	42	140
Abreu,Jose	43	139
Cespedes,Yoenis	43	139
Hairston,Scott	51	139
Young,Chris	50	138
Uggla,Dan	45	135
Arencibia,J.P.	46	134
Gyorko,Jedd	41	134
Kubel,Jason	42	132
Murphy,Donnie	44	131
Reddick,Josh	47	131
Duda,Lucas	46	130
Norris,Derek	42	130
Shoppach,Kelly	48	130
Wieters,Matt	41	130

Top PX, FB% under 35%

NAME	FB%	PX
Gonzalez,Carlos	34	162
Votto,Joey	32	155
Carp,Mike	34	154
Puig,Yasiel	32	145
Myers,Wil	34	143
Jones,Adam	33	141
Harper,Bryce	33	140
Wallace,Brett	34	137
Cano,Robinson	29	136
Cuddyer,Michael	31	133
Avila,Alex	32	129
Heyward,Jason	34	127
Headley,Chase	32	126
Krauss,Marc	33	126
Castro,Jason	33	125
Morales,Kendrys	32	125
Zimmerman,Ryan	34	125
Bradley,Jackie	30	124
Desmond,Ian	34	124
Morse,Michael	32	124
Pence,Hunter	34	123
Marte,Starling	30	121
Kipnis,Jason	32	120

BATTER SKILLS RANKING - SPEED

TOP Spd, 400+ AB

NAME	POS	Spd
Marte,Starling	7	184
Segura,Jean	6	181
Jackson,Austin	8	174
Gardner,Brett	8	161
Revere,Ben	8	161
Fowler,Dexter	8	160
Young Jr.,Eric	7 9	158
Bourn,Michael	8	157
Simmons,Andrelton	6	153
Trout,Mike	7 8	153
Lagares,Juan	8	148
Escobar,Alcides	6	147
Jennings,Desmond	8	147
Pagan,Angel	8	147
Gomez,Carlos	8	146
Gregorius,Didi	6	146
Maybin,Cameron	8	144
Miller,Bradley	6	142
Cabrera,Everth	6	141
Garcia,Avisail	8 9	141
Hechavarria,Adeiny	6	141
Aoki,Norichika	9	140
McCutchen,Andrew	8	140
LeMahieu,DJ	4	139
Andrus,Elvis	6	137
Span,Denard	8	137
Suzuki,Ichiro	9	137
Villar,Jonathan	6	137
Eaton,Adam	7 8	136
Venable,Will	8 9	136
Granderson,Curtis	8	135
Stubbs,Drew	8 9	133
Cain,Lorenzo	8 9	132
Castro,Starlin	6	132
Martin,Leonys	8 9	131
Crawford,Carl	7	129
Reyes,Jose	6	129
Machado,Manny	5	128
Infante,Omar	4	127
De Aza,Alejandro	7 8	126

TOP Spd, 300 or fewer AB

NAME	POS	Spd
Hamilton,Billy	8	168
Ozuna,Marcell	8 9	160
Gentry,Craig	7 8	159
Garcia,Leury	4	158
Gose,Anthony	8	154
Weeks,Jemile	4	153
Gordon,Dee	6	152
Hicks,Aaron	8	151
Robinson,Derrick	7	150
Kawasaki,Munenori	6	149
Bloomquist,Willie	4	148
Beltre,Engel	9	146
Campana,Tony	8	146
Fuld,Sam	7 8 9	144
Arias,Joaquin	5 6	141
Johnson,Elliot	4	140
Mastroianni,Darin	7	140
Urrutia,Henry	0	140
Ciriaco,Pedro	6	138
Hernandez,Cesar	8	138
Lake,Junior	7 8	138
Reimold,Nolan	0	138
Robinson,Shane	7 8 9	136

POSITIONAL SCARCITY

NAME	POS	Spd
Urrutia,Henry	DH	140
Reimold,Nolan	2	138
Crisp,Coco	3	120
Cespedes,Yoenis	4	117
Dickerson,Chris	5	108
Hamilton,Josh	6	104
Zunino,Mike	CA	112
Lucroy,Jonathan	2	110
Hundley,Nick	3	108
Herrmann,Chris	4	106
Vogt,Stephen	5	104
Gomes,Yan	6	102
Norris,Derek	7	97
Cruz,Tony	8	94
Young,Michael	1B	116
Belt,Brandon	2	111
Hart,Corey	3	108
Satin,Josh	4	106
Frandsen,Kevin	5	105
Baker,Jeff	6	102
Hosmer,Eric	7	100
Pacheco,Jordan	8	98
Keppinger,Jeff	9	97
Rodriguez,Sean	10	97
Garcia,Leury	2B	158
Weeks,Jemile	2	153
Bloomquist,Willie	3	148
Bonifacio,Emilio	4	141
Green,Grant	5	140
Johnson,Elliot	6	140
LeMahieu,DJ	7	139
Rutledge,Josh	8	137
Arias,Joaquin	3B	141
Escobar,Eduardo	2	135
Kelly,Don	3	129
Machado,Manny	4	128
Iglesias,Jose	5	123
Lawrie,Brett	6	122
Asche,Cody	7	120
Bogaerts,Xander	8	118
Gillaspie,Conor	9	117
Nelson,Chris	10	117
Segura,Jean	SS	181
Simmons,Andrelton	2	153
Gordon,Dee	3	152
Kawasaki,Munenori	4	149
Escobar,Alcides	5	147
Gregorius,Didi	6	146
Miller,Bradley	7	142
Arias,Joaquin	8	141
Marte,Starling	OF	184
Jackson,Austin	2	174
Dyson,Jarrod	3	168
Hamilton,Billy	4	168
Bourjos,Peter	5	166
Gardner,Brett	6	161
Revere,Ben	7	161
Fowler,Dexter	8	160
Ozuna,Marcell	9	160
Gentry,Craig	10	159
Young Jr.,Eric	11	158
Bourn,Michael	12	157
Gose,Anthony	13	154
Trout,Mike	14	153
Hicks,Aaron	15	151
Robinson,Derrick	16	150

TOP Spd, .340+ OBP

NAME	OBP	Spd
Jackson,Austin	354	174
Gardner,Brett	350	161
Fowler,Dexter	383	160
Gentry,Craig	349	159
Trout,Mike	400	153
Yelich,Christian	340	149
Blanco,Gregor	340	144
Miller,Bradley	346	142
Aoki,Norichika	354	140
McCutchen,Andrew	393	140
Andrus,Elvis	340	137
Eaton,Adam	346	136
Reyes,Jose	362	129
Victorino,Shane	343	124
Pence,Hunter	340	122
Braun,Ryan	376	121
Puig,Yasiel	363	120
Scutaro,Marco	351	119
Bogaerts,Xander	342	118
Hoes,L.J.	349	117
Pedroia,Dustin	364	117
Jeter,Derek	342	114
Carpenter,Matt	370	112
Upton,Justin	356	112
Belt,Brandon	359	111
Utley,Chase	358	111
Lucroy,Jonathan	342	110
Rendon,Anthony	348	110
Wright,David	381	110
Bradley,Jackie	342	109
Cuddyer,Michael	352	108
Gonzalez,Carlos	372	107
Jay,Jon	348	107
Kipnis,Jason	344	107
Zobrist,Ben	363	107
Prado,Martin	341	106
Markakis,Nick	340	105
Gordon,Alex	350	104
Kinsler,Ian	342	104
Heyward,Jason	352	103

TOP Spd, OBP under .300

NAME	OBP	Spd
Ozuna,Marcell	293	160
Garcia,Leury	272	158
Gose,Anthony	291	154
Weeks,Jemile	298	153
Robinson,Derrick	288	150
Kawasaki,Munenori	296	149
Lagares,Juan	290	148
Escobar,Alcides	290	147
Beltre,Engel	287	146
Campana,Tony	293	146
Fuld,Sam	295	144
Arias,Joaquin	279	141
Hechavarria,Adeiny	276	141
Green,Grant	284	140
Johnson,Elliot	272	140
Ciriaco,Pedro	273	138
Casilla,Alexi	298	135
Escobar,Eduardo	285	135
Nunez,Eduardo	296	135
Lough,David	297	134
Amarista,Alexi	282	132
Schafer,Jordan	292	130
Gennett,Scooter	293	129

Top Spd, SBO% over 20%

NAME	SBO%	Spd
Marte,Starling	43%	184
Segura,Jean	31%	181
Dyson,Jarrod	49%	168
Hamilton,Billy	85%	168
Gardner,Brett	33%	161
Revere,Ben	30%	161
Gentry,Craig	34%	159
Garcia,Leury	32%	158
Young Jr.,Eric	33%	158
Bourn,Michael	29%	157
Gose,Anthony	39%	154
Trout,Mike	21%	153
Weeks,Jemile	26%	153
Gordon,Dee	44%	152
Hicks,Aaron	23%	151
Robinson,Derrick	26%	150
Escobar,Alcides	21%	147
Jennings,Desmond	23%	147
Beltre,Engel	27%	146
Campana,Tony	45%	146
Gomez,Carlos	37%	146
Fuld,Sam	27%	144
Maybin,Cameron	25%	144
Bonifacio,Emilio	35%	141
Cabrera,Everth	37%	141
Johnson,Elliot	37%	140
Mastroianni,Darin	28%	140
LeMahieu,DJ	25%	139
Ciriaco,Pedro	28%	138
Hernandez,Cesar	23%	138
Lake,Junior	23%	138
Andrus,Elvis	26%	137
Villar,Jonathan	38%	137
Venable,Will	24%	136
Casilla,Alexi	26%	135
Nunez,Eduardo	27%	135
Stubbs,Drew	22%	133
Fuentes,Reymond	31%	132
Martin,Leonys	36%	131
Schafer,Jordan	39%	130

Top Spd, SBO% under 15%

NAME	SBO%	Spd
Jackson,Austin	12%	174
Ozuna,Marcell	8%	160
Simmons,Andrelton	9%	153
Bloomquist,Willie	14%	148
Gregorius,Didi	5%	146
Dickerson,Corey	12%	142
Miller,Bradley	11%	142
Arias,Joaquin	6%	141
Garcia,Avisail	14%	141
Green,Grant	9%	140
Urrutia,Henry	9%	140
Reimold,Nolan	6%	138
Robinson,Shane	12%	136
Escobar,Eduardo	11%	135
Amarista,Alexi	13%	132
Denorfia,Chris	13%	131
Gennett,Scooter	12%	129
Kelly,Don	7%	129
Johnson,Reed	3%	128
Machado,Manny	7%	128
Infante,Omar	6%	127
Owings,Christopher	14%	126
Ackley,Dustin	8%	124

BATTER SKILLS RANKING - BATTING AVERAGE

TOP Ct%, 400+ AB

NAME	ct%	BA
Scutaro,Marco	92	294
Aoki,Norichika	91	287
Martinez,Victor	90	315
Prado,Martin	90	289
Simmons,Andrelton	90	261
Callaspo,Alberto	89	263
Infante,Omar	89	290
Molina,Yadier	89	302
Pedroia,Dustin	89	296
Perez,Salvador	89	299
Revere,Ben	89	289
Reyes,Jose	89	303
Suzuki,Ichiro	89	267
Aybar,Erick	88	278
Barney,Darwin	88	246
Brantley,Michael	88	281
Kinsler,Ian	88	268
Markakis,Nick	88	277
Ramirez,Alexei	88	277
Span,Denard	88	282
Altuve,Jose	87	281
Arenado,Nolan	87	279
Beltre,Adrian	87	302
Crisp,Coco	87	264
Loney,James	87	281
Pujols,Albert	87	287
Cabrera,Melky	86	290
Cano,Robinson	86	315
Encarnacion,Edwin	86	284
Escobar,Alcides	86	258
Escobar,Yunel	86	264
Hardy,J.J.	86	256
Hill,Aaron	86	284
Murphy,Daniel	86	291
Pagan,Angel	86	284
Pierzynski,A.J.	86	277
Rollins,Jimmy	86	252
Victorino,Shane	86	280
Andrus,Elvis	85	276
Ellsbury,Jacoby	85	283

TOP Ct%, 300 or fewer AB

NAME	Ct%	BA
Pierre,Juan	92	266
Polanco,Placido	92	272
Keppinger,Jeff	91	275
Getz,Chris	90	245
Izturis,Cesar	90	230
Chavez,Endy	89	245
Frandsen,Kevin	89	244
Shuck,J.B.	89	271
Bloomquist,Willie	88	291
Hairston,Jerry	88	234
Hanigan,Ryan	88	259
Lombardozzi,Steve	88	272
Pena,Brayan	88	271
Harrison,Josh	87	258
Pacheco,Jordan	87	273
Taveras,Oscar	87	275
Herrera,Jonathan	86	271
Robinson,Shane	86	243
Arias,Joaquin	85	256
Betancourt,Yuniesky	85	236
Fuld,Sam	85	225
Carroll,Jamey	84	243
Elmore,Jake	84	246

LOW Ct%, 400+ AB

NAME	ct%	BA
Carter,Chris	61	222
Dunn,Adam	62	224
Napoli,Mike	64	262
Davis,Chris	66	276
Alvarez,Pedro	67	242
Howard,Ryan	67	256
Stanton,Giancarlo	67	261
Stubbs,Drew	67	229
Saltalamacchia,Jarrod	68	251
Villar,Jonathan	68	238
Arcia,Oswaldo	69	250
Arencibia,J.P.	69	205
Moss,Brandon	69	250
Upton,B.J.	69	236
Willingham,Josh	69	241
Duda,Lucas	71	233
Franklin,Nick	71	238
Granderson,Curtis	71	249
Saunders,Michael	71	246
Bruce,Jay	72	255
Davis,Ike	72	234
Myers,Wil	72	270
Rasmus,Colby	72	256
Trumbo,Mark	72	246
Weeks,Rickie	72	233
Gomez,Carlos	73	260
Marte,Starling	73	272
Soriano,Alfonso	73	258
Adams,Matt	74	272
Belt,Brandon	74	279
Castro,Jason	74	264
Drew,Stephen	74	258
Fowler,Dexter	74	282
Gonzalez,Carlos	74	309
Hamilton,Josh	74	269
Headley,Chase	74	265
Kemp,Matt	74	296
Middlebrooks,Will	74	256
Montero,Miguel	74	269
Asche,Cody	75	259
Cruz,Nelson	75	263
Goldschmidt,Paul	75	290
Gyorko,Jedd	75	251
Hart,Corey	75	272
Jackson,Austin	75	286
Johnson,Chris	75	285
LaRoche,Adam	75	252
Puig,Yasiel	75	287
Smoak,Justin	75	240
Swisher,Nick	75	263
Upton,Justin	75	276
Venable,Will	75	262
Bourn,Michael	76	270
Choo,Shin-Soo	76	284
D Arnaud,Travis	76	262
Frazier,Todd	76	251
Freese,David	76	273
Longoria,Evan	76	266
Rosario,Wilin	76	273
Trout,Mike	76	302
Bogaerts,Xander	77	277
Byrd,Marlon	77	269
Cain,Lorenzo	77	254
De Aza,Alejandro	77	266
Desmond,Ian	77	273
Gordon,Alex	77	281

TOP Ct%, bb% over 10%

NAME	bb%	ct%
Hanigan,Ryan	12	88
Encarnacion,Edwin	13	86
Cabrera,Miguel	13	84
Mauer,Joe	12	84
Zobrist,Ben	12	83
Fielder,Prince	12	82
Jaso,John	13	82
Ortiz,David	13	82
Abreu,Jose	11	81
Bautista,Jose	15	81
Carpenter,Matt	11	81
Holliday,Matt	12	81
McCutchen,Andrew	12	81
Sanchez,Gaby	12	81
Wright,David	11	81
Berkman,Lance	15	80
Helton,Todd	12	80
Teixeira,Mark	12	80
Barton,Daric	13	79
Ellis,A.J.	11	79
Ethier,Andre	11	79
Heyward,Jason	11	79
Santana,Carlos	15	79
Valbuena,Luis	12	79
Harper,Bryce	11	78
Joyce,Matt	13	77
Martin,Russell	12	77
Punto,Nick	12	77
Votto,Joey	18	77
Werth,Jayson	12	77
Blanco,Gregor	11	76
Choo,Shin-Soo	14	76
Grandal,Yasmani	11	76
Longoria,Evan	11	76
Trout,Mike	14	76
Goldschmidt,Paul	13	75
LaRoche,Adam	12	75
Smoak,Justin	11	75
Swisher,Nick	13	75
Youkilis,Kevin	11	75

TOP Ct%, bb% under 6%

NAME	bb%	Ct%
Pierre,Juan	5	92
Keppinger,Jeff	5	91
Izturis,Cesar	5	90
Chavez,Endy	5	89
Frandsen,Kevin	4	89
Infante,Omar	4	89
Perez,Salvador	4	89
Suzuki,Ichiro	4	89
Aybar,Erick	5	88
Bloomquist,Willie	5	88
Lombardozzi,Steve	4	88
Pena,Brayan	4	88
Ramirez,Alexei	4	88
Altuve,Jose	5	87
Arenado,Nolan	5	87
Aviles,Mike	4	87
Harrison,Josh	4	87
Pacheco,Jordan	5	87
Taveras,Oscar	5	87
Escobar,Alcides	4	86
Murphy,Daniel	5	86
Pierzynski,A.J.	4	86
Amarista,Alexi	5	85

Top Ct%, GB% over 50%

NAME	GB%	ct%
Pierre,Juan	51	92
Aoki,Norichika	58	91
Izturis,Cesar	51	90
Chavez,Endy	55	89
Frandsen,Kevin	56	89
Revere,Ben	60	89
Shuck,J.B.	51	89
Suzuki,Ichiro	54	89
Bloomquist,Willie	51	88
Span,Denard	54	88
Altuve,Jose	51	87
Cabrera,Melky	51	86
Escobar,Yunel	55	86
Furcal,Rafael	51	86
Young,Michael	51	86
Andrus,Elvis	56	85
Jeter,Derek	63	85
LeMahieu,DJ	55	85
Segura,Jean	60	85
Carroll,Jamey	53	84
Hosmer,Eric	52	84
Ramos,Wilson	58	84
Solano,Jhonatan	67	84
Tabata,Jose	60	84
Casilla,Alexi	53	83
Denorfia,Chris	57	83
Hoes,LJ	54	83
Kawasaki,Munenori	55	83
Schumaker,Skip	54	83
Casilla,Alexi	53	83
Ciriaco,Pedro	53	82
Eaton,Adam	57	82
Iglesias,Jose	57	82
Jay,Jon	52	82
Nieves,Wil	63	82
Ciriaco,Pedro	53	82
Eaton,Adam	57	82
Borbon,Julio	52	81
Presley,Alex	57	81
Young Jr.,Eric	54	81

Top Ct%, GB% under 40%

NAME	GB%	Ct%
Kinsler,Ian	37	88
Beltre,Adrian	39	87
Suzuki,Kurt	39	87
Encarnacion,Edwin	35	86
Hill,Aaron	38	86
Rollins,Jimmy	39	86
Sogard,Eric	36	86
Kelly,Don	38	84
Konerko,Paul	38	84
Ramirez,Aramis	39	84
Stewart,Chris	38	84
Beckham,Gordon	37	83
Lowrie,Jed	32	83
Roberts,Brian	36	83
Tracy,Chad	35	83
Beltran,Carlos	38	82
Gillaspie,Conor	37	82
Gregorius,Didi	39	82
McCann,Brian	37	82
Ortiz,David	38	82
Beltran,Carlos	38	82
Abreu,Jose	35	81
Bautista,Jose	39	81

PITCHER SKILLS RANKINGS - Starting Pitchers

Top Command (k/bb)

NAME	Cmd
Lee,Cliff	7.0
Wainwright,Adam	4.4
Hamels,Cole	4.2
Haren,Dan	4.1
Salazar,Danny	4.0
Sale,Chris	4.0
Estrada,Marco	3.9
Hernandez,Felix	3.9
Kershaw,Clayton	3.9
Price,David	3.8
Slowey,Kevin	3.8
Medlen,Kris	3.7
Petit,Yusmeiro	3.7
Scherzer,Max	3.7
Strasburg,Stephen	3.7
Zimmermann,Jordan	3.7
Fister,Doug	3.6
Greinke,Zack	3.6
Bailey,Homer	3.5
Peavy,Jake	3.5
Wacha,Michael	3.5
Bumgarner,Madison	3.4
Corbin,Patrick	3.4
Darvish,Yu	3.4
Gausman,Kevin	3.4
Milone,Tommy	3.4
Nolasco,Ricky	3.4
Verlander,Justin	3.4
Arroyo,Bronson	3.3
Colon,Bartolo	3.3
Iwakuma,Hisashi	3.3

Top Control (bb/9)

NAME	Ctl
Lee,Cliff	1.3
Slowey,Kevin	1.6
Arroyo,Bronson	1.7
Colon,Bartolo	1.7
McCarthy,Brandon	1.7
Jordan,Taylor	1.8
Albers,Andrew	1.9
Fister,Doug	1.9
Haren,Dan	1.9
Lohse,Kyle	1.9
Petit,Yusmeiro	1.9
Wainwright,Adam	1.9
Zimmermann,Jordan	1.9
Buehrle,Mark	2.0
Hamels,Cole	2.0
Kuroda,Hiroki	2.0
Medlen,Kris	2.0
Lyons,Tyler	2.1
Milone,Tommy	2.1
Nolasco,Ricky	2.1
Price,David	2.1
Capuano,Chris	2.2
Corbin,Patrick	2.2
Estrada,Marco	2.2
Iwakuma,Hisashi	2.2
Peavy,Jake	2.2
Weaver,Jered	2.2
Bailey,Homer	2.3
Baker,Scott	2.3
Correia,Kevin	2.3
Greinke,Zack	2.3

Top Dominance (k/9)

NAME	Dom
Darvish,Yu	11.0
Strasburg,Stephen	10.0
Cingrani,Tony	9.9
Scherzer,Max	9.8
Salazar,Danny	9.7
Smith,Burch	9.6
Fernandez,Jose	9.5
Sale,Chris	9.3
Kershaw,Clayton	9.0
Lee,Cliff	9.0
Lincecum,Tim	9.0
Samardzija,Jeff	9.0
Sanchez,Anibal	9.0
Verlander,Justin	9.0
Gonzalez,Gio	8.9
Hernandez,Felix	8.9
Jimenez,Ubaldo	8.9
Walker,Taijuan	8.9
Burnett,A.J.	8.8
Liriano,Francisco	8.8
Moore,Matt	8.8
Kazmir,Scott	8.7
Miller,Shelby	8.7
Lynn,Lance	8.6
Gausman,Kevin	8.5
Morrow,Brandon	8.5
Bedard,Erik	8.4
Bumgarner,Madison	8.4
Estrada,Marco	8.4
Hamels,Cole	8.4
Wood,Alex	8.4

Top Ground Ball Rate

NAME	GB
Morton,Charlie	60
Deduno,Samuel	59
Anderson,Brett	58
Britton,Zach	57
Masterson,Justin	57
Westbrook,Jake	57
Cahill,Trevor	56
Chatwood,Tyler	56
Cobb,Alex	56
Hudson,Tim	56
Garcia,Jaime	55
Hernandez,Roberto	55
Paxton,James	55
Alvarez,Henderson	54
Burnett,A.J.	54
Jordan,Taylor	54
Keuchel,Dallas	54
Lannan,John	54
Porcello,Rick	54
Gray,Sonny	53
Harrell,Lucas	53
Mejia,Jenrry	53
Cosart,Jarred	52
Fife,Stephen	52
Locke,Jeff	52
Pettibone,Jonathan	52
Ross,Robbie	52
Fister,Doug	51
Hernandez,Felix	51
Kelly,Joe	51
Marquis,Jason	51

Top Fly Ball Rate

NAME	FB
Smith,Burch	52
Redmond,Todd	51
Baker,Scott	49
Chen,Bruce	49
Matsuzaka,Daisuke	48
Straily,Dan	48
Slowey,Kevin	47
Hughes,Phil	46
Odorizzi,Jake	46
Petit,Yusmeiro	46
Weaver,Jered	46
Bauer,Trevor	45
Cingrani,Tony	45
Estrada,Marco	45
Griffin,A.J.	45
Peacock,Brad	45
Santana,Johan	45
Wood,Travis	45
Happ,J.A.	44
Harang,Aaron	44
Moore,Matt	44
Peavy,Jake	44
Scherzer,Max	44
Beachy,Brandon	43
Hanson,Tommy	43
Marcum,Shaun	43
Chen,Wei-Yin	42
Cloyd,Tyler	42
Karns,Nathan	42
McDonald,James	42
Minor,Mike	42

High GB, Low Dom

NAME	GB	Dom
Morton,Charlie	60	5.5
Deduno,Samuel	59	6.1
Britton,Zach	57	5.2
Westbrook,Jake	57	4.3
Cahill,Trevor	56	6.4
Hudson,Tim	56	6.2
Chatwood,Tyler	56	6.0
Hernandez,Roberto	55	5.9
Keuchel,Dallas	54	6.4
Jordan,Taylor	54	5.3
Alvarez,Henderson	54	4.9
Lannan,John	54	4.5
Harrell,Lucas	53	5.4
Cosart,Jarred	52	5.9
Pettibone,Jonathan	52	5.8
Fife,Stephen	52	5.7
Kelly,Joe	51	5.9
Marquis,Jason	51	5.2
Richard,Clayton	51	5.0
Maholm,Paul	50	6.0
Roark,Tanner	50	5.8
Drabek,Kyle	50	5.7
Tepesch,Nicholas	49	6.3
Diamond,Scott	49	4.3
Miley,Wade	48	6.4
Perez,Martin	48	5.9
Leake,Mike	48	5.8
Harrison,Matt	48	5.7
Rusin,Chris	48	4.7
de la Rosa,Jorge	47	6.4
Feldman,Scott	47	6.3

High GB, High Dom

NAME	GB	Dom
Masterson,Justin	57	8.0
Cobb,Alex	56	8.0
Burnett,A.J.	54	8.8
Hernandez,Felix	51	8.9
Ryu,Hyun-Jin	51	8.2
Wainwright,Adam	50	8.2
Ventura,Yordano	49	8.3
Strasburg,Stephen	48	10.0
Liriano,Francisco	48	8.8
Gallardo,Yovani	48	8.0
Bumgarner,Madison	47	8.4
Wood,Alex	47	8.4
Price,David	47	8.0
Fernandez,Jose	46	9.5
Sale,Chris	46	9.3
Samardzija,Jeff	46	9.0
Lynn,Lance	46	8.6
Gausman,Kevin	46	8.5
Greinke,Zack	46	8.3
Kershaw,Clayton	45	9.0
Lee,Cliff	45	9.0
Lincecum,Tim	45	9.0
Sanchez,Anibal	45	9.0
Gonzalez,Gio	45	8.9
Wacha,Michael	45	8.3
Doubront,Felix	45	8.1
Johnson,Josh	45	8.1
Latos,Mat	45	8.0
Shields,James	45	8.0
Jimenez,Ubaldo	44	8.9
Hamels,Cole	44	8.4

Lowest xERA

NAME	xERA
Strasburg,Stephen	2.76
Lee,Cliff	2.78
Darvish,Yu	2.80
Hernandez,Felix	2.87
Kershaw,Clayton	2.89
Wainwright,Adam	2.90
Sale,Chris	2.91
Fernandez,Jose	2.95
Cobb,Alex	3.10
Hamels,Cole	3.10
Burnett,A.J.	3.11
Salazar,Danny	3.11
Bumgarner,Madison	3.12
Greinke,Zack	3.12
Price,David	3.16
Scherzer,Max	3.16
Sanchez,Anibal	3.17
Ryu,Hyun-Jin	3.18
Gausman,Kevin	3.19
Medlen,Kris	3.20
Wood,Alex	3.24
Ross,Robbie	3.27
Verlander,Justin	3.27
Wacha,Michael	3.27
Masterson,Justin	3.29
Iwakuma,Hisashi	3.30
Porcello,Rick	3.31
Bailey,Homer	3.33
Fister,Doug	3.33
Corbin,Patrick	3.34
Shields,James	3.34

Top BPV, 180+ IP

NAME	BPV
Lee,Cliff	149
Strasburg,Stephen	134
Darvish,Yu	130
Hernandez,Felix	129
Sale,Chris	129
Wainwright,Adam	126
Kershaw,Clayton	123
Hamels,Cole	120
Scherzer,Max	120
Fernandez,Jose	115
Greinke,Zack	111
Price,David	111
Sanchez,Anibal	111
Bumgarner,Madison	110
Verlander,Justin	107
Ryu,Hyun-Jin	106
Medlen,Kris	105
Burnett,A.J.	104
Bailey,Homer	102
Corbin,Patrick	100
Fister,Doug	100
Shields,James	99
Iwakuma,Hisashi	98
Zimmermann,Jordan	98
Porcello,Rick	96
Latos,Mat	95
Nolasco,Ricky	94
Samardzija,Jeff	93
Kuroda,Hiroki	91
Lynn,Lance	91
Kluber,Corey	89

Top BPV, <150 IP

NAME	BPV
Gausman,Kevin	110
Smith,Burch	101
Ross,Robbie	92
Capuano,Chris	90
Garcia,Jaime	89
Blanton,Joe	87
Hudson,Daniel	87
Petit,Yusmeiro	87
Ventura,Yordano	85
Lyons,Tyler	84
Erlin,Robert	81
Marcum,Shaun	81
McCarthy,Brandon	79
Beckett,Josh	78
Jordan,Taylor	78
Anderson,Brett	77
Morrow,Brandon	77
Baker,Scott	76
Mejia,Jenrry	76
Billingsley,Chad	75
Hudson,Tim	75
Skaggs,Tyler	75
Slowey,Kevin	75
Taillon,Jameson	75
Luebke,Cory	74
Phelps,David	71
Tepesch,Nicholas	71
Roark,Tanner	70
Floyd,Gavin	69
Redmond,Todd	69
Hefner,Jeremy	68

PITCHER SKILLS RANKINGS - Relief Pitchers

Top Command (k/bb)

NAME	Cmd
Uehara,Koji	8.6
Mujica,Edward	5.7
Kimbrel,Craig	5.3
Romo,Sergio	5.2
Jansen,Kenley	4.8
Papelbon,Jonathan	4.8
Otero,Dan	4.6
Doolittle,Sean	4.4
Melancon,Mark	4.4
Perkins,Glen	4.3
O Day,Darren	4.2
Tazawa,Junichi	4.2
Street,Huston	4.1
Hochevar,Luke	4.0
Chapman,Aroldis	3.9
Fien,Casey	3.9
Janssen,Casey	3.9
Rosenthal,Trevor	3.9
Herrera,Kelvin	3.8
Holland,Greg	3.8
McGee,Jake	3.8
Belisle,Matt	3.7
Maness,Seth	3.7
Robertson,David	3.7
Smyly,Drew	3.7
Hunter,Tommy	3.6
Marshall,Sean	3.6
Nathan,Joe	3.6
Loup,Aaron	3.5
Motte,Jason	3.5
Hawkins,LaTroy	3.4

Top Control (bb/9)

NAME	Ctl
Mujica,Edward	1.2
Otero,Dan	1.3
Uehara,Koji	1.3
Maness,Seth	1.4
Hunter,Tommy	1.7
Hawkins,LaTroy	1.8
Doolittle,Sean	1.9
Melancon,Mark	1.9
Romo,Sergio	1.9
Badenhop,Burke	2.0
Belisle,Matt	2.0
Lopez,Wilton	2.0
Loup,Aaron	2.0
O Day,Darren	2.0
Papelbon,Jonathan	2.0
Street,Huston	2.1
Tazawa,Junichi	2.1
Janssen,Casey	2.2
Johnson,Jim	2.2
Hochevar,Luke	2.3
Kintzler,Brandon	2.3
Patton,Troy	2.3
Perkins,Glen	2.3
Smyly,Drew	2.3
Watson,Tony	2.3
Fien,Casey	2.4
Swarzak,Anthony	2.4
Figaro,Alfredo	2.5
Ortiz,Joseph	2.5
Parnell,Bobby	2.5
Scheppers,Tanner	2.5

Top Dominance (k/9)

NAME	Dom
Chapman,Aroldis	15.2
Kimbrel,Craig	14.3
Jansen,Kenley	13.8
Alburquerque,Al	12.3
Frieri,Ernesto	12.3
Holland,Greg	12.2
Delabar,Steve	12.1
Marmol,Carlos	11.6
Bastardo,Antonio	11.5
Robertson,David	11.4
Grilli,Jason	11.1
Uehara,Koji	11.0
Rosenthal,Trevor	10.9
Brothers,Rex	10.8
Hanrahan,Joel	10.7
Rodriguez,Paco	10.7
McGee,Jake	10.5
Nathan,Joe	10.5
Fujikawa,Kyuji	10.4
Perez,Oliver	10.4
Hernandez,David	10.3
Walden,Jordan	10.3
Allen,Cody	10.2
Henderson,Jim	10.2
Pryor,Stephen	10.2
Crain,Jesse	10.1
Farquhar,Daniel	10.1
Ramos,A.J.	10.1
Santos,Sergio	10.1
Soria,Joakim	10.1
Axford,John	10.0

Top Ground Ball Rate

NAME	GB
Ziegler,Brad	70
Venters,Jonny	68
Downs,Scott	63
Maness,Seth	63
Belisario,Ronald	62
Lopez,Javier	61
Affeldt,Jeremy	60
Johnson,Jim	60
Qualls,Chad	59
Albers,Matt	58
Kintzler,Brandon	58
Rzepczynski,Marc	58
League,Brandon	57
Wright,Jamey	57
Loup,Aaron	56
McFarland,T.J.	56
Melancon,Mark	56
Machi,Jean	55
Otero,Dan	55
Strop,Pedro	55
Avilan,Luis	54
Howell,J.P.	54
Marshall,Sean	54
Morris,Bryan	54
Rodney,Fernando	54
Stammen,Craig	54
Webb,Ryan	54
Badenhop,Burke	53
Casilla,Santiago	53
Cishek,Steve	53
Gomez,Jeanmar	53

Top Fly Ball Rate

NAME	FB
Frieri,Ernesto	57
Sipp,Tony	55
Kohn,Michael	54
Peralta,Joel	54
Thielbar,Caleb	53
Bastardo,Antonio	52
Clippard,Tyler	52
Uehara,Koji	50
Bailey,Andrew	49
Doolittle,Sean	49
Feliz,Neftali	49
Fields,Joshua	49
Kelley,Shawn	49
Parker,Blake	49
Russell,James	49
Salas,Fernando	49
Aardsma,David	48
Clemens,Paul	48
Morales,Franklin	48
Perez,Oliver	48
Black,Victor	47
Blevins,Jerry	47
Hernandez,David	47
Hoover,J.J.	47
Rosenberg,B.J.	47
Withrow,Chris	47
Allen,Cody	45
Collmenter,Josh	45
Delabar,Steve	45
Fien,Casey	45
Street,Huston	45

High GB, Low Dom

NAME	GB	Dom
Ziegler,Brad	70	5.8
Maness,Seth	63	5.1
Johnson,Jim	60	6.4
Qualls,Chad	59	6.3
Kintzler,Brandon	58	6.4
Albers,Matt	58	6.1
League,Brandon	57	5.9
McFarland,T.J.	56	5.7
Otero,Dan	55	6.0
Avilan,Luis	54	6.2
Webb,Ryan	54	6.2
Morris,Bryan	54	5.4
Lopez,Wilton	53	6.4
Richards,Garrett	53	6.3
Badenhop,Burke	53	6.2
Gomez,Jeanmar	53	5.9
Hawkins,LaTroy	52	6.1
Boggs,Mitchell	52	5.5
Mendoza,Luis	52	5.3
Thornton,Matt	51	6.4
Figaro,Alfredo	49	5.6
Mazzaro,Vin	48	5.9
Hand,Donovan	48	5.3
Wolf,Ross	47	5.2
Roenicke,Josh	46	6.4
Pressly,Ryan	46	5.7
Rosario,Sandy	44	6.0
Bass,Anthony	43	6.2
Guerrier,Matt	43	5.9
Swarzak,Anthony	43	5.9
Breslow,Craig	42	6.4

High GB, High Dom

NAME	GB	Dom
Venters,Jonny	68	9.4
Melancon,Mark	56	8.3
Strop,Pedro	55	9.2
Marshall,Sean	54	9.5
Rodney,Fernando	54	9.5
Howell,J.P.	54	8.0
Stammen,Craig	54	8.0
Cishek,Steve	53	9.3
Medina,Yoervis	53	9.1
Parnell,Bobby	53	8.3
Herrera,Kelvin	51	9.8
Rondon,Bruce	51	9.7
Aumont,Phillippe	51	9.1
Crow,Aaron	51	8.5
De La Rosa,Dane	51	8.2
Wright,Wesley	50	9.1
Gearrin,Cory	50	8.4
Jones,Nate	49	9.6
Shaw,Bryan	49	8.0
Kimbrel,Craig	48	14.3
Robertson,David	48	11.4
Brothers,Rex	48	10.8
Outman,Josh	48	8.4
Santos,Sergio	47	10.1
Axford,John	47	10.0
Miller,Andrew	47	9.9
Diekman,Jake	47	9.4
Cook,Ryan	47	9.1
Harris,Will	47	8.8
Janssen,Casey	47	8.7
Ottavino,Adam	47	8.2

Lowest xERA

NAME	xERA
Kimbrel,Craig	1.78
Chapman,Aroldis	2.11
Jansen,Kenley	2.12
Uehara,Koji	2.45
Holland,Greg	2.49
Robertson,David	2.59
Melancon,Mark	2.68
Rosenthal,Trevor	2.69
Herrera,Kelvin	2.70
Marshall,Sean	2.73
Romo,Sergio	2.79
Venters,Jonny	2.84
McGee,Jake	2.87
Perkins,Glen	2.89
Rodriguez,Paco	2.91
Janssen,Casey	2.93
Fujikawa,Kyuji	2.96
Santos,Sergio	2.97
Cishek,Steve	2.99
Parnell,Bobby	2.99
Grilli,Jason	3.01
Jones,Nate	3.01
Soria,Joakim	3.02
Tazawa,Junichi	3.03
Delabar,Steve	3.04
Farquhar,Daniel	3.06
Nathan,Joe	3.06
Putz,J.J.	3.06
Rondon,Bruce	3.06
Harris,Will	3.07
Papelbon,Jonathan	3.08

Top BPV, 10+ Saves

NAME	BPV
Kimbrel,Craig	210
Jansen,Kenley	186
Chapman,Aroldis	184
Uehara,Koji	178
Holland,Greg	153
Robertson,David	148
Romo,Sergio	144
Rosenthal,Trevor	142
Melancon,Mark	134
Papelbon,Jonathan	133
Perkins,Glen	133
Nathan,Joe	122
Janssen,Casey	121
Grilli,Jason	118
Frieri,Ernesto	115
Mujica,Edward	113
Parnell,Bobby	113
Street,Huston	113
Farquhar,Daniel	112
Cishek,Steve	111
Bell,Heath	110
Doolittle,Sean	110
Benoit,Joaquin	105
Allen,Cody	102
Reed,Addison	98
Scheppers,Tanner	98
Johnson,Jim	95
Cook,Ryan	93
Balfour,Grant	91
Brothers,Rex	91
Strop,Pedro	86

Top BPV, 9- Saves

NAME	BPV
Herrera,Kelvin	137
McGee,Jake	136
Marshall,Sean	131
Tazawa,Junichi	122
Rodriguez,Paco	121
Hochevar,Luke	120
Putz,J.J.	120
Fujikawa,Kyuji	119
Soria,Joakim	119
Santos,Sergio	118
Motte,Jason	116
Delabar,Steve	115
Fien,Casey	115
O Day,Darren	112
Harris,Will	111
Jones,Nate	111
Smyly,Drew	111
Rodriguez,Francisco	110
Belisle,Matt	108
Thatcher,Joe	108
Gregerson,Luke	107
Hanrahan,Joel	106
Otero,Dan	106
Rondon,Bruce	106
Siegrist,Kevin	106
Loup,Aaron	105
Kelley,Shawn	102
Lecure,Sam	101
Vincent,Nick	101
Walden,Jordan	101
Bastardo,Antonio	100

RISK MANAGEMENT

GRADE "F" in HEALTH (proj. R$ > $0)

Pitchers	Batters
Alburquerque,Al	Berkman,Lance
Alvarez,Henderson	Betemit,Wilson
Anderson,Brett	Blackmon,Charlie
Baker,Scott	Blanks,Kyle
Beachy,Brandon	Bloomquist,Willie
Beckett,Josh	Bourjos,Peter
Billingsley,Chad	Castro,Jason
Buchholz,Clay	Cervelli,Francisco
Cashner,Andrew	Chavez,Eric
Casilla,Santiago	Coghlan,Chris
Chacin,Jhoulys	Crawford,Carl
Cobb,Alex	Crowe,Trevor
Cotts,Neal	D Arnaud,Travis
Crain,Jesse	DeRosa,Mark
Cueto,Johnny	Drew,Stephen
De Fratus,Justin	Ellsbury,Jacoby
de la Rosa,Jorge	Furcal,Rafael
Estrada,Marco	Gardner,Brett
Feliz,Neftali	Granderson,Curtis
Fujikawa,Kyuji	Gutierrez,Franklin
Garcia,Jaime	Hart,Corey
Halladay,Roy	Howard,Ryan
Hammel,Jason	Jeter,Derek
Hanrahan,Joel	Kemp,Matt
Harrison,Matt	Lowrie,Jed
Hawkins,LaTroy	Ludwick,Ryan
Howell,J.P.	Martinez,Victor
Hudson,Daniel	Mastroianni,Darin
Hudson,Tim	Maybin,Cameron
Johnson,Josh	Morales,Kendrys
Kazmir,Scott	Morrison,Logan
Kelley,Shawn	Pagan,Angel
Kintzler,Brandon	Pearce,Steve
Lackey,John	Pena,Ramiro
Luebke,Cory	Quentin,Carlos
Marcum,Shaun	Ramos,Wilson
Marshall,Sean	Reimold,Nolan
McCarthy,Brandon	Reyes,Jose
Mejia,Jenrry	Roberts,Brian
Morrow,Brandon	Rodriguez,Alex
Motte,Jason	Romine,Austin
Nicasio,Juan	Scott,Luke
Niemann,Jeff	Sizemore,Scott
Ogando,Alexi	Sweeney,Ryan
Peavy,Jake	Teixeira,Mark
Pryor,Stephen	Tulowitzki,Troy
Putz,J.J.	Utley,Chase
Rodriguez,Wandy	Youkilis,Kevin
Santos,Sergio	
Soria,Joakim	
Stauffer,Tim	
Street,Huston	
Tazawa,Junichi	
Uehara,Koji	

Highest Reliability Grades - Health / Experience / Consistency (Min. Grade = BBB)

CA	POS	Rel
Martin,Russell	2	BBA
Molina,Yadier	2	ABB
Santana,Carlos	203	AAB
Wieters,Matt	2	AAA

1B/DH	POS	Rel
Goldschmidt,Paul	3	AAB
Moreland,Mitch	3	BBB
Reynolds,Mark	35	ABB
Santana,Carlos	203	AAB
Swisher,Nick	39	AAB
Trumbo,Mark	3	AAB

2B	POS	Rel
Altuve,Jose	4	ABB
Barney,Darwin	4	AAB
Beckham,Gordon	4	BBA
Callaspo,Alberto	45	ABB
Cano,Robinson	4	AAB
Green,Grant	4	ABA
Johnson,Kelly	47	ABA
Kendrick,Howie	4	BAB
Kipnis,Jason	4	AAB
Pedroia,Dustin	4	BAB
Phillips,Brandon	4	AAB
Scutaro,Marco	4	AAB
Uggla,Dan	4	AAB
Walker,Neil	4	BBA
Zobrist,Ben	469	AAB

SS	POS	Rel
Andrus,Elvis	6	AAA
Aybar,Erick	6	BAA
Cabrera,Asdrubal	6	BAB
Cozart,Zack	6	BBA
Ramirez,Alexei	6	AAB
Rollins,Jimmy	6	BAA
Zobrist,Ben	469	AAB

3B	POS	Rel
Beltre,Adrian	5	BAB
Callaspo,Alberto	45	ABB
Moustakas,Mike	5	ABA
Plouffe,Trevor	5	BBA
Reynolds,Mark	35	ABB
Seager,Kyle	5	AAA

OF	POS	Rel
Beltre,Engel	9	ABB
Bourn,Michael	8	BAB
Brantley,Michael	7	AAA
Bruce,Jay	9	AAA
Cruz,Nelson	9	BBB
De Aza,Alejandro	78	AAA
Ethier,Andre	89	AAA
Gindl,Caleb	7	ABB
Gonzalez,Carlos	7	BBB
Gordon,Alex	7	AAB
Gose,Anthony	8	ABB
Holliday,Matt	7	BAA
Hunter,Torii	9	AAB
Ibanez,Raul	07	ABA
Jay,Jon	8	BBA
Jennings,Desmond	8	BBA
Johnson,Kelly	47	ABA
Jones,Adam	8	AAA
Joyce,Matt	079	BBB
Marte,Starling	7	BBB
Parra,Gerardo	89	ABB
Reddick,Josh	9	BBA
Smith,Seth	07	ABB
Soriano,Alfonso	7	AAB
Stubbs,Drew	89	AAB
Suzuki,Ichiro	9	AAB
Swisher,Nick	39	AAB
Upton,Justin	79	AAB
Vicciedo,Dayan	7	ABA
Young,Chris	789	ABB
Zobrist,Ben	469	AAB

RP	Rel
Axford,John	ABA
Balfour,Grant	BBA
Bell,Heath	ABB
Chapman,Aroldis	BBB
Clippard,Tyler	ABB
Collmenter,Josh	BBA
Duensing,Brian	ABA
Frieri,Ernesto	ABB
Jansen,Kenley	BBA
Johnson,Jim	AAA
Kimbrel,Craig	AAB
League,Brandon	ABB
Marmol,Carlos	BBA
Nathan,Joe	BBB
Papelbon,Jonathan	AAB
Perkins,Glen	BBA
Valverde,Jose	BBB
Villanueva,Carlos	BBA

SP	Rel
Arroyo,Bronson	AAA
Bailey,Homer	BAB
Buehrle,Mark	AAA
Bumgarner,Madison	AAA
Burnett,A.J.	BAA
Cain,Matt	BAA
Corbin,Patrick	ABB
Dempster,Ryan	BAA
Dickey,R.A.	AAB
Doubront,Felix	BBB
Fister,Doug	BAA
Gallardo,Yovani	BAA
Garcia,Freddy	BBB
Gonzalez,Gio	AAA
Guthrie,Jeremy	BAA
Hamels,Cole	AAA
Harrell,Lucas	ABB
Hellickson,Jeremy	AAA
Hernandez,Felix	AAA
Holland,Derek	BAA
Iwakuma,Hisashi	AAA
Jackson,Edwin	AAA
Kendrick,Kyle	AAA
Kennedy,Ian	AAA
Kershaw,Clayton	AAA
Kuroda,Hiroki	BAA
Latos,Mat	AAA
Leake,Mike	AAA
Lee,Cliff	AAA
Lester,Jon	AAA
Lincecum,Tim	AAA
Locke,Jeff	ABA
Masterson,Justin	AAB
Mendoza,Luis	ABB
Miley,Wade	AAA
Milone,Tommy	ABA
Minor,Mike	AAA
Nolasco,Ricky	BAB
Norris,Bud	BAA
Parker,Jarrod	ABA
Porcello,Rick	AAA
Price,David	BAA
Ryu,Hyun-Jin	AAB
Sabathia,CC	AAA
Sale,Chris	AAA
Samardzija,Jeff	AAA
Santana,Ervin	BAB
Saunders,Joe	BAA
Scherzer,Max	AAA
Shields,James	AAA
Tanaka,Masahiro	AAB
Verlander,Justin	AAA
Wainwright,Adam	BAA
Wilson,C.J.	AAA
Wood,Travis	ABB

RISK MANAGEMENT

GRADE "A" in CONSISTENCY

Pitchers (min 120 IP)

Arrieta,Jake	Peavy,Jake
Arroyo,Bronson	Perez,Martin
Blanton,Joe	Petit,Yusmeiro
Buehrle,Mark	Porcello,Rick
Bumgarner,Madison	Price,David
Burnett,A.J.	Quintana,Jose
Cahill,Trevor	Rodriguez,Wandy
Cain,Matt	Sabathia,CC
Cashner,Andrew	Salazar,Danny
Chen,Bruce	Sale,Chris
Colon,Bartolo	Samardzija,Jeff
Correia,Kevin	Sanchez,Anibal
Cosart,Jarred	Santiago,Hector
Cueto,Johnny	Saunders,Joe
Deduno,Samuel	Scherzer,Max
Delgado,Randall	Shields,James
Dempster,Ryan	Straily,Dan
Detwiler,Ross	Strasburg,Stephen
Duffy,Danny	Turner,Jacob
Erlin,Robert	Vargas,Jason
Estrada,Marco	Verlander,Justin
Feldman,Scott	Vogelsong,Ryan
Fister,Doug	Volquez,Edinson
Gallardo,Yovani	Wainwright,Adam
Garza,Matt	Weaver,Jered
Gonzalez,Gio	Wilson,C.J.
Greinke,Zack	Zimmermann,Jordan
Guthrie,Jeremy	Zito,Barry
Hamels,Cole	**Batters (min 425 AB)**
Harrison,Matt	Alonso,Yonder
Hellickson,Jeremy	Andrus,Elvis
Hernandez,Felix	Aybar,Erick
Holland,Derek	Beckham,Gordon
Hughes,Phil	Brantley,Michael
Iwakuma,Hisashi	Bruce,Jay
Jackson,Edwin	Chisenhall,Lonnie
Johnson,Josh	Cozart,Zack
Kelly,Joe	Crisp,Coco
Kendrick,Kyle	De Aza,Alejandro
Kennedy,Ian	Ethier,Andre
Kershaw,Clayton	Hart,Corey
Keuchel,Dallas	Holliday,Matt
Kuroda,Hiroki	Jay,Jon
Latos,Mat	Jennings,Desmond
Leake,Mike	Jones,Adam
Lee,Cliff	LeMahieu,DJ
Lester,Jon	Longoria,Evan
Lincecum,Tim	Machado,Manny
Locke,Jeff	McLouth,Nate
Lohse,Kyle	Morales,Kendrys
Lyles,Jordan	Moustakas,Mike
Lynn,Lance	Murphy,Daniel
Maholm,Paul	Plouffe,Trevor
McAllister,Zach	Ramos,Wilson
Medlen,Kris	Revere,Ben
Miley,Wade	Rollins,Jimmy
Milone,Tommy	Schierholtz,Nate
Minor,Mike	Scutaro,Marco
Nicasio,Juan	Seager,Kyle
Niese,Jon	Viciedo,Dayan
Norris,Bud	Villar,Jonathan
Nova,Ivan	Walker,Neil
Ogando,Alexi	Wieters,Matt
Parker,Jarrod	Zimmerman,Ryan

TOP COMBINATION OF SKILLS AND RELIABILITY
Maximum of one "C" in Reliability Grade

BATTING POWER

PX 125+	PX	Rel
Carter,Chris	185	ACB
Goldschmidt,Paul	177	AAB
Alvarez,Pedro	165	BBC
Saltalamacchia,Jarrod	165	ACB
Bruce,Jay	163	AAA
Gonzalez,Carlos	162	BBB
Encarnacion,Edwin	158	BAC
Reynolds,Mark	156	ABB
Braun,Ryan	154	ABC
Cabrera,Miguel	153	AAC
Rasmus,Colby	151	BBC
Upton,Justin	150	AAB
Soriano,Alfonso	148	AAB
Belt,Brandon	147	ACB
Hamilton,Josh	144	AAC
Myers,Wil	143	ABC
Trumbo,Mark	143	AAB
Jones,Adam	141	AAA
Swisher,Nick	140	AAB
Wallace,Brett	137	ACB
Cano,Robinson	136	AAB
Holliday,Matt	136	BAA
Ibanez,Raul	135	ABA
Uggla,Dan	135	AAB
Arencibia,J.P.	134	BCB
Gyorko,Jedd	134	BCB
Cruz,Nelson	132	BBB
Fielder,Prince	132	AAC
Moreland,Mitch	132	BBB
Reddick,Josh	131	BBA
Freeman,Freddie	130	AAC
Wieters,Matt	130	AAA
Lind,Adam	129	BBC
Santana,Carlos	129	AAB
Gindl,Caleb	128	ABB
Pena,Carlos	128	BBC
Sanchez,Jorge Tony	127	ACB
Krauss,Marc	126	ACA
Beltre,Adrian	125	BAB
Espinosa,Danny	125	ABC
Joyce,Matt	125	BBB
Mayberry,John	125	ACB

RUNNER SPEED

Spd 110+	SX	Rel
Marte,Starling	184	BBB
Segura,Jean	181	ACB
Bourn,Michael	157	BAB
Gose,Anthony	154	ABB
Robinson,Derrick	150	ACA
Jennings,Desmond	147	BBA
Beltre,Engel	146	ABB
Blanco,Gregor	144	ACB
Hechavarria,Adeiny	141	ABC
Aoki,Norichika	140	AAC
Green,Grant	140	ABA
LeMahieu,DJ	139	ACA
Pollock IV,A.J.	139	ABC
Presley,Alex	138	ACB
Andrus,Elvis	137	AAA
Span,Denard	137	CBB
Suzuki,Ichiro	137	AAB
Villar,Jonathan	137	ACA
Venable,Will	136	ACB
Stubbs,Drew	133	AAB
Castro,Starlin	132	AAC
Denorfia,Chris	131	ACB
Machado,Manny	128	ACA
Infante,Omar	127	CAB
De Aza,Alejandro	126	AAA
Ackley,Dustin	124	ABC
Ramirez,Alexei	124	AAB
Victorino,Shane	124	BAC
Paredes,Jimmy	122	ACA
Reddick,Josh	122	BBA
Braun,Ryan	121	ABC
Cozart,Zack	119	BBA
Scutaro,Marco	119	BBA
Aybar,Erick	118	BAA
Gillaspie,Conor	117	ACB
Hoes,LJ	117	ACB
Pedroia,Dustin	117	BAB
Ryan,Brendan	115	ACB
Upton,B.J.	114	BAC
Lombardozzi,Steve	113	ACA
Barnes,Brandon	112	ACB
Upton,Justin	112	AAB
Altuve,Jose	111	ABB
Belt,Brandon	111	ACB
Brantley,Michael	111	AAA
DeJesus,David	111	CBA

OVERALL PITCHING SKILL

BPV over 85	BPV	Rel
Kimbrel,Craig	216	ABB
Romo,Sergio	172	BCB
Papelbon,Jonathan	163	AAB
Chapman,Aroldis	157	BCB
Marshall,Sean	148	ACA
Lee,Cliff	143	BAA
Jansen,Kenley	143	BCB
Robertson,David	140	BCB
Motte,Jason	136	ABA
Lopez,Wilton	125	BCA
Hamels,Cole	122	AAA
Sabathia,CC	122	AAA
Scherzer,Max	122	AAA
Halladay,Roy	122	CAA
Shields,James	121	AAA
Greinke,Zack	121	AAB
Dotel,Octavio	121	BCA
Mujica,Edward	119	ACA
Sale,Chris	118	ABA
Hernandez,Felix	117	AAA
Peralta,Joel	117	ACB
Verlander,Justin	116	AAA
Thornton,Matt	116	ACA
Kershaw,Clayton	115	AAA
Betancourt,Rafael	112	BCB
Hernandez,David	111	ACB
Belisle,Matt	110	ACA
Axford,John	108	AAA
Price,David	107	AAA
Bumgarner,Madison	107	AAB
Milone,Tommy	106	ABB
Oliver,Darren	106	ACA
Lincoln,Brad	105	ACB
Darvish,Yu	102	AAC
Walden,Jordan	102	BCB
Venters,Jonny	101	ACA
Haren,Dan	100	AAA
Estrada,Marco	100	BCA
Gallardo,Yovani	99	BAA
Davis,Wade	99	AAB
Garza,Matt	97	CAB
Latos,Mat	96	AAA
Kuroda,Hiroki	96	BAA
Garcia,Jaime	96	CBA
Parnell,Bobby	96	BCA
Clippard,Tyler	96	ABB
Fister,Doug	95	CAA
Lecure,Sam	95	ACB
Sanchez,Anibal	93	CAA
Rodriguez,Francisco	93	BBA
Niese,Jon	92	CAA
Dickey,R.A.	92	AAB
Takahashi,Hisanori	92	ACA
Balfour,Grant	92	BCA
Lincecum,Tim	90	AAA
Nolasco,Ricky	88	AAA
Kennedy,Ian	88	AAB
Affeldt,Jeremy	88	BCA
Capuano,Chris	87	AAA
Dempster,Ryan	87	BAA
Lynn,Lance	87	BCA
Weaver,Jered	86	AAA

LIMA Plan Targets

LIMA	1B	3B	2B	SS	CA	DH	OF
A	Abreu,Jose Pujols,Albert Votto,Joey	Arenado,Nolan §Beltre,Adrian Sandoval,Pablo	Hill,Aaron Infante,Omar Kinsler,Ian §Pedroia,Dustin §Scutaro,Marco Utley,Chase	Hardy,J.J. Simmons,Andrelton	§Santana,Carlos		§Brantley,Michael §Holliday,Matt Pagan,Angel Span,Denard
B+	Fielder,Prince Gonzalez,Adrian Hosmer,Eric Morrison,Logan Teixeira,Mark	Ramirez,Aramis	Carpenter,Matt Murphy,Daniel Prado,Martin	§Aybar,Erick Lowrie,Jed §Ramirez,Alexei Tulowitzki,Troy §Zobrist,Ben	Lucroy,Jonathan Mauer,Joe McCann,Brian Posey,Buster	Ortiz,David	Aoki,Norichika Bautista,Jose Cabrera,Melky Crisp,Coco Markakis,Nick McLouth,Nate Murphy,David Quentin,Carlos Victorino,Shane
B			§Altuve,Jose	§Andrus,Elvis Furcal,Rafael Jeter,Derek	§Molina,Yadier	Butler,Billy	Revere,Ben §Suzuki,Ichiro

LIMA	STARTING PITCHERS			RELIEF PITCHERS			
A	Haren,Dan Kazmir,Scott §Porcello,Rick §Samardzija,Jeff			§Bell,Heath Carpenter,David Cook,Ryan Cotts,Neal Crain,Jesse Delabar,Steve	Fien,Casey Furbush,Charlie Harris,Will Jones,Nate Lecure,Sam McGee,Jake	Motte,Jason Otero,Dan Putz,J.J. Robertson,David Rondon,Bruce Rosenthal,Trevor	Santos,Sergio Tazawa,Junichi Thayer,Dale Vincent,Nick Walden,Jordan
B+	Chen,Wei-Yin Cueto,Johnny Estrada,Marco §Fister,Doug	Garcia,Jaime Gausman,Kevin Hudson,Daniel Luebke,Cory	§Milone,Tommy Ross,Robbie Skaggs,Tyler Ventura,Yordano	Allen,Cody Cecil,Brett §Collmenter,Josh Gorzelanny,Tom Gregerson,Luke	Herrera,Kelvin Kontos,George Loup,Aaron Machi,Jean O Day,Darren	Rodriguez,Francisco Rodriguez,Paco Scheppers,Tanner Siegrist,Kevin Smyly,Drew	Stammen,Craig Stauffer,Tim Torres,Alexander §Villanueva,Carlos
B	§Burnett,A.J. §Cain,Matt Cobb,Alex §Dickey,R.A. Erlin,Robert	§Hamels,Cole Kluber,Corey §Lester,Jon Lynn,Lance §Nolasco,Ricky	Peavy,Jake §Verlander,Justin Wacha,Michael Walker,Taijuan Wood,Alex	Farquhar,Daniel Hawkins,LaTroy	Hochevar,Luke Kintzler,Brandon	Parnell,Bobby Perez,Chris	Watson,Tony

§ Indicates players that carry a lower risk score

BATTERS
Contact rate + Walk rate of at least 90%
PX or Spd level of at least 100
Regular playing time
Projected Rotisserie value between $10 and $30

PITCHERS
Command ratio (K/BB) of 2.5 or better
Strikeout rate of 7.0 or better (unless ground ball rate is greater than 50%)
Fly ball rate of 40% or less
Projected Rotisserie value between $1 and $29

PORTFOLIO 3 PLAN

TIER 1

High Skill, Low Risk				Filters:	BBB	80	one of 100	100
BATTERS	Age	Bats	Pos	REL	Ct%	PX	Spd	R$
Cano,Robinson	31	L	4	AAB	86	136	80	$35
Holliday,Matt	34	R	7	BAA	81	136	81	$29
Andrus,Elvis	25	R	6	AAA	85	50	137	$29
Beltre,Adrian	35	R	5	BAB	87	125	69	$28
Pedroia,Dustin	30	R	4	BAB	89	99	117	$27
Kendrick,Howie	30	R	4	BAB	80	94	104	$23
Ramirez,Alexei	32	R	6	AAB	88	71	124	$22
Altuve,Jose	24	R	4	ABB	87	65	111	$22
Aybar,Erick	30	B	6	BAA	88	79	118	$21
Molina,Yadier	31	R	2	ABB	89	103	64	$21
Seager,Kyle	26	L	5	AAA	81	118	80	$20
Zobrist,Ben	33	B	486	AAB	83	109	107	$20
Wieters,Matt	28	B	2	AAA	80	130	67	$18
Walker,Neil	28	B	4	BBA	81	114	96	$18
Cabrera,Asdrubal	28	B	6	BAB	80	110	87	$18
Brantley,Michael	27	L	7	AAA	88	73	111	$18
Jay,Jon	29	L	9	BBA	82	75	107	$17
Scutaro,Marco	38	R	4	BBA	92	57	119	$17
Parra,Gerardo	27	L	89	ABB	82	90	107	$13
Suzuki,Ichiro	40	L	8	AAB	89	53	137	$13
Moustakas,Mike	25	L	5	ABA	81	114	69	$12
Cozart,Zack	28	R	6	BBA	81	83	119	$11
Beckham,Gordon	27	R	4	BBA	83	82	104	$11

TIER 2

High Skill, Mod Risk				Filters:	BBB	80	one of 100	100	<$20
BATTERS	Age	Bats	Pos	REL	Ct%	PX	Spd	R$	
Phillips,Brandon*	33	R	4	AAB	85	90	95	$23	
Jennings,Desmond*	27	R	9	BBA	78	108	147	$22	
Hunter,Torii*	38	R	8	AAB	79	103	98	$21	
De Aza,Alejandro	30	L	97	AAA	77	95	126	$20	
Trumbo,Mark	28	R	3	AAB	72	143	86	$19	
Santana,Carlos	28	B	203	AAB	79	129	74	$19	
Swisher,Nick	33	B	38	AAB	75	140	76	$18	
Viciedo,Dayan	25	R	7	ABA	78	120	81	$14	
Plouffe,Trevor	28	R	5	BBA	77	115	105	$10	

TIER 3

High Skill, High Risk				Filters:	N/A	80	one of 100	100	<$10
BATTERS	Age	Bats	Pos	REL	Ct%	PX	Spd	R$	
DeJesus,David	34	L	97	CBA	81	100	111	$9	
Descalso,Daniel	27	L	645	ACB	82	86	109	$9	
Gentry,Craig	30	R	97	BFC	82	67	159	$9	
Wong,Kolten	23	L	4	ADB	83	58	128	$9	
Gennett,Scooter	24	L	4	ADA	81	89	129	$8	
Mercer,Jordy	27	R	64	ACC	81	99	104	$8	
Shuck,J.B.	27	L	7	ACC	89	49	130	$8	
Bloomquist,Willie	36	R	4	FDB	88	47	148	$7	
Gregorius,Didi	24	L	6	ADB	82	79	146	$7	
Harrison,Josh	26	R	8	ADB	87	96	119	$7	
Urrutia,Henry	27	L	0	AFF	82	68	140	$7	
Amarista,Alexi	25	L	94	ADA	85	69	132	$6	
Berkman,Lance	38	B	0	FDD	80	102	80	$6	
Chavez,Eric	36	L	5	FFC	80	123	80	$6	
Getz,Chris	30	L	4	DDB	90	40	127	$6	
Hechavarria,Adeiny	25	R	6	ABC	81	60	141	$6	
Lough,David	28	L	8	ACC	84	68	134	$6	
Ozuna,Marcell	23	R	89	CFF	80	97	160	$6	
Flores,Wilmer	22	R	5	AFC	82	101	87	$5	
Gordon,Dee	26	L	6	CDB	80	43	152	$5	
Casilla,Alexi	29	B	4	BDB	83	64	135	$4	
Galvis,Freddy	24	B	4	DCA	80	98	110	$4	
Hernandez,Cesar	24	B	9	ADA	80	50	138	$4	
Herrera,Jonathan	29	B	64	BFB	86	50	116	$4	
Lombardozzi,Steve	25	B	47	ACA	88	60	113	$4	
Pastornicky,Tyler	24	R	4	BDB	82	68	122	$4	
Pierre,Juan	36	L	7	ABD	92	42	119	$4	

TIER 1

High Skill, Low Risk			Filters:	BBB	75
PITCHERS	Age	Thrw	REL	BPV	R$
Kershaw,Clayton	26	L	AAA	123	$38
Jansen,Kenley	26	R	BBA	186	$32
Kimbrel,Craig	26	R	AAB	210	$32
Bumgarner,Madison	24	L	AAA	110	$27
Chapman,Aroldis	26	L	BBB	184	$27
Lee,Cliff	35	L	AAA	149	$25
Sale,Chris	25	L	AAA	129	$25
Verlander,Justin	31	R	AAA	107	$25
Hamels,Cole	30	L	AAA	120	$23
Wainwright,Adam	32	R	BAA	126	$23
Price,David	28	L	BAA	111	$22
Scherzer,Max	29	R	AAA	120	$22
Hernandez,Felix	28	R	AAA	129	$21
Perkins,Glen	31	L	BBA	133	$21
Bailey,Homer	28	R	BAB	102	$20
Johnson,Jim	31	R	AAA	95	$20
Nathan,Joe	39	R	BBB	122	$20
Papelbon,Jonathan	33	R	AAB	133	$20
Balfour,Grant	36	R	BBA	91	$19
Latos,Mat	26	R	AAA	95	$19
Cain,Matt	29	R	BAA	82	$18
Iwakuma,Hisashi	33	R	AAA	98	$18
Shields,James	32	R	AAA	99	$18
Frieri,Ernesto	28	R	ABB	115	$17
Gonzalez,Gio	28	L	AAA	85	$17
Ryu,Hyun-Jin	27	L	AAB	106	$17
Minor,Mike	26	L	AAA	88	$16
Corbin,Patrick	24	L	ABB	100	$14
Dickey,R.A.	39	R	AAB	86	$14
Kuroda,Hiroki	39	R	BAA	91	$13
Burnett,A.J.	37	R	BAA	104	$12
Samardzija,Jeff	29	R	AAA	93	$12
Tanaka,Masahiro	25	R	AAB	94	$12
Arroyo,Bronson	37	R	AAA	75	$11
Fister,Doug	30	R	BAA	100	$11
Nolasco,Ricky	31	R	BAB	94	$11
Porcello,Rick	25	R	AAA	96	$11
Holland,Derek	27	L	BAA	85	$10
Kennedy,Ian	29	R	AAA	84	$10
Lester,Jon	30	L	AAA	86	$10
Masterson,Justin	29	R	AAB	82	$10
Gallardo,Yovani	28	R	BAA	77	$9
Lincecum,Tim	30	R	AAA	85	$9
Clippard,Tyler	29	R	ABB	99	$8
Milone,Tommy	27	L	ABA	88	$8
Sabathia,CC	33	L	AAA	84	$8
Bell,Heath	36	R	ABB	110	$6
Collmenter,Josh	28	R	BBA	86	$4
Villanueva,Carlos	30	R	BBA	78	$3
Axford,John	31	R	ABA	97	$2

TIER 2

High Skill, Mod Risk			Filters:	BBB	50	<$20
PITCHERS	Age	Thrw	REL	BPV	R$	
Wilson,C.J.	33	L	AAA	67	$11	
Miley,Wade	27	L	AAA	68	$9	
Parker,Jarrod	25	R	ABA	55	$9	
Santana,Ervin	31	R	BAB	69	$9	
Buehrle,Mark	35	L	AAA	69	$7	
Hellickson,Jeremy	27	R	AAA	64	$7	
Leake,Mike	26	R	AAA	69	$7	
Wood,Travis	27	L	ABB	50	$6	
Dempster,Ryan	37	R	BAA	61	$2	
Doubront,Felix	26	L	BBB	62	$1	
Jackson,Edwin	30	R	AAA	72	$1	
Norris,Bud	29	R	BAA	69	$1	

PORTFOLIO 3 PLAN

TIER 3 (cont.)

High Skill, High Risk

BATTERS	Age	Bats	Pos	REL	Ct%	PX	Spd	R$
						one of		
				N/A	80	100	100	<$10
Robinson,Shane	29	R	897	AFA	86	52	136	$4
Tejada,Ruben	24	R	6	CCC	85	51	110	$4
Valencia,Danny	29	R	0	ACD	80	118	91	$4
Elmore,Jake	27	R	6	ACC	84	63	117	$3
Fuld,Sam	32	L	798	DFB	85	43	144	$3
Kelly,Don	34	L	795	AFC	84	62	129	$3
Pennington,Cliff	30	B	64	ACB	80	65	104	$3
Pill,Brett	29	R	3	ADB	82	110	95	$3
Sweeney,Ryan	29	L	9	FFB	82	83	102	$3
Arias,Joaquin	29	R	56	BDC	85	58	141	$2
Borbon,Julio	28	L	9	ADA	81	56	127	$2
Carroll,Jamey	40	R	5	ACC	84	40	113	$2
Chavez,Endy	36	L	89	BFF	89	42	115	$2
Coghlan,Chris	29	L	7	FDB	80	64	108	$2
Frandsen,Kevin	32	R	34	ADB	89	66	105	$2
Pena,Ramiro	28	B	5	FFD	80	70	110	$2
Ciriaco,Pedro	28	R	6	ADD	82	57	138	$1
Santiago,Ramon	34	B	455	AFC	83	55	113	$1
Schafer,Logan	27	L	79	ADA	81	80	118	$1

TIER 3

High Skill, High Risk

PITCHERS	Age	Thrw	REL	BPV	R$
			N/A	75	<$10
Colon,Bartolo	41	R	DAA	76	$9
Haren,Dan	33	R	CAB	106	$9
Kluber,Corey	28	R	CCC	89	$9
Gregerson,Luke	30	R	BCA	107	$8
Ross,Tyson	27	R	DCC	79	$8
Tazawa,Junichi	28	R	FDB	122	$8
Niese,Jon	27	L	DAA	86	$7
Nova,Ivan	27	R	CBA	77	$7
Walker,Taijuan	21	R	ADC	83	$7
Erlin,Robert	23	L	ADA	81	$6
Fien,Casey	30	R	ADF	115	$6
Gee,Dillon	28	R	DAB	78	$6
Herrera,Kelvin	24	R	ADB	137	$6
Hochevar,Luke	30	R	CAB	120	$6
Hoover,J.J.	26	R	ADF	92	$6
O Day,Darren	31	R	DDC	112	$6
Peralta,Joel	38	R	ACB	75	$6
Ramirez,Erasmo	24	R	DDC	83	$6
Soria,Joakim	30	R	FDA	119	$6
Stammen,Craig	30	R	ACC	93	$6
Storen,Drew	26	R	CCA	100	$6
Bastardo,Antonio	28	L	ADA	100	$5
Delabar,Steve	30	R	BDB	115	$5
Gausman,Kevin John	23	R	AFF	110	$5
Hawkins,LaTroy	41	R	FCB	91	$5
Hudson,Tim	38	R	FAB	75	$5
Marshall,Sean	31	L	FCA	131	$5
McGee,Jake	27	L	ADC	136	$5
Rodriguez,Francisco	32	R	BCB	110	$5
Rodriguez,Paco	23	L	ADB	121	$5
Rondon,Bruce	23	R	AFA	106	$5
Siegrist,Kevin	24	L	AFF	106	$5
Vincent,Nick	27	R	ADB	101	$5
Walden,Jordan	26	R	DCA	101	$5
Watson,Tony	29	L	ADA	90	$5
Baker,Scott	32	R	FDC	76	$4
Furbush,Charlie	28	L	BDB	100	$4
Hunter,Tommy	27	R	DCC	82	$4
Jones,Nate	28	R	ADB	111	$4
Loup,Aaron	26	L	ADB	105	$4
McCarthy,Brandon	30	R	FBB	79	$4
Morrow,Brandon	29	R	FBB	77	$4
Motte,Jason	32	R	FCA	116	$4
Perez,Chris	29	R	CBB	80	$4

TIER 3 (cont.)

High Skill, High Risk

PITCHERS	Age	Thrw	REL	BPV	R$
			N/A	75	<$10
Putz,J.J.	37	R	FBA	120	$4
Ross,Robbie	25	L	BDA	92	$4
Santos,Sergio	30	R	FDF	118	$4
Thayer,Dale	33	R	ADA	94	$4
Alburquerque,Al	28	R	FDA	88	$3
Belisle,Matt	34	R	ACA	108	$3
Burton,Jared	33	R	DDC	83	$3
Cecil,Brett	27	L	ACB	100	$3
Crain,Jesse	32	R	FDA	94	$3
Dunn,Mike	29	L	ADC	80	$3
Garcia,Jaime	27	L	FBB	89	$3
Hernandez,David	29	R	ACB	100	$3
Howell,J.P.	31	L	FDA	79	$3
Jordan,Taylor	25	R	CFF	78	$3
Kintzler,Brandon	29	R	FDD	90	$3
Petit,Yusmeiro	29	R	ADA	87	$3
Pryor,Stephen	24	R	FFC	83	$3
Shaw,Bryan	26	R	ADB	81	$3
Smith,Burch	24	R	AFF	101	$3
Torres,Alexander	26	L	ADF	88	$3
Anderson,Brett	26	L	FDA	77	$2
Capuano,Chris	35	L	DAA	90	$2
Cotts,Neal	34	L	FFF	100	$2
Gorzelanny,Tom	31	L	DCA	79	$2
Harris,Will	29	R	ADB	111	$2
Kelley,Shawn	30	R	FDA	102	$2
Lecure,Sam	30	R	BCA	101	$2
Lopez,Javier	36	L	ADA	82	$2
Machi,Jean	32	R	AFF	87	$2
Maness,Seth	25	R	ADA	96	$2
Mejia,Jenrry	24	R	FDF	76	$2
Skaggs,Tyler	22	L	ADB	75	$2
Stauffer,Tim	32	R	FCB	79	$2
Veras,Jose	33	R	ACA	75	$2
Beckett,Josh	34	R	FBA	78	$1
Billingsley,Chad	29	R	FBB	75	$1
Capps,Carter	23	R	ADC	98	$1
Carpenter,David	28	R	ADF	98	$1
Frasor,Jason	36	R	DDA	82	$1
Fujikawa,Kyuji	33	R	FCB	119	$1
Hanrahan,Joel	32	R	FBD	106	$1
Hudson,Daniel	27	R	FCB	87	$1
Johnson,Josh	30	R	FBA	80	$1
Kontos,George	29	R	ADF	81	$1
Lindstrom,Matt	34	R	DDA	77	$1
Lopez,Wilton	30	R	CCB	91	$1
Marcum,Shaun	32	R	FBA	81	$1
Otero,Dan	29	R	ADD	106	$1
Patton,Troy	28	L	CDA	85	$1
Ventura,Yordano	23	R	ADB	85	$1
Wright,Jamey	39	R	ACA	75	$1

*Tier 2 players should generally be less than $20. If you're going to spend more than $20, be aware of the added risk.

**Tier 3 players should generally be less than $10. If you're going to spend more than $10, be aware of the added risk.

RANDOM VARIANCE - Rebounds/Corrections

Rebounds/Improvements — BATTERS

BATTERS	POS	+
Barney,Darwin	4	+5
Murphy,David	7	+5
Mayberry,John	89	+5
Morse,Michael	9	+5
Arencibia,J.P.	2	+4
Davis,Ike	3	+4
Rizzo,Anthony	3	+4
Konerko,Paul	3	+4
Uggla,Dan	4	+4
Weeks,Rickie	4	+4
Middlebrooks,Will	5	+4
Pierre,Juan	7	+4
Ruggiano,Justin	78	+4
Young,Chris	789	+4
Wieters,Matt	2	+3
Moreland,Mitch	3	+3
Encarnacion,Edwin	3	+3
Pujols,Albert	3	+3
Jones,Garrett	39	+3
Walker,Neil	4	+3
Izturis,Maicer	456	+3
Frazier,Todd	5	+3
Valbuena,Luis	5	+3
Joyce,Matt	79	+3
Heyward,Jason	89	+3
Hamilton,Josh	9	+3

Corrections/Declines — BATTERS

BATTERS	POS	-
Castillo,Welington	2	-5
Castro,Jason	2	-5
Saltalamacchia,Jarrod	2	-5
Mauer,Joe	2	-5
Freeman,Freddie	3	-5
Donaldson,Josh	5	-5
Johnson,Chris	5	-5
Uribe,Juan	5	-5
Peralta,Jhonny	6	-5
Ramirez,Hanley	6	-5
Nava,Daniel	79	-5
Rasmus,Colby	8	-5
Byrd,Marlon	9	-5
Cuddyer,Michael	9	-5
Werth,Jayson	9	-5
Craig,Allen	379	-4
Infante,Omar	4	-4
Carpenter,Matt	45	-4
Shuck,J.B.	7	-4
Gomez,Carlos	8	-4
Lough,David	9	-4
Rosario,Wilin	2	-3
Hosmer,Eric	3	-3
Lind,Adam	3	-3
Lucas,Edward	345	-3
Hill,Aaron	4	-3
Mercer,Jordy	46	-3
Cabrera,Miguel	5	-3
Cabrera,Everth	6	-3
Tulowitzki,Troy	6	-3
Trout,Mike	78	-3
Ellsbury,Jacoby	8	-3
McCutchen,Andrew	8	-3
Revere,Ben	8	-3
Myers,Wil	9	-3
Victorino,Shane	9	-3

Rebounds/Improvements — PITCHERS

PITCHERS	+
Blanton,Joe	+5
Hernandez,Roberto	+5
Keuchel,Dallas	+5
Volquez,Edinson	+5
Davis,Wade	+4
Lyles,Jordan	+4
Saunders,Joe	+4
Axelrod,Dylan	+3
Harang,Aaron	+3
Hellickson,Jeremy	+3
Hughes,Phil	+3
Jackson,Edwin	+3
Kluber,Corey	+3
Porcello,Rick	+3
Rogers,Esmil	+3
Vogelsong,Ryan	+3
Zito,Barry	+3

Corrections/Declines — PITCHERS

PITCHERS	-
Buchholz,Clay	-5
Fernandez,Jose	-5
Kershaw,Clayton	-5
Chen,Bruce	-4
Colon,Bartolo	-4
Kelly,Joe	-4
Wood,Travis	-4
Iwakuma,Hisashi	-3
Ogando,Alexi	-3

Minimum 300 AB (batters), 100 IP (pitchers), in 2013.

SPECIAL BONUS COVERAGE!

It was during the final editing process in which we first heard it—the slow, chant-like refrain of "Fear the Beard." Quietly—and ignorable—at first, but then the words slowly gained momentum and volume until clarity struck us all at once—it was the ghost of Brian Wilson, calling out for a player box. After briefly discussing the merits of eliminating (and wiping forever from the record) Chris Withrow, we found this corner to share our thoughts on this important reliever. And our consciences are now clear.

Either that, or we just plumb forgot him.

(Note that Wilson's projection is not a part of any of the previous charts.)

Wilson,Brian						Health		F		LIMA Plan		C+	Missed nearly two full seasons following 2012 TJ surgery (his second). Small sample-size skills weren't quite
Age:	32	Th:	R	Role	RP	PT/Exp		D		Rand Var		-5	vintage in Aug-Sept with LA, but he turned in a solid post-season run (6 IP, 0 ER, 2 BB, 8 K). That may be
Ht:	6' 2"	Wt:	205	Type	Pwr	Consist		F		MM		5520	enough to lure some team into signing him as a closer. Health and 2011 struggles elevate the risk.

Yr	Tm	W	L	Sv	IP	K	ERA	xERA	WHIP	oOPS	vL	vR	BF/G	Ctl	Dom	Cmd	SwK	G	L	F	H%	S%	hr/f	GS	APC	DOM%	DIS%	Sv%	LI	RAR	BPV	BPX	R$
09	SF	5	6	38	72	83	2.74	3.29	1.20	595	532	657	4.5	3.4	10.3	3.1	9%	46	18	36	32%	77%	4%	0	19			84	1.73	14.1	119	223	$23
10	SF	3	3	48	75	93	1.81	2.97	1.18	597	607	587	4.4	3.1	11.2	3.6	11%	49	13	38	33%	86%	4%	0	19			91	1.50	20.9	144	233	$28
11	SF	6	4	36	55	54	3.11	3.84	1.47	660	599	720	4.3	5.1	8.8	1.7	7%	53	17	30	32%	78%	4%	0	18			88	1.54	5.7	53	80	$16
12	SF	0	0	1	2	2	9.00	7.66	3.00	1100	933	1143	6.0	9.0	9.0	1.0	7%	25	38	38	52%	67%	0%	0	28			100	0.39	-1.2	-78	-102	-$5
13	LA	2	1	0	14	13	0.66	2.66	0.88	467	413	485	2.7	2.6	8.6	3.3	10%	56	19	25	24%	92%	0%	0	12			0	1.00	5.4	117	152	$0
1st Half																																	
2nd Half		2	1	0	14	13	0.66	2.66	0.88	467	413	485	2.7	2.6	8.6	3.3	10%	56	19	25	24%	92%	0%	0	12			0	1.00	5.4	117	152	$0
14	Proj	4	4	12	58	65	2.95	3.13	1.22	612	554	666	4.2	3.9	10.0	2.6	9%	49	16	35	30%	78%	9%	0						6.6	102	133	$9

Universal Draft Grid

Most publications and websites provide cheat sheets with ranked player lists for different fantasy draft formats. The biggest problem with these tools is that they perpetuate the myth that players can be ranked in a linear fashion.

Since rankings are based on highly variable projections, it is foolhardy to draw conclusions that a $24 player is better than a $23 player is better than a $22 player. Yes, a first round pick is better than a 10th round pick, but within most rounds, all players are pretty much interchangeable commodities.

But typical cheat sheets don't reflect that reality. Auction sheets rank players by dollar value. Snake draft sheets rank players within round, accounting for position and categorical scarcity. But just as ADPs have a ridiculously low success rate, these cheat sheets are similarly flawed.

We have a tool at BaseballHQ.com called the Rotisserie Grid. It is a chart—that can be customized to your league parameters—which organizes players into pockets of skill, by position. It is one of the most popular tools on the site. One of the best features of this grid is that its design provides immediate insight into position scarcity.

So in the *Forecaster*, we recently transitioned to this format as a sort of Universal Draft Grid.

How to use the chart

Across the top of the grid, players are sorted by position. First and third base, and second and shortstop are presented side-by-side for easy reference when considering corner and middle infielders, respectively.

The vertical axis separates each group of players into tiers based on potential fantasy impact. At the top are the Elite players; at the bottom are the Fringe players.

Auction leagues: The tiers in the grid represent rough break-points for dollar values. Elite players could be considered those that are purchased for $30 and up. Each subsequent tier is a step down of approximately $5.

Snake drafters: Tiers can be used to rank players similarly, though most tiers will encompass more than one round. Any focus on position scarcity will bump some players up a bit. For instance, with the dearth of Elite shortstops and the wealth of Elite outfielders, one might opt to draft Troy Tulowitzki (from the Gold tier) before the Elite level Carlos Gonzalez. The reason we target scarce positions early is that there will be plenty of solid outfielders and starting pitchers later on.

To build the best foundation, you should come out of the first 10 rounds with all your middle infielders, all your corner infielders, one outfielder, at least one catcher and two pitchers (at least one closer).

The players are listed at the position where they both qualify and provide the most fantasy value. Additional position eligibility (20 games) is listed in parentheses. Listings in bold are players with high reliability grades (minimum "B" across the board).

Each player is presented with his 7-character Mayberry score. The first four digits (all on a 0-5 scale) represent skill: power, speed, batting average and playing time for batters; ERA, dominance, saves potential and playing time for pitchers. The last four alpha characters are the reliability grade (A-F): health, experience and consistency.

Within each tier, players are sorted by the first character of their Mayberry score. This means that batters are sorted by power; pitchers by ERA potential. If you need to prospect for the best skill sets among players in a given tier, target those with 4s and 5s in whatever skill you need.

CAVEATS and DISCLAIMERS

The placement of players in tiers does not represent average draft positions (ADP) or average auction values (AAV). It represents where each player's true value may lie. It is the variance between this true value and the ADP/AAV market values—or better, the value that your league-mates place on each player—where you will find your potential for profit or loss.

That means **you cannot take this chart right into your draft with you**. You have to compare these rankings with your ADPs and AAVs, and build your draft list from there. In other words, if we project Alex Rios as a "Gold" level pick but you know the other owners (or your ADPs) see him as a fourth-rounder, you can probably wait to pick him up in round 3. If you are in an auction league with owners who overvalue Yankees and Mark Teixeira (projected at $20) gets bid past $25, you will likely take a loss should you decide to chase the bidding.

Finally, this chart is intended as a preliminary look based on current factors. For Draft Day, you will need to make your own adjustments based upon many different criteria that will impact the world between now and then. Daily updates appear online at BaseballHQ.com. A free projections update is available in March at **http://www.baseballhq.com/content/ron-shandlers-baseball-forecaster-2014**

Universal Draft Grid

TIER	FIRST BASE	THIRD BASE	SECOND BASE	SHORTSTOP
Elite	Goldschmidt,Paul (5245 AAB) Encarnacion,Edwin (4255 BAC)	Cabrera,Miguel (4155 AAC) Wright,David (4335 DBC)	Cano,Robinson (4255 AAB)	Reyes,Jose (2545 FAC)
Gold	Votto,Joey (4145 BAF) Davis,Chris (5125 ABF) Fielder,Prince (4045 AAC) Freeman,Freddie (4235 AAC) Gonzalez,Adrian (3235 AAC) Hosmer,Eric (3335 AAF) Pujols,Albert (4135 CAC)	Beltre,Adrian (4145 BAB)	Kipnis,Jason (4435 AAB) Pedroia,Dustin (2445 BAB) Murphy,Daniel (2335 CAA)	Andrus,Elvis (1525 AAA) Ramirez,Hanley (4345 DBF) Tulowitzki,Troy (4145 FCD) Cabrera,Everth (1515 BCC)
Stars	Morales,Kendrys (4035 FCA) Craig,Allen (O) (3335 CCB) Belt,Brandon (4325 ACB) Rizzo,Anthony (4125 ABF)	Longoria,Evan (4125 DBA) Zimmerman,Ryan (4335 CAA) Donaldson,Josh (3225 ABF) Ramirez,Aramis (4135 CBB) Sandoval,Pablo (3035 CBC) Seager,Kyle (3225 AAA)	Kinsler,Ian (2335 CAB) Carpenter,Matt (3) (3235 ABD) Kendrick,Howie (2335 BAB) Phillips,Brandon (2225 AAB) Altuve,Jose (1425 ABB) Hill,Aaron (3235 DBF) Prado,Martin (3O) (2245 AAD)	Desmond,Ian (4425 AAD) Castro,Starlin (2425 AAC) Ramirez,Alexei (1435 AAB) Segura,Jean (1525 ACB) Aybar,Erick (1435 BAA) Zobrist,Ben (2O) (3335 AAB)
Regulars	Napoli,Mike (5115 BBF) Trumbo,Mark (4115 AAB) Hart,Corey (4225 FCA) Swisher,Nick (O) (4125 AAB) Abreu,Jose (4235 ADF) Teixeira,Mark (4135 FCC) Adams,Matt (4025 ACC) LaRoche,Adam (4215 CBF) Alonso,Yonder (2125 BCA) Lind,Adam (4225 BBC) Moss,Brandon (O) (5125 ACC)	Middlebrooks,Will (4225 CCF) Alvarez,Pedro (5215 BBC) Frazier,Todd (4225 ACD) Headley,Chase (4225 BAD) Lawrie,Brett (3425 DCC) Arenado,Nolan (3145 ADB) Johnson,Chris (3225 ABC)	Infante,Omar (1435 CAB) Walker,Neil (3125 BBA) Scutaro,Marco (1325 BBA) Utley,Chase (3425 FCA) Bonifacio,Emilio (O) (1503 CCB) LeMahieu,DJ (1535 ACA) Gyorko,Jedd (4125 BCB)	Miller,Bradley (2415 AFB) Cabrera,Asdrubal (3225 BAB) Escobar,Alcides (1525 AAD) Simmons,Andrelton (2535 BDB) Villar,Jonathan (1505 ACA) Hardy,J.J. (3225 BAC) Rollins,Jimmy (2325 BAA)
Mid-Level	Howard,Ryan (5115 FCC) Morneau,Justin (3325 DBC) Loney,James (1135 ABF) Dunn,Adam (5005 AAD) Moreland,Mitch (4025 BBB) Morrison,Logan (3225 FDB) Davis,Ike (4215 DCD) Ruf,Darin (O) (5113 ADF) Jones,Garrett (O) (4223 ABD) Smoak,Justin (4205 BCB)	Asche,Cody (3315 AFB) Bogaerts,Xander (4335 AFD) Freese,David (2025 CBC) Chisenhall,Lonnie (4325 BDA) Moustakas,Mike (3015 ABA) Rodriguez,Alex (4213 FCA) Dominguez,Matt (3025 ACB) Machado,Manny (3325 ACA) Young,Michael (1) (1333 AAD) Plouffe,Trevor (3115 BBA)	Rendon,Anthony (3225 AFF) Rutledge,Josh (3533 ADC) Profar,Jurickson (2325 ADD) Beckham,Gordon (2315 BBA) Callaspo,Alberto (3) (1025 ABB) Dozier,Brian (3315 ACC) Ackley,Dustin (O) (1315 ABC) Ellis,Mark (1215 DBB) Franklin,Nick (3305 ADB)	Lowrie,Jed (2) (4225 FBB) Peralta,Jhonny (3015 ABF) Drew,Stephen (4315 FCC) Jeter,Derek (1335 FBF) Cozart,Zack (2415 BBA) Escobar,Yunel (1225 AAC) Nunez,Eduardo (1513 CDC) Furcal,Rafael (1433 FDB) Iglesias,Jose (3) (0405 ADB)
Bench	Carter,Chris (O) (5205 ACB) Duda,Lucas (O) (4005 BCC) Wallace,Brett (4103 ACB) Carp,Mike (O) (4121 CDF) Blanks,Kyle (O) (4203 FFD) Colabello,Chris (4103 ADC) Guzman,Jesus (O) (3213 ADA) Konerko,Paul (2023 BAD) Overbay,Lyle (3213 ADA) Baker,Jeff (O) (3311 CFD) Parmelee,Chris (O) (3103 ACF)	Francisco,Juan (1) (4003 ADA) Gillaspie,Conor (3025 ACB) Reynolds,Mark (1) (4103 ABB) Uribe,Juan (3213 CDD) Valbuena,Luis (3015 ACA) Youkilis,Kevin (3213 FCC) Chavez,Eric (4331 FFC) Olt,Mike (4203 AFF) Flores,Wilmer (3021 AFC)	Weeks,Rickie (4315 DBC) Wong,Kolten (1523 ADB) Barney,Darwin (1325 AAB) Gennett,Scooter (2313 ADA) Johnson,Kelly (O) (3303 ABA) Sogard,Eric (1313 BDA) Bloomquist,Willie (0321 FDB) Espinosa,Danny (4303 ABC) Schumaker,Skip (O) (1133 CDA) Uggla,Dan (4205 AAB) Amarista,Alexi (O) (1413 ADA) Getz,Chris (0521 DDB) Sizemore,Scott (4311 FFF) Flaherty,Ryan (3203 ADA) Forsythe,Logan (2411 DDC) Green,Grant (2203 ABA) Keppinger,Jeff (31) (1031 CCF) Roberts,Brian (2213 FFD) Solano,Donovan (1323 BDB) Weeks,Jemile (1501 ACC)	Aviles,Mike (3) (1213 BCA) Crawford,Brandon (1115 ACB) Descalso,Daniel (23) (2323 ACB) Mercer,Jordy (2) (2123 ACC) Gregorius,Didi (1113 ADB) Hechavarria,Adeiny (1315 ABC) Izturis,Maicer (23) (0223 CCB) Gordon,Dee (0501 CDB)
Fringe	Pacheco,Jordan (1331 ADF) Rodriguez,Sean (O) (3201 ADB) Singleton,Jonathan (3203 ADD) Barton,Daric (1201 ADA) Freiman,Nathan (1011 ADB) Pena,Carlos (4001 BBC) Pill,Brett (3121 ADB) Sanchez,Gaby (2111 ACD) Satin,Josh (2001 ACB) Helton,Todd (3030 DCB)	Betancourt,Yuniesky (1) (2011 BCA) Nelson,Chris (2311 CDF) Polanco,Placido (0321 DCA) Davidson,Matthew (4001 ADB) Jimenez,Luis (1201 ACB) Kelly,Don (O) (1401 AFC) Murphy,Donnie (4201 DFD) Carroll,Jamey (0321 ACC) Pena,Ramiro (1211 FFD) Tracy,Chad (2001 CFF) Hairston,Jerry (O) (1111 DDC) Hannahan,Jack (1001 ADB) Turner,Justin (2121 BDA)	Casilla,Alexi (1511 BDB) Dietrich,Derek (4311 AFC) Galvis,Freddy (2313 DCA) Garcia,Leury (1501 AFC) Johnson,Elliot (1501 ADC) Lombardozzi,Steve (O) (1321 ACA) Pastornicky,Tyler (1411 BDB) DeRosa,Mark (3) (1001 FFC) Abreu,Tony (3121 DDB) Frandsen,Kevin (1) (1231 ADB) Giavotella,Johnny (1211 ACA) Goins,Ryan (1211 ADB) Roberts,Ryan (2201 ACC) Lucas,Edward (31) (1103 ACC) Santiago,Ramon (3) (1111 AFC)	Florimon Jr.,Pedro (1303 ACB) Herrera,Jonathan (2) (1311 BFB) Nix,Jayson (3) (2301 DFB) Owings,Christopher (2411 ADC) Punto,Nick (23) (1211 DFB) Tejada,Ruben (1213 CCC) Bianchi,Jeff (3) (1201 BDC) Cedeno,Ronny (1311 BDA) Elmore,Jake (1311 ACC) Escobar,Eduardo (3) (1311 ADC) Pennington,Cliff (2) (1301 ACB) Arias,Joaquin (3) (1511 BDC) Gonzalez,Marwin (1221 BDA) Ryan,Brendan (1303 ACB) Ciriaco,Pedro (1511 ADD)

Universal Draft Grid

Elite

CATCHER	DH	OUTFIELD		OUTFIELD	
		Trout,Mike	(4535 ABD)	Jones,Adam	**(4345 AAA)**
		McCutchen,Andrew	(4545 AAD)	Ellsbury,Jacoby	(2535 FAF)
		Braun,Ryan	(4445 ABC)	Gomez,Carlos	(4515 BCC)
		Gonzalez,Carlos	**(5435 BBB)**	Kemp,Matt	(5335 FBF)

Gold

CATCHER	DH	OUTFIELD		OUTFIELD	
	Martinez,Victor (2035 FCC)	**Holliday,Matt**	**(4245 BAA)**	Marte,Starling	(4525 BBB)
	Ortiz,David (5155 DBC)	Rios,Alex	(3535 AAF)	Cespedes,Yoenis	(4325 BBD)
		Upton,Justin	**(4325 AAB)**	**Gardner,Brett**	**(2515 FCB)**
		Choo,Shin-Soo	(3325 BAC)	Gordon,Alex	(4325 AAB)
		Harper,Bryce	(4335 BCC)	Puig,Yasiel	(4335 AFF)
		Pence,Hunter	(4435 AAD)	Jackson,Austin	(3515 BAD)

Stars

CATCHER	DH	OUTFIELD		OUTFIELD	
Lucroy,Jonathan (3335 BBF)	Butler,Billy (3025 AAC)	Beltran,Carlos	(4235 CAB)	Crawford,Carl	(3535 FCC)
Posey,Buster (1) (3135 CBF)		**Bourn,Michael**	**(1515 BAB)**	**Jennings,Desmond**	**(3515 BBA)**
Molina,Yadier **(3145 ABB)**		**Bruce,Jay**	**(5225 AAA)**	**Soriano,Alfonso**	**(4225 AAB)**
Rosario,Wilin (4125 ACC)		Fowler,Dexter	(4515 BBD)	Werth,Jayson	(4325 DBD)
		Myers,Wil	(4325 ABC)	**Hunter,Torii**	**(3225 AAB)**
		Revere,Ben	(0535 CCA)	Venable,Will	(3525 ACB)
		Stanton,Giancarlo	(5225 CBD)	Young Jr.,Eric	(1515 CCF)
		Crisp,Coco	(2525 DBA)	**De Aza,Alejandro**	**(2415 AAA)**
		Cuddyer,Michael	(4335 CBC)	Hamilton,Billy	(1503 AFC)
		Martin,Leonys	(2525 ADD)	Hamilton,Josh	(4325 AAC)
		Victorino,Shane	(2535 BAC)	Heyward,Jason	(4335 CBC)
		Aoki,Norichika	(1435 AAC)	Pagan,Angel	(2535 FBB)
		Bautista,Jose	(4235 DBD)	Upton,B.J.	(3405 BAC)

Regulars

CATCHER	DH	OUTFIELD		OUTFIELD	
Mauer,Joe (3045 DBC)		Brown,Domonic	(3325 ACC)	**Jay,Jon**	**(1335 BBA)**
Santana,Carlos (1) **(4125 AAB)**		**Cruz,Nelson**	**(4115 BBB)**	Markakis,Nick	(1135 BAD)
Wieters,Matt **(4225 AAA)**		Granderson,Curtis	(4515 FBC)	Rasmus,Colby	(4215 BBC)
Perez,Salvador (2035 CCB)		Span,Denard	(1535 CBB)	Eaton,Adam	(1425 DDF)
McCann,Brian (3025 BBC)		**Brantley,Michael**	**(1335 AAA)**	**Ethier,Andre**	**(3235 AAA)**
Pierzynski,A.J. (2035 BBC)		Cabrera,Melky	(2335 CBF)	Maybin,Cameron	(2515 FCC)
Ramos,Wilson (3025 FDA)		Davis,Rajai	(2513 CCB)	Ross,Cody	(4125 DCB)
		Dyson,Jarrod	(1513 BDB)	Cain,Lorenzo	(2515 DCB)
		Garcia,Avisail	(2315 BFC)	Murphy,David	(3235 ABF)

Mid-Level

CATCHER	DH	OUTFIELD		OUTFIELD	
Saltalamacchia,Jarrod (5215 ACB)		Bourjos,Peter	(2503 FDC)	Dickerson,Corey	(4333 AFA)
Castro,Jason (4125 FDC)		Saunders,Michael	(4315 ACC)	Hoes,LJ	(1313 ACB)
Gattis,Evan (O) (4123 AFB)		**Viciedo,Dayan**	**(3125 ABA)**	**Joyce,Matt**	**(4213 BBB)**
Gomes,Yan (4423 ADC)		Byrd,Marlon	(3025 BCF)	Morse,Michael	(4013 DCD)
Montero,Miguel (3005 BBC)		McLouth,Nate	(2415 CCA)	**Reddick,Josh**	**(4415 BBA)**
Avila,Alex (4213 BCD)		**Parra,Gerardo**	**(2333 ABB)**	Springer,George	(4303 AFF)
D Arnaud,Travis (3113 FDC)		Quentin,Carlos	(4033 FCA)	Taveras,Oscar	(3333 AFD)
Doumit,Ryan (O) (3125 CCB)		Schierholtz,Nate	(3225 BCA)	Almonte,Abraham	(2313 ADB)
Jaso,John (2223 DDF)		**Stubbs,Drew**	**(3505 AAB)**	Calhoun,Kole	(3323 AFD)
Ruiz,Carlos (2233 CCF)		**Suzuki,Ichiro**	**(1533 AAB)**	Denorfia,Chris	(2433 ACB)
		Arcia,Oswaldo Celestino	(4205 AFD)	Dirks,Andy	(2323 BCD)
		Blackmon,Charlie	(3433 FDA)	Lake,Junior	(3513 ADB)
		Blanco,Gregor	(1503 ACB)	Ludwick,Ryan	(3013 FCF)
		Pollock IV,A.J.	(2523 ABC)	Presley,Alex	(2433 ACB)
		Willingham,Josh	(4105 CBD)	Raburn,Ryan	(4113 BDF)
		Yelich,Christian S.	(3523 AFF)	**Young,Chris**	**(4413 ABB)**
		Davis,Khristopher	(4223 AFF)		

Bench

CATCHER	DH	OUTFIELD		OUTFIELD	
Martin,Russell **(3115 BBA)**	Scott,Luke (4113 FDA)	DeJesus,David	(2223 CBA)	Mastroianni,Darin	(1501 FFD)
Castillo,Welington (3203 CDB)	Urrutia,Henry (1421 AFF)	Gentry,Craig	(1511 BFC)	Mayberry,John	(4213 ACB)
Mesoraco,Devin (2015 ADB)	Berkman,Lance (3111 FDD)	Gomes,Jonny	(4203 ADD)	Moore,Tyler	(4311 ADD)
Montero,Jesus (3023 ACC)	Reimold,Nolan (3313 FFF)	**Ibanez,Raul**	**(4223 ABA)**	**Smith,Seth**	**(3113 ABB)**
Norris,Derek (4313 ADC)		Lagares,Juan	(1403 ACC)	Van Slyke,Scott	(4111 ACD)
Phegley,Joshua (2213 ACB)		Nava,Daniel	(3123 BCC)	Wells,Vernon	(2213 CCA)
Suzuki,Kurt (1213 ACB)		Ruggiano,Justin	(4213 ADF)	Barnes,Brandon	(2303 ACB)
Bethancourt,Christian (2211 AFD)		Tabata,Jose	(1433 CDC)	Hicks,Aaron	(3501 ADD)
Conger,Hank (3013 AFB)		Bradley,Jackie	(4323 AFB)	Lough,David	(1411 ACC)
Navarro,Dioner (2221 AFD)		Castellanos,Nick	(2213 ADC)	Marisnick,Jake	(3411 AFC)
Zunino,Mike (2403 BFF)		Heisey,Chris	(3413 CDB)	Ozuna,Marcell	(2511 CFF)
Cervelli,Francisco (2213 FFF)		Kubel,Jason	(4003 BCD)	Bernadina,Roger	(2501 BDF)
Ellis,A.J. (2005 ACD)		Maxwell,Justin	(4503 DDB)	Brown,Andrew	(4201 ADB)
Iannetta,Chris (3003 CDB)		Shuck,J.B.	(0323 ACD)	Danks,Jordan	(3301 ACD)
Pinto,Josmil (3021 AFA)		Young,Delmon	(2013 BCA)	Den Dekker,Matthew	(2303 ADA)
Ross,David (4101 DFB)		Bogusevic,Brian	(2411 CDC)	**Gose,Anthony**	**(2501 ABB)**
Soto,Geovany (4011 CDD)		**Gindl,Caleb**	**(4123 ABB)**	Hairston,Scott	(4201 BFC)
		Grossman,Robert	(2303 ADA)	Schafer,Jordan	(1501 CDA)
		Harrison,Josh	(2431 ADB)	Sierra,Moises	(3201 ACA)

Fringe

CATCHER	DH	OUTFIELD		OUTFIELD	
Flowers,Tyler (4103 AFB)	Valencia,Danny (3021 ACD)	Campana,Tony	(0501 ADB)	Nieuwenhuis,Kirk	(3201 ADB)
Grandal,Yasmani (3011 DFD)	Betemit,Wilson (4201 FDF)	Choice,Michael	(2201 ADA)	Ramirez,Wilkin	(2301 DDA)
Kratz,Erik (4003 BFB)	Pearce,Steve (2201 FFC)	Fuentes,Reymond	(1501 ADF)	Sweeney,Ryan	(2223 FFB)
Lavarnway,Ryan (2101 ADB)	Dickerson,Chris (2401 BFF)	Hernandez,Cesar	(1411 ADA)	Torres,Andres	(1401 DCA)
Lobaton,Jose (2003 CFC)	Hafner,Travis (3201 DDC)	Lambo,Andrew	(4101 ADB)	Tuiasosopo,Matt	(3101 ACC)
Pena,Brayan (1021 AFC)		Martinez,J.D.	(2103 CCC)	**Beltre,Engel**	**(0521 ABB)**
Arencibia,J.P. (4003 BCB)		Paul,Xavier	(3211 ADC)	Borbon,Julio	(1511 ADA)
Buck,John (2001 ACA)		Pierre,Juan	(0531 ABD)	Chavez,Endy	(0321 BFF)
Federowicz,Tim (3001 ADB)		Robinson,Shane	(1511 AFA)	Coghlan,Chris	(1311 FDB)
Hanigan,Ryan (0013 CDC)		Snider,Travis	(3101 CDD)	Crowe,Trevor	(1301 FFB)
Hundley,Nick (3103 DDF)		Almonte,Zoilo	(1211 BDB)	Francoeur,Jeff	(1301 ABD)
Kottaras,George (4201 AFA)		Bay,Jason	(3301 DDD)	Gutierrez,Franklin	(3303 FFC)
Nieves,Wil (1111 BFD)		Cowgill,Collin	(2401 ADC)	Johnson,Reed	(2211 CFC)
Sanchez,Hector (1011 AFC)		Fuld,Sam	(0521 DFB)	Paredes,Jimmy	(1401 ACA)
Brantly,Rob (1013 AFF)		Krauss,Marc	(4111 ACA)	Robinson,Derrick	(0501 ACA)

Universal Draft Grid

TIER	STARTING PITCHERS				RELIEF PITCHERS			
Elite	Kershaw,Clayton	(5405 AAA)			Jansen,Kenley	(5531 BBA)		
					Kimbrel,Craig	(5530 AAB)		
Gold	Darvish,Yu	(5505 BAC)	Lee,Cliff	(5405 AAA)	Chapman,Aroldis	(5530 BBB)	Uehara,Koji	(5530 FCA)
	Bumgarner,Madison	(5305 AAA)	Sale,Chris	(5405 AAA)	Holland,Greg	(5530 BBC)		
	Strasburg,Stephen	(5505 CBA)	Verlander,Justin	(4405 AAA)	Robertson,David	(5530 BCA)		
	Fernandez,Jose	(5505 ADF)			Rosenthal,Trevor	(5531 ADA)		
Stars	Hamels,Cole	(5405 AAA)	Hernandez,Felix	(5405 AAA)	Cishek,Steve	(5431 ACB)	Romo,Sergio	(5530 BCB)
	Medlen,Kris	(5305 CBA)	Salazar,Danny	(5503 ADA)	Perkins,Glen	(5530 BBA)		
	Wainwright,Adam	(5305 BAA)	Bailey,Homer	(4305 BAB)	Janssen,Casey	(5430 CBA)		
	Greinke,Zack	(5305 DAA)			Johnson,Jim	(5231 AAA)		
	Price,David	(5305 BAA)			Nathan,Joe	(5530 BBB)		
	Scherzer,Max	(5505 AAA)			Papelbon,Jonathan	(5431 AAB)		
Regulars	Latos,Mat	(4305 AAA)	Weaver,Jered	(3205 CAA)	Balfour,Grant	(4530 BBA)	Grilli,Jason	(5530 DCA)
	Cain,Matt	(4305 AAA)	Zimmermann,Jordan	(4205 DAA)	Parnell,Bobby	(5330 DCA)	Henderson,Jim	(4530 BDB)
	Iwakuma,Hisashi	(4205 AAA)	Cingrani,Tony	(4503 BDC)	Reed,Addison	(4430 ABC)	Rodney,Fernando	(4530 CBC)
	Shields,James	(4305 AAA)	Cole,Gerrit	(4205 ADB)	Benoit,Joaquin	(4530 ACA)	Soriano,Rafael	(3330 DBA)
	Gonzalez,Gio	(4405 AAA)	Minor,Mike	(4305 AAA)	Brothers,Rex	(5530 ACA)	Street,Huston	(4430 FBB)
	Ryu,Hyun-Jin	(5305 AAB)	Miller,Shelby	(4405 ACD)	Cashner,Andrew	(4305 FCA)		
	Sanchez,Anibal	(5405 CAA)	Wacha,Michael	(4303 AFF)	Frieri,Ernesto	(5530 ABB)		
Mid-Level	Cobb,Alex	(5303 FCB)	Archer,Chris	(4303 ADC)	Cook,Ryan	(4420 ACB)		
	Corbin,Patrick	(4305 ABB)	Arroyo,Bronson	(3105 AAA)	Farquhar,Daniel	(5530 ADC)		
	Cueto,Johnny	(4203 FAA)	Fister,Doug	(4205 BAA)	Mujica,Edward	(4230 ACA)		
	Dickey,R.A.	(4205 AAB)	Gray,Sonny	(4205 ADD)	Ziegler,Brad	(5121 ACA)		
	Estrada,Marco	(4403 FBA)	Kazmir,Scott	(4403 FDF)	Allen,Cody	(4520 ADA)		
	Straily,Dan	(3303 ADA)	Nolasco,Ricky	(4205 BAB)	Melancon,Mark	(5321 ACC)		
	Buchholz,Clay	(3203 FBB)	Porcello,Rick	(4205 AAA)	Doolittle,Sean	(4321 ACA)		
	Kuroda,Hiroki	(4205 BAA)	Teheran,Julio	(3303 ABD)	Scheppers,Tanner	(4320 ADD)		
	Lohse,Kyle	(3105 DAA)	Wilson,C.J.	(3305 AAA)	Smyly,Drew	(4411 BDD)		
	Lynn,Lance	(4405 CAA)	Holland,Derek	(3305 AAA)	Strop,Pedro	(5420 BDB)		
	Wheeler,Zack	(3305 ADC)	Jimenez,Ubaldo	(4405 AAC)				
	Burnett,A.J.	(5405 BAA)	Kennedy,Ian	(3305 AAA)				
	Garza,Matt	(4305 DBA)	Lackey,John	(3205 FBC)				
	Griffin,A.J.	(3205 BCD)	Lester,Jon	(4305 AAA)				
	Liriano,Francisco	(4405 DBB)	Masterson,Justin	(4305 AAB)				
	Samardzija,Jeff	(4405 AAA)	Peavy,Jake	(3303 FBA)				
	Tanaka,Masahiro	(4303 AAB)	Quintana,Jose	(3205 ACA)				
	Wood,Alex	(4403 AFF)	Tillman,Chris	(3305 ABC)				
Bench	Colon,Bartolo	(3103 DAA)	Rodriguez,Wandy	(3103 FAA)	Clippard,Tyler	(4511 ABB)	Watson,Tony	(4201 ADA)
	Gallardo,Yovani	(4305 BAA)	Wood,Travis	(2205 ABB)	Gregerson,Luke	(5410 BCA)		
	Haren,Dan	(4303 CAB)	Cahill,Trevor	(3205 DAA)	Tazawa,Junichi	(5411 FDB)		
	Kluber,Corey	(4305 CCC)	Eovaldi,Nathan	(3203 DCC)	Black,Victor	(3510 AFA)		
	Lincecum,Tim	(4405 AAA)	Gausman,Kevin	(5401 AFF)	Bell,Heath	(5410 ABB)		
	Miley,Wade	(3205 AAA)	Hudson,Tim	(4101 FAB)	Fien,Casey	(4510 ADF)		
	Parker,Jarrod	(3205 ABA)	Luebke,Cory	(3201 FDB)	Herrera,Kelvin	(5510 ADB)		
	Santana,Ervin	(3205 BAB)	Paxton,James	(3203 ADC)	Hochevar,Luke	(5411 CAB)		
	de la Rosa,Jorge	(3203 FCF)	Richards,Garrett	(3103 ACB)	Hoover,J.J.	(4510 ADF)		
	Milone,Tommy	(3203 ABA)	Vargas,Jason	(2105 DAA)	O Day,Darren	(5410 DDC)		
	Moore,Matt	(3403 CBC)			Peralta,Joel	(3511 ACB)		
	Ross,Tyson	(4303 DCC)			Soria,Joakim	(5510 FDA)		
	Sabathia,CC	(4305 AAA)			Stammen,Craig	(4301 ACC)		
	Buehrle,Mark	(3105 AAA)			Storen,Drew	(4311 CCA)		
	Chacin,Jhoulys	(3105 FAC)			Bastardo,Antonio	(4510 ADA)		
	Chen,Wei-Yin	(3203 CAB)			Delabar,Steve	(5510 BDB)		
	Hellickson,Jeremy	(3205 AAA)			Hawkins,LaTroy	(4110 FCB)		
	Leake,Mike	(3105 AAA)			Marshall,Sean	(5510 FCA)		
	Niese,Jon	(4203 DAA)			McGee,Jake	(5510 ADC)		
	Nova,Ivan	(4203 CBA)			Rodriguez,Francisco	(5510 BCB)		
	Ogando,Alexi	(3201 FCA)			Rodriguez,Paco	(5510 ADB)		
	Walker,Taijuan	(3403 ADC)			Rondon,Bruce	(5510 AFA)		
	Beachy,Brandon	(3303 FCB)			Siegrist,Kevin	(5500 AFF)		
	Erlin,Robert	(3303 ADA)			Smith,Joe	(4210 BCA)		
	Gee,Dillon	(3203 DAB)			Vincent,Nick	(4400 ADB)		
	Ramirez,Erasmo	(3203 DDC)			Walden,Jordan	(4511 DCA)		

Universal Draft Grid

Fringe

STARTING PITCHERS

Player	Code	Player	Code
Alvarez,Henderson	(3003 FBB)	Nicasio,Juan	(3303 FCA)
Baker,Scott	(3201 FDC)	Skaggs,Tyler	(3301 ADB)
Feldman,Scott	(3103 DBA)	Beckett,Josh	(3301 FBA)
McCarthy,Brandon	(3103 FBB)	Billingsley,Chad	(3301 FBB)
Morrow,Brandon	(3403 FBB)	Chatwood,Tyler	(3103 CDC)
Oberholtzer,Brett	(2103 ADC)	Chen,Bruce	(1103 CAA)
Peacock,Brad	(2303 ADD)	**Doubront,Felix**	**(3303 BBB)**
Ross,Robbie	(4201 BDA)	**Guthrie,Jeremy**	**(2005 BAA)**
Delgado,Randall	(3203 ACA)	Halladay,Roy	(2203 FAB)
Garcia,Jaime	(4201 FBB)	Hudson,Daniel	(3300 FCB)
Gonzalez,Miguel M	(2203 BCF)	Hughes,Phil	(2203 DBA)
Harrison,Matt	(2103 FBA)	**Jackson,Edwin**	**(3205 AAA)**
Jordan,Taylor	(3001 CFF)	Johnson,Josh	(3303 FBA)
Kelly,Joe	(3103 ACA)	Marcum,Shaun	(3301 FBA)
McAllister,Zach	(2203 DCA)	Maurer,Brandon	(3201 CDC)
Morton,Charlie	(3105 DCB)	Niemann,Jeff	(3201 FDA)
Odorizzi,Jake	(2201 ADB)	**Norris,Bud**	**(3303 BAA)**
Peralta,Wily	(3205 ACC)	Perez,Martin	(3105 CDA)
Petit,Yusmeiro	(3203 ADA)	Ventura,Yordano	(3301 ADB)
Roark,Tanner	(3101 ADD)	Correia,Kevin	(2003 CAA)
Smith,Burch	(3501 AFF)	Danks,John	(2103 FCB)
Stults,Eric	(2105 DCD)	Deduno,Samuel	(2103 CDA)
Anderson,Brett	(4201 FDA)	Floyd,Gavin	(3301 FBA)
Capuano,Chris	(4201 DAA)	Hanson,Tommy	(2203 DBB)
Dempster,Ryan	**(3303 BAA)**	**Kendrick,Kyle**	**(2003 AAA)**
Gonzalez,Miguel A	(2101 ADF)	Lyons,Tyler	(3200 ADC)
Hammel,Jason	(3203 FAC)	Redmond,Todd	(2201 ADC)
Maholm,Paul	(3103 DAA)	Thornburg,Tyler	(2301 ADA)
Mejia,Jenrry	(4301 FDF)		

RELIEF PITCHERS

Player	Code	Player	Code
Collmenter,Josh	**(3301 BBA)**	Belisario,Ronald	(4200 ADB)
De La Rosa,Dane	(4311 ADC)	Blevins,Jerry	(3300 ADA)
Furbush,Charlie	(4510 BDB)	Casilla,Santiago	(3210 FCA)
Hunter,Tommy	(3111 DCC)	Cotts,Neal	(5500 FFF)
Jones,Nate	(5511 ADB)	Feliz,Neftali	(3410 FCA)
Loup,Aaron	(5211 ADB)	Gorzelanny,Tom	(3301 DCA)
Martinez,Carlos	(3201 ADA)	Harris,Will	(5400 ADB)
Motte,Jason	(5510 FCA)	Kelley,Shawn	(4500 FDA)
Perez,Chris	(3420 CBB)	Lecure,Sam	(5400 BCA)
Putz,J.J.	(5510 FBA)	Lopez,Javier	(4210 ADA)
Santos,Sergio	(5500 FDF)	Machi,Jean	(4200 AFF)
Thayer,Dale	(4310 ADA)	Maness,Seth	(4001 ADA)
Alburquerque,Al	(5500 FDA)	Medina,Yoervis	(4410 ADB)
Belisle,Matt	(5311 ACA)	Stauffer,Tim	(4201 FCB)
Burton,Jared	(4310 DDC)	Thielbar,Caleb	(3300 AFF)
Cecil,Brett	(4510 ACB)	Torres,Carlos	(3201 ADB)
Crain,Jesse	(4500 FDA)	Veras,Jose	(3410 ACA)
Dunn,Mike	(4510 ADC)	Wilson,Justin	(3201 ADB)
Fields,Joshua	(2420 ADA)	Albers,Matt	(3100 BCA)
Hernandez,David	(4510 ACB)	Breslow,Craig	(3200 CCB)
Howell,J.P.	(4310 FDA)	Capps,Carter	(4510 ADC)
Kintzler,Brandon	(5210 FDD)	Carpenter,David	(4400 ADF)
Pryor,Stephen	(4510 FFC)	De Fratus,Justin	(3300 FDC)
Ramos,A.J.	(3511 ADD)	Frasor,Jason	(4400 DDA)
Santiago,Hector	(2403 ACA)	Fujikawa,Kyuji	(5510 FCB)
Shaw,Bryan	(4310 ADB)	Gregg,Kevin	(2320 ACA)
Torres,Alexander	(4501 ADF)	Hanrahan,Joel	(5510 FBD)
Villanueva,Carlos	**(3301 BBA)**	Kontos,George	(4201 ADF)
Axford,John	**(4510 ABA)**	Lindstrom,Matt	(4210 DDA)
Lopez,Wilton	(4101 CCB)	Figaro,Alfredo	(3101 CCA)
Otero,Dan	(4100 ADD)	Gaudin,Chad	(3301 FCC)
Ottavino,Adam	(3301 ADB)	Matusz,Brian	(4400 CDD)
Patton,Troy	(3200 CDA)	Mazzaro,Vin	(3101 ACB)
Withrow,Chris	(3400 BDC)	Parker,Blake	(3400 DFD)
Wright,Jamey	(4301 ACA)	Perez,Oliver	(3510 DDD)
Affeldt,Jeremy	(4300 FDB)	Pestano,Vinnie	(3500 BCB)
Avilan,Luis	(3100 ADB)	Qualls,Chad	(4100 BCB)
Badenhop,Burke	(4100 ACA)	Rosenberg,B.J.	(2200 ADC)
Bailey,Andrew	(3510 FDD)	Simon,Alfredo	(3201 DCB)
Chavez,Jesse	(3300 ADC)	Thatcher,Joe	(4500 FDB)
Collins,Tim	(3400 ACC)	Webb,Ryan	(3100 CCA)
Crow,Aaron	(4400 ACA)	Wilhelmsen,Tom	(3310 ABC)
Downs,Scott	(4200 ADB)	Wright,Wesley	(4400 ADA)

Below Fringe

STARTING PITCHERS

Player	Code	Player	Code
Cloyd,Tyler	(2101 ADC)	Blanton,Joe	(3203 FBA)
Davis,Wade	(3301 BBC)	Diamond,Scott	(2001 ACD)
Detwiler,Ross	(2103 FCA)	Drabek,Kyle	(2101 FDB)
Duffy,Danny	(2303 FDA)	Koehler,Tom	(2103 ADC)
Keuchel,Dallas	(3103 ACA)	Marquis,Jason	(1000 FBB)
Locke,Jeff	**(3203 ABA)**	McDonald,James	(1201 FBB)
Santana,Johan	(2201 FDF)	**Mendoza,Luis**	**(2000 ABB)**
Slowey,Kevin	(2101 FDC)	Nelson,Jimmy	(1300 ADA)
Taillon,Jameson	(3200 AFF)	Noesi,Hector	(2100 ADB)
Tepesch,Nicholas	(3101 DDF)	Ohlendorf,Ross	(2101 FDC)
Turner,Jacob	(2103 ACA)	Rienzo,Andre	(2200 ADC)
Albers,Andrew	(2001 ADC)	Webster,Allen	(2300 ADB)
Bedard,Erik	(2401 FBA)	Britton,Zach	(1000 DDB)
Carrasco,Carlos	(3210 FDB)	Cosart,Jarred	(1103 ADA)
Garcia,Freddy	**(2001 BBB)**	Gibson,Kyle	(2103 DDC)
Happ,J.A.	(2301 FBB)	Richard,Clayton	(2001 FBB)
Harang,Aaron	(2201 DAB)	Rusin,Chris	(2001 ACC)
Hernandez,Roberto	(3103 BBD)	Sanabia,Alex	(1000 FDB)
Karns,Nathan	(2300 AFF)	Volquez,Edinson	(2203 DAA)
Lee,Zach	(3200 AFB)	Westbrook,Jake	(2001 DAB)
Phelps,David	(3201 DCC)	White,Alex	(1100 FDA)
Alvarez,Jose	(2100 ADB)	Worley,Vance	(2003 CCD)
Familia,Jeurys	(3300 FDB)	Axelrod,Dylan	(1101 ACB)
Grimm,Justin	(2100 ADC)	Fife,Stephen	(2100 DDB)
Hefner,Jeremy	(3100 DCA)	Hernandez,Pedro	(1000 ADC)
Holmberg,David	(2100 ADB)	Lannan,John	(1000 FBC)
Lyles,Jordan	(2103 ACA)	Matsuzaka,Daisuke	(0201 FDB)
Pettibone,Jonathan	(3101 DDB)	Pelfrey,Mike	(2101 FBB)
Vogelsong,Ryan	(2103 FAA)	**Saunders,Joe**	**(2003 BAA)**
Williams,Jerome	(2101 CBB)	Zito,Barry	(1103 DBA)
Arrieta,Jake	(2203 CCA)	**Harrell,Lucas**	**(1001 ABB)**

RELIEF PITCHERS

Player	Code	Player	Code
Broxton,Jonathan	(3300 FCC)	Rondon,Hector	(3300 FFF)
Diekman,Jake	(4400 ADA)	Russell,James	(1100 ACA)
Duensing,Brian	**(3200 ACA)**	**Valverde,Jose**	**(3310 BBB)**
Gearrin,Cory	(4400 ADB)	Aardsma,David	(1300 FFC)
Gomez,Jeanmar	(3101 BCB)	Blackley,Travis	(2200 BDC)
Krol,Ian	(3300 AFF)	Chamberlain,Joba	(3400 FDB)
League,Brandon	**(4100 ABB)**	Cisnero,Jose	(2400 ADF)
Morales,Franklin	(2300 FDA)	Gonzalez,Michael	(3510 DDA)
Ondrusek,Logan	(3200 ADC)	Gutierrez,Juan	(2300 DDF)
Parra,Manny	(4500 FDC)	Jennings,Dan	(2300 ADB)
Pressly,Ryan	(2100 ADA)	Kohn,Michael	(2400 FDA)
Ramos,Cesar	(3200 ADA)	Lo,Chia-Jen	(1310 FFF)
Rzepczynski,Marc	(4200 BDB)	Morris,Bryan	(2001 ADA)
Salas,Fernando	(3300 CCB)	Outman,Josh	(3300 BDC)
Swarzak,Anthony	(3101 CCA)	Rosario,Sandy	(3100 DDB)
Venters,Jonny	(5400 FDA)	Sipp,Tony	(2400 ADA)
Warren,Adam	(2201 ACC)	Thornton,Matt	(3200 CCA)
Claiborne,Preston	(3200 ADA)	Varvaro,Anthony	(2200 ADB)
Francisco,Frank	(3500 FCB)	Bass,Anthony	(2100 DCC)
Germen,Gonzalez	(3300 ADB)	Bettis,Chad	(2201 FFF)
Guerrier,Matt	(2100 FDA)	Coke,Phil	(2200 CCB)
Hagadone,Nick	(2400 ADC)	Hand,Donovan	(2000 ADB)
Jepsen,Kevin	(3300 FDF)	Wolf,Ross	(2000 ADB)
Lincoln,Brad	(2200 ADB)	Aumont,Phillippe	(2400 ADB)
Marmol,Carlos	**(3510 BBA)**	Boggs,Mitchell	(2100 ADF)
McFarland,T.J.	(3100 ADB)	Roenicke,Josh	(1100 ACA)
Mijares,Jose	(3400 DCC)	Clemens,Paul	(1101 ADD)
Miller,Andrew	(4500 FDC)	Rogers,Esmil	(2201 DCD)
Ortiz,Joseph	(3100 AFA)		

Rotisserie 500 (version 3)

This is a modified Rotisserie format that incorporates some of the rules variations discussed in the Encyclopedia, and adds a few more. Its intent is to resolve several incongruities in the original game. The format has proven very popular in trial leagues. Version 3 modifies some of the previous rules in order to make it more feasible to conduct an online draft.

1. Stat categories: Roto500 uses a modified 4x4 format. It keeps HR, SB, Strikeouts and ERA. **On base average** replaces batting average as a more accurate measure of that element of skill. **Runs Produced** (R + RBI − HR) reduces the impact of situation-dependent stats, from 40% to 25%. **(Wins + Quality Starts)** provides more equitable value for good pitchers on bad teams. And **(Saves + Holds)** provides value to more members of the bullpen.

Perhaps the biggest change is the elimination of WHIP. While WHIP is a good category in its own right, few fantasy leaguers use it to manage their pitching staffs. Its elimination allows us to have a single ratio category on each of the batting and pitching sides, and a balance that has always been missing in Rotisserie. Despite scaling back to eight categories, Roto500 captures just as much performance, if not more. In addition, with fewer moving parts, it becomes easier to manage your roster, which in turn provides more control over running your team.

2. Valuing of players: Within an individual league, there are several different "currencies" that measure the value of a player. For the active roster in an auction league, the currency is a $260 budget. For the reserve roster, the currency is snake picks. For free agents, the currency might be FAAB dollars or first owner to the computer.

Roto500 suggests that we should use a common currency to value and roster players no matter how we acquire them. After all, a player is a player is a player. George Springer shouldn't be valued using one unit of measure if he's drafted, another if he's a reserve pick and yet another if he's FAABed. There should be a standard, consistent unit of measure used for all players, for every aspect of the game.

In Roto500, that unit of measure is dollars, and this is used for every aspect of player acquisition, all season long. Every owner gets a $500 budget at the beginning of the season. This goes to pay for everything—the draft roster, reserves and free agents acquired during the season.

There is no $260 limit for the draft. This means you have to decide how you are going to budget your money. If you spend $260 on your active roster, that will leave you $240 for reserve players and free agents. You can opt to stock up with the very best players for your active roster—perhaps $300 worth, or more—but that will limit your options for reserves and free agents. If you excel at in-season management, perhaps you draft

a $200 team, or less, and leave yourself with more money during the season. Each owner has to decide how he is going to play it.

3. Selection of players: Roto500 starts as a 12-team mixed league with 23 man active rosters and 17-man reserves. (While this is the recommended player pool, Roto500 can also be played as an AL-only or NL-only league, with a shallower reserve list.)

Each player has a pre-set list price, calculated as the average of his end-of-season values from the past two years (rounded up, if necessary). Seasons in which a player maintained his rookie eligibility are valued at $10. Negative valued years revert to $0, but every player must have a list price for the upcoming season of at least $1. **The following pages contain the Roto500 price list for 2014 drafts.**

The draft is conducted as a standard snake draft. Players are selected one-by-one, but as owners fill their rosters, they use up some portion of their $500 budget. One might think that the draft would simply proceed in ranked order of each player's price, however, there is more strategy involved. For example:

Perhaps you have the 17th pick and both Alex Rios and Ryan Braun would be the natural selections based on their $25 price tags. However, you are worried about Rios' inconsistency and Braun's PED rebound season. You believe Bryce Harper is going to have a breakout season and he still out there at $19. In a traditional snake draft, you could select Harper and just hope you made the right choice. In Roto500, you've just bought yourself $6 more to spend later in the draft or during the season.

It's nice to be able to quantify your decisions.

The draft continues for 40 rounds, with the only positional requirement that all 23 active spots have eligible players selected by the end of the draft. Reserve rosters constitute each team's bench as well as its disabled list.

4. In-season. Intra-roster moves can be made once weekly. Free agent drafts take place once monthly (e.g. the first Sunday of each month, etc.). Players are acquired by means of a reverse-order-of-the-standings snake draft with all players having list prices. These list prices will be each player's current Rotisserie value to-date, with a minimum price of $10.

A player's acquisition price becomes his list price for the remainder of the season and is deducted from the owner's $500 balance.

It is important to note that every dollar is precious. Once a dollar is spent, it is gone from your $500 budget. You cannot reclaim dollars for players who are cut. The only way a player's salary can re-fund the budget is if he is deemed out for the season. If you make a trade with another owner, you assume the salaries of the players acquired (and can remove the salaries of the players traded). And once you've spent that 500th dollar, the free agent pool is then closed off to you.

ROTISSERIE 500   2014 Draft - List Prices   Batters

BATTERS	'12	'13	R$
Trout,Mike	46	53	50
Cabrera,Miguel	38	48	43
McCutchen,Andrew	36	40	38
Votto,Joey	24	41	33
Goldschmidt,Paul	20	43	32
Encarnacion,Edwin	32	30	31
Choo,Shin-Soo	20	37	29
Cano,Robinson	26	30	28
Wright,David	28	25	27
Holliday,Matt	24	28	26
Kipnis,Jason	18	33	26
Gonzalez,Carlos	24	27	26
Fielder,Prince	29	22	26
Rios,Alex	21	29	25
Braun,Ryan	41	8	25
Davis,Chris	11	36	24
Ortiz,David	16	31	24
Beltre,Adrian	22	25	24
Mauer,Joe	25	19	22
Posey,Buster	27	17	22
Headley,Chase	32	12	22
Gomez,Carlos	12	30	21
Freeman,Freddie	14	28	21
Pedroia,Dustin	15	27	21
Upton,Justin	19	23	21
Zobrist,Ben	23	19	21
Butler,Billy	21	20	21
Jones,Adam	18	22	20
Pence,Hunter	11	28	20
Hamilton,Josh	29	10	20
Crisp,Coco	14	24	19
Bruce,Jay	17	21	19
Beltran,Carlos	21	17	19
Andrus,Elvis	12	25	19
Desmond,Ian	16	21	19
Harper,Bryce	16	21	19
Zimmerman,Ryan	17	20	19
Reyes,Jose	22	15	19
Bourn,Michael	23	14	19
Santana,Carlos	14	22	18
Ramirez,Hanley	15	21	18
Fowler,Dexter	16	20	18
Stanton,Giancarlo	19	17	18
Ellsbury,Jacoby	0	35	18
Gordon,Alex	18	17	18
Jackson,Austin	21	14	18
Kinsler,Ian	15	19	17
Aoki,Norichika	15	19	17
Werth,Jayson	3	30	17
Bautista,Jose	11	22	17
Soriano,Alfonso	13	20	17
Molina,Yadier	18	15	17
Victorino,Shane	13	19	16
Craig,Allen	14	18	16
Dunn,Adam	18	14	16
Altuve,Jose	13	18	16
Gonzalez,Adrian	13	18	16
De Aza,Alejandro	13	18	16
Hunter,Torii	16	15	16
Swisher,Nick	17	14	16
Cuddyer,Michael	3	27	15
Cabrera,Everth	8	22	15
Puig,Yasiel	10	20	15
Davis,Rajai	11	19	15
LaRoche,Adam	17	13	15
Prado,Martin	17	13	15
Ramirez,Aramis	21	9	15
Hill,Aaron	22	8	15
Jennings,Desmond	10	19	15
Heyward,Jason	20	9	15
Donaldson,Josh	0	28	14
Carpenter,Matt	1	27	14
Pujols,Albert	19	9	14
Cespedes,Yoenis	17	10	14
Willingham,Josh	21	6	14
Hosmer,Eric	4	22	13
Seager,Kyle	8	18	13
Segura,Jean	0	25	13
Longoria,Evan	4	21	13
Venable,Will	8	17	13
Cruz,Nelson	11	14	13
Ethier,Andre	12	13	13

BATTERS	'12	'13	R$
Tulowitzki,Troy	0	24	12
Murphy,Daniel	5	19	12
Napoli,Mike	5	19	12
Belt,Brandon	7	17	12
Brantley,Michael	8	16	12
Trumbo,Mark	10	14	12
Granderson,Curtis	21	3	12
Pagan,Angel	16	7	12
Marte,Starling	0	22	11
Jay,Jon	8	14	11
Myers,Wil	10	12	11
Moss,Brandon	4	17	11
Utley,Chase	4	17	11
Lucroy,Jonathan	5	16	11
Span,Denard	7	14	11
Phillips,Brandon	10	11	11
Revere,Ben	11	10	11
Freese,David	14	7	11
Kemp,Matt	15	6	11
Alvarez,Pedro	8	12	10
Saunders,Michael	8	12	10
Reddick,Josh	12	8	10
Cabrera,Melky	18	2	10
Castellanos,Nick	10	10	10
Hamilton,Billy	10	10	10
Taylor,Michael	10	10	10
Decker,Jaff	10	10	10
Lambo,Andrew	10	10	10
Beltre,Engel	10	10	10
Bogaerts,Xander	10	10	10
Owings,Christopher	10	10	10
Urrutia,Henry	10	10	10
Wong,Kolten	10	10	10
Pinto,Josmil	10	10	10
Davidson,Matthew	10	10	10
Bradley,Jackie	10	10	10
D Arnaud,Travis	10	10	10
Marisnick,Jake	10	10	10
Young Jr.,Eric	0	19	10
McLouth,Nate	0	19	10
Gardner,Brett	0	19	10
Pollock IV,A.J.	10	9	10
Scutaro,Marco	11	8	10
Martinez,Victor	1	17	9
Rosario,Wilin	7	11	9
Yelich,Christian S.	10	8	9
Adams,Matt	10	8	9
Shuck,J.B.	10	8	9
Martin,Leonys	0	17	9
Lind,Adam	0	17	9
Brown,Domonic	0	17	9
Morales,Kendrys	4	13	9
Denorfia,Chris	4	13	9
Johnson,Chris	4	13	9
Blanco,Gregor	6	11	9
Gyorko,Jedd	10	7	9
Uggla,Dan	11	6	9
Konerko,Paul	14	3	9
Montero,Miguel	14	3	9
Nava,Daniel	0	16	8
Ramirez,Alexei	1	15	8
Joyce,Matt	4	12	8
Markakis,Nick	6	10	8
Walker,Neil	8	8	8
Suzuki,Ichiro	8	8	8
Byrd,Marlon	0	15	8
Lowrie,Jed	0	15	8
Rizzo,Anthony	1	14	8
Dyson,Jarrod	2	13	8
Sandoval,Pablo	4	11	8
Kendrick,Howie	5	10	8
Ruggiano,Justin	6	9	8
Morneau,Justin	6	9	8
Wieters,Matt	8	7	8
Cabrera,Asdrubal	8	7	8
Villar,Jonathan	10	5	8
Ruf,Darin	10	5	8
Calhoun,Kole	10	5	8
Franklin,Nick	10	5	8
Loney,James	0	14	7
Rollins,Jimmy	1	13	7
Infante,Omar	3	11	7

BATTERS	'12	'13	R$
Parra,Gerardo	3	11	7
Miller,Bradley	10	4	7
Gattis,Evan	10	4	7
Iglesias,Jose	10	4	7
Davis,Khristopher	10	4	7
Mercer,Jordy	10	4	7
Pierre,Juan	10	4	7
Gennett,Scooter	10	4	7
Rodriguez,Alex	11	3	7
Castro,Jason	0	13	7
Carter,Chris	0	13	7
Gentry,Craig	0	13	7
Dozier,Brian	0	13	7
Rasmus,Colby	1	12	7
Stubbs,Drew	3	10	7
Frazier,Todd	5	8	7
Gomes,Jonny	5	8	7
Reynolds,Mark	6	7	7
Ross,Cody	8	5	7
Satin,Josh	10	3	7
Rendon,Anthony	10	3	7
Grossman,Robert	10	3	7
Dominguez,Matt	10	3	7
Gillaspie,Conor	10	3	7
Saltalamacchia,Jarrod	0	12	6
Drew,Stephen	0	12	6
Peralta,Jhonny	0	12	6
Davis,Ike	7	5	6
Gregorius,Didi	10	2	6
Arenado,Nolan	10	2	6
Barnes,Brandon	10	2	6
Lough,David	10	2	6
Arcia,Oswaldo Celestino	10	2	6
Kawasaki,Munenori	10	2	6
Garcia,Avisail	10	2	6
Lake,Junior	10	2	6
Weeks,Rickie	10	2	6
Escobar,Alcides	11	1	6
Machado,Manny	0	11	6
Alonso,Yonder	4	7	6
Aybar,Erick	5	6	6
Jaso,John	6	5	6
DeJesus,David	6	5	6
Jones,Garrett	9	2	6
Hoes,LJ	10	1	6
Van Slyke,Scott	10	1	6
Gindl,Caleb	10	1	6
Dickerson,Corey	10	1	6
Eaton,Adam	10	1	6
Crawford,Carl	0	10	5
Hardy,J.J.	0	10	5
Schafer,Jordan	0	10	5
Martin,Russell	0	10	5
Smoak,Justin	0	10	5
Callaspo,Alberto	2	8	5
Johnson,Kelly	4	6	5
Lawrie,Brett	4	6	5
Pierzynski,A.J.	7	3	5
Bonifacio,Emilio	0	9	5
Ibanez,Raul	0	9	5
Escobar,Yunel	0	9	5
McCann,Brian	0	9	5
Raburn,Ryan	0	9	5
Dirks,Andy	2	7	5
Ellis,A.J.	5	4	5
Uribe,Juan	0	8	4
Iannetta,Chris	0	8	4
Schierholtz,Nate	0	8	4
Quentin,Carlos	1	7	4
Young,Michael	1	7	4
Navarro,Dioner	1	7	4
Perez,Salvador	0	7	4
Cain,Lorenzo	0	7	4
LeMahieu,DJ	0	7	4
Duda,Lucas	0	7	4
Doumit,Ryan	2	5	4
Carp,Mike	0	6	3
Moreland,Mitch	0	6	3
Norris,Derek	0	6	3
Simmons,Andrelton	0	6	3
Gomes,Yan	0	6	3
Helton,Todd	0	6	3

BATTERS	'12	'13	R$
Sanchez,Gaby	0	6	3
Castillo,Welington	0	5	3
Sogard,Eric	0	5	3
Smith,Seth	1	4	3
Avila,Alex	1	4	3
Maxwell,Justin	1	4	3
Vicieido,Dayan	2	3	3
Ramos,Wilson	0	4	2
Valbuena,Luis	0	4	2
Florimon Jr.,Pedro	0	4	2
Blackmon,Charlie	0	4	2
Chavez,Eric	0	4	2
Tabata,Jose	0	4	2
Plouffe,Trevor	0	4	2
Baker,Jeff	0	4	2
Rutledge,Josh	0	4	2
Ellis,Mark	0	4	2
Young,Chris	0	4	2
Pena,Carlos	3	1	2
Howard,Ryan	0	3	2
Overbay,Lyle	0	3	2
Nix,Jayson	0	3	2
Roberts,Brian	0	3	2
Aviles,Mike	0	3	2
Nunez,Eduardo	0	3	2
Beckham,Gordon	0	3	2
Getz,Chris	0	3	2
Berkman,Lance	0	3	2
Scott,Luke	0	3	2
Francisco,Juan	0	3	2
Johnson,Elliot	0	3	2
Tuiasosopo,Matt	1	2	2
Ackley,Dustin	1	2	2
Morrison,Logan	0	2	1
Wells,Vernon	0	2	1
Robinson,Shane	0	2	1
Crawford,Brandon	0	2	1
Lobaton,Jose	0	2	1
Punto,Nick	0	2	1
Paul,Xavier	0	2	1
DeRosa,Mark	0	2	1
Soto,Geovany	0	2	1
Mayberry,John	0	2	1
Cozart,Zack	0	1	1
Valencia,Danny	0	1	1
Middlebrooks,Will	0	1	1
Hafner,Travis	0	1	1
Descalso,Daniel	0	1	1
Bay,Jason	0	1	1
Schumaker,Skip	0	1	1
Murphy,Donnie	0	1	1
Young,Delmon	0	1	1
Danks,Jordan	0	1	1
Bourjos,Peter	0	1	1
Buck,John	0	1	1
Guzman,Jesus	0	1	1
Kelly,Don	0	1	1

ROTISSERIE 500 — 2014 Draft - List Prices — Pitchers

PITCHERS	'12	'13	R$	PITCHERS	'12	'13	R$	PITCHERS	'12	'13	R$	PITCHERS	'12	'13	R$
Kershaw,Clayton	32	32	32	Familia,Jeurys	10	10	10	Wood,Alex	10	1	6	Maholm,Paul	6	0	3
Verlander,Justin	35	14	25	Fujikawa,Kyuji	10	10	10	Santana,Ervin	0	10	6	Marshall,Sean	6	0	3
Price,David	34	9	22	Ventura,Yordano	10	10	10	Avilan,Luis	0	10	5	Capuano,Chris	6	0	3
Gonzalez,Gio	30	12	21	Bauer,Trevor	10	10	10	Cashner,Andrew	0	10	5	Kennedy,Ian	6	0	3
Hernandez,Felix	23	17	20	Lo,Chia-Jen	10	10	10	Leake,Mike	0	10	5	Hanrahan,Joel	6	0	3
Dickey,R.A.	35	5	20	Rasmus,Cory	10	10	10	Lester,Jon	0	10	5	Dunn,Mike	0	5	3
Scherzer,Max	15	24	20	Wilson,Alex	10	10	10	Oberholtzer,Brett	10	0	5	Tazawa,Junichi	0	5	3
Medlen,Kris	25	14	20	Odorizzi,Jake	10	10	10	Farquhar,Daniel	10	0	5	Pettitte,Andy	0	5	3
Sale,Chris	22	16	19	Cleto,Maikel	10	10	10	Cosart,Jarred	10	0	5	Vincent,Nick	0	5	3
Kimbrel,Craig	19	18	19	Figueroa,Pedro	10	10	10	Salazar,Danny	10	0	5	Breslow,Craig	0	5	3
Bumgarner,Madison	17	18	18	Holmberg,David	10	10	10	Kohn,Michael	10	0	5	Howell,J.P.	0	5	3
Hamels,Cole	25	9	17	Betances,Dellin	10	10	10	Pettibone,Jonathan	10	0	5	Hoover,J.J.	0	5	3
Darvish,Yu	11	22	17	Karns,Nathan	10	10	10	Erlin,Robert	10	0	5	Hawkins,LaTroy	0	5	3
Lee,Cliff	13	20	17	Smith,Burch	10	10	10	Hand,Donovan	10	0	5	Kluber,Corey	0	5	3
Greinke,Zack	16	17	17	Alvarez,Jose	10	10	10	Figaro,Alfredo	10	0	5	Garza,Matt	0	5	3
Shields,James	17	16	17	Bettis,Chad	10	10	10	McFarland,T.J.	10	0	5	Kazmir,Scott	1	4	3
Zimmermann,Jordan	16	16	16	Surkamp,Eric	10	10	10	Pressly,Ryan	10	0	5	Gonzalez,Miguel	0	5	3
Chapman,Aroldis	20	12	16	Dyson,Sam	10	10	10	Koehler,Tom	10	0	5	Feldman,Scott	0	5	3
Weaver,Jered	24	8	16	Omogrosso,Brian	10	10	10	Jimenez,Cesar	10	0	5	Vargas,Jason	4	1	3
Fernandez,Jose	10	21	16	Hynes,Colt	10	10	10	Claiborne,Preston	10	0	5	O Flaherty,Eric	5	0	3
Strasburg,Stephen	18	13	16	Magill,Matthew	10	10	10	Jordan,Taylor	10	0	5	Lopez,Javier	0	4	2
Lohse,Kyle	21	9	15	Burgos,Hiram	10	10	10	Rondon,Hector	10	0	5	Downs,Scott	0	4	2
Cain,Matt	27	3	15	Hellweg,John	10	10	10	Albers,Andrew	10	0	5	Crow,Aaron	0	4	2
Wainwright,Adam	6	23	15	Webster,Allen	10	10	10	Peacock,Brad	10	0	5	Cecil,Brett	0	4	2
Rodney,Fernando	22	7	15	McHugh,Collin	10	10	10	Tepesch,Nicholas	10	0	5	Lecure,Sam	0	4	2
Cueto,Johnny	28	1	15	Tanaka,Masahiro	10	10	10	O Sullivan,Sean	10	0	5	Gregg,Kevin	0	4	2
Latos,Mat	13	15	14	Harvey,Matt	0	19	10	Wolf,Ross	10	0	5	Qualls,Chad	0	4	2
Kuroda,Hiroki	16	10	13	Bailey,Homer	8	11	10	Gausman,Kevin John	10	0	5	Veras,Jose	0	4	2
Jansen,Kenley	9	16	13	Romo,Sergio	10	9	10	Lyons,Tyler	10	0	5	Loup,Aaron	0	4	2
Iwakuma,Hisashi	4	20	12	Cook,Ryan	11	7	9	Rienzo,Andre	10	0	5	Mazzaro,Vin	0	4	2
Ryu,Hyun-Jin	10	14	12	Moore,Matt	5	12	9	Clemens,Paul	10	0	5	Shaw,Bryan	0	4	2
Sanchez,Anibal	2	20	11	Johnson,Jim	8	9	9	Burke,Greg	10	0	5	Simon,Alfredo	0	4	2
Holland,Greg	5	17	11	Papelbon,Jonathan	11	6	9	Gibson,Kyle	10	0	5	Chen,Bruce	0	4	2
Nathan,Joe	5	16	11	Gallardo,Yovani	14	3	9	Maurer,Brandon	10	0	5	Stults,Eric	0	4	2
Wilson,C.J.	6	15	11	Uehara,Koji	0	16	8	Henderson,Jim	0	9	5	Guthrie,Jeremy	0	4	2
Lynn,Lance	12	9	11	Robertson,David	3	13	8	Smith,Joe	1	8	5	Ross,Robbie	1	3	2
Miley,Wade	14	7	11	Balfour,Grant	8	8	8	Rosenthal,Trevor	0	9	5	Burton,Jared	2	2	2
Hembree,Heath	10	10	10	Soriano,Rafael	9	7	8	Smyly,Drew	0	9	5	Ross,Tyson	0	4	2
Davis,Erik	10	10	10	Frieri,Ernesto	9	7	8	de la Rosa,Jorge	0	9	5	Niese,Jon	1	3	2
Burns,Cory	10	10	10	Cole,Gerrit	10	6	8	Chacin,Jhoulys	0	9	5	Hernandez,David	4	0	2
Freeman,Sam	10	10	10	Peavy,Jake	13	3	8	Nolasco,Ricky	0	9	5	Rodriguez,Wandy	4	0	2
Caminero,Arquimedes	10	10	10	Sabathia,CC	16	0	8	Peralta,Joel	1	8	5	Lopez,Wilton	4	0	2
Stinson,Josh	10	10	10	Harrison,Matt	16	0	8	Lackey,John	1	8	5	Broxton,Jonathan	4	0	2
Savery,Joe	10	10	10	Liriano,Francisco	0	15	8	Parnell,Bobby	3	6	5	Detwiler,Ross	4	0	2
Britton,Drake	10	10	10	Miller,Shelby	0	15	8	Arroyo,Bronson	3	6	5	Bastardo,Antonio	0	3	2
Boxberger,Brad	10	10	10	Cishek,Steve	4	11	8	Mcgee,Jake	5	4	5	Rodriguez,Francisco	0	3	2
Roe,Chaz	10	10	10	Torres,Alexander	10	5	8	Wilhelmsen,Tom	9	0	5	Thayer,Dale	0	3	2
Paterson,Joe	10	10	10	Maness,Michael	10	5	8	Dempster,Ryan	9	0	5	Ottavino,Adam	0	3	2
Dwyer,Christopher	10	10	10	Medina,Yoervis	10	5	8	Hellickson,Jeremy	9	0	5	Ramos,A.J.	0	3	2
Cabral,Cesar	10	10	10	Melancon,Mark	0	14	7	Kelly,Joe	0	8	4	Collmenter,Josh	0	3	2
Robles,Mauricio	10	10	10	Buchholz,Clay	0	14	7	Janssen,Casey	0	8	4	Gaudin,Chad	0	3	2
Cabrera,Alberto	10	10	10	Minor,Mike	0	14	7	Mujica,Edward	0	8	4	Ogando,Alexi	0	3	2
Castro,Simon	10	10	10	Teheran,Julio	0	14	7	Hunter,Tommy	0	8	4	Chatwood,Tyler	0	3	2
Dominguez,Jose	10	10	10	Burnett,A.J.	1	13	7	Nova,Ivan	0	8	4	Morton,Charlie	0	3	2
Layne,Tom	10	10	10	Fister,Doug	5	9	7	Gee,Dillon	0	8	4	Perez,Martin	0	3	2
Spruill,Ezekiel	10	10	10	Casilla,Santiago	6	8	7	Griffin,A.J.	0	8	4	McAllister,Zach	0	3	2
Gast,John	10	10	10	Roark,Tanner	10	4	7	Quintana,Jose	0	8	4	Santiago,Hector	0	3	2
Langwell,Matt	10	10	10	Jimenez,Ubaldo	0	13	7	Grilli,Jason	2	6	4	Straily,Dan	0	3	2
Raley,Brooks	10	10	10	Masterson,Justin	0	13	7	Milone,Tommy	5	3	4	Porcello,Rick	0	3	2
Garcia,Onelki	10	10	10	Clippard,Tyler	2	11	7	Belisario,Ronald	7	1	4	Lincecum,Tim	0	3	2
Belfiore,Michael	10	10	10	Perkins,Glen	4	9	7	Boggs,Mitchell	8	0	4	Jones,Nate	2	1	2
Cedeno,Xavier	10	10	10	Gregerson,Luke	5	8	7	Carpenter,David	0	7	4	Strop,Pedro	3	0	2
De la Rosa,Eury	10	10	10	Rivera,Mariano	0	12	6	Allen,Cody	0	7	4	Billingsley,Chad	3	0	2
Colon,Bartolo	2	18	10	Corbin,Patrick	0	12	6	Hochevar,Luke	0	7	4	Harang,Aaron	3	0	2
Siegrist,Kevin	10	10	10	Benoit,Joaquin	1	11	6	Wilson,Justin	0	7	4	Hughes,Phil	3	0	2
Thielbar,Caleb	10	10	10	Scheppers,Tanner	0	12	6	Watson,Tony	0	7	4	Diamond,Scott	3	0	2
Withrow,Chris	10	10	10	Cobb,Alex	0	12	6	De La Rosa,Dane	0	7	4	Harrell,Lucas	3	0	2
Paxton,James	10	10	10	O Day,Darren	5	7	6	Cingrani,Tony	0	7	4	Frasor,Jason	0	2	1
Rosario,Sandy	10	10	10	Stammen,Craig	6	6	6	Buehrle,Mark	4	3	4	Machi,Jean	0	2	1
Black,Victor	10	10	10	Parker,Jarrod	8	4	6	Hudson,Tim	6	1	4	Perez,Chris	0	2	1
Rondon,Bruce	10	10	10	Gray,Sonny	10	2	6	Cahill,Trevor	6	1	4	Delabar,Steve	0	2	1
Cisnero,Jose	10	10	10	Wheeler,Zack	10	2	6	Pestano,Vinnie	7	0	4	Lindstrom,Matt	0	2	1
Pryor,Stephen	10	10	10	Vogelsong,Ryan	12	0	6	Morrow,Brandon	7	0	4	Fien,Casey	0	2	1
Nelson,Jimmy	10	10	10	Brothers,Rex	0	11	6	Reed,Addison	0	6	3	Axford,John	0	2	1
Walker,Taijuan	10	10	10	Wood,Travis	0	11	6	Rodriguez,Paco	0	6	3	Bell,Heath	0	2	1
Aumont,Phillippe	10	10	10	Tillman,Chris	0	11	6	Street,Huston	0	6	3	Thornburg,Tyler	0	2	1
Rosenberg,B.J.	10	10	10	Holland,Derek	0	11	6	Doolittle,Sean	0	6	3	Swarzak,Anthony	0	2	1
Krol,Ian	10	10	10	Cotts,Neal	1	10	6	Kintzler,Brandon	0	6	3	Norris,Bud	0	2	1
Martinez,Carlos	10	10	10	Ziegler,Brad	1	10	6	Archer,Chris	0	6	3	Estrada,Marco	0	2	1
Germen,Gonzalez	10	10	10	Herrera,Kelvin	7	4	6	Locke,Jeff	0	6	3	Doubront,Felix	0	2	1
Fields,Joshua	10	10	10	Rice,Scott	10	1	6	Crain,Jesse	0	6	3	Burnett,Sean	2	0	1
Ortiz,Joseph	10	10	10	Wacha,Michael	10	1	6	Samardzija,Jeff	3	3	3	Beachy,Brandon	2	0	1

Simulation League Cheat Sheet
Using Runs Above Replacement creates a more real-world ranking of player value, which serves simulation gamers well. Batters and pitchers are integrated, and value break-points are delineated.

SIMULATION LEAGUE DRAFT — TOP 500+

NAME	POS	RAR
Cabrera,Miguel	5	78.1
Cano,Robinson	4	61.8
Trout,Mike	78	56.5
Votto,Joey	3	52.9
McCutchen,Andrew	8	50.0
Braun,Ryan	7	49.3
Tulowitzki,Troy	6	49.1
Ortiz,David	0	47.0
Gonzalez,Carlos	7	46.9
Goldschmidt,Paul	3	44.7
Wright,David	5	44.4
Holliday,Matt	7	43.2
Encarnacion,Edwin	3	42.7
Ramirez,Hanley	6	42.6
Kershaw,Clayton	P	41.5
Mauer,Joe	2	41.1
Beltre,Adrian	5	39.8
Reyes,Jose	6	38.8
Pedroia,Dustin	4	38.4
Kemp,Matt	8	37.5
Posey,Buster	23	37.4
Carpenter,Matt	45	36.1
Fielder,Prince	3	34.8
Longoria,Evan	5	34.0
Upton,Justin	79	33.7
Santana,Carlos	23	33.3
Harper,Bryce	7	31.9
Stanton,Giancarlo	9	31.2
Choo,Shin-Soo	8	30.9
Ramirez,Aramis	5	30.4
Davis,Chris	3	30.1
Martinez,Victor	0	30.1
Zimmerman,Ryan	5	29.9
Freeman,Freddie	3	29.2
Zobrist,Ben	469	28.7
Bautista,Jose	9	28.3
Kipnis,Jason	4	28.3
Hill,Aaron	4	28.2
Fowler,Dexter	8	28.0
Lucroy,Jonathan	2	27.9
Molina,Yadier	2	27.3
Werth,Jayson	9	27.1
Gordon,Alex	7	26.8
Desmond,Ian	6	25.7
Butler,Billy	0	25.5
Pujols,Albert	3	25.3
Donaldson,Josh	5	25.2
Jones,Adam	8	25.2
Bumgarner,Madison	P	25.0
Medlen,Kris	P	25.0
Cuddyer,Michael	9	24.9
Sandoval,Pablo	5	23.7
Sale,Chris	P	23.3
Darvish,Yu	P	23.2
Gonzalez,Adrian	3	22.9
Utley,Chase	4	22.5
Cespedes,Yoenis	7	22.3
Jackson,Austin	8	22.3
Bogaerts,Xander	5	22.1
Lowrie,Jed	46	22.1
Puig,Yasiel	9	22.1
Verlander,Justin	P	22.1
Abreu,Jose	3	22.0

NAME	POS	RAR
Walker,Neil	4	21.9
Belt,Brandon	3	21.8
Strasburg,Stephen	P	21.8
Murphy,Daniel	4	21.7
Beltran,Carlos	9	21.6
Napoli,Mike	3	21.6
Perez,Salvador	2	21.4
Miller,Bradley	6	21.2
Pence,Hunter	9	21.0
Headley,Chase	5	20.1
Kinsler,Ian	4	20.0
Wieters,Matt	2	20.0
Kendrick,Howie	4	19.4
Lee,Cliff	P	19.4
Prado,Martin	457	19.3
Rendon,Anthony	4	19.0
Fernandez,Jose	P	18.9
Price,David	P	18.9
Greinke,Zack	P	18.8
Drew,Stephen	6	18.5
Ethier,Andre	89	17.5
Rosario,Wilin	2	17.4
Wainwright,Adam	P	17.4
Castro,Jason	2	17.0
McCann,Brian	2	17.0
Craig,Allen	379	16.7
Swisher,Nick	39	16.7
Cabrera,Asdrubal	6	16.6
Montero,Miguel	2	16.6
Quentin,Carlos	7	16.5
Bruce,Jay	9	16.4
Hernandez,Felix	P	16.4
Iwakuma,Hisashi	P	16.4
Scutaro,Marco	4	16.3
Sanchez,Anibal	P	16.3
Myers,Wil	9	16.1
Hamels,Cole	P	15.9
Infante,Omar	4	15.8
Morales,Kendrys	3	15.8
Salazar,Danny	P	15.8
Kimbrel,Craig	P	15.7
Bailey,Homer	P	15.6
Jansen,Kenley	P	15.6
Seager,Kyle	5	15.5
Ross,Cody	79	15.4
Uehara,Koji	P	15.3
Hamilton,Josh	9	15.2
Simmons,Andrelton	6	15.2
Cingrani,Tony	P	15.1
Cobb,Alex	P	15.1
Granderson,Curtis	8	15.0
Ellsbury,Jacoby	8	14.9
Hardy,J.J.	6	14.9
Rizzo,Anthony	3	14.9
Phillips,Brandon	4	14.8
Johnson,Chris	5	14.7
Cain,Matt	P	14.7
Crawford,Carl	7	14.4
Aybar,Erick	6	14.3
Gomez,Carlos	8	14.3
Saltalamacchia,Jarrod	2	14.3
Heyward,Jason	89	14.2
Gonzalez,Gio	P	14.1

NAME	POS	RAR
Latos,Mat	P	14.1
Brown,Domonic	7	14.0
Jaso,John	2	14.0
Alvarez,Pedro	5	13.9
Willingham,Josh	7	13.8
Shields,James	P	13.7
Pagan,Angel	8	13.6
Ryu,Hyun-Jin	P	13.5
Avila,Alex	2	13.4
Teixeira,Mark	3	13.4
Andrus,Elvis	6	13.3
Cabrera,Melky	7	13.2
Castro,Starlin	6	13.2
Peralta,Jhonny	6	13.2
Robertson,David	P	13.2
Murphy,David	7	13.1
Soriano,Alfonso	7	13.0
Hosmer,Eric	3	12.8
Ramos,Wilson	2	12.8
Hart,Corey	3	12.7
Lind,Adam	3	12.7
Holland,Greg	P	12.7
Gomes,Yan	2	12.5
Rasmus,Colby	8	12.4
Arenado,Nolan	5	12.3
Gyorko,Jedd	4	12.3
Chapman,Aroldis	P	12.2
Ramirez,Alexei	6	12.1
Cueto,Johnny	P	12.1
Gomes,Jonny	7	12.0
Jeter,Derek	6	12.0
Scherzer,Max	P	11.8
Cole,Gerrit	P	11.7
Rollins,Jimmy	6	11.6
Zimmermann,Jordan	P	11.6
Escobar,Yunel	6	11.4
Pierzynski,A.J.	2	11.3
Cashner,Andrew	P	11.2
Cishek,Steve	P	11.1
Wacha,Michael	P	11.1
Crisp,Coco	8	10.8
Furcal,Rafael	6	10.6
Rutledge,Josh	4	10.4
Freese,David	5	10.2
Weaver,Jered	P	10.2
Joyce,Matt	79	10.1
Rios,Alex	9	10.1
Middlebrooks,Will	5	10.0
Ruiz,Carlos	2	10.0
Rosenthal,Trevor	P	10.0
Brantley,Michael	7	9.9
Moss,Brandon	39	9.9
Buchholz,Clay	P	9.9
Melancon,Mark	P	9.9
Wood,Alex	P	9.7
Tanaka,Masahiro	P	9.6
Ziegler,Brad	P	9.6
D Arnaud,Travis	2	9.4
Frazier,Todd	5	9.4
Gregerson,Luke	P	9.4
Victorino,Shane	9	9.3
Balfour,Grant	P	9.2
Straily,Dan	P	9.2

NAME	POS	RAR
Gattis,Evan	27	9.1
Dickerson,Corey	7	9.0
Siegrist,Kevin	P	9.0
Marte,Starling	7	8.9
Cook,Ryan	P	8.6
Clippard,Tyler	P	8.5
Loup,Aaron	P	8.5
Parnell,Bobby	P	8.5
Herrera,Kelvin	P	8.4
Perkins,Glen	P	8.4
Gardner,Brett	8	8.2
Adams,Matt	3	8.1
Davis,Khristopher	7	8.1
Lohse,Kyle	P	8.1
Romo,Sergio	P	8.1
Jennings,Desmond	8	8.0
Mercer,Jordy	46	8.0
Montero,Jesus	2	7.9
Chisenhall,Lonnie	5	7.8
Miller,Shelby	P	7.8
Wheeler,Zack	P	7.8
Cruz,Nelson	9	7.7
Papelbon,Jonathan	P	7.7
Quintana,Jose	P	7.7
Altuve,Jose	4	7.6
Stammen,Craig	P	7.6
Benoit,Joaquin	P	7.5
Franklin,Nick	4	7.4
Hunter,Torii	9	7.4
Chavez,Eric	5	7.2
Lawrie,Brett	5	7.2
Corbin,Patrick	P	7.2
Crain,Jesse	P	7.2
Fister,Doug	P	7.2
Arcia,Oswaldo Celesti	79	7.1
Profar,Jurickson	4	7.1
Rodriguez,Alex	5	7.1
Marshall,Sean	P	7.1
Doolittle,Sean	P	7.0
Nathan,Joe	P	7.0
LaRoche,Adam	3	6.9
Soria,Joakim	P	6.9
Cabrera,Everth	6	6.8
Norris,Derek	2	6.8
Viciedo,Dayan	7	6.8
Hoover,J.J.	P	6.8
Johnson,Jim	P	6.8
Rondon,Bruce	P	6.8
Howard,Ryan	3	6.7
Janssen,Casey	P	6.7
Mujica,Edward	P	6.7
Smyly,Drew	P	6.7
Wilson,C.J.	P	6.7
Maness,Seth	P	6.6
O Day,Darren	P	6.6
Carp,Mike	37	6.5
Rodriguez,Paco	P	6.5
Scheppers,Tanner	P	6.5
Watson,Tony	P	6.5
Gindl,Caleb	7	6.4
Kuroda,Hiroki	P	6.4
Pinto,Josmil	2	6.3
Sizemore,Scott	4	6.3

SIMULATION LEAGUE DRAFT — TOP 500+

NAME	POS	RAR	NAME	POS	RAR	NAME	POS	RAR	NAME	POS	RAR
Estrada,Marco	P	6.3	Archer,Chris	P	4.2	Storen,Drew	P	2.8	Jordan,Taylor	P	1.3
Asche,Cody	5	6.2	Black,Victor	P	4.2	Forsythe,Logan	4	2.7	Lopez,Wilton	P	1.3
Castillo,Welington	2	6.2	Cotts,Neal	P	4.1	Alburquerque,Al	P	2.7	Gentry,Craig	78	1.2
Gray,Sonny	P	6.2	Liriano,Francisco	P	4.1	Belisario,Ronald	P	2.7	Mesoraco,Devin	2	1.2
Yelich,Christian S.	7	6.0	LeMahieu,DJ	4	4.0	Niese,Jon	P	2.7	Hanigan,Ryan	2	1.1
Howell,J.P.	P	6.0	Morneau,Justin	3	4.0	Strop,Pedro	P	2.7	Frasor,Jason	P	1.1
Navarro,Dioner	2	5.9	Dunn,Adam	3	3.9	Cozart,Zack	6	2.6	Hanrahan,Joel	P	1.1
Span,Denard	8	5.8	Lindstrom,Matt	P	3.9	Denorfia,Chris	789	2.6	Ramirez,Erasmo	P	1.1
Van Slyke,Scott	7	5.7	Martinez,Carlos	P	3.9	Young Jr.,Eric	79	2.6	Betemit,Wilson	0	1.0
Young,Michael	35	5.7	Masterson,Justin	P	3.9	Badenhop,Burke	P	2.6	Bogusevic,Brian	7	1.0
Miley,Wade	P	5.7	Minor,Mike	P	3.9	Chacin,Jhoulys	P	2.6	Nunez,Eduardo	6	1.0
Samardzija,Jeff	P	5.7	Aoki,Norichika	9	3.8	Soriano,Rafael	P	2.6	Pastornicky,Tyler	4	1.0
Tazawa,Junichi	P	5.7	Youkilis,Kevin	5	3.8	Pollock IV,A.J.	8	2.5	Punto,Nick	456	1.0
Hawkins,LaTroy	P	5.6	McGee,Jake	P	3.8	Schierholtz,Nate	9	2.5	Sweeney,Ryan	8	1.0
Pryor,Stephen	P	5.6	Putz,J.J.	P	3.8	Feliz,Neftali	P	2.5	Eovaldi,Nathan	P	1.0
Vincent,Nick	P	5.6	Stauffer,Tim	P	3.8	Henderson,Jim	P	2.5	Smith,Burch	P	1.0
Eaton,Adam	78	5.4	Ackley,Dustin	48	3.7	Motte,Jason	P	2.5	Davis,Rajai	79	0.9
Ibanez,Raul	7	5.4	Street,Huston	P	3.7	Veras,Jose	P	2.5	Laird,Gerald	2	0.9
Burnett,A.J.	P	5.4	Thayer,Dale	P	3.7	Belisle,Matt	P	2.4	Morse,Michael	9	0.9
Rodriguez,Francisco	P	5.4	Iannetta,Chris	2	3.6	Gausman,Kevin	P	2.4	Olt,Mike	5	0.9
Dickey,R.A.	P	5.3	Taveras,Oscar	9	3.6	Hochevar,Luke	P	2.4	Billingsley,Chad	P	0.9
Kintzler,Brandon	P	5.3	Venable,Will	89	3.6	Thatcher,Joe	P	2.4	Brach,Brad	P	0.9
Machi,Jean	P	5.3	Albers,Matt	P	3.6	Torres,Alexander	P	2.4	Matusz,Brian	P	0.9
Santos,Sergio	P	5.3	Burton,Jared	P	3.6	Beckham,Gordon	4	2.3	Ondrusek,Logan	P	0.9
Raburn,Ryan	9	5.2	Casilla,Santiago	P	3.6	Martin,Russell	2	2.3	Hundley,Nick	2	0.8
Grilli,Jason	P	5.2	Collmenter,Josh	P	3.6	Patton,Troy	P	2.3	Lavarnway,Ryan	2	0.8
Duda,Lucas	37	5.1	Jimenez,Ubaldo	P	3.6	Venters,Jonny	P	2.3	Morrison,Logan	3	0.8
Soto,Geovany	2	5.1	Markakis,Nick	9	3.5	Affeldt,Jeremy	P	2.2	Turner,Justin	5	0.8
Allen,Cody	P	5.1	Moore,Tyler	7	3.5	Bastardo,Antonio	P	2.2	Hunter,Tommy	P	0.8
Frieri,Ernesto	P	5.1	Breslow,Craig	P	3.5	Downs,Scott	P	2.2	Lackey,John	P	0.8
Ross,Robbie	P	5.1	Delabar,Steve	P	3.5	Nova,Ivan	P	2.2	Moreland,Mitch	3	0.7
Smith,Joe	P	5.1	Shaw,Bryan	P	3.4	Davis,Ike	3	2.1	Moustakas,Mike	5	0.7
Dirks,Andy	7	5.0	Walden,Jordan	P	3.4	Herrera,Jonathan	46	2.1	Garcia,Jaime	P	0.7
Kottaras,George	2	5.0	Grandal,Yasmani	2	3.3	Bell,Heath	P	2.1	Gearrin,Cory	P	0.7
Nava,Daniel	79	5.0	Anderson,Brett	P	3.3	Young,Chris	789	2.0	Nolasco,Ricky	P	0.7
Dunn,Mike	P	4.9	Colon,Bartolo	P	3.3	Holland,Derek	P	2.0	Reed,Addison	P	0.7
Fien,Casey	P	4.9	Parker,Jarrod	P	3.3	Kazmir,Scott	P	2.0	Blackmon,Charlie	89	0.6
Lopez,Javier	P	4.9	Gregorius,Didi	6	3.2	Mejia,Jenrry	P	2.0	Dozier,Brian	4	0.6
Luebke,Cory	P	4.8	Cecil,Brett	P	3.2	Wilson,Justin	P	2.0	Loney,James	3	0.6
Alonso,Yonder	3	4.7	Wright,Jamey	P	3.2	Keppinger,Jeff	345	1.9	Odorizzi,Jake	P	0.6
Berkman,Lance	0	4.7	Ludwick,Ryan	7	3.1	Avilan,Luis	P	1.9	Espinosa,Danny	4	0.5
Descalso,Daniel	456	4.7	Farquhar,Daniel	P	3.1	Crow,Aaron	P	1.9	Heisey,Chris	7	0.5
Brothers,Rex	P	4.7	Furbush,Charlie	P	3.1	Calhoun,Kole	9	1.8	Collins,Tim	P	0.5
Ross,David	2	4.6	Jones,Nate	P	3.1	DeJesus,David	78	1.8	Kontos,George	P	0.5
De La Rosa,Dane	P	4.6	Kelly,Joe	P	3.1	de la Rosa,Jorge	P	1.8	Krol,Ian	P	0.5
Porcello,Rick	P	4.6	Ross,Tyson	P	3.1	Lynn,Lance	P	1.8	Lester,Jon	P	0.5
Rodney,Fernando	P	4.6	Bradley,Jackie	8	3.0	Parker,Blake	P	1.8	Salas,Fernando	P	0.5
Saunders,Michael	789	4.5	Crawford,Brandon	6	3.0	Bloomquist,Willie	4	1.7	Almonte,Abraham	8	0.4
Garza,Matt	P	4.5	De Aza,Alejandro	78	3.0	Gennett,Scooter	4	1.7	Axford,John	P	0.4
Lecure,Sam	P	4.5	Schumaker,Skip	478	3.0	Bourn,Michael	8	1.6	Bailey,Andrew	P	0.4
Medina,Yoervis	P	4.5	Harris,Will	P	3.0	Ellis,Mark	4	1.6	Lyons,Tyler	P	0.4
Otero,Dan	P	4.5	Kelley,Shawn	P	3.0	Reddick,Josh	9	1.6	Baker,Jeff	37	0.3
Teheran,Julio	P	4.5	Peralta,Joel	P	3.0	Machado,Manny	5	1.5	Bay,Jason	79	0.3
Callaspo,Alberto	45	4.4	Webb,Ryan	P	3.0	Gorzelanny,Tom	P	1.5	Flores,Wilmer	5	0.3
Ellis,A.J.	2	4.4	Wright,Wesley	P	3.0	Paxton,James	P	1.5	Gillaspie,Conor	5	0.3
Jay,Jon	8	4.4	Cervelli,Francisco	2	2.9	Qualls,Chad	P	1.5	Kratz,Erik	2	0.3
Uggla,Dan	4	4.4	Plouffe,Trevor	5	2.9	Rzepczynski,Marc	P	1.5	Lake,Junior	78	0.3
Valbuena,Luis	5	4.4	Ruf,Darin	379	2.9	Withrow,Chris	P	1.5	Lombardozzi,Steve	47	0.3
Weeks,Rickie	4	4.4	Carpenter,David	P	2.9	Owings,Christopher	6	1.4	Paul,Xavier	7	0.3
Ogando,Alexi	P	4.4	Kluber,Corey	P	2.9	Segura,Jean	6	1.4	Pena,Brayan	2	0.3
Ottavino,Adam	P	4.4	Doumit,Ryan	29	2.8	De Fratus,Justin	P	1.4	Broxton,Jonathan	P	0.3
Pestano,Vinnie	P	4.4	Kubel,Jason	7	2.8	Fujikawa,Kyuji	P	1.4	Hernandez,David	P	0.3
Thielbar,Caleb	P	4.3	Blevins,Jerry	P	2.8	Conger,Hank	2	1.3	Wilhelmsen,Tom	P	0.3

2014 FANTASY BASEBALL WINNERS RESOURCE GUIDE

orders.baseballhq.com

10 REASONS

why winners rely on BASEBALL HQ PRODUCTS for fantasy baseball information

1 NO OTHER RESOURCE provides you with more vital intelligence to help you win. Compare the depth of our offerings in these pages with any other information product or service.

2 NO OTHER RESOURCE provides more exclusive information, like cutting-edge component skills analyses, revolutionary strategies like the LIMA Plan, and innovative gaming formats like Rotisserie 500. *You won't find these anywhere else on the internet, guaranteed.*

3 NO OTHER RESOURCE has as long and consistent a track record of success in top national competitions... Our writers and readers have achieved 33 first place finishes, plus another 31 second and third place finishes since 1997. *No other resource comes remotely close.*

4 NO OTHER RESOURCE has as consistent a track record in projecting impact performances. In 2013, our readers had surprises like Domonic Brown, Chris Davis, Josh Donaldson, Stephen Drew, Adam Lind, Jonathan Lucroy, Starling Marte, Leonys Martin, Jean Segura, Andrew Cashner, Tyler Chatwood, Alex Cobb, Patrick Corbin, Ubaldo Jimenez, Corey Kluber, John Lackey, Ivan Nova, Anibal Sanchez and Max Scherzer on their teams, *and dozens more.*

5 NO OTHER RESOURCE is supported by more than 50 top writers and analysts — all paid professionals and proven winners, not weekend hobbyists or corporate staffers.

6 NO OTHER RESOURCE has a wider scope, providing valuable information not only for Rotisserie, but for alternative formats like simulations, salary cap contests, daily games, points, head-to-head, dynasty leagues and others.

7 NO OTHER RESOURCE is as highly regarded by its peers in the industry. Baseball HQ is the *only* three-time winner of the Fantasy Sports Trade Association's "Best Fantasy Baseball Online Content" award and Ron Shandler has won two lifetime achievement awards.

8 NO OTHER RESOURCE is as highly regarded *outside* of the fantasy industry. Many Major League general managers are regular customers. We were advisors to the St. Louis Cardinals in 2004 and our former Minor League Director is now a scout for the organization.

9 NO OTHER RESOURCE has been creating fantasy baseball winners for as long as we have. Our 28 years of stability *guarantees your investment.*

10 Year after year, more than 90% of our customers report that Baseball HQ products and services have helped them improve their performance in their fantasy leagues. That's the bottom line.

TO ORDER
MAIL check or money order to:
Baseball HQ/USA Today Sports Media Group, 1440 Broadway, 17th Floor, New York, NY 10018
PHONE 1-800-422-7820
FAX: 540-772-1969
ONLINE secure order form: *http://orders.baseballhq.com/*

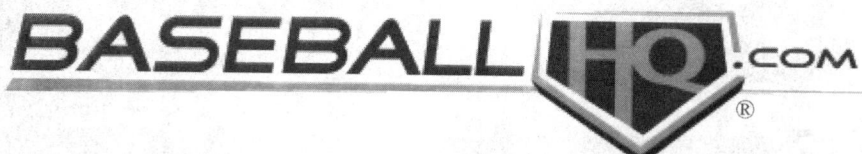

2014 CHEATER'S BOOKMARK

BATTING STATISTICS			BENCHMARKS			
Abbrv	Term	Formula / Desc.	BAD UNDER	'13 LG AVG AL	'13 LG AVG NL	BEST OVER
Avg	Batting Average	h/ab	235	256	258	290
xBA	Expected Batting Average	See glossary		267	273	
OB	On Base Average	(h+bb)/(ab+bb)	290	318	318	350
Slg	Slugging Average	total bases/ab	350	406	401	475
OPS	On Base plus Slugging	OB+Slg	650	724	719	800
bb%	Walk Rate	bb/(ab+bb)	5%	8%	8%	10%
ct%	Contact Rate	(ab-k) / ab	75%	78%	79%	85%
Eye	Batting Eye	bb/k	0.40	0.41	0.42	0.80
PX	Power Index	Normalized power skills	80	100	100	120
Spd	Statistically Scouted Speed	Normalized speed skills	80	100	100	120
SBO	Stolen Base Opportunity %	(sb+cs)/(singles+bb)		9%	9%	
G/F	Groundball/Flyball Ratio	gb / fb		1.3	1.4	
G	Ground Ball Per Cent	gb / balls in play		43%	45%	
L	Line Drive Per Cent	ld / balls in play		21%	21%	
F	Fly Ball Per Cent	fb / balls in play		36%	34%	
BPV	Base Performance Value	See glossary	10	41	44	50
RC/G	Runs Created per Game	See glossary	3.00	4.41	4.36	6.00
RAR	Runs Above Replacement	See glossary	0.0			6.00

PITCHING STATISTICS			BENCHMARKS			
Abbrv	Term	Formula / Desc.	BAD OVER	'13 LG AVG AL	'13 LG AVG NL	BEST UNDER
ERA	Earned Run Average	er*9/ip	4.75	3.99	3.74	3.00
xERA	Expected ERA	See glossary		3.85	3.74	
WHIP	Baserunners per Inning	(h+bb)/ip	1.50	1.32	1.28	1.15
BF/G	Batters Faced per Game	((ip*2.82)+h+bb)/g	28.0			
PC	Pitch Counts per Start		120	96	94	
OBA	Opposition Batting Avg	Opp. h/ab	290	256	251	240
OOB	Opposition On Base Avg	Opp. (h+bb)/(ab+bb)	350	316	311	290
BABIP	BatAvg on balls in play	(h-hr)/((ip*2.82)+h-k-hr)		296	292	
Ctl	Control Rate	bb*9/ip		3.1	3.0	2.8
hr/9	Homerun Rate	hr*9/ip		1.0	0.9	1.0
hr/f	Homerun per Fly ball	hr/fb		11%	10%	10%
S%	Strand Rate	(h+bb-er)/(h+bb-hr)		73%	73%	
DIS%	PQS Disaster Rate	% GS that are PQS 0/1		22%	20%	20%

			BAD UNDER	'13 LG AVG AL	'13 LG AVG NL	BEST OVER
RAR	Runs Above Replacement	See glossary	-0.0			+25.0
Dom	Dominance Rate	k*9/ip		7.7	7.5	7.0
Cmd	Command Ratio	k/bb		2.5	2.5	2.5
G/F	Groundball/Flyball Ratio	gb / fb		1.22	1.38	
SwK%	Swinging Strike Percentage	See essay on p. 60	7%	8%	8%	10%
BPV	Base Performance Value	See glossary	50	76	78	100
DOM%	PQS Dominance Rate	% GS that are PQS 4/5		47%	50%	50%
Sv%	Saves Conversion Rate	(saves / save opps)		73%	73%	80%
REff%	Relief Effectiveness Rate	See glossary		66%	66%	80%

NOTES

ESSENTIALS

Home page for year-round fanalytic coverage:

www.BaseballHQ.com

For March projections update and any other information related to this book:

www.baseballhq.com/content/ ron-shandlers-baseball-forecaster-2014

For the schedule of dates and cities on our Spring 2014 First Pitch tour, including registration information:

www.FirstPitchForums.com

Facebook: **www.facebook.com/baseballhq**
Twitter: **www.twitter.com/baseballhq**
HQ staffers on Twitter:
www.twitter.com/BaseballHQ/lists/hq-staff